Distances and j[...]

The mileage chart shows distances in [...] AA-recommended routes. Using motor[...] normally the fastest route, though not [...]

The journey times, shown in hours and minutes, are average off-peak driving times along AA-recommended routes. These times should be used as a guide only and do not allow for unforeseen traffic delays, rest breaks or fuel stops.

For example, the 378 miles (608 km) journey between Glasgow and Norwich should take approximately 7 hours 28 minutes.

Journey times

(Upper-right triangle of the chart shows journey times in hours and minutes; lower-left triangle shows distances in miles. City labels run along the diagonal: Aberdeen, Aberystwyth, Barnstaple, Birmingham, Brighton, Bristol, Cambridge, Cardiff, Carlisle, Carmarthen, Dorchester, Dover, Edinburgh, Exeter, Fort William, Glasgow, Gloucester, Guildford, Hereford, Holyhead, Hull, Inverness, Kendal, Leeds, Lincoln, Liverpool, Maidstone, Manchester, Middlesbrough, Newcastle, Northampton, Norwich, Nottingham, Oxford, Penzance, Perth, Peterborough, Plymouth, Portsmouth, Preston, Salisbury, Sheffield, Shrewsbury, Southampton, Stoke-on-Trent, Stranraer, Taunton, Wick, York, LONDON.)

Distances in miles (one mile equals 1.6093 km)

GREAT BRITAIN
ROAD ATLAS

32nd edition June 2017

© AA Media Limited 2017

Original edition printed 1986.

Cartography: All cartography in this atlas edited, designed and produced by the Mapping Services Department of AA Publishing (A05507).

This atlas contains Ordnance Survey data © Crown copyright and database right 2017 and Royal Mail data © Royal Mail copyright and database right 2017.

This atlas is based upon Crown Copyright and is reproduced with the permission of Land & Property Services under delegated authority from the Controller of Her Majesty's Stationery Office,© Crown copyright and database right 2017, PMLPA No.100497

© Ordnance Survey Ireland/ Government of Ireland. Copyright Permit No. MP000717

Publisher's Notes: Published by AA Publishing (a trading name of AA Media Limited, whose registered office is Fanum House, Basing View, Basingstoke, Hampshire RG21 4EA, UK. Registered number 06112600).

ISBN: 978 0 7495 7859 6 (leather)
ISBN: 978 0 7495 7858 9 (standard)

A CIP catalogue record for this book is available from The British Library.

Disclaimer: The contents of this atlas are believed to be correct at the time of the latest revision, it will not contain any subsequent amended, new or temporary information including diversions and traffic control or enforcement systems. The publishers cannot be held responsible or liable for any loss or damage occasioned to any person acting or refraining from action as a result of any use or reliance on material in this atlas, nor for any errors, omissions or changes in such material. This does not affect your statutory rights.

The publishers would welcome information to correct any errors or omissions and to keep this atlas up to date. Please write to the Atlas Editor, AA Publishing, The Automobile Association, Fanum House, Basing View, Basingstoke, Hampshire RG21 4EA, UK.
E-mail: roadatlasfeedback@theaa.com

Acknowledgements: AA Publishing would like to thank the following for their assistance in producing this atlas: Crematoria data provided by the Cremation Society of Great Britain. Cadw, English Heritage, Forestry Commission, Historic Scotland, Johnsons, National Trust and National Trust for Scotland, RSPB, The Wildlife Trust, Scottish Natural Heritage, Natural England, The Countryside Council for Wales (road maps). Award winning beaches from 'Blue Flag' and 'Keep Scotland Beautiful' (summer 2016 data): for latest information visit www.blueflag.org and www.keepscotlandbeautiful.org

Road signs are © Crown Copyright 2017. Reproduced under the terms of the Open Government Licence.

Transport for London (Central London Map), Nexus (Newcastle district map).

Printer: Printed in Italy by G. Canale & C. S.p.A.

Atlas contents

Map pages and distance chart	**inside front cover**
Route planning	**II–XVII**
Route planner	II–VII
Channel hopping and the Isle of Wight	VIII–IX
Ferries to Ireland and the Isle of Man	X
Scotland and North Sea ferries	XI
Caravan and camping sites in Britain	XII–XV
Traffic signs	XVI–XVII
Motorways	**XVIII–XXV**
Restricted junctions	XVIII–XXI
M25 London Orbital motorway	XXII
M6 Toll motorway	XXIII
Smart motorways	XXIV–XXV
Map pages	**XXVI**
Road map symbols	**1**
Road maps	**2–173**
Britain 1:200,000 scale Some islands are shown at slightly smaller scales	2–169
Ireland 1:1,000,000 scale	170–173
District maps	**174–185**
Birmingham	174–175
Glasgow	176–177
London	178–181
Manchester	182–183
Tyne & Wear	184–185
Street map symbols	**186**
Towns, ports and airports	**187–237**
Town plans	188–234
Major airports	235–237
Port plans	VIII–XI
Channel Tunnel terminals	27
Central London	**238–253**
Central London street map	238–247
Central London index	248–253
Index to place names	**254–302**
County, administrative area map	254
Place name index	255–302
Map pages and distance chart	**inside back cover**

Scale 1:200,000
or 3.16 miles to 1 inch

REPUBLIC
OF
IRELAND

Holyhead Anglesey Llandudno Colwyn Rhyl Widnes Mar
Bangor Conwy Bay Holywell John Lennon Runcorn Knutsfo
Caernarfon Bethesda Abergele Queensferry Ellesmere Northwich Mac
Denbigh Mold Port Chester
66 Betws-y- Ruthin Crewe Kidsgr
SNOWDONIA Coed Wrexham Nantwich **70** S
68 Newcastle-
Pwllheli Porthmadog Langollen Whitchurch under-Lyme
Abersoch Bala Oswestry Market
Drayton
Newport A518
Barmouth Dolgellau Shrewsbury Can
54 Welshpool **56** Telford **5**
Machynlleth WOLVERHAMPTON
Cardigan Bay Newtown Church Bridgnorth
Stretton
Aberystwyth WALES Stourbridge Haleso
Llangurig Ludlow Kidderminster
Rhayader Knighton Bromsgro

42 Aberaeron Tregaron Llandrindod Leominster Worcester
44 Wells Kington **46**
Cardigan Lampeter Builth Great
Newcastle Wells Malvern
40 Emlyn Hay-on-Wye Hereford Ledbury
St Davids Fishguard Llandovery Brecon Ross-on-Wye Tewke
Carmarthen Llandeilo BRECON BEACONS Abergavenny Gloucester
PEMBROKESHIRE St Clears Monmouth Stroud
COAST **28** Merthyr **30** Chepstow **32**
Haverfordwest Llanelli Neath Tydfil Cwmbran
Milford Haven Swansea Cwmbran
Pembroke Dock Tenby Port Pontypridd Newport
Pembroke Talbot Avonmouth
Bridgend CARDIFF BRISTOL
Cardiff Clevedon Bath
Bristol **20**
Bristol Weston- Cheddar Frome
18 super-Mare Wells Shepton
Channel Glastonbury Mallet
16 Ilfracombe Lynton Minehead Bridgwater
Lundy EXMOOR Taunton Wincanton
Barnstaple Yeovil Shaftesb
Bideford South A303
Great Molton Ilminster Sherborne
Torrington Chard Crewkerne Blandford
Bude Tiverton Axminster Forum
Holsworthy **8** Hatherleigh Crediton Exeter Honiton Bridport
4 Okehampton Exeter Lyme Dorchester
Regis
DARTMOOR Weymouth
Wadebridge Tavistock Exmouth Fortuneswell
Cornwall Bodmin Dawlish
Newquay Buckfastleigh Teignmouth
Newquay **6** Plymouth Newton Abbot
Liskeard Torquay
Lostwithiel Saltash PLYMOUTH Totnes Paignton Channel Islands
2 Isles of St Austell Torpoint Dartmouth inset
Scilly inset Kingsbridge
Redruth Truro Guernsey
Camborne Jersey
Penzance St-Malo
Land's Falmouth Santander Roscoff
End Helston (Apr–Oct) St-Malo (Nov–Mar)
Lizard E N G L I S H

Legend

Motorway
Toll motorway
Primary route
dual carriageway
Primary route
single carriageway
Other A road
or Ⓥ Vehicle ferry
Fast vehicle ferry
or catamaran
National Park
16 Atlas page
number

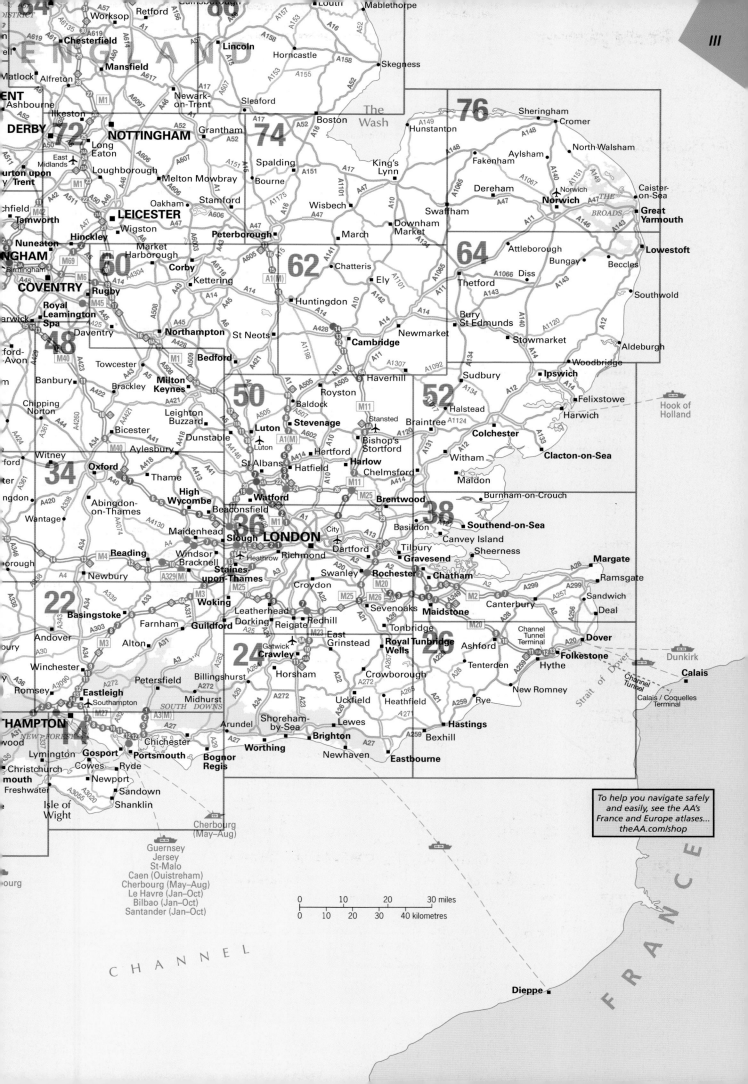

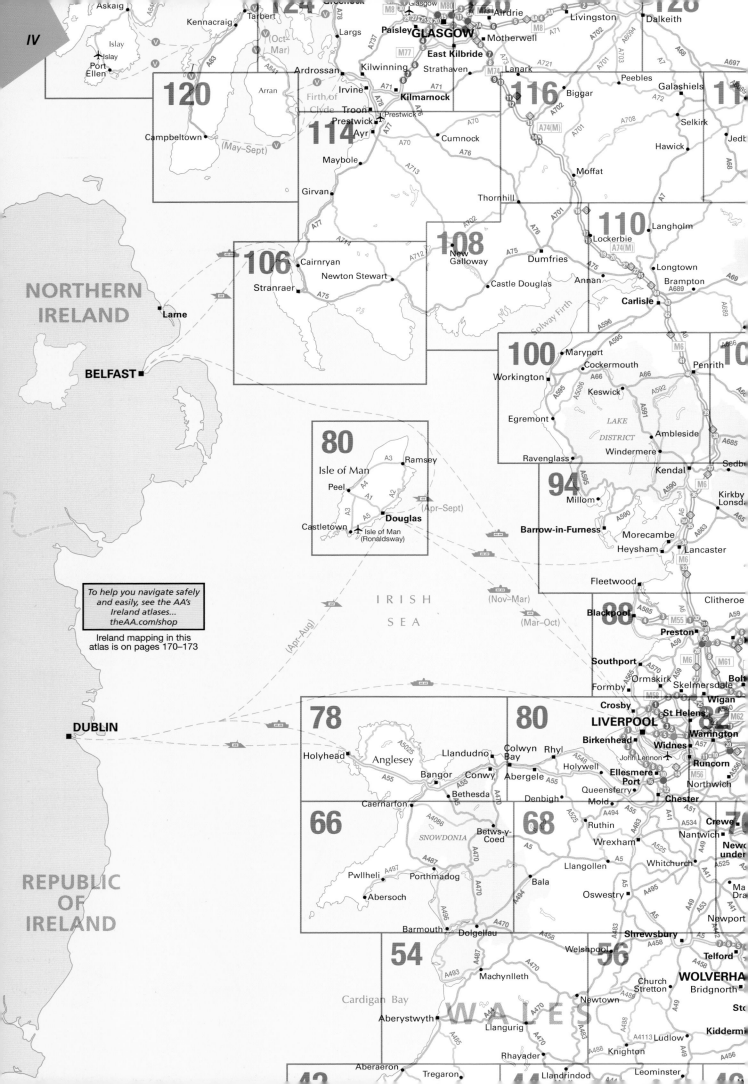

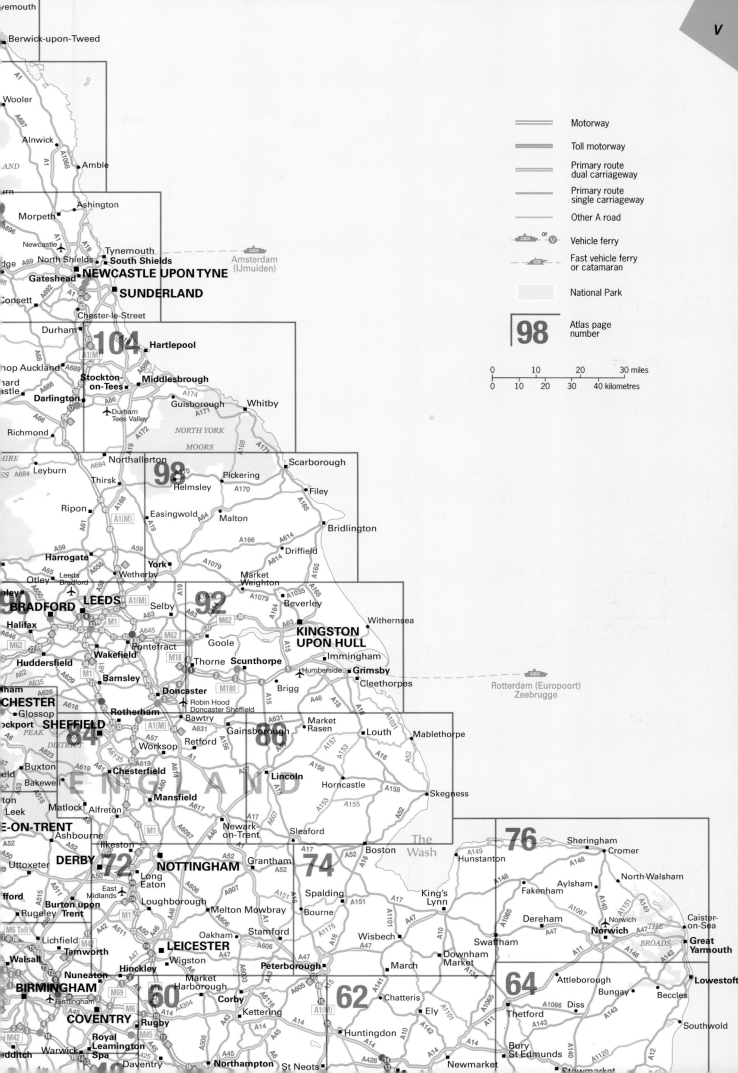

v

Motorway

Toll motorway

Primary route dual carriageway

Primary route single carriageway

Other A road

or V   Vehicle ferry

Fast vehicle ferry or catamaran

National Park

98 Atlas page number

0   10   20   30 miles
0 10 20 30 40 kilometres

Berwick-upon-Tweed

Wooler

Alnwick

Amble

AND

Morpeth

Ashington

Newcastle

North Shields

Tynemouth

South Shields

Amsterdam (IJmuiden)

Gateshead

NEWCASTLE UPON TYNE

SUNDERLAND

Consett

Chester-le-Street

Durham

hop Auckland

104

Hartlepool

Stockton-on-Tees

Middlesbrough

Darlington

Durham Tees Valley

Guisborough

Whitby

Richmond

NORTH YORK MOORS

HIRE

Leyburn

Northallerton

Scarborough

Thirsk

98

Helmsley

Pickering

Filey

Ripon

Easingwold

Malton

Bridlington

Driffield

Harrogate

Otley

Leeds Bradford

Market Weighton

York

Wetherby

90

BRADFORD

LEEDS

Selby

92

Beverley

Halifax

KINGSTON UPON HULL

Withernsea

Goole

Huddersfield

Wakefield

Pontefract

Thorne

Scunthorpe

Immingham

Barnsley

Humberside

Grimsby

Rotterdam (Europoort) Zeebrugge

Doncaster

Brigg

Cleethorpes

CHESTER

Glossop

Rotherham

Robin Hood Doncaster Sheffield

ckport

SHEFFIELD

84

Bawtry

Market Rasen

Louth

Mablethorpe

PEAK DISTRICT

Worksop

Retford

Gainsborough

86

Buxton

Chesterfield

Bakewell

Lincoln

Horncastle

Skegness

ton

Matlock

Alfreton

Mansfield

Leek

Ashbourne

Ilkeston

Newark-on-Trent

Sleaford

Boston

The Wash

Sheringham

Cromer

DERBY

72

Long Eaton

Grantham

74

Hunstanton

A149

North Walsham

Uttoxeter

East Midlands

NOTTINGHAM

Loughborough

Spalding

King's Lynn

Fakenham

Aylsham

Burton upon Trent

Melton Mowbray

Bourne

76

Dereham

Norwich

Caister-on-Sea

Rugeley

Lichfield

Oakham

Stamford

Wisbech

Swaffham

THE BROADS

Walsall

Tamworth

LEICESTER

Wigston

Peterborough

March

Downham Market

Great Yarmouth

BIRMINGHAM

Nuneaton

Hinckley

Market Harborough

60

Corby

62

Chatteris

Ely

64

Attleborough

Bungay

Lowestoft

Thetford

Diss

Beccles

COVENTRY

Rugby

Kettering

Huntingdon

Bury St Edmunds

Southwold

Warwick

Royal Leamington Spa

Daventry

Northampton

St Neots

Newmarket

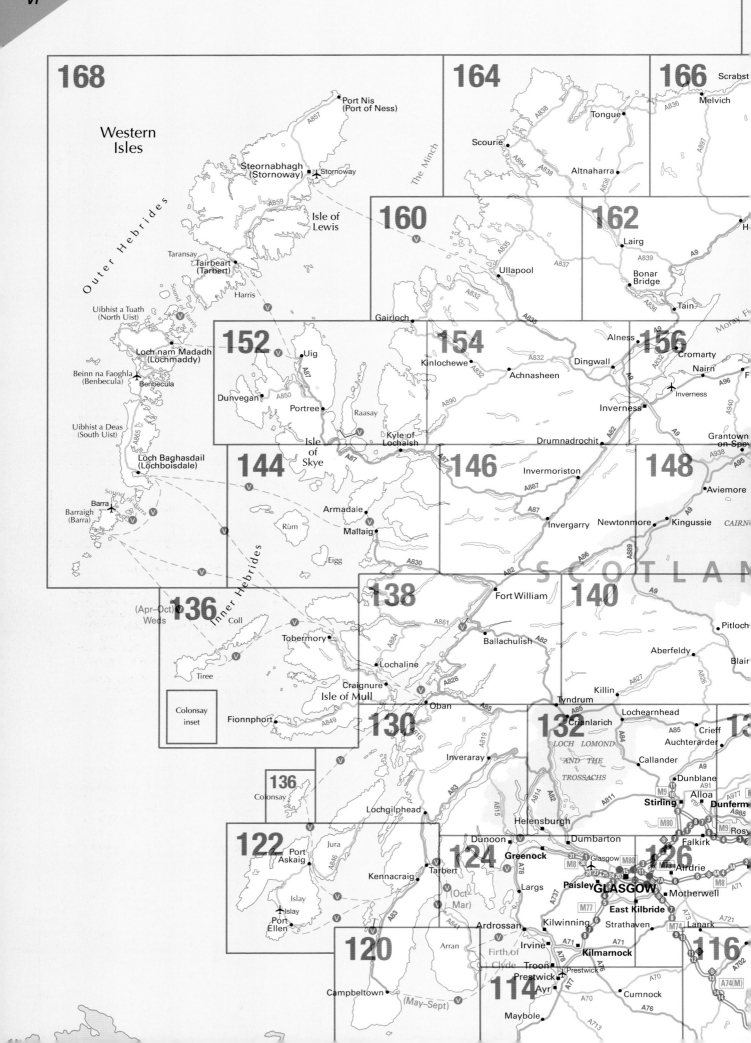

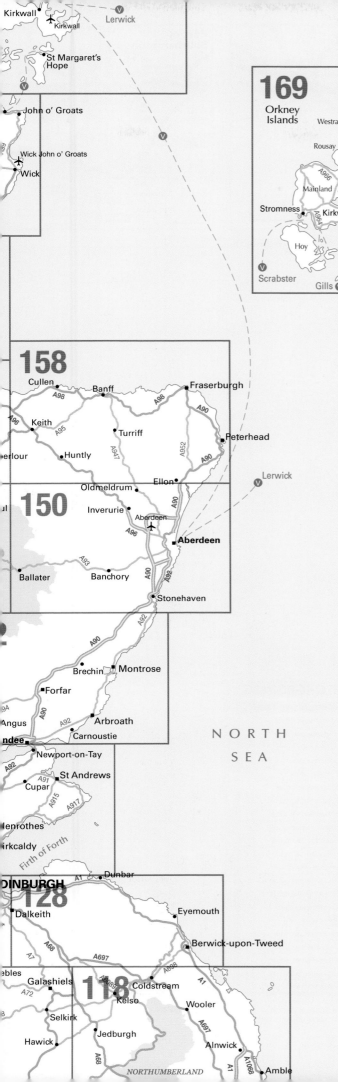

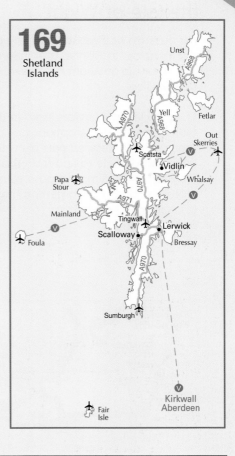

169 Orkney Islands

Papa Westray

North Ronaldsay

Westray

Rousay

Eday

Sanday

Stronsay

Mainland

Shapinsay

Stromness

Kirkwall

Kirkwall

Lerwick

A966

A964

A960

Hoy

St Margaret's Hope

Aberdeen

Scrabster

South Ronaldsay

Gills

169 Shetland Islands

Unst

A968

Yell

Fetlar

Scatsta

A970

Out Skerries

Papa Stour

A971

Vidlin

Whalsay

Mainland

A970

Tingwall

Foula

Scalloway

Lerwick

Bressay

A970

Sumburgh

Fair Isle

Kirkwall Aberdeen

158

Cullen

Banff

Fraserburgh

A98

A98

A90

A96

Keith

A95

Turriff

Peterhead

A947

A952

A90

erlour

Huntly

Ellon

A90

Oldmeldrum

Lerwick

150

Inverurie

Aberdeen

A96

Aberdeen

A93

Ballater

Banchory

A90

A92

Stonehaven

A92

A90

Brechin

Montrose

Forfar

A92

Angus

Arbroath

A94

A90

Carnoustie

ndee

Newport-on-Tay

A92

A91

St Andrews

Cupar

A915

A917

lenrothes

irkcaldy

Firth of Forth

FERRY INFORMATION

Information on ferry routes and operators can be found on pages *VIII–XI*.

EMERGENCY DIVERSION ROUTES

In an emergency it may be necessary to close a section of motorway or other main road to traffic, so a temporary sign may advise drivers to follow a diversion route. To help drivers navigate the route, black symbols on yellow patches may be permanently displayed on existing direction signs, including motorway signs. Symbols may also be used on separate signs with yellow backgrounds.

For further information see *theaa.com/motoring_advice/ general-advice/emergency-diversion-routes.html*

NORTH SEA

DINBURGH

Dunbar

A1

128

Dalkeith

Eyemouth

A68

A7

A697

Berwick-upon-Tweed

eebles

Galashiels

A7

A698

A1

A72

118

Coldstream

Selkirk

Kelso

Wooler

Hawick

Jedburgh

A697

Alnwick

A68

A1

A1068

Amble

NORTHUMBERLAND

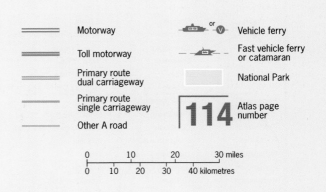

Motorway		Vehicle ferry
Toll motorway		Fast vehicle ferry or catamaran
Primary route dual carriageway		National Park
Primary route single carriageway	**114**	Atlas page number
Other A road		

0   10   20   30 miles
0 10 20 30   40 kilometres

Channel hopping and the Isle of Wight

For business or pleasure, hopping on a ferry across to France, the Channel Islands or Isle of Wight has never been easier.

The vehicle ferry services listed in the table give you all the options, together with detailed port plans to help you navigate to and from the ferry terminals. Simply choose your preferred route, not forgetting the fast sailings (see 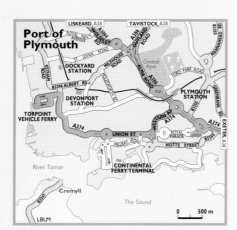). Bon voyage!

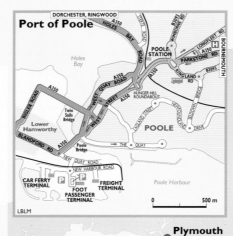

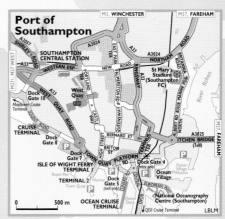

ENGLISH

Plymouth

Aldern

St Peter Port

Herm

Guernsey

Sark

Channel Islands

Jersey

St Helier

Roscoff

St-Malo

ENGLISH CHANNEL AND ISLE OF WIGHT FERRY CROSSINGS

From	To	Journey time	Operator website
Dover	Calais	1 hr 30 mins	dfdsseaways.co.uk
Dover	Calais	1 hr 30 mins	poferries.com
Dover	Dunkirk	2 hrs	dfdsseaways.co.uk
Folkestone	Calais (Coquelles)	35 mins	eurotunnel.com
Lymington	Yarmouth (IOW)	40 mins	wightlink.co.uk
Newhaven	Dieppe	4 hrs	dfdsseaways.co.uk
Plymouth	Roscoff	6–8 hrs	brittany-ferries.co.uk
Plymouth	St-Malo	10 hrs 15 mins (Nov–Mar)	brittany-ferries.co.uk
Poole	Cherbourg	4 hrs 15 mins	brittany-ferries.co.uk
Poole	Guernsey	3 hrs	condorferries.co.uk
Poole	Jersey	4 hrs 30 mins	condorferries.co.uk
Poole	St-Malo	7–12 hrs (via Channel Is.)	condorferries.co.uk
Portsmouth	Caen (Ouistreham)	6–7 hrs	brittany-ferries.co.uk
Portsmouth	Cherbourg	3 hrs (May–Aug)	brittany-ferries.co.uk
Portsmouth	Cherbourg	5 hrs 30 mins (May–Aug)	condorferries.co.uk
Portsmouth	Fishbourne (IOW)	45 mins	wightlink.co.uk
Portsmouth	Guernsey	7 hrs	condorferries.co.uk
Portsmouth	Jersey	8–11 hrs	condorferries.co.uk
Portsmouth	Le Havre	8 hrs (Jan–Oct)	brittany-ferries.co.uk
Portsmouth	St-Malo	9–11 hrs	brittany-ferries.co.uk
Southampton	East Cowes (IOW)	60 mins	redfunnel.co.uk

The information listed is provided as a guide only, as services are liable to change at short notice. Services shown are for vehicle ferries only, operated by conventional ferry unless indicated as a fast ferry service ( ). Please check sailings before planning your journey.

Travelling further afield? For ferry services to Northern Spain see brittany-ferries.co.uk.

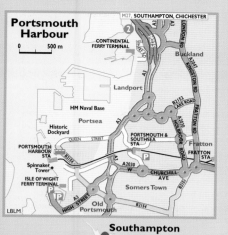

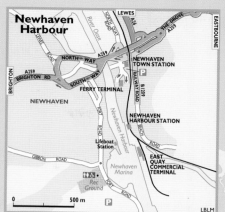

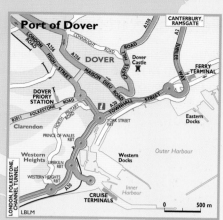

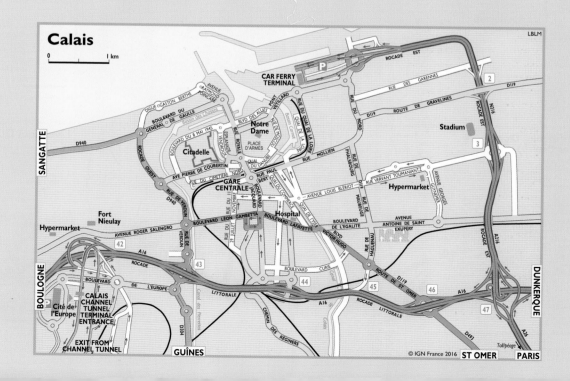

With so many sea crossings to Ireland and the Isle of Man the information provided in the table to the right will help you make the right choice.

IRISH SEA FERRY CROSSINGS

From	To	Journey time	Operator website
Cairnryan	Belfast	2 hrs 15 mins 🚢	stenaline.co.uk
Cairnryan	Larne	2 hrs	poferries.com
Douglas	Belfast	2 hrs 45 mins (April–Sept) 🚢	steam-packet.com
Douglas	Dublin	2 hrs 55 mins (April–Aug) 🚢	steam-packet.com
Fishguard	Rosslare	3 hrs 30 mins – 4 hrs	stenaline.co.uk
Heysham	Douglas	3 hrs 30 mins	steam-packet.com
Holyhead	Dublin	1 hr 50 mins 🚢	irishferries.com
Holyhead	Dublin	3 hrs 30 mins	irishferries.com
Holyhead	Dublin	3 hrs 30 mins	stenaline.co.uk
Liverpool	Douglas	2 hrs 45 mins (Mar–Oct) 🚢	steam-packet.com
Liverpool	Dublin	7 hrs 30 mins – 8 hrs 30 mins	poferries.com
Liverpool (Birkenhead)	Belfast	8 hrs	stenaline.co.uk
Liverpool (Birkenhead)	Douglas	4 hrs 15 mins (Nov–Mar)	steam-packet.com
Pembroke Dock	Rosslare	4 hrs	irishferries.com

The information listed is provided as a guide only, as services are liable to change at short notice. Services shown are for vehicle ferries only, operated by conventional ferry unless indicated as a fast ferry service (🚢). Please check sailings before planning your journey.

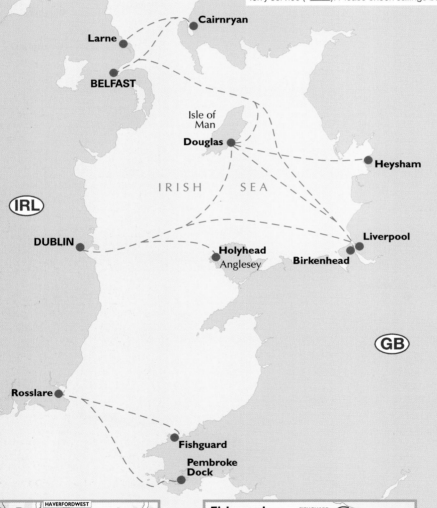

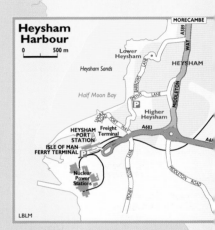

Heysham Harbour

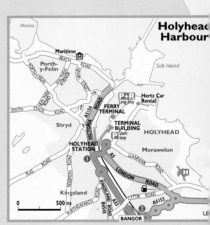

Holyhead Harbour

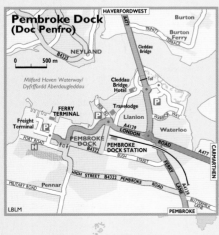

Pembroke Dock (Doc Penfro)

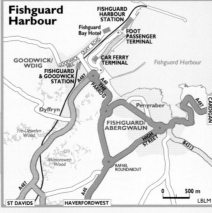

Fishguard Harbour

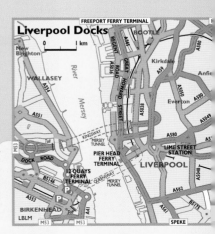

Liverpool Docks

SCOTLAND FERRIES

rom	To	Journey time	Operator website
Scottish Islands/west coast of Scotland			
ourock	Dunoon	20 mins	*western-ferries.co.uk*
enelg	Skye	20 mins (Easter–Oct)	*skyeferry.co.uk*

umerous and varied sailings from the west coast of Scotland to Scottish islands are provided by Caledonian acBrayne. Please visit *calmac.co.uk* for all ferry information, including those of other operators.

		Orkney Islands	
erdeen	Kirkwall	6 hrs	*northlinkferries.co.uk*
lls	St Margaret's Hope	1 hr	*pentlandferries.co.uk*
crabster	Stromness	1 hr 30 mins	*northlinkferries.co.uk*
rwick	Kirkwall	5 hrs 30 mins	*northlinkferries.co.uk*

er-island services are operated by Orkney Ferries. Please see *orkneyferries.co.uk* for details.

		Shetland Islands	
erdeen	Lerwick	12 hrs 30 mins	*northlinkferries.co.uk*
rkwall	Lerwick	7 hrs 45 mins	*northlinkferries.co.uk*

er-island services are operated by Shetland Island Council Ferries. Please see *shetland.gov.uk/ferries* for details.

ase note that some smaller island services are day dependent and reservations are uired for some routes. Book and confirm sailing schedules by contacting the operator.

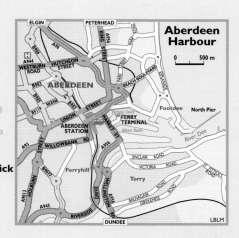

Aberdeen Harbour

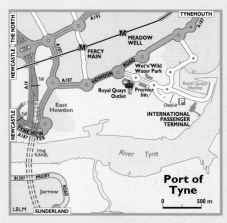

Port of Tyne

Port of Hull

For a port plan of Harwich see atlas page 53

NORTH SEA FERRY CROSSINGS

rom	To	Journey time	Operator website
arwich	Hook of Holland	7–8 hrs	*stenaline.co.uk*
ngston upon Hull	Rotterdam (Europoort)	10 hrs 45 mins	*poferries.com*
ngston upon Hull	Zeebrugge	13 hrs 15 mins	*poferries.com*
ewcastle upon Tyne	Amsterdam (IJmuiden)	15 hrs 30 mins	*dfdsseaways.co.uk*

e information listed on this page is provided as a guide only, as services are liable to ange at short notice. Services shown are for vehicle ferries only, operated by conventional y. Please check sailings before planning your journey.

Caravan and camping sites in Britain

These pages list the top 300 AA-inspected Caravan and Camping (C & C) sites in the Pennant rating scheme. **Five Pennant Premier sites are shown in green,**
Four Pennant sites are shown in blue.
Listings include addresses, telephone numbers and websites together with page and grid references to locate the sites in the atlas. The total number of touring pitches is also included for each site, together with the type of pitch available. The following abbreviations are used: **C = Caravan CV = Campervan T = Tent**
To find out more about the AA's Pennant rating scheme and other rated caravan and camping sites not included on these pages please visit ***theAA.com***

ENGLAND

Alders Caravan Park
Home Farm, Alne, York
YO61 1RY
Tel: 01347 838722 **97 R7**
alderscaravanpark.co.uk
Total Pitches: 87 (C, CV & T)

Andrewshayes Holiday Park
Dalwood, Axminster
EX13 7DY
Tel: 01404 831225 **10 E5**
andrewshayes.co.uk
Total Pitches: 150 (C, CV & T)

Apple Tree Park C & C Site
A38, Claypits, Stonehouse
GL10 3AL
Tel: 01452 742362 **32 E3**
appletreepark.co.uk
Total Pitches: 65 (C, CV & T)

Appuldurcombe Gardens Holiday Park
Appuldurcombe Road, Wroxall,
Isle of Wight
PO38 3EP
Tel: 01983 852597 **14 F10**
appuldurcombegardens.co.uk
Total Pitches: 130 (C, CV & T)

Atlantic Bays Holiday Park
St Merryn, Padstow
PL28 8PY
Tel: 01841 520855 **4 D7**
atlanticbaysholidaypark.co.uk
Total Pitches: 70 (C, CV & T)

Ayr Holiday Park
St Ives, Cornwall
TR26 1EJ
Tel: 01736 795855 **2 E5**
ayrholidaypark.co.uk
Total Pitches: 40 (C, CV & T)

Back of Beyond Touring Park
234 Ringwood Road,
St Leonards, Dorset
BH24 2SB
Tel: 01202 876968 **13 J4**
backofbeyondtouringpark.co.uk
Total Pitches: 80 (C, CV & T)

Bagwell Farm Touring Park
Knights in the Bottom, Chickerell,
Weymouth
DT3 4EA
Tel: 01305 782575 **11 N8**
bagwellfarm.co.uk
Total Pitches: 320 (C, CV & T)

Bardsea Leisure Park
Priory Road, Ulverston
LA12 9QE
Tel: 01229 584712 **94 F5**
bardsealeisure.co.uk
Total Pitches: 83 (C & CV)

Barlings Country Holiday Park
Barlings Lane, Langworth
LN3 5DF
Tel: 01522 753200 **86 E5**
barlingscountrypark.co.uk
Total Pitches: 84 (C, CV & T)

Barn Farm Campsite
Barn Farm, Birchover, Matlock
DE4 2BL
Tel: 01629 650245 **84 B8**
barnfarmcamping.com
Total Pitches: 62 (C, CV & T)

Bath Chew Valley Caravan Park
Ham Lane, Bishop Sutton
BS39 5TZ
Tel: 01275 332127 **19 Q3**
bathchewvalley.co.uk
Total Pitches: 45 (C, CV & T)

Bay View Holiday Park
Bolton le Sands, Carnforth
LA5 9TN
Tel: 01524 732854 **95 K7**
holgates.co.uk
Total Pitches: 100 (C, CV & T)

Beaconsfield Farm Caravan Park
Battlefield, Shrewsbury
SY4 4AA
Tel: 01939 210370 **69 P11**
beaconsfieldholidaypark.co.uk
Total Pitches: 60 (C & CV)

Beech Croft Farm
Beech Croft, Blackwell in the
Peak, Buxton
SK17 9TQ
Tel: 01298 85330 **83 P10**
beechcroftfarm.co.uk
Total Pitches: 30 (C, CV & T)

Bellingham C & C Club Site
Brown Rigg, Bellingham
NE48 2JY
Tel: 01434 220175 **112 B4**
campingandcaravanningclub.
co.uk/bellingham
Total Pitches: 64 (C, CV & T)

Beverley Parks C & C Park
Goodrington Road, Paignton
TQ4 7JE
Tel: 01803 661961 **7 M7**
beverley-holidays.co.uk
Total Pitches: 172 (C, CV & T)

Bingham Grange Touring & Camping Park
Melplash, Bridport
DT6 3TT
Tel: 01308 488234 **11 K5**
binghamgrange.co.uk
Total Pitches: 150 (C, CV & T)

Blackmore Vale C & C Park
Sherborne Causeway,
Shaftesbury
SP7 9PX
Tel: 01747 851523 **20 F10**
blackmorevalecaravanpark.co.uk
Total Pitches: 13 (C, CV & T)

Blue Rose Caravan Country Park
Star Carr Lane, Brandesburton
YO25 8RU
Tel: 01964 543366 **99 N11**
bluerosepark.com
Total Pitches: 58 (C & CV)

Briarfields Motel & Touring Park
Gloucester Road, Cheltenham
GL51 0SX
Tel: 01242 235324 **46 H10**
briarfields.net
Total Pitches: 72 (C, CV & T)

Broadhembury C & C Park
Steeds Lane, Kingsnorth, Ashford
TN26 1NQ
Tel: 01233 620859 **26 H4**
broadhembury.co.uk
Total Pitches: 110 (C, CV & T)

Brokerswood Country Park
Brokerswood, Westbury
BA13 4EH
Tel: 01373 822238 **20 F4**
brokerswoodcountrypark.co.uk
Total Pitches: 69 (C, CV & T)

Brompton Caravan Park
Brompton-on-Swale, Richmond
DL10 7EZ
Tel: 01748 824629 **103 N10**
bromptoncaravanpark.co.uk
Total Pitches: 177 (C, CV & T)

Budemeadows Touring Park
Widemouth Bay, Bude
EX23 0NA
Tel: 01288 361646 **16 C11**
budemeadows.com
Total Pitches: 145 (C, CV & T)

Burrowhayes Farm C & C Site & Riding Stables
West Luccombe, Porlock,
Minehead
TA24 8HT
Tel: 01643 862463 **18 A5**
burrowhayes.co.uk
Total Pitches: 120 (C, CV & T)

Burton Constable Holiday Park & Arboretum
Old Lodges, Sproatley, Hull
HU11 4LJ
Tel: 01964 562508 **93 L3**
burtonconstable.co.uk
Total Pitches: 105 (C, CV & T)

Cakes & Ale
Abbey Lane, Theberton, Leiston
IP16 4TE
Tel: 01728 831655 **65 N9**
cakesandale.co.uk
Total Pitches: 55 (C, CV & T)

Calloose C & C Park
Leedstown, Hayle
TR27 5ET
Tel: 01736 850431 **2 F7**
calloose.co.uk
Total Pitches: 109 (C, CV & T)

Camping Caradon Touring Park
Trelawne, Looe
PL13 2NA
Tel: 01503 272388 **5 L11**
campingcaradon.co.uk
Total Pitches: 75 (C, CV & T)

Capesthorne Hall
Congleton Road, Siddington,
Macclesfield
SK11 9JY
Tel: 01625 861221 **82 H10**
capesthorne.com
Total Pitches: 50 (C & CV)

Carlyon Bay C & C Park
Bethesda, Cypress Avenue,
Carlyon Bay
PL25 3RE
Tel: 01726 812735 **3 R3**
carlyonbay.net
Total Pitches: 180 (C, CV & T)

Carnon Downs C & C Park
Carnon Downs, Truro
TR3 6JJ
Tel: 01872 862283 **3 L5**
carnon-downs-caravanpark.co.uk
Total Pitches: 150 (C, CV & T)

Carvynick Country Club
Summercourt,
Newquay
TR8 5AF
Tel: 01872 510716 **4 D10**
carvynick.co.uk
Total Pitches: 47 (C & CV)

Castlerigg Hall C & C Park
Castlerigg Hall,
Keswick
CA12 4TE
Tel: 017687 74499 **101 J6**
castlerigg.co.uk
Total Pitches: 68 (C, CV & T)

Cayton Village Caravan Park
Mill Lane, Cayton Bay,
Scarborough
YO11 3NN
Tel: 01723 583171 **99 M4**
caytontouring.co.uk
Total Pitches: 310 (C, CV & T)

Charris C & C Park
Candy's Lane, Corfe Mullen,
Wimborne
BH21 3EF
Tel: 01202 885970 **12 G5**
charris.co.uk
Total Pitches: 45 (C, CV & T)

Cheddar Mendip Heights C & C Club Site
Townsend,
Priddy, Wells
BA5 3BP
Tel: 01749 870241 **19 P4**
campingandcaravanningclub.
co.uk/cheddar
Total Pitches: 90 (C, CV & T)

Chy Carne Holiday Park
Kuggar, Ruan Minor,
Helston
TR12 7LX
Tel: 01326 290200 **3 J10**
chycarne.co.uk
Total Pitches: 30 (C, CV & T)

Clippesby Hall
Hall Lane, Clippesby,
Great Yarmouth
NR29 3BL
Tel: 01493 367800 **77 N9**
clippesby.com
Total Pitches: 120 (C, CV & T)

Cofton Country Holidays
Starcross,
Dawlish
EX6 8RP
Tel: 01626 890111 **9 N8**
coftonholidays.co.uk
Total Pitches: 450 (C, CV & T)

Concierge Camping
Ratham Estate, Ratham Lane,
West Ashling, Chichester
PO18 8DL
Tel: 01243 573118 **15 M5**
conciergecamping.co.uk
Total Pitches: 15 (C, CV & T)

Concierge Glamping
Ratham Estate, Ratham Lane,
West Ashling, Chichester
PO18 8DL
Tel: 01243 573118 **15 M5**
conciergecamping.co.uk
Total Pitches: 4 (T)

Coombe Touring Park
Race Plain
Netherhampton,
Salisbury
SP2 8PN
Tel: 01722 328451 **21 L9**
coombecaravanpark.co.uk
Total Pitches: 50 (C, CV & T)

Corfe Castle C & C Club Site
Bucknowle, Wareham
BH20 5PQ
Tel: 01929 480280 **12 F8**
campingandcaravanningclub.co.uk/
corfecastle
Total Pitches: 80 (C, CV & T)

Cornish Farm Touring Park
Shoreditch, Taunton
TA3 7BS
Tel: 01823 327746 **18 H10**
cornishfarm.com
Total Pitches: 50 (C, CV & T)

Cosawes Park
Perranarworthal, Truro
TR3 7QS
Tel: 01872 863724 **3 K6**
cosawestouringandcamping.co.uk
Total Pitches: 59 (C, CV & T)

Cote Ghyll C & C Park
Osmotherley, Northallerton
DL6 3AH
Tel: 01609 883425 **104 E11**
coteghyll.com
Total Pitches: 77 (C, CV & T)

Country View Holiday Park
Sand Road, Sand Bay,
Weston-super-Mare
BS22 9UJ
Tel: 01934 627595 **19 K2**
cvhp.co.uk
Total Pitches: 190 (C, CV & T)

Crafty Camping
Woodland Workshop,
Yonder Hill, Holditch
TA20 4NL
Tel: 01460 221102 **10 G4**
mallinson.co.uk
Total Pitches: 8 (T)

Crealy Meadows C & C Park
Sidmouth Road, Clyst St Mary,
Exeter
EX5 1DR
Tel: 01395 234888 **9 P6**
crealymeadows.co.uk
Total Pitches: 120 (C, CV & T)

Crows Nest Caravan Park
Gristhorpe, Filey
YO14 9PS
Tel: 01723 582206 **99 M4**
crowsnestcaravanpark.com
Total Pitches: 49 (C, CV & T)

Dell Touring Park
Beyton Road, Thurston,
Bury St Edmunds
IP31 3RB
Tel: 01359 270121 **64 C9**
thedellcaravanpark.co.uk
Total Pitches: 50 (C, CV & T)

Dolbeare Park C & C
St Ive Road, Landrake, Saltash
PL12 5AF
Tel: 01752 851332 **5 P9**
dolbeare.co.uk
Total Pitches: 60 (C, CV & T)

Dornafield
Dornafield Farm, Two Mile Oak,
Newton Abbot
TQ12 6DD
Tel: 01803 812732 **7 L5**
dornafield.com
Total Pitches: 135 (C, CV & T)

Dorset Country Holidays
Sherborne Causeway, Shaftesbury
SP7 9PX
Tel: 01747 851523 **20 F10**
blackmorevalecaravanand
campingpark.co.uk
Total Pitches: 7 (T)

East Fleet Farm Touring Park
Chickerell, Weymouth
DT3 4DW
Tel: 01305 785768 **11 N9**
eastfleet.co.uk
Total Pitches: 400 (C, CV & T)

Eden Valley Holiday Park
Lanlivery,
Nr Lostwithiel
PL30 5BU
Tel: 01208 872277 **4 H10**
edenvalleyholidaypark.co.uk
Total Pitches: 56 (C, CV & T)

Eskdale C & C Club Site
Boot, Holmrook
CA19 1TH
Tel: 019467 23253 **100 G10**
campingandcaravanningclub.co.uk/
eskdale
Total Pitches: 100 (CV & T)

Exe Valley Caravan Site
Mill House, Bridgetown,
Dulverton
TA22 9JR
Tel: 01643 851432 **18 B**
exevalleycamping.co.uk
Total Pitches: 48 (C, CV & T)

Fields End Water Caravan Park & Fishery
Benwick Road, Doddington,
March
PE15 0TY
Tel: 01354 740199 **62 E**
fieldsendcaravans.co.uk
Total Pitches: 52 (C, CV & T)

Flusco Wood
Flusco,
Penrith
CA11 0JB
Tel: 017684 80020 **101 N**
fluscowood.co.uk
Total Pitches: 36 (C & CV)

Globe Vale Holiday Park
Radnor, Redruth
TR16 4BH
Tel: 01209 891183 **3 J**
globevale.co.uk
Total Pitches: 138 (C, CV & T)

Golden Cap Holiday Park
Seatown, Chideock,
Bridport
DT6 6JX
Tel: 01308 422139 **11 J**
wdlh.co.uk
Total Pitches: 108 (C, CV & T)

Golden Square C & C Park
Oswaldkirk, Helmsley
YO62 5YQ
Tel: 01439 788269 **98 C**
goldensquarecaravanpark.co.uk
Total Pitches: 129 (C, CV & T)

Goosewood Holiday Park
Sutton-on-the-Forest,
York
YO61 1ET
Tel: 01347 810829 **98 B**
flowerofmay.com
Total Pitches: 100 (C & CV)

Green Acres Caravan Park
High Knells, Houghton,
Carlisle
CA6 4JW
Tel: 01228 675418 **110 H**
caravanpark-cumbria.com
Total Pitches: 35 (C, CV & T)

Greenacres Touring Park
Haywards Lane, Chelston,
Wellington
TA21 9PH
Tel: 01823 652844 **18 G1**
greenacres-wellington.co.uk
Total Pitches: 40 (C & CV)

Greenhill Farm C & C Park
Greenhill Farm, New Road,
Landford,
Salisbury
SP5 2AZ
Tel: 01794 324117 **21 Q1**
greenhillfarm.co.uk
Total Pitches: 160 (C, CV & T)

Greenhill Leisure Park
Greenhill Farm, Station Road,
Bletchingdon,
Oxford
OX5 3BQ
Tel: 01869 351600 **48 E1**
greenhill-leisure-park.co.uk
Total Pitches: 92 (C, CV & T)

Grouse Hill Caravan Park
Flask Bungalow Farm,
Fylingdales,
Robin Hood's Bay
YO22 4QH
Tel: 01947 880543 **105 P1**
grousehill.co.uk
Total Pitches: 175 (C, CV & T)

Gunvenna Holiday Park
St Minver,
Wadebridge
PL27 6QN
Tel: 01208 862405 **4 F**
gunvenna.com
Total Pitches: 75 (C, CV & T)

Gwithian Farm Campsite
Gwithian Farm, Gwithian,
Hayle
TR27 5BX
Tel: 01736 753127 **2 F**
gwithianfarm.co.uk
Total Pitches: 87 (C, CV & T)

Harbury Fields
Harbury Fields Farm, Harbury,
Nr Leamington Spa
CV33 9JN
Tel: 01926 612457   **48 C2**
harburyfields.co.uk
Total Pitches: 59 (C & CV)

Haw Wood Farm Caravan Park
Hinton,
Saxmundham
IP17 3QT
Tel: 01502 359550   **65 N7**
hawwoodfarm.co.uk
Total Pitches: 60 (C, CV & T)

Heathfield Farm Camping
Heathfield Road, Freshwater,
Isle of Wight
PO40 9SH
Tel: 01983 407822   **13 P7**
heathfieldcamping.co.uk
Total Pitches: 75 (C, CV & T)

Heathland Beach Caravan Park
London Road,
Kessingland
NR33 7PJ
Tel: 01502 740337   **65 Q4**
heathlandbeach.co.uk
Total Pitches: 63 (C, CV & T)

Hele Valley Holiday Park
Hele Bay,
Ilfracombe
EX34 9RD
Tel: 01271 862460   **17 J2**
helevalley.co.uk
Total Pitches: 50 (C, CV & T)

Hendra Holiday Park
Newquay
TR8 4NY
Tel: 01637 875778   **4 C9**
hendra-holidays.com
Total Pitches: 548 (C, CV & T)

Herding Hill Farm
Shield Hill,
Haltwhistle
NE49 9NW
Tel: 01434 320175   **111 P7**
herdinghillfarm.co.uk
Total Pitches: 22 (C, CV & T)

**Herding Hill Farm
Glamping Site**
Shield Hill, Haltwhistle
NE49 9NW
Tel: 01434 320175   **111 P7**
herdinghillfarm.co.uk
Total Pitches: 24 (T)

Hidden Valley Park
West Down, Braunton,
Ilfracombe
EX34 8NU
Tel: 01271 813837   **17 J3**
hiddenvalleypark.com
Total Pitches: 100 (C, CV & T)

High Moor Farm Park
Skipton Road,
Harrogate
HG3 2LT
Tel: 01423 563637   **97 K9**
highmoorfarmpark.co.uk
Total Pitches: 320 (C & CV)

Highfield Farm Touring Park
Long Road, Comberton,
Cambridge
CB23 7DG
Tel: 01223 262308   **62 E9**
highfieldfarmtouringpark.co.uk
Total Pitches: 120 (C, CV & T)

Highlands End Holiday Park
Eype, Bridport,
Dorset
DT6 6AR
Tel: 01308 422139   **11 K6**
wdlh.co.uk
Total Pitches: 195 (C, CV & T)

Hill Cottage Farm C & C Park
Sandleheath Road, Alderholt,
Fordingbridge
SP6 3EG
Tel: 01425 650513   **13 K2**
*hillcottagefarmcampingand
caravanpark.co.uk*
Total Pitches: 95 (C, CV & T)

Hill Farm Caravan Park
Branches Lane,
Sherfield English,
Romsey
SO51 6FH
Tel: 01794 340402   **21 Q10**
hillfarmpark.com
Total Pitches: 100 (C, CV & T)

Hill of Oaks & Blakeholme
Windermere
LA12 8NR
Tel: 015395 31578   **94 H3**
hillofoaks.co.uk
Total Pitches: 43 (C & CV)

Hillside Caravan Park
Canvas Farm, Moor Road,
Knayton,
Thirsk
YO7 4BR
Tel: 01845 537349   **97 P3**
hillsidecaravanpark.co.uk
Total Pitches: 50 (C & CV)

Hollins Farm C & C
Far Arnside,
Carnforth
LA5 0SL
Tel: 01524 701767   **95 J5**
holgates.co.uk
Total Pitches: 12 (C, CV & T)

Holmans Wood Holiday Park
Harcombe Cross,
Chudleigh
TQ13 0DZ
Tel: 01626 853785   **9 L8**
holmanswood.co.uk
Total Pitches: 73 (C, CV & T)

Honeybridge Park
Honeybridge Lane,
Dial Post,
Horsham
RH13 8NX
Tel: 01403 710923   **24 E7**
honeybridgepark.co.uk
Total Pitches: 130 (C, CV & T)

Hurley Riverside Park
Park Office,
Hurley,
Nr Maidenhead
SL6 5NE
Tel: 01628 824493   **35 M8**
hurleyriversidepark.co.uk
Total Pitches: 200 (C, CV & T)

Hylton Caravan Park
Eden Street,
Silloth
CA7 4AY
Tel: 016973 31707   **109 P10**
stanwix.com
Total Pitches: 90 (C, CV & T)

Island Lodge C & C Site
Stumpy Post Cross,
Kingsbridge
TQ7 4BL
Tel: 01548 852956   **7 J9**
islandlodgesite.co.uk
Total Pitches: 30 (C, CV & T)

**Isle of Avalon Touring
Caravan Park**
Godney Road,
Glastonbury
BA6 9AF
Tel: 01458 833618   **19 N7**
avaloncaravanpark.co.uk
Total Pitches: 120 (C, CV & T)

Jacobs Mount Caravan Park
Jacobs Mount,
Stepney Road,
Scarborough
YO12 5NL
Tel: 01723 361178   **99 L3**
jacobsmount.com
Total Pitches: 156 (C, CV & T)

Jasmine Caravan Park
Cross Lane, Snainton,
Scarborough
YO13 9BE
Tel: 01723 859240   **99 J4**
jasminepark.co.uk
Total Pitches: 68 (C, CV & T)

Juliot's Well Holiday Park
Camelford,
Cornwall
PL32 9RF
Tel: 01840 213302   **4 H5**
*southwestholidayparks.co.uk/
parks/juliots-well*
Total Pitches: 39 (C, CV & T)

Kenneggy Cove Holiday Park
Higher Kenneggy,
Rosudgeon,
Penzance
TR20 9AU
Tel: 01736 763453   **2 F8**
kenneggycove.co.uk
Total Pitches: 40 (C, CV & T)

Kings Down Tail C & C Park
Salcombe Regis,
Sidmouth
EX10 0PD
Tel: 01297 680313   **10 D6**
kingsdowntail.co.uk
Total Pitches: 80 (C, CV & T)

King's Lynn C & C Park
New Road,
North Runcton,
King's Lynn
PE33 0RA
Tel: 01553 840004   **75 M7**
kl-cc.co.uk
Total Pitches: 150 (C, CV & T)

Kits Coty Glamping
84 Collingwood Road,
Kits Coty Estate, Aylesford
ME20 7ER
Tel: 01634 685862   **38 B9**
kitscotyglamping.co.uk
Total Pitches: 4 (T)

Kneps Farm Holiday Park
River Road, Stanah,
Thornton-Cleveleys,
Blackpool
FY5 5LR
Tel: 01253 823632   **88 D2**
knepsfarm.co.uk
Total Pitches: 40 (C & CV)

**Knight Stainforth Hall
Caravan & Campsite**
Stainforth, Settle
BD24 0DP
Tel: 01729 822200   **96 B7**
knightstainforth.co.uk
Total Pitches: 100 (C, CV & T)

**Ladycross Plantation
Caravan Park**
Egton, Whitby
YO21 1UA
Tel: 01947 895502   **105 M9**
ladycrossplantation.co.uk
Total Pitches: 130 (C, CV & T)

Lady's Mile Holiday Park
Dawlish, Devon
EX7 0LX
Tel: 01626 863411   **9 N9**
ladysmile.co.uk
Total Pitches: 570 (C, CV & T)

Lamb Cottage Caravan Park
Dalefords Lane, Whitegate,
Northwich
CW8 2BN
Tel: 01606 882302   **82 D11**
lambcottage.co.uk
Total Pitches: 45 (C & CV)

Langstone Manor C & C Park
Moortown, Tavistock
PL19 9JZ
Tel: 01822 613371   **6 E4**
langstone-manor.co.uk
Total Pitches: 40 (C, CV & T)

Lanyon Holiday Park
Loscombe Lane, Four Lanes,
Redruth
TR16 6LP
Tel: 01209 313474   **2 H6**
lanyonholidaypark.co.uk
Total Pitches: 25 (C, CV & T)

Lebberston Touring Park
Filey Road, Lebberston,
Scarborough
YO11 3PE
Tel: 01723 585723   **99 M4**
lebberstontouring.co.uk
Total Pitches: 125 (C & CV)

Lee Valley Campsite
Sewardstone Road,
Chingford,
London
E4 7RA
Tel: 020 8529 5689   **51 J11**
visitleevalley.org.uk/wheretostay
Total Pitches: 81 (C, CV & T)

Lickpenny Caravan Site
Lickpenny Lane, Tansley,
Matlock
DE4 5GF
Tel: 01629 583040   **84 D9**
lickpennycaravanpark.co.uk
Total Pitches: 80 (C & CV)

Lime Tree Park
Dukes Drive, Buxton
SK17 9RP
Tel: 01298 22988   **83 N10**
limetreeparkbuxton.com
Total Pitches: 106 (C, CV & T)

**Lincoln Farm Park
Oxfordshire**
High Street,
Standlake
OX29 7RH
Tel: 01865 300239   **34 C4**
lincolnfarmpark.co.uk
Total Pitches: 90 (C, CV & T)

Long Acres Touring Park
Station Road, Old Leake,
Boston
PE22 9RF
Tel: 01205 871555   **87 L10**
long-acres.co.uk
Total Pitches: 40 (C, CV & T)

Longnor Wood Holiday Park
Newtown, Longnor,
Nr Buxton
SK17 0NG
Tel: 01298 83648   **71 K2**
longnorwood.co.uk
Total Pitches: 47 (C, CV & T)

Lower Polladras Touring Park
Carleen, Breage, Helston
TR13 9NX
Tel: 01736 762220   **2 G7**
lower-polladras.co.uk
Total Pitches: 39 (C, CV & T)

Lowther Holiday Park
Eamont Bridge, Penrith
CA10 2JB
Tel: 01768 863531   **101 P5**
lowther-holidaypark.co.uk
Total Pitches: 180 (C, CV & T)

Manor Farm Holiday Centre
Charmouth, Bridport
DT6 6QL
Tel: 01297 560226   **10 H6**
manorfarmholidaycentre.co.uk
Total Pitches: 400 (C, CV & T)

**Manor Wood Country
Caravan Park**
Manor Wood, Coddington,
Chester
CH3 9EN
Tel: 01829 782990   **69 N3**
cheshire-caravan-sites.co.uk
Total Pitches: 45 (C, CV & T)

Mayfield Park
Cheltenham Road, Cirencester
GL7 7BH
Tel: 01285 831301   **33 K3**
mayfieldpark.co.uk
Total Pitches: 105 (C, CV & T)

Meadowbank Holidays
Stour Way, Christchurch
BH23 2PQ
Tel: 01202 483597   **13 K6**
meadowbank-holidays.co.uk
Total Pitches: 41 (C & CV)

Middlewick Farm
Wick Lane, Glastonbury
BA6 8JW
Tel: 01458 832351   **19 P7**
middlewickholidaycottages.co.uk
Total Pitches: 3 (T)

**Middlewood Farm
Holiday Park**
Middlewood Lane, Fylingthorpe,
Robin Hood's Bay, Whitby
YO22 4UF
Tel: 01947 880414   **105 P10**
middlewoodfarm.com
Total Pitches: 100 (C, CV & T)

Minnows Touring Park
Holbrook Lane,
Sampford Peverell
EX16 7EN
Tel: 01884 821770   **18 D11**
minnowstouringpark.co.uk
Total Pitches: 59 (C, CV & T)

Moon & Sixpence
Newbourn Road, Waldringfield,
Woodbridge
IP12 4PP
Tel: 01473 736650   **53 N2**
moonandsixpence.eu
Total Pitches: 50 (C & CV)

Moor Lodge Park
Blackmoor Lane, Bardsey, Leeds
LS17 9DZ
Tel: 01937 572424   **91 K2**
moorlodgecaravanpark.co.uk
Total Pitches: 12 (C & CV)

Moss Wood Caravan Park
Crimbles Lane, Cockerham
LA2 0ES
Tel: 01524 791041   **95 K11**
mosswood.co.uk
Total Pitches: 25 (C, CV & T)

Naburn Lock Caravan Park
Naburn
YO19 4RU
Tel: 01904 728697   **98 C11**
naburnlock.co.uk
Total Pitches: 100 (C, CV & T)

New Lodge Farm C & C Site
New Lodge Farm,
Bulwick, Corby
NN17 3DU
Tel: 01780 450493   **73 P11**
newlodgefarm.com
Total Pitches: 72 (C, CV & T)

Newberry Valley Park
Woodlands,
Combe Martin
EX34 0AT
Tel: 01271 882334   **17 K2**
newberryvalleypark.co.uk
Total Pitches: 110 (C, CV & T)

Newlands Holidays
Charmouth, Bridport
DT6 6RB
Tel: 01297 560259   **10 H6**
newlandsholidays.co.uk
Total Pitches: 240 (C, CV & T)

Newperran Holiday Park
Rejerrah,
Newquay
TR8 5QJ
Tel: 01872 572407   **3 K3**
newperran.co.uk
Total Pitches: 357 (C, CV & T)

Ninham Country Holidays
Ninham, Shanklin,
Isle of Wight
PO37 7PL
Tel: 01983 864243   **14 G10**
ninham-holidays.co.uk
Total Pitches: 135 (C, CV & T)

North Morte Farm C & C Park
North Morte Road, Mortehoe,
Woolacombe
EX34 7EG
Tel: 01271 870381   **16 H2**
northmortefarm.co.uk
Total Pitches: 180 (C, CV & T)

**Northam Farm Caravan &
Touring Park**
Brean,
Burnham-on-Sea
TA8 2SE
Tel: 01278 751244   **19 K3**
northamfarm.co.uk
Total Pitches: 350 (C, CV & T)

**Oakdown Country
Holiday Park**
Gatedown Lane, Weston,
Sidmouth
EX10 0PT
Tel: 01297 680387   **10 D6**
oakdown.co.uk
Total Pitches: 150 (C, CV & T)

Old Hall Caravan Park
Capernwray, Carnforth
LA6 1AD
Tel: 01524 733276   **95 L6**
oldhallcaravanpark.co.uk
Total Pitches: 38 (C & CV)

Orchard Park
Frampton Lane,
Hubbert's Bridge, Boston
PE20 3QU
Tel: 01205 290328   **74 E2**
orchardpark.co.uk
Total Pitches: 87 (C, CV & T)

Ord House Country Park
East Ord,
Berwick-upon-Tweed
TD15 2NS
Tel: 01289 305288   **129 P9**
ordhouse.co.uk
Total Pitches: 79 (C, CV & T)

Oxon Hall Touring Park
Welshpool Road,
Shrewsbury
SY3 5FB
Tel: 01743 340868   **56 H2**
morris-leisure.co.uk
Total Pitches: 105 (C, CV & T)

Padstow Touring Park
Padstow
PL28 8LE
Tel: 01841 532061   **4 E7**
padstowtouringpark.co.uk
Total Pitches: 150 (C, CV & T)

Park Cliffe C & C Estate
Birks Road, Tower Wood,
Windermere
LA23 3PG
Tel: 015395 31344   **94 H2**
parkcliffe.co.uk
Total Pitches: 60 (C, CV & T)

Parkers Farm Holiday Park
Higher Mead Farm,
Ashburton, Devon
TQ13 7LJ
Tel: 01364 654869   **7 K4**
parkersfarmholidays.co.uk
Total Pitches: 100 (C, CV & T)

Parkland C & C Site
Sorley Green Cross,
Kingsbridge
TQ7 4AF
Tel: 01548 852723   **7 J9**
parklandsite.co.uk
Total Pitches: 50 (C, CV & T)

Penrose Holiday Park
Goonhavern, Truro
TR4 9QF
Tel: 01872 573185   **3 K3**
penroseholidaypark.com
Total Pitches: 110 (C, CV & T)

Pentire Haven Holiday Park
Stibb Road,
Kilkhampton,
Bude
EX23 9QY
Tel: 01288 321601   **16 C9**
pentirehaven.co.uk
Total Pitches: 120 (C, CV & T)

Petwood Caravan Park
Off Stixwould Road,
Woodhall Spa
LN10 6QH
Tel: 01526 354799 **86 G8**
petwoodcaravanpark.com
Total Pitches: 98 (C, CV & T)

Polmanter Touring Park
Halsetown,
St Ives
TR26 3LX
Tel: 01736 795640 **2 E6**
polmanter.co.uk
Total Pitches: 270 (C, CV & T)

Porlock Caravan Park
Porlock, Minehead
TA24 8ND
Tel: 01643 862269 **18 A5**
porlockcaravanpark.co.uk
Total Pitches: 40 (C, CV & T)

Porthtowan Tourist Park
Mile Hill, Porthtowan, Truro
TR4 8TY
Tel: 01209 890256 **2 H4**
porthtowantouristpark.co.uk
Total Pitches: 80 (C, CV & T)

**Quantock Orchard
Caravan Park**
Flaxpool, Crowcombe, Taunton
TA4 4AW
Tel: 01984 618618 **18 F7**
quantock-orchard.co.uk
Total Pitches: 60 (C, CV & T)

Ranch Caravan Park
Station Road, Honeybourne,
Evesham
WR11 7PR
Tel: 01386 830744 **47 M6**
ranch.co.uk
Total Pitches: 120 (C & CV)

Riddings Wood C & C Park
Bullock Lane, Riddings,
Alfreton
DE55 4BP
Tel: 01773 605160 **84 F10**
riddingswoodcaravanand
campingpark.co.uk
Total Pitches: 75 (C, CV & T)

Ripley Caravan Park
Knaresborough Road, Ripley,
Harrogate
HG3 3AU
Tel: 01423 770050 **97 L8**
ripleycaravanpark.com
Total Pitches: 60 (C, CV & T)

River Dart Country Park
Holne Park, Ashburton
TQ13 7NP
Tel: 01364 652511 **7 J5**
riverdart.co.uk
Total Pitches: 170 (C, CV & T)

River Valley Holiday Park
London Apprentice,
St Austell
PL26 7AP
Tel: 01726 73533 **3 Q3**
rivervalleyholidaypark.co.uk
Total Pitches: 45 (C, CV & T)

Riverside C & C Park
Marsh Lane,
North Molton Road,
South Molton
EX36 3HQ
Tel: 01769 579269 **17 N6**
exmoorriverside.co.uk
Total Pitches: 58 (C, CV & T)

Riverside Caravan Park
High Bentham,
Lancaster
LA2 7FJ
Tel: 015242 61272 **95 P7**
riversidecaravanpark.co.uk
Total Pitches: 61 (C & CV)

Riverside Caravan Park
Leigham Manor Drive,
Marsh Mills,
Plymouth
PL6 8LL
Tel: 01752 344122 **6 E7**
riversidecaravanpark.com
Total Pitches: 259 (C, CV & T)

**Riverside Meadows Country
Caravan Park**
Ure Bank Top, Ripon
HG4 1JD
Tel: 01765 602964 **97 M6**
flowerofmay.com
Total Pitches: 80 (C, CV & T)

Robin Hood C & C Park
Green Dyke Lane,
Slingsby
YO62 4AP
Tel: 01653 628391 **98 E6**
robinhoodcaravan.co.uk
Total Pitches: 32 (C, CV & T)

**Rose Farm Touring &
Camping Park**
Stepshort, Belton,
Nr Great Yarmouth
NR31 9JS
Tel: 01493 780896 **77 P11**
rosefarmtouring.co.uk
Total Pitches: 145 (C, CV & T)

Rosedale C & C Park
Rosedale Abbey,
Pickering
YO18 8SA
Tel: 01751 417272 **105 K11**
flowerofmay.com
Total Pitches: 100 (C, CV & T)

Ross Park
Park Hill Farm, Ipplepen,
Newton Abbot
TQ12 5TT
Tel: 01803 812983 **7 L5**
rossparkcaravanpark.co.uk
Total Pitches: 110 (C, CV & T)

Rudding Holiday Park
Follifoot,
Harrogate
HG3 1JH
Tel: 01423 870439 **97 M10**
ruddingholidaypark.co.uk
Total Pitches: 86 (C, CV & T)

Run Cottage Touring Park
Alderton Road, Hollesley,
Woodbridge
IP12 3RQ
Tel: 01394 411309 **53 Q3**
runcottage.co.uk
Total Pitches: 45 (C, CV & T)

Rutland C & C
Park Lane, Greetham,
Oakham
LE15 7FN
Tel: 01572 813520 **73 N8**
rutlandcaravanandcamping.co.uk
Total Pitches: 130 (C, CV & T)

St Helens Caravan Park
Wykeham, Scarborough
YO13 9QD
Tel: 01723 862771 **99 K4**
sthelenscaravanpark.co.uk
Total Pitches: 250 (C, CV & T)

St Mabyn Holiday Park
Longstone Road, St Mabyn,
Wadebridge
PL30 3BY
Tel: 01208 841677 **4 H7**
stmabynholidaypark.co.uk
Total Pitches: 120 (C, CV & T)

Sandy Balls Holiday Village
Sandy Balls Estate Ltd, Godshill,
Fordingbridge
SP6 2JZ
Tel: 0844 693 1336 **13 L2**
sandyballs.co.uk
Total Pitches: 225 (C, CV & T)

**Seaview International
Holiday Park**
Boswinger,
Mevagissey
PL26 6LL
Tel: 01726 843425 **3 P5**
seaviewinternational.com
Total Pitches: 201 (C, CV & T)

Severn Gorge Park
Bridgnorth Road, Tweedale,
Telford
TF7 4JB
Tel: 01952 684789 **57 N3**
severngorgepark.co.uk
Total Pitches: 12 (C & CV)

Shamba Holidays
East Moors Lane, St Leonards,
Ringwood
BH24 2SB
Tel: 01202 873302 **13 K4**
shambaholidays.co.uk
Total Pitches: 150 (C, CV & T)

Shrubbery Touring Park
Rousdon,
Lyme Regis
DT7 3XW
Tel: 01297 442227 **10 F6**
shrubberypark.co.uk
Total Pitches: 120 (C, CV & T)

Silverbow Park
Perranwell, Goonhavern
TR4 9NX
Tel: 01872 572347 **3 K3**
silverbowpark.co.uk
Total Pitches: 90 (C, CV & T)

Silverdale Caravan Park
Middlebarrow Plain, Cove Road,
Silverdale, Nr Carnforth
LA5 0SH
Tel: 01524 701508 **95 K5**
holgates.co.uk
Total Pitches: 80 (C, CV & T)

Skelwith Fold Caravan Park
Ambleside, Cumbria
LA22 0HX
Tel: 015394 32277 **101 L10**
skelwith.com
Total Pitches: 150 (C & CV)

Somers Wood Caravan Park
Somers Road, Meriden
CV7 7PL
Tel: 01676 522978 **59 K8**
somerswood.co.uk
Total Pitches: 48 (C & CV)

**South Lytchett Manor
C & C Park**
Dorchester Road,
Lytchett Minster, Poole
BH16 6JB
Tel: 01202 622577 **12 G6**
southlytchettmanor.co.uk
Total Pitches: 150 (C, CV & T)

South Meadows Caravan Park
South Road, Belford
NE70 7DP
Tel: 01668 213326 **119 M4**
southmeadows.co.uk
Total Pitches: 83 (C, CV & T)

Stanmore Hall Touring Park
Stourbridge Road,
Bridgnorth
WV15 6DT
Tel: 01746 761761 **57 N6**
morris-leisure.co.uk
Total Pitches: 129 (C, CV & T)

Stowford Farm Meadows
Berry Down,
Combe Martin
EX34 0PW
Tel: 01271 882476 **17 K3**
stowford.co.uk
Total Pitches: 700 (C, CV & T)

Stroud Hill Park
Fen Road, Pidley,
St Ives
PE28 3DE
Tel: 01487 741333 **62 D5**
stroudhillpark.co.uk
Total Pitches: 60 (C, CV & T)

**Sumners Ponds Fishery &
Campsite**
Chapel Road, Barns Green,
Horsham
RH13 0PR
Tel: 01403 732539 **24 D5**
sumnersponds.co.uk
Total Pitches: 86 (C, CV & T)

Sun Valley Resort
Pentewan Road, St Austell
PL26 6DJ
Tel: 01726 843266 **3 Q4**
sunvalleyresort.co.uk
Total Pitches: 29 (C, CV & T)

**Swiss Farm Touring &
Camping**
Marlow Road,
Henley-on-Thames
RG9 2HY
Tel: 01491 573419 **35 L8**
swissfarmcamping.co.uk
Total Pitches: 140 (C, CV & T)

**Tanner Farm Touring
C & C Park**
Tanner Farm, Goudhurst Road,
Marden
TN12 9ND
Tel: 01622 832399 **26 B3**
tannerfarmpark.co.uk
Total Pitches: 120 (C, CV & T)

Tattershall Lakes Country Park
Sleaford Road,
Tattershall
LN4 4LR
Tel: 01526 348800 **86 H9**
tattershall-lakes.com
Total Pitches: 186 (C, CV & T)

Tehidy Holiday Park
Harris Mill, Illogan,
Portreath
TR16 4JQ
Tel: 01209 216489 **2 H5**
tehidy.co.uk
Total Pitches: 18 (C, CV & T)

Teversal C & C Club Site
Silverhill Lane, Teversal
NG17 3JJ
Tel: 01623 551838 **84 G8**
campingandcaravanningclub.co.uk/
teversal
Total Pitches: 126 (C, CV & T)

The Inside Park
Down House Estate,
Blandford Forum
DT11 9AD
Tel: 01258 453719 **12 E4**
theinsidepark.co.uk
Total Pitches: 125 (C, CV & T)

The Laurels Holiday Park
Padstow Road, Whitecross,
Wadebridge
PL27 7JQ
Tel: 01209 313474 **4 F7**
thelaurelsholidaypark.co.uk
Total Pitches: 30 (C, CV & T)

The Old Brick Kilns
Little Barney Lane, Barney,
Fakenham
NR21 0NL
Tel: 01328 878305 **76 E5**
old-brick-kilns.co.uk
Total Pitches: 65 (C, CV & T)

The Old Oaks Touring Park
Wick Farm, Wick, Glastonbury
BA6 8JS
Tel: 01458 831437 **19 P7**
theoldoaks.co.uk
Total Pitches: 98 (C, CV & T)

**The Orchards Holiday
Caravan Park**
Main Road, Newbridge,
Yarmouth,
Isle of Wight
PO41 0TS
Tel: 01983 531331 **14 D9**
orchards-holiday-park.co.uk
Total Pitches: 160 (C, CV & T)

The Quiet Site
Ullswater, Watermillock
CA11 0LS
Tel: 07768 727016 **101 M6**
thequietsite.co.uk
Total Pitches: 100 (C, CV & T)

The Ranch Caravan Park
Cliffe Common, Selby
YO8 6PA
Tel: 01757 638984 **91 R4**
theranchcaravanpark.co.uk
Total Pitches: 44 (C, CV & T)

Treago Farm Caravan Site
Crantock, Newquay
TR8 5QS
Tel: 01637 830277 **4 B9**
treagofarm.co.uk
Total Pitches: 90 (C, CV & T)

Tregoad Park
St Martin, Looe
PL13 1PB
Tel: 01503 262718 **5 M10**
tregoadpark.co.uk
Total Pitches: 200 (C, CV & T)

Treloy Touring Park
Newquay
TR8 4JN
Tel: 01637 872063 **4 D9**
treloy.co.uk
Total Pitches: 223 (C, CV & T)

Trencreek Holiday Park
Hillcrest, Higher Trencreek,
Newquay
TR8 4NS
Tel: 01637 874210 **4 C9**
trencreekholidaypark.co.uk
Total Pitches: 194 (C, CV & T)

Trethem Mill Touring Park
St Just-in-Roseland,
Nr St Mawes, Truro
TR2 5JF
Tel: 01872 580504 **3 M6**
trethem.com
Total Pitches: 84 (C, CV & T)

Trevalgan Touring Park
Trevalgan, St Ives
TR26 3BJ
Tel: 01736 791892 **2 D6**
trevalgantouringpark.co.uk
Total Pitches: 135 (C, CV & T)

Trevella Park
Crantock, Newquay
TR8 5EW
Tel: 01637 830308 **4 C10**
trevella.co.uk
Total Pitches: 165 (C, CV & T)

Trevornick
Holywell Bay, Newquay
TR8 5PW
Tel: 01637 830531 **4 B10**
trevornick.co.uk
Total Pitches: 688 (C, CV & T)

Truro C & C Park
Truro
TR4 8QN
Tel: 01872 560274 **3 K4**
trurocaravanandcampingpark.co.uk
Total Pitches: 51 (C, CV & T)

Tudor C & C
Shepherds Patch, Slimbridge,
Gloucester
GL2 7BP
Tel: 01453 890483 **32 D4**
tudorcaravanpark.com
Total Pitches: 75 (C, CV & T)

Two Mills Touring Park
Yarmouth Road,
North Walsham
NR28 9NA
Tel: 01692 405829 **77 K6**
twomills.co.uk
Total Pitches: 81 (C, CV & T)

Ulwell Cottage Caravan Park
Ulwell Cottage, Ulwell,
Swanage
BH19 3DG
Tel: 01929 422823 **12 H8**
ulwellcottagepark.co.uk
Total Pitches: 77 (C, CV & T)

Vale of Pickering Caravan Park
Carr House Farm, Allerston,
Pickering
YO18 7PQ
Tel: 01723 859280 **98 H4**
valeofpickering.co.uk
Total Pitches: 120 (C, CV & T)

Wagtail Country Park
Cliff Lane, Marston,
Grantham
NG32 2HU
Tel: 01400 251955 **73 M2**
wagtailcountrypark.co.uk
Total Pitches: 76 (C & CV)

Warcombe Farm C & C Park
Station Road, Mortehoe,
Woolacombe
EX34 7EJ
Tel: 01271 870690 **16 H2**
warcombefarm.co.uk
Total Pitches: 250 (C, CV & T)

Wareham Forest Tourist Park
North Trigon,
Wareham
BH20 7NZ
Tel: 01929 551393 **12 E6**
warehamforest.co.uk
Total Pitches: 200 (C, CV & T)

Waren C & C Park
Waren Mill, Bamburgh
NE70 7EE
Tel: 01668 214366 **119 N4**
meadowhead.co.uk
Total Pitches: 150 (C, CV & T)

Watergate Bay Touring Park
Watergate Bay,
Tregurrian
TR8 4AD
Tel: 01637 860387 **4 D8**
watergatebaytouringpark.co.uk
Total Pitches: 171 (C, CV & T)

Waterrow Touring Park
Wiveliscombe,
Taunton
TA4 2AZ
Tel: 01984 623464 **18 E9**
waterrowpark.co.uk
Total Pitches: 44 (C, CV & T)

Wayfarers C & C Park
Relubbus Lane, St Hilary,
Penzance
TR20 9EF
Tel: 01736 763326 **2 F7**
wayfarerspark.co.uk
Total Pitches: 32 (C, CV & T)

Wells Touring Park
Haybridge,
Wells
BA5 1AJ
Tel: 01749 676869 **19 P5**
wellstouringpark.co.uk
Total Pitches: 72 (C, CV & T)

Wheathill Touring Park
Wheathill,
Bridgnorth
WV16 6QT
Tel: 01584 823456 **57 L8**
wheathillpark.co.uk
Total Pitches: 25 (C & CV)

Whitefield Forest Touring Park
Brading Road, Ryde,
Isle of Wight
PO33 1QL
Tel: 01983 617069 **14 H9**
whitefieldforest.co.uk
Total Pitches: 90 (C, CV & T)

**Widdicombe Farm
Touring Park**
Marldon, Paignton
TQ3 1ST
Tel: 01803 558325 **7 M6**
widdicombefarm.co.uk
Total Pitches: 180 (C, CV & T)

Widemouth Fields C & C Park
Park Farm, Poundstock,
Bude
EX23 0NA
Tel: 01288 361351 **16 C11**
peterbullresorts.co.uk/
widemouth-fields
Total Pitches: 156 (C, CV & T)

Wight Glamping Holidays
Iverland, Long Lane,
Newport,
Isle of Wight
PO30 2NW
Tel: 01983 532507 **14 F9**
wightglampingholidays.co.uk
Total Pitches: 4 (T)

Wild Rose Park
Ormside,
Appleby-in-Westmorland
CA16 6EJ
Tel: 017683 51077 **102 C7**
harrisonholidayhomes.co.uk
Total Pitches: 226 (C & CV)

**Wilksworth Farm
Caravan Park**
Cranborne Road,
Wimborne Minster
BH21 4HW
Tel: 01202 885467 **12 H4**
wilksworthfarmcaravanpark.co.uk
Total Pitches: 85 (C, CV & T)

**Willowbank Holiday Home &
Touring Park**
Coastal Road, Ainsdale,
Southport
PR8 3ST
Tel: 01704 571566 **88 C8**
willowbankcp.co.uk
Total Pitches: 87 (C & CV)

Wolds View Touring Park
115 Brigg Road,
Caistor
LN7 6RX
Tel: 01472 851099 **93 K10**
woldsviewtouringpark.co.uk
Total Pitches: 60 (C, CV & T)

Wood Farm C & C Park
Axminster Road,
Charmouth
DT6 6BT
Tel: 01297 560697 **10 H6**
woodfarm.co.uk
Total Pitches: 175 (C, CV & T)

Wooda Farm Holiday Park
Poughill,
Bude
EX23 9HJ
Tel: 01288 352069 **16 C10**
wooda.co.uk
Total Pitches: 200 (C, CV & T)

Woodclose Caravan Park
High Casterton,
Kirkby Lonsdale
LA6 2SE
Tel: 015242 71597 **95 N5**
woodclosepark.com
Total Pitches: 22 (C, CV & T)

Woodhall Country Park
Stixwold Road,
Woodhall Spa
LN10 6UJ
Tel: 01526 353710 **86 G8**
woodhallcountrypark.co.uk
Total Pitches: 115 (C, CV & T)

**Woodland Springs Adult
Touring Park**
Venton,
Drewsteignton
EX6 6PG
Tel: 01647 231695 **8 G6**
woodlandsprings.co.uk
Total Pitches: 81 (C, CV & T)

Woodlands Grove C & C Park
Blackawton,
Dartmouth
TQ9 7DQ
Tel: 01803 712598 **7 L8**
woodlands-caravanpark.com
Total Pitches: 350 (C, CV & T)

Woodovis Park
Gulworthy, Tavistock
PL19 8NY
Tel: 01822 832968 **6 C4**
woodovis.com
Total Pitches: 50 (C, CV & T)

**Yeatheridge Farm Caravan
Park**
East Worlington,
Crediton
EX17 4TN
Tel: 01884 860330 **9 J2**
yeatheridge.co.uk
Total Pitches: 103 (C, CV & T)

SCOTLAND

Aviemore Glamping
Eriskay,
Craignagower Avenue,
Aviemore
PH22 1RW
Tel: 01479 810717 **148 F5**
aviemoreglamping.com
Total Pitches: 4 (T)

Banff Links Caravan Park
Inverboyndie, Banff
AB45 2JJ
Tel: 01261 812228 **158 G5**
banfflinkscaravanpark.co.uk
Total Pitches: 55 (C, CV & T)

Beecraigs C & C Site
Beecraigs Country Park,
The Visitor Centre,
Linlithgow
EH49 6PL
Tel: 01506 844516 **127 J3**
beecraigs.co.uk
Total Pitches: 36 (C, CV & T)

Blair Castle Caravan Park
Blair Atholl, Pitlochry
PH18 5SR
Tel: 01796 481263 **141 L4**
blaircastlecaravanpark.co.uk
Total Pitches: 226 (C, CV & T)

Brighouse Bay Holiday Park
Brighouse Bay, Borgue,
Kirkcudbright
DG6 4TS
Tel: 01557 870267 **108 D11**
gillespie-leisure.co.uk
Total Pitches: 190 (C, CV & T)

Cairnsmill Holiday Park
Largo Road,
St Andrews
KY16 8NN
Tel: 01334 473604 **135 M5**
cairnsmill.co.uk
Total Pitches: 62 (C, CV & T)

**Craigtoun Meadows
Holiday Park**
Mount Melville,
St Andrews
KY16 8PQ
Tel: 01334 475959 **135 M4**
craigtounmeadows.co.uk
Total Pitches: 56 (C, CV & T)

Gart Caravan Park
The Gart, Callander
FK17 8LE
Tel: 01877 330002 **133 J6**
theholidaypark.co.uk
Total Pitches: 128 (C & CV)

Glen Nevis C & C Park
Glen Nevis, Fort William
PH33 6SX
Tel: 01397 702191 **139 L3**
glen-nevis.co.uk
Total Pitches: 380 (C, CV & T)

Glenearly Caravan Park
Dalbeattie
DG5 4NE
Tel: 01556 611393 **108 H8**
glenearlycaravanpark.co.uk
Total Pitches: 39 (C, CV & T)

Hoddom Castle Caravan Park
Hoddom, Lockerbie
DG11 1AS
Tel: 01576 300251 **110 C6**
hoddomcastle.co.uk
Total Pitches: 200 (C, CV & T)

Huntly Castle Caravan Park
The Meadow, Huntly
AB54 4UJ
Tel: 01466 794999 **158 D9**
huntlycastle.co.uk
Total Pitches: 90 (C, CV & T)

Linnhe Lochside Holidays
Corpach, Fort William
PH33 7NL
Tel: 01397 772376 **139 K2**
linnhe-lochside-holidays.co.uk
Total Pitches: 85 (C, CV & T)

Loch Ken Holiday Park
Parton, Castle Douglas
DG7 3NE
Tel: 01644 470282 **108 E6**
lochkenholidaypark.co.uk
Total Pitches: 40 (C, CV & T)

Loch Shin Wigwams
Forge Cottage, Achfrish,
Shinness, Lairg
IV27 4DN
Tel: 01549 402936 **162 D4**
wigwamholidays.com
Total Pitches: 2 (T)

Lomond Woods Holiday Park
Old Luss Road, Balloch,
Loch Lomond
G83 8QP
Tel: 01389 755000 **132 D11**
holiday-parks.co.uk
Total Pitches: 115 (C & CV)

Milton of Fonab Caravan Park
Bridge Road, Pitlochry
PH16 5NA
Tel: 01796 472882 **141 M6**
fonab.co.uk
Total Pitches: 154 (C, CV & T)

River Tilt Caravan Park
Blair Atholl, Pitlochry
PH18 5TE
Tel: 01796 481467 **141 L4**
rivertiltpark.co.uk
Total Pitches: 30 (C, CV & T)

Runach Arainn
The Old Manse, Kilmory,
Isle of Arran
KA27 8PH
Tel: 01770 870515 **121 J7**
runacharainn.com
Total Pitches: 3 (T)

Sands of Luce Holiday Park
Sands of Luce, Sandhead,
Stranraer
DG9 9JN
Tel: 01776 830456 **106 F7**
sandsofluceholidaypark.co.uk
Total Pitches: 80 (C, CV & T)

Seaward Caravan Park
Dhoon Bay, Kirkcudbright
DG6 4TJ
Tel: 01557 870267 **108 E11**
gillespie-leisure.co.uk
Total Pitches: 25 (C, CV & T)

Shieling Holidays
Craignure, Isle of Mull
PA65 6AY
Tel: 01680 812496 **138 C10**
shielingholidays.co.uk
Total Pitches: 90 (C, CV & T)

Silver Sands Holiday Park
Covesea, West Beach,
Lossiemouth
IV31 6SP
Tel: 01343 813262 **157 N3**
silver-sands.co.uk
Total Pitches: 140 (C, CV & T)

Skye C & C Club Site
Loch Greshornish, Borve,
Arnisort, Edinbane,
Isle of Skye
IV51 9PS
Tel: 01470 582230 **152 E7**
campingandcaravanningclub.co.uk/
skye
Total Pitches: 105 (C, CV & T)

Strathfillan Wigwam Village
Auchtertyre Farm, Tyndrum,
Crianlarich
FK20 8RU
Tel: 01838 400251 **132 D2**
wigwamholidays.com
Total Pitches: 23 (T)

Thurston Manor Leisure Park
Innerwick, Dunbar
EH42 1SA
Tel: 01368 840643 **129 J5**
thurstonmanor.co.uk
Total Pitches: 120 (C & CV)

Trossachs Holiday Park
Aberfoyle
FK8 3SA
Tel: 01877 382614 **132 G8**
trossachsholidays.co.uk
Total Pitches: 66 (C, CV & T)

Witches Craig C & C Park
Blairlogie, Stirling
FK9 5PX
Tel: 01786 474497 **133 N8**
witchescraig.co.uk
Total Pitches: 60 (C, CV & T)

WALES

**Bron Derw Touring
Caravan Park**
Llanrwst
LL26 0YT
Tel: 01492 640494 **67 P2**
bronderw-wales.co.uk
Total Pitches: 48 (C & CV)

Bron-Y-Wendon Caravan Park
Wern Road, Llanddulas,
Colwyn Bay
LL22 8HG
Tel: 01492 512903 **80 C9**
northwales-holidays.co.uk
Total Pitches: 130 (C & CV)

Bryn Gloch C & C Park
Betws Garmon,
Caernarfon
LL54 7YY
Tel: 01286 650216 **67 J3**
campwales.co.uk
Total Pitches: 160 (C, CV & T)

**Caerfai Bay Caravan &
Tent Park**
Caerfai Bay, St Davids,
Haverfordwest
SA62 6QT
Tel: 01437 720274 **40 E6**
caerfaibay.co.uk
Total Pitches: 106 (C, CV & T)

Cenarth Falls Holiday Park
Cenarth, Newcastle Emlyn
SA38 9JS
Tel: 01239 710345 **41 Q2**
cenarth-holipark.co.uk
Total Pitches: 30 (C, CV & T)

Daisy Bank Caravan Park
Snead, Montgomery
SY15 6EB
Tel: 01588 620471 **56 E6**
daisy-bank.co.uk
Total Pitches: 80 (C, CV & T)

**Deucoch Touring &
Camping Park**
Sarn Bach, Abersoch
LL53 7LD
Tel: 01758 713293 **66 E9**
deucoch.com
Total Pitches: 70 (C, CV & T)

Dinlle Caravan Park
Dinas Dinlle,
Caernarfon
LL54 5TW
Tel: 01286 830324 **66 G3**
thornleyleisure.co.uk
Total Pitches: 175 (C, CV & T)

Eisteddfa
Eisteddfa Lodge, Pentrefelin,
Criccieth
LL52 0PT
Tel: 01766 522696 **67 J7**
eisteddfapark.co.uk
Total Pitches: 100 (C, CV & T)

Erwlon C & C Park
Brecon Road, Llandovery
SA20 0RD
Tel: 01550 721021 **43 Q8**
erwlon.co.uk
Total Pitches: 75 (C, CV & T)

Fforest Fields C & C Park
Hundred House, Builth Wells
LD1 5RT
Tel: 01982 570406 **44 G4**
fforestfields.co.uk
Total Pitches: 120 (C, CV & T)

**Hendre Mynach Touring
C & C Park**
Llanaber Road, Barmouth
LL42 1YR
Tel: 01341 280262 **67 L11**
hendremynach.co.uk
Total Pitches: 240 (C, CV & T)

Home Farm Caravan Park
Marian-Glas,
Isle of Anglesey
LL73 8PH
Tel: 01248 410614 **78 H8**
homefarm-anglesey.co.uk
Total Pitches: 102 (C, CV & T)

Islawrffordd Caravan Park
Tal-y-bont, Barmouth
LL43 2AQ
Tel: 01341 247269 **67 K10**
islawrffordd.co.uk
Total Pitches: 105 (C, CV & T)

Llys Derwen C & C Site
Ffordd Bryngwyn, Llanrug,
Caernarfon
LL55 4RD
Tel: 01286 673322 **67 J2**
llysderwen.co.uk
Total Pitches: 20 (C, CV & T)

Moelfryn C & C Park
Ty-Cefn, Pant-y-Bwlch,
Newcastle Emlyn
SA38 9JE
Tel: 01559 371231 **42 F7**
moelfryncaravanpark.co.uk
Total Pitches: 25 (C, CV & T)

Pencelli Castle C & C Park
Pencelli, Brecon
LD3 7LX
Tel: 01874 665451 **44 F10**
pencelli-castle.com
Total Pitches: 80 (C, CV & T)

Penhein Glamping
Penhein, Llanvair Discoed,
Chepstow
NP16 6RB
Tel: 01633 400581 **31 N6**
penhein.co.uk
Total Pitches: 6 (T)

Penisar Mynydd Caravan Park
Caerwys Road, Rhuallt, St Asaph
LL17 0TY
Tel: 01745 582227 **80 F9**
penisarmynydd.co.uk
Total Pitches: 71 (C, CV & T)

Plas Farm Caravan Park
Betws-yn-Rhos, Abergele
LL22 8AU
Tel: 01492 680254 **80 B10**
plasfarmcaravanpark.co.uk
Total Pitches: 54 (C, CV & T)

Plassey Holiday Park
The Plassey, Eyton, Wrexham
LL13 0SP
Tel: 01978 780277 **69 L5**
plassey.com
Total Pitches: 90 (C, CV & T)

Pont Kemys C & C Park
Chainbridge, Abergavenny
NP7 9DS
Tel: 01873 880688 **31 K3**
pontkemys.com
Total Pitches: 65 (C, CV & T)

Red Kite Touring Park
Van Road, Llanidloes
SY18 6NG
Tel: 01686 412122 **55 L7**
redkitetouringpark.co.uk
Total Pitches: 66 (C & CV)

River View Touring Park
The Dingle, Llanedi,
Pontarddulais
SA4 0FH
Tel: 01635 844876 **28 G3**
riverviewtouringpark.com
Total Pitches: 60 (C, CV & T)

Riverside Camping
Seiont Nurseries, Pont Rug,
Caernarfon
LL55 2BB
Tel: 01286 678781 **67 J2**
riversidecamping.co.uk
Total Pitches: 73 (C, CV & T)

St David's Park
Red Wharf Bay, Pentraeth,
Isle of Anglesey
LL75 8RJ
Tel: 01248 852341 **79 J8**
stdavidspark.com
Total Pitches: 45 (C, CV & T)

The Little Yurt Meadow
Bay Tree Barns, Mill Road,
Bronington
SY13 3HJ
Tel: 01948 780136 **69 N7**
thelittleyurtmeadow.co.uk
Total Pitches: 3 (T)

Trawsdir Touring C & C Park
Llanaber, Barmouth
LL42 1RR
Tel: 01341 280999 **67 K11**
barmouthholidays.co.uk
Total Pitches: 70 (C, CV & T)

Trefalun Park
Devonshire Drive, St Florence,
Tenby
SA70 8RD
Tel: 01646 651514 **41 L10**
trefalunpark.co.uk
Total Pitches: 90 (C, CV & T)

Tyddyn Isaf Caravan Park
Lligwy Bay, Dulas,
Isle of Anglesey
LL70 9PQ
Tel: 01248 410203 **78 H7**
tyddynisaf.co.uk
Total Pitches: 80 (C, CV & T)

White Tower Caravan Park
Llandwrog, Caernarfon
LL54 5UH
Tel: 01286 830649 **66 H3**
whitetowerpark.co.uk
Total Pitches: 52 (C & CV)

CHANNEL ISLANDS

Beuvelande Camp Site
Beuvelande, St Martin,
Jersey
JE3 6EZ
Tel: 01534 853575 **11 c1**
campingjersey.com
Total Pitches: 150 (C, CV & T)

Durrell Wildlife Camp
Les Augres Manor, La Profonde
Rue, Trinity,
Jersey
JE3 5BP
Tel: 01534 860095 **11 c1**
durrell.org/camp
Total Pitches: 12 (T)

Fauxquets Valley Campsite
Castel,
Guernsey
GY5 7QL
Tel: 01481 255460 **10 b2**
fauxquets.co.uk
Total Pitches: 120 (CV & T)

Rozel Camping Park
Summerville Farm,
St Martin,
Jersey
JE3 6AX
Tel: 01534 855200 **11 c1**
rozelcamping.com
Total Pitches: 100 (C, CV & T)

Signs giving orders

**Signs with red circles are mostly prohibitive.
Plates below signs qualify their message.**

Entry to
20mph zone

End of
20mph zone

Maximum
speed

National speed
limit applies

School crossing
patrol

Stop and
give way

Give way to
traffic on
major road

Manually operated temporary
STOP and GO signs

No entry for
vehicular traffic

No vehicles
except bicycles
being pushed

No cycling

No motor
vehicles

No buses
(over 8
passenger
seats)

No
overtaking

No
towed
caravans

No vehicles
carrying
explosives

No vehicle or
combination of
vehicles over
length shown

No vehicles
over
height shown

No vehicles
over
width shown

Give priority to
vehicles from
opposite
direction

No right turn

No left turn

No
U-turns

No goods vehicles
over maximum
gross weight
shown (in tonnes)
except for loading
and unloading

WEAK BRIDGE
No vehicles
over maximum
gross weight
shown
(in tonnes)

Permit
holders
only
Parking
restricted to
permit holders

RED ROUTE
No stopping during
period indicated
except for buses

URBAN CLEARWAY
No stopping during
times shown
except for as long
as necessary to set
down or pick up
passengers

No waiting

No stopping
(Clearway)

**Signs with blue circles but no red border mostly give
positive instruction.**

Ahead only

Turn left ahead
(right if symbol
reversed)

Turn left
(right if symbol
reversed)

Keep left
(right if symbol
reversed)

Vehicles may
pass either
side to reach
same
destination

Mini-roundabout
(roundabout
circulation – give
way to vehicles
from the
immediate right)

Route to be
used by pedal
cycles only

Segregated
pedal cycle
and pedestrian
route

Minimum speed

End of minimum
speed

Buses and
cycles only

Trams only

Pedestrian
crossing
point over
tramway

One-way traffic
(note: compare
circular 'Ahead
only' sign)

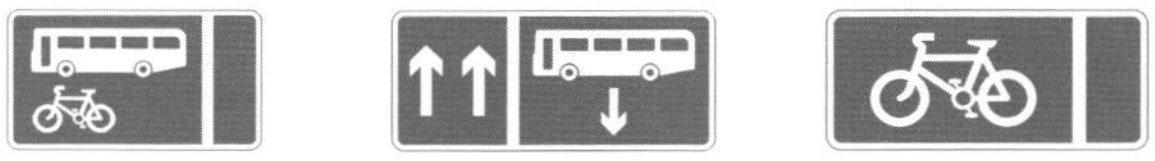

With-flow bus and
cycle lane

Contraflow bus lane

With-flow pedal cycle lane

Warning signs

Mostly triangular

Distance to
'STOP' line
ahead

Dual
carriageway
ends

Road narrows on
right (left if
symbol reversed)

Road
narrows on
both sides

Distance to
'Give Way'
line ahead

Crossroads

Junction on
bend ahead

T-junction with
priority over
vehicles from
the right

Staggered
junction

Traffic merging
from left ahead

The priority through route is indicated by the broader line.

Double bend first
to left (symbol
may be reversed)

Bend to right
(or left if symbol
reversed)

Roundabout

Uneven road

REDUCE
SPEED
NOW
Plate below
some signs

Two-way
traffic crosses
one-way road

Two-way traffic
straight ahead

Opening or
swing bridge
ahead

Low-flying aircraft
or sudden
aircraft noise

Falling or
fallen rocks

Traffic signals
not in use

Traffic signals

Slippery road

Steep hill
downwards

Steep hill
upwards

Gradients may be shown as a ratio i.e. 20% = 1

Tunnel ahead

Trams crossing ahead

Level crossing with barrier or gate ahead

Level crossing without barrier or gate ahead

Level crossing without barrier

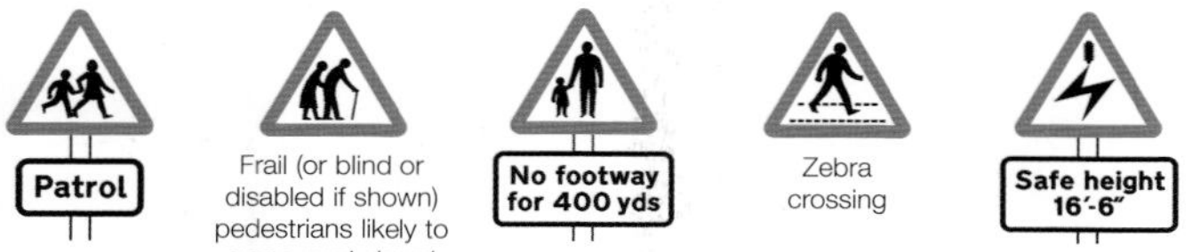
Patrol
No footway for 400 yds
Safe height 16'-6"

chool crossing patrol ahead (some signs have amber hts which flash hen crossings are in use)

Frail (or blind or disabled if shown) pedestrians likely to cross road ahead

Pedestrians in road ahead

Zebra crossing

Overhead electric cable; plate indicates maximum height of vehicles which can pass safely

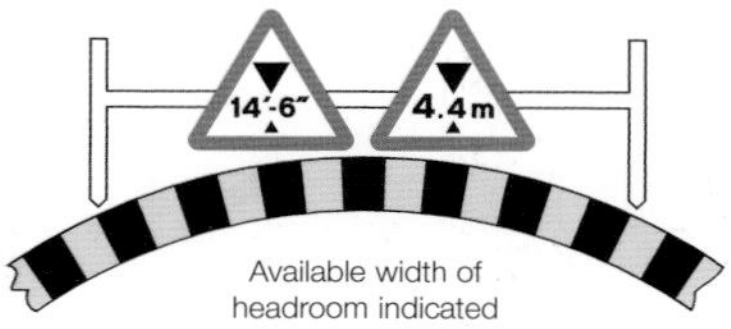
14'-6"
4.4 m

Available width of headroom indicated

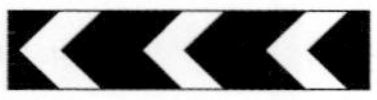

Sharp deviation of route to left (or right if chevrons reversed)

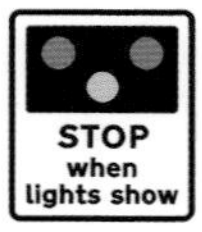
STOP
when
lights show

Light signals ahead at level crossing, airfield or bridge

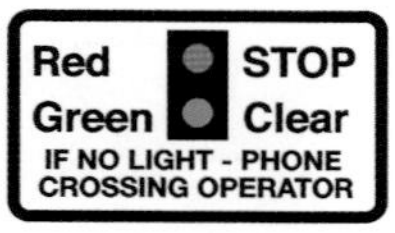
Red
STOP
Green
Clear
IF NO LIGHT - PHONE
CROSSING OPERATOR

Miniature warning lights at level crossings

Cattle

Wild animals

Wild horses or ponies

Accompanied horses or ponies

Cycle route ahead

Ice
Queues likely
Humps for ½ mile
Hidden dip
Soft verges for 2 miles

Risk of ice

Traffic queues likely ahead

Distance over which road humps extend

Other danger; plate indicates nature of danger

Soft verges

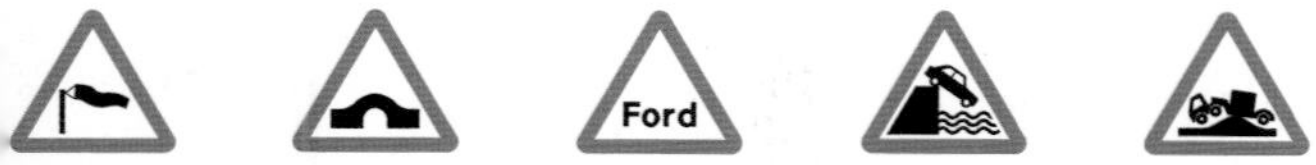
Ford

Side winds

Hump bridge

Worded warning sign

Quayside or river bank

Risk of grounding

Direction signs

Mostly rectangular

Signs on motorways – blue backgrounds

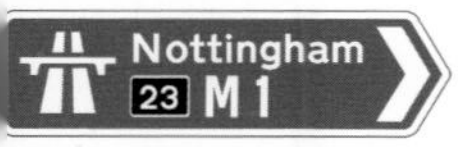
Nottingham
23 M1

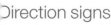

At a junction leading directly into a motorway (junction number may be shown on a black background)

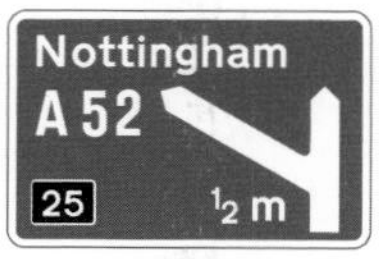
Nottingham
A 52
25
½ m

On approaches to junctions (junction number on black background)

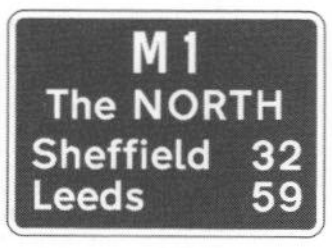
M1
The NORTH
Sheffield 32
Leeds 59

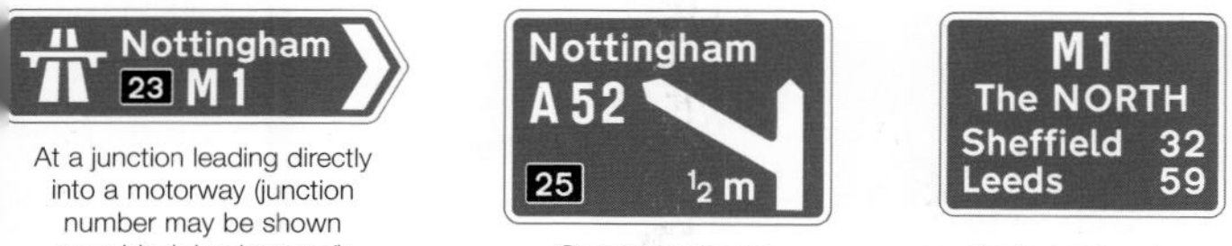

Route confirmatory sign after junction

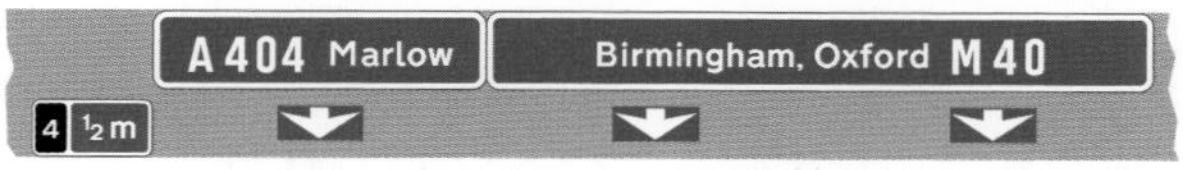
A404 Marlow
Birmingham, Oxford M40
4 ½ m

Downward pointing arrows mean 'Get in lane'
The left-hand lane leads to a different destination from the other lanes.

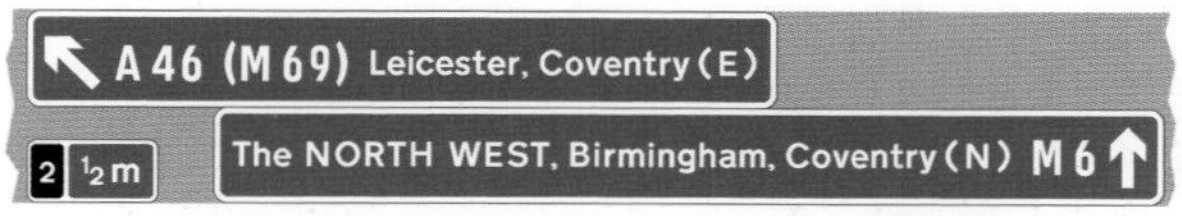
A46 (M69) Leicester, Coventry (E)
2 ½ m
The NORTH WEST, Birmingham, Coventry (N) M6

The panel with the inclined arrow indicates the destinations which can be reached by leaving the motorway at the next junction

Signs on primary routes - green backgrounds

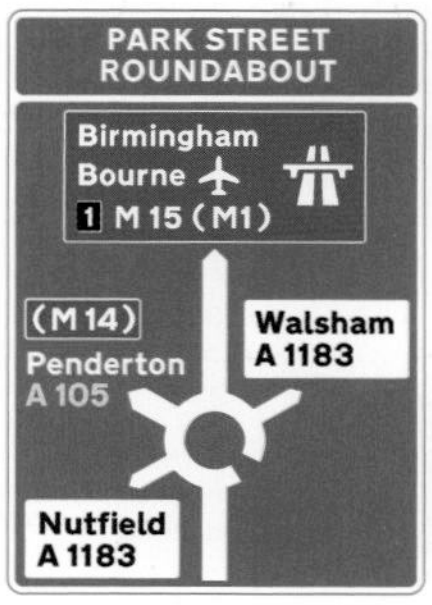
PARK STREET
ROUNDABOUT
Birmingham
Bourne
1 M 15 (M1)
(M14)
Penderton
A 105
Walsham
A 1183
Nutfield
A 1183

On approaches to junctions

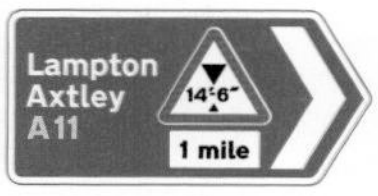
Lampton
Axtley
A11
14'6"
1 mile

At the junction

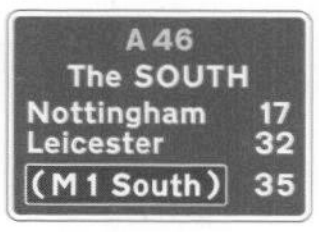
A 46
The SOUTH
Nottingham 17
Leicester 32
(M1 South) 35

Route confirmatory sign after junction

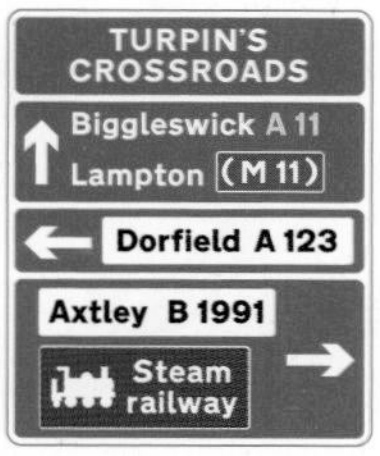
TURPIN'S
CROSSROADS
Biggleswick A 11
Lampton (M 11)
Dorfield A 123
Axtley B 1991
Steam
railway

On approaches to junctions

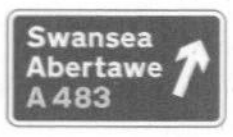
Swansea
Abertawe
A 483

On approach to a junction in Wales (bilingual)

Blue panels indicate that the motorway starts at the junction ahead.
Motorways shown in brackets can also be reached along the route indicated.
White panels indicate local or non-primary routes leading from the junction ahead.
Brown panels show the route to tourist attractions.
The name of the junction may be shown at the top of the sign.
The aircraft symbol indicates the route to an airport.
A symbol may be included to warn of a hazard or restriction along that route.

Signs on non-primary and local routes - black borders

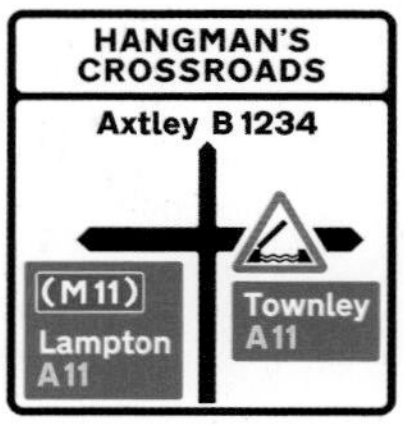
HANGMAN'S
CROSSROADS
Axtley B 1234
(M11)
Lampton
A 11
Townley
A 11

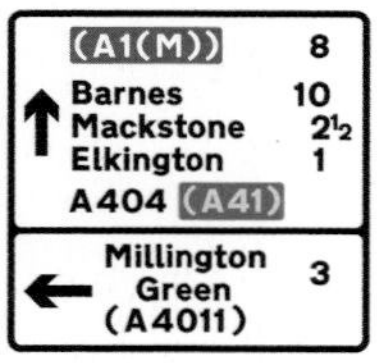
(A1(M)) 8
Barnes 10
Mackstone 2½
Elkington 1
A404 (A41)
Millington
Green 3
(A4011)

On approaches to junctions

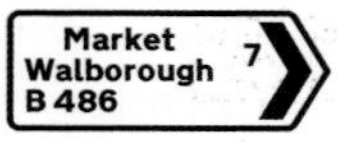
Market
Walborough 7
B 486

At the junction

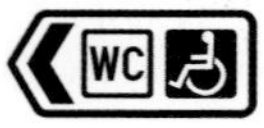
WC

Direction to toilets with access for the disabled

Green panels indicate that the primary route starts at the junction ahead.
Route numbers on a blue background show the direction to a motorway.
Route numbers on a green background show the direction to a primary route.

Emergency diversion routes

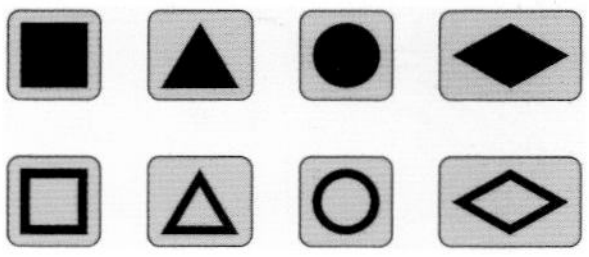

In an emergency it may be necessary to close a section of motorway or other main road to traffic, so a temporary sign may advise drivers to follow a diversion route. To help drivers navigate the route, black symbols on yellow patches may be permanently displayed on existing direction signs, including motorway signs. Symbols may also be used on separate signs with yellow backgrounds.

For further information see www.theaa.com/motoring_advice/general-advice/emergency-diversion-routes.html

AA
The Highway Code
AA
Know Your Road Signs

Note: The signs shown in this road atlas are those most commonly in use and are not all drawn to the same scale. In Scotland and Wales bilingual versions of some signs are used, showing both English and Gaelic or Welsh spellings. Some older designs of signs may still be seen on the roads. A comprehensive explanation of the signing system illustrating the vast majority of road signs can be found in the AA's handbook *Know Your Road Signs*. Where there is a reference to a rule number, this refers to *The Highway Code*. Both of these publications are on sale at theaa.com/shop and booksellers.

Restricted junctions

Motorway and Primary Route junctions which have access or exit restrictions are shown on the map pages thus:

M1 London - Leeds

Northbound
Access only from A1 (northbound)

Southbound
Exit only to A1 (southbound)

Northbound
Access only from A41 (northbound)

Southbound
Exit only to A41 (southbound)

Northbound
Access only from M25 (no link from A405)

Southbound
Exit only to M25 (no link from A405)

Northbound
Access only from A414

Southbound
Exit only to A414

Northbound
Exit only to M45

Southbound
Access only from M45

Northbound
Exit only to M6 (northbound)

Southbound
Exit only to A14 (southbound)

Northbound
Exit only, no access

Southbound
Access only, no exit

Northbound
Access only from A42

Southbound
No restriction

Northbound
No exit, access only

Southbound
Exit only, no access

Northbound
Exit only, no access

Southbound
Access only, no exit

Northbound
Exit only to M621

Southbound
Access only from M621

Northbound
Exit only to A1(M) (northbound)

Southbound
Access only from A1(M) (southbound)

M2 Rochester - Faversham

Westbound
No exit to A2 (eastbound)

Eastbound
No access from A2 (westbound)

M3 Sunbury - Southampton

Northeastbound
Access only from A303, no exit

Southwestbound
Exit only to A303, no access

Northbound
Exit only, no access

Southbound
Access only, no exit

Northeastbound
Access from M27 only, no exit

Southwestbound
No access to M27 (westbound)

M4 London - South Wales

For junctions 1 & 2 see London district map on pages 178–181

Westbound
Exit only to M48

Eastbound
Access only from M48

Westbound
Access only from M48

Eastbound
Exit only to M48

Westbound
Exit only, no access

Eastbound
Access only, no exit

Westbound
Exit only, no access

Eastbound
Access only, no exit

Westbound
Exit only to A48(M)

Eastbound
Access only from A48(M)

Westbound
Exit only, no access

Eastbound
No restriction

Westbound
Access only, no exit

Eastbound
No access or exit

M5 Birmingham - Exeter

Northeastbound
Access only, no exit

Southwestbound
Exit only, no access

Northeastbound
Access only from A417 (westbound)

Southwestbound
Exit only to A417 (eastbound)

Northeastbound
Exit only to M49

Southwestbound
Access only from M49

Northeastbound
No access, exit only

Southwestbound
No exit, access only

M6 Toll Motorway

See M6 Toll motorway map on page *XXIII*

M6 Rugby - Carlisle

Northbound
Exit only to M6 Toll

Southbound
Access only from M6 Toll

Northbound
Exit only to M42 (southbound) and A446

Southbound
Exit only to A446

Northbound
Access only from M42 (southbound)

Southbound
Exit only to M42

Northbound
Exit only, no access

Southbound
Access only, no exit

Northbound
Exit only to M54

Southbound
Access only from M54

Northbound
Access only from M6 Toll

Southbound
Exit only to M6 Toll

Westbound
Exit only to A483

Eastbound
Access only from A483

Northbound
No restriction

Southbound
Access only from M5 (eastbound)

Northbound
Exit only to M56 (westbound)

Southbound
Access only from M5 (eastbound)

Northbound
Access only, no exit

Southbound
Exit only, no access

Northbound
Exit only, no access

Southbound
Access only, no exit

Northbound
Access only from M6

Southbound
Exit only to M61

Northbound
Exit only, no access

Southbound
Access only, no exit

Northbound
Exit only, no access

Southbound
Access only, no exit

M8 Edinburgh - Bishopton

For junctions 7A to 28A see Glasgow district map on pages 176–177

Westbound
Exit only, no access

Eastbound
Access only, no exit

Westbound
Access only, no exit

Eastbound
Exit only, no access

Westbound
Access only, no exit

Eastbound
Exit only, no access

M9 Edinburgh - Dunblane

Northwestbound
Access only, no exit

Southeastbound
Exit only, no access

Northwestbound
Exit only, no access

Southeastbound
Access only, no exit

Northwestbound
Access only, no exit

Southeastbound
Exit only to A905

Northwestbound
Exit only to M876
(southwestbound)

Southeastbound
Access only from M876
(northeastbound)

M11 London - Cambridge

Northbound
Access only from A406
(eastbound)

Southbound
Exit only to A406

Northbound
Exit only, no access

Southbound
Access only, no exit

Northbound
Exit only, no access

Southbound
No direct access,
use jct 8

Northbound
Exit only to A11

Southbound
Access only from A11

Northbound
Exit only, no access

Southbound
Access only, no exit

Northbound
Exit only, no access

Southbound
Access only, no exit

M20 Swanley - Folkestone

Northwestbound
Staggered junction; follow
signs - access only

Southeastbound
Staggered junction; follow
signs - exit only

Northwestbound
Exit only to M26
(westbound)

Southeastbound
Access only from M26
(eastbound)

Northwestbound
Access only from A20

Southeastbound
For access follow signs -
exit only to A20

Northwestbound
No restriction

Southeastbound
For exit follow signs

Northwestbound
Access only, no exit

Southeastbound
Exit only, no access

M23 Hooley - Crawley

Northbound
Exit only to A23
(northbound)

Southbound
Access only from A23
(southbound)

Northbound
Access only, no exit

Southbound
Exit only, no access

M25 London Orbital Motorway

See M25 London Orbital motorway map on
page *XXII*

M26 Sevenoaks - Wrotham

Westbound
Exit only to clockwise
M25 (westbound)

Eastbound
Access only from
anticlockwise M25
(eastbound)

Westbound
Access only from M20
(northwestbound)

Eastbound
Exit only to M20
(southeastbound)

M27 Cadnam - Portsmouth

Westbound
Staggered junction; follow
signs - access only from
M3 (southbound). Exit
only to M3 (northbound)

Eastbound
Staggered junction; follow
signs - access only from
M3 (southbound). Exit
only to M3 (northbound)

Westbound
Exit only, no access

Eastbound
Access only, no exit

Westbound
Staggered junction; follow
signs - exit only to M275
(southbound)

Eastbound
Staggered junction; follow
signs - access only from
M275 (northbound)

M40 London - Birmingham

Northwestbound
Exit only, no access

Southeastbound
Access only, no exit

Northwestbound
Exit only, no access

Southeastbound
Access only, no exit

Northwestbound
Exit only to M40/A40

Southeastbound
Access only from
M40/A40

Northwestbound
Exit only, no access

Southeastbound
Access only, no exit

Northwestbound
Access only, no exit

Southeastbound
Exit only, no access

Northwestbound
Access only, no exit

Southeastbound
Exit only, no access

M42 Bromsgrove - Measham

See Birmingham district map on pages
174–175

M45 Coventry - M1

Westbound
Access only from A45
(northbound)

Eastbound
Exit only, no access

Westbound
Access only from M1
(northbound)

Eastbound
Exit only to M1
(southbound)

M48 Chepstow

Westbound
Access only from M4
(westbound)

Eastbound
Exit only to M4
(eastbound)

Westbound
No exit to M4 (eastbound)

Eastbound
No access from M4
(westbound)

M53 Mersey Tunnel - Chester

Northbound
Access only from M56
(westbound). Exit only to
M56 (eastbound)

Southbound
Access only from M56
(westbound). Exit only to
M56 (eastbound)

M54 Telford - Birmingham

Westbound
Access only from M6
(northbound)

Eastbound
Exit only to M6
(southbound)

M56 Chester - Manchester

For junctions 1,2,3,4 & 7 see Manchester
district map on pages 182–183

Westbound
Access only, no exit

Eastbound
No access or exit

Westbound
No exit to M6
(southbound)

Eastbound
No access from M6
(northbound)

Westbound
Exit only to M53

Eastbound
Access only from M53

Westbound
No access or exit

Eastbound
No restriction

M57 Liverpool Outer Ring Road

Northwestbound
Access only, no exit

Southeastbound
Exit only, no access

Northwestbound
Access only from A580
(westbound)

Southeastbound
Exit only, no access

M58 Liverpool - Wigan

Westbound
Exit only, no access

Eastbound
Access only, no exit

M60 Manchester Orbital

See Manchester district map on pages
182–183

M61 Manchester - Preston

Northwestbound
No access or exit

Southeastbound
Exit only, no access

Northwestbound
Exit only to M6
(northbound)

Southeastbound
Access only from M6
(southbound)

M62 Liverpool - Kingston upon Hull

Westbound
Access only, no exit

Eastbound
Exit only, no access

Westbound
No access to A1(M)
(southbound)

Eastbound
No restriction

M65 Preston - Colne

Northeastbound
Exit only, no access

Southwestbound
Access only, no exit

Northeastbound
Access only, no exit

Southwestbound
Exit only, no access

M66 Bury

Northbound
Exit only to A56
(northbound)

Southbound
Access only from A56
(southbound)

Northbound
Exit only, no access

Southbound
Access only, no exit

M67 Hyde Bypass

Westbound
Access only, no exit

Eastbound
Exit only, no access

Westbound
Exit only, no access

Eastbound
Access only, no exit

Westbound
Exit only, no access

Eastbound
No restriction

M69 Coventry - Leicester

Northbound
Access only, no exit

Southbound
Exit only, no access

M73 East of Glasgow

Northbound
No exit to A74 and A721

Southbound
No exit to A74 and A721

Northbound
No access from or exit to
A89. No access from M8
(eastbound)

Southbound
No access from or exit to
A89. No exit to M8
(westbound)

M74 and A74(M) Glasgow - Gretna

Northbound
Exit only, no access

Southbound
Access only, no exit

Northbound
Access only, no exit

Southbound
Exit only, no access

Northbound
No access from A74 and
A721

Southbound
Access only, no exit to
A74 and A721

Northbound
Access only, no exit

Southbound
Exit only, no access

Northbound
No access or exit

Southbound
Exit only, no access

Northbound
No restriction

Southbound
Access only, no exit

Northbound
Access only, no exit

Southbound
Exit only, no access

Northbound
Exit only, no access

Southbound
Access only, no exit

Northbound
Exit only, no access

Southbound
Access only, no exit

M77 Glasgow - Kilmarnock

Northbound
No exit to M8
(westbound)

Southbound
No access from M8
(eastbound)

Northbound
Access only, no exit

Southbound
Exit only, no access

Northbound
Access only, no exit

Southbound
Exit only, no access

Northbound
Access only, no exit

Southbound
No restriction

Northbound
Exit only, no access

Southbound
Exit only, no access

M80 Glasgow - Stirling

For junctions 1 & 4 see Glasgow district map on pages 176–177

Northbound
Exit only, no access

Southbound
Access only, no exit

Northbound
Access only, no exit

Southbound
Exit only, no access

Northbound
Exit only to M876
(northeastbound)

Southbound
Access only from M876
(southwestbound)

M90 Edinburgh - Perth

Northbound
No exit, access only

Southbound
Exit only to A90
(eastbound)

Northbound
Exit only to A92
(eastbound)

Southbound
Access only from A92
(westbound)

Northbound
Access only, no exit

Southbound
Exit only, no access

Northbound
Exit only, no access

Southbound
Access only, no exit

Northbound
No access from A912
No exit to A912
(southbound)

Southbound
No access from A912
(northbound).
No exit to A912

M180 Doncaster - Grimsby

Westbound
Access only, no exit

Eastbound
Exit only, no access

M606 Bradford Spur

Northbound
Exit only, no access

Southbound
No restriction

M621 Leeds - M1

Clockwise
Access only, no exit

Anticlockwise
Exit only, no access

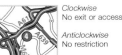

Clockwise
No exit or access

Anticlockwise
No restriction

Clockwise
Access only, no exit

Anticlockwise
Exit only, no access

Clockwise
Exit only, no access

Anticlockwise
Access only, no exit

Clockwise
Exit only to M1
(southbound)

Anticlockwise
Access only from M1
(northbound)

M876 Bonnybridge - Kincardine Bridge

Northeastbound
Access only from M80
(northbound)

Southwestbound
Exit only to M80
(southbound)

Northeastbound
Exit only to M9
(eastbound)

Southwestbound
Access only from M9
(westbound)

A1(M) South Mimms - Baldock

Northbound
Exit only, no access

Southbound
Access only, no exit

Northbound
No restriction

Southbound
Exit only, no access

Northbound
Access only, no exit

Southbound
No access or exit

(M) Pontefract - Bedale

Northbound
No access to M62
(eastbound)

Southbound
No restriction

Northbound
Access only from M1
(northbound)

Southbound
Exit only to M1
(southbound)

A1(M) Scotch Corner - Newcastle upon Tyne

Northbound
Exit only to A66(M)
(eastbound)

Southbound
Access only from A66(M)
(westbound)

Northbound
No access. Exit only to
A194(M) & A1
(northbound)

Southbound
No exit. Access only from
A194(M) & A1
(southbound)

3(M) Horndean - Havant

Northbound
Access only from A3

Southbound
Exit only to A3

Northbound
Exit only, no access

Southbound
Access only, no exit

A38(M) Birmingham
ctoria Road (Park Circus)

Northbound
No exit

Southbound
No access

A48(M) Cardiff Spur

Westbound
Access only from M4
(westbound)

Eastbound
Exit only to M4
(eastbound)

Westbound
Exit only to A48
(westbound)

Eastbound
Access only from A48
(eastbound)

A57(M) Manchester
Brook Street (A34)

Westbound
No exit

Eastbound
No access

A58(M) Leeds
Park Lane and Westgate

Northbound
No restriction

Southbound
No access

A64(M) Leeds
Clay Pit Lane (A58)

Westbound
No exit (to Clay Pit Lane)

Eastbound
No access (from Clay Pit
Lane)

A66(M) Darlington Spur

Westbound
Exit only to A1(M)
(southbound)

Eastbound
Access only from A1(M)
(northbound)

A74(M) Gretna - Abington

Northbound
Exit only, no access

Southbound
No exit

A194(M)
Newcastle upon Tyne

Northbound
Access only from A1(M)
(northbound)

Southbound
Exit only to A1(M)
(southbound)

A12 M25 - Ipswich

Northeastbound
Access only, no exit

Southwestbound
No restriction

Northeastbound
Exit only, no access

Southwestbound
Access only, no exit

Northeastbound
Exit only, no access

Southwestbound
Access only, no exit

Northeastbound
Access only, no exit

Southwestbound
Exit only, no access

Northeastbound
No restriction

Southwestbound
Access only, no exit

Northeastbound
Exit only, no access

Southwestbound
Access only, no exit

Northeastbound
Access only, no exit

Southwestbound
Exit only, no access

Northeastbound
Exit only, no access

Southwestbound
Access only, no exit

Northeastbound
Exit only (for Stratford
St Mary and Dedham)

Southwestbound
Access only

A14 M1 - Felixstowe

Westbound
Exit only to M6 & M1
(northbound)

Eastbound
Access only from M6 &
M1 (southbound)

Westbound
Exit only, no access

Eastbound
Access only, no exit

Westbound
Exit only to M11
(for London)

Eastbound
Access only, no exit

Westbound
Exit only to A14
(northbound)

Eastbound
Access only, no exit

Northeastbound
Exit only, no access

Southwestbound
Access only, no exit

Westbound
Access only, no exit

Eastbound
Exit only, no access

Westbound
Exit only to A11
Access only from A1303

Eastbound
Access only from A11

Westbound
Access only from A11

Eastbound
Exit only to A11

Westbound
Exit only, no access

Eastbound
Access only, no exit

Westbound
Access only, no exit

Eastbound
Exit only, no access

A55 Holyhead - Chester

Westbound
Exit only, no access

Eastbound
Access only, no exit

Westbound
Access only, no exit

Eastbound
Exit only, no access

Westbound
Exit only, no access

Eastbound
No access or exit.

Westbound
No restriction

Eastbound
No access or exit

Westbound
Exit only, no access

Eastbound
No access or exit

Westbound
Exit only, no access

Eastbound
Access only, no exit

Westbound
Exit only to A5104

Eastbound
Access only from A5104

Refer also to atlas pages 36–37 and 50–51

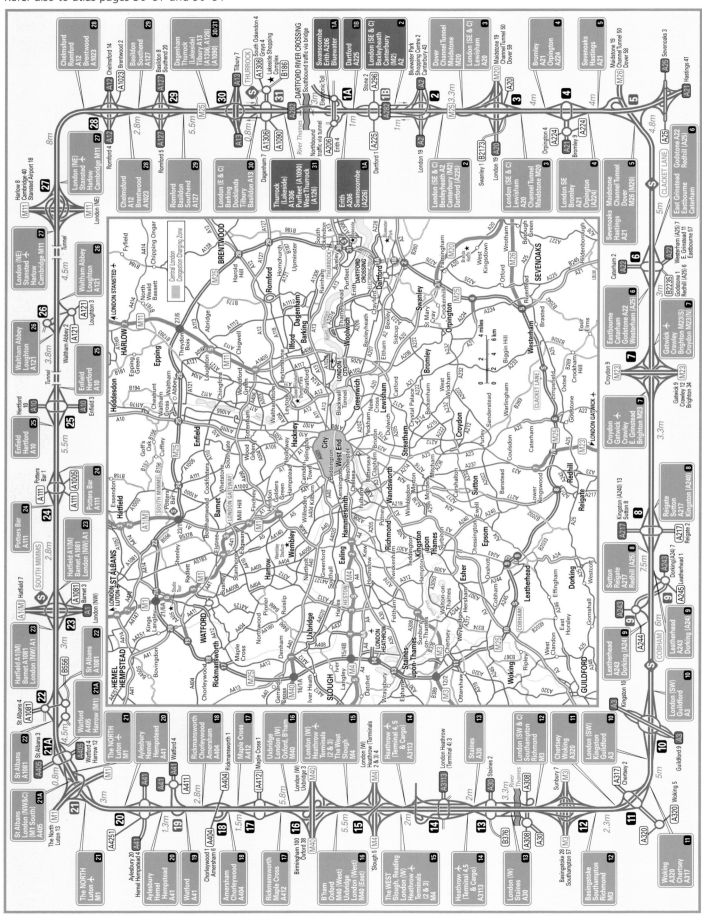

Refer also to atlas pages 58–59

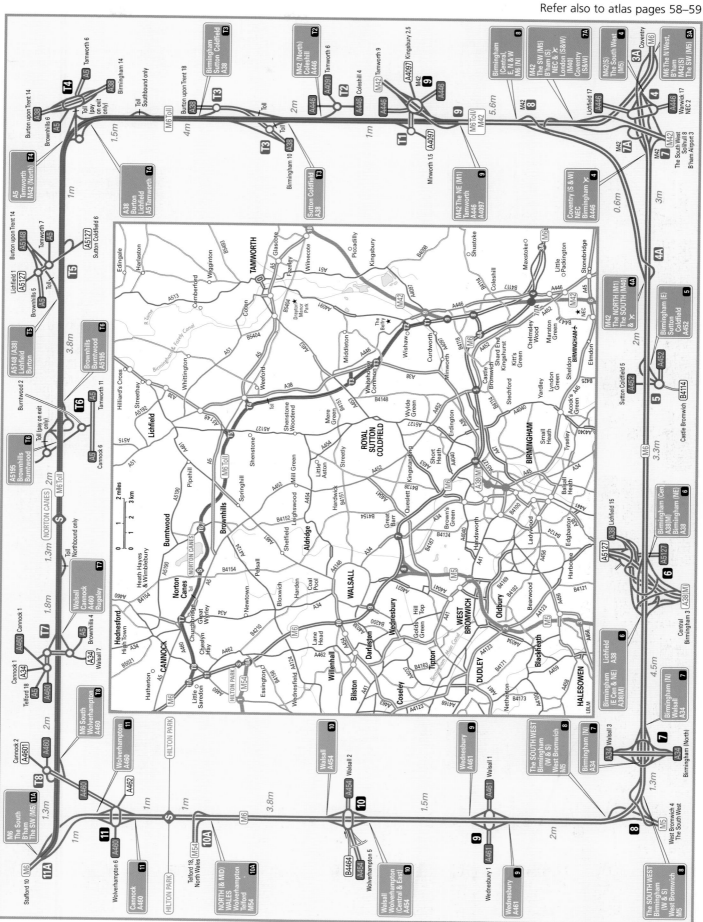

Smart motorways

Since Britain's first motorway (the Preston Bypass) opened in 1958, motorways have changed significantly. A vast increase in car journeys over the last 60 years has meant that motorways quickly filled to capacity. To combat this, the recent development of **smart motorways** uses technology to monitor and actively manage traffic flow and congestion

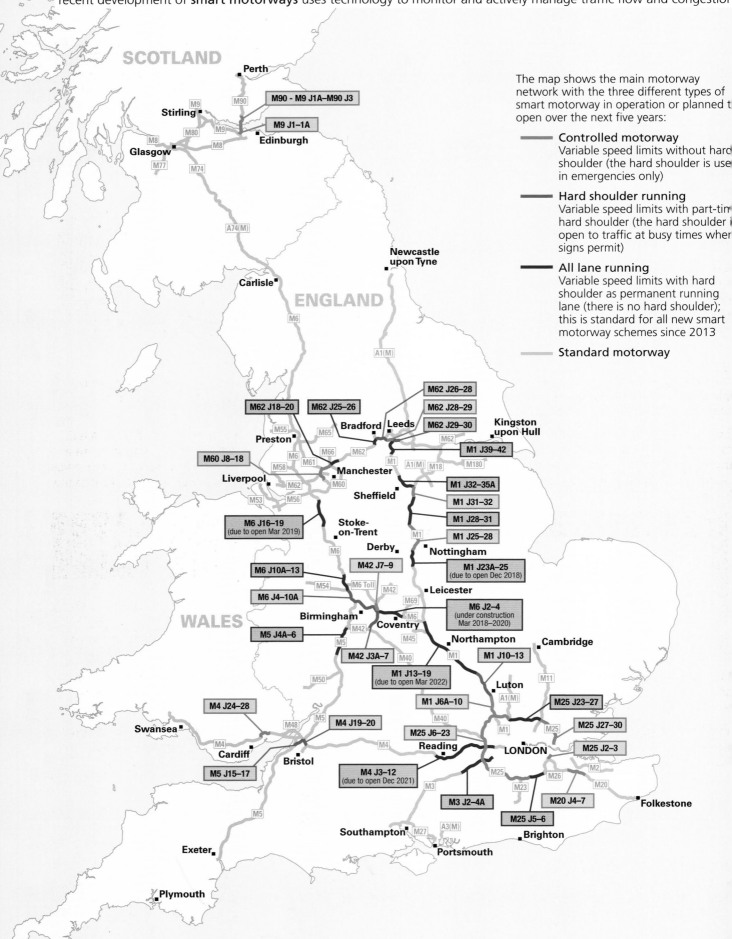

The map shows the main motorway network with the three different types of smart motorway in operation or planned t open over the next five years:

Controlled motorway
Variable speed limits without hard shoulder (the hard shoulder is use in emergencies only)

Hard shoulder running
Variable speed limits with part-tim hard shoulder (the hard shoulder open to traffic at busy times wher signs permit)

All lane running
Variable speed limits with hard shoulder as permanent running lane (there is no hard shoulder); this is standard for all new smart motorway schemes since 2013

Standard motorway

Smart motorways (*Intelligent Transport Systems* in Scotland) are the responsibility of Highways England, Transport Scotland and Transport for Wa

ow they work

art motorways utilise various active traffic management methods, monitored through a regional traffic control centre:

Traffic flow is monitored using CCTV

Speed limits are changed to smooth traffic flow and reduce stop-start driving

Capacity of the motorway can be increased by either temporarily or permanently opening the hard shoulder to traffic

- Warning signs and messages alert drivers to hazards and traffic jams ahead
- Lanes can be closed in the case of an accident or emergency by displaying a red X sign
- Emergency refuge areas are located regularly along the motorway where there is no hard shoulder available

an emergency

a smart motorway there is often no hard shoulder so in an emergency you will need to make your ay to the nearest **emergency refuge area** or motorway service area.

ergency refuge areas are lay-bys marked with blue signs featuring an orange SOS telephone symbol. e telephone connects to the regional control centre and pinpoints your location. The control centre ll advise you on what to do, send help and assist you in returning to the motorway.

you are unable to reach an emergency refuge area or hard shoulder (if there is one) move as close to e nearside (left hand) boundary or verge as you can.

t is not possible to get out of your vehicle safely, or there is no other place of relative safety to wait, y in your vehicle with your seat-belt on and dial 999 if you have a mobile phone. If you don't have a one, sit tight and wait to be rescued. Once the regional traffic control centre is aware of your uation, via the police or CCTV, they will use the smart motorway technology to set overhead signs and se the lane to keep traffic away from you. They will also send a traffic officer or the police to help you.

Sign indicating presence of emergency refuge areas ahead

This sign is located at each emergency refuge area

gns

otorway signals and messages advise of abnormal traffic conditions ahead and may indicate speed limits. They may ply to individual lanes when mounted overhead or, when located on the central reservation or at the side of the otorway, to the whole carriageway.

here traffic is allowed to use the hard shoulder as a traffic lane, each lane will have overhead signals and signs. A red oss (with no signals) displayed above the hard shoulder indicates when it is closed. When the hard shoulder is in use as raffic lane the red cross will change to a speed limit. Should it be necessary to close any lane, a red cross with red lamps shing in vertical pairs will be shown above that lane. Prior to this, the signal will show an arrow directing traffic into the jacent lane.

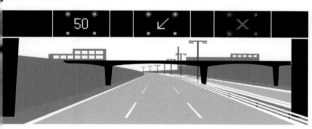

These signals are mounted above the carriageway with a signal for each traffic lane; each signal has two pairs of lamps that flash. You should obey the signal for your lane

Move to adjacent lane (arrow may point downwards to the right)

Leave motorway at next exit

Red lamps flashing from side to side in pairs, together with a red cross, mean 'do not proceed in the traffic lane directly below'. More than one lane may be closed to traffic

here variable speed limit signs are mounted over individual lanes and the speed limit is shown in a red ring, the limit is andatory. You will be at risk of a driving offence if you do not keep to the speed limit. Speed limits that do not include e red ring are the maximum speeds advised for the prevailing conditions.

eed limits of 60, 50 and 40mph are used on all types of smart motorways. When no speed limit is shown the national eed limit of 70mph is in place (this is reduced to 60mph for particular vehicles such as heavy or articulated goods icles and vehicles towing caravans or trailers).

Quick tips

- Never drive in a lane closed by a red X
- Keep to the speed limit shown on the gantries
- A solid white line indicates the hard shoulder – do not drive in it unless directed or in the case of an emergency
- A broken white line indicates a normal running lane

- Exit the smart motorway where possible if your vehicle is in difficulty. In an emergency, move onto the hard shoulder where there is one, or the nearest emergency refuge area
- Put on your hazard lights if you break down

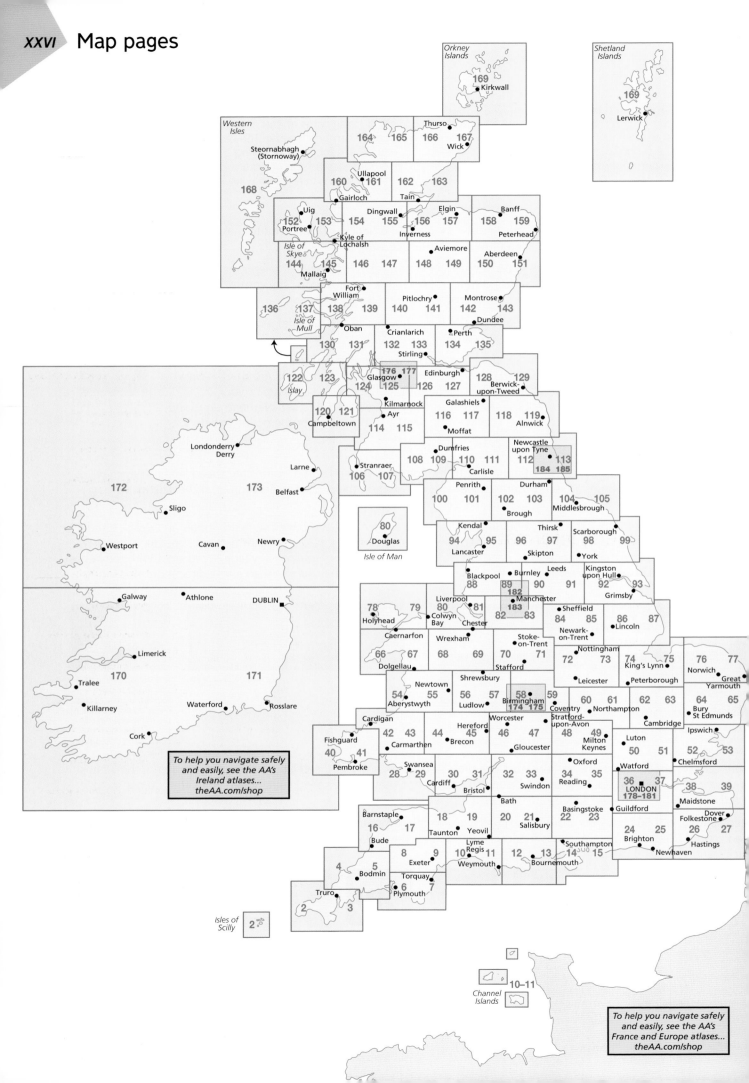

Orkney Islands

169 Kirkwall

Shetland Islands

169 Lerwick

Western Isles

Steornabhagh (Stornoway)

Thurso

164 165 166 167 Wick

168

160 Ullapool 161 162 163
Gairloch Tain

Uig Dingwall Elgin Banff
152 153 154 155 156 157 158 159
Portree Inverness Peterhead
Kyle of
Lochalsh Aviemore Aberdeen
Isle of
Skye 144 145 146 147 148 149 150 151
Mallaig

Fort
William
136 137 138 139 140 141 142 143 Montrose
Isle of Pitlochry
Mull Dundee
Oban Crianlarich Perth
130 131 132 133 134 135
Stirling
176 177
122 123 Glasgow Edinburgh 128 129
Islay 124 125 126 127 Berwick-
upon-Tweed
Kilmarnock Galashiels
120 121 Ayr 116 117 118 119
Campbeltown 114 115 Moffat Alnwick

Dumfries Newcastle
upon Tyne
Londonderry 108 109 110 111 112 113
Derry Carlisle 184 185

Larne Penrith Durham
100 101 102 103 104 105
Belfast Brough Middlesbrough
172 173
Sligo Kendal Thirsk Scarborough
94 95 96 97 98 99
Westport Cavan Newry Lancaster Skipton York

80 Blackpool Burnley Leeds Kingston
upon Hull
Galway Athlone DUBLIN Douglas 88 89 90 91 92 93
182
Isle of Man Liverpool Manchester Grimsby
78 79 80 81 183 90
Colwyn 82 83 Sheffield
Holyhead Bay Chester 84 85 86 87
Limerick Caernarfon Stoke- Newark- Lincoln
on-Trent on-Trent
170 171 Wrexham Nottingham
66 67 68 69 70 71 72 73 74 75 76 77
Tralee Dolgellau King's Lynn Norwich
Stafford Great
Killarney Waterford Shrewsbury Leicester Peterborough Yarmouth
Rosslare Newtown 58 Birmingham 59
Cork 54 55 56 57 174 175 60 61 62 63 64 65
Aberystwyth Ludlow Coventry Northampton Cambridge Bury
Stratford- St Edmunds
Fishguard Hereford upon-Avon 48 49 Ipswich
Cardigan 42 43 44 45 46 47 Milton 52 53
40 41 Carmarthen Brecon Gloucester Keynes Luton
Pembroke Worcester 50 51 Chelmsford
Swansea 30 31 Oxford Watford 38 39
28 29 Cardiff 32 33 34 35 36 37 Maidstone
Bristol Swindon Reading LONDON Dover
Bath 178-181 Folkestone
Barnstaple 18 19 20 21 Basingstoke 22 23 24 25 Hastings
16 17 Salisbury Guildford Brighton 26 27
Bude Taunton Yeovil Southampton Newhaven
Lyme 12 13 14
8 9 Regis 10 11 Bournemouth 15
4 5 Exeter Weymouth
Truro 6 Torquay
2 3 7 Plymouth

Isles of
Scilly 2

To help you navigate safely
and easily, see the AA's
Ireland atlases...
theAA.com/shop

10-11
Channel
Islands

To help you navigate safely
and easily, see the AA's
France and Europe atlases...
theAA.com/shop

Motoring information

M4	Motorway with number	Primary route service area	Road tunnel	International freight terminal
Toll T4	Toll motorway with toll station	BATH — Primary route destination	Road toll, steep gradient (arrows point downhill)	24-hour Accident & Emergency hospital
11	Motorway junction with and without number	A1123 — Other A road single/dual carriageway	Distance in miles between symbols	Crematorium
3	Restricted motorway junctions	B2070 — B road single/dual carriageway	Vehicle ferry	Park and Ride (at least 6 days per week)
Fleet	Motorway service area	Minor road more than 4 metres wide, less than 4 metres wide	Fast vehicle ferry or catamaran	City, town, village or other built-up area
	Motorway and junction under construction	Roundabout	Railway line, in tunnel	628 637 Lecht Summit — Height in metres, mountain pass
A3	Primary route single/dual carriageway	Interchange/junction	Railway station and level crossing	Sandy beach
	Primary route junction with and without number	Narrow primary/other A/B road with passing places (Scotland)	Tourist railway	National boundary
3	Restricted primary route junctions	Road under construction/approved	Airport, heliport	County, administrative boundary

Touring information To avoid disappointment, check opening times before visiting

Scenic route	Garden	Waterfall	Motor-racing circuit
Tourist Information Centre	Arboretum	Hill-fort	Air show venue
Tourist Information Centre (seasonal)	Country park	Roman antiquity	Ski slope (natural, artificial)
Visitor or heritage centre	Agricultural showground	Prehistoric monument	National Trust property
Picnic site	Theme park	Battle site with year 1066	National Trust for Scotland property
Caravan site (AA inspected)	Farm or animal centre	Steam railway centre	English Heritage site
Camping site (AA inspected)	Zoological or wildlife collection	Cave	Historic Scotland site
Caravan & camping site (AA inspected)	Bird collection	Windmill, monument	Cadw (Welsh heritage) site
Abbey, cathedral or priory	Aquarium	Beach (award winning)	Other place of interest
Ruined abbey, cathedral or priory	RSPB site	Lighthouse	Boxed symbols indicate attractions within urban areas
Castle	National Nature Reserve (England, Scotland, Wales)	Golf course (AA listed)	World Heritage Site (UNESCO)
Historic house or building	Local nature reserve	Football stadium	National Park
Museum or art gallery	Wildlife Trust reserve	County cricket ground	National Scenic Area (Scotland)
Industrial interest	Forest drive	Rugby Union national stadium	Forest Park
Aqueduct or viaduct	National trail	International athletics stadium	Heritage coast
Vineyard, Brewery or distillery	Viewpoint	Horse racing, show jumping	Major shopping centre

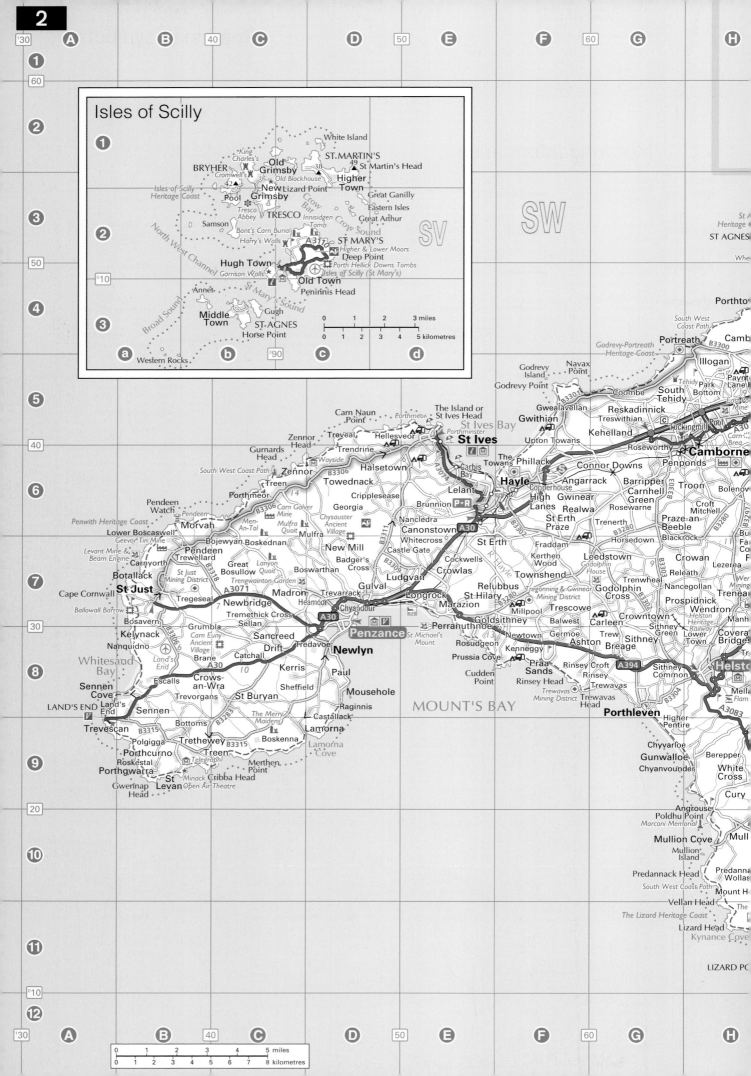

Isles of Scilly

White Island

ST.MARTIN'S
St Martin's Head
King Charles's
BRYHER
Old Grimsby
Cromwell's
Old Blockhouse
42
New Grimsby
Lizard Point
Higher Town
Pool
Isles-of-Scilly Heritage Coast
Tresco Abbey
TRESCO
Great Ganilly
Eastern Isles
Great Arthur
Innisidgen Tomb
Samson
Bant's Carn Burial
Harry's Walls
A3117
ST MARY'S
North West Channel
Higher & Lower Moors
Deep Point
Hugh Town
Porth Hellick Downs Tombs
Garrison Walls
Isles of Scilly (St Mary's)
Old Town
Peninnis Head
Annet
St Mary's Sound
Broad Sound
Middle Town
Gugh
ST.AGNES
Horse Point

SV
SW

Western Rocks

0   1   2   3 miles
0 1 2 3 4 5 kilometres

Porthto
South West Coast Path
Portreath
B3300
Illogan
Godrevy-Portreath Heritage-Coast
Paynt
Navax Point
South
Tehidy Park Bottom
Godrevy Island
Godrevy Point
Coombe
Tehidy
Reskadinnick
Treswithian
Kehelland
Tuckingmill
A30
Gwithian
Upton Towans
Roseworthy
Camborne
Carn Naun Point
Porthmeor
The Island or St Ives Head
St Ives Bay
Gwealavellan
Penponds
Zennor Head
Treveal
Hellesveor
Porthminster
St Ives
The Towans
Phillack
Connor Downs
Troon
Bolenov
Gurnards Head
Trendrine
Carbis Bay
Hayle
Copperhouse
Angarrack
Barripper
Carnhell Green
South West Coast Path
Zennor
Halsetown
Lelant
High Gwinear
Rosewarne
Praze-an-Beeble
Towednack
Brunnion
P•R
Lanes
St Erth
Trenerth
Horsedown
Blackrock
Treen
B3306
Cripplesease
Nancledra
Praze
Porthmeor
Carn Galver Mine
Georgia
Canonstown
A30
St Erth
Fraddam
Leedstown
Crowan
Pendeen Watch
Chysauster Ancient Village
Whitecross
Kerthen Wood
Townshend
Nancegollan
Penwith Heritage Coast
Men-An-Tol
Mulfra
Castle Gate
Cockwells
Trenwheal
Releath
Lower Boscaswell
Morvah
Mulfra Quoit
New Mill
B3311
Crowlas
Godolphin House
Trewneal
Geevor Tin Mine
Bojewyan
Boskednan
Badger's Cross
Ludgvan
Relubbus
Godolphin Cross
Prospidnick
Levant Mine & Beam Engine
Pendeen
Trewellard
Great Bosullow
Boswarthan
B3309
St Hilary
Tregonning & Gwinear Mining District
Millpool
Trescowe
Crowntown
Wendron
Carnyorth
Lanyon Quoit
Gulval
Trevarrack
Longrock
Balwest
Carleen
Crownton
Helston Heritage Railway
Botallack
St Just Mining District
Trengwainton Garden
Madron
Heamoor
Marazion
Goldsithney
Newtown
Germoe
Ashton
Trew
Sithney Green
Lower Town
Covera Bridge
Cape Cornwall
St Just
A3071
Newbridge
Chyandour
A30
Perranuthnoe
Rosudgeon
Kenneggy
Breage
Sithney
Ballowall Barrow
Tregeseal
Tremethick Cross
St Michael's Mount
Prussia Cove
A394
Helsto
Bosavern
Sellan
Grumbla
Penzance
Praa Sands
Rinsey Croft
Sithney Common
Kelynack
Carn Euny Ancient Village
Sancreed
Drift
Tredavoe
Newlyn
Cudden Point
Rinsey Head
Rinsey
Trewavas
Mella
Nanquidno
Brane
Catchall
Prussia Cove
Trewavas Head
B3304
Whitesand Bay
Land's End
Kerris
Paul
Trewavas Mining District
Porthleven
Escalls
Crows-an-Wra
A30
Sheffield
Mousehole
Higher Pentire
Sennen Cove
Land's End
Sennen
Trevorgans
St Buryan
Raginnis
Chyvarloe
LAND'S END
The Merry Maidens
Castallack
Gunwalloe
Berepper
Trevescan
Bottoms
Boskenna
Lamorna
Chyanvounder
White Cross
Polgigga
Trethewey
Treen
Lamorna Cove
MOUNT'S BAY
Cury
Porthcurno
Telegraph
Merthen Point
Roskestal
Porthgwarra
St Levan
Cribba Head
Angrouse
Gwennap Head
Minack Open Air Theatre
Poldhu Point
Marconi Memorial
Mullion Cove
Mull
Mullion Island
Predannack Head
Predanna Wollas
South West Coast Path
Mount H
Vellan Head
The Lizard Heritage Coast
Lizard Head
Kynance Cove
LIZARD PO

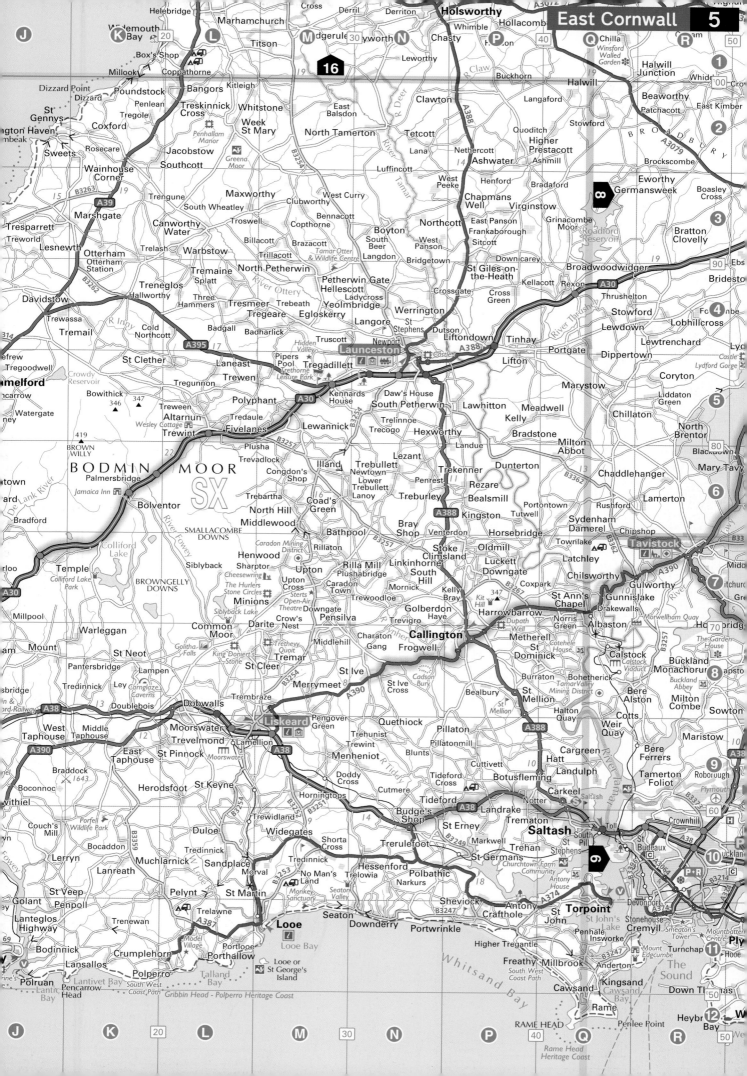

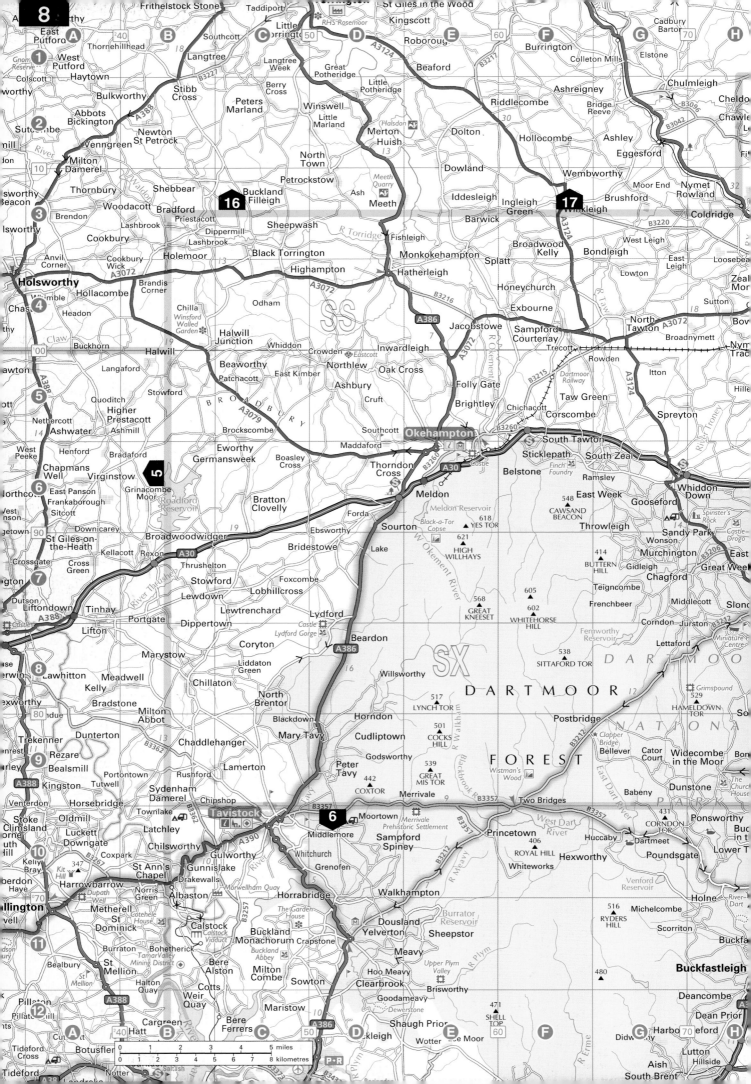

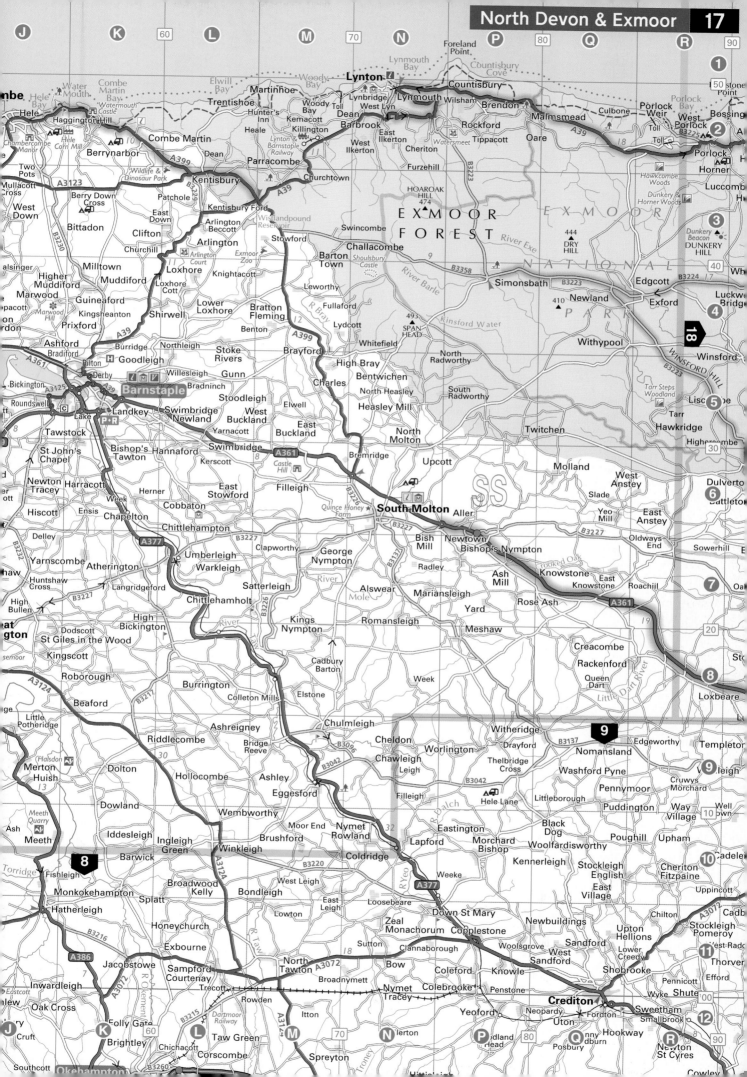

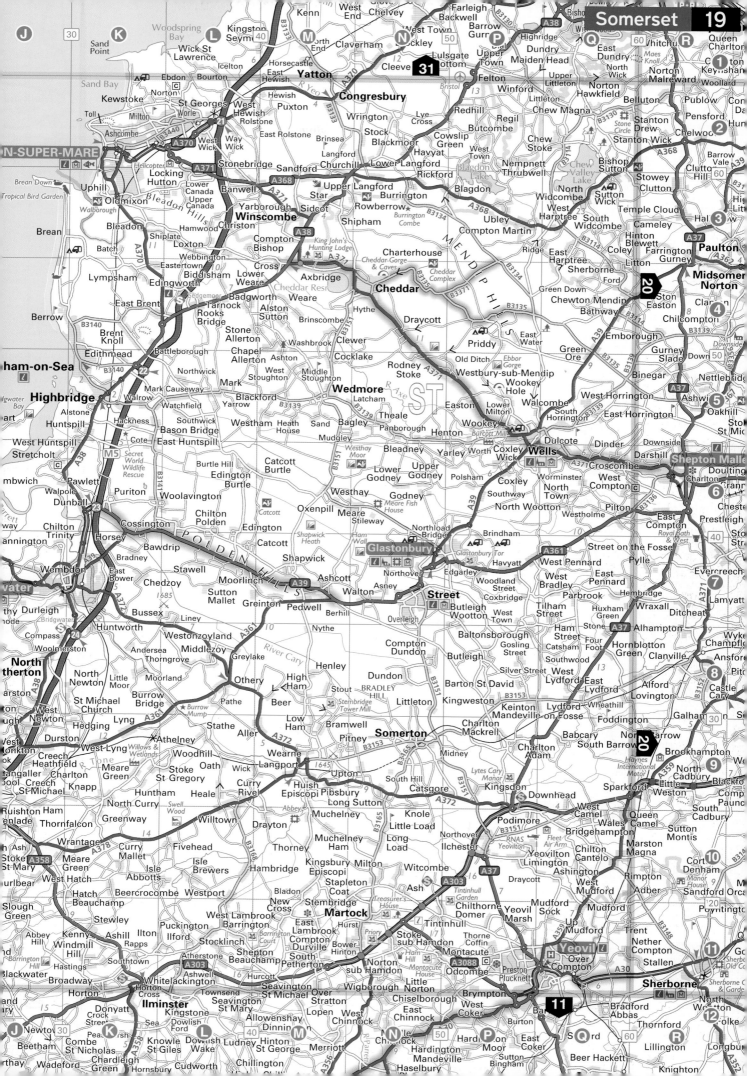

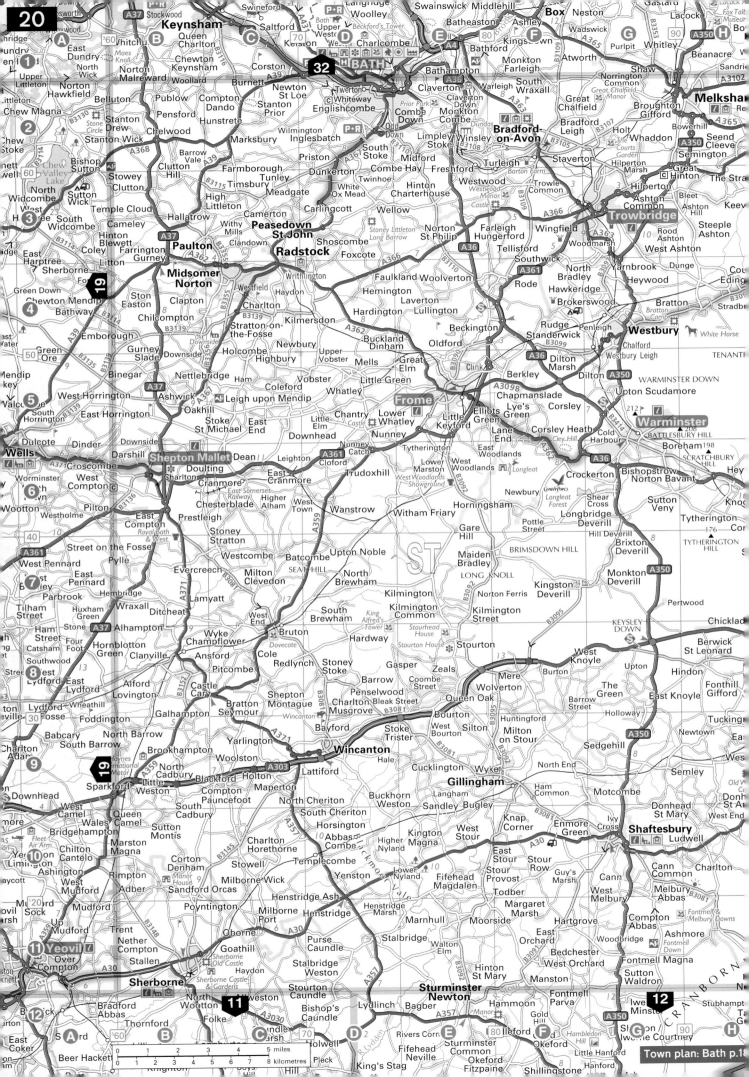

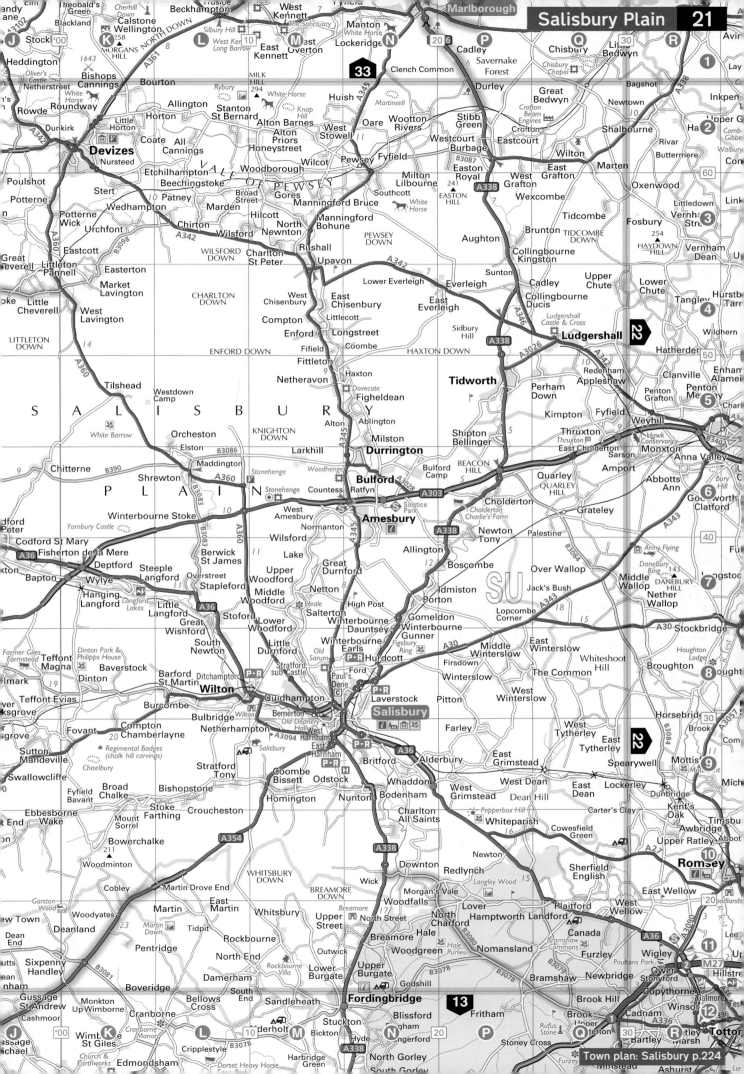

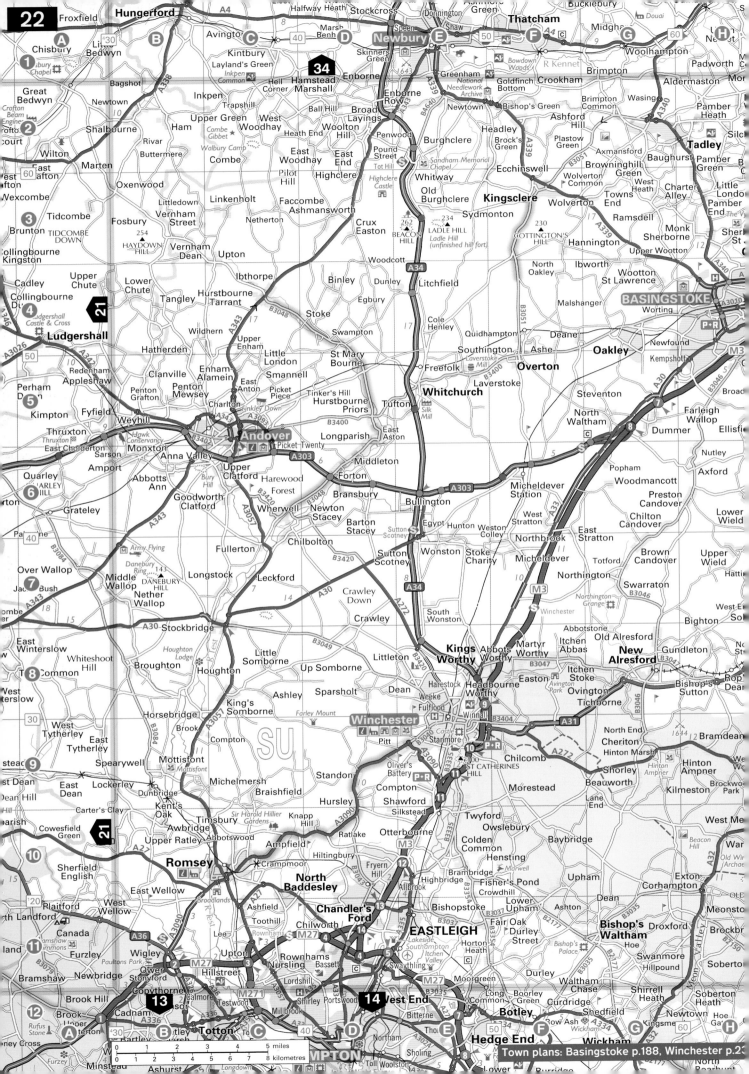

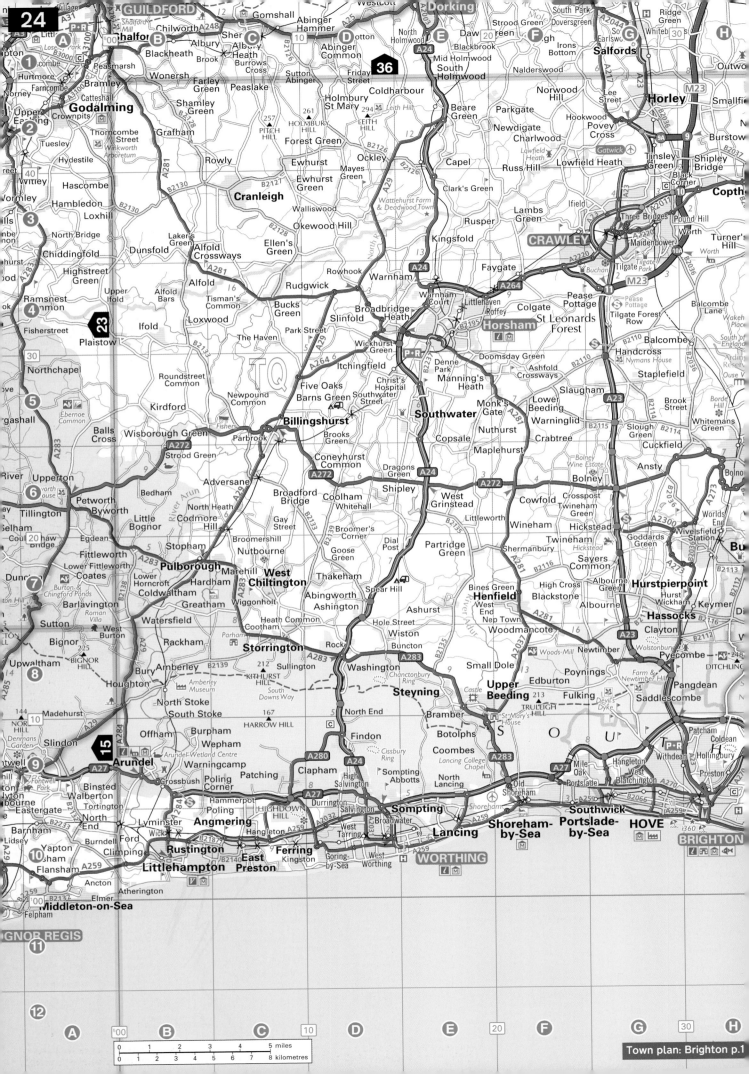

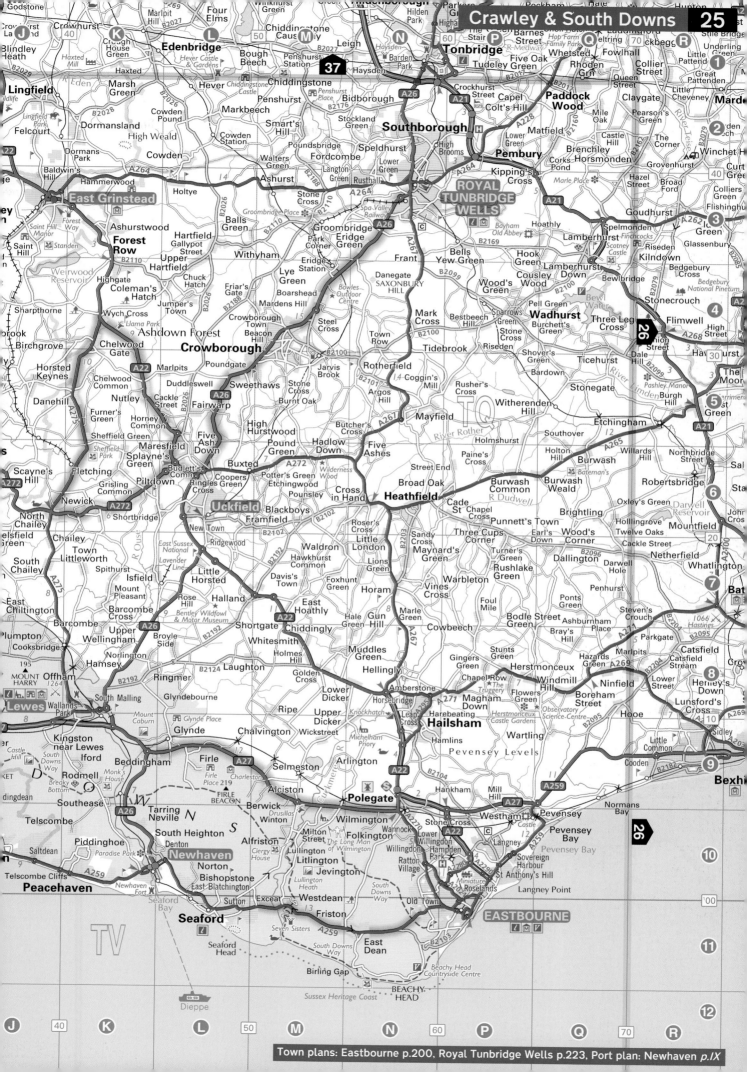

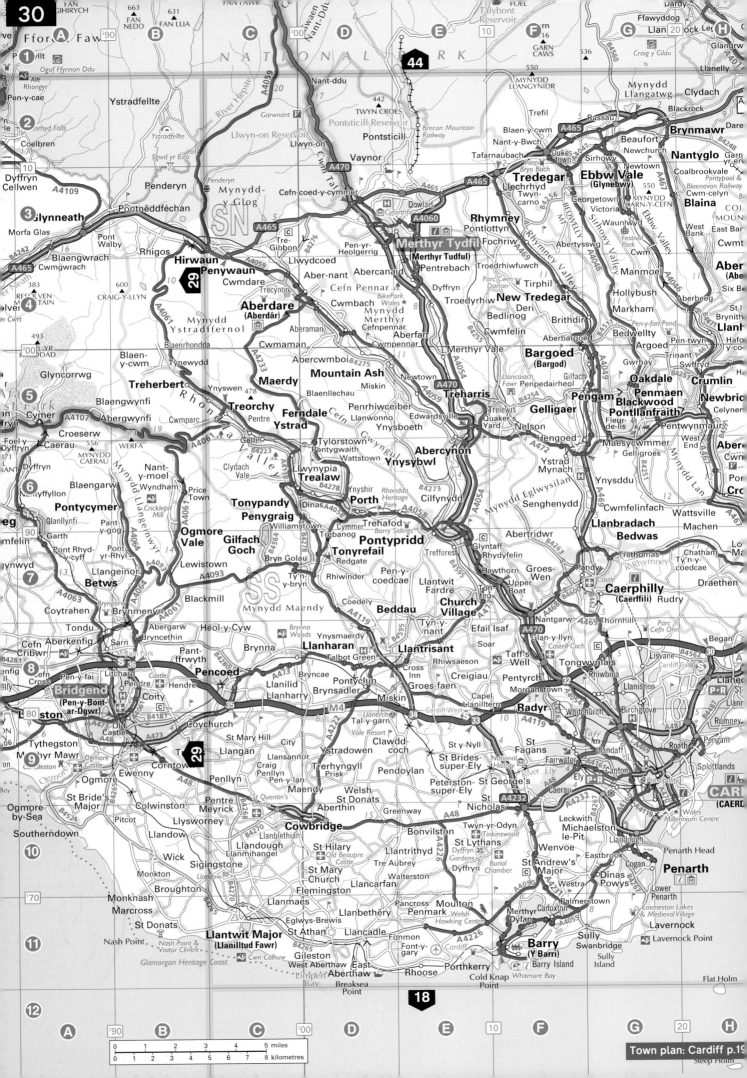

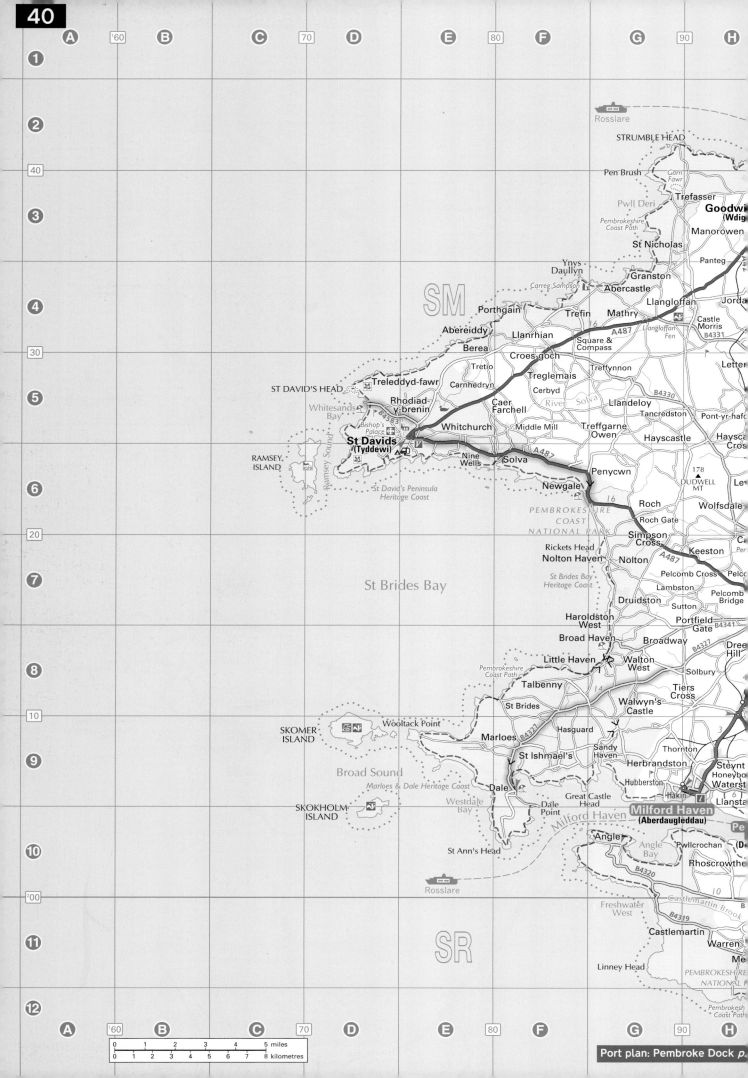

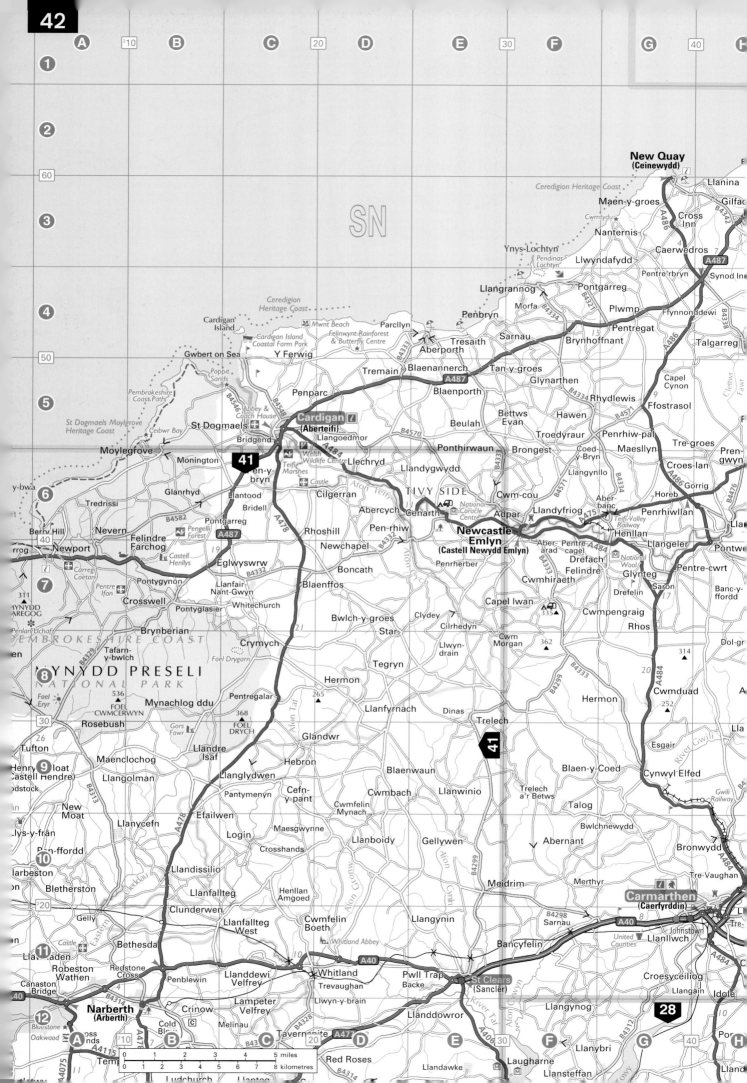

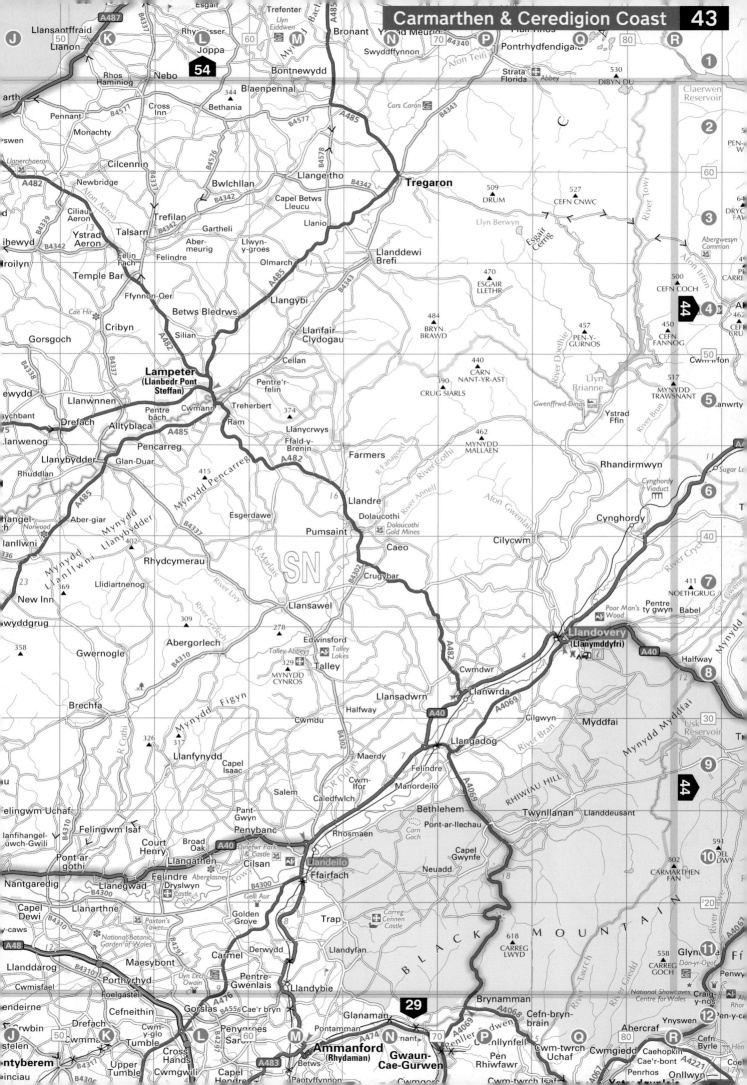

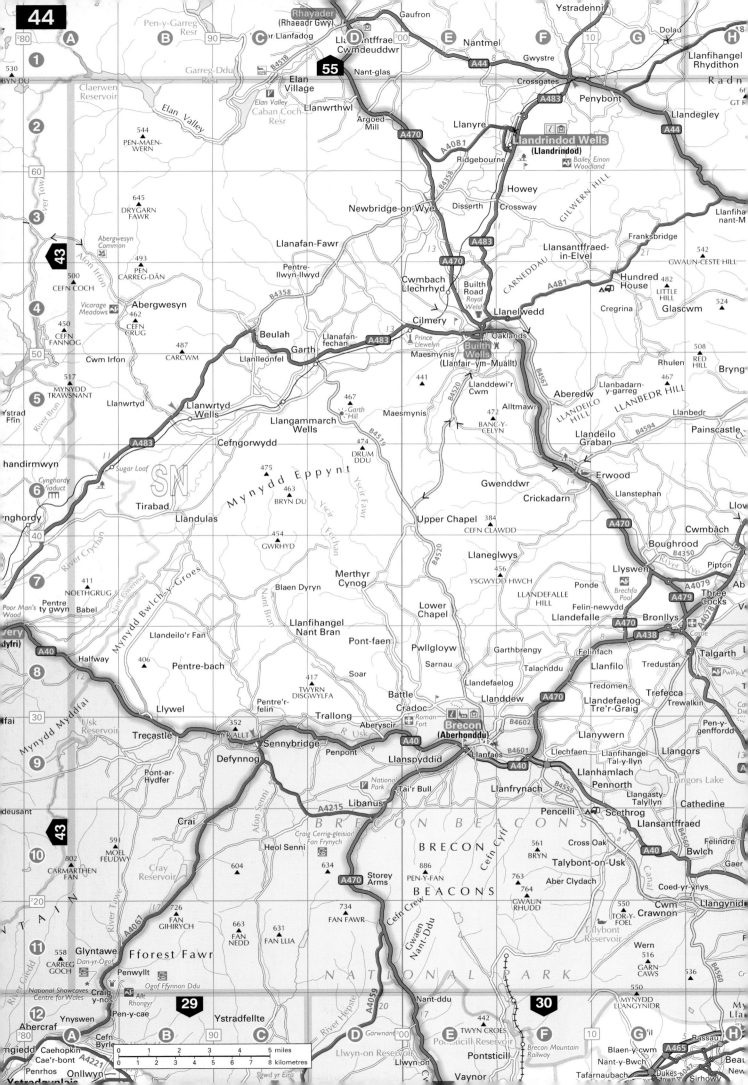

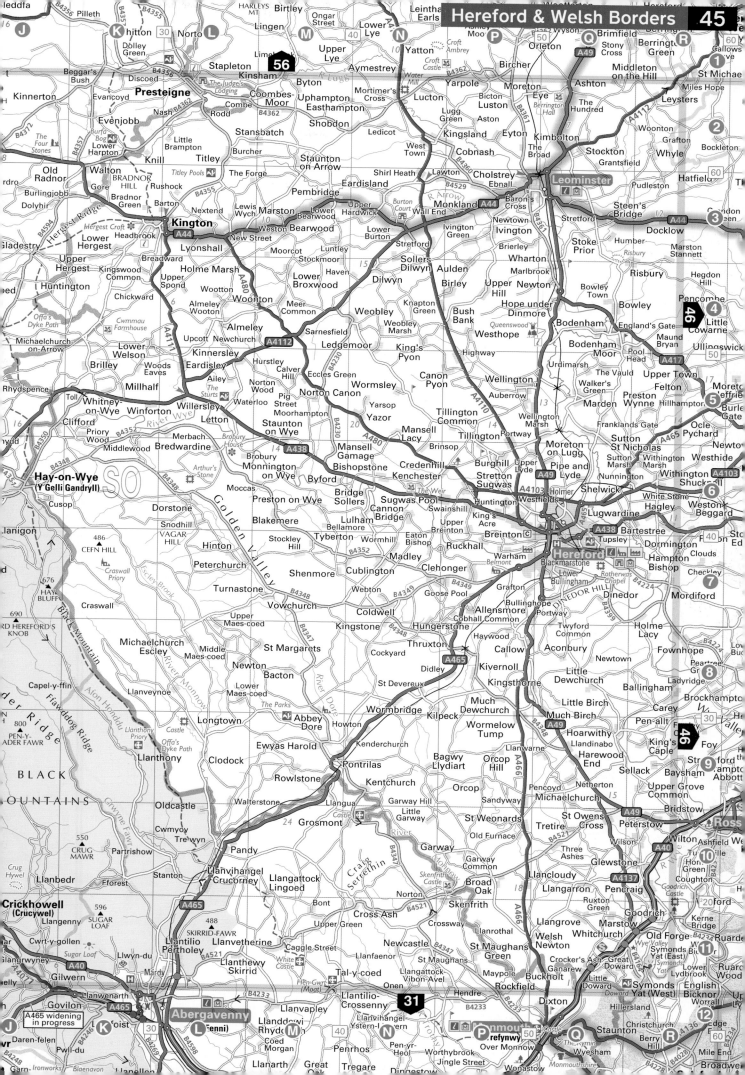

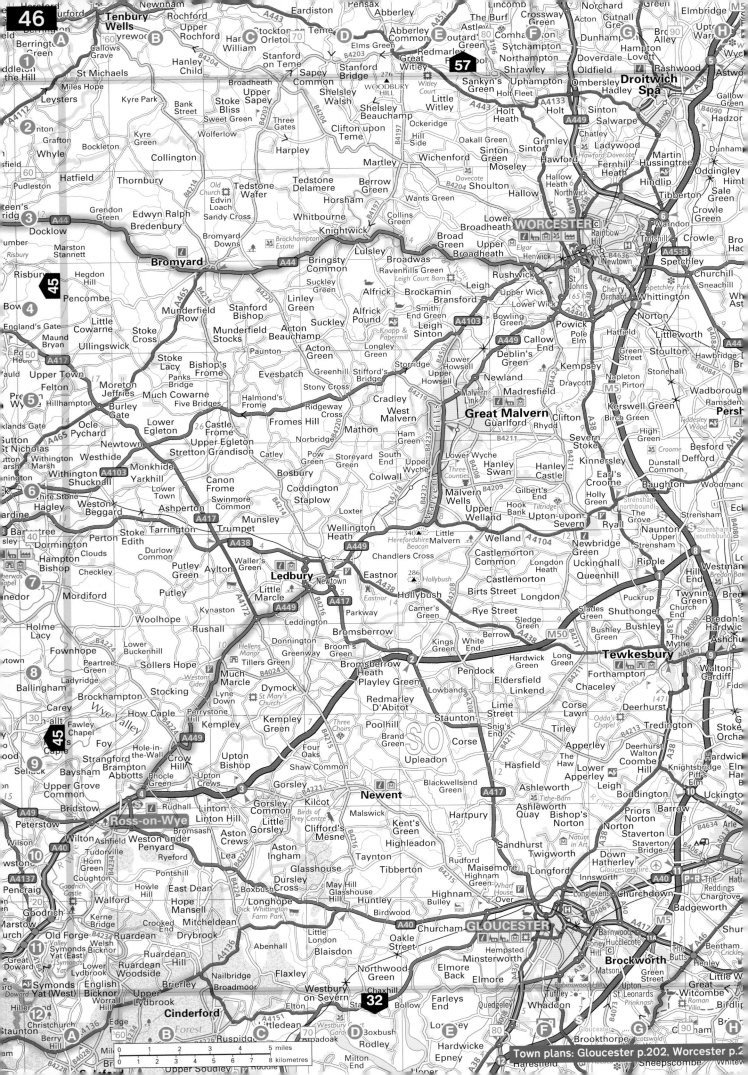

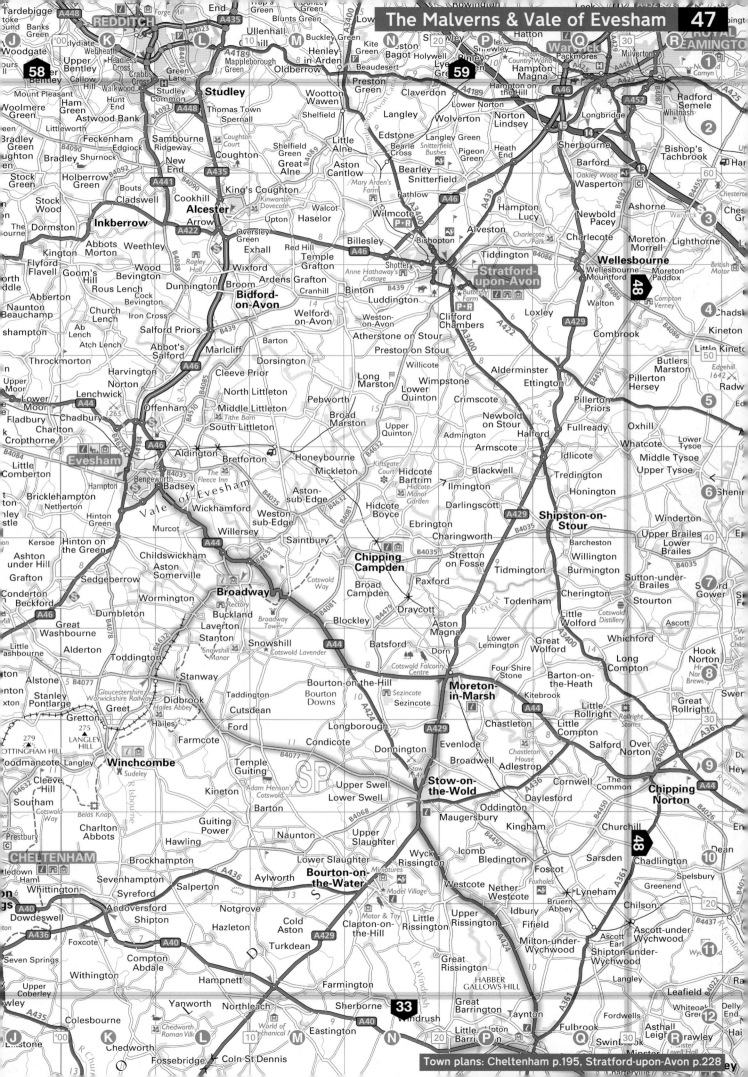

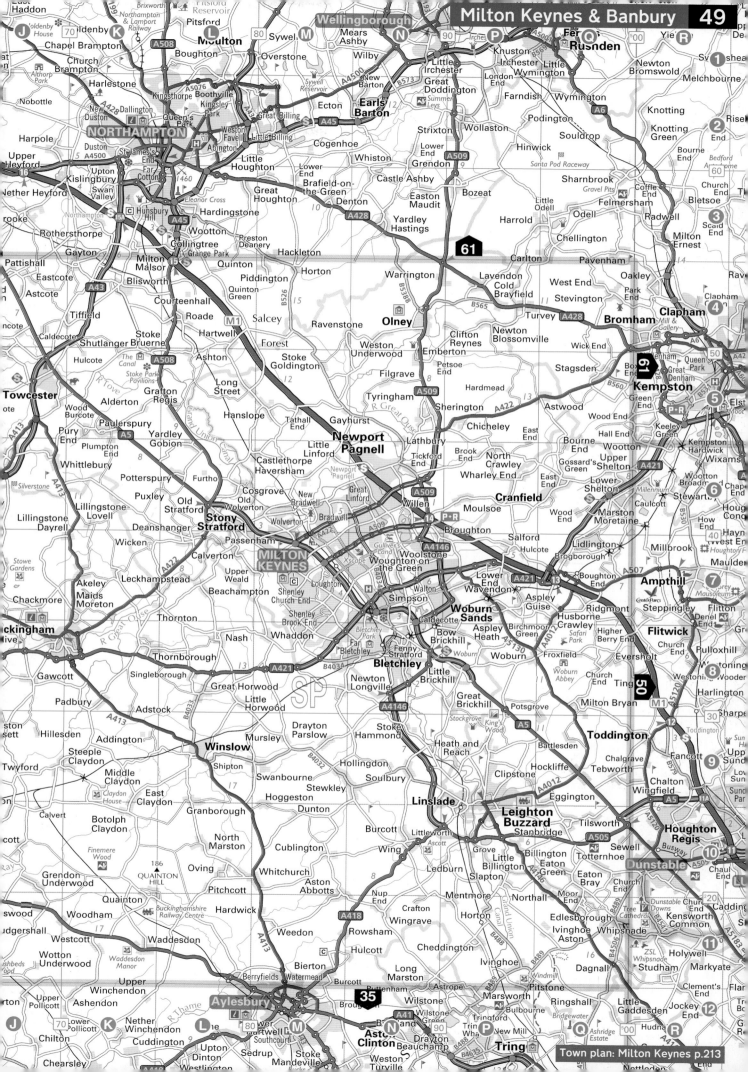

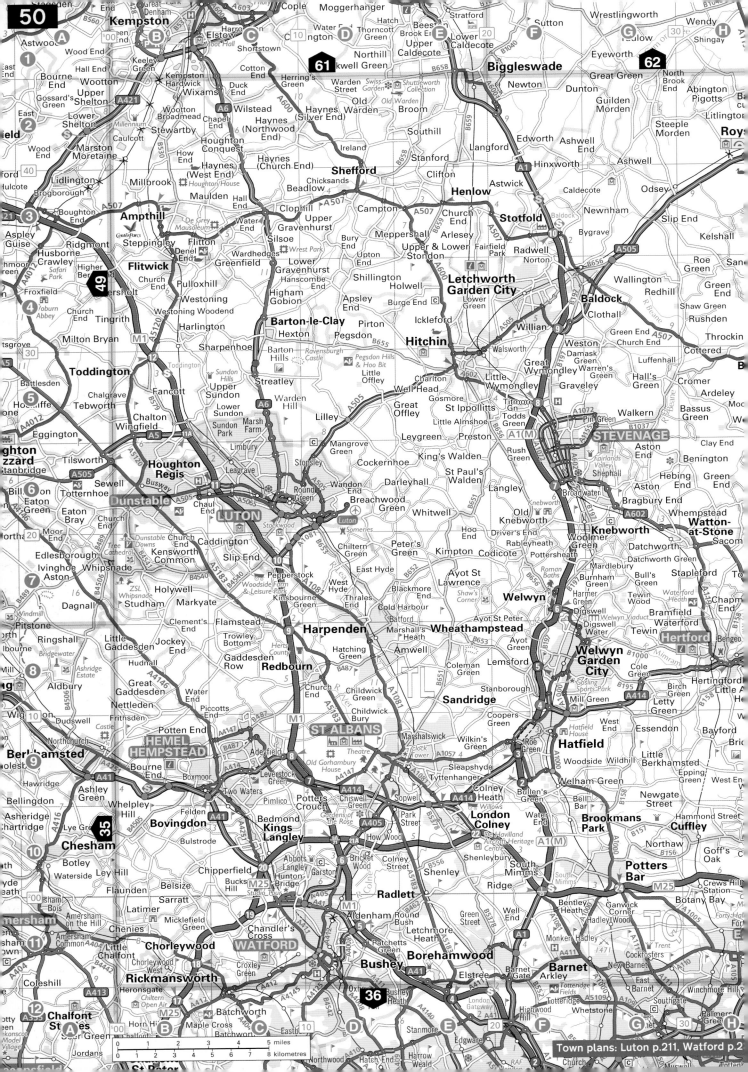

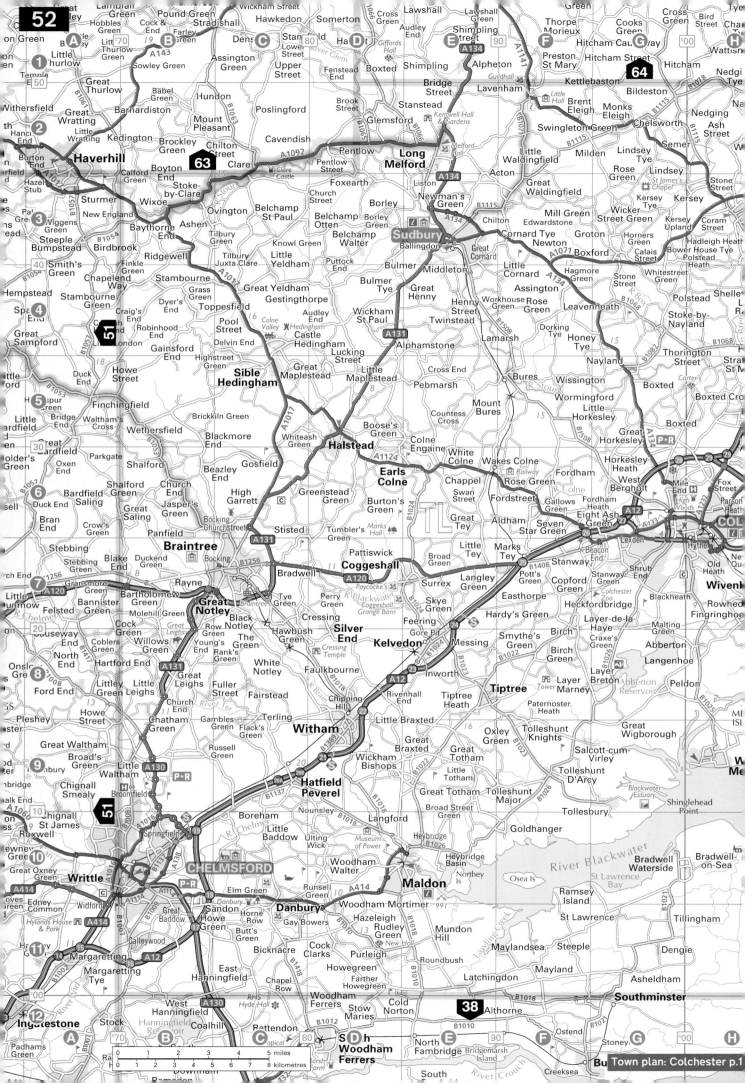

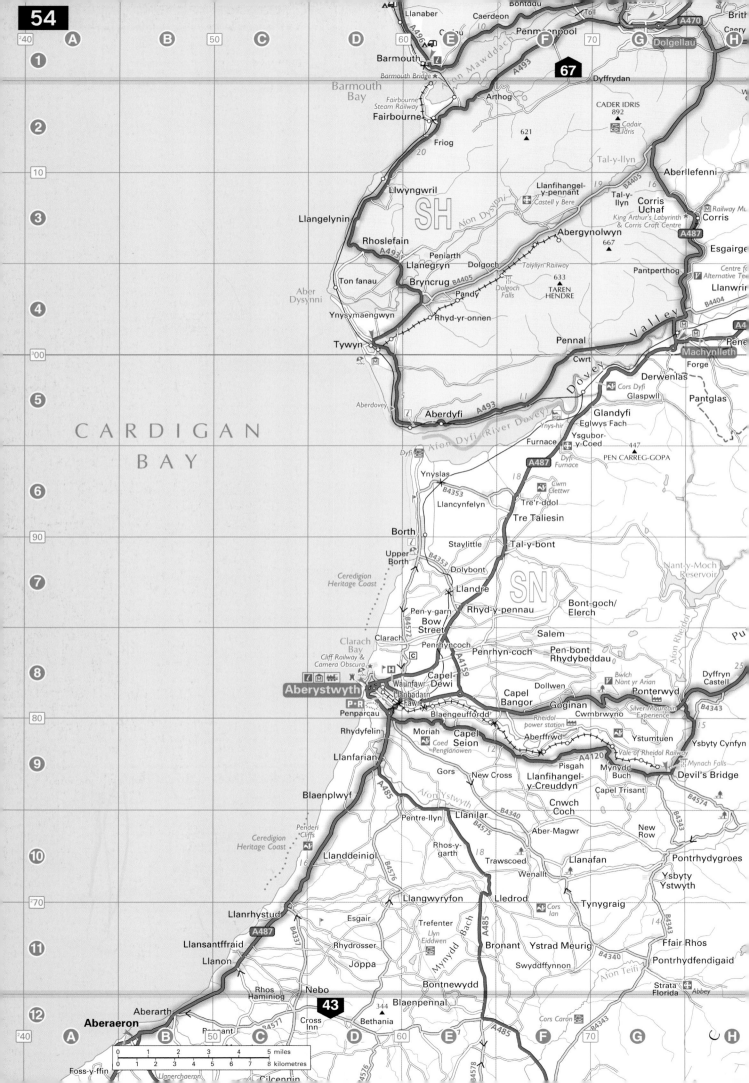

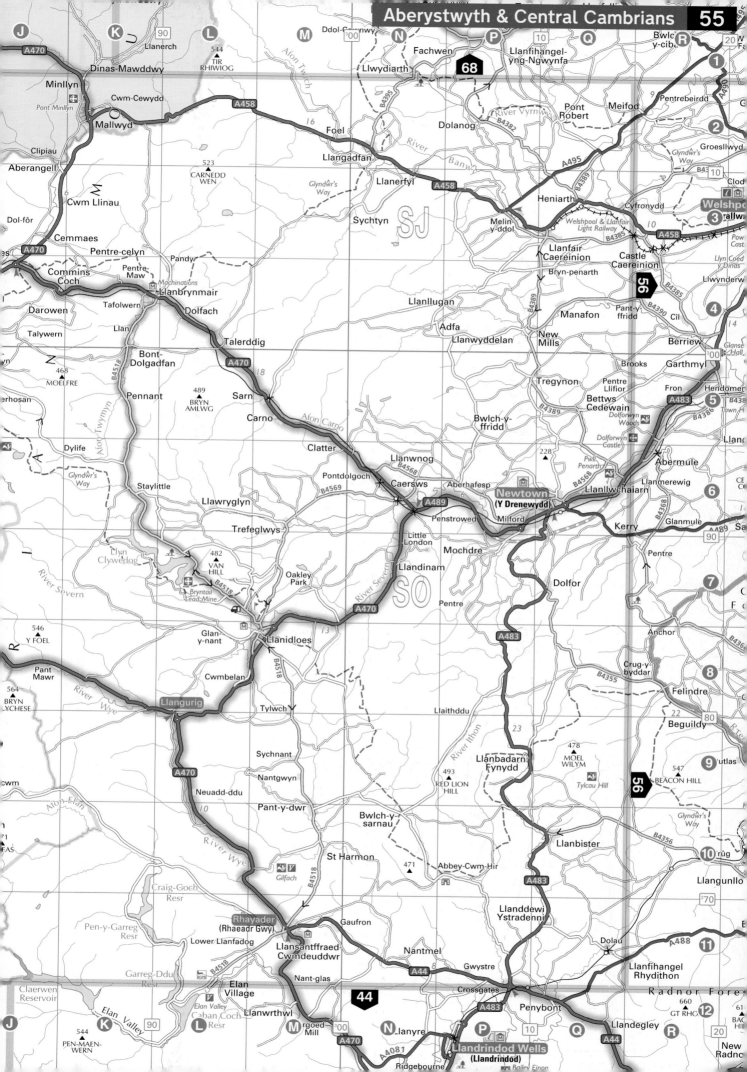

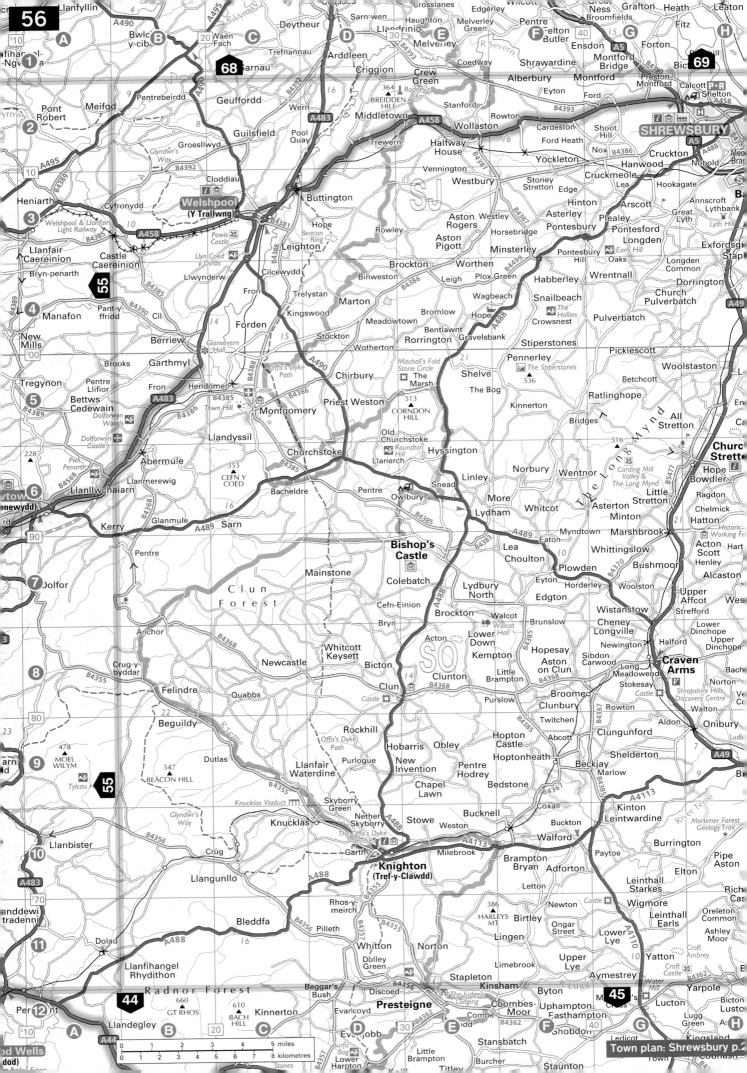

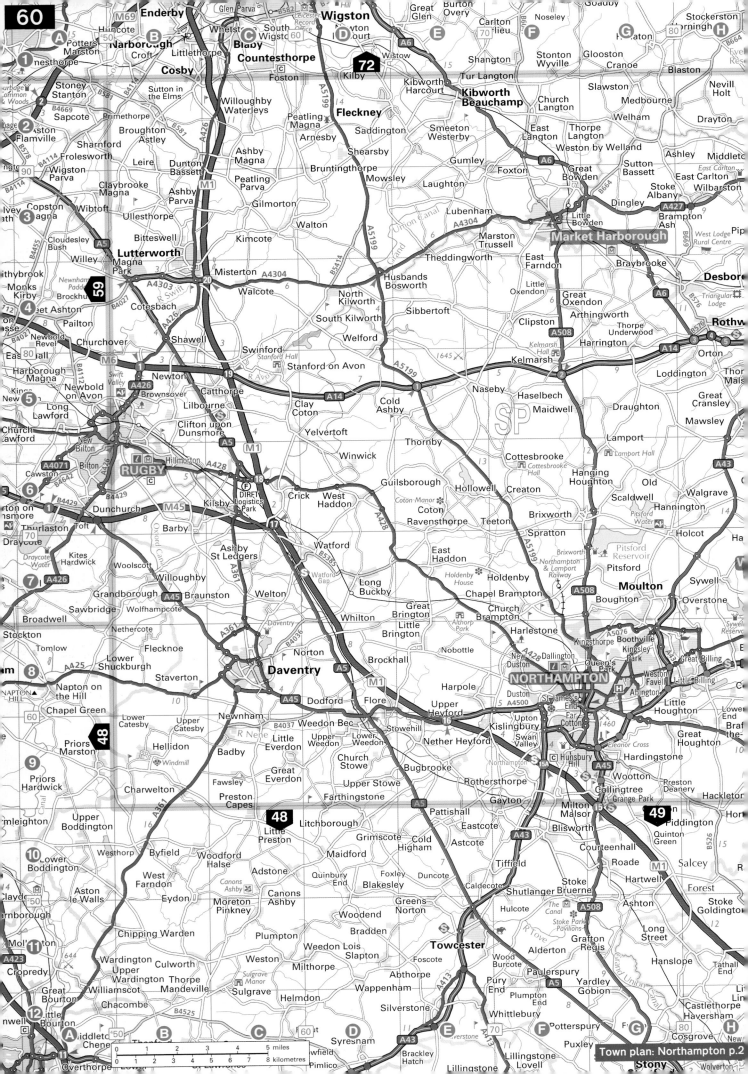

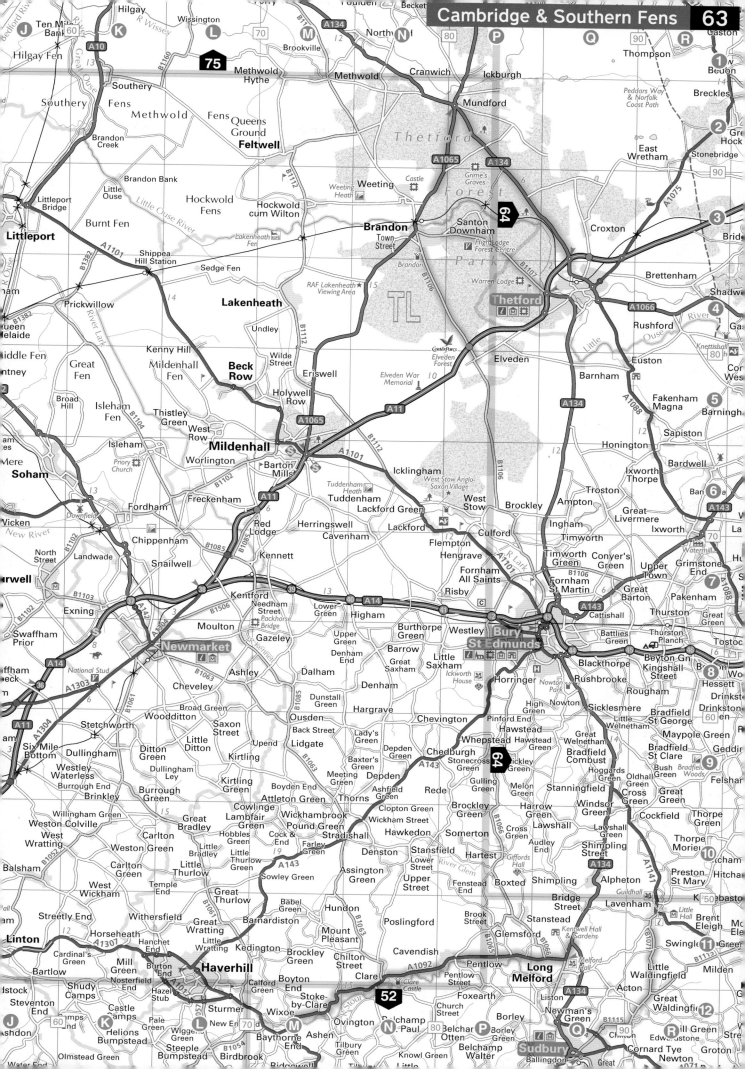

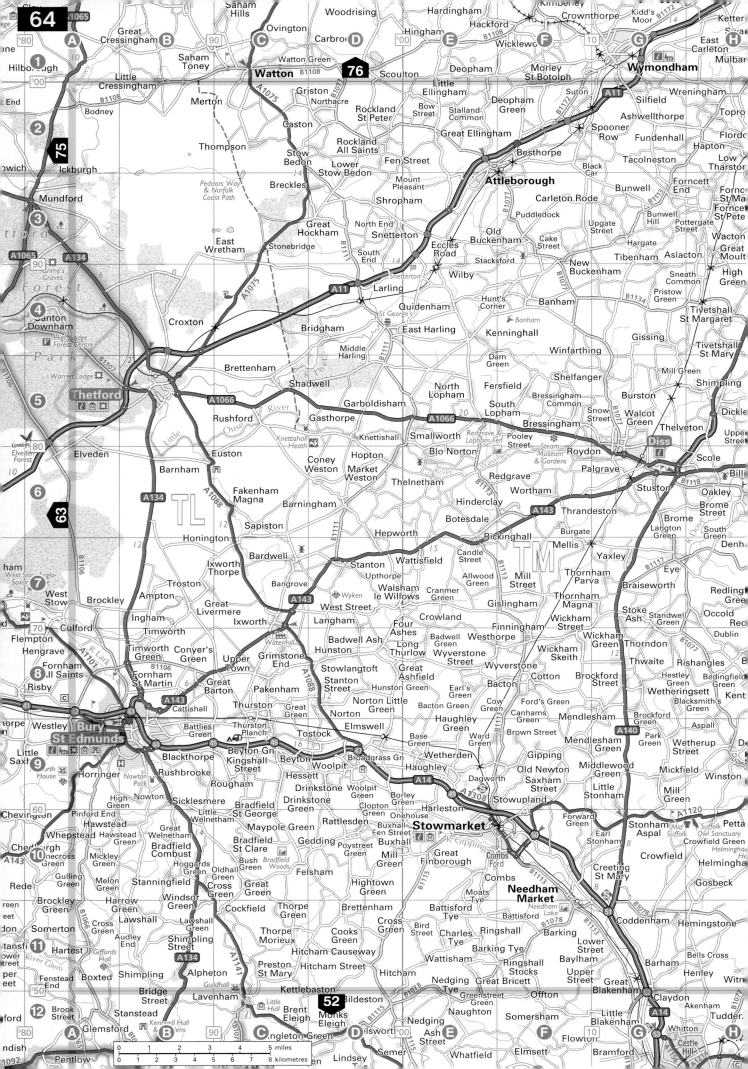

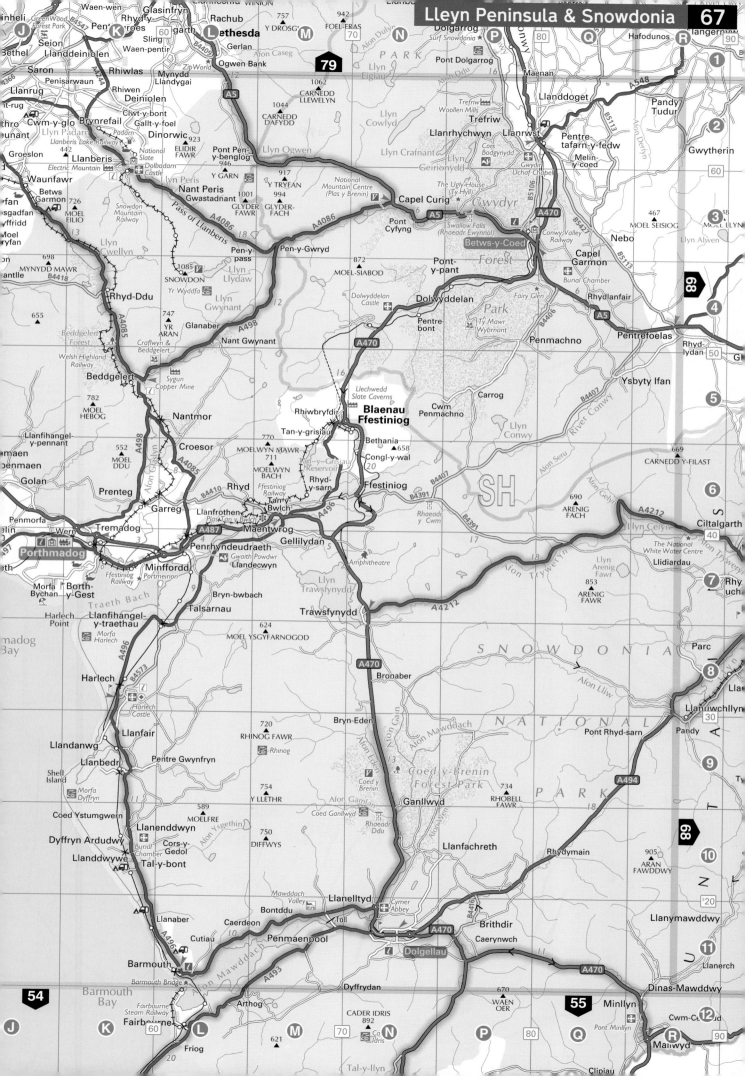

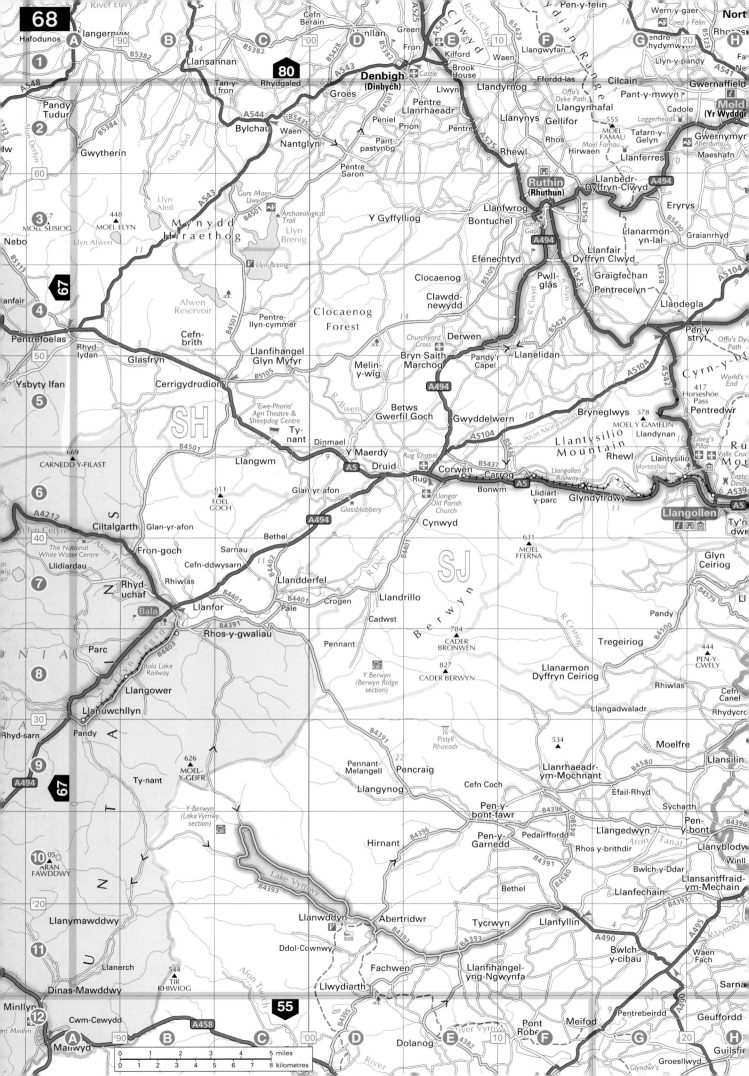

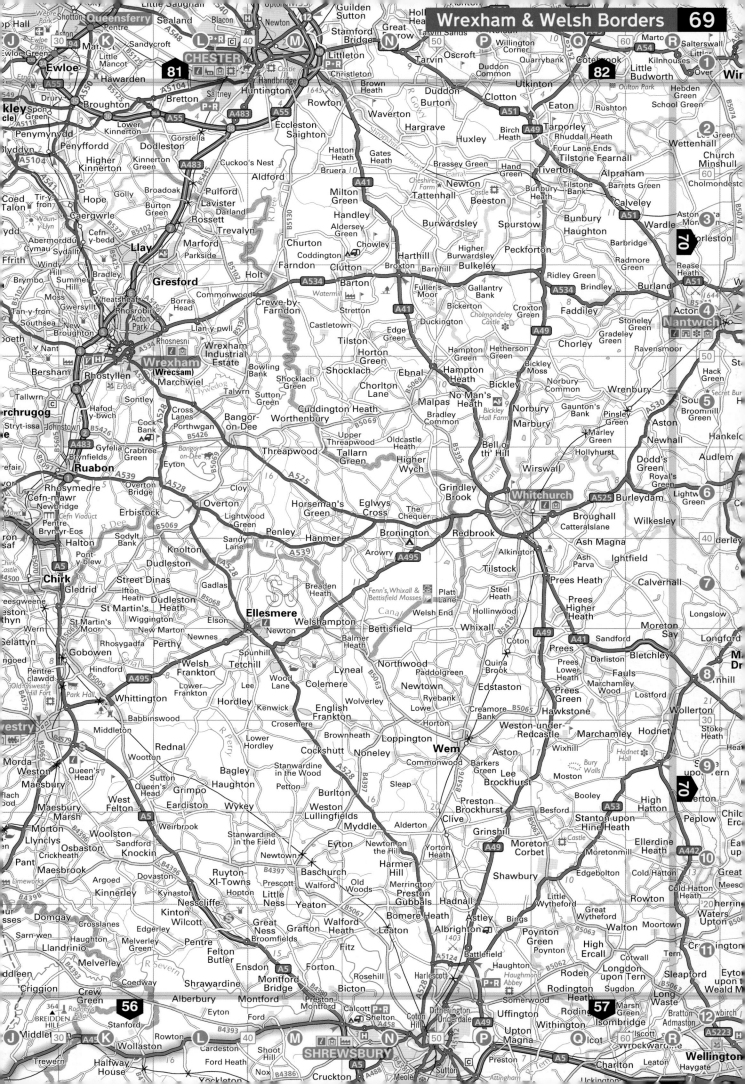

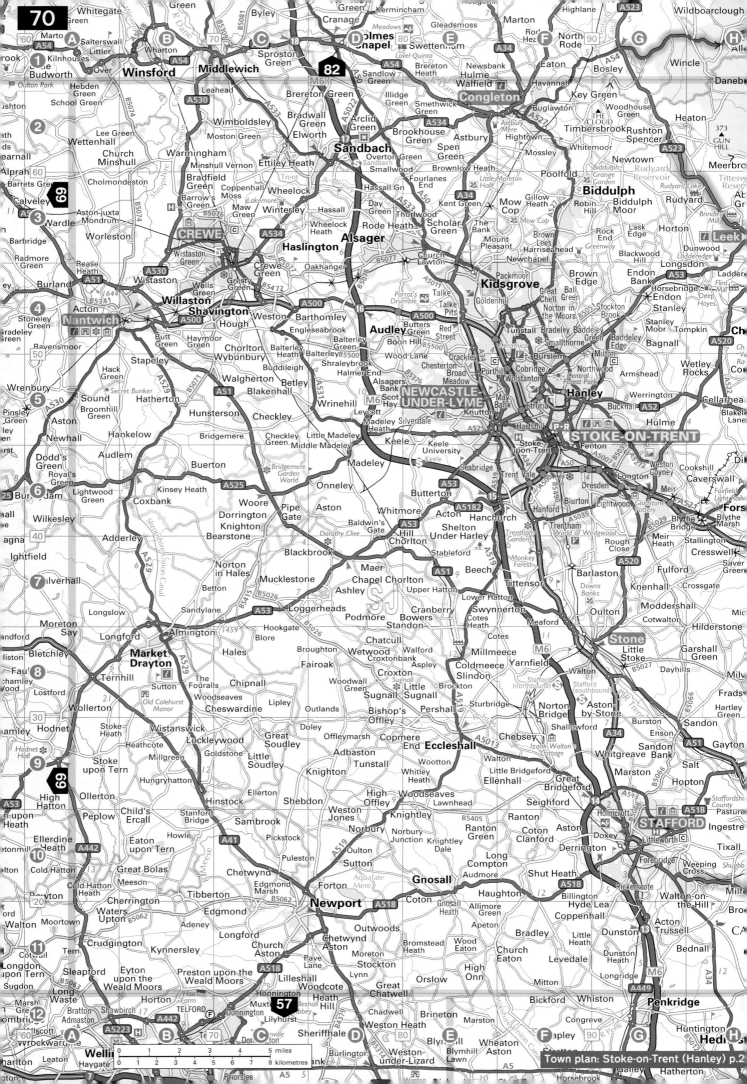

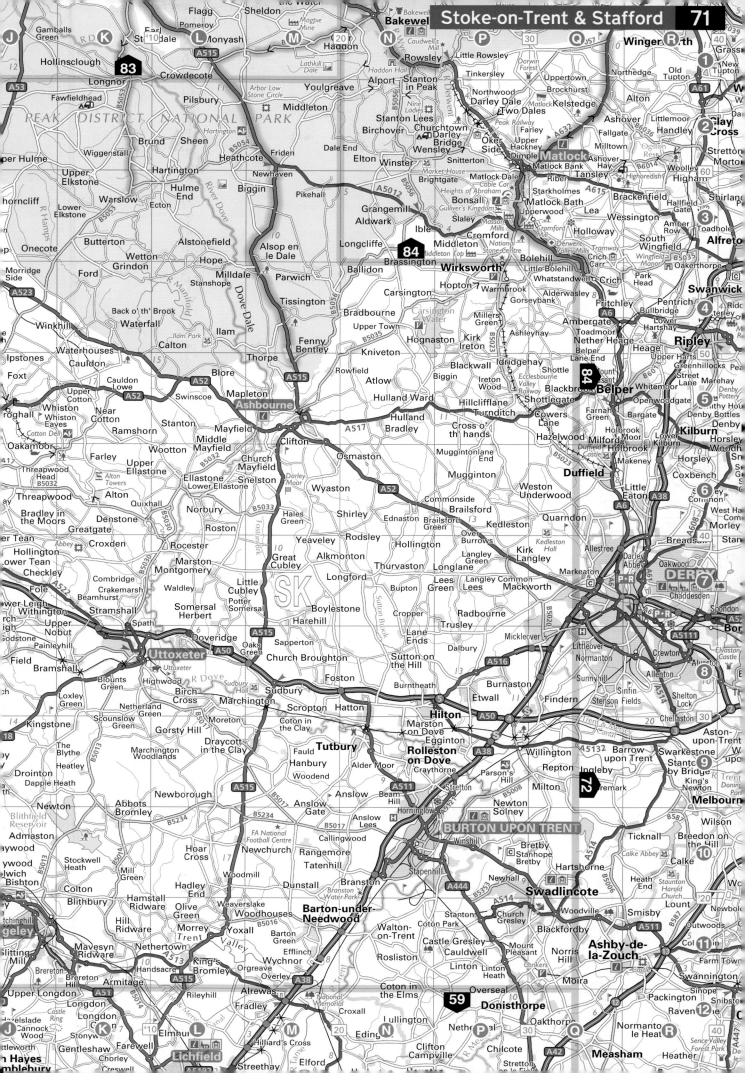

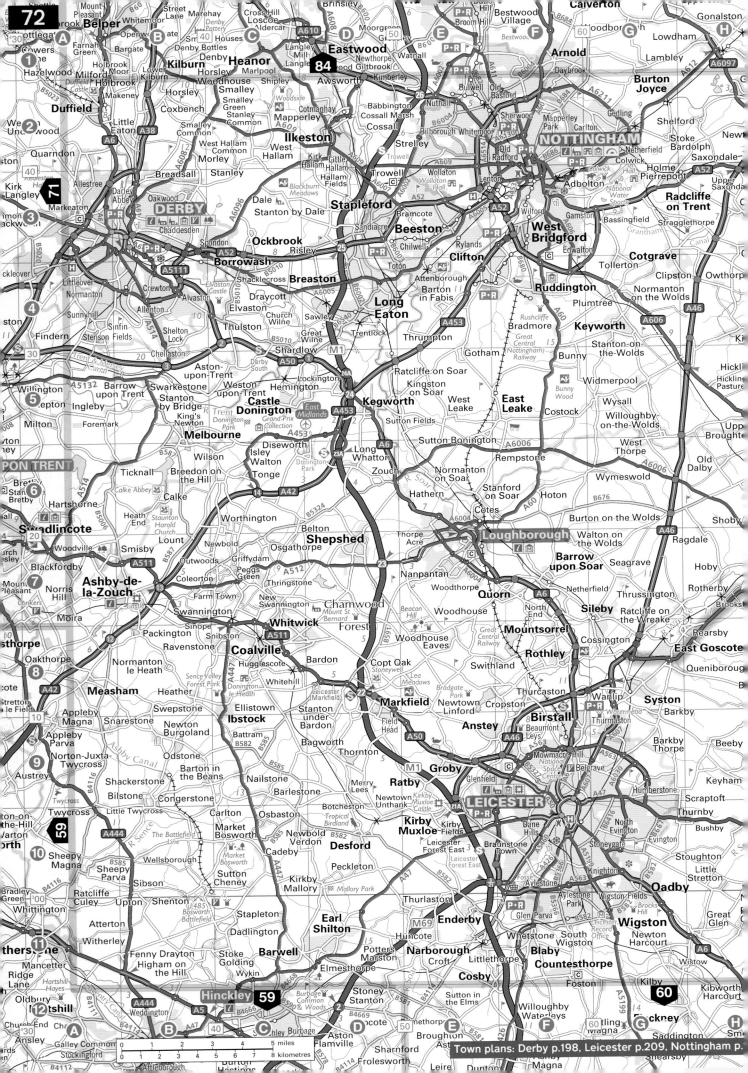

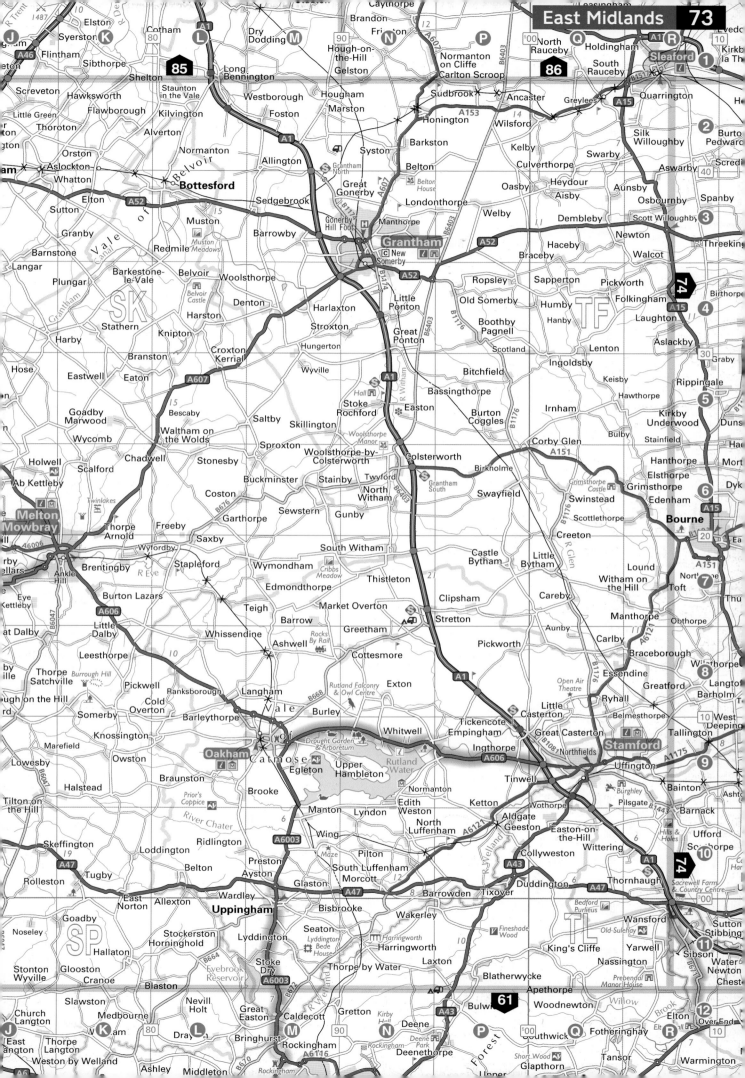

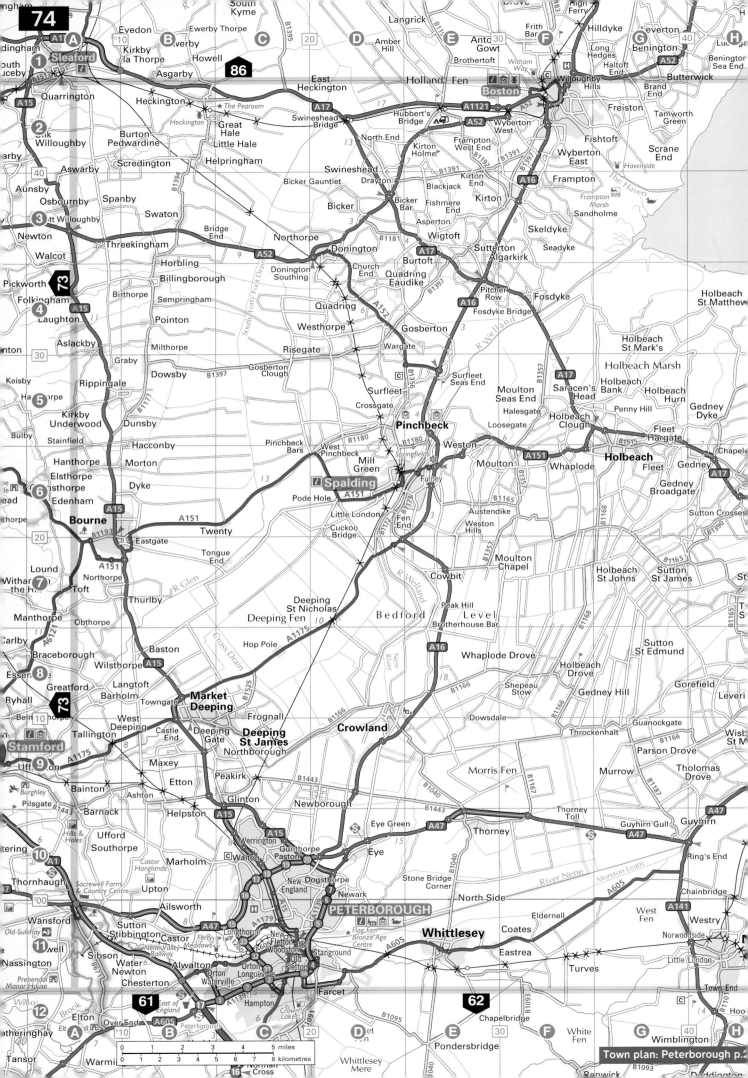

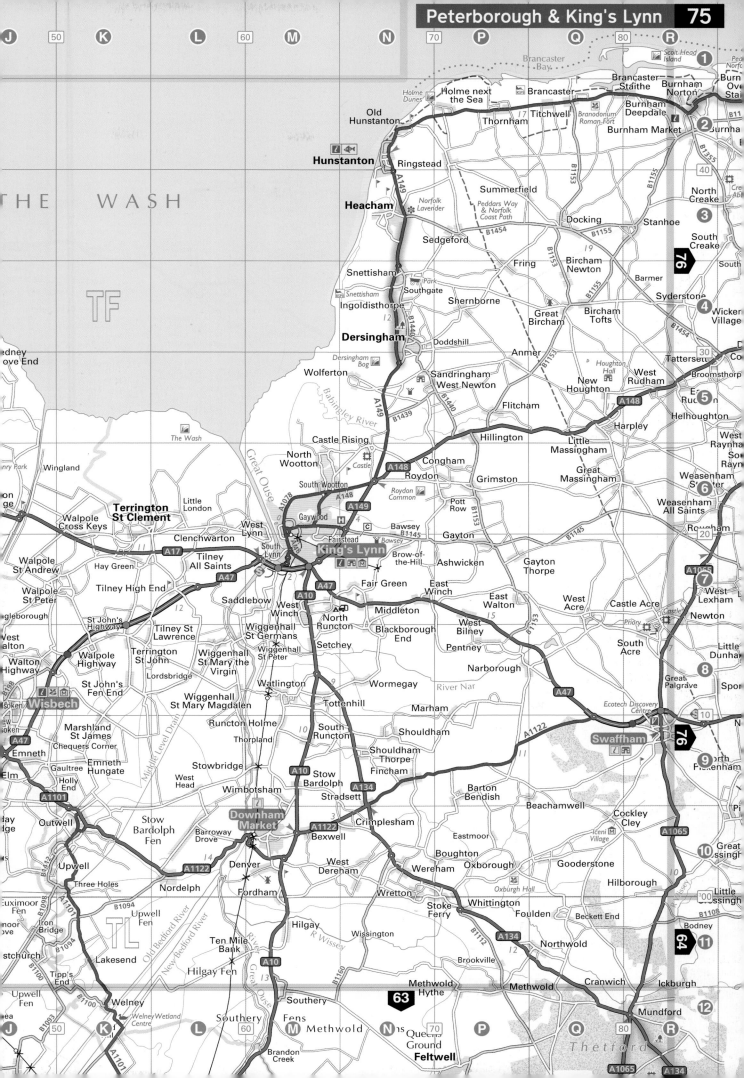

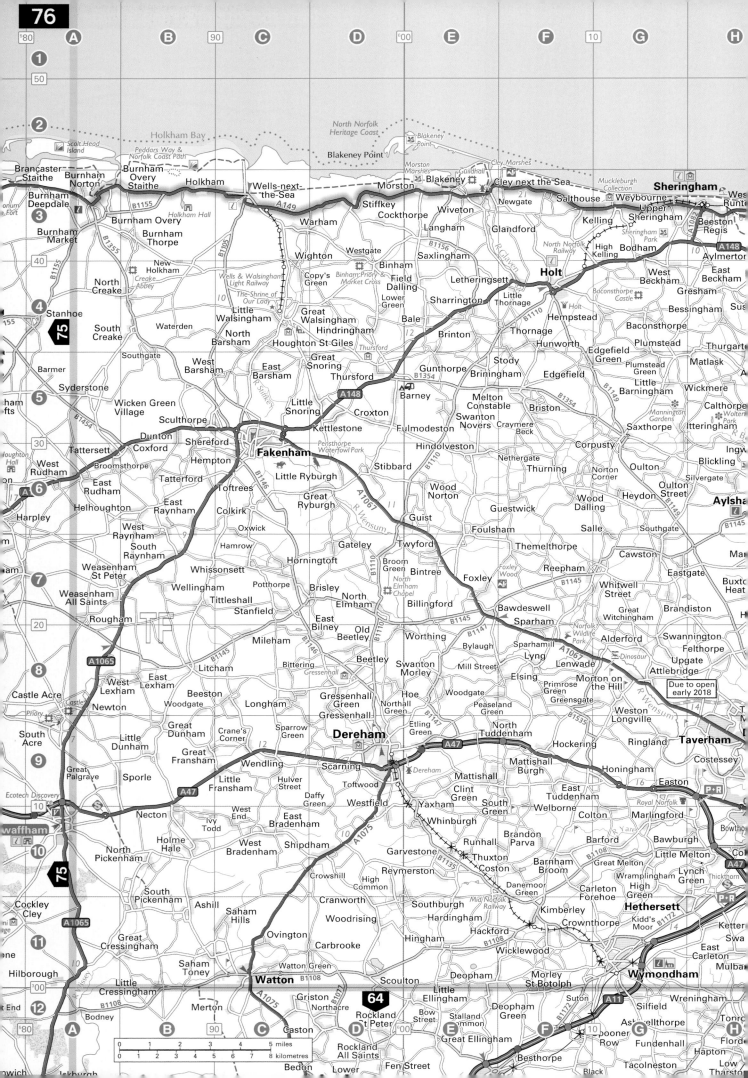

Holyhead Harbour

Marina
Maritime
Porth-y-Felin
BEACH ROAD
Porth-y-Felin
WALTHEW AVENUE
NEW PARK ROAD
PRINCE STREET
VICTORIA ROAD
A5154
SOUTH STACK ROAD
P+R Long stay
Hertz Car Rental
FERRY TERMINAL
TERMINAL BUILDING
P Short stay
HOLYHEAD
HOLYHEAD STATION
Morawelon
Stryd
PLAS ROAD
RESERVOIR ROAD
Kingsland
KINGSLAND ROAD B545
PORTH-Y-FELIN
A55
A5
A5
LONDON ROAD
LLANFAWR ROAD
CYTTIR ROAD
A5153
A5
Kingsland
BANGOR
Salt Island
H
LBLM
0   500 m

The Skerries
North Anglesey Heritage Coast
Wylfa Head
Cemaes Bay
Llanbadrig
Porth Wen
Bull Bay
Bull Bay
Amlwch
Llaneilian
Hen Borth
Cemlyn Bay
Cemaes
A5025
Burwen
Peng
CARMEL HEAD
Tregele
Pentrefelin
Llanfairynghornwy
Llanfechell
Rhosbeirio
Bodewryd
Penysarn
Nebo
Swtan Folk
17
Rhosgoch
Gadfa
City Dulas
Llanrhyddlad
Llanfflewyn
Carreglefn
Rhosybol
Holyhead Bay
Church Bay
Dublin
Llanfaethlu
Llanbabo
Llyn Alaw
Capel Parc
Brynrefail
B5111
Llandyfrydog
Dublin
Llanddeusant
Gwredog
Llanerchymedd
Maenaddv
Porth Tywynmawr
Llynnon Mill
Elim
Llantrisant
Hebron
Bachau
North Stack
Breakwater
Llanfwrog
Stryd-y-Facsen
Pen-llyn
Llanfigael
Capel Coch
Bry
Gogarth Bay
Holyhead Mountain Hut Circles
Holyhead (Caergybi)
Llanfachraeth
Cors Erddreiniog
Llaingoch
Penrhos
Llyn Llywenan
ANGLESEY
Tregaian
South Stack
Ellins Tower
Penrhos Feilw
Kingsland
Llanynghenedl
Llanfigael
Llechcynfarwy
Llangwyllog
B5111
Holyhead Mountain Heritage Coast
3
A5
B5112
Trefor
B5109
B5110
Rhosm
Penrhyn Mawr
Trefignath
Valley
A5025
Bodedern
Llechcynfarwy
Llyn Llywenan
Presaddfed
B5109
Cefni Reservoir
Oriel Ynys Môn
A55
B4545
Trearddur Bay
Caergeiliog
Bryngwran
Llynfaes
Bodffordd
21
HOLY ISLAND
Four Mile Bridge
Llanfihangel yn Nhowyn
4
Gwalchmai
Langwyllog
Llange
Llanfair-yn-Neubwll
Llechylched
5
Heneglwys
A5
Rhoscolyn
Valley
Capel Gwyn
10
Anglesey
A4080
Dothan
A55
Llangristiolus
Rhoscolyn Head
Plas Cymyran
Ty Newydd
Cerrigceinwen
18
Llangaffo
SH
Cymyran Bay
Pencarnisiog
Din-Dryfol
Rhosneigr
Llanfaelog
Bryn Du
Henblas
Pentre Berw
Barclodiad y Gawres
Ty Croes
Bethel
Capel Mawr
Trefdraeth
Gaerwen
Porth Trecastell
Llanddani
Aberffraw
Anglesey Circuit
Llangadwaladr
Hermon
Malltraeth
A4080
Llangaffo
B4419
Brynsien
Aberffraw Bay
Bodorgan
Bodwyr Burial Chamber
Ca
Castell Bryn Gwyn
Angles Sea
Foel Farm Park
Dwyran
Newborough
Pen-lôn
Aberffraw Bay Heritage Coast
Malltraeth Bay
Newborough W
Caernarfo
Llanddwyn Island
Llanddwyn Bay
Abermenai Point
Caernarfon Castle
Welsh Highland Railway

0 1 2 3 4 5 miles
0 1 2 3 4 5 6 7 8 kilometres

Llandudno

0   200 m

Llandudno Bay

TABOR HILL
Great Orme Tramway
HILL TERRACE
The Grand Hotel
North Shore Beach

The Old Bank Gallery
War Memorial

Travelodge
GLODDAETH STREET
MOSTYN STREET
SOUTH PARADE
A546
The Promenade

Town Hall
St John's
THE PARADE
A546
B5115

DEGANWY

Our Lady Star of the Sea
Victoria
Holy Trinity
Mostyn Gallery
Medical Centre
MOSTYN BROADWAY
Swimming Pool
Venue Cymru
St Paul's
MOSTYN AVE

Conwy Archive Service
LLANDUDNO STATION
CONWAY ROAD
Parc Llandudno Retail Park
CYLCH-TUDUR
Mostyn Champneys Retail Park
CLARENCE CRESCENT
CAE CLYD
PEN CLYD

Ysgol Tudno
Police Station
Magistrates' Court
Fire & Ambulance Station
CLARENCE DRIVE

Ysgol Ffordd Dyffryn
Superstore
Ysgol Craig Y Don

Coach
Ysgol Morfa Rhianedd
CONWAY ROAD
A470

LBLM
Llandudno FC
Ysgol John Bright
A55, BETWS-Y-COED

SH

Seawatch Centre

Moelfre
lgo
n-glas

Great Orme Heritage Coast
GREAT ORMES HEAD
Great Orme Tramway
Toll
Little Ormes Head
Penrhyn Bay

Rhôs-on-Sea
Colwyn B 80
(Bae Colwyn)

Benllech
Red Wharf Bay
Puffin Island
Black Point
Conwy Bay
Llandudno
Penrhyn-side
Llandrillo-yn-Rhos
llanddi

Red Wharf Bay
Glan-yr-afon
Caim
Toll
Penmon
Llanrhos
Pydew
Deganwy
Esgyryn
Llysfaen Rh

Llanddona
Llangoed
B5109
Tywyn
Mochdre
Old Colwyn
A55

Pentraeth
Llanfaes
Beaumaris Castle
Dwygyfylchi
Conwy
Llandudno Junction
Llanelian-yn-Rhôs
9 llanddi

Beaumaris
Gaol
Penmaenan
Conwy Castle
Bryn-y-Maen
B5383
Dolwen

Llansadwrn
Courthouse
Penmaenmawr
Capelulo
Llansanffraid Glan Conwy
Betws-yn-Rhô

Llandegfan
A5545
Llanfairfechan
Garizim
Henryd
A470
80
Dawn
Betws yn-Rho

Menai Bridge
(Porthaethwy)
A55
Nant-y-pandy
Bangor
Gorddinog
S N O W D O N I A
610
TAL-Y-FAN
Rowen
Caerhun
Castell
B5106
Graig
Eglwysbach
Bodnant
Tal-y-Cafn
Trofarth

Igwyngyll
Britannia Bridge
Penrhyn Castle
Spinnies Abergowen
Abergwyngregyn
Coedydd Aber
Aber Falls
Ty'n-y-Groes
Pentre'r Felin
River Elwy

Plas Newydd
Cae'r garnedd
Tal-y-bont
Afon Anafon
Llanbedr-y-Cennin
Tal-y-Bont
N A T I O N A L
Dolgarrog
Surf Snowdonia
Maenan
Hafodunos
Llang yw

Cap'el-y-graig
Llandygai
580
MOEL WNION
Pont Dolgarrog
Llanddoget

Waen-wen
Glasinfryn
Rhyd-y-groes
Llanllechid
Rachub
Pentir
Bethesda
Gerlan
Y DROSGL 757
942 FOEL-FRAS
1062 CARNEDD LLEWELYN
Afon Dulyn
P A R K
Llyn Eigiau
Trefriw Woollen Mills
Pandy Tudur
Gwytherin

Seion
Llanddeiniolen
Saron
Mynydd Llandygai
ZipWorld
Ogwen Bank
Afon Caseg
67
Trefafan-y-fedw
B538

Penisarwaun
Rhiwlas
Rhiwen
Deiniolen
1044 CARNEDD DAFYDD
923
442
A5
Llanrhychwyn
Melin
Pentre-tafarn-y-fedw

Cwm-y-glo
Brynrefail
Gallt-y-foel
Dinorwic
National Slate
ELIDIR FAWR
Llyn Ogwen
Cors Bodgynydd
Llanrwst
Q
R
B5113
Gwytherin

roeslon
Llanberis Lake Railway
Pont Pen-y-benglog
Llyn Crafnant

Isle of Man

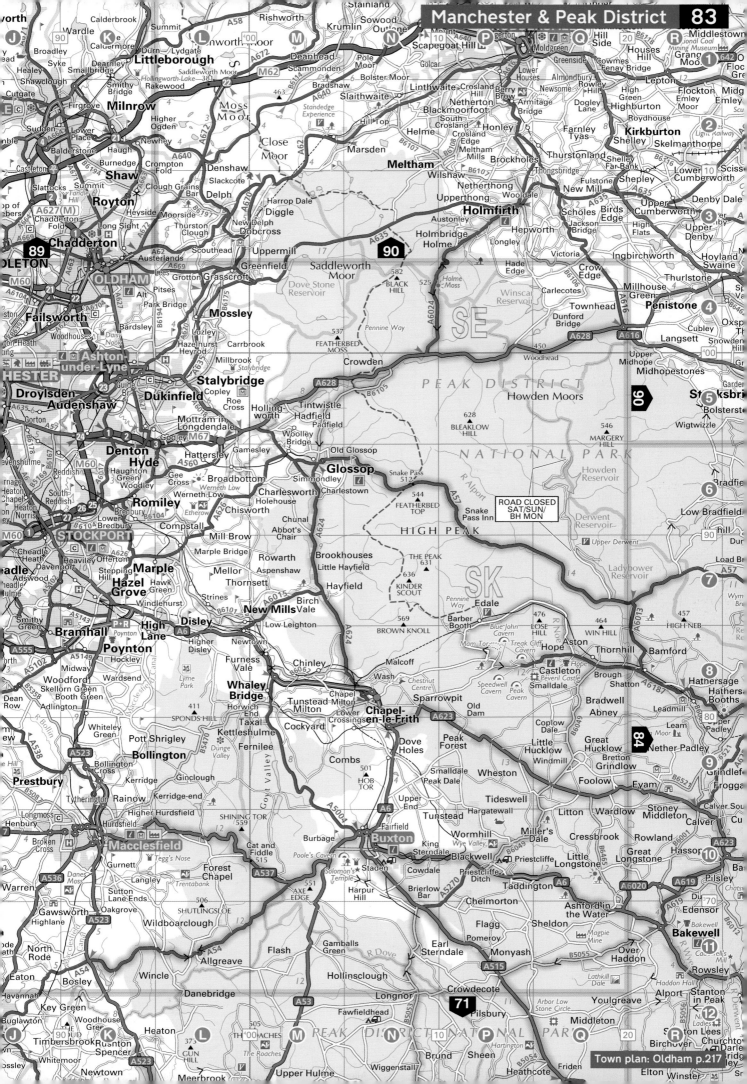

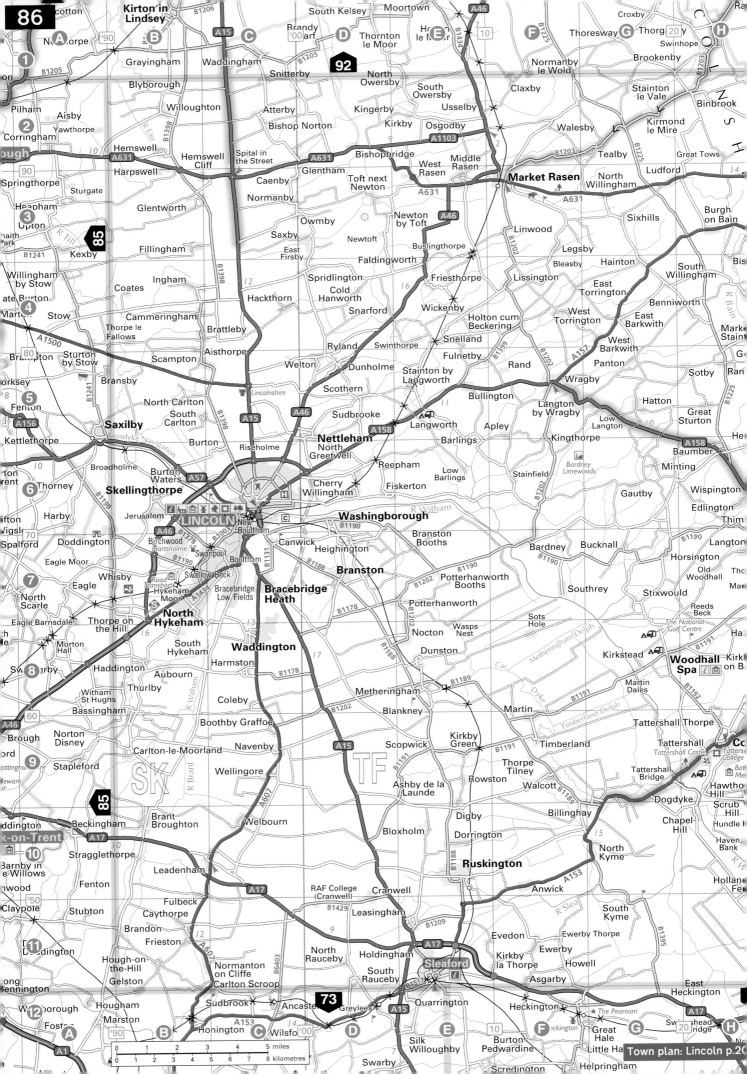

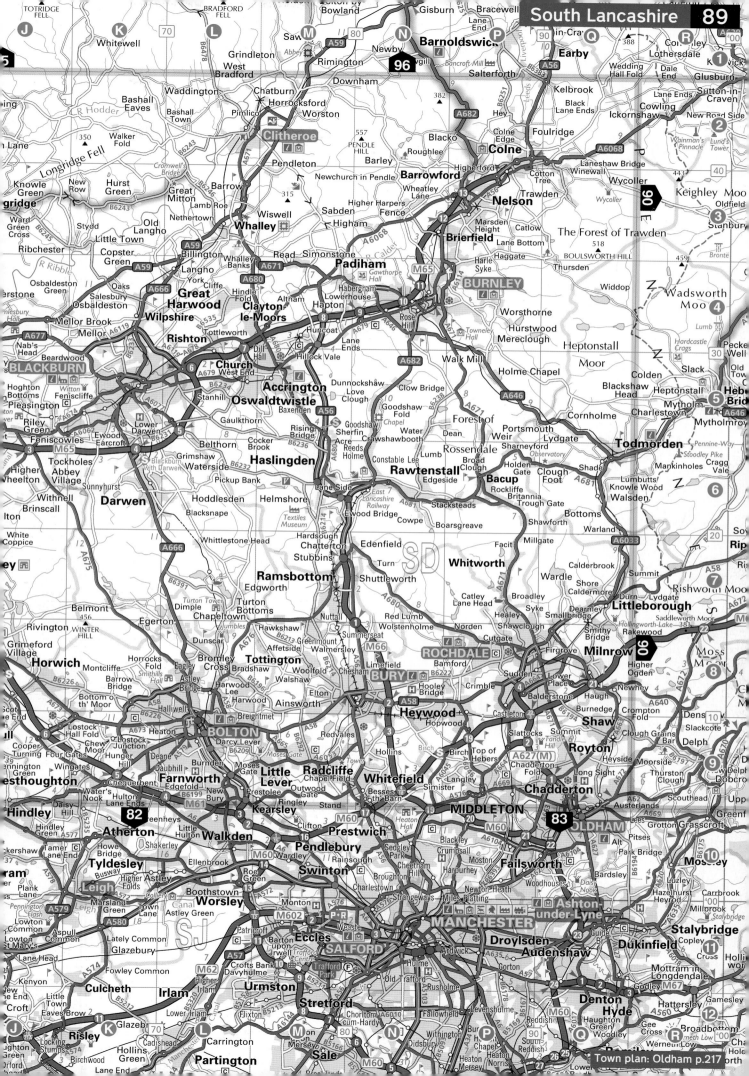

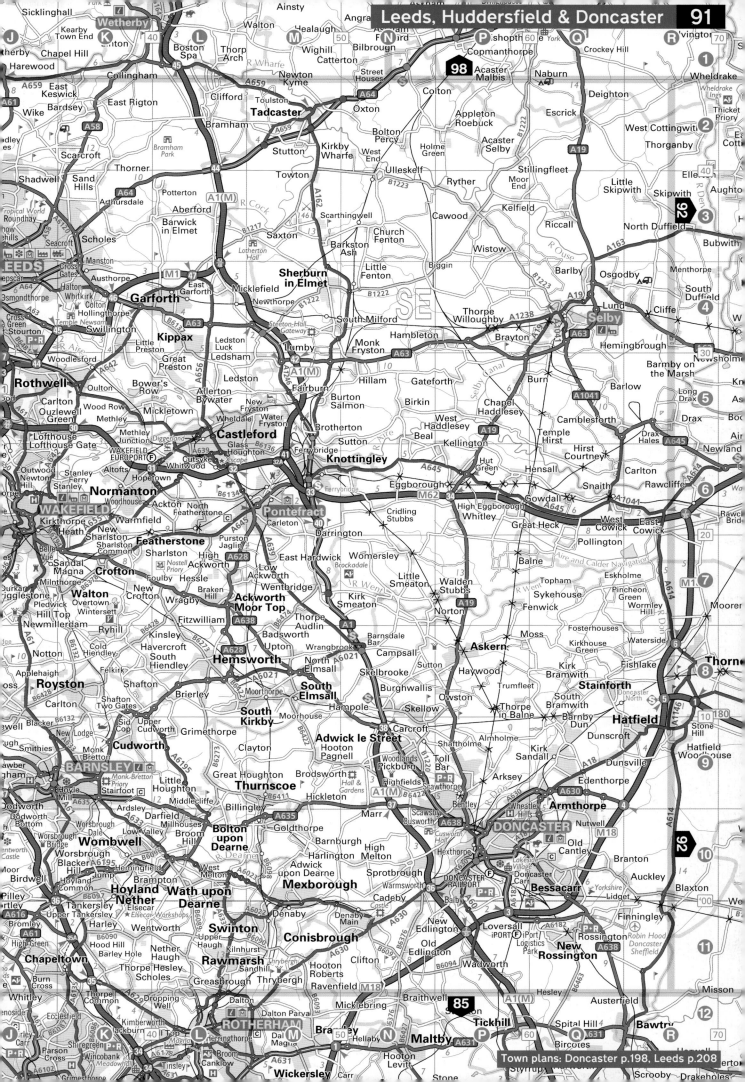

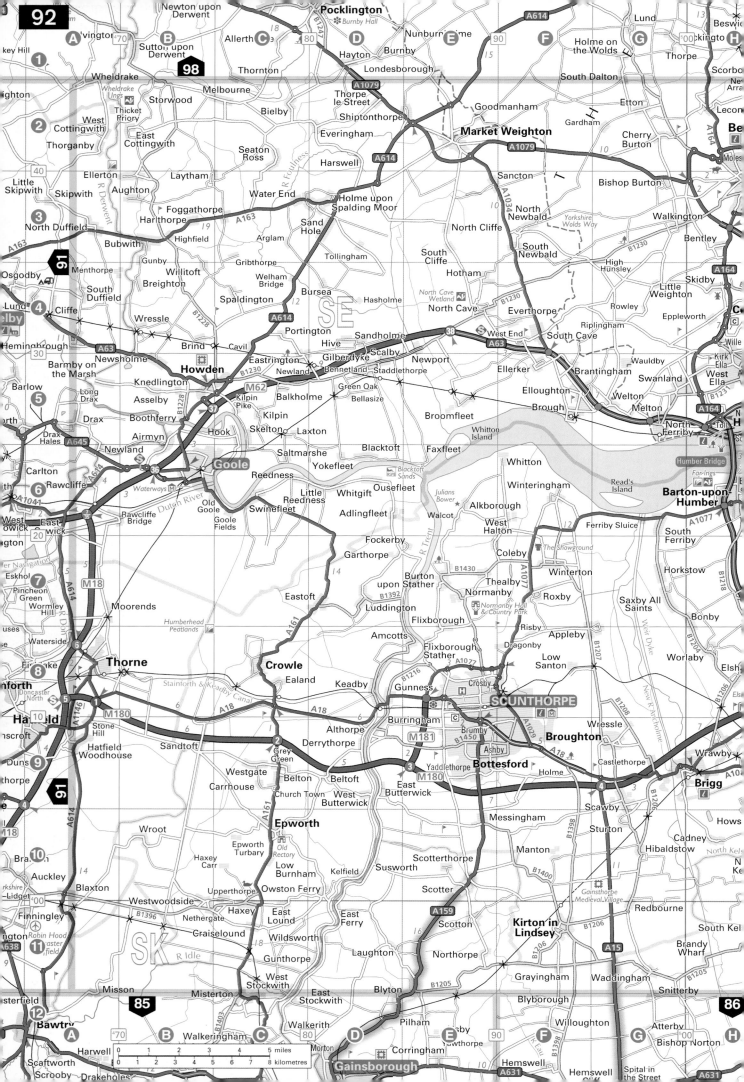

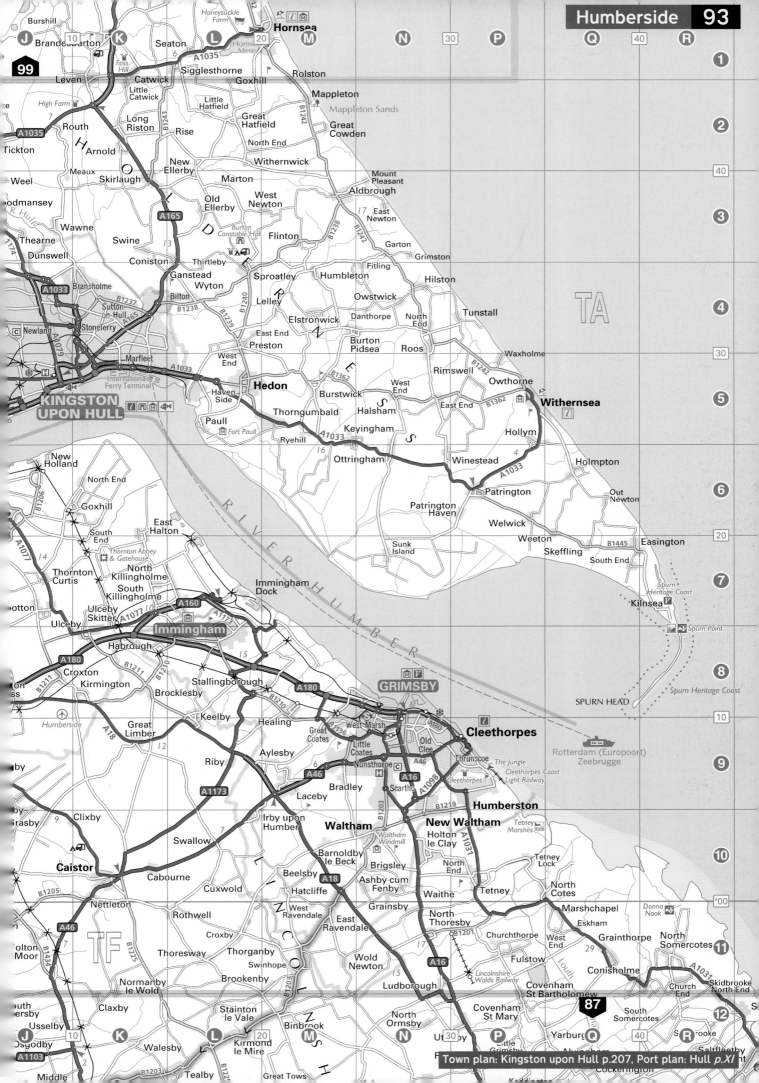

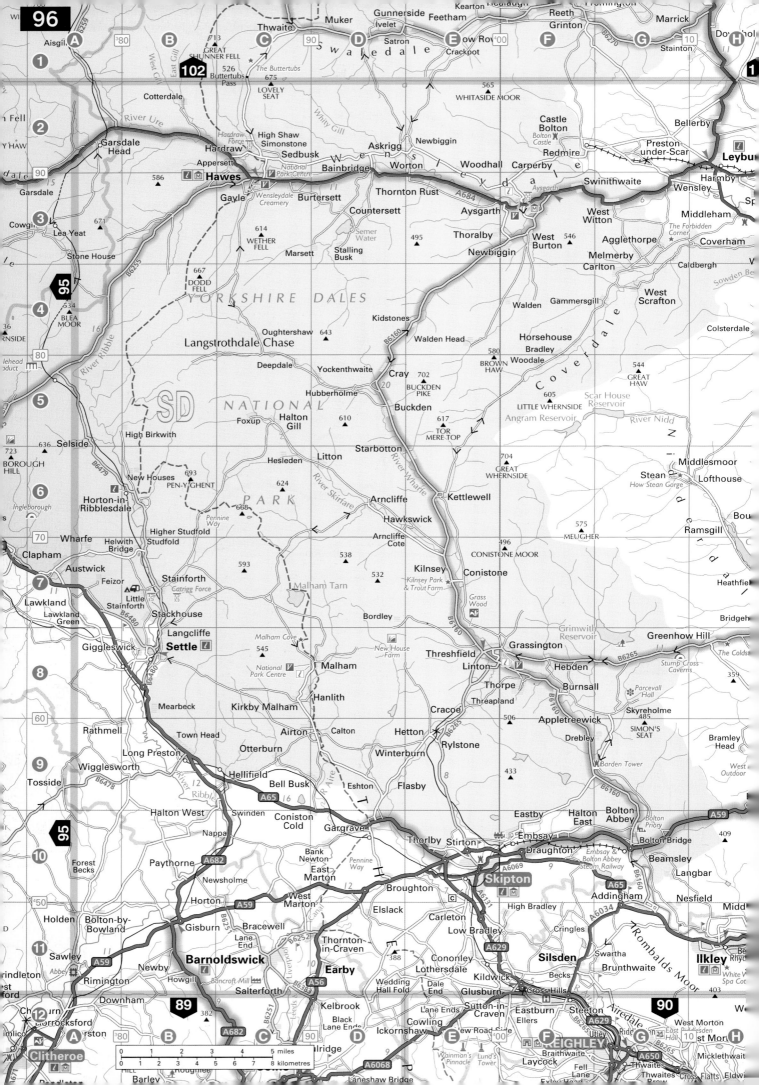

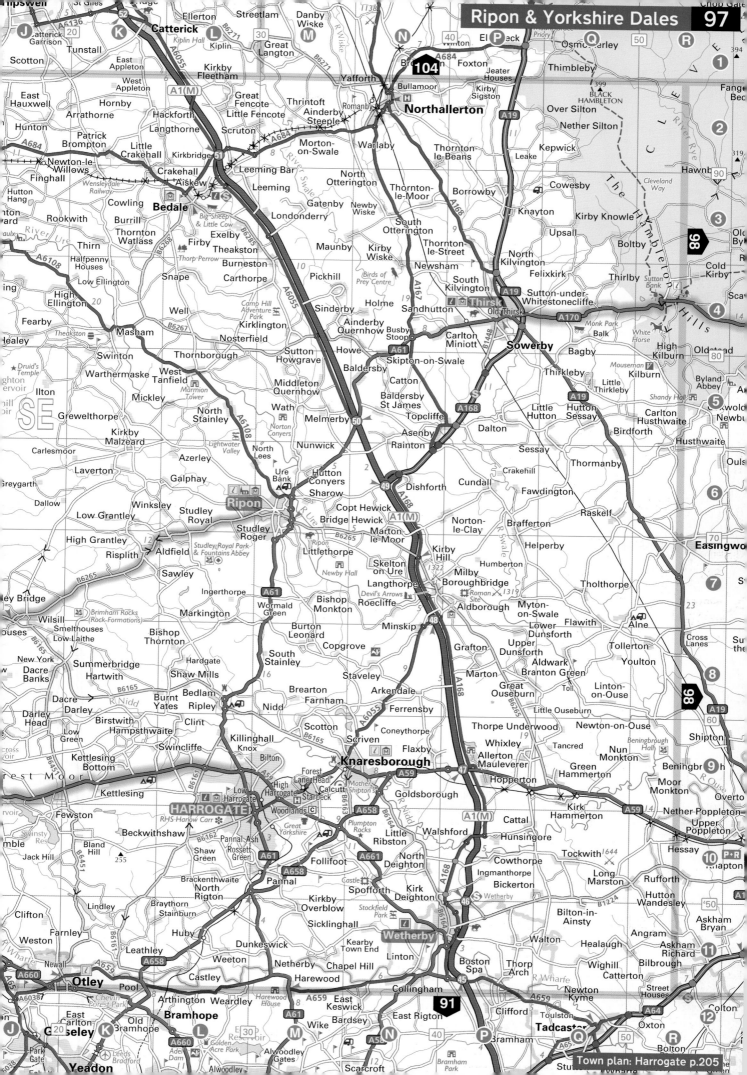

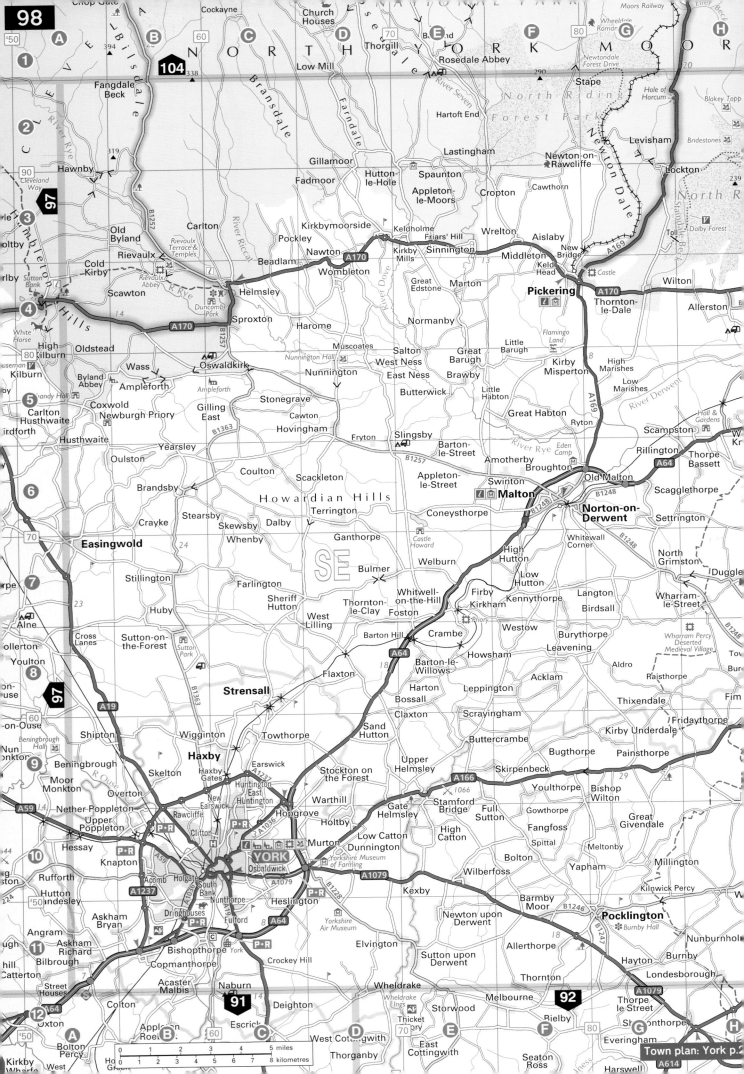

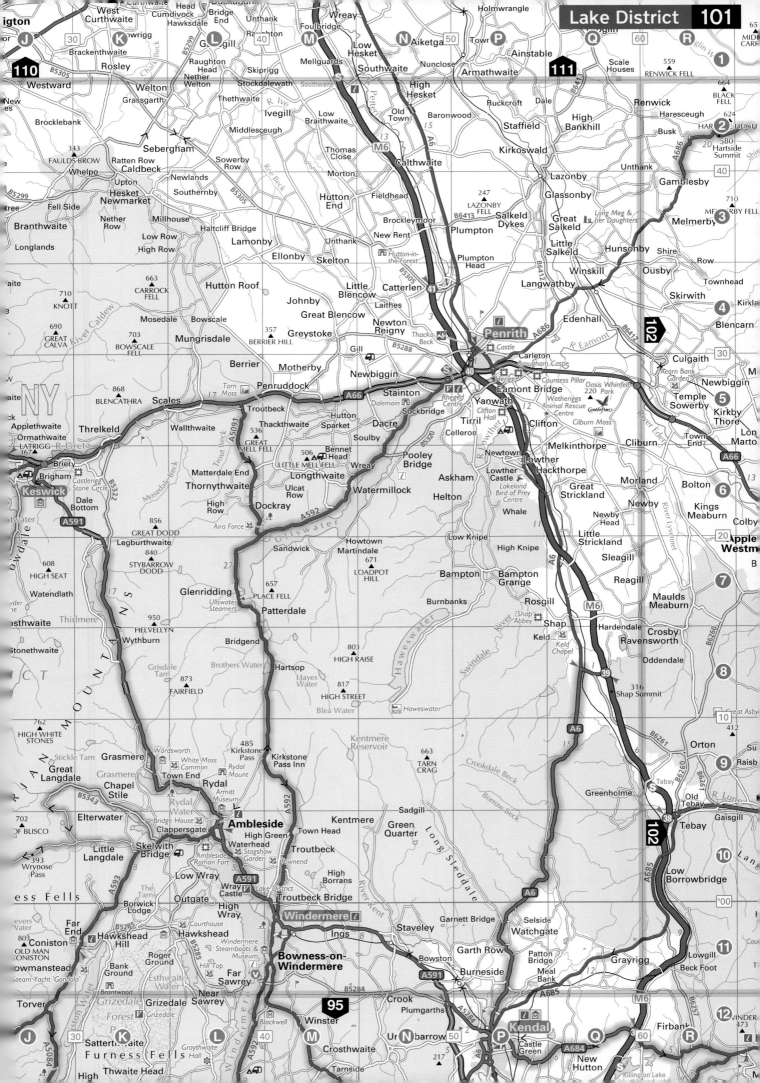

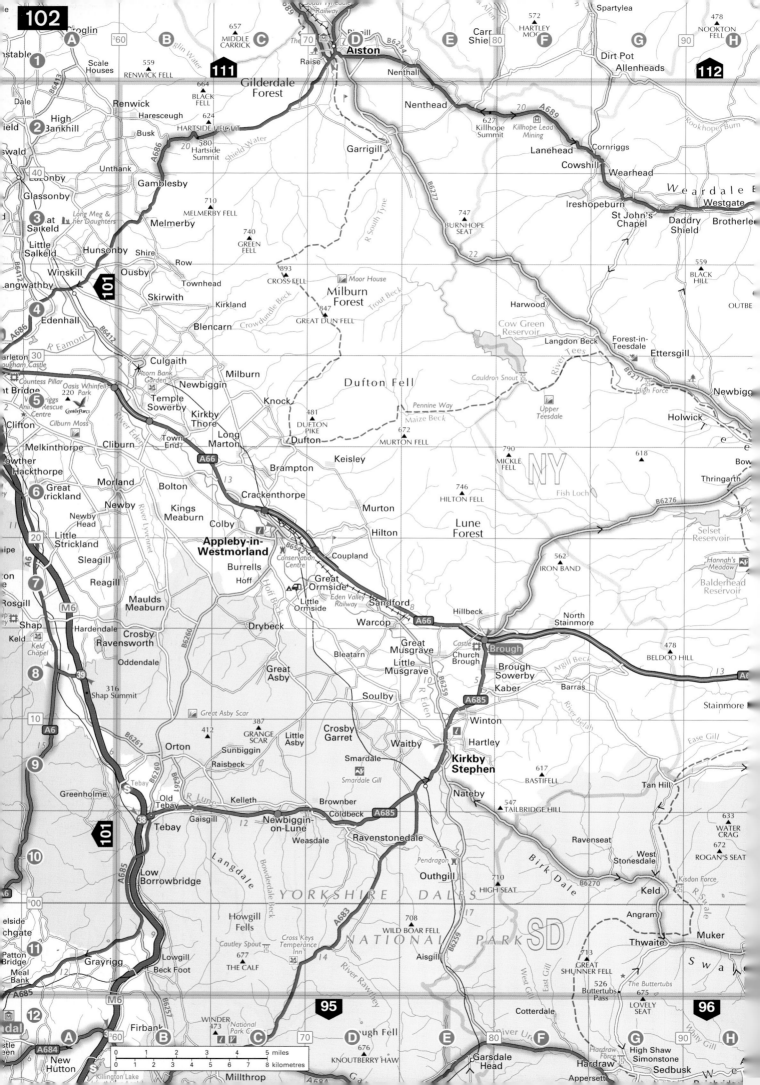

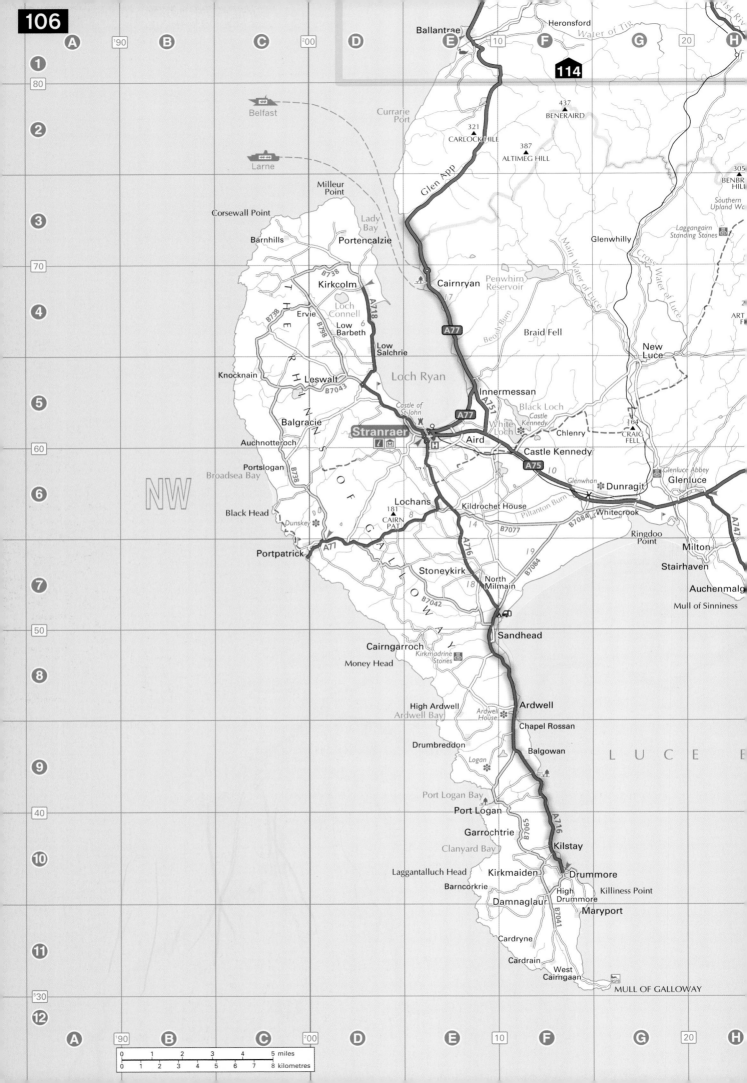

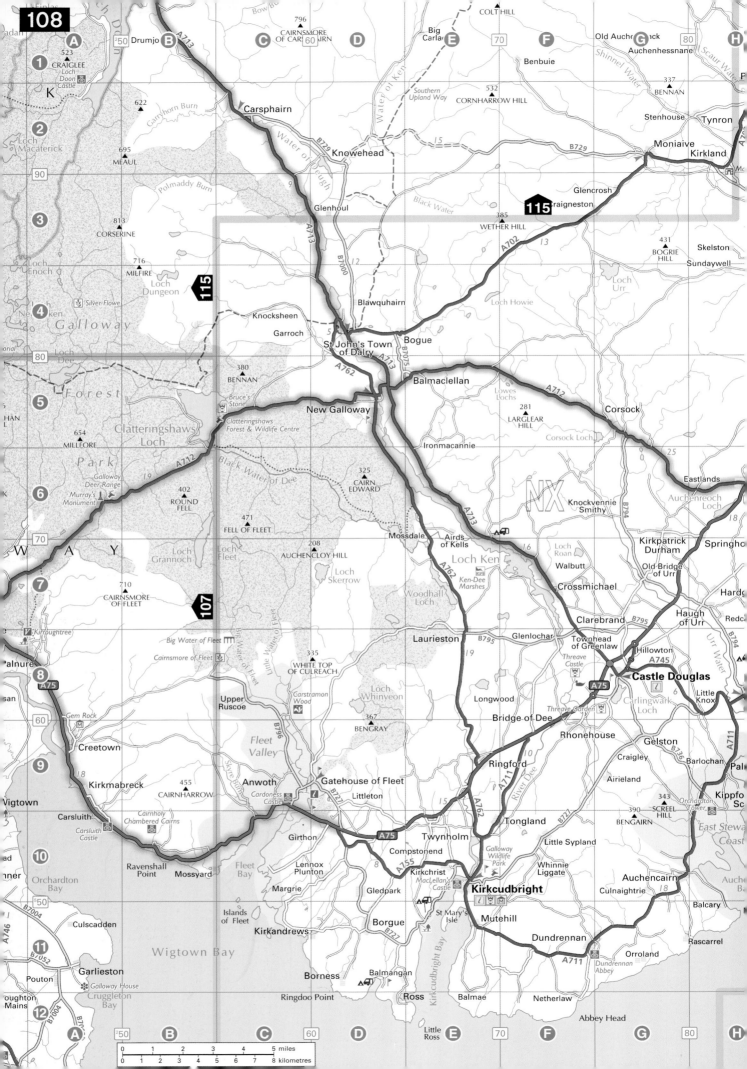

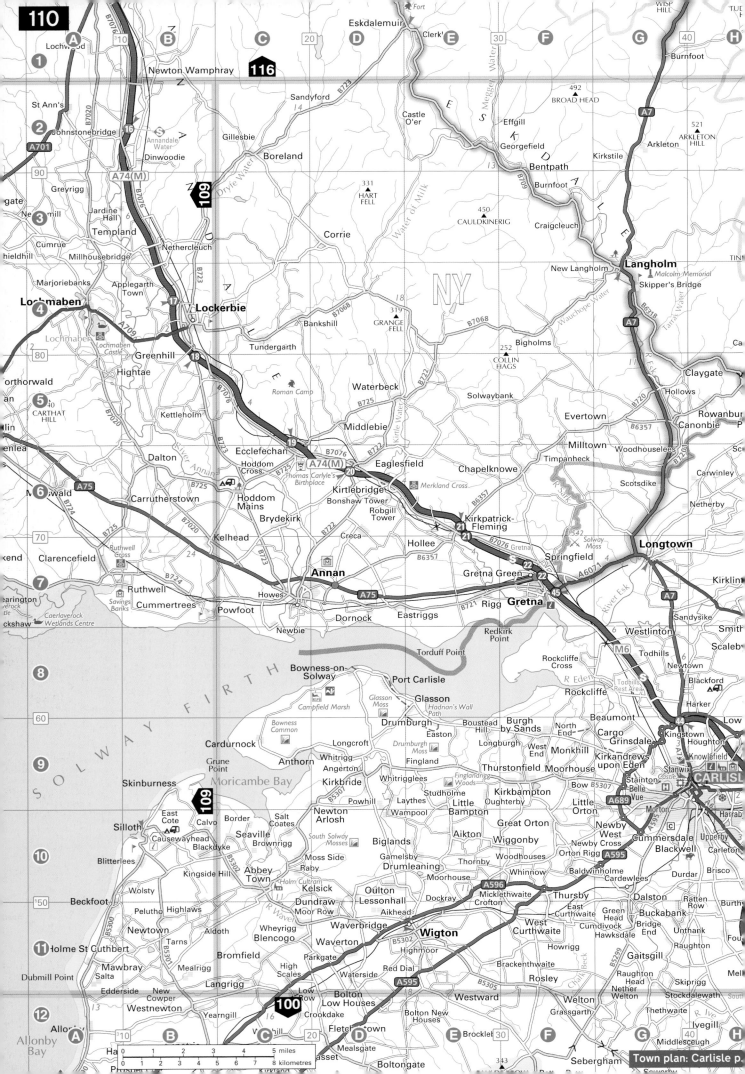

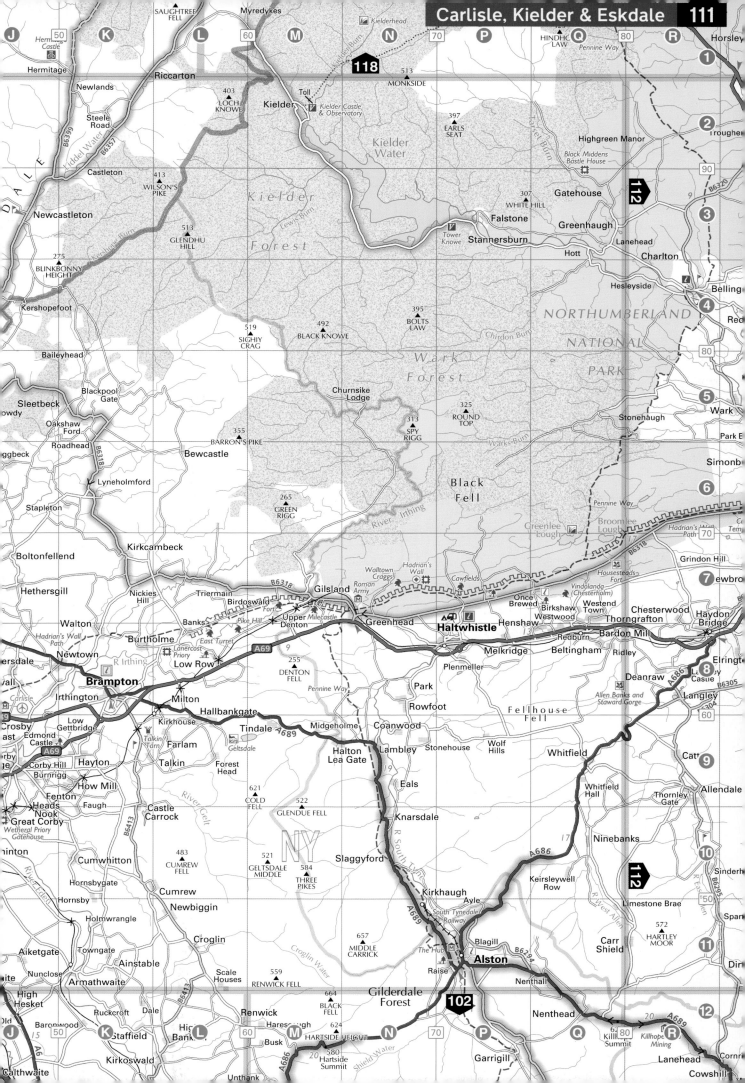

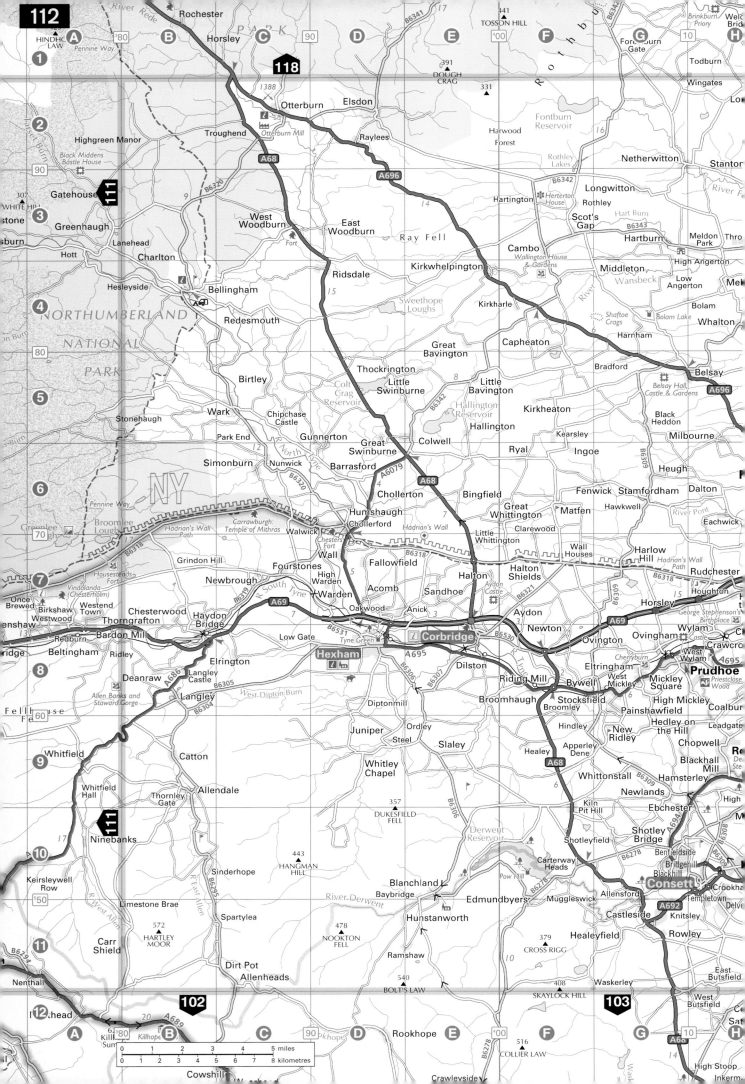

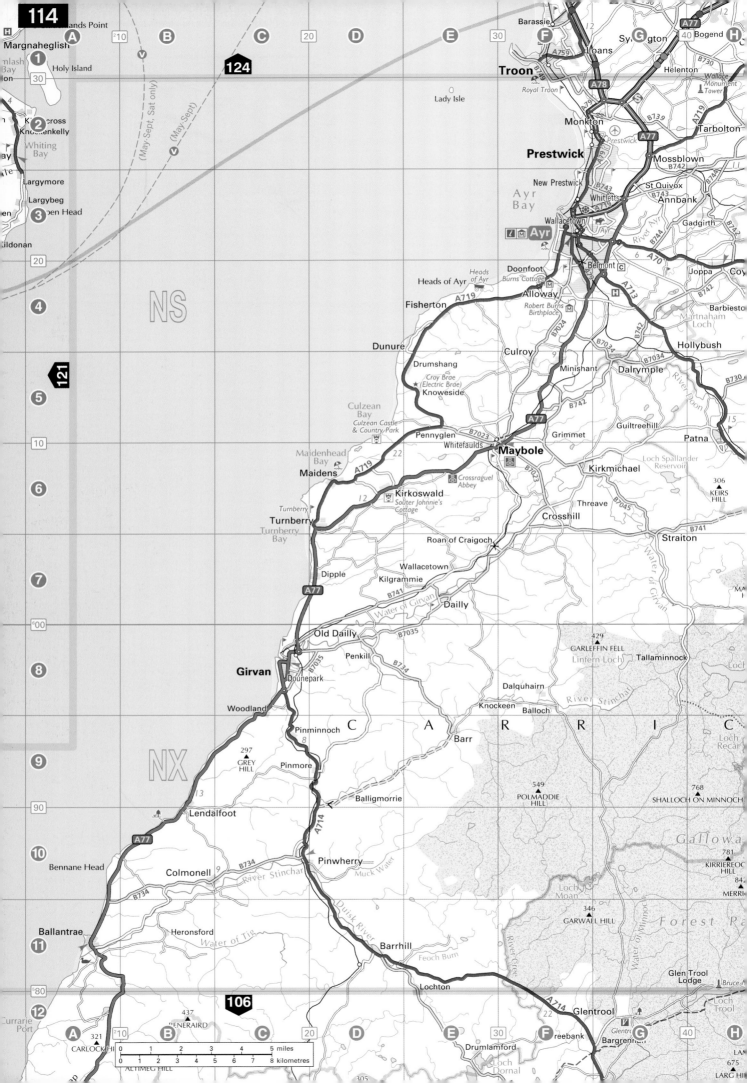

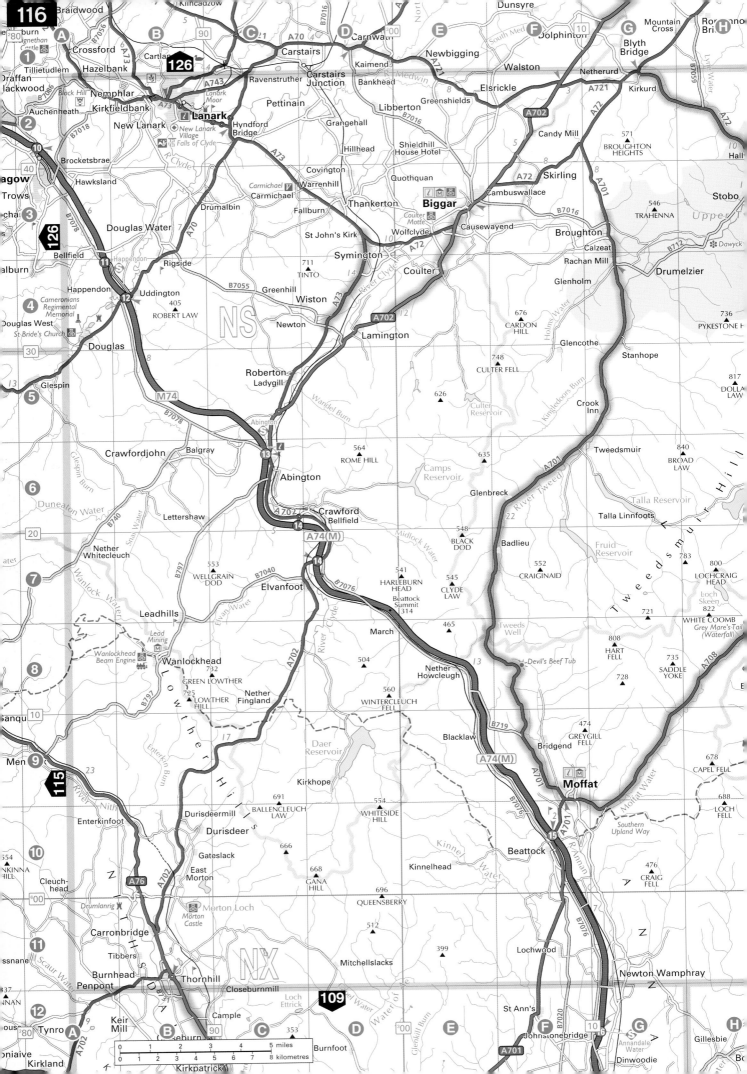

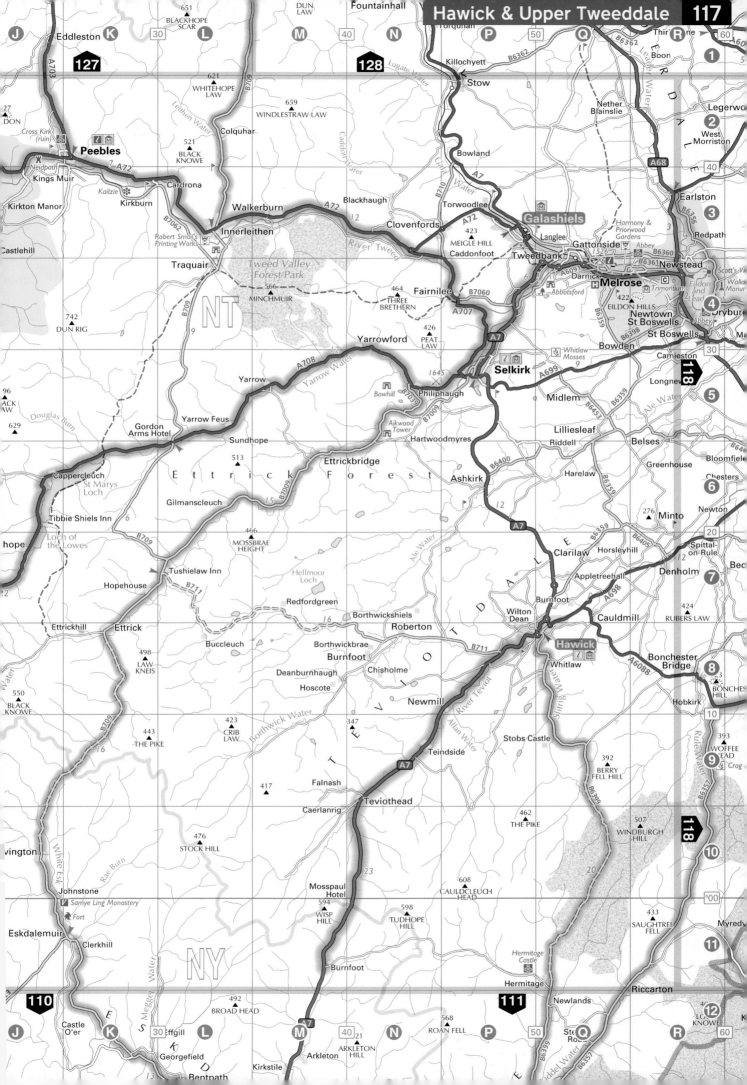

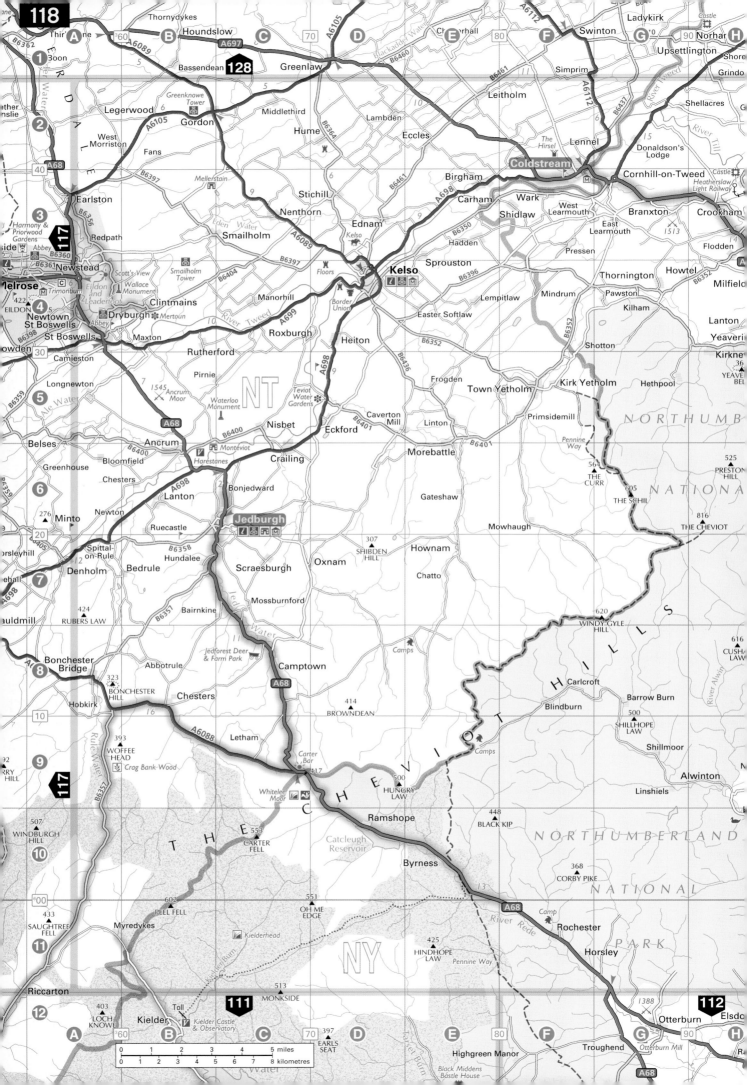

ound of Bute

J · 200 · K · L · 10 · M · N · P · Q · R

St Blane's Church
Garrochty
Garroch Head
Little Cumbrae Island
Fairlie Roads
Hunterston Power Station

124

Sannox

Corrie

874 GOATFELL

Glen Rosa

Merkland Point
Brodick Castle, Garden & Country Park
Brodick Bay
Brodick
Strathwhillan

124

Corriegills

RUACH

Lamlash

A841

Margnaheglish

Lamlash Bay
Cordon

Clauchlands Point

Holy Island

Auchencairn

Kingscross
Knockenkelly

Whiting Bay

Whiting Bay

Glen Ashdale

Carn Ban

Largymore

Dippen
Largybeg
Dippen Head

Bennan

Kildonan

nan Head

Pladda

Ailsa Craig
340

FIRTH

OF

CLYDE

v

v (May-Sept, Sat only)

v (May-Sept)

NS

NX

Drakemyre
Highfield
Dalry
Auchen de
Bu
Glengarnock
B784
B30
A737
B707

Portencross
Farland Head
B7048
Blackshaw
Munnoch
Dalgarven Mill
B781
B780
B780
B714
B780
West Kilbride
Seamill
B7047

Kilwinning
Fergushill
B785
slie

Ardrossan
Horse Isle
A78
B780
A738
Eglinton
Stevenston
Ardeer
B719
A78
Girdle Toll
40
Per

Saltcoats
Cunn

Irvine
Maritime
Fullarton
Dreghorn
Spring
4
B708
Gailes
Dryb

Irvine Bay
Castle
Barassie
B746
B749
12
Troon
A759
Loans
30
A78
Royal Troon
A78
M ton

Lady Isle
Prestwick
New Prestwick
B743
Whitlet
A719

Ayr Bay
Wallace
7
Ayr
20
Belmon

Doonfoot
Burns Cottage
Heads of Ayr
Heads of Ayr
Alloway
Robert Burns Birthplace
B7024
8
B703

Fisherton
A719

Dunure
Culroy
Minishant

Drumshang
Croy Brae (Electric Brae)
Knoweside
9

Culzean Bay
Culzean Castle & Country Park
Pennyglen
B7023
Whitefaulds
Maybole
Grimmet
10

114

Maidenhead Bay
Maidens
A719

Crossraguel Abbey
Kirkoswald
Souter Johnnie's Cottage
B7023
Kirkm

Turnberry
Turnberry
Turnberry Bay
Roan of Craigoch
Crosshill
Threave
10

Dipple
Wallacetown
Kilgrammie
11

A77
Dailly
B741
Water of Girvan

Old Dailly
B7035
Penkill
A 00
Linfern Lo
R
12
EFFIN

Girvan
20
Dounepark
B734
Q
Dalquhairn
River Sti

Woodland
Knockeen
Balloch

J · 700 · K · L · 10 · M · N · P · Q · R

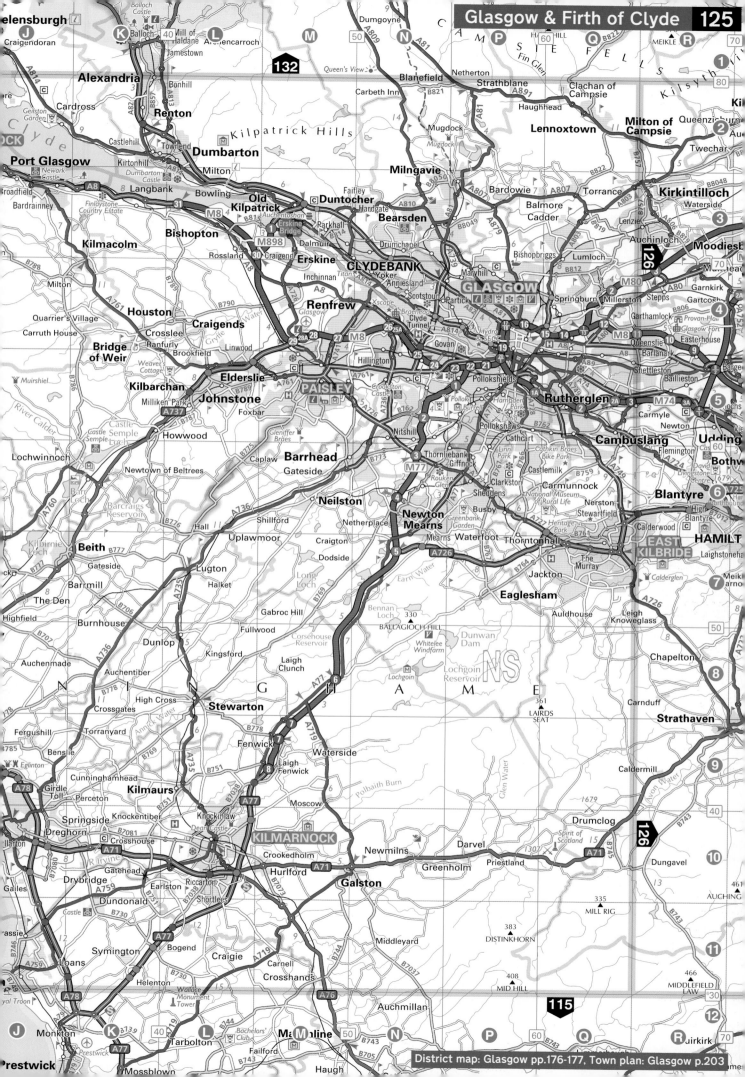

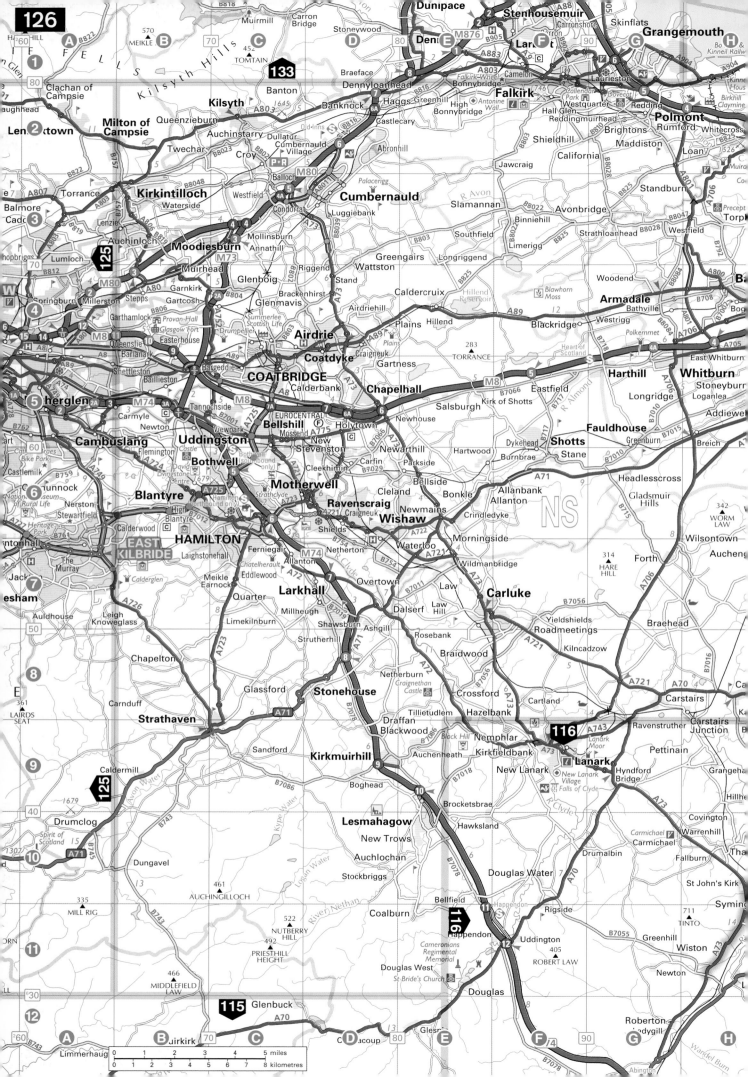

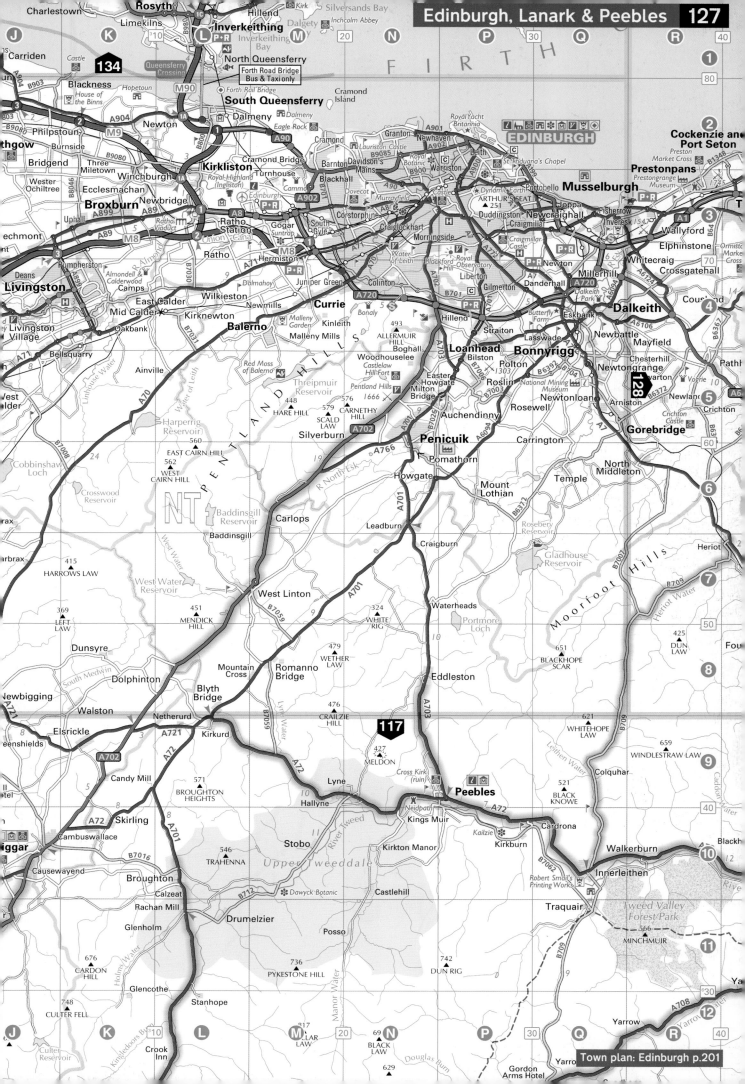

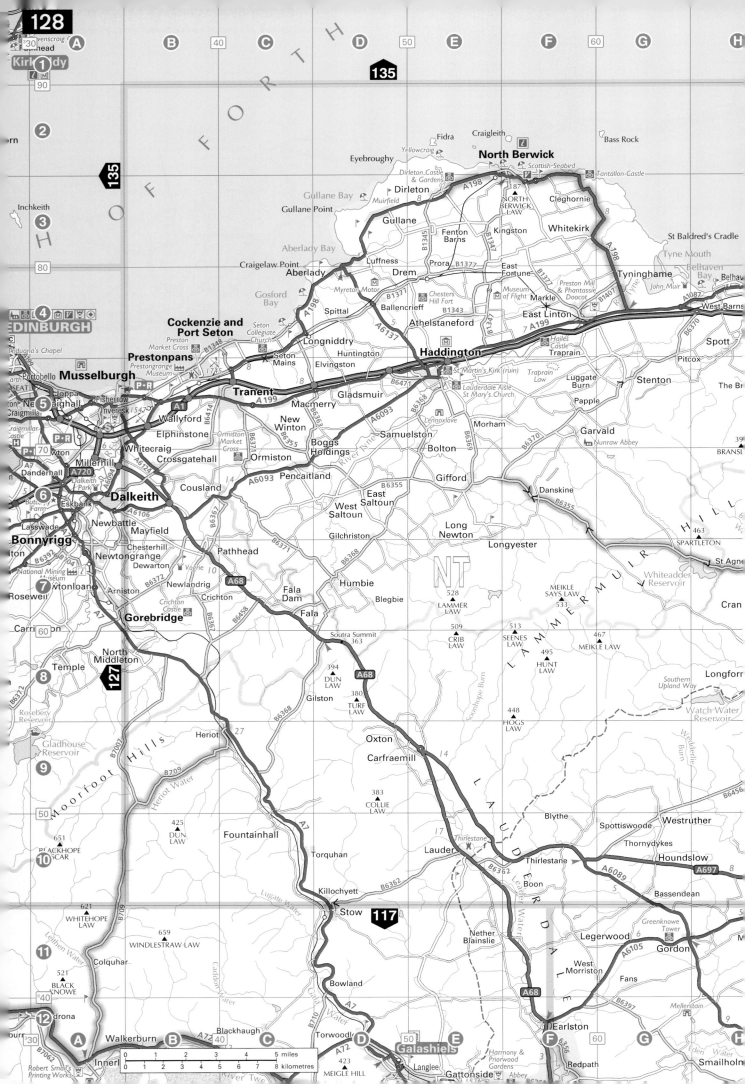

J   K   80   L   M   90   N   P   '00   Q   R   10

① 90
②
③
④ 80
⑤
⑥ 70
⑦ 60
⑧
⑨ 50
⑩
⑪
⑫ 40

NU

Barns Ness
East Barns
Chapel Point
Skateraw
Torness Power Station
Thorntonloch
Crowhill
Reed Point
Cove
Pease Bay
Siccar Point
Fast Castle Head
Dunglass Collegiate Church
Cockburnspath
amstocks
Pease Dean
A1107
196 ▲ BROWN RIG
Coldingham Loch
ST ABB'S HEAD
St Abbs
LAW LL
9
Ecclaw
Grantshouse
Coldingham
Coldingham Bay
Southern Upland Way
Butterdean
Eye Water
21
Houndwood
Heugh Head
B6438
22
A1107
Eyemouth
bbey St Bathans
Quixwood
262 ▲ HORSELEY HILL
Reston
Cairncross
A1
Ayton
B6355
Burnmouth
ord
Edin's Hall Broch
14
B6438
Auchencrow
325 ▲ COCKBURN LAW
Marygold
Lamberton
Marshall Meadows Bay
B6355
A6112
Lintlaw
Preston
Chirnside
B6437
B6355
North Northumberland Heritage Coast
Primrosehill
B6365
Cumledge
Edrom Church
Chirnsidebridge
Foulden
1333
×
A6105
Berwick-upon-Tweed
Edrom
15
Broadhaugh
Edington
Foulden Tithe Barn
Castle
Barracks & Main Guard
Manderston
A6105
Allanton
Hutton
Whiteadder Water
Town Ramparts
Duns
B6437
Paxton
A6461
Tweedmouth
Gavinton
Blackadder
B6460
Paxton
Spittal
Huds Head
olwarth
Nisbet Hill
Sinclair's Hill
Whitsome
Hilton
13
Loanend
East Ord
A167
Scremerston
7
Fogo
A6112
6
B6437
Horndean
Horncliffe
Murton
Unthank
A1
Charterhall
Blackadder Water
Swinton
B6461
Ladykirk
Castle
Norham
A698
Thornton
Cheswick
B6460
11
B6461
Simprim
A6112
Upsettlington
Shoreswood
Grindon
West Allerdean
Ancroft
Goswick
18
10
Leitholm
6
15
River Tweed
Felkington
119
B6354
Haggerston
CAUSEWAY FLOODED AT HIGH TIDE
Lambden
Eccles
Shellacres
Grindonrigg
Duddo
Bowsden
B6525
Berrington
15
Beal
⑪
The Hirsel
Lennel
River Till
Donaldson's Lodge
15
Goswick
Fenham
Lindis Prie
Birgham
Coldstream
Cornhill-on-Tweed
Castle
Etal
Lowick
West Kyloe
B6353
Fenwick
B6461
Carham
Wark
Heatherslaw Light Railway
Heatherslaw Corn Mill
Lady Waterford Hall
Buckton
Ednam
hidlaw
West Learmouth
90
Crookt
Ford
R
10
Kelso
B6350
Hadden
East Learmouth
E M xton
1513 ×
14
Flodden
Kimmerston
Detchant
Holburn
Pressen
St Cuthbert's
Middleton

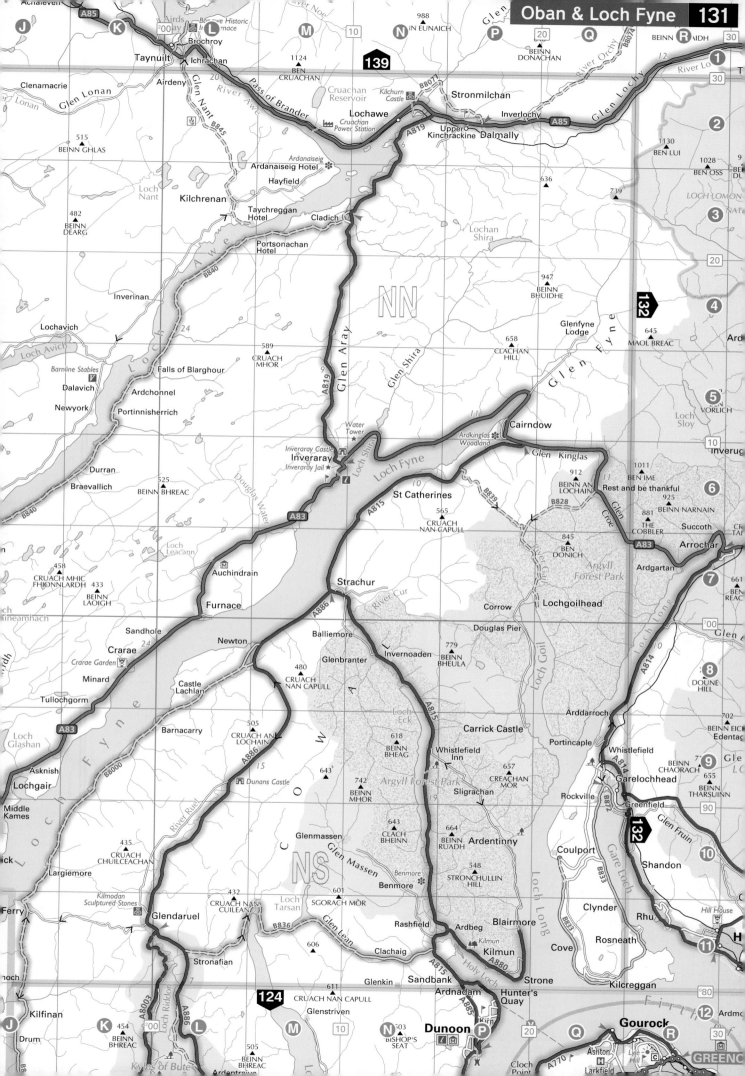

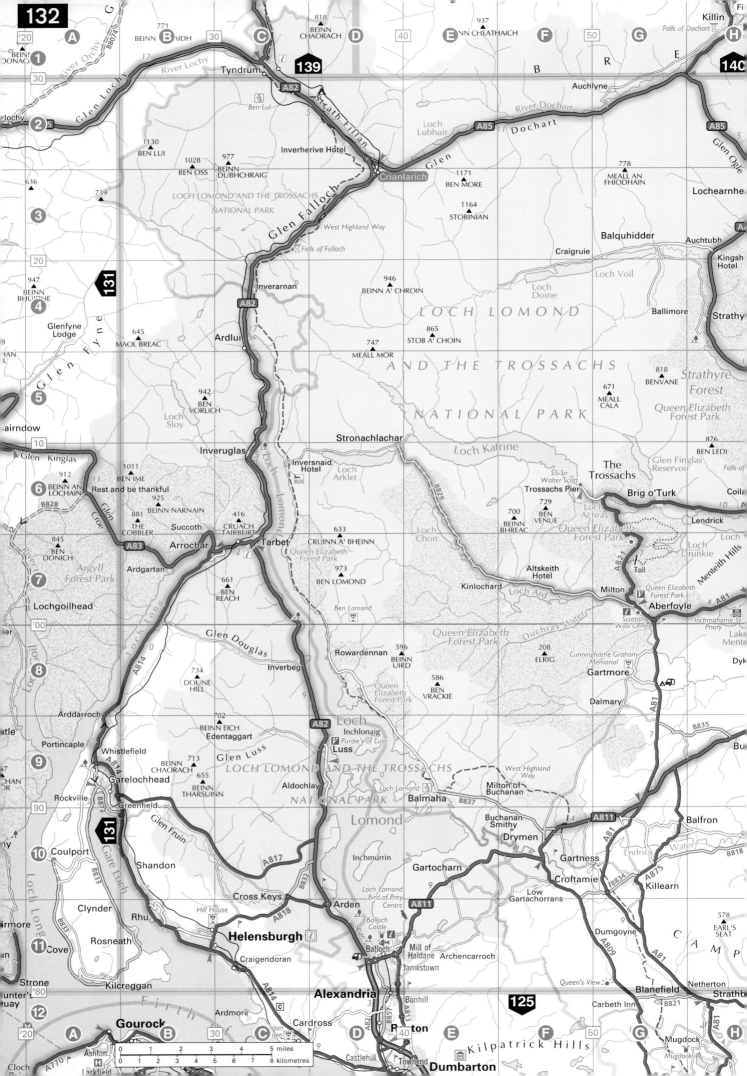

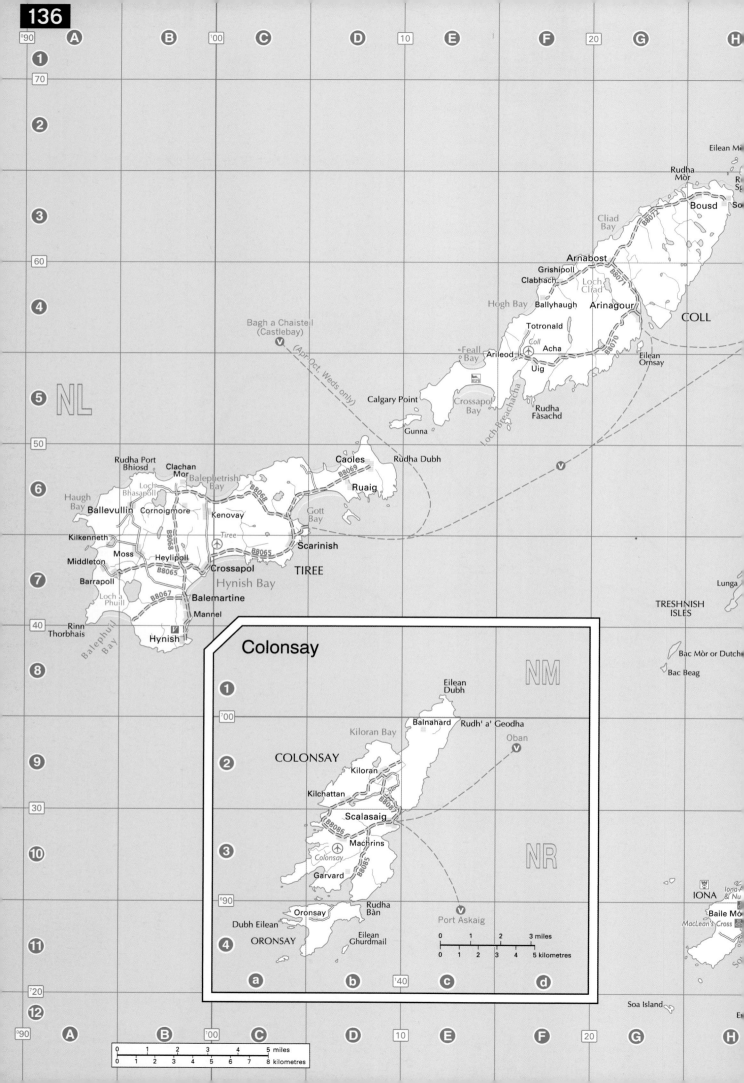

NL

NM

NR

Colonsay

COLL

Eilean Mò

Rudha
Mòr

R
Sg

Bousd

So

Cliad
Bay

Arnabost

Grishipoll

Clabhach

Loch
Cliad

Hogh Bay

Ballyhaugh

Arinagour

Totronald

Coll

Acha

Arileod

Uig

Rudha
Fàsachd

Eilean
Ornsay

Bagh a Chaisteil
(Castlebay)

(Apr.-Oct. Weds only)

Feall
Bay

Calgary Point

Crossapol
Bay

Gunna

Loch Breachacha

Caoles

Rudha Dubh

Ruaig

B8069

NL

Rudha Port
Bhiosd

Clachan
Mor

Balephetrish
Bay

Haugh
Bay

Loch
Bhasapoll

B8068

Ballevullin

Cornoigmore

Kenovay

Gott
Bay

Tiree

Kilkenneth

B8068

Moss

Heylipoll

B8065

Scarinish

Middleton

B8065

Crossapol

TIREE

Barrapoll

Hynish Bay

Loch a
Phuill

B8067

Balemartine

Mannel

Rinn
Thorbhais

Balephuill
Bay

Hynish

TRESHNISH
ISLES

Lunga

Bac Mòr or Dutch

Bac Beag

Eilean
Dubh

Balnahard

Rudh' a' Geodha

Kiloran Bay

COLONSAY

Oban

Kiloran

Kilchattan

B8087

Scalasaig

B8086

Machrins

Colonsay

B8085

Garvard

IONA

Iona
& Nu

Baile Mò

MacLean's Cross

Oronsay

Rudha
Bàn

Dubh Eilean

ORONSAY

Eilean
Ghurdmail

Port Askaig

0   1   2   3 miles

0   1   2   3   4   5 kilometres

Soa Island

En

J   K   40   L   M   50   N   P   60   Q   R   70

Rudha Aird Druimnich
Morar, Moidart and
Ardnamurchan
239 Ardmolic
BEINN
BHREAC **1**

Sanna Point
Kilmory   Ockle Point   Ardtoe   Shielfoot
D 70 breck
Sanna Bay
Portuairk   Achnaha   Branault   Ockle
Kentra   Blain   Mingarry
Sanna Bay
356
BEINN
BHREAC
Arevegaig
Acharacle **2**
Ardnamurchan Point   Achosnich   436
MEALL NAN CON   ARDNAMURCHAN
437

342
BEINN
NA SEILG   Kilchoan
Ormsaigmore Mingary
527
BEN
HIANT
19   Glenbeg
Glenborrodale   Laga
512
BEN
LAGA   Salen **3**
GEARR

Ardslignish

Carna **138**   60 **4**

Ardmore Point
Sorne Point   Auliston Point   Oronsay
571
BEINN
LADAIN

Quinish Point   Glengorm Castle
Loch Teacuis
Drimnin
437
BEINN
BHUIDHE
Loch Arienas **5**

Caliach Point   **Tobermory**   Calve Island
550
SÌTHEAN NA RAPLAICH
Ach
G
Clag

292
'S AIRDE BEINN   Dervaig   Achnadrish House
Larachbeg
50
A884 **6**
Loch Aline
Ra
Ac

Calgary
B8073
Calgary Bay   Ensay   342
CÀRN MÒR   444
SPEINNE MÒR   10
Fuinary
Lochaline

nish Point   Burg   Loch Frisa   Glen Aros   Aros   B8849

a' Chaoil   Fanmore   390
CNOC AN DÀ CHINN
Glenaros House   Fishnish Point   Fishnish Pier **7**

Gometra   Ballygown   Eas Fors   333
BEINN NAN CÀRN   Killiechronan   Salen   A849   11

Loch Tuath   ULVA   Oskamull   B8073   Gruline   B8035   2   408
BEINN NAN LUS   Glen Forsa   Scanastle Bay   40

Little Colonsay   Eorsa   Macquarie Mausoleum   ISLE   636
BEINN MHEADHON   Altcreich

Staffa   Inch Kenneth   591
BEINN A' GHRÀIG   Loch Bà   OF   766
DUN DA GHAOITHE   Craign **8**

gal's Cave   Loch na Keal, Isle of Mull   Inchkenneth Chapel (ruin)

Balnahard   966
BEN MORE   704
CRUACHAN DEARG   MULL   Lochd
Loc **9**

519
BEIN-NA-SREINE   A849
Strathcoil   30

491
CREACH BHEINN   Tiroran   Aird of Kinloch   Glen More   717
BEN BUIE   698
BEN CREACH   **10**
Cro

Rudha nan Cearc   Fossil Tree   Burg   Pennycross   Pennyghael   Loch Fuaran   Lochbuie   Loch lve

ntra   Loch na Lathaich   A849   Leidle Water   503
BEINN NA CROISE   Loch Buie   **130**   337
MAOL BÀN

Ardhglas   6   Bunessan   Loch Assapol   Carsaig   Rudha Dubh   Loch Uisg   377
DRUIM FADA   **11**

ROSS OF MULL   376
CRUACHAN MIN   376
BEINN CHREAGACH   20

Ardchiavaig   Uisken   Malcolm's Point   **12**
FIRTH

Rudha nam Braithrean
Rudha Ardalanish

J   K   40   L   M   50   N   P   60   Q   R   70

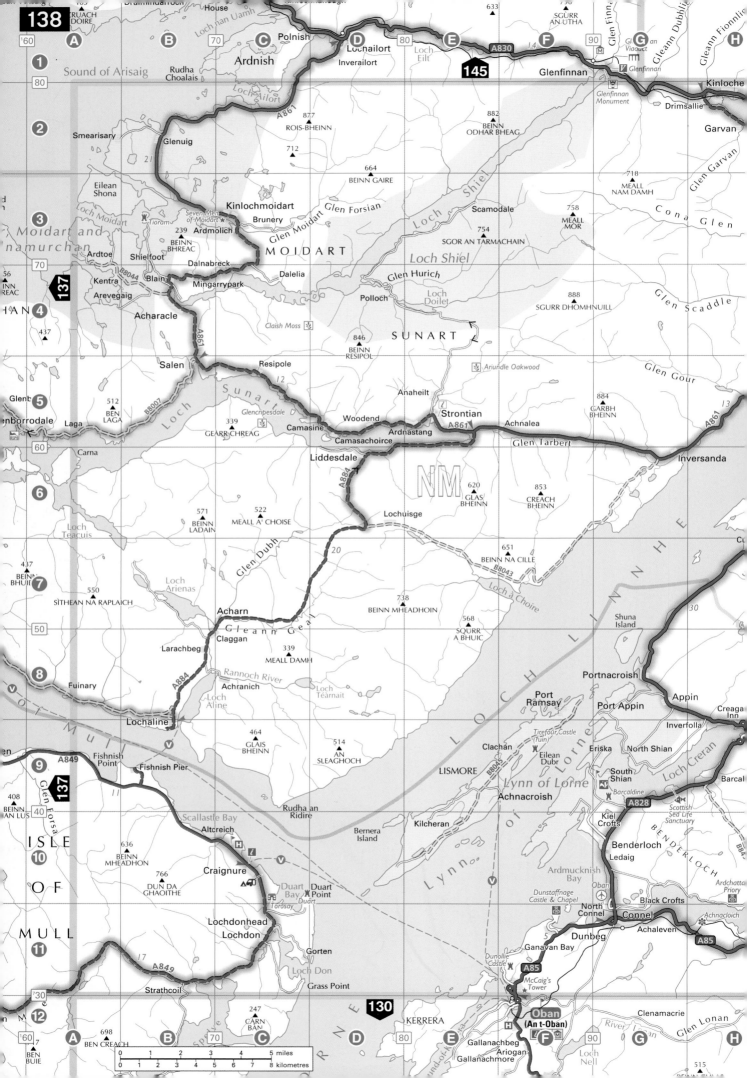

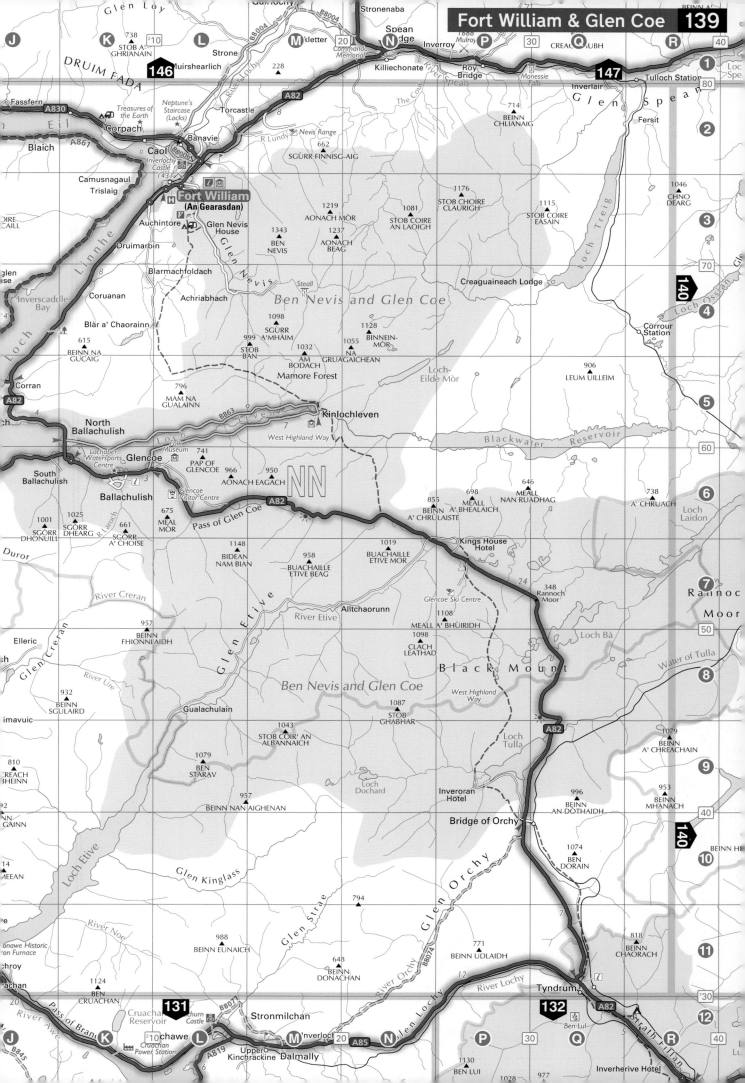

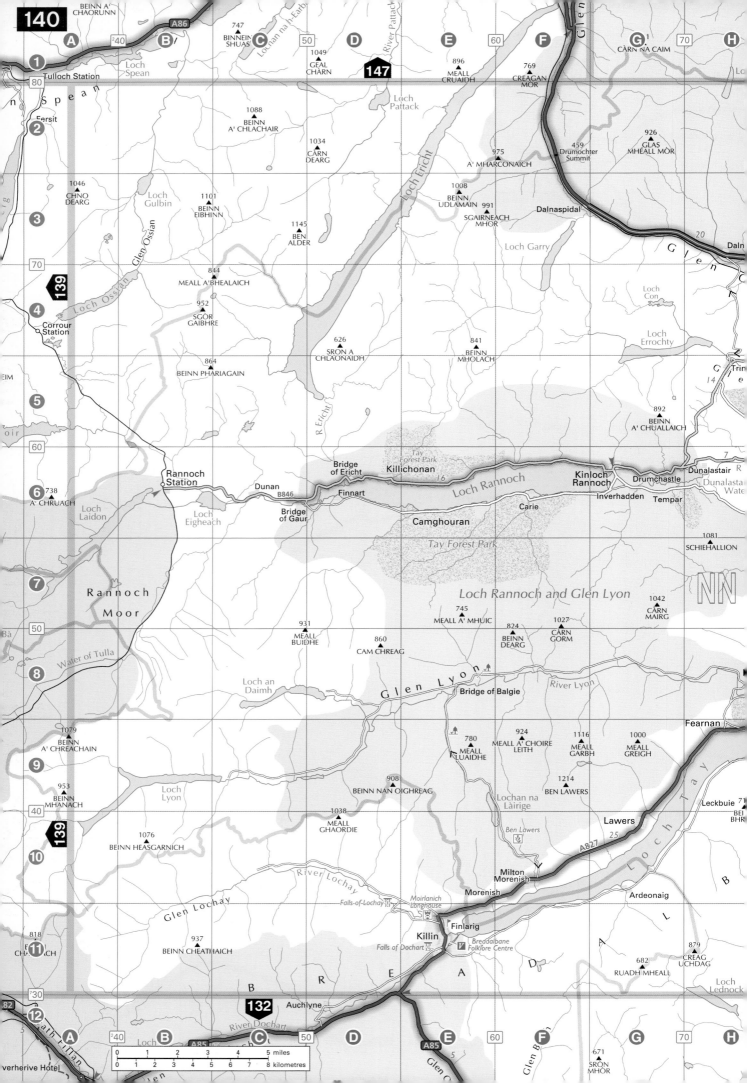

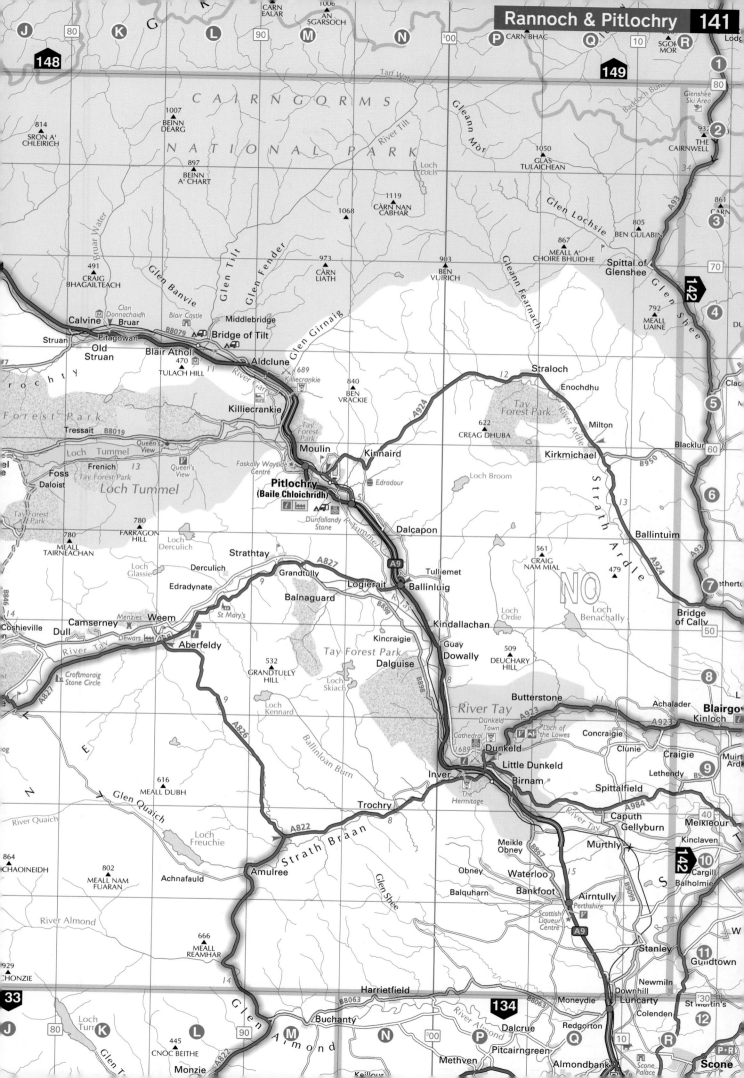

J 80 K G L 90 M N 300 P **CARN BHAC** Q 10 R SGOR MOR
148 149

CAIRNGORMS
Glenshee Ski Area
CARN EALAR
CARN AN SGARSACH

NATIONAL PARK 142
814 SRON A' CHLEIRICH
1007 BEINN DEARG
Tarf Water
1006
300
933 THE CAIRNWELL 2

897 BEINN A' CHART
River Tilt
Gleann Mor
1050 GLAS TULAICHEAN
A93 861 CARN 3

1068
1119 CARN NAN CABHAR
Loch Loch
805 BEN GULABIN
Glen Lochsie
70 5

491 CRAIG BHAGAILTEACH
Glen Banvie
Glen Tilt
Glen Fender
973 CARN LIATH
903 BEN VUIRICH
Gleann Fearnach
867 MEALL A' CHOIRE BHUIDHE
Spittal of Glenshee
Glen Shee
792 MEALL UAINE
4

Calvine Bruar
Clan Donnachaidh
Blair Castle
Middlebridge
Bridge of Tilt
Glen Girnaig
Straloch
12
Enochdhu
Tay Forest Park
River Ardle
Milton
Blacklur 60 5

Struan Pitagowan Old Struan
Blair Atholl
B8079
470 TULACH HILL
Aldclune
1689 Killiecrankie
840 BEN VRACKIE
622 CREAG DHUBA
Kirkmichael
Strath Ardle
B950
6

Trochty
Forest Park
Tressait B8019
Killiecrankie
RSPB
Tay Forest Park
Moulin
Kinnaird
Loch Broom
13
Ballintuim
A924
A93
7

Loch Tummel
Queen's View
Frenich 13
Tay Forest Park
Queen's View
Faskally Wayside Centre
Pitlochry (Baile Chloichridh)
Edradour
Dalcapon
561 CRAIG NAM MIAL
479
Netherton
Bridge of Cally

Foss Daloist
Loch Tummel
Dunfallandy Stone
River Tummel
A9
NO
50

Tay Forest Park
780 FARRAGON HILL
Loch Derculich
Strathtay
A827
Grantully
Logierait
Ballinluig
Tulliemet
Loch Ordie
Loch Benachally
Bridge of Cally

780
MEALL TAIRNEACHAN
Loch Glassie
Derculich
Edradynate
Balnaguard
River Tay
B898
Kindallachan
509 DEUCHARY HILL
8

B846
14
Camserney Weem
Menzies
St Mary's
532 GRANTULLY HILL
Tay Forest Park
Kincraigie
Kincraigie
Guay Dowally
8

Coshieville Dull
Dewars
Aberfeldy
River Tay
Loch Kennard
Loch Skiach
Dalguise
B898
Butterstone
River Tay
A923
Achalader
Blairgo
Kinloch
8

Croftmoraig Stone Circle
A826
9
Ballinloan Burn
Dunkeld Town
Cathedral
1689
Loch of the Lowes
Concraigie
Clunie
Craigie
Muirt Ard
9

A827
616 MEALL DUBH
Glen Quaich
Loch Kennard
Tay Forest Park
Dunkeld
Little Dunkeld
Lethendy
B9
Spittalfield
9

River Quaich
Loch Freuchie
Trochry
Inver Birnam
The Hermitage
A984
Caputh Gellyburn
Kinclaven
Meikleour

og
Glen Quaich
A822
Strath Braan
8
Meikle Obney
A923
River Tay
Murthly
142
10

864 CHAOINEIDH
802 MEALL NAM FUARAN
Achnafauld
Amulree
Glen Shee
Obney
Waterloo
Bankfoot
B867
B9099
Cargill
Balholmie
10

River Almond
666 MEALL REAMHAR
A822
Balquharn
Airntully
Perthshire
Scottish Liqueur Centre
A9

929 CHONZIE
Harrietfield
B8063
134
River Almond
Dalcrue
Moneydie
Downhill
Luncarty
Newmiln
Colenden
St Martin's
11

J 80 K L 90 M N 300 P Q 10 R
33
Loch Turr
CNOC BEITHE 445
Glen Almond
Buchanty
Methven
Keillour
Pitcairngreen
Almondbank
Scone Palace
Scone
Stanley
Guildtown
12

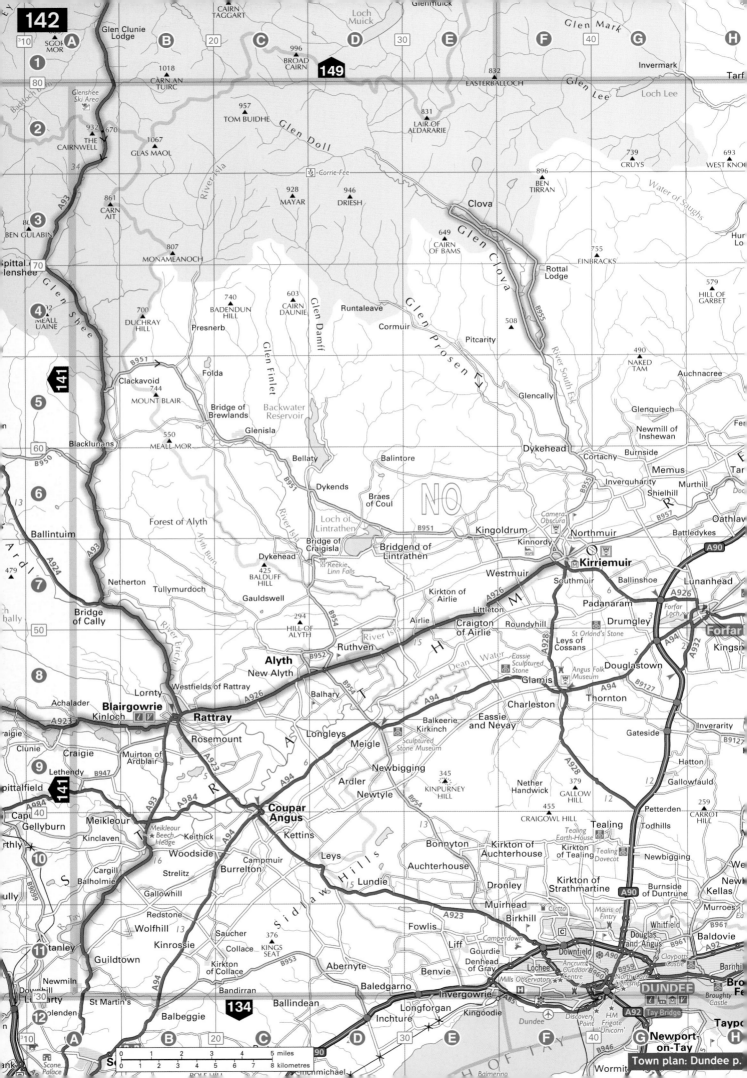

J **K** 60 **L** **M** 465 GOYLE 70 **N** **P** 80 **Q** **R** 90

MOUNT
BATTOCK

475
HILL OF
FINGRAY

454
Cairn
O'Mount

B974

465
GOYLE
HILL

Water

Glenbervie

Drumlithie

New Mill

Temple
of Fiddes

151

10

Crawton **1** 80

sk Folk

544
STURDY
HILL

414
FINELLA
HILL

Auchenblae

Mondynes

Fowlsheugh
Trelong
Bay

Kinneff

Catterline **2**

Todhead Point

k Esk

605
BULG

Mains of
Balnakette

B966

Fordoun

B967

Arbuthnott

A92

77
OF
REN

Fettercairn

Pittarrow

Redmyre

Inverbervie

Bervie
Bay **3**

B9120

Mains of
Haulkerton

Gannachy

Edzell Castle
& Garden

Bogmuir

Sauchieburn

Edzell
Woods
Luthermuir

Laurencekirk

B9120

Redford

Gourdon

70

ridgend

Balfield

Dunlappie

Edzell

A90

B974

North

A937

Dykelands

Benholm

4

Brown
Caterthun

River

Esk

Johnshaven

13

White
Caterthun

Inchbare

Newtonmill

Logie Pert

Marykirk

Lochside

Bush

Milton Ness

on
muir

Tigerton

Keithock

Craigo

Logie

Morphie

St Cyrus

Mains of
alhall

Little
Brechin

Lochty

Trinity

Logie

5

reston

Maison
Dieu Chapel
(ruin)

Brechin

ℹ

Dun

Hillside

A92

60

R South Esk

Brechin Castle
& Pictavia

A935

9

House of
Dun

Montrose Air Station

Montrose

Netherton

A933

Caledonian
Railway

Haughs of
Kinnaird

Barnhead

Montrose
Basin

Scurdie Ness

NO **6**

Aberlemno

Sculptured Stones

8

Farnell

Maryton

A934

Craig

Ferryden

Mains of
Melgunds

B9113

Westerton
of Rossie

Usan

Bolshan

132
WUDDY
LAW

Braehead

Boddin Point

7

A932

Guthrie

Glasterlaw

Kinnell

Lunan

Lunan Bay

50

Pitmuies

Friockheim
C

B965

Boysack

Inverkeilor

Letham

Leysmill

Chapelton

13

8

A933

Cauldcots

Letham
Grange

Red Head

Colliston

Marywell

Condor

St Vigeans

Auchmithie

Redford

6

Carlingheugh
Bay **9**

Greystone

Carmyllie

B9127

The Deil's
Head

Bonnington

Arbirlot

Arbroath

40

Kirkton
of Monikie

B961

Elliot Water

A92

ℹ

10

aigton

Muirdrum

East Haven

B9128

A92

17

Upper
Victoria

7

Panbride

Barry Mill

11

Barry

West Haven

th

Carnoustie

BUDDON
NESS

135

12 730

s Point

J **K** 60 **L** **M** 70 **N** **P** 80 **Q** **R** 90

J 60 K CALPAY L CROWLIN ISLANDS 70 M N Plockton P 80 Q 90 R

Eyre Point

67 Longay

153

Port-an-Eorna

Drumbuie   Duirinish

447   BEINN RAIMH   154   1

396   MULLACH NA CARN   27 Pabay   Badicaul   Balmacara   Conchra   Auchtertyre   Killilan   30

Dunan   Badicaul   Kyle of Lochalsh (Caol Loch Aillse)   Nostie   Carndu   Camas Luinie   2

Luib   Caolas Scalpay   Lochalsh Woodland Garden   Kirkton   Ardelve   Bundalloch   Loch nan Eun

708 BEINN NA CAILLICH   732   Corry H   Skye Bridge   Kyleakin   Carndu   Dornie   Loch Long

BEINN DEORG MHÒR   Broadford   Lower Breakish   Eilean Donan   Keppoch   840   SGÙRR A' BHÀRGID   3

Harrapool   Waterloo   A87   840   SGÙRR A'BHÀRGID   Inverinate

rrin   B8083   14   Skulamus   Upper Breakish   732 SGURR NA COINNICH   Bernera   603 BEINN A'CHUIRN   Letterfearn   20 Ault a'   Invershiel Shiel Bri

Loch Slapin   Otter Haven   Galltair   Loch Duich   4

300 BEINN NAN CARN   Heast   605 BEN ASLAK   Kylerhea (Apr-Oct) V   Glenelg Bay   408 BEINN A' CHAOINICH   Moyle   350 Màm Ratàgan   FIVE

Rudha Suisnish   Suisnish   561 BEINN NA SEAMRAIG   Bernera   Glenelg   Balvraid   Moyle   1011 THE SADDLE   5

298 SGORACH BREAC   Drumfearn   Eilanreach   Glenelg Brochs   Glean Beag   Balvraid   945 SGÙRR NA SGINE   10

Tokavaig   Ord River   Duisdalemore   Isleornsay   Sandaig Island   974 BEINN SGRITHEAL   773 BEINN NAN CAORACH   Arnisdale

Loch Eishort   Ornsay   Rudha Buidhe   Loch Hourn   Glen Arnisdale   6

kavaig   Achnacloich   Loch na Dal   Rudh' Ard Slisneach   Corran   614   709 DRUM FADA   Kinloc Hourr

aig Bay   Teangue   Loch nam Uamph   Knock   Inverguseran   784 BEINN NA CAILLICH   KNOYDART   7

Ferrindonald   Kilmore   Knock Bay   Glen Guseran   518 DRUIM NA CLUAIN-AIRIDHE   1019 LADHAR BHEINN   00

Kilbeg   Armadale Castle   SOUND OF SLEAT   Sandaig   Knoydart   940 LUINNE BHEINN   8

Ardvasar   Clan Donald V   Armadale   Sandaig Bay   Inverie   KNOYDART   00

Aird of Sleat   A851   Calligarry   Inverie Bay   854 BEINN BHUIDHE   1039 SGURR NA CICHE   SGU

Ard Thurinish   V   Courteachan   Mallaigvaig   Rudha Raonuill   Loch Nevis   Kylesmorar   859 SGURR NAH-AIDE   Glen De

Mallaig (Malaig) V   547 CARN A'GHOBHAIR   437 SGÙRR BHUIDHE   Bracorina   723 SGURR BREAC   9

Glasnacardoch Bay   Loch an Nostaire   Beoraidbeg   Bracora   Tarbet   Glen Pean

Morar   Swordland   90

Glenancross   Loch Morar   Lettermorar   Meoble   716 AN STAC   146

A830   503 CARN A' MHÀDAIDH-RUAIDH   Meoble   949 SGURR NAN COIREACHAN   964   10

Eilean Ighe   Bunacaimh   710 MEITH BHEINN   SG THU

Luinga Mhòr   Back of Keppoch   600 SIDHEAN MÒR   796 SGÙRR AN UTHA   11

103 CRUACH DOIRE   Arisaig   Prince Charlie's Cairn   633   Glen Finnan   Glenfinnan Viaduct

Rudh' Arisaig   Druimindarroch   Arisaig House   Kinlochnanuagh   A830 14   Glenfinnan V Glenfinnan   12

Polnish   Loch Eilt   Glenfinnan Monument   sallie

Sound of Arisaig   Ardnish   Lochailort   Inverailort   882 BEINN ODHAR BHEAG

Rudha Choalais   A861   138   Glenfinnan

Smearisary   Glenuig   877 ROIS-BHEINN   712   BEINN ODHAR BHEAG

J 60 K 70 L M 70 N 80 P Q 90 R

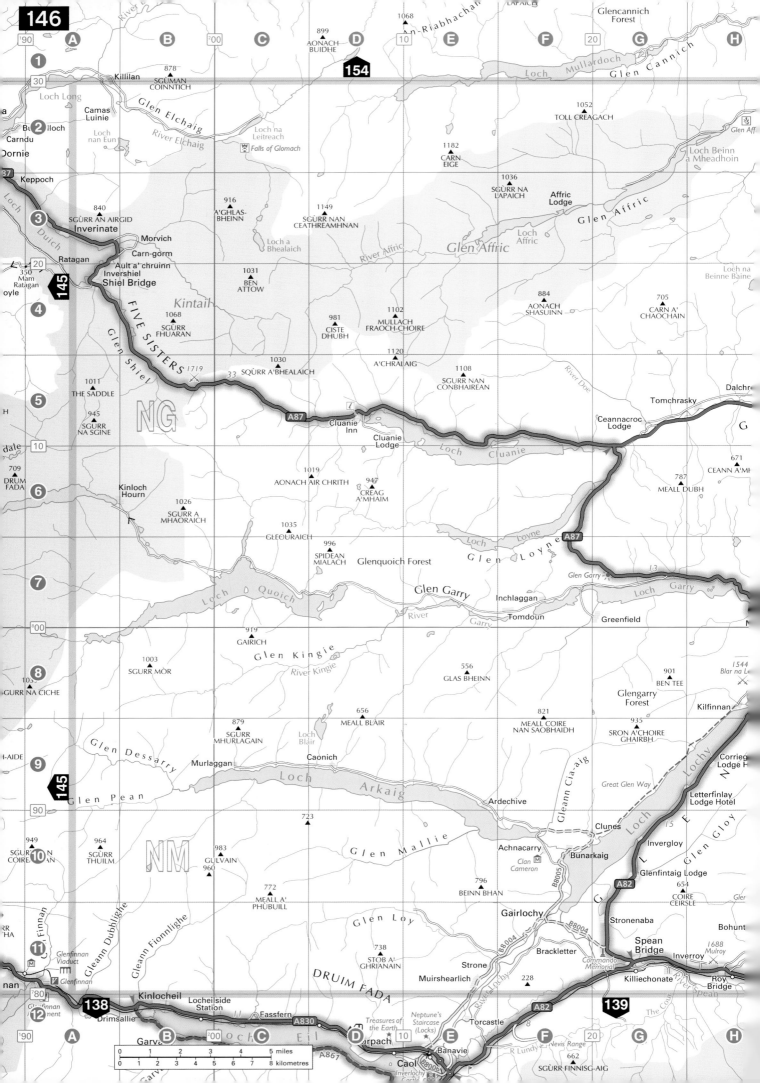

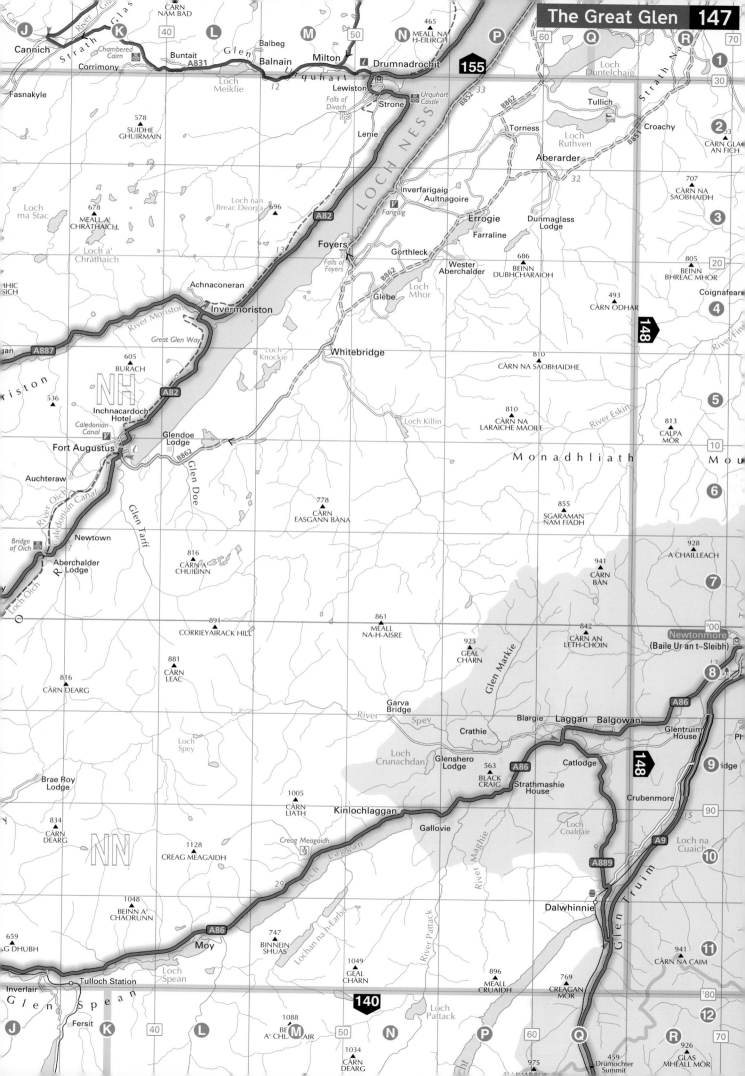

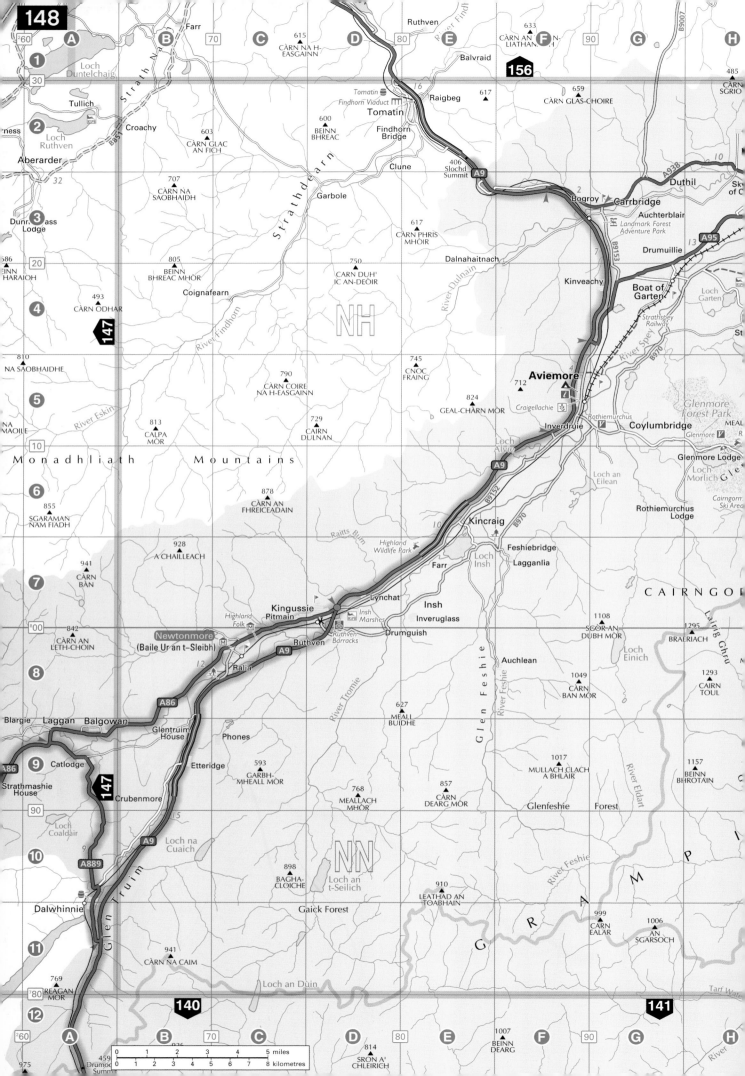

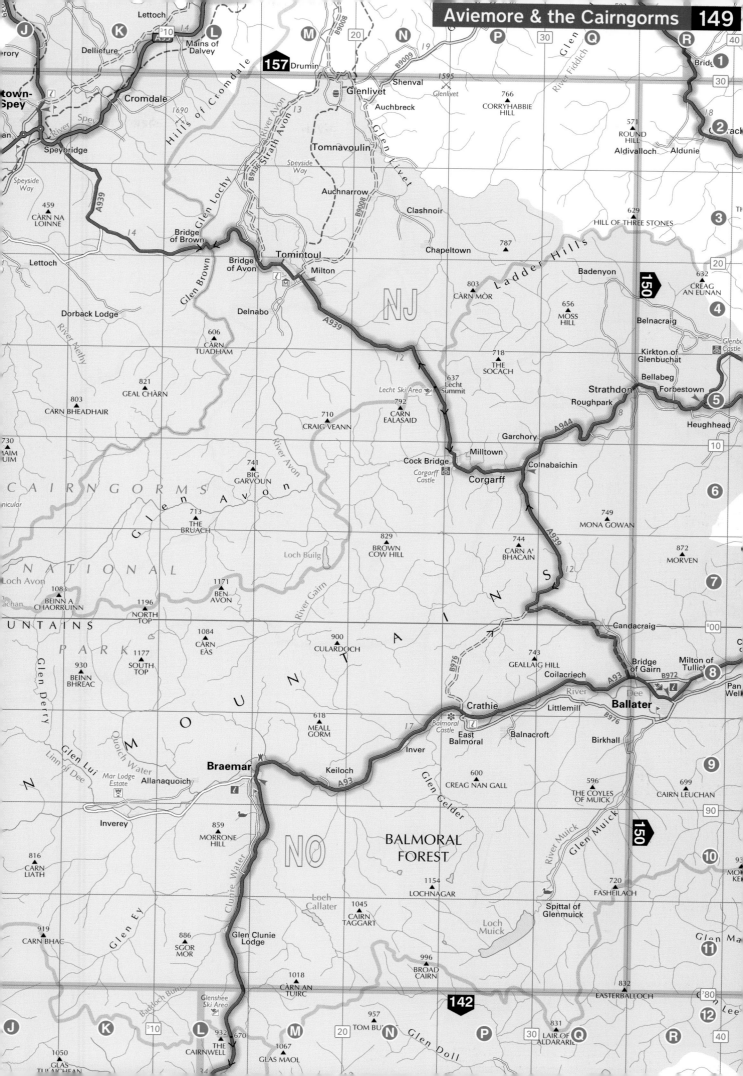

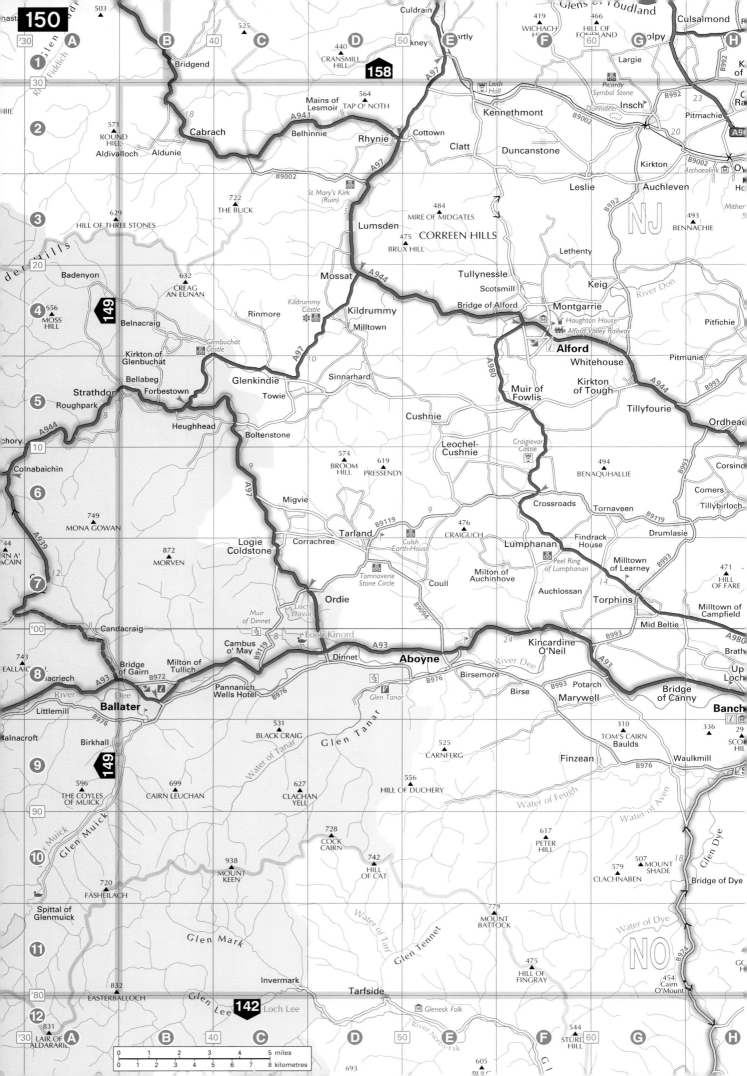

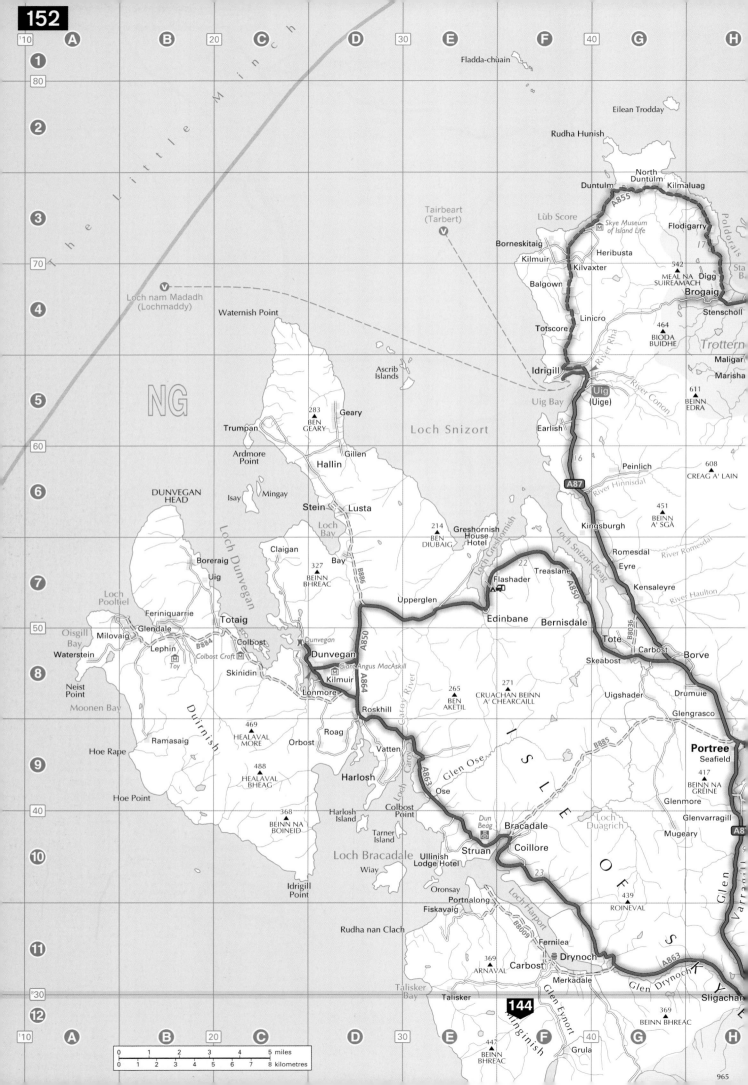

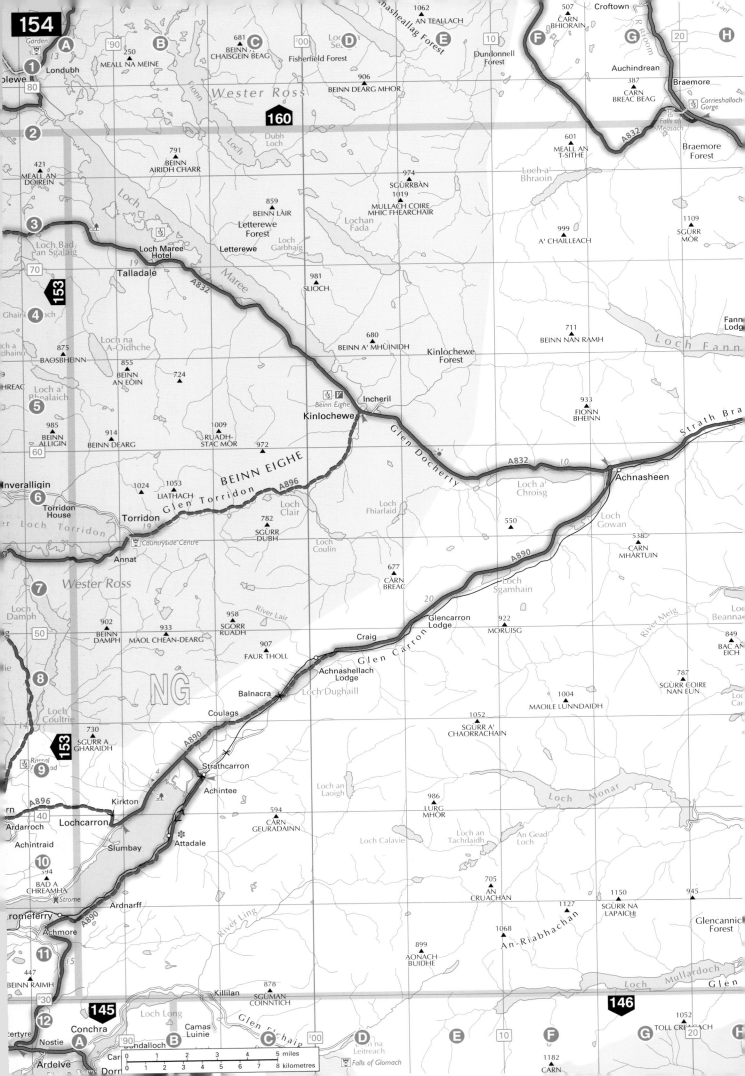

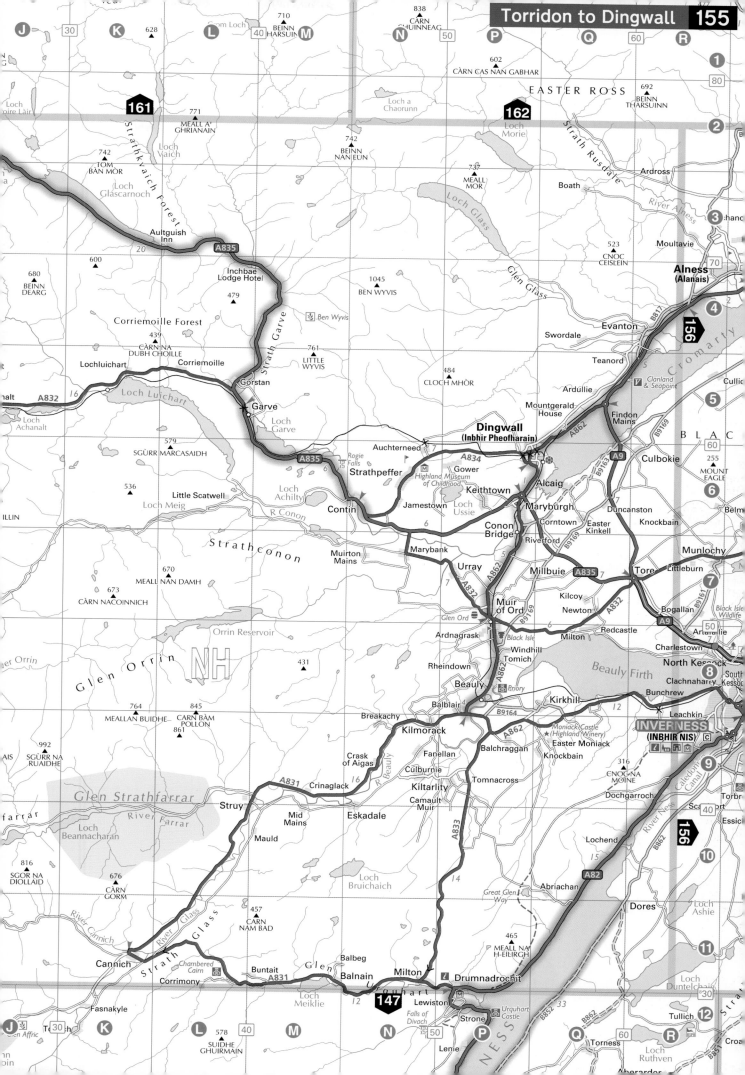

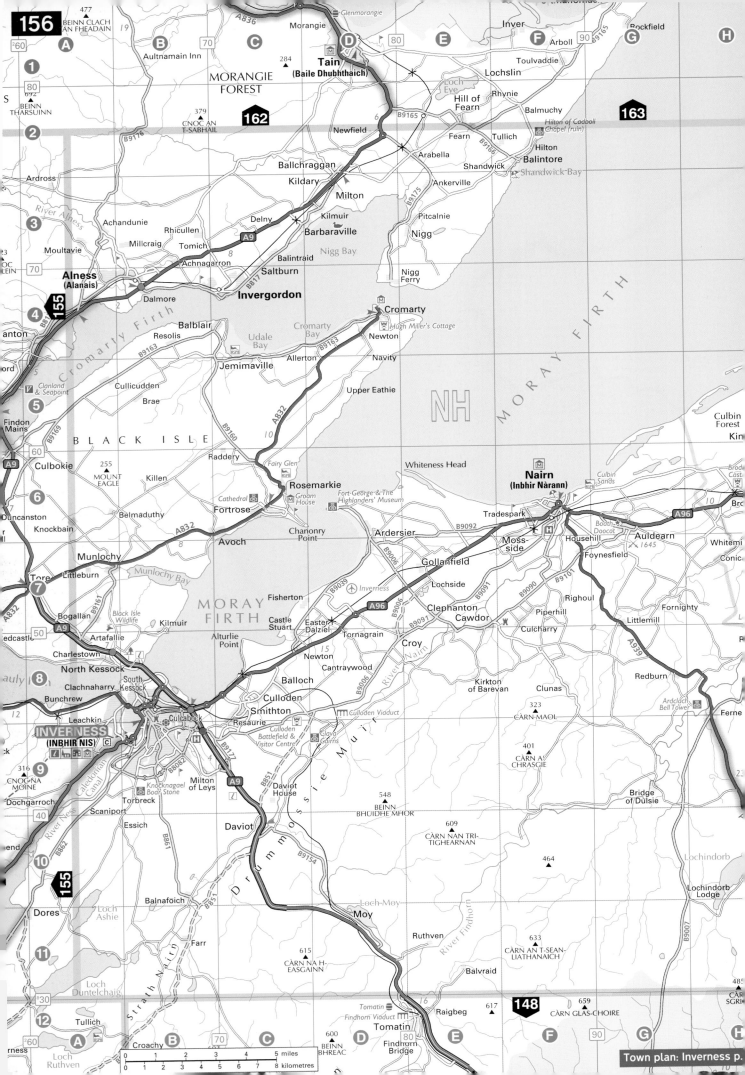

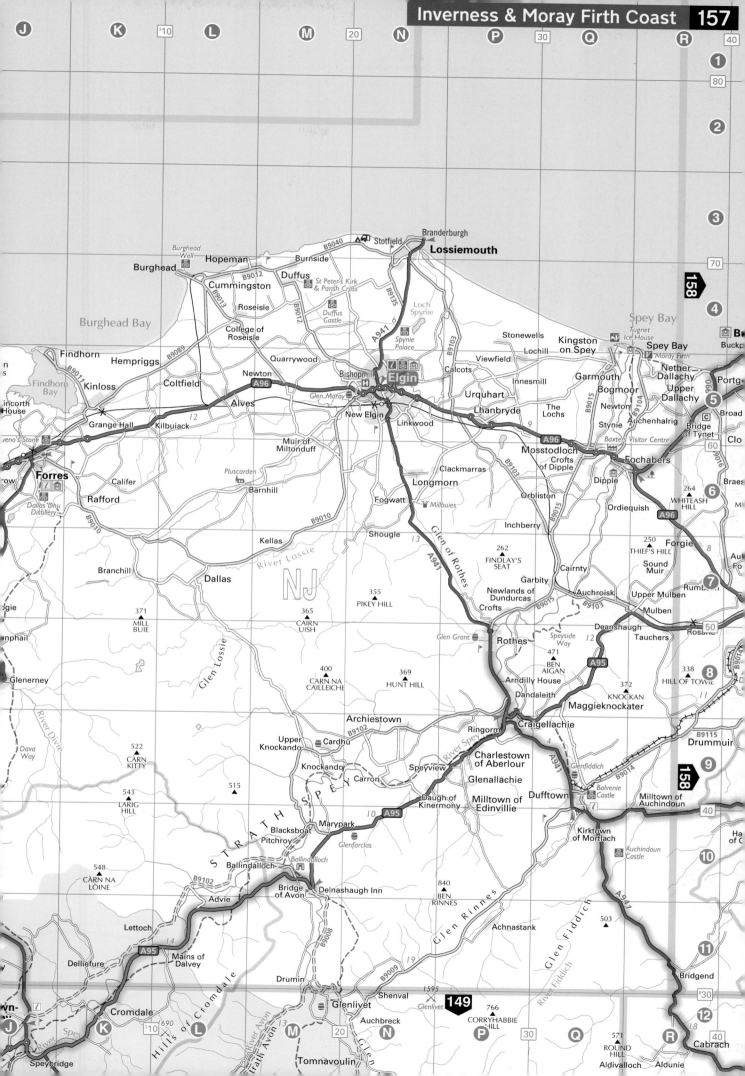

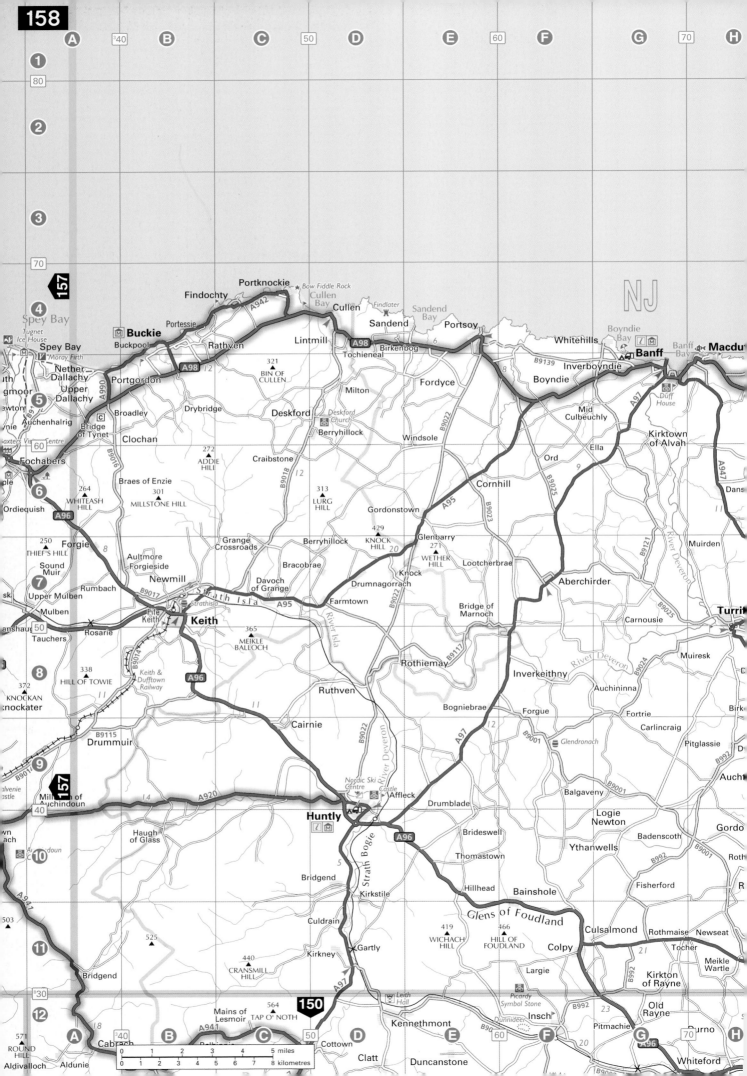

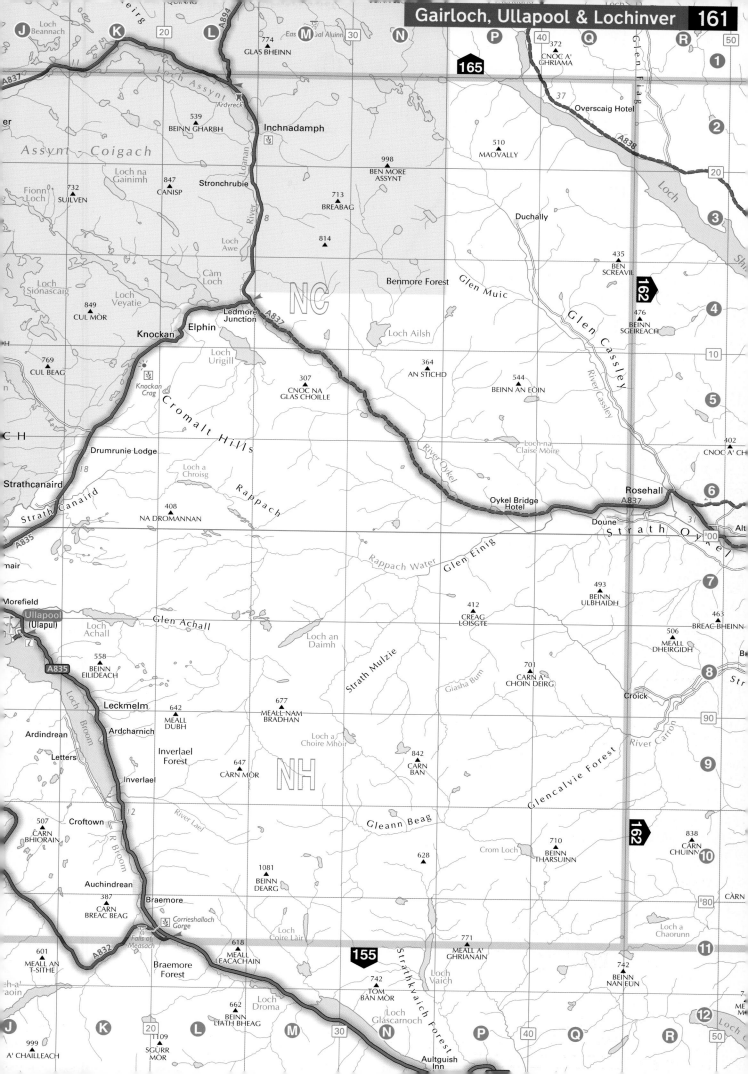

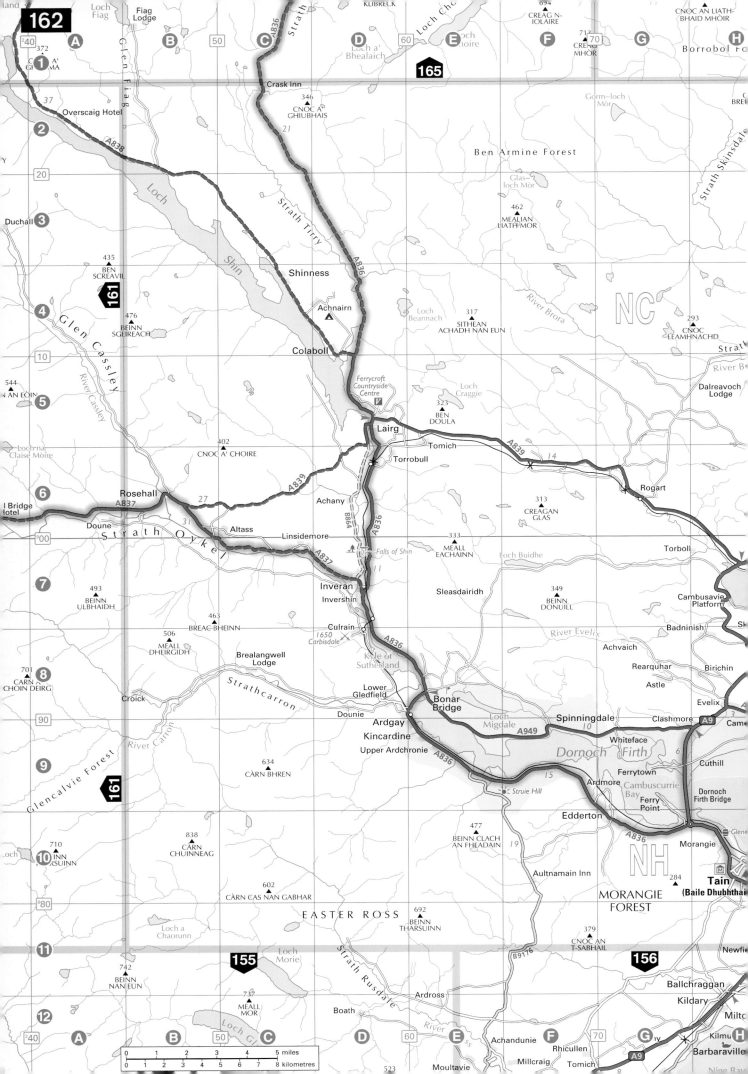

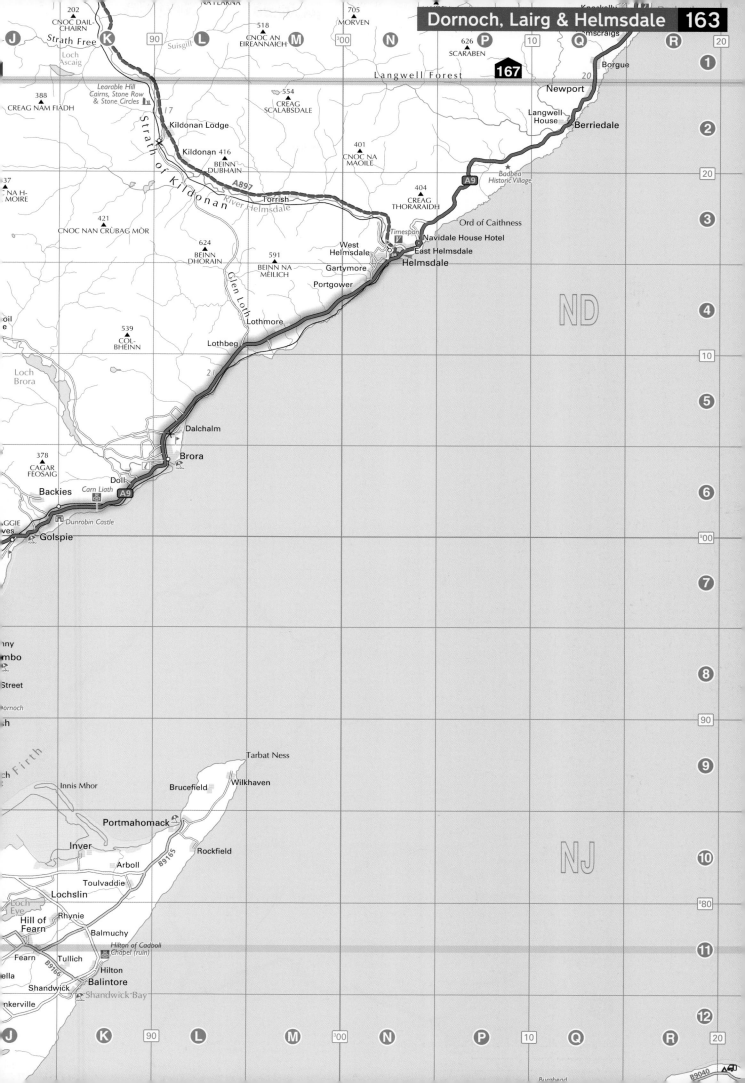

167

J
K
90 Suisgill
L
M
300
N
P
SCARABEN
626
Q
R
20

1

202
CNOC DAIL-CHAIRN
Strath Free
Loch Ascaig
518
CNOC AN EIREANNAICH
705
MORVEN

Langwell Forest
Knockelly
mscraigs
Borgue
20
Newport

388
CREAG NAM FIADH
Learable Hill
Cairns, Stone Row
& Stone Circles
17
Kildonan Lodge
554
CREAG SCALABSDALE

Langwell House
Berriedale

2

20

37
NA H-MOIRE
Kildonan 416
BEINN DUBHAIN
A897
Torrish
River Helmsdale
401
CNOC NA MAOILE
404
CREAG THORARAIDH
A9
Badbea Historic Village

20

3

421
CNOC NAN CRÙBAG MÒR
624
BEINN DHORAIN
Glen Loth
591
BEINN NA MEILICH
West Helmsdale
Gartymore
Portgower
Timespan
Navidale House Hotel
East Helmsdale
Helmsdale
Ord of Caithness

ND

4

539
COL-BHEINN
Lothmore
Lothbeg
21

10

5

Loch Brora
Dalchalm
Brora
Doll

6

378
CAGAR FEOSAIG
Backies
Carn Liath
A9
Doll

GGIE
ves
Golspie
Dunrobin Castle
900

7

nny
mbo
Street
ornoch
h

8

90

ch Firth
Tarbat Ness

9

Innis Mhor
Brucefield
Wilkhaven
Portmahomack
Inver
B9165
Rockfield

NJ

10

Arboll
Toulvaddie
Lochslin
Loch Eye
880

Hill of Fearn
Rhynie
Balmuchy
Hilton of Cadboll
Chapel (ruin)

11

Fearn
Tullich
Hilton
B9166
Shandwick
Balintore
ella
nkerville
Shandwick Bay

12

J
K
90
L
M
300
N
P
10
Q
R
20

B9040

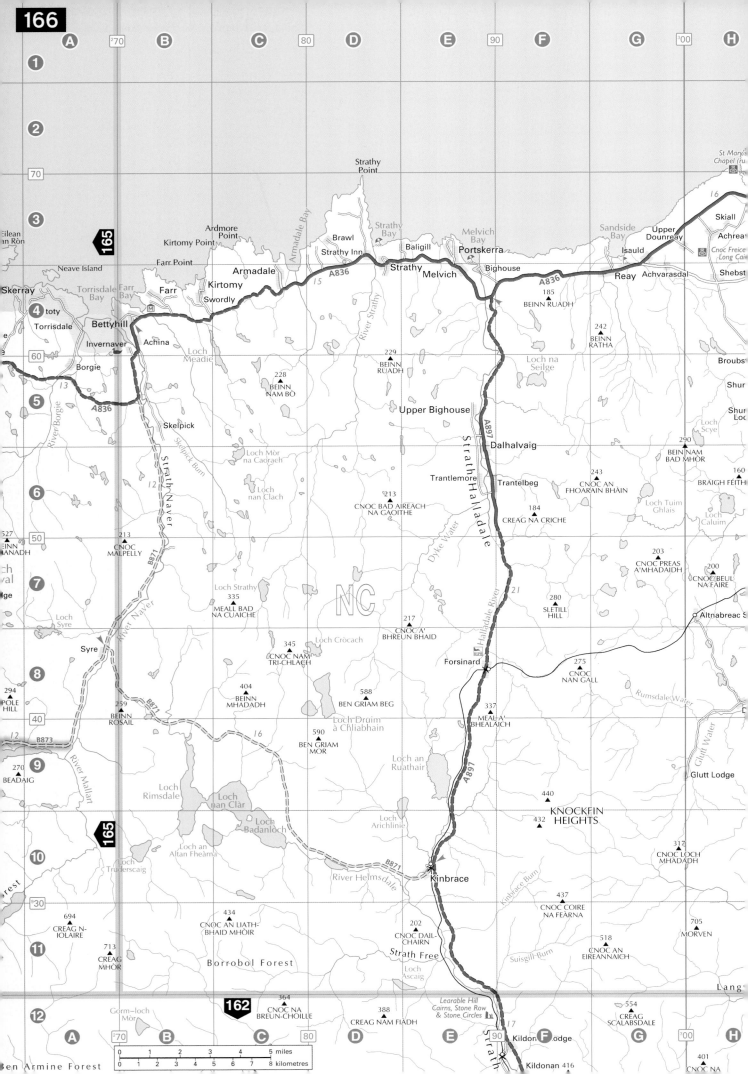

J 10 K L 20 M N 30 P Q 40 R

PENTLAND FIRTH

Langaton Point
Nethertown
Uppertown
Mell Head
St John's Point

ISLAND OF STROMA

St Margaret's Hope

DUNNET HEAD
Briga Head

Scarfskerry
Castle of Mey

A836
Gills Bay

Huna
Kirkstyle
Canisby

DUNCANSBY HEAD

John o' Groats
Muckle Stack

121
DUNNET HILL

Brough
St John's Loch

Loch of Mey
15

Rattar
Mey
Gills

Stacks of Duncansby

Stromness

Holborn Head

West Dunnet
Dunnet

Barrock

A99

Skirza
Skirza Head

Clarden Head
Scrabster

A9
Thurso Bay
Thurso

Castlehill
Murkle
A836
5

Dunnet Bay

Inkstack

Brabstermire

Freswick
Freswick Bay

Ness Head

70

Glengolly
Westfield

B874
A9
Weydale

Castletown

Greenland

Slickly

Auckengill

Broch
Nybster

Olrig House

Tain

Hilliclay

B876

Bowermadden

Sortat

Howe

Brough Head

Sordale

Bower

Lyth

Keiss

60

Roadside
B874

Knockdee
Clayock

Loch Scarmclate

Halcro

Kirk

16

Mireland
A99

Halkirk

Gillock

Loch of Wester

Killimster

Sinclair Bay

Georgemas Junction Station
A882
21

B874

B870

Reiss

Scotscalder Station

Harpsdale

176
SPITTAL HILL

Loch Watten

Winless

Sibster

Castle Girnigoe & Sinclair
Noss Head

Olgrinmore

Spittal

Watten
B870

Bilbster
A882

Ackergill
Wick
John o' Groats

Staxigoe

River Thurso
MA'
MAIRNIE

Mybster
Loch of Toftingall

Haster
Milton

Janetstown
A99

Papigoe

Westerdale
23

Wick
Wick Bay

Strath Beg

136
BEINN CHÀITEAG

Badlipster

Newton

Old Wick
South Head
Castle of Old Wick

Whiterow

50

ND

Tannach

Loch Hempriggs

A9

145
BALLHARN HILL

Grey Cairns of Camster

Thrumster

Loch More

Loch Ruard

Loch Stemster

212
HILL OF YARROWS

Loch of Yarrows

A99
17

Sarclet

Achavanich

248
STEMSTER HILL

Cairn o' Get

Ulbster

Loch Sand

Loch an Thulachan

Loch Rangag

Whaligoe

40

226
COIRE NA BEINN

Roster

Whaligoe Steps

Bruan

287
BEN-A-CHIELT

Upper Lybster

Hill o'Many Stanes

Mid Clyth

Halberry Head

264
CNOCAN CONACHREAG

Swiney

Occumster

Clyth Ness

Houstry

Invershore
Lybster

Landhallow

Forse

Lybster Bay

Smerral

Latheron

Dunbeath Water

Latheronwheel

A9
Janetstown

Laidhay Croft

Dunbeath

30

Knockally

Dunbeath Bay

Ramscraigs

11

Borgue

20

163

Newport

Langwell House

J 10 K riedale L 20 M N 30 P Q 40 R

1 2 3 4 5 6 7 8 9 10 11 12

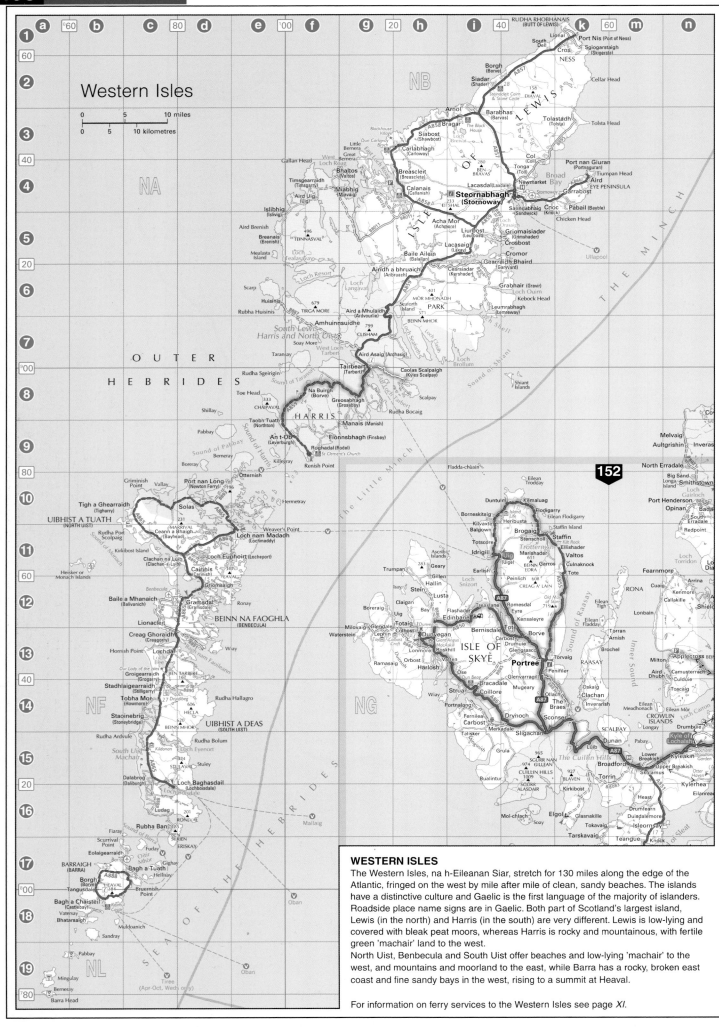

Western Isles

0   5   10 miles
0   5   10 kilometres

WESTERN ISLES

The Western Isles, na h-Eileanan Siar, stretch for 130 miles along the edge of the Atlantic, fringed on the west by mile after mile of clean, sandy beaches. The islands have a distinctive culture and Gaelic is the first language of the majority of islanders. Roadside place name signs are in Gaelic. Both part of Scotland's largest island, Lewis (in the north) and Harris (in the south) are very different. Lewis is low-lying and covered with bleak peat moors, whereas Harris is rocky and mountainous, with fertile green 'machair' land to the west.

North Uist, Benbecula and South Uist offer beaches and low-lying 'machair' to the west, and mountains and moorland to the east, while Barra has a rocky, broken east coast and fine sandy bays in the west, rising to a summit at Heaval.

For information on ferry services to the Western Isles see page XI.

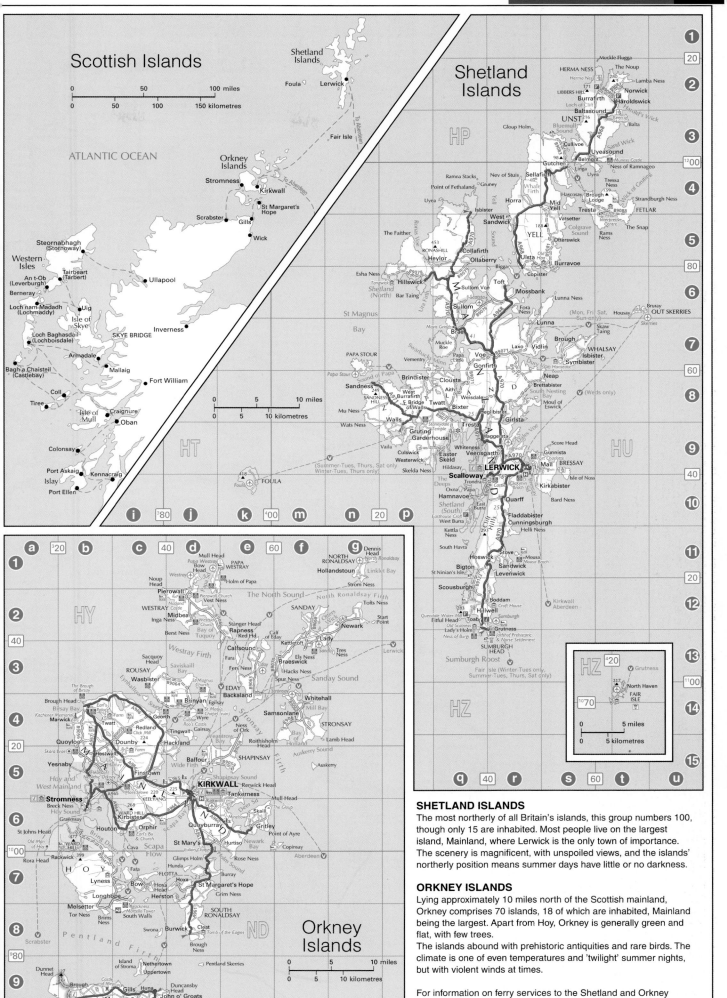

SHETLAND ISLANDS

The most northerly of all Britain's islands, this group numbers 100, though only 15 are inhabited. Most people live on the largest island, Mainland, where Lerwick is the only town of importance. The scenery is magnificent, with unspoiled views, and the islands' northerly position means summer days have little or no darkness.

ORKNEY ISLANDS

Lying approximately 10 miles north of the Scottish mainland, Orkney comprises 70 islands, 18 of which are inhabited, Mainland being the largest. Apart from Hoy, Orkney is generally green and flat, with few trees.

The islands abound with prehistoric antiquities and rare birds. The climate is one of even temperatures and 'twilight' summer nights, but with violent winds at times.

For information on ferry services to the Shetland and Orkney Islands see page XI.

IRISH SEA

Legend

M1	Toll-free motorway
M1 Toll	Toll motorway and plaza
3	Motorway junctions with and without number
3	Restricted motorway junctions
S Gorey	Motorway service area
N7	National primary route (Republic of Ireland)
N81	National secondary route (Republic of Ireland)
R116	Regional road (Republic of Ireland)
7	Distance in kilometres between symbols (Republic of Ireland)
A2	Primary route (Northern Ireland)
A42	A road (Northern Ireland)
B176	B road (Northern Ireland)
7	Distance in miles between symbols (Northern Ireland)
	Minor road
	Road under construction
	Scenic route
	International boundary
Roscoff	Vehicle ferry
Cairnryan	Fast vehicle ferry or catamaran
	National Park
	Gaeltacht (Irish language area)

To reflect the distances shown on road signs, distances are shown in miles in Northern Ireland and kilometres in the Republic of Ireland.

16 kilometres = 10 miles

For key to touring information see page 1

Ireland index

Abbeydorney....C12
Abbeyfeale....D12
Abbeyleix....G11
Adamstown....H12
Adare....D12
Adrigole....C14
Aghadowey....H4
Ahascragh....E9
Ahoghill....J4
Allihies....B15
Anascaul....B13
An Bun Beag....E4
An Charraig....E5
An Clochán Liath....E4
An Coireán....B14
An Daingean....B13
An Fhairche....C9
Annalong....J7
Annestown....G13
An Rinn....G13
An Spidéal....D9
Antrim....J5
Ardagh....D12
Ardara....E5
Ardee....H8
Ardfert....C12
Ardfinnan....F12
Ardglass....K6
Ardgroom....B14
Ardmore....F14
Arklow....J11
Arless....H11
Armagh....H6
Armoy....J3
Arthurstown....H13
Arvagh....G7
Ashbourne....J9
Ashford....J10
Askeaton....D12
Athboy....H8
Athea....D12
Athenry....E9
Athleague....E8
Athlone....F9
Athy....H10
Augher....G6
Aughnacloy....H6
Aughrim....J11
Avoca....J11

Bagenalstown....H11
Baile Mhic Íre....D14
Bailieborough....H7
Balbriggan....J8
Balla....D8
Ballaghaderreen....E7
Ballina....D7
Ballina....E11
Ballinafad....E7
Ballinagh....G7
Ballinakill....G11
Ballinalee....F8
Ballinamallard....G6
Ballinamore....F7
Ballinascarty....D14
Ballinasloe....E9
Ballincollig....E14
Ballindine....D8
Ballineen....D14
Ballingarry....D12
Ballingarry....G12
Ballingeary....D14
Ballinhassig....E14
Ballinlough....E8
Ballinrobe....D8
Ballinspittle....E15
Ballintober....E8
Ballintra....F5
Ballivor....H9
Ballon....H11
Ballybaun....E9
Ballybay....H7
Ballybofey....F5
Ballybunion....C12
Ballycanew....J11
Ballycarry....K5
Ballycastle....J3
Ballycastle....C6
Ballyclare....J5
Ballycolla....G11
Ballyconneely....B9
Ballyconnell....G7
Ballycotton....F14
Ballycumber....F9
Ballydehob....C15
Ballydesmond....D13
Ballyduff....C12
Ballyduff....F13
Ballyfarnon....E7
Ballygalley....J4
Ballygar....E9
Ballygawley....E6
Ballygawley....H6
Ballygowan....K5
Ballyhack....H13
Ballyhaise....G7
Ballyhale....G12
Ballyhaunis....E8
Ballyhean....D8
Ballyheige....C12
Ballyjamesduff....G8
Ballykeeran....F9
Ballylanders....E12
Ballylickey....C14
Ballyliffin....G3
Ballylongford....C12
Ballylooby....F12
Ballylynan....H10
Ballymacarbry....F13
Ballymahon....F8
Ballymakeery....D14
Ballymena....J4
Ballymoe....E8
Ballymoney....H4
Ballymore....F8
Ballymore Eustace....H10

Ballymote....E7
Ballynahinch....J6
Ballynure....J5
Ballyporeen....F13
Ballyragget....G11
Ballyronan....H5
Ballysadare....E6
Ballyshannon....F5
Ballyvaughan....D10
Ballywalter....K5
Balrothery....J8
Baltimore....C15
Baltinglass....H10
Banagher....F10
Banbridge....J6
Bandon....E14
Bangor....K5
Bangor Erris....C7
Bansha....F12
Banteer....D13
Bantry....C14
Barna....D9
Béal an Mhuirhead....B6
Béal Átha an Ghaorthaidh....D14
Bearna....D9
Beaufort....C13
Belcoo....F6
Belfast....J5
Belgooly....E14
Bellaghy....H4
Belleek....F6
Belmullet....B6
Belturbet....G7
Belview Port....H13
Benburb....H6
Bennettsbridge....G12
Beragh....G5
Bettystown....J8
Birr....F10
Blacklion....F6
Blackrock....J9
Blackwater....J12
Blarney....E14
Blessington....H10
Boherbue....D13
Borris....H11
Borris-in-Ossory....F10
Borrisokane....F10
Borrisoleigh....F11
Boyle....E7
Bracknagh....G10
Bray....J10
Bridgetown....H13
Brittas....J9
Broadford....E11
Broadford....D12
Broughshane....J4
Bruff....E12
Bruree....E12
Bunbeg....E4
Bunclody....H11
Buncrana....G3
Bundoran....E6
Bunmahon....G13
Bun na hAbhna....C6
Bunnahowen....C6
Bunnyconnellan....D7
Bunratty....D11
Burnfort....E13
Bushmills....H3
Buttevant....E13

Cadamstown....F10
Caherconlish....E12
Caherdaniel....B14
Cahersiveen....B14
Cahir....F12
Caledon....H6
Callan....G12
Caltra....E9
Camp....B13
Campile....H13
Cappagh White....F12
Cappamore....E11
Cappoquin....F13
Carlanstown....H8
Carlingford....J7
Carlow....H11
Carna....C9
Carndonagh....G3
Carnew....J11
Carnlough....J4
Carracastle....E7
Carraig Airt....F3
Carrick....E5
Carrickart....F3
Carrickfergus....K5
Carrickmacross....H7
Carrickmore....G5
Carrick-on-Shannon....F7
Carrick-on-Suir....G12
Carrigahorig....F10
Carrigaline....E14
Carrigallen....F7
Carriganimmy....D14
Carrigans....G4
Carrigtohill....E14
Carryduff....J5
Cashel....C9
Cashel....F12
Castlebellingham....J7
Castleblayney....H7
Castlebridge....J12
Castlecomer....G11
Castleconnell....E11
Castlederg....F5
Castledermot....H11
Castlegregory....B13
Castleisland....C13
Castlemaine....C13
Castlemartyr....F14

Castleplunket....E8
Castlepollard....G8
Castlerea....E8
Castlerock....H3
Castleshane....H6
Castletown....G10
Castletownbere....B15
Castletownroche....E13
Castletownshend....D15
Castlewellan....J6
Cathair Dónall....B14
Causeway....C12
Cavan....G7
Celbridge....H9
Charlestown....D7
Charleville....E12
Cheekpoint....H13
Cill Charthaigh....E5
Cill Chiaráin....C9
Clady....G5
Clane....H9
Clara....G9
Clarecastle....D11
Claremorris....D8
Clarinbridge....D10
Clashmore....F13
Claudy....G4
Clifden....B9
Cliffony....E6
Clogh....G11
Cloghan....F10
Clogheen....F13
Clogher....G6
Clohamon....H11
Clonakilty....D15
Clonard....H9
Clonaslee....G10
Clonbulloge....G9
Clonbur....C9
Clondalkin....J9
Clones....G7
Clonlara....E11
Clonmany....G3
Clonmel....F12
Clonmellon....H8
Clonmore....F11
Clonony....F10
Clonoulty....F12
Clonroche....H12
Clontibret....H6
Cloondara....F8
Clough....K6
Cloughjordan....F10
Cloyne....F14
Coachford....D14
Coagh....H5
Coalisland....H5
Cobh....E14
Coleraine....H3
Collinstown....G8
Collon....H8
Collooney....E6
Comber....K5
Cong....D9
Conna....F13
Cookstown....H5
Coole....G8
Cooraclare....C11
Cootehill....G7
Cork....E14
Cornamona....C9
Corr na Móna....C9
Corrofin....D10
Courtmacsherry....E15
Courtown....J11
Craigavon....J6
Craughwell....E10
Crawfordsburn....K5
Creegs....E8
Creeslough....F4
Croagh....D12
Croithlí....E4
Crookedwood....G8
Crookhaven....C15

Crookstown....D14
Croom....E12
Crossakeel....H8
Cross Barry....E14
Crosshaven....E14
Crossmaglen....H7
Crossmolina....D7
Crumlin....J5
Crusheen....D10
Culdaff....G3
Cullybackey....J4
Curracloe....J12
Curraghboy....F9
Curry....E7
Cushendall....J4
Cushendun....J3

Daingean....G9
Daingean Uí Chúis....B13
Delgany....J10
Delvin....G8
Derry....G4
Derrygonnelly....F6
Derrylin....G6
Dervock....H3
Dingle....B13
Doagh....J5
Donaghadee....K5
Donaghmore....G11
Donard....H10
Donegal....F5
Doneraile....E13
Doolin....C10
Doon....E12
Doonbeg....C11
Doon Cross Roads....F9
Douglas....E14
Downpatrick....K6
Dowra....F6
Draperstown....H5
Drimoleague....D15
Drogheda....J8
Dromahair....E6
Dromcolliher....D12
Dromore....J6
Dromore....G5
Dromore West....D6
Drumcliff....E6
Drumcondra....H8
Drumkeeran....F7
Drumlish....F8
Drumod....F8
Drumquin....G5
Drumshanbo....F7
Drumsna....F7
Duagh....C12
Dublin....J9
Duleek....J8
Dunboyne....J9
Dún Chaoin....A13
Duncormick....H13
Dundalk....J7
Dunderrow....E14
Dundonald....K5
Dundrum....K6
Dundrum....F12
Dunfanaghy....F3
Dungannon....H5
Dungarvan....G12
Dungarvan....G13
Dungiven....G4
Dunglow....E4
Dungourney....F14
Dunkineely....E5
Dún Laoghaire....J9
Dunlavin....H10
Dunleer....J8
Dunloy....J4
Dunmanway....D14
Dunmore....E8
Dunmore East....H13
Dunmurry....J5
Dunquin....A13
Dunshaughlin....H9

Durrow....G11
Durrus....C15
Dysart....E9

Easky....D6
Edenderry....H9
Edgeworthstown....G8
Eglinton....G4
Elphin....F8
Emyvale....H5
Enfield....H9
Ennis....D11
Enniscorthy....H12
Enniscrone....D6
Enniskean....D14
Enniskillen....F6
Ennistymon....D10
Eyrecourt....F10

Fahan....G4
Farranfore....C13
Feakle....E10
Fenagh....F7
Ferbane....F9
Fermoy....E13
Ferns....J12
Fethard....F12
Fethard....H13
Finnea....G8
Fintona....G6
Fivemiletown....G6
Fontstown....H10
Foulkesmill....H12
Foxford....D7
Foynes....D11
Freemount....D13
Frenchpark....E8
Freshford....G11
Fuerty....E8

Galbally....E12
Galway....D9
Garrison....F6
Garristown....J8
Garryvoe....F14
Garvagh....H4
Geashill....G10
Gilford....J6
Glandore....D15
Glanmire....E14
Glanworth....E13
Glaslough....H6
Glassan....F9
Gleann Cholm Cille....E5
Glenarm....J4
Glenavy....J5
Glenbeigh....B13
Glencolumbkille....E5
Glenealy....J10
Glengarriff....C14
Glenmore....H12
Glennamaddy....E8
Glenties....E5
Glin....D12
Glinsce....C9
Glinsk....C9
Golden....F12
Goleen....C15
Goresbridge....H11
Gorey....J11
Gort....D10
Gortin....G5
Gowran....H11
Graiguenamanagh....H12
Granard....G8
Grange....E6
Greenore....J7
Greyabbey....K5
Greystones....J10
Gulladuff....H4

Hacketstown....H11
Headford....D9
Herbertstown....E12

Hillsborough....J6
Hilltown....J6
Holycross....F11
Holywood....K5
Horse & Jockey....F11
Horseleap....G9
Hospital....E12
Howth....J9

Inch....B13
Inchigeelagh....D14
Inishannon....E14
Inishcrone....D6
Inistioge....H12
Irvinestown....F6

Johnstown....G11

Kanturk....D13
Keadew....F7
Keady....H6
Keel....B7
Keenagh....F8
Kells....J4
Kells....H8
Kenmare....C14
Kesh....G6
Kilbeggan....G9
Kilberry....H8
Kilbrittain....E14
Kilcar....E5
Kilcock....H9
Kilcolgan....D10
Kilconnell....E9
Kilcoole....J10
Kilcormac....F10
Kilcullen....H10
Kilcurry....J7
Kildare....H10
Kildavin....H11
Kildorrery....E13
Kilfenora....D10
Kilgarvan....C14
Kilkee....C11
Kilkeel....J7
Kilkelly....E8
Kilkenny....G11
Kilkieran....C9
Kilkinlea Lower....C12
Kill....H9
Kill....G13
Killadysert....D11
Killala....D6
Killaloe....E11
Killarney....C13
Killashandra....G7
Killeagh....F14
Killeigh....G10
Killenaule....F12
Killimer....C11
Killimor....E10
Killiney....J9
Killinick....J13
Killorglin....C13
Killough....K6
Killucan....G9
Killybegs....E5
Killyleagh....K6
Kilmacanoge....J10
Kilmacrenan....F4
Kilmacthomas....G13
Kilmaganny....G12
Kilmaine....D8
Kilmallock....E12
Kilmanagh....G11
Kilmeage....H9
Kilmeedy....D12
Kilmichael....D14
Kilmore Quay....H13
Kilmuckridge....J12
Kilnaleck....G8
Kilrea....H4
Kilrush....C11
Kilsheelan....G12
Kiltealy....H12

Kiltegan....H11
Kiltimagh....D8
Kiltoom....F9
Kingscourt....H7
Kinlough....E6
Kinnegad....G9
Kinnitty....F10
Kinsale....E14
Kinvarra....D10
Kircubbin....K5
Knock....D8
Knockcroghery....F8
Knocklofty....F12
Knocktopher....G12

Lahinch....C10
Lanesborough....F8
Laragh....J10
Larne....K4
Lauragh....C14
Laurencetown....E10
Leap....D15
Leenaun....C8
Leighlinbridge....H11
Leitrim....F7
Leixlip....J9
Lemybrien....G13
Letterfrack....B8
Letterkenny....F4
Lifford....G4
Limavady....G4
Limerick....E11
Lisbellaw....G6
Lisburn....J5
Liscannor....C10

Liscarroll....D13
Lisdoonvarna....D10
Lismore....F13
Lisnaskea....G6
Lisryan....F8
Listowel....C12
Loghill....D12
Londonderry....G4
Longford....F8
Loughbrickland....J6
Loughgall....H6
Loughglinn....E8
Loughrea....E10
Louisburgh....C8
Lucan....J9
Lurgan....J6
Lusk....J8

Machair Loiscthe....F4
Macroom....D14
Maghera....H4
Magherafelt....H5
Maguiresbridge....G6
Malahide....J9
Malin....G3
Malin More....E5
Manorhamilton....F6
Mallow....E13
Markethill....H6
Martinstown....J4
Maynooth....H9
Mazetown....J5
Middletown....H6
Midleton....F14

...ford	F4	Mulrany	C7
...street	D13	Myshall	H11
...town	C13		
...town Malbay	C11	Naas	H10
...chelstown	E13	Naul	J8
...ate	F9	Navan	H8
...hill	F7	Neale	D8
...naghan	H6	Nenagh	E11
...nasterevin	G10	Newbliss	G7
...neygall	F11	Newbridge	H10
...neymore	H5	Newcastle	J6
...nivea	E9	Newcastle West	D12
...oncoin	G13	New Inn	F12
...orfields	J4	Newmarket	D13
...ntbellew	E9	Newmarket on	
...ntcharles	F5	Fergus	D11
...ntmellick	G10	Newport	C7
...ntollagh	G10	Newport	E11
...ntshannon	E10	New Ross	H12
...ville	G3	Newry	J6
...y	H6	Newtown	G11
...ynalty	H8	Newtownabbey	J5
...yore	F9	Newtownards	K5
...ckross	C13	Newtownbutler	F7
...ff	G4	Newtownhamilton	H6
...llaghmore	E6	Newtownmount-	
...llinavat	G12	kennedy	J10
...llingar	G9		
Newtownstewart	G5	Portglenone	H4
Nobber	H8	Portlaoise	G10
		Portmagee	B14
Ogonnelloe	E11	Portmarnock	J9
Oilgate	H12	Portnoo	E4
Oldcastle	G8	Portraine	J9
Omagh	G5	Portroe	E11
Omeath	J7	Portrush	H3
Oola	E12	Portstewart	H3
Oranmore	D9	Portumna	E11
Oughterard	D9	Poulgorm Bridge	C13
		Poyntz Pass	J6
Pallas Green	E12		
Parknasilla	B14	Raharney	G9
Partry	D8	Ramelton	F4
Passage East	H13	Ramsgrange	J5
Passage West	E14	Randalstown	H4
Patrickswell	E12	Rasharkin	H4
Paulstown	H11	Rathangan	H10
Pettigo	F5	Rathcoole	J9
Plumbridge	G5	Rathcormac	E13
Pomeroy	H5	Rathdowney	G11
Pontoon	D7	Rathdrum	J10
Portadown	H6	Rathfriland	J6
Portaferry	K6	Rathkeale	D12
Portarlington	H10	Rathmolyon	H9
Portavogie	K6	Rathmore	D13
Portballintrae	H3	Rathmullan	G4
		Rathnew	J10
Rathowen	G8	Salthill	D9
Rathvilly	H11	Scarriff	E11
Ratoath	J9	Scartaglin	C13
Ray	G4	Scarva	J6
Recess	C9	Schull	C15
Renvyle	B8	Scramoge	G5
Ringaskiddy	E14	Seskinore	G5
Ringville	G13	Shanagarry	E14
Rockcorry	H7	Shanagolden	D12
Roosky	F8	Shankill	J9
Rosapenna	F3	Shannon	D11
Rosbercon	H12	Shannonbridge	F9
Roscommon	F8	Shercock	H7
Roscrea	F10	Shillelagh	H11
Rosscarbery	D15	Shinrone	F10
Rosses Point	E6	Shrule	D9
Rosslare	J13	Silvermines	E11
Rosslare Harbour	J13	Sion Mills	G5
Rosslea	G6	Sixmilebridge	D11
Rossnowlagh	F5	Skerries	J8
Rostrevor	J7	Skibbereen	D15
Roundstone	B9	Slane	H8
Roundwood	J10	Sligo	E6
Rush	J9	Smithborough	G6
		Sneem	B14
Saintfield	K6	Spanish Point	C11
St Johnston	G4	Spiddal	D9
Sallins	H9	Sraith Salach	C9
Stewartstown	H5	Tobercurry	E7
Stillorgan	J9	Tobermore	H4
Stonyford	G12	Toomyvara	F11
Strabane	G4	Toormore	C15
Stradbally	G10	Tralee	C13
Stradone	G7	Tramore	G13
Straffan	H9	Trim	H8
Strandhill	E6	Tuam	D9
Strangford	K6	Tuamgraney	E11
Stranorlar	F5	Tubbercurry	E7
Strokestown	F8	Tulla	D11
Summerhill	H9	Tullamore	G10
Swanlinbar	F6	Tullow	H11
Swatragh	H4	Tulsk	E8
Swinford	D7	Turlough	D7
Swords	J9	Tyrrellspass	G9
Taghmon	H12	Urlingford	G11
Tagoat	J13		
Tahilla	C14	Virginia	G8
Tallaght	J9		
Tallow	F13	Warrenpoint	J7
Tallowbridge	F13	Waterford	G13
Tandragee	J6	Watergrasshill	E13
Tang	F9	Waterville	B14
Tarbert	C12	Wellingtonbridge	H13
Templemore	F11	Westport	C8
Templetouhy	F11	Wexford	J12
Termonfeckin	J8	Whitegate	E14
Termon Rock	G5	Whitehead	K5
Thomastown	G12	Wicklow	J10
Thurles	F11	Woodenbridge	J11
Timahoe	G10	Woodford	E10
Timoleague	D15		
Tinahely	J11	Youghal	F14
Tipperary	F12		

179

For Central London see pages 238–247

St Mary's Lighthouse
St Mary's Island

Seaton Delaval
Bates Cottages
Holywell

Whitley Bay C

East Holywell
Earsdon
Whitley Bay

Monkseaton

WHITLEY BAY

West Monkseaton
Shiremoor
Murton
West Monkseaton

Shiremoor Station
Backworth

CULLERCOATS
Marden
Cullercoats

West Allotment
New York
Marden Park Nature Reserve

Blue Reef
Longsands South

Willington Square
North Tyneside General
Preston
Tynemouth

King Edwards Bay
Tynemouth Priory & Castle
TYNEMOUTH

Billy Mill
Tynemouth

Stephenson Railway Museum
West Chirton
NORTH SHIELDS

Amsterdam (IJmuiden)

Willington Square
Silverlink Roundabout
North Tyneside Steam Railway
Howdon Interchange
Waterville Road
NORTH SHIELDS

Arbeia Roman Fort & Museum
The Lawe
Tyne Road
Sandhaven

NORTH

SEA

Howdon
Percy Main
SOUTH SHIELDS

Willington
Howdon
Meadow Well
SOUTH SHIELDS

Royal Quays
Mill Dam

Archer Street

Point Pleasant
East Howdon
Tyne Tunnel

Westoe
Chichester
Cauldwell

Harton
Marsden Road
Marsden Rock

Arbeia Roman & Baths
River Tyne

JARROW
Bede's World
St Paul's Monastery
East Jarrow
Tyne Dock

Marsden
Marsden Bay

Hebburn-Jarrow Colliery

Simonside
West Harton
South Tyneside General

Souter Lighthouse & The Leas

HEBBURN
Monkton
Primrose
Brockley Whins
BROCKLEY WHINS
Biddick Hall

Cleadon Park

Primrose
Lindisfarne Roundabout
South Shields
Whiteleas

Hedworth
FELLGATE
Boldon Colliery
Cleadon

Fellgate
Whitburn

Wardley
West Boldon
East Boldon
EAST BOLDON

South Bents

Folingsby
Testos Roundabout
NEWCASTLE ROAD
Dipe Lane
Greyhound Stadium

Seaburn

Fulwell
Seaburn

Downhill
Witherwack
Carley Hill
Roker

Marley Pots
High Southwick
Roker

Hylton Castle
Castletown
North Hylton Road
Southwick
Monkwearmouth
STADIUM OF LIGHT
National Glass Centre

Sunderland Harbour

Concord
Sulgrave
Hylton Plantation
Low Southwick
Queen Alexandra Bridge
Deptford
Stadium of Light (Sunderland AFC)

Hertburn
PALLION
Ayre's Quay
ST PETER'S

Washington Wetland Centre
South Hylton
Pallion
Millfield
Bishopwearmouth
SUNDERLAND

Barmston
Teal Farm
SOUTH HYLTON
Ford
Sunderland Royal
UNIVERSITY
PARK LANE

Washington Village
Pennywell
Sunderland
High Barnes
Barnes Park
SUNDERLAND

Columbia
Fatfield
Hastings Hill
Grindon
Springwell
Humbledon
Ashbrooke
Hendon

Penshaw Monument
Herrington Country Park

Hillview
Sunderland Eye Infirmary
Grangetown

Mount Pleasant
Penshaw
Middle Herrington
Thorney Close
Plains Farm
Silksworth Sports Complex & Ski Centre
Farringdon

Biddick Gill Wood
Shiney Row
New Herrington
East Herrington
Silksworth
New Silksworth
Tunstall
Ryhope

Street map symbols

Town, port and airport plans

Motorway and junction	One-way, gated/ closed road	Railway station	P Car park
Primary road single/ dual carriageway	Restricted access road	Light rapid transit system station	P+R Park and Ride (at least 6 days per week)
A road single/ dual carriageway	Pedestrian area	Level crossing	Bus/coach station
B road single/ dual carriageway	Footpath	Tramway	H Hospital
Local road single/ dual carriageway	Road under construction	Ferry route	H 24-hour Accident & Emergency hospital
Other road single/ dual carriageway, minor road	Road tunnel	Airport, heliport	Petrol station, 24 hour Major suppliers only
Building of interest	Lighthouse	Railair terminal	City wall
Ruined building	Castle	Theatre or performing arts centre	Escarpment
Tourist Information Centre	Castle mound	Cinema	Cliff lift
Visitor or heritage centre	Monument, statue	Abbey, chapel, church	River/canal, lake
World Heritage Site (UNESCO)	Post Office	Synagogue	Lock, weir
Museum	Public library	Mosque	Viewpoint
English Heritage site	Shopping centre	Golf course	Park/sports ground
Historic Scotland site	Shopmobility	Racecourse	Cemetery
Cadw (Welsh heritage) site	Football stadium	Nature reserve	Woodland
National Trust site	Rugby stadium	Aquarium	Built-up area
National Trust Scotland site	County cricket ground	Toilet, with facilities for the less able	Beach

Central London street map (see pages 238–247)

London Underground station	London Overground station	Docklands Light Railway (DLR) station	Central London Congestion Charging Zone

Royal Parks

Green Park	Park open 24 hours. Constitution Hill and The Mall closed to traffic Sundays and public holidays
Hyde Park	Park open 5am–midnight. Park roads closed to traffic midnight–5am.
Kensington Gardens	Park open 6am–dusk.
Regent's Park	Park open 5am–dusk. Park roads closed to traffic midnight–7am.
St James's Park	Park open 5am–midnight. The Mall closed to traffic Sundays and public holidays.

Traffic regulations in the City of London include security checkpoints and restrict the number of entry and exit points.

Note: Oxford Street is closed to through-traffic (except buses & taxis) 7am–7pm Monday–Saturday.

Central London Congestion Charging Zone

The daily charge for driving or parking a vehicle on public roads in the Congestion Charging Zone (CCZ), during operating hours, is £11.50 per vehicle per day in advance or on the day of travel. Alternatively you can pay £10.50 by registering with CC Auto Pay, an automated payment system. Drivers can also pay the next charging day after travelling in the zone but this will cost £14. Payment permits entry, travel within and exit from the CCZ by the vehicle as often as required on that day.

The CCZ operates between 7am and 6pm, Mon–Fri only. There is no charge at weekends, on public holidays or between 25th Dec and 1st Jan inclusive.

For up to date information on the CCZ, exemptions, discounts or ways to pay, visit tfl.gov.uk/modes/driving/congestion-charge or write to Congestion Charging, P.O. Box 4782, Worthing BN11 9PS. Textphone users can call 020 7649 9123.

Town Plans

Aberdeen 188
Basingstoke 188
Bath 189
Birmingham 190
Blackpool 189
Bournemouth 191
Bradford 191
Brighton 192
Bristol 192
Cambridge 193
Canterbury 194
Cardiff 194
Carlisle 195
Cheltenham 195
Chester 196
Colchester 196
Coventry 197
Darlington 197
Derby 198
Doncaster 198
Dover 199
Dundee 199
Durham 200
Eastbourne 200
Edinburgh 201
Exeter 202
Glasgow 203
Gloucester 202
Great Yarmouth 204

Guildford 204
Harrogate 205
Huddersfield 205
Inverness 206
Ipswich 206
Kingston upon Hull 207
Lancaster 207
Leeds 208
Leicester 209
Lincoln 209
Liverpool 210
Llandudno 79
LONDON 238-247
Luton 211
Maidstone 211
Manchester 212
Margate 39
Middlesbrough 214
Milton Keynes 213
Newcastle upon Tyne 215
Newport 214
Newquay 4
Northampton 216
Norwich 216
Nottingham 217
Oldham 217
Oxford 218
Perth 219
Peterborough 219

Plymouth 220
Poole 222
Portsmouth 221
Preston 222
Ramsgate 39
Reading 223
Royal Tunbridge Wells 223
Salisbury 224
Sheffield 224
Shrewsbury 225
Southampton 226
Southend-on-Sea 225
Stirling 227
Stockton-on-Tees 227
Stoke-on-Trent (Hanley) 228
Stratford-upon-Avon 228
Sunderland 229
Swansea 230
Swindon 230
Taunton 231
Torquay 231
Warwick 232
Watford 232
Winchester 233
Wolverhampton 233
Worcester 234
York 234

Central London

PADDINGTON 238 239 240 241 FINSBURY CITY STEPNEY
SOHO 246 247
KENSINGTON 242 243 244 245 SOUTHWARK BERMONDSEY
CHELSEA WESTMINSTER KENNINGTON

Ferry Ports

Aberdeen Harbour XI
Calais IX
Dover, Port of IX
Fishguard Harbour X
Harwich International Port 53
Heysham Harbour X
Holyhead Harbour X
Hull, Port of XI
Liverpool Docks X
Newhaven Harbour IX
Pembroke Dock X
Plymouth, Port of VIII
Poole, Port of VIII
Port of Tyne XI
Portsmouth Harbour IX
Southampton, Port of VIII

Channel Tunnel

Folkestone Terminal 27
Calais / Coquelles Terminal 27

Airports

Aberdeen 237
Birmingham 236
East Midlands 236
Edinburgh 237
Glasgow 237
Leeds Bradford 237
London City 236
London Gatwick 235
London Heathrow 235
London Luton 235
London Stansted 235
Manchester 236

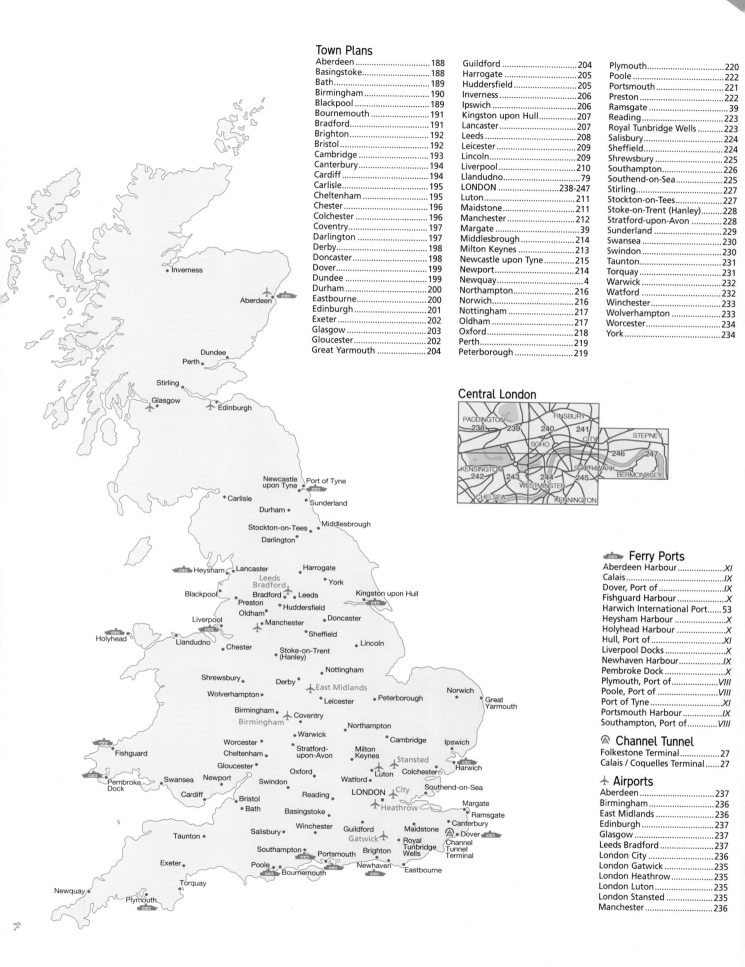

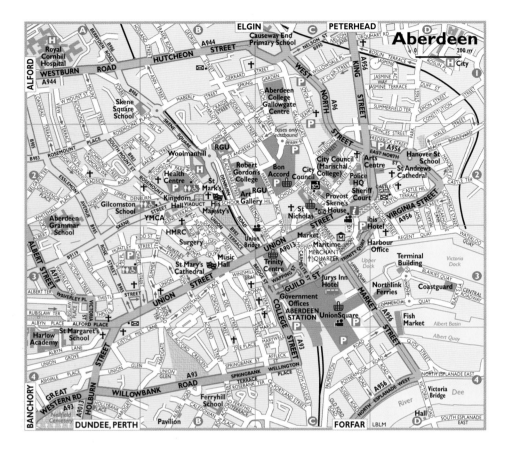

Aberdeen

Aberdeen is found on atlas page **151 N6**

Affleck Street C4	Maberly Street ....
Albert Street A3	Marischal Street ....
Albury Road B4	Market Street ....
Alford Place A3	Nelson Street ....
Ann Street B1	Palmerston Road ....
Beach Boulevard D2	Park Street ....
Belgrave Terrace A2	Portland Street ....
Berryden Road A1	Poynernook Road ....
Blackfriars Street B2	Regent Quay ....
Blaikies Quay D3	Richmond Street ....
Bon Accord Crescent B4	Rose Place ....
Bon Accord Street B3	Rose Street ....
Bridge Street C3	Rosemount Place ....
Caledonian Place B4	Rosemount Viaduct ......
Carmelite Street C3	St Andrew Street ....
Chapel Street A3	St Clair Street ....
Charlotte Street B1	School Hill ....
College Street C3	Skene Square ....
Constitution Street D1	Skene Street ....
Crimon Place B3	Skene Terrace ....
Crown Street B3	South College Street .....
Dee Street B3	South Esplanade East ....
Denburn Road B2	South Mount Street ......
Diamond Street B3	Spa Street ....
East North Street D2	Springbank Street ....
Esslemont Avenue A2	Springbank Terrace ......
Gallowgate C1	Summer Street ....
George Street B1	Summerfield Terrace .....
Gilcomston Park B2	Thistle Lane ....
Golden Square B3	Thistle Place ....
Gordon Street B3	Thistle Street ....
Great Western Road A4	Trinity Quay ....
Guild Street C3	Union Bridge ....
Hadden Street C3	Union Grove ....
Hanover Street D2	Union Street ....
Hardgate B4	Union Terrace ....
Harriet Street C2	Upper Denburn ....
Holburn Street A4	Victoria Road ....
Huntly Street A3	Victoria Street ....
Hutcheon Street B1	View Terrace ....
Jasmine Terrace D1	Virginia Street ....
John Street B2	Wapping Street ....
Justice Mill Lane A4	Waverley Place ....
King Street C1	Wellington Place ....
Langstane Place B3	West North Street ....
Leadside Road A2	Westburn Road ....
Loanhead Terrace A1	Whitehall Place ....
Loch Street C1	Willowbank Road ....

Basingstoke

Basingstoke is found on atlas page **22 H4**

Alencon Link C1	London Street ....
Allnutt Avenue D2	Lower Brook Street ....
Basing View C1	Lytton Road ....
Beaconsfield Road C4	Market Place ....
Bounty Rise A4	May Place ....
Bounty Road A4	Montague Place ....
Bramblys Close A3	Mortimer Lane ....
Bramblys Drive A3	New Road ....
Budd's Close A3	New Road ....
Castle Road C4	New Street ....
Chapel Hill B1	Penrith Road ....
Chequers Road C2	Rayleigh Road ....
Chester Place A4	Red Lion Lane ....
Churchill Way B2	Rochford Road ....
Churchill Way East D1	St Mary's Court ....
Churchill Way West A2	Sarum Hill ....
Church Square B2	Seal Road ....
Church Street B2	Solby's Road ....
Church Street B3	Southend Road ....
Cliddesden Road C4	Southern Road ....
Clifton Terrace C1	Stukeley Road ....
Cordale Road A4	Sylvia Close ....
Council Road B4	Timberlake Road ....
Crossborough Gardens .. D3	Victoria Street ....
Crossborough Hill D3	Victory Roundabout .....
Cross Street B3	Vyne Road ....
Devonshire Place A4	Winchcombe Road ....
Eastfield Avenue D2	Winchester Road ....
Eastrop Lane D2	Winchester Street ....
Eastrop Roundabout C1	Winterthur Way ....
Eastrop Way D2	Worting Road ....
Essex Road A2	Wote Street ....
Fairfields Road B4	
Festival Way C2	
Flaxfield Court A2	
Flaxfield Road A3	
Flaxfield Road B3	
Frances Road A4	
Frescade Crescent A4	
Goat Lane C2	
Hackwood Road C4	
Hamelyn Road A4	
Hardy Lane A4	
Hawkfield Lane A4	
Haymarket Yard C3	
Joices Yard B3	
Jubilee Road B4	
London Road D3	

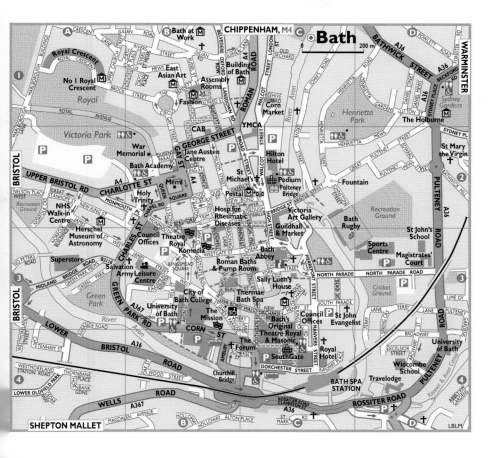

Bath

Bath is found on atlas page **20 D2**

Archway Street	D4	Lower Borough Walls	B3
Argyle Street	C2	Lower Bristol Road	A3
Avon Street	B3	Lower Oldfield Park	A4
Bartlett Street	B1	Manvers Street	C3
Barton Street	B2	Midland Bridge Road	A3
Bathwick Street	D1	Milk Street	B3
Beauford Square	B2	Milsom Street	B2
Beau Street	B3	Monmouth Place	A2
Beckford Road	D1	Monmouth Street	B2
Bennett Street	B1	New Bond Street	B2
Bridge Street	C2	New King Street	A2
Broad Street	C2	New Orchard Street	C3
Broadway	D4	Norfolk Buildings	A3
Brock Street	A1	North Parade	C3
Chapel Road	B2	North Parade Road	D3
Charles Street	A3	Old King Street	B2
Charlotte Street	A2	Oxford Row	B1
Cheap Street	C3	Pierrepont Street	C3
Cheltenham Street	A4	Princes Street	B2
Circus Mews	B1	Pulteney Road	D2
Claverton Street	C4	Queen Square	B2
Corn Street	B4	Queen Street	B2
Daniel Street	D1	Railway Place	C4
Dorchester Street	C4	Rivers Street	B1
Edward Street	D2	Roman Road	C1
Ferry Lane	D3	Rossiter Road	C4
Gay Street	B1	Royal Avenue	A1
George Street	B2	Royal Crescent	A1
Great Pulteney Street	C2	St James's Parade	B3
Great Stanhope Street	A2	St John's Road	C1
Green Park Road	A3	Saw Close	B3
Green Street	B2	Southgate Street	C4
Grove Street	C2	South Parade	C3
Guinea Lane	B1	Stall Street	C3
Henrietta Gardens	D1	Sutton Street	D1
Henrietta Mews	C2	Sydney Place	D1
Henrietta Road	C1	The Circus	B1
Henrietta Street	C2	Thornbank Place	A4
Henry Street	C3	Union Street	B2
High Street	C2	Upper Borough Walls	C2
Hot Bath Street	B3	Upper Bristol Road	A2
James Street West	B3	Upper Church Street	A1
John Street	B2	Walcot Street	C2
Julian Road	B1	Wells Road	A4
Kingsmead North	B3	Westgate Buildings	B3
Kingston Road	C3	Westgate Street	B3
Lansdown Road	B1	Westmoreland Station Road	A4
London Street	C1	York Street	C3

Blackpool

Blackpool is found on atlas page **88 C3**

Abingdon Street	B1	Havelock Street	C4
Adelaide Street	B3	High Street	C1
Albert Road	B3	Hornby Road	B3
Albert Road	C3	Hornby Road	D3
Alfred Street	C2	Hull Road	B3
Ashton Road	D4	Kay Street	C4
Bank Hey Street	B2	Kent Road	C4
Banks Street	B1	King Street	C2
Belmont Avenue	C4	Leamington Road	D2
Bennett Avenue	D3	Leicester Road	D2
Bethesda Road	C4	Leopold Grove	C2
Birley Street	B2	Lincoln Road	D2
Blenheim Avenue	D4	Livingstone Road	C3
Bonny Street	B4	Lord Street	B1
Buchanan Street	C1	Louise Street	C4
Butler Street	C1	Milbourne Street	C1
Caunce Street	D1	Montreal Avenue	D3
Cedar Square	C2	New Bonny Street	B3
Central Drive	C4	New Larkhill Street	C1
Chapel Street	B4	Palatine Road	C4
Charles Street	C1	Palatine Road	D3
Charnley Road	C3	Park Road	D2
Cheapside	B2	Park Road	D4
Church Street	B2	Peter Street	D2
Church Street	C2	Pier Street	B4
Church Street	D2	Princess Parade	B1
Clifton Street	B2	Promenade	B1
Clinton Avenue	D4	Queen Street	B1
Cookson Street	C2	Raikes Parade	D2
Coop Street	B4	Reads Avenue	C3
Coronation Street	C3	Reads Avenue	D3
Corporation Street	B2	Regent Road	C2
Dale Street	B4	Ribble Road	C4
Deansgate	B2	Ripon Road	D3
Dickson Road	B1	Seasiders Way	B4
Edward Street	C2	Selbourne Road	D1
Elizabeth Street	D1	South King Street	C2
Fairhurst Street	D1	Springfield Road	B1
Fisher Street	C1	Stanley Road	C3
Fleet Street	C3	Talbot Road	B2
Foxhall Road	B4	Talbot Road	C1
Freckleton Street	D4	Topping Street	C2
General Street	B1	Vance Road	B3
George Street	C1	Victoria Street	B2
Gorton Street	D1	Victory Road	D1
Granville Road	D2	West Street	B2
Grosvenor Street	C1	Woolman Road	D4
Harrison Street	D4	York Street	B4

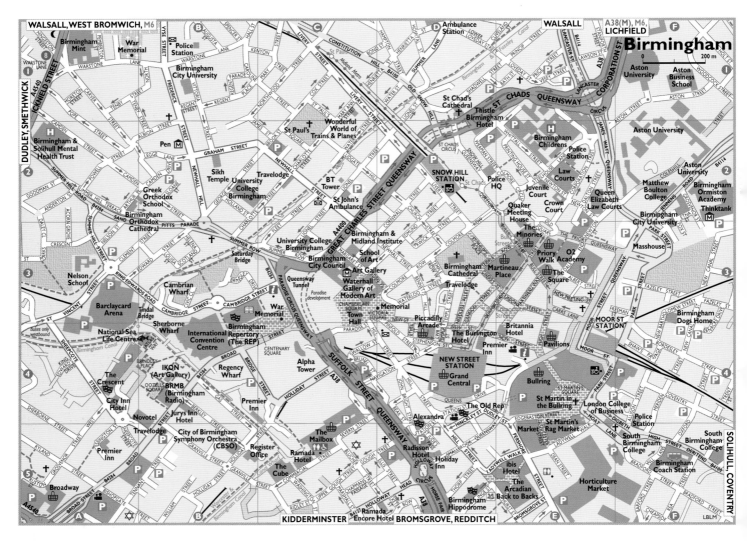

Birmingham

Birmingham is found on atlas page **58 G7**

Acorn Grove....................A2	Caroline Street.................B1	Etna Street.......................F2	Kenyon Street..................B1	Oozells Square.................B4	Spencer Street..................B1
Albert Street.....................E3	Carrs Lane........................E3	Exeter Street....................D5	King Edward's Drive..........A4	Oxford Street....................F5	Staniforth Street...............E1
Albert Street.....................F3	Carver Street....................A1	Fazeley Street..................F3	King Edwards Road...........A3	Paradise Circus	Station Street...................D5
Albion Street....................B2	Chamberlain Square..........C3	Fleet Street......................C3	Ladywell Walk..................D5	Queensway...................C3	Steelhouse Lane...............E2
Allison Street...................F4	Chapmans Passage..........C5	Fox Street........................F3	Lancaster Circus...............E1	Paradise Street.................C4	Stephenson Street.............D4
Anderton Street................A2	Charlotte Street................B3	Frederick Street................B1	Lancaster Street...............E1	Park Street.......................E4	Suffolk Street Queensway...C4
Arthur Place.....................A2	Cheapside........................F5	Freeman Street................E3	Lawson Street..................E1	Pemberton Street.............A1	Summer Hill Road..............A2
Aston Street.....................F1	Cherry Street...................D3	Gas Street.......................B4	Legge Lane......................B2	Pershore Street................E5	Summer Hill Street.............A2
Atlas Way.........................B4	Church Street...................D2	George Street...................B2	Lighthouse Avenue...........A3	Pinfold Street...................D4	Summer Hill Terrace...........A2
Banbury Street.................F3	Civic Close.......................B3	Gloucester Street.............E5	Lionel Street....................C3	Pope Street......................A1	Summer Lane...................D1
Barford Street..................F5	Clement Street.................A3	Goodman Street...............A2	Livery Street....................C1	Powell Street....................A2	Summer Row....................B3
Bartholomew Street...........F3	Cliveland Street................D1	Gough Street....................C5	Louisa Street....................B3	Price Street......................E1	Swallow Street..................C4
Barwick Street..................D3	Coleshill Street.................F2	Graham Street..................B2	Loveday Street.................E1	Princip Street...................E1	Temple Row.....................D3
Bath Street.......................E1	Colmore Circus	Granville Street.................B5	Lower Loveday Street.........D1	Printing House Street.........E2	Temple Row West..............D3
Beak Street......................D4	Queensway...................E2	Great Charles Street	Lower Temple Street..........D4	Queens Drive...................D4	Temple Street...................D3
Benacre Drive...................F4	Colmore Row....................D3	Queensway...................C3	Ludgate Hill.....................C3	Queensway Tunnel............C3	Tenby Street....................A1
Bennetts Hill....................D3	Commercial Street.............C5	Grosvenor Street..............F2	Margaret Street................C3	Rea Street.......................F5	Tenby Street North............A1
Berkley Street..................B4	Constitution Hill................C1	Grosvenor Street West.......A5	Marshall Street.................C5	Regent Parade..................B1	Tennant Street..................A5
Bishopgate Street.............A5	Cornwall Street.................D3	Hall Street........................B1	Martineau Way..................E1	Regent Place....................B1	The Priory Queensway........E2
Blucher Street..................C5	Corporation Street.............E1	Hampton Street.................D1	Mary Ann Street...............C1	Regent Street...................B1	Thorp Street....................D5
Bond Street......................C1	Corporation Street.............E3	Helena Street....................B3	Mary Street......................C1	Ridley Street.....................C5	Tindal Bridge....................B3
Bordesley Street...............F4	Coventry Street.................F4	Henrietta Street................C1	Meriden Street..................F4	Ruston Street...................A5	Trent Street......................F4
Bow Street.......................D5	Cox Street.......................C1	High Street.......................E4	Mill Lane..........................F5	Ryland Street...................A5	Union Street.....................E3
Bradford Street.................F5	Dale End..........................E3	High Street Deritend..........F5	Moat Lane.......................E4	St Chads Queensway.........E1	Upper Gough Street...........C5
Bridge Street....................B4	Daley Close......................A3	Hill Street.........................C4	Moor Street......................E4	St Jude's Pass..................D5	Vesey Street....................E1
Brindley Drive...................B3	Dalton Street....................E2	Hinckley Street.................D4	Moor Street	St Marks Crescent............A3	Victoria Square.................D3
Brindley Place...................B4	Dean Street......................E5	Hingeston Street...............A1	Queensway...................E4	St Martin's Square.............E4	Vittoria Street...................B1
Broad Street.....................A5	Digbeth...........................E4	Holland Street...................B2	Moreton Street.................A1	St Paul's Square................C1	Vyse Street......................B1
Bromsgrove Bireet.............E5	Dudley Street...................D4	Holliday Street..................B5	Navigation Street...............C4	St Philip's Place................D3	Warstone Lane..................A1
Brook Street.....................C2	Eden Place.......................C3	Holloway Circus................D5	Needless Alley..................D3	St Vincent Street...............A3	Washington Street.............B4
Brunel Street....................C4	Edgbaston Street...............E4	Holloway Head..................C5	Nelson Street...................A3	Sand Pitts Parade..............A2	Waterloo Street.................D3
Bull Street........................E3	Edmund Street..................D3	Holt Street........................F1	New Bartholomew Street....F4	Saturday Bridge................B3	Water Street.....................C2
Cambridge Street..............B3	Edward Street..................B3	Horse Fair........................D5	New Canal Street...............F4	Scotland Street.................B3	Weaman Street.................D2
Camden Drive...................B2	Ellis Street.......................D5	Hospital Street..................D1	Newhall Hill.....................B2	Severn Street...................C5	Whittall Street..................D2
Camden Street..................A2	Essington Street...............A5	Hurst Street......................E5	Newhall Street..................C2	Shadwell Street.................D1	William Street...................B5
Cannon Street..................D3	Ethel Street......................D4	Icknield Street..................A1	New Meeting Street...........E3	Shaw's Passage...............F4	Woodcock Street...............F1
		Inge Street.......................D5	New Street.......................D3	Sheepcote Street..............A4	
		James Street....................B2	Newton Street..................E2	Sherborne Street..............A4	
		James Watt Queensway.....E2	Northwood Hill..................D1	Sloane Street....................B2	
		Jennens Road...................F2	Old Snow Hill...................D1	Smallbrook Queensway......D5	
		John Bright Street.............D4	Old Square.......................E3	Snow Hill Queensway.........D2	

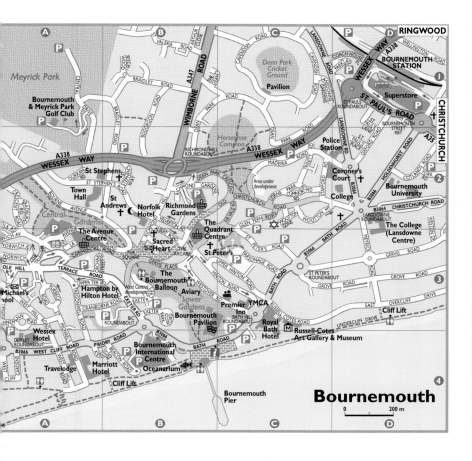

Bournemouth

Bournemouth is found on atlas page **13 J6**

Albert Road	B3	Old Christchurch Road	C2
Avenue Lane	A3	Orchard Street	A3
Avenue Road	A3	Oxford Road	D2
Bath Hill Roundabout	C3	Park Road	D1
Bath Road	B4	Parsonage Road	C3
Beacon Road	B4	Poole Hill	A3
BIC Roundabout	B3	Priory Road	A4
Bodorgon Road	B2	Purbeck Road	A3
Bourne Avenue	A2	Richmond Gardens	B2
Bournemouth Street		Richmond Hill	B3
Roundabout	D1	Richmond Hill Roundabout	B2
Bradburne Road	A2	Russell Cotes Road	C3
Braidley Road	B1	St Michael's Road	A3
Cavendish Road	C1	St Paul's Lane	D1
Central Drive	A1	St Paul's Place	D2
Christchurch Road	D2	St Paul's Road	D1
Coach House Place	D1	St Pauls Roundabout	D1
Commercial Road	A3	St Peter's Road	C3
Cotlands Road	D2	St Peter's Roundabout	C3
Cranborne Road	A3	St Stephen's Road	A2
Crescent Road	A2	St Stephen's Way	B2
Cumnor Road	C2	St Valerie Road	B1
Dean Park Crescent	B2	Stafford Road	C2
Dean Park Road	B2	Suffolk Road	A2
Durley Road	A3	Terrace Road	A3
Durley Roundabout	A4	The Arcade	B3
Durrant Road	A2	The Deans	B1
East Overcliff Drive	D3	The Square	B3
Exeter Crescent	B3	The Triangle	A3
Exeter Park Road	B3	Tregonwell Road	A3
Exeter Road	B3	Trinity Road	C2
Fir Vale Road	C2	Undercliff Drive	D3
Gervis Place	B3	Upper Hinton Road	C3
Gervis Road	D3	Upper Norwich Road	A3
Glen Fern Road	C2	Upper Terrace Road	A3
Grove Road	C3	Wellington Road	D1
Hahnemann Road	A3	Wessex Way	A2
Hinton Road	B3	West Cliff Gardens	A4
Holdenhurst Road	D2	West Cliff Road	A4
Kerley Road	A4	West Hill Road	A3
Lansdowne Gardens	C1	Weston Drive	D2
Lansdowne Road	C1	Westover Road	B3
Lansdowne Roundabout	D2	Wimborne Road	B1
Lorne Park Road	C2	Wootton Gardens	C2
Madeira Road	C2	Wootton Mount	C2
Meyrick Road	D3	Wychwood Close	B1
Norwich Avenue	A3	Yelverton Road	B2
Norwich Road	A3	York Road	D2

Bradford

Bradford is found on atlas page **90 F4**

Aldermanbury	B3	Lower Kirkgate	C2
Bank Street	B2	Lumb Lane	A1
Barkerend Road	D2	Manchester Road	B4
Barry Street	B2	Manningham Lane	A1
Bolling Road	C4	Manor Row	B1
Bolton Road	C2	Market Street	B3
Bridge Street	C3	Midland Road	B1
Broadway	C3	Morley Street	A4
Burnett Street	D2	Nelson Street	B4
Canal Road	C1	North Brook Street	C1
Carlton Street	A3	Northgate	B2
Centenary Square	B3	North Parade	B1
Chandos Street	C4	North Street	C2
Chapel Street	D3	North Wing	D1
Cheapside	B2	Otley Road	D1
Chester Street	A4	Paradise Street	A2
Church Bank	C2	Peckover Street	D2
Claremont	A4	Piccadilly	B2
Croft Street	C4	Pine Street	C2
Darfield Street	A1	Princes Way	B3
Darley Street	B2	Randall Well Street	A3
Drewton Road	A2	Rawson Road	A2
Dryden Street	D4	Rawson Square	B2
Duke Street	B2	Rebecca Street	A2
East Parade	D3	St Blaise Way	C1
Edmund Street	A4	Sawrey Place	A4
Edward Street	C4	Senior Way	B4
Eldon Place	A1	Shipley Airedale Road	C1
Filey Street	D3	Stott Hill	C2
George Street	C3	Sunbridge Road	A2
Godwin Street	B2	Sunbridge Street	B3
Grattan Road	A2	Tetley Street	A3
Great Horton Road	A4	Thornton Road	A3
Grove Terrace	A4	Trafalgar Street	B1
Hallfield Road	A1	Tyrrel Street	B2
Hall Ings	B4	Upper Park Gate	D2
Hamm Strasse	B1	Upper Piccadilly	B2
Holdsworth Street	C1	Valley Road	C1
Houghton Place	A1	Vicar Lane	C3
Howard Street	A4	Wakefield Road	D4
Hustlergate	B3	Wapping Road	D1
Infirmary Street	A1	Water Lane	A2
John Street	B2	Wellington Street	C2
Lansdowne Place	A4	Westgate	A2
Leeds Road	D3	Wharf Street	C1
Little Horton	A4	White Abbey Road	A1
Little Horton Lane	B4	Wigan Street	A2
Longcroft Link	A2	Wilton Street	A4

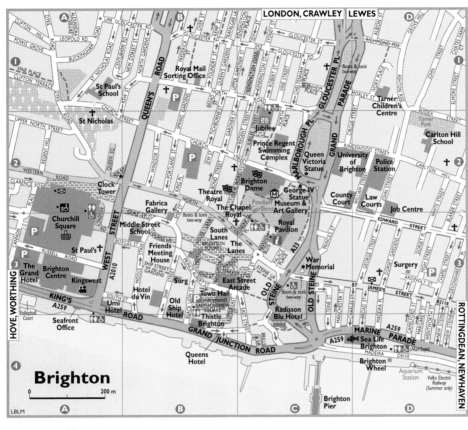

Brighton

Brighton is found on atlas page **24 H10**

Ardingly Street	D3	Madeira Place	
Ashton Rise	D1	Manchester Street	
Bartholomew Square	B3	Margaret Street	
Black Lion Street	B3	Marine Parade	
Blaker Street	D3	Market Street	
Bond Street	B2	Marlborough Place	
Boyces Street	A3	Meeting House Lane	
Brighton Place	B3	Middle Street	
Broad Street	D4	Morley Street	
Buckingham Road	A1	New Dorset Street	
Camelford Street	D4	New Road	
Cannon Place	A3	New Steine	
Carlton Hill	D2	Nile Street	
Centurion Road	A1	North Gardens	
Chapel Street	D3	North Place	
Charles Street	C4	North Road	
Cheltenham Place	C1	North Street	
Church Street	A1	Old Steine	
Church Street	B2	Portland Street	
Circus Street	C2	Powis Grove	
Clifton Hill	A1	Prince Albert Street	
Clifton Terrace	A1	Prince's Street	
Devonshire Place	D3	Queen's Gardens	
Dukes Lane	B3	Queen Square	
Duke Street	B2	Queen's Road	
East Street	C3	Regency Road	
Edward Street	C2	Regent Hill	
Elmore Street	D1	Regent Street	
Foundry Street	B1	Robert Street	
Frederick Street	B1	St James's Street	
Gardner Street	B2	St Nicholas Road	
George Street	D3	Ship Street	
Gloucester Place	C1	Spring Gardens	
Gloucester Road	B1	Steine Street	
Gloucester Street	C1	Sussex Street	
Grand Junction Road	B4	Sydney Street	
Grand Parade	C2	Tichborne Street	
High Street	D3	Tidy Street	
Ivory Place	D1	Upper Gardner Street	
John Street	D2	Upper Gloucester Road	
Jubilee Street	C2	Upper North Street	
Kensington Gardens	C1	Vine Street	
Kensington Street	C1	Wentworth Street	
Kew Street	B1	Western Road	
King's Road	A3	West Street	
Kingswood Street	C2	White Street	
Leopold Road	A1	William Street	
Little East Street	B4	Windsor Street	

Bristol

Bristol is found on atlas page **31 Q10**

Anchor Road	A3	Passage Street	
Avon Street	D3	Pembroke Street	
Baldwin Street	B2	Penn Street	
Bath Bridge	D4	Pero's Bridge	
Bond Street	C1	Perry Road	
Bond Street	D2	Philadelphia Street	
Broadmead	C1	Portwall Lane	
Broad Plain	D2	Prewett Street	
Broad Quay	B3	Prince Street	
Broad Street	B2	Queen Charlotte Street	
Broad Weir	C2	Queen Square	
Canons Way	A3	Redcliffe Hill	
Canynge Street	C3	Redcliffe Parade West	
Castle Street	C2	Redcliffe Way	
College Green	A3	Redcliff Mead Lane	
Colston Avenue	B2	Redcliff Street	
Colston Street	B2	Royal Fort Road	
Commercial Road	B4	Rupert Street	
Corn Street	B2	St Augustine's Parade	
Countership	C3	St George's Road	
Cumberland Road	A4	St Matthias Park	
Deanery Road	A3	St Michael's Hill	
Denmark Street	A3	St Stephen's Street	
Explore Lane	A3	St Thomas Street	
Fairfax Street	C2	Small Street	
Ferry Street	C3	Somerset Street	
Friary	D3	Southwell Street	
Frogmore Street	A2	Tankards Close	
Great George Street	A3	Telephone Avenue	
Great George Street	D1	Temple Back	
Guinea Street	B4	Temple Back East	
Haymarket	C1	Temple Gate	
Hill Street	A2	Temple Street	
Horfield Road	B1	Temple Way	
Houlton Street	D1	The Grove	
Jacob Street	D2	The Horsefair	
King Street	B3	The Pithay	
Lewins Mead	B2	Tower Hill	
Lodge Street	A2	Trenchard Street	
Lower Castle Street	D2	Tyndall Avenue	
Lower Church Lane	A2	Union Street	
Lower Maudlin Street	B1	Upper Maudlin Street	
Marlborough Hill	B1	Victoria Street	
Marlborough Street	B1	Wapping Road	
Marsh Street	B3	Welsh Back	
Newgate	C2	Whitson Street	
Old Market Street	D2	Wine Street	
Park Street	A2	Woodland Road	

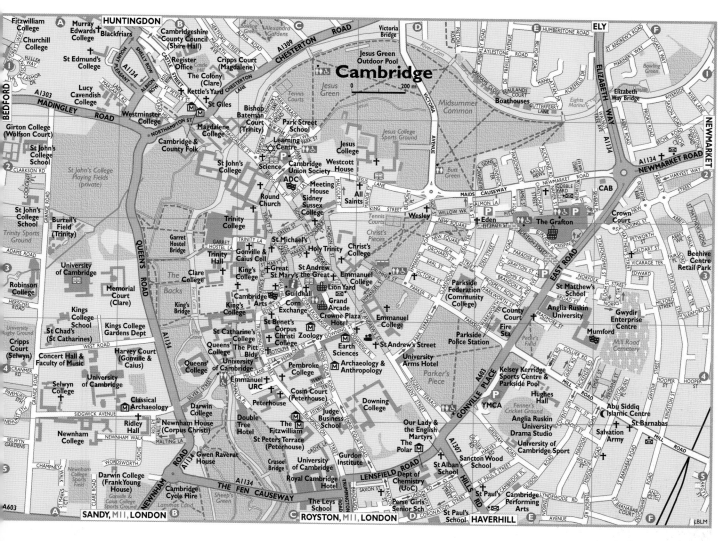

Cambridge

Cambridge is found on atlas page **62 G9**

Abbey Road	F1
Abbey Street	F2
Abbey Walk	F3
Acrefield Drive	E1
Adam and Eve Street	E3
Albion Row	B1
Alpha Road	C1
Auckland Road	E2
Aylestone Road	E1
Bailey Mews	E2
Banhams Close	D1
Beaulands Court	E1
Beche Road	F2
Belmont Place	D2
Belvoir Road	E1
Bene't Street	C3
Bloom Street	F3
Bradmore Street	E3
Brandon Place	E3
Bridge Street	C2
Broad Street	E3
Brookside	D5
Brunswick Gardens	E2
Brunswick Terrace	E2
Burleigh Place	E3
Burleigh Street	E3
Cambridge Place	E5
Castle Row	B1
Castle Street	B1
Champneys Walk	A5
Chesterton Lane	B1
Chesterton Road	C1
Christchurch Street	E2
City Road	E3
Clarendon Street	D3
Cobble Yard	E2

Collier Road	E4
Corn Exchange Street	C3
Coronation Street	D5
Covent Garden	E4
Crispin Place	E3
Cross Street	E4
Crusoe Bridge	B5
Cutler Ferry Close	E1
Cutterferry Lane	E1
De Freville Avenue	E1
Devonshire Road	F5
Ditchburn Place	F4
Downing Place	C4
Downing Street	C4
Drosier Road	D5
Drummer Street	D3
Earl Street	D3
East Road	E3
Eden Street	E3
Eden Street Back	E3
Edward Street	F3
Elizabeth Way	F1
Elm Street	D3
Emery Street	E3
Emmanuel Road	D3
Emmanuel Street	D3
Evening Court	E2
Fairsford Place	F3
Fair Street	D2
Fitzroy Lane	E2
Fitzroy Street	E2
Fitzwilliam Street	C4
Garret Hostel Bridge	B3
Garret Hostel Lane	B3
Geldart Street	F3
George IV Street	D5

Glisson Road	E5
Godstone Road	F2
Gonville Place	D4
Grange Road	A3
Grange Road	A4
Granta Place	B4
Green Street	C3
Gresham Road	E5
Gwydir Street	F4
Harvest Way	F2
Harvey Road	E5
Hertford Street	B1
Hills Road	D5
Hobson Street	C3
Humberstone Road	E1
James Street	E2
Jesus Lane	C2
Jesus Terrace	D3
John Street	E3
Kimberley Road	E1
King's Bridge	B3
King's Parade	C3
Kingston Street	F4
King Street	D2
Lady Margaret Road	A1
Lensfield Road	D5
Logan's Way	F1
Lwr Park Street	C2
Lyndewode Road	E5
Mackenzie Road	E4
Madingley Road	A1
Magdalene Street	B2
Magrath Avenue	B1
Maids Causeway	D2
Malcolm Street	C2
Malting Lane	B5
Manhattan Drive	E1
Manor Street	D2
Mariner's Way	F1
Market Street	C3
Mawson Road	E5

Milford Street	F3
Mill Lane	C4
Mill Road	E4
Mill Street	E4
Mortimer Road	E4
Mount Pleasant	B1
Napier Street	E2
Newmarket Road	E2
Newnham Road	B5
Newnham Walk	A5
New Park Street	C2
New Square	D3
New Street	F2
Norfolk Street	E3
Norfolk Terrace	F3
Northampton Street	B2
Occupation Road	F2
Orchard Street	D3
Panton Street	D5
Paradise Street	E3
Parker Street	D3
Park Parade	C1
Parkside	D3
Park Street	C2
Park Terrace	D4
Parsonage Street	E2
Peas Hill	C3
Pembroke Street	C4
Perowne Street	F4
Petworth Street	F3
Pound Hill	B1
Priory Road	F1
Prospect Row	E3
Queen's Road	B3
Regent Street	D4
Regent Terrace	D4
River Lane	F1
Riverside	F1
St Andrew's Road	F1
St Andrew's Street	D3
St Barnabas Road	F5

St Mary's Street	C3
St Matthew's Gardens	F2
St Matthew's Street	F3
St Paul's Street	E5
St Peter's Street	B1
Salmon Lane	E2
Saxon Road	F1
Saxon Street	D5
Severn Place	F2
Shelly Row	B1
Shop Street	D2
Sidgwick Avenue	A4
Sidney Street	C2
Silver Street	B4
Staffordshire Street	F3
Sturton Street	F3
Sussex Street	C3
Tenison Avenue	E5
Tenison Road	E5
Tennis Court Road	C4
Tennis Court Terrace	C4
The Fen Causeway	B5
Thompson's Lane	C2
Trinity Lane	C3
Trinity Street	C3
Trumpington Road	C5
Trumpington Street	C4
Union Road	D5
Vicarage Terrace	F3
Victoria Avenue	D1
Victoria Bridge	D1
Victoria Road	D1
Victoria Street	D3
Warkworth Street	E3
Warkworth Terrace	E3
Wellington Street	E2
West Road	A4
Wilkin Street	E5
Willis Road	E4
Willow Walk	D2
Wordsworth Grove	A5
Young Street	F3

University Colleges

Christ's College	C3
Clare College	A3
Clare College	B1
Clare College	B3
Corpus Christi College	C4
Darwin College	B4
Downing College	D4
Emmanuel College	C3
Emmanuel College	D3
Fitzwilliam College	A1
Girton College (Wolfson Court)	A2
Gonville & Caius College	C3
Gonville & Caius College	B4
Jesus College	C2
King's College	B3
Lucy Cavendish College	A1
Magdalene College	B2
Murray Edwards College	A1
Newnham College	A5
Pembroke College	C4
Peterhouse	C4
Queens' College	B4
Robinson College	A3
St Catharine's College	C4
St Edmund's College	A1
St John's College	B2
Selwyn College	A4
Sidney Sussex College	C2
Trinity College	B3
Westminster College	B1

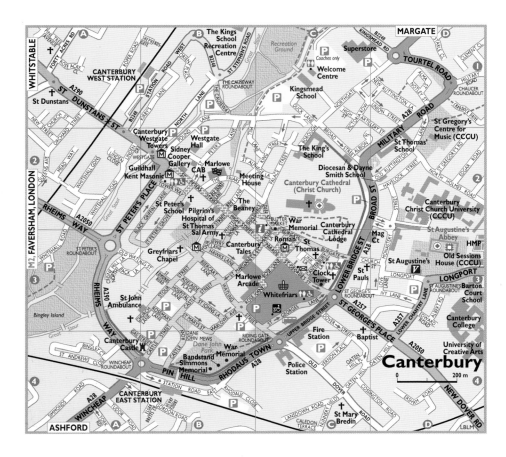

Canterbury

Canterbury is found on atlas page **39 K10**

Adelaide Place	B3	Notley Street	
Albert Road	D3	Nunnery Fields	
Albion Place	C2	Oaten Hill	
Alma Street	D1	Old Dover Road	
Artillery Street	C1	Old Ruttington Lane	
Beercart Lane	B3	Orchard Street	
Best Lane	B2	Palace Street	
Black Griffin Lane	A3	Parade	
Borough	C2	Pin Hill	
Broad Street	D2	Pound Lane	
Burgate	C3	Queens Avenue	
Butter Market	C2	Rheims Way	
Canterbury Lane	C3	Rhodaus Town	
Castle Row	B4	Rose Lane	
Castle Street	B3	Rosemary Lane	
Cossington Road	C4	St Alphege Lane	
Dover Street	C3	St Dunstans Street	
Duck Lane	C1	St Edmunds Road	
Edgar Road	D2	St George's Lane	
Edward Road	D3	St George's Place	
Ersham Road	D4	St George's Street	
Gas Street	A4	St Gregory's Road	
Gordon Road	B4	St Johns Lane	
Guildhall Street	B2	St Margaret's Street	
Havelock Street	D2	St Marys Street	
Hawks Lane	B3	St Peter's Grove	
High Street	B2	St Peter's Lane	
Hospital Lane	B3	St Peter's Place	
Ivy Lane	C3	St Peters Street	
Jewry Lane	B3	Station Road East	
King Street	C2	Station Road West	
Kirby's Lane	B1	Stour Street	
Lansdown Road	C4	Sturry Road	
Linden Grove	A2	Sun Street	
Longport	D3	The Causeway	
Love Lane	D3	The Friars	
Lower Bridge Street	C3	Tourtel Road	
Lower Chantry Lane	D4	Tower Way	
Marlowe Avenue	B3	Tudor Road	
Mead Way	A2	Union Street	
Mercery Lane	C3	Upper Bridge Street	
Military Road	D2	Vernon Place	
Mill Lane	B1	Victoria Row	
Monastery Street	D3	Watling Street	
New Dover Road	D4	Whitehall Gardens	
New Ruttington Lane	D1	Whitehall Road	
North Lane	B1	Wincheap	
Northgate	C1	York Road	

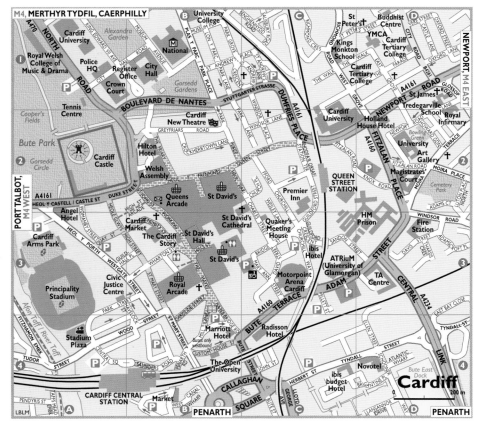

Cardiff

Cardiff is found on atlas page **30 G9**

Adam Street	D3	Moira Terrace	
Adams Court	D2	Museum Avenue	
Adamscroft Place	D3	Museum Place	
Atlantic Wharf	D4	Newport Road Lane	
Boulevard de Nantes	B2	North Luton Place	
Bridge Street	C3	North Road	
Brigantine Place	D4	Oxford Lane	
Bute Street	C4	Oxford Street	
Bute Terrace	C3	Park Grove	
Callaghan Square	B4	Park Lane	
Caroline Street	B3	Park Place	
Castle Lane	D1	Park Street	
Castle Street	A2	Pellett Street	
Central Link	D3	Pendyris Street	
Charles Street	B2	Quay Street	
Churchill Way	C2	Queen Street	
City Hall Road	A1	Richmond Crescent	
City Road	D1	Richmond Road	
Crockherbtown Lane	B2	St Andrew's Crescent	
Custom House Street	B4	St Andrew's Lane	
David Street	C3	St Andrew's Place	
Davis Street	D3	St John Street	
Duke Street	A2	St Mary Street	
Dumfries Place	C2	St Peter's Street	
East Bay Close	D3	Salisbury Road	
East Grove	D1	Sandon Street	
Ellen Street	D4	Saunders Road	
Fford Churchill	C2	Schooner Way	
Fitzalan Place	D2	Stuttgarter Strasse	
Fitzalan Road	D2	The Friary	
Fitzhamon Embankment	A4	The Hayes	
Glossop Road	D1	The Parade	
Greyfriars Road	B2	The Walk	
Guildford Street	C3	Trinity Street	
Guildhall Place	A3	Tudor Street	
Havelock Street	B3	Tyndall Street	
Hayes Bridge Road	B3	Vere Street	
Heol Siarl	B2	Wesley Lane	
Herbert Street	C4	West Canal Wharf	
High Street	B3	West Grove	
High Street Arcade	B2	Westgate Street	
Hills Street	B3	Wharton Street	
King Edward VII Avenue	A1	Windsor Lane	
Knox Road	D2	Windsor Place	
Lloyd George Avenue	C4	Windsor Road	
Mary Ann Street	C3	Womanby Street	
Mill Lane	B4	Wood Street	
Moira Place	D2	Working Street	

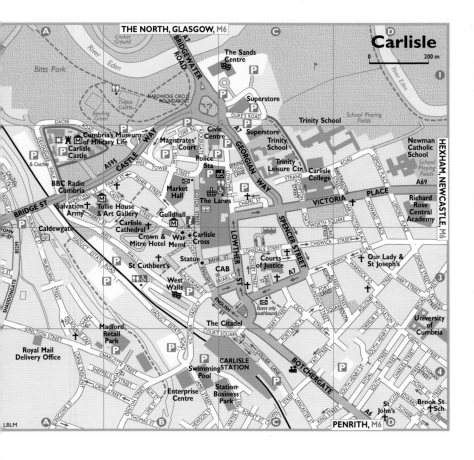

Carlisle

Carlisle is found on atlas page **110 G9**

Abbey Street	A2	Howard Place	D2
Aglionby Street	D3	Howe Street	D4
Annetwell Street	A2	James Street	B4
Bank Street	B3	John Street	A3
Blackfriars Street	B3	Junction Street	A4
Blencowe Street	A4	King Street	C4
Botchergate	C4	Lancaster Street	C4
Bridge Lane	A2	Lime Street	B4
Bridge Street	A2	Lismore Place	D2
Bridgewater Road	B1	Lismore Street	D3
Broad Street	D3	Lonsdale Street	C3
Brunswick Street	C3	Lorne Crescent	A4
Caldew Maltings	A2	Lorne Street	A4
Castle Street	B2	Lowther Street	C2
Castle Way	B2	Mary Street	C3
Cecil Street	C3	Mayor's Drive	A1
Chapel Place	A3	Milbourne Crescent	A3
Chapel Street	C2	Milbourne Street	A3
Charles Street	D4	Myddleton Street	D3
Charlotte Street	A4	North Alfred Street	D3
Chatsworth Square	C2	Orfeur Street	D3
Chiswick Street	C3	Peter Street	B2
Close Street	D4	Petteril Street	D3
Collier Lane	C4	Portland Place	C4
Compton Street	C2	Portland Square	C3
Corp Road	B2	Randall Street	B4
Court Square	B4	Rickergate	B2
Crosby Street	C3	Rigg Street	A3
Crown Street	C4	Robert Street	C4
Currie Street	C3	Rydal Street	D4
Dacre Road	A1	Scotch Street	B2
Denton Street	B4	Shaddongate	A3
Devonshire Walk	A2	Sheffield Street	A4
Duke's Road	C1	South Alfred Street	D3
Edward Street	D4	South Henry Street	D4
Elm Street	B4	Spencer Street	C2
English Street	B3	Spring Gardens Lane	C2
Finkle Street	B2	Strand Road	C2
Fisher Street	B2	Tait Street	C4
Flower Street	D4	Thomas Street	B4
Friars Court	C3	Viaduct Estate Road	A3
Fusehill Street	D4	Victoria Place	C2
Georgian Way	C2	Victoria Viaduct	B4
Grey Street	D4	Warwick Road	D3
Hartington Place	D2	Warwick Square	D3
Hartington Street	D2	Water Street	C4
Hart Street	D3	West Tower Street	B2
Hewson Street	B4	West Walls	B3

Cheltenham

Cheltenham is found on atlas page **46 H10**

Albion Street	C2	Montpellier Parade	B4
All Saints' Road	D2	Montpellier Spa Road	B4
Ambrose Street	B1	Montpellier Street	A4
Argyll Road	D4	Montpellier Terrace	A4
Back Montpellier Terrace	A4	Montpellier Walk	A4
Bath Road	B4	New Street	A1
Bath Street	C3	North Street	B2
Bayshill Road	A3	Old Bath Road	D4
Bayshill Villas Lane	A3	Oriel Road	B3
Bennington Street	B1	Parabola Lane	A3
Berkeley Street	C3	Parabola Road	A3
Burton Street	A1	Park Street	A1
Carlton Street	D3	Pittville Circus	D1
Church Street	B2	Pittville Circus Road	D1
Clarence Parade	B2	Pittville Street	B2
Clarence Road	C1	Portland Street	C1
Clarence Street	B2	Prestbury Road	C1
College Road	C4	Priory Street	D3
Crescent Terrace	B2	Promenade	B3
Devonshire Street	A1	Queens Parade	A3
Duke Street	D3	Regent Street	B2
Dunalley Street	B1	Rodney Road	B3
Evesham Road	C1	Royal Well	B2
Fairview Road	C2	Royal Well Lane	A2
Fairview Street	D2	St Anne's Road	D2
Fauconberg Road	A3	St Anne's Terrace	D2
Glenfall Street	D1	St George's Place	B2
Grosvenor Street	C3	St George's Road	A2
Grove Street	A1	St George's Street	B1
Henrietta Street	B1	St James' Square	A2
Hewlett Road	D3	St James Street	C3
High Street	A1	St Johns Avenue	C2
High Street	C2	St Margaret's Road	B1
Imperial Lane	B3	St Paul's Street South	B1
Imperial Square	B3	Sandford Street	C3
Jersey Street	D1	Selkirk Street	D1
Jessop Avenue	A2	Sherborne Street	C2
Keynsham Road	D4	Station Street	A1
King Street	A1	Suffolk Parade	B4
Knapp Road	A1	Swindon Road	B1
Lansdown Road	A4	Sydenham Villas Road	D3
Leighton Road	D2	Trafalgar Street	B4
London Road	D3	Union Street	D2
Malden Road	D1	Wellington Street	C3
Market Street	A1	Winchcombe Street	C2
Milsom Street	A1	Winstonian Road	D2
Monson Avenue	B1	Witcombe Place	C3
Montpellier Grove	B4	York Street	D1

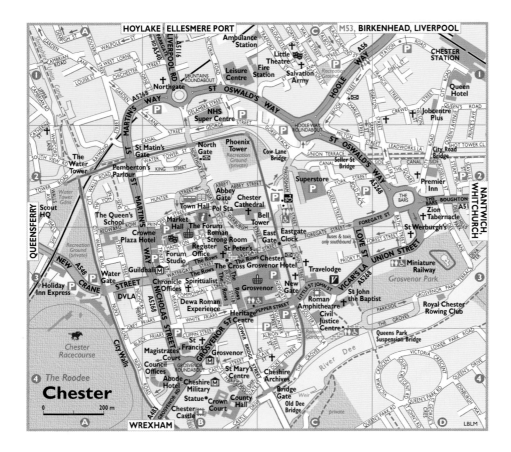

Chester

Chester is found on atlas page **81 N11**

Albion Street	C4	Nicholas Street	
Bath Street	D2	Northgate Street	
Black Diamond Street	C1	Nun's Road	
Boughton	D2	Parkgate Road	
Bouverie Street	A1	Park Street	
Bridge Street	B3	Pepper Street	
Brook Street	C1	Princess Street	
Canal Side	C2	Priory Place	
Castle Street	B4	Queen's Park Road	
Charles Street	C1	Queen's Road	
Chichester Street	A1	Queen Street	
City Road	D2	Raymond Street	
City Walls Road	A2	Russell Street	
Commonhall Street	B3	St Anne Street	
Cornwall Street	C1	St John's Road	
Crewel Street	D1	St John Street	
Cuppin Street	B4	St Martin's Way	
Dee Hills Park	D2	St Mary's Hill	
Dee Lane	D2	St Olave Street	
Delamere Street	B1	St Oswald's Way	
Duke Street	C4	St Werburgh Street	
Eastgate Street	B3	Samuel Street	
Egerton Street	C1	Seller Street	
Foregate Street	C2	Shipgate Street	
Forest Street	C3	Souter's Lane	
Francis Street	D1	South View Road	
Frodsham Street	C2	Stanley Street	
Garden Lane	A1	Station Road	
George Street	B2	Steam Mill Street	
Gloucester Street	C1	Steele Street	
Gorse Stacks	C2	Talbot Street	
Grosvenor Park Terrace	D3	Tower Road	
Grosvenor Road	B4	Trafford Street	
Grosvenor Street	B4	Trinity Street	
Hamilton Place	B3	Union Street	
Hoole Way	C1	Union Terrace	
Hunter Street	B2	Upper Cambrian Road	
King Street	B2	Vicar's Lane	
Leadworks Lane	D2	Victoria Crescent	
Little St John Street	C3	Victoria Road	
Liverpool Road	B1	Volunteer Street	
Lorne Street	A1	Walpole Street	
Love Street	C3	Walter Street	
Lower Bridge Street	B4	Watergate Street	
Lower Park Road	D4	Water Tower Street	
Milton Street	C2	Weaver Street	
New Crane Street	A3	White Friars	
Newgate Street	C3	York Street	

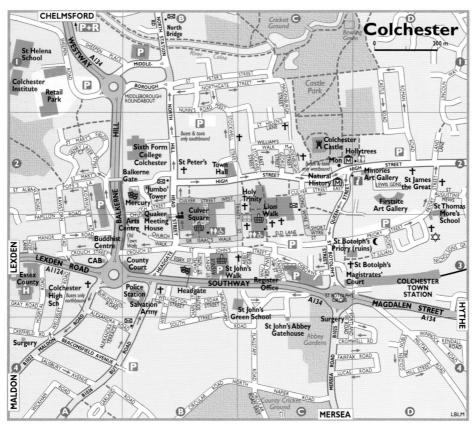

Colchester

Colchester is found on atlas page **52 G6**

Abbey Gates	C3	Middleborough	
Alexandra Road	A3	Middleborough Roundabout	
Alexandra Terrace	A4	Military Road	
Balkerne Hill	A3	Mill Street	
Beaconsfield Avenue	A4	Napier Road	
Burlington Road	A3	Nicholsons Green	
Butt Road	A4	North Bridge	
Castle Road	D1	Northgate Street	
Cedar Street	B3	North Hill	
Chapel Street North	B3	North Station Road	
Chapel Street South	B3	Nunn's Road	
Church Street	B3	Osborne Street	
Church Walk	B3	Papillon Road	
Circular Road East	C4	Pope's Lane	
Circular Road North	B4	Portland Road	
Creffield Road	A4	Priory Street	
Cromwell Road	C4	Queen Street	
Crouch Street	A3	Rawstorn Road	
Crouch Street	B3	Roman Road	
Crowhurst Road	A2	St Alban's Road	
Culver Street East	C2	St Augustine Mews	
Culver Street West	B2	St Botolph's Circus	
East Hill	D2	St Botolph's Street	
East Stockwell Street	C2	St Helen's Lane	
Essex Street	B3	St John's Avenue	
Fairfax Road	C4	St John's Street	
Flagstaff Road	B4	St Julian Grove	
Garland Road	A4	St Mary's Fields	
George Street	C2	St Peter's Street	
Golden Noble Hill	D4	Salisbury Avenue	
Gray Road	A3	Sheepen Place	
Headgate	B3	Sheepen Road	
Head Street	B2	Short Wyre Street	
Henry Laver Court	A2	Sir Isaac's Walk	
High Street	B2	South Street	
Hospital Road	A4	Southway	
Hospital Lane	A3	Stanwell Street	
Land Lane	D2	Trinity Street	
Lewis Gardens	D2	Walsingham Road	
Lexden Road	A3	Wellesley Road	
Lincoln Way	D1	Wellington Street	
Long Wyre Street	C2	West Stockwell Street	
Lucas Road	C4	West Street	
Magdalen Street	D3	Westway	
Maidenburgh Street	C1	Whitewell Road	
Maldon Road	A4	Wickham Road	
Manor Road	A3	William's Walk	
Mersea Road	C4	Winnock Road	

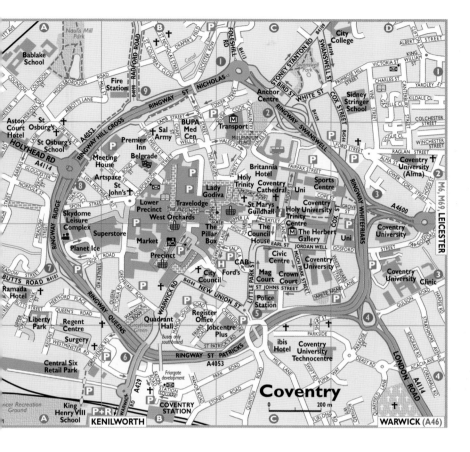

Coventry

Coventry is found on atlas page **59 M9**

Abbots Lane	A1	Much Park Street	C3
Acacia Avenue	D4	New Union Street	B3
Alma Street	D2	Norfolk Street	A2
Barras Lane	A2	Paradise Street	D4
Bayley Lane	C2	Park Road	B4
Bird Street	C1	Parkside	C4
Bishop Street	B1	Primrose Hill Street	D1
Broadgate	B2	Priory Row	C2
Butts Road	A3	Priory Street	C2
Butts Street	A3	Puma Way	C4
Canterbury Street	D1	Quaryfield Lane	D4
Chester Street	A2	Queen's Road	A3
Cheylesmore	C3	Queen Victoria Road	B3
Cornwall Road	D4	Quinton Road	C4
Corporation Street	B2	Radford Road	B1
Coundon Road	A1	Raglan Street	D2
Cox Street	D1	Regent Street	A4
Cox Street	D2	Ringway Hill Cross	A2
Croft Road	A3	Ringway Queens	A3
Earl Street	C3	Ringway Rudge	A3
Eaton Road	B4	Ringway St Nicholas	B1
Fairfax Street	C2	Ringway St Patricks	B4
Foleshill Road	C1	Ringway Swanswell	C1
Gloucester Street	A2	Ringway Whitefriars	D2
Gosford Street	D3	St Johns Street	C3
Greyfriars Lane	B3	St Nicholas Street	B1
Greyfriars Road	B3	Salt Lane	C3
Grosvenor Road	A4	Seagrave Road	D4
Gulson Road	D3	Spon Street	A2
Hales Street	C2	Stanley Road	A3
Hertford Place	A3	Stoney Road	B4
High Street	C3	Stoney Stanton Road	C1
Hill Street	B2	Strathmore Avenue	D3
Holyhead Road	A2	Swanswell Street	C1
Jordan Well	C3	The Burges	B2
Lamb Street	B2	Tower Street	B1
Leicester Row	B1	Trinity Street	C2
Little Park Street	C3	Upper Hill Street	B2
London Road	D4	Upper Wells Street	A4
Lower Ford Street	D2	Victoria Street	D1
Lower Holyhead Road	A2	Vine Street	D1
Manor House Road	B4	Warwick Road	B3
Manor Road	B4	Warwick Road	B4
Meadow Street	A3	Westminster Road	A4
Meriden Street	A1	White Friars Street	D3
Middleborough Road	A1	White Street	C1
Mile Lane	C4	Windsor Street	A3
Mill Street	A1	Yardley Street	D1

Darlington

Darlington is found on atlas page **103 Q8**

Abbey Road	A3	Maude Street	A2
Albert Street	D4	Neasham Road	D4
Appleby Close	D4	Northgate	C2
Barningham Street	B1	North Lodge Terrace	B2
Bartlett Street	B1	Northumberland Street	B4
Beaumont Street	B3	Oakdene Avenue	A4
Bedford Street	C4	Outram Street	A2
Beechwood Avenue	A4	Parkgate	D3
Blackwellgate	B3	Park Lane	D4
Bondgate	B3	Park Place	C4
Borough Road	D3	Pendower Street	B1
Brunswick Street	C3	Pensbury Street	D4
Brunton Street	D4	Polam Lane	B4
Chestnut Street	C1	Portland Place	A3
Cleveland Terrace	A4	Powlett Street	B3
Clifton Road	C4	Priestgate	C3
Commercial Street	B2	Raby Terrace	B3
Coniscliffe Road	A4	Russell Street	C2
Corporation Road	B1	St Augustine's Way	B2
Crown Street	C2	St Cuthbert's Way	C2
Dodds Street	B1	St Cuthbert's Way	C4
Duke Street	A3	St James Place	D4
Easson Road	B1	Salisbury Terrace	A1
East Mount Road	D1	Salt Yard	B3
East Raby Street	B3	Scarth Street	A4
East Street	C3	Skinnergate	B3
Elms Road	A2	South Arden Street	B4
Feethams	C4	Southend Avenue	A4
Fife Road	A3	Stanhope Road North	A2
Four Riggs	B2	Stanhope Road South	A3
Freeman's Place	C2	Stonebridge	C3
Gladstone Street	B2	Sun Street	B2
Grange Road	B4	Swan Street	C4
Greenbank Road	A1	Swinburne Road	A3
Greenbank Road	B2	Trinity Road	A2
Green Street	D3	Tubwell Row	B3
Hargreave Terrace	C4	Uplands Road	A2
Haughton Road	D2	Valley Street North	C2
High Northgate	C1	Vane Terrace	A2
High Row	B3	Victoria Embankment	C4
Hollyhurst Road	A1	Victoria Road	B4
Houndgate	B3	Victoria Road	C4
Jack Way Steeple	D3	West Crescent	A2
John Street	C1	West Powlett Street	A3
Kendrew Street	B2	West Row	B3
Kingston Street	B1	West Street	B4
Langholm Crescent	A4	Woodland Road	A2
Larchfield Street	A3	Yarm Road	D3

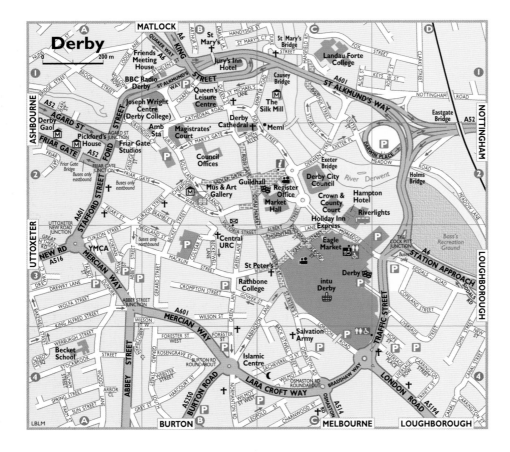

Derby

Derby is found on atlas page **72 B3**

Abbey Street	A4	King Alfred Street	
Agard Street	A1	King Street	
Albert Street	C3	Lara Croft Way	
Babington Lane	B4	Leopold Street	
Back Sitwell Street	C4	Liversage Row	
Becket Street	B3	Liversage Street	
Bold Lane	B2	Lodge Lane	
Bradshaw Way	C4	London Road	
Bramble Street	B2	Macklin Street	
Bridge Street	A1	Mansfield Road	
Brook Street	A1	Meadow Lane	
Burton Road	B4	Meadow Road	
Canal Street	D4	Mercian Way	
Carrington Street	D4	Morledge	
Cathedral Road	B1	Newland Street	
Cavendish Court	A2	New Road	
Chapel Street	B1	New Street	
Clarke Street	D1	Nottingham Road	
Copeland Street	D3	Osmaston Road	
Corn Market	B2	Phoenix Street	
Crompton Street	B3	Queen Street	
Curzon Street	A2	Robert Street	
Curzon Street	A3	Rosengrave Street	
Darwin Place	C2	Sacheverel Street	
Derwent Street	C2	Sadler Gate	
Drewry Lane	A3	St Alkmund's Way	
Duke Street	C1	St Helen's Street	
Dunkirk	A3	St Mary's Gate	
East Street	C3	St Peter's Street	
Exchange Street	C3	Siddals Road	
Exeter Place	C2	Sowter Road	
Exeter Street	C2	Spring Street	
Ford Street	A2	Stafford Street	
Forester Street West	B4	Station Approach	
Forman Street	A3	Stockbrook Street	
Fox Street	C1	Strand	
Friary Street	A2	Stuart Street	
Full Street	B1	Sun Street	
Gerard Street	B3	The Cock Pitt	
Gower Street	B3	Thorntree Lane	
Green Lane	B3	Traffic Street	
Grey Street	A4	Trinity Street	
Handyside Street	B1	Victoria Street	
Harcourt Street	B4	Wardwick	
Iron Gate	B2	Werburgh Street	
John Street	D4	Wilmot Street	
Jury Street	B2	Wolfa Street	
Keys Street	D1	Woods Lane	

Doncaster

Doncaster is found on atlas page **91 P10**

Alderson Drive	D3	Nelson Street	
Apley Road	B3	Nether Hall Road	
Balby Road Bridge	A4	North Bridge Road	
Beechfield Road	B3	North Street	
Broxholme Lane	C1	Palmer Street	
Carr House Road	C4	Park Road	
Carr Lane	B4	Park Terrace	
Chamber Road	B3	Prince's Street	
Chequer Avenue	C4	Priory Place	
Chequer Road	C3	Prospect Place	
Childers Street	C4	Queen's Road	
Christ Church Road	B1	Rainton Road	
Church View	A1	Ravensworth Road	
Church Way	B1	Rectory Gardens	
Clark Avenue	C4	Regent Square	
Cleveland Street	A4	Roman Road	
College Road	B3	Royal Avenue	
Cooper Street	C4	St Georges Gate	
Coopers Terrace	B2	St James Street	
Copley Road	B1	St Mary's Road	
Cunningham Road	B3	St Sepulchre Gate	
Danum Road	D3	St Sepulchre Gate West	
Dockin Hill Road	B1	St Vincent Avenue	
Duke Street	A2	St Vincent Road	
East Laith Gate	B2	Scot Lane	
Elmfield Road	C3	Silver Street	
Firbeck Road	D3	Somerset Road	
Frances Street	B2	South Parade	
Glyn Avenue	C1	South Street	
Green Dyke Lane	A4	Spring Gardens	
Grey Friars' Road	A1	Stirling Street	
Hall Cross Hill	C2	Stockil Road	
Hall Gate	B2	Theobald Avenue	
Hamilton Road	D4	Thorne Road	
Hannington Street	B1	Thorne Road	
High Street	A2	Town Fields	
Highfield Road	C1	Town Moor Avenue	
Jarratt Street	B4	Trafford Way	
King's Road	C1	Vaughan Avenue	
Lawn Avenue	C2	Waterdale	
Lawn Road	C2	Welbeck Road	
Lime Tree Avenue	D4	Welcome Way	
Manor Drive	D3	West Laith Gate	
Market Place	A2	West Street	
Market Road	B1	Whitburn Road	
Milbanke Street	B1	White Rose Way	
Milton Walk	B4	Windsor Road	
Montague Street	B1	Wood Street	

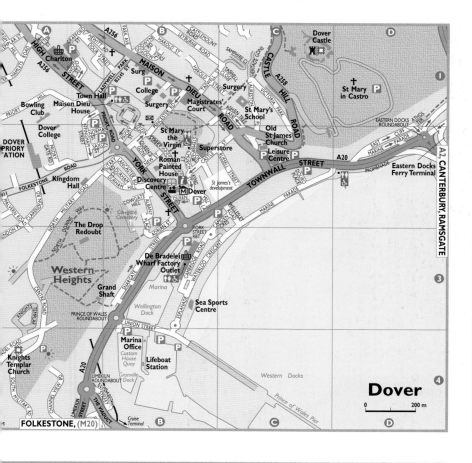

Dover

Dover is found on atlas page **27 P3**

Adrian Street	B3		Marine Parade	D2
Albany Place	B2		Military Road	B2
Ashen Tree Lane	C1		Mill Lane	B2
Athol Terrace	D1		New Street	B2
Biggin Street	B2		Norman Street	A2
Burgh Hill	A1		North Downs Way	A3
Cambridge Road	B3		North Military Road	A3
Camden Crescent	C2		Park Avenue	B1
Castle Hill Road	C1		Park Street	B1
Castlemount Road	B1		Pencester Road	B2
Castle Street	B2		Peter Street	A1
Centre Road	A3		Princes of Wales	
Channel View Road	A4		Roundabout	B3
Church Street	B2		Priory Gate Road	A2
Citadel Road	A4		Priory Hill	A1
Clarendon Place	A3		Priory Road	A1
Clarendon Road	A2		Priory Street	B2
Cowgate Hill	B2		Promenade	D2
Crafford Street	A1		Queen's Gate	B2
Douro Place	C2		Queen Street	B2
Dour Street	A1		Russell Street	B2
Durham Close	B2		Samphire Close	C1
Durham Hill	B2		Saxon Street	A2
East Cliff	D2		Snargate Street	B3
Eastern Docks			South Military Road	A4
Roundabout	D2		Stembrook	B2
Effingham Street	A2		Taswell Close	C1
Elizabeth Street	A4		Taswell Street	B1
Esplanade	B3		Templar Street	A1
Folkestone Road	A2		The Viaduct	A4
Godwyne Close	B1		Tower Hamlets Road	A1
Godwyne Road	B1		Townwall Street	C2
Harold Street	B1		Union Street	B3
Harold Street	B1		Victoria Park	C1
Heritage Gardens	C1		Waterloo Crescent	B3
Hewitt Road	A1		Wellesley Road	C2
High Street	A1		Wood Street	A1
King Street	B2		York Street	B2
Knights Templar	A3		York Street Roundabout	B3
Ladywell	A1			
Lancaster Road	B2			
Laureston Place	C1			
Leyburne Road	B1			
Limekiln Roundabout	A4			
Limekiln Street	A4			
Maison Dieu Road	B1			
Malvern Road	A2			
Marine Parade	C2			

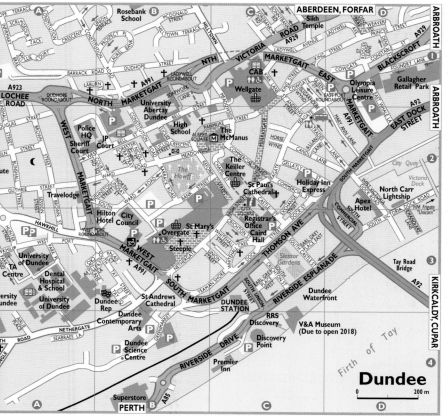

Dundee

Dundee is found on atlas page **142 G11**

Albert Square	B2		Ladywell Avenue	C1
Bank Street	B2		Laurel Bank	B1
Barrack Road	A1		Lochee Road	A1
Barrack Road	B2		McDonald Street	D2
Bell Street	B2		Meadowside	B2
Blackscroft	D1		Miln Street	A2
Blinshall Street	A1		Murraygate	C2
Blinshall Street	A2		Nethergate	A4
Bonnybank Road	C1		Nicoll Street	B2
Brown Street	A2		North Lindsay Street	B2
Candle Lane	C2		North Marketgait	B1
Castle Street	C2		North Victoria Road	C1
Chapel Street	C2		Old Hawkhill	A3
City Square	C3		Panmure Street	B2
Commercial Street	C2		Perth Road	A4
Constable Street	D1		Princes Street	D1
Constitution Crescent	A1		Prospect Place	B1
Constitution Road	A1		Queen Street	C1
Constitution Road	B2		Reform Street	B2
Court House Square	A2		Riverside Drive	B4
Cowgate	C1		Riverside Esplanade	C3
Cowgate	D1		Roseangle	A4
Crichton Street	C3		St Andrews Street	C1
Dock Street	C3		Scrimgeour Place	A1
Douglas Street	A2		Seabraes Lane	A4
Dudhope Street	B1		Seagate	C2
East Dock Street	D2		Session Street	A2
East Marketgait	C1		South Commercial Street	D3
East Whale Lane	D1		South Marketgait	B3
Euclid Crescent	B2		South Tay Street	B3
Euclid Street	B2		South Union Street	C3
Exchange Street	C3		South Victoria Dock Road	D3
Forebank Road	C1		South Ward Road	B2
Forester Street	B2		Sugarhouse Wynd	C1
Foundry Lane	D1		Tay Road Bridge	D3
Gellatly Street	C2		Tay Square	B3
Greenmarket	B4		Thomson Avenue	C3
Guthrie Street	A2		Trades Lane	C2
Hawkhill	A3		Union Street	B3
High Street	C3		Union Terrace	B1
Hilltown	B1		Ward Road	B2
Hilltown Terrace	B1		Weavers Yard	D1
Hunter Street	A3		West Marketgait	A2
Infirmary Brae	A1		West Port	A3
Johnston Street	B2		West Victoria Dock Road	D2
King Street	C1		Whitehall Crescent	C3
Kirk Lane	C1		Whitehall Street	C3
Laburn Street	A1		Yeaman Shore	B3

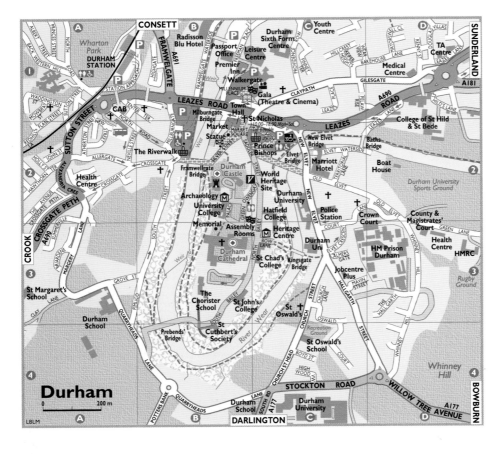

Durham

Durham is found on atlas page **103 Q2**

Albert Street	A1	Mayorswell Close	
Alexandria Crescent	A2	Milburngate Bridge	
Allergate	A2	Millburngate	
Atherton Street	A2	Millennium Place	
Back Western Hill	A1	Mowbray Street	
Bakehouse Lane	C1	Neville Street	
Baths Bridge	C2	New Elvet	
Bow Lane	C3	New Elvet Bridge	
Boyd Street	C4	New Street	
Briardene	A3	North Bailey	
Church Lane	C3	North Road	
Church Street	C4	Old Elvet	
Church Street Head	C4	Oswald Court	
Clay Lane	A3	Owengate	
Claypath	C1	Palace Green	
Court Lane	C3	Palmers Gate	
Crossgate	A2	Pelaw Rise	
Crossgate Peth	A3	Pimlico	
Douglas Villas	D1	Potters Bank	
Elvet Bridge	C2	Prebends' Bridge	
Elvet Crescent	C3	Princes' Street	
Elvet Waterside	C2	Providence Row	
Finney Terrace	C1	Quarryheads Lane	
Flass Street	A2	Redhills Lane	
Framwelgate	B1	Renny Street	
Framwelgate Bridge	B2	Saddler Street	
Framwelgate Waterside	B1	St Hild's Lane	
Freeman Place	B1	Silver Street	
Gilesgate	C1	South Bailey	
Green Lane	D3	South Road	
Grove Street	A3	South Street	
Hallgarth Street	C3	Station Approach	
Hawthorn Terrace	A2	Stockton Road	
Highgate	B1	Summerville	
High Road View	C4	Sutton Street	
High Street	C2	Tenter Terrace	
Hillcrest	C1	Territorial Lane	
Holly Street	A2	The Avenue	
John Street	A2	The Hall Garth	
Keiper Heights	C1	Waddington Street	
Kingsgate Bridge	C3	Wear View	
Leazes Lane	D1	Whinney Hill	
Leazes Lane	D2	Willow Tree Avenue	
Leazes Place	C1		
Leazes Road	B1		
Margery Lane	A3		
Market Square	B2		
Mavin Street	C3		

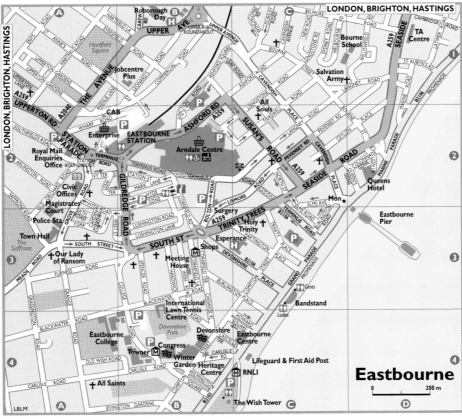

Eastbourne

Eastbourne is found on atlas page **25 P11**

Arlington Road	A2	Langney Road	
Ashford Road	B2	Langney Road	
Ashford Road	C1	Lascelles Terrace	
Ashford Square	B1	Latimer Road	
Avenue Lane	A1	Leaf Road	
Belmore Road	C1	Lismore Road	
Blackwater Road	A4	Longstone Road	
Bolton Road	B3	Lushington Road	
Bourne Street	C1	Marine Parade	
Burlington Place	B3	Marine Road	
Burlington Road	C3	Mark Lane	
Camden Road	A3	Meads Road	
Carew Road	B1	Melbourne Road	
Carlisle Road	A4	Old Orchard Road	
Carlisle Road	B4	Old Wish Road	
Cavendish Avenue	C1	Pevensey Road	
Cavendish Place	C1	Promenade	
Ceylon Place	C2	Queen's Gardens	
Chiswick Place	B3	Saffrons Road	
College Road	B3	St Anne's Road	
Colonnade Gardens	D2	St Aubyn's Road	
Commercial Road	B1	St Leonard's Road	
Compton Street	B4	Seaside	
Compton Street	C3	Seaside Road	
Cornfield Lane	B3	Southfields Road	
Cornfield Road	B2	South Street	
Cornfield Terrace	B3	South Street	
Devonshire Place	B3	Spencer Road	
Dursley Road	C1	Station Parade	
Elms Road	C3	Station Street	
Enys Road	A1	Susan's Road	
Eversfield Road	A1	Sutton Road	
Furness Road	A3	Sydney Road	
Gildredge Road	B2	Terminus Road	
Grand Parade	C3	Terminus Road	
Grange Road	A3	The Avenue	
Grassington Road	A3	Tideswell Road	
Grove Road	A3	Trinity Place	
Hardwick Road	B3	Trinity Trees	
Hartfield Lane	A1	Upper Avenue	
Hartfield Road	A1	Upperton Gardens	
Hartington Place	C3	Upperton Road	
Howard Square	C4	West Street	
Hyde Gardens	B2	West Terrace	
Hyde Road	A2	Willowfield Road	
Ivy Terrace	A2	Wilmington Square	
Jevington Gardens	A4	Wish Road	
Junction Road	B2	York Road	

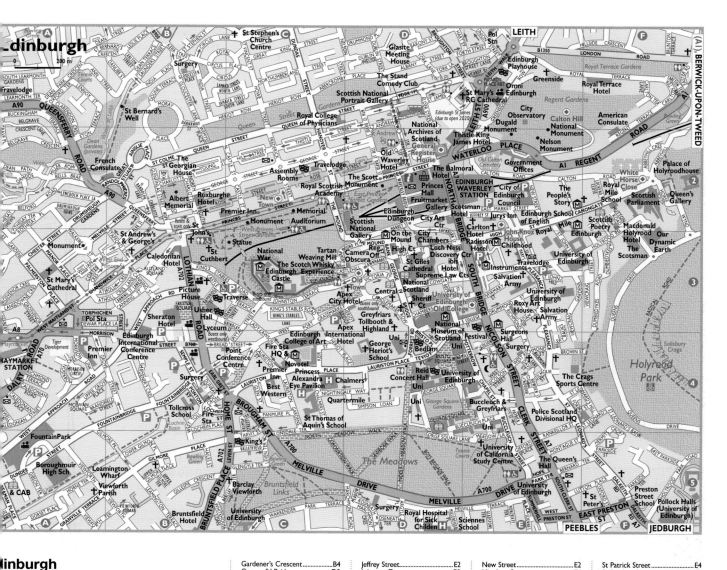

Edinburgh

Edinburgh is found on atlas page **127 P3**

Abbeyhill	F2	Chapel Street	E4	Gardener's Crescent	B4	Jeffrey Street	E2	New Street	E2	St Patrick Street	E4
Abercromby Place	C1	Charlotte Square	B2	George IV Bridge	D3	Johnston Terrace	C3	Nicolson Square	E4	St Stephen Street	B1
Adam Street	E3	Chester Street Gardens	A3	George Square	D4	Keir Street	C4	Nicolson Street	E4	St Vincent Street	C1
Ann Street	A1	Circus Lane	B1	George Square Lane	D5	Kerr Street	B1	Nightingale Way	C4	Saunders Street	B1
Argyle Place	D5	Circus Place	B1	George Street	B2	King's Stables Road	B3	North Bridge	D2	Sciennes	E5
Atholl Crescent Lane	A3	Clarendon Crescent	A1	George Street	C2	Lady Lawson Street	C3	North Castle Street	C2	Semple Street	B4
Bank Street	D3	Clerk Street	E4	Gifford Place	E5	Lansdowne Crescent	A3	North Meadow Walk	C5	Shandwick Place	A3
Barclay Terrace	C5	Cockburn Street	D2	Gillespie Crescent	B5	Lauriston Gardens	C4	North St Andrew Street	D1	Simpson Loan	D4
Belford Road	A2	Coronation Walk	C5	Gilmore Park	A5	Lauriston Place	C4	North St David Street	D1	South Bridge	E3
Belgrave Crescent	A2	Cowan's Close	E4	Gilmore Place	B5	Lauriston Street	C4	Northumberland Street	C1	South Charlotte Street	B2
Boys Brigade Walk	D5	Cowgate	D3	Gilmour Street	E4	Lawnmarket	D3	Oxford Street	F5	South Clerk Street	E5
Brandfield Street	A4	Dalkeith Road	F5	Glenfinlas Street	B2	Leamington Terrace	B5	Palmerston Place	A3	South Learmonth Gardens	A1
Bread Street	B4	Dalry Road	A4	Gloucester Lane	B1	Leith Street	E1	Panmure Place	C4	South St Andrew Street	D2
Bristo Place	D4	Danube Street	B1	Granville Terrace	A5	Leith Walk	E1	Pleasance	E3	South St David Street	D2
Brougham Street	C4	Davie Street	E4	Great King Street	C1	Lennox Street	A1	Ponton Street	B4	Spittal Street	C4
Broughton Street	D1	Dean Park Crescent	A1	Great Stuart Street	B2	Leven Place	C5	Potterrow	E4	Stafford Street	B3
Broughton Street Lane	E1	Dean Street	A1	Greenmarket	C3	Lochrin Place	B4	Princes Street	C2	Tarvit Street	C5
Brunton Terrace	F1	Dewar Place Lane	A3	Greenside Row	E1	Lochrin Street	B4	Queens Drive	F3	The Mound	C2
Bruntsfield Place	B5	Douglas Gardens	A3	Grindlay Street	B3	London Road	E1	Queensferry Road	A1	Thistle Street	C2
Buccleuch Place	D4	Doune Terrace	B1	Grosvenor Street	A3	Lothian Road	B3	Queensferry Street	B2	Torphichen Street	A3
Buccleuch Street	E4	Drummond Street	E3	Grove Street	A4	Lower Gilmore Place	B5	Queen Street	B2	Union Street	E1
Caledonian Place	A4	Dublin Street	D1	Haddon's Court	E4	Lutton Place	E5	Radical Road	F3	Upper Gilmore Place	B5
Caledonian Road	A4	Dumbiedykes Road	F3	Hanover Street	C2	Lynedoch Place Lane	A2	Ramsay Lane	C3	Victoria Street	D3
Caledonian Street	A4	Dunbar Street	B4	Haymarket Terrace	A4	Manor Place	A3	Randolph Crescent	B2	Viewcraig Gardens	E4
Calton Road	E2	Dundas Street	C1	Heriot Row	C1	Marchmont Crescent	D5	Randolph Lane	B2	Viewcraig Street	F3
Candlemaker Row	D3	Dundee Street	A5	Hermits Croft	F5	Marchmont Road	D5	Rankeillor Street	E5	Viewforth	A5
Canning Street	B3	Earl Grey Street	B4	High Street	D3	Market Street	D2	Regent Road	E2	Walker Street	A3
Canongate	E2	Easter Road	F1	High Street	E3	Meadow Lane	E5	Richmond Place	E3	Warrender Park Terrace	C5
Carlton Terrace	F1	East Market Street	E2	Hillside Crescent	E1	Melville Drive	C5	Rose Street	B2	Waterloo Place	D2
Castle Hill	C3	East Parkside	F5	Hill Street	C2	Melville Street	A3	Rosneath Place	D5	Waverley Bridge	D2
Castle Terrace	B3	East Preston Street	F5	Holyrood Park Road	F5	Melville Terrace	D5	Rothesay Place	A3	West Approach Road	A3
Chalmers Street	C4	Elder Street	D1	Holyrood Road	E3	Middle Meadow Walk	D5	Royal Circus	B1	West Maitland Street	A3
Chambers Street	D3	Forrest Road	D4	Home Street	C4	Millerfield Place	D5	Royal Terrace	E1	West Nicolson Street	E4
		Forth Street	D1	Hope Street	B2	Miller Row	A2	St Andrew Square	D1	West Port	C4
		Fountainbridge	A4	Horse Wynd	F2	Moncrieff Terrace	E5	St Bernard's Crescent	A1	West Richmond Street	E4
		Frederick Street	C2	Howden Street	E4	Montague Street	E5	St Colme Street	B2	West Toll Cross	B4
				Howe Street	C1	Moray Place	B1	St James Place	D1	William Street	A3
				India Place	B1	Morrison Link	A4	St Leonard's Bank	F4	Yeaman Place	A5
				India Street	B1	Morrison Street	A4	St Leonard's Hill	E4	York Lane	D1
				Jamaica Street South Lane	B1	Mound Place	D3	St Leonard's Lane	F4	York Place	D1
				Jawbone Walk	D5	Nelson Street	C1	St Leonard's Street	E4	Young Street	B2

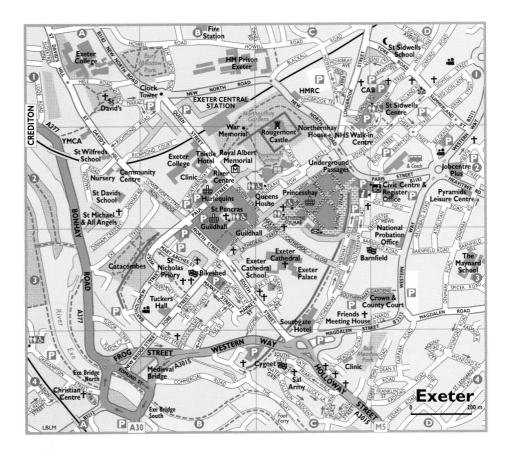

Exeter

Exeter is found on atlas page **9 M6**

Acland Road	D1	King William Street	
Archibald Road	D3	Longbrook Street	
Athelstan Road	D3	Lower North Street	
Bailey Street	C2	Magdalen Road	
Bampfylde Lane	C2	Magdalen Street	
Bampfylde Street	D2	Market Street	
Barnfield Road	D3	Martins Lane	
Bartholomew Street West	B3	Mary Arches Street	
Bear Street	C3	Musgrave Row	
Bedford Street	C2	New Bridge Street	
Belgrave Road	D2	New North Road	
Blackall Road	C1	Northernhay Street	
Bonhay Road	A2	North Street	
Bude Street	D2	Old Park Road	
Bull Meadow Road	C4	Oxford Road	
Castle Street	C2	Palace Gate	
Cathedral Close	C3	Paris Street	
Cathedral Yard	B3	Paul Street	
Cedars Road	D4	Preston Street	
Cheeke Street	D1	Princesshay	
Chichester Mews	C3	Queens Crescent	
Commercial Road	B4	Queen's Terrace	
Coombe Street	B3	Queen Street	
Deanery Place	C3	Radford Road	
Dean Street	D4	Red Lion Lane	
Denmark Road	D3	Richmond Court	
Dinham Crescent	A3	Richmond Road	
Dinham Road	A2	Roberts Road	
Dix's Field	D2	Roman Walk	
Eastgate	C2	St David's Hill	
Edmund Street	A4	Sidwell Street	
Elm Grove Road	B1	Sidwell Street	
Exe Street	A3	Smythen Street	
Fairpark Road	D4	Southernhay East	
Fore Street	B3	Southernhay Gardens	
Franklin Street	D4	Southernhay West	
Friernhay Street	B3	South Street	
Frog Street	A4	Spicer Road	
George Street	B3	Summerland Street	
Guinea Street	B3	Temple Road	
Haldon Road	A2	Tudor Court	
Heavitree Road	D2	Tudor Street	
Hele Road	A1	Verney Street	
High Street	C2	Well Street	
Holloway Street	C4	Western Way	
Howell Road	B1	West Street	
Iron Bridge	B2	Wonford Road	
King Street	B3	York Road	

Gloucester

Gloucester is found on atlas page **46 F11**

Albert Street	D4	Millbrook Street	
Albion Street	B4	Montpellier	
All Saints' Road	D4	Napier Street	
Alvin Street	C2	Nettleton Road	
Archdeacon Street	B2	New Inn Lane	
Arthur Street	C4	Norfolk Street	
Barbican Road	B3	Northgate Street	
Barrack Square	B3	Old Tram Road	
Barton Street	D4	Over Causeway	
Bedford Street	C3	Oxford Road	
Belgrave Road	C4	Oxford Street	
Berkeley Street	B3	Park Road	
Black Dog Way	C2	Park Street	
Blenheim Road	D4	Parliament Street	
Brunswick Road	B4	Pembroke Street	
Brunswick Square	B4	Pitt Street	
Bruton Way	D3	Priory Road	
Bull Lane	B3	Quay Street	
Castle Meads Way	A2	Royal Oak Road	
Clarence Street	C3	Russell Street	
Clare Street	B2	St Aldate Street	
College Court	B2	St Catherine Street	
Commercial Road	B3	St John's Lane	
Cromwell Street	C4	St Mark Street	
Cross Keys Lane	B3	St Mary's Square	
Deans Walk	C1	St Mary's Street	
Eastgate Street	C3	St Michael's Square	
Gouda Way	B1	St Oswald's Road	
Great Western Road	D2	Sebert Street	
Greyfriars	B3	Severn Road	
Hampden Way	C3	Sherborne Street	
Hare Lane	C2	Sinope Street	
Heathville Road	D2	Southgate Street	
Henry Road	D1	Spa Road	
Henry Street	D2	Station Road	
High Orchard Street	A4	Swan Road	
Honyatt Road	D1	Sweetbriar Street	
Kings Barton Street	C4	The Cross	
Kingsholm Road	C1	The Oxebode	
King's Square	C3	The Quay	
Ladybellegate Street	B3	Union Street	
Llanthony Road	A4	Upper Quay Street	
London Road	D2	Vauxhall Road	
Longsmith Street	B3	Wellington Street	
Market Parade	C3	Westgate Street	
Merchants' Road	A4	Widden Street	
Mercia Road	B1	Worcester Parade	
Metz Way	D3	Worcester Street	

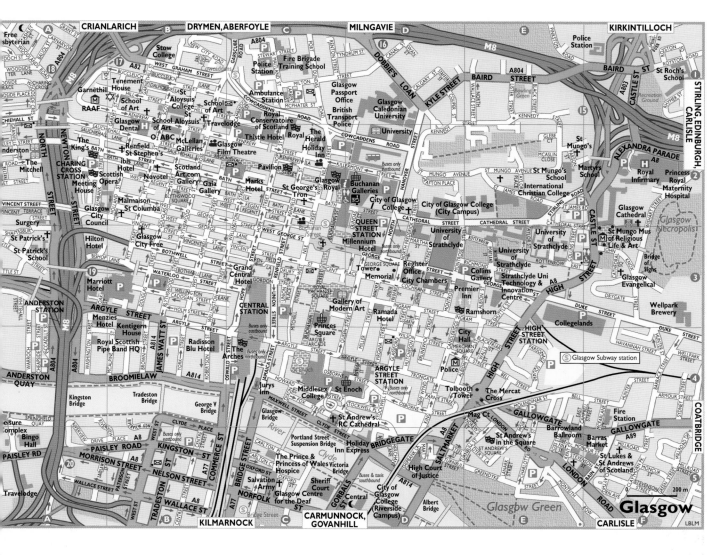

asgow

gow is found on atlas page **125 P4**

Albert Bridge.....................D5	Candleriggs.....................D4	Garnethill Street.....................B1
Albion Street.....................D4	Carlton Place.....................C5	Garnet Street.....................B2
Albion Street.....................E3	Carnarvon Street.....................A1	Garscube Road.....................C1
Alexandra Parade.....................F2	Castle Street.....................F1	Garth Street.....................D3
Anderston Quay.....................A4	Castle Street.....................F2	George Square.....................D3
Argyle Arcade.....................C4	Cathedral Square.....................F3	George Street.....................E3
Argyle Street.....................A3	Cathedral Street.....................D2	George V Bridge.....................B4
Armour Street.....................F4	Centre Street.....................B5	Glasgow Bridge.....................C5
Ashley Street.....................A1	Chalmer Street.....................F5	Glassford Street.....................D4
Bain Street.....................F5	Charing Cross.....................A1	Glebe Court.....................E2
Baird Street.....................E1	Charlotte Street.....................E5	Gorbals Street.....................C5
Baliol Street.....................A1	Cheapside Street.....................A4	Gordon Street.....................C3
Barrack Street.....................F4	Claythorn Avenue.....................F5	Grafton Place.....................D2
Bath Lane.....................B2	Claythorn Park.....................F5	Granville Street.....................A2
Bath Street.....................A2	Clyde Place.....................B4	Greendyke Street.....................E5
Bell Street.....................E4	Clyde Street.....................C4	Green Street.....................F5
Berkeley Street.....................A2	Cochrane Street.....................D3	Hanover Street.....................D3
Blackfriars Street.....................E4	Collins Street.....................E3	High Street.....................E4
Black Street.....................E1	Commerce Street.....................B5	Hill Street.....................B1
Blythswood Square.....................B2	Couper Street.....................D1	Holland Street.....................B2
Blythswood Street.....................B3	Cowcaddens Road.....................C1	Holm Street.....................B3
Bothwell Lane.....................B3	Dalhousie Lane.....................B1	Hope Street.....................C3
Bothwell Street.....................B3	Dixon Street.....................C4	Howard Street.....................C4
Bridgegate.....................D5	Dobbie's Loan.....................D1	Hunter Street.....................F4
Bridge of Sighs.....................F3	Dorset Street.....................A2	Hutcheson Street.....................D4
Bridge Street.....................C5	Douglas Street.....................B3	Hydepark Street.....................A4
Broomielaw.....................B4	Drury Lane.....................C3	Ingram Street.....................D3
Brown Street.....................B4	Drygate.....................F3	Jamaica Street.....................C4
Brunswick Street.....................D4	Duke Street.....................F3	James Watt Street.....................B4
Buccleuch Lane.....................B1	Dundas Street.....................D3	John Knox Street.....................F3
Buccleuch Street.....................B1	Dunlop Street.....................D4	John Street.....................D3
Buchanan Street.....................C4	Dyer's Lane.....................E5	Kennedy Street.....................D2
Cadogan Street.....................B3	East Campbell Street.....................E4	Kennedy Street.....................E1
Calgary Street.....................D1	Elmbank Street.....................A2	Kent Road.....................A2
Cambridge Street.....................C1	Fox Street.....................C4	Kent Street.....................E5
Canal Street.....................D1	Gallowgate.....................E4	Killermont Street.....................C2

Garnethill Street.....................B1	Larbert Street.....................C1
Garnet Street.....................B2	Lister Street.....................E1
Garscube Road.....................C1	London Road.....................E4
Garth Street.....................D3	Maitland Street.....................C1
George Square.....................D3	Martha Street.....................D3
George Street.....................E3	Mart Street.....................D5
George V Bridge.....................B4	Maxwell Street.....................C4
Glasgow Bridge.....................C5	McAlpine Street.....................B4
Glassford Street.....................D4	McAslin Close.....................E2
Glebe Court.....................E2	McFarlane Street.....................F4
Gorbals Street.....................C5	McPhater Street.....................C1
Gordon Street.....................C3	Merchant Lane.....................D5
Grafton Place.....................D2	Miller Street.....................D4
Granville Street.....................A2	Millroad Drive.....................F5
Greendyke Street.....................E5	Millroad Street.....................F5
Green Street.....................F5	Milton Street.....................C1
Hanover Street.....................D3	Mitchell Street.....................C4
High Street.....................E4	Moir Street.....................E5
Hill Street.....................B1	Molendinar Street.....................E5
Holland Street.....................B2	Moncur Street.....................E5
Holm Street.....................B3	Monteith Row.....................E5
Hope Street.....................C3	Montrose Street.....................D3
Howard Street.....................C4	Morrison Street.....................B5
Hunter Street.....................F4	Nelson Street.....................B5
Hutcheson Street.....................D4	New City Road.....................B1
Hydepark Street.....................A4	Newton Street.....................A2
Ingram Street.....................D3	New Wynd.....................D4
Jamaica Street.....................C4	Norfolk Street.....................C5
James Watt Street.....................B4	North Frederick Street.....................D3
John Knox Street.....................F3	North Hanover Street.....................D3
John Street.....................D3	North Portland Street.....................E3
Kennedy Street.....................D2	North Street.....................A2
Kennedy Street.....................E1	North Wallace Street.....................E1
Kent Road.....................A2	Osborne Street.....................C4
Kent Street.....................E5	Oswald Street.....................C4
Killermont Street.....................C2	Oxford Street.....................C5
Kingston Bridge.....................A5	Paisley Road.....................A5
Kingston Street.....................B5	Parnie Street.....................D4
King Street.....................D4	Parsonage Square.....................E4
Kyle Street.....................D1	Parson Street.....................E2
Lanark Street.....................E5	Paterson Street.....................B5

Pinkston Road.....................E1	Stafford Street.....................D1
Pitt Street.....................B2	Steel Street.....................D5
Port Dundas Road.....................C1	Stevenson Street.....................F5
Portland Street Suspension Bridge.....................C5	Stewart Street.....................C1
Queen Street.....................C4	Stirling Road.....................E2
Renfield Lane.....................C3	Stockwell Place.....................D4
Renfield Street.....................C3	Stockwell Street.....................D4
Renfrew Lane.....................C2	Suffolk Street.....................E5
Renfrew Street.....................B1	Sydney Street.....................F4
Renton Street.....................C1	Taylor Place.....................E2
Rhymer Street.....................F1	Taylor Street.....................E2
Richmond Street.....................E3	Tradeston Bridge.....................B4
Riverview Drive.....................A4	Tradeston Street.....................B5
Robertson Street.....................B4	Trongate.....................D4
Rose Street.....................B2	Turnbull Street.....................D5
Ross Street.....................E5	Tyndrum Street.....................C1
Rottenrow.....................E3	Union Street.....................C3
Rottenrow East.....................E3	Virginia Street.....................D4
Royal Exchange Square.....................C3	Wallace Street.....................A5
Royston Road.....................F1	Walls Street.....................E4
Royston Square.....................F1	Warroch Street.....................A4
St Andrew's Square.....................E5	Washington Street.....................A4
St Andrew's Street.....................E4	Waterloo Street.....................B3
St James Road.....................E2	Wellington Lane.....................B3
St Mungo Avenue.....................D2	Wellington Street.....................B3
St Vincent Lane.....................B3	Wellpark Street.....................F4
St Vincent Place.....................C3	West Campbell Street.....................B3
St Vincent Street.....................A2	West George Lane.....................B2
St Vincent Terrace.....................A2	West George Street.....................B2
Saltmarket.....................D5	West Graham Street.....................B1
Sauchiehall Lane.....................A2	West Nile Street.....................C3
Sauchiehall Street.....................A1	West Regent Lane.....................C2
Sauchiehall Street.....................B2	West Regent Street.....................B2
Scott Street.....................B1	West Street.....................B5
Shaftesbury Street.....................A3	Wilson Street.....................D4
Shipbank Lane.....................D5	Wishart Street.....................F3
Shuttle Street.....................E3	Woodlands Road.....................A1
South Frederick Street.....................D3	Woodside Crescent.....................A1
Springburn Road.....................F1	Woodside Terrace.....................A1
Springfield Quay.....................A4	Woodside Terrace Lane.....................A1
	York Street.....................B4

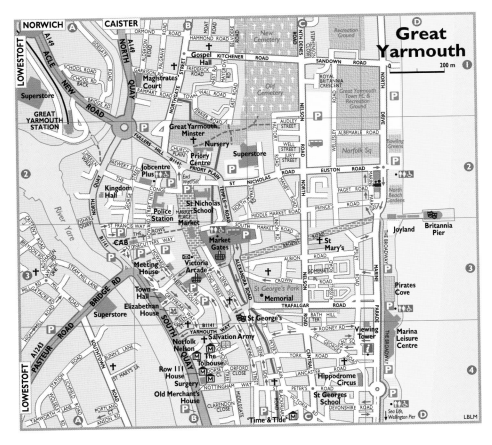

Great Yarmouth

Great Yarmouth is found on atlas page **77 Q10**

Acle New Road	A1	North Drive	D
Albemarle Road	C2	North Market Road	C
Albion Road	C3	North Quay	A
Alderson Road	B1	Northgate Street	B
Alexandra Road	B3	Nottingham Way	B
Apsley Road	C3	Ormond Road	B
Belvidere Road	B1	Paget Road	B
Blackfriars Road	C4	Palgrave Road	B
Brewery Street	A2	Pasteur Road	A
Breydon Road	A3	Prince's Road	C
Bridge Road	A1	Priory Plain	B
Bridge Road	A3	Queen Street	B
Bunn's Lane	A4	Rampart Road	B
Church Plain	B2	Regent Road	C
Critten's Road	A3	Rodney Road	C
Crown Road	C3	Russell Road	C
Dene Side	B3	St Francis Way	A
Devonshire Road	C4	St George's Road	A
East Road	B1	St Nicholas Road	B
Euston Road	C2	St Peter's Plain	C
Factory Road	C2	St Peter's Road	C
Ferrier Road	B1	Sandown Road	C
Fishers Quay	A2	Saw Mill Lane	A
Frederick Road	B1	School Road	A
Fullers Hill	B2	School Road Back	A
Garrison Road	B1	Sidegate Road	A
Gatacre Road	A3	South Market Road	C
George Street	A2	South Quay	A
Greyfriars Way	B3	Southtown Road	A
Hammond Road	B1	Station Road	A
High Mill Road	A3	Steam Mill Lane	A
Howard Street North	B2	Stephenson Close	C
Howard Street South	B3	Stonecutters Way	A
King Street	B3	Tamworth Lane	A
Kitchener Road	B1	Temple Road	B
Ladyhaven Road	A3	The Broadway	D
Lancaster Road	C4	The Conge	B
Lichfield Road	A4	The Rows	A
Limekiln Walk	A2	Tolhouse Street	B
Manby Road	C2	Town Wall Road	B
Marine Parade	D3	Trafalgar Road	C
Maygrove Road	B1	Union Road	B
Middle Market Road	C2	Victoria Road	C
Middlegate	B4	Wellesley Road	C
Moat Road	B1	West Road	B
Nelson Road Central	C3	Wolseley Road	C
Nelson Road North	C1	Yarmouth Way	B
North Denes Road	C1	York Road	C

Guildford

Guildford is found on atlas page **23 Q5**

Abbot Road	C4	Millmead Terrace	D
Angel Gate	B3	Mount Pleasant	C
Artillery Road	B1	Nightingale Road	D
Artillery Terrace	C1	North Street	B
Bedford Road	A2	Onslow Road	A
Bridge Street	A3	Onslow Street	B
Bright Hill	C3	Oxford Road	C
Brodie Road	D3	Pannells Court	C
Bury Fields	B4	Park Street	A
Bury Street	B4	Pewley Bank	D
Castle Hill	C4	Pewley Fort Inner Court	D
Castle Street	C3	Pewley Hill	C
Chapel Street	B3	Pewley Way	D
Chertsey Street	C2	Phoenix Court	C
Cheselden Road	D2	Porridge Pot Alley	B
Church Road	B1	Portsmouth Road	A
College Road	B2	Poyle Road	D
Commercial Road	B2	Quarry Street	B
Dene Road	D2	Sandfield Terrace	C
Denmark Road	D2	Semaphore Road	D
Drummond Road	B1	South Hill	C
Eagle Road	C1	Springfield Road	C
Epsom Road	D2	Station Approach	A
Falcon Road	C1	Stoke Fields	C
Fort Road	C4	Stoke Grove	C
Foxenden Road	D1	Stoke Road	C
Friary Bridge	A3	Swan Lane	B
Friary Street	B3	Sydenham Road	C
George Road	B1	Testard Road	A
Guildford Park Road	A2	The Bars	C
Harvey Road	D3	The Mount	A
Haydon Place	C2	The Shambles	B
High Pewley	D4	Tunsgate	B
High Street	B3	Upperton Road	A
Jeffries Passage	C2	Victoria Road	C
Jenner Road	D2	Walnut Tree Close	A
Laundry Road	B2	Ward Street	C
Leapale Lane	B2	Warwicks Bench	C
Leapale Road	B2	Wherwell Road	A
Leas Road	B1	William Road	C
London Road	D2	Wodeland Avenue	A
Mareschal Road	A4	Woodbridge Road	B
Market Street	C3	York Road	C
Martyr Road	C2		
Mary Road	A1		
Millbrook	B3		
Mill Lane	B3		
Millmead	B3		

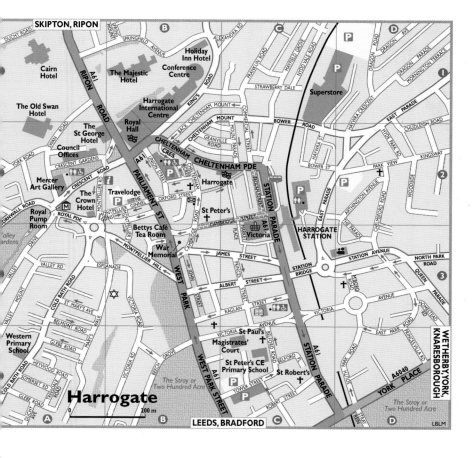

Harrogate

Harrogate is found on atlas page **97 M9**

Albert Street	C3
Alexandra Road	B1
Arthington Avenue	D2
Back Cheltenham Mount	B2
Beech Grove	B4
Belford Place	C4
Belford Road	C4
Belmont Road	A3
Beulah Street	C2
Bower Road	C1
Bower Street	C2
Cambridge Road	B3
Cambridge Street	C2
Chelmsford Road	D3
Cheltenham Crescent	B2
Cheltenham Mount	B2
Cheltenham Parade	B2
Chudleigh Road	D2
Cold Bath Road	A3
Commercial Street	C1
Cornwall Road	A2
Crescent Gardens	A2
Crescent Road	A2
Dragon Avenue	D1
Dragon Parade	D1
Dragon Road	D1
Duchy Avenue	A4
Duchy Road	A1
East Parade	C2
East Park Road	D4
Esplanade	A3
Franklin Road	C1
Glebe Road	A4
Granville Road	B2
Haywra Street	C2
Heywood Road	A4
Homestead Road	D3
Hyde Park Road	D2
Hywra Crescent	D2
James Street	B3
John Street	B3
King's Road	B1
Kingsway	D2
Market Place	C3
Marlborough Road	D3
Mayfield Grove	C1
Montpellier Gardens	B2
Montpellier Hill	B3

Montpellier Road	A2
Montpellier Street	B2
Mornington Terrace	D1
Mount Parade	C2
North Park Road	D3
Nydd Vale Road	C1
Oxford Street	B2
Park View	D2
Parliament Street	B2
Princes Street	C3
Princes Villa Road	D4
Queen Parade	D3
Raglan Street	C3
Ripon Road	A1
Robert Street	C4
Royal Parade	A2
St Mary's Avenue	A3
St Mary's Walk	A4
Somerset Road	A4
South Park Road	D4
Springfield Avenue	B1
Spring Mount	B1
Station Avenue	D3
Station Bridge	C3
Station Parade	C2
Strawberry Dale	C1
Stray Rein	D4
Swan Road	A2
The Ginnel	B2
The Parade	D2
Tower Street	C4
Treesdale Road	A4
Union Street	B2
Valley Drive	A3
Valley Mount	A3
Valley Road	A3
Victoria Avenue	B4
Victoria Road	B3
West Park	B3
West Park Street	B4
Woodside	D2
York Place	D4
York Road	A2

Huddersfield

Huddersfield is found on atlas page **90 E7**

Albion Street	B4
Alfred Street	C4
Back Union Street	C1
Bankfield Road	A4
Bath Street	B1
Belmont Street	A1
Brook Street	C2
Byram Street	C2
Cambridge Road	B1
Carforth Street	D4
Castlegate	B1
Chancery Lane	B3
Chapel Hill	B4
Chapel Street	B4
Church Street	C2
Clare Hill	B1
Claremont Street	B1
Cloth Hall Street	B3
Cross Church Street	C3
Dundas Lane	B3
Elizabeth Queen Gardens	A2
Elmwood Avenue	A1
Firth Street	D4
Fitzwilliam Street	A2
Fitzwilliam Street	B2
Gasworks Street	D1
Great Northern Street	C1
Greenhead Road	A3
Half Moon Street	B3
High Street	B3
Highfields Road	A1
John William Street	B2
King Street	C3
King's Mill Lane	D4
Kirkgate	C3
Leeds Road	C2
Lincoln Street	D3
Lord Street	C2
Lower Fitzwilliam Street	C1
Lynton Avenue	A3
Manchester Road	A3
Market Place	C3
Market Street	B3
Merton Street	A3
Milford Street	B4
Mountjoy Road	A1
New North Parade	B2
New North Road	A1

New North Road	A2
New Street	B4
Northgate	C1
Northumberland Street	C2
Old Leeds Road	D2
Old South Street	B3
Outcote Bank	B4
Oxford Street	C1
Page Street	C4
Park Avenue	A2
Park Drive South	A2
Peel Street	C4
Portland Street	A2
Princess Street	B4
Prospect Street	A4
Quay Street	D2
Queen Street	C3
Queen Street South	C4
Queensgate	C4
Railway Street	B2
Ramsden Street	B3
Rook Street	B1
St Andrew's Road	D2
St George's Square	B2
St John's Road	B1
St Peter's Street	C2
Southgate	C2
Spring Grove Street	A4
Spring Street	A3
Springwood Avenue	A3
Stadium Way	D1
Station Street	B2
Trinity Street	A2
Turnbridge Road	D2
Union Street	C1
Upper George Street	A3
Upperhead Row	B3
Viaduct Street	B2
Victoria Lane	C3
Wakefield Road	D3
Water Street	A3
Watergate	D2
Waverley Road	A2
Wentworth Street	A2
Westgate	B3
William Street	C1
Wood Street	C2
Zetland Street	C3

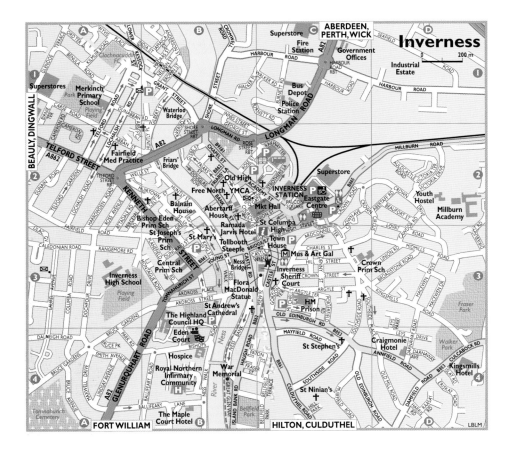

Inverness

Inverness is found on atlas page **156 B8**

Abertaff Road D2	Gordon Terrace ....
Academy Street B2	Grant Street ....
Anderson Street B1	Great Glen Way ....
Annfield Road D4	Harbour Road ....
Ardconnel Terrace C3	Harris Road ....
Ardross Street B3	Harrowden Road ....
Argyle Street C3	Haugh Road ....
Argyle Terrace C3	High Street ....
Ballifeary Lane A4	Hill Park ....
Ballifeary Road B4	Hill Street ....
Bank Street B2	Huntly Street ....
Bellfield Terrace C4	Innes Street ....
Benula Road A1	Islay Road ....
Birnie Terrace A1	Kenneth Street ....
Bishops Road B4	King Street ....
Bridge Street B3	Kingsmills Road ....
Broadstone Road D3	Laurel Avenue ....
Bruce Gardens A4	Lindsay Avenue ....
Bruce Park A4	Lochalsh Road ....
Burnett Road C1	Longman Road ....
Caledonian Road A3	Lovat Road ....
Cameron Road A2	Lower Kessock Street ....
Cameron Square A2	Maxwell Drive ....
Carse Road A1	Mayfield Road ....
Castle Road B3	Midmills Road ....
Castle Street C3	Millburn Road ....
Chapel Street B2	Mitchell's Lane ....
Charles Street C3	Muirfield Road ....
Columba Road A4	Ness Bank ....
Crown Circus C2	Old Edinburgh Road ....
Crown Drive D2	Park Road ....
Crown Road C2	Planefield Road ....
Crown Street C3	Porterfield Road ....
Culcabock Road D4	Raasay Road ....
Dalneigh Road A4	Rangemore Road ....
Damfield Road D4	Ross Avenue ....
Darnaway Road D4	Seafield Road ....
Denny Street C3	Shore Street ....
Dochfour Drive A3	Smith Avenue ....
Dunabban Road A1	Southside Place ....
Dunain Road A2	Southside Road ....
Duncraig Street B3	Telford Gardens ....
Eriskay Road D4	Telford Road ....
Fairfield Road A3	Telford Street ....
Falcon Square C2	Tomnahurich Street ....
Friars' Lane B2	Union Road ....
Glendoe Terrace A1	Walker Road ....
Glenurquhart Road A4	Young Street ....

Ipswich

Ipswich is found on atlas page **53 L3**

Alderman Road A3	Key Street ....
Anglesea Road B1	King Street ....
Argyle Street D2	London Road ....
Austin Street C4	Lower Brook Street ....
Barrack Lane A1	Lower Orwell Street ....
Belstead Road B4	Museum Street ....
Berners Street B1	Neale Street ....
Black Horse Lane B2	Neptune Quay ....
Blanche Street D2	New Cardinal Street ....
Bolton Lane C1	Newson Street ....
Bond Street D3	Northgate Street ....
Bramford Road A1	Norwich Road ....
Bridge Street C4	Old Foundry Road ....
Burlington Road A2	Orchard Street ....
Burrell Road B4	Orford Street ....
Cardigan Street A1	Orwell Place ....
Carr Street C2	Orwell Quay ....
Cecil Road B1	Portman Road ....
Cemetery Road D1	Princes Street ....
Chancery Road A4	Quadling Street ....
Charles Street B1	Queen Street ....
Christchurch Street D1	Ranelagh Road ....
Civic Drive B2	Russell Road ....
Clarkson Street A1	St George's Street ....
Cobbold Street C2	St Helen's Street ....
College Street C3	St Margaret's Street ....
Commercial Road A4	St Matthews Street ....
Constantine Road A3	St Nicholas Street ....
Crown Street B2	St Peter's Street ....
Cumberland Street A1	Silent Street ....
Dalton Road A2	Sir Alf Ramsey Way ....
Dock Street D3	Soane Street ....
Duke Street D4	South Street ....
Eagle Street C3	Star Lane ....
Elm Street B2	Stoke Quay ....
Falcon Street B3	Suffolk Road ....
Fonnereau Road B1	Tacket Street ....
Foundation Street C3	Tavern Street ....
Franciscan Way B3	Tower Ramparts ....
Geneva Road A1	Tuddenham Avenue ....
Grafton Way B3	Turret Lane ....
Great Gipping Street A2	Upper Orwell Street ....
Great Whip Street C4	Vernon Street ....
Grey Friars Road B3	West End Road ....
Grimwade Street D3	Westgate Street ....
Handford Road A2	Willoughby Road ....
Hervey Street D1	Wolsey Street ....
High Street B1	Woodbridge Road ....

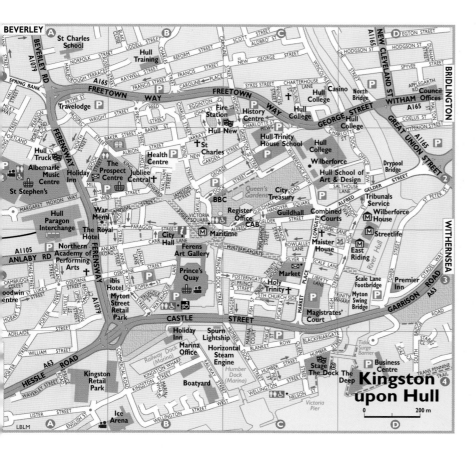

Kingston upon Hull

Kingston upon Hull is found on atlas page **93 J5**

Adelaide Street	A4	Market Place	C3
Albion Street	B2	Mill Street	A2
Alfred Gelder Street	C2	Myton Street	B3
Anlaby Road	A3	New Cleveland Street	D1
Baker Street	B2	New Garden Street	B2
Beverley Road	A1	New George Street	C1
Blackfriargate	C4	Norfolk Street	A1
Blanket Row	C4	Osborne Street	B3
Bond Street	B2	Osborne Street	A3
Brook Street	A2	Paragon Street	B2
Caroline Street	B1	Percy Street	B1
Carr Lane	B3	Porter Street	A3
Castle Street	B3	Portland Place	A2
Chapel Lane	C2	Portland Street	A2
Charles Street	B1	Postergate	C3
Charterhouse Lane	C1	Princes Dock Street	B3
Citadel Way	D3	Prospect Street	A1
Commercial Road	B4	Queen Street	C4
Dagger Lane	C3	Railway Street	B4
Dock Office Row	D2	Raywell Street	B1
Dock Street	B2	Reform Street	B1
Durham Street	D1	Russell Street	A1
Egginton Street	B1	St Luke's Street	A3
Ferensway	A2	St Peter Street	D2
Freetown Way	A1	Saville Street	B2
Gandhi Way	D2	Scale Lane	C3
Garrison Road	D3	Scott Street	C1
George Street	B2	Silver Street	C3
George Street	D1	South Bridge Road	D4
Great Union Street	D1	South Church Side	C3
Grimston Street	C2	South Street	B2
Guildhall Road	C2	Spring Bank	A1
Hanover Square	C2	Spyvee Street	D1
Hessle Road	A4	Sykes Street	C1
High Street	C3	Tower Street	D3
Hodgson Street	D1	Upper Union Street	A3
Humber Dock Street	C4	Victoria Square	B2
Humber Street	C4	Waterhouse Lane	B3
Hyperion Street	D1	Wellington Street	C4
Jameson Street	B2	Wellington Street West	B4
Jarratt Street	B2	West Street	A2
King Edward Street	B2	Whitefriargate	C3
Kingston Street	B4	Wilberforce Drive	C2
Liddell Street	B1	William Street	A4
Lime Street	C1	Wincolmlee	C1
Lister Street	A4	Witham	D1
Lowgate	C3	Worship Street	C1
Margaret Moxon Way	A2	Wright Street	A1

Lancaster

Lancaster is found on atlas page **95 K8**

Aberdeen Road	D4	Lincoln Road	A3
Aldcliffe Road	B4	Lindow Street	B4
Alfred Street	C2	Lodge Street	C2
Ambleside Road	D1	Long Marsh Lane	A2
Balmoral Road	D4	Lune Street	B1
Bath Street	D3	Market Street	B3
Blades Street	A3	Meeting House Lane	A3
Bond Street	D3	Middle Street	B3
Borrowdale Road	D2	Moor Gate	D3
Brewery Lane	C3	Moor Lane	C3
Bridge Lane	B2	Morecambe Road	B1
Brock Street	C3	Nelson Street	C3
Bulk Road	D2	North Road	C2
Bulk Street	C3	Owen Road	C1
Cable Street	B2	Park Road	D3
Castle Hill	B3	Parliament Street	C2
Castle Park	A3	Patterdale Road	D2
Caton Road	C2	Penny Street	B4
Cheapside	C3	Portland Street	B4
China Street	B3	Primrose Street	D4
Church Street	B2	Prospect Street	D4
Common Garden Street	B3	Quarry Road	C4
Dale Street	D4	Queen Street	B4
Dallas Road	B3	Regent Street	B4
Dalton Road	D2	Ridge Lane	D1
Dalton Square	C3	Ridge Street	D1
Damside Street	B2	Robert Street	C3
Derby Road	C1	Rosemary Lane	C2
De Vitre Street	C2	St George's Quay	A1
Dumbarton Road	D4	St Leonard's Gate	C2
East Road	D3	St Peter's Road	C4
Edward Street	C3	Sibsey Street	A3
Fairfield Road	A3	South Road	C4
Fenton Street	B3	Station Road	A3
Gage Street	C3	Stirling Road	D4
Garnet Street	D2	Sulyard Street	C3
George Street	C3	Sun Street	B3
Grasmere Road	D3	Thurnham Street	C4
Great John Street	C3	Troutbeck Road	D2
Gregson Road	D4	Ulleswater Road	D3
Greyhound Bridge Road	B1	West Road	A3
High Street	B4	Westbourne Road	A3
Kelsey Street	A3	Wheatfield Street	A3
Kentmere Road	D2	Williamson Road	D3
King Street	B3	Wingate-Saul Road	A3
Kingsway	C1	Wolseley Street	D2
Kirkes Road	D4	Woodville Street	D3
Langdale Road	D1	Wyresdale Road	D3

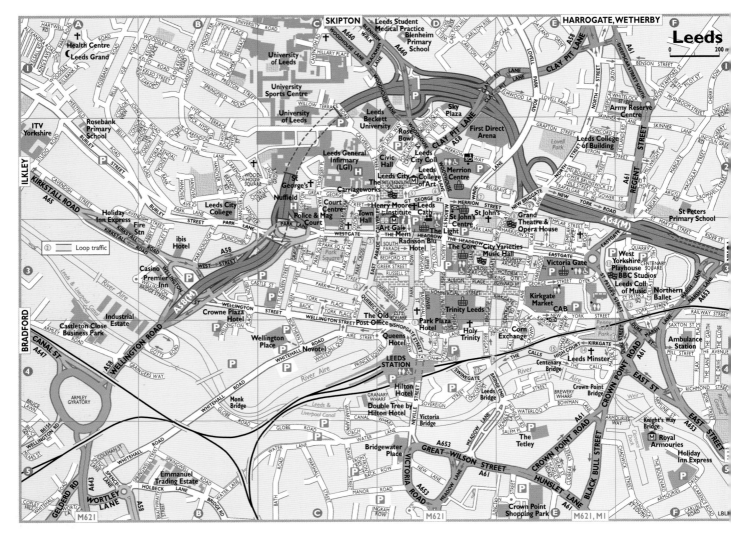

Leeds

Leeds is found on atlas page **90 H4**

Abbey Street	B3	Calverley Street	C2
Aire Street	C4	Canal Street	A4
Albion Place	D3	Canal Wharf	C4
Albion Street	D2	Carlton Carr	D1
Alexandra Road	A1	Carlton Hill	D1
Argyle Road	F2	Carlton Rise	D1
Armley Gyratory	A4	Castle Street	B3
Armley Road	A4	Cavendish Road	C1
Armouries Drive	F5	Cavendish Street	A2
Armouries Way	E4	Centenary Square	F3
Back Hyde Terrace	B2	Central Road	E3
Back Row	C5	Chadwick Street	F5
Bath Road	C5	Cherry Row	F1
Bedford Street	D3	Chorley Lane	B2
Belgrave Street	D2	City Square	D3
Belle Vue Road	A1	Claremont	B2
Belmont Grove	C2	Clarence Road	F5
Benson Street	F1	Clarendon Road	B1
Bingley Street	B3	Clay Pit Lane	D2
Bishopgate Street	D4	Cloberry Street	B1
Black Bull Street	E5	Commercial Street	D3
Blackman Lane	C1	Concord Street	E2
Blenheim Walk	C1	Consort Street	B2
Boar Lane	D4	Consort View	A1
Bowman Lane	E4	County Arcade	E3
Bow Street	F4	Cromer Terrace	B1
Brandon Road	B2	Cromwell Street	F2
Bridge End	D4	Cross Arcade	D3
Bridge Road	B5	Cross Kelso Road	B1
Bridge Street	E2	Cross Stamford Street	F1
Bridge Street	E3	Crown Point Road	E5
Briggate	D4	Crown Street	E4
Burley Street	A2	Cudbear Street	E5
Butts Court	D3	David Street	C5
Byron Street	E2	Dock Street	E4
Call Lane	E4	Duke Street	F4

Duke Street	F4	King's Avenue	A1
Duncan Street	D4	King Street	C3
Duncombe Street	B3	Kirkgate	E3
Dyer Street	E3	Kirkstall Road	A2
Eastgate	E3	Lady Lane	E3
East Parade	C3	Lands Lane	D3
East Street	F4	Leighton Street	C2
Elmwood Lane	E1	Leylands Road	F2
Flax Place	F4	Lifton Place	B1
Front Street	C5	Lincoln Green Road	F2
Geldred Road	A5	Lisbon Street	B3
George Street	E3	Little Queen Street	C3
Globe Road	B4	Lovell Park Hill	E1
Gotts Road	B4	Lovell Park Road	E1
Gower Street	E2	Lower Basinghall Street	D3
Grace Street	C3	Lower Brunswick Street	E2
Grafton Street	E2	Lyddon Terrace	B1
Graingers Way	A4	Mabgate	F2
Great George Street	C2	Macaulay Street	F2
Great Wilson Street	D5	Manor Road	C5
Greek Street	D3	Mark Lane	D3
Hanover Avenue	B2	Marlborough Street	B3
Hanover Lane	B2	Marshall Street	C5
Hanover Square	B2	Marsh Lane	F4
Harewood Street	E3	Maude Street	E4
Harper Street	E4	Meadow Lane	D5
Harrison Street	E3	Melbourne Street	E2
Hartwell Road	A1	Merrion Street	D2
High Court	E4	Merrion Way	D2
Holbeck Lane	B5	Millennium Square	D2
Hope Road	F2	Mill Street	F4
Hunslet Lane	E4	Millwright Street	F2
Hunslet Road	E5	Mount Preston Street	B1
Hyde Park Road	A1	Mushroom Street	F1
Hyde Street	B2	Neptune Street	F4
Hyde Terrace	B1	Neville Street	D4
Infirmary Street	D3	New Briggate	E3
Junction Street	D5	New Lane	D5
Kelso Road	B1	New Station Street	D4
Kendal Lane	B2	New York Road	E2
King Edward Street	E3	New York Street	E3

King's Avenue	A1	Northern Street	C4
King Street	C3	North Street	E2
Kirkgate	E3	Oxford Place	C3
Kirkstall Road	A2	Oxford Row	C3
Lady Lane	E3	Park Cross Street	C3
Lands Lane	D3	Park Lane	B2
Leighton Street	C2	Park Place	C3
Leylands Road	F2	Park Row	D3
Lifton Place	B1	Park Square East	C3
Lincoln Green Road	F2	Park Square North	C3
Lisbon Street	B3	Park Square West	C3
Little Queen Street	C3	Park Street	C3
Lovell Park Hill	E1	Pilot Street	F1
Lovell Park Road	E1	Portland Crescent	C2
Lower Basinghall Street	D3	Portland Way	D2
Lower Brunswick Street	E2	Princes Square	C4
Lyddon Terrace	B1	Quarry Hill	F3
Mabgate	F2	Quebec Street	D2
Macaulay Street	F2	Queen Square	D2
Manor Road	C5	Queen Square Court	D2
Mark Lane	D3	Queen Street	C3
Marlborough Street	B3	Railway Street	F3
Marshall Street	C5	Regent Street	F2
Marsh Lane	F4	Richmond Street	F4
Maude Street	E4	Rider Street	F3
Meadow Lane	D5	Rillbank Lane	A1
Melbourne Street	E2	Rosebank Road	A1
Merrion Street	D2	St Cecilia Street	F3
Merrion Way	D2	St John's Road	A1
Millennium Square	D2	St Mary's Street	F3
Mill Street	F4	St Paul's Street	C3
Millwright Street	F2	St Peter's Square	F3
Mount Preston Street	B1	St Peter's Street	E3
Mushroom Street	F1	Salem Place	E5
Neptune Street	F4	Saxton Lane	F4
Neville Street	D4	Sheepscar Grove	E1
New Briggate	E3	Sheepscar Street South	F1
New Lane	D5	Skinner Lane	E1
New Station Street	D4	South Parade	D3
New York Road	E2	Sovereign Street	D4
New York Street	E3	Spence Lane	A5

Springfield Mount	
Springwell Road	
Springwell Street	
Studio Road	
Swinegate	
Templar Street	
The Avenue	
The Boulevard	
The Calls	
The Headrow	
Thoresby Place	
Trafalgar Street	
Upper Basinghall Street	
Vicar Lane	
Victoria Road	
Victoria Street	
Victoria Terrace	
Wade Lane	
Water Lane	
Waterloo Street	
Wellington Bridge Street	
Wellington Road	
Wellington Road	
Wellington Street	
Westfield Road	
Westgate	
West Street	
Wharf Approach	
Wharf Street	
Whitehall Quay	
Whitehall Road	
Whitehall Road	
Whitelock Street	
Willow Terrace Road	
Woodhouse Lane	
Woodhouse Square	
Woodsley Road	
Wortley Lane	
Wortley Lane	
York Place	
York Street	

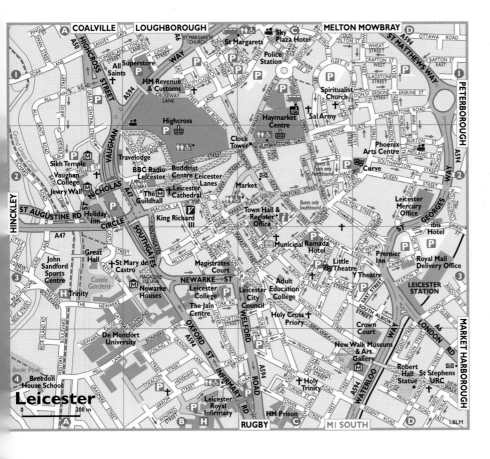

Leicester

Leicester is found on atlas page **72 F10**

Albion Street	C3	Infirmary Road	B4
All Saints Road	A1	Jarrom Street	B4
Bath Lane	A2	Jarvis Street	A1
Bedford Street	C1	King Street	C3
Belgrave Gate	C1	Lee Street	C1
Belvoir Street	C3	London Road	D3
Bishop Street	C3	Lower Brown Street	B3
Bonners Lane	B4	Magazine Square	B3
Bowling Green Street	C3	Mansfield Street	B1
Burgess Street	B1	Market Place South	B2
Burton Street	D2	Market Street	C3
Calais Hill	C3	Mill Lane	A4
Campbell Street	D3	Morledge Street	D1
Cank Street	B2	Newarke Street	B3
Castle Street	A3	New Walk	C3
Charles Street	C1	Oxford Street	B3
Chatham Street	C3	Peacock Lane	B2
Cheapside	C2	Pocklington Walk	B3
Church Gate	B1	Princess Road East	D4
Clyde Street	D1	Princess Road West	C4
Colton Street	C2	Queen Street	D2
Conduit Street	D3	Regent Road	C4
Crafton Street West	D1	Regent Street	D4
Deacon Street	B4	Richard III Road	A2
De Montfort Street	D4	Rutland Street	C2
Dover Street	C3	St Augustine Road	A2
Duke Street	C3	St George Street	D2
Duns Lane	A3	St Georges Way	D2
East Bond Street Lane	B1	St James Street	C1
Erskine Street	D1	St Matthews Way	D1
Fleet Street	C1	St Nicholas Circle	A2
Friar Lane	B3	Sanvey Gate	A1
Gallowtree Gate	C2	Soar Lane	A1
Gateway Street	A3	South Albion Street	D3
Granby Street	C2	Southampton Street	D2
Grasmere Street	A4	Southgates	B3
Gravel Street	B1	Station Street	D3
Great Central Street	A1	The Newarke	A3
Greyfriars	B2	Tower Street	C4
Halford Street	C2	Vaughan Way	A2
Haymarket	C1	Waterloo Way	D4
Highcross Street	A1	Welford Road	C3
Highcross Street	B2	Welles Street	A2
High Street	B2	Wellington Street	C3
Hill Street	C1	Western Boulevard	A4
Horsefair Street	B3	West Street	C4
Humberstone Gate	C2	Wharf Street South	D1
Humberstone Road	D1	Yeoman Street	C2

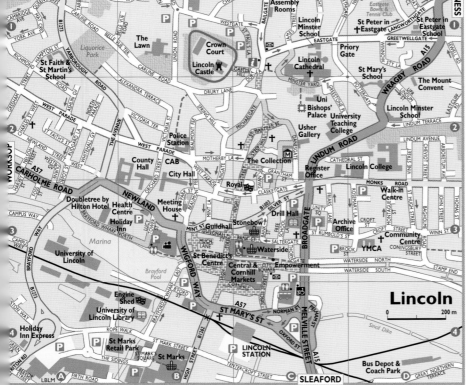

Lincoln

Lincoln is found on atlas page **86 C6**

Alexandra Terrace	B2	Montague Street	D3
Arboretum Avenue	D2	Motherby Lane	B2
Bagholme Road	D3	Nelson Street	A2
Bailgate	C1	Newland	B3
Bank Street	C3	Newland Street West	A2
Beaumont Fee	B3	Norman Street	C4
Belle Vue Terrace	A1	Northgate	C1
Brayford Way	A3	Orchard Street	B3
Brayford Wharf East	B4	Oxford Street	C4
Brayford Wharf North	A3	Park Street	B3
Broadgate	C3	Pelham Street	C4
Burton Road	B1	Pottergate	D2
Carholme Road	A2	Queen's Crescent	A1
Carline Road	A1	Richmond Road	A1
Cathedral Street	C2	Rope Walk	A4
Chapel Lane	B1	Rosemary Lane	D3
Charles Street West	A2	Rudgard Lane	A2
Cheviot Street	D2	St Hugh Street	D3
City Square	C3	St Mark Street	B4
Clasketgate	C3	St Martin's Street	C2
Cornhill	B4	St Mary's Street	B4
Croft Street	D3	St Rumbold's Street	C3
Danesgate	C2	Saltergate	C3
Depot Street	A3	Silver Street	C3
Drury Lane	B2	Sincil Street	C4
East Bight	C1	Spring Hill	B2
Eastgate	C1	Steep Hill	C2
Free School Lane	C3	Swan Street	C3
Friars Lane	C3	Tentercroft Street	B4
Grantham Street	C2	The Avenue	A2
Greetwellgate	D1	Thorngate	C3
Gresham Street	A2	Triton Road	A4
Guildhall Street	B3	Union Road	B1
Hampton Street	A1	Unity Square	C3
High Street	B3	Victoria Street	B2
Hungate	B3	Victoria Terrace	B2
John Street	D3	Vine Street	D2
Langworthgate	D1	Waterside North	C3
Lindum Road	C2	Waterside South	C3
Lindum Terrace	D2	Westgate	B1
Lucy Tower Street	B3	West Parade	A2
May Crescent	A1	Whitehall Grove	A2
Melville Street	C4	Wigford Way	B3
Michaelgate	C2	Winnow Sty Lane	D1
Minster Yard	C2	Winn Street	D3
Mint Lane	B3	Wragby Road	D2
Mint Street	B3	Yarborough Road	A1
Monks Road	D3	York Avenue	A1

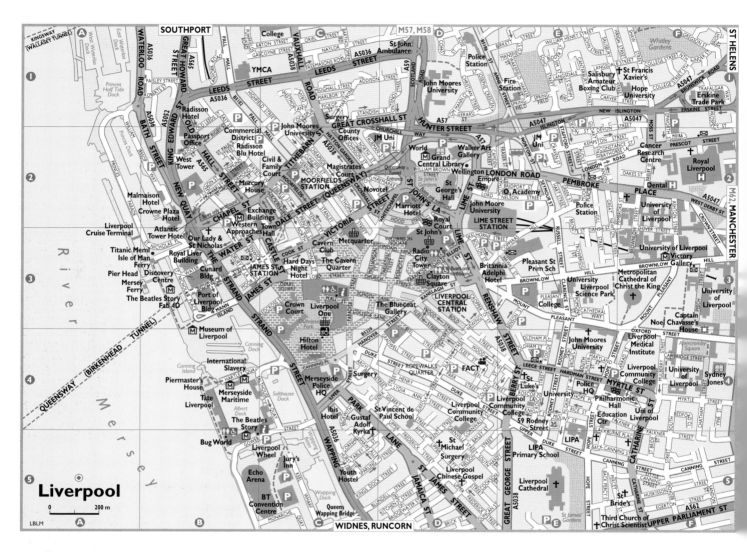

Liverpool

Liverpool is found on atlas page **81 L6**

Addison Street C1
Anson Street E2
Argyle Street C4
Arrad Street F4
Ashton Street F2
Audley Street E2
Back Canning Street E5
Baltimore Street E4
Bath Street B2
Beckwith Street C4
Bedford Street South F5
Benson Street E3
Berry Street E4
Bidder Street E1
Birkett Street D1
Bixteth Street B2
Blackburne Place E5
Blundell Street C5
Bold Street D3
Bosnett Street D3
Bridgewater Street D5
Bridport Street E2
Brook Street B2
Brownlow Hill E3
Brownlow Street F3
Brunswick Road F1
Brunswick Street B3
Cambridge Street F4
Camden Street D2
Canning Place C4
Canning Street E5
Canterbury Street E1
Carver Street E1
Castle Street C3
Catharine Street F5
Cathedral Way E3

Chapel Street B2
Chatham Street F4
Cheapside C2
Christian Street D1
Churchill Way D2
Church Street C3
Clarence Street E3
Cockspur Street C1
College Lane C3
College Street North F1
College Street South F1
Colquitt Street D4
Constance Street E1
Cook Street C3
Copperas Hill E3
Cornhill C5
Cornwallis Street D5
Craven Street E2
Cropper Street D3
Crosshall Street C2
Crown Street F2
Dale Street (Queensway) C3
Dansie Street E3
Daulby Street F2
Derby Square C3
Devon Street E2
Dover Street F3
Drury Lane B3
Duke Street D4
East Street B1
Eaton Street B1
Eberle Street C2
Edmund Street B2
Egerton Street F5
Elliot Street D3
Epworth Street F1

Erskine Street F1
Falkner Street E4
Fazakerley Street B2
Fenwick Street B3
Fleet Street D3
Fontenoy Street D1
Fraser Street E2
Gascoyne Street B1
Gilbert Street D4
Gildart Street E2
Gill Street E2
Gower Street B5
Gradwell Street D4
Great Crosshall Street C1
Great George Street E5
Great Howard Street B1
Great Newton Street E2
Greek Street E2
Gregson Street F1
Grenville Street South D5
Hackins Hey C2
Hanover Street C4
Hardman Street E4
Harker Street E1
Hartley Quay B4
Hart Street E2
Hatton Garden C2
Hawke Street E3
Henry Street D4
Highfield Street B1
Hood Street D2
Hope Place E4
Hope Street E5
Hotham Street E2
Hunter Street D1
Huskisson Street F5
Islington E2
Jamaica Street D5
James Street B3
Johnson Street C2
Keel Wharf C5

Kempston Street E2
Kent Street D5
Kinder Street F1
King Edward Street B2
Kingsway (Wallasey Tunnel) A1
Kitchen Street D5
Knight Street E4
Langsdale Street E1
Leece Street E4
Leeds Street B1
Lime Street D2
Liver Street C4
London Road D2
London Road E2
Lord Nelson Street D2
Lord Street C3
Lydia Ann Street D4
Mann Island B3
Mansfield Street E1
Marybone C1
Maryland Street E4
Midghall Street C1
Moorfields B2
Moor Street B3
Moss Street F1
Mount Pleasant E3
Mount Street E4
Mulberry Street F4
Myrtle Street E4
Naylor Street C1
Nelson Street D5
Newington D4
New Islington E1
New Quay B2
North John Street C3
Norton Street E2
Old Hall Street B2
Oldham Street E4
Old Haymarket C2
Old Leeds Street B1
Ormond Street B2

Oxford Street F4
Paisley Street B1
Pall Mall B1
Paradise Street C3
Parker Street D3
Parr Street D4
Peech Street F3
Pembroke Place E2
Pembroke Street F2
Percey Street E5
Pilgrim Street E4
Pleasant Street E3
Pomona Street E3
Prescot Street F2
Princes Parade A2
Prospect Street F1
Queensway
  (Birkenhead Tunnel) A4
Ranelagh Street D3
Redcross Street C3
Renshaw Street D3
Richmond Lane C3
Rigby Street B2
Rodney Street E4
Roscoe Street E4
Rose Hill D1
Russell Street E3
St Anne Street D1
St James Street D5
St John's Lane D2
St Josephs Crescent D1
St Nicholas Place B3
St Paul's Street B2
Salisbury Street E1
Salthouse Quay C4
Sandon Street F5
School Lane C3
Scotland Road D1
Seel Street D4
Seymour Street E2

Shaw Street F1
Sir Thomas Street C2
Skelhorne Street D2
Slater Street D4
Soho Street E1
Sparling Street C4
Springfield E2
Stafford Street C2
Stanley Street C2
Strand Street B3
Suffolk Street D5
Tabley Street D4
Tarleton Street D3
Temple Street C2
The Strand B3
Tithe Barn Street C1
Trafalgar Way E1
Trowbridge Street E3
Trueman Street C2
Upper Duke Street E5
Upper Frederick Street D4
Upper Parliament Street E5
Upper Pitt Street D4
Vauxhall Road C1
Vernon Street C2
Victoria Street C3
Wakefield Street E1
Wall Street C2
Wapping C4
Waterloo Road A1
Water Street B3
West Derby Street F2
Westmorland Drive B2
Whitechapel C3
William Brown Street D2
William Henry Street E1
William Jessop Way A2
Williamson Square D3
Williamson Street D3
Wood Street D3
York Street C4

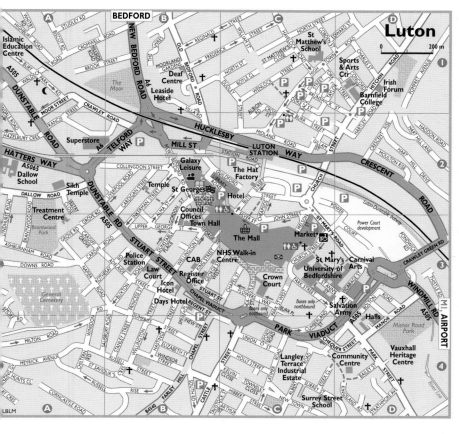

Luton

Luton is found on atlas page **50 C6**

Adelaide Street	B3	Hibbert Street	C4
Albert Road	C4	Highbury Road	A1
Alma Street	B2	High Town Road	C1
Arthur Street	C4	Hitchin Road	D1
Ashburnham Road	A3	Holly Street	C4
Biscot Road	A1	Hucklesby Way	B2
Brantwood Road	A3	Inkerman Street	B3
Brunswick Street	C1	John Street	C3
Burr Street	C2	King Street	B3
Bury Park Road	A1	Latimer Road	C4
Buxton Road	B3	Liverpool Road	B2
Cardiff Road	A3	Manor Road	D4
Cardigan Street	B2	Meyrick Avenue	A4
Castle Street	B4	Midland Road	C2
Chapel Street	B4	Mill Street	B2
Chapel Viaduct	B3	Milton Road	A4
Charles Street	D1	Moor Street	A1
Chequer Street	C4	Napier Road	A3
Chiltern Road	A4	New Bedford Road	B1
Church Street	C2	New Town Street	C4
Church Street	C3	Old Bedford Road	B1
Cobden Street	C1	Park Street	C3
Collingdon Street	B2	Park Street West	C3
Concorde Street	D1	Park Viaduct	C4
Crawley Green Road	D3	Princess Street	B3
Crawley Road	A1	Regent Street	B3
Crescent Road	D2	Reginald Street	B1
Cromwell Road	A1	Rothesay Road	A3
Cumberland Street	C4	Russell Rise	A4
Dallow Road	A2	Russell Street	B4
Dudley Street	C1	St Mary's Road	C3
Dumfries Street	B4	St Saviour's Crescent	A4
Dunstable Road	A1	Salisbury Road	A4
Farley Hill	B4	Stanley Street	B4
Flowers Way	C3	Station Road	C2
Frederick Street	B1	Strathmore Avenue	D4
George Street	B3	Stuart Street	B3
George Street West	B3	Surrey Street	C4
Gordon Street	B3	Tavistock Street	B4
Grove Road	A3	Telford Way	B2
Guildford Street	B2	Upper George Street	B3
Hart Hill Drive	D2	Vicarage Street	D3
Hart Hill Lane	D2	Waldeck Road	A1
Hartley Road	D2	Wellington Street	B4
Hastings Street	B4	Wenlock Street	C1
Hatters Way	A2	Windmill Road	D3
Havelock Road	C1	Windsor Street	B4
Hazelbury Crescent	A2	Winsdon Road	A4

Maidstone

Maidstone is found on atlas page **38 C10**

Albany Street	D1	Market Buildings	B2
Albion Place	D2	Marsham Street	C2
Allen Street	D1	Meadow Walk	D4
Ashford Road	D3	Medway Street	B3
Bank Street	B3	Melville Road	C4
Barker Road	B4	Mill Street	B3
Bedford Place	A3	Mote Avenue	D3
Bishops Way	B3	Mote Road	D3
Brewer Street	C2	Old School Place	D2
Broadway	A3	Orchard Street	C4
Broadway	B3	Padsole Lane	C3
Brunswick Street	C4	Palace Avenue	B3
Buckland Hill	A2	Princes Street	D1
Buckland Road	A2	Priory Road	C4
Camden Street	C1	Pudding Lane	B2
Chancery Lane	D3	Queen Anne Road	D2
Charles Street	A4	Reginald Road	A4
Church Street	C2	Rocky Hill	A3
College Avenue	B4	Romney Place	C3
College Road	C4	Rose Yard	B2
County Road	C1	Rowland Close	A4
Crompton Gardens	D4	St Anne Court	A2
Cromwell Road	D2	St Faith's Street	B2
Douglas Road	A4	St Luke's Avenue	D1
Earl Street	B2	St Luke's Road	D1
Elm Grove	D4	St Peters Street	A2
Fairmeadow	B1	Sandling Road	B1
Florence Road	A4	Sittingbourne Road	D1
Foley Street	D1	Square Hill Road	D3
Foster Street	C4	Stacey Street	B1
Gabriel's Hill	C3	Station Road	B1
George Street	C4	Terrace Road	A3
Greenside	D4	Tonbridge Road	A4
Hart Street	A4	Tufton Street	C2
Hastings Road	D4	Union Street	C2
Hayle Road	C4	Upper Stone Street	C4
Heathorn Street	D1	Victoria Street	A3
Hedley Street	C1	Vinters Road	D2
High Street	B3	Wat Tyler Way	C3
Holland Road	D1	Week Street	B1
James Street	C1	Well Road	C1
Jeffrey Street	C1	Westree Road	A4
King Street	C2	Wheeler Street	C1
Kingsley Road	D4	Woollett Street	C1
Knightrider Street	C4	Wyatt Street	C2
Lesley Place	A1		
London Road	A3		
Lower Stone Street	C3		

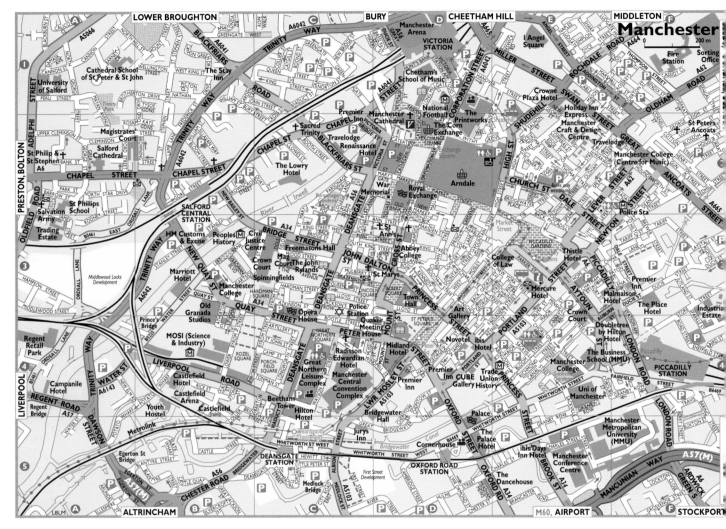

Manchester

Manchester is found on atlas page **82 H5**

Abingdon Street	E4
Addington Street	E1
Adelphi Street	A2
Albion Street	C5
Angel Street	E1
Ardwick Green South	F5
Artillery Street	C4
Atherton Street	B4
Atkinson Street	C3
Auburn Street	E4
Aytoun Street	E3
Back Piccadilly	E3
Bank Street	A2
Baring Street	F4
Barton Street	C4
Berry Street	F4
Blackfriars Road	B1
Blackfriars Street	C2
Blantyre Street	B5
Bloom Street	B2
Bloom Street	E4
Blossom Street	F2
Boad Street	F4
Boond Street	C1
Booth Street	D3
Bootle Street	C4
Brancaster Road	E5
Brazennose Street	C3
Brewer Street	F3
Bridge Street	C3
Bridgewater Place	E2
Bridgewater Street	B4
Bridgewater Viaduct	B5
Brook Street	E5
Brotherton Drive	A1
Browncross Street	B2

Browning Street	B2
Brown Street	D3
Bury Street	B1
Byrom Street	B4
Cable Street	E1
Cambridge Street	D5
Camp Street	C4
Canal Street	E4
Cannon Street	A1
Canon Green Drive	B1
Castle Street	B5
Cathedral Street	D2
Chadderton Street	F1
Chapel Street	A2
Charles Street	E5
Charlotte Street	D3
Chatham Street	E3
Cheapside	D3
Chester Road	B5
China Lane	E3
Chorlton Street	E4
Church Street	E2
City Road East	C5
Cleminson Street	A2
College Land	C2
Collier Street	C1
Commercial Street	C4
Copperas Street	E2
Cornell Street	F2
Corporation Street	D2
Cotton Street	F2
Crosskeys Street	F1
Cross Street	C2
Cross Street	D3
Dale Street	E2
Dantzic Street	D2

Dawson Street	A5
Deansgate	C4
Dickinson Street	D4
Duke Street	B4
Dulcie Street	F3
East Ordsall Lane	A3
Egerton Street	A5
Exchange Square	D2
Fairfield Street	F4
Faulkner Street	D4
Fennel Street	D1
Ford Street	A2
Fountain Street	D3
Frederick Street	B2
Garden Lane	B1
Gartside Street	B3
George Leigh Street	F2
George Street	D4
Gore Street	B2
Granby Row	E5
Gravel Lane	C1
Great Ancoats Street	F2
Great Bridgewater Street	C5
Great Ducie Street	D1
Great George Street	A2
Great Jackson Street	B5
Great John Street	B4
Greengate	C1
Greengate West	B1
Gun Street	F2
Hanover Street	D1
Hardman Street	C3
Hewitt Street	C5
High Street	D2
Hood Street	F2
Hope Street	E3
Houndsworth Street	F2
Hulme Street	D5
James Street	A3
Jersey Street	F2
John Dalton Street	C3

John Street	D1
John Street	E2
Joiner Street	E2
Jutland Street	F3
Kennedy Street	D3
King Street	C1
King Street	C3
King Street West	C3
Lamb Lane	B2
Laystall Street	F3
Left Bank	B3
Lena Street	F3
Lever Street	E2
Little Lever Street	E3
Little Peter Street	C5
Liverpool Road	B4
Lloyd Street	C3
London Road	F4
Long Millgate	D1
Longworth Street	C4
Lower Byrom Street	B4
Lower Mosley Street	C4
Lower Ormond Street	D5
Ludgate Street	E1
Major Street	E4
Mancunian Way	E5
Marble Street	D3
Market Street	D2
Marsden Street	D3
Marshall Street	E1
Mason Street	E1
Mayan Avenue	A1
Medlock Street	C5
Middlewood Street	A3
Miller Street	E1
Minshull Street	E3
Mirabel Street	C1
Mosley Street	D3
Mount Street	B1
Mount Street	D4
Museum Street	C4

Nathan Drive	B1
New Bailey Street	B2
New Bridge Street	C1
New Cathedral Street	D2
New Elm Road	A4
New George Street	E2
New Quay Street	B3
Newton Street	E3
New York Street	E3
Nicholas Street	D3
North George Street	A1
North Hill Street	A1
North Star Drive	A2
Norton Street	C1
Oldfield Road	A3
Oldham Road	F1
Oldham Street	E2
Ordsall Lane	A4
Oxford Road	D5
Oxford Street	D4
Pall Mall	D3
Parker Street	E3
Peru Street	A1
Peter Street	C4
Piccadilly	E3
Piccadilly Gardens	E3
Portland Street	D4
Port Street	F3
Potato Wharf	A5
Princess Street	D3
Quay Street	B3
Queen Street	C1
Queen Street	C3
Redhill Street	F2
Regent Road	A4
Reyner Street	D4
Rice Street	B4
Richmond Street	E4
Rochdale Road	E1
Rodney Street	A3
Rosamond Drive	A2

Sackville Street	
St Anns Square	
St Ann Street	
St James Square	
St James Street	
St Mary's Parsonage	
St Stephen Street	
Store Street	
Sharp Street	
Shudehill	
Silk Street	
Simpson Street	
South King Street	
Spear Street	
Spring Gardens	
Station Approach	
Swan Street	
Tariff Street	
Thomas Street	
Thompson Street	
Tib Lane	
Tib Street	
Todd Street	
Tonman Street	
Travis Street	
Trinity Way	
Turner Street	
Victoria Bridge Street	
Victoria Station Approach	
Victoria Street	
Warwick Street	
Watson Street	
Well Street	
West King Street	
West Mosley Street	
Whitworth Street	
Whitworth Street West	
Windmill Street	
Wood Street	
York Street	

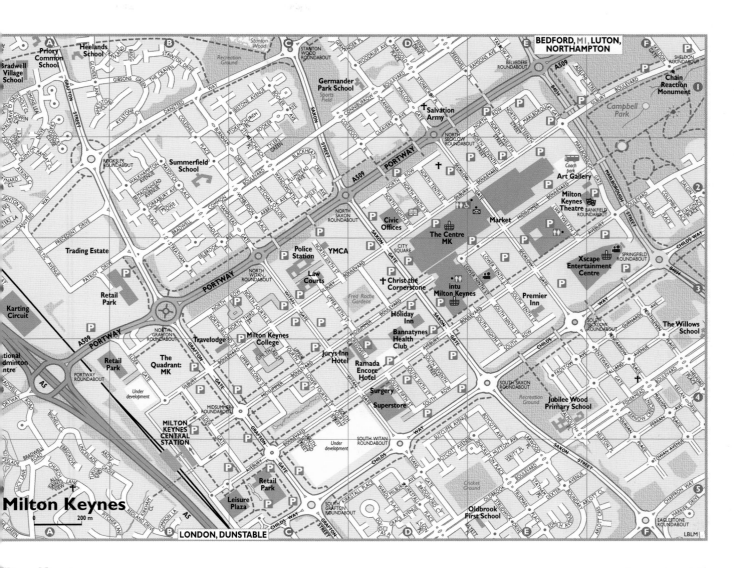

Milton Keynes

Milton Keynes is found on atlas page **49 N7**

Adelphi Street E1	Craddocks Close A1	Ibistone Avenue C1	North Saxon Roundabout C2	Silbury Roundabout B4	Tylers Green C2
Albion Place F2	Cranesbill Place D1	Kellan Drive F4	North Secklow	Simons Lea A1	Tyson Place D5
All Saints View A5	Cresswell Lane D3	Kernow Crescent F4	Roundabout D1	Skeldon Gate F1	Ulyett Place D5
Arbrook Avenue C2	Dalgin Place F2	Kirkham Close B5	North Second Street B3	South Eighth Street E3	Upper Fifth Street C3
Ardys Court A2	Dansteed Way A2	Kirkstall Place C5	North Sixth Street C3	South Fifth Street D4	Upper Fourth Street C4
Arlott Close E5	Dansteed Way B1	Larwood Place E5	North Third Street C3	South Fourth Street C4	Upper Second Street C4
Arlott Crescent F5	Deltic Avenue A3	Leasowe Place B2	North Tenth Street D2	South Grafton Roundabout C5	Upper Third Street C4
Atkins Close A2	Dexter Avenue E5	Linceslade Grove A5	North Thirteenth Street E1	South Ninth Street E3	Verity Place E5
Audley Mews A2	Douglas Place D5	Loughton Road A2	North Twelfth Street E1	South Row D4	Walgrave Drive A1
Avebury Boulevard C5	Eaglestone Roundabout F5	Lower Fourth Street C4	Oldbrook Boulevard E5	South Saxon Roundabout E4	Walkhampton Avenue B2
Bankfield Roundabout E2	Ebbsgrove A5	Lower Ninth Street E3	Overend Close A1	South Secklow Roundabout C5	Wandsworth Place C2
Belvedere Roundabout E1	Edrich Avenue E5	Lower Tenth Street E3	Padstow Avenue E4	South Second Street C5	Wardle Place D5
Bignell Close A4	Elder Gate B4	Lower Twelfth Street E2	Patriot Drive A3	South Seventh Street D4	Whetstone Close A1
Blackheath Crescent C2	Evans Gate D5	Lucy Lane A5	Pencarrow Place F3	South Sixth Street D4	Wimbledon Place C2
Booker Avenue C1	Falmouth Place E4	Maidenhead Avenue B2	Pentewan Gate F4	South Tenth Street E3	Wisely Avenue C2
Boycott Avenue D5	Fennel Drive D1	Mallow Gate D1	Perran Avenue F4	South Witan Roundabout D5	Witan Gate C4
Boycott Avenue E4	Fishermead Boulevard F4	Marigold Place D1	Pitcher Lane A5	Speedwell Place D1	Woodruff Avenue D1
Bradwell Common	Forrabury Avenue B2	Marlborough Gate E1	Plumstead Avenue C2	Springfield Roundabout F3	Yarrow Place E1
Boulevard B2	Fosters Lane A2	Marlborough Gate E2	Polruan Place F4	Stainton Drive B1	
Bradwell Road A4	Garrat Drive A3	Marlborough Street F2	Porthleven Place F3	Stanton Wood	
Bradwell Road A5	Germander Place C1	Mayditch Place B2	Portway A4	Roundabout C1	
Bridgeford Court D5	Gibsons Green B1	Maynard Close A2	Portway Roundabout A4	Statham Place E5	
Brill Place B2	Glovers Lane A1	Midsummer Boulevard C4	Precedent Drive A3	Stokenchurch Place D1	
Burnham Drive B1	Grace Avenue D5	Midsummer Boulevard E2	Quinton Drive A2	Stonecrop Place D1	
Chaffron Way F5	Grafton Gate B4	Midsummer Roundabout B4	Ramsay Close A2	Streatham Place B3	
Childs Way C5	Grafton Street A1	Milburn Avenue D5	Ramsons Avenue E1	Strudwick Drive E5	
Childs Way F3	Grafton Street C5	Mitcham Close C2	Redland Drive B5	Sutcliffe Avenue D4	
Church Lane A5	Gurnards Avenue F3	Mullion Place F4	Rooksley Roundabout A2	Talland Avenue F4	
City Square D3	Hadley Place B2	North Eighth Street D2	Rylstone Close B1	The Boundary F3	
Cleavers Avenue D1	Hampstead Gate B2	North Eleventh Street E1	Saxon Gate D2	The Close A1	
Coleshill Place B1	Harrier Drive F5	North Fourth Street C3	Saxon Street C1	The Craven B1	
Coltsfoot Place C1	Helford Place F4	North Grafton	Secklow Gate D2	The Green A5	
Columbia Place F2	Helston Place F4	Roundabout B3	Shackleton Place E5	Towan Avenue F5	
Common Lane B5	Holy Close A1	North Ninth Street D2	Sheldon Roundabout F1	Tranlands Brigg B1	
Conniburrow Boulevard C1	Hutton Avenue E5	North Row B3	Silbury Boulevard B4	Trueman Place E5	
Coppin Lane A2		North Row D2		Turvil End A5	

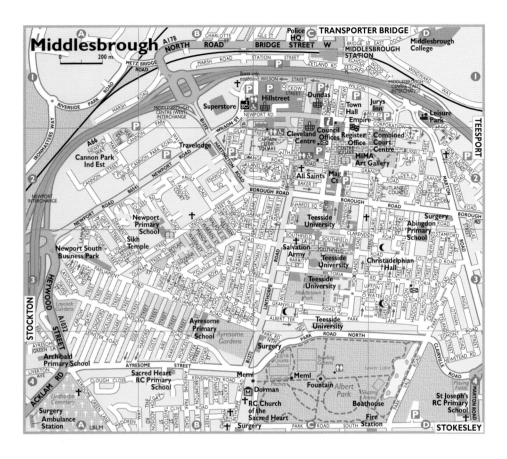

Middlesbrough

Middlesbrough is found on atlas page **104 E7**

Acklam Road	A4	Heywood Street	
Acton Street	C3	Ironmasters Way	
Aire Street	B4	Kensington Road	
Albert Road	C2	Kildare Street	
Amber Street	C2	Laurel Street	
Athol Street	B3	Lees Road	
Aubrey Street	D3	Linthorpe Road	
Ayresome Park Road	B4	Longford Street	
Ayresome Street	A4	Lorne Street	
Borough Road	C2	Lothian Road	
Bretnall Street	B2	Marsh Street	
Bridge Street East	C1	Marton Road	
Bridge Street West	C1	Melrose Street	
Bush Street	B4	Metz Bridge Road	
Cadogen Street	B3	Myrtle Street	
Camden Street	D2	Newlands Road	
Cannon Park Road	A2	Newport Road	
Cannon Park Way	A2	Palm Street	
Cannon Street	A2	Park Lane	
Carlow Street	A3	Park Road North	
Centre Square	C2	Park Vale Road	
Clairville Road	D4	Parliament Road	
Clarendon Road	C3	Pearl Street	
Clifton Street	B3	Pelham Street	
Corporation Road	D1	Portman Street	
Costa Street	B4	Princes Road	
Craven Street	B3	Riverside Park Road	
Crescent Road	A3	Ruby Street	
Croydon Road	D3	Russell Street	
Derwent Street	A2	St Pauls Road	
Diamond Road	B3	Southfield Road	
Egmont Road	D4	Station Street	
Emily Street	C2	Stowe Street	
Errol Street	D3	Tavistock Street	
Essex Street	A4	Tennyson Street	
Fairbridge Street	C2	Union Street	
Falmouth Street	D3	Victoria Road	
Finsbury Street	B3	Victoria Street	
Fleetham Street	B2	Warren Street	
Garnet Street	B2	Waterloo Road	
Glebe Road	B3	Waverley Street	
Grange Road	B2	Wembley Street	
Grange Road	D2	Wilson Street	
Granville Road	C3	Wilton Street	
Gresham Road	B3	Windsor Street	
Harewood Street	B3	Woodlands Road	
Harford Street	B4	Worcester Street	
Hartington Road	B2	Zetland Road	

Newport

Newport is found on atlas page **31 K7**

Albert Terrace	B3	Jones Street	
Allt-Yr-Yn Avenue	A2	Keynsham Avenue	
Bailey Street	B3	King Street	
Bedford Road	D2	Kingsway	
Blewitt Street	B3	Kingsway	
Bond Street	C1	Llanthewy Road	
Bridge Street	B2	Locke Street	
Bryngwyn Road	A3	Lower Dock Street	
Brynhyfryd Avenue	A4	Lucas Street	
Brynhyfryd Road	A4	Market Street	
Caerau Crescent	A4	Mellon Street	
Caerau Road	A3	Mill Street	
Cambrian Road	B2	North Street	
Caroline Street	D3	Oakfield Road	
Cedar Road	D2	Park Square	
Charles Street	C3	Pugsley Street	
Chepstow Road	D1	Queen's Hill	
Clarence Place	C1	Queen's Hill Crescent	
Clifton Place	B4	Queen Street	
Clifton Road	B4	Queensway	
Clyffard Crescent	A3	Risca Road	
Clytha Park Road	A2	Rodney Road	
Clytha Square	C4	Rudry Street	
Colts Foot Close	A1	Ruperra Lane	
Commercial Street	C4	Ruperra Street	
Corelli Street	D1	St Edward Street	
Corn Street	C2	St Julian Street	
Corporation Road	D2	St Mark's Crescent	
Devon Place	B2	St Mary Street	
Dewsland Park Road	B4	St Vincent Road	
Dumfries Place	D4	St Woolos Road	
East Street	B3	School Lane	
East Usk Road	C1	Serpentine Road	
Factory Road	B1	Skinner Street	
Fields Road	A2	Sorrel Drive	
Friars Field	B4	Spencer Road	
Friars Road	B4	Stow Hill	
Friar Street	C3	Stow Hill	
George Street	D4	Stow Park Avenue	
Godfrey Road	A2	Talbot Lane	
Gold Tops	A2	Tregare Street	
Grafton Road	C2	Tunnel Terrace	
Granville Lane	D4	Upper Dock Street	
Granville Street	D4	Upper Dock Street	
High Street	B2	Usk Way	
Hill Street	C3	Victoria Crescent	
John Frost Square	C3	West Street	
John Street	D4	York Place	

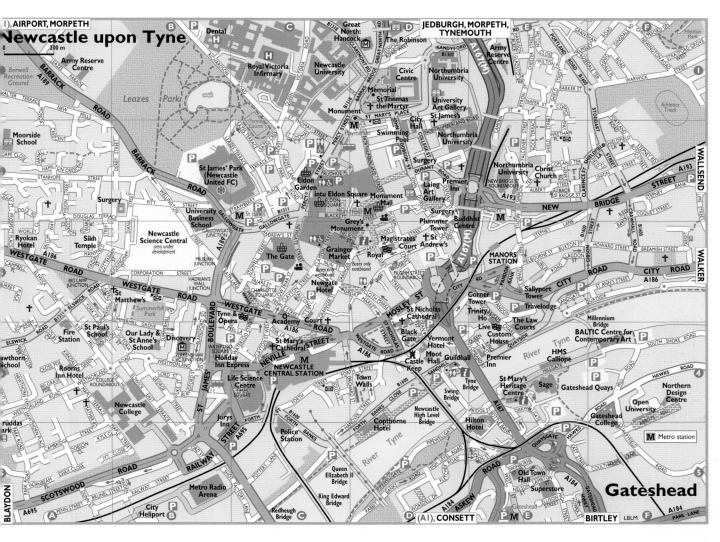

ewcastle upon Tyne

ewcastle upon Tyne is found on atlas page **113 K8**

Abbots Hill	F4	
Albert Street	E2	
Argyle Street	E2	
Askew Road	D5	
Avision Street	A2	
Back New Bridge Street	E2	
Barker Street	E1	
Barrack Road	A1	
Barras Bridge	D1	
Bath Lane	B3	
Belgrave Parade	A4	
Big Lamp Junction	A3	
Blackett Street	C2	
Blagdon Street	E3	
Blandford Square	B4	
Blandford Street	B4	
Bottle Bank	E4	
Boyd Street	F2	
Breamish Street	F3	
Bridge Street	E4	
Broad Chare	E3	
Brunel Street	A5	
Buckingham Street	B3	
Buxton Street	E3	
Byron Street	E1	
Cambridge Street	A5	
Camden Street	E2	
Campbell Place	A3	
Carliol Square	D3	
Charlotte Square	C3	
Chelmsford Green	F1	
Chester Street	E1	
City Road	E3	
Claremont Road	D1	
Clarence Street	E2	
Clayton Street	C3	

Clayton Street West	C4	
Cloth Market	D3	
Colby Court	A4	
College Roundabout	A4	
College Street	D2	
Cookson Close	A3	
Copland Terrace	E2	
Coppice Way	E1	
Coquet Street	F2	
Corporation Street	B3	
Cottenham Street	A3	
Coulthards Lane	F5	
Crawhall Road	F2	
Cross Parade	A4	
Cross Street	C3	
Darnell Place	A2	
Dean Street	D3	
Derby Street	B2	
Diana Street	B3	
Dinsdale Place	F1	
Dinsdale Road	F1	
Dobson Close	A5	
Douglas Terrace	A2	
Duke Street	B4	
Dunn Street	A5	
Durant Road	D2	
East Street	E5	
Edward Place	A3	
Eldon Square	C2	
Ellison Street	E5	
Elswick East Terrace	B4	
Elswick Road	A3	
Elswick Row	A3	
Essex Close	A5	
Falconar's Court	C3	
Falconer Street	E2	

Fenkle Street	C3	
Field Close	F2	
Fletcher Road	D5	
Forth Banks	C4	
Forth Banks Close	D5	
Forth Street	C4	
Friars Street	C3	
Gallowgate	B2	
Gallowgate Junction	B3	
Gateshead Highway	E5	
George Street	B4	
Gibson Street	F3	
Gladstone Terrace	E1	
Gloucester Terrace	A4	
Grainger Street	C3	
Grantham Road	E1	
Great North Road	D1	
Grey Street	D3	
Groat Market	C3	
Hamilton Crescent	A2	
Hanover Street	C4	
Harrison Place	E1	
Hawks Road	E5	
Hawthorn Place	A4	
Hawthorn Road	A4	
Helmsley Road	E1	
Henry Square	E1	
High Bridge	D3	
High Level Road	D5	
High Street	E5	
Hillgate	E4	
Hood Street	D3	
Hopper Street	E5	
Hornbeam Place	A5	
Houston Street	A4	
Howard Street	F3	
Hudson Street	E5	
Ivy Close	A5	
Jesmond Road West	D1	
John Dobson Street	D2	
Jubilee Road	E3	

King Edward Bridge	C5	
King Street	E4	
Kirkdale Green	A4	
Kyle Close	A5	
Lambton Street	E5	
Leazes Crescent	C2	
Leazes Lane	C2	
Leazes Park Road	C2	
Leazes Terrace	C2	
Liddle Road	A2	
Lime Street	F2	
Lombard Street	E4	
Longley Street	A2	
Lord Street	B4	
Low Friar Street	C3	
Maiden Street	B5	
Mansfield Street	A3	
Maple Street	B5	
Maple Terrace	A4	
Market Street	D3	
Mather Road	A4	
Melbourne Street	E3	
Mill Road	F4	
Milton Close	E1	
Milton Place	E1	
Monday Crescent	A1	
Mosley Street	D3	
Naper Street	E1	
Nelson Street	C3	
Nelson Street	E5	
Neville Street	C4	
New Bridge Street	E2	
Newgate Street	C3	
Newington Road	F1	
New Mills	A1	
Northumberland Road	D2	
Northumberland Street	D2	
Nun Street	C3	
Oakwellgate	E4	
Orchard Street	C4	
Ord Street	B5	

Oxford Street	D2	
Pandon	E3	
Pandon Bank	E3	
Park Lane	F5	
Park Road	A5	
Peel Lane	B4	
Penn Street	A5	
Percy Street	C2	
Pilgrim Street	D2	
Pink Lane	C4	
Pipewellgate	D5	
Pitt Street	B2	
Portland Road	E1	
Portland Road	F1	
Pottery Lane	C5	
Prospect Place	A2	
Prudhoe Place	C2	
Quarryfield Road	F5	
Quayside	E5	
Quayside	E4	
Queen Street	E4	
Queen Victoria Road	C1	
Rabbit Banks Road	D5	
Railway Street	B5	
Red Barnes	F2	
Richardson Road	B1	
Rock Terrace	E2	
Rosedale Terrace	E1	
Rye Hill	A4	
St Andrew's Street	C3	
St Ann's Street	F3	
St James' Boulevard	B4	
St Mary's Place	D1	
St Nicholas Street	D4	
St Thomas' Court	E2	
St Thomas' Street	C1	
Sandgate	E3	
Sandhill	D4	
Sandyford Road	D1	
Scotswood Road	A5	

Shieldfield Lane	F2	
Shield Street	E2	
Shot Factory Lane	B5	
Simpson Terrace	E2	
Somerset Place	A4	
South Shore Road	F4	
South Street	C4	
Stanhope Street	A2	
Stepney Bank	F2	
Stepney Lane	E3	
Stepney Road	F2	
Stoddart Street	F1	
Stowell Street	C3	
Stratford Grove West	F1	
Strawberry Place	C2	
Summerhill Grove	B3	
Summerhill Road	A3	
Summerhill Terrace	B4	
Swinburne Street	E5	
Tarset Road	F3	
Terrace Place	C2	
Thorpe Close	A2	
Tindal Street	A3	
Tower Street	E3	
Tyne Bridge	E4	
Union Street	F2	
Vallum Way	A3	
Victoria Street	B4	
Walter Terrace	A1	
Warwick Street	F1	
Waterloo Square	B4	
Waterloo Street	C4	
Wellington Street	B2	
Westgate Road	A3	
Westmorland Road	A4	
West Street	E5	
West Walls	C3	
Worley Close	A3	
Worsdell Drive	D5	
Wretham Place	E2	
York Street	A3	

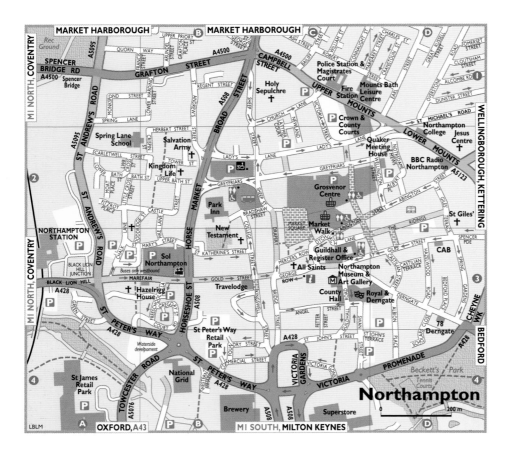

Northampton

Northampton

Northampton is found on atlas page **60 G8**

Abington Street	C2
Albert Place	D2
Albion Place	D3
Angel Street	C3
Arundel Street	B1
Ash Street	C1
Bailiff Street	C1
Black Lion Hill	A3
Bradshaw Street	B2
Bridge Street	C3
Broad Street	B1
Campbell Street	C1
Castilian Street	D3
Castle Street	B2
Chalk Lane	A3
Cheyne Walk	D3
Church Lane	C1
College Street	B2
Commercial Street	B4
Connaught Street	C1
Court Road	B3
Cranstoun Street	D1
Crispin Street	B2
Derngate	D3
Doddridge Street	A3
Drapery	C3
Dunster Street	D1
Dychurch Lane	C3
Earl Street	D1
Fetter Street	C3
Fitzroy Place	A2
Foundry Street	B4
Francis Street	A1
Freeschool Lane	B3
George Row	C3
Gold Street	B3
Grafton Street	A1
Great Russell Street	D1
Green Street	A3
Gregory Street	B3
Greyfriars	B2
Guildhall Road	C3
Hazelwood Road	D3
Herbert Street	B2
Horse Market	B3
Horseshoe Street	B3
Kingswell Street	C3
Lady's Lane	B2

Little Cross Street	
Lower Bath Street	
Lower Cross Street	
Lower Harding Street	
Lower Mounts	
Marefair	
Margaret Street	
Market Square	
Mercers Row	
Moat Place	
Monkspond Street	
Newland	
Notredame Mews	
Overstone Road	
Pike Lane	
Quorn Way	
Regent Street	
Robert Street	
St Andrew's Road	
St Andrew's Street	
St Giles Street	
St Giles' Terrace	
St John's Street	
St Katherine's Street	
St Mary's Street	
St Michael's Road	
St Peter's Way	
Scarletwell Street	
Scholars Close	
Sheep Street	
Sheep Street	
Spencer Bridge Road	
Spencer Parade	
Spring Gardens	
Spring Lane	
Swan Street	
Tanner Street	
The Ridings	
Towcester Road	
Tower Street	
Upper Bath Street	
Upper Mounts	
Upper Priory Street	
Victoria Gardens	
Victoria Promenade	
Victoria Street	
Wellington Street	
Western Wharf	

Norwich

Norwich is found on atlas page **77 J10**

All Saints Green	B4
Bank Plain	C2
Barn Road	A1
Bedding Lane	C1
Bedford Street	B2
Ber Street	C4
Bethel Street	A3
Bishopgate	D1
Brigg Street	B3
Calvert Street	B1
Castle Meadow	C2
Cathedral Street	D2
Cattle Market Street	C3
Chantry Road	B3
Chapelfield East	A3
Chapelfield North	A3
Chapelfield Road	A3
Cleveland Road	A3
Colegate	B1
Convent Road	A3
Coslany Street	B2
Cow Hill	A2
Davey Place	B3
Dove Street	B2
Duke Street	B1
Elm Hill	C2
Exchange Street	B2
Farmers Avenue	C3
Ferry Lane	D2
Fishergate	C1
Friars Quay	B1
Gentlemans Walk	B3
Goldenball Street	C3
Grapes Hill	A2
Haymarket	B3
Heigham Street	A1
King Street	C2
London Street	B2
Lower Goat Lane	B2
Magdalen Street	C1
Market Avenue	C3
Mills Yard	A1
Mountergate	D3
Music House Lane	D4
Muspole Street	B1
Norfolk Street	A4
Oak Street	A1
Palace Street	C1

Pottergate	
Prince of Wales Road	
Princes Street	
Quay Side	
Queens Road	
Queen Street	
Rampant Horse Street	
Recorder Road	
Red Lion Street	
Riverside Road	
Riverside Walk	
Rose Lane	
Rouen Road	
Rupert Street	
St Andrews Street	
St Benedicts Street	
St Faiths Lane	
St Georges Street	
St Giles Street	
St Julians Alley	
St Marys Plain	
St Peters Street	
St Stephens Road	
St Stephens Square	
St Stephens Street	
St Swithins Road	
St Verdast Street	
Surrey Street	
Ten Bell Lane	
Theatre Street	
Thorn Lane	
Tombland	
Unicorn Yard	
Union Street	
Unthank Road	
Upper Goat Lane	
Upper King Street	
Upper St Giles Street	
Vauxhall Street	
Walpole Street	
Wensum Street	
Wessex Street	
Westlegate	
Westwick Street	
Wherry Road	
Whitefriars	
White Lion Street	
Willow Lane	

Norwich

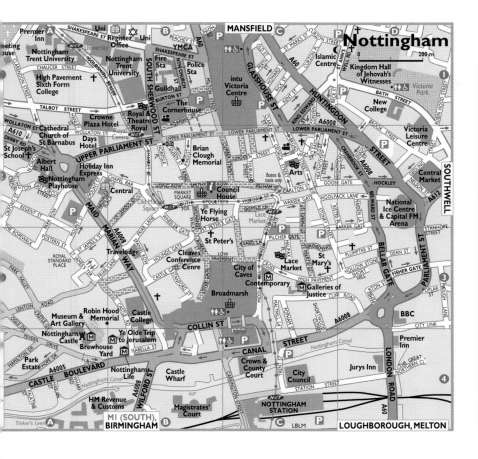

Nottingham

Nottingham is found on atlas page **72 F3**

Albert Street	B3	Lenton Road	A3
Barker Gate	D2	Lincoln Street	C2
Bath Street	D1	Lister Gate	B3
Bellar Gate	D3	London Road	D4
Belward Street	D2	Long Row	B2
Broad Street	C2	Lower Parliament Street	C2
Broadway	C3	Low Pavement	B3
Bromley Place	A2	Maid Marian Way	A2
Brook Street	D1	Market Street	B2
Burton Street	B1	Middle Hill	C3
Canal Street	C4	Milton Street	B1
Carlton Street	C2	Mount Street	A3
Carrington Street	C4	Norfolk Place	B2
Castle Boulevard	A4	North Circus Street	A2
Castle Gate	B3	Park Row	A3
Castle Road	B3	Parliament Street	D3
Chapel Bar	B2	Pelham Street	C2
Chaucer Street	A1	Peveril Drive	A4
Clarendon Street	A1	Pilcher Gate	C3
Cliff Road	C3	Popham Street	C3
Collin Street	B4	Poultry	B2
Cranbrook Street	D2	Queen Street	B2
Cumber Street	C2	Regent Street	A2
Curzon Place	C1	St Ann's Well Road	D1
Derby Road	A2	St James's Street	A3
Exchange Walk	B2	St Marks Gate	C3
Fisher Gate	D3	St Marks Street	C1
Fletcher Gate	C3	St Mary's Gate	C3
Forman Street	B1	St Peter's Gate	B3
Friar Lane	A3	Shakespeare Street	A1
Gedling Street	D2	Smithy Row	B2
George Street	C2	South Parade	B2
Glasshouse Street	C1	South Sherwood Street	B1
Goldsmith Street	A1	Spaniel Row	B3
Goose Gate	C2	Station Street	C4
Halifax Place	C3	Stoney Street	C2
Heathcote Street	C2	Talbot Street	A1
High Cross Street	C2	Thurland Street	C2
High Pavement	C3	Trent Street	C4
Hockley	D2	Upper Parliament Street	A2
Hollow Stone	D3	Victoria Street	C2
Hope Drive	A4	Warser Gate	C2
Hounds Gate	B3	Weekday Cross	C3
Howard Street	C1	Wellington Circus	A2
Huntingdon Street	C1	Wheeler Gate	B2
Kent Street	C1	Wilford Street	B4
King Edward Street	C1	Wollaton Street	A1
King Street	B2	Woolpack Lane	C2

Oldham

Oldham is found on atlas page **83 K4**

Ascroft Street	B3	Napier Street East	A4
Bar Gap Road	B1	New Radcliffe Street	A2
Barlow Street	D4	Oldham Way	A3
Barn Street	B3	Park Road	B4
Beever Street	D2	Park Street	A4
Bell Street	D2	Peter Street	B3
Belmont Street	B1	Prince Street	D3
Booth Street	A3	Queen Street	C3
Bow Street	C3	Radcliffe Street	B1
Brook Street	D2	Raleigh Close	B1
Brunswick Street	B3	Ramsden Street	A1
Cardinal Street	C2	Regent Street	D2
Chadderton Way	A1	Rhodes Bank	C3
Chaucer Street	B3	Rhodes Street	C2
Clegg Street	C3	Rifle Street	B1
Coldhurst Street	B1	Rochdale Road	A1
Crossbank Street	B4	Rock Street	B2
Curzon Street	B2	Roscoe Street	C3
Dunbar Street	A1	Ruskin Street	A1
Eden Street	B2	St Hilda's Drive	A1
Egerton Street	C2	St Marys Street	B1
Emmott Way	C4	St Mary's Way	B2
Firth Street	C3	Shaw Road	D1
Fountain Street	B2	Shaw Street	C1
Franklin Street	B1	Siddall Street	C1
Gower Street	D2	Silver Street	B3
Grange Street	A2	Southgate Street	C3
Greaves Street	C3	South Hill Street	D4
Greengate Street	D4	Spencer Street	D2
Hardy Street	D4	Sunfield Road	B1
Harmony Street	C4	Thames Street	D1
Henshaw Street	B2	Trafalgar Street	A1
Higginshaw Road	C1	Trinity Street	B1
Highfield Street	A2	Tulbury Street	A1
High Street	B3	Union Street	B3
Hobson Street	B3	Union Street West	A4
Hooper Street	D4	Union Street West	B3
Horsedge Street	C1	University Way	B4
John Street	A3	Wallshaw Street	D2
King Street	B3	Wall Street	B4
Lemnos Street	D2	Ward Street	A1
Malby Street	C1	Waterloo Street	C3
Malton Street	A4	Wellington Street	B4
Manchester Street	A3	West End Street	A2
Market Place	B3	West Street	B3
Marlborough Street	C4	Willow Street	D2
Middleton Road	A3	Woodstock Street	C4
Mortimer Street	D1	Yorkshire Street	C3

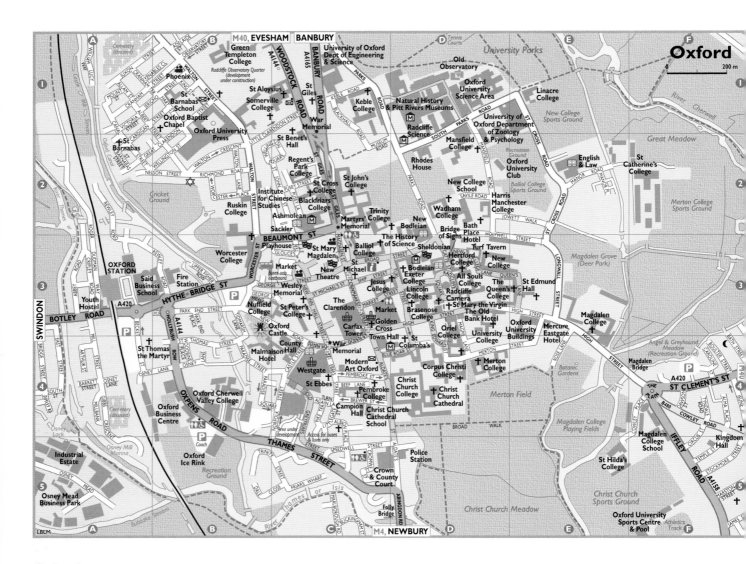

Oxford

Oxford is found on atlas page **34 F3**

Abbey Road	A3
Abingdon Road	D5
Adelaide Street	B1
Albert Street	A1
Albion Place	C4
Allam Street	A1
Alma Place	F4
Arthur Street	A4
Banbury Road	C1
Barrett Street	A4
Bath Street	F4
Beaumont Street	C3
Becket Street	A3
Beef Lane	C4
Blackhall Road	C1
Blue Boar Street	C4
Bonn Square	C4
Botley Road	A3
Boulter Street	F4
Brewer Street	C4
Bridge Street	A4
Broad Street	C3
Broad Walk	D4
Buckingham Street	C5
Canal Street	A1
Cardigan Street	A2
Caroline Street	F4
Castle Street	C4
Catte Street	D3
Circus Street	F5
Cornmarket Street	C3
Cowley Place	F4
Cowley Road	F4
Cranham Street	A1
Cranham Terrace	A1
Cripley Road	A3

Cromwell Street	C5
Dale Close	B5
Dawson Street	F4
East Street	A4
Folly Bridge	C5
Friars Wharf	C5
George Street	B3
George Street Mews	B3
Gibbs Crescent	A4
Gloucester Street	C3
Great Clarendon Street	A2
Hart Street	B1
High Street	D3
High Street	E4
Hollybush Row	B3
Holywell Street	D2
Hythe Bridge Street	B3
Iffley Road	F4
James Street	F5
Jericho Street	A1
Jowett Walk	D2
Juxon Street	A1
Keble Road	C1
King Edward Street	D3
King Street	B1
Little Clarendon Street	B2
Littlegate Street	C4
Longwall Street	E3
Magdalen Bridge	E4
Magdalen Street	C3
Magpie Lane	D3
Manor Place	E2
Manor Road	E2
Mansfield Road	D2
Market Street	C3
Marlborough Road	C5

Marston Street	F5
Merton Street	D4
Millbank	A4
Mill Street	A4
Mount Street	A1
Museum Road	C2
Nelson Street	A2
New College Lane	D3
New Inn Hall Street	C3
New Road	B3
Norfolk Street	C4
Observatory Street	B1
Old Greyfriars Street	C4
Osney Lane	A4
Osney Lane	B4
Osney Mead	A5
Oxpens Road	B4
Paradise Square	B4
Paradise Street	B4
Park End Street	B3
Parks Road	C1
Parks Road	D2
Pembroke Street	C4
Pike Terrace	C4
Pusey Lane	C2
Pusey Street	C2
Queen's Lane	D3
Queen Street	C4
Radcliffe Square	D3
Rewley Road	A2
Rewley Road	B3
Richmond Road	B2
Roger Dudman Way	A3
Rose Lane	E4
St Aldate's	C4
St Aldate's	D5

St Barnabas Street	A2
St Clement's Street	F4
St Cross Road	E1
St Cross Road	E2
St Ebbes Street	C4
St Giles	C2
St John Street	C2
St Michael's Street	C3
St Thomas' Street	B4
Savile Road	D2
Ship Street	C3
South Parks Road	D2
South Street	A4
Speedwell Street	C5
Stockmore Street	F5
Temple Street	F5
Thames Street	C5
The Plain	F4
Tidmarsh Lane	B3
Trinity Street	B5
Turl Street	D3
Turn Again Lane	C4
Tyndale Road	F4
Upper Fisher Row	B3
Venables Close	A1
Victoria Street	A1
Walton Crescent	B2
Walton Lane	B2
Walton Street	B1
Wellington Square	B2
Wellington Street	B2
William Lucy Way	A1
Woodbine Place	B4
Woodstock Road	C1
Worcester Place	B2
Worcester Street	B3

University Colleges

All Souls College	D3
Balliol College	C3
Brasenose College	D3
Christ Church College	D4
Corpus Christi College	D4
Exeter College	D3
Harris Manchester College	D2
Hertford College	D3
Jesus College	C3
Keble College	C1
Linacre College	E1
Lincoln College	D3
Magdalen College	E3
Mansfield College	D2
Merton College	D4
New College	D3
Nuffield College	B3
Oriel College	D3
Pembroke College	C4
Ruskin College	B2
St Catherine's College	F2
St Cross College	C2
St Hilda's College	E5
St John's College	C2
St Peter's College	C3
Somerville College	B1
The Queen's College	D3
Trinity College	C2
University College	D3
Wadham College	D2
Worcester College	B3

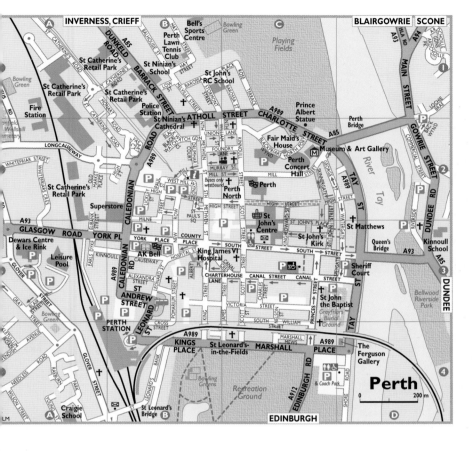

Perth

Perth is found on atlas page **134 E3**

Albert Place	B3	Marshall Place	C4
Alexandra Street	B3	Melville Street	B1
Ardchoille Park	D1	Mill Street	B2
Atholl Street	B1	Mill Street	C2
Back Wynd	D2	Milne Street	B2
Balhousie Street	B1	Monart Road	A1
Barossa Place	B1	Murray Street	B2
Barrack Street	B1	Needless Road	A4
Blackfriars Wynd	C2	New Row	B3
Black Watch Garden	B2	North Methven Street	B2
Caledonian Road	B2	North Port	C2
Caledonian Road	B3	North William Street	B2
Canal Street	C3	Old Market Place	A2
Cavendish Avenue	A4	Paul Street	B2
Charles Street	C3	Perth Bridge	D2
Charlotte Street	C2	Pickletullum Road	A4
Charterhouse Lane	B3	Pomarium Street	B3
Commercial Street	D2	Princes Street	C3
County Place	B3	Queen's Bridge	D3
Cross Street	B4	Raeburn Park	A4
Dundee Road	D3	Riggs Road	A2
Dunkeld Road	B1	Riverside	D3
Earls Dyke	A3	Rose Terrace	C1
Edinburgh Road	C4	St Andrew Street	B3
Elibank Street	A3	St Catherine's Road	A1
Feus Road	A2	St John's Place	C3
Foundry Lane	B2	St John Street	C3
George Street	C2	St Leonard's Bank	B4
Glasgow Road	A3	St Paul's Square	B2
Glover Street	A3	Scott Street	C3
Glover Street	A4	Shore Road	D4
Gowrie Street	D2	Skinnergate	C2
Gray Street	A3	South Methven Street	B2
Hay Street	B1	South Street	C3
High Street	B2	South William Street	C4
High Street	C2	Speygate	D3
Hospital Street	B3	Stormont Street	B1
Isla Road	D1	Tay Street	D2
James Street	C3	Tay Street	D4
King Edward Street	C3	Union Lane	B2
Kings Place	B4	Victoria Street	C3
King Street	B3	Watergate	D2
Kinnoull Causeway	A3	West Mill Wynd	B2
Kinnoull Street	C2	Whitefriars Crescent	A2
Leonard Street	B3	Whitefriar Street	A2
Lochie Brae	D1	Wilson Street	A4
Longcauseway	A2	York Place	A3
Main Street	D1	York Place	B3

Peterborough

Peterborough is found on atlas page **74 C11**

Albert Place	B3	New Road	C1
Bishop's Road	C3	Northminster	C1
Boongate	D1	North Street	B1
Bourges Boulevard	A1	Oundle Road	B4
Bridge Street	B3	Park Road	B1
Bright Street	A1	Peet Street	B1
Broadway	B2	Pipe Lane	D2
Brook Street	C1	Priestgate	A2
Cathedral Square	B2	Rivergate	B3
Cattle Market Street	B1	River Lane	A2
Chapel Street	C1	Russell Street	A1
Church Street	B2	St John's Street	C2
Church Walk	C1	St Peters Road	B3
City Road	C2	South Street	D2
Cowgate	B2	Star Road	D2
Craig Street	B1	Station Road	A2
Crawthorne Road	C1	Thorpe Lea Road	A3
Cromwell Road	A1	Thorpe Road	A2
Cross Street	B2	Trinity Street	B3
Cubitt Way	B4	Viersen Platz	B3
Deacon Street	A1	Vineyard Road	C3
Dickens Street	D1	Wake Road	D2
Eastfield Road	D1	Wareley Road	A4
Eastgate	D2	Wellington Street	D1
East Station Road	C4	Wentworth Street	B3
Embankment Road	C3	Westgate	A1
Exchange Street	B2		
Fengate Close	D2		
Field Walk	D1		
Fitzwilliam Street	B1		
Frank Perkins Parkway	D4		
Geneva Street	B1		
Gladstone Street	A1		
Granby Street	C2		
Hawksbill Way	B4		
Hereward Close	D2		
Hereward Road	D2		
King Street	B2		
Laxton Square	C2		
Lea Gardens	A3		
Lincoln Road	B1		
London Road	B4		
Long Causeway	B2		
Manor House Street	B1		
Mayor's Walk	A1		
Midgate	B2		
Morris Street	D1		
Nene Street	D2		

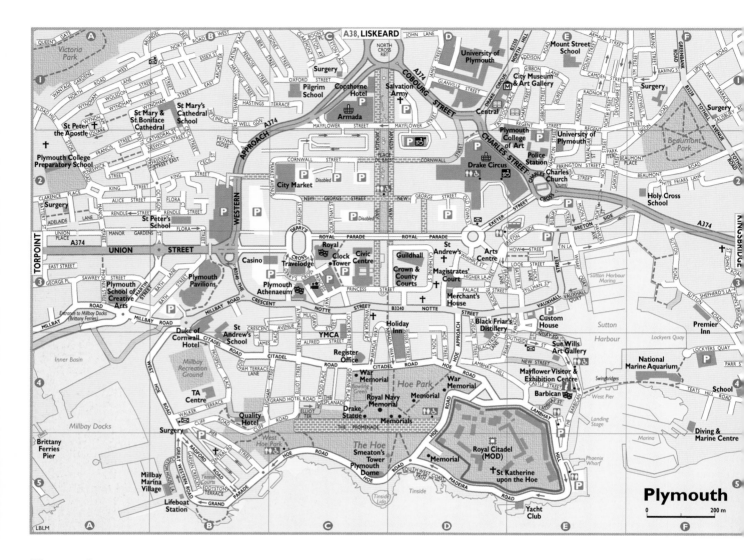

Plymouth

Plymouth is found on atlas page **6 D8**

Addison Road	E1
Adelaide Lane	A2
Alfred Street	C4
Alice Street	A2
Anstis Street	A2
Archer Terrace	B1
Armada Street	E1
Armada Way	C2
Armada Way	C4
Arundel Crescent	A1
Athenaeum Street	C3
Baring Street	F1
Bath Lane	B3
Bath Street	B3
Batter Street	E3
Battery Street	A2
Beaumont Avenue	F1
Beaumont Place	E2
Beaumont Road	F2
Bilbury Street	E2
Blackfriars Lane	D4
Boon's Place	C1
Breton Side	D3
Buckwell Street	D3
Camden Street	E1
Castle Street	E4
Cathedral Street	A2
Catherine Street	D3
Cecil Street	B1
Central Road	B5
Chapel Street	E1
Charles Cross	E2
Charles Street	D2
Citadel Road	B4
Citadel Road	C4
Claremont Street	C1

Clarence Place	A2
Cliff Road	B4
Cobourg Street	D1
Cornwall Street	C2
Courtenay Street	C3
Crescent Avenue	B3
Custom House Lane	B5
Derry's Cross	C3
Devonshire Street	E1
Drake Circus	D1
East Street	A3
Ebrington Street	E2
Eddystone Terrace	B5
Eldad Hill	A1
Elliot Street	C4
Elliot Terrace	C4
Essex Street	B1
Eton Avenue	C1
Eton Place	C1
Exeter Street	D2
Flora Court	B2
Flora Street	B2
Francis Street	A2
Frederick Street East	B2
Friar's Parade	D4
Garden Crescent	B5
Gasking Street	E2
George Place	A3
Gibbon Lane	E1
Gibbons Street	E1
Gilwell Street	E1
Glanville Street	D1
Grand Hotel Road	C4
Grand Parade	B5
Great Western Road	B5
Greenbank Road	F1

Hampton Street	E2
Harwell Street	B1
Hastings Street	B1
Hastings Terrace	B1
Hawkers Avenue	E2
Hetling Close	B1
Hicks Lane	E3
Higher Lane	D3
Hill Street	E2
Hoe Approach	D4
Hoegate Street	D3
Hoe Road	C5
Hoe Street	D3
Holyrood Place	C4
How Street	E3
Ilbert Street	B1
James Street	D1
John Lane	D1
King Street	A2
Ladywell Place	F1
Lambhay Hill	D4
Lambhay Street	E4
Leigham Street	B4
Leigham Terrace Lane	B4
Lipson Road	F1
Lockyers Quay	F4
Lockyer Street	C3
Looe Street	E3
Madeira Road	D5
Manor Gardens	A3
Manor Street	A2
Market Avenue	C2
Martin Street	A3
Mayflower Street	C1
Mayflower Street	D1
May Terrace	F1

Millbay Road	A3
Moon Street	E2
Mount Street	E1
Mulgrave Street	C3
Neswick Street	A2
New George Street	C2
New Street	E4
North Cross Roundabout	C1
North Hill	E1
North Road West	A1
North Street	E2
Notte Street	C3
Octagon Street	B2
Old Town Street	D2
Osborne Place	C4
Oxford Street	C1
Palace Street	D3
Park Terrace	E2
Parr Street	F4
Patna Place	B1
Peacock Lane	D3
Penrose Street	B1
Phoenix Street	A3
Pier Street	B5
Place de Brest	C2
Plym Street	F1
Princess Street	C3
Princess Way	C3
Prospect Place	B4
Prynne Close	B2
Quay Road	E4
Queen's Gate	A1
Radford Road	B5
Radnor Place	E1
Radnor Street	E1
Raleigh Street	C2

Regent Street	E1
Rendle Street	A2
Royal Parade	C3
St James Place	B4
St John's Bridge Road	F3
St John's Road	F3
Salisbury Road	F1
Sawrey Street	A3
Shepherd's Lane	F3
Southside Street	D4
South West Coast Path	D5
Stillman Street	E3
Stoke Road	A2
Sussex Street	D3
Sutton Road	F3
Sydney Street	B1
Tavistock Place	D1
Teats Hill Road	F4
The Barbican	E4
The Crescent	B3
The Esplanade	C4
The Promenade	C4
Tin Lane	E3
Tothill Avenue	F1
Tothill Road	F2
Trafalgar Street	E2
Union Place	A3
Union Street	A3
Vauxhall Quay	E3
Vauxhall Street	E3
Walker Terrace	B4
Wantage Gardens	A1
Well Garden	B1
Western Approach	B2
West Hoe Road	A4
Wharf Quay	E3

Whimple Street	D
White Friars Lane	F
Windsor Place	C
Wolsdon Street	A
Wyndham Lane	A
Wyndham Mews	A
Wyndham Square	A
Wyndham Street East	A
Zion Street	D

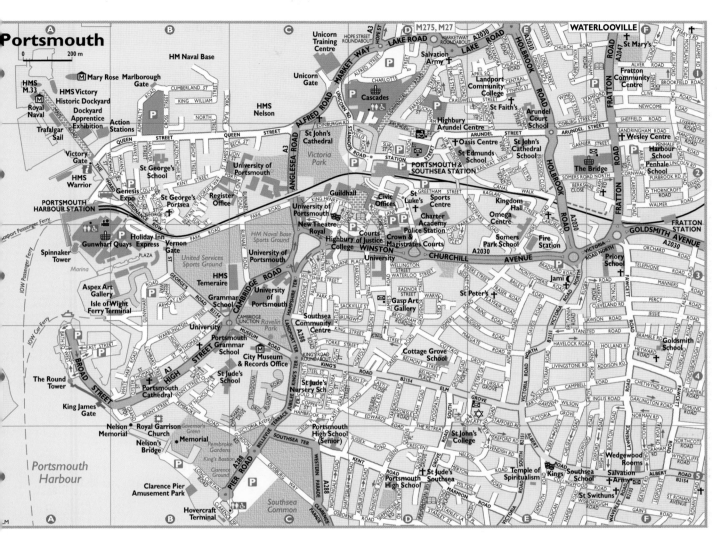

Portsmouth

Portsmouth is found on atlas page **14 H7**

Addison Road	F4	Cavendish Road	E5	Foster Road	E1
Admiralty Road	B2	Central Street	E1	Fratton Road	F2
Albany Road	E5	Charlotte Street	D1	Gain's Road	F5
Albert Grove	E5	Chelsea Road	E5	Garnier Street	E2
Albert Road	E5	Chester Place	E5	Goldsmith Avenue	F3
Alec Rose Lane	D3	Chetwynd Road	F4	Gold Street	C4
Alexandra Road	E1	Church Road	E1	Goodwood Road	E5
Alfred Road	C1	Claremont Road	F2	Gordon Road	C5
Alfred Street	D1	Clarence Parade	C5	Great Southsea Street	C4
Alver Road	F1	Cleveland Road	F3	Green Road	D4
Anglesea Road	C2	Clive Road	F1	Greetham Street	D2
Ariel Road	F2	Clock Street	B2	Grosvenor Street	D3
Armory Lane	B3	College Street	B2	Grove Road North	D4
Arundel Street	D2	Collingwood Road	E5	Grove Road South	D5
Arundel Street	E2	Commercial Road	D1	Guildford Road	F1
Ashburton Road	D5	Cornwall Road	F2	Guildhall Walk	C2
Bailey's Road	E3	Cottage Grove	D4	Gunwharf Road	B3
Bath Square	A4	Cottage View	E2	Hambrook Street	C4
Bellevue Terrace	C5	Crasswell Street	D1	Hampshire Terrace	C3
Belmont Place	D4	Cross Street	B2	Harold Road	F5
Bishop Street	B2	Cumberland Street	B1	Havant Street	B2
Blackfriars Road	E2	Curzon Howe Road	B2	Havelock Road	E4
Blount Road	C4	Darlington Road	F4	Hawke Street	B2
Boulton Road	F5	Drummond Road	E1	Hereford Road	E5
Bramble Road	F4	Duisburg Way	C5	Highbury Street	B4
Brideside Close	E2	Duncan Road	E5	High Street	B4
Britain Street	B2	Earlsdon Street	D3	Holbrook Road	E1
Broad Street	A4	East Street	A4	Holland Road	F4
Brookfield Road	F1	Edinburgh Road	C2	Hudson Road	E3
Brunswick Street	C3	Eldon Street	D4	Hyde Park Road	D3
Buckingham Street	D1	Elm Grove	D4	Inglis Road	F4
Cambridge Road	C3	Elphinstone Road	D5	Jessie Road	F3
Campbell Road	E4	Exmouth Road	E5	Jubilee Terrace	C4
Canal Walk	E2	Fawcett Road	F3	Kent Road	C4
Carlisle Road	E2	Fawcett Road	F4	Kent Street	B2
Castle Road	C4	Flint Street	C4	King Albert Street	E1
				King Henry I Street	C2
				King's Road	C4
				King's Terrace	C4
				King Street	C4
				King William Street	B1

Lake Road	D1	Palmerston Road	D5	Stamford Street	E1
Landport Street	E1	Paradise Street	D1	Stanhope Road	D2
Landport Terrace	C3	Park Road	B3	Stansted Road	E4
Landsdowne Street	C3	Pelham Road	D4	Station Street	D2
Lawrence Road	F5	Pembroke Road	B4	Steel Street	C4
Lawson Road	F3	Penhale Road	F2	Stone Street	C4
Leopold Street	F5	Penny Street	B4	Sussex Road	D5
Lincoln Road	F2	Percy Road	F3	Sutherland Road	F4
Little Southsea Street	C4	Pier Road	C5	Talbot Road	F4
Livingstone Road	E4	Playfair Road	E3	Telephone Road	F3
Lombard Street	B4	Portland Road	D5	Temple Street	D1
Londesborough Road	F4	Purbrook Road	F2	The Hard	A2
Lords Street	E1	Queens Crescent	D5	The Retreat	D5
Lorne Road	F4	Queen Street	B2	The Thicket	D4
Main Road	A1	Raglan Street	E2	Thorncroft Road	F2
Manners Road	F3	Railway View	D1	Tottenham Road	F1
Margate Road	D4	Richmond Place	D5	Trevor Road	F4
Market Way	C1	Rivers Street	D3	Unicorn Road	C1
Marmion Road	D5	Rugby Road	E3	Upper Arundel Street	D2
Mary Rose Street	D2	Sackville Street	C3	Victoria Avenue	C5
Melbourne Place	C3	St Andrews Road	E4	Victoria Grove	E4
Merton Road	D5	St Bartholomews Gardens	E4	Victoria Road North	E4
Middle Street	D3	St Davids Road	D4	Victoria Road North	F3
Milford Road	E2	St Edwards Road	D4	Victoria Road South	E5
Montgomerie Road	E3	St Faith's Road	D1	Vivash Road	F2
Moorland Road	F1	St George's Road	B3	Walmer Road	F2
Museum Road	C4	St George's Square	B2	Warblington Street	B4
Napier Road	E5	St George's Way	B2	Warwick Crescent	D3
Nelson Road	D5	St James's Road	D3	Waterloo Street	D3
Newcome Road	F1	St James's Street	B2	Waverley Road	F5
Nightingale Road	C5	St Nicholas Street	B4	Western Parade	C5
Norfolk Street	D4	St Paul's Road	C3	West Street	A4
Norman Road	F4	St Peters Grove	E4	White Hart Road	B4
Olinda Street	F1	St Thomas's Street	B4	Wilson Grove	E4
Orchard Road	F3	Sandringham Road	F2	Wiltshire Street	C3
Ordnance Row	B2	Shaftesbury Road	C5	Winston Churchill Avenue	D3
Osborne Road	C5	Somers Road	D4	Wisborough Road	E5
Outram Road	E4	Somers Road	E3	Woodpath	D4
Oxford Road	F5	Somers Road North	E3	Woodville Drive	C4
Oyster Street	B4	Southsea Terrace	C5	Yarborough Road	D4
Pains Road	E3	Stafford Road	E4	Yorke Street	C4

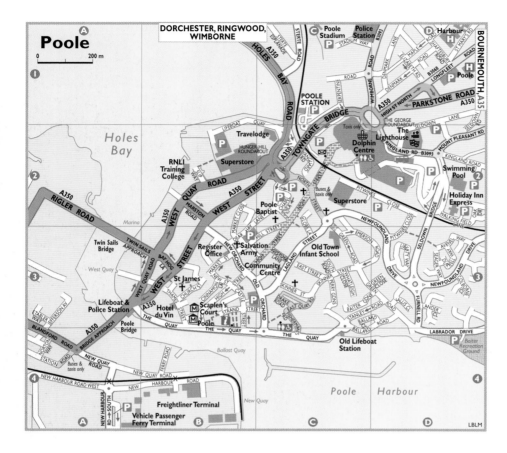

Poole

Poole is found on atlas page **12 H6**

Avenel Way	D3	New Orchard	
Baiter Gardens	C3	New Quay Road	
Ballard Close	C3	New Street	
Ballard Road	C4	North Street	
Bay Hog Lane	B3	Norton Way	
Blandford Road	A3	Oak Drive	
Bridge Approach	A4	Old Orchard	
Castle Street	B3	Parkstone Road	
Chapel Lane	C2	Perry Gardens	
Church Street	B3	Pitwines Close	
Cinnamon Lane	B3	Poole Bridge	
Colborne Close	D3	Rigler Road	
Dear Hay Lane	B3	St Mary's Road	
Denmark Lane	D1	Seager Way	
Denmark Road	D1	Seldown Bridge	
Drake Road	C3	Seldown Lane	
Durrell Way	D3	Seldown Road	
East Quay Road	C3	Serpentine Road	
East Street	C3	Shaftesbury Road	
Elizabeth Road	D1	Skinner Street	
Emerson Road	C3	Slip Way	
Ferry Road	B4	South Road	
Fisherman's Road	C3	Stabler Way	
Furnell Road	D3	Stadium Way	
Globe Lane	C2	Stanley Road	
Green Close	D3	Sterte Esplanade	
Green Road	C3	Sterte Road	
High Street	B3	Strand Street	
High Street North	D1	Thames Street	
Hill Street	C3	The Quay	
Holes Bay Road	C1	Towngate Bridge	
Jefferson Avenue	A3	Twin Sails Approach	
Kingland Road	D2	Twin Sails Bridge	
Labrador Drive	D4	Vallis Close	
Lagland Street	C3	Vanguard Road	
Lander Close	D3	Walking Field Lane	
Liberty Way	D3	Westons Lane	
Lifeboat Quay	B2	West Quay Road	
Longfleet Road	D1	West Street	
Maple Road	D1	Whatleigh Close	
Market Close	B2	Wimborne Road	
Market Street	B3		
Marston Road	B2		
Mount Pleasant Road	D2		
Newfoundland Drive	C2		
New Harbour Road	A4		
New Harbour Road South	A4		
New Harbour Road West	A4		

Preston

Preston is found on atlas page **88 G5**

Adelphi Street	A1	Holstein Street	
Arthur Street	A3	Hopwood Street	
Avenham Lane	C4	Jutland Street	
Avenham Road	C3	Lancaster Road	
Avenham Street	C3	Lancaster Road North	
Berwick Road	C4	Latham Street	
Birley Street	C2	Lawson Street	
Boltons Court	C3	Leighton Street	
Bow Lane	A3	Lund Street	
Butler Street	B3	Lune Street	
Cannon Street	C3	Main Sprit Weind	
Carlisle Street	C2	Manchester Road	
Chaddock Street	C4	Market Street	
Chapel Street	B3	Market Street West	
Charlotte Street	D4	Marsh Lane	
Cheapside	C3	Maudland Road	
Christ Church Street	A3	Meadow Street	
Church Street	C3	Moor Lane	
Clarendon Street	D4	Mount Street	
Corporation Street	B2	North Road	
Corporation Street	B3	Oak Street	
Craggs Row	B1	Ormskirk Road	
Cross Street	C3	Oxford Street	
Crown Street	B1	Pedder Street	
Deepdale Road	D1	Percy Street	
Derby Street	D2	Pitt Street	
Earl Street	C2	Pole Street	
East Cliff	B4	Pump Street	
East Street	D1	Queen Street	
Edmund Street	D2	Ribblesdale Place	
Edward Street	A2	Ring Way	
Elizabeth Street	B1	Rose Street	
Fishergate	B3	St Austin's Road	
Fishergate Hill	A4	St Paul's Road	
Fleet Street	B3	St Paul's Square	
Fox Street	B3	St Peter's Street	
Friargate	B2	Sedgwick Street	
Friargate	C2	Selborne Street	
Fylde Road	A1	Shepherd Street	
Glover's Court	C3	Snow Hill	
Glover Street	C3	Syke Street	
Great Avenham Street	C4	Tithebarn Street	
Great Shaw Street	B2	Walker Street	
Grimshaw Street	D2	Walton's Parade	
Guildhall Street	C3	Ward's End	
Harrington Street	B1	Warwick Street	
Heatley Street	B2	West Cliff	
Herschell Street	D4	Winkley Square	

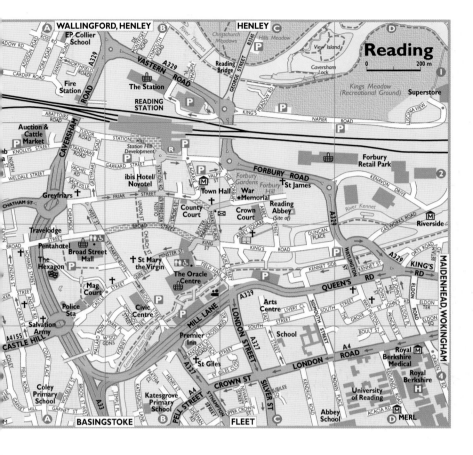

Reading

Reading is found on atlas page **35 K10**

Abbey Square	C3	King's Road	D3
Abbey Street	C2	King Street	B3
Addison Road	A1	Knollys Street	A2
Anstey Road	A3	Livery Close	C3
Baker Street	A3	London Road	C4
Blagrave Street	B2	London Street	C3
Boult Street	D4	Mallard Row	A4
Bridge Street	B3	Market Place	B2
Broad Street	A3	Mill Lane	B4
Brook Street West	A4	Minster Street	B3
Buttermarket	B3	Napier Road	C1
Cardiff Road	A1	Newark Street	C4
Carey Street	A3	Northfield Road	A1
Castle Hill	A4	Parthia Close	B4
Castle Street	A3	Pell Street	B4
Caversham Road	A2	Prince's Street	D3
Chatham Street	A2	Queen's Road	C3
Cheapside	A2	Queen Victoria Street	B2
Church Street	B3	Redlands Road	D4
Church Street	B4	Ross Road	A1
Coley Place	A4	Sackville Street	A2
Craven Road	D4	St Giles Close	B4
Crossland Road	B4	St John's Road	D3
Cross Street	B2	St Mary's Butts	B3
Crown Street	C4	Sidmouth Street	C3
Deansgate Road	B4	Silver Street	C4
Duke Street	C3	Simmonds Street	B3
Duncan Place	C3	Southampton Street	B4
East Street	C3	South Street	C3
Eldon Road	D3	Station Hill	B2
Field Road	A4	Station Road	B2
Fobney Street	B4	Swan Place	B3
Forbury Road	C2	Swansea Road	A1
Friar Street	B2	The Forbury	C2
Garnet Street	A4	Tudor Road	A2
Garrard Street	B2	Union Street	B2
Gas Works Road	D3	Upper Crown Street	C4
George Street	C1	Vachel Road	A2
Greyfriars Road	A2	Valpy Street	B2
Gun Street	B3	Vastern Road	B1
Henry Street	B4	Waterside Gardens	B4
Howard Street	A3	Watlington Street	D3
Katesgrove Lane	B4	Weldale Street	A2
Kenavon Drive	D2	West Street	A2
Kendrick Road	C4	Wolseley Street	A4
Kennet Side	C3	Yield Hall Place	B3
Kennet Street	D3	York Road	A1
King's Meadow Road	C1	Zinzan Street	A3

Royal Tunbridge Wells

Royal Tunbridge Wells is found on atlas page **25 N3**

Albert Street	C1	High Street	B4
Arundel Road	C4	Lansdowne Road	C2
Bayhall Road	D2	Lime Hill Road	B1
Belgrave Road	C1	Linden Park Road	A4
Berkeley Road	B4	Little Mount Sion	B4
Boyne Park	A1	London Road	A2
Buckingham Road	C4	Lonsdale Gardens	B2
Calverley Gardens	C3	Madeira Park	B4
Calverley Park	C2	Major York's Road	A4
Calverley Park Gardens	D2	Meadow Road	B1
Calverley Road	C2	Molyneux Park Road	A1
Calverley Street	C1	Monson Road	C2
Cambridge Gardens	D4	Monson Way	B2
Cambridge Street	D3	Mount Edgcumbe Road	A3
Camden Hill	D3	Mount Ephraim	A2
Camden Park	D3	Mount Ephraim Road	B1
Camden Road	C1	Mountfield Gardens	C3
Carlton Road	D2	Mountfield Road	C3
Castle Place	A2	Mount Pleasant Avenue	B2
Castle Street	B3	Mount Pleasant Road	B2
Chapel Place	B4	Mount Sion	B4
Christchurch Avenue	B3	Nevill Street	B4
Church Road	A2	Newton Road	B1
Civic Way	B2	Norfolk Road	C4
Claremont Gardens	C4	North Street	D2
Claremont Road	C4	Oakfield Court Road	D3
Clarence Road	B2	Park Street	D3
Crescent Road	B2	Pembury Road	D2
Culverden Street	B1	Poona Road	C4
Dale Street	C1	Prince's Street	D3
Dudley Road	B1	Prospect Road	D3
Eden Road	B4	Rock Villa Road	B1
Eridge Road	A4	Royal Chase	A1
Farmcombe Lane	C4	St James' Road	D1
Farmcombe Road	C4	Sandrock Road	D1
Ferndale	D1	Somerville Gardens	A1
Frant Road	A4	South Green	B3
Frog Lane	B4	Station Approach	B3
Garden Road	C1	Stone Street	D1
Garden Street	C1	Sutherland Road	C3
George Street	D3	Tunnel Road	C1
Goods Station Road	B1	Upper Grosvenor Road	B1
Grecian Road	C4	Vale Avenue	B3
Grosvenor Road	B1	Vale Road	B3
Grove Hill Gardens	C3	Victoria Road	C1
Grove Hill Road	C3	Warwick Park	B4
Guildford Road	C3	Wood Street	C1
Hanover Road	B1	York Road	B2

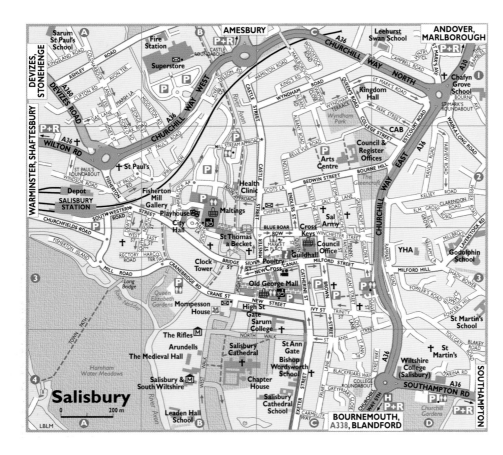

Salisbury

Salisbury is found on atlas page **21 M9**

Albany Road	C1	Kingsland Road
Ashley Road	A1	King's Road
Avon Approach	B2	Laverstock Road
Bedwin Street	C2	Malthouse Lane
Belle Vue Road	C2	Manor Road
Blackfriars Way	C4	Marlborough Road
Blue Boar Row	C3	Meadow Road
Bourne Avenue	D1	Middleton Road
Bourne Hill	C2	Milford Hill
Bridge Street	B3	Milford Street
Brown Street	C3	Mill Road
Campbell Road	D1	Minster Street
Castle Street	B1	Nelson Road
Catherine Street	C3	New Canal
Chipper Lane	C2	New Street
Churchfields Road	A2	North Street
Churchill Way East	D3	Park Street
Churchill Way North	C1	Pennyfarthing Street
Churchill Way South	C4	Queen's Road
Churchill Way West	B2	Queen Street
Clarendon Road	D2	Rampart Road
Clifton Road	A1	Rectory Road
Coldharbour Lane	A1	Rollestone Street
College Street	C1	St Ann Street
Cranebridge Road	B3	St Edmund's Church Street
Crane Street	B3	St Mark's Avenue
Devizes Road	A1	St Mark's Road
Dew's Road	A3	St Paul's Road
East Street	B3	Salt Lane
Elm Grove	D2	Scots Lane
Elm Grove Road	D2	Sidney Street
Endless Street	C2	Silver Street
Estcourt Road	D2	Southampton Road
Exeter Street	C4	South Street
Eyres Way	D4	South Western Road
Fairview Road	D2	Spire View
Fisherton Street	A2	Summerlock Approach
Fowler's Road	D3	Tollgate Road
Friary Lane	C4	Trinity Street
Gas Lane	A1	Wain-A-Long Road
George Street	A1	Wessex Road
Gigant Street	C3	West Street
Greencroft Street	C2	Wilton Road
Guilder Lane	C3	Winchester Street
Hamilton Road	C1	Windsor Road
High Street	B3	Woodstock Road
Ivy Street	C3	Wyndham Road
Kelsey Road	D2	York Road

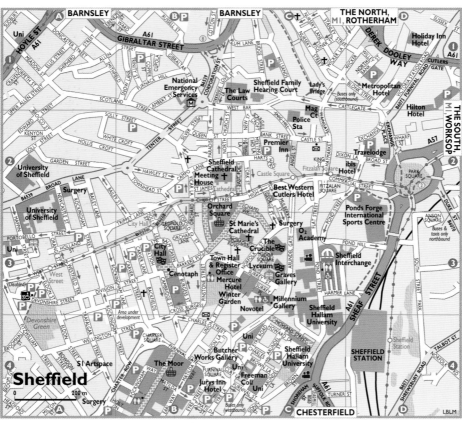

Sheffield

Sheffield is found on atlas page **84 E3**

Angel Street	C2	Howard Street
Arundel Gate	C3	Hoyle Street
Arundel Street	C4	King Street
Backfields	B3	Lambert Street
Bailey Street	A2	Leopold Street
Balm Green	B3	Mappin Street
Bank Street	C2	Matilda Street
Barkers Pool	B3	Meetinghouse Lane
Broad Lane	A2	Mulberry Street
Broad Street	D2	Newcastle Street
Brown Street	C4	New Street
Cambridge Street	B3	Norfolk Street
Campo Lane	B2	North Church Street
Carver Street	B3	Orchard Street
Castlegate	C1	Paradise Street
Castle Street	C2	Pinstone Street
Charles Street	B4	Pond Hill
Charter Row	A4	Pond Street
Church Street	B2	Portobello Street
Commercial Street	C2	Queen Street
Corporation Street	B1	Rockingham Street
Cross Burgess Street	B3	St James Street
Cutlers Gate	D1	Scargill Croft
Derek Dooley Way	D1	Scotland Street
Devonshire Street	A3	Sheaf Street
Division Street	A3	Shoreham Street
Dixon Lane	C2	Shrewsbury Road
Duke Street	D2	Silver Street
Exchange Street	D2	Smithfield
Eyre Street	B4	Snig Hill
Fig Tree Lane	C2	Solly Street
Fitzwilliam Street	A4	South Street Park
Flat Street	C3	Suffolk Road
Furnace Hill	B1	Surrey Street
Furnival Gate	B4	Talbot Street
Furnival Road	D1	Tenter Street
Furnival Street	C4	Townhead Street
Garden Street	A2	Trafalgar Street
George Street	C2	Trippet Lane
Gibralter Street	B1	Union Street
Harmer Lane	C3	Vicar Lane
Harts Head	C2	Victoria Station Road
Hawley Street	B2	Waingate
Haymarket	C2	Wellington Street
High Street	C2	West Bar
Holland Street	A3	West Street
Hollis Croft	A2	White Croft
Holly Street	B3	York Street

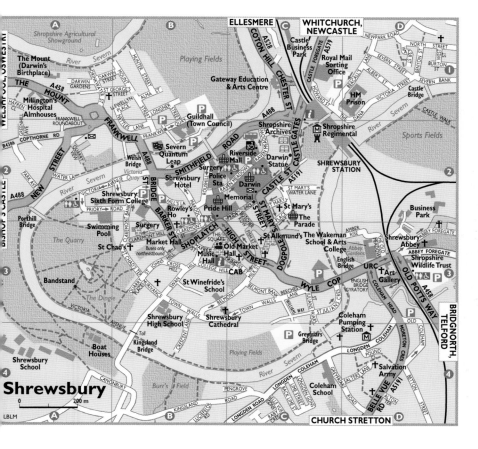

Shrewsbury

Shrewsbury is found on atlas page **56 H2**

Abbey Foregate	D3	Mardol	B2
Albert Street	D1	Market Street	B3
Alma Street	B1	Milk Street	C3
Amber Rise	D3	Moreton Crescent	D4
Barker Street	B2	Mount Street	B1
Beacall's Lane	D1	Murivance	B3
Beeches Lane	C3	Nettles Lane	B1
Belle Vue Gardens	C4	Newpark Road	D1
Belle Vue Road	D4	New Street	A2
Belmont	B3	North Street	D1
Belmont Bank	C3	Old Coleham	D3
Benyon Street	D1	Old Potts Way	D3
Betton Street	D4	Park Avenue	A2
Bridge Street	B2	Pengrove	C4
Burton Street	D1	Pound Close	D4
Butcher Row	C2	Pride Hill	C2
Canonbury	A4	Princess Street	B3
Castle Foregate	C1	Priory Road	A2
Castle Gates	C2	Quarry Place	B3
Castle Street	C2	Quarry View	A2
Chester Street	C1	Raven Meadows	B2
Claremont Bank	B3	Roushill	B2
Claremont Hill	B3	St Chad's Terrace	B3
Claremont Street	B3	St George's Street	A1
Coleham Head	D3	St Johns Hill	B3
College Hill	B3	St Julians Friars	C3
Copthorne Road	A2	St Julians Crescent	C3
Coton Hill	C1	St Mary's Place	C2
Crescent Lane	B4	St Mary's Street	C2
Cross Hill	B3	St Mary's Water Lane	C2
Darwin Gardens	A1	Salters Lane	D4
Darwin Street	A1	Severn Bank	D1
Dogpole	C3	Severn Street	D1
Drinkwater Street	A1	Shoplatch	B3
Fish Street	C3	Smithfield Road	B2
Frankwell	A2	Swan Hill	B3
Frankwell Quay	B2	The Dana	D1
Greenhill Avenue	A2	The Mount	A1
Greyfriars Road	C4	The Old Meadow	D3
High Street	C3	The Square	B3
Hill's Lane	B2	Town Walls	B3
Howard Street	C1	Victoria Avenue	A2
Hunter Street	B1	Victoria Street	D1
Kingsland Road	B4	Water Lane	A2
Lime Street	C4	Water Street	D1
Longden Coleham	C4	West Street	D1
Longden Road	C4	Williams Way	C3
Longner Street	B1	Wyle Cop	C3

Southend-on-Sea

Southend-on-Sea is found on atlas page **38 E4**

Albert Road	C3	Kursaal Way	D4
Alexandra Road	A3	Lancaster Gardens	C2
Alexandra Street	A3	Leamington Road	D2
Ambleside Drive	D2	London Road	A2
Ashburnham Road	A2	Lucy Road	C4
Baltic Avenue	B3	Luker Road	A2
Baxter Avenue	A1	Marine Parade	C4
Beach Road	D4	Milton Street	B1
Beresford Road	D4	Napier Avenue	A2
Boscombe Road	C1	Nelson Street	A3
Bournemouth Park Road	D1	Oban Road	D1
Cambridge Road	A3	Old Southend Road	D3
Capel Terrace	A3	Outing Close	D3
Chancellor Road	B3	Pitmans Close	B2
Cheltenham Road	D2	Pleasant Road	C3
Chichester Road	B1	Portland Avenue	B3
Christchurch Road	D1	Princes Street	A2
Church Road	B3	Prittlewell Square	A3
Clarence Road	A3	Quebec Avenue	C2
Clarence Street	B3	Queen's Road	A2
Clifftown Parade	A4	Queensway	A1
Clifftown Road	B3	Royal Terrace	B4
Coleman Street	B1	Runwell Terrace	A3
Cromer Road	C2	St Ann's Road	B1
Devereux Road	A4	St Leonard's Road	C3
Eastern Esplanade	D4	Scratton Road	A3
Elmer Approach	A2	Short Street	B1
Elmer Avenue	A2	Southchurch Avenue	C2
Essex Street	B1	Southchurch Road	B2
Ferndown Close	D1	Stanier Close	D2
Fowler Close	D2	Stanley Road	C3
Gordon Place	A2	Sutton Road	C1
Gordon Road	A2	Swanage Road	C1
Grange Gardens	C2	Toledo Road	C2
Grover Street	B3	Tylers Avenue	B3
Guildford Road	B1	Tyrel Drive	C2
Hamlet Road	A3	Victoria Avenue	A1
Hartington Place	C4	Warrior Square East	B2
Hartington Road	C3	Warrior Square North	B2
Hastings Road	C2	Warrior Square	B2
Hawtree Close	D4	Wesley Road	C3
Herbert Grove	C3	Western Esplanade	A4
Heygate Avenue	B3	Weston Road	B3
High Street	B2	Whitegate Road	B2
Hillcrest Road	C2	Wimborne Road	C1
Honiton Road	D2	Windermere Road	D2
Horace Road	C3	Woodgrange Drive	D3
Kilworth Avenue	C2	York Road	B3

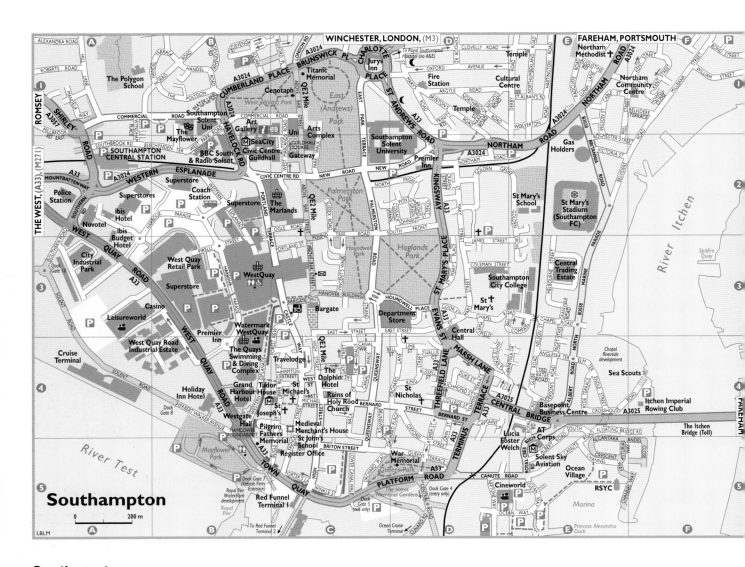

Southampton

Southampton is found on atlas page **14 D4**

Above Bar Street	C1	Channel Way	E5	Hartington Road	E1	Northumberland Road	E1	South Front	C2
Albert Road North	E4	Chapel Road	D3	Havelock Road	B1	Ocean Way	D5	Strand	C3
Albert Road South	E5	Charlotte Place	C1	Herbert Walker Avenue	B4	Ogle Road	C2	Sussex Road	C2
Alcantara Crescent	E5	Civic Centre Road	B2	High Street	C4	Orchard Place	C5	Ted Bates Road	E4
Alexandra Road	A1	Clovelly Road	D1	Hill Lane	A1	Oxford Avenue	D1	Terminus Terrace	D5
Anderson's Road	E4	Coleman Street	D3	Houndwell Place	D3	Oxford Street	D4	The Compass	D3
Andes Close	F5	College Street	D4	Howell Close	F1	Paget Street	E4	The Polygon	B1
Anglesea Terrace	E4	Commercial Road	A1	Itchen Bridge	F4	Palmerston Road	C2	Threefield Lane	D4
Argyle Road	D1	Cook Street	D3	James Street	D3	Park Walk	C2	Town Quay	B5
Asturias Way	E5	Cossack Green	D2	Johnson Street	D2	Peel Street	E1	Trinity Road	D1
Augustine Road	E1	Craven Street	D2	John Street	D5	Pirelli Street	B3	Upper Bugle Street	C4
Back Of The Walls	C4	Crosshouse Road	E4	Kent Street	F1	Platform Road	C5	Victoria Street	E2
Bargate Street	C3	Cumberland Place	B1	King Street	D4	Porter's Lane	C5	Vincent's Walk	C3
Bedford Place	C1	Cunard Road	D5	Kingsway	D2	Portland Street	C3	Water Lane	B1
Bell Street	D4	Derby Road	E1	Latimer Street	D5	Portland Terrace	B2	Western Esplanade	A2
Belvidere Road	E2	Devonshire Road	B1	Lime Street	D4	Pound Tree Road	C3	Western Esplanade	B4
Belvidere Terrace	F1	Duke Street	D4	London Road	C1	Queens Terrace	D5	West Marlands Road	C2
Bernard Street	C4	Eastgate Street	C4	Lower Canal Walk	C5	Queensway	D2	West Park Road	B2
Blechynden Terrace	B2	East Park Terrace	C1	Lumpy Lane	E1	Radcliffe Road	E1	West Quay Road	A2
Bond Street	F1	East Street	C3	Mandela Way	A1	Richmond Street	D4	West Street	C4
Brinton's Road	D1	Elm Terrace	E4	Marine Parade	E3	Roberts Road	A1	White Star Place	D4
Britannia Road	E1	Endle Street	E4	Marsh Lane	D4	Rochester Street	E2	William Street	F1
Briton Street	C5	Evans Street	D3	Maryfield	D3	Royal Crescent Road	E5	Wilson Street	E1
Broad Green	D2	Exmoor Road	D1	Mayflower Roundabout	B4	Russell Street	D4	Winkle Street	C5
Brunswick Place	C1	Floating Bridge Road	E4	Melbourne Street	E3	Ryde Terrace	E5	Winton Street	D2
Brunswick Square	C4	Forest View	D4	Millbank Street	F1	St Alban's Road	E1	Wolverton Road	E1
Bugle Street	C5	French Street	C5	Millbrook Road East	A1	St Andrews Road	D1	Wyndham Place	A1
Cable Street	E1	Glebe Road	E4	Morris Road	B1	St Marks Road	D1	
Canal Walk	C4	Golden Grove	D2	Mountbatten Way	A2	St Mary's Place	D3	
Canute Road	D5	Granville Road	E3	Nelson Street	E4	St Mary's Road	D1	
Captains Place	D4	Grosvenor Square	B1	Neptune Way	D5	St Mary Street	D2	
Carpathia Drive	D4	Hamtun Street	C4	New Road	C2	St Michael Street	C4	
Castle Way	C3	Handel Road	B1	Nichols Road	D1	Shirley Road	A1	
Central Bridge	D4	Handel Terrace	B1	Northam Road	D2	Solent Road	A3	
Central Road	D5	Hanover Buildings	C3	Northbrook Road	D1	Southbrook Road	A2	
Challis Court	D4	Harbour Parade	B2	North Front	C2	Southern Road	A2	

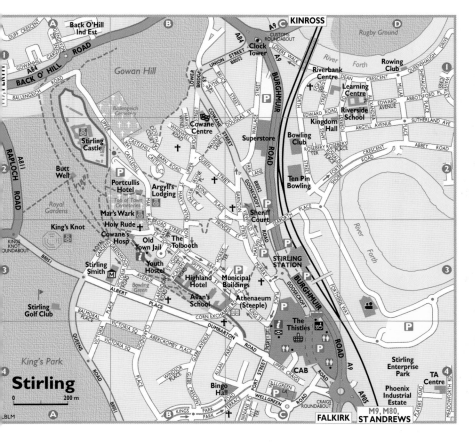

Stirling

Stirling is found on atlas page **133 M9**

Abbey Road	D2	Kings Park Road	B4
Abbotsford Place	D1	King Street	C3
Abercromby Place	B4	Lovers Walk	C1
Academy Road	B3	Lower Bridge Street	B1
Albert Place	A3	Lower Castlehill	B2
Alexandra Place	D1	Mar Place	B2
Allan Park	B4	Maxwell Place	C3
Argyll Avenue	D2	Meadowforth Road	D4
Back O' Hill Road	A1	Millar Place	D1
Baker Street	B3	Morris Terrace	B3
Ballengeich Road	A1	Murray Place	C3
Balmoral Place	A3	Ninians Road	C4
Bank Street	B3	Park Lane	C2
Barn Road	B2	Park Terrace	B4
Barnton Street	C2	Pitt Terrace	C4
Bayne Street	B1	Players Road	D4
Bow Street	B3	Port Street	C4
Broad Street	B3	Princes Street	B3
Bruce Street	B1	Queenshaugh Drive	D1
Burghmuir Road	C1	Queens Road	A4
Castle Court	B2	Queen Street	B2
Clarendon Place	B4	Raploch Road	A2
Clarendon Road	B3	Ronald Place	C2
Corn Exchange Road	B3	Rosebery Place	C2
Cowane Street	B1	Rosebery Terrace	C2
Craigs Roundabout	C4	Royal Gardens	A3
Crofthead Court	B2	St John Street	B3
Customs Roundabout	C1	St Mary's Wynd	B2
Dean Crescent	D1	Seaforth Place	C3
Douglas Street	C2	Shiphaugh Place	D1
Duff Crescent	A1	Shore Road	C2
Dumbarton Road	B4	Spittal Street	B3
Edward Avenue	D1	Sutherland Avenue	D2
Edward Road	C1	Tannery Lane	B2
Forrest Road	D2	Union Street	B1
Forth Crescent	C2	Upper Bridge Street	B2
Forth Street	C1	Upper Castlehill	A2
Forth View	C1	Upper Craigs	C4
Glebe Avenue	B4	Victoria Place	A4
Glebe Crescent	B4	Victoria Road	B3
Glendevon Drive	A1	Victoria Square	A4
Goosecroft Road	C2	Viewfield Street	C2
Gowanhill Gardens	A1	Wallace Street	C2
Greenwood Avenue	A3	Waverley Crescent	D1
Harvey Wynd	B1	Wellgreen Lane	C4
Irvine Place	B2	Wellgreen Road	C4
James Street	C2	Whinwell Road	B2
Kings Knot Roundabout	A3	Windsor Place	B4

Stockton-on-Tees

Stockton-on-Tees is found on atlas page **104 D7**

1825 Way	B4	Massey Road	D3
Allison Street	B1	Melbourne Street	A2
Alma Street	B1	Middle Street	B2
Bath Lane	C1	Mill Street West	A2
Bedford Street	A1	Nelson Terrace	B2
Bishop Street	B2	North Shore Road	D2
Bishopton Lane	A1	Northport Road	D1
Bishopton Road	A1	Northshore Link	C2
Bowesfield Lane	A4	Norton Road	B1
Bridge Road	B3	Palmerston Street	A2
Bridge Road	C4	Park Road	A4
Bright Street	B2	Park Terrace	C3
Britannia Road	A1	Parkfield Road	B4
Brunswick Street	B3	Parliament Street	B4
Bute Street	A2	Portrack Lane	D1
Church Road	D1	Prince Regent Street	B3
Clarence Row	C1	Princess Avenue	C1
Corporation Street	A2	Princeton Drive	D4
Council of Europe		Quayside Road	C3
Boulevard	C2	Raddcliffe Crescent	D3
Cromwell Avenue	B1	Ramsgate	B3
Dixon Street	A2	Riverside	C3
Dovecot Street	A3	Russell Street	B2
Dugdale Street	D1	St Paul's Street	A1
Durham Road	A1	Silver Street	B3
Durham Street	A2	Skinner Street	B3
Edwards Street	A4	Station Street	D4
Farrer Street	B2	Sydney Street	B2
Finkle Street	C3	The Square	D2
Frederick Street	B1	Thistle Green	C2
Fudan Way	D3	Thomas Street	B1
Gooseport Road	D1	Thompson Street	B1
Hartington Road	A3	Tower Street	B4
Harvard Avenue	D3	Union Street East	C1
High Street	B2	University Boulevard	C3
Hill Street East	D1	Vane Street	B2
Hume Street	B1	Vicarage Street	A1
Hutchinson Street	A2	Wellington Street	A2
John Street	B2	West Row	B3
King Street	B2	Westbourne Street	A4
Knightport Road	D1	Westpoint Road	C3
Knowles Street	C2	Wharf Street	B4
Laing Street	B1	William Street	B3
Leeds Street	B2	Woodland Street	A4
Lobdon Street	B2	Worthing Street	A3
Lodge Street	B3	Yale Crescent	C4
Mandale Road	D4	Yarm Lane	A4
Maritime Road	C1	Yarm Road	A4

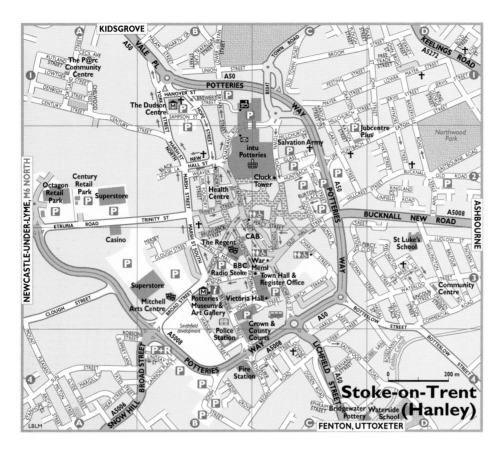

Stoke-on-Trent (Hanley)

Stoke-on-Trent (Hanley) is found on atlas page **70 F5**

Albion Street	B3	Lichfield Street	C
Bagnall Street	B3	Linfield Road	D
Balfour Street	D3	Lower Mayer Street	D
Baskerville Road	D1	Lowther Street	A
Bathesda Street	B4	Ludlow Street	B
Bernard Street	C4	Malam Street	B
Bethesda Street	B3	Marsh Street	B
Birch Terrace	C3	Marsh Street North	B
Botteslow Street	C3	Marsh Street South	B
Broad Street	B4	Mayer Street	C
Broom Street	C1	Mersey Street	B
Brunswick Street	B3	Milton Street	C
Bryan Street	B1	Mount Pleasant	A
Bucknall New Road	C2	Mynors Street	A
Bucknall Old Road	D2	New Hall Street	B
Cardiff Grove	B4	Ogden Road	C
Century Street	A1	Old Hall Street	C
Charles Street	C3	Old Town Road	C
Cheapside	B3	Pall Mall	B
Chelwood Street	A1	Percy Street	C
Clough Street	A3	Piccadilly	B
Clyde Street	A4	Portland Street	A
Commercial Road	D3	Potteries Way	B
Denbigh Street	A1	Quadrant Road	B
Derby Street	C4	Regent Road	B
Dyke Street	D2	Rutland Street	A
Eastwood Road	C4	St John Street	A
Eaton Street	D2	St Luke Street	D
Etruria Road	A2	Sampson Street	A
Festing Street	C1	Sheaf Street	A
Foundry Street	B2	Slippery Lane	A
Garth Street	C2	Snow Hill	B
Gilman Street	C3	Stafford Street	B
Goodson Street	C2	Sun Street	A
Grafton Street	C1	Tontine Street	C
Hanover Street	B1	Town Road	B
Harley Street	C4	Trafalgar Street	B
Hillchurch	C2	Trinity Street	B
Hillcrest Street	C2	Union Street	B
Hinde Street	B4	Upper Hillchurch Street	C
Hope Street	B1	Upper Huntbach Street	C
Hordley Street	C3	Warner Street	B
Huntbach Street	C2	Waterloo Street	D
Jasper Street	C4	Well Street	D
Jervis Street	D1	Wellington Road	C
John Bright Street	D1	Wellington Street	D
John Street	B3	Yates Street	A
Keelings Road	D1	York Street	A

Stratford-upon-Avon

Stratford-upon-Avon is found on atlas page **47 P3**

Albany Road	A3	New Street	B
Alcester Road	A2	Old Red Hen Court	C
Arden Street	B2	Old Town	C
Avenue Road	C1	Orchard Way	C
Bancroft Place	C2	Payton Street	C
Birmingham Road	B1	Percy Street	C
Brewery Street	B1	Rother Street	B
Bridge Foot	D2	Rowley Crescent	C
Bridge Street	C2	Ryland Street	B
Bridgeway	D2	St Andrew's Crescent	A
Broad Street	B4	St Gregory's Road	C
Brookvale Road	A4	St Martin's Close	A
Bull Street	B4	Sanctus Drive	A
Cedar Close	D1	Sanctus Road	A
Chapel Lane	C3	Sanctus Street	A
Chapel Street	C3	Sandfield Road	B
Cherry Orchard	A4	Scholars Lane	B
Cherry Street	B4	Seven Meadows Road	A
Chestnut Walk	B3	Shakespeare Street	C
Church Street	B3	Sheep Street	C
Clopton Bridge	D3	Shipston Road	D
Clopton Road	B1	Shottery Road	A
College Lane	B4	Shrieves Walk	C
College Mews	B4	Southern Lane	C
College Street	B4	Station Road	B
Ely Gardens	B3	Swan's Nest	D
Ely Street	B3	The Willows	A
Evesham Place	B4	Tiddington Road	D
Evesham Road	A4	Town Square	B
Garrick Way	A4	Tramway Bridge	D
Great William Street	C1	Tyler Street	C
Greenhill Street	B2	Union Street	C
Grove Road	B3	Warwick Court	C
Guild Street	C2	Warwick Crescent	D
Henley Street	B2	Warwick Road	C
High Street	C3	Waterside	C
Holtom Street	B4	Welcombe Road	C
John Street	C2	Wellesbourne Grove	A
Kendall Avenue	B1	Western Road	B
Lock Close	C2	West Street	C
Maidenhead Road	C1	Willows Drive North	A
Mansell Street	B2	Windsor Street	C
Mayfield Avenue	C1	Wood Street	C
Meer Street	B2		
Mill Lane	C4		
Mulberry Street	C1		
Narrow Lane	B4		
New Broad Street	B4		

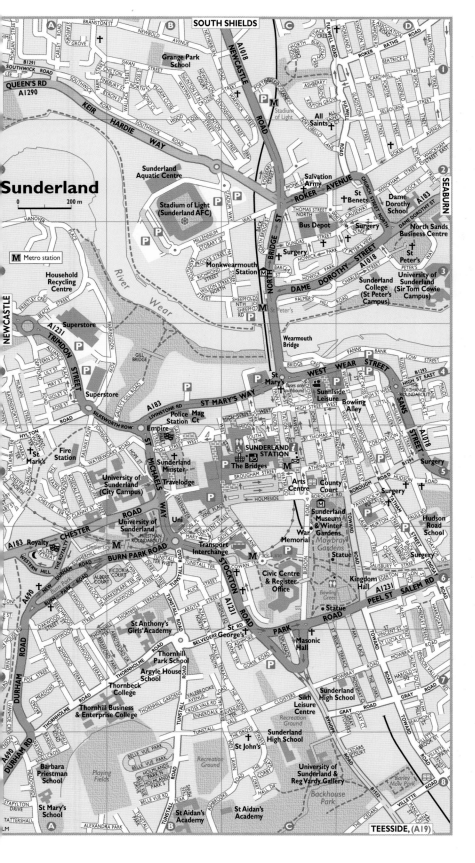

Sunderland

Sunderland is found on atlas page **113 N9**

Abbotsford Green	B7		Meadowside	A8
Abbs Street	C2		Middle Street	C5
Albion Place	B6		Milburn Street	A4
Alice Street	B6		Millennium Way	B3
Alliance Place	A4		Monk Street	C2
Amberley Street	D6		Moreland Street	D1
Argyle Square	B6		Morgan Street	A1
Argyle Street	B6		Mowbray Road	D7
Ashbrooke Road	B8		Netherburn Road	B1
Ashmore Street	C7		Newbold Avenue	B1
Ashwood Street	A7		Newcastle Road	C1
Ashwood Terrace	A7		New Durham Road	A6
Association Road	D1		Nile Street	D4
Athenaeum Street	C5		Norfolk Street	D5
Azalea Terrace North	B6		North Bridge Street	C3
Azalea Terrace South	B7		Northcote Avenue	D6
Back North Bridge Street	C3		North Street	B1
Beach Street	A3		Oakwood Street	A6
Beatrice Street	D1		Olive Street	B6
Beaumont Street	D7		Otto Terrace	A7
Bedford Street	C4		Palmer's Hill Road	C3
Beechwood Street	A6		Panns Bank	D4
Beechwood Terrace	A7		Park Lane	C5
Belvedere Road	B7		Park Place	D6
Beresford Park	A7		Park Road	C6
Birchfield Road	A7		Pauls Road	D5
Borough Road	D5		Peel Street	D6
Bridge Crescent	C4		Portobello Lane	C1
Bridge Street	C4		Queen's Road	A1
Briery Vale Road	C7		Railway Row	A5
Bright Street	D1		Ravensworth Street	A4
Brooke Street	B3		Richmond Street	B3
Brougham Street	C5		Ripon Street	D1
Burdon Road	C5		Roker Avenue	C2
Burn Park Road	B6		Roker Baths Road	D1
Cardwell Street	D1		Rosedale Street	A5
Carley Road	A1		Ross Street	B1
Charles Street	D3		Russell Street	D4
Chester Road	A6		Ryhope Road	C7
Churchill Street	D6		St Bede's Terrace	D7
Church Street North	D2		St Michaels Way	B5
Clanny Street	A5		St Peter's View	D3
Cork Street	D4		St Thomas' Street	C5
Coronation Street	D5		St Vincent Street	D7
Cowan Terrace	C6		Salem Road	D6
Cross Vale Road	B7		Salem Street	D6
Crozier Street	B1		Salem Street South	D7
Dame Dorothy Street	C3		Salisbury Street	D6
Deptford Road	A4		Sans Street	D4
Derby Street	B6		Selbourne Street	D1
Derwent Street	B6		Shakespeare Terrace	A6
Devonshire Street	B1		Shallcross	A8
Dock Street	D2		Sheepfolds Road	C3
Dundas Street	C3		Silksworth Row	A4
Durham Road	A7		South Street	C5
Easington Street	B3		Southwick Road	A1
East Cross Street	D4		Stadium Way	C2
Eden House Road	A7		Stansfield Street	D1
Egerton Street	D6		Station Street	C4
Eglinton Street	B1		Stobart Street	B3
Eglinton Street North	B1		Stockton Road	C6
Elmwood Street	A6		Swan Street	B1
Ennerdale	B7		Tatham Street	D5
Farm Street	A1		Tatham Street Back	D5
Farringdon Row	B4		The Avenue	C7
Fawcett Street	C4		The Cloisters	C7
Forster Street	D1		The Royalty	A6
Fox Street	A7		Thomas Street North	C2
Foyle Street	D5		Thornhill Terrace	B6
Frederick Street	D5		Thornholme Road	A7
Fulwell Road	C1		Toward Road	D5
Galley's Gill Road	B4		Trimdon Street	A4
Gladstone Street	D1		Tunstall Road	B7
Gorse Road	C7		Tunstall Terrace	B6
Gray Road	D7		Tunstall Terrace West	B6
Green Terrace	B5		Tunstall Vale	B8
Hampden Road	D1		Union Street	C4
Hanover Place	A2		Valebrooke Avenue	B7
Harlow Street	A5		Villette Road	D8
Harrogate Street	D6		Villiers Street	D4
Hartington Street	D1		Vine Place	B5
Havelock Terrace	A6		Wallace Street	B1
Hay Street	C3		Warwick Street	C1
Hendon Valley Road	D7		Waterloo Place	C5
High Street East	D4		Waterworks Road	A5
High Street West	B5		Wayman Street	B1
Holmeside	C5		Wearhead Drive	A7
Hope Street	B5		Westbourne Road	A5
Howick Park	C3		Western Hill	A6
Hudson Road	D5		West Lawn	C8
Hylton Road	A5		West Street	C5
Johnson Street	A5		West Sunniside	D4
John Street	C4		West Wear Street	C4
Keir Hardie Way	A1		Wharncliffe Street	A5
Laura Street	D5		Whickham Street	D2
Lime Street	A4		Whickham Street East	D2
Lindsay Road	D6		Whitburn Street	D3
Little Villiers Street	D4		William Street	D4
Low Street	D4		Wilson Street North	B3
Mary Street	B6		York Street	C4
Mauds Lane	D4		Zetland Street	D2

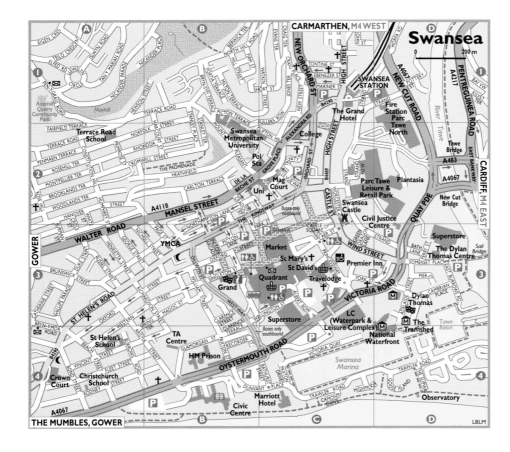

Swansea

Swansea is found on atlas page **29 J6**

Adelaide Street............................D3	New Orchard Street............................
Alexandra Road............................C2	New Street............................
Argyle Street............................A4	Nicander Parade............................
Bath Lane............................D3	Nicholl Street............................
Beach Street............................A4	Norfolk Street............................
Bond Street............................A4	North Hill Road............................
Brunswick Street............................A3	Northampton Lane............................
Burrows Road............................A4	Orchard Street............................
Caer Street............................C3	Oxford Street............................
Carlton Terrace............................B2	Oystermouth Road............................
Castle Street............................C2	Page Street............................
Catherine Street............................A3	Park Street............................
Clarence Street............................B3	Paxton Street............................
Clifton Hill............................C2	Pentreguinea Road............................
Constituion Hill............................A2	Pen-Y-Graig Road............................
Cradock Street............................B2	Picton Lane............................
Craig Place............................C1	Pier Street............................
Cromwell Street............................A2	Primrose Street............................
De La Beche Street............................B2	Princess Way............................
Dillwyn Street............................B3	Quay Parade............................
Duke Street............................A3	Recorder Street............................
Dunvant Place............................B4	Rhondda Street............................
East Bank Way............................D2	Richardson Street............................
East Burrows Road............................D3	Rodney Street............................
Ebenezer Street............................C1	Rose Hill............................
Elfed Road............................A1	Russel Street............................
Ferry Street............................D3	St Helen's Road............................
Firm Street............................B1	Short Street............................
Fleet Street............................A4	Singleton Street............................
George Street............................A3	Somerset Place............................
Glamorgan Street............................B4	Strand............................
Green Lane Dragon............................C3	Tan Y Marian Road............................
Grove Place............................C2	Teilo Crescent............................
Hanover Street............................A2	Terrace Road............................
Harcourt Street............................B2	The Kingsway............................
Heathfield............................B2	Tontine Street............................
Henrietta Street............................A3	Trawler Road............................
Hewson Street............................A1	Victoria Quay............................
High Street............................C2	Victoria Road............................
Hill Street............................B1	Vincent Street............................
Humphrey Street............................A2	Walter Road............................
Islwyn Road............................A1	Watkin Street............................
Llewelyn Circle............................A1	Wellington Street............................
Madoc Street............................B3	West Way............................
Mansel Street............................B2	Western Street............................
Mariner Street............................C1	William Street............................
Mount Pleasant............................B2	Wind Street............................
New Cut Road............................D1	York Street............................

Swindon

Swindon is found on atlas page **33 M8**

Albion Street............................A4	Islington Street............................
Alfred Street............................C2	John Street............................
Ashford Road............................B4	King Street............................
Aylesbury Street............................B2	London Street............................
Bathurst Road............................C2	Manchester Road............................
Beckhampton Street............................C3	Market Street............................
Bridge Street............................B2	Maxwell Street............................
Bristol Street............................A3	Medgbury Road............................
Broad Street............................C2	Milford Street............................
Cambria Bridge Road............................A4	Milton Road............................
Canal Walk............................B3	Morley Street............................
Carfax Street............................C2	Morse Street............................
Carr Street............................B3	Newcastle Street............................
Chester Street............................A3	Newcombe Drive............................
Church Place............................A3	Newhall Street............................
Cirencester Way............................D1	Northampton Street............................
Clarence Street............................C3	North Star Avenue............................
College Street............................B3	Ocotal Way............................
Commercial Road............................B3	Park Lane............................
Corporation Street............................C2	Plymouth Street............................
County Road............................D2	Polaris Way............................
Crombey Street............................B4	Ponting Street............................
Curtis Street............................A4	Portsmouth Street............................
Deacon Street............................B4	Princes Street............................
Dixon Street............................B4	Prospect Hill............................
Dover Street............................C4	Queen Street............................
Dowling Street............................B4	Radnor Street............................
Drove Road............................D4	Regent Place............................
Dryden Street............................A4	Regent Street............................
Eastcott Hill............................C4	Rosebery Street............................
East Street............................B2	Salisbury Street............................
Edgeware Road............................B3	Sanford Street............................
Elmina Road............................C1	Sheppard Street............................
Emlyn Square............................A3	Southampton Street............................
Euclid Street............................C3	Stafford Street............................
Faringdon Road............................A3	Stanier Street............................
Farnsby Street............................B3	Station Road............................
Fleet Street............................B2	Swindon Road............................
Fleming Way............................C3	Tennyson Street............................
Gladstone Street............................C2	Theobald Street............................
Gooch Street............................C2	Victoria Road............................
Graham Street............................C2	Villett Street............................
Great Western Way............................A1	Westcott Place............................
Groundwell Road............................C3	Western Street............................
Havelock Street............................B3	Whitehead Street............................
Hawksworth Way............................A1	Whitney Street............................
Haydon Street............................C2	William Street............................
Holbrook Way............................B2	York Road............................

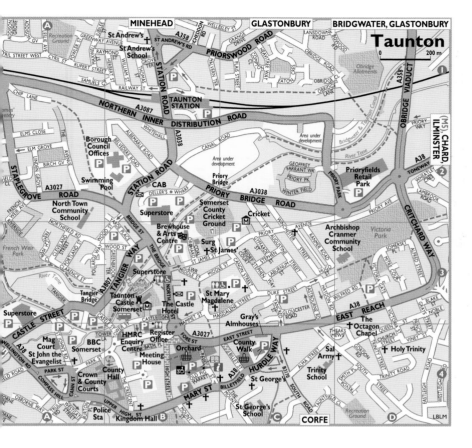

Taunton

Taunton is found on atlas page **18 H10**

Albemarle Road	B2	Northern Inner	
Alfred Street	D3	Distribution Road	A1
Alma Street	C4	Northfield Road	A3
Belvedere Road	B2	North Street	B3
Billetfield	C4	Obridge Road	C1
Billet Street	C4	Obridge Viaduct	D2
Bridge Street	B2	Old Pig Market	B4
Canal Road	B2	Parkfield Road	A4
Cann Street	A4	Park Street	A4
Canon Street	C3	Paul Street	B4
Castle Street	A4	Plais Street	C1
Cheddon Road	B1	Portland Street	A3
Chip Lane	A1	Priorswood Road	B1
Church Street	D4	Priory Avenue	C3
Clarence Street	A3	Priory Bridge Road	C2
Cleveland Street	A3	Queen Street	D4
Compass Hill	A4	Railway Street	B1
Critchard Way	D2	Ranmer Road	C3
Cyril Street	A1	Raymond Street	A1
Deller's Wharf	B2	Rupert Street	A1
Duke Street	C3	St Andrew's Road	B1
Eastbourne Road	C3	St Augustine Street	C3
Eastleigh Road	D4	St James Street	B3
East Reach	D3	St John's Road	A4
East Street	C4	Samuels Court	A1
Fore Street	B4	South Road	C4
Fowler Street	A1	South Street	D4
French Weir Avenue	A2	Staplegrove Road	A2
Gloucester Road	C3	Station Road	B2
Grange Drive	C1	Stephen Street	C3
Grays Street	D3	Stephen Way	C3
Greenway Avenue	A1	Tancred Street	C3
Gyffarde Street	C3	The Avenue	A2
Hammet Street	B4	The Bridge	B3
Haydon Road	C3	The Crescent	B4
Herbert Street	B1	Thomas Street	B1
High Street	B4	Toneway	D2
Hugo Street	C3	Tower Street	B4
Hurdle Way	C4	Trinity Street	D4
Laburnum Street	C3	Upper High Street	B4
Lansdowne Road	C1	Victoria Gate	D3
Leslie Avenue	A1	Victoria Street	D3
Linden Grove	A2	Viney Street	D4
Lower Middle Street	B3	Wellington Road	A4
Magdalene Street	B3	Wilfred Road	C3
Mary Street	B4	William Street	B1
Maxwell Street	A1	Winchester Street	C2
Middle Street	B3	Wood Street	B3

Torquay

Torquay is found on atlas page **7 N6**

Abbey Road	B1	Middle Warbury Road	D1
Alexandra Road	C1	Mill Lane	A1
Alpine Road	C2	Montpellier Road	D3
Ash Hill Road	C1	Morgan Avenue	B1
Avenue Road	A1	Museum Road	D3
Bampfylde Road	A2	Palm Road	B1
Beacon Hill	D4	Parkhill Road	D4
Belgrave Road	A1	Pembroke Road	C1
Braddons Hill Road East	D3	Pennsylvania Road	D1
Braddons Hill Road West	C2	Pimlico	C2
Braddons Street	D2	Potters Hill	C1
Bridge Road	A1	Princes Road	C1
Camden Road	D1	Queen Street	C2
Cary Parade	C3	Rathmore Road	A2
Cary Road	C3	Rock Road	C2
Castle Lane	C1	Rosehill Road	D1
Castle Road	C1	St Efride's Road	A1
Cavern Road	D1	St Luke's Road	B2
Chestnut Avenue	A2	St Marychurch Road	C1
Church Lane	A1	Scarborough Road	B2
Church Street	A1	Seaway Lane	A4
Cleveland Road	A1	Shedden Hill Road	B3
Croft Hill	B2	Solbro Road	A3
Croft Road	B2	South Hill Road	D3
East Street	A1	South Street	A1
Ellacombe Road	C1	Stentiford Hill Road	C2
Falkland Road	A2	Strand	D3
Fleet Street	C3	Sutherland Road	D1
Grafton Road	D2	Temperance Street	C2
Hennapyn Road	A4	The Terrace	D3
Higher Union Lane	B1	Torbay Road	A4
Hillesdon Road	D2	Tor Church Road	A1
Hoxton Road	D1	Tor Hill Road	B1
Hunsdon Road	D3	Torwood Street	D3
King's Drive	A3	Trematon Ave	B1
Laburnum Street	A1	Trinity Hill	D3
Lime Avenue	A2	Union Street	B1
Lower Ellacombe		Upper Braddons Hill	D2
Church Road	D1	Vanehill Road	D4
Lower Union Lane	C2	Vansittart Road	A1
Lower Warbury Road	D2	Vaughan Parade	C3
Lucius Street	A1	Victoria Parade	D4
Lymington Road	B1	Victoria Road	C1
Magdalene Road	B1	Vine Road	A1
Market Street	C2	Walnut Road	A2
Meadfoot Lane	D4	Warberry Road West	C1
Melville Lane	C2	Warren Road	B2
Melville Street	C2	Wellington Road	C1

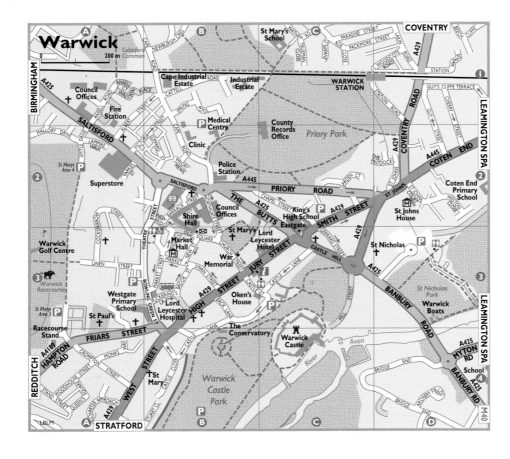

Warwick

Warwick is found on atlas page **59 L11**

Albert Street.....................A2	Packmore Street.....................
Ansell Court.......................A1	Paradise Street.....................
Ansell Road........................A1	Parkes Street.....................
Archery Fields...................D4	Priory Mews.....................
Back Lane.........................B3	Priory Road.....................
Banbury Road....................D3	Puckering's Lane.....................
Barrack Street....................B2	Queen's Square.....................
Beech Cliffe......................D1	Roe Close.....................
Bowling Green Street.........B3	St Johns.....................
Bridge End........................D4	St Johns Court.....................
Brook Street......................B3	Saltisford.....................
Cape Road.........................B1	Sharpe Close.....................
Castle Close.......................B4	Smith Street.....................
Castle Hill.........................C3	Spring Pool.....................
Castle Lane........................B4	Stand Street.....................
Castle Street......................B3	Station Avenue.....................
Cattell Road........................B1	Station Road.....................
Chapel Street......................C2	Stuart Close.....................
Charter Approach................A4	Swan Street.....................
Cherry Street......................D1	Theatre Street.....................
Church Street......................B3	The Butts.....................
Cocksparrow Street.............A3	The Paddocks.....................
Coten End........................D2	Trueman Close.....................
Coventry Road...................D2	Victoria Street.....................
Crompton Street.................A4	Vittle Drive.....................
Edward Street.....................B2	Wallwin Place.....................
Friars Street.......................A4	Wathen Road.....................
Garden Court......................C2	Weston Close.....................
Gerrard Street....................C3	West Street.....................
Guy's Cliffe Terrace.............D1	Woodcote Road.....................
Guy Street.........................D1	Woodhouse Street.....................
Hampton Road....................A4	
High Street.........................B3	
Jury Street.........................B3	
Lakin Road..........................D1	
Lammas Walk......................A2	
Linen Street.......................A3	
Mallory Drive......................A2	
Market Place......................B3	
Market Street......................B3	
Mill Street.........................C3	
Monks Way........................A4	
Myton Road.......................D4	
New Bridge........................B2	
Newburgh Crescent.............B1	
New Street.........................B3	
Northgate Street.................B2	
Old Square.........................B3	

Watford

Watford is found on atlas page **50 D11**

Addiscombe Road................B3	Market Street.....................
Albert Road North...............B2	Marlborough Road.....................
Albert Road South...............B2	Merton Road.....................
Alexandra Road...................A1	Mildred Avenue.....................
Anglian Close......................D1	Monica Close.....................
Beechen Grove...................C3	Nascot Street.....................
Brocklesbury Close..............D2	New Road.....................
Burton Avenue....................A4	New Street.....................
Cassiobury Drive.................A2	Orphanage Road.....................
Cassio Road........................A3	Park Avenue.....................
Charter Way.......................C3	Peace Prospect.....................
Chester Road......................A4	Percy Road.....................
Chester Street.....................A4	Pretoria Road.....................
Clarendon Road...................C1	Prince Street.....................
Cross Street.......................C2	Queen's Road.....................
Denmark Street...................A1	Queen Street.....................
Derby Road.........................C3	Radlett Road.....................
Duke Street........................C2	Raphael Drive.....................
Durban Road East................A4	Reeds Crescent.....................
Durban Road West...............A4	Rickmansworth Road.....................
Earl Street.........................C3	Rosslyn Road.....................
Ebury Road.........................D2	St Albans Road.....................
Essex Road.........................A1	St John's Road.....................
Estcourt Road.....................C2	St Mary's Road.....................
Exchange Road....................B3	St Pauls Way.....................
Farraline Road.....................B4	Shady Lane.....................
Feranley Street....................B4	Shaftesbury Road.....................
Francis Street......................B3	Smith Street.....................
Franklin Road......................B1	Sotheron Road.....................
Gartlet Road.......................C2	Southsea Avenue.....................
Gaumont Approach...............B2	Stanley Road.....................
George Street......................C4	Station Road.....................
Gladstone Road...................D3	Stephenson Way.....................
Granville Road.....................C4	Sutton Road.....................
Grosvenor Road...................C3	The Avenue.....................
Halsey Road........................B2	The Broadway.....................
Harwoods Road...................A4	The Crescent.....................
Hempstead Road..................A1	The Parade.....................
High Street.........................C3	Upton Road.....................
Hyde Road.........................A2	Vicarage Road.....................
Keele Close........................C1	Water Lane.....................
King Street.........................C4	Wellington Road.....................
Lady's Close........................C4	Wellstone Road.....................
Link Road...........................D1	Westland Road.....................
Loates Lane........................C3	West Street.....................
Lord Street.........................C3	Whippendell Road.....................
Lower High Street................D4	Wiggenhall Road.....................
Malden Road.......................A1	Woodford Road.....................

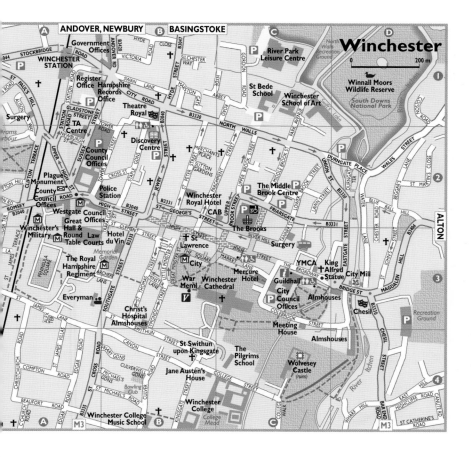

Winchester

Winchester is found on atlas page **22 E9**

Alex Terrace	A3	Market Lane	C3
Alison Way	A1	Marston Gate	B1
Andover Road	B1	Merchants Place	B2
Archery Lane	A3	Mews Lane	A3
Bar End Road	D4	Middle Brook Street	C2
Beaufort Road	A4	Minster Lane	B3
Beggar's Lane	D2	Newburgh Street	A2
Blue Ball Hill	D2	North Walls	C1
Bridge Street	D3	Parchment Street	B2
Canon Street	B4	Park Avenue	C2
Canute Road	D4	Romsey Road	A2
Chesil Street	D3	St Clement Street	B2
Chester Road	D2	St Cross Road	A4
Christchurch Road	A4	St George's Street	B2
City Road	B1	St James' Lane	A3
Clifton Hill	A2	St James Terrace	A3
Clifton Road	A1	St James' Villas	A4
Clifton Terrace	A2	St John's Street	D3
Colebrook Street	C3	St Martin's Close	D2
College Street	B4	St Michael's Gardens	B4
College Walk	C4	St Michael's Road	B4
Colson Road	D1	St Paul's Hill	A1
Compton Road	A4	St Peter Street	B2
Cross Street	B2	St Swithun Street	B3
Crowder Terrace	A3	St Thomas Street	B3
Culver Road	B4	Silchester Way	B1
Culverwell Gardens	B4	Silver Hill	C3
Durngate Place	D2	Southgate Street	B3
Durngate Terrace	D2	Staple Gardens	B2
Eastgate Street	D3	Station Road	A1
East Hill	D4	Stockbridge Road	A1
Edgar Road	A4	Sussex Street	A2
Friarsgate	C2	Sutton Gardens	B2
Friary Gardens	B4	Swan Lane	B1
Gladstone Street	A1	Symonds Street	B3
Gordon Road	C1	Tanner Street	C3
Great Minster Street	B3	The Broadway	C3
Highcliffe Road	D4	The Square	B3
High Street	B2	Tower Road	A1
Hyde Abbey Road	B1	Tower Street	A2
Hyde Close	B1	Trafalgar Street	B3
Hyde Street	B1	Union Street	C2
Jewry Street	B2	Upper Brook Street	C2
Kingsgate Street	B4	Upper High Street	A2
Lawn Street	C2	Victoria Road	B1
Little Minster Street	B3	Wales Street	D2
Lower Brook Street	C2	Water Lane	D3
Magdalen Hill	D3	Wharf Hill	D4

Wolverhampton

Wolverhampton is found on atlas page **58 D5**

Bath Avenue	A1	Peel Street	B3
Bath Road	A2	Penn Road	B4
Bell Street	B3	Piper's Row	D2
Berry Street	C2	Pitt Street	B3
Bilston Road	D3	Powlett Street	D4
Bilston Street	C3	Princess Street	C2
Birch Street	B2	Queen Square	B2
Broad Street	C2	Queen Street	C2
Castle Street	C3	Raby Street	D4
Chapel Ash	A3	Raglan Street	A3
Church Lane	B4	Railway Drive	D2
Church Street	B4	Red Lion Street	B2
Clarence Road	B2	Retreat Street	A4
Clarence Street	B2	Ring Road St Andrews	A2
Cleveland Road	D4	Ring Road St Davids	D2
Cleveland Street	B3	Ring Road St Georges	C4
Corn Hill	D2	Ring Road St Johns	B4
Culwell Street	D1	Ring Road St Marks	B3
Dale Street	A4	Ring Road St Patricks	C1
Darlington Street	B3	Ring Road St Peters	B2
Dudley Road	C4	Russell Street	A4
Dudley Street	C2	St George's Parade	C3
Fold Street	B3	St John's Square	C4
Fryer Street	C2	St Mark's Road	A3
Garrick Street	C3	St Mark's Street	A3
Graiseley Street	A4	Salop Street	B3
Great Brickkiln Street	A4	School Street	B3
Great Western Street	C1	Skinner Street	B3
Grimstone Street	D1	Snow Hill	B3
Horseley Fields	D2	Stafford Street	C1
Hospital Street	D4	Stephenson Street	A3
Lansdown Road	A1	Stewart Street	B4
Lever Street	C4	Summer Row	B3
Lichfield Street	C2	Tempest Street	C3
Little's Lane	C1	Temple Street	B3
Long Street	C2	Thomas Street	B4
Lord Street	A3	Tower Street	C2
Mander Street	A4	Vicarage Road	D4
Market Street	C3	Victoria Street	B3
Merridale Street	A4	Warwick Street	D3
Middle Cross	D3	Waterloo Road	B1
Mitre Fold	B2	Wednesfield Road	D1
Molineux Street	B1	Westbury Street	C2
New Hampton Road East	A1	Whitemore Hill	B1
North Street	B2	Whitmore Street	B4
Park Avenue	A1	Worcester Street	B4
Park Road East	B1	Wulfruna Street	C2
Park Road West	A2	Zoar Street	A4

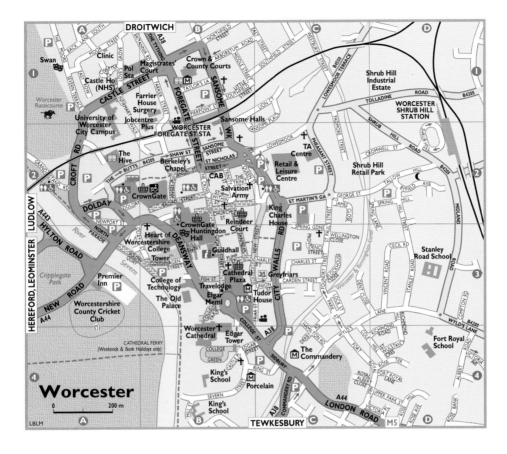

Worcester

Worcester is found on atlas page **46 G4**

Albert Road	D4	Middle Street
Angel Street	B2	Midland Road
Arboretum Road	B1	Mill Street
Back Lane South	A1	Moor Street
Blockhouse Close	C3	Newport Street
Britannia Road	A1	New Road
Broad Street	B2	New Street
Byfield Rise	D2	Northfield Street
Carden Street	C3	North Parade
Castle Street	A1	Padmore Street
Cathedral Ferry	A4	Park Street
Cecil Road	D3	Pheasant Street
Charles Street	C3	Pierpoint Street
Charter Place	A1	Providence Street
Church Street	B2	Pump Street
City Walls Road	C3	Quay Street
Cole Hill	C4	Queen Street
College Street	B3	Richmond Road
Commandery Road	C4	Rose Hill
Compton Road	D3	Rose Terrace
Copenhagen Street	B3	St Martin's Gate
Croft Road	A2	St Nicholas Street
Cromwell Street	D2	St Paul's Street
Deansway	B3	St Swithin Street
Dent Close	C3	Sansome Walk
Derby Road	C4	Severn Street
Dolday	A2	Severn Terrace
East Street	B1	Shaw Street
Edgar Street	B4	Shrub Hill Road
Farrier Street	B1	Sidbury
Fish Street	B3	Southfield Street
Foregate Street	B1	Spring Hill
Fort Royal Hill	C4	Stanley Road
Foundry Street	C3	Tallow Hill
Friar Street	C3	Taylor's Lane
George Street	C2	The Butts
Grandstand Road	A2	The Cross
Hamilton Road	C3	The Moors
High Street	B3	The Shambles
Hill Street	D2	The Tything
Hylton Road	A3	Tolladine Road
King Street	B4	Trinity Street
Little Southfield Street	B1	Union Street
Lock Street	C3	Upper Park Street
London Road	C4	Vincent Road
Love's Grove	A1	Wellington Close
Lowesmoor	C2	Westbury Street
Lowesmoor Terrace	C1	Wyld's Lane

York

York is found on atlas page **98 C10**

Aldwark	C2	Lower Ousegate
Barbican Road	D4	Lower Priory Street
Bishopgate Street	B4	Low Petergate
Bishophill Senior	B3	Margaret Street
Black Horse Lane	D2	Market Street
Blake Street	B2	Micklegate
Blossom Street	A4	Minster Yard
Bootham	B1	Monkgate
Bridge Street	B3	Museum Street
Buckingham Street	B3	Navigation Road
Cemetery Road	D4	New Street
Church Street	C2	North Street
Clifford Street	C3	Nunnery Lane
College Street	C1	Ogleforth
Colliergate	C2	Palmer Lane
Coney Street	B2	Palmer Street
Coppergate	C3	Paragon Street
Cromwell Road	B4	Parliament Street
Davygate	B2	Pavement
Deangate	C1	Peasholme Green
Dove Street	B4	Percy's Lane
Duncombe Place	B2	Piccadilly
Dundas Street	D2	Price's Lane
Fairfax Street	B3	Priory Street
Fawcett Street	D4	Queen Street
Feasegate	C2	Rougier Street
Fetter Lane	B3	St Andrewgate
Finkle Street	C2	St Denys' Road
Fishergate	C4	St Leonard's Place
Foss Bank	D1	St Martins Lane
Fossgate	C2	St Maurice's Road
Foss Islands Road	D2	St Saviourgate
George Street	D3	St Saviours Place
Gillygate	B1	Scarcroft Road
Goodramgate	C2	Shambles
Hampden Street	B4	Skeldergate
High Ousegate	C3	Spen Lane
High Petergate	B1	Spurriergate
Holgate Road	A4	Station Road
Hope Street	D4	Stonegate
Hungate	D2	Swinegate
Jewbury	D1	The Stonebow
Kent Street	D4	Toft Green
King Street	C3	Tower Street
Kyme Street	B4	Trinity Lane
Lendal	B2	Victor Street
Long Close Lane	D4	Walmgate
Lord Mayor's Walk	C1	Wellington Road

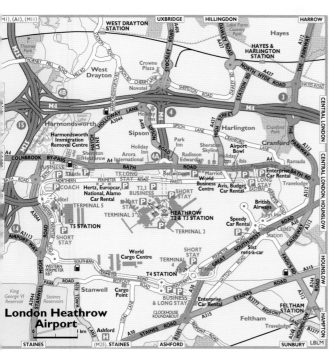

London Heathrow Airport – 17 miles west of central London, M25 junction 14 and M4 junction 4A

Satnav Location: TW6 1EW (Terminal 2), TW6 1QG (T3), TW6 3XA (T4), TW6 2GA (T5)
Information: visit *www.heathrow.com*
Parking: short-stay, long-stay and business parking is available.
Public Transport: coach, bus, rail and London Underground.
There are several 4-star and 3-star hotels within easy reach of the airport.
Car hire facilities are available.

London Gatwick Airport – 29 miles south of central London, M23 junction 9A

Satnav Location: RH6 0NP (South terminal), RH6 0PJ (North terminal)
Information: visit *www.gatwickairport.com*
Parking: short and long-stay parking is available at both the North and South terminals.
Public Transport: coach, bus and rail.
There are several 4-star and 3-star hotels within easy reach of the airport.
Car hire facilities are available.

London Stansted Airport – 36 miles north-east of central London, M11 junction 8/8A

Satnav Location: CM24 1RW
Information: visit *www.stanstedairport.com*
Parking: short, mid and long-stay open-air parking is available.
Public Transport: coach, bus and direct rail link to London on the Stansted Express.
There are several hotels within easy reach of the airport.
Car hire facilities are available.

London Luton Airport – 34 miles north of central London

Satnav Location: LU2 9QT
Information: visit *www.london-luton.co.uk*
Parking: short-term, mid-term and long-stay parking is available.
Public Transport: coach, bus and rail.
There are several hotels within easy reach of the airport.
Car hire facilities are available.

London City Airport – 8 miles east of central London

Satnav Location: E16 2PX
Information: visit *www.londoncityairport.com*
Parking: short and long-stay open-air parking is available.
Public Transport: easy access to the rail network, Docklands Light Railway and the London Underground.
There are 5-star, 4-star and 3-star hotels within easy reach of the airport.
Car hire facilities are available.

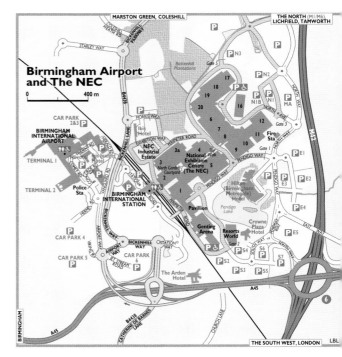

Birmingham Airport – 10 miles east of Birmingham, M42 junction

Satnav Location: B26 3QJ
Information: visit *www.birminghamairport.co.uk*
Parking: short and long-stay parking is available.
Public Transport: Air-Rail Link service operates every 2 minutes to and from Birmingham International Railway Station & Interchange.
There is one 3-star hotel adjacent to the airport and several 4 and 3-star hotels within easy reach of the airport. Car hire facilities are available.

East Midlands Airport – 14 miles south-west of Nottingham, M1 junction 23A/24

Satnav Location: DE74 2SA
Information: visit *www.eastmidlandsairport.com*
Parking: short and long-stay parking is available.
Public Transport: bus and coach services to major towns and cities in the East Midlands.
There are several 3-star hotels within easy reach of the airport.
Car hire facilities are available.

Manchester Airport – 10 miles south of Manchester, M56 junction 5

Satnav Location: M90 1QX
Information: visit *www.manchesterairport.co.uk*
Parking: short and long-stay parking is available.
Public Transport: coach, bus and rail.
There are several 4-star and 3-star hotels within easy reach of the airport. Car hire facilities are available.

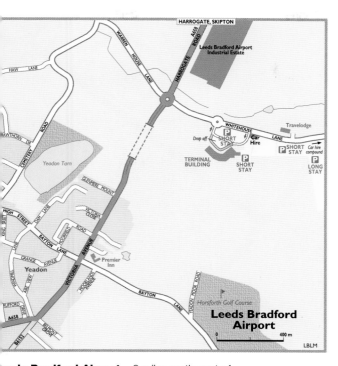

Leeds Bradford Airport – 8 miles north-east of
Bradford and 8 miles north-west of Leeds

Satnav Location: LS19 7TU
Information: visit www.leedsbradfordairport.co.uk
Parking: short, mid-term and long-stay parking is available.
Public Transport: bus service operates every 30 minutes from Bradford, Leeds and Otley.
There are several 4-star and 3-star hotels within easy reach of the airport.
Car hire facilities are available.

Aberdeen Airport – 7 miles north-west of Aberdeen

Satnav Location: AB21 7DU
Information: visit www.aberdeenairport.com
Parking: short and long-stay parking is available.
Public Transport: regular bus service to central Aberdeen.
There are several 4-star and 3-star hotels within easy reach of the airport.
Car hire facilities are available.

Edinburgh Airport – 9 miles west of Edinburgh

Satnav Location: EH12 9DN
Information: visit www.edinburghairport.com
Parking: short and long-stay parking is available.
Public Transport: regular bus services to central Edinburgh, Glasgow and Fife
and a tram service to Edinburgh.
There are several 4-star and 3-star hotels within easy reach of the airport.
Car hire and valet parking facilities are available.

Glasgow Airport – 10 miles west of Glasgow, M8 junction 28/29

Satnav Location: PA3 2SW
Information: visit www.glasgowairport.com
Parking: short and long-stay parking is available.
Public Transport: regular coach services operate direct to central Glasgow and Edinburgh.
There are several 3-star hotels within easy reach of the airport.
Car hire facilities are available.

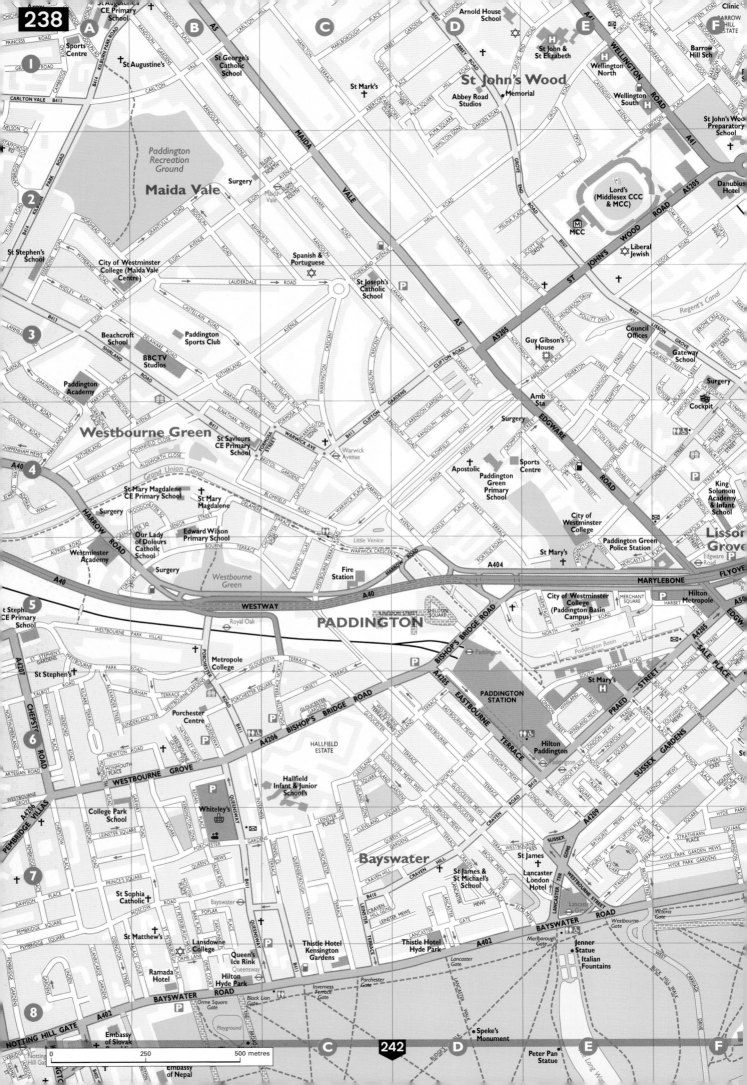

This index lists street and station names, and top places of tourist interest shown in red. Names are listed in alphabetical order and written in full, but may be abbreviated on the map. Each entry is followed by its Postcode District and then the page number and grid reference to the square in which the name is found. Names are asterisked (*) in the index where there is insufficient space to show them on the map.

A

Abbey Gardens NW8	238	C1
Abbey Orchard Street SW1P	244	B4
Abbey Road NW8	238	D1
Abbey Street SE1	246	B7
Abchurch Lane EC4N	241	L7
Abercorn Close NW8	238	C1
Abercorn Place NW8	238	C1
Aberdeen Place NW8	238	E3
Abingdon Road W8	242	A4
Abingdon Street SW1P	244	C3
Abingdon Villas W8	242	A4
Ackroyd Drive E3	247	L1
Acorn Walk SE16	247	K5
Acton Street WC1X	240	E2
Adam and Eve Mews W8	242	A3
Adam Street WC2N	240	D8
Adam's Row W1K	239	K8
Addle Hill EC4V	241	H7
Adelina Grove E1	246	F1
Adeline Place WC1B	240	B5
Adler Street E1	246	C2
Admiral Place SE16	247	K5
Admiral Walk W9	238	C4
Adpar Street W2	238	E4
Agdon Street EC1V	241	H3
Agnes Street E14	247	L2
Ainsty Street SE16	247	G6
Air Street W1B	240	A8
Alaska Street SE1	244	F2
Albany Road SE5	245	L8
Albany Street NW1	239	L1
Albemarle Street W1S	239	L8
Albermarle Way EC1V	241	H4
Alberta Street SE17	245	H7
Albert Bridge SW3	243	G8
Albert Embankment SE1	244	D7
Albert Gardens E1	247	H3
Albert Gate SW1X	243	G3
Albert Place W8	242	C3
Albion Gate W2	239	G7
Albion Place EC1M	241	H4
Albion Street SE16	247	G7
Albion Street W2	239	G7
Aldenham Street NW1	240	A1
Aldermanbury EC2V	241	K6
Alderney Mews SE1	245	K4
Alderney Street SW1V	243	L6
Aldersgate Street EC1A	241	J4
Aldford Street W1K	239	J8
Aldgate ◎ EC3M	246	B3
Aldgate EC3N	246	B3
Aldgate East ◎ E1	246	C2
Aldgate High Street EC3N	246	B3
Aldsworth Close W9	238	B4
Aldwych WC2E	240	E7
Alexander Place SW7	242	F5
Alexander Street W2	238	A6
Alexandra Gate SW7	242	E3
Alfred Mews WC1E	240	B4
Alfred Place WC1E	240	B4
Alfred Road W2	238	A5
Alice Street SE1	245	M4
Alie Street E1	246	C3
Allen Street W8	242	A4
Allhallows Lane EC4R	241	L8
Allington Street SW1E	243	L4
Allitsen Road NW8	238	F1
Allsop Place NW1	239	H4
Alma Square NW8	238	D1
Alpha Place SW3	243	G8
Alsace Street SE17	245	M7
Alscot Road SE1	246	C8
Alvey Street SE17	245	M6
Ambergate Street SE17	245	H7
Amberley Road W9	238	A4
Ambrosden Avenue SW1P	244	A4
Amelia Street SE17	245	J6
America Square EC3N	246	B3
America Street SE1	245	J2
Ampton Street WC1X	240	E2
Amwell Street EC1R	240	F2
Anchorage Point E14	247	M6
Andover Place NW6	238	B1
Angel ◎ N1	241	G1
Angel Junction N1	241	G1
Angel Street EC1A	241	J6
Ann Moss Way SE16	246	F8
Ann's Close SW1X	243	J3
Ansdell Street W8	242	B4
Antill Terrace E1	247	H2
Antizan Street E1	246	B2
Apple Tree Yard SW1Y	240	A8
Appold Street EC2A	241	M4
Apsley Gate W1J	243	J2
Apsley House & Wellington Museum W1J	243	K2
Aquinas Street SE1	245	G1
Arbour Square E1	247	H2
Archangels SE16	247	J7
Archer Street W1B	240	A7
Arch Street SE1	245	J4
Arden Estate N1	241	M1
Argyle Square WC1H	240	D2
Argyle Street WC1H	240	D2
Argyll Road W8	242	A3
Argyll Street W1F	239	M6
Arlington Street SW1A	243	M1
Arlington Way EC1R	241	G2
Arne Street WC2H	240	D6
Arnhem Place E14	247	M8
Arnold Estate SE1	246	C7
Arnside Street SE17	245	K8
Artesian Road W11	238	A6
Arthur Street EC4V	241	L7
Artichoke Hill E1W	246	E4
Artillery Lane E1	246	A1
Artillery Row SW1P	244	B4
Arundel Street WC2R	240	F7
Ashbridge Street NW8	238	F3
Ashburn Gardens SW7	242	C5
Ashburn Place SW7	242	C5
Ashby Street EC1V	241	H2
Asher Way E1W	246	D4
Ashfield Street E1	246	E2
Ashford Street N1	241	M2
Ashley Place SW1P	243	M4
Ashmill Street NW1	238	F4
Ashmole Street SW8	244	F8
Ashworth Road W9	238	B2
Assam Street E1	246	C2
Assembly Place E1	247	G1
Astell Street SW3	243	G6
Aston Street E14	247	K1
Astwood Mews SW7	242	C5
Atherstone Mews SW7	242	D5
Atterbury Street SW1P	244	C6
Attneave Street WC1X	240	F3
Aulton Place SE11	245	G7
Austin Friars EC2N	241	L6
Australia Gate SW1A	243	M3
Austral Street SE11	245	H5
Aveline Street SE11	244	F7
Ave Maria Lane EC1A	241	H6
Avenue Dock Hill SE16	247	J6
Avery Farm Row SW1W	243	K6
Avery Row W1K	239	L7
Aybrook Street W1U	239	J5
Aylesbury Road SE17	245	L7
Aylesbury Street EC1R	241	H4
Aylesford Street SW1V	244	B7
Aylward Street E1	247	G2
Ayres Street SE1	245	K2

B

Babmaes Street SW1Y	240	B8
Bache's Street N1	241	L2
Back Church Lane E1	246	D3
Back Hill EC1R	241	G4
Bacon Grove SE1	246	B7
Bainbridge Street WC1A	240	C6
Bakers Mews W1U	239	J6
Baker's Row EC1R	241	G4
Baker Street NW1	239	H4
Baker Street W1U	239	J5
Baker Street ◎ NW1	239	H4
Balcombe Street NW1	239	G3
Balderton Street W1K	239	J7
Baldwin's Gardens EC1N	240	F5
Baldwin Street EC1V	241	L2
Bale Road E1	247	J1
Balfe Street N1	240	D1
Balfour Mews W1K	239	K8
Balfour Place W1K	239	J8
Balfour Street SE17	245	K5
Baltic Square East E1	241	J3
Baltic Street West EC1Y	241	J4
Bank ◎ EC2R	241	L6
Bank End SE1	245	K1
Bankside SE1	241	J8
Banner Street EC1Y	241	K3
Banqueting House SW1A	244	C2
Banyard Road SE16	246	E8
Barbican ◎ EC1A	241	J4
Barbican Estate EC2Y	241	J5
Barge House Street SE1	245	G1
Bark Place W2	238	B7
Barkston Gardens SW5	242	B6
Barley Corn Way E14	247	L4
Barlow/Congreve Estate SE17	245	M5
Barlow Place W1J	239	L7
Barlow Street SE17	245	L5
Barnardo Street E1	247	H3
Barnby Street NW1	240	A1
Barnes Street E14	247	J2
Barnham Street SE1	246	A6
Baron's Place SE1	245	G3
Baron Street N1	241	G1
Barrett Street W1U	239	K6
Barrow Hill Estate NW8	238	F1
Barrow Hill Road NW8	238	F1
Barter Street WC1A	240	D5
Bartholomew Close EC1A	241	J5
Bartholomew Lane EC2R	241	L6
Bartholomew Street SE1	245	L5
Bartlett Court EC4A	241	G6
Barton Street SW1P	244	C4
Basil Street SW3	243	H4
Basin Approach E14	247	K3
Basinghall Lane EC2V	241	K5
Basinghall Street EC2V	241	K5
Bastwick Street EC1V	241	J3
Bateman's Buildings W1D	240	B6
Bateman Street W1D	240	B6
Bath Street EC1V	241	K2
Bath Terrace SE1	245	J4
Bathurst Mews W2	238	E7
Bathurst Street W2	238	E7
Battle Bridge Lane SE1	245	M1
Batty Street E1	246	D2
Bayley Street WC1B	240	B5
Baylis Road SE1	244	F3
Bayswater ◎ W2	238	B7
Bayswater Road W2	238	E7
Baythorne Street E3	247	L1
Beaconsfield Road SE17	245	M7
Beak Street W1F	240	A7
Bear Grove SE1	241	J8
Bear Lane SE1	245	H1
Beauchamp Place SW3	243	G4
Beaufort Gardens SW3	243	G4
Beaufort Street SW3	242	E8
Beaumont Place W1T	240	A3
Beaumont Street W1G	239	K4
Beccles Street E14	247	M3
Beckett Street SE1	245	L3
Beckway Street SE17	245	M6
Bedale Street SE1	245	L1
Bedford Avenue WC1B	240	C5
Bedfordbury WC2N	240	C7
Bedford Gardens W8	242	A2
Bedford Row WC1N	240	E4
Bedford Square WC1B	240	B5
Bedford Street WC2E	240	D7
Bedford Way WC1H	240	C3
Bedlow Close NW8	238	F3
Beech Street EC2Y	241	J4
Beeston Place SW1W	243	L4
Belgrave Mews North * SW1X	243	J3
Belgrave Mews South * SW1X	243	K4
Belgrave Place SW1X	243	K4
Belgrave Road SW1V	243	L5
Belgrave Road SW1V	244	A6
Belgrave Square SW1X	243	J3
Belgrave Street E1	247	J2
Bell Lane E1	246	B1
Bell Street NW1	238	F4
Bell Yard WC2A	240	F6
Belvedere Road SE1	244	E2
Benjamin Street EC1M	241	H4
Ben Jonson Road E1	247	J1
Bennett Street SW1A	243	M1
Ben Smith Way SE16	246	D7
Benson Quay E1W	246	F4
Bentinck Mews W1U	239	K6
Bentinck Street W1U	239	K6
Bere Street E1W	247	H3
Bergen Square SE16	247	K8
Berkeley Mews W1H	239	H6
Berkeley Square W1J	239	L8
Berkeley Street W1J	239	L8
Bermondsey ◎ SE16	246	E7
Bermondsey Spa SE16	246	C8
Bermondsey Square SE1	246	A8
Bermondsey Street SE1	246	A6
Bermondsey Wall East SE16	246	E7
Bermondsey Wall Estate SE16	246	D7
Bermondsey Wall West SE16	246	C6
Bernard Street WC1N	240	D4
Berners Mews W1T	240	A5
Berners Place W1F	240	A6
Berners Street W1T	240	A5
Berryfield Road SE17	245	J6
Berry Street EC1V	241	H3
Berwick Street W1F	240	A6
Bessborough Gardens SW1V	244	B6
Bessborough Street SW1V	244	B6
Betterton Street WC2H	240	D6
Bevenden Street N1	241	L2
Bevin Close SE16	247	J5
Bevington Street SE16	246	D7
Bevin Way WC1X	240	F1
Bevis Marks EC3A	246	A2
Bewley Street E1	246	F3
Bickenhall Street W1U	239	H4
Bidborough Street WC1H	240	C2
Biddulph Road W9	238	B2
Big Ben (Elizabeth Tower) * SW1A	244	D3
Bigland Street E1	246	E3
Billiter Square EC3M	246	A3
Billiter Street EC3M	246	A3
Bina Gardens SW5	242	C6
Bingham Place W1U	239	J4
Binney Street W1K	239	K7
Birchfield Street E14	247	M3
Birchin Lane EC3V	241	L7
Birdcage Walk SW1H	244	A3
Birde Lane EC4Y	241	H6
Bird Street W1C	239	K6
Birkenhead Street N1	240	D1
Bishop's Bridge Road W2	238	C6
Bishopsgate EC2M	246	A2
Bishops Square E1	246	B1
Bishop's Terrace SE11	245	G5
Bittern Street SE1	245	J3
Blackall Street EC2A	241	M3
Blackburne's Mews W1K	239	J7
Black Friars ◎ EC4V	241	H7
Blackfriars Bridge SE1	241	H8
Black Friars Lane EC4V	241	H7
Blackfriars Road SE1	245	H3
Blackhorse Court SE1	245	L4
Black Lion Gate W2	238	B8
Black Prince Road SE11	244	E6
Blackwood Street SE17	245	K6
Blandford Street W1U	239	H5
Blenheim Street W1S	239	L7
Bletchley Street N1	241	K1
Blomfield Road W9	238	C4
Blomfield Street EC2M	241	M5
Blomfield Villas W2	238	C5
Bloomfield Terrace SW1W	243	J6
Bloomsbury Square WC1A	240	D5
Bloomsbury Street WC1B	240	C5
Bloomsbury Way WC1A	240	C5
Blount Street E14	247	K2
Blue Ball Yard SW1A	243	M1
Bohn Road E1	247	J1
Bolsover Street W1W	239	L4
Bolton Gardens SW5	242	B6
Bolton Street W1J	243	L1
Bond Street ◎ W1C	239	K6
Bondway SW8	244	D8
Bonhill Street EC2A	241	L4
Bonnington Square SW8	244	E8
Boot Street N1	241	M2
Borough ◎ SE1	245	K3
Borough High Street SE1	245	K3
Borough Road SE1	245	H3
Boscobel Place SW1W	243	K5
Boscobel Street NW8	238	E4
Boss Street SE1	246	B6
Boston Place NW1	239	G3
Botolph Lane EC3R	241	M7
Boundary Lane SE17	245	K8
Boundary Row SE1	245	H2
Bourdon Street W1K	239	L7
Bourlet Close W1W	239	M5
Bourne Estate EC1N	240	F4
Bourne Street SW1W	243	J6
Bourne Terrace W2	238	B5
Bouverie Place W2	238	F6
Bouverie Street EC4Y	241	G6
Bowland Yard * SW1X	243	J3
Bow Lane EC4M	241	K6
Bowling Green Lane EC1R	241	G3
Bowling Green Place SE1	245	L2
Bowling Green Street SE11	244	F8
Bowling Green Walk N1	241	M2
Bowsell Street WC1N	240	D4
Bow Street WC2E	240	D7
Boyd Street E1	246	D3
Boyfield Street SE1	245	H3
Boyle Street W1S	239	M7
Boyson Road SE17	245	K8
Brackland Terrace SW3	243	H6
Brackley Street EC1Y	241	J4
Bradenham Close SE17	245	K8
Brad Street SE1	245	G2
Braganza Street SE17	245	H7
Braham Street E1	246	C3
Bramerton Street SW3	242	F7
Bramham Gardens SW5	242	B6
Branch Road E14	247	J3
Brandon Estate SE17	245	H8
Brandon Street SE17	245	K6
Brangton Road SE11	244	F7
Bray Crescent SE16	247	H6
Bray Place SW3	243	H6
Bread Street EC4M	241	K7
Bream's Buildings EC4A	240	F6
Brechin Place SW7	242	D6
Breezer's Hill E1W	246	D4
Brendon Street W1H	239	G5
Bressenden Place SW1W	243	L4
Brettell Street SE17	245	L7
Brewers Green SW1H	244	A3
Brewer Street W1F	240	A7
Brewhouse Lane E1W	246	F6
Brewhouse Walk SE16	247	J5
Brick Court WC2R	240	F7
Brick Street W1J	243	K2
Bridewell Place EC4V	241	H7
Bridgeman Street NW8	238	F1
Bridge Place SW1V	243	L5
Bridgeport Place E1W	246	D4
Bridge Street EC4V	241	J7
Bridge Street SW1A	244	D3
Bridgewater Street EC2Y	241	J4
Bridgeway Street NW1	240	A1
Bridle Lane W1F	240	A7
Bridstow Place W2	238	A6
Brightlingsea Place E14	247	L4
Brill Place NW1	240	C1
Briset Street EC1M	241	H4
Bristol Gardens W9	238	B4
Britannia Street WC1X	240	E2
Britannia Walk N1	241	L2
Britannia Way N1	241	K2
Britten Street SW3	242	F7
Britton Street EC1M	241	H4
Broadbent Street W1K	239	L7
Broadgate Circle EC2M	241	M5
Broadley Street NW8	238	F4
Broadley Terrace NW1	238	F4
Broadstone Place W1U	239	J5
Broad Walk NW1	239	K1
Broad Walk W2	239	H7
Broadwall SE1	245	G1
Broadway SW1H	244	B4
Broadwick Street W1F	240	A7
Brockham Street SE1	245	K4
Brodlove Lane E1W	247	H3
Bromley Street E1	247	J2
Brompton Road SW3	243	G4
Brompton Road SW7	242	F5
Brompton Square SW3	242	F4
Bronti Close SE17	245	K7
Brook Drive SE11	245	G5
Brooke Street EC1N	240	F5
Brook Gate W2	239	H8
Brook Mews North W2	238	D7
Brook's Mews W1K	239	K7
Brook Street W1K	239	K7
Brook Street W2	238	E7
Brown Heart Gardens W1K	239	K7
Browning Mews W1G	239	K5
Browning Street SE17	245	K6
Brownlow Mews WC1N	240	E3
Brownlow Street WC1V	240	E5
Brown Street W1H	239	G6
Brunel Road SE16	247	G6
Brune Street E1	246	B1
Brunswick ◎ WC1N	240	D3
Brunswick Gardens W8	242	A2
Brunswick Place N1	241	L2
Brunswick Quay SE16	247	J8
Brunswick Square WC1N	240	D3
Brunswick Street WC1N	240	D3
Brunton Place E14	247	K3
Brushfield Street E1	246	B1
Bruton Lane W1J	239	L8
Bruton Place W1J	239	L8
Bruton Street W1J	239	L8
Bryan Road SE16	247	K6
Bryanston Mews West W1H	239	G5
Bryanston Mews East W1H	239	H5
Bryanston Place W1H	239	G5
Bryanston Square W1H	239	H5
Bryanston Street W1C	239	H7
Buck Hill Walk W2	238	E8
Buckingham Gate SW1E	243	L3
Buckingham Mews SW1E	243	L3
Buckingham Palace SW1A	243	L3
Buckingham Palace Road SW1W	243	L5
Buckingham Place SW1E	243	M4
Buckland Street N1	241	L1
Buckle Street E1	246	C2
Bucknall Street WC2H	240	C6
Buckters Rents SE16	247	J5
Budge's Walk W2	242	D2
Bulleid Way SW1V	243	L5
Bulstrode Street W1U	239	K5
Bunhill Row EC1Y	241	L3
Burdett Estate E14	247	M1
Burdett Road E14	247	L2
Burdett Street SE1	244	F3
Burgess Street E14	247	M1
Burge Street SE1	245	L4
Burlington Arcade W1J	239	M8
Burlington Gardens W1S	239	M8
Burnhouse Place SW1W	243	J6
Burnsall Street SW3	243	G7
Burnside Close SE16	247	J5
Burrell Street SE1	245	H1
Burslem Street E1	246	D3
Burton Grove SE17	245	L7
Burton Street WC1H	240	C2
Burwood Place W2	239	G6
Bury Close SE16	247	H5
Bury Court EC3A	246	A2
Bury Place WC1A	240	D5
Bury Street EC3A	246	A2
Bury Street SW1Y	244	A1
Bury Walk SW3	242	F6
Bushell Street E1W	246	D5
Bush Lane EC4V	241	L7
Butcher Row E1	247	J3
Bute Street SW7	242	E5
Butler Place SW1H	244	B4
Butler's Wharf SE1	246	C6
Buttesland Street N1	241	L2
Byefield Close SE16	247	K6
Bylands Close SE16	247	J5
Byng Place WC1E	240	B4
Byng Street E14	247	M6
Byward Street EC3R	246	A4
Bywater Place SE16	247	K5
Bywater Street SW3	243	G6

C

Cabbell Street NW1	238	F5
Cable Street E1	246	F3
Cadiz Street SE17	245	K7
Cadogan Gardens SW3	243	H5
Cadogan Gate SW1X	243	H5
Cadogan Lane SW1X	243	J4
Cadogan Place SW1X	243	J4
Cadogan Square SW1X	243	H5
Cadogan Street SW3	243	G6
Caledonian Road N1	240	D1
Caledonia Street N1	240	D1
Cale Street SW3	242	F6
Callow Street SW3	242	D7
Calshot Street N1	240	E1
Calthorpe Street WC1X	240	E3
Cambridge Circus WC2H	240	C7
Cambridge Gardens NW6	238	A1
Cambridge Gate NW1	239	L3
Cambridge Road NW6	238	A2
Cambridge Road NW6	238	A2
Cambridge Square W2	238	F6
Cambridge Street SW1V	243	L6
Cambridge Terrace NW1	239	L2
Cambridge Terrace Mews NW1	239	L3
Camdenhurst Street E14	247	K2
Camera Place SW10	242	D8
Camomile Street EC3A	246	A2
Campden Grove W8	242	A2
Campden Hill Road W8	242	A2
Campden Street W8	242	A1
Camperdown Street E1	246	C3
Canada Estate SE16	247	G7
Canada Gate SW1A	243	M3
Canada Street SE16	247	H7
Canada Water ◎ ● SE16	247	G7
Canada Wharf SE16	247	L5
Canal Street SE5	245	L8
Canary Riverside E14	247	L4
Candle Street E1	247	K1
Canning Place W8	242	C4
Cannon Drive E14	247	M4
Cannon Street EC4N	241	K7
Cannon Street ◎ ● EC4R	241	K7
Cannon Street Road E1	246	E3
Canon Beck Road SE16	247	G6
Canon Row SW1A	244	D3
Canton Street E14	247	M3
Capeners Close * SW1X	243	J3
Capland Street NW8	238	E3
Capper Street WC1E	240	A4
Capstan Way SE16	247	K5
Carbis Road E14	247	L2
Carburton Street W1W	239	L4
Cardigan Street SE11	244	F6
Cardington Street NW1	240	A2
Carey Street WC2A	240	F6
Carlisle Avenue EC3N	246	B3
Carlisle Lane SE1	244	F4
Carlisle Place SW1P	243	M5
Carlisle Street W1D	240	B6
Carlos Place W1K	239	K7
Carlton Gardens SW1Y	244	B2
Carlton Hill NW6	238	B1
Carlton House Terrace SW1Y	244	B1
Carlton Street W1J	243	L1
Carlton Vale NW6	238	A1
Carlton Vale NW6	238	B1
Carlyle Square SW3	242	F7
Carmelite Street EC4Y	241	G7
Carnaby Street W1F	239	M7
Caroline Place W2	238	B7
Caroline Street E1	247	H3
Caroline Terrace SW1W	243	J5
Carpenter Street W1K	239	K7
Carrington Street W1J	243	L1
Carr Street E14	247	K1
Carteret Street SW1H	244	B3
Carter Lane EC4V	241	H7
Carter Place SE17	245	K7
Carter Street SE17	245	J7
Carthusian Street EC1M	241	J4
Carting Lane WC2R	240	D8
Cartwright Gardens WC1H	240	C2
Cartwright Street E1	246	C4
Casey Close NW8	238	F3
Casson Street E1	246	C1
Castellain Road W9	238	B3
Castlebrook Close SE11	245	G5
Castle Lane SW1E	243	M4
Catesby Street SE17	245	L6
Cathay Street SE16	246	F7
Cathcart Road SW10	242	C8
Cathedral Walk SW1E	243	M4
Catherine Place SW1E	243	M4
Catherine Street WC2E	240	E7
Cato Street W1H	239	G5
Causton Street SW1P	244	B6
Cavell Street E1	246	F1

Cavendish Avenue NW8 238 E1
Cavendish Place W1G 239 L6
Cavendish Square W1G 239 L6
Cavendish Street N1 241 L1
Caversham Street SW3 243 G8
Caxton Street SW1H 244 B4
Cayton Street EC1V 241 K2
Centaur Street SE1 244 F4
Central Street EC1V 241 J2
Chadwell Street EC1R 241 G1
Chadwick Street SW1P 244 B4
Chagford Street NW1 239 H4
Chalton Street NW1 240 B1
Chambers Street SE16 246 D7
Chamber Street E1 246 C3
Chambers Wharf SE16 246 D6
Chancel Street SE1 245 H1
Chancery Lane WC2A 240 F5
Chancery Lane WC1V 240 F5
Chandos Place WC2N 240 C8
Chandos Street W1G 239 L5
Chantry Square W8 242 B4
Chapel Market N1 240 F1
Chapel Street NW1 238 F5
Chapel Street SW1X 243 K3
Chaplin Close SE1 245 G3
Chapman Street E1 246 E3
Chapter Road SE17 245 H7
Chapter Street SW1P 244 B6
Chargrove Close SE16 247 H6
Charing Cross ⇌ WC2N 244 D1
Charing Cross Road WC2H 240 B6
Charing Cross Road WC2N 240 C7
Charlbert Street NW8 238 F1
Charles II Street SW1Y 240 B8
Charles Square N1 241 M2
Charles Street W1J 243 K1
Charleston Street SE17 245 K6
Charlotte Road EC2A 241 M3
Charlotte Street W1T 240 A4
Charlwood Place SW1V 244 A6
Charlwood Road SW1V 243 M7
Charlwood Street SW1V 244 A6
Charrington Street NW1 240 B1
Charterhouse Square EC1M 241 H4
Charterhouse Street EC1M 241 G5
Chart Street N1 241 L2
Chaseley Street E14 247 J2
Chatham Street SE17 245 L5
Cheapside EC2V 241 K6
Chelsea Bridge SW1W 243 K8
Chelsea Bridge Road SW1W 243 J8
Chelsea Embankment SW3 243 G8
Chelsea Manor Gardens SW3 242 F7
Chelsea Manor Street SW3 242 G7
Chelsea Park Gardens SW3 242 E8
Chelsea Physic Garden SW3 243 H8
Chelsea Square SW3 242 E7
Cheltenham Terrace SW3 243 H6
Chenies Mews WC1E 240 B4
Chenies Street WC1E 240 B4
Cheniston Gardens W8 242 A4
Chepstow Place W2 238 A7
Chepstow Road W2 238 A6
Chequer Street EC1Y 241 K3
Cherbury Street N1 241 L1
Cherry Garden Street SE16 246 E7
Chesham Close SW1X 243 J4
Chesham Place SW1X 243 J4
Chesham Street SW1X 243 J4
Chester Close SW1X 243 K3
Chester Close North NW1 239 L2
Chester Close South NW1 239 L2
Chesterfield Gardens W1J 243 K1
Chesterfield Hill W1J 239 K8
Chesterfield Street W1J 243 K1
Chester Gate NW1 239 L2
Chester Mews SW1X 243 K3
Chester Place NW1 239 L1
Chester Road NW1 239 K2
Chester Row SW1W 243 K5
Chester Square SW1W 243 K5
Chester Square Mews SW1W 243 K4
Chester Street SW1X 243 K4
Chester Terrace NW1 239 L2
Chester Way SE11 245 G6
Cheval Place SW7 243 G4
Cheval Street E14 247 M7
Cheyne Gardens SW3 243 G8
Cheyne Row SW3 242 F8
Cheyne Walk SW3 242 F8
Chicheley Street SE1 244 E2
Chichester Road NW6 238 A1
Chichester Road W2 238 C5
Chichester Street SW1V 244 A7
Chicksand Street E1 246 C1
Chigwell Hill E1W 246 E4
Child's Place SW5 242 A5
Child's Street SW5 242 A5
Chiltern Street W1U 239 J4
Chilworth Mews W2 238 D6
Chilworth Street W2 238 D6
China Hall Mews SE16 247 G8
Chinatown W1D 240 B7
Chippenham Mews W9 238 A4
Chiswell Street EC1Y 241 K4
Chitty Street W1T 240 A4
Christchurch Street SW3 243 G8
Christian Street E1 246 D3
Christina Street EC2A 241 M3
Christopher Close SE16 247 H6
Christopher Street EC2A 241 L4
Chudleigh Street E1 247 H2
Chumleigh Street SE5 245 M8
Churchill Gardens
Road SW1V 243 L7
Churchill War Rooms SW1A 244 C3
Church Street NW8 238 F4
Church Way NW1 240 B2
Churchyard Row SE11 245 H5
Churton Place SW1V 244 A6
Churton Street SW1V 244 A6
Circus Road NW8 238 E1
Cirencester Square W2 238 A5
City Garden Row N1 241 J1
City Road EC1V 241 J1
City Road EC1Y 241 L3
Clabon Mews SW1X 243 H5
Clack Street SE16 247 G7
Clanricarde Gardens W2 238 A8
Claremont Square N1 240 F1
Clarence Gardens NW1 239 L2
Clarence Mews SE16 247 G6
Clarendon Gardens W9 238 D4
Clarendon Gate W2 238 F7
Clarendon Place W2 238 F7

Clarendon Street SW1V 243 L6
Clareville Grove SW7 242 D6
Clareville Street SW7 242 D6
Clarges Mews W1J 243 L1
Clarges Street W1J 243 L1
Clark Street E1 246 F2
Claverton Street SW1V 244 A7
Clave Street E1W 246 F5
Clayton Street SE11 244 F8
Cleaver Square SE11 245 G7
Cleaver Street SE11 245 G7
Clegg Street E1W 246 F5
Clemence Street E14 247 L2
Clements Lane EC4N 241 L7
Clement's Road SE16 246 E8
Clenston Mews W1H 239 H6
Clere Street EC2A 241 L3
Clerkenwell Close EC1R 241 G3
Clerkenwell Green EC1R 241 G4
Clerkenwell Road EC1M 241 G4
Cleveland Gardens W2 238 C6
Cleveland Mews W1T 239 M4
Cleveland Place SW1Y 244 A1
Cleveland Row SW1A 244 A2
Cleveland Square W2 238 C6
Cleveland Street W1T 239 M4
Cleveland Terrace W2 238 D6
Clifford Street W1S 239 M7
Clifton Gardens W9 238 C4
Clifton Place SE16 247 G6
Clifton Place W2 238 E7
Clifton Road W9 238 D3
Clifton Street EC2A 241 M3
Clifton Villas W9 238 C4
Clink Street SE1 245 K1
Clipper Close SE16 247 H6
Clipstone Mews W1W 239 M4
Clipstone Street W1W 239 L4
Cliveden Place SW1W 243 J5
Cloak Lane EC4R 241 K7
Cloth Fair EC1A 241 J5
Cloth Street EC1A 241 J5
Cluny Place SE1 246 A8
Cobb Street E1 246 B2
Coburg Street NW1 240 A2
Coburg Close SW1P 244 A5
Cochrane Mews NW8 238 E1
Cochrane Street NW8 238 E1
Cock Lane EC1A 241 H5
Cockspur Street SW1Y 244 C1
Codling Close * E1W 246 D5
Coin Street SE1 245 G1
Coke Street E1 246 D2
Colbeck Mews SW7 242 C6
Coleborn Row N1 241 H1
Coleherne Road SW10 242 B7
Coleman Street EC2R 241 L6
Cole Street SE1 245 K3
Coley Street WC1X 240 F3
College Hill EC4R 241 K7
College Street EC4R 241 K7
Collett Road SE16 246 D8
Collier Street N1 240 E1
Collingham Gardens SW5 242 B6
Collingham Place SW5 242 B6
Collingham Road SW5 242 B5
Colnbrook Street SE1 245 H4
Colombo Street SE1 245 H1
Colonnade WC1N 240 D4
Coltman Street E14 247 K2
Commercial Road E1 246 D2
Commercial Road E14 247 K3
Commercial Street E1 246 B2
Compton Street EC1V 241 H3
Concert Hall Approach SE1 244 E2
Conder Street E14 247 K2
Conduit Mews W2 238 E6
Conduit Place W2 238 E6
Conduit Street W1S 239 L7
Congreve Street SE17 245 M5
Connaught Close W2 238 F7
Connaught Place W2 239 G7
Connaught Square W2 239 G6
Connaught Street W2 239 G6
Cons Street SE1 245 G2
Constitution Hill SW1A 243 L3
Content Street SE17 245 K5
Conway Street W1T 239 M4
Cookham Crescent SE16 247 H6
Cook's Road SE17 245 H8
Coombs Street N1 241 J1
Cooper's Lane Estate NW1 240 B1
Cooper's Road SE3N 246 B3
Copenhagen Place E14 247 L2
Cope Place W8 242 A4
Copley Court SE17 245 J8
Copley Street E1 247 H2
Copperfield Road E3 247 K1
Copperfield Street SE1 245 J2
Copthall Avenue EC2R 241 L6
Coptic Street WC1A 240 C5
Coral Street SE1 245 G3
Coram Street WC1H 240 C3
Cork Square E1W 246 E5
Cork Street W1S 239 M8
Corlett Street NW1 238 F5
Cornhill EC3V 241 L6
Cornwall Gardens SW7 242 C4
Cornwall Mews South SW7 242 C5
Cornwall Road SE1 244 F1
Cornwall Road SE1 245 G2
Cornwall Street E1 246 E3
Cornwall Terrace Mews NW1 239 H4
Cornwood Drive E1 247 G2
Coronet Street N1 241 M2
Corporation Row EC1R 241 G3
Corsham Street N1 241 L2
Cosser Street SE1 244 F4
Cosway Street NW1 239 G4
Cottage Place SW3 242 F4
Cottesmore Gardens W8 242 B4
Cottons Lane SE1 245 M1
Coulson Street SW3 243 H6
Counter Street SE1 245 M1
County Street SE1 245 K5
Courtenay Square SE11 244 F7
Courtenay Street SE11 244 F6
Courtfield Gardens SW5 242 B5
Courtfield Road SW7 242 C5
Court Street E1 246 E1
Cousin Lane EC4R 241 K8
Covent Garden WC2E 240 D7
Covent Garden WC2E 240 D7
Coventry Street W1D 240 B8
Cowcross Street EC1M 241 H4
Cowper Street EC2A 241 L3

Crail Row SE17 245 L5
Cramer Street W1U 239 J5
Crampton Street SE17 245 J6
Cranbourn Street WC2H 240 C7
Cranleigh Street NW1 240 A1
Cranley Gardens SW7 242 D6
Cranley Mews SW7 242 D6
Cranley Place SW7 242 E6
Cranston Estate N1 241 L1
Cranwood Street EC1V 241 L2
Craven Hill W2 238 C7
Craven Hill Gardens W2 238 C7
Craven Road W2 238 D7
Craven Street WC2N 244 D1
Craven Terrace W2 238 D7
Crawford Passage EC1R 241 G3
Crawford Place W1H 239 G5
Crawford Street W1H 239 G5
Creechurch Lane EC3A 246 A3
Creed Lane EC4V 241 H7
Cresswell Place SW10 242 D6
Cressy Place E1 247 G1
Crestfield Street WC1H 240 D2
Crimscott Street SE1 246 A8
Crispin Street E1 246 B1
Cromer Street WC1H 240 D2
Crompton Street W2 238 D4
Cromwell Place SW7 242 E5
Cromwell Road SW5 242 B5
Cromwell Road SW7 242 E5
Crondall Court N1 241 M1
Crondall Street N1 241 L1
Cropley Street N1 241 K1
Crosby Row SE1 245 L3
Cross Lane EC3R 246 A4
Crosswall EC3N 246 B3
Crowder Street E1 246 E3
Crucifix Lane SE1 246 A6
Cruikshank Street WC1X 240 F1
Crutched Friars EC3N 246 A3
Cuba Street E14 247 M6
Cubitt Street WC1X 240 E2
Culford Gardens SW3 243 H6
Culling Road SE16 246 F7
Cullum Street EC3M 246 A3
Culross Street W1K 239 J8
Culworth Street NW8 238 F1
Cumberland Gardens WC1X 240 F2
Cumberland Gate W2 239 H7
Cumberland Market NW1 239 L2
Cumberland Street SW1V 243 L6
Cumberland Terrace NW1 239 L1
Cumberland Terrace
Mews NW1 239 L1
Cumberland Wharf SE16 247 G6
Cumming Street N1 240 E1
Cundy Street SW1W 243 K6
Cunningham Place NW8 238 E3
Cureton Street SW1P 244 C6
Curlew Street SE1 246 B6
Cursitor Street EC4A 240 F6
Curtain Road EC2A 241 M3
Curtain Road EC2A 241 M4
Curzon Gate W2 243 K2
Curzon Street W1J 243 K1
Cuthbert Street W2 238 E4
Cutler Street EC3A 246 A2
Cynthia Street N1 240 F1
Cypress Place W1T 240 A4
Cyrus Street EC1V 241 H3

D

Dacre Street SW1H 244 B3
Dakin Place E1 247 J1
Dallington Street EC1V 241 H3
Damien Street E1 246 F2
Dane Street WC1R 240 E5
Dansey Place W1D 240 B7
Dante Road SE11 245 H5
Danvers Street SW3 242 F8
D'Arblay Street W1F 240 A6
Dartford Street SE17 245 K8
Dartmouth Street SW1H 244 B3
Darwin Street SE17 245 L5
Date Street SE17 245 K7
Davenant Street E1 246 D1
Daventry Street NW1 238 F4
Davidge Street SE1 245 H3
Davies Mews W1K 239 K7
Davies Street W1K 239 K7
Dawes Street SE17 245 L6
Dawson Place W2 238 A7
Deacon Way SE17 245 J5
Deal Porters Way SE16 247 G8
Deal Street E1 246 D1
Dean Bradley Street SW1P 244 C5
Dean Close SE16 247 H6
Deancross Street E1 246 F3
Deanery Street W1K 243 K1
Dean Farrar Street SW1H 244 C4
Dean Ryle Street SW1P 244 C5
Dean's Buildings SE17 245 L6
Dean Stanley Street SW1P 244 C4
Dean Street W1D 240 B6
Dean's Yard SW1P 244 C4
Decima Street SE1 245 M4
Deck Close SE16 247 J6
Defoe Close SE16 247 K7
Delamere Terrace W2 238 B4
De Laune Street SE17 245 H7
Delaware Road W9 238 B3
Dellow Street E1 246 F3
Delverton Road SE17 245 H7
Denbigh Place SW1V 243 M6
Denbigh Street SW1V 243 M6
Denbigh Street SW1V 244 A6
Denman Street W1D 240 B7
Denmark Street WC2H 240 C6
Denny Close SE11 245 G6
Denyer Street SW3 243 G5
Derby Gate SW1A 244 D3
Derby Street W1J 243 K1
Dering Street W1S 239 L6
Derry Street W8 242 B3
De Vere Gardens W8 242 C3
Deverell Street SE1 245 L4
Devonport Street E1 247 G3
Devonshire Close W1G 239 K4
Devonshire Mews
South W1G 239 K4
Devonshire Mews West W1G 239 K4
Devonshire Place W1G 239 K4
Devonshire Place Mews W1G 239 K4

Devonshire Row EC2M 246 A2
Devonshire Square EC2M 246 A2
Devonshire Street W1G 239 K4
Devonshire Terrace W2 238 D7
De Walden Street W1G 239 K5
Dickens Estate SE16 246 D7
Dickens Square SE1 245 K4
Dilke Street SW3 243 H8
Dingley Place EC1V 241 K2
Dingley Road EC1V 241 J2
Discovery Walk E1W 246 F5
Disney Place SE1 245 K2
Distaff Lane EC4V 241 J7
Distin Street SE11 244 F6
Dockhead SE1 246 C7
Dockley Road SE16 246 D8
Dock Street E1 246 D4
Doddington Grove SE17 245 H7
Doddington Place SE17 245 H8
Dodson Street SE1 245 G3
Dod Street E14 247 M2
Dolben Street SE1 245 H2
Dolland Street SE11 244 E7
Dolphin Square SW1V 244 A7
Dolphin Square SW1V 244 B7
Dombey Street WC1N 240 E4
Dominion Street EC2A 241 L5
Donegal Street N1 240 F1
Dongola Road E1 247 J1
Donne Place SW3 243 G5
Doon Street SE1 244 F1
Dora Street E14 247 L2
Doric Way NW1 240 B2
Dorset Rise EC4Y 241 G7
Dorset Square NW1 239 H4
Dorset Street W1U 239 H5
Doughty Mews WC1N 240 E3
Doughty Street WC1N 240 E3
Douglas Street SW1P 244 B6
Douro Place W8 242 C3
Douthwaite Square * E1W 246 D5
Dovehouse Street SW3 242 E6
Dover Street W1J 243 L1
Dover Street W1S 239 L8
Dowgate Hill EC4R 241 K7
Downfield Close W9 238 B3
Downing Street SW1A 244 C2
Down Street W1J 243 K2
Downtown Road SE16 247 K6
D'Oyley Street SW1X 243 J5
Draco Street SE17 245 J8
Drake Close SE16 247 H6
Draycott Avenue SW3 243 G5
Draycott Place SW3 243 H6
Draycott Terrace SW3 243 H5
Drayson Mews W8 242 A3
Drayton Gardens SW10 242 D6
Druid Street SE1 246 A6
Druid Street SE1 246 B6
Drummond Crescent NW1 240 B2
Drummond Road SE16 246 E8
Drummond Street NW1 240 A3
Drury Lane WC2B 240 D6
Dryden Court SE11 245 G5
Dryden Street WC2B 240 D6
Duchess Mews W1G 239 L5
Duchess Street W1B 239 L5
Duchy Street SE1 245 G1
Duckett Street E1 247 J1
Duck Lane W1F 240 B6
Dufferin Street EC1Y 241 K4
Duke of Wellington
Place SW1W 243 K3
Duke of York Square SW3 243 H6
Duke of York Street SW1Y 244 A1
Duke Shore Wharf E14 247 K4
Duke's Lane W8 242 A2
Duke's Place EC3A 246 B2
Duke's Road WC1H 240 C2
Duke Street W1K 239 K7
Duke Street W1U 239 J6
Duke Street St James's SW1Y 244 A1
Dunbar Wharf E14 247 L4
Duncannon Street WC2N 240 C8
Duncan Terrace N1 241 H1
Dundee Street E1W 246 E5
Dundee Wharf E14 247 L4
Dunelm Street E1 247 H2
Dunlop Place SE16 246 C8
Dunraven Street W1K 239 J7
Dunster Court EC3R 246 A3
Duplex Ride SW1X 243 H3
Durand's Wharf SE16 247 L6
Durham Row E1 247 J1
Durham Street SE11 244 E7
Durham Terrace W2 238 A6
Dyott Street WC1A 240 C6
Dysart Street EC2A 241 M4

E

Eagle Close EC1M 241 H4
Eagle Street WC1R 240 E5
Eardley Crescent SW5 242 A7
Earlham Street WC2H 240 C7
Earl's Court ⊖ SW5 242 A6
Earl's Court Gardens SW5 242 B6
Earl's Court Road SW5 242 A6
Earl's Court Square SW5 242 A6
Earlstoke Street EC1V 241 H2
Earl Street EC2A 241 M4
Earnshaw Street WC2H 240 C6
East Arbour Street E1 247 H2
Eastbourne Mews W2 238 D6
Eastbourne Terrace W2 238 D6
Eastcastle Street W1W 240 A6
Eastcheap EC3M 241 M7
Eastfield Street E14 247 K1
East India Dock Road E14 247 M3
East Lane SE16 246 D7
East Poultry Avenue EC1A 241 H5
East Road N1 241 L2
East Smithfield E1W 246 C4
East Street SE17 245 L6
Eaton Close SW1W 243 J5
Eaton Gate SW1W 243 J5
Eaton Lane SW1W 243 L4
Eaton Mews North SW1W 243 K5
Eaton Mews South SW1W 243 K5
Eaton Mews West SW1W 243 K5
Eaton Place SW1X 243 J4
Eaton Row SW1W 243 K4
Eaton Square SW1W 243 K5

Eaton Terrace SW1W 243 J5
Ebbisham Drive SW8 244 E8
Ebury Bridge SW1W 243 K6
Ebury Bridge Road SW1W 243 K7
Ebury Mews SW1W 243 K5
Ebury Square SW1W 243 K6
Ebury Street SW1W 243 K5
Eccleston Bridge SW1W 243 L5
Eccleston Mews SW1X 243 K4
Eccleston Place SW1W 243 L5
Eccleston Square SW1V 243 L5
Eccleston Street SW1X 243 K4
Edbrooke Road W9 238 A3
Edge Street W8 242 A1
Edgware Road W2 238 F5
Edgware Road ⊖ NW1 238 F5
Edinburgh Gate SW1X 243 H3
Edith Grove SW10 242 C8
Edwards Mews W1H 239 J6
Egerton Crescent SW3 242 F5
Egerton Gardens SW3 242 F5
Egerton Terrace SW3 243 G4
Eglinton Court SE17 245 J7
Elba Place SE17 245 K5
Eldon Place EC2M 241 L5
Eldon Road W8 242 B4
Eleanor Close SE16 247 H6
Elephant & Castle SE1 245 J4
Elephant & Castle ⇌ ⊖ SE1 245 J5
Elephant Lane SE16 246 F6
Elephant Road SE17 245 J5
Elf Row E1W 247 G3
Elgar Street SE16 247 K7
Elgin Avenue W9 238 B2
Elgin Mews North W9 238 C2
Elgin Mews South W9 238 C2
Elia Mews N1 241 H1
Elia Street N1 241 H1
Elim Estate SE1 245 M3
Elim Street SE1 245 M3
Elizabeth Street SW1W 243 K5
Ellen Street E1 246 D3
Elliott's Row SE11 245 H5
Ellis Street SW1X 243 J5
Elmfield Way W9 238 A4
Elm Park Gardens SW10 242 E7
Elm Park Lane SW3 242 E7
Elm Park Road SW3 242 E8
Elm Place SW7 242 E7
Elms Mews W2 238 D7
Elm Street WC1X 240 F4
Elm Tree Road NW8 238 E2
Elnathan Mews W9 238 B4
Elsa Street E1 247 J1
Elsted Street SE17 245 L6
Elvaston Mews SW7 242 D4
Elvaston Place SW7 242 D4
Elverton Street SW1P 244 B5
Ely Place EC1N 241 G5
Elystan Place SW3 243 G6
Elystan Street SW3 242 F6
Embankment ⊖ WC2N 244 D1
Embankment Gardens SW3 243 H8
Embankment Place WC2N 244 D1
Emba Street SE16 246 D7
Emerald Street WC1N 240 E4
Emerson Street SE1 241 J1
Emery Hill Street SW1P 244 A5
Emery Street SE1 245 G3
Emperor's Gate SW7 242 C5
Empire Square SE1 245 L3
Empress Place SW6 242 A7
Endell Street WC2H 240 C6
Endsleigh Gardens WC1H 240 B3
Endsleigh Place WC1H 240 B3
Endsleigh Street WC1H 240 B3
Enford Street W1H 239 G5
English Grounds SE1 245 M1
Enid Street SE1 246 C8
Ennismore Gardens SW7 242 F3
Ennismore Gardens
Mews SW7 242 F3
Ennismore Mews SW7 242 F3
Ennismore Street SW7 242 F4
Enny Street SE11 245 G6
Ensign Street E1 246 D4
Epworth Street EC2A 241 L3
Erasmus Street SW1P 244 C6
Errol Street EC1Y 241 K4
Essendine Road W9 238 A3
Essex Street WC2R 240 F7
Essex Villas W8 242 A3
Europa Place EC1V 241 J2
Euston ⊖ NW1 240 B2
Euston Road NW1 240 B3
Euston Road NW1 240 A3
Euston Square NW1 240 A3
Euston Street NW1 240 A3
Evelyn Gardens SW7 242 D7
Evelyn Way N1 241 L1
Evershot Street NW1 240 A1
Everton Buildings NW1 239 M2
Ewer Street SE1 245 J2
Ewhurst Close E1 247 G1
Exchange Square EC2A 241 M4
Exeter Street WC2E 240 D7
Exhibition Road SW7 242 E3
Exmouth Market EC1R 241 G3
Exon Street SE17 245 M6
Exton Street SE1 244 F2
Eyre Street Hill EC1R 240 F4

F

Fairclough Street E1 246 D3
Fair Street SE1 246 B6
Falmouth Road SE1 245 K4
Fann Street EC1M 241 J4
Fanshaw Street N1 241 M1
Fareham Street W1D 240 B6
Farmer Street W8 242 A1
Farm Lane SW6 242 A8
Farm Street W1K 239 K8
Farnham Place SE1 245 J1
Farrance Street E14 247 M3
Farringdon ⇌ ⊖ EC1M 241 G4
Farringdon Lane EC1R 241 G4
Farringdon Road EC1R 241 G3
Farringdon Street EC1M 241 H5
Farrins Rents SE16 247 J6
Farrow Place SE16 247 K7
Farthing Fields * E1W 246 F5
Fashion Street E1 246 B1
Faunce Street SE17 245 H7
Fawcett Street SW10 242 C8

Featherstone Street EC1Y 241 L3
Fenchurch Avenue EC3M 246 A3
Fenchurch Buildings EC3M 246 A3
Fenchurch Place EC3M 246 A3
Fenchurch Street EC3M 246 A3
Fenchurch Street ⇌ EC3M 246 A3
Fendall Street SE1 ..... 246 B8
Fenning Street SE1 ..... 245 M2
Fentiman Road SW8 ..... 244 D8
Fernsbury Street WC1X 240 F2
Fetter Lane EC4A 241 G6
Fieldgate Street E1 ..... 246 D2
Fielding Street SE17 ..... 245 J7
Field Street WC1X 240 E1
Finborough Road SW10 ..... 242 B8
Finch Lane EC3V 241 L6
Finland Street SE16 ..... 247 K8
Finsbury Circus EC2M 241 L5
Finsbury Estate EC1R 241 G3
Finsbury Market EC2A 241 M4
Finsbury Square EC2A 241 L4
Finsbury Street EC2Y 241 L4
First Street SW3 ..... 243 G5
Fishermans Drive SE16 ..... 247 J6
Fisher Street WC1R 240 D5
Fisherton Street NW8 ..... 238 E3
Fish Street Hill EC3R 241 L7
Fitzalan Street SE11 ..... 244 F5
Fitzhardinge Street W1H 239 J6
Fitzroy Square W1T 239 M4
Fitzroy Street W1T 239 M4
Flamborough Street E14 ..... 247 J3
Flank Street E1 ..... 246 C4
Flaxman Terrace WC1H 240 C3
Fleet Street EC4A 241 G6
Fleming Road SE17 ..... 245 H8
Fletcher Street E1 ..... 246 D3
Flint Street SE17 ..... 245 L6
Flitcroft Street WC2H 240 C6
Flockton Street SE16 ..... 246 D7
Flood Street SW3 ..... 243 G7
Flood Walk SW3 ..... 243 G7
Floral Street WC2E 240 D7
Forbes Street E1 ..... 246 D3
Fordham Street E1 ..... 246 D2
Ford Square E1 ..... 246 F2
Fore Street EC2Y 241 K5
Formosa Street W9 ..... 238 C4
Forset Street W1H 239 G6
Forsyth Gardens SE17 ..... 245 H8
Fort Street E1 ..... 246 B1
Fortune Street EC1Y 241 K4
Foster Lane EC2V 241 J6
Foulis Terrace SW7 ..... 242 E6
Foundry Close SE16 ..... 247 J5
Fournier Street E1 ..... 246 B1
Fowey Close E1W 246 E5
Frampton Street NW8 ..... 238 E4
Francis Street SW1P 244 A5
Frankland Close SE16 ..... 246 F8
Franklin's Row SW3 ..... 243 H6
Frazier Street SE1 ..... 245 G3
Frean Street SE16 ..... 246 C8
Frederick Close W2 ..... 239 G7
Frederick Street WC1X 240 E2
Frederic Mews * SW1X 243 J5
Freemantle Street SE17 ..... 245 M6
Friend Street EC1V 241 H2
Frith Street W1D 240 B6
Fulbourne Street E1 ..... 246 E1
Fulford Street SE16 ..... 246 F7
Fulham Road SW10 ..... 242 D8
Fulham Road SW3 ..... 242 F6
Furnival Street EC4A 240 F5
Fynes Street SW1P 244 B5

G

Gabriel's Wharf SE1 ..... 245 G1
Gainsford Street SE1 ..... 246 B6
Galleon Close SE16 ..... 247 G6
Galsworthy Avenue E14 ..... 247 K2
Galway Street EC1V 241 K2
Gambia Street SE1 ..... 245 G2
Garden Road NW8 ..... 238 D1
Garden Row SE1 ..... 245 H4
Garden Street E1 ..... 247 H1
Garden Walk EC2A 241 M3
Gard Street EC1V 241 J2
Garford Street E14 ..... 247 M4
Garnault Place EC1R 241 G3
Garnet Street E1W 246 F4
Garrett Street EC1Y 241 K3
Garrick Street WC2E 240 C7
Garterway SE16 ..... 247 H7
Garway Road W2 ..... 238 B6
Gataker Street * SE16 ..... 246 E8
Gate Mews SW7 ..... 242 F3
Gateforth Street NW8 ..... 238 F3
Gate Mews NW1 ..... 239 L3
Gatesborough Street * EC2A 241 M3
Gate Street WC2A 240 E5
Gatliff Road SW1W 243 K7
Gaunt Street SE1 ..... 245 J4
Gayfere Street SW1P 244 C4
Gaywood Street SE1 ..... 245 H4
Gaza Street SE17 ..... 245 H7
Gedling Place SE1 ..... 246 C7
Gee Street EC1V 241 J3
George Mathers Road SE11 ..... 245 H5
George Row SE16 ..... 246 C7
George Street W1H 239 H6
George Yard W1K 239 K7
Geraldine Street SE11 ..... 245 H4
Gerald Road SW1W 243 K5
Gerridge Street SE1 ..... 245 G3
Gertrude Street SW10 ..... 242 D8
Gibson Road SE11 ..... 244 E5
Gilbert Place WC1A 240 C5
Gilbert Road SE11 ..... 245 G5
Gilbert Street W1K 239 K7
Gildea Street W1W 239 L5
Gillingham Street SW1V 243 M5
Gill Street E14 ..... 247 L3
Gilston Road SW10 ..... 242 D7
Giltspur Street EC1A 241 H5
Gladstone Street SE1 ..... 245 H4
Glamis Place E1W 247 G4
Glamis Road E1W 247 G4
Glasgow Terrace SW1V 243 M7
Glasshill Street SE1 ..... 245 J3
Glasshouse Street W1B 240 A8
Glasshouse Walk SE11 ..... 244 D6

Glebe Place SW3 ..... 242 F7
Gledhow Road SW5 ..... 242 C6
Glentworth Street NW1 ..... 239 H4
Globe Pond Road SE16 ..... 247 J5
Globe Street SE1 ..... 245 K4
Gloucester Court * EC3R 246 A4
Gloucester Gardens W2 ..... 238 C6
Gloucester Mews W2 ..... 238 D6
Gloucester Mews West W2 ..... 238 C6
Gloucester Place NW1 ..... 239 H3
Gloucester Place W1U 239 H5
Gloucester Place Mews W1U 239 H5
Gloucester Road SW7 ..... 242 C4
Gloucester Road SW7 ..... 242 D6
Gloucester Road ⊖ SW7 ..... 242 C5
Gloucester Square W2 ..... 238 F6
Gloucester Street SW1V 243 M7
Gloucester Terrace W2 ..... 238 B5
Gloucester Terrace W2 ..... 238 D6
Gloucester Walk W8 ..... 242 A2
Gloucester Way EC1R 241 G2
Glyn Street SE11 ..... 244 E7
Godfrey Street SW3 ..... 243 G6
Goding Street SE11 ..... 244 D7
Godliman Street EC4V 241 J7
Godwin Close N1 ..... 241 K1
Golden Hinde II SE1 ..... 245 L1
Golden Jubilee Bridge WC2N 244 D1
Golden Lane EC1Y 241 J4
Golden Square W1F 240 A7
Golding Street E1 ..... 246 E3
Goldney Road W9 ..... 238 A4
Goldsmith Street EC2V 241 K6
Gomm Road SE16 ..... 247 G8
Goodge Place W1T 240 A5
Goodge Street W1T 240 A5
Goodge Street ⊖ W1T 240 B5
Goodwin Close SE16 ..... 246 C8
Gordon Place W8 ..... 242 A2
Gordon Square WC1H 240 B3
Gordon Street WC1H 240 B3
Gore Street SW7 ..... 242 D4
Goring Street * EC3A 246 A2
Gosfield Street W1W 239 L5
Goslett Yard WC2H 240 B6
Goswell Road EC1V 241 H1
Gough Street WC1X 240 F3
Goulston Street E1 ..... 246 B2
Gower Mews WC1E 240 B5
Gower Place NW1 ..... 240 A3
Gower Street WC1E 240 B3
Gower's Walk E1 ..... 246 D2
Gracechurch Street EC3V 241 M7
Grafton Place NW1 ..... 240 B2
Grafton Street W1S 239 L8
Grafton Way W1T 240 A4
Graham Street N1 ..... 241 J1
Graham Terrace SW1W 243 J6
Granby Terrace NW1 ..... 239 M1
Grand Avenue EC1A 241 H5
Grange Road SE1 ..... 246 B8
Grange Walk SE1 ..... 246 B8
Grange Yard SE1 ..... 246 B8
Grantully Road W9 ..... 238 B2
Granville Place W1H 239 J6
Granville Road NW6 ..... 238 A1
Granville Square WC1X 240 F2
Grape Street WC2H 240 C6
Gravel Lane E1 ..... 246 B2
Gray's Inn Road WC1X 240 D2
Gray's Inn Square WC1R 240 F5
Gray Street SE1 ..... 245 G3
Great Castle Street W1G 239 L6
Great Central Street NW1 ..... 239 G4
Great Chapel Street W1D 240 B6
Great College Street SW1P 244 C4
Great Cumberland
    Place W1H 239 H6
Great Dover Street SE1 ..... 245 K3
Great Eastern Street EC2A 241 M3
Great George Street SW1P 244 C3
Great Guildford Street SE1 ..... 245 J1
Great James Street WC1N 240 E4
Great Marlborough
    Street W1F 239 M7
Great Maze Pond SE1 ..... 245 L2
Great New Portland
    Street WC2H 240 C7
Greatorex Street E1 ..... 246 D1
Great Ormond Street WC1N 240 D4
Great Percy Street WC1X 240 F2
Great Peter Street SW1P 244 B4
Great Portland Street W1W 239 L4
Great Portland
    Street ⊖ W1W 239 L4
Great Pulteney Street W1F 240 A7
Great Queen Street WC2B 240 D6
Great Russell Street WC1B 240 C5
Great Scotland Yard SW1A 244 C1
Great Smith Street SW1P 244 C4
Great Suffolk Street SE1 ..... 245 H2
Great Sutton Street EC1V 241 J4
Great Swan Alley EC2R 241 L6
Great Titchfield Street W1W 239 M4
Great Tower Street EC3M 241 M7
Great Tower Street EC3R 246 A4
Great Winchester
    Street EC2N 241 L6
Great Windmill Street W1D 240 B7
Greek Street W1D 240 B6
Greenacre Square SE16 ..... 247 J6
Green Bank E1W 246 E5
Greenberry Street NW8 ..... 238 F1
Greencoat Place SW1P 244 A5
Green Coat Row SW1P 244 A4
Greenfield Road E1 ..... 246 D2
Greenham Close SE1 ..... 244 F3
Green Park ⊖ W1J 243 M1
Green Street W1K 239 J7
Greenwell Street W1W 239 L4
Greet Street SE1 ..... 245 G2
Grenade Street E14 ..... 247 L4
Grendon Street NW8 ..... 238 F3
Grenville Place SW7 ..... 242 C5
Gresham Street EC2V 241 J6
Gresse Street W1T 240 B5
Greville Street EC1N 241 G5
Greycoat Place SW1P 244 B4
Greycoat Street SW1P 244 B4
Grigg's Place * SE1 ..... 246 A8
Grosvenor Bridge SW8 ..... 243 L8
Grosvenor Crescent SW1X 243 J3
Grosvenor Crescent
    Mews SW1X 243 J3
Grosvenor Gardens SW1W 243 L4
Grosvenor Gardens Mews
    East SW1W 243 L4

Grosvenor Gardens Mews
    North SW1W 243 L4
Grosvenor Gardens Mews
    South * SW1W 243 L4
Grosvenor Gate W2 ..... 239 H8
Grosvenor Hill W1K 239 L7
Grosvenor Place SW1X 243 K3
Grosvenor Road SW1V 243 L8
Grosvenor Square W1K 239 J7
Grosvenor Street W1K 239 K7
Grosvenor Terrace SE5 ..... 245 J8
Grove End Road NW8 ..... 238 D2
Guildhouse Street SW1V 243 M5
Guilford Street WC1N 240 D4
Guinness Square SE1 ..... 245 M5
Gulliver Street SE16 ..... 247 K8
Gunpowder Square EC4A 241 G6
Gun Street E1 ..... 246 B1
Gunthorpe Street E1 ..... 246 C2
Gutter Lane EC2V 241 J6
Guy Street SE1 ..... 245 L3

H

Haberdasher Street N1 ..... 241 L2
Haddonhall Estate SE1 ..... 245 M4
Hainton Close E1 ..... 246 F3
Halcrow Street * E1 ..... 246 F2
Half Moon Street W1J 243 L1
Halford Road W14 ..... 242 A8
Halkin Place SW1X 243 J4
Halkin Street SW1X 243 K3
Hallam Street W1W 239 L5
Halley Street E14 ..... 247 K1
Hallfield Estate W2 ..... 238 C6
Hall Place W2 ..... 238 E4
Hall Road NW8 ..... 238 D2
Hall Street EC1V 241 H2
Halpin Place SE17 ..... 245 M6
Halsey Street SW3 ..... 243 G5
Hamilton Close NW8 ..... 238 D2
Hamilton Close SE16 ..... 247 K7
Hamilton Gardens NW8 ..... 238 D2
Hamilton Place W1J 243 K2
Hamilton Terrace NW8 ..... 238 C1
Hamlet Way SE1 ..... 245 L3
Hammett Street EC3N 246 B4
Hampden Close NW1 ..... 240 B1
Hampden Gurney Street W2 ..... 239 G6
Hampstead Road NW1 ..... 239 M2
Hampton Street SE17 ..... 245 J6
Hanbury Street E1 ..... 246 C1
Hand Court WC1V 240 E5
Handel Street WC1N 240 D3
Hankey Place SE1 ..... 245 L3
Hannibal Road E1 ..... 247 G1
Hanover Square W1S 239 L6
Hanover Street W1S 239 L7
Hans Crescent SW3 ..... 243 H3
Hanson Street W1W 239 M4
Hans Place SW1X 243 H4
Hans Road SW3 ..... 243 G4
Hans Street SW1X 243 H4
Hanway Place W1T 240 B6
Hanway Street W1T 240 B6
Harbet Road W2 ..... 238 F5
Harbour Street WC1N 240 E4
Harcourt Street W1H 239 G5
Harcourt Terrace SW10 ..... 242 C7
Hardinge Street E1W 247 G3
Hardwick Street EC1R 241 G2
Hardwidge Street SE1 ..... 245 M2
Hardy Close SE16 ..... 247 H6
Harewood Place W1G 239 L6
Harewood Row NW1 ..... 239 G4
Harewood Avenue NW1 ..... 239 G4
Harford Street E1 ..... 247 J1
Harleyford Road SE11 ..... 244 E8
Harley Gardens SW10 ..... 242 D7
Harley Street W1G 239 K4
Harmsworth Street SE17 ..... 245 G7
Harold Estate SE1 ..... 246 A8
Harper Road SE1 ..... 245 K4
Harriet Walk SW1X 243 H3
Harrington Gardens SW7 ..... 242 C6
Harrington Road SW7 ..... 242 E5
Harrington Square NW1 ..... 239 M1
Harrington Street NW1 ..... 239 M2
Harrison Street WC1H 240 D2
Harrods SW1X 243 G4
Harrowby Street W1H 239 G6
Harrow Place E1 ..... 246 B2
Harrow Road W2 ..... 238 A4
Hart Street EC3R 246 A3
Hasker Street SW3 ..... 243 G5
Hastings Street WC1H 240 C2
Hatfields SE1 ..... 245 G1
Hatherley Grove W2 ..... 238 B6
Hatteraick Road SE16 ..... 247 G6
Hatton Garden EC1N 241 G4
Hatton Street W2 ..... 238 E4
Hatton Wall EC1N 241 G4
Havering Street E1 ..... 247 H3
Haverstock Street N1 ..... 241 J1
Hawke Place * SE16 ..... 247 H6
Haydon Street EC3N 246 B3
Hayes Place NW1 ..... 239 G4
Hay Hill W1J 239 L8
Hayles Street SE11 ..... 245 H5
Haymarket SW1Y 240 B8
Hayne Street EC1A 241 J4
Hay's Lane SE1 ..... 245 M1
Hay's Mews W1J 239 L8
Haywood Place EC1R 241 H3
Headfort Place SW1X 243 K3
Head Street E1 ..... 247 H2
Hearnshaw Street E14 ..... 247 K2
Hearn Street EC2A 241 M4
Heathcote Street WC1N 240 E3
Heddon Street W1B 239 M7
Heddon Street W1S 240 A7
Hedger Street SE11 ..... 245 H5
Heiron Street SE17 ..... 245 J8
Hellings Street E1W 246 D5
Helmet Row EC1V 241 K3
Helsinki Square SE16 ..... 247 L8
Henderson Drive NW8 ..... 238 E3
Heneage Lane EC3A 246 A3
Heneage Street E1 ..... 246 C1
Henrietta Place W1G 239 L6
Henrietta Street WC2E 240 D7
Henriques Street E1 ..... 246 D2
Henshaw Street SE17 ..... 245 L5
Herbal Hill EC1R 241 G4

Herbert Crescent SW1X 243 H4
Herbrand Street WC1H 240 C3
Hercules Road SE1 ..... 244 F4
Hereford Road W2 ..... 238 A6
Hereford Square SW7 ..... 242 D6
Hermitage Street W2 ..... 238 E5
Hermitage Wall E1W 246 D5
Hermit Street EC1V 241 H2
Heron Place SE16 ..... 247 K5
Heron Quay E14 ..... 247 M5
Herrick Street SW1P 244 C6
Hertford Street W1J 243 K2
Hertsmere Road E14 ..... 247 M4
Hesper Mews SW5 ..... 242 B6
Hessel Street E1 ..... 246 E3
Hewett Street EC2A 241 M3
Heygate Estate SE17 ..... 245 J5
Heygate Street SE17 ..... 245 J5
Hide Place SW1P 244 B6
High Holborn WC1V 240 E5
High Street
    Kensington ⊖ W8 ..... 242 A3
Hildyard Road SW6 ..... 242 A8
Hilliards Court E1W 246 F5
Hillingdon Street SE17 ..... 245 J8
Hill Road NW8 ..... 238 D1
Hills Place W1F 239 M6
Hill Street W1J 239 K8
Hinde Street W1U 239 K6
Hind Grove E14 ..... 247 M3
Hindgrove Area E14 ..... 247 M3
Hithe Grove SE16 ..... 247 G8
HMS Belfast SE1 ..... 246 A5
Hobart Place SW1W 243 K4
Hobury Street SW10 ..... 242 D8
Hogarth Road SW5 ..... 242 B6
Holbein Mews SW1W 243 J6
Holbein Place SW1W 243 J6
Holborn EC1N 241 G5
Holborn ⊖ EC1N 240 E5
Holborn Circus EC1N 241 G5
Holborn Viaduct EC1A 241 G5
Holford Street WC1X 240 F2
Holland Street SE1 ..... 245 H1
Holland Street W8 ..... 242 A3
Hollen Street W1F 240 A6
Holles Street W1C 239 L6
Hollywood Road SW10 ..... 242 C8
Holyoak Road SE11 ..... 245 H5
Holyrood Street SE1 ..... 246 M2
Holyrood Street SE1 ..... 246 A6
Holywell Row EC2A 241 M4
Homefield Street * N1 ..... 241 M1
Homer Row W1H 239 G5
Homer Street W1H 239 G5
Hooper Street E1 ..... 246 D3
Hopetown Street E1 ..... 246 C1
Hopkins Street W1F 240 A7
Hopton Street SE1 ..... 245 H1
Hopwood Road SE17 ..... 245 L8
Hornton Place W8 ..... 242 A3
Hornton Street W8 ..... 242 A2
Horse & Dolphin Yard W1D 240 B7
Horseferry Road E14 ..... 247 J3
Horseferry Road SW1P 244 B4
Horse Guards Avenue SW1A 244 C2
Horse Guards Parade SW1A 244 C2
Horse Guards Road SW1A 244 C2
Horselydown Lane SE1 ..... 246 B6
Horsley Street SE17 ..... 245 K8
Hosier Lane EC1A 241 H5
Hothfield Place SE16 ..... 247 G8
Hotspur Street SE11 ..... 244 F6
Houghton Street WC2A 240 E6
Houndsditch EC3A 246 A2
Houses of Parliament SW1A 244 D3
Howick Place SW1E 244 A4
Howland Street W1T 240 A4
Howland Way SE16 ..... 247 K7
Howley Place W2 ..... 238 D5
Hoxton Square N1 ..... 241 M2
Hoxton Street N1 ..... 241 M1
Hugh Mews SW1V 243 L6
Hugh Street SW1V 243 L6
Hugh Street SW1V 243 L6
Hull Close SE16 ..... 247 J6
Hull Street EC1V 241 J2
Hungerford Bridge SE1 ..... 244 E1
Hunter Close SE1 ..... 245 M4
Hunter Street WC1N 240 D3
Huntley Street WC1E 240 A4
Huntsman Street SE17 ..... 245 M6
Huntsworth Mews NW1 ..... 239 H3
Hurley Crescent SE16 ..... 247 H6
Hutching's Street E14 ..... 247 M7
Hutton Street EC4Y 241 G7
Hyde Park W2 ..... 243 G1
Hyde Park Corner SW1X 243 K2
Hyde Park Corner ⊖ W1J 243 K2
Hyde Park Court SW7 ..... 242 D3
Hyde Park Crescent W2 ..... 238 F6
Hyde Park Garden Mews W2 ..... 238 F7
Hyde Park Gardens W2 ..... 238 F7
Hyde Park Gate SW7 ..... 242 C3
Hyde Park Gate SW7 ..... 242 D3
Hyde Park Square W2 ..... 238 F7
Hyde Park Street W2 ..... 238 F7

I

Idol Lane EC3R 241 M7
Ifield Road SW10 ..... 242 B8
Iliffe Street SE17 ..... 245 J6
Iliffe Yard SE17 ..... 245 J6
Imperial College Road SW7 ..... 242 D4
Imperial War Museum SE1 ..... 245 G4
India Street EC3N 246 B3
Ingestre Place W1F 240 A7
Inglebert Street EC1R 240 F2
Ingram Close SE11 ..... 244 E5
Inner Circle NW1 ..... 239 J2
Inverness Terrace W2 ..... 238 B6
Inverness Terrace Gate W2 ..... 238 C8
Invicta Plaza SE1 ..... 245 H1
Inville Road SE17 ..... 245 L7
Ironmonger Lane EC2V 241 K6
Ironmonger Row EC1V 241 K2
Irving Street WC2N 240 C8
Isambard Place SE16 ..... 247 G6
Island Row E14 ..... 247 K3
Iverna Court W8 ..... 242 A4
Iverna Gardens W8 ..... 242 A4
Ives Street SW3 ..... 243 G5
Ivor Place NW1 ..... 239 G4
Ixworth Place SW3 ..... 242 F6

J

Jacob Street SE1 ..... 246 C6
Jamaica Gate SE16 ..... 246 F8
Jamaica Road SE1 ..... 246 C7
Jamaica Road SE16 ..... 246 E7
Jamaica Street E1 ..... 247 G2
Jamaica Wharf SE1 ..... 246 C6
James Street W1U 239 K6
James Street WC2E 240 D7
Jameson Street W8 ..... 242 A1
Jamuna Close E14 ..... 247 K1
Janeway Street SE16 ..... 246 D7
Jardine Road E1W 247 J4
Java Wharf SE1 ..... 246 C6
Jay Mews SW7 ..... 242 D3
Jermyn Street SW1Y 240 A8
Jerome Crescent NW8 ..... 238 F3
Jewery Street EC3N 246 B3
Joan Street SE1 ..... 245 G2
Jockey's Fields WC1R 240 E4
Johanna Street SE1 ..... 244 F3
John Adam Street WC2N 240 D8
John Carpenter Street EC4Y 241 G7
John Felton Road SE16 ..... 246 D7
John Fisher Street E1 ..... 246 C4
John Islip Street SW1P 244 C5
John Prince's Street W1G 239 L6
John Roll Way SE16 ..... 246 D7
John Ruskin Street SE5 ..... 245 J8
John Slip Street SW1P 244 C6
John's Mews WC1N 240 E4
Johnson's Place SW1V 244 A7
Johnson Street * E1 ..... 247 G3
Johnson Street WC1N 240 E4
Joiner Street SE1 ..... 245 L1
Jonathan Street SE11 ..... 244 E6
Jubilee Place SW3 ..... 243 G6
Jubilee Street E1 ..... 247 G2
Jubilee Walk SW3 ..... 242 B1
Judd Street WC1H 240 C2
Junction Mews W2 ..... 238 F5
Juxon Street SE11 ..... 244 E5

K

Katherine Close SE16 ..... 247 H5
Kean Street WC2B 240 E6
Keel Close SE16 ..... 247 J6
Keeley Street WC2B 240 E6
Keeton's Road SE16 ..... 246 E7
Kell Street SE1 ..... 245 H3
Kelso Place W8 ..... 242 B4
Kemble Street WC2B 240 E6
Kempsford Gardens SW5 ..... 242 A7
Kempsford Road SE11 ..... 245 G5
Kendall Place W1U 239 J5
Kendal Street W2 ..... 239 G6
Kennet Street E1W 246 D5
Kenning Street SE16 ..... 247 H6
Kennings Way SE11 ..... 245 G7
Kennington ⊖ SE11 ..... 245 H7
Kennington Lane SE11 ..... 244 E7
Kennington Oval SE11 ..... 244 E8
Kennington Park
    Gardens SE11 ..... 245 G8
Kennington Park Place SE11 ..... 245 G7
Kennington Park Road SE11 ..... 245 G7
Kennington Road SE1 ..... 244 F4
Kennington Road SE11 ..... 245 G5
Kennington Oval SE11 ..... 244 F8
Kenrick Place W1U 239 J5
Kensington Church Street W8 ..... 242 A1
Kensington Court W8 ..... 242 B3
Kensington Gardens W2 ..... 242 C1
Kensington Gardens
    Square W2 ..... 238 B6
Kensington Gate W8 ..... 242 C4
Kensington Gore SW7 ..... 242 D3
Kensington High Street W8 ..... 242 A4
Kensington Palace
    Gardens W8 ..... 242 B1
Kensington Palace
    Gardens W8 ..... 242 B2
Kensington Place W8 ..... 242 A1
Kensington Road SW7 ..... 243 G3
Kensington Road W8 ..... 242 B3
Kensington Square W8 ..... 242 B3
Kenton Street WC1H 240 C3
Kenway Road SW5 ..... 242 A6
Keystone Close N1 ..... 240 D1
Keyworth Street SE1 ..... 245 H4
Kilburn Park Road NW6 ..... 238 A2
Kildare Terrace W2 ..... 238 A6
Killick Street N1 ..... 240 E1
Kinburn Street SE16 ..... 247 H6
Kinder Street E1 ..... 246 E2
King & Queen Wharf SE16 ..... 247 H5
King and Queen Street SE17 ..... 245 K6
King Charles Street SW1A 244 C2
Kingdom Street W2 ..... 238 C5
King Edward Street EC1A 241 J6
King Edward Walk SE1 ..... 245 G4
King James Street SE1 ..... 245 H3
Kingly Street W1F 239 M7
King's Arms Yard EC2R 241 L6
King's Bench Street SE1 ..... 245 H2
Kingscote Street EC4V 241 H7
King's Cross ⇌ N1C 240 D1
King's Cross Road WC1X 240 E2
King's Cross St
    Pancras ⊖ N1C 240 D1
King's Head Yard SE1 ..... 245 L1
King's Mews WC1N 240 F4
Kingsmill Terrace NW8 ..... 238 E1
King Square EC1V 241 J2
King's Road SW3 ..... 242 E8
King's Scholars
    Passage SW1P 243 M5
King's Stairs Close SE16 ..... 246 F6
King Street EC2V 241 K6
King Street WC2E 240 D7
King Street SW1Y 244 A1
King Street W6 ..... 242 A1
Kingsway WC2B 240 E6
King William Street EC4N 241 L7
Kinnerton Place
    North * SW1X 243 J3
Kinnerton Place
    South * SW1X 243 J3
Kinnerton Street SW1X 243 J3
Kinnerton Yard * SW1X 243 J3
Kipling Estate SE1 ..... 245 L3
Kipling Street SE1 ..... 245 L3

Kirby Estate SE16.......... 246 D7
Kirby Grove SE1.......... 245 M3
Kirby Street EC1N.......... 241 G4
Knaresborough Place SW5.......... 242 B5
Knightrider Street EC4V.......... 241 H7
Knightsbridge SW1X.......... 243 H3
Knightsbridge ⊖ SW3.......... 243 H3
Knox Street W1H.......... 239 H4
Kynance Mews SW7.......... 242 C4
Kynance Place SW7.......... 242 C4

L

Lackington Street EC2A.......... 241 L4
Lafone Street SE1.......... 246 B6
Lagado Mews SE16.......... 247 H5
Lambeth Bridge SW1P.......... 244 D5
Lambeth High Street SE1.......... 244 E5
Lambeth Hill EC4V.......... 241 J7
Lambeth North ⊖ SE1.......... 244 F3
Lambeth Palace Road SE1.......... 244 F4
Lambeth Road SE1.......... 244 F4
Lambeth Walk SE11.......... 244 F5
Lamb's Conduit Street WC1N.......... 240 D4
Lamb's Passage EC1Y.......... 241 K4
Lamb Street E1.......... 246 B1
Lamb Way SE1.......... 246 A7
Lamlash Street SE11.......... 245 H5
Lanark Place W9.......... 238 D3
Lanark Road W9.......... 238 B1
Lancaster Gate W2.......... 238 D7
Lancaster Gate W2.......... 238 D8
Lancaster Gate ⊖ W2.......... 238 E7
Lancaster Mews W2.......... 238 D7
Lancaster Place WC2E.......... 240 E7
Lancaster Street SE1.......... 245 H3
Lancaster Terrace W2.......... 238 E7
Lancaster Walk W2.......... 238 D8
Lancelot Place SW7.......... 243 G3
Lancing Street NW1.......... 240 B2
Lanesborough Place * SW1X.......... 243 J3
Langdale Street E1.......... 246 E3
Langford Place NW8.......... 238 D1
Langham Place W1B.......... 239 L5
Langham Street W1W.......... 239 L5
Langham Street W1W.......... 239 M5
Langley Lane SW8.......... 244 D8
Langley Street WC2H.......... 240 C7
Langton Close WC1X.......... 240 E3
Lanhill Road W9.......... 238 A3
Lansdowne Place SE1.......... 245 L4
Lant Street SE1.......... 245 J3
Larcom Street SE17.......... 245 K6
Lauderdale Road W9.......... 238 B3
Laud Street SE11.......... 244 E7
Launcelot Street SE1.......... 244 F3
Launceston Place W8.......... 242 C4
Laurence Pountney
    Lane EC4V.......... 241 L7
Lavender Road SE16.......... 247 K5
Lavender Wharf SE16.......... 247 K4
Lavington Street SE1.......... 245 J1
Lawn Lane SW8.......... 244 D8
Lawrence Street SW3.......... 242 F8
Lawrence Wharf SE16.......... 247 L6
Law Street SE1.......... 245 L4
Laxton Place NW1.......... 239 L3
Laystall Street EC1R.......... 240 F4
Leadenhall Street EC3A.......... 246 A3
Leadenhall Street EC3V.......... 241 M6
Leake Street SE1.......... 244 F2
Leather Lane EC1N.......... 241 G4
Leathermarket Street SE1.......... 245 M3
Leeke Street WC1X.......... 240 E2
Lees Place W1K.......... 239 J7
Leicester Square ⊖ WC2H.......... 240 C7
Leicester Square WC2H.......... 240 C7
Leicester Street WC2H.......... 240 B7
Leigh Street WC1H.......... 240 C3
Leinster Gardens W2.......... 238 C6
Leinster Mews W2.......... 238 C7
Leinster Place W2.......... 238 C7
Leinster Square W2.......... 238 A7
Leinster Terrace W2.......... 238 C7
Leman Street E1.......... 246 C3
Lennox Gardens SW1X.......... 243 G4
Lennox Gardens Mews SW1X.......... 243 G5
Leonard Street EC2A.......... 241 L3
Leopold Estate E3.......... 247 M1
Leopold Street E3.......... 247 L1
Leroy Street SE1.......... 245 M5
Lever Street EC1V.......... 241 J2
Lewisham Street SW1H.......... 244 B3
Lexham Gardens W8.......... 242 A5
Lexham Mews W8.......... 242 A5
Lexington Street W1F.......... 240 A7
Leyden Street E1.......... 246 B2
Leydon Close SE16.......... 247 H5
Library Street SE1.......... 245 H3
Lidlington Place NW1.......... 240 A1
Lilestone Street NW8.......... 238 F3
Lilley Close E1W.......... 246 D5
Lillie Road SW6.......... 242 A7
Lillie Yard SW6.......... 242 A7
Limeburner Lane EC4M.......... 241 H6
Lime Close E1W.......... 246 D5
Limehouse Causeway E14.......... 247 L4
Limehouse Link E14.......... 247 L3
Limehouse ≥ ⊖ E14.......... 247 J3
Limerston Street SW10.......... 242 D8
Lime Street EC3M.......... 241 M7
Lincoln's Inn Fields WC2A.......... 240 E6
Linden Gardens W2.......... 238 A8
Lindley Street E1.......... 246 F1
Lindsay Square SW1V.......... 244 B7
Lindsey Street EC1A.......... 241 H4
Linhope Street NW1.......... 239 G3
Linsey Street SE16.......... 246 D8
Lisle Street WC2H.......... 240 B7
Lisson Green Estate NW8.......... 238 F3
Lisson Grove NW8.......... 239 G4
Lisson Grove NW8.......... 238 F3
Lisson Street NW1.......... 238 F4
Litchfield Street WC2H.......... 240 C7
Little Argyll Street W1F.......... 239 M6
Little Britain EC1A.......... 241 J5
Little Chester Street SW1X.......... 243 K4
Little George Street SW1P.......... 244 C3
Little Marlborough
    Street W1F.......... 240 A7
Little New Street EC4A.......... 241 G6
Little Portland Street W1G.......... 239 L6
Little Russell Street WC1A.......... 240 C5
Little St James's Street SW1A.......... 243 M2
Little Sanctuary SW1A.......... 244 C3

Little Somerset Street E1.......... 246 B3
Little Titchfield Street W1W.......... 239 M5
Liverpool Grove SE17.......... 245 K7
Liverpool Street EC2M.......... 241 M5
Liverpool Street ≥ ⊖ EC2M.......... 241 M5
Lizard Street EC1V.......... 241 K3
Llewellyn Street SE16.......... 246 D7
Lloyd Baker Street WC1X.......... 240 F2
Lloyd's Avenue EC3N.......... 246 B3
Lloyd Square WC1X.......... 240 F2
Lloyds Row EC1R.......... 241 G2
Lloyd's Street WC1X.......... 240 F2
Locksley Estate E14.......... 247 L2
Locksley Street E14.......... 247 L1
Lockyer Street SE1.......... 245 L3
Lodge Road NW8.......... 238 F3
Loftie Street SE16.......... 246 D7
Logan Place W8.......... 242 A5
Lolesworth Close E1.......... 246 B1
Lollard Street SE11.......... 244 F5
Lollard Street SE11.......... 244 F6
Loman Street SE1.......... 245 J2
Lomas Street E1.......... 246 D1
Lombard Lane EC4Y.......... 241 G6
Lombard Street EC3V.......... 241 L7
London Bridge EC4R.......... 241 L8
London Bridge ≥ ⊖ SE1.......... 245 L1
London Bridge Street SE1.......... 245 L1
London Dungeon SE1.......... 244 E2
London Eye SE1.......... 244 E2
London Mews W2.......... 238 E6
London Road SE1.......... 245 H4
London Street EC3R.......... 246 A3
London Street W2.......... 238 E6
London Transport
    Museum WC2E.......... 240 D7
London Wall EC2M.......... 241 K5
London Zoo ZSL NW1.......... 239 J1
Long Acre WC2E.......... 240 D7
Longford Street NW1.......... 239 L3
Long Lane EC1A.......... 241 J5
Long Lane SE1.......... 245 L3
Longmoore Street SW1V.......... 243 M6
Longridge Road SW5.......... 242 A5
Longville Road SE11.......... 245 H5
Long Walk SE1.......... 246 A8
Long Yard WC1N.......... 240 E4
Lord North Street SW1P.......... 244 C4
Lord's Cricket Ground NW8.......... 238 E2
Lorenzo Street WC1X.......... 240 E2
Lorrimore Road SE17.......... 245 J8
Lorrimore Square SE17.......... 245 H8
Lothbury EC2R.......... 241 L6
Loughborough Street SE11.......... 244 F7
Lovat Lane EC3R.......... 241 M7
Love Lane EC2V.......... 241 K6
Lovell Place SE16.......... 247 K7
Lowell Street E14.......... 247 K2
Lower Belgrave Street SW1W.......... 243 K4
Lower Grosvenor Place SW1W.......... 243 L4
Lower James Street W1F.......... 240 A7
Lower John Street W1F.......... 240 A7
Lower Marsh SE1.......... 244 F3
Lower Road SE16.......... 247 G7
Lower Sloane Street SW1W.......... 243 J6
Lower Thames Street EC3R.......... 246 A4
Lower Thames Street EC3R.......... 241 M8
Lowndes Close * SW1X.......... 243 J4
Lowndes Place SW1X.......... 243 J4
Lowndes Square SW1X.......... 243 H3
Lowndes Street SW1X.......... 243 J4
Lucan Place SW3.......... 242 F5
Lucey Road SE16.......... 246 C8
Ludgate Circus EC4M.......... 241 H6
Ludgate Hill EC4M.......... 241 H6
Luke Street EC2A.......... 241 M3
Lukin Street E1.......... 247 G3
Lumley Street W1K.......... 239 K7
Lupus Street SW1V.......... 243 L7
Lupus Street SW1V.......... 244 B7
Luton Street NW8.......... 238 E4
Luxborough Street W1U.......... 239 J4
Lyall Mews SW1X.......... 243 J4
Lyall Street SW1X.......... 243 J4
Lyons Place NW8.......... 238 E3
Lytham Street SE17.......... 245 K7

M

Macclesfield Road EC1V.......... 241 J2
Macclesfield Street * W1D.......... 240 B7
Mace Close E1W.......... 246 E5
Macklin Street WC2B.......... 240 D6
Mackworth Street NW1.......... 239 M2
Macleod Street SE17.......... 245 K7
Madame Tussauds NW1.......... 239 J4
Maddox Street W1S.......... 239 M7
Magdalen Street SE1.......... 245 M2
Magee Street SE11.......... 244 F8
Maguire Street SE1.......... 246 C6
Maida Avenue W9.......... 238 D4
Maida Vale W9.......... 238 C2
Maida Vale ⊖ W9.......... 238 C2
Maiden Lane SE1.......... 245 K1
Maiden Lane WC2E.......... 240 D7
Major Road SE16.......... 246 D7
Makins Street SW3.......... 243 G6
Malet Street WC1E.......... 240 B4
Mallord Street SW3.......... 242 E8
Mallory Street NW8.......... 238 F3
Mallow Street EC1Y.......... 241 L3
Malta Street EC1V.......... 241 H3
Maltby Street SE1.......... 246 B7
Manchester Square W1U.......... 239 J6
Manchester Street W1U.......... 239 J5
Manciple Street SE1.......... 245 L3
Mandeville Place W1U.......... 239 K6
Manette Street W1D.......... 240 B6
Manilla Street E14.......... 247 M6
Manningford Close EC1V.......... 241 H2
Manor Place SE17.......... 245 J7
Manresa Road SW3.......... 242 F7
Mansell Street E1.......... 246 C3
Mansfield Mews W1G.......... 239 K5
Mansfield Street W1G.......... 239 L5
Mansion House ⊖ EC4V.......... 241 K7
Manson Mews SW7.......... 242 D5
Manson Place SW7.......... 242 D6
Mapleleaf Square SE16.......... 247 J6
Maples Place E1.......... 246 F1
Maple Street W1T.......... 239 M4
Marble Arch W1C.......... 239 H7
Marble Arch ⊖ W1C.......... 239 H7
Marchmont Street WC1H.......... 240 C3
Margaret Street W1W.......... 239 L6
Margaretta Terrace SW3.......... 242 F8

Margery Street WC1X.......... 240 F3
Marigold Street SE16.......... 246 E7
Marine Street SE16.......... 246 C7
Market Mews W1J.......... 243 K1
Market Place W1W.......... 239 M6
Markham Square SW3.......... 243 G6
Markham Street SW3.......... 243 G6
Mark Lane EC3R.......... 246 A4
Marlborough Gate W2.......... 238 E7
Marlborough Place NW8.......... 238 C1
Marlborough Road SW1A.......... 244 A2
Marlborough Street SW3.......... 242 F6
Marloes Road W8.......... 242 B4
Marlow Way SE16.......... 247 H6
Maroon Street E14.......... 247 K2
Marshall Street W1F.......... 240 A7
Marshalsea Road SE1.......... 245 J2
Marsham Street SW1P.......... 244 C5
Marsh Wall E14.......... 247 M5
Martha's Buildings EC1V.......... 241 K3
Martha Street E1.......... 246 F3
Martin Lane EC4V.......... 241 L7
Maryland Road W9.......... 238 A4
Marylands Road W9.......... 238 A4
Marylebone ≥ ⊖ NW1.......... 239 G4
Marylebone Flyover W2.......... 238 F5
Marylebone High Street W1U.......... 239 K5
Marylebone Lane W1U.......... 239 K6
Marylebone Road NW1.......... 239 G4
Marylebone Street W1G.......... 239 K5
Marylee Way SE11.......... 244 F6
Masjid Lane E14.......... 247 M2
Mason Street SE17.......... 245 M5
Massinger Street SE17.......... 245 M6
Masters Street E1.......... 247 J1
Matlock Street E14.......... 247 J2
Matthew Parker Street SW1H.......... 244 C3
Maunsel Street SW1P.......... 244 B5
Mayfair Place W1J.......... 243 L1
Mayflower Street SE16.......... 246 F7
Mayford Estate NW1.......... 240 A1
Maynards Quay E1W.......... 246 F4
May's Street WC2N.......... 240 C8
McAuley Close SE1.......... 244 F4
McLeod's Mews SW7.......... 242 C5
Meadcroft Road SE11.......... 245 G8
Meadcroft Road SE11.......... 245 H8
Meadow Road SW8.......... 244 D8
Meadow Row SE1.......... 245 J5
Mead Row SE1.......... 244 F4
Meakin Estate SE1.......... 245 M4
Mecklenburgh Square WC1N.......... 240 E3
Medway Street SW1P.......... 244 B5
Meeting House Alley E1W.......... 246 E5
Melcombe Place NW1.......... 239 G4
Melcombe Street W1U.......... 239 H4
Melina Place NW8.......... 238 D2
Melior Street SE1.......... 245 M2
Melton Street NW1.......... 240 A2
Memorial Gates SW1W.......... 243 K3
Mepham Street SE1.......... 244 F2
Mercer Street WC2H.......... 240 C7
Merchant Square W2.......... 238 E5
Merlin Street EC1R.......... 240 F2
Mermaid Court SE1.......... 245 K2
Merrick Square SE1.......... 245 K4
Merrow Street SE17.......... 245 L7
Merrington Road SW6.......... 242 A8
Methley Street SE11.......... 245 G7
Meymott Street SE1.......... 245 G2
Micawber Street N1.......... 241 K1
Micklethwaite Lane SW6.......... 242 A8
Middlesex Street E1.......... 246 A1
Middlesex Street E1.......... 246 B2
Middle Street EC1A.......... 241 J5
Middle Temple WC2R.......... 240 F7
Middle Temple Lane EC4Y.......... 240 F7
Middleton Drive SE16.......... 247 H6
Midland Road NW1.......... 240 C1
Midship Close SE16.......... 247 H6
Milborne Grove SW10.......... 242 D7
Milcote Street SE1.......... 245 H3
Miles Street SW8.......... 244 D8
Milford Lane WC2R.......... 240 F7
Milk Street EC2V.......... 241 K6
Milk Yard E1W.......... 247 G4
Millbank SW1P.......... 244 D4
Millennium Bridge SE1.......... 241 J8
Millennium Harbour E14.......... 247 M6
Milligan Street E14.......... 247 L4
Millman Mews WC1N.......... 240 E4
Millman Street WC1N.......... 240 E4
Mill Place E14.......... 247 K3
Millstream Road SE1.......... 246 B7
Mill Street SE1.......... 246 C6
Mill Street W1S.......... 239 L7
Milner Street SW3.......... 243 G5
Milton Street EC2Y.......... 241 K4
Milverton Street SE11.......... 245 G7
Mincing Lane EC3M.......... 246 A4
Minera Mews SW1W.......... 243 J5
Minories EC3N.......... 246 B3
Mitchell Street EC1V.......... 241 J3
Mitre Road SE1.......... 245 G2
Mitre Street EC3A.......... 246 A3
Molyneux Street W1H.......... 239 G5
Monck Street SW1P.......... 244 C4
Monkton Street SE11.......... 245 G5
Monkwell Square EC2Y.......... 241 K5
Monmouth Place W2.......... 238 A6
Monmouth Road W2.......... 238 A6
Monmouth Street WC2H.......... 240 C6
Montague Close SE1.......... 245 L1
Montague Place EC3R.......... 246 A4
Montague Street WC1B.......... 240 C5
Montagu Mansions W1H.......... 239 H5
Montagu Mews North W1H.......... 239 H5
Montagu Mews West W1H.......... 239 H6
Montagu Place W1H.......... 239 H5
Montagu Row W1U.......... 239 H5
Montagu Square W1H.......... 239 H5
Montagu Street W1H.......... 239 H6
Montford Place SE11.......... 244 F7
Monthorpe Road E1.......... 246 C1
Montpelier Place SW7.......... 243 G3
Montpelier Street SW7.......... 243 G3
Montpelier Walk SW7.......... 242 G3
Montrose Place SW1X.......... 243 K3
Monument EC4R.......... 241 L7
Monument ⊖ EC4R.......... 241 L7
Monument Street EC3R.......... 241 L7
Monument Street EC3R.......... 241 M7
Monza Street E1W.......... 247 G4
Moodkee Street SE16.......... 247 G7
Moore Street SW3.......... 243 H5
Moorfields EC2Y.......... 241 L5
Moorgate EC2R.......... 241 L6
Moorgate ≥ ⊖ EC2Y.......... 241 L5

Moor Lane EC2Y.......... 241 K5
Moor Street W1D.......... 240 C7
Mora Street EC1V.......... 241 K2
Morecambe Street SE17.......... 245 K6
Moreland Street EC1V.......... 241 H2
More London SE1.......... 246 A5
Moreton Place SW1V.......... 244 A6
Moreton Street SW1V.......... 244 B6
Moreton Terrace SW1V.......... 244 A6
Morgan's Lane SE1.......... 245 M2
Morgan's Lane SE1.......... 246 A6
Morley Street SE1.......... 245 G3
Mornington Crescent NW1.......... 239 M1
Mornington Place NW1.......... 239 L1
Mornington Terrace NW1.......... 239 L1
Morocco Street SE1.......... 245 M3
Morpeth Terrace SW1P.......... 243 M5
Morris Street E1.......... 246 F3
Morshead Road W9.......... 238 A2
Mortimer Market WC1E.......... 240 A4
Mortimer Street W1T.......... 240 A5
Mortimer Street W1W.......... 239 M5
Morton Place SE1.......... 244 F4
Morwell Street WC1B.......... 240 B5
Moscow Place W2.......... 238 B7
Moscow Road W2.......... 238 B7
Mossop Street SW3.......... 243 G5
Motcomb Street SW1X.......... 243 J4
Mount Gate W2.......... 242 E2
Mount Mills EC1V.......... 241 J3
Mount Pleasant WC1X.......... 240 F4
Mount Row W1K.......... 239 K8
Mount Street W1K.......... 239 K8
Mount Street Mews W1K.......... 239 K8
Mount Terrace E1.......... 246 E1
Moxon Street W1U.......... 239 J5
Mulberry Street E1.......... 246 D2
Mulberry Walk SW3.......... 242 E8
Mulready Street NW8.......... 238 F4
Mundy Street N1.......... 241 M2
Munster Square W1.......... 239 L3
Munton Road SE17.......... 245 K5
Murphy Street SE1.......... 244 F3
Murray Grove N1.......... 241 K1
Musbury Street E1.......... 247 G2
Muscovy Street EC3N.......... 246 A4
Museum of London EC2Y.......... 241 J5
Museum Street WC1A.......... 240 C5
Myddelton Passage EC1R.......... 241 G2
Myddelton Square EC1R.......... 241 G1
Myddelton Street EC1R.......... 241 G2
Myrdle Street E1.......... 246 D2

N

Naoroji Street WC1X.......... 240 F2
Napier Grove N1.......... 241 K1
Narrow Street E14.......... 247 K4
Nash Street NW1.......... 239 L2
Nassau Street W1W.......... 239 M5
Nathaniel Close * E1.......... 246 C2
National Portrait
    Gallery WC2H.......... 240 C8
Natural History
    Museum SW7.......... 242 E4
Neal Street WC2H.......... 240 C6
Neckinger SE1.......... 246 C8
Needleman Street SE16.......... 247 H7
Nelson Close NW6.......... 238 A1
Nelson Place N1.......... 241 H1
Nelson Square SE1.......... 245 H2
Nelson Street E1.......... 246 E2
Nelson Terrace N1.......... 241 H1
Neptune Street SE16.......... 247 G7
Nesham Street E1W.......... 246 D4
Netherton Grove SW10.......... 242 D8
Netley Street NW1.......... 239 M2
Nevern Place SW5.......... 242 A6
Nevern Square SW5.......... 242 A6
Neville Street SW7.......... 242 E6
Newark Street E1.......... 246 E2
New Atlas Wharf E14.......... 247 M8
New Bond Street W1S.......... 239 L7
New Bond Street W1S.......... 239 L8
New Bridge Street EC4V.......... 241 H6
New Broad Street EC2M.......... 241 M5
New Burlington
    Street W1S.......... 239 M7
Newburn Street SE11.......... 244 F7
Newbury Street EC1A.......... 241 J5
Newcastle Place W2.......... 238 E5
New Cavendish Street W1G.......... 239 K5
New Change EC4M.......... 241 J6
New Church Road SE5.......... 245 L8
Newcomen Street SE1.......... 245 K2
New Compton Street WC2H.......... 240 C6
Newcourt Street NW8.......... 238 F1
Newell Street E14.......... 247 L3
New Fetter Lane EC4A.......... 241 G6
Newgate Street EC1A.......... 241 J6
New Goulston Street E1.......... 246 B2
Newham's Row SE1.......... 246 A7
Newington Butts SE1.......... 245 H6
Newington Causeway SE1.......... 245 J4
New Kent Road SE1.......... 245 K5
Newlands Quay E1W.......... 246 F4
Newman Street W1T.......... 240 A5
New North Place EC2A.......... 241 M3
New North Road N1.......... 241 L1
New North Street WC1N.......... 240 D4
New Oxford Street WC1A.......... 240 C6
Newport Street SE11.......... 244 E5
New Quebec Street W1H.......... 239 H6
New Ride SW7.......... 242 E3
New Road E1.......... 246 E2
New Row WC2N.......... 240 C7
New Spring
    Gardens Walk SE1.......... 244 D7
New Square WC2A.......... 240 F6
New Street EC2M.......... 246 A2
New Street Square EC4A.......... 241 G6
Newton Road W2.......... 238 A6
Newton Street WC2B.......... 240 D5
New Union Street EC2Y.......... 241 K5
Nicholas Lane EC3V.......... 241 L7
Nicholson Street SE1.......... 245 H1
Nightingale Place SW10.......... 242 D8
Nile Street N1.......... 241 K2
Nine Elms Lane SW8.......... 244 C8
Noble Street EC2V.......... 241 J6
Noel Road N1.......... 241 J1
Noel Street W1F.......... 240 A6
Norbiton Road E14.......... 247 L2
Norfolk Crescent W2.......... 239 G6

Norfolk Place W2.......... 238 E6
Norfolk Square W2.......... 238 E6
Norman Street EC1V.......... 241 J3
Norris Street SW1Y.......... 240 B8
Northampton Road EC1R.......... 241 G3
Northampton Square EC1V.......... 241 H2
North Audley Street W1K.......... 239 J7
North Bank NW8.......... 238 F2
Northburgh Street EC1V.......... 241 H3
North Carriage Drive W2.......... 238 F7
Northdown Street N1.......... 240 D1
Northey Street E14.......... 247 K4
North Gower Street NW1.......... 240 A2
North Mews WC1N.......... 240 E4
North Ride W2.......... 239 G7
North Row W1K.......... 239 J7
North Tenter Street E1.......... 246 C3
North Terrace SW3.......... 242 F4
Northumberland Alley EC3N.......... 246 B3
Northumberland
    Avenue WC2N.......... 244 C1
Northumberland Place W2.......... 238 A6
Northumberland
    Street WC2N.......... 244 C1
North Wharf Road W2.......... 238 E5
Northwick Terrace NW8.......... 238 D3
Norway Gate SE16.......... 247 K7
Norway Place E14.......... 247 L3
Norwich Street EC4A.......... 240 F5
Nottingham Place W1U.......... 239 J4
Nottingham Street W1U.......... 239 J4
Notting Hill Gate W11.......... 238 A8
Notting Hill Gate ⊖ W11.......... 242 A1
Nugent Terrace NW8.......... 238 D1
Nutford Place W1H.......... 239 G6

O

Oakden Street SE11.......... 245 G5
Oakington Road W9.......... 238 A3
Oak Lane E14.......... 247 L3
Oakley Close EC1V.......... 241 H1
Oakley Gardens SW3.......... 243 G8
Oakley Square NW1.......... 240 A1
Oakley Street SW3.......... 242 F8
Oak Tree Road NW8.......... 238 F2
Oat Lane EC2V.......... 241 J5
Occupation Road SE17.......... 245 J6
Ocean Square E1.......... 247 J1
Odessa Street SE16.......... 247 L7
Ogle Street W1W.......... 239 M5
Old Bailey EC4M.......... 241 H6
Old Barrack Yard SW1X.......... 243 J3
Old Bond Street W1S.......... 239 M8
Old Broad Street EC2N.......... 241 M6
Old Brompton Road SW5.......... 242 B6
Old Brompton Road SW7.......... 242 D6
Old Burlington Street W1S.......... 239 M7
Oldbury Place W1U.......... 239 J4
Old Castle Street E1.......... 246 B2
Old Cavendish Street W1G.......... 239 L6
Old Church Road E1.......... 247 H2
Old Church Street SW3.......... 242 E7
Old Compton Street W1D.......... 240 B7
Old Court Place W8.......... 242 B2
Old Gloucester Street WC1N.......... 240 D4
Old Jamaica Road SE16.......... 246 C7
Old Jewry EC2R.......... 241 K6
Old Kent Road SE1.......... 245 M5
Old Marylebone Road NW1.......... 239 G5
Old Montague Street E1.......... 246 C1
Old North Street WC1X.......... 240 E5
Old Paradise Street SE11.......... 244 E5
Old Park Lane W1J.......... 243 K2
Old Pye Street SW1P.......... 244 B4
Old Queen Street SW1H.......... 244 B3
Old Square WC2A.......... 240 F6
Old Street EC1V.......... 241 J3
Old Street ⊖ ≥ EC1Y.......... 241 L3
Old Street Junction EC1Y.......... 241 L3
Oliver's Yard EC1Y.......... 241 L3
Olney Road SE17.......... 245 J8
O'Meara Street SE1.......... 245 K2
Omega Place N1.......... 240 D1
Onega Gate SE16.......... 247 J8
Ongar Road SW6.......... 242 A8
Onslow Gardens SW7.......... 242 D6
Onslow Square SW7.......... 242 E6
Onslow Square SW7.......... 242 E6
Ontario Street SE1.......... 245 J4
Ontario Way E14.......... 247 M4
Opal Street SE1.......... 245 H6
Orange Place SE16.......... 247 G8
Orange Square SW1W.......... 243 K6
Orange Street E1.......... 246 D5
Orange Street WC2B.......... 240 B8
Orb Street SE17.......... 245 L6
Orchardson Street NW8.......... 238 E4
Orchard Street W1H.......... 239 J6
Ordehall Street WC1N.......... 240 E4
Orient Street SE11.......... 245 H5
Orme Court W2.......... 238 B8
Orme Lane W2.......... 238 B8
Orme Square Gate W2.......... 238 B8
Ormond Close WC1N.......... 240 D4
Ormonde Gate SW3.......... 243 H7
Ormond Yard SW1Y.......... 240 A8
Orsett Street SE11.......... 244 E6
Orsett Terrace W2.......... 238 C5
Orton Street E1W.......... 246 D5
Osbert Street SW1V.......... 244 B6
Osborn Street E1.......... 246 C2
Oslo Square SE16.......... 247 K7
Osnaburgh Street NW1.......... 239 L3
Osnaburgh Terrace NW1.......... 239 L3
Ossington Buildings W1U.......... 239 J5
Ossington Street W2.......... 238 A8
Ossulston Street NW1.......... 240 B1
Oswin Street SE11.......... 245 H5
Othello Close SE1.......... 245 H6
Otto Street SE17.......... 245 H8
Outer Circle NW1.......... 239 H3
Outer Circle NW1.......... 239 K1
Oval SE11.......... 244 F8
Oval Way SE11.......... 244 E7
Ovington Square SW3.......... 243 G4
Ovington Street SW3.......... 243 G5
Owen Street EC1V.......... 241 G1
Oxenden Street SW1Y.......... 240 B8
Oxford Circus ⊖ W1B.......... 239 M6
Oxford Road NW6.......... 238 A1
Oxford Square W2.......... 238 F6
Oxford Street W1C.......... 239 L6
Oxford Street WC1A.......... 240 A6

P

Pace Place E1 .... 246 E3
Pacific Wharf SE16 .... 247 H5
Paddington ⇌ ⊖ W2 .... 238 D6
Paddington Green W2 .... 238 E5
Paddington Street W1U 239 J5
Pageant Crescent SE16 .... 247 K5
Page Street SW1P 244 B5
Paget Street EC1V 241 H2
Pakenham Street WC1X 240 E3
Palace Avenue W8 .... 238 B2
Palace Court W2 .... 238 A7
Palace Gardens Terrace W8 .. 242 A1
Palace Gate W8 .... 242 C3
Palace Green W8 .... 238 B2
Palace Place SW1E 243 M4
Palace Street SW1E 243 M4
Pall Mall SW1Y 244 A1
Pall Mall East SW1Y 244 B1
Palmer Street SW1H 244 B3
Pancras Lane EC4N 241 K6
Pancras Road N1C 240 C1
Panton Street SW1Y 240 B8
Paradise Street SE16 .... 246 E7
Paradise Walk SW3 .... 243 H8
Pardoner Street SE1 .... 245 L4
Pardon Street EC1V 241 H3
Parfett Street E1 .... 246 D2
Paris Garden SE1 .... 245 G1
Park Crescent W1B 239 K4
Parker's Row SE1 .... 246 C7
Parker Street WC2B 240 D6
Park Lane W1K 239 H7
Park Lane W2 .... 243 J1
Park Place SW1A 243 M1
Park Road NW1 .... 239 H3
Park Square East NW1 .... 239 L3
Park Square Mews NW1 .... 239 K3
Park Square West NW1 .... 239 K3
Park Street SE1 .... 245 K1
Park Street W1K 239 J7
Park Village East NW1 .... 239 L1
Park Walk SW10 .... 242 D8
Park West Place W2 .... 239 G6
Parliament Street SW1A 244 C2
Parry Street SW8 .... 244 D8
Passmore Street SW1W 243 J6
Paternoster Square EC1 .... 241 J6
Pater Street W8 .... 242 A4
Pattina Walk SE16 .... 247 K5
Paul Street EC2A 241 M3
Paultons Square SW3 .... 242 E8
Paveley Street NW1 .... 239 G3
Pavilion Road SW1X 243 H3
Pavilion Road SW1X 243 H4
Paxton Terrace SW1V 243 L7
Peabody Avenue SW1V 243 L7
Peabody Estate SE1 .... 245 J1
Peacock Street SE17 .... 245 J6
Pearl Street E1W 246 F5
Pearman Street SE1 .... 245 G3
Pear Tree Court EC1R 241 G3
Peartree Lane E1W 247 G4
Pear Tree Street EC1V 241 J3
Peel Street W8 .... 242 A1
Peerless Street EC1V 241 K2
Pelham Crescent SW7 .... 242 F6
Pelham Place SW7 .... 242 F5
Pelham Street SW7 .... 242 F5
Pelier Street SE17 .... 245 K8
Pemberton Row EC4A 241 G6
Pembridge Gardens W2 .... 238 A8
Pembridge Place W2 .... 238 A7
Pembridge Square W2 .... 238 A7
Pembridge Villas W11 .... 238 A7
Pembroke Close SW1X 243 J3
Penang Street E1W 246 F5
Penfold Place NW8 .... 238 F5
Penfold Street NW8 .... 238 E4
Pennant Mews W8 .... 242 B5
Pennington Street E1W 246 D4
Pennyfields E14 .... 247 M4
Penrose Grove SE17 .... 245 J7
Penrose Street SE17 .... 245 J7
Penryn Road SE16 .... 246 E7
Penton Place SE17 .... 245 H6
Penton Rise WC1X 240 E2
Penton Street N1 .... 240 F1
Pentonville Road N1 .... 240 E1
Penywern Road SW5 .... 242 A6
Pepper Street SE1 .... 245 J2
Pepys Street EC3N 246 A4
Percival Street EC1V 241 H3
Percy Circus WC1X 240 F2
Percy Street W1T 240 B5
Perkin's Rent SW1P 244 B4
Petersham Mews SW7 .... 242 D4
Petersham Place SW7 .... 242 C4
Peter Street W1F 240 B7
Peto Place NW1 .... 239 L3
Petticoat Lane E1 .... 246 B2
Petty France SW1H 244 A3
Petty Wales EC3R 246 A4
Petyward SW3 .... 243 G6
Phelp Street SE17 .... 245 L7
Phene Street SW3 .... 243 G8
Phillimore Walk W8 .... 242 A3
Philpot Lane EC3M 241 M7
Philpot Street E1 .... 246 E2
Phipp's Mews SW1W 243 L5
Phipp Street EC2A 241 M3
Phoenix Place WC1X 240 F3
Phoenix Road NW1 .... 240 B1
Phoenix Street WC2H 240 C6
Piccadilly W1J 243 L2
Piccadilly Arcade SW1Y 243 M1
Piccadilly Circus W1B 240 A8
Piccadilly Circus ⊖ W1J 240 B8
Pickard Street EC1V 241 J2
Picton Place W1U 239 K6
Pier Head E1W 246 E6
Pigott Street E14 .... 247 M3
Pilgrimage Street SE1 .... 245 L3
Pimlico ⊖ SW1V 244 B6
Pimlico Road SW1W 243 J6
Pinchin Street E1 .... 246 D3
Pindar Street EC2A 241 M4
Pindock Mews W9 .... 238 B3
Pine Street EC1R 240 F3
Pitfield Street N1 .... 241 M1
Pitsea Street E1 .... 247 H3
Pitt's Head Mews W1J 243 K2
Pitt Street W8 .... 242 A2
Pixley Street E14 .... 247 L2
Platina Street * EC2A 241 L3

Plover Way SE16 .... 247 K8
Plumbers Row E1 .... 246 D2
Plumtree Court EC4A 241 G5
Plympton Street NW8 .... 238 F4
Pocock Street SE1 .... 245 H2
Pollen Street W1S 239 L7
Pollitt Drive NW8 .... 238 E3
Polperro Mews W9 .... 238 B2
Polygon Road NW1 .... 240 B1
Pond Place SW3 .... 242 F6
Ponler Street E1 .... 246 E3
Ponsonby Place SW1P 244 C6
Ponsonby Terrace SW1P 244 C6
Ponton Road SW8 .... 244 B8
Pont Street SW1X 243 H4
Poolmans Street SE16 .... 247 H6
Pope Street SE1 .... 246 B7
Poplar Place W2 .... 238 B7
Poppin's Court EC4A 241 H6
Porchester Gardens W2 .... 238 B7
Porchester Gate W2 .... 238 C8
Porchester Place W2 .... 239 G6
Porchester Road W2 .... 238 B5
Porchester Square W2 .... 238 B6
Porchester Terrace W2 .... 238 C7
Porchester Terrace
  North W2 .... 238 C6
Porlock Street SE1 .... 245 L3
Porter Street SE1 .... 245 K2 *[see note]*
Porteus Road W2 .... 238 D5
Portland Place W1B 239 L4
Portland Place W1B 239 L5
Portland Square E1W 246 E5
Portland Street SE17 .... 245 L7
Portman Close W1H 239 J6
Portman Mews South W1H ... 239 J6
Portman Square W1H 239 J6
Portman Street W1H 239 J6
Portpool Lane EC1N 240 F4
Portsea Place W2 .... 239 G6
Portsmouth Street WC2A 240 E6
Portsoken Street E1 .... 246 B3
Portugal Street WC2A 240 E6
Potier Street SE1 .... 245 L4
Potters Fields SE1 .... 246 B6
Pottery Street SE16 .... 246 E7
Poultry EC2V 241 K6
Powis Place WC1N 240 D4
Praed Mews W2 .... 238 E6
Praed Street W2 .... 238 E6
Pratt Walk SE1 .... 244 E5
Premier Place E14 .... 247 M4
Prescot Street E1 .... 246 C3
Preston Close SW1 .... 245 M5
Price's Street SE1 .... 245 H1
Prideaux Place WC1X 240 F2
Primrose Street EC2A 246 A1
Prince Albert Road NW8 .... 238 F1
Prince Consort Road SW7 .... 242 D3
Princelet Street E1 .... 246 C1
Prince of Wales Gate SW7 ... 242 F3
Princes Arcade SW1Y 240 A8
Prince's Gardens SW7 .... 242 E3
Prince's Gate Mews SW7 ..... 242 E4
Princes Riverside Road SE16 . 247 H5
Prince's Square W2 .... 238 A7
Princess Road NW6 .... 238 A1
Princess Street SE1 .... 245 H4
Princes Street W1B 239 L6
Prince's Street EC2R 241 L6
Princeton Street WC1R 240 E5
Prioress Street SE1 .... 245 L4
Priory Green Estate N1 .... 240 E1
Priory Walk SW10 .... 242 D7
Proctor Street WC1V 240 E5
Prospect Place E1W 247 G5
Prospect Street SE16 .... 246 E7
Provident Court W1K 239 J7
Provost Street N1 .... 241 L1
Prusom Street E1W 246 F5
Pudding Lane EC3R 241 M7
Pumphouse Mews E1W 246 D3
Purbrook Street SE1 .... 246 A7
Purcell Street N1 .... 241 M1
Purchese Street NW1 .... 240 B1

Q

Quebec Way SE16 .... 247 J7
Queen Anne's Gate SW1H 244 B3
Queen Anne Street W1G 239 K5
Queen Elizabeth Street SE1 .. 246 B6
Queen Mother Gate W2 .... 243 J2
Queensborough Terrace W2 . 238 C7
Queensberry Place SW7 .... 242 E5
Queen's Gardens W2 .... 238 C7
Queen's Gate SW7 .... 242 D3
Queen's Gate SW7 .... 242 D4
Queen's Gate Gardens SW7 . 242 D5
Queen's Gate Mews SW7 ..... 242 D4
Queen's Gate Place SW7 ..... 242 D4
Queen's Gate Place
  Mews SW7 .... 242 D4
Queen's Gate Terrace SW7 .. 242 C4
Queen's Mews W2 .... 238 B7
Queen Square WC1N 240 D4
Queen's Row SE17 .... 245 K7
Queen Street EC4N 241 K7
Queen Street W1J 243 L1
Queen Street Place EC4R 241 K7
Queen's Walk SE1 .... 246 A5
Queen's Walk SW1A 243 M2
Queensway ⊖ W2 .... 238 B6
Queensway W2 .... 238 B8
Queen Victoria Street EC4V .. 241 J7
Quick Street N1 .... 241 H1

R

Raby Street E14 .... 247 K2
Radcliffe Road SE1 .... 246 B8
Radcot Street SE11 .... 245 G7
Radnor Mews W2 .... 238 E6
Radnor Place W2 .... 238 F6
Radnor Street EC1V 241 K3
Radnor Walk SW3 .... 243 G7
Railway Approach SE1 .... 245 L1
Railway Avenue SE16 .... 247 G6
Railway Street N1 .... 240 D1
Raine Street E1W 246 F5
Ralston Street SW3 .... 243 H7
Ramillies Place W1F 239 M6

Ramillies Street W1F 239 M6
Rampart Street E1 .... 246 E2
Rampayne Street SW1V 244 B6
Randall Road SE11 .... 244 D6
Randall Row SE11 .... 244 E6
Randolph Avenue W9 .... 238 B1
Randolph Crescent W9 .... 238 C3
Randolph Gardens NW6 .... 238 B1
Randolph Mews W9 .... 238 D4
Randolph Road W9 .... 238 C4
Ranelagh Grove SW1W 243 K6
Ranelagh Road SW1V 244 A7
Rangoon Street * EC3N 246 B3
Ranston Street NW8 .... 238 F4
Raphael Street SW7 .... 243 G3
Ratcliffe Cross Street E1W ... 247 J3
Ratcliffe Lane E14 .... 247 J3
Rathbone Place W1T 240 B5
Rathbone Street W1T 240 A5
Raven Row E1 .... 246 F1
Ravensdon Street SE11 .... 245 G7
Ravey Street EC2A 241 M3
Rawlings Street SW3 .... 243 G5
Rawstone Street EC1V 241 H2
Ray Street EC1R 241 G4
Reardon Place E1W 246 F5
Reardon Street E1W 246 E5
Rectory Square E1 .... 247 H1
Redan Place W2 .... 238 B6
Redburn Street SW3 .... 243 G7
Redcastle Close E1W 247 G4
Redcliffe Gardens SW10 ...... 242 B7
Redcliffe Mews SW10 .... 242 C7
Redcliffe Place SW10 .... 242 C8
Redcliffe Road SW10 .... 242 D7
Redcliffe Square SW10 .... 242 B7
Redcliffe Street SW10 .... 242 B8
Redcross Way SE1 .... 245 K2
Redesdale Street SW3 .... 243 G7
Redfield Lane SW5 .... 242 A5
Redhill Street NW1 .... 239 L1
Red Lion Row SE5 .... 245 K8
Red Lion Square WC1R 240 E5
Red Lion Street WC2B 240 E5
Redman's Road E1 .... 247 G1
Red Place W1K 239 J7
Redriff Road SE16 .... 247 J8
Reedworth Street SE11 .... 245 G6
Reeves Mews W1K 239 J8
Regal Close SE1 .... 246 D1
Regan Way N1 .... 241 M1
Regency Street SW1P 244 B5
Regent Place W1B 240 A7
Regent's Park ⊖ W1B 239 L4
Regent's Park W1 .... 239 J1
Regent's Park Estate NW1 ... 239 L2
Regent Square WC1N 240 D2
Regent Street SW1Y 240 B8
Regent Street W1S 239 M7
Relton Mews SW7 .... 243 G4
Remington Street N1 .... 241 H1
Remnant Street WC2A 240 E6
Renforth Street SE16 .... 247 G7
Renfrew Road SE11 .... 245 H5
Rennie Street SE1 .... 245 H1
Rephidim Street SE1 .... 245 M4
Repton Street E14 .... 247 K2
Reveley Square SE16 .... 247 K7
Rex Place W1K 239 J8
Rhodeswell Road E14 .... 247 L2
Rich Street E14 .... 247 M3
Rickett Street SW6 .... 242 A8
Ridgemount Street WC1E 240 B4
Ridgmount Gardens WC1E ... 240 B4
Riding House Street W1W 239 M5
Riley Road SE1 .... 246 B7
Ripley's Believe It
  or Not! W1J 240 B8
Risborough Street SE1 .... 245 J2
Risdon Street SE16 .... 247 G7
Rissinghill Street N1 .... 240 F1
River Street EC1R 240 F2
Rivington Street EC2A 241 M3
Robert Adam Street W1U 239 J6
Roberts Close SE16 .... 247 J7
Robert Street NW1 .... 239 L2
Rochester Row SW1P 244 A5
Rochester Street SW1P 244 B5
Rockingham Street SE1 .... 245 J4
Rocliffe Street N1 .... 241 H1
Roding Mews E1W 246 D5
Rodmarton Street W1U 239 H5
Rodney Place SE17 .... 245 K5
Rodney Road SE17 .... 245 K5
Rodney Street N1 .... 240 E1
Roger Street WC1N 240 E4
Roland Gardens SW7 .... 242 D6
Roland Way SE17 .... 245 L7
Romford Street E1 .... 246 E2
Romilly Street W1D 240 B7
Romney Street SW1P 244 C5
Rood Lane EC3M 241 M7
Ropemaker Road SE16 .... 247 K7
Ropemaker Street EC2Y 241 L4
Roper Lane SE1 .... 246 B7
Rope Street SE16 .... 247 K8
Rope Walk Gardens E1 .... 246 E2
Rosary Gardens SW7 .... 242 D6
Roscoe Street EC1Y 241 K3
Rose Alley SE1 .... 241 K8
Rosebery Avenue EC1R 240 F3
Rosemoor Street SW3 .... 243 G6
Rose Street WC2E 240 C7
Rossmore Road NW1 .... 239 G3
Rotary Street SE1 .... 245 H3
Rotherhithe ⊖ SE16 .... 247 G6
Rotherhithe Street SE16 ...... 247 G6
Rotherhithe Street SE16 ...... 247 J4
Rotherhithe Tunnel SE16 ..... 247 H5
Rothsay Street SE1 .... 245 M4
Rotten Row W2 .... 242 F2
Rouel Road SE16 .... 246 D8
Roupell Street SE1 .... 245 G2
Royal Albert Hall SW7 .... 242 E3
Royal Avenue SW3 .... 243 H6
Royal Hospital Road SW3 .... 243 H7
Royal Mint Street E1 .... 246 C4
Royal Oak ⊖ W2 .... 238 B5
Royal Oak Yard SE1 .... 246 A7
Royal Opera House WC2E 240 D7
Royal Road SE17 .... 245 H8
Royal Street SE1 .... 244 E4
Rudolph Road NW6 .... 238 A1
Rugby Street WC1N 240 E4
Rum Close E1W 246 F4
Rupack Street SE16 .... 246 F7
Rupert Street W1D 240 B7

Ramillies Street W1F 239 M6
Rushworth Street SE1 .... 245 H2
Russell Court SW1A 244 A2
Russell Square WC1B 240 C4
Russell Square ⊖ WC1B 240 D4
Russell Street WC2B 240 D7
Russia Dock Road SE16 .... 247 K6
Rutherford Street SW1P 244 B5
Rutland Gardens SW7 .... 243 G3
Rutland Gate SW7 .... 242 F3
Rutland Mews SW7 .... 242 F4
Rutland Street SW7 .... 242 F4
Ryder Street SW1Y 244 A1

S

Sackville Street W1S 240 A8
Saffron Hill EC1N 241 G4
Saffron Street EC1N 241 G4
Sail Street SE11 .... 244 F5
St Agnes Place SE11 .... 245 G8
St Alban's Grove W8 .... 242 B4
St Alban's Street SW1Y 240 B8
St Alphage Garden EC2Y 241 K5
St Andrews Hill EC4V 241 H7
St Andrew's Place NW1 .... 239 L3
St Andrew Street EC4A 241 G5
St Anne's Court W1F 240 B6
St Ann's Street SW1P 244 C4
St Anselm's Place W1K 239 K7
St Barnabas Street SW1W ... 243 K6
St Botolph Street EC3N 246 B2
St Bride Street EC4A 241 G6
St Chad's Street WC1H 240 D2
St Clare Street EC3N 246 B3
St Clements Lane WC2A 240 E6
St Cross Street EC1N 241 G4
St Dunstan's Hill EC3R 241 M8
St Dunstan's Lane EC3R 241 M7
St Elmos Road SE16 .... 247 J7
St Ermin's Hill SW1H 244 B3
St George's Circus SE1 .... 245 H3
St George's Drive SW1V 243 M6
St George's Estate E1 .... 246 D3
St George's Lane * EC3R 241 M7
St George's Road SE1 .... 245 G4
St George's Square SW1V 244 B7
St George Street W1S 239 L7
St Giles High Street WC2H ... 240 C6
St Helen's Place EC3A 246 A2
St James Market * SW1Y 240 B8
St James's Park ⊖ SW1H 244 B3
St James's Park SW1A 244 B3
St James's Place SW1A 243 M2
St James's Road SE16 .... 246 D8
St James's Square SW1Y 244 A1
St James's Street SW1A 243 M1
St James Walk EC1R 241 G3
St John's Lane EC1M 241 H4
St John's Place EC1M 241 H4
St John Square EC1V 241 H4
St John Street EC1V 241 H2
St John's Wood High
  Street NW8 .... 238 F1
St John's Wood Road NW8 ... 238 E3
St Katharine's Way E1W 246 C5
St Leonard's Terrace SW3 .... 243 H7
St Loo Avenue SW3 .... 243 G8
St Luke's Close EC1V 241 K3
St Luke's Street SW3 .... 242 F6
St Manningtree E1 .... 246 C2
St Mark Street E1 .... 246 C3
St Martin's Lane WC2N 240 C7
St Martin's le Grand EC1A 241 J6
St Martin's Place WC2N 240 C8
St Mary at Hill EC3R 241 M8
St Mary Axe EC3A 246 A3
St Mary Church Street SE16 . 246 F7
St Mary's Gardens SE11 ...... 245 G5
St Mary's Terrace W2 .... 238 D4
St Mary's Walk SE11 .... 245 G5
St Matthew Street SW1P 244 B4
St Michael's Street W2 .... 238 F6
St Olav's Square SE16 .... 246 F7
St Oswald's Place SE11 .... 244 E7
St Pancras
  International ⇌ N1C 240 C1
St Paul's ⊖ EC1A 241 J6
St Paul's Avenue SE16 .... 247 J5
St Paul's Cathedral EC4M 241 J6
St Paul's Churchyard EC4M .. 241 J6
St Paul's Way SE1 .... 247 L1
St Petersberg Mews W2 ...... 238 B7
St Petersburgh Place W2 ..... 238 B7
St Saviours Wharf SE1 .... 246 C6
St Stephen's Gardens W2 .... 238 A5
St Swithin's Lane EC4N 241 L7
St Thomas Street SE1 .... 245 L2
St Vincent Street W1U 239 J5
Salamanca Street SE1 .... 244 D6
Salem Road W2 .... 238 B7
Sale Place W2 .... 238 F5
Salisbury Court EC4Y 241 G6
Salisbury Place W1H 239 H4
Salisbury Street NW8 .... 238 F4
Salmon Lane E14 .... 247 J2
Salter Road SE16 .... 247 J5
Salter Street E14 .... 247 M4
Samford Street NW8 .... 238 F4
Sampson Street E1W 246 D5
Sancroft Street SE11 .... 244 F6
Sandford Row SE17 .... 245 L6
Sandland Street WC1R 240 E5
Sandpiper Close SE16 .... 247 L6
Sandwich Street WC1H 240 C2
Sandy's Row E1 .... 246 B1
Sans Walk EC1R 241 G3
Sardinia Street WC2A 240 E6
Savage Gardens EC3N 246 B3
Savile Row W1S 239 M7
Savoy Hill WC2R 240 E8
Savoy Place WC2R 240 D8
Savoy Street WC2E 240 E7
Sawyer Street SE1 .... 245 J2
Scala Street W1T 240 A5
Scandrett Street E1W 246 E5
Scarborough Street E1 .... 246 C3
Scarsdale Villas W8 .... 242 A4
Schooner Close * SE16 .... 247 H6
Science Museum SW7 .... 242 E4
Scoresby Street SE1 .... 245 H2
Scotch House
  Junction SW1X 243 H3
Scotland Place SW1A 244 C1
Scott Ellis Grove NW8 .... 238 E2
Scott Lidgett Crescent SE16 . 246 D7

Scrutton Street EC2A 241 M3
Seaford Street WC1H 240 D2
Seagrave Road SW6 .... 242 A8
Sea Life London
  Aquarium SE1 .... 244 E3
Searles Road SE1 .... 245 L5
Sebastian Street EC1V 241 H2
Secker Street SE1 .... 244 F2
Sedan Way SE17 .... 245 M6
Sedding Street SW1X 243 J5
Seddon Street WC1X 240 E3
Seething Lane EC3N 246 A4
Sekforde Street EC1R 241 H3
Selfridges W1A 239 J6
Selsey Street E14 .... 247 M1
Selwood Place SW7 .... 242 E6
Semley Place SW1W 243 K6
Senior Street W2 .... 238 B4
Senrab Street E1 .... 247 H2
Serle Street WC2A 240 F6
Serpentine Bridge W2 .... 242 E1
Serpentine Road W2 .... 242 F2
Seth Street SE16 .... 247 G7
Settles Street E1 .... 246 D2
Seven Dials WC2H 240 C6
Seville Street SW1X 243 H3
Sevington Street W9 .... 238 A3
Seward Street EC1V 241 J3
Seymour Mews W1H 239 J6
Seymour Place W1H 239 G5
Seymour Street W1H 239 H6
Seymour Street W2 .... 239 G7
Seymour Walk SW10 .... 242 C7
Shad Thames SE1 .... 246 B6
Shad Thames SE1 .... 246 C6
Shadwell ⊖ E1 .... 246 F3
Shadwell Gardens E1 .... 246 F3
Shaftesbury
  Avenue W1D 240 B7
Shaftesbury
  Avenue WC2H 240 C6
Shaftesbury Street N1 .... 241 K1
Shakespeare's Globe SE1 ... 241 K8
Shand Street SE1 .... 246 A6
Sharsted Street SE17 .... 245 H7
Shaw Crescent E14 .... 247 K2
Shawfield Street SW3 .... 243 G7
Sheffield Terrace W8 .... 242 A2
Sheldon Square W2 .... 238 D5
Shelmerdine Close E3 .... 247 M1
Shelton Street WC2H 240 D6
Shepherdess Walk N1 .... 241 K1
Shepherd Street W1J 243 K1
Sheraton Street W1F 240 B6
Sherborne Lane EC4N 241 L7
Ship and Mermaid Row SE1 . 245 M2
Shipwright Road SE16 .... 247 K7
Shirland Road W9 .... 238 A3
Shoe Lane EC4A 241 G5
Shorter Street EC3N 246 B4
Shorts Gardens WC2H 240 C6
Short Street SE1 .... 245 G2
Shoulder of Mutton
  Alley E14 .... 247 K4
Shouldham Street W1H 239 G5
Shroton Street NW1 .... 238 F4
Siddons Lane W1H 239 H4
Sidmouth Street WC1N 240 D3
Sidney Square E1 .... 246 F2
Sidney Street E1 .... 246 F1
Silex Street SE1 .... 245 H3
Silk Street EC2Y 241 K4
Silver Walk SE16 .... 247 K5
Silvester Street SE1 .... 245 K3
Singer Street EC2A 241 L3
Sir John Soane's
  Museum WC2A 240 E5
Skinner Place * SW1W 243 J6
Skinners Lane EC4V 241 K7
Skinner Street EC1R 241 G3
Slippers Place SE16 .... 246 F8
Sloane Avenue SW3 .... 243 G6
Sloane Court SW3 .... 243 J6
Sloane Court East SW3 .... 243 J6
Sloane Gardens SW1W 243 J6
Sloane Square ⊖ SW1W 243 J5
Sloane Square SW1X 243 J6
Sloane Street SW1X 243 H3
Sloane Terrace SW1X 243 J5
Smeaton Street E1W 246 E5
Smithfield Street EC1A 241 H5
Smith Square SW1P 244 C4
Smith Street SW3 .... 243 G7
Smith Terrace SW3 .... 243 G7
Smithy Street E1 .... 247 G1
Snowden Street EC2A 241 M4
Snow Hill EC1A 241 H5
Snowsfields SE1 .... 245 L2
Soho Square W1D 240 B6
Soho Street W1D 240 B6
Somerford Way SE16 .... 247 K7
Somers Crescent W2 .... 238 F6
Somerset House WC2R 240 E7
Somers Estate NW1 .... 240 A1
Sondes Street SE17 .... 245 L7
South & West Africa
  Gate SW1A 244 A3
Southall Place SE1 .... 245 L3
Southampton
  Buildings WC2A 240 F5
Southampton Place WC1A ... 240 D5
Southampton Row WC1B 240 D4
Southampton Street WC2E ... 240 D7
South Audley Street W1K 239 K8
South Carriage Drive SW1X .. 243 H3
South Carriage Drive SW7 ... 242 F3
South Eaton Place SW1W 243 J5
Southern Street N1 .... 240 E1
South Kensington ⊖ SW7 .... 242 E4
South Kensington ⊖ SW7 .... 242 E4
South Lambeth Road SW8 ... 244 D8
South Molton Lane W1K 239 K7
South Molton Street W1K 239 K7
South Parade SW3 .... 242 E7
South Place EC2M 241 L5
South Sea Street SE16 .... 247 L8
South Square WC1R 240 F5
South Tenter Street E1 .... 246 C3
South Terrace SW7 .... 242 F5
Southwark ⊖ SE1 .... 245 H2
Southwark Bridge SE1 .... 241 K8
Southwark Bridge
  Road SE1 .... 245 J3
Southwark Park
  Road SE16 .... 246 E8
Southwark Street SE1 .... 245 H1

outhwell Gardens SW7 ...... 242 C5
outh Wharf Road W2 ...... 238 E6
outhwick Mews W2 ...... 238 F6
outhwick Place W2 ...... 238 F6
outhwick Street W2 ...... 238 F6
overeign Close E1W 246 F4
overeign Crescent SE16 ...... 247 H6
panish Place W1U 239 J5
pa Road SE16 ...... 246 C8
pear Mews SW5 ...... 242 A6
pelman Street E1 ...... 246 C1
pence Close SE16 ...... 247 K7
pencer Street EC1V 241 H2
penser Street SW1E 244 A4
pert Street E14 ...... 247 J4
pital Square E1 ...... 246 A1
pring Gardens SW1A 244 C1
pring Street W2 ...... 238 E6
purgeon Street SE1 ...... 245 L4
pur Road SE1 ...... 244 F3
tables Way SE11 ...... 244 F7
table Yard Road SW1A 244 A2
tacey Street WC2H 240 C6
tafford Road SW1E 243 M3
tafford Road NW6 ...... 238 E4
tafford Road W1S 239 M8
tafford Terrace W8 ...... 242 A3
tainer Street SE1 ...... 245 L2
tainsby Road E14 ...... 247 M2
talham Street SE16 ...... 246 F8
tamford Street SE1 ...... 245 G1
tanford Place SE1 ...... 245 M6
tanford Road W8 ...... 242 B4
tanhope Close * SE16 ...... 247 H6
tanhope Gardens SW7 ...... 242 D5
tanhope Gate W1K 243 K1
tanhope Mews SW7 ...... 242 D5
tanhope Mews East SW7 ...... 242 D5
tanhope Mews West SW7 ...... 242 D5
tanhope Place W2 ...... 239 G7
tanhope Place Gate W2 ...... 239 G7
tanhope Row W1J 243 K1
tanhope Street NW1 ...... 239 M1
tanhope Terrace W2 ...... 238 E7
tannary Street SE11 ...... 245 G7
taples Close SE16 ...... 247 J5
taple Street SE1 ...... 245 L3
tarcross Street NW1 ...... 240 A2
tar Street W2 ...... 238 F6
tation Approach Road SE1 ...... 244 F3
tave Yard Road SE16 ...... 247 J5
tead Street SE17 ...... 245 K6
teedman Street SE17 ...... 245 J5
teel's Lane E1 ...... 247 G3
teeres Way SE16 ...... 247 K7
tephenson Way NW1 ...... 240 A3
tephen Street W1T 240 B5
tepney Green E1 ...... 247 H1
tepney High Street E1 ...... 247 J1
tepney Way E1 ...... 246 E1
terling Street SW7 ...... 243 G3
tevedore Street E1W 246 E5
tevens Street SE1 ...... 246 A7
teward Street * E1 ...... 246 B1
tewart's Grove SW3 ...... 242 F6
tew Lane EC4V 241 J7
tillington Street SW1P 244 A5
tockholm Way E1W 246 D5
tocks Place E14 ...... 247 M3
tone Buildings WC2A 240 F5
tonecutter Street EC4A 241 G6
toney Lane E1 ...... 246 B2
toney Street SE1 ...... 245 K1
topford Road SE17 ...... 245 J7
tore Street WC1E 240 B5
torey's Gate SW1H 244 C3
torks Road SE16 ...... 246 D8
toughton Close SE11 ...... 244 E6
tourcliffe Street W1H 239 G6
trafford Street E14 ...... 247 M4
trand WC2R 240 D8
tratford Place W1C 239 K6
tratford Road W8 ...... 242 A5
tratheam Place W2 ...... 238 F7
tratton Street W1J 243 L1
trype Street E1 ...... 246 B2
tuart Road NW6 ...... 238 A2
tukeley Street WC2B 240 D6
turgeon Road SE17 ...... 245 J7
turge Street SE1 ...... 245 J3
turt Street N1 ...... 241 K1
tutfield Street E1 ...... 246 D3
udley Street N1 ...... 241 H1
udrey Street SE1 ...... 245 J3
uffolk Lane EC4V 241 L7
uffolk Street SW1Y 240 B8
ugar Quay Walk EC3R 246 A4
ullivan Road SE11 ...... 245 G5
ummercourt Road E1 ...... 247 G2
ummer Place SW7 ...... 242 E6
ummers Street EC1R 240 F4
umner Street SE1 ...... 245 J1
underland Terrace W2 ...... 238 A6
un Passage SE16 ...... 246 D8
un Street EC2M 241 M4
urrendale Place W9 ...... 238 A4
urrey Quays Road SE16 ...... 247 H7
urrey Row SE1 ...... 245 H2
urrey Square SE17 ...... 245 M6
urrey Street WC2E 240 E7
urrey Water Road SE16 ...... 247 H6
ussex Gardens W2 ...... 238 E6
ussex Mews East W2 ...... 238 E7
ussex Place NW1 ...... 239 H3
ussex Place W2 ...... 238 E6
ussex Square W2 ...... 238 E7
ussex Street SW1V 243 L7
utherland Avenue W9 ...... 238 A4
utherland Row SW1V 243 L6
utherland Square SE17 ...... 245 J7
utherland Street SW1V 243 L7
utton Row W1D 240 B6
utton Street E1 ...... 247 G3
uttons Way EC1Y 241 K4
wain Street NW8 ...... 238 F3
wallow Place W1B 239 L6
wallow Street W1B 240 A8
wan Lane EC4R 241 L8
wan Mead SE1 ...... 245 M4
wan Road SE16 ...... 247 G6
wan Street SE1 ...... 245 K3
wan Walk SW3 ...... 243 H8
wedenborg Gardens E1 ...... 246 E4
weeney Crescent SE1 ...... 246 C7
winton Street WC1X 240 E2
ydney Street SW3 ...... 242 F6
ymons Street SW3 ...... 243 H6

T

Tabard Gardens Estate SE1 ...... 245 L3
Tabard Street SE1 ...... 245 L3
Tabernacle Street EC2A 241 L3
Tachbrook Street SW1V 244 A6
Talbot Road W2 ...... 238 A6
Talbot Square W2 ...... 238 E6
Talbot Yard SE1 ...... 245 L2
Tallis Street EC4Y 241 G7
Tamworth Street SW6 ...... 242 A8
Tanner Street SE1 ...... 246 A7
Taplow Street N1 ...... 241 K1
Tarling Street E1 ...... 246 F3
Tarver Road SE17 ...... 245 H7
Tate Britain SW1P 244 C6
Tate Modern SE1 ...... 241 J8
Tatum Street SE17 ...... 245 M6
Taunton Place NW1 ...... 239 G3
Tavistock Place WC1H 240 C3
Tavistock Square WC1H 240 C3
Tavistock Street WC2E 240 D7
Taviton Street WC1H 240 B3
Teak Close SE16 ...... 247 K6
Tedworth Square SW3 ...... 243 G7
Telford Terrace SW1V 243 M7
Temeraire Street SE16 ...... 247 G6
Temple WC2R 240 F7
Temple Avenue EC4Y 241 G7
Temple Lane EC4Y 241 G7
Temple Place WC2R 240 F7
Templeton Place SW5 ...... 242 A5
Tench Street E1W 246 E5
Tenniel Close W2 ...... 238 C7
Tennis Street SE1 ...... 245 L2
Tenterden Street W1S 239 L6
Teredo Street SE16 ...... 247 J8
Terminus Place SW1V 243 L4
Thame Road SE16 ...... 247 H6
Thanet Street WC1H 240 C2
Thavies Inn EC4A 241 G6
Thayer Street W1U 239 K5
The Arches WC2N 240 D8
The Boltons SW10 ...... 242 C7
The British Library NW1 ...... 240 C2
The British Museum WC1B 240 C5
The Broad Walk W2 ...... 238 B8
The Broad Walk W8 ...... 242 C2
The Cut SE1 ...... 245 G2
The Flower Walk W2 ...... 242 D3
The Grange SE1 ...... 246 B8
The Highway E1W 246 E4
The Little Boltons SW10 ...... 242 C7
The Mall SW1A 244 B2
The Mitre E14 ...... 247 L3
The Monument EC3R 241 L7
The National Gallery WC2N 240 C8
The Oval (Surrey County
   Cricket Ground) SE11 ...... 244 F8
The Shard SE1 ...... 245 L2
The Vale SW3 ...... 242 E8
Thirleby Road SW1P 244 A4
Thomas More Street E1W 246 D4
Thomas Road E14 ...... 247 M2
Thoresby Street N1 ...... 241 K1
Thorney Street SW1P 244 C5
Thornton Place W1H 239 H4
Thrale Street SE1 ...... 245 K1
Thrawl Street E1 ...... 246 C1
Threadneedle Street EC2R 241 L6
Three Colt Street E14 ...... 247 L3
Three Oak Lane SE1 ...... 246 B6
Throgmorton Avenue EC2N 241 L6
Throgmorton Street EC2N 241 L6
Thurland Road SE16 ...... 246 D8
Thurloe Place SW7 ...... 242 F5
Thurloe Square SW7 ...... 242 F5
Thurloe Street SW7 ...... 242 F5
Thurlow Street SE17 ...... 245 M7
Tichbourne Row W2 ...... 238 F6
Tiller Road E14 ...... 247 M8
Tillman Street E1 ...... 246 E3
Tilney Street W1J 243 K1
Timber Pond Road SE16 ...... 247 J6
Tinsley Street E1 ...... 247 G1
Tinworth Street SE11 ...... 244 D6
Tisdall Place SE17 ...... 245 L6
Tite Street SW3 ...... 243 H8
Tiverton Street SE1 ...... 245 J4
Token House Yard EC2R 241 L6
Tolmer's Square NW1 ...... 240 A3
Tomlin's Terrace E14 ...... 247 K2
Tonbridge Street WC1H 240 D2
Tooley Street SE1 ...... 245 L1
Tooley Street SE1 ...... 246 B6
Tor Gardens W8 ...... 242 A2
Torquay Street W2 ...... 238 A5
Torrens Street EC1V 241 G1
Torrington Place E1W 246 D5
Torrington Place WC1E 240 B4
Torrington Square WC1E 240 B4
Tothill Street SW1H 244 B3
Tottenham Court Road W1T 240 A4
Tottenham Court
   Road W1D 240 B6
Tottenham Street W1T 240 A5
Toulmin Street SE1 ...... 245 J3
Tower Bridge EC3N 246 B5
Tower Bridge
   Approach EC3N 246 B5
Tower Bridge Road SE1 ...... 246 A7
Tower Bridge Wharf E1W 246 C5
Tower Gateway EC3N 246 B4
Tower Hill EC3N 246 B4
Tower Hill EC3N 246 B4
Tower of London EC3N 246 B4
Tower Place EC3R 246 A4
Tower Street WC2H 240 C7
Townsend Street SE17 ...... 245 M5
Toynbee Street E1 ...... 246 B1
Trafalgar Gardens E1 ...... 247 H1
Trafalgar Square WC2N 240 C8
Trafalgar Street SE17 ...... 245 L7
Transept Street NW1 ...... 238 F5
Trebeck Street W1J 243 L1
Trebovir Road SW5 ...... 242 A6
Tregunter Road SW10 ...... 242 C7
Trenton Road SE16 ...... 246 E8
Tresham Crescent NW8 ...... 238 F3
Trevor Place SW7 ...... 243 G3
Trevor Square SW7 ...... 243 G3
Trevor Street SW7 ...... 243 G3

Trinidad Street E14 ...... 247 M4
Trinity Church Square SE1 ...... 245 K3
Trinity Square EC3N 246 B4
Trinity Street SE1 ...... 245 K3
Trump Street EC2V 241 K6
Tudor Street EC4Y 241 G7
Tufton Street SW1P 244 C4
Tunnel Road SE16 ...... 247 G6
Turks Row SW3 ...... 243 J6
Turner's Road E3 ...... 247 L2
Turner Street E1 ...... 246 E2
Turnmill Street EC1N 241 G4
Turpentine Lane SW1V 243 L7
Turquand Street SE17 ...... 245 K6
Tyers Gate SE1 ...... 245 M3
Tyers Street SE11 ...... 244 E7
Tyers Terrace SE11 ...... 244 E7
Tyron Street SW3 ...... 243 H6
Tysoe Street EC1R 241 G3

U

Udall Street SW1P 244 A5
Ufford Street SE1 ...... 245 G3
Ulster Place NW1 ...... 239 K4
Umberston Street E1 ...... 246 E2
Undershaft EC3A 246 A2
Underwood Road N1 ...... 241 K2
Underwood Street N1 ...... 241 K1
Union Street SE1 ...... 245 H2
University Street WC1E 240 A4
Upbrook Mews W2 ...... 238 D6
Upper Belgrave Street SW1X 243 K4
Upper Berkeley Street W1H 239 H6
Upper Brook Street W1K 239 J7
Upper Cheyne Row SW3 ...... 242 F8
Upper Grosvenor Street W1K 239 J8
Upper Ground SE1 ...... 244 F1
Upper Harley Street NW1 ...... 239 K3
Upper James Street W1F 240 A7
Upper John Street W1F 240 A7
Upper Marsh SE1 ...... 244 E3
Upper Montagu Street W1H 239 H5
Upper St Martin's WC2H 240 C7
Upper Tachbrook
   Street SW1V 244 A5
Upper Thames Street EC4V 241 J7
Upper Wimpole Street W1G 239 K4
Upper Woburn Place WC1H 240 B2
Urlwin Street SE5 ...... 245 J8
Uxbridge Street W8 ...... 242 A1

V

Valentine Place SE1 ...... 245 G3
Vandon Passage SW1H 244 A3
Vandon Street SW1H 244 A4
Vandy Street EC2A 241 M4
Varden Street E1 ...... 246 E2
Varndell Street NW1 ...... 239 M2
Vauban Street SE16 ...... 246 C8
Vaughan Street SE16 ...... 247 L7
Vaughan Way E1W 246 D5
Vauxhall SW8 ...... 244 D7
Vauxhall Bridge SW1V 244 C7
Vauxhall Bridgefoot SE1 ...... 244 D7
Vauxhall Bridge Road SW1V 243 M5
Vauxhall Cross SE1 ...... 244 D7
Vauxhall Grove SW8 ...... 244 D8
Vauxhall Street SE11 ...... 244 E6
Vauxhall Walk SE11 ...... 244 E6
Venables Street W2 ...... 238 E4
Vere Street W1G 239 K6
Vernon Place WC1A 240 D5
Vernon Rise WC1X 240 E2
Verulam Street WC1X 240 F4
Vestry Street N1 ...... 241 L2
Vicarage Gate W8 ...... 242 B2
Victoria SW1V 243 L5
Victoria & Albert
   Museum SW7 ...... 242 F4
Victoria Embankment SW1A 244 D2
Victoria Embankment WC2R 240 F7
Victoria Gate W2 ...... 238 F7
Victoria Road W8 ...... 242 C4
Victoria Square SW1W 243 L4
Victoria Street SW1E 244 A4
Victoria Yard SE17 ...... 245 K5
Victory Place SE17 ...... 245 L5
Victory Way SE16 ...... 247 K7
Vigo Street W1S 239 M8
Villa Street SE17 ...... 245 L7
Villiers Street WC2N 240 D8
Vincent Close SE16 ...... 247 K7
Vincent Square SW1P 244 B5
Vincent Street SW1P 244 B5
Vincent Terrace N1 ...... 241 H1
Vince Street EC1V 241 L2
Vine Court E1 ...... 246 D1
Vinegar Street E1W 246 E5
Vine Hill EC1R 240 F4
Vine Lane SE1 ...... 246 A6
Vine Street EC3N 246 B3
Violet Hill NW8 ...... 238 C1
Virgil Street SE1 ...... 244 F4
Virginia Street E1 ...... 246 D4
Viscount Street EC2Y 241 J4

W

Wadding Street SE17 ...... 245 K6
Wakefield Street WC1H 240 D3
Wakeling Street E14 ...... 247 J3
Wakley Street EC1V 241 H2
Walbrook EC4N 241 L7
Walburgh Street E1 ...... 246 E3
Walcorde Avenue SE17 ...... 245 K6
Walcot Square SE11 ...... 245 G5
Walden Street E1 ...... 246 E2
Wallwood Street E14 ...... 247 M1
Walnut Tree Walk SE11 ...... 244 F5
Walpole Street SW3 ...... 243 H6
Walter Terrace E1 ...... 247 H2
Walton Street SW3 ...... 243 G4
Walworth Place SE17 ...... 245 K7
Walworth Road SE17 ...... 245 J5
Wandsworth Road SW8 ...... 244 C8
Wansey Street SE17 ...... 245 J6
Wapping E1W 246 F5
Wapping High Street E1W 246 E6
Wapping Lane E1W 246 F4
Wapping Wall E1W 247 G5
Warden's Grove SE1 ...... 245 J2

Wardour Street W1F 240 B6
Warner Street EC1R 240 F4
Warren Street W1T 239 M4
Warren Street NW1 ...... 239 M3
Warrington Crescent W9 ...... 238 C3
Warrington Gardens W9 ...... 238 C4
Warwick Avenue W9 ...... 238 B3
Warwick Avenue W9 ...... 238 C4
Warwick Crescent W2 ...... 238 C5
Warwick House Street SW1Y 244 B1
Warwick Lane EC4M 241 H6
Warwick Place W9 ...... 238 C4
Warwick Row SW1E 243 M4
Warwick Square SW1V 243 M6
Warwick Street W1B 240 A7
Warwick Way SW1V 243 L6
Waterhouse Square EC1N 241 G5
Waterloo Bridge SE1 ...... 240 F2
Waterloo Bridge WC2R 240 E8
Waterloo East SE1 ...... 245 G2
Waterloo Place SW1Y 244 B1
Waterloo Road SE1 ...... 244 F1
Waterloo Road SE1 ...... 245 G2
Waterman Way E1W 246 E5
Waterside Close SE16 ...... 246 D7
Watling Street EC4N 241 K7
Watney Street E1 ...... 246 F3
Watts Street E1 ...... 246 E5
Waveney Close E1W 246 D5
Waverton Street W1J 239 K8
Weavers Lane SE1 ...... 246 A6
Webber Row SE1 ...... 245 G3
Webber Street SE1 ...... 245 H3
Webb Street SE1 ...... 246 A8
Webster Road SE16 ...... 246 D8
Weigh House Street W1K 239 K7
Welbeck Street W1G 239 K5
Welbeck Way W1G 239 K6
Welland Mews E1W 246 E5
Wellclose Square E1 ...... 246 D4
Wellesley Street E1 ...... 247 H2
Wellesley Terrace N1 ...... 241 K2
Wellington Arch W1J 243 K2
Wellington Square SW3 ...... 243 H6
Wellington Place NW8 ...... 238 E2
Wellington Road NW8 ...... 238 E1
Wellington Street WC2E 240 D7
Wells Mews W1T 240 A5
Wells Street W1T 240 A5
Wells Way SE5 ...... 245 M8
Wenlock Road N1 ...... 241 K1
Wenlock Street N1 ...... 241 K1
Wentworth Street E1 ...... 246 B2
Werrington Street NW1 ...... 240 A1
Wesley Street W1G 239 K5
West Arbour Street E1 ...... 247 G2
Westbourne Crescent W2 ...... 238 D7
Westbourne Gardens W2 ...... 238 B6
Westbourne Gate W2 ...... 238 E7
Westbourne Grove W2 ...... 238 A6
Westbourne Grove
   Terrace W2 ...... 238 B6
Westbourne Park Road W2 ...... 238 A5
Westbourne Park Villas W2 ...... 238 A5
Westbourne Street W2 ...... 238 E7
Westbourne Terrace W2 ...... 238 D6
Westbourne Terrace
   Mews W2 ...... 238 C6
Westbourne Terrace
   Road W2 ...... 238 C5
West Brompton SW5 ...... 242 A7
West Carriage Drive W2 ...... 242 E2
Westcott Road SE17 ...... 245 H8
West Cromwell Road SW5 ...... 242 A5
Western Place SE16 ...... 247 G6
Westferry E14 ...... 247 M4
Westferry Circus E14 ...... 247 M5
Westferry Road E14 ...... 247 M5
West Gardens E1W 246 F4
Westgate Terrace SW10 ...... 242 B7
West Halkin Street SW1X 243 J4
West India Avenue E14 ...... 247 M5
West India Dock Road E14 ...... 247 M3
Westland Place N1 ...... 241 K2
West Lane SE16 ...... 246 E7
Westminster SW1A 244 D3
Westminster Abbey SW1P 244 C3
Westminster Bridge SW1A 244 D3
Westminster Bridge
   Road SE1 ...... 244 F3
Westmoreland Place SW1V 243 L7
Westmoreland Road SE17 ...... 245 K8
Westmoreland Street W1G 239 K5
Westmoreland Terrace SW1V 243 L7
Weston Rise WC1X 240 E1
Weston Street SE1 ...... 245 M2
Weston Street SE1 ...... 245 M3
Westport Street E1 ...... 247 H2
West Poultry Avenue EC1A 241 H5
West Road SW3 ...... 243 H7
West Smithfield EC1A 241 H5
West Square SE11 ...... 245 H4
West Street WC2H 240 C7
West Tenter Street E1 ...... 246 C3
West Warwick Place SW1V 243 M6
Westway W2 ...... 238 B5
Wetherby Gardens SW5 ...... 242 C6
Weyhill Road E1 ...... 246 D2
Weymouth Mews W1G 239 L5
Weymouth Street W1G 239 K5
Wharfdale Road N1 ...... 240 D1
Wharfedale Street SW10 ...... 242 B7
Wharf Road N1 ...... 241 J1
Wharton Street WC1X 240 F2
Wheatley Street W1G 239 K5
Whetstone Park WC2A 240 E5
Whidborne Street WC1H 240 D2
Whiskin Street EC1R 241 G2
Whitcomb Street WC2H 240 B8
Whitechapel E1 ...... 246 E1
Whitechapel Estate E1 ...... 246 C4
Whitechapel High Street E1 ...... 246 C2
Whitechapel Road E1 ...... 246 D1
Whitecross Street EC1Y 241 K3
Whitefriars Street EC4Y 241 G6
Whitehall SW1A 244 C2
Whitehall Court SW1A 244 D2
Whitehall Place SW1A 244 D1
White Hart Street SE11 ...... 245 G6
White Hart Yard SE1 ...... 245 L2
Whitehaven Street NW8 ...... 238 F4
Whitehead's Grove SW3 ...... 243 G6
White Horse Lane E1 ...... 247 H1
Whitehorse Road E1 ...... 247 J1
Whitehorse Road E1 ...... 247 J3

White Horse Street W1J 243 L1
White Kennett Street E1 ...... 246 B2
White Lion Hill EC4V 241 H7
White Lion Street N1 ...... 240 F1
White's Grounds SE1 ...... 246 A7
White's Row E1 ...... 246 B1
White Tower Way E1 ...... 247 J1
Whitfield Place W1T 240 A4
Whitfield Street W1T 240 A4
Whitgift Street SE11 ...... 244 E5
Whittaker Street SW1W 243 J6
Whittlesey Street SE1 ...... 245 G2
Wicker Street E1 ...... 246 E3
Wickham Close E1 ...... 247 G1
Wickham Street SE11 ...... 244 E7
Wicklow Street WC1X 240 E2
Widegate Street E1 ...... 246 A1
Widley Road W9 ...... 238 A3
Wigmore Place W1G 239 K5
Wigmore Street W1U 239 K6
Wigton Place SE11 ...... 245 G7
Wilbraham Place SW1X 243 J5
Wild Court WC2B 240 E6
Wild's Rents SE1 ...... 245 M4
Wild Street WC2B 240 D6
Wilfred Street SW1E 243 M4
Wilkes Street E1 ...... 246 B1
William IV Street WC2N 240 C8
William Mews SW1X 243 H3
William Road NW1 ...... 239 M3
Willow Place SW1P 244 A5
Willow Street EC2A 241 M3
Wilmington Square WC1X 240 F3
Wilmington Street WC1X 240 F2
Wilson Grove SE16 ...... 246 E7
Wilson Street EC2A 241 L4
Wilton Crescent SW1X 243 J3
Wilton Mews SW1X 243 K4
Wilton Place SW1X 243 J3
Wilton Road SW1V 243 L4
Wilton Row SW1X 243 J3
Wilton Street SW1X 243 K4
Wimpole Mews W1G 239 K5
Wimpole Street W1G 239 K5
Winchester Street SW1V 243 L6
Winchester Walk SE1 ...... 245 K1
Wincott Street SE11 ...... 245 G5
Windmill Road SE11 ...... 244 F7
Windmill Street W1T 240 B5
Windrose Close SE16 ...... 247 H6
Windsor Terrace N1 ...... 241 K1
Wine Close E1W 246 F5
Winnett Street W1D 240 B7
Winsland Mews W2 ...... 238 E6
Winsland Street W2 ...... 238 E6
Winsley Street W1W 240 A6
Winthrop Street E1 ...... 246 E1
Woburn Place WC1H 240 C3
Woburn Square WC1H 240 C4
Wodeham Gardens E1 ...... 246 E1
Wolfe Crescent SE16 ...... 247 H7
Wolseley Street SE1 ...... 246 C6
Woodbridge Street EC1R 241 G3
Woodchester Square W9 ...... 238 A4
Woodfall Street SW3 ...... 243 H7
Woodland Crescent SE16 ...... 247 H7
Woodseer Street E1 ...... 246 C1
Woods Mews W1K 239 J7
Woods Place SE1 ...... 246 A8
Woodstock Street W1C 239 K6
Wood Street EC2V 241 K6
Woolaston Close SE1 ...... 245 J5
Wooler Street SE17 ...... 245 L7
Wootton Street SE1 ...... 245 G2
Worgan Street SE11 ...... 244 E6
Worgan Street SE16 ...... 247 H8
Wormwood Street EC2M 241 M5
Worship Street EC2A 241 M4
Wren Street WC1X 240 E3
Wright's Lane W8 ...... 242 A3
Wyatt Close SE16 ...... 247 L7
Wyclif Street EC1V 241 H2
Wymering Road W9 ...... 238 A2
Wynard Terrace SE11 ...... 244 F7
Wyndham Place W1H 239 H5
Wyndham Street W1H 239 G4
Wynnstay Gardens W8 ...... 242 A4
Wynyat Street EC1V 241 H2
Wythburn Place W1H 239 H6

Y

Yalding Road SE16 ...... 246 C8
Yardley Street WC1X 240 F2
Yeomans Row SW3 ...... 243 G4
York Boulevard WC2N 240 D8
York Bridge NW1 ...... 239 J3
York Gate NW1 ...... 239 J4
York Road SE1 ...... 244 E2
Yorkshire Road E14 ...... 247 K3
York Square E14 ...... 247 J2
York Street W1H 239 G5
York Street W1U 239 H5
York Terrace East NW1 ...... 239 J4
York Terrace West NW1 ...... 239 J4
York Way N1 ...... 240 D1

Z

Zoar Street SE1 ...... 245 J1
ZSL London Zoo NW1 ...... 239 J1

This index lists places appearing in the main-map section of the atlas in alphabetical order. The reference following each name gives the atlas page number and grid reference of the square in which the place appears. The map shows counties, unitary authorities and administrative areas, together with a list of the abbreviated name forms used in the index. The top 100 places of tourist interest are indexed in **red**, World Heritage sites in **green**, motorway service areas in **blue**, airports in blue *italic* and National Parks in green *italic*

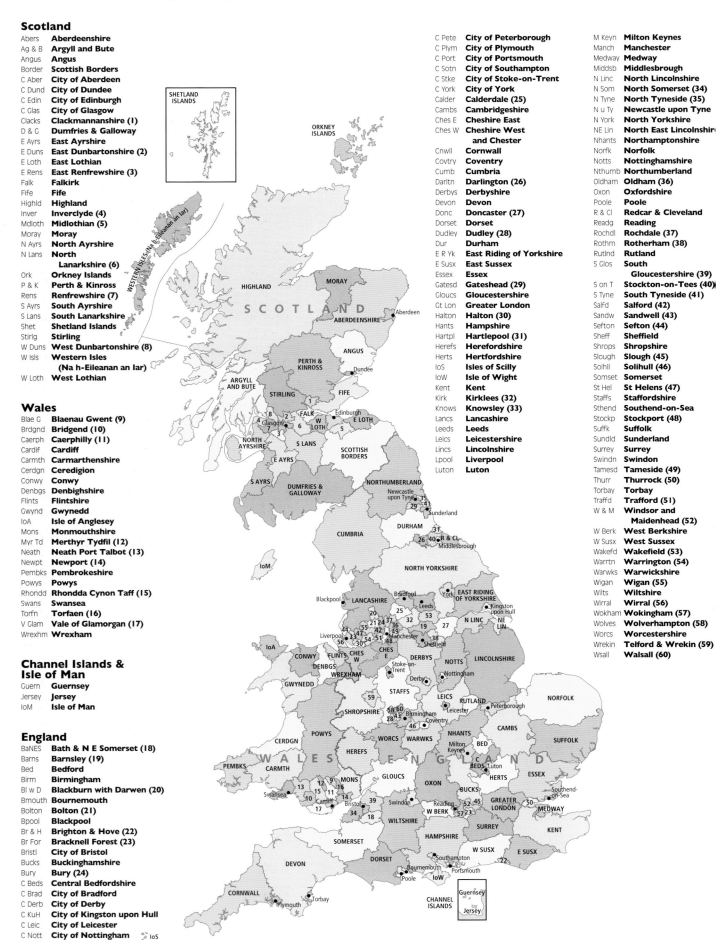

Scotland

Abers	**Aberdeenshire**
Ag & B	**Argyll and Bute**
Angus	**Angus**
Border	**Scottish Borders**
C Aber	**City of Aberdeen**
C Dund	**City of Dundee**
C Edin	**City of Edinburgh**
Clacks	**Clackmannanshire (1)**
D & G	**Dumfries & Galloway**
E Ayrs	**East Ayrshire**
E Duns	**East Dunbartonshire (2)**
E Loth	**East Lothian**
E Rens	**East Renfrewshire (3)**
Falk	**Falkirk**
Fife	**Fife**
Highld	**Highland**
Inver	**Inverclyde (4)**
Mdloth	**Midlothian (5)**
Moray	**Moray**
N Ayrs	**North Ayrshire**
N Lans	**North Lanarkshire (6)**
Ork	**Orkney Islands**
P & K	**Perth & Kinross**
Rens	**Renfrewshire (7)**
S Ayrs	**South Ayrshire**
S Lans	**South Lanarkshire**
Shet	**Shetland Islands**
Stirlg	**Stirling**
W Duns	**West Dunbartonshire (8)**
W Isls	**Western Isles (Na h-Eileanan an Iar)**
W Loth	**West Lothian**

Wales

Blae G	**Blaenau Gwent (9)**
Brdgnd	**Bridgend (10)**
Caerph	**Caerphilly (11)**
Cardif	**Cardiff**
Carmth	**Carmarthenshire**
Cerdgn	**Ceredigion**
Conwy	**Conwy**
Denbgs	**Denbighshire**
Flints	**Flintshire**
Gwynd	**Gwynedd**
IoA	**Isle of Anglesey**
Mons	**Monmouthshire**
Myr Td	**Merthyr Tydfil (12)**
Neath	**Neath Port Talbot (13)**
Newpt	**Newport (14)**
Pembks	**Pembrokeshire**
Powys	**Powys**
Rhondd	**Rhondda Cynon Taff (15)**
Swans	**Swansea**
Torfn	**Torfaen (16)**
V Glam	**Vale of Glamorgan (17)**
Wrexhm	**Wrexham**

Channel Islands & Isle of Man

Guern	**Guernsey**
Jersey	**Jersey**
IoM	**Isle of Man**

England

BaNES	**Bath & N E Somerset (18)**
Barns	**Barnsley (19)**
Bed	**Bedford**
Birm	**Birmingham**
Bl w D	**Blackburn with Darwen (20)**
Bmouth	**Bournemouth**
Bolton	**Bolton (21)**
Bpool	**Blackpool**
Br & H	**Brighton & Hove (22)**
Br For	**Bracknell Forest (23)**
Bristl	**City of Bristol**
Bucks	**Buckinghamshire**
Bury	**Bury (24)**
C Beds	**Central Bedfordshire**
C Brad	**City of Bradford**
C Derb	**City of Derby**
C KuH	**City of Kingston upon Hull**
C Leic	**City of Leicester**
C Nott	**City of Nottingham**
C Pete	**City of Peterborough**
C Plym	**City of Plymouth**
C Port	**City of Portsmouth**
C Sotn	**City of Southampton**
C Stke	**City of Stoke-on-Trent**
C York	**City of York**
Calder	**Calderdale (25)**
Cambs	**Cambridgeshire**
Ches E	**Cheshire East**
Ches W	**Cheshire West and Chester**
Cnwll	**Cornwall**
Covtry	**Coventry**
Cumb	**Cumbria**
Darltn	**Darlington (26)**
Derbys	**Derbyshire**
Devon	**Devon**
Donc	**Doncaster (27)**
Dorset	**Dorset**
Dudley	**Dudley (28)**
Dur	**Durham**
E R Yk	**East Riding of Yorkshire**
E Susx	**East Sussex**
Essex	**Essex**
Gatesd	**Gateshead (29)**
Gloucs	**Gloucestershire**
Gt Lon	**Greater London**
Halton	**Halton (30)**
Hants	**Hampshire**
Hartpl	**Hartlepool (31)**
Herefs	**Herefordshire**
Herts	**Hertfordshire**
IoS	**Isles of Scilly**
IoW	**Isle of Wight**
Kent	**Kent**
Kirk	**Kirklees (32)**
Knows	**Knowsley (33)**
Lancs	**Lancashire**
Leeds	**Leeds**
Leics	**Leicestershire**
Lincs	**Lincolnshire**
Lpool	**Liverpool**
Luton	**Luton**
M Keyn	**Milton Keynes**
Manch	**Manchester**
Medway	**Medway**
Middsb	**Middlesbrough**
N Linc	**North Lincolnshire**
N Som	**North Somerset (34)**
N Tyne	**North Tyneside (35)**
N u Ty	**Newcastle upon Tyne**
N York	**North Yorkshire**
NE Lin	**North East Lincolnshire**
Nhants	**Northamptonshire**
Norfk	**Norfolk**
Notts	**Nottinghamshire**
Nthumb	**Northumberland**
Oldham	**Oldham (36)**
Oxon	**Oxfordshire**
Poole	**Poole**
R & Cl	**Redcar & Cleveland**
Readg	**Reading**
Rochdl	**Rochdale (37)**
Rothm	**Rotherham (38)**
Rutlnd	**Rutland**
S Glos	**South Gloucestershire (39)**
S on T	**Stockton-on-Tees (40)**
S Tyne	**South Tyneside (41)**
Salfd	**Salford (42)**
Sandw	**Sandwell (43)**
Sefton	**Sefton (44)**
Sheff	**Sheffield**
Shrops	**Shropshire**
Slough	**Slough (45)**
Solhll	**Solihull (46)**
Somset	**Somerset**
St Hel	**St Helens (47)**
Staffs	**Staffordshire**
Sthend	**Southend-on-Sea**
Stockp	**Stockport (48)**
Suffk	**Suffolk**
Sundld	**Sunderland**
Surrey	**Surrey**
Swindn	**Swindon**
Tamesd	**Tameside (49)**
Thurr	**Thurrock (50)**
Torbay	**Torbay**
Traffd	**Trafford (51)**
W & M	**Windsor and Maidenhead (52)**
W Berk	**West Berkshire**
W Susx	**West Sussex**
Wakefd	**Wakefield (53)**
Warrtn	**Warrington (54)**
Warwks	**Warwickshire**
Wigan	**Wigan (55)**
Wirral	**Wirral (56)**
Wokham	**Wokingham (57)**
Wolves	**Wolverhampton (58)**
Worcs	**Worcestershire**
Wrekin	**Telford & Wrekin (59)**
Wsall	**Walsall (60)**

Abbas Combe – Anslow Gate 255

A

ɪas Combe Somset 20 D10
ɪerley Worcs 57 P11
ɪerley Common
Vorcs 57 N11
ɪerton Essex 52 H8
ɪerton Worcs 47 J4
ɪerwick Nthumb 119 M8
ɪess Roding Essex 51 N8
ɪey Devon 10 C2
ɪey-Cwm-Hir Powys 55 P10
ɪeydale Sheff 84 D4
ɪey Dore Herefs 45 M8
ɪey Green Staffs 70 H3
ɪey Hill Somset 19 J11
ɪey St Bathans
Border 129 K7
ɪeystead Lancs 95 M10
ɪey Town Cumb 110 C10
ɪey Valley
Crematorium Derbys 84 F10
ɪey Village Lancs 89 J6
ɪey Wood Gt Lon 37 L5
ɪotrule Border 118 B8
ɪots Bickington
Devon 16 F9
ɪots Bromley Staffs 71 K10
ɪotsbury Dorset 11 M7
ɪot's Chair Derbys 83 M6
ɪots Deuglie P & K 134 E5
ɪots Leigh N Som 31 P10
ɪotsham Devon 16 G6
ɪotskerswell Devon 7 M5
ɪots Langley Herts 50 C10
ɪotsleigh Devon 7 L9
ɪots Leigh N Som 31 P10
ɪotsley Cambs 62 B9
ɪots Morton Worcs 47 K3
ɪots Ripton Cambs 62 B5
ɪot's Salford Warwks 47 L4
ɪotstone Hants 22 G8
ɪotswood Hants 22 C10
ɪots Worthy Hants 22 E8
ɪotts Ann Hants 22 B6
ɪott Street Dorset 12 G4
ɪott Shrops 56 F9
ɪon Shrops 57 K7
ɪnhall Gloucs 46 C11
ɪraeron Cerdgn 43 J2
ɪraman Rhondd 30 D4
ɪrangell Gwynd 55 J2
ɪr-arad Carmth 42 F6
ɪrarder Highld 147 Q2
ɪrargie P & K 134 F4
ɪrarth Cerdgn 43 J2
ɪravon Neath 29 K7
ɪr-banc Cerdgn 42 G6
ɪrbargoed Caerph 30 G4
ɪrbeeg Blae G 30 H4
ɪrcanaid Myr Td 30 E4
ɪrcarn Caerph 30 H6
ɪrcastle Pembks 40 G4
ɪrcegir Powys 55 J4
ɪrchalder Lodge
Highld 147 J7
ɪrchirder Abers 158 F7
ɪr Clydach Powys 44 G10
ɪrcraf Powys 29 M2
ɪrcregan Neath 29 M5
ɪrcwmboi Rhondd 30 D5
ɪrcych Pembks 41 P2
ɪrcynon Rhondd 30 E6
ɪrdalgie P & K 134 D3
ɪrdare Rhondd 30 D4
ɪrdaron Gwynd 66 B9
ɪrdeen C Aber 151 N6
ɪrdeen Airport C Aber 151 M5
ɪrdeen
Crematorium C Aber 151 M6
ɪrdesach Gwynd 66 G4
ɪrdour Fife 134 F10
ɪrdulais Neath 29 L5
ɪrdyfi Gwynd 54 E5
ɪredw Powys 44 F5
ɪreiddy Pembks 40 E4
ɪrerch Gwynd 66 F7
ɪrfan Myr Td 30 E4
ɪrfeldy P & K 141 L8
ɪrffraw IoA 78 F11
ɪrffrwd Cerdgn 54 F9
ɪrford Leeds 91 L3
ɪrfoyle Stirlg 132 G7
ɪrgarw Brdgnd 29 P8
ɪrgarwed Neath 29 M4
ɪrgavenny Mons 31 J2
ɪrgele Conwy 80 C9
ɪr-giar Carmth 43 K6
ɪrgorlech Carmth 43 L8
ɪrgwesyn Powys 44 B4
ɪrgwili Carmth 42 H10
ɪrgwydol Powys 54 H4
ɪrgwynfi Neath 29 N5
ɪrgwyngregyn Gwynd 79 M10
ɪrgynolwyn Gwynd 54 F3
ɪrhafesp Powys 55 P6
ɪrhosan Powys 55 J5
ɪrkenfig Brdgnd 29 N8
ɪrlady E Loth 128 D4
ɪrlemno Angus 143 J6
ɪrllefenni Gwynd 54 H3
ɪrllynfi Powys 44 H7
ɪrlour, Charlestown
of Moray 157 P9
ɪr-Magwr Cerdgn 54 F10
ɪr-meurig Cerdgn 43 L3
ɪrmorddu Flints 69 K3
ɪrmule Powys 56 B6
ɪrnant Carmth 42 F10
ɪr-nant Rhondd 30 D4
ɪrnethy P & K 134 F4
ɪrnyte P & K 142 D11
ɪrporth Cerdgn 42 E4
ɪrsoch Gwynd 66 E9
ɪrsychan Torfn 31 J4
ɪrthin V Glam 30 D10
ɪrtillery Blae G 30 H4
ɪrtridwr Caerph 30 F7
ɪrtridwr Powys 68 D11
ɪrtysswg Caerph 30 F3
ɪruthven P & K 134 B4
ɪryscir Powys 44 D9
ɪrystwyth Cerdgn 54 D8
ɪrystwyth
Crematorium Cerdgn 54 E8
ɪngdon-on-Thames
Oxon 34 E5
ɪnger Common Surrey 36 D11
ɪnger Hammer Surrey 36 C11
ɪngton Nhants 60 G8
ɪngton S Lans 116 C6
Abington Pigotts Cambs 50 H2
Abington Services S Lans 116 C6
Abingworth W Susx 24 D7
Ab Kettleby Leics 73 J6
Ab Lench Worcs 47 K4
Ablington Gloucs 33 M3
Ablington Wilts 21 N5
Abney Derbys 83 Q8
Above Church Staffs 71 J4
Aboyne Abers 150 E8
Abram Wigan 82 D4
Abriachan Highld 155 Q10
Abridge Essex 51 L11
Abronhill N Lans 126 D2
Abson S Glos 32 D10
Abthorpe Nhants 48 H5
Aby Lincs 87 M5
Acaster Malbis C York 98 B11
Acaster Selby N York 91 P2
Accrington Lancs 89 M5
Accrington
Crematorium Lancs 89 M5
Acha Ag & B 136 F5
Achahoish Ag & B 123 N4
Achalader P & K 141 R8
Achaleven Ag & B 138 G11
Acha Mor W Isls 168 i5
Achanalt Highld 155 J5
Achandunie Highld 156 A3
Achany Highld 162 D6
Acharacle Highld 138 B4
Acharn Highld 138 C7
Acharn P & K 141 J9
Achavanich Highld 167 L8
Achduart Highld 160 G6
Achfary Highld 164 G9
A'Chill Highld 144 C6
Achiltibuie Highld 160 G5
Achina Highld 166 B4
Achinhoan Ag & B 120 E8
Achintee Highld 154 B9
Achintraid Highld 153 Q10
Achmelvich Highld 160 H2
Achmore Highld 153 R11
Achmore W Isls 168 i5
Achnacarnin Highld 164 B10
Achnacarry Highld 146 F10
Achnacloich Highld 145 J6
Achnaconeran Highld 147 L4
Achnacroish Ag & B 138 F9
Achnadrish House
Ag & B 137 M5
Achnafauld P & K 141 L10
Achnagarron Highld 156 B3
Achnaha Highld 137 M2
Achnahaird Highld 160 G4
Achnahannet Highld 148 H2
Achnairn Highld 162 D4
Achnalea Highld 138 F5
Achnamara Ag & B 130 F10
Achnasheen Highld 154 G6
Achnashellach Lodge
Highld 154 D8
Achnastank Moray 157 P11
Achosnich Highld 137 L2
Achranich Highld 138 C8
Achreamie Highld 166 H3
Achriabhach Highld 139 L4
Achriesgill Highld 164 G6
Achtoty Highld 165 Q4
Achurch Nhants 61 M4
Achvaich Highld 162 G8
Achvarasdal Highld 166 G4
Ackergill Highld 167 Q6
Acklam Middsb 104 E7
Acklam N York 98 F8
Ackleton Shrops 57 P5
Acklington Nthumb 119 P10
Ackton Wakefd 91 L6
Ackworth Moor Top
Wakefd 91 L7
Acle Norfk 77 N9
Acock's Green Birm 58 H8
Acol Kent 39 P8
Acomb C York 98 B10
Acomb Nthumb 112 D7
Acombe Somset 10 D2
Aconbury Herefs 45 Q8
Acre Lancs 89 M6
Acrefair Wrexhm 69 J6
Acton Ches E 70 A4
Acton Dorset 12 G9
Acton Gt Lon 36 F4
Acton Shrops 56 E8
Acton Staffs 70 E6
Acton Suffk 52 E2
Acton Worcs 58 B11
Acton Beauchamp
Herefs 46 C4
Acton Bridge Ches W 82 C9
Acton Burnell Shrops 57 J4
Acton Green Herefs 46 C4
Acton Park Wrexhm 69 K4
Acton Pigott Shrops 57 J4
Acton Round Shrops 57 L5
Acton Scott Shrops 56 H7
Acton Trussell Staffs 70 G11
Acton Turville S Glos 32 F8
Adbaston Staffs 70 D9
Adber Dorset 19 Q10
Adbolton Notts 72 F3
Adderbury Oxon 48 E7
Adderley Shrops 70 B7
Adderstone Nthumb 119 M4
Addiewell W Loth 126 H5
Addingham C Brad 96 G11
Addington Bucks 49 K9
Addington Gt Lon 37 J8
Addington Kent 37 Q9
Addiscombe Gt Lon 36 H7
Addlestone Surrey 36 C8
Addlestonemoor Surrey 36 C7
Addlethorpe Lincs 87 P7
Adeney Wrekin 70 B11
Adeyfield Herts 50 C9
Adfa Powys 55 P4
Adforton Herefs 56 G10
Adisham Kent 39 M11
Adlestrop Gloucs 47 P9
Adlingfleet E R Yk 92 D6
Adlington Ches E 83 K8
Adlington Lancs 89 J8
Admaston Staffs 71 J10
Admaston Wrekin 57 L2
Admington Warwks 47 P5
Adpar Cerdgn 42 F6
Adsborough Somset 19 J9
Adscombe Somset 18 G7
Adstock Bucks 49 K9
Adstone Nhants 48 G4
Adswood Stockp 83 J7
Adversane W Susx 24 C6
Advie Highld 157 L11
Adwalton Leeds 90 G5
Adwell Oxon 35 J5
Adwick le Street Donc 91 N9
Adwick upon Dearne
Donc 91 M10
Ae D & G 109 L3
Ae Bridgend D & G 109 M3
Afan Forest Park Neath 29 N5
Affetside Bury 89 M8
Affleck Abers 158 E9
Affpuddle Dorset 12 D6
Affric Lodge Highld 146 F3
Afon-wen Flints 80 G10
Afton Devon 7 L6
Afton IoW 13 P7
Agecroft Crematorium
Salfd 82 H4
Agglethorpe N York 96 G3
Aigburth Lpool 81 M7
Aike E R Yk 99 L11
Aiketgate Cumb 111 J11
Aikhead Cumb 110 D11
Aikton Cumb 110 E10
Ailby Lincs 87 M5
Ailey Herefs 45 L5
Ailsworth C Pete 74 B11
Ainderby Quernhow
N York 97 M4
Ainderby Steeple N York 97 M2
Aingers Green Essex 53 K7
Ainsdale Sefton 88 C8
Ainsdale-on-Sea Sefton 88 B8
Ainstable Cumb 111 K11
Ainsworth Bury 89 M8
Ainthorpe N York 105 K9
Aintree Sefton 81 M5
Ainville W Loth 127 L5
Aird Ag & B 130 F7
Aird D & G 106 E5
Aird W Isls 168 k4
Aird a Mhulaidh W Isls 168 g6
Aird Asaig W Isls 168 g7
Aird Dhubh Highld 153 N9
Airdeny Ag & B 131 K2
Aird of Kinloch Ag & B 137 N10
Aird of Sleat Highld 145 J7
Airdrie N Lans 126 D4
Airdriehill N Lans 126 D4
Airds of Kells D & G 108 E6
Aird Uig W Isls 168 f4
Airidh a bhruaich W Isls 168 h6
Airieland D & G 108 G9
Airlie Angus 142 E7
Airmyn E R Yk 92 B6
Airntully P & K 141 Q10
Airor Highld 145 M6
Airth Falk 133 Q10
Airton N York 96 D9
Aisby Lincs 73 Q3
Aisby Lincs 85 Q2
Aisgill Cumb 102 E11
Aish Devon 6 H6
Aish Devon 7 L7
Aisholt Somset 18 G7
Aiskew N York 97 L3
Aislaby N York 98 F3
Aislaby N York 105 N9
Aislaby S on T 104 D8
Aisthorpe Lincs 86 B4
Aith Shet 169 q8
Akeld Nthumb 119 J5
Akeley Bucks 49 K7
Akenham Suffk 53 K2
Albaston Cnwll 5 Q7
Alberbury Shrops 56 F2
Albourne W Susx 24 G7
Albourne Green W Susx 24 G7
Albrighton Shrops 57 Q4
Albrighton Shrops 69 N11
Alburgh Norfk 65 K4
Albury Herts 51 K6
Albury Oxon 35 J3
Albury Surrey 36 B11
Albury End Herts 51 K6
Albury Heath Surrey 36 C11
Alby Hill Norfk 76 H5
Alcaig Highld 155 Q6
Alcaston Shrops 56 H7
Alcester Warwks 47 L3
Alcester Lane End Birm 58 G8
Alciston E Susx 25 M9
Alcombe Somset 18 C5
Alcombe Wilts 32 F11
Alconbury Cambs 61 Q5
Alconbury Weston
Cambs 61 Q5
Aldborough N York 97 P7
Aldborough Norfk 76 H5
Aldbourne Wilts 33 Q9
Aldbrough E R Yk 93 M3
Aldbrough St John
N York 103 P8
Aldbury Herts 35 Q2
Aldcliffe Lancs 95 K8
Aldclune P & K 141 L5
Aldeburgh Suffk 65 P10
Aldeby Norfk 65 N3
Aldenham Herts 50 D11
Alderbury Wilts 21 N9
Aldercar Derbys 84 F11
Alderford Norfk 76 G8
Alderholt Dorset 13 K2
Alderley Gloucs 32 E6
Alderley Edge Ches E 82 H9
Aldermans Green Covtry 59 N8
Aldermaston W Berk 34 G11
Alderminster Warwks 47 P5
Alder Moor Staffs 71 N9
Aldersey Green Ches W 69 N3
Aldershot Hants 23 N4
Alderton Gloucs 47 K8
Alderton Nhants 49 K5
Alderton Shrops 69 N10
Alderton Suffk 53 P3
Alderton Wilts 32 F8
Alderwasley Derbys 71 Q4
Aldfield N York 97 L7
Aldford Ches W 69 M3
Aldgate Rutlnd 73 P10
Aldham Essex 52 F6
Aldham Suffk 52 J2
Aldingbourne W Susx 15 P5
Aldingham Cumb 94 F6
Aldington Kent 27 J4
Aldington Worcs 47 L6
Aldington Corner Kent 27 J4
Aldivalloch Moray 150 B2
Aldochlay Ag & B 132 D9
Aldon Shrops 56 G9
Aldoth Cumb 109 P11
Aldreth Cambs 62 F6
Aldridge Wsall 58 G4
Aldringham Suffk 65 N9
Aldro N York 98 G8
Aldsworth Gloucs 33 N3
Aldsworth W Susx 15 L5
Aldunie Moray 150 B2
Aldwark Derbys 84 B9
Aldwark N York 97 Q8
Aldwick W Susx 15 P7
Aldwincle Nhants 61 M4
Aldworth W Berk 34 G9
Alexandria W Duns 125 K2
Aley Somset 18 G7
Alfardisworthy Devon 16 D9
Alfington Devon 10 C5
Alfold Surrey 24 B4
Alfold Bars W Susx 24 B4
Alfold Crossways Surrey 24 B3
Alford Abers 150 F4
Alford Lincs 87 N5
Alford Somset 20 B8
Alford Crematorium
Lincs 87 M5
Alfreton Derbys 84 F9
Alfrick Worcs 46 D4
Alfrick Pound Worcs 46 D4
Alfriston E Susx 25 M10
Algarkirk Lincs 74 E3
Alhampton Somset 20 B8
Alkborough N Linc 92 E6
Alkerton Gloucs 32 E3
Alkerton Oxon 48 C6
Alkham Kent 27 N3
Alkington Shrops 69 P7
Alkmonton Derbys 71 M7
Allaleigh Devon 7 L8
Allanaquoich Abers 149 L9
Allanbank N Lans 126 E6
Allanton Border 129 M9
Allanton N Lans 126 E6
Allanton S Lans 126 C7
Allaston Gloucs 32 B4
Allbrook Hants 22 E10
All Cannings Wilts 21 L2
Allendale Nthumb 112 B9
Allen End Warwks 59 J5
Allenheads Nthumb 112 C11
Allensford Dur 112 G10
Allen's Green Herts 51 L7
Allensmore Herefs 45 P7
Allenton C Derb 72 B4
Aller Devon 17 P6
Aller Somset 19 M9
Allerby Cumb 100 E3
Allercombe Devon 9 P6
Allerford Somset 18 B5
Allerston N York 98 H4
Allerthorpe E R Yk 98 F11
Allerton C Brad 90 E4
Allerton Highld 156 D4
Allerton Lpool 81 M7
Allerton Bywater Leeds 91 L5
Allerton Mauleverer
N York 97 P9
Allesley Covtry 59 M8
Allestree C Derb 72 A3
Allet Common Cnwll 3 K4
Allexton Leics 73 L10
Allgreave Ches E 83 L11
Allhallows Medway 38 D6
Allhallows-on-Sea
Medway 38 D6
Alligin Shuas Highld 153 Q6
Allimore Green Staffs 70 F11
Allington Dorset 11 K6
Allington Kent 38 C10
Allington Lincs 73 M2
Allington Wilts 21 L2
Allington Wilts 21 P7
Allington Wilts 32 G9
Allithwaite Cumb 94 H5
Alloa Clacks 133 P9
Allonby Cumb 100 E2
Allostock Ches W 82 F10
Alloway S Ayrs 114 F4
Allowenshay Somset 10 H2
All Saints South
Elmham Suffk 65 L5
Allscott Shrops 57 N5
Allscott Wrekin 57 L2
All Stretton Shrops 56 H5
Alltami Flints 81 K11
Alltchaorunn Highld 139 M7
Alltmawr Powys 44 F5
Alltwalis Carmth 42 H8
Alltwen Neath 29 K5
Alltyblaca Cerdgn 43 K5
Allweston Dorset 11 P2
Allwood Green Suffk 64 E7
Almeley Herefs 45 L4
Almeley Wooton Herefs 45 L4
Almer Dorset 12 F5
Almholme Donc 91 P9
Almington Staffs 70 C8
Almodington W Susx 15 M7
Almondbank P & K 134 D2
Almondbury Kirk 90 F8
Almondsbury S Glos 32 B8
Alne N York 97 Q7
Alness Highld 156 B4
Alnham Nthumb 119 J8
Alnmouth Nthumb 119 P8
Alnwick Nthumb 119 N8
Alperton Gt Lon 36 E4
Alphamstone Essex 52 E4
Alpheton Suffk 64 B11
Alphington Devon 9 M6
Alpington Norfk 77 K11
Alport Derbys 84 B8
Alpraham Ches E 69 Q3
Alresford Essex 53 J7
Alrewas Staffs 59 J2
Alsager Ches E 70 D3
Alsagers Bank Staffs 70 D5
Alsop en le Dale Derbys 71 M4
Alston Cumb 111 P11
Alston Devon 10 G4
Alstone Gloucs 47 J8
Alstone Somset 19 K5
Alstonefield Staffs 71 L3
Alston Sutton Somset 19 M4
Alswear Devon 17 N7
Alt Oldham 83 K4
Altandhu Highld 160 F4
Altarnun Cnwll 5 L5
Altass Highld 162 C6
Altcreich Ag & B 138 B10
Altgaltraig Ag & B 124 C3
Altham Lancs 89 M4
Althorne Essex 38 F2
Althorpe N Linc 92 D9
Altnabreac Station
Highld 166 H7
Altnaharra Highld 165 N9
Altofts Wakefd 91 K6
Alton Derbys 84 E8
Alton Hants 23 K7
Alton Staffs 71 K6
Alton Wilts 21 N5
Alton Barnes Wilts 21 M2
Alton Pancras Dorset 11 Q4
Alton Priors Wilts 21 M2
Alton Towers Staffs 71 K6
Altrincham Traffd 82 G7
Altrincham
Crematorium Traffd 82 F7
Altskeith Hotel Stirlg 132 F7
Alva Clacks 133 P8
Alvanley Ches W 81 P10
Alvaston C Derb 72 B4
Alvechurch Worcs 58 F10
Alvecote Warwks 59 K4
Alvediston Wilts 21 J10
Alveley Shrops 57 P8
Alverdiscott Devon 17 J6
Alverstoke Hants 14 H7
Alverstone IoW 14 G9
Alverthorpe Wakefd 91 J6
Alverton Notts 73 K2
Alves Moray 157 L5
Alvescot Oxon 33 Q4
Alveston S Glos 32 B7
Alveston Warwks 47 P3
Alvingham Lincs 87 L2
Alvington Gloucs 32 B4
Alwalton C Pete 74 B11
Alwinton Nthumb 118 H9
Alwoodley Leeds 90 H2
Alwoodley Gates Leeds 91 J2
Alyth P & K 142 C8
Ambergate Derbys 84 D10
Amber Hill Lincs 86 H11
Amberley Gloucs 32 G4
Amberley W Susx 24 B8
Amber Row Derbys 84 E9
Amberstone E Susx 25 N8
Amble Nthumb 119 Q10
Amblecote Dudley 58 C7
Ambler Thorn C Brad 90 D5
Ambleside Cumb 101 L10
Ambleston Pembks 41 K5
Ambrosden Oxon 48 H11
Amcotts N Linc 92 E8
America Cambs 62 F5
Amersham Bucks 35 Q5
Amersham Common
Bucks 35 Q5
Amersham Old Town
Bucks 35 Q5
Amersham on the Hill
Bucks 35 Q5
Amerton Staffs 70 H9
Amesbury Wilts 21 N6
Amhuinnsuidhe W Isls 168 f7
Amington Staffs 59 K4
Amisfield D & G 109 M4
Amlwch IoA 78 G6
Ammanford Carmth 28 H2
Amotherby N York 98 E6
Ampfield Hants 22 D10
Ampleforth N York 98 B5
Ampney Crucis Gloucs 33 L4
Ampney St Mary Gloucs 33 L4
Ampney St Peter Gloucs 33 L4
Amport Hants 22 B6
Ampthill C Beds 50 B3
Ampton Suffk 64 B7
Amroth Pembks 41 N9
Amulree P & K 141 L10
Amwell Herts 50 E8
Anaheilt Highld 138 E5
Ancaster Lincs 73 P2
Anchor Shrops 56 B7
Ancroft Nthumb 129 P11
Ancrum Border 118 B6
Ancton W Susx 15 Q6
Anderby Lincs 87 P5
Andersea Somset 19 K8
Andersfield Somset 18 H8
Anderson Dorset 12 E5
Anderton Ches W 82 D9
Anderton Cnwll 6 C8
Andover Hants 22 C5
Andoversford Gloucs 47 K11
Andreas IoM 80 f2
Anelog Gwynd 66 B9
Anerley Gt Lon 36 H7
Anfield Lpool 81 M6
Anfield Crematorium
Lpool 81 M6
Angarrack Cnwll 2 F6
Angarrick Cnwll 3 K6
Angelbank Shrops 57 K9
Angersleigh Somset 18 G11
Angerton Cumb 110 D9
Angle Pembks 40 G10
Anglesey IoA 78 G8
Anglesey Abbey Cambs 62 H8
Angmering W Susx 24 C10
Angram N York 97 R11
Angram N York 102 G11
Angrouse Cnwll 2 H10
Anick Nthumb 112 D7
Ankerville Highld 156 E3
Ankle Hill Leics 73 K7
Anlaby E R Yk 92 H5
Anmer Norfk 75 P5
Anmore Hants 15 J4
Annan D & G 110 C7
Annandale Water
Services D & G 109 P2
Annaside Cumb 94 B3
Annat Highld 154 A7
Annathill N Lans 126 C3
Anna Valley Hants 22 C6
Annbank S Ayrs 114 H3
Anne Hathaway's
Cottage Warwks 47 N4
Annesley Notts 84 H10
Annesley Woodhouse
Notts 84 G10
Annfield Plain Dur 113 J10
Anniesland C Glas 125 N4
Annitsford N Tyne 113 L6
Annscroft Shrops 56 H3
Ansdell Lancs 88 C5
Ansford Somset 20 B8
Ansley Warwks 59 M6
Anslow Staffs 71 N9
Anslow Gate Staffs 71 M10

Anslow Lees Staffs....71 N10
Ansteadbrook Surrey....23 P8
Anstey Hants....23 K6
Anstey Herts....51 K4
Anstey Leics....72 F9
Anstruther Fife....135 P7
Ansty W Susx....24 G6
Ansty Warwks....59 P8
Ansty Wilts....21 J9
Ansty Cross Dorset....12 C4
Anthill Common Hants....14 H4
Anthonys Surrey....36 B8
Anthorn Cumb....110 C9
Antingham Norfk....77 K5
An t-Ob W Isls....168 f9
Antonine Wall....126 E2
Anton's Gowt Lincs....87 K11
Antony Cnwll....5 Q11
Antrobus Ches W....82 D9
Anvil Corner Devon....16 F11
Anvil Green Kent....27 K2
Anwick Lincs....86 F10
Anwoth D & G....108 C9
Aperfield Gt Lon....37 K9
Apes Dale Worcs....58 E10
Apethorpe Nhants....73 Q11
Apeton Staffs....70 F11
Apley Lincs....86 F5
Apperknowle Derbys....84 E5
Apperley Gloucs....46 G9
Apperley Bridge C Brad....90 F3
Apperley Dene Nthumb....112 C9
Appersett N York....96 C2
Appin Ag & B....138 G8
Appleby N Linc....92 G8
Appleby-in-
  Westmorland Cumb....102 C6
Appleby Magna Leics....59 M3
Appleby Parva Leics....59 M3
Appleby Street Herts....50 H10
Applecross Highld....153 N9
Appledore Devon....9 Q2
Appledore Devon....16 H5
Appledore Kent....26 G6
Appledore Heath Kent....26 G5
Appleford Oxon....34 F6
Applegarth Town D & G....109 P4
Applehaigh Wakefd....91 K8
Appleshaw Hants....22 B5
Applethwaite Cumb....101 J5
Appleton Halton....81 Q7
Appleton Oxon....34 D4
Appleton Warrtn....82 D8
Appleton-le-Moors
  N York....98 E3
Appleton-le-Street
  N York....98 E6
Appleton Roebuck
  N York....91 P2
Appleton Thorn Warrtn....82 D8
Appleton Wiske N York....104 C10
Appletreehall Border....117 Q7
Appletreewick N York....96 G8
Appley Somset....18 E10
Appley Bridge Lancs....88 G9
Apse Heath IoW....14 G10
Apsley End C Beds....50 D4
Apuldram W Susx....15 M6
Arabella Highld....156 E2
Arbirlot Angus....143 L9
Arboll Highld....163 K10
Arborfield Wokham....35 L11
Arborfield Cross
  Wokham....35 L11
Arbourthorne Sheff....84 E3
Arbroath Angus....143 L9
Arbuthnott Abers....143 P2
Arcadia Kent....26 E4
Archddu Carmth....28 D4
Archdeacon Newton
  Darltn....103 Q7
Archencarroch W Duns....132 E11
Archiestown Moray....157 N9
Archirondel Jersey....11 c1
Arclid Green Ches E....70 D2
Ardallie Abers....159 P10
Ardanaiseig Hotel Ag & B....131 M3
Ardaneaskan Highld....153 Q10
Ardarroch Highld....153 Q10
Ardbeg Ag & B....122 F10
Ardbeg Ag & B....124 D4
Ardbeg Ag & B....131 P11
Ardcharnich Highld....161 K9
Archiavaig Ag & B....137 K12
Ardchonnel Ag & B....131 K5
Ardchullarie More Stirlg....132 H5
Arddarroch Ag & B....131 Q9
Arddleen Powys....69 J11
Ardechive Highld....146 E9
Ardeer N Ayrs....124 H9
Ardelve Highld....145 Q2
Arden Ag & B....132 D11
Ardens Grafton Warwks....47 M4
Ardentallen Ag & B....130 G3
Ardentinny Ag & B....131 P10
Ardentraive Ag & B....120 C3
Ardeonaig Stirlg....140 G10
Ardersier Highld....156 D7
Ardessie Highld....160 H9
Ardfern Ag & B....130 G7
Ardfernal Ag & B....123 J3
Ardgartan Ag & B....132 B7
Ardgay Highld....162 D8
Ardgour Highld....139 J5
Ardgowan Inver....124 G2
Ardhallow Ag & B....124 F3
Ardhasig W Isls....168 g7
Ardheslaig Highld....153 P6
Ardindrean Highld....161 K9
Ardingly W Susx....24 H5
Ardington Oxon....34 D7
Ardington Wick Oxon....34 D7
Ardlamont Ag & B....124 B4
Ardleigh Essex....53 J6
Ardleigh Heath Essex....52 H5
Ardler P & K....142 D9
Ardley Oxon....48 F9
Ardley End Essex....51 M8
Ardlui Ag & B....132 C4
Ardlussa Ag & B....130 C10
Ardmair Highld....161 J7
Ardmaleish Ag & B....124 D4
Ardminish Ag & B....123 K10
Ardmolich Highld....138 C3
Ardmore Ag & B....125 J2
Ardmore Highld....162 G9
Ardnadam Ag & B....131 P11
Ardnagrask Highld....155 P9
Ardnamurchan Highld....137 P2
Ardnarff Highld....154 A10

Ardnastang Highld....138 E5
Ardpatrick Ag & B....123 N8
Ardrishaig Ag & B....130 H10
Ardross Highld....155 R3
Ardrossan N Ayrs....124 G9
Ardsley Barns....91 K9
Ardsley East Leeds....91 J5
Ardslignish Highld....137 P3
Ardtalla Ag & B....122 G9
Ardtoe Highld....138 A3
Arduaine Ag & B....130 F5
Ardullie Highld....155 Q5
Ardvasar Highld....145 K7
Ardvorlich P & K....133 J3
Ardvourlie W Isls....168 g6
Ardwell D & G....106 F8
Ardwick Manch....83 J5
Areley Kings Worcs....57 P10
Arevegaig Highld....138 B4
Arford Hants....23 M7
Argam E R Yk....92 C3
Argoed Caerph....30 G5
Argoed Shrops....69 K10
Argoed Mill Powys....44 D2
Argos Hill E Susx....25 N5
Argyll Forest Park
  Ag & B....131 Q7
Aribruach W Isls....168 h6
Aridhglas Ag & B....137 J11
Arileod Ag & B....136 F5
Arinagour Ag & B....136 G4
Ariogan Ag & B....130 H2
Arisaig Highld....145 L10
Arisaig House Highld....145 L11
Arkendale N York....97 N8
Arkesden Essex....51 L4
Arkleby Cumb....100 F3
Arkleton D & G....110 G2
Arkle Town N York....103 K10
Arkley Gt Lon....50 F11
Arksey Donc....91 P9
Arkwright Town Derbys....84 F6
Arle Gloucs....46 H10
Arlecdon Cumb....100 D7
Arlescote Warwks....48 C5
Arlesey C Beds....50 E3
Arleston Wrekin....57 M2
Arley Ches E....82 E8
Arley Warwks....59 L6
Arlingham Gloucs....32 D2
Arlington Devon....17 L3
Arlington E Susx....25 M9
Arlington Gloucs....33 M3
Arlington Beccott Devon....17 L3
Armadale Highld....145 K7
Armadale Highld....166 C4
Armadale W Loth....126 G4
Armaside Cumb....100 G5
Armathwaite Cumb....111 K11
Arminghall Norfk....77 K11
Armitage Staffs....71 K11
Armitage Bridge Kirk....90 E8
Armley Leeds....90 H4
Armscote Warwks....47 P6
Armshead Staffs....70 G5
Armston Nhants....61 N3
Armthorpe Donc....91 Q10
Arnabost Ag & B....136 G3
Arnaby Cumb....94 D4
Arncliffe N York....96 D6
Arncliffe Cote N York....96 D6
Arncroach Fife....135 N6
Arndilly House Moray....157 N7
Arne Dorset....12 G7
Arnesby Leics....60 E2
Arngask P & K....134 E5
Arnisdale Highld....145 P5
Arnish Highld....153 K8
Arniston Mdloth....127 Q5
Arnol W Isls....168 i3
Arnold E R Yk....93 K2
Arnold Notts....85 J11
Arnprior Stirlg....133 J3
Arnside Cumb....95 K5
Aros Ag & B....137 P6
Arowry Wrexhm....69 N7
Arrad Foot Cumb....94 G4
Arram E R Yk....92 H2
Arran N Ayrs....120 H4
Arrathorne N York....97 K2
Arreton IoW....14 F9
Arrina Highld....153 N6
Arrington Cambs....62 D10
Arrochar Ag & B....132 B7
Arrow Warwks....47 L3
Arrowfield Top Worcs....58 F10
Arscott Shrops....56 G3
Artafallie Highld....156 A8
Arthington Leeds....90 H2
Arthingworth Nhants....60 G4
Arthog Gwynd....54 E2
Arthrath Abers....159 N10
Arthursdale Leeds....91 K3
Artrochie Abers....159 P11
Arundel W Susx....24 B9
Asby Cumb....100 E6
Ascog Ag & B....124 E5
Ascot W & M....35 P11
Ascott Warwks....48 B8
Ascott Earl Oxon....48 B11
Ascott-under-
  Wychwood Oxon....48 B11
Asenby N York....97 N5
Asfordby Leics....73 J7
Asfordby Hill Leics....73 J7
Asgarby Lincs....86 F11
Asgarby Lincs....87 K7
Ash Devon....7 L9
Ash Devon....17 J10
Ash Dorset....12 E2
Ash Kent....37 P8
Ash Kent....39 N10
Ash Somset....19 J10
Ash Somset....19 N10
Ash Surrey....23 P4
Ashampstead W Berk....34 G9
Ashampstead Green
  W Berk....34 G9
Ashbocking Suffk....64 H11
Ashbourne Derbys....71 M5
Ashbrittle Somset....18 E10
Ashburnham Place
  E Susx....25 Q8
Ashburton Devon....7 K4
Ashbury Devon....8 D5
Ashbury Oxon....33 Q7
Ashby N Linc....92 E9
Ashby by Partney Lincs....87 M7
Ashby cum Fenby NE Lin....93 N10
Ashby de la Launde Lincs....86 E9

Ashby-de-la-Zouch Leics....72 B7
Ashby Folville Leics....73 J8
Ashby Magna Leics....60 C2
Ashby Parva Leics....60 B3
Ashby Puerorum Lincs....87 K6
Ashby St Ledgers Nhants....60 C7
Ashby St Mary Norfk....77 L11
Ashchurch Gloucs....46 H8
Ashcombe Devon....9 M9
Ashcombe N Som....19 K2
Ashcott Somset....19 M7
Ashdon Essex....51 N2
Ashdown Forest E Susx....25 L4
Ashe Hants....22 F4
Asheldham Essex....52 G11
Ashen Essex....52 B3
Ashendon Bucks....35 K2
Asheridge Bucks....35 P4
Ashfield Hants....22 C11
Ashfield Herefs....46 A10
Ashfield Stirlg....133 M7
Ashfield cum Thorpe
  Suffk....65 J9
Ashfield Green Suffk....63 N9
Ashfield Green Suffk....65 K7
Ashfold Crossways
  W Susx....24 F5
Ashford Devon....6 H9
Ashford Devon....17 J4
Ashford Kent....26 H3
Ashford Surrey....36 C6
Ashford Bowdler Shrops....57 J10
Ashford Carbonell
  Shrops....57 J10
Ashford Hill Hants....22 G2
Ashford in the Water
  Derbys....83 Q11
Ashgill S Lans....126 D7
Ash Green Surrey....23 P5
Ash Green Warwks....59 M8
Ashill Devon....10 B2
Ashill Norfk....76 B11
Ashill Somset....19 K11
Ashingdon Essex....38 E3
Ashington Nthumb....113 L3
Ashington Poole....12 H5
Ashington Somset....19 Q10
Ashington W Susx....24 D7
Ashkirk Border....117 P6
Ashlett Hants....14 E6
Ashleworth Gloucs....46 F9
Ashleworth Quay Gloucs....46 F9
Ashley Cambs....63 L8
Ashley Ches E....82 G8
Ashley Devon....17 M9
Ashley Dorset....13 K4
Ashley Gloucs....32 H6
Ashley Hants....13 N5
Ashley Hants....22 C8
Ashley Kent....27 P2
Ashley Nhants....60 G2
Ashley Staffs....70 D7
Ashley Wilts....32 F11
Ashley Green Bucks....35 Q3
Ashleyhay Derbys....71 P4
Ashley Heath Dorset....13 K4
Ashley Moor Herefs....56 H11
Ash Magna Shrops....69 Q7
Ashmansworth Hants....22 D3
Ashmansworthy Devon....16 E8
Ashmead Green Gloucs....32 E5
Ashmill Devon....5 P2
Ash Mill Devon....17 P7
Ashmore Dorset....20 H11
Ashmore Green W Berk....34 F11
Ashorne Warwks....48 B3
Ashover Derbys....84 D8
Ashow Warwks....59 M10
Ash Parva Shrops....69 Q7
Ashperton Herefs....46 B6
Ashprington Devon....7 L7
Ash Priors Somset....18 G9
Ashreigney Devon....17 L9
Ash Street Suffk....52 H2
Ashtead Surrey....36 E9
Ash Thomas Devon....9 P2
Ashton C Pete....74 B9
Ashton Ches W....81 Q11
Ashton Cnwll....2 G8
Ashton Devon....9 L8
Ashton Hants....22 F11
Ashton Herefs....45 Q2
Ashton Inver....124 G2
Ashton Nhants....49 L5
Ashton Nhants....61 N3
Ashton Somset....19 M5
Ashton Common Wilts....20 G3
Ashton Hill Wilts....20 H3
Ashton-in-Makerfield
  Wigan....82 C5
Ashton Keynes Wilts....33 K6
Ashton under Hill Worcs....47 J7
Ashton-under-Lyne
  Tamesd....83 K5
Ashton upon Mersey
  Traffd....82 G6
Ashurst Hants....13 P2
Ashurst Kent....25 M3
Ashurst Lancs....88 F9
Ashurst W Susx....24 E7
Ashurst Wood W Susx....25 K3
Ash Vale Surrey....23 N4
Ashwater Devon....5 P2
Ashwell Herts....50 G3
Ashwell Rutlnd....73 M8
Ashwell End Herts....50 G2
Ashwellthorpe Norfk....64 G2
Ashwick Somset....20 B5
Ashwicken Norfk....75 P7
Ashwood Staffs....58 C7
Askam in Furness Cumb....94 E5
Askern Donc....91 N8
Askerswell Dorset....11 L6
Askett Bucks....35 M3
Askham Cumb....101 P6
Askham Notts....85 M6
Askham Bryan C York....98 B11
Askham Richard C York....98 A11
Asknish Ag & B....131 J9
Askrigg N York....96 E3
Askwith N York....97 J11
Aslackby Lincs....74 A4
Aslacton Norfk....64 H3
Aslockton Notts....73 J2
Asney Somset....19 N7
Aspall Suffk....64 H9
Aspatria Cumb....100 F2
Aspenden Herts....51 J5
Aspenshaw Derbys....83 M7

Asperton Lincs....74 E3
Aspley Staffs....70 E8
Aspley Guise C Beds....49 P7
Aspley Heath C Beds....49 P8
Aspley Heath Warwks....58 G10
Aspull Wigan....89 J9
Aspull Common Wigan....82 D5
Asselby E R Yk....92 D5
Asserby Lincs....87 N5
Asserby Turn Lincs....87 N5
Assington Suffk....52 F4
Assington Green Suffk....63 N10
Astbury Ches E....70 E2
Astcote Nhants....49 J4
Asterby Lincs....87 J5
Asterley Shrops....56 F6
Asterton Shrops....56 F5
Asthall Oxon....33 Q2
Asthall Leigh Oxon....34 B2
Astle Highld....162 G8
Astley Shrops....69 P11
Astley Warwks....59 M7
Astley Wigan....82 F4
Astley Worcs....57 P11
Astley Abbotts Shrops....57 N5
Astley Bridge Bolton....89 L8
Astley Cross Worcs....57 Q11
Astley Green Wigan....82 F5
Aston Birm....58 G7
Aston Ches E....69 R5
Aston Ches W....82 C9
Aston Derbys....83 Q8
Aston Flints....81 L11
Aston Herefs....45 P2
Aston Herts....50 G6
Aston Oxon....34 B4
Aston Rothm....84 G3
Aston Shrops....57 Q6
Aston Shrops....69 P9
Aston Staffs....70 D6
Aston Staffs....70 F10
Aston Wokham....35 L8
Aston Wrekin....57 L3
Aston Abbotts Bucks....49 M10
Aston Botterell Shrops....57 L8
Aston-by-Stone Staffs....70 G8
Aston Cantlow Warwks....47 M2
Aston Clinton Bucks....35 N2
Aston Crews Herefs....46 C10
Aston Cross Gloucs....46 H8
Aston End Herts....50 G6
Aston-Eyre Shrops....57 M6
Aston Fields Worcs....58 E11
Aston Flamville Leics....59 Q6
Aston Heath Ches W....82 C9
Aston Ingham Herefs....46 C10
Aston juxta Mondrum
  Ches E....70 A3
Aston le Walls Nhants....48 E4
Aston Magna Gloucs....47 N7
Aston Munslow Shrops....57 J7
Aston-on-Carrant Gloucs....46 H8
Aston on Clun Shrops....56 F8
Aston Pigott Shrops....56 E3
Aston Rogers Shrops....56 E3
Aston Rowant Oxon....35 K5
Aston Sandford Bucks....35 L3
Aston Somerville Worcs....47 K7
Aston-sub-Edge Gloucs....47 M6
Aston Tirrold Oxon....34 G7
Aston-upon-Trent
  Derbys....72 C5
Aston Upthorpe Oxon....34 G7
Astrop Nhants....48 F7
Astrope Herts....35 N2
Astwick C Beds....50 F3
Astwith Derbys....84 F8
Astwood M Keyn....49 Q5
Astwood Worcs....58 D11
Astwood Bank Worcs....58 F2
Aswarby Lincs....73 R3
Aswardby Lincs....87 L6
Atcham Shrops....57 J3
Atch Lench Worcs....47 K4
Athelhampton Dorset....12 C6
Athelington Suffk....65 J7
Athelney Somset....19 K9
Athelstaneford E Loth....128 E4
Atherfield Green IoW....14 E11
Atherington Devon....17 K7
Atherington W Susx....24 B10
Atherstone Somset....19 L11
Atherstone Warwks....59 M5
Atherstone on Stour
  Warwks....47 P4
Atherton Wigan....82 E4
Atley Hill N York....103 Q10
Atlow Derbys....71 N5
Attadale Highld....154 B10
Attenborough Notts....72 E4
Atterby Lincs....86 C2
Attercliffe Sheff....84 E3
Atterley Shrops....57 L5
Atterton Leics....72 B11
Attingham Park Shrops....57 J3
Attleborough Norfk....64 E2
Attleborough Warwks....59 N6
Attlebridge Norfk....76 G8
Attleton Green Suffk....63 M10
Atwick E R Yk....99 P10
Atworth Wilts....32 G11
Auberrow Herefs....45 P5
Aubourn Lincs....86 B8
Auchbreck Moray....149 N2
Auchedly Abers....159 L11
Auchenblae Abers....143 N2
Auchenbowie Stirlg....133 M10
Auchencairn D & G....108 G10
Auchencairn D & G....109 L4
Auchencairn N Ayrs....121 K6
Auchencrow Border....129 M7
Auchendinny Mdloth....127 P5
Auchengray S Lans....126 H7
Auchenhalrig Moray....157 R5
Auchenheath S Lans....126 E9
Auchenhessnane D & G....115 R8
Auchenlochan Ag & B....124 B3
Auchenmade N Ayrs....125 K8
Auchenmalg D & G....106 H7
Auchentiber N Ayrs....125 K8
Auchindrain Ag & B....131 L7
Auchindrean Highld....161 K10
Auchininna Abers....158 G8
Auchinleck E Ayrs....115 L3
Auchinloch N Lans....126 B3
Auchinstarry N Lans....126 C2
Auchintore Highld....139 K3
Auchiries Abers....159 Q10
Auchlean Highld....148 F8
Auchlee Abers....151 M8
Auchleven Abers....150 G3

Auchlochan S Lans....126 E...
Auchlossan Abers....150 ...
Auchlyne Stirlg....132 ...
Auchmillan E Ayrs....115 ...
Auchmithie Angus....143 ...
Auchnacree Angus....142 ...
Auchnagatt Abers....159 ...
Auchnarrow Moray....149 ...
Auchroisk Moray....157 ...
Auchterarder P & K....133 ...
Auchteraw Highld....147 ...
Auchterblair Highld....148 ...
Auchtercairn Highld....153 ...
Auchterderran Fife....134 ...
Auchterhouse Angus....142 E...
Auchterless Abers....158 ...
Auchtermuchty Fife....134 ...
Auchterneed Highld....155 ...
Auchtertool Fife....134 ...
Auchtertyre Highld....145 ...
Auchtubh Stirlg....132 ...
Auckengill Highld....167 ...
Auckley Donc....91 Q...
Audenshaw Tamesd....83 ...
Audlem Ches E....70 ...
Audley Staffs....70 ...
Audley End Essex....51 M...
Audley End Essex....52 ...
Audley End Suffk....64 B...
Audley End House &
  Gardens Essex....51 M...
Audmore Staffs....70 E...
Audnam Dudley....58 ...
Aughertree Cumb....101 ...
Aughton E R Yk....92 ...
Aughton Lancs....88 ...
Aughton Lancs....95 ...
Aughton Rothm....84 ...
Aughton Wilts....21 ...
Aughton Park Lancs....88 ...
Auldearn Highld....156 ...
Aulden Herefs....45 ...
Auldgirth D & G....109 ...
Auldhouse S Lans....125 ...
Ault a' chruinn Highld....146 ...
Aultbea Highld....160 ...
Aultgrishin Highld....160 ...
Aultguish Inn Highld....155 ...
Ault Hucknall Derbys....84 ...
Aultmore Moray....158 ...
Aultnagoire Highld....147 ...
Aultnamain Inn Highld....162 ...
Aunby Lincs....73 ...
Aunk Devon....9 ...
Aunsby Lincs....73 ...
Aust S Glos....31 ...
Austendike Lincs....74 ...
Austerfield Donc....85 ...
Austerlands Oldham....83 ...
Austhorpe Leeds....91 ...
Austonley Kirk....90 ...
Austrey Warwks....59 ...
Austwick N York....95 ...
Authorpe Lincs....87 ...
Authorpe Row Lincs....87 ...
Avebury Wilts....33 M...
Avebury Trusloe Wilts....33 L...
Aveley Thurr....37 ...
Avening Gloucs....32 ...
Averham Notts....85 M...
Aveton Gifford Devon....6 ...
Aviemore Highld....148 ...
Avington W Berk....34 ...
Avoch Highld....156 ...
Avon Hants....13 ...
Avonbridge Falk....126 ...
Avon Dassett Warwks....48 ...
Avonmouth Bristl....31 ...
Avonwick Devon....7 ...
Awbridge Hants....22 B...
Awkley S Glos....31 ...
Awliscombe Devon....10 ...
Awre Gloucs....32 ...
Awsworth Notts....72 ...
Axborough Worcs....58 ...
Axbridge Somset....19 ...
Axford Hants....22 ...
Axford Wilts....33 P...
Axmansford Hants....22 ...
Axminster Devon....10 ...
Axmouth Devon....10 ...
Axton Flints....80 ...
Aycliffe Dur....103 ...
Aydon Nthumb....112 ...
Aylburton Gloucs....32 ...
Ayle Nthumb....111 P...
Aylesbeare Devon....9 ...
Aylesbury Bucks....35 ...
Aylesbury
  Crematorium Bucks....49 M...
Aylesby NE Lin....93 ...
Aylesford Kent....38 B...
Aylesham Kent....39 M...
Aylestone C Leic....72 F...
Aylestone Park C Leic....72 F...
Aylmerton Norfk....76 ...
Aylsham Norfk....76 ...
Aylton Herefs....46 ...
Aylworth Gloucs....47 M...
Aymestrey Herefs....56 ...
Aynho Nhants....48 ...
Ayot Green Herts....50 ...
Ayot St Lawrence Herts....50 ...
Ayot St Peter Herts....50 ...
Ayr S Ayrs....114 ...
Aysgarth N York....96 ...
Ayshford Devon....18 ...
Ayside Cumb....94 ...
Ayston Rutlnd....73 M...
Aythorpe Roding Essex....51 ...
Ayton Border....129 ...
Azerley N York....97 ...

B

Babbacombe Torbay....7 ...
Babbington Notts....72 ...
Babbinswood Shrops....69 ...
Babbs Green Herts....51 ...
Babcary Somset....19 ...
Babel Carmth....44 ...
Babel Green Suffk....63 ...
Babell Flints....80 ...
Babeny Devon....6 ...
Bablock Hythe Oxon....34 ...
Babraham Cambs....62 ...

Babworth – Bearley 257

worth Notts 85 L4
hau IoA 78 G8
he Shrops 56 H8
heldre Powys 56 C6
helor's Bump E Susx 26 D9
kaland Ork 169 e3
kbarrow Cumb 94 H4
ke Carmth 41 Q7
kfolds Abers 159 P7
kford Ches W 81 M10
kford Cross Ches W 81 M10
kies Highld 163 J6
k of Keppoch Highld 145 L10
k o' th' Brook Staffs 71 K4
k Street Suffk 63 M9
kwell N Som 31 N11
kworth N Tyne 113 M6
on's End Solhll 59 J7
onsthorpe Norfk 76 G4
ton Herefs 45 M8
ton Norfk 77 L5
ton Suffk 64 F8
ton Green Suffk 64 E8
up Lancs 89 P6
lachro Highld 153 P3
lbury Swindn 33 N8
lby Nhants 60 C9
lcall Highld 164 E8
lcall Highld 164 F5
lcaul Highld 160 G8
ldeley Edge C Stke 70 G4
ldeley Green C Stke 70 G4
ldesley Clinton
Warwks 59 K10
ldesley Ensor Warwks 59 L5
ldidarrach Highld 160 H2
ldinsgill Border 127 L7
lenscoth Abers 158 G10
lentarbet Highld 160 G5
lenyon Abers 149 Q4
lgall Cnwll 5 L4
lgeney Cambs 74 H11
lger Shrops 57 P5
lger's Cross Cnwll 2 D7
lgers Mount Kent 37 L8
lgeworth Gloucs 46 H11
lgworth Somset 19 L4
lharlick Cnwll 5 M4
licaul Highld 145 N2
lingham Suffk 65 L8
lesmere Kent 38 H11
llieu Border 116 F7
llipster Highld 167 M7
lluarach Highld 160 F8
lninish Highld 162 H8
lrallach Highld 160 H8
lsey Worcs 47 L6
lshot Lea Surrey 23 N5
lsworth Wakefd 91 M8
lwell Ash Suffk 64 D8
lwell Green Suffk 64 E8
lber Dorset 12 C2
lby N York 97 Q4
Enderby Lincs 87 L6
lendon Gloucs 33 K3
lginswood Shrops 57 M8
lgrow Cumb 100 G2
h a Chaisteil W Isls 168 b18
lham Kent 39 J11
h a Tuath W Isls 168 c17
lilt Flints 81 J9
linton Warwks 59 M10
lan Neath 29 K6
ley Leeds 90 G3
ley Shrops 69 M9
ley Somset 19 N5
more Hants 23 J6
nall Staffs 70 G4
nor W Berk 34 E11
shot Surrey 23 P2
shot Wilts 34 B11
stone S Glos 32 C7
thorpe Notts 84 G10
worth Leics 72 C9
wy Llydiart Herefs 45 N9
don C Brad 90 F3
don Green C Brad 90 E3
e Ailein W Isls 168 h5
e a Mhanaich W Isls 168 c12
e Mòr Ag & B 136 H11
ey Green Hants 23 J9
eyhead Cumb 111 K5
iff Bridge Calder 90 E5
lieston C Glas 126 B5
rigg Lancs 95 K9
bridge N York 96 D2
shole Abers 158 F10
nton C Pete 74 A9
nton E R Yk 99 K10
nton Oxon 48 G9
town Fife 135 K7
nkine Border 118 C7
er's End Herts 51 J7
er Street Thurr 37 P4
ewell Derbys 84 B7
a Gwynd 68 B7
allan W Isls 168 h5
beg Highld 155 M11
beggie P & K 134 F2
blair Highld 155 P8
blair Highld 156 C4
by Donc 91 P10
cary D & G 108 H11
chraggan Highld 155 P9
chreick Highld 164 E4
combe W Susx 24 H4
combe Lane W Susx 24 H4
comie Links Fife 135 Q6
dersby N York 97 N5
dersby St James
N York 97 N5
derstone Lancs 89 J4
derstone Rochdl 89 Q8
derton Notts 85 P10
dhu Cnwll 3 K5
dinnie Fife 135 L5
dinnies P & K 134 C4
dock Herts 50 F4
dock Services Herts 50 F3
dovie C Dund 142 H11
drine IoM 80 f5
dslow E Susx 26 D9
dwin IoM 80 e5
dwinholme Cumb 110 F10
dwin's Gate Staffs 70 D7
dwin's Hill W Susx 25 J3
e Norfk 76 E4
edgarno P & K 142 D11
emartine Ag & B 136 B7
erno C Edin 127 M4
farg Fife 134 H7
Balfield Angus 143 J4
Balfour Ork 169 d5
Balfron Stirlg 132 G10
Balgaveny Abers 158 G9
Balgonar Fife 134 C9
Balgowan D & G 106 F9
Balgowan Highld 147 Q9
Balgown Highld 152 F4
Balgracie D & G 106 C5
Balgray S Lans 116 B6
Balham Gt Lon 36 G6
Balhary P & K 142 D8
Balholmie P & K 142 A10
Baligill Highld 166 E3
Balintore Angus 142 D6
Balintore Highld 156 F2
Balintraid Highld 156 C3
Balivanich W Isls 168 c12
Balk N York 97 Q4
Balkeerie Angus 142 E9
Balkholme E R Yk 92 C5
Ballabeg IoM 80 c7
Ballachulish Highld 139 K6
Ballafesson IoM 80 b7
Ballajora IoM 80 g3
Ballakilpheric IoM 80 b7
Ballamodha IoM 80 c7
Ballanlay Ag & B 124 C5
Ballantrae S Ayrs 114 A11
Ballards Gore Essex 38 F3
Ballards Green Warwks 59 L6
Ballasalla IoM 80 c7
Ballater Abers 150 B8
Ballaugh IoM 80 d3
Ballchraggan Highld 156 D2
Ballencrieff E Loth 128 D4
Ballevullin Ag & B 136 B6
Ball Green C Stke 70 F4
Ball Haye Green Staffs 70 H3
Ball Hill Hants 22 D2
Ballidon Derbys 71 N4
Balliekine N Ayrs 120 G4
Balliemore Ag & B 131 N8
Balligmorrie S Ayrs 114 D9
Ballimore Stirlg 132 G4
Ballindalloch Moray 157 M10
Ballindean P & K 134 H2
Ballingdon Suffk 52 E3
Ballinger Common Bucks 35 P4
Ballingham Herefs 46 A8
Ballingry Fife 134 F8
Ballinluig P & K 141 N7
Ballinshoe Angus 142 G7
Ballintuim P & K 141 R6
Balloch Highld 156 C8
Balloch N Lans 126 C3
Balloch P & K 133 N4
Balloch S Ayrs 114 F8
Balloch W Duns 132 D11
Balls Cross W Susx 23 Q9
Balls Green E Susx 25 L3
Ball's Green Gloucs 32 G5
Ballygown Ag & B 137 L7
Ballygrant Ag & B 122 E6
Ballyhaugh Ag & B 136 F4
Balmacara Highld 145 P2
Balmaclellan D & G 108 E5
Balmae D & G 108 E12
Balmaha Stirlg 132 E9
Balmalcolm Fife 135 J6
Balmangan D & G 108 D11
Balmedie Abers 151 P4
Balmer Heath Shrops 69 M8
Balmerino Fife 135 K3
Balmerlawn Hants 13 P4
Balmichael N Ayrs 120 H5
Balmore E Duns 125 P3
Balmuchy Highld 163 K11
Balmule Fife 134 G10
Balmullo Fife 135 L3
Balnacoil Lodge Highld 163 J4
Balnacra Highld 154 C8
Balnacroft Abers 149 P9
Balnafoich Highld 156 B10
Balnaguard P & K 141 M7
Balnahard Ag & B 136 c2
Balnahard Ag & B 137 M9
Balnain Highld 155 M11
Balnakeil Highld 165 J3
Balne N York 91 P7
Balquharn P & K 141 P10
Balquhidder Stirlg 132 G3
Balsall Common Solhll 59 K9
Balsall Heath Birm 58 G8
Balsall Street Solhll 59 K9
Balscote Oxon 48 C6
Balsham Cambs 63 J10
Baltasound Shet 169 t3
Balterley Staffs 70 D4
Balterley Green Staffs 70 D4
Balterley Heath Staffs 70 C4
Baltersan D & G 107 M5
Balthangie Abers 159 K7
Baltonsborough Somset 19 P8
Balvicar Ag & B 130 F4
Balvraid Highld 145 P4
Balvraid Highld 156 E11
Balwest Cnwll 2 F7
Bamber Bridge Lancs 88 H5
Bamber's Green Essex 51 N6
Bamburgh Nthumb 119 N4
Bamburgh Castle
Nthumb 119 N3
Bamford Derbys 84 B4
Bamford Rochdl 89 P8
Bampton Cumb 101 P7
Bampton Devon 18 C10
Bampton Oxon 34 B4
Bampton Grange Cumb 101 P7
Banavie Highld 139 L2
Banbury Oxon 48 E6
Banbury Crematorium
Oxon 48 E6
Bancffosfelen Carmth 28 E2
Banchory Abers 150 H8
Banchory-Devenick
Abers 151 N7
Bancycapel Carmth 28 D2
Bancyfelin Carmth 42 F11
Banc-y-ffordd Carmth 42 H7
Bandirran P & K 142 C11
Bandrake Head Cumb 94 G3
Banff Abers 158 G5
Bangor Gwynd 79 K10
Bangor Crematorium
Gwynd 79 K10
Bangor-on-Dee Wrexhm 69 L5
Bangors Cnwll 5 L2
Bangor's Green Lancs 88 D9
Bangrove Suffk 64 C7
Banham Norfk 64 F4
Bank Hants 13 N3
Bankend D & G 109 M7
Bankfoot P & K 141 Q10
Bankglen E Ayrs 115 L5
Bank Ground Cumb 101 K11
Bankhead C Aber 151 N6
Bankhead S Lans 116 D2
Bank Newton N York 96 D10
Banknock Falk 126 D2
Banks Cumb 111 L8
Banks Lancs 88 D6
Banks Green Worcs 58 E11
Bankshill D & G 110 C4
Bank Street Worcs 46 B2
Bank Top Calder 90 E6
Bank Top Lancs 88 G9
Banningham Norfk 77 J6
Bannister Green Essex 51 Q6
Bannockburn Stirlg 133 N9
Banstead Surrey 36 G9
Bantham Devon 6 H10
Banton N Lans 126 C2
Banwell N Som 19 L3
Bapchild Kent 38 F9
Bapton Wilts 21 J7
Barabhas W Isls 168 i3
Barassie S Ayrs 125 J11
Barbaraville Highld 156 C3
Barber Booth Derbys 83 P8
Barber Green Cumb 94 H4
Barbieston S Ayrs 114 H4
Barbon Cumb 95 N4
Barbridge Ches E 69 R3
Barbrook Devon 17 N2
Barby Nhants 60 B6
Barcaldine Ag & B 138 H9
Barcheston Warwks 47 Q7
Barclose Cumb 110 H8
Barcombe E Susx 25 K8
Barcombe Cross E Susx 25 K7
Barcroft C Brad 90 C3
Barden N York 96 H2
Barden Park Kent 37 N11
Bardfield End Green
Essex 51 P4
Bardfield Saling Essex 51 Q5
Bardney Lincs 86 F7
Bardon Leics 72 C8
Bardon Mill Nthumb 111 Q8
Bardowie E Duns 125 P3
Bardown E Susx 25 Q5
Bardrainney Inver 125 J3
Bardsea Cumb 94 G6
Bardsey Leeds 91 K2
Bardsey Island Gwynd 66 A10
Bardsley Oldham 83 K4
Bardwell Suffk 64 C7
Bare Lancs 95 K8
Bareppa Cnwll 3 K8
Barfad D & G 107 K4
Barford Norfk 76 G10
Barford Warwks 47 Q2
Barford St John Oxon 48 D8
Barford St Martin Wilts 21 L8
Barford St Michael Oxon 48 D8
Barfrestone Kent 39 N11
Bargate Derbys 84 E11
Bargeddie N Lans 126 B5
Bargoed Caerph 30 G5
Bargrennan D & G 107 L2
Barham Cambs 61 P5
Barham Kent 39 M11
Barham Suffk 64 G11
Barham Crematorium
Kent 27 M2
Bar Hill Cambs 62 E8
Barholm Lincs 74 A8
Barkby Leics 72 G9
Barkby Thorpe Leics 72 G9
Barkers Green Shrops 69 P9
Barkestone-le-Vale Leics 73 K4
Barkham Wokham 35 L11
Barking Gt Lon 37 K4
Barking Suffk 64 F11
Barkingside Gt Lon 37 K3
Barking Tye Suffk 64 F11
Barkisland Calder 90 D7
Barkla Shop Cnwll 3 J3
Barkston Lincs 73 N2
Barkston Ash N York 91 M3
Barkway Herts 51 J3
Barlanark C Glas 126 B5
Barlaston Staffs 70 F7
Barlavington W Susx 23 Q11
Barlborough Derbys 84 G5
Barlby N York 91 Q4
Barlestone Leics 72 C9
Barley Herts 51 K3
Barley Lancs 89 N2
Barleycroft End Herts 51 K5
Barley Hole Rothm 91 K11
Barleythorpe Rutlnd 73 L9
Barling Essex 38 F4
Barlings Lincs 86 E6
Barlochan D & G 108 H9
Barlow Derbys 84 D6
Barlow Gatesd 113 J8
Barlow N York 91 Q5
Barmby Moor E R Yk 98 F11
Barmby on the Marsh
E R Yk 92 A5
Barmer Norfk 75 R4
Barming Heath Kent 38 B10
Barmollack Ag & B 120 F3
Barmouth Gwynd 67 L11
Barmpton Darltn 104 B7
Barmston E R Yk 99 P9
Barnaby Green Suffk 65 P5
Barnacarry Ag & B 131 L9
Barnack C Pete 74 A9
Barnacle Warwks 59 N8
Barnard Castle Dur 103 L7
Barnard Gate Oxon 34 D2
Barnardiston Suffk 63 M11
Barnbarroch D & G 108 H9
Barnburgh Donc 91 M10
Barnby Suffk 65 P4
Barnby Dun Donc 91 Q9
Barnby in the Willows
Notts 85 Q10
Barnby Moor Notts 85 L4
Barncorkrie D & G 106 E10
Barnehurst Gt Lon 37 L5
Barnes Gt Lon 36 F5
Barnes Street Kent 37 P11
Barnet Gt Lon 50 F11
Barnetby le Wold N Linc 93 J9
Barnet Gate Gt Lon 50 F11
Barney Norfk 76 D5
Barnham Suffk 64 B6
Barnham W Susx 15 Q6
Barnham Broom Norfk 76 F10
Barnhead Angus 143 M6
Barnhill C Dund 142 H11
Barnhill Ches W 69 N4
Barnhill Moray 157 L6
Barnhills D & G 106 C3
Barningham Dur 103 L8
Barningham Suffk 64 D6
Barnoldby le Beck NE Lin 93 M10
Barnoldswick Lancs 96 C11
Barnsdale Bar Donc 91 N8
Barns Green W Susx 24 D5
Barnsley Barns 91 J9
Barnsley Gloucs 33 L4
Barnsley Crematorium
Barns 91 K9
Barnsole Kent 39 N10
Barnstaple Devon 17 K5
Barnston Essex 51 P7
Barnston Wirral 81 K8
Barnstone Notts 73 J3
Barnt Green Worcs 58 F10
Barnton C Edin 127 M3
Barnton Ches W 82 D10
Barnwell All Saints
Nhants 61 M4
Barnwell St Andrew
Nhants 61 N4
Barnwood Gloucs 46 G11
Baron's Cross Herefs 45 P3
Baronwood Cumb 101 P2
Barr S Ayrs 114 E9
Barra W Isls 168 b17
Barra Airport W Isls 168 c17
Barrachan D & G 107 L8
Barraigh W Isls 168 b17
Barrapoll Ag & B 136 A7
Barras Cumb 102 F8
Barrasford Nthumb 112 D6
Barregarrow IoM 80 d4
Barrets Green Ches E 69 Q3
Barrhead E Rens 125 M6
Barrhill S Ayrs 114 D11
Barrington Cambs 62 E11
Barrington Somset 19 L11
Barripper Cnwll 2 G6
Barrmill N Ayrs 125 K7
Barrock Highld 167 N2
Barrow Gloucs 46 G10
Barrow Lancs 89 L3
Barrow Rutlnd 73 M7
Barrow Shrops 57 M4
Barrow Somset 20 D8
Barrow Suffk 63 N8
Barroway Drove Norfk 75 L10
Barrow Bridge Bolton 89 K8
Barrow Burn Nthumb 118 G8
Barrowby Lincs 73 M3
Barrowden Rutlnd 73 N10
Barrowford Lancs 89 P3
Barrow Gurney N Som 31 P11
Barrow Haven N Linc 93 J6
Barrow Hill Derbys 84 F5
Barrow-in-Furness
Cumb 94 E7
Barrow Island Cumb 94 D7
Barrow Nook Lancs 81 N4
Barrow's Green Ches E 70 B3
Barrow Street Wilts 20 F8
Barrow-upon-Humber
N Linc 93 J6
Barrow upon Soar Leics 72 F7
Barrow upon Trent
Derbys 72 B5
Barrow Vale BaNES 20 B2
Barry Angus 143 J11
Barry V Glam 30 F11
Barry Island V Glam 30 F11
Barsby Leics 72 H8
Barsham Suffk 65 M4
Barston Solhll 59 K9
Bartestree Herefs 45 R6
Barthol Chapel Abers 159 K11
Bartholomew Green
Essex 52 B7
Barthomley Ches E 70 D4
Bartley Hants 13 P2
Bartley Green Birm 58 F8
Bartlow Cambs 63 J11
Barton Cambs 62 F9
Barton Ches W 69 M4
Barton Gloucs 47 L9
Barton Herefs 45 K3
Barton Lancs 88 D9
Barton Lancs 88 G3
Barton N York 103 P9
Barton Oxon 34 G3
Barton Torbay 7 N5
Barton Warwks 47 M4
Barton Bendish Norfk 75 P9
Barton End Gloucs 32 F5
Barton Green Staffs 71 M11
Barton Hartshorn Bucks 48 H8
Barton Hill N York 98 E8
Barton in Fabis Notts 72 E4
Barton in the Beans
Leics 72 B9
Barton-le-Clay C Beds 50 C4
Barton-le-Street N York 98 E6
Barton-le-Willows
N York 98 E8
Barton Mills Suffk 63 M6
Barton-on-Sea Hants 13 M6
Barton-on-the-Heath
Warwks 47 Q8
Barton Park Services
N York 103 P9
Barton St David Somset 19 P8
Barton Seagrave Nhants 61 J5
Barton Stacey Hants 22 D6
Barton Town Devon 17 M3
Barton Turf Norfk 77 M7
Barton-under-
Needwood Staffs 71 M11
Barton-upon-Humber
N Linc 92 H6
Barton upon Irwell Salfd 82 G5
Barton Waterside N Linc 92 H6
Barugh Barns 91 J9
Barugh Green Barns 91 J9
Barvas W Isls 168 i3
Barway Cambs 63 J5
Barwell Leics 72 C11
Barwick Devon 17 K10
Barwick Herts 51 J7
Barwick Somset 11 M2
Barwick in Elmet Leeds 91 L3
Baschurch Shrops 69 M10
Bascote Warwks 48 D2
Bascote Heath Warwks 48 C2
Base Green Suffk 64 E9
Basford Green Staffs 70 H4
Bashall Eaves Lancs 89 K2
Bashall Town Lancs 89 L2
Bashley Hants 13 M5
Basildon Essex 38 B4
Basildon & District
Crematorium Essex 38 C4
Basingstoke Hants 22 H4
Basingstoke
Crematorium Hants 22 G5
Baslow Derbys 84 C6
Bason Bridge Somset 19 K5
Bassaleg Newpt 31 J7
Bassendean Border 128 G10
Bassenthwaite Cumb 100 H4
Bassett C Sotn 22 D11
Bassingbourn-cum-
Kneesworth Cambs 50 H2
Bassingfield Notts 72 G3
Bassingham Lincs 86 B9
Bassingthorpe Lincs 73 P5
Bassus Green Herts 50 H5
Basted Kent 37 P9
Baston Lincs 74 B8
Bastwick Norfk 77 N8
Batch Somset 19 K3
Batchworth Herts 36 C2
Batchworth Heath Herts 36 C2
Batcombe Dorset 11 N4
Batcombe Somset 20 C7
Bate Heath Ches E 82 E9
Batford Herts 50 D7
Bath BaNES 20 D2
Bathampton BaNES 32 E11
Bath, City of BaNES 20 E2
Bathealton Somset 18 E10
Batheaston BaNES 32 E11
Bathford BaNES 32 E11
Bathgate W Loth 126 H4
Bathley Notts 85 N9
Bathpool Cnwll 5 M7
Bathpool Somset 19 J9
Bath Side Essex 53 N5
Bathville W Loth 126 G4
Bathway Somset 19 Q4
Batley Kirk 90 G6
Batsford Gloucs 47 N8
Batson Devon 7 J11
Battersby N York 104 G9
Battersea Gt Lon 36 G5
Battisborough Cross
Devon 6 F9
Battisford Suffk 64 F11
Battisford Tye Suffk 64 E11
Battle E Susx 26 C8
Battle Powys 44 E8
Battleborough Somset 19 K4
Battledown Gloucs 47 J10
Battledykes Angus 142 H6
Battlefield Shrops 69 P11
Battlesbridge Essex 38 C3
Battlesden C Beds 49 Q9
Battleton Somset 18 B9
Battlies Green Suffk 64 C9
Battram Leics 72 C9
Battramsley Cross Hants 13 P5
Batt's Corner Hants 23 M6
Baughton Worcs 46 G6
Baughurst Hants 22 G2
Baulds Abers 150 G9
Baulking Oxon 34 B6
Baumber Lincs 86 H6
Baunton Gloucs 33 K4
Baveney Wood Shrops 57 M9
Baverstock Wilts 21 K8
Bawburgh Norfk 76 H10
Bawdeswell Norfk 76 E7
Bawdrip Somset 19 K7
Bawdsey Suffk 53 P3
Bawsey Norfk 75 N6
Bawtry Donc 85 K2
Baxenden Lancs 89 M5
Baxterley Warwks 59 L5
Baxter's Green Suffk 63 N9
Bay Highld 152 D7
Bayble W Isls 168 k4
Baybridge Hants 22 F10
Baybridge Nthumb 112 E10
Baycliff Cumb 94 F6
Baydon Wilts 33 Q9
Bayford Herts 50 H9
Bayford Somset 20 D9
Bayhead W Isls 168 c11
Bay Horse Lancs 95 K10
Bayley's Hill Kent 37 M10
Baylham Suffk 64 G11
Baynard's Green Oxon 48 F9
Baysdale Abbey N York 104 H9
Baysham Herefs 45 R9
Bayston Hill Shrops 56 H3
Baythorne End Essex 52 B3
Bayton Worcs 57 M10
Bayton Common Worcs 57 N10
Bayworth Oxon 34 E4
Beach S Glos 32 D10
Beachampton Bucks 49 L7
Beachamwell Norfk 75 Q9
Beachley Gloucs 31 Q6
Beachy Head E Susx 25 N11
Beacon Devon 10 D3
Beacon End Essex 52 G7
Beacon Hill E Susx 25 M4
Beacon Hill Kent 26 D5
Beacon Hill Notts 85 P10
Beacon Hill Surrey 23 N7
Beacon's Bottom Bucks 35 L5
Beaconsfield Bucks 35 P6
Beaconsfield Services
Bucks 35 Q7
Beadlam N York 98 D4
Beadlow C Beds 50 D3
Beadnell Nthumb 119 P5
Beaford Devon 17 K8
Beal N York 91 N5
Beal Nthumb 119 L2
Bealbury Cnwll 5 P8
Bealsmill Cnwll 5 P6
Beam Hill Staffs 71 N9
Beamhurst Staffs 71 K7
Beaminster Dorset 11 K4
Beamish Dur 113 K10
Beamish Museum Dur 113 K10
Beamsley N York 96 G10
Bean Kent 37 N6
Beanacre Wilts 32 H11
Beanley Nthumb 119 L7
Beardon Devon 8 D8
Beardwood Bl w D 89 K5
Beare Devon 9 N4
Beare Green Surrey 24 E2
Bearley Warwks 47 N2

Bearley Cross Warwks 47 N2
Bearpark Dur 103 P2
Bearsden E Duns 125 N3
Bearsted Kent 38 D10
Bearstone Shrops 70 C7
Bearwood Birm 58 F7
Bearwood Herefs 45 M3
Bearwood Poole 12 H5
Beattock D & G 116 F10
Beauchamp Roding Essex 51 N9
Beauchief Sheff 84 D4
Beaudesert Warwks 59 J11
Beaufort Blae G 30 G2
Beaulieu Hants 14 C6
Beaulieu Road Station Hants 13 P3
Beauly Highld 155 P8
Beaumaris IoA 79 L9
Beaumaris Castle IoA 79 L9
Beaumont Cumb 110 F9
Beaumont Essex 53 L7
Beaumont Jersey 11 b2
Beaumont Hill Darltn 103 Q7
Beaumont Leys C Leic 72 F9
Beausale Warwks 59 K10
Beauworth Hants 22 G9
Beaworthy Devon 8 C5
Beazley End Essex 52 B6
Bebington Wirral 81 L8
Bebside Nthumb 113 L4
Beccles Suffk 65 N4
Becconsall Lancs 88 F6
Beckbury Shrops 57 P4
Beckenham Gt Lon 37 J7
Beckenham Crematorium Gt Lon 37 J7
Beckermet Cumb 100 D9
Beckett End Norfk 75 Q11
Beckfoot Cumb 94 D3
Beckfoot Cumb 100 G10
Beck Foot Cumb 102 B11
Beckford Cumb 109 N11
Beckford Worcs 47 J7
Beckhampton Wilts 33 L11
Beck Hole N York 105 M10
Beckingham Lincs 85 Q10
Beckingham Notts 85 N3
Beckington Somset 20 F4
Beckjay Shrops 56 F9
Beckley E Susx 26 E7
Beckley Hants 13 M5
Beckley Oxon 34 G2
Beck Row Suffk 63 L5
Becks C Brad 96 F11
Beck Side Cumb 94 E4
Beck Side Cumb 94 H4
Beckton Gt Lon 37 K4
Beckwithshaw N York 97 L10
Becontree Gt Lon 37 L3
Bedale N York 97 L3
Bedburn Dur 103 L4
Bedchester Dorset 20 G11
Beddau Rhondd 30 E7
Beddgelert Gwynd 67 K5
Beddingham E Susx 25 K9
Beddington Gt Lon 36 H7
Beddington Corner Gt Lon 36 G7
Bedfield Suffk 65 J8
Bedfield Little Green Suffk 65 J8
Bedford Bed 61 M11
Bedford Crematorium Bed 61 N10
Bedgebury Cross Kent 26 B5
Bedham W Susx 24 B6
Bedhampton Hants 15 K5
Bedingfield Suffk 64 H8
Bedingfield Green Suffk 64 H8
Bedlam N York 97 L8
Bedlington Nthumb 113 L4
Bedlinog Myr Td 30 E4
Bedminster Bristl 31 Q10
Bedminster Down Bristl 31 Q10
Bedmond Herts 50 C10
Bednall Staffs 70 H11
Bedrule Border 118 B7
Bedstone Shrops 56 F9
Bedwas Caerph 30 G7
Bedwellty Caerph 30 G4
Bedworth Warwks 59 N7
Bedworth Woodlands Warwks 59 M7
Beeby Leics 72 H9
Beech Hants 23 J7
Beech Staffs 70 F7
Beech Hill W Berk 23 J2
Beechingstoke Wilts 21 L3
Beedon W Berk 34 E9
Beedon Hill W Berk 34 E9
Beeford E R Yk 99 N10
Beeley Derbys 84 C7
Beelsby NE Lin 93 M10
Beenham W Berk 34 G11
Beenham's Heath W & M 35 M9
Beeny Cnwll 5 J3
Beer Devon 10 E7
Beer Somset 19 M8
Beercrocombe Somset 19 K10
Beer Hackett Dorset 11 N2
Beesands Devon 7 L10
Beesby Lincs 87 N4
Beeson Devon 7 L10
Beeston C Beds 61 Q11
Beeston Ches W 69 P3
Beeston Leeds 90 H4
Beeston Norfk 76 C8
Beeston Notts 72 E3
Beeston Regis Norfk 76 H3
Beeswing D & G 109 J7
Beetham Cumb 95 K5
Beetham Somset 10 F2
Beetley Norfk 76 D8
Began Cardif 30 H8
Begbroke Oxon 34 E2
Begdale Cambs 75 J9
Begelly Pembks 41 M9
Beggarington Hill Leeds 90 H6
Beggar's Bush Powys 45 K2
Beguildy Powys 56 B9
Beighton Norfk 77 N10
Beighton Sheff 84 F4
Beinn Na Faoghla W Isls 168 d12
Beith N Ayrs 125 J6
Bekesbourne Kent 39 L10
Bekesbourne Hill Kent 39 L10
Belaugh Norfk 77 K8
Belbroughton Worcs 58 D9
Belchalwell Dorset 12 C3

Belchalwell Street Dorset 12 C3
Belchamp Otten Essex 52 D3
Belchamp St Paul Essex 52 C3
Belchamp Walter Essex 52 D3
Belchford Lincs 87 J5
Belford Nthumb 119 M4
Belgrave C Leic 72 F9
Belhelvie Abers 151 N4
Belhinnie Abers 150 D2
Bellabeg Abers 150 B5
Bellamore Herefs 45 M6
Bellanoch Ag & B 130 F9
Bellasize E R Yk 92 D5
Bellaty Angus 142 C6
Bell Bar Herts 50 G9
Bell Busk N York 96 D9
Belleau Lincs 87 M5
Bell End Worcs 58 D9
Bellerby N York 96 H2
Bellever Devon 8 G9
Belle Vue Cumb 110 G9
Belle Vue Wakefd 91 J7
Bellfield S Lans 116 D6
Bellfield S Lans 126 E11
Bell Heath Worcs 58 D9
Bell Hill Hants 23 K10
Bellingdon Bucks 35 P3
Bellingham Nthumb 112 B4
Belloch Ag & B 120 C4
Bellochantuy Ag & B 120 C5
Bell o' th' Hill Ches W 69 P5
Bellows Cross Dorset 13 J2
Bells Cross Suffk 64 H11
Bellshill N Lans 126 C5
Bellshill Nthumb 119 M4
Bellside N Lans 126 E6
Bellsquarry W Loth 127 J4
Bells Yew Green E Susx 25 P3
Belluton BaNES 20 B2
Belmaduthy Highld 156 A6
Belmesthorpe Rutlnd 73 Q8
Belmont Bl w D 89 K7
Belmont Gt Lon 36 G8
Belmont S Ayrs 114 F4
Belmont Shet 169 s3
Belnacraig Abers 150 B4
Belowda Cnwll 4 F9
Belper Derbys 84 D11
Belper Lane End Derbys 84 D11
Belph Derbys 84 H5
Belsay Nthumb 112 G5
Belses Border 117 R5
Belsford Devon 7 K7
Belsize Herts 50 B10
Belstead Suffk 53 K3
Belstone Devon 8 F6
Belthorn Lancs 89 L6
Beltinge Kent 39 L8
Beltingham Nthumb 111 Q8
Beltoft N Linc 92 D9
Belton Leics 72 C6
Belton Lincs 73 N3
Belton N Linc 92 C9
Belton Norfk 77 P11
Belton Rutlnd 73 L10
Belton House Lincs 73 N3
Beltring Kent 37 Q11
Belvedere Gt Lon 37 L5
Belvoir Leics 73 L4
Bembridge IoW 14 H9
Bemerton Wilts 21 M8
Bempton E R Yk 99 P6
Benacre Suffk 65 Q5
Benbecula W Isls 168 d12
Benbecula Airport W Isls 168 c12
Benbuie D & G 115 P8
Benderloch Ag & B 138 G10
Benenden Kent 26 D5
Benfieldside Dur 112 G10
Bengates Norfk 77 L6
Bengeo Herts 50 H8
Bengeworth Worcs 47 K6
Benhall Green Suffk 65 M9
Benhall Street Suffk 65 M9
Benholm Abers 143 Q4
Beningbrough N York 98 A9
Benington Herts 50 G6
Benington Lincs 87 L11
Benington Sea End Lincs 87 M11
Benllech IoA 79 J8
Benmore Ag & B 131 N10
Bennacott Cnwll 5 M3
Bennan N Ayrs 121 J7
Bennet Head Cumb 101 M6
Bennetland E R Yk 92 D5
Bennett End Bucks 35 L5
Ben Nevis Highld 139 M3
Benniworth Lincs 86 H4
Benover Kent 26 B2
Ben Rhydding C Brad 96 H11
Benslie N Ayrs 125 J9
Benson Oxon 34 H6
Bentfield Green Essex 51 M5
Benthall Shrops 57 M4
Bentham Gloucs 46 H11
Benthoul C Aber 151 L7
Bentlawnt Shrops 56 E4
Bentley Donc 91 P9
Bentley E R Yk 92 H3
Bentley Hants 23 L6
Bentley Suffk 53 K4
Bentley Warwks 59 L5
Bentley Crematorium Essex 51 N11
Bentley Heath Herts 50 G11
Bentley Heath Solhll 59 J9
Benton Devon 17 M4
Bentpath D & G 110 F2
Bentwichen Devon 17 N5
Bentworth Hants 23 J6
Benvie Angus 142 E11
Benville Dorset 11 L4
Benwick Cambs 62 D2
Beoley Worcs 58 G11
Beoraidbeg Highld 145 L9
Bepton W Susx 23 N11
Berden Essex 51 L5
Berea Pembks 40 E4
Bere Alston Devon 6 C5
Bere Ferrers Devon 6 D6
Berepper Cnwll 2 H9
Bere Regis Dorset 12 D6
Bergh Apton Norfk 77 L11
Berhill Somset 19 M7
Berinsfield Oxon 34 G5
Berkeley Gloucs 32 C5
Berkeley Heath Gloucs 32 C5
Berkeley Road Gloucs 32 D4
Berkhamsted Herts 35 Q3

Berkley Somset 20 F5
Berkswell Solhll 59 K9
Bermondsey Gt Lon 36 H5
Bermuda Warwks 59 N7
Bernera Highld 145 P3
Bernisdale Highld 152 G7
Berrick Prior Oxon 34 H6
Berrick Salome Oxon 34 H6
Berriedale Highld 163 Q2
Berrier Cumb 101 L5
Berriew Powys 56 B4
Berrington Nthumb 119 K2
Berrington Shrops 57 J3
Berrington Worcs 57 K11
Berrington Green Worcs 57 K11
Berrow Somset 19 J4
Berrow Worcs 46 E8
Berrow Green Worcs 46 D3
Berry Brow Kirk 90 E8
Berry Cross Devon 16 H9
Berry Down Cross Devon 17 K3
Berryfields Bucks 49 L11
Berry Hill Gloucs 31 Q2
Berry Hill Pembks 41 L2
Berryhillock Moray 158 D5
Berryhillock Moray 158 D7
Berrynarbor Devon 17 K2
Berry Pomeroy Devon 7 L6
Berry's Green Gt Lon 37 K9
Bersham Wrexhm 69 K5
Berstead W Susx 15 P6
Berthengam Flints 80 G9
Berwick E Susx 25 M9
Berwick Bassett Wilts 33 L10
Berwick Hill Nthumb 113 J5
Berwick St James Wilts 21 L7
Berwick St John Wilts 20 H10
Berwick St Leonard Wilts 20 H8
Berwick-upon-Tweed Nthumb 129 P9
Bescaby Leics 73 L5
Bescar Lancs 88 D8
Besford Shrops 69 Q9
Besford Worcs 46 H6
Bessels Leigh Oxon 34 E4
Besses o' th' Barn Bury 89 N9
Bessingby E R Yk 99 P7
Bessingham Norfk 76 H4
Bestbeech Hill E Susx 25 P4
Besthorpe Norfk 64 F2
Besthorpe Notts 85 P8
Bestwood Village Notts 85 J11
Beswick E R Yk 99 L11
Betchcott Shrops 56 G5
Betchworth Surrey 36 F10
Bethania Cerdgn 43 L2
Bethania Gwynd 67 N6
Bethel Gwynd 68 C7
Bethel Gwynd 79 J11
Bethel IoA 78 F10
Bethel Powys 68 F10
Bethersden Kent 26 F3
Bethesda Gwynd 79 L11
Bethesda Pembks 41 L7
Bethlehem Carmth 43 N9
Bethnal Green Gt Lon 36 H4
Betley Staffs 70 D5
Betsham Kent 37 P6
Betteshanger Kent 39 P11
Bettiscombe Dorset 10 H4
Bettisfield Wrexhm 69 N7
Betton Shrops 70 B7
Betton Strange Shrops 57 J3
Bettws Newpt 31 J6
Bettws Cedewain Powys 55 Q5
Bettws Evan Cerdgn 42 F5
Bettws-Newydd Mons 31 L3
Bettyhill Highld 166 B4
Betws Brdgnd 29 P7
Betws Carmth 28 H4
Betws Bledrws Cerdgn 43 L4
Betws Garmon Gwynd 67 J3
Betws Gwerfil Goch Denbgs 68 D5
Betws-y-Coed Conwy 67 P3
Betws-yn-Rhos Conwy 80 C10
Beulah Cerdgn 42 E5
Beulah Powys 44 C4
Bevendean Br & H 24 H9
Bevercotes Notts 85 M6
Beverley E R Yk 92 H3
Beverston Gloucs 32 G6
Bevington Gloucs 32 C5
Bewaldeth Cumb 100 H4
Bewcastle Cumb 111 L6
Bewdley Worcs 57 P9
Bewerley N York 97 J7
Bewholme E R Yk 99 P11
Bewlbridge Kent 25 Q4
Bexhill E Susx 26 B10
Bexley Gt Lon 37 L6
Bexleyheath Gt Lon 37 L5
Bexleyhill W Susx 23 P9
Bexon Kent 38 E10
Bexwell Norfk 75 M10
Beyton Suffk 64 C9
Beyton Green Suffk 64 C9
Bhaltos W Isls 168 f4
Bhatarsaigh W Isls 168 b18
Bibstone S Glos 32 C6
Bibury Gloucs 33 M3
Bicester Oxon 48 G10
Bickenhill Solhll 59 J8
Bicker Lincs 74 D3
Bicker Bar Lincs 74 D3
Bicker Gauntlet Lincs 74 D3
Bickershaw Wigan 82 D4
Bickerstaffe Lancs 81 N4
Bickerton Ches W 69 P4
Bickerton Devon 7 L11
Bickerton N York 97 Q10
Bickerton Nthumb 119 J10
Bickford Staffs 58 C2
Bickington Devon 7 L4
Bickington Devon 17 J5
Bickleigh Devon 6 E6
Bickleigh Devon 9 M3
Bickleton Devon 17 J5
Bickley Ches W 69 P5
Bickley Gt Lon 37 K7
Bickley N York 99 J2
Bickley Worcs 57 L10
Bickley Moss Ches W 69 P5
Bicknoller Somset 18 F7
Bicknor Kent 38 E10
Bickton Hants 13 L3
Bicton Herefs 45 P2
Bicton Shrops 56 H2
Bicton Shrops 56 M11

Bidborough Kent 25 N2
Bidden Hants 23 K5
Biddenden Kent 26 E4
Biddenden Green Kent 26 E3
Biddenham Bed 61 M10
Biddestone Wilts 32 G10
Biddisham Somset 19 L4
Biddlesden Bucks 48 H7
Biddlestone Nthumb 119 J9
Biddulph Staffs 70 F3
Biddulph Moor Staffs 70 G3
Bideford Devon 16 H6
Bidford-on-Avon Warwks 47 M4
Bidston Wirral 81 K6
Bielby E R Yk 92 C2
Bieldside C Aber 151 M7
Bierley IoW 14 F11
Bierton Bucks 49 M11
Big Balcraig D & G 107 L9
Bigbury Devon 6 H9
Bigbury-on-Sea Devon 6 H10
Bigby Lincs 93 J9
Big Carlae D & G 115 N8
Biggar Cumb 94 D7
Biggar S Lans 116 E3
Biggin Derbys 71 M3
Biggin Derbys 71 P5
Biggin N York 91 N4
Biggin N York 97 Q11
Biggin Hill Gt Lon 37 K9
Biggin Hill Airport Gt Lon 37 K8
Biggleswade C Beds 50 E2
Bigholms D & G 110 F4
Bighouse Highld 166 E4
Bighton Hants 22 H8
Biglands Cumb 110 E10
Bignor W Susx 15 Q4
Bigrigg Cumb 100 D8
Big Sand Highld 160 B11
Bigton Shet 169 q11
Bilborough C Nott 72 E2
Bilbrook Somset 18 D6
Bilbrook Staffs 58 C4
Bilbrough N York 98 A11
Bilbster Highld 167 N6
Bildershaw Dur 103 P6
Bildeston Suffk 52 G2
Billacott Cnwll 5 M3
Billericay Essex 37 Q2
Billesdon Leics 73 J10
Billesley Warwks 47 M3
Billingborough Lincs 74 B4
Billinge St Hel 82 B4
Billingford Norfk 64 H6
Billingford Norfk 76 E7
Billingham S on T 104 E6
Billinghay Lincs 86 G10
Billingley Barns 91 L10
Billingshurst W Susx 24 C5
Billingsley Shrops 57 N8
Billington C Beds 49 P10
Billington Lancs 89 L3
Billington Staffs 70 F10
Billockby Norfk 77 N9
Billy Row Dur 103 N3
Bilsborrow Lancs 88 G3
Bilsby Lincs 87 N5
Bilsham W Susx 15 Q6
Bilsington Kent 27 J4
Bilsthorpe Notts 85 K8
Bilsthorpe Moor Notts 85 L8
Bilston Mdloth 127 P5
Bilston Wolves 58 E5
Bilstone Leics 72 B9
Bilting Kent 27 J2
Bilton E R Yk 93 L4
Bilton N York 97 M9
Bilton Nthumb 119 P8
Bilton Warwks 59 Q10
Bilton-in-Ainsty N York 97 Q11
Bilton Banks Nthumb 119 P8
Binbrook Lincs 86 H2
Binchester Blocks Dur 103 P4
Bincombe Dorset 11 P8
Binegar Somset 20 B5
Bines Green W Susx 24 E7
Binfield Br For 35 M10
Binfield Heath Oxon 35 K9
Bingfield Nthumb 112 E6
Bingham Notts 73 J3
Bingham's Melcombe Dorset 12 C4
Bingley C Brad 90 E3
Bings Shrops 69 P11
Binham Norfk 76 D4
Binley Covtry 59 N9
Binley Hants 22 D4
Binley Woods Warwks 59 N9
Binnegar Dorset 12 E7
Binniehill Falk 126 F3
Binscombe Surrey 23 Q5
Binsey Oxon 34 E3
Binstead IoW 14 G8
Binsted Hants 23 L6
Binsted W Susx 15 Q5
Binton Warwks 47 M4
Bintree Norfk 76 E7
Binweston Shrops 56 E4
Birch Essex 52 F8
Birch Rochdl 89 P9
Bircham Newton Norfk 75 Q4
Bircham Tofts Norfk 75 Q4
Birchanger Essex 51 M6
Birchanger Green Services Essex 51 M6
Birch Cross Staffs 71 L8
Birchencliffe Kirk 90 E7
Bircher Herefs 45 H11
Birchfield Birm 58 G6
Birch Green Essex 52 F8
Birch Green Herts 50 G8
Birch Green Worcs 46 G5
Birchgrove Cardif 30 G9
Birchgrove Swans 29 K5
Birchgrove W Susx 25 K5
Birch Heath Ches W 69 P2
Birch Hill Ches W 81 Q10
Birchington Kent 39 N8
Birchington-on-Sea Kent 39 N8
Birchley Heath Warwks 59 L6
Birchmoor Warwks 59 L4
Birchmoor Green C Beds 49 Q8
Birchover Derbys 84 B8
Birch Services Rochdl 89 N9
Birch Vale Derbys 83 M7
Birchwood Lincs 86 B7
Birchwood Somset 10 E2
Birchwood Warrtn 82 E6
Bircotes Notts 85 K2
Birdbrook Essex 52 B3
Birdforth N York 97 Q5
Birdham W Susx 15 M6

Birdingbury Warwks 59 P11
Birdlip Gloucs 32 H2
Birdoswald Cumb 111 M8
Birdsall N York 98 G8
Birds Edge Kirk 90 G9
Birds Green Essex 51 N9
Birdsgreen Shrops 57 P7
Birdsmoorgate Dorset 10 H4
Bird Street Suffk 64 E11
Birdwell Barns 91 J11
Birdwood Gloucs 46 D11
Birgham Border 118 E3
Birichin Highld 162 H9
Birkacre Lancs 88 H7
Birkby N York 104 B9
Birkdale Sefton 88 C7
Birkenbog Abers 158 C4
Birkenhead Wirral 81 L7
Birkenhead (Queensway) Tunnel Lpool 81 L7
Birkenhills Abers 158 H8
Birkenshaw Kirk 90 G5
Birkhall Abers 149 Q6
Birkhill Angus 142 F11
Birkhill D & G 117 J4
Birkholme Lincs 73 N6
Birkin N York 91 P5
Birks Leeds 90 H4
Birley Herefs 45 P3
Birley Carr Sheff 84 D3
Birling Kent 37 Q7
Birling Nthumb 119 P9
Birling Gap E Susx 25 N11
Birlingham Worcs 46 H6
Birmingham Birm 58 G7
Birmingham Airport Solhll 59 J8
Birnam P & K 141 P8
Birness Abers 159 N11
Birse Abers 150 G8
Birsemore Abers 150 G8
Birstall Kirk 90 G5
Birstall Leics 72 F9
Birstwith N York 97 L8
Birthorpe Lincs 74 B4
Birtley Gatesd 113 L9
Birtley Herefs 56 F11
Birtley Nthumb 112 D5
Birtley Crematorium Gatesd 113 L9
Birts Street Worcs 46 E7
Bisbrooke Rutlnd 73 M11
Biscathorpe Lincs 86 H4
Biscovey Cnwll 3 R3
Bisham W & M 35 M8
Bishampton Worcs 47 J3
Bish Mill Devon 17 N7
Bishop Auckland Dur 103 P5
Bishopbridge Lincs 86 D3
Bishopbriggs E Duns 125 P3
Bishop Burton E R Yk 92 G3
Bishop Middleham Dur 104 B4
Bishopmill Moray 157 N5
Bishop Monkton N York 97 M7
Bishop Norton Lincs 86 C3
Bishopsbourne Kent 39 L11
Bishops Cannings Wilts 21 L2
Bishop's Castle Shrops 56 F6
Bishop's Caundle Dorset 11 Q3
Bishop's Cleeve Gloucs 47 J9
Bishop's Frome Herefs 46 C5
Bishops Gate Surrey 35 Q11
Bishop's Green Essex 51 Q7
Bishop's Green Hants 22 F2
Bishop's Hull Somset 18 H10
Bishop's Itchington Warwks 48 C3
Bishops Lydeard Somset 18 G9
Bishop's Norton Gloucs 46 F10
Bishop's Nympton Devon 17 P7
Bishop's Offley Staffs 70 D9
Bishop's Stortford Herts 51 L6
Bishop's Sutton Hants 22 H7
Bishop's Tachbrook Warwks 48 B2
Bishop's Tawton Devon 17 K6
Bishopsteignton Devon 7 N3
Bishopstoke Hants 22 E10
Bishopston Swans 28 G7
Bishopstone Bucks 35 M2
Bishopstone E Susx 25 L10
Bishopstone Herefs 45 N5
Bishopstone Swindn 33 P8
Bishopstone Wilts 21 L9
Bishopstrow Wilts 20 G7
Bishop Sutton BaNES 19 Q3
Bishop's Waltham Hants 22 F11
Bishopswood Somset 10 F2
Bishop's Wood Staffs 58 B3
Bishopsworth Bristl 31 Q11
Bishop Thornton N York 97 L7
Bishopthorpe C York 98 B11
Bishopton Darltn 104 B6
Bishopton Rens 125 L3
Bishopton Warwks 47 P3
Bishop Wilton E R Yk 98 F9
Bishton Newpt 31 L7
Bishton Staffs 71 J10
Bisley Gloucs 32 H3
Bisley Surrey 23 Q3
Bisley Camp Surrey 23 Q3
Bispham Bpool 88 C2
Bispham Green Lancs 88 F8
Bissoe Cnwll 3 K5
Bisterne Hants 13 L4
Bitchet Green Kent 37 N10
Bitchfield Lincs 73 N6
Bittadon Devon 17 J3
Bittaford Devon 6 H7
Bittering Norfk 76 C8
Bitterley Shrops 57 K9
Bitterne C Sotn 14 E5
Bitteswell Leics 59 Q7
Bitton S Glos 32 C11
Bix Oxon 35 K8
Bixter Shet 169 q8
Blaby Leics 72 F11
Blackadder Border 129 J10
Blackawton Devon 7 L8
Blackbeck Cumb 100 D9
Blackborough Devon 10 D3
Blackborough End Norfk 75 M8
Black Bourton Oxon 33 Q4
Blackboys E Susx 25 M6
Blackbrook Derbys 84 D11
Blackbrook St Hel 81 Q4
Blackbrook Staffs 70 D7

Blackbrook – Boyton Cross 259

ackbrook Surrey 36 E11
ackburn Abers 151 L5
ackburn Bl w D 89 K5
ackburn Rothm 84 E2
ackburn W Loth 126 H4
ackburn with Darwen Services Bl w D 89 K6
ack Callerton N u Ty 113 J7
ack Car Norfk 64 F2
ack Corner W Susx 24 G3
ackcraig E Ayrs 115 M6
ack Crofts Ag & B 138 G11
ack Cross Cnwll 4 E9
ackden Heath Ches E 82 G10
ackdog Abers 151 P5
ack Dog Devon 9 K3
ackdown Devon 8 D9
ackdown Dorset 10 H4
ackdyke Cumb 109 P10
acker Barns 91 J9
acker Hill Barns 91 K10
ackfen Gt Lon 37 L6
ackfield Hants 14 D6
ackford Cumb 110 G8
ackford P & K 133 P6
ackford Somset 19 M5
ackford Somset 20 C9
ackfordby Leics 72 A7
ackgang IoW 14 E11
ackhall C Edin 127 M2
ackhall Dur 104 E3
ackhall Colliery Dur 104 E3
ackhall Mill Gatesd 112 H9
ackhaugh Border 117 N3
ackheath Essex 52 H7
ackheath Gt Lon 37 J5
ackheath Sandw 58 E7
ackheath Suffk 65 N7
ackheath Surrey 36 B11
ack Heddon Nthumb 112 G5
ackhill Abers 159 Q6
ackhill Abers 159 Q9
ackhill Dur 112 G10
ackhill of Clackriach Abers 159 M8
ackhorse Devon 9 N6
ackjack Lincs 74 E3
ackland Wilts 33 K11
ack Lane Ends Lancs 89 Q2
acklaw D & G 116 E9
ackley Manch 83 J4
ackley Crematorium Manch 82 H4
acklunans P & K 142 A5
ackmarstone Herefs 45 Q7
ackmill Brdgnd 29 P7
ackmoor Hants 23 L8
ack Moor Leeds 90 H3
ackmoor N Som 19 N2
ackmoorfoot Kirk 90 D8
ackmore Essex 51 P10
ackmore End Essex 52 B5
ackmore End Herts 50 E7
ack Mountains 45 K9
ackness Falk 127 K2
acknest Hants 23 L6
acknest W & M 35 Q11
ack Notley Essex 52 C7
acko Lancs 89 P2
ack Pill Swans 28 H6
ackpool Bpool 88 C3
ackpool Devon 7 L4
ackpool Devon 7 M9
ackpool Airport Lancs 88 C4
ackpool Gate Cumb 111 K5
ackpool Zoo Bpool 88 C3
ackridge W Loth 126 F4
ackrock Cnwll 2 H7
ackrock Mons 30 H2
ackrod Bolton 89 J8
acksboat Moray 157 M10
ackshaw D & G 109 M7
ackshaw Head Calder 90 B5
acksmith's Green Suffk 64 G8
acksnape Bl w D 89 L6
ackstone W Susx 24 F7
ack Street Suffk 65 Q4
ack Tar Pembks 41 J9
ackthorn Oxon 48 H11
ackthorpe Suffk 64 C9
acktoft E R Yk 92 D6
acktop C Aber 151 M7
ack Torrington Devon 8 C3
ackwall Derbys 71 P5
ackwall Tunnel Gt Lon 37 J4
ackwater Cnwll 3 J4
ackwater Hants 23 M3
ackwater IoW 14 F9
ackwater Somset 19 J11
ackwaterfoot N Ayrs 120 H6
ackwell Cumb 110 H10
ackwell Darltn 103 Q8
ackwell Derbys 83 P10
ackwell Derbys 84 F9
ackwell Warwks 47 P6
ackwell Worcs 58 E10
ackwellsend Green Gloucs 46 E9
ackwood Caerph 30 G5
ackwood D & G 109 K3
ackwood S Lans 126 D9
ackwood Hill Staffs 70 G3
acon Ches W 81 M11
adbean Kent 27 L2
adnoch D & G 107 M7
adon Oxon 34 E2
adon Somset 19 M10
aenannerch Cerdgn 42 D5
aenau Ffestiniog Gwynd 67 N5
aenavon Torfn 31 J3
aenavon Industrial Landscape Torfn 30 H3
aen Dyryn Powys 44 C7
aenffos Pembks 41 N3
aengarw Brdgnd 29 P6
aengeuffordd Cerdgn 54 E8
aengwrach Neath 29 N3
aengwynfi Neath 29 N5
aenllechau Rhondd 30 D5
aenpennal Cerdgn 43 M2
aenplwyf Cerdgn 54 D9
aenporth Cerdgn 42 E5
aenrhondda Rhondd 29 P5
aenwaun Carmth 41 P5
aen-y-Coed Carmth 42 F9
aen-y-cwm Blae G 30 F2
aenycwm Cerdgn 55 J9
aen-y-cwm Rhondd 29 P5
agdon N Som 19 P3
Blagdon Somset 18 H11
Blagdon Torbay 7 M6
Blagdon Hill Somset 18 H11
Blagill Cumb 111 P11
Blaguegate Lancs 88 F9
Blaich Highld 139 J2
Blain Highld 138 B4
Blaina Blae G 30 H3
Blair Atholl P & K 141 L4
Blair Drummond Stirlg 133 L8
Blairgowrie P & K 142 B8
Blairhall Fife 134 B10
Blairingone P & K 134 B8
Blairlogie Stirlg 133 N8
Blairmore Ag & B 131 P11
Blairmore Highld 164 E5
Blair's Ferry Ag & B 124 B4
Blaisdon Gloucs 46 D11
Blakebrook Worcs 57 Q9
Blakedown Worcs 58 C9
Blake End Essex 52 B7
Blakeley Lane Staffs 70 H5
Blakemere Ches W 82 C10
Blakemere Herefs 45 M6
Blakemore Devon 7 K6
Blakenall Heath Wsall 58 F4
Blakeney Gloucs 32 C3
Blakeney Norfk 76 E3
Blakenhall Ches E 70 C5
Blakenhall Wolves 58 D5
Blakeshall Worcs 58 B8
Blakesley Nhants 48 H4
Blanchland Nthumb 112 E10
Blandford Camp Dorset 12 F3
Blandford Forum Dorset 12 E3
Blandford St Mary Dorset 12 E3
Bland Hill N York 97 K10
Blanefield Stirlg 125 N2
Blankney Lincs 86 E8
Blantyre S Lans 126 B6
Blàr a' Chaorainn Highld 139 L4
Blargie Highld 147 Q9
Blarmachfoldach Highld 139 K4
Blashford Hants 13 L3
Blaston Leics 73 L11
Blatherwycke Nhants 73 P11
Blawith Cumb 94 F3
Blawquhairn D & G 108 D4
Blaxhall Suffk 65 M10
Blaxton Donc 91 R10
Blaydon Gatesd 113 J8
Bleadney Somset 19 N5
Bleadon N Som 19 K3
Bleak Street Somset 20 E8
Blean Kent 39 K9
Bleasby Lincs 86 F4
Bleasby Notts 85 M11
Bleasdale Lancs 95 M11
Bleatarn Cumb 102 D8
Bleathwood Herefs 57 K10
Blebocraigs Fife 135 L4
Bleddfa Powys 56 C11
Bledington Gloucs 47 P10
Bledlow Bucks 35 L4
Bledlow Ridge Bucks 35 L5
Bleet Wilts 20 G3
Blegbie E Loth 128 D7
Blencarn Cumb 102 B4
Blencogo Cumb 110 C11
Blendworth Hants 15 K4
Blenheim Palace Oxon 48 D11
Blennerhasset Cumb 100 G2
Bletchingdon Oxon 48 F11
Bletchingley Surrey 36 H10
Bletchley M Keyn 49 N8
Bletchley Shrops 69 R8
Bletchley Park Museum M Keyn 49 N8
Bletherston Pembks 41 L6
Bletsoe Bed 61 M9
Blewbury Oxon 34 F7
Blickling Norfk 76 H6
Blidworth Notts 85 J9
Blidworth Bottoms Notts 85 J10
Blindburn Nthumb 118 F8
Blindcrake Cumb 100 F4
Blindley Heath Surrey 37 J11
Blisland Cnwll 5 J7
Blissford Hants 13 L2
Bliss Gate Worcs 57 N10
Blisworth Nhants 49 K4
Blithbury Staffs 71 K11
Blitterlees Cumb 109 P10
Blockley Gloucs 47 N8
Blofield Norfk 77 L10
Blofield Heath Norfk 77 L9
Blo Norton Norfk 64 E6
Bloomfield Border 118 A6
Blore Staffs 70 C8
Blore Staffs 71 L5
Blounce Hants 23 K5
Blounts Green Staffs 71 K8
Blowick Sefton 88 D7
Bloxham Oxon 48 D7
Bloxholm Lincs 86 E10
Bloxwich Wsall 58 E4
Bloxworth Dorset 12 E6
Blubberhouses N York 97 J9
Blue Anchor Cnwll 4 E10
Blue Anchor Somset 18 D6
Blue Bell Hill Kent 38 B9
Blue John Cavern Derbys 83 P8
Blundellsands Sefton 81 L5
Blundeston Suffk 65 Q2
Blunham C Beds 61 Q10
Blunsdon St Andrew Swindn 33 M7
Bluntington Worcs 58 D10
Bluntisham Cambs 62 E6
Blunts Cnwll 5 N9
Blunts Green Warwks 58 H11
Blurton C Stke 70 F6
Blyborough Lincs 86 B2
Blyford Suffk 65 N6
Blymhill Staffs 57 Q2
Blymhill Lawn Staffs 57 Q2
Blyth Notts 85 K3
Blyth Nthumb 113 M4
Blyth Bridge Border 127 L8
Blythburgh Suffk 65 N6
Blyth Crematorium Nthumb 113 M4
Blythe Border 128 F10
Blythe Bridge Staffs 70 H6
Blythe End Warwks 59 K6
Blythe Marsh Staffs 70 H6
Blyth Services Notts 85 K3
Blyton Lincs 85 Q2
Boarhills Fife 135 P5
Boarhunt Hants 14 H5
Boarley Kent 38 C10
Boarsgreave Lancs 89 N6
Boarshead E Susx 25 M4
Boar's Head Wigan 88 H9
Boars Hill Oxon 34 E4
Boarstall Bucks 34 H2
Boasley Cross Devon 8 D6
Boath Highld 155 Q3
Boat of Garten Highld 148 G4
Bobbing Kent 38 E8
Bobbington Staffs 57 Q6
Bobbingworth Essex 51 M9
Bocaddon Cnwll 5 K10
Bocking Essex 52 C7
Bocking Churchstreet Essex 52 C6
Bockleton Worcs 46 A2
Boconnoc Cnwll 5 J9
Boddam Abers 159 R9
Boddam Shet 169 q12
Boddington Gloucs 46 G9
Bodedern IoA 78 E8
Bodelwyddan Denbgs 80 E9
Bodenham Herefs 45 Q4
Bodenham Wilts 21 N9
Bodenham Moor Herefs 45 Q4
Bodewryd IoA 78 G6
Bodfari Denbgs 80 F10
Bodffordd IoA 78 G9
Bodfuan Gwynd 66 E7
Bodham Norfk 76 G3
Bodiam E Susx 26 C6
Bodicote Oxon 48 E7
Bodieve Cnwll 4 F7
Bodinnick Cnwll 5 J11
Bodle Street Green E Susx 25 Q8
Bodmin Cnwll 4 H8
Bodmin Moor Cnwll 5 K6
Bodney Norfk 64 A2
Bodorgan IoA 78 F11
Bodsham Kent 27 K2
Bodwen Cnwll 4 G9
Bodymoor Heath Warwks 59 J5
Bogallan Highld 156 A7
Bogbrae Abers 159 P10
Bogend S Ayrs 125 L11
Boggs Holdings E Loth 128 C5
Boghall Mdloth 127 N4
Boghall W Loth 126 H4
Boghead S Lans 126 D9
Bogmoor Moray 157 R5
Bogmuir Abers 143 L3
Bogniebrae Abers 158 E8
Bognor Regis W Susx 15 P7
Bogroy Highld 148 G3
Bogue D & G 108 D4
Bohetherick Cnwll 5 Q8
Bohortha Cnwll 3 M7
Bohuntine Highld 146 H11
Bojewyan Cnwll 2 B7
Bokiddick Cnwll 4 H9
Bolam Dur 103 N6
Bolam Nthumb 112 H4
Bolberry Devon 6 H11
Bold Heath St Hel 82 B7
Boldmere Birm 58 H6
Boldon Colliery S Tyne 113 M8
Boldre Hants 13 P5
Boldron Dur 103 K8
Bole Notts 85 N3
Bolehill Derbys 84 C9
Bole Hill Derbys 84 D6
Bolenowe Cnwll 2 H6
Bolham Devon 18 C11
Bolham Water Devon 10 D2
Bolingey Cnwll 3 K3
Bollington Ches E 83 K9
Bollington Cross Ches E 83 K9
Bollow Gloucs 32 D2
Bolney W Susx 24 G6
Bolnhurst Bed 61 N9
Bolnore W Susx 24 H6
Bolshan Angus 143 L7
Bolsover Derbys 84 G6
Bolster Moor Kirk 90 D7
Bolsterstone Sheff 90 H11
Boltby N York 97 Q3
Boltenstone Abers 150 C5
Bolter End Bucks 35 L6
Bolton Bolton 89 L9
Bolton Cumb 102 B6
Bolton E Loth 128 E6
Bolton E R Yk 98 F10
Bolton Nthumb 119 M8
Bolton Abbey N York 96 G10
Bolton Bridge N York 96 G10
Bolton-by-Bowland Lancs 96 A11
Boltonfellend Cumb 111 J7
Boltongate Cumb 100 H2
Bolton-le-Sands Lancs 95 K7
Bolton Low Houses Cumb 100 H2
Bolton New Houses Cumb 100 H2
Bolton-on-Swale N York 103 Q11
Bolton Percy N York 91 N2
Bolton Town End Lancs 95 K7
Bolton upon Dearne Barns 91 M10
Bolventor Cnwll 5 K6
Bomarsund Nthumb 113 L4
Bomere Heath Shrops 69 N11
Bonar Bridge Highld 162 E8
Bonawe Ag & B 139 J11
Bonby N Linc 92 H7
Boncath Pembks 41 P3
Bonchester Bridge Border 118 A8
Bonchurch IoW 14 G11
Bondleigh Devon 8 G4
Bonds Lancs 88 F2
Bonehill Devon 8 H9
Bonehill Staffs 59 J4
Bo'ness Falk 134 C11
Boney Hay Staffs 58 F2
Bonhill W Duns 125 K2
Boningale Shrops 57 Q4
Bonjedward Border 118 C6
Bonkle N Lans 126 E6
Bonnington Angus 143 K10
Bonnington Kent 27 J4
Bonnybank Fife 135 K7
Bonnybridge Falk 126 E2
Bonnykelly Abers 159 L7
Bonnyrigg Mdloth 127 Q4
Bonnyton Angus 142 E10
Bonsall Derbys 84 C9
Bonshaw Tower D & G 110 D6
Bont Mons 45 M11
Bontddu Gwynd 67 M11
Bont-Dolgadfan Powys 55 K4
Bont-goch Cerdgn 54 F7
Bonthorpe Lincs 87 N6
Bontnewydd Cerdgn 54 E11
Bontnewydd Gwynd 66 H3
Bontuchel Denbgs 68 E3
Bonvilston V Glam 30 E10
Bonwm Denbgs 68 F6
Bon-y-maen Swans 29 J5
Boode Devon 17 J4
Booker Bucks 35 M6
Booley Shrops 69 Q9
Boon Border 128 F10
Boon Hill Staffs 70 E4
Boorley Green Hants 14 F4
Boosbeck R & Cl 105 J7
Boose's Green Essex 52 D5
Boot Cumb 100 G10
Booth Calder 90 C5
Boothby Graffoe Lincs 86 C9
Boothby Pagnell Lincs 73 P4
Boothferry E R Yk 92 B5
Booth Green Ches E 83 K8
Boothstown Salfd 82 F4
Booth Town Calder 90 D5
Boothville Nhants 60 G8
Bootle Cumb 94 C3
Bootle Sefton 81 L5
Boots Green Ches W 82 G10
Boot Street Suffk 53 M2
Booze N York 103 K10
Boraston Shrops 57 L11
Bordeaux Guern 10 c1
Borden Kent 38 E9
Borden W Susx 23 M10
Border Cumb 110 C10
Borders Crematorium Border 117 R4
Bordley N York 96 D7
Boreham Essex 52 C10
Boreham Wilts 20 G6
Boreham Street E Susx 25 Q8
Borehamwood Herts 50 E11
Boreland D & G 110 C2
Boreraig Highld 152 B7
Boreton Shrops 57 J3
Borgh W Isls 168 b17
Borgh W Isls 168 j2
Borgie Highld 165 Q5
Borgue D & G 108 D11
Borgue Highld 167 K11
Borley Essex 52 D3
Borley Green Essex 52 D3
Borley Green Suffk 64 D9
Borneskitaig Highld 152 F3
Borness D & G 108 D11
Boroughbridge N York 97 N7
Borough Green Kent 37 P9
Borras Head Wrexhm 69 L4
Borrowash Derbys 72 C4
Borrowby N York 97 P3
Borrowby N York 105 L7
Borrowstoun Falk 134 B11
Borstal Medway 38 B8
Borth Cerdgn 54 E6
Borthwickbrae Border 117 N8
Borthwickshiels Border 117 N7
Borth-y-Gest Gwynd 67 K7
Borve Highld 152 G8
Borve W Isls 168 b17
Borve W Isls 168 f8
Borve W Isls 168 j2
Borwick Lancs 95 L6
Borwick Lodge Cumb 101 K11
Borwick Rails Cumb 94 D5
Bosavern Cnwll 2 B7
Bosbury Herefs 46 C6
Boscarne Cnwll 4 G8
Boscastle Cnwll 4 H3
Boscombe Bmouth 13 K6
Boscombe Wilts 21 P7
Boscoppa Cnwll 3 Q3
Bosham W Susx 15 M6
Bosham Hoe W Susx 15 M6
Bosherston Pembks 41 J12
Boskednan Cnwll 2 C7
Boskenna Cnwll 2 C9
Bosley Ches E 83 K11
Bosoughan Cnwll 4 D9
Bossall N York 98 E8
Bossiney Cnwll 4 H4
Bossingham Kent 27 L2
Bossington Somset 18 A5
Bostock Green Ches W 82 E11
Boston Lincs 74 F2
Boston Crematorium Lincs 87 K11
Boston Spa Leeds 97 P11
Boswarthan Cnwll 2 C7
Boswinger Cnwll 3 P5
Botallack Cnwll 2 B7
Botany Bay Gt Lon 50 G11
Botcheston Leics 72 D10
Botesdale Suffk 64 E6
Bothal Nthumb 113 K3
Bothampstead W Berk 34 F9
Bothamsall Notts 85 L6
Bothel Cumb 100 G3
Bothenhampton Dorset 11 K6
Bothwell S Lans 126 C6
Bothwell Services S Lans 126 C6
Botley Bucks 35 Q4
Botley Hants 14 F4
Botley Oxon 34 E3
Botolph Claydon Bucks 49 K10
Botolphs W Susx 24 E9
Botolph's Bridge Kent 27 K5
Bottesford Leics 73 L3
Bottesford N Linc 92 E9
Bottisham Cambs 62 H8
Bottomcraig Fife 135 K3
Bottom of Hutton Lancs 88 F5
Bottom o' th' Moor Bolton 89 K8
Bottoms Calder 89 Q6
Bottoms Cnwll 2 B9
Botts Green Warwks 59 K6
Botusfleming Cnwll 5 Q9
Botwnnog Gwynd 66 D8
Bough Beech Kent 37 L11
Boughrood Powys 44 G7
Boughspring Gloucs 31 Q5
Boughton Nhants 60 G7
Boughton Norfk 75 P10
Boughton Notts 85 L7
Boughton Aluph Kent 26 H2
Boughton End C Beds 49 Q7
Boughton Green Kent 38 C11
Boughton Malherbe Kent 26 E2
Boughton Monchelsea Kent 38 C11
Boughton Street Kent 39 J10
Boulby R & Cl 105 L7
Boulder Clough Calder 90 C6
Bouldnor IoW 14 C9
Bouldon Shrops 57 J7
Boulmer Nthumb 119 Q8
Boulston Pembks 41 J8
Boultham Lincs 86 C7
Bourn Cambs 62 D9
Bourne Lincs 74 A6
Bournebridge Essex 37 M2
Bournebrook Birm 58 F8
Bourne End Bed 61 M8
Bourne End Bucks 35 N7
Bourne End C Beds 49 Q6
Bourne End Herts 50 B9
Bournemouth Bmouth 13 J6
Bournemouth Airport Dorset 13 K5
Bournemouth Crematorium Bmouth 13 K6
Bournes Green Gloucs 32 H4
Bournes Green Sthend 38 F4
Bournheath Worcs 58 E10
Bournmoor Dur 113 M10
Bournstream Gloucs 32 D6
Bournville Birm 58 F8
Bourton Dorset 20 E8
Bourton N Som 19 L2
Bourton Oxon 33 P7
Bourton Shrops 57 K5
Bourton Wilts 21 K2
Bourton on Dunsmore Warwks 59 P10
Bourton-on-the-Hill Gloucs 47 N8
Bourton-on-the-Water Gloucs 47 N10
Bousd Ag & B 136 H3
Boustead Hill Cumb 110 E9
Bouth Cumb 94 G3
Bouthwaite N York 96 H6
Bouts Worcs 47 K3
Boveney Bucks 35 P9
Boveridge Dorset 13 J2
Bovey Tracey Devon 9 K9
Bovingdon Herts 50 B10
Bovingdon Green Bucks 35 M7
Bovinger Essex 51 M9
Bovington Dorset 12 D7
Bovington Camp Dorset 12 D7
Bow Cumb 110 F9
Bow Devon 7 L7
Bow Devon 8 H4
Bow Gt Lon 37 J4
Bow Ork 169 c7
Bowbank Dur 102 H6
Bow Brickhill M Keyn 49 P8
Bowbridge Gloucs 32 G3
Bowburn Dur 104 B3
Bowcombe IoW 14 E9
Bowd Devon 10 C6
Bowden Border 117 R4
Bowden Devon 7 L9
Bowden Hill Wilts 32 H11
Bowdon Traffd 82 G7
Bower Highld 167 M4
Bower Ashton Bristl 31 Q10
Bowerchalke Wilts 21 K10
Bowerhill Wilts 20 H2
Bower Hinton Somset 19 N11
Bower House Tye Suffk 52 G3
Bowermadden Highld 167 M4
Bowers Staffs 70 E7
Bowers Gifford Essex 38 C4
Bowershall Fife 134 D9
Bower's Row Leeds 91 L5
Bowes Dur 103 J8
Bowgreave Lancs 88 F2
Bowhouse D & G 109 M7
Bowithick Cnwll 5 K5
Bowker's Green Lancs 81 N4
Bowland Border 117 P2
Bowland Bridge Cumb 95 J3
Bowley Herefs 45 Q4
Bowley Town Herefs 45 Q4
Bowlhead Green Surrey 23 P7
Bowling C Brad 90 F4
Bowling W Duns 125 L3
Bowling Bank Wrexhm 69 L5
Bowling Green Worcs 46 F4
Bowmanstead Cumb 101 K11
Bowmore Ag & B 122 D8
Bowness-on-Solway Cumb 110 D8
Bowness-on-Windermere Cumb 101 M11
Bow of Fife Fife 135 J5
Bowriefauld Angus 143 J8
Bowscale Cumb 101 L4
Bowsden Nthumb 119 J2
Bowston Cumb 101 N11
Bow Street Cerdgn 54 E7
Bow Street Norfk 64 E2
Bowthorpe Norfk 76 H10
Box Gloucs 32 G4
Box Wilts 32 F11
Boxbush Gloucs 32 D2
Boxbush Gloucs 46 C10
Box End Bed 61 M11
Boxford Suffk 52 G3
Boxford W Berk 34 D10
Boxgrove W Susx 15 P5
Box Hill Surrey 36 E10
Boxley Kent 38 C10
Boxmoor Herts 50 B9
Box's Shop Cnwll 16 C11
Boxted Essex 52 G5
Boxted Essex 52 H5
Boxted Suffk 64 A11
Boxted Cross Essex 52 H5
Boxwell Gloucs 32 F6
Boxworth Cambs 62 D8
Boyden End Suffk 63 M9
Boyden Gate Kent 39 M8
Boylestone Derbys 71 M7
Boyndie Abers 158 F5
Boyndlie Abers 159 M5
Boynton E R Yk 99 N7
Boysack Angus 143 L8
Boys Hill Dorset 11 P2
Boythorpe Derbys 84 E7
Boyton Cnwll 5 N3
Boyton Suffk 53 Q2
Boyton Wilts 21 J7
Boyton Cross Essex 51 P9

Boyton End Suffk....52 B3
Bozeat Nhants....61 K9
Braaid IoM....80 d6
Brabling Green Suffk....65 K9
Brabourne Kent....27 K3
Brabourne Lees Kent....27 J3
Brabstermire Highld....167 P3
Bracadale Highld....152 F10
Braceborough Lincs....74 A8
Bracebridge Heath Lincs....86 C7
Bracebridge Low Fields
  Lincs....86 C7
Braceby Lincs....73 Q3
Bracewell Lancs....96 C11
Brackenfield Derbys....84 E9
Brackenhirst N Lans....126 C4
Brackenthwaite Cumb....110 E11
Brackenthwaite N York....97 L10
Bracklesham W Susx....15 M7
Brackletter Highld....146 F11
Brackley Nhants....48 G7
Brackley Hatch Nhants....48 H6
Bracknell Br For....35 N11
Braco P & K....133 N6
Bracobrae Moray....158 D7
Bracon Ash Norfk....64 H2
Bracora Highld....145 M9
Bracorina Highld....145 M9
Bradaford Devon....5 P3
Bradbourne Derbys....71 N4
Bradbury Dur....104 B5
Bradden Nhants....48 H5
Braddock Cnwll....5 K9
Bradeley C Stke....70 F4
Bradenham Bucks....35 M5
Bradenstoke Wilts....33 K9
Bradfield Devon....9 Q3
Bradfield Essex....53 K5
Bradfield Norfk....77 K5
Bradfield Sheff....84 C2
Bradfield W Berk....34 H10
Bradfield Combust Suffk....64 B10
Bradfield Green Ches E....70 B3
Bradfield Heath Essex....53 K5
Bradfield St Clare Suffk....64 C10
Bradfield St George
  Suffk....64 C10
Bradford C Brad....90 F4
Bradford Cnwll....5 J6
Bradford Devon....16 G10
Bradford Nthumb....112 G5
Bradford Nthumb....119 N4
Bradford Abbas Dorset....11 M2
Bradford Leigh Wilts....20 F2
Bradford-on-Avon Wilts....20 F2
Bradford-on-Tone
  Somset....18 G10
Bradford Peverell Dorset....11 P6
Bradiford Devon....17 K5
Brading IoW....14 H9
Bradley Derbys....71 N5
Bradley Hants....22 H6
Bradley Kirk....90 F6
Bradley N York....96 F4
Bradley NE Lin....93 M9
Bradley Staffs....70 F11
Bradley Wolves....58 E5
Bradley Worcs....47 J2
Bradley Wrexhm....69 K4
Bradley Common
  Ches W....69 P5
Bradley Green Somset....19 J7
Bradley Green Warwks....59 L4
Bradley Green Worcs....47 J2
Bradley in the Moors
  Staffs....71 K6
Bradley Stoke S Glos....32 B8
Bradmore Notts....72 F4
Bradney Somset....19 K7
Bradninch Devon....9 N4
Bradninch Devon....17 L5
Bradnop Staffs....71 J3
Bradnor Green Herefs....45 K3
Bradpole Dorset....11 K6
Bradshaw Bolton....89 L8
Bradshaw Calder....90 D5
Bradshaw Kirk....90 D8
Bradstone Devon....5 P5
Bradwall Green Ches E....70 D2
Bradwell Derbys....83 Q8
Bradwell Devon....17 J3
Bradwell Essex....52 D7
Bradwell M Keyn....49 M6
Bradwell Norfk....77 Q11
Bradwell Crematorium
  Staffs....70 F5
Bradwell-on-Sea Essex....52 H10
Bradwell Waterside
  Essex....52 G10
Bradworthy Devon....16 E9
Brae Highld....156 B5
Brae Shet....169 q7
Braeface Falk....133 M11
Braehead Angus....143 M7
Braehead D & G....107 M7
Braehead S Lans....126 H7
Braemar Abers....149 M9
Braemore Highld....161 K11
Braemore Highld....167 J11
Brae Roy Lodge Highld....147 J9
Braeside Inver....124 G3
Braes of Coul Angus....142 D6
Braes of Enzie Moray....158 A6
Braeswick Ork....169 f3
Braevallich Ag & B....131 K6
Brafferton Darltn....103 Q6
Brafferton N York....97 P6
Brafield-on-the-Green
  Nhants....60 H9
Bragar W Isls....168 h3
Bragbury End Herts....50 G6
Braidwood S Lans....126 E8
Brailsford Derbys....71 P6
Brailsford Green Derbys....71 P6
Brain's Green Gloucs....32 C3
Braintree Essex....52 C7
Braiseworth Suffk....64 G7
Braishfield Hants....22 C9
Braithwaite C Brad....90 C2
Braithwaite Cumb....100 H6
Braithwaite Donc....84 H2
Braithwell Donc....91 L7
Braken Hill Wakefd....91 L7
Bramber W Susx....24 E8
Brambridge Hants....22 E10
Bramcote Notts....72 E3
Bramcote Warwks....59 P7
Bramcote
  Crematorium Notts....72 E3
Bramdean Hants....22 H9
Bramerton Norfk....77 K11
Bramfield Herts....50 G7

Bramfield Suffk....65 M7
Bramford Suffk....53 K2
Bramhall Stockp....83 J8
Bramham Leeds....91 L2
Bramhope Leeds....90 H2
Bramley Hants....23 J3
Bramley Leeds....90 G3
Bramley Rothm....84 G2
Bramley Surrey....24 B2
Bramley Corner Hants....22 H3
Bramley Green Hants....23 J3
Bramley Head N York....96 H9
Bramling Kent....39 M10
Brampford Speke Devon....9 M5
Brampton Cambs....62 B6
Brampton Cumb....102 C6
Brampton Cumb....111 K8
Brampton Lincs....85 P5
Brampton Norfk....77 J7
Brampton Rothm....91 L10
Brampton Suffk....65 N5
Brampton Abbotts
  Herefs....46 B9
Brampton Ash Nhants....60 G3
Brampton Bryan Herefs....56 F10
Brampton-en-le-
  Morthen Rothm....84 G3
Bramshall Staffs....71 K8
Bramshaw Hants....21 Q11
Bramshill Hants....23 K2
Bramshott Hants....23 M8
Bramwell Somset....19 M9
Branault Highld....137 N2
Brancaster Norfk....75 Q2
Brancaster Staithe Norfk....75 Q2
Brancepeth Dur....103 P3
Branchill Moray....157 K7
Brand End Lincs....87 L11
Branderburgh Moray....157 N3
Brandesburton E R Yk....99 N11
Brandeston Suffk....65 J9
Brand Green Gloucs....46 D9
Brandis Corner Devon....16 G11
Brandiston Norfk....76 G7
Brandon Dur....103 P2
Brandon Lincs....86 B11
Brandon Nthumb....119 K7
Brandon Suffk....63 N3
Brandon Warwks....59 P9
Brandon Bank Norfk....63 K3
Brandon Creek Norfk....63 K2
Brandon Parva Norfk....76 F10
Brandsby N York....98 B6
Brandy Wharf Lincs....92 H11
Brane Cnwll....2 C8
Bran End Essex....51 Q5
Branksome Poole....12 H6
Branksome Park Poole....13 J6
Bransbury Hants....22 D6
Bransby Lincs....85 Q5
Branscombe Devon....10 D7
Bransford Worcs....46 E4
Bransgore Hants....13 L5
Bransholme C KuH....93 K4
Bransley Shrops....57 M9
Branson's Cross Worcs....58 G10
Branston Leics....73 L5
Branston Lincs....86 D7
Branston Staffs....71 N10
Branston Booths Lincs....86 E7
Branstone IoW....14 G10
Brant Broughton Lincs....86 B10
Brantham Suffk....53 K5
Branthwaite Cumb....100 E6
Branthwaite Cumb....101 J3
Brantingham E R Yk....92 F5
Branton Donc....91 Q10
Branton Nthumb....119 K7
Branton Green N York....97 P8
Branxton Nthumb....118 G3
Brassey Green Ches W....69 P2
Brassington Derbys....71 N4
Brasted Kent....37 L9
Brasted Chart Kent....37 L10
Brathens Abers....150 H8
Bratoft Lincs....87 N8
Brattleby Lincs....86 B4
Bratton Somset....18 B5
Bratton Wilts....20 H4
Bratton Wrekin....57 L2
Bratton Clovelly Devon....8 C6
Bratton Fleming Devon....17 L4
Bratton Seymour
  Somset....20 C9
Braughing Herts....51 J5
Braughing Friars Herts....51 K6
Braunston Nhants....60 B7
Braunston Rutlnd....73 L9
Braunstone Town Leics....72 F10
Braunton Devon....16 H4
Brawby N York....98 E5
Brawl Highld....166 D3
Braworth N York....104 F9
Bray W & M....35 P9
Braybrooke Nhants....60 G4
Braydon Wilts....33 K7
Braydon Brook Wilts....33 J6
Braydon Side Wilts....33 K7
Brayford Devon....17 M5
Bray's Hill E Susx....25 Q8
Bray Shop Cnwll....5 N7
Braystones Cumb....100 D9
Braythorn N York....97 K11
Brayton N York....91 Q4
Braywick W & M....35 N9
Braywoodside W & M....35 N9
Brazacott Cnwll....5 M3
Breach Kent....27 L2
Breach Kent....38 D8
Breachwood Green
  Herts....50 E6
Breaden Heath Shrops....69 M7
Breadsall Derbys....72 B3
Breadstone Gloucs....32 D4
Breadward Herefs....45 K4
Breage Cnwll....2 G8
Breakachy Highld....155 N10
Breakspear
  Crematorium Gt Lon....36 C3
Brealangwell Lodge
  Highld....162 C8
Bream Gloucs....32 B3
Breamore Hants....21 N11
Brean Somset....19 J3
Breanais W Isls....168 e5
Brearley Calder....90 C5
Brearton N York....97 M8
Breascleit W Isls....168 h4
Breasclete W Isls....168 h4
Breaston Derbys....72 D4
Brechfa Carmth....43 K8

Brechin Angus....143 L5
Breckles Norfk....64 D3
Brecon Powys....44 F5
Brecon Beacons
  National Park....44 E10
Bredbury Stockp....83 K6
Brede E Susx....26 D8
Bredenbury Herefs....46 B3
Bredfield Suffk....65 K11
Bredgar Kent....38 E9
Bredhurst Kent....38 C9
Bredon Worcs....46 H7
Bredon's Hardwick
  Worcs....46 H7
Bredon's Norton Worcs....46 H7
Bredwardine Herefs....45 L6
Breedon on the Hill Leics....72 C6
Breich W Loth....126 H5
Breightmet Bolton....89 L9
Breighton E R Yk....92 B4
Breinton Herefs....45 P7
Bremhill Wilts....33 J10
Bremridge Devon....17 M6
Brenchley Kent....25 Q2
Brendon Devon....16 F10
Brendon Devon....17 P2
Brendon Hill Somset....18 D8
Brenfield Ag & B....123 P3
Brenish W Isls....168 e5
Brenkley N u Ty....113 K5
Brent Cross Gt Lon....36 F3
Brent Eleigh Suffk....52 F2
Brentford Gt Lon....36 E5
Brentingby Leics....73 K7
Brent Knoll Somset....19 K4
Brent Mill Devon....6 H7
Brent Pelham Herts....51 K4
Brentwood Essex....37 N2
Brenzett Kent....26 H6
Brenzett Green Kent....26 H6
Brereton Staffs....71 K11
Brereton Green Ches E....70 D2
Brereton Heath Ches E....82 H11
Brereton Hill Staffs....71 K11
Bressay Shet....169 s9
Bressingham Norfk....64 F5
Bressingham Common
  Norfk....64 F5
Bretby Derbys....71 P10
Bretby Crematorium
  Derbys....71 P10
Bretford Warwks....59 P9
Bretforton Worcs....47 L6
Bretherton Lancs....88 F6
Brettabister Shet....169 r8
Brettenham Norfk....64 C5
Brettenham Suffk....64 D11
Bretton Derbys....84 B5
Bretton Flints....69 L2
Brewers End Essex....51 N6
Brewer Street Surrey....36 H10
Brewood Staffs....58 C3
Briantspuddle Dorset....12 D6
Brick End Essex....51 N5
Brickendon Herts....50 H9
Bricket Wood Herts....50 D10
Brick Houses Sheff....84 D4
Brickkiln Green Essex....52 B5
Bricklehampton Worcs....47 J6
Bride IoM....80 f1
Bridekirk Cumb....100 F4
Bridell Pembks....41 N2
Bridestowe Devon....8 D7
Brideswell Abers....158 E10
Bridford Devon....9 K7
Bridge Kent....39 L11
Bridge End Cumb....94 D4
Bridge End Cumb....110 G11
Bridge End Devon....6 H9
Bridge End Dur....103 K3
Bridge End Essex....51 Q4
Bridge End Lincs....74 B3
Bridgefoot Cumb....100 E5
Bridge Green Essex....51 L3
Bridgehampton Somset....19 Q10
Bridge Hewick N York....97 M6
Bridgehill Dur....112 G10
Bridgehouse Gate N York....97 J7
Bridgemary Hants....14 G6
Bridgemere Ches E....70 C5
Bridgend Abers....158 D10
Bridgend Ag & B....120 E4
Bridgend Ag & B....122 D7
Bridgend Angus....143 J4
Bridgend Brdgnd....29 P9
Bridgend Cerdgn....42 C5
Bridgend Cumb....101 M8
Bridgend D & G....116 F9
Bridgend Devon....6 F9
Bridgend Fife....135 K5
Bridgend Moray....158 A11
Bridgend Moray....157 M10
Bridgend P & K....134 E3
Bridgend W Loth....127 J2
Bridgend of Lintrathen
  Angus....142 D7
Bridge of Alford Abers....150 F4
Bridge of Allan Stirlg....133 M8
Bridge of Avon Moray....149 M3
Bridge of Avon Moray....157 M10
Bridge of Balgie P & K....140 E8
Bridge of Brewlands
  Angus....142 B5
Bridge of Brown Highld....149 L3
Bridge of Cally P & K....142 A7
Bridge of Canny Abers....150 H8
Bridge of Craigisla
  Angus....142 D7
Bridge of Dee D & G....108 F9
Bridge of Don C Aber....151 N6
Bridge of Dulsie Highld....156 G9
Bridge of Dye Abers....150 H10
Bridge of Earn P & K....134 E4
Bridge of Ericht P & K....140 D6
Bridge of Feugh Abers....151 J9
Bridge of Forss Highld....166 H3
Bridge of Gairn Abers....150 B8
Bridge of Gaur P & K....140 D6
Bridge of Marnoch
  Abers....158 E7
Bridge of Muchalls Abers....151 M9
Bridge of Orchy Ag & B....139 Q6
Bridge of Tilt P & K....141 L4
Bridge of Tynet Moray....158 A5
Bridge of Walls Shet....169 p8
Bridge of Weir Rens....125 K4
Bridge Reeve Devon....17 M9
Bridgerule Devon....16 D10
Bridges Shrops....56 F5
Bridge Sollers Herefs....45 N6
Bridge Street Suffk....52 E2
Bridgetown Cnwll....5 N4

Bridgetown Somset....18 B8
Bridge Trafford Ches W....81 P10
Bridge Yate S Glos....32 C10
Bridgham Norfk....64 D4
Bridgnorth Shrops....57 N6
Bridgwater Somset....19 J7
Bridgwater Services
  Somset....19 K8
Bridlington E R Yk....99 P7
Bridport Dorset....11 K6
Bridstow Herefs....46 A10
Brierfield Lancs....89 N3
Brierley Barns....91 L8
Brierley Gloucs....46 B11
Brierley Herefs....45 P3
Brierley Hill Dudley....58 D7
Brierlow Bar Derbys....83 N11
Brierton Hartpl....104 E4
Briery Cumb....101 J6
Brigg N Linc....92 H9
Briggate Norfk....77 L6
Briggswath N York....105 N9
Brigham Cumb....100 E4
Brigham Cumb....101 J6
Brigham E R Yk....99 M10
Brighouse Calder....90 E6
Brighstone IoW....14 D10
Brightgate Derbys....84 C9
Brighthampton Oxon....34 C4
Brightholmlee Sheff....90 H11
Brightley Devon....8 F5
Brightling E Susx....25 Q6
Brightlingsea Essex....53 J8
Brighton Br & H....24 H10
Brighton Cnwll....3 N3
Brighton le Sands Sefton....81 L5
Brightons Falk....126 G2
Brightwalton W Berk....34 D9
Brightwalton Green
  W Berk....34 D9
Brightwalton Holt
  W Berk....34 D9
Brightwell Suffk....53 N3
Brightwell Baldwin Oxon....35 J5
Brightwell-cum-
  Sotwell Oxon....34 G6
Brightwell Upperton
  Oxon....35 J6
Brignall Dur....103 L8
Brig o'Turk Stirlg....132 G6
Brigsley NE Lin....93 N10
Brigsteer Cumb....95 K3
Brigstock Nhants....61 K3
Brill Bucks....35 J2
Brill Cnwll....3 J8
Brilley Herefs....45 K5
Brimfield Herefs....57 J11
Brimfield Cross Herefs....57 J11
Brimington Derbys....84 F6
Brimley Devon....9 K9
Brimpsfield Gloucs....32 H2
Brimpton W Berk....22 G2
Brimpton Common
  W Berk....22 G2
Brimscombe Gloucs....32 G4
Brimstage Wirral....81 L8
Brincliffe Sheff....84 D4
Brind E R Yk....92 B4
Brindham Somset....19 P7
Brindister Shet....169 p8
Brindle Lancs....88 H6
Brindley Ches E....69 Q4
Brineton Staffs....57 Q2
Bringhurst Leics....60 H2
Bringsty Common
  Herefs....46 D3
Brington Cambs....61 N5
Briningham Norfk....76 E5
Brinkely Notts....85 M10
Brinkhill Lincs....87 L6
Brinkley Cambs....63 K10
Brinklow Warwks....59 P9
Brinkworth Wilts....33 K8
Brinscall Lancs....89 J6
Brinscombe Somset....19 M4
Brinsea N Som....19 M2
Brinsley Notts....84 G11
Brinsop Herefs....45 N6
Brinsworth Rothm....84 F3
Brinton Norfk....76 E4
Brinyan Ork....169 d4
Brisco Cumb....110 H10
Brisley Norfk....76 C7
Brislington Bristl....32 B10
Brissenden Green Kent....26 F4
Bristol Bristl....31 Q10
Bristol Airport N Som....31 P11
Bristol Zoo Gardens
  Bristl....31 Q10
Briston Norfk....76 F5
Brisworthy Devon....6 F5
Britannia Lancs....89 P6
Britford Wilts....21 N9
Brithdir Caerph....30 F4
Brithdir Gwynd....67 P11
British Legion Village
  Kent....38 B10
Briton Ferry Neath....29 K6
Britwell Salome Oxon....35 J6
Brixham Torbay....7 N7
Brixton Devon....6 F8
Brixton Gt Lon....36 H5
Brixton Deverill Wilts....20 G7
Brixworth Nhants....60 F6
Brize Norton Oxon....33 Q3
Brize Norton Airport
  Oxon....33 Q3
Broad Alley Worcs....58 C11
Broad Blunsdon Swindn....33 M6
Broadbottom Tamesd....83 L6
Broadbridge W Susx....15 M5
Broadbridge Heath
  W Susx....24 D4
Broad Campden Gloucs....47 N7
Broad Carr Calder....90 D7
Broad Chalke Wilts....21 L9
Broad Clough Lancs....89 P6
Broadclyst Devon....9 N5
Broadfield Pembks....41 M10
Broadford Highld....145 K3
Broad Ford Kent....26 B4
Broadford Bridge
  W Susx....24 C6
Broadgairhill Border....117 J7
Broadgrass Green Suffk....64 D9
Broad Green Cambs....63 K9
Broad Green Essex....52 E7
Broad Green Worcs....46 E4
Broad Green Worcs....58 E10
Broadhaugh Border....129 M9

Broad Haven Pembks....40 G...
Broadheath Traffd....82 G...
Broadheath Worcs....57 M1...
Broadhembury Devon....10 ...
Broadhempston Devon....7 ...
Broad Hill Cambs....63 J...
Broad Hinton Wilts....33 M...
Broadholme Lincs....85 Q...
Broadland Row E Susx....26 D...
Broad Layings Hants....51 ...
Broadley Essex....51 K...
Broadley Lancs....89 P...
Broadley Moray....158 ...
Broadley Common Essex....51 K...
Broad Marston Worcs....47 M...
Broadmayne Dorset....12 ...
Broad Meadow Staffs....70 D...
Broadmere Hants....22 H...
Broadmoor Gloucs....46 B1...
Broadmoor Pembks....41 L...
Broadnymett Devon....8 ...
Broad Oak Carmth....43 L1...
Broad Oak Cumb....94 ...
Broadoak Dorset....11 J...
Broad Oak E Susx....25 ...
Broad Oak E Susx....26 D...
Broadoak Gloucs....32 C...
Broad Oak Hants....23 L...
Broad Oak Herefs....45 P1...
Broad Oak Kent....39 L...
Broadoak St Hel....82 B...
Broadoak Wrexhm....69 L...
Broad Road Suffk....65 K...
Broad's Green Essex....51 Q...
Broadstairs Kent....39 Q...
Broadstone Mons....31 P...
Broadstone Poole....12 H...
Broadstone Shrops....57 J...
Broad Street E Susx....26 D...
Broad Street Essex....51 N...
Broad Street Kent....27 M...
Broad Street Kent....38 D1...
Broad Street Medway....38 C...
Broad Street Wilts....21 M...
Broad Street Green
  Essex....52 E1...
Broad Town Wilts....33 L...
Broadwas Worcs....46 E...
Broadwater Herts....50 F...
Broadwater W Susx....24 D1...
Broadwaters Worcs....58 C...
Broadway Carmth....28 C...
Broadway Carmth....41 Q...
Broadway Pembks....40 G...
Broadway Somset....19 K1...
Broadway Suffk....65 M...
Broadway Worcs....47 L...
Broadwell Gloucs....31 Q...
Broadwell Gloucs....47 P...
Broadwell Oxon....33 P...
Broadwell Warwks....59 Q1...
Broadwey Dorset....11 P...
Broadwindsor Dorset....11 J...
Broadwood Kelly Devon....8 ...
Broadwoodwidger
  Devon....5 Q...
Brobury Herefs....45 L...
Brochel Highld....153 L...
Brochroy Ag & B....139 J1...
Brock Lancs....88 G...
Brockamin Worcs....46 E...
Brockbridge Hants....22 H1...
Brockdish Norfk....65 J...
Brockencote Worcs....58 C1...
Brockenhurst Hants....13 P...
Brocketsbrae S Lans....126 E1...
Brockford Green Suffk....64 G...
Brockford Street Suffk....64 G...
Brockhall Nhants....60 D...
Brockham Surrey....36 E...
Brockhampton Gloucs....47 K1...
Brockhampton Hants....15 K5
Brockhampton Herefs....46 A...
Brockhampton Green
  Dorset....11 Q...
Brockholes Kirk....90 F...
Brockhurst Derbys....84 F...
Brockhurst Warwks....59 Q...
Brocklebank Cumb....101 K...
Brocklesby Lincs....93 K...
Brockley N Som....31 N1...
Brockley Suffk....64 A...
Brockley Green Suffk....63 M1...
Brockley Green Suffk....64 B...
Brockleymoor Cumb....101 N...
Brockmoor Dudley....58 D...
Brockscombe Devon....8 ...
Brock's Green Hants....22 E...
Brockton Shrops....56 F...
Brockton Shrops....57 J...
Brockton Shrops....57 L...
Brockton Shrops....57 N...
Brockton Staffs....70 D...
Brockweir Gloucs....31 P...
Brockwood Park Hants....22 H...
Brockworth Gloucs....46 G1...
Brocton Cnwll....4 ...
Brocton Staffs....70 H1...
Brodick N Ayrs....121 H...
Brodie Moray....156 H...
Brodsworth Donc....91 N...
Brogaig Highld....152 H...
Brogborough C Beds....49 Q...
Brokenborough Wilts....32 H...
Broken Cross Ches E....82 H...
Broken Cross Ches W....82 E1...
Brokerswood Wilts....20 G...
Bromborough Wirral....81 M...
Brome Suffk....64 G...
Brome Street Suffk....64 G...
Bromeswell Suffk....65 L1...
Bromfield Cumb....110 C1...
Bromfield Shrops....56 H...
Bromham Bed....61 M1...
Bromham Wilts....33 J...
Bromley Barns....91 J...
Bromley Dudley....58 D...
Bromley Gt Lon....37 K...
Bromley Shrops....57 N...
Bromley Common
  Gt Lon....37 K...
Bromley Cross Bolton....89 L...
Bromley Cross Essex....53 J...
Bromley Green Kent....26 F...
Bromlow Shrops....56 F...
Brompton Medway....38 C...
Brompton N York....104 F1...
Brompton-by-Sawdon
  N York....

ompton-on-Swale N York ... 103 P11
ompton Ralph Somset ... 18 C8
ompton Regis Somset ... 18 C8
omsash Herefs ... 46 C10
omsberrow Gloucs ... 46 D8
omsberrow Heath Gloucs ... 46 D8
omsgrove Worcs ... 58 K10
omstead Heath Staffs ... 70 D11
omyard Herefs ... 46 C4
omyard Downs Herefs ... 46 C3
onaber Gwynd ... 67 N8
onant Cerdgn ... 54 E11
oncroft Shrops ... 57 J7
ongest Cerdgn ... 42 F5
onington Wrexhm ... 69 N7
onllys Powys ... 44 G8
onwydd Carmth ... 42 H10
onydd Powys ... 45 J5
onygarth Shrops ... 69 J7
ook Carmth ... 41 Q9
ook Hants ... 13 N2
ook Hants ... 22 B9
ook IoW ... 14 C10
ook Kent ... 27 J3
ook Surrey ... 23 P7
ook Surrey ... 36 C11
ooke Norfk ... 65 K2
ooke Rutlnd ... 73 L9
ookenby Lincs ... 93 M11
ook End Bed ... 61 N8
ook End C Beds ... 61 Q11
ook End Cambs ... 61 N6
ook End M Keyn ... 49 P6
ookfield Rens ... 125 L5
ookhampton Oxon ... 34 H5
ookhampton Somset ... 20 B9
ook Hill Hants ... 13 N2
ook House Denbgs ... 80 F11
ookhouse Lancs ... 95 L8
ookhouse Rothm ... 84 H3
ookhouse Green Ches E ... 70 E2
ookhouses Derbys ... 83 M7
ookland Kent ... 26 G6
ooklands Traffd ... 82 G6
ookmans Park Herts ... 50 F10
ooks Powys ... 55 Q5
ooksby Leics ... 72 H7
ooks End Kent ... 39 N8
ooks Green W Susx ... 24 D6
ook Street Essex ... 37 N2
ook Street Kent ... 26 F5
ook Street Suffk ... 52 D2
ook Street W Susx ... 24 H5
ookthorpe Gloucs ... 32 F2
ookville Nthumb ... 75 P11
ookwood Surrey ... 23 Q3
oom C Beds ... 50 E2
oom Rothm ... 84 F2
oom Warwks ... 47 L4
oome Norfk ... 65 M3
oome Shrops ... 56 G8
oome Worcs ... 58 D9
oomedge Warrtn ... 82 F7
oome Park Nthumb ... 119 M8
oomer's Corner W Susx ... 24 D6
oomershill W Susx ... 24 C7
oomfield Essex ... 52 B9
oomfield Kent ... 38 D11
oomfield Kent ... 39 L8
oomfield Somset ... 18 H8
oomfields Shrops ... 69 M11
oomfleet E R Yk ... 92 E5
oom Green Norfk ... 76 D7
oomhall W & M ... 35 Q11
oomhaugh Nthumb ... 112 F8
oom Hill Barns ... 91 L10
oom Hill Dorset ... 12 H4
oom Hill Notts ... 84 H11
oomhill Nthumb ... 119 P10
oom Hill Worcs ... 58 D9
oomhill Green Ches E ... 70 A5
oomley Nthumb ... 112 F8
oompark Dur ... 103 P2
oom's Green Gloucs ... 46 D8
oomsthorpe Norfk ... 76 A6
oom Street Kent ... 38 H9
ora Highld ... 163 L6
oseley Shrops ... 57 M4
otherhouse Bar Lincs ... 74 E8
otherlee Dur ... 102 H3
othertoft Lincs ... 87 J11
otherton N York ... 91 M5
otton R & Cl ... 105 J7
oubster Highld ... 166 H5
ough Cumb ... 102 E8
ough Derbys ... 83 Q8
ough E R Yk ... 92 F5
ough Highld ... 167 M2
ough Notts ... 85 P9
ough Shet ... 169 s7
oughall Shrops ... 69 Q6
ough Lodge Shet ... 169 s4
ough Sowerby Cumb ... 102 E8
oughton Border ... 116 G3
oughton Bucks ... 35 M2
oughton Cambs ... 62 C5
oughton Flints ... 69 K2
oughton Hants ... 22 B8
oughton Lancs ... 88 G4
oughton M Keyn ... 49 N7
oughton N Linc ... 92 G9
oughton N York ... 96 D10
oughton N York ... 98 F6
oughton Nhants ... 60 H5
oughton Oxon ... 48 D7
oughton Salfd ... 82 H4
oughton Staffs ... 70 D8
oughton V Glam ... 29 P10
oughton Astley Leics ... 60 B2
oughton Beck Cumb ... 94 F4
oughton Gifford Wilts ... 20 G2
oughton Green Worcs ... 47 J2
oughton Hackett Worcs ... 46 H4
oughton-in-Furness Cumb ... 94 E3
oughton Mains D & G ... 107 J8
oughton Mills Cumb ... 94 E2
oughton Moor Cumb ... 100 E4
oughton Poggs Oxon ... 33 P4
oughton Tower Cumb ... 94 E3
oughty Ferry C Dund ... 142 H11
ough with St Giles N York ... 103 P11
ow End Cumb ... 94 F6
ownber Cumb ... 102 D9
own Candover Hants ... 22 G7

Brown Edge Lancs ... 88 D8
Brown Edge Staffs ... 70 G4
Brown Heath Ches W ... 69 N2
Brownheath Shrops ... 69 N9
Brownhill Abers ... 159 L10
Brownhills Fife ... 135 N4
Brownhills Wsall ... 58 F3
Brownieside Nthumb ... 119 N6
Browninghill Green Hants ... 22 G3
Brown Lees Staffs ... 70 F3
Brownlow Heath Ches E ... 70 E2
Brownrigg Cumb ... 100 D6
Brownrigg Cumb ... 110 C10
Brownsea Island Dorset ... 12 H7
Brown's Green Birm ... 58 G6
Brownsham Devon ... 16 D6
Browns Hill Gloucs ... 32 G4
Brownsover Warwks ... 60 B5
Brownston Devon ... 6 H8
Brown Street Suffk ... 64 F9
Brow-of-the-Hill Norfk ... 75 N7
Browston Green Norfk ... 77 P11
Broxa N York ... 99 J2
Broxbourne Herts ... 51 J9
Broxburn E Loth ... 128 H4
Broxburn W Loth ... 127 K3
Broxfield Nthumb ... 119 P7
Broxted Essex ... 51 N5
Broxton Ches W ... 69 N4
Broyle Side E Susx ... 25 L8
Bruan Highld ... 167 P9
Bruar P & K ... 141 K4
Brucefield Highld ... 163 L9
Bruchag Ag & B ... 124 E6
Bruera Ches W ... 69 M2
Bruern Abbey Oxon ... 47 Q10
Bruichladdich Ag & B ... 122 C7
Bruisyard Suffk ... 65 L8
Bruisyard Street Suffk ... 65 L8
Brumby N Linc ... 92 E9
Brund Staffs ... 71 L2
Brundall Norfk ... 77 L10
Brundish Suffk ... 65 K8
Brundish Street Suffk ... 65 K7
Brunery Highld ... 138 C3
Brunnion Cnwll ... 2 E6
Brunslow Shrops ... 56 F9
Brunswick Village N u Ty ... 113 K6
Bruntcliffe Leeds ... 90 H5
Brunthwaite C Brad ... 96 G11
Bruntingthorpe Leics ... 60 D3
Brunton Fife ... 135 J3
Brunton Nthumb ... 119 P6
Brunton Wilts ... 21 P3
Brushford Devon ... 17 M10
Brushford Somset ... 18 B9
Bruton Somset ... 20 C7
Bryan's Green Worcs ... 58 C11
Bryanston Dorset ... 12 E3
Bryant's Bottom Bucks ... 35 N5
Brydekirk D & G ... 110 C6
Bryher IoS ... 2 b2
Brymbo Wrexhm ... 69 J4
Brympton Somset ... 19 P11
Bryn Carmth ... 28 F4
Bryn Ches W ... 82 D10
Bryn Neath ... 29 M6
Bryn Shrops ... 56 D7
Bryn Wigan ... 82 C4
Brynamman Carmth ... 29 K2
Brynberian Pembks ... 41 M3
Brynbryddan Neath ... 29 L6
Bryn-bwbach Gwynd ... 67 L2
Bryncae Rhondd ... 30 C8
Bryncethin Brdgnd ... 29 P8
Bryncir Gwynd ... 66 H6
Bryn-côch Neath ... 29 K5
Bryncroes Gwynd ... 66 C8
Bryncrug Gwynd ... 54 E4
Bryn Du IoA ... 78 E10
Bryn-Eden Gwynd ... 67 N9
Bryneglwys Denbgs ... 68 F5
Brynfields Wrexhm ... 69 K6
Brynford Flints ... 80 H10
Bryn Gates Wigan ... 82 C4
Bryn Golau Rhondd ... 30 D7
Bryngwran IoA ... 78 F9
Bryngwyn Mons ... 31 L3
Bryngwyn Powys ... 44 H5
Bryn-Henllan Pembks ... 41 K3
Brynhoffnant Cerdgn ... 42 F4
Bryning Lancs ... 88 E5
Brynithel Blae G ... 30 H4
Brynmawr Blae G ... 30 G2
Bryn-mawr Gwynd ... 66 C8
Brynmenyn Brdgnd ... 29 P8
Brynmill Swans ... 28 H6
Brynna Rhondd ... 30 C8
Bryn-penarth Powys ... 55 Q4
Brynrefail Gwynd ... 67 K2
Brynrefail IoA ... 78 H7
Brynsadler Rhondd ... 30 D8
Bryn Saith Marchog Denbgs ... 68 E4
Brynsiencyn IoA ... 78 H11
Brynteg IoA ... 78 H8
Bryn-y-bal Flints ... 69 J2
Bryn-y-Maen Conwy ... 79 Q9
Bryn-yr-Eos Wrexhm ... 69 J6
Bualintur Highld ... 144 F3
Buarth-draw Flints ... 80 H9
Bubbenhall Warwks ... 59 N10
Bubwith E R Yk ... 92 B3
Buccleuch Border ... 117 L8
Buchanan Smithy Stirlg ... 132 F10
Buchanhaven Abers ... 159 R8
Buchanty P & K ... 133 Q2
Buchany Stirlg ... 133 L7
Buchlyvie Stirlg ... 132 H9
Buckabank Cumb ... 110 G11
Buckden Cambs ... 61 Q7
Buckden N York ... 96 D5
Buckenham Norfk ... 77 M10
Buckerell Devon ... 10 C4
Buckfast Devon ... 7 J5
Buckfastleigh Devon ... 7 J5
Buckhaven Fife ... 135 K8
Buckholt Mons ... 45 Q11
Buckhorn Devon ... 5 P2
Buckhorn Weston Dorset ... 20 E10
Buckhurst Hill Essex ... 37 K2
Buckie Moray ... 158 B4
Buckingham Bucks ... 49 J8
Buckland Bucks ... 35 N2
Buckland Devon ... 6 H10
Buckland Gloucs ... 47 L7
Buckland Hants ... 13 P5
Buckland Herts ... 51 J4
Buckland Kent ... 27 P3

Buckland Oxon ... 34 B5
Buckland Surrey ... 36 F10
Buckland Brewer Devon ... 16 G7
Buckland Common Bucks ... 35 P3
Buckland Dinham Somset ... 20 E4
Buckland Filleigh Devon ... 16 H10
Buckland in the Moor Devon ... 7 J4
Buckland Monachorum Devon ... 6 D5
Buckland Newton Dorset ... 11 P3
Buckland Ripers Dorset ... 11 P8
Buckland St Mary Somset ... 10 F2
Buckland-Tout-Saints Devon ... 7 K9
Bucklebury W Berk ... 34 G10
Bucklers Hard Hants ... 14 D6
Bucklesham Suffk ... 53 M3
Buckley Flints ... 69 J2
Buckley Green Warwks ... 59 J11
Bucklow Hill Ches E ... 82 F8
Buckminster Leics ... 73 M6
Bucknall C Stke ... 70 G5
Bucknall Lincs ... 86 G7
Bucknell Oxon ... 48 G9
Bucknell Shrops ... 56 F10
Buckpool Moray ... 158 B4
Bucksburn C Aber ... 151 M6
Buck's Cross Devon ... 16 F7
Bucks Green W Susx ... 24 C4
Buckshaw Village Lancs ... 88 H6
Bucks Hill Herts ... 50 C10
Bucks Horn Oak Hants ... 23 M6
Buck's Mills Devon ... 16 F7
Buckton E R Yk ... 99 P6
Buckton Herefs ... 56 F10
Buckton Nthumb ... 119 L3
Buckworth Cambs ... 61 P5
Budby Notts ... 85 K7
Buddileigh Staffs ... 70 C5
Bude Cnwll ... 16 C10
Budge's Shop Cnwll ... 5 N10
Budlake Devon ... 9 N4
Budle Nthumb ... 119 N3
Budleigh Salterton Devon ... 9 Q8
Budlett's Common E Susx ... 25 L6
Budock Water Cnwll ... 3 K7
Buerton Ches E ... 70 B6
Bugbrooke Nhants ... 60 E9
Bugford Devon ... 7 L8
Buglawton Ches E ... 70 F2
Bugle Cnwll ... 4 G10
Bugley Somset ... 20 E10
Bugthorpe E R Yk ... 98 F9
Buildwas Shrops ... 57 L4
Builth Road Powys ... 44 E4
Builth Wells Powys ... 44 E4
Bulbourne Herts ... 35 P2
Bulbridge Wilts ... 21 L8
Bulby Lincs ... 73 R5
Bulford Wilts ... 21 N6
Bulford Camp Wilts ... 21 N6
Bulkeley Ches E ... 69 P4
Bulkington Warwks ... 59 N7
Bulkington Wilts ... 20 H3
Bulkworthy Devon ... 16 F9
Bullamoor N York ... 97 N2
Bull Bay IoA ... 78 G6
Bullbridge Derbys ... 84 E10
Bullbrook Br For ... 35 N11
Bullen's Green Herts ... 50 F9
Bulley Gloucs ... 46 E11
Bullgill Cumb ... 100 D3
Bullinghope Herefs ... 45 Q7
Bullington Hants ... 22 E6
Bullington Lincs ... 86 E5
Bullockstone Kent ... 39 L8
Bull's Green Herts ... 50 G7
Bull's Green Norfk ... 65 N3
Bulmer Essex ... 52 D3
Bulmer N York ... 98 D7
Bulmer Tye Essex ... 52 D4
Bulphan Thurr ... 37 P3
Bulstone Devon ... 10 D7
Bulstrode Herts ... 50 B10
Bulverhythe E Susx ... 26 C10
Bulwark Abers ... 159 M8
Bulwell C Nott ... 72 E2
Bulwick Nhants ... 61 L2
Bumble's Green Essex ... 51 K9
Bunacaimb Highld ... 145 L10
Bunarkaig Highld ... 146 F10
Bunbury Ches E ... 69 Q3
Bunbury Heath Ches E ... 69 Q3
Bunchrew Highld ... 155 R8
Buncton W Susx ... 24 D8
Bundalloch Highld ... 145 Q2
Bunessan Ag & B ... 137 K11
Bungay Suffk ... 65 L4
Bunker's Hill Lincs ... 87 J10
Bunnahabhain Ag & B ... 122 F5
Bunny Notts ... 72 F5
Buntait Highld ... 155 M11
Buntingford Herts ... 51 J6
Bunwell Norfk ... 64 G3
Bunwell Hill Norfk ... 64 G3
Bupton Derbys ... 71 N7
Burbage Derbys ... 83 M10
Burbage Leics ... 59 P6
Burbage Wilts ... 21 P2
Burcher Herefs ... 45 L2
Burchett's Green E Susx ... 25 Q4
Burchett's Green W & M ... 35 M8
Burcombe Wilts ... 21 L8
Burcot Oxon ... 34 G5
Burcot Worcs ... 58 E10
Burcote Shrops ... 57 N5
Burcott Bucks ... 49 M11
Burcott Bucks ... 49 N10
Burdale N York ... 98 H8
Bures Essex ... 52 F5
Burford Oxon ... 33 Q2
Burford Shrops ... 57 K11
Burg Ag & B ... 137 K6
Burgate Suffk ... 64 F6
Burgates Hants ... 23 L9
Burge End Herts ... 50 D4
Burgess Hill W Susx ... 24 H7
Burgh Suffk ... 65 J11
Burgh by Sands Cumb ... 110 F9
Burgh Castle Norfk ... 77 P10
Burghclere Hants ... 22 E3
Burghead Moray ... 157 L4
Burghfield W Berk ... 35 J11

Burghfield Common W Berk ... 35 J11
Burgh Heath Surrey ... 36 F9
Burgh Hill E Susx ... 26 B6
Burghill Herefs ... 45 P6
Burgh Island Devon ... 6 G10
Burgh le Marsh Lincs ... 87 P7
Burgh next Aylsham Norfk ... 77 J6
Burgh on Bain Lincs ... 86 H3
Burgh St Margaret Norfk ... 77 N9
Burgh St Peter Norfk ... 65 P3
Burghwallis Donc ... 91 N8
Burham Kent ... 38 B9
Buriton Hants ... 23 K11
Burland Ches E ... 69 R4
Burlawn Cnwll ... 4 F7
Burleigh Gloucs ... 32 G4
Burlescombe Devon ... 18 E11
Burleston Dorset ... 12 C6
Burlestone Devon ... 7 L9
Burley Hants ... 13 M4
Burley Rutlnd ... 73 M8
Burley Shrops ... 56 H8
Burleydam Ches E ... 69 R6
Burley Gate Herefs ... 46 A5
Burley in Wharfedale C Brad ... 97 J11
Burley Lawn Hants ... 13 M4
Burley Street Hants ... 13 M4
Burley Wood Head C Brad ... 90 F2
Burlingham Green Norfk ... 77 M9
Burlingjobb Powys ... 45 K3
Burlington Shrops ... 57 P2
Burlton Shrops ... 69 N9
Burmarsh Kent ... 27 K5
Burmington Warwks ... 47 Q7
Burn N York ... 91 P5
Burnage Manch ... 83 J6
Burnaston Derbys ... 71 P8
Burnbanks Cumb ... 101 P7
Burnbrae N Lans ... 126 F6
Burnby E R Yk ... 98 G11
Burn Cross Sheff ... 91 J11
Burndell W Susx ... 15 Q6
Burnden Bolton ... 89 L9
Burnedge Rochdl ... 89 Q8
Burneside Cumb ... 101 P11
Burness Ork ... 169 f2
Burneston N York ... 97 M4
Burnett BaNES ... 32 C11
Burnfoot Border ... 117 N8
Burnfoot Border ... 117 Q7
Burnfoot D & G ... 109 L2
Burnfoot D & G ... 110 F3
Burnfoot D & G ... 117 M11
Burnfoot P & K ... 134 B7
Burnham Bucks ... 35 P8
Burnham N Linc ... 93 J7
Burnham Deepdale Norfk ... 75 R2
Burnham Green Herts ... 50 G7
Burnham Market Norfk ... 76 A3
Burnham Norton Norfk ... 76 A3
Burnham-on-Crouch Essex ... 38 F2
Burnham-on-Sea Somset ... 19 K5
Burnham Overy Norfk ... 76 A3
Burnham Overy Staithe Norfk ... 76 A3
Burnham Thorpe Norfk ... 76 B3
Burnhaven Abers ... 159 R9
Burnhead D & G ... 116 B11
Burnhervie Abers ... 151 J4
Burnhill Green Staffs ... 57 P4
Burnhope Dur ... 113 J11
Burnhouse N Ayrs ... 125 K7
Burniston N York ... 99 L2
Burnley Lancs ... 89 N4
Burnley Crematorium Lancs ... 89 N4
Burnmouth Border ... 129 P7
Burn Naze Lancs ... 88 C2
Burn of Cambus Stirlg ... 133 L7
Burnopfield Dur ... 113 J9
Burnrigg Cumb ... 111 J9
Burnsall N York ... 96 F7
Burnside Angus ... 142 G6
Burnside Angus ... 143 J7
Burnside Fife ... 134 F6
Burnside Moray ... 157 M4
Burnside W Loth ... 127 K2
Burnside of Duntrune Angus ... 142 G11
Burntcommon Surrey ... 36 B10
Burnthreath Derbys ... 71 N8
Burnt Heath Essex ... 53 J6
Burnt Hill W Berk ... 34 G10
Burnthouse Cnwll ... 3 K6
Burnt Houses Dur ... 103 M6
Burntisland Fife ... 134 G10
Burnt Oak E Susx ... 25 M5
Burnton E Ayrs ... 115 J6
Burntwood Staffs ... 58 G3
Burntwood Green Staffs ... 58 G3
Burnt Yates N York ... 97 L8
Burnworthy Somset ... 18 G11
Burpham Surrey ... 36 B10
Burpham W Susx ... 24 B9
Burradon N Tyne ... 113 L6
Burradon Nthumb ... 119 J9
Burrafirth Shet ... 169 t2
Burras Cnwll ... 2 H7
Burraton Cnwll ... 5 Q8
Burravoe Shet ... 169 s5
Burrells Cumb ... 102 C7
Burrelton P & K ... 142 C10
Burridge Devon ... 10 G3
Burridge Devon ... 17 K4
Burridge Hants ... 14 F4
Burrill N York ... 97 K3
Burringham N Linc ... 92 D9
Burrington Devon ... 17 L6
Burrington Herefs ... 56 G10
Burrington N Som ... 19 N3
Burrough End Cambs ... 63 K9
Burrough Green Cambs ... 63 K9
Burrough on the Hill Leics ... 73 K8
Burrow Lancs ... 95 N6
Burrow Somset ... 18 B6
Burrow Bridge Somset ... 19 L8
Burrowhill Surrey ... 23 Q2
Burrows Cross Surrey ... 36 C11
Burry Swans ... 28 E6
Burry Green Swans ... 28 E6
Burry Port Carmth ... 28 D4
Burscough Lancs ... 88 E8
Burscough Bridge Lancs ... 88 E8
Bursea E R Yk ... 92 D4
Burshill E R Yk ... 99 M11

Bursledon Hants ... 14 E5
Burslem C Stke ... 70 F5
Burstall Suffk ... 53 J3
Burstock Dorset ... 11 J4
Burston Norfk ... 64 G5
Burston Staffs ... 70 G8
Burstow Surrey ... 24 H2
Burstwick E R Yk ... 93 M5
Burtersett N York ... 96 C3
Burtholme Cumb ... 111 K8
Burthorpe Green Suffk ... 63 N8
Burthwaite Cumb ... 110 H11
Burthy Cnwll ... 4 E9
Burtle Hill Somset ... 19 L6
Burtoft Lincs ... 74 E3
Burton Ches W ... 69 P2
Burton Ches W ... 81 L10
Burton Dorset ... 11 P6
Burton Dorset ... 13 L6
Burton Lincs ... 86 C6
Burton Nthumb ... 119 N4
Burton Pembks ... 41 J9
Burton Somset ... 11 L2
Burton Somset ... 18 G6
Burton Wilts ... 20 F8
Burton Wilts ... 32 F9
Burton Agnes E R Yk ... 99 N8
Burton Bradstock Dorset ... 11 K7
Burton Coggles Lincs ... 73 P5
Burton Dassett Warwks ... 48 C4
Burton End Essex ... 51 M6
Burton End Suffk ... 63 L11
Burton Fleming E R Yk ... 99 M6
Burton Green Warwks ... 59 L9
Burton Green Wrexhm ... 69 K3
Burton Hastings Warwks ... 59 P7
Burton-in-Kendal Cumb ... 95 L5
Burton-in-Kendal Services Cumb ... 95 L5
Burton in Lonsdale N York ... 95 P6
Burton Joyce Notts ... 72 G2
Burton Latimer Nhants ... 61 K6
Burton Lazars Leics ... 73 K7
Burton Leonard N York ... 97 M8
Burton on the Wolds Leics ... 72 F6
Burton Overy Leics ... 72 H11
Burton Pedwardine Lincs ... 74 B2
Burton Pidsea E R Yk ... 93 M4
Burton Salmon N York ... 91 M5
Burton's Green Essex ... 52 D6
Burton upon Stather N Linc ... 92 E7
Burton upon Trent Staffs ... 71 N10
Burton Waters Lincs ... 86 B6
Burtonwood Warrtn ... 82 C6
Burtonwood Services Warrtn ... 82 C6
Burwardsley Ches W ... 69 P3
Burwarton Shrops ... 57 L7
Burwash E Susx ... 25 Q6
Burwash Common E Susx ... 25 P6
Burwash Weald E Susx ... 25 Q6
Burwell Cambs ... 63 J7
Burwell Lincs ... 87 L5
Burwen IoA ... 78 G6
Burwick Ork ... 169 d8
Bury Bury ... 89 N8
Bury Cambs ... 62 C4
Bury Somset ... 18 B9
Bury W Susx ... 24 B8
Bury End C Beds ... 50 D3
Bury Green Herts ... 51 L6
Bury St Edmunds Suffk ... 64 B9
Burythorpe N York ... 98 F8
Busby E Rens ... 125 P6
Busby Stoop N York ... 97 N4
Buscot Oxon ... 33 P5
Bush Abers ... 143 P4
Bush Cnwll ... 16 C10
Bush Bank Herefs ... 45 P4
Bushbury Wolves ... 58 D4
Bushbury Crematorium Wolves ... 58 D4
Busby Leics ... 72 H10
Bushey Herts ... 50 D11
Bushey Heath Herts ... 36 D2
Bush Green Norfk ... 65 J4
Bush Green Suffk ... 64 D9
Bushley Worcs ... 46 G8
Bushley Green Worcs ... 46 G8
Bushmead Bed ... 61 P8
Bushmoor Shrops ... 56 G7
Bushton Wilts ... 33 L9
Busk Cumb ... 102 B2
Buslingthorpe Lincs ... 86 E3
Bussage Gloucs ... 32 G4
Bussex Somset ... 19 L7
Butcher's Cross E Susx ... 25 N5
Butcombe N Som ... 19 P2
Bute Ag & B ... 124 C4
Butleigh Somset ... 19 P8
Butleigh Wootton Somset ... 19 P7
Butler's Cross Bucks ... 35 M3
Butler's Hill Notts ... 84 H11
Butlers Marston Warwks ... 48 B4
Butley Suffk ... 65 M11
Butley High Corner Suffk ... 53 Q2
Buttercrambe N York ... 98 E9
Butterdean Border ... 129 K7
Butterknowle Dur ... 103 M5
Butterleigh Devon ... 9 N3
Butterley Derbys ... 84 F10
Buttermere Cumb ... 100 H6
Buttermere Wilts ... 22 B2
Butters Green Staffs ... 70 E4
Buttershaw C Brad ... 90 E5
Butterstone P & K ... 141 Q8
Butterton Staffs ... 70 E6
Butterton Staffs ... 71 K3
Butterwick Dur ... 104 C4
Butterwick Lincs ... 87 L11
Butterwick N York ... 99 K6
Butterwick N York ... 98 H5
Butt Green Ches E ... 70 B4
Buttington Powys ... 56 C3
Buttonbridge Shrops ... 57 N9
Buttonoak Shrops ... 57 N8
Buttsash Hants ... 14 D5
Buttsbear Cross Cnwll ... 16 D11
Butt's Green Essex ... 52 C11
Buxhall Suffk ... 64 E10
Buxhall Fen Street Suffk ... 64 E10
Buxted E Susx ... 25 L6
Buxton Derbys ... 83 N10
Buxton Norfk ... 77 J7

Buxton Heath Norfk....76 H7
Bwlch Powys....44 H10
Bwlchgwyn Wrexhm....69 J4
Bwlchilan Cerdgn....43 L3
Bwlchnewydd Carmth....42 G10
Bwlchtocyn Gwynd....66 E9
Bwlch-y-cibau Powys....68 G11
Bwlch-y-Ddar Powys....68 G10
Bwlchyfadfa Cerdgn....42 H5
Bwlch-y-ffridd Powys....55 P5
Bwlch-y-groes Pembks....41 P3
Bwlchymyrdd Swans....28 G5
Bwlch-y-sarnau Powys....55 N10
Byermoor Gatesd....113 J9
Byers Green Dur....103 P4
Byfield Nhants....48 F4
Byfleet Surrey....36 C8
Byford Herefs....45 M6
Bygrave Herts....50 G3
Byker N u Ty....113 L8
Byland Abbey N York....98 A5
Bylaugh Norfk....76 E8
Bylchau Conwy....68 C2
Byley Ches W....82 F11
Bynea Carmth....28 F5
Byrness Nthumb....118 E10
Bystock Devon....9 P8
Bythorn Cambs....61 N5
Byton Herefs....45 M2
Bywell Nthumb....112 F8
Byworth W Susx....23 Q10

C

Cabbacott Devon....16 G7
Cabourne Lincs....93 K10
Cabrach Ag & B....122 G7
Cabrach Moray....150 B2
Cabus Lancs....95 K11
Cackle Street E Susx....25 L5
Cackle Street E Susx....25 Q7
Cackle Street E Susx....26 D8
Cadbury Devon....9 M3
Cadbury Barton Devon....17 M8
Cadbury World Birm....58 F8
Cadder E Duns....125 Q3
Caddington C Beds....50 C7
Caddonfoot Border....117 P3
Cadeby Donc....91 N10
Cadeby Leics....72 C10
Cadeleigh Devon....9 M3
Cade Street E Susx....25 P6
Cadgwith Cnwll....3 J11
Cadham Fife....134 H7
Cadishead Salfd....82 F6
Cadle Swans....28 H5
Cadley Lancs....88 G4
Cadley Wilts....21 P4
Cadley Wilts....33 P11
Cadmore End Bucks....35 L6
Cadnam Hants....13 P2
Cadney N Linc....92 H10
Cadole Flints....68 H2
Cadoxton V Glam....30 F11
Cadoxton Juxta-Neath
   Neath....29 L5
Cadwst Denbgs....68 D7
Caeathro Gwynd....67 J2
Caehopkin Powys....29 M2
Caenby Lincs....86 C3
Caeo Carmth....43 N6
Caerau,Brdgnd Devon....29 N6
Caerau Cardif....30 F9
Cae'r-bont Powys....29 M2
Cae'r bryn Carmth....28 G2
Caerdeon Gwynd....67 M11
Caer Farchell Pembks....40 E5
Caergeiliog IoA....78 E9
Caergwrle Flints....69 K3
Caerhun Conwy....79 P10
Caerlanrig Border....117 M10
Caerleon Newpt....31 K6
Caernarfon Gwynd....66 H2
Caernarfon Castle
   Gwynd....66 H2
Caerphilly Caerph....30 G7
Caersws Powys....55 N6
Caerwedros Cerdgn....42 G3
Caerwent Mons....31 N6
Caerwys Flints....80 G10
Caerynwch Gwynd....67 P11
Caggle Street Mons....45 M11
Caim IoA....79 L8
Cairinis W Isls....168 d11
Cairnbaan Ag & B....130 G9
Cairnbulg Abers....159 P4
Cairncross Border....129 M7
Cairncurran Inver....125 J3
Cairndow Ag & B....131 P5
Cairneyhill Fife....134 C10
Cairngarroch D & G....106 E8
Cairngorms National
   Park....149 K7
Cairnie Abers....158 C9
Cairnorrie Abers....159 L9
Cairnryan D & G....106 E4
Cairnty Moray....157 Q7
Caister-on-Sea Norfk....77 Q9
Caistor Lincs....93 K10
Caistor St Edmund Norfk....77 J11
Cakebole Worcs....58 C10
Cake Street Norfk....64 F3
Calais Street Suffk....52 G4
Calanais W Isls....168 h4
Calbourne IoW....14 D9
Calceby Lincs....87 L5
Calcot Flints....80 H10
Calcot Gloucs....33 L2
Calcot W Berk....35 J10
Calcot Row W Berk....35 J10
Calcots Moray....157 P5
Calcott Kent....39 L9
Calcott Shrops....56 G2
Calcutt N York....97 M9
Calcutt Wilts....33 M6
Caldbeck Cumb....101 K2
Caldbergh N York....96 G3
Caldecote Cambs....61 P3
Caldecote Cambs....62 D9
Caldecote Herts....50 F3
Caldecote Nhants....49 J4
Caldecote Highfields
   Cambs....62 E9
Caldecott Nhants....61 L7
Caldecott Rutlnd....61 J2
Caldecott M Keyn....49 N7
Calder Cumb....100 D10
Calderbank N Lans....126 D5

Calder Bridge Cumb....100 D9
Calderbrook Rochdl....89 Q7
Caldercruix N Lans....126 E4
Calder Grove Wakefd....91 J7
Caldermill S Lans....126 B9
Caldermore Rochdl....89 Q7
Calder Vale Lancs....95 L11
Caldey Island Pembks....41 M11
Caldicot Mons....31 N7
Caldmore Wsall....58 F5
Caldwell N York....103 N8
Caldy Wirral....81 J7
Caledfwlch Carmth....43 N9
Calenick Cnwll....3 L5
Calf of Man IoM....80 a8
Calford Green Suffk....63 M11
Calfsound Ork....169 e3
Calgary Ag & B....137 K5
Califer Moray....157 K6
California Falk....126 G2
California Norfk....77 Q8
California Cross Devon....7 J7
Calke Derbys....72 B6
Calke Abbey Derbys....72 B6
Callakille Highld....153 M6
Callander Stirlg....133 J6
Callanish W Isls....168 h4
Callaughton Shrops....57 L5
Callestick Cnwll....3 K3
Calligarry Highld....145 K7
Callington Cnwll....5 P8
Callingwood Staffs....71 M10
Callow Herefs....45 P8
Callow End Worcs....46 F4
Callow Hill Wilts....33 K8
Callow Hill Wilts....47 K2
Callow Hill Worcs....57 N10
Callows Grave Worcs....57 K11
Calmore Hants....13 P2
Calmsden Gloucs....33 K3
Calne Wilts....33 J10
Calow Derbys....84 F6
Calshot Hants....14 E6
Calstock Cnwll....6 C5
Calstone Wellington
   Wilts....33 K11
Calthorpe Norfk....76 H5
Calthorpe Street Norfk....77 N2
Calthwaite Cumb....101 N2
Calton N York....96 D9
Calton Staffs....71 L5
Calveley Ches E....69 Q3
Calver Derbys....84 B6
Calverhall Shrops....69 R7
Calver Hill Herefs....45 M5
Calverleigh Devon....9 M2
Calverley Leeds....90 G3
Calver Sough Derbys....84 B6
Calvert Bucks....49 J10
Calverton M Keyn....49 L7
Calverton Notts....85 K11
Calvine P & K....141 K4
Calvo Cumb....109 P10
Calzeat Border....116 G3
Cam Gloucs....32 E5
Camasachoirce Highld....138 D5
Camasine Highld....138 D5
Camas Luinie Highld....146 A2
Camastianavaig Highld....153 J10
Camault Muir Highld....155 P9
Camber E Susx....26 G8
Camberley Surrey....23 N2
Camberwell Gt Lon....36 H5
Camblesforth N York....91 Q5
Cambo Nthumb....112 F3
Cambois Nthumb....113 M4
Camborne Cnwll....2 G5
Camborne & Redruth
   Mining District Cnwll....2 G5
Cambourne Cambs....62 D9
Cambridge Cambs....62 G9
Cambridge Gloucs....32 D4
Cambridge Airport
   Cambs....62 G9
Cambridge City
   Crematorium Cambs....62 E8
Cambrose Cnwll....2 H4
Cambus Clacks....133 P9
Cambusavie Platform
   Highld....162 H7
Cambusbarron Stirlg....133 M9
Cambuskenneth Stirlg....133 N9
Cambuslang S Lans....125 Q5
Cambus o' May Abers....150 C8
Cambuswallace S Lans....116 E3
Camden Town Gt Lon....36 G4
Cameley BaNES....20 B3
Camelford Cnwll....5 J5
Camelon Falk....133 P11
Camerory Highld....157 J11
Camer's Green Worcs....46 E7
Camerton BaNES....20 C3
Camerton Cumb....100 D4
Camghouran P & K....140 E6
Camieston Border....117 N4
Cammachmore Abers....151 N8
Cammeringham Lincs....86 B4
Camore Highld....162 H9
Campbeltown Ag & B....120 D7
Campbeltown Airport
   Ag & B....120 C7
Camperdown N Tyne....113 L6
Cample D & G....109 J2
Campmuir P & K....142 C10
Camps W Loth....127 K4
Campsall Donc....91 N8
Campsea Ash Suffk....65 L10
Camps End Cambs....51 P2
Campton C Beds....50 D4
Camptown Border....118 C8
Camrose Pembks....40 H6
Camserney P & K....141 K8
Camusnagaul Highld....139 K3
Camusnagaul Highld....160 H9
Camusteel Highld....153 M9
Camusterrach Highld....153 N9
Canada Hants....21 Q11
Canal Foot Cumb....94 G5
Canaston Bridge Pembks....41 L7
Candacraig Abers....149 Q8
Candlesby Lincs....87 N7
Candle Street Suffk....64 E7
Candover Green Shrops....57 J3
Candy Mill Border....116 F2
Cane End Oxon....35 J9
Canewdon Essex....38 F3
Canford Bottom Dorset....13 H4
Canford Cliffs Poole....13 J7
Canford Crematorium
   Bristl....31 Q9

Canford Heath Poole....12 H6
Canford Magna Poole....12 H5
Canhams Green Suffk....64 F9
Canisbay Highld....167 P2
Canklow Rothm....84 F2
Canley Covtry....59 M9
Canley Crematorium
   Covtry....59 M9
Cann Dorset....20 G10
Canna Highld....144 B6
Cann Common Dorset....20 G10
Cannich Highld....155 K11
Cannington Somset....19 J7
Canning Town Gt Lon....37 K4
Cannock Staffs....58 E2
Cannock Chase Staffs....70 H11
Cannock Wood Staffs....58 F2
Cannon Bridge Herefs....45 N6
Canonbie D & G....110 G5
Canon Frome Herefs....46 B6
Canon Pyon Herefs....45 P5
Canons Ashby Nhants....48 G4
Canonstown Cnwll....2 E6
Canterbury Kent....39 K10
Canterbury Cathedral
   Kent....39 L10
Cantley Norfk....77 M11
Cantlop Shrops....57 J3
Canton Cardif....30 G9
Cantraywood Highld....156 D8
Cantsfield Lancs....95 N6
Canvey Island Essex....38 C5
Canwick Lincs....86 C7
Canworthy Water Cnwll....5 L3
Caol Highld....139 L2
Caolas Scalpaigh W Isls....168 h8
Caoles Ag & B....136 D6
Caonich Highld....146 D9
Capel Kent....25 P2
Capel Surrey....24 E2
Capel Bangor Cerdgn....54 F8
Capel Betws Lleucu
   Cerdgn....43 M3
Capel Coch IoA....78 H8
Capel Curig Conwy....67 N3
Capel Cynon Cerdgn....42 G5
Capel Dewi Carmth....43 J10
Capel Dewi Cerdgn....43 J6
Capel-Dewi Cerdgn....54 E8
Capel Garmon Conwy....67 Q3
Capel Green Suffk....53 Q2
Capel Gwyn Carmth....43 J10
Capel Gwyn IoA....78 E9
Capel Gwynfe Carmth....43 P10
Capel Hendre Carmth....28 G2
Capel Isaac Carmth....43 L9
Capel Iwan Carmth....41 Q3
Capel le Ferne Kent....27 N4
Capelles Guern....10 C1
Capel Llanilltern Cardif....30 E9
Capel Mawr IoA....78 G10
Capel Parc IoA....78 G7
Capel St Andrew Suffk....53 Q2
Capel St Mary Suffk....53 J4
Capel Seion Cerdgn....54 E9
Capel Trisant Cerdgn....54 G9
Capeluchaf Gwynd....66 G5
Capelulo Conwy....79 N9
Capel-y-ffin Powys....45 K8
Capel-y-graig Gwynd....79 J11
Capenhurst Ches W....81 M10
Capernwray Lancs....95 L6
Cape Wrath Highld....164 G1
Capheaton Nthumb....112 H4
Caplaw E Rens....125 L6
Capon's Green Suffk....65 K8
Cappercleuch Border....117 J6
Capstone Medway....38 C8
Capton Devon....7 L8
Capton Somset....18 E7
Caputh P & K....141 Q9
Caradon Mining
   District Cnwll....5 M7
Caradon Town Cnwll....5 M7
Carbeth Inn Stirlg....125 N2
Carbis Cnwll....4 G10
Carbis Bay Cnwll....2 E6
Carbost Highld....152 F11
Carbost Highld....152 G8
Carbrook Sheff....84 E3
Carbrooke Norfk....76 C11
Carburton Notts....85 K6
Carclaze Cnwll....3 Q3
Car Colston Notts....73 J2
Carcroft Donc....91 N9
Cardenden Fife....134 G8
Cardeston Shrops....56 F2
Cardewlees Cumb....110 G10
Cardiff Cardif....30 G9
Cardiff Airport V Glam....30 E11
Cardiff & Glamorgan
   Crematorium Cardif....30 G8
Cardiff Gate Services
   Cardif....30 H8
Cardiff West Services
   Cardif....30 E9
Cardigan Cerdgn....42 C5
Cardinal's Green Cambs....63 K11
Cardington Bed....61 N11
Cardington Shrops....57 J5
Cardinham Cnwll....5 J8
Cardrain D & G....106 F11
Cardrona Border....117 J3
Cardross Ag & B....125 J2
Cardross Crematorium
   Ag & B....125 J2
Cardryne D & G....106 F11
Cardurnock Cumb....110 C9
Careby Lincs....73 Q7
Careston Angus....143 J5
Carew Pembks....41 K10
Carew Cheriton Pembks....41 K10
Carew Newton Pembks....41 K10
Carey Herefs....45 R8
Carfin N Lans....126 D6
Carfraemill Border....128 E3
Cargate Green Norfk....77 M9
Cargenbridge D & G....109 L6
Cargill P & K....142 B10
Cargo Cumb....110 G9
Cargreen Cnwll....6 C6
Cargurrel Cnwll....3 M6
Carham Nthumb....118 E3
Carhampton Somset....18 D6
Carharrack Cnwll....3 J5
Carie P & K....140 F6
Carinish W Isls....168 d11
Carisbrooke IoW....14 F9
Cark Cumb....94 H5
Carkeel Cnwll....5 Q9

Carlabhagh W Isls....168 h3
Carland Cross Cnwll....3 M3
Carlby Lincs....73 Q8
Carlcroft Nthumb....118 F8
Carlecotes Barns....83 Q4
Carleen Cnwll....2 G7
Carlesmoor N York....97 K6
Carleton Cumb....100 D9
Carleton Cumb....101 P5
Carleton Cumb....110 H10
Carleton Lancs....88 C3
Carleton N York....96 E11
Carleton Wakefd....91 M6
Carleton Crematorium
   Bpool....88 C3
Carleton Forehoe Norfk....76 F10
Carleton Rode Norfk....64 G3
Carleton St Peter Norfk....77 L11
Carlidnack Cnwll....3 K8
Carlincraig Abers....158 G9
Carlingcott BaNES....20 C3
Carlin How R & Cl....105 K7
Carlisle Cumb....110 G9
Carlisle Airport Cumb....111 J8
Carlisle Crematorium
   Cumb....110 G10
Carloggas Cnwll....4 D8
Carlops Border....127 M6
Carloway W Isls....168 h3
Carlton Barns....91 K8
Carlton Bed....61 L9
Carlton Cambs....63 K10
Carlton Leeds....91 J5
Carlton Leics....72 B10
Carlton N York....91 Q6
Carlton N York....96 G4
Carlton N York....98 C3
Carlton Notts....72 G2
Carlton S on T....104 C6
Carlton Suffk....65 M9
Carlton Colville Suffk....65 Q4
Carlton Curlieu Leics....72 H11
Carlton Green Cambs....63 K10
Carlton Husthwaite
   N York....97 Q5
Carlton-in-Cleveland
   N York....104 F10
Carlton in Lindrick Notts....85 J4
Carlton-le-Moorland
   Lincs....86 B9
Carlton Miniott N York....97 N4
Carlton-on-Trent Notts....85 N8
Carlton Scroop Lincs....86 B11
Carluke S Lans....126 E7
Carlyon Bay Cnwll....3 R3
Carmacoup S Lans....115 Q2
Carmarthen Carmth....42 H10
Carmel Carmth....43 L11
Carmel Flints....80 H9
Carmel Gwynd....66 H4
Carmichael S Lans....116 C3
Carmountside
   Crematorium C Stke....70 G5
Carmunnock C Glas....125 P6
Carmyle C Glas....125 Q5
Carmyllie Angus....143 J9
Carnaby E R Yk....99 N7
Carnbee Fife....135 N6
Carnbo P & K....134 D7
Carn Brea Cnwll....2 H5
Carnbrogie Abers....151 M2
Carndu Highld....145 Q2
Carnduff S Lans....126 B8
Carne Cnwll....3 K9
Carne Cnwll....3 M6
Carne Cnwll....4 F10
Carnewas Cnwll....4 D8
Carnforth Lancs....95 K6
Carn-gorm Highld....146 B3
Carnhedryn Pembks....40 F5
Carnhell Green Cnwll....2 G6
Carnie Abers....151 L6
Carnkie Cnwll....2 H5
Carnkie Cnwll....3 J7
Carnkiet Cnwll....3 K3
Carno Powys....55 M5
Carnock Fife....134 C10
Carnon Downs Cnwll....3 K5
Carnousie Abers....158 G7
Carnoustie Angus....143 K11
Carnsmerry Cnwll....4 G10
Carnwath S Lans....126 H8
Carnyorth Cnwll....2 B7
Carol Green Solhll....59 L9
Carpalla Cnwll....3 P3
Carperby N York....96 F3
Carr Rothm....84 H2
Carradale Ag & B....120 F4
Carrbridge Highld....148 G3
Carrbrook Tamesd....83 L4
Carrefour Jersey....11 b1
Carreglefn IoA....78 F7
Carr Gate Wakefd....91 J6
Carrhouse N Linc....92 C9
Carrick Ag & B....131 J10
Carrick Castle Ag & B....131 P9
Carriden Falk....134 C11
Carrington Lincs....87 K9
Carrington Mdloth....127 Q5
Carrington Traffd....82 F6
Carrog Conwy....67 P3
Carrog Denbgs....68 F6
Carron Falk....133 P11
Carron Moray....157 N9
Carronbridge D & G....116 B11
Carron Bridge Stirlg....133 L11
Carronshore Falk....133 P11
Carrow Hill Mons....31 M6
Carr Shield Nthumb....112 B11
Carrutherstown D & G....109 P6
Carruth House Inver....125 K4
Carr Vale Derbys....84 G7
Carrville Dur....104 B2
Carsaig Ag & B....137 N11
Carscreugh D & G....107 K4
Carsethorn D & G....109 L9
Carshalton Gt Lon....36 G8
Carsington Derbys....71 P4
Carskey Ag & B....120 C10
Carsluith D & G....107 N6
Carsphairn D & G....115 L9
Carstairs S Lans....126 H7
Carstairs Junction S Lans....126 H8
Carswell Marsh Oxon....34 C5
Carter's Clay Hants....22 B10
Carters Green Essex....51 M8
Carterton Oxon....33 Q3
Carterway Heads
   Nthumb....112 F10

Carthew Cnwll....4 G10
Carthorpe N York....97 M4
Cartington Nthumb....119 K11
Cartland S Lans....126 F7
Cartledge Derbys....84 D5
Cartmel Cumb....94 H5
Cartmel Fell Cumb....95 J4
Carway Carmth....28 D2
Carwinley Cumb....110 H6
Cashe's Green Gloucs....32 F3
Cashmoor Dorset....12 H2
Cassington Oxon....34 D2
Cassop Colliery Dur....104 C3
Castallack Cnwll....2 D8
Castel Guern....10 b2
Castell Conwy....79 P11
Castell-y-bwch Torfn....31 J5
Casterton Cumb....95 N5
Castle Cnwll....4 H11
Castle Acre Norfk....75 Q8
Castle Ashby Nhants....61 J9
Castlebay W Isls....168 b18
Castle Bolton N York....96 F2
Castle Bromwich Solhll....58 H7
Castle Bytham Lincs....73 P7
Castlebythe Pembks....41 K5
Castle Caereinion Powys....56 B3
Castle Camps Cambs....51 P2
Castle Carrock Cumb....111 K9
Castlecary Falk....126 E2
Castle Cary Somset....20 B7
Castle Combe Wilts....32 F9
Castle Donington Leics....72 C5
Castle Douglas D & G....108 G8
Castle Eaton Swindn....33 M5
Castle Eden Dur....104 D4
Castleford Wakefd....91 L5
Castle Frome Herefs....46 C6
Castle Gate Cnwll....2 D7
Castle Green Cumb....95 L2
Castle Green Surrey....23 R2
Castle Gresley Derbys....71 P11
Castle Hedingham Essex....52 C4
Castlehill Border....117 J4
Castlehill Highld....167 M3
Castle Hill Kent....25 P2
Castlehill S Duns....53 L4
Castlehill W Duns....125 L3
Castle Howard N York....98 F6
Castle Kennedy D & G....106 F6
Castle Lachlan Ag & B....131 L6
Castlemartin Pembks....40 H11
Castlemilk C Glas....125 P5
Castle Morris Pembks....40 H4
Castlemorton Worcs....46 E7
Castlemorton Common
   Worcs....46 E7
Castle O'er D & G....110 D3
Castle Rising Norfk....75 N6
Castleside Dur....112 G11
Castle Stuart Highld....156 C8
Castlethorpe M Keyn....49 M6
Castlethorpe N Linc....92 F9
Castleton Border....111 L3
Castleton Derbys....83 Q8
Castleton N York....105 J9
Castleton Newpt....31 J7
Castleton Rochdl....89 P8
Castletown Ches W....69 M3
Castletown Dorset....11 P11
Castletown Highld....167 L3
Castletown IoM....80 c8
Castletown Sundld....113 N9
Castley N York....97 L11
Caston Norfk....64 B2
Castor C Pete....74 B11
Caswell Bay Swans....28 G7
Catacol N Ayrs....123 R10
Cat and Fiddle Derbys....83 M10
Catbrain S Glos....31 Q8
Catbrook Mons....31 N3
Catch Flints....81 J10
Catchall Cnwll....2 C8
Catchem's Corner Solhll....59 L8
Catchgate Dur....113 J10
Catcliffe Rothm....84 F3
Catcomb Wilts....33 K9
Catcott Somset....19 L7
Catcott Burtle Somset....19 L6
Caterham Surrey....36 H9
Catfield Norfk....77 M7
Catfield Common Norfk....77 M7
Catford Gt Lon....37 J6
Catforth Lancs....88 F4
Cathcart C Glas....125 P5
Cathedine Powys....44 G9
Catherine-de-Barnes
   Solhll....59 J8
Catherine Slack C Brad....90 D4
Catherington Hants....15 J5
Catherston Leweston
   Dorset....10 H6
Catherton Shrops....57 M9
Catisfield Hants....14 G5
Catley Herefs....45 R7
Catley Lane Head Rochdl....89 P7
Catlodge Highld....147 Q7
Catlow Lancs....89 P3
Catlowdy Cumb....111 J6
Catmere End Essex....51 L4
Catmore W Berk....34 E8
Caton Devon....7 J4
Caton Lancs....95 L8
Caton Green Lancs....95 L7
Cator Court Devon....8 G8
Catrine E Ayrs....115 K2
Cat's Ash Newpt....31 L6
Catsfield E Susx....26 B9
Catsfield Stream E Susx....26 B9
Catsgore Somset....19 N10
Catsham Somset....19 Q9
Catshill Worcs....58 E10
Catstree Shrops....57 N4
Cattadale Ag & B....120 C3
Cattal N York....97 P10
Cattawade Suffk....53 K5
Catterall Lancs....88 F2
Catteralslane Shrops....69 P5
Catterick N York....103 P12
Catterick Bridge N York....103 P11
Catterick Garrison
   N York....103 N12
Catterlen Cumb....101 N4
Catterline Abers....143 R3
Catterton N York....97 R11
Catteshall Surrey....23 P5
Catthorpe Leics....60 C6
Cattishall Suffk....64 A8
Cattistock Dorset....11 M5
Catton N York....97 N5

...tton Nthumb 112 B9
...twick E R Yk 99 N11
...tworth Cambs 61 N6
...udle Green Gloucs 32 H2
...ulcott C Beds 50 B2
...ulcott Oxon 48 F10
...uldhame Stirlg 133 J9
...uldcots Angus 143 M8
...uldmill Border 117 Q7
...uldon Staffs 71 K5
...uldon Lowe Staffs 71 K5
...uldwell Derbys 71 P11
...ulkerbush D & G 109 K9
...ulside D & G 110 H4
...undle Marsh Dorset 11 P2
...unsall Worcs 58 C8
...unton Notts 85 M8
...useway Hants 23 K10
...useway End Cumb 95 K3
...useway End D & G 107 M6
...useway End Essex 51 Q7
...usewayend S Lans 116 E3
...usewayhead Cumb 109 P10
...usewayhead Stirlg 133 N8
...useyend Nthumb 151 N4
...usey Park Nthumb 113 J2
...usey Park Bridge Nthumb 113 J2
...vendish Suffk 63 P11
...venham Suffk 63 N6
...versfield Oxon 48 G9
...versham Readg 35 K10
...verswall Staffs 70 H6
...verton Mill Border 118 D5
...vil E R Yk 96 C4
...vkwell Lincs 87 J5
...vwood N York 91 P3
...vsand Cnwll 6 C8
...vston Norfk 76 G7
...vston Warwks 59 Q10
...vthorn N York 98 F3
...vthorne Barns 90 H9
...vton N York 98 C5
...xton Cambs 62 D9
...xton End Cambs 62 D9
...xton Gibbet C Beds 62 C8
...ynham Shrops 57 K10
...ythorpe Lincs 86 B11
...ythorpe Notts 85 L11
...yton N York 99 M4
...annacroc Lodge Highld 146 G5
...arsiadar W Isls 168 I5
...ciliford Mons 31 P4
...in Newpt 31 J7
...in Berain Conwy 80 D11
...in-brith Conwy 68 B4
...in-bryn-brain Carmth 29 K2
...in Byrle Powys 29 M2
...in Canel Powys 68 H8
...in Coch Powys 68 F9
...in-coed-y-cymmer Myr Td 30 D3
...in Cribwr Brdgnd 29 N8
...in Cross Brdgnd 29 N8
...in-ddwysarn Gwynd 68 C7
...in-Einion Shrops 56 D7
...ineithin Carmth 28 G2
...ingorwydd Powys 44 C5
...in-mawr Wrexhm 69 J6
...inpennar Rhondd 30 D4
...in-y-bedd Flints 69 K3
...in-y-pant Carmth 41 N5
...nt IoA 78 H9
...lan Cerdgn 43 M5
...lardyke Fife 135 P7
...larhead Staffs 70 H5
...leron Cumb 101 N5
...ynen Caerph 30 H5
...naes IoA 78 F6
...nmaes Powys 55 J3
...nmaes Road Powys 55 J4
...narth Cerdgn 41 Q2
...rbyd Pembks 40 F5
...es Fife 135 L5
...ne Abbas Dorset 11 P4
...ney Wick Gloucs 33 L5
...rigceinwen IoA 78 G10
...rigydrudion Conwy 68 C5
...ss Norfk 77 N8
...unant Gwynd 67 J2
...aceley Gloucs 46 G8
...acewater Cnwll 3 K5
...ackmore Bucks 49 J7
...acombe Nhants 48 E6
...adbury Worcs 47 K5
...adderton Oldham 89 Q9
...adderton Fold Oldham 89 Q9
...addesden C Derb 72 B3
...addesley Corbett Worcs 58 C10
...addlehanger Devon 8 C9
...addleworth W Berk 34 D9
...adlington Oxon 48 B10
...adshunt Warwks 48 B4
...adwell Leics 73 K6
...adwell Derbys 57 P2
...adwell End Bed 61 N7
...adwell Heath Gt Lon 37 L3
...adwell St Mary Thurr 37 P5
...adwick Worcs 58 B11
...adwick End Solhll 59 K10
...adwick Green St Hel 82 B5
...affcombe Somset 10 H2
...afford Hundred Thurr 37 P5
...agford Devon 8 H7
...ailey E Susx 25 J7
...ainbridge Cambs 74 H10
...ainhurst Kent 26 B2
...albury Kent 12 H3
...albury Common Dorset 12 H3
...aldon Surrey 36 H9
...ale IoW 14 E11
...ale Green IoW 14 E11
...alfont Common Bucks 36 B2
...alfont St Giles Bucks 35 Q6
...alfont St Peter Bucks 36 B2
...alford Gloucs 32 G4
...alford Oxon 35 K4
...alford Wilts 20 B5
...algrove Oxon 34 H5
...alk End Essex 51 P8
...alkhouse Green Oxon 35 K9
...alkway Somset 10 H3
...alkwell Kent 38 E9

Challaborough Devon 6 H10
Challacombe Devon 17 M3
Challoch D & G 107 L4
Challock Kent 38 H11
Chalmington Dorset 11 M4
Chalton C Beds 50 B5
Chalton C Beds 61 P10
Chalton Hants 23 K11
Chalvey Slough 35 Q9
Chalvington E Susx 25 M9
Chambers Green Kent 26 F3
Chandler's Cross Herts 50 C11
Chandlers Cross Worcs 46 E7
Chandler's Ford Hants 22 D11
Channel's End Bed 61 P9
Channel Tunnel Terminal Kent 27 L4
Chanterlands Crematorium C KuH 93 J12
Chantry Somset 20 D5
Chantry Suffk 53 K3
Chapel Cumb 100 H4
Chapel Fife 134 H9
Chapel Allerton Leeds 91 J3
Chapel Allerton Somset 19 M4
Chapel Amble Cnwll 4 F6
Chapel Brampton Nhants 60 F7
Chapelbridge Cambs 62 C2
Chapel Choriton Staffs 70 E7
Chapel Cross E Susx 25 P6
Chapel End Bed 61 P9
Chapel End C Beds 50 C2
Chapel End Cambs 61 P4
Chapel End Warwks 59 M6
Chapelend Way Essex 52 B4
Chapel-en-le-Frith Derbys 83 N8
Chapel Field Bury 89 M9
Chapelgate Lincs 74 H6
Chapel Green Warwks 48 G2
Chapel Green Warwks 59 L7
Chapel Haddlesey N York 91 P5
Chapelhall N Lans 126 D5
Chapel Hill Abers 159 Q10
Chapel Hill Lincs 86 H10
Chapel Hill Mons 31 P5
Chapel Hill N York 97 M11
Chapelhope Border 117 J7
Chapelknowe D & G 110 F6
Chapel Lawn Shrops 56 F9
Chapel-le-Dale N York 95 Q5
Chapel Leigh Somset 18 F9
Chapel Milton Derbys 83 N8
Chapel of Garioch Abers 151 J3
Chapel Rossan D & G 106 F9
Chapel Row E Susx 25 P8
Chapel Row W Berk 34 G11
Chapels Cumb 94 L4
Chapel St Leonards Lincs 87 Q6
Chapel Stile Cumb 101 K9
Chapelton Angus 143 L8
Chapelton Devon 17 K6
Chapelton S Lans 126 B8
Chapeltown Bl w D 89 L7
Chapel Town Cnwll 4 D10
Chapeltown Moray 149 N3
Chapeltown Sheff 91 K11
Chapmanslade Wilts 20 F5
Chapmans Well Devon 5 P3
Chapmore End Herts 50 H7
Chappel Essex 52 E6
Charaton Cnwll 5 N8
Chard Somset 10 G3
Chard Junction Somset 10 G4
Chardleigh Green Somset 10 G2
Chardstock Devon 10 G4
Charfield S Glos 32 D6
Chargrove Gloucs 46 H11
Charing Kent 26 G2
Charing Crematorium Kent 26 G2
Charing Heath Kent 26 F2
Charing Hill Kent 38 G11
Charingworth Gloucs 47 N7
Charlbury Oxon 48 C11
Charlcombe BaNES 32 D11
Charlcutt Wilts 33 J9
Charlecote Warwks 47 Q3
Charlemont Sandw 58 F6
Charles Devon 17 M5
Charleshill Surrey 23 N6
Charleston Angus 142 F8
Charlestown C Aber 151 N7
Charlestown C Brad 90 F3
Charlestown Calder 90 B5
Charlestown Cnwll 3 Q3
Charlestown Cnwll 3 Q3
Charlestown Derbys 83 M6
Charlestown Dorset 11 P9
Charlestown Highld 153 Q3
Charlestown Highld 156 A8
Charlestown Salfd 82 H4
Charlestown of Aberlour Moray 157 P9
Charles Tye Suffk 64 E11
Charlesworth Derbys 83 M6
Charlinch Somset 18 H8
Charlottetown Fife 134 H4
Charlton Gt Lon 37 K5
Charlton Hants 22 C5
Charlton Herts 50 E5
Charlton Nhants 48 F7
Charlton Nthumb 112 B4
Charlton Oxon 34 D7
Charlton Somset 19 J9
Charlton Somset 20 B6
Charlton Somset 20 C4
Charlton Surrey 36 C7
Charlton W Susx 15 N4
Charlton Wilts 20 H10
Charlton Wilts 33 J7
Charlton Worcs 47 K5
Charlton Worcs 58 B10
Charlton Wrekin 57 K2
Charlton Abbots Gloucs 47 K10
Charlton Adam Somset 19 P9
Charlton All Saints Wilts 21 N10
Charlton Down Dorset 11 P5
Charlton Hill Shrops 57 K2
Charlton Horethorne Somset 20 C10
Charlton Kings Gloucs 47 J10
Charlton Mackrell Somset 19 P9
Charlton Marshall Dorset 12 F4
Charlton Musgrove Somset 20 D9

Charlton-on-Otmoor Oxon 48 G11
Charlton on the Hill Dorset 12 E4
Charlton St Peter Wilts 21 M3
Charlwood Hants 23 J8
Charlwood Surrey 24 F2
Charminster Dorset 11 P6
Charmouth Dorset 10 H6
Charndon Bucks 49 J10
Charney Bassett Oxon 34 C6
Charnock Green Lancs 88 H7
Charnock Richard Lancs 88 H7
Charnock Richard Crematorium Lancs 88 H7
Charnock Richard Services Lancs 88 G7
Charsfield Suffk 65 K10
Chart Corner Kent 38 C11
Charter Alley Hants 22 G3
Charterhall Border 129 K11
Charterhouse Somset 19 N3
Chartershall Stirlg 133 M9
Charterville Allotments Oxon 34 B2
Chartham Kent 39 K11
Chartham Hatch Kent 39 K10
Chart Hill Kent 26 C2
Chartridge Bucks 35 P4
Chart Sutton Kent 26 D2
Chartway Street Kent 38 D11
Charvil Wokham 35 L9
Charwelton Nhants 60 B9
Chase Terrace Staffs 58 F3
Chasetown Staffs 58 F3
Chastleton Oxon 47 P9
Chasty Devon 16 E11
Chatburn Lancs 89 M2
Chatcull Staffs 70 D8
Chatham Caerph 30 H7
Chatham Medway 38 C7
Chatham Green Essex 52 B8
Chathill Nthumb 119 N5
Chatley Worcs 46 G2
Chatsworth House Derbys 84 C6
Chattenden Medway 38 C7
Chatter End Essex 51 L5
Chatteris Cambs 62 E3
Chatterton Lancs 89 M7
Chattisham Suffk 53 J3
Chatto Border 118 E7
Chatton Nthumb 119 L5
Chaul End C Beds 50 C6
Chawleigh Devon 17 N9
Chawley Oxon 34 E4
Chawston Bed 61 Q9
Chawton Hants 23 K7
Chaxhill Gloucs 32 D2
Chazey Heath Oxon 35 J9
Cheadle Staffs 71 J6
Cheadle Stockp 83 J7
Cheadle Heath Stockp 83 J7
Cheadle Hulme Stockp 83 J7
Cheam Gt Lon 36 F8
Cheapside W & M 35 P11
Chearsley Bucks 35 K2
Chebsey Staffs 70 F9
Checkendon Oxon 35 J8
Checkley Ches E 70 C5
Checkley Herefs 46 A7
Checkley Staffs 71 J7
Checkley Green Ches E 70 C5
Chedburgh Suffk 63 N9
Cheddar Somset 19 N4
Cheddington Bucks 49 P10
Cheddleton Staffs 70 H4
Cheddleton Heath Staffs 70 H4
Cheddon Fitzpaine Somset 18 H9
Chedglow Wilts 32 H6
Chedgrave Norfk 65 N2
Chedington Dorset 11 K3
Chediston Suffk 65 M6
Chediston Green Suffk 65 M6
Chedworth Gloucs 33 L2
Chedzoy Somset 19 K7
Cheeseman's Green Kent 26 H4
Cheetham Hill Manch 82 H4
Cheldon Devon 8 H2
Chelford Ches E 82 H10
Chellaston C Derb 72 B4
Chellington Bed 61 L9
Chelmarsh Shrops 57 N7
Chelmick Shrops 56 H6
Chelmondiston Suffk 53 M4
Chelmorton Derbys 83 P11
Chelmsford Essex 52 B10
Chelmsford Crematorium Essex 51 Q8
Chelmsley Wood Solhll 59 J7
Chelsea Gt Lon 36 G5
Chelsfield Gt Lon 37 L8
Chelsham Surrey 37 J9
Chelston Somset 18 G10
Chelsworth Suffk 52 G2
Cheltenham Gloucs 46 H10
Cheltenham Crematorium Gloucs 47 J10
Chelveston Nhants 61 L7
Chelvey N Som 31 N11
Chelwood BaNES 20 B2
Chelwood Common E Susx 25 K5
Chelwood Gate E Susx 25 K4
Chelworth Wilts 33 J6
Chelworth Lower Green Wilts 33 L6
Chelworth Upper Green Wilts 33 L6
Cheney Longville Shrops 56 G8
Chenies Bucks 50 B11
Chepstow Mons 31 P6
Chequerbent Bolton 89 K9
Chequers Corner Norfk 75 J9
Cherhill Wilts 33 K10
Cherington Gloucs 32 H5
Cherington Warwks 47 Q7
Cheriton Devon 17 N2
Cheriton Hants 22 G9
Cheriton Kent 27 M4
Cheriton Pembks 41 J11
Cheriton Swans 28 E6
Cheriton Bishop Devon 9 J6
Cheriton Fitzpaine Devon 9 L3
Cherrington Wrekin 70 B10
Cherry Burton E R Yk 92 G2
Cherry Hinton Cambs 62 G9
Cherry Orchard Worcs 46 G4
Cherry Willingham Lincs 86 D6

Chertsey Surrey 36 B7
Cherwell Valley Services Oxon 48 F9
Cheselbourne Dorset 12 C5
Chesham Bucks 35 Q4
Chesham Bury 89 N8
Chesham Bois Bucks 35 Q5
Cheshunt Herts 51 J10
Chesil Beach Dorset 11 N9
Chesley Kent 38 E9
Cheslyn Hay Staffs 58 E3
Chessetts Wood Warwks 59 J10
Chessington Gt Lon 36 E8
Chessington World of Adventures Gt Lon 36 E8
Chester Ches W 81 N11
Chesterblade Somset 20 C6
Chester Crematorium Ches W 81 M11
Chester-le-Street Dur 113 L10
Chester Moor Dur 113 L11
Chesters Border 118 B6
Chesters Border 118 B8
Chester Services Ches W 81 P10
Chesterton Cambs 62 G8
Chesterton Cambs 74 B11
Chesterton Gloucs 33 K4
Chesterton Oxon 48 G10
Chesterton Shrops 57 P5
Chesterton Staffs 70 E5
Chesterton Green Warwks 48 C3
Chesterwood Nthumb 112 B7
Chester Zoo Ches W 81 N10
Chestfield Kent 39 K8
Chestnut Street Kent 38 E9
Cheston Devon 6 H7
Cheswardine Shrops 70 C8
Cheswick Nthumb 129 Q10
Cheswick Green Solhll 58 H9
Chetnole Dorset 11 N3
Chettiscombe Devon 9 N2
Chettisham Cambs 62 H4
Chettle Dorset 12 G2
Chetton Shrops 57 M6
Chetwode Bucks 48 H9
Chetwynd Wrekin 70 C10
Chetwynd Aston Wrekin 70 D11
Cheveley Cambs 63 L8
Chevening Kent 37 L9
Cheverton IoW 14 E10
Chevington Suffk 63 N9
Cheviot Hills 118 E9
Chevithorne Devon 18 C11
Chew Magna BaNES 19 Q2
Chew Moor Bolton 89 K9
Chew Stoke BaNES 19 Q2
Chewton Keynsham BaNES 32 C11
Chewton Mendip Somset 19 Q4
Chichacott Devon 8 F5
Chicheley M Keyn 49 P5
Chichester W Susx 15 N6
Chichester Crematorium W Susx 15 N5
Chickerell Dorset 11 N8
Chickering Suffk 65 J6
Chicklade Wilts 20 H8
Chicksands C Beds 50 D3
Chickward Herefs 45 K4
Chidden Hants 23 J11
Chiddingfold Surrey 23 Q7
Chiddingly E Susx 25 M8
Chiddingstone Kent 25 M2
Chiddingstone Causeway Kent 37 M11
Chideock Dorset 11 J6
Chidham W Susx 15 L6
Chidswell Kirk 90 H6
Chieveley W Berk 34 E10
Chieveley Services W Berk 34 E10
Chignall St James Essex 51 Q8
Chignall Smealy Essex 51 Q8
Chigwell Essex 37 K2
Chigwell Row Essex 37 L2
Chilbolton Hants 22 C6
Chilcomb Hants 22 F9
Chilcombe Dorset 11 L6
Chilcompton Somset 20 B4
Chilcote Leics 59 L2
Childer Thornton Ches W 81 M9
Child Okeford Dorset 12 D2
Childrey Oxon 34 C7
Child's Ercall Shrops 70 B9
Childswickham Worcs 47 L7
Childwall Lpool 81 N6
Childwick Bury Herts 50 D8
Childwick Green Herts 50 D8
Chilfrome Dorset 11 M5
Chilgrove W Susx 15 M4
Chilham Kent 39 J11
Chilla Devon 8 B4
Chillaton Devon 8 B8
Chillenden Kent 39 N11
Chillerton IoW 14 E10
Chillesford Suffk 65 M11
Chillingham Nthumb 119 L5
Chillington Devon 7 K10
Chillington Somset 10 H2
Chilmark Wilts 21 J8
Chilmington Green Kent 26 G3
Chilson Oxon 48 B11
Chilsworthy Cnwll 5 Q7
Chilsworthy Devon 16 E9
Chiltern Green C Beds 50 D7
Chiltern Hills 35 L5
Chilterns Crematorium Bucks 35 P5
Chilthorne Domer Somset 19 P11
Chilton Bucks 35 J2
Chilton Devon 9 J4
Chilton Dur 103 Q5
Chilton Kent 27 N3
Chilton Oxon 34 E7
Chilton Suffk 52 F2
Chilton Candover Hants 22 G6
Chilton Cantelo Somset 19 Q10
Chilton Foliat Wilts 34 B10
Chilton Polden Somset 19 L6
Chilton Street Suffk 63 N11
Chilton Trinity Somset 19 J7
Chilwell Notts 72 E3
Chilworth Hants 22 D11

Chilworth Surrey 36 B11
Chimney Oxon 34 C4
Chineham Hants 23 J3
Chingford Gt Lon 37 J2
Chinley Derbys 83 M8
Chinnor Oxon 35 L4
Chipchase Castle Nthumb 112 C5
Chipnall Shrops 70 C8
Chippenham Cambs 63 L7
Chippenham Wilts 32 H10
Chipperfield Herts 50 B10
Chipping Herts 51 J4
Chipping Lancs 89 J2
Chipping Campden Gloucs 47 N7
Chipping Hill Essex 52 D8
Chipping Norton Oxon 48 B9
Chipping Ongar Essex 51 N10
Chipping Sodbury S Glos 32 D8
Chipping Warden Nhants 48 C5
Chipshop Devon 8 B9
Chipstable Somset 18 D9
Chipstead Kent 37 M9
Chipstead Surrey 36 G9
Chirbury Shrops 56 D5
Chirk Wrexhm 69 J7
Chirnside Border 129 M8
Chirnsidebridge Border 129 M8
Chirton Wilts 21 L3
Chisbury Wilts 33 Q11
Chiselborough Somset 11 K2
Chiseldon Swindn 33 N8
Chiselhampton Oxon 34 G5
Chisholme Border 117 N8
Chislehurst Gt Lon 37 K6
Chislet Kent 39 M9
Chisley Calder 90 C5
Chiswell Green Herts 50 D10
Chiswick Gt Lon 36 F5
Chiswick End Cambs 62 E11
Chisworth Derbys 83 L6
Chitcombe E Susx 26 D7
Chithurst W Susx 23 M10
Chittering Cambs 62 G7
Chitterne Wilts 21 J6
Chittlehamholt Devon 17 M7
Chittlehampton Devon 17 L6
Chittoe Wilts 33 J11
Chivelstone Devon 7 K11
Chivenor Devon 17 J5
Chiverton Cross Cnwll 3 J4
Chlenry D & G 106 F5
Chobham Surrey 23 Q2
Cholderton Wilts 21 P6
Cholesbury Bucks 35 P3
Chollerford Nthumb 112 D6
Chollerton Nthumb 112 D6
Cholmondeston Ches E 70 A3
Cholsey Oxon 34 G7
Cholstrey Herefs 45 P3
Chop Gate N York 104 G11
Choppington Nthumb 113 L4
Chopwell Gatesd 112 H9
Chorley Ches E 69 Q4
Chorley Lancs 88 H7
Chorley Shrops 57 M8
Chorley Staffs 58 G2
Chorleywood Herts 50 B11
Chorleywood West Herts 50 B11
Chorlton Ches E 70 C4
Chorlton-cum-Hardy Manch 82 H6
Chorlton Lane Ches W 69 N5
Choulton Shrops 56 F7
Chowley Ches W 69 N3
Chrishall Essex 51 K3
Chrisswell Inver 124 G3
Christchurch Cambs 75 J11
Christchurch Dorset 13 L6
Christchurch Gloucs 31 Q2
Christchurch Newpt 31 K7
Christian Malford Wilts 33 J9
Christleton Ches W 81 N11
Christmas Common Oxon 35 K6
Christmas Pie Surrey 23 P5
Christon N Som 19 L3
Christon Bank Nthumb 119 P6
Christow Devon 9 K7
Christ's Hospital W Susx 24 D5
Chuck Hatch E Susx 25 L4
Chudleigh Devon 9 L9
Chudleigh Knighton Devon 9 K9
Chulmleigh Devon 17 M9
Chunal Derbys 83 M6
Church Lancs 89 L5
Churcham Gloucs 46 E11
Church Aston Wrekin 70 C11
Church Brampton Nhants 60 F7
Church Brough Cumb 102 E8
Church Broughton Derbys 71 N8
Church Cove Cnwll 3 J11
Church Crookham Hants 23 M4
Churchdown Gloucs 46 G11
Church Eaton Staffs 70 E11
Church End Bed 61 N9
Church End Bed 61 P9
Church End Bucks 35 K3
Church End C Beds 49 Q10
Church End C Beds 49 Q8
Church End C Beds 50 B4
Church End C Beds 50 B7
Church End C Beds 50 E3
Church End Cambs 61 N6
Church End Cambs 62 B4
Church End Cambs 62 D5
Churchend Essex 51 P6
Church End Essex 51 P6
Church End Essex 52 B8
Church End Gloucs 46 G7
Church End Gt Lon 36 F2
Church End Herts 50 D8
Church End Herts 50 K6
Church End Lincs 74 D4
Church End Lincs 93 R11
Church End Warwks 59 K6
Church End Warwks 59 L6
Church Enstone Oxon 48 C9
Church Fenton N York 91 N3
Churchfield Sandw 58 F6
Churchgate Herts 51 H10
Churchgate Street Essex 51 L8
Church Green Devon 10 D5

Church Gresley Derbys....71 P11
Church Hanborough
  Oxon....34 D2
Church Hill Staffs....58 F2
Church Houses N York....105 H3
Churchill Devon....10 F4
Churchill Devon....17 K3
Churchill N Som....19 M3
Churchill Oxon....47 Q10
Churchill Worcs....46 H4
Churchill Worcs....58 C9
Churchinford Somset....10 E2
Church Knowle Dorset....12 F8
Church Laneham Notts....85 P5
Church Langton Leics....60 F2
Church Lawford Warwks....59 Q9
Church Lawton Ches E....70 E3
Church Leigh Staffs....71 J7
Church Lench Worcs....47 K4
Church Mayfield Staffs....71 M6
Church Minshull Ches E....70 B2
Church Norton W Susx....15 N7
Churchover Warwks....60 B4
Church Preen Shrops....57 J5
Church Pulverbatch
  Shrops....56 G4
Churchstanton Somset....10 D2
Churchstoke Powys....56 D6
Churchstow Devon....7 J9
Church Stowe Nhants....60 D9
Church Street Essex....52 C3
Church Street Kent....38 B7
Church Street Suffk....52 P5
Church Stretton Shrops....56 H6
Churchthorpe Lincs....93 P11
Churchtown Bpool....88 C2
Churchtown Cnwll....4 H6
Churchtown Derbys....84 C8
Churchtown Devon....17 M3
Churchtown IoM....80 f3
Churchtown Lancs....88 F2
Church Town N Linc....92 C9
Churchtown Sefton....88 D7
Church Village Rhondd....30 E7
Church Warsop Notts....85 J7
Church Wilne Derbys....72 C4
Churnsike Lodge
  Nthumb....111 N5
Churston Ferrers Torbay....7 N7
Churt Surrey....23 N7
Churton Ches W....69 M3
Churwell Leeds....90 H5
Chwilog Gwynd....66 G7
Chyandour Cnwll....2 D7
Chyanvounder Cnwll....2 H9
Chyeowling Cnwll....3 K5
Chyvarloe Cnwll....2 H9
Cil Powys....56 B4
Cilcain Flints....80 H11
Cilcennin Cerdgn....43 K2
Cilcewydd Powys....56 C4
Cilfrew Neath....29 L4
Cilfynydd Rhondd....30 E6
Cilgerran Pembks....41 N2
Cilgwyn Carmth....43 P9
Cilgwyn Gwynd....66 H4
Ciliau-Aeron Cerdgn....43 K3
Cilmaengwyn Neath....29 K3
Cilmery Powys....44 E4
Cilrhedyn Pembks....41 Q4
Cilsan Carmth....43 L10
Ciltalgarth Gwynd....68 A6
Cilycwm Carmth....43 Q7
Cimla Neath....29 L5
Cinderford Gloucs....32 C2
Cinder Hill Wolves....58 D6
Cippenham Slough....35 Q8
Cirencester Gloucs....33 K4
Citadilla N York....103 P11
City Gt Lon....36 H4
City V Glam....30 C9
City Airport Gt Lon....37 K4
City Dulas IoA....78 H7
City of London
  Crematorium Gt Lon....37 K3
Clabhach Ag & B....136 F4
Clachaig Ag & B....131 N11
Clachan Ag & B....123 N8
Clachan Ag & B....130 F4
Clachan Ag & B....138 F9
Clachan Highld....153 J10
Clachan-a-Luib W Isls....168 d11
Clachan Mor Ag & B....136 B6
Clachan na Luib W Isls....168 d11
Clachan of Campsie
  E Duns....125 Q2
Clachan-Seil Ag & B....130 F4
Clachnaharry Highld....156 A8
Clachtoll Highld....164 B11
Clackavoid P & K....142 A5
Clacket Lane Services
  Surrey....37 K10
Clackmannan Clacks....133 Q9
Clackmannanshire
  Bridge Fife....133 Q10
Clackmarras Moray....157 N6
Clacton-on-Sea Essex....53 L8
Cladich Ag & B....131 M3
Cladswell Worcs....47 L3
Claggan Highld....138 C8
Claigan Highld....152 C7
Clandown BaNES....20 C3
Clanfield Hants....15 J11
Clanfield Oxon....33 Q4
Clannaborough Devon....8 H4
Clanville Hants....22 B5
Clanville Somset....20 B8
Claonaig Ag & B....123 Q8
Clapgate Dorset....12 H4
Clapgate Herts....51 K6
Clapham Bed....61 M10
Clapham Devon....9 L7
Clapham Gt Lon....36 G5
Clapham N York....95 Q7
Clapham W Susx....24 B9
Clapham Green Bed....61 M10
Clap Hill Kent....27 J4
Clappersgate Cumb....101 L10
Clapton Somset....11 J3
Clapton Somset....20 B4
Clapton-in-Gordano
  N Som....31 N10
Clapton-on-the-Hill
  Gloucs....47 N11
Clapworthy Devon....17 M7
Clarach Cerdgn....54 E8
Claravale Gatesd....112 H8
Clarbeston Pembks....41 L6
Clarbeston Road Pembks....41 K6
Clarborough Notts....85 M4
Clare Suffk....63 N11

Clarebrand D & G....108 G7
Clarencefield D & G....109 N7
Clarewood Nthumb....112 F7
Clarilaw Border....117 Q7
Clark's Green Surrey....24 L3
Clarkston E Rens....125 P6
Clashmore Highld....162 G9
Clashmore Highld....164 B10
Clashnessie Highld....164 C10
Clashnoir Moray....149 N3
Clathy P & K....134 B3
Clathymore P & K....134 C3
Clatt Abers....150 E2
Clatter Powys....55 M6
Clatterford End Essex....51 P8
Clatworthy Somset....18 E8
Claughton Lancs....88 G2
Claughton Lancs....95 M7
Claughton Wirral....81 L7
Clavelshay Somset....19 J3
Claverdon Warwks....59 J11
Claverham N Som....31 N11
Clavering Essex....51 L4
Claverley Shrops....57 P6
Claverton BaNES....20 E2
Claverton Down BaNES....20 E2
Clawdd-coch V Glam....30 E9
Clawdd-newydd Denbgs....68 E4
Clawthorpe Cumb....95 L5
Clawton Devon....5 P2
Claxby Lincs....86 F2
Claxby Lincs....87 N6
Claxton N York....98 D9
Claxton Norfk....77 L11
Claybrooke Magna Leics....59 Q7
Clay Common Suffk....65 P5
Clay Coton Nhants....60 C5
Clay Cross Derbys....84 E8
Claydon Oxon....48 E5
Claydon Suffk....53 K2
Clay End Herts....50 H6
Claygate D & G....110 G5
Claygate Kent....26 B3
Claygate Surrey....36 E8
Claygate Cross Kent....37 P9
Clayhall Gt Lon....37 K2
Clayhanger Devon....18 D10
Clayhanger Wsall....58 F4
Clayhidon Devon....18 G11
Clayhill E Susx....26 D7
Clayhill Hants....13 P3
Clayhithe Cambs....62 H8
Clayock Highld....167 L5
Claypit Hill Cambs....62 E10
Claypits Gloucs....32 E3
Claypole Lincs....85 P11
Claythorpe Lincs....87 M5
Clayton C Brad....90 E4
Clayton Donc....91 M9
Clayton W Susx....24 G8
Clayton Green Lancs....88 H6
Clayton-le-Moors Lancs....89 M4
Clayton-le-Woods Lancs....88 H6
Clayton West Kirk....90 H8
Clayworth Notts....85 M3
Cleadale Highld....144 G10
Cleadon S Tyne....113 N8
Clearbrook Devon....6 E5
Clearwell Gloucs....31 Q3
Clearwell Meend Gloucs....31 Q3
Cleasby N York....103 Q8
Cleat Ork....169 d8
Cleatlam Dur....103 M7
Cleator Cumb....100 D8
Cleator Moor Cumb....100 D7
Cleckheaton Kirk....90 F5
Cleedownton Shrops....57 K8
Cleehill Shrops....57 K6
Cleekhimin N Lans....126 D6
Clee St Margaret Shrops....57 K8
Cleestanton Shrops....57 K9
Cleethorpes NE Lin....93 P9
Cleeton St Mary Shrops....57 L9
Cleeve N Som....31 N11
Cleeve Oxon....34 H8
Cleeve Hill Gloucs....47 J9
Cleeve Prior Worcs....47 L5
Cleghornie E Loth....128 F3
Clehonger Herefs....45 N7
Cleish P & K....134 D8
Cleland N Lans....126 D6
Clement's End C Beds....50 B8
Clement Street Kent....37 M6
Clenamacrie Ag & B....131 J2
Clench Common Wilts....33 N11
Clenchwarton Norfk....75 L6
Clenerty Abers....159 J5
Clent Worcs....58 D9
Cleobury Mortimer
  Shrops....57 M9
Cleobury North Shrops....57 L7
Cleongart Ag & B....120 C5
Clephanton Highld....156 E7
Clerkhill P & K....117 K11
Cleuch-head D & G....115 R7
Clevancy Wilts....33 L9
Clevedon N Som....31 M10
Cleveley Oxon....48 C10
Cleveleys Lancs....88 C2
Cleverton Wilts....33 J7
Clewer Somset....19 M4
Cley next the Sea Norfk....76 E3
Cliburn Cumb....101 Q6
Cliddesden Hants....22 H5
Cliff Warwks....59 L4
Cliffe Lancs....89 L4
Cliffe Medway....38 B6
Cliffe N York....91 R4
Cliffe N York....103 P7
Cliff End E Susx....26 E9
Cliffe Woods Medway....38 B7
Clifford Herefs....45 J5
Clifford Leeds....91 L2
Clifford Chambers
  Warwks....47 N4
Clifford's Mesne Gloucs....46 D10
Cliffsend Kent....39 P9
Clifton Bristl....31 Q10
Clifton C Beds....50 E3
Clifton C Nott....72 E4
Clifton C York....98 B10
Clifton Calder....90 F6
Clifton Cumb....101 P5
Clifton Derbys....71 M6
Clifton Devon....17 L3
Clifton Donc....91 N11
Clifton Lancs....88 F4
Clifton N York....97 J11
Clifton Nthumb....113 K4
Clifton Oxon....48 E8
Clifton Salfd....82 G4

Clifton Worcs....46 F5
Clifton Campville Staffs....59 L2
Clifton Hampden Oxon....34 F5
Clifton Reynes M Keyn....49 P4
Clifton upon Dunsmore
  Warwks....60 B5
Clifton upon Teme
  Worcs....46 D2
Cliftonville Kent....39 Q7
Climping W Susx....15 Q6
Clink Somset....20 E5
Clint N York....97 L9
Clinterty C Aber....151 L5
Clint Green Norfk....76 E9
Clintmains Border....118 B4
Clipiau Gwynd....55 J2
Clippesby Norfk....77 N9
Clipsham Rutlnd....73 P7
Clipston Nhants....60 F4
Clipston Notts....72 G4
Clipstone C Beds....49 P9
Clipstone Notts....85 J8
Clitheroe Lancs....89 L2
Clive Shrops....69 P10
Clixby Lincs....93 J10
Cloatley Wilts....33 J6
Clocaenog Denbgs....68 E4
Clochan Moray....158 B5
Clock Face St Hel....82 B6
Cloddiau Powys....56 C3
Clodock Herefs....45 L9
Cloford Somset....20 D6
Clola Abers....159 P9
Clophill C Beds....50 C3
Clopton Nhants....61 N4
Clopton Suffk....65 J11
Clopton Corner Suffk....65 J11
Clopton Green Suffk....63 N10
Clopton Green Suffk....64 D10
Clos du Valle Guern....10 C1
Closeburn D & G....109 J2
Closeburnmill D & G....109 K2
Closeclark IoM....80 c6
Closworth Somset....11 M2
Clothall Herts....50 G4
Clotton Ches W....69 P2
Cloudesley Bush Warwks....59 Q7
Clouds Herefs....46 A7
Clough Oldham....89 Q9
Clough Foot Calder....89 Q6
Clough Head Calder....90 D7
Cloughton N York....99 L2
Cloughton Newlands
  N York....105 R11
Clousta Shet....169 q8
Clova Angus....142 E3
Clovelly Devon....16 E7
Clovenfords Border....117 P3
Clovulin Highld....139 J5
Clow Bridge Lancs....89 N5
Clowne Derbys....84 G5
Clows Top Worcs....57 N10
Cloy Wrexhm....69 L6
Cluanie Inn Highld....146 D5
Cluanie Lodge Highld....146 D5
Clubworthy Cnwll....5 M3
Clugston D & G....107 L6
Clun Shrops....56 E8
Clunas Highld....156 F8
Clunbury Shrops....56 F8
Clunderwen Carmth....41 M7
Clune Highld....148 D2
Clunes Highld....146 F10
Clunie P & K....141 R9
Clunton Shrops....56 E8
Cluny Fife....134 G8
Clutton BaNES....20 B3
Clutton Ches W....69 N4
Clutton Hill BaNES....20 B3
Clwt-y-bont Gwynd....67 J2
Clydach Mons....30 H2
Clydach Swans....29 J4
Clydach Vale Rhondd....30 C6
Clydebank W Duns....125 M3
Clydebank
  Crematorium W Duns....125 M3
Clydey Pembks....41 Q3
Clyffe Pypard Wilts....33 L9
Clynder Ag & B....131 Q11
Clyne Neath....29 M4
Clynnog-fawr Gwynd....66 G5
Clyro Powys....45 J6
Clyst Honiton Devon....9 N6
Clyst Hydon Devon....9 P4
Clyst St George Devon....9 N7
Clyst St Lawrence Devon....9 P4
Clyst St Mary Devon....9 N6
Cnoc W Isls....168 j4
Cnwch Coch Cerdgn....54 F10
Coad's Green Cnwll....5 M6
Coal Aston Derbys....84 E5
Coalbrookvale Blae G....30 G3
Coalburn S Lans....126 E11
Coalburns Gatesd....112 H8
Coaley Gloucs....32 E4
Coalhill Essex....38 C2
Coalmoor Wrekin....57 M3
Coalpit Heath S Glos....32 C8
Coal Pool Wsall....58 E4
Coalport Wrekin....57 M4
Coalsnaughton Clacks....133 Q8
Coal Street Suffk....65 J7
Coaltown of Balgonie
  Fife....134 H8
Coaltown of Wemyss
  Fife....135 J8
Coalville Leics....72 C8
Coanwood Nthumb....111 N9
Coat Somset....19 N10
Coatbridge N Lans....126 C4
Coatdyke N Lans....126 C4
Coate Swindn....33 N8
Coate Wilts....21 K2
Coates Cambs....74 F11
Coates Gloucs....33 J4
Coates Lincs....86 B4
Coates Notts....85 P4
Coates W Susx....23 Q11
Coatham R & Cl....104 G5
Coatham Mundeville
  Darltn....103 Q6
Cobbaton Devon....17 L6
Coberley Gloucs....47 J11
Cobhall Common Herefs....45 P7
Cobham Kent....37 Q7
Cobham Surrey....36 D8
Cobham Services Surrey....36 D9
Coblers Green Essex....51 Q7
Cobley Dorset....21 K10

Cobnash Herefs....45 P2
Cobo Guern....10 b1
Cobridge C Stke....70 F5
Coburby Abers....159 M5
Cock Alley Derbys....84 F6
Cockayne N York....104 H11
Cockayne Hatley C Beds....62 C11
Cock Bank Wrexhm....69 L5
Cock Bevington Warwks....47 L4
Cock Bridge Abers....149 P6
Cockburnspath Border....129 K5
Cock Clarks Essex....52 D11
Cock & End Suffk....63 M10
Cockenzie and Port
  Seton E Loth....128 C4
Cocker Bar Lancs....88 G6
Cocker Brook Lancs....89 L5
Cockerham Lancs....95 K10
Cockermouth Cumb....100 F4
Cockernhoe Herts....50 D6
Cockersdale Leeds....90 G5
Cockett Swans....28 H6
Cockfield Dur....103 M6
Cockfield Suffk....64 C11
Cockfosters Gt Lon....50 G11
Cock Green Essex....51 Q7
Cocking W Susx....23 N11
Cocking Causeway
  W Susx....23 N11
Cockington Torbay....7 M6
Cocklake Somset....19 M5
Cockley Beck Cumb....100 H10
Cockley Cley Norfk....75 Q10
Cock Marling E Susx....26 E8
Cockpole Green Wokham....35 L8
Cocks Cnwll....3 K3
Cockshutford Shrops....57 K7
Cockshutt Shrops....69 M9
Cock Street Kent....38 C11
Cockthorpe Norfk....76 D3
Cockwells Cnwll....2 E7
Cockwood Devon....9 N8
Cockwood Somset....18 H6
Cockyard Derbys....83 M9
Cockyard Herefs....45 N8
Coddenham Suffk....64 G11
Coddington Ches W....69 N3
Coddington Herefs....46 D6
Coddington Notts....85 P10
Codford St Mary Wilts....21 J7
Codford St Peter Wilts....21 J7
Codicote Herts....50 F7
Codmore Hill W Susx....24 C6
Codnor Derbys....84 F11
Codrington S Glos....32 D9
Codsall Staffs....58 C4
Codsall Wood Staffs....58 B4
Coedely Rhondd....30 D7
Coedkernew Newpt....31 J8
Coed Morgan Mons....31 L2
Coedpoeth Wrexhm....69 J4
Coed Talon Flints....69 J3
Coedway Powys....69 K11
Coed-y-Bryn Cerdgn....42 G5
Coed-y-caerau Newpt....31 L6
Coed-y-paen Mons....31 K5
Coed-yr-ynys Powys....44 H10
Coed Ystumgwern
  Gwynd....67 K10
Coelbren Powys....29 N2
Coffinswell Devon....7 M5
Coffle End Bed....61 M9
Cofton Devon....9 N8
Cofton Hackett Worcs....58 F9
Cogan V Glam....30 G10
Cogenhoe Nhants....60 H8
Cogges Oxon....34 C3
Coggeshall Essex....52 E7
Coggin's Mill E Susx....25 N5
Coignafearn Highld....148 C4
Coilacriech Abers....149 Q8
Coilantogle Stirlg....132 H6
Coillore Highld....152 F10
Coity Brdgnd....29 P8
Col W Isls....168 j4
Colaboll Highld....162 D4
Colan Cnwll....4 D9
Colaton Raleigh Devon....10 B7
Colbost Highld....152 C8
Colburn N York....103 N11
Colby Cumb....102 C6
Colby IoM....80 b7
Colby Norfk....77 J5
Colchester Essex....52 G6
Colchester
  Crematorium Essex....52 G7
Colchester Zoo Essex....52 G7
Cold Ash W Berk....34 F11
Cold Ashby Nhants....60 E5
Cold Ashton S Glos....32 E10
Cold Aston Gloucs....47 M11
Coldbackie Highld....165 P4
Coldbeck Cumb....102 D10
Cold Blow Pembks....41 M8
Cold Brayfield M Keyn....49 P4
Cold Cotes N York....95 Q6
Coldean Br & H....24 H9
Coldeast Devon....7 L4
Colden Calder....90 B5
Colden Common Hants....22 E10
Coldfair Green Suffk....65 N9
Coldham Cambs....74 H10
Cold Hanworth Lincs....86 D4
Coldharbour Cnwll....3 K4
Coldharbour Devon....9 Q2
Coldharbour Gloucs....31 Q4
Cold Harbour Herts....50 D7
Coldharbour Oxon....34 H9
Coldharbour Surrey....24 D2
Cold Harbour Wilts....20 G5
Cold Hatton Wrekin....70 A10
Cold Hatton Heath
  Wrekin....70 A10
Cold Hesledon Dur....113 P11
Cold Hiendley Wakefd....91 K8
Cold Higham Nhants....49 M4
Coldingham Border....129 N6
Cold Kirby N York....98 H3
Coldmeece Staffs....70 F8
Cold Newton Leics....73 J9
Cold Northcott Cnwll....5 L4
Cold Norton Essex....52 E11
Cold Overton Leics....73 L8
Coldred Kent....27 N2
Coldridge Devon....8 H3
Coldstream Border....118 H3
Coldwaltham W Susx....24 B7
Coldwell Herefs....45 N7
Coldwells Abers....159 N10
Cold Weston Shrops....57 K8
Cole Somset....20 C8

Colebatch Shrops....56 E
Colebrook C Plym....6 E
Colebrook Devon....9 J
Colebrooke Devon....9 J
Coleby Lincs....86 C
Coleby N Linc....92 E
Cole End Warwks....59 J
Coleford Devon....9 J
Coleford Gloucs....31 Q
Coleford Somset....20 D
Coleford Water Somset....18 F
Colegate End Norfk....64 H
Cole Green Herts....50 G
Cole Green Herts....51 J
Cole Henley Hants....22 E
Colehill Dorset....12 H
Coleman Green Herts....50 E
Coleman's Hatch E Susx....25 M
Colemere Shrops....69 N
Colemore Hants....23 J
Colemore Green Shrops....57 N
Colenden P & K....134 E
Coleorton Leics....72 C
Colerne Wilts....32 F
Colesbourne Gloucs....33 K
Cole's Cross Devon....7
Coles Cross Dorset....10 H
Colesden Bed....61 N
Coles Green Suffk....53 K
Coleshill Bucks....35 Q
Coleshill Oxon....33 Q
Coleshill Warwks....59 J
Colestocks Devon....10 B
Coley BaNES....20
Colgate W Susx....24 E
Colinsburgh Fife....135 M
Colinton C Edin....127 N
Colintraive Ag & B....124 D
Colkirk Norfk....76
Coll Ag & B....136 C
Coll W Isls....168
Collace P & K....142 C11
Collafirth Shet....169
Coll Airport Ag & B....136
Collaton Devon....7
Collaton St Mary Torbay....7
College of Roseisle
  Moray....157
College Town Br For....23 N
Collessie Fife....134 H
Colleton Mills Devon....17
Collier Row Gt Lon....37 M
Collier's End Herts....51
Collier's Green E Susx....26 C
Colliers Green Kent....26
Collier Street Kent....26
Colliery Row Sundld....113 M1
Collieston Abers....151
Collin D & G....109
Collingbourne Ducis
  Wilts....21 P
Collingbourne
  Kingston Wilts....21 P
Collingham Leeds....97 N1
Collingham Notts....85 P
Collington Herefs....46
Collingtree Nhants....60
Collins Green Warrtn....82 C
Collins Green Worcs....46 D
Colliston Angus....143 L1
Colliton Devon....10
Collyweston Nhants....73 P1
Colmonell S Ayrs....114 B1
Colmworth Bed....61
Colnabaichin Abers....149
Colnbrook Slough....36
Colne Cambs....62
Colne Lancs....89
Colne Bridge Kirk....90
Colne Edge Lancs....89
Colne Engaine Essex....52
Colney Norfk....76 H1
Colney Heath Herts....50
Colney Street Herts....50 E
Coln Rogers Gloucs....33
Coln St Aldwyns Gloucs....33
Coln St Dennis Gloucs....33
Colonsay Ag & B....136
Colpy Abers....158 F
Colquhar Border....117
Colquite Cnwll....4
Colscott Devon....16
Colsterdale N York....96
Colsterworth Lincs....73
Colston Bassett Notts....73
Coltfield Moray....157
Colt Hill Hants....23
Coltishall Norfk....77
Colton Cumb....94
Colton Leeds....91
Colton N York....97
Colton Norfk....76 G1
Colton Staffs....71 J
Colt's Hill Kent....25
Columbjohn Devon....9
Colva Powys....44
Colvend D & G....109 J1
Colwall Herefs....46
Colwell Nthumb....112
Colwich Staffs....71 J
Colwick Notts....72
Colworth W Susx....15
Colwyn Bay Conwy....80
Colwyn Bay
  Crematorium Conwy....79
Colyford Devon....10
Colyton Devon....10
Combe Devon....7 J
Combe Herefs....45
Combe Oxon....48 D
Combe W Berk....22
Combe Almer Dorset....12
Combe Common Surrey....23
Combe Down BaNES....20
Combe Fishacre Devon....7
Combe Florey Somset....18
Combe Hay BaNES....20
Combeinteignhead
  Devon....7
Combe Martin Devon....17
Combe Raleigh Devon....10
Comberbach Ches W....82
Comberford Staffs....59
Comberton Cambs....62
Comberton Herefs....56 H
Combe St Nicholas
  Somset....10
Combpyne Devon....10
Combridge Staffs....71

Combrook – Croachy 265

ombrook Warwks 48 B4
ombs Derbys 83 M9
ombs Suffk 64 E10
ombs Ford Suffk 64 E10
ombwich Somset 19 J6
omers Abers 150 H6
omhampton Worcs 58 B11
ommercial End Cambs 63 J8
ommins Coch Powys 55 J4
ommondale N York 105 J8
ommon Edge Bpool 88 C4
ommon End Cumb 100 D6
ommon Moor Cnwll 5 L8
ommon Platt Wilts 33 M7
ommonside Ches W 82 B10
ommonside Derbys 71 N6
ommon Side Derbys 84 D5
ommonwood Shrops 69 N9
ommonwood Wrexhm 69 L4
ompass Somset 19 J8
ompstall Stockp 83 L6
ompstonend D & G 108 E10
ompton Devon 7 M6
ompton Hants 22 B9
ompton Hants 22 E9
ompton Staffs 57 Q8
ompton Surrey 23 Q5
ompton W Berk 34 F8
ompton W Susx 15 L4
ompton Wilts 21 M4
ompton Abbas Dorset 20 G11
ompton Abdale Gloucs 47 L11
ompton Bassett Wilts 33 K10
ompton Beauchamp Oxon 33 Q7
ompton Bishop Somset 19 L3
ompton Chamberlayne Wilts 21 K9
ompton Dando BaNES 20 B2
ompton Dundon Somset 19 N8
ompton Durville Somset 19 M11
ompton Greenfield S Glos 31 Q8
ompton Martin BaNES 19 P3
ompton Pauncefoot Somset 20 B9
ompton Valence Dorset 11 M6
omrie Fife 134 C10
omrie P & K 133 M3
onaglen House Highld 139 J4
onchra Highld 145 Q2
oncraigie P & K 141 Q9
onder Green Lancs 95 K9
onderton Worcs 47 J7
ondicote Gloucs 47 N9
ondorrat N Lans 126 C3
ondover Shrops 56 H3
oney Hill Gloucs 46 G11
oneyhurst Common W Susx 24 D6
oneysthorpe N York 98 E6
oneythorpe N York 97 N9
oney Weston Suffk 64 D6
onford Hants 23 M8
ongdon's Shop Cnwll 5 M6
ongerstone Leics 72 B9
ongham Norfk 75 P6
ongleton Ches E 70 F2
ongl-y-wal Gwynd 67 N6
ongresbury N Som 19 M2
ongreve Staffs 58 D2
onheath D & G 109 L7
onicavel Moray 156 H7
oningsby Lincs 86 H9
onington Cambs 61 Q3
onington Cambs 62 D7
onisbrough Donc 91 N11
onisholme Lincs 93 R11
oniston Cumb 101 K11
oniston E R Yk 93 L3
oniston Cold N York 96 D10
onistone N York 96 E7
onnah's Quay Flints 81 K11
onnel Ag & B 138 G11
onnel Park E Ayrs 115 M5
onnor Downs Cnwll 2 F6
onon Bridge Highld 155 P6
ononley N York 96 E11
onsall Staffs 70 H5
onsett Dur 112 H10
onstable Burton N York 97 J2
onstable Lee Lancs 89 N6
onstantine Cnwll 3 J8
onstantine Bay Cnwll 4 D7
ontin Highld 155 N6
onwy Conwy 79 P9
onwy Castle Conwy 79 P9
onyer Kent 38 G9
onyer's Green Suffk 64 B8
ooden E Susx 26 B10
ookbury Devon 16 G10
ookbury Wick Devon 16 F10
ookham W & M 35 N7
ookham Dean W & M 35 N7
ookham Rise W & M 35 N7
ookhill Worcs 47 L3
ookley Suffk 65 L6
ookley Worcs 58 B8
ookley Green Oxon 35 J6
ookney Abers 151 M9
ooksbridge E Susx 25 K8
ooksey Green Worcs 58 D11
ook's Green Essex 53 L8
ooks Green Suffk 64 D11
ookshill Staffs 70 G6
ooksland Cnwll 4 H8
ooksmill Green Essex 51 P9
ookson Green Ches W 82 C10
oolham W Susx 24 D6
ooling Medway 38 C6
ooling Street Medway 38 B7
oombe Cnwll 2 G5
oombe Cnwll 3 L5
oombe Cnwll 3 N3
oombe Devon 7 N4
oombe Devon 9 K8
oombe Devon 10 C6
oombe Gloucs 32 E6
oombe Hants 23 J10
oombe Wilts 21 M4
oombe Abbey Warwks 59 N9
oombe Bissett Wilts 21 M9
oombe Cellars Devon 7 N4
oombe Cross Hants 23 J10
oombe Hill Gloucs 46 G9
oombe Keynes Dorset 12 D8
oombe Pafford Torbay 7 N5
oombes W Susx 24 E9
oombes-Moor Herefs 45 M2
Coombe Street Somset 20 E8
Coombeswood Dudley 58 E7
Coopersale Common Essex 51 L10
Coopersale Street Essex 51 L10
Cooper's Corner Kent 37 L11
Coopers Green E Susx 25 L6
Coopers Green Herts 50 E9
Cooper Street Kent 39 P9
Cooper Turning Bolton 89 J9
Cootham W Susx 24 C8
Copdock Suffk 53 K3
Copford Green Essex 52 F7
Copgrove N York 97 M8
Copister Shet 169 r6
Cople Bed 61 P11
Copley Calder 90 D6
Copley Dur 103 L5
Copley Tamesd 83 L5
Coplow Dale Derbys 83 Q9
Copmanthorpe C York 98 B11
Copmere End Staffs 70 E9
Copp Lancs 88 E3
Coppathorne Cnwll 16 C11
Coppenhall Staffs 70 G11
Coppenhall Moss Ches E 70 C3
Copperhouse Cnwll 2 F6
Coppicegate Shrops 57 N8
Coppingford Cambs 61 Q5
Coppins Corner Kent 26 F2
Copplestone Devon 9 J4
Coppull Lancs 88 H8
Coppull Moor Lancs 88 H8
Copsale W Susx 24 E6
Copster Green Lancs 89 K4
Copston Magna Warwks 59 Q7
Cop Street Kent 39 N9
Copthall Green Essex 51 K10
Copt Heath Solhll 59 J9
Copt Hewick N York 97 M6
Copthorne Cnwll 5 M3
Copthorne W Susx 24 H3
Copt Oak Leics 72 D8
Copy's Green Norfk 76 C4
Copythorne Hants 13 P2
Coram Street Suffk 52 H3
Corbets Tey Gt Lon 37 N3
Corbière Jersey 11 a2
Corbridge Nthumb 112 E8
Corby Nhants 61 J3
Corby Glen Lincs 73 Q6
Corby Hill Cumb 111 J9
Cordon N Ayrs 121 K5
Cordwell Derbys 84 D5
Coreley Shrops 57 L10
Cores End Bucks 35 P7
Corfe Somset 18 H11
Corfe Castle Dorset 12 G8
Corfe Mullen Dorset 12 G5
Corfton Shrops 56 H7
Corgarff Abers 149 P6
Corhampton Hants 22 H10
Corks Pond Kent 25 Q2
Corley Warwks 59 M7
Corley Ash Warwks 59 L7
Corley Moor Warwks 59 L8
Corley Services Warwks 59 M7
Cormuir Angus 142 E4
Cornard Tye Suffk 52 F3
Corndon Devon 8 G7
Corner Row Lancs 88 E4
Corney Cumb 94 C2
Cornforth Dur 104 B4
Cornhill Abers 158 E6
Cornhill-on-Tweed Nthumb 118 G3
Cornholme Calder 89 Q5
Cornish Hall End Essex 51 Q3
Cornoigmore Ag & B 136 B6
Cornriggs Dur 102 F2
Cornsay Dur 103 M2
Cornsay Colliery Dur 103 N2
Corntown Highld 155 Q6
Corntown V Glam 29 P9
Cornwall Airport Newquay Cnwll 4 D9
Cornwell Oxon 47 Q9
Cornwood Devon 6 G7
Cornworthy Devon 7 L7
Corpach Highld 139 K2
Corpusty Norfk 76 G6
Corrachree Abers 150 D7
Corran Highld 139 J5
Corran Highld 145 P6
Corrany IoM 80 g4
Corrie D & G 110 D3
Corrie N Ayrs 121 K3
Corriecravie N Ayrs 120 H7
Corriegills N Ayrs 121 K4
Corriegour Lodge Hotel Highld 146 H9
Corriemoille Highld 155 L5
Corrimony Highld 155 L11
Corringham Lincs 85 Q2
Corringham Thurr 38 B5
Corris Gwynd 54 H3
Corris Uchaf Gwynd 54 G3
Corrow Ag & B 131 P7
Corry Highld 145 K3
Corscombe Devon 8 F5
Corscombe Dorset 11 L3
Corse Gloucs 46 E9
Corse Lawn Gloucs 46 F8
Corsham Wilts 32 G10
Corsindae Abers 150 H6
Corsley Wilts 20 F5
Corsley Heath Wilts 20 F5
Corsock D & G 108 G5
Corston BaNES 32 C11
Corston Wilts 32 H8
Corstorphine C Edin 127 M3
Cors-y-Gedol Gwynd 67 L10
Cortachy Angus 142 F6
Corton Suffk 65 Q2
Corton Wilts 20 H6
Corton Denham Somset 20 B10
Coruanan Highld 139 K4
Corwen Denbgs 68 E6
Coryates Dorset 11 N7
Coryton Devon 8 C8
Coryton Thurr 38 B5
Cosby Leics 72 E11
Coseley Dudley 58 D6
Cosford Shrops 57 Q3
Cosgrove Nhants 49 L6
Cosham C Port 15 J5
Cosheston Pembks 41 K10
Coshieville P & K 141 J8
Cossall Notts 72 D2
Cossall Marsh Notts 72 D2
Cossington Leics 72 G8
Cossington Somset 19 L6
Costessey Norfk 76 H9
Costock Notts 72 F5
Coston Leics 73 L6
Coston Norfk 76 F10
Cote Oxon 34 C4
Cote Somset 19 K6
Cotebrook Ches W 82 C11
Cotehill Cumb 111 J10
Cotes Cumb 95 K3
Cotes Leics 72 F6
Cotes Staffs 70 E8
Cotesbach Leics 60 B4
Cotes Heath Staffs 70 E8
Cotford St Luke Somset 18 G9
Cotgrave Notts 72 G3
Cothal Abers 151 M4
Cotham Notts 85 N11
Cothelstone Somset 18 G8
Cotherstone Dur 103 K7
Cothill Oxon 34 E5
Cotleigh Devon 10 E4
Cotmanhay Derbys 72 D2
Coton Cambs 62 F9
Coton Nhants 60 E6
Coton Shrops 69 P8
Coton Staffs 59 J4
Coton Staffs 70 E10
Coton Staffs 70 H8
Coton Clanford Staffs 70 F10
Coton Hayes Staffs 70 H8
Coton Hill Shrops 56 H2
Coton in the Clay Staffs 71 M9
Coton in the Elms Derbys 71 N11
Coton Park Derbys 71 P11
Cotswolds 33 J3
Cotswold Wildlife Park & Gardens Oxon 33 P3
Cott Devon 7 K6
Cottam E R Yk 99 K7
Cottam Lancs 88 G4
Cottam Notts 85 P5
Cottenham Cambs 62 F7
Cotterdale N York 96 B2
Cottered Herts 50 H5
Cotteridge Birm 58 F8
Cotterstock Nhants 61 M2
Cottesbrooke Nhants 60 F6
Cottesmore Rutlnd 73 N8
Cottingham E R Yk 92 H4
Cottingham Nhants 60 H2
Cottingley C Brad 90 E3
Cottingley Hall Crematorium Leeds 90 H4
Cottisford Oxon 48 G8
Cotton Suffk 64 F8
Cotton End Bed 61 N11
Cotton Tree Lancs 89 Q3
Cottown Abers 150 E2
Cottown Abers 151 K4
Cottown of Gight Abers 159 K9
Cotts Devon 6 C5
Cotwall Wrekin 69 R11
Cotwalton Staffs 70 G8
Couch's Mill Cnwll 5 J10
Coughton Herefs 46 A10
Coughton Warwks 47 L2
Coulaghailtro Ag & B 123 M6
Coulags Highld 154 C9
Coulderton Cumb 100 C9
Coull Abers 150 E7
Coulport Ag & B 131 Q10
Coulsdon Gt Lon 36 G9
Coulston Wilts 21 J4
Coulter S Lans 116 E4
Coultershaw Bridge W Susx 23 Q11
Coultings Somset 18 H6
Coulton N York 98 C6
Coultra Fife 135 K3
Cound Shrops 57 K3
Coundlane Shrops 57 K4
Coundon Dur 103 P5
Coundon Grange Dur 103 P5
Countersett N York 96 D3
Countess Wilts 21 N6
Countess Cross Essex 52 E5
Countess Wear Devon 9 M7
Countesthorpe Leics 72 F11
Counties Crematorium Nhants 60 F9
Countisbury Devon 17 N2
Coupar Angus P & K 142 C10
Coup Green Lancs 88 H5
Coupland Cumb 102 D7
Coupland Nthumb 118 H4
Cour Ag & B 123 P10
Court-at-Street Kent 27 J4
Courteachan Highld 145 L8
Courteenhall Nhants 49 L4
Court Henry Carmth 43 L10
Courtsend Essex 38 H3
Courtway Somset 18 H8
Cousland Mdloth 128 B6
Cousley Wood E Susx 25 Q4
Cove Ag & B 131 Q11
Cove Border 129 K5
Cove Devon 18 C11
Cove Hants 23 N3
Cove Highld 160 C8
Cove Bay C Aber 151 P7
Cove Bottom Suffk 65 P6
Covehithe Suffk 65 Q5
Coven Staffs 58 D3
Coveney Cambs 62 G4
Covenham St Bartholomew Lincs 87 K2
Covenham St Mary Lincs 87 K2
Coven Heath Staffs 58 D3
Coventry Covtry 59 M9
Coventry Airport Warwks 59 N10
Coverack Cnwll 3 K10
Coverack Bridges Cnwll 2 H7
Coverham N York 96 H3
Covington Cambs 61 N6
Covington S Lans 116 D3
Cowan Bridge Lancs 95 N5
Cowbeech E Susx 25 P8
Cowbit Lincs 74 E7
Cowbridge V Glam 30 C10
Cowdale Derbys 83 N10
Cowden Kent 25 L2
Cowdenbeath Fife 134 F9
Cowden Pound Kent 25 L2
Cowden Station Kent 25 L2
Cowers Lane Derbys 71 Q5
Cowes IoW 14 E7
Cowesby N York 97 Q3
Cowesfield Green Wilts 21 Q10
Cowfold W Susx 24 F6
Cowgill Cumb 95 R3
Cow Green Suffk 64 F8
Cowhill S Glos 32 B6
Cowie Stirlg 133 N10
Cowlam E R Yk 99 K7
Cowley Devon 9 M5
Cowley Gloucs 33 J2
Cowley Gt Lon 36 C4
Cowley Oxon 34 F4
Cowling Lancs 88 H7
Cowling N York 90 B2
Cowling N York 97 K3
Cowlinge Suffk 63 M10
Cowmes Kirk 90 F7
Cowpe Lancs 89 N6
Cowpen Nthumb 113 L4
Cowpen Bewley S on T 104 E6
Cowplain Hants 15 J4
Cowshill Dur 102 G2
Cowslip Green N Som 19 N2
Cowthorpe N York 97 P10
Coxall Herefs 56 F10
Coxbank Ches E 70 B6
Coxbench Derbys 72 B2
Coxbridge Somset 19 P7
Cox Common Suffk 65 N5
Coxford Cnwll 5 K2
Coxford Norfk 76 B6
Coxgreen Staffs 57 Q7
Coxheath Kent 38 B11
Coxhoe Dur 104 B3
Coxley Somset 19 P6
Coxley Wakefd 90 H7
Coxley Wick Somset 19 P6
Coxpark Cnwll 5 Q7
Coxtie Green Essex 51 N11
Coxwold N York 98 A5
Coychurch Brdgnd 29 P9
Coychurch Crematorium Brdgnd 29 P8
Coylton S Ayrs 114 H4
Coylumbridge Highld 148 G5
Coytrahen Brdgnd 29 N7
Crabbs Cross Worcs 58 F11
Crab Orchard Dorset 13 J3
Crabtree W Susx 24 F5
Crabtree Green Wrexhm 69 K6
Crackenthorpe Cumb 102 C6
Crackington Haven Cnwll 5 J2
Crackley Staffs 70 E4
Crackley Warwks 59 L10
Crackleybank Shrops 57 P2
Crackpot N York 103 J11
Cracoe N York 96 E8
Craddock Devon 10 B2
Cradle End Herts 51 L6
Cradley Dudley 58 D7
Cradley Herefs 46 D5
Cradley Heath Sandw 58 D7
Cradoc Powys 44 E8
Crafthole Cnwll 5 P11
Crafton Bucks 49 N11
Crag Foot Lancs 95 K6
Craggan Highld 149 J2
Cragg Hill Leeds 90 G3
Cragg Vale Calder 90 C6
Craghead Dur 113 K10
Cragside House & Garden Nthumb 119 L10
Crai Powys 44 B10
Craibstone Moray 158 C6
Craichie Angus 143 J8
Craig Angus 143 M6
Craig Highld 154 D8
Craigbank E Ayrs 115 L5
Craigburn Border 127 N7
Craigcefnparc Swans 29 J4
Craigcleuch D & G 110 F3
Craigdam Abers 159 K11
Craigdhu Ag & B 130 G6
Craigearn Abers 151 J5
Craigellachie Moray 157 P9
Craigend P & K 134 E3
Craigend Rens 125 M3
Craigendoran Ag & B 132 C11
Craigends Rens 125 L4
Craighlaw D & G 107 K5
Craighouse Ag & B 122 H6
Craigie P & K 141 R9
Craigie S Ayrs 125 L11
Craigiefold Abers 159 M4
Craigley D & G 108 G9
Craig Llangiwg Neath 29 K4
Craiglockhart C Edin 127 N3
Craigmillar C Edin 127 Q3
Craignant Shrops 69 J7
Craigneston D & G 115 Q10
Craigneuk N Lans 126 D4
Craigneuk N Lans 126 D6
Craignure Ag & B 138 C10
Craigo Angus 143 M5
Craig Penllyn V Glam 30 C9
Craigrothie Fife 135 K5
Craigruie Stirlg 132 F3
Craig's End Essex 52 B4
Craigton Angus 143 J10
Craigton C Aber 151 L7
Craigton E Rens 125 M7
Craigton Crematorium C Glas 125 N5
Craigton of Airlie Angus 142 E7
Craig-y-Duke Neath 29 K4
Craig-y-nos Powys 44 A11
Crail Fife 135 Q6
Crailing Border 118 C6
Craiselound N Linc 92 C11
Crakehall N York 97 K3
Crakehill N York 97 P6
Crakemarsh Staffs 71 K7
Crambe N York 98 E8
Cramlington Nthumb 113 L5
Cramond C Edin 127 M2
Cramond Bridge C Edin 127 M2
Crampmoor Hants 22 C10
Cranage Ches E 82 G11
Cranberry Staffs 70 E7
Cranborne Dorset 13 J2
Cranbourne Br For 35 P10
Cranbrook Devon 9 N6
Cranbrook Kent 26 C4
Cranbrook Common Kent 26 C4
Crane Moor Barns 91 J10
Crane's Corner Norfk 76 C9
Cranfield C Beds 49 Q6
Cranford Devon 16 E7
Cranford Gt Lon 36 D5
Cranford St Andrew Nhants 61 K5
Cranford St John Nhants 61 K5
Cranham Gloucs 32 G2
Cranham Gt Lon 37 N3
Cranhill Warwks 47 M4
Crank St Hel 81 Q5
Cranleigh Surrey 24 C3
Cranmer Green Suffk 64 E7
Cranmore IoW 14 C8
Cranmore Somset 20 C6
Cranoe Leics 73 K11
Cransford Suffk 65 L9
Cranshaws Border 128 H7
Cranstal IoM 80 g1
Cranswick E R Yk 99 L10
Crantock Cnwll 4 B9
Cranwell Lincs 86 D11
Cranwich Norfk 63 N2
Cranworth Norfk 76 D11
Craobh Haven Ag & B 130 F6
Crapstone Devon 6 E5
Crarae Ag & B 131 K8
Crask Inn Highld 162 C2
Crask of Aigas Highld 155 N9
Craster Nthumb 119 Q7
Craswall Herefs 45 K7
Crateford Staffs 58 D3
Cratfield Suffk 65 L6
Crathes Abers 151 K8
Crathes Crematorium Abers 151 K8
Crathie Abers 149 P8
Crathie Highld 147 P9
Crathorne N York 104 D9
Craven Arms Shrops 56 G8
Crawcrook Gatesd 112 H8
Crawford Lancs 81 P4
Crawford S Lans 116 D6
Crawfordjohn S Lans 116 B6
Crawley Hants 22 D8
Crawley Oxon 34 B2
Crawley W Susx 24 G3
Crawley Down W Susx 24 H3
Crawleyside Dur 103 J2
Crawshawbooth Lancs 89 N5
Crawton Abers 143 R2
Craxe's Green Essex 52 F8
Cray N York 96 D5
Crayford Gt Lon 37 M5
Crayke N York 98 B6
Craymere Beck Norfk 76 F5
Crays Hill Essex 38 B3
Cray's Pond Oxon 34 H8
Craythorne Staffs 71 N9
Craze Lowman Devon 9 N2
Crazies Hill Wokham 35 L8
Creacombe Devon 17 Q8
Creagan Inn Ag & B 138 H9
Creag Ghoraidh W Isls 168 c13
Creagorry W Isls 168 c13
Creaguaineach Lodge Highld 139 Q4
Creamore Bank Shrops 69 P8
Creaton Nhants 60 F6
Creca D & G 110 D6
Credenhill Herefs 45 P6
Crediton Devon 9 K4
Creebank D & G 107 K2
Creebridge D & G 107 M4
Creech Dorset 12 F8
Creech Heathfield Somset 19 J9
Creech St Michael Somset 19 J9
Creed Cnwll 3 N4
Creekmoor Poole 12 H6
Creekmouth Gt Lon 37 L4
Creeksea Essex 38 F2
Creeting St Mary Suffk 64 F10
Creeton Lincs 73 Q6
Creetown D & G 107 N6
Cregneash IoM 80 a8
Creg ny Baa IoM 80 e5
Cregrina Powys 44 G4
Creich Fife 135 J3
Creigiau Cardif 30 E8
Cremyll Cnwll 6 D8
Cressage Shrops 57 K4
Cressbrook Derbys 83 Q10
Cresselly Pembks 41 L9
Cressex Bucks 35 M6
Cressing Essex 52 C7
Cresswell Nthumb 113 L2
Cresswell Pembks 41 L9
Cresswell Staffs 70 H7
Creswell Derbys 84 H6
Creswell Green Staffs 58 G2
Cretingham Suffk 65 J9
Cretshengan Ag & B 123 M6
Crewe Ches E 70 C3
Crewe-by-Farndon Ches W 69 M4
Crewe Crematorium Ches E 70 C3
Crewe Green Ches E 70 C3
Crew Green Powys 69 K11
Crewkerne Somset 11 J3
Crews Hill Station Gt Lon 50 H10
Crewton C Derb 72 B4
Crianlarich Stirlg 132 D2
Cribyn Cerdgn 43 K4
Criccieth Gwynd 66 H7
Crich Derbys 84 D10
Crich Carr Derbys 84 D10
Crichton Mdloth 128 B7
Crick Mons 31 N6
Crick Nhants 60 C6
Crickadarn Powys 44 F6
Cricket St Thomas Somset 10 H3
Crickheath Shrops 69 J10
Crickhowell Powys 45 J11
Cricklade Wilts 33 L6
Cricklewood Gt Lon 36 F3
Cridling Stubbs N York 91 N6
Crieff P & K 133 P3
Criggan Cnwll 4 G9
Criggion Powys 69 J11
Crigglestone Wakefd 91 J7
Crimble Rochdl 89 P8
Crimond Abers 159 Q6
Crimplesham Norfk 75 N10
Crimscote Warwks 47 P5
Crinaglack Highld 155 M9
Crinan Ag & B 130 F9
Crindledyke N Lans 126 E6
Cringleford Norfk 76 H10
Cringles C Brad 96 F11
Crinow Pembks 41 M8
Cripplesease Cnwll 2 E6
Cripplestyle Dorset 13 J2
Cripp's Corner E Susx 26 C7
Croachy Highld 148 B2

266 Croanford – Ddol

Croanford Cnwll 4 G7
Crockenhill Kent 37 M7
Crocker End Oxon 35 K7
Crockerhill W Susx 15 P5
Crockernwell Devon 9 J6
Crocker's Ash Herefs 45 Q11
Crockerton Wilts 20 G6
Crocketford D & G 108 H6
Crockey Hill C York 98 C11
Crockham Hill Kent 37 K10
Crockhurst Street Kent 37 P11
Crockleford Heath Essex 52 H6
Crock Street Somset 10 G2
Croeserw Neath 29 N5
Croes-goch Pembks 40 F4
Croes-lan Cerdgn 42 G6
Croesor Gwynd 67 L6
Croesyceiliog Carmth 42 H11
Croesyceiliog Torfn 31 K5
Croes-y-mwyalch Torfn 31 K6
Croes-y-pant Mons 31 K4
Croft Leics 72 E11
Croft Lincs 87 P8
Croft Warrtn 82 D6
Croftamie Stirlg 132 F10
Croft Mitchell Cnwll 2 H6
Crofton Cumb 110 F10
Crofton Wakefd 91 K7
Crofton Wilts 21 Q2
Croft-on-Tees N York 103 Q9
Croftown Highld 161 K10
Crofts Moray 157 P7
Crofts Bank Traffd 82 G5
Crofts of Dipple Moray 157 Q6
Crofts of Savoch Abers 159 P5
Crofty Swans 28 F6
Crogen Gwynd 68 D7
Croggan Ag & B 130 E2
Croglin Cumb 111 L11
Croick Highld 162 B8
Cromarty Highld 156 D4
Crombie Fife 134 D11
Cromdale Highld 149 K2
Cromer Herts 50 G5
Cromer Norfk 77 J3
Cromford Derbys 84 C9
Cromhall S Glos 32 C6
Cromhall Common
S Glos 32 C7
Cromor W Isls 168 j5
Crompton Fold Oldham 89 Q9
Cromwell Notts 85 N8
Cronberry E Ayrs 115 M3
Crondall Hants 23 L5
Cronkbourne IoM 80 e6
Cronk-y-Voddy IoM 80 d4
Cronton Knows 81 P7
Crook Cumb 101 N11
Crook Dur 103 N3
Crookdake Cumb 100 G2
Crooke Wigan 88 H9
Crooked End Gloucs 46 B11
Crookedholm E Ayrs 125 M10
Crooked Soley Wilts 34 B10
Crookes Sheff 84 D3
Crookhall Dur 112 H10
Crookham Nthumb 118 H3
Crookham W Berk 22 F2
Crookham Village Hants 23 L4
Crook Inn Border 116 G5
Crooklands Cumb 95 L4
Crook of Devon P & K 134 C7
Cropper Derbys 71 N7
Cropredy Oxon 48 E5
Cropston Leics 72 F8
Cropthorne Worcs 47 J5
Cropton N York 98 F3
Cropwell Bishop Notts 72 H3
Cropwell Butler Notts 72 H3
Cros W Isls 168 k1
Crosbost W Isls 168 i5
Crosby Cumb 100 E3
Crosby IoM 80 d6
Crosby N Linc 92 E8
Crosby Sefton 81 L5
Crosby Garret Cumb 102 D9
Crosby Ravensworth
Cumb 102 B8
Crosby Villa Cumb 100 E3
Croscombe Somset 19 Q6
Crosemere Shrops 69 M9
Crosland Edge Kirk 90 E8
Crosland Hill Kirk 90 E8
Cross Somset 19 M4
Crossaig Ag & B 123 P9
Crossapol Ag & B 136 B7
Cross Ash Mons 45 N11
Cross-at-Hand Kent 26 C2
Crossbush W Susx 24 B9
Crosscanonby Cumb 100 E3
Cross Coombe Cnwll 3 J3
Crossdale Street Norfk 77 J4
Cross End Bed 61 N9
Cross End Essex 52 E5
Crossens Sefton 88 D6
Cross Flatts C Brad 90 E2
Crossford Fife 134 D10
Crossford S Lans 126 E8
Crossgate Cnwll 5 N4
Crossgate Lincs 74 D5
Crossgate Staffs 70 G7
Crossgatehall E Loth 128 B6
Crossgates E Ayrs 125 K9
Crossgates Fife 134 E10
Cross Gates Leeds 91 K4
Crossgates N York 99 L4
Crossgates Powys 44 F2
Crossgill Lancs 95 M8
Cross Green Devon 5 P4
Cross Green Leeds 91 J4
Cross Green Staffs 58 D3
Cross Green Suffk 64 A11
Cross Green Suffk 64 B10
Cross Green Suffk 64 D11
Cross Hands Carmth 28 G2
Crosshands Carmth 41 N6
Crosshands E Ayrs 125 M11
Cross Hands Pembks 41 L8
Cross Hill Derbys 84 F11
Crosshill Fife 134 F8
Crosshill S Ayrs 114 F6
Cross Hills N York 96 F11
Crosshouse E Ayrs 125 K10
Cross Houses Shrops 57 J3
Cross Houses Shrops 57 M6
Cross in Hand E Susx 25 N6
Cross Inn Cerdgn 42 G3
Cross Inn Cerdgn 43 K2
Cross Inn Pembks 41 M9
Cross Inn Rhondd 30 E8
Cross Keys Ag & B 132 C10
Crosskeys Caerph 30 H6
Cross Keys Wilts 32 G10
Crosskirk Highld 166 H3
Crosslands Cumb 94 G3
Cross Lane IoW 14 F9
Cross Lane Head Shrops 57 N5
Cross Lanes Cnwll 2 H9
Cross Lanes Cnwll 3 K5
Cross Lanes N York 98 A8
Crosslanes Shrops 69 K11
Cross Lanes Wrexhm 69 L5
Crosslee Rens 125 L4
Crossley Kirk 90 G6
Crossmichael D & G 108 F7
Cross Oak Powys 44 G10
Cross of Jackston Abers 158 H11
Cross o' th' hands
Derbys 71 P5
Crosspost W Susx 24 G6
Crossroads Abers 150 F6
Crossroads Abers 151 K9
Cross Roads C Brad 90 D3
Cross Street Suffk 64 H6
Crosston Angus 143 J6
Cross Town Ches E 82 G9
Crossway Mons 45 N11
Crossway Powys 44 F3
Crossway Green Mons 31 P6
Crossway Green Worcs 58 B11
Crossways Dorset 12 C7
Crosswell Pembks 41 M3
Crosthwaite Cumb 95 J2
Croston Lancs 88 F7
Crostwick Norfk 77 K8
Crostwight Norfk 77 L6
Crouch Kent 37 P9
Crouch Kent 39 J10
Crouch End Gt Lon 36 H3
Croucheston Wilts 21 L9
Crouch Hill Dorset 11 Q2
Crough House Green
Kent 37 K11
Croughton Nhants 48 F8
Crovie Abers 159 K4
Crow Hants 13 L4
Crowan Cnwll 2 G7
Crowborough E Susx 25 M4
Crowborough Town
E Susx 25 M4
Crowcombe Somset 18 F7
Crowdecote Derbys 83 P11
Crowden Derbys 83 N5
Crowden Devon 8 C5
Crowdhill Hants 22 E10
Crowdleham Kent 37 N9
Crow Edge Barns 83 Q4
Crowell Oxon 35 K5
Crow End Cambs 62 D9
Crowfield Nhants 48 H6
Crowfield Suffk 64 G10
Crowfield Green Suffk 64 G10
Crowgate Street Norfk 77 L7
Crow Green Essex 51 N11
Crowhill E Loth 129 J5
Crow Hill Herefs 46 B9
Crowhole Derbys 84 D5
Crowhurst E Susx 26 C9
Crowhurst Surrey 37 J11
Crowhurst Lane End
Surrey 37 J11
Crowland Lincs 74 D8
Crowland Suffk 64 E7
Crowlas Cnwll 2 E7
Crowle N Linc 92 C8
Crowle Worcs 46 H3
Crowle Green Worcs 46 H3
Crowmarsh Gifford
Oxon 34 H7
Crown Corner Suffk 65 K7
Crownhill C Plym 6 D7
Crownhill Crematorium
M Keyn 49 M7
Crownpits Surrey 23 Q6
Crownthorpe Norfk 76 F11
Crowntown Cnwll 2 G7
Crows-an-Wra Cnwll 2 B8
Crow's Green Essex 51 Q5
Crowshill Norfk 76 D10
Crow's Nest Cnwll 5 M8
Crowsnest Shrops 56 F4
Crowthorne Wokham 23 M2
Crowton Ches W 82 C10
Croxall Staffs 59 J2
Croxby Lincs 93 L11
Croxdale Dur 103 Q3
Croxden Staffs 71 K7
Croxley Green Herts 50 C11
Croxteth Lpool 81 N5
Croxton Cambs 62 B8
Croxton N Linc 93 J8
Croxton Norfk 64 B4
Croxton Norfk 76 D5
Croxton Staffs 70 D8
Croxtonbank Staffs 70 D8
Croxton Green Ches E 69 Q4
Croxton Kerrial Leics 73 L5
Croy Highld 156 D8
Croy N Lans 126 C2
Croyde Devon 16 G4
Croyde Bay Devon 16 G4
Croydon Cambs 62 D11
Croydon Gt Lon 36 H7
Croydon Crematorium
Gt Lon 36 H7
Crubenmore Highld 148 B9
Cruckmeole Shrops 56 G3
Cruckton Shrops 56 G2
Cruden Bay Abers 159 Q10
Crudgington Wrekin 70 A11
Crudwell Wilts 33 J6
Cruft Devon 8 D5
Crûg Powys 56 B10
Crugmeer Cnwll 4 E6
Crugybar Carmth 43 N7
Crug-y-byddar Powys 56 B8
Crumlin Caerph 30 H5
Crumplehorn Cnwll 5 L11
Crumpsall Manch 82 H4
Crundale Kent 27 J2
Crundale Pembks 41 J7
Crunwear Pembks 41 N8
Cruwys Morchard Devon 9 L2
Crux Easton Hants 22 D3
Cruxton Dorset 11 N5
Crwbin Carmth 28 E2
Cryers Hill Bucks 35 N5
Crymych Pembks 41 N4
Crynant Neath 29 L4
Crystal Palace Gt Lon 36 H6
Cuaig Highld 153 N6
Cuan Ag & B 130 F5
Cubbington Warwks 59 M11
Cubert Cnwll 4 B10
Cubley Barns 90 G10
Cublington Bucks 49 M10
Cublington Herefs 45 N7
Cuckfield W Susx 24 H5
Cucklington Somset 20 E9
Cuckney Notts 85 J6
Cuckoo Bridge Lincs 74 D6
Cuckoo's Corner Hants 23 K6
Cuckoo's Nest Ches W 69 L2
Cuddesdon Oxon 34 G4
Cuddington Bucks 35 K2
Cuddington Ches W 82 C10
Cuddington Heath
Ches W 69 N5
Cuddy Hill Lancs 88 F3
Cudham Gt Lon 37 K9
Cudliptown Devon 8 D9
Cudnell Bmouth 13 J5
Cudworth Barns 91 K9
Cudworth Somset 10 H2
Cuerdley Cross Warrtn 82 B7
Cufaude Hants 23 J3
Cuffley Herts 50 H10
Cuil Highld 138 H6
Culbokie Highld 155 R6
Culbone Somset 17 Q2
Culburnie Highld 155 N9
Culcabock Highld 156 B9
Culcharry Highld 156 F7
Culcheth Warrtn 82 E6
Culdrain Abers 158 D11
Culduie Highld 153 N9
Culford Suffk 64 A7
Culgaith Cumb 102 B5
Culham Oxon 34 F5
Culkein Highld 164 B10
Culkein Drumbeg Highld 164 D10
Culkerton Gloucs 32 H5
Cullen Moray 158 D4
Cullercoats N Tyne 113 N6
Cullerlie Abers 151 K7
Cullicudden Highld 156 A5
Cullingworth C Brad 90 D3
Cuillin Hills Highld 144 G3
Cullipool Ag & B 130 E5
Cullivoe Shet 169 s3
Culloden Highld 156 C8
Cullompton Devon 9 P3
Cullompton Services
Devon 9 P3
Culm Davy Devon 18 F11
Culmington Shrops 56 H8
Culmstock Devon 10 C2
Culnacraig Highld 160 H6
Culnaightrie D & G 108 G10
Culnaknock Highld 153 J5
Culpho Suffk 53 M2
Culrain Highld 162 D8
Culross Fife 134 B10
Culroy S Ayrs 114 F5
Culsalmond Abers 158 G11
Culscadden D & G 107 N8
Culshabbin D & G 107 K7
Culswick Shet 169 p9
Cultercullen Abers 151 N3
Cults C Aber 151 M7
Culverstone Green Kent 37 P8
Culverthorpe Lincs 73 Q2
Culworth Nhants 48 F5
Culzean Castle &
Country Park S Ayrs 114 D5
Cumbernauld N Lans 126 D3
Cumbernauld Village
N Lans 126 D2
Cumberworth Lincs 87 P6
Cumdivock Cumb 110 F11
Cuminestown Abers 159 K7
Cumledge Border 129 K8
Cummersdale Cumb 110 G10
Cummertrees D & G 109 P7
Cummingston Moray 157 L4
Cumnock E Ayrs 115 L3
Cumnor Oxon 34 E4
Cumrew Cumb 111 L10
Cumrue D & G 109 N3
Cumwhinton Cumb 111 J10
Cumwhitton Cumb 111 K10
Cundall N York 97 P6
Cunninghamhead N Ayrs 125 K9
Cunningsburgh Shet 169 r10
Cupar Fife 135 K5
Cupar Muir Fife 135 K5
Curbar Derbys 84 C6
Curbridge Hants 14 F4
Curbridge Oxon 34 B3
Curdridge Hants 14 F4
Curdworth Warwks 59 J6
Curland Somset 19 J11
Curridge W Berk 34 E10
Currie C Edin 127 M4
Curry Mallet Somset 19 K10
Curry Rivel Somset 19 L9
Curteis Corner Kent 26 E4
Curtisden Green Kent 26 B3
Curtisknowle Devon 7 J8
Cury Cnwll 2 H9
Cushnie Abers 150 E5
Cushuish Somset 18 G8
Cusop Herefs 45 J6
Cusworth Donc 91 N10
Cutcloy D & G 107 N11
Cutcombe Somset 18 B7
Cutgate Rochdl 89 P8
Cuthill Highld 162 H9
Cutiau Gwynd 67 L11
Cutler's Green Essex 51 N4
Cutmadoc Cnwll 4 H9
Cutmere Cnwll 5 N9
Cutnall Green Worcs 58 C11
Cutsdean Gloucs 47 L8
Cutsyke Wakefd 91 L6
Cutthorpe Derbys 84 D6
Cuttivett Cnwll 5 P9
Cuxham Oxon 35 J5
Cuxton Medway 38 B8
Cuxwold Lincs 93 L10
Cwm Blae G 30 G3
Cwm Denbgs 80 F9
Cwmafan Neath 29 L6
Cwmaman Rhondd 30 D5
Cwmann Carmth 43 L5
Cwmavon Torfn 31 J3
Cwm-bach Carmth 28 E4
Cwmbach Carmth 41 Q5
Cwmbach Powys 44 H7
Cwmbach Rhondd 30 D4
Cwmbach Llechrhyd
Powys 44 E4
Cwmbelan Powys 55 L8
Cwmbran Torfn 31 J6
Cwmbrwyno Cerdgn 54 G8
Cwm Capel Carmth 28 E4
Cwmcarn Caerph 30 H6
Cwmcarvan Mons 31 N3
Cwm-celyn Blae G 30 H3
Cwm-Cewydd Gwynd 55 K2
Cwm-cou Cerdgn 41 Q2
Cwm Crawnon Powys 44 G11
Cwmdare Rhondd 30 C4
Cwmdu Carmth 43 M8
Cwmdu Powys 44 H10
Cwmdu Swans 28 H6
Cwmduad Carmth 42 G8
Cwm Dulais Swans 28 H4
Cwmdwr Carmth 43 P8
Cwmfelin Brdgnd 29 N7
Cwmfelin Myr Td 30 E4
Cwmfelin Boeth Carmth 41 N7
Cwmfelinfach Caerph 30 G6
Cwmfelin Mynach
Carmth 41 P6
Cwmffrwd Carmth 42 H11
Cwmgiedd Powys 29 L2
Cwmgorse Carmth 29 K2
Cwmgwili Carmth 28 G2
Cwmgwrach Neath 29 N4
Cwmhiraeth Carmth 42 F7
Cwm-Ifor Carmth 43 N9
Cwm Irfon Powys 44 B5
Cwmisfael Carmth 43 J11
Cwm Llinau Powys 55 J3
Cwmllynfell Neath 29 K2
Cwmmawr Carmth 28 F2
Cwm Morgan Carmth 41 Q4
Cwmparc Rhondd 29 P5
Cwmpengraig Carmth 42 G7
Cwm Penmachno Conwy 67 P5
Cwmpennar Rhondd 30 D4
Cwmrhos Powys 44 H10
Cwmrhydyceirw Swans 29 J5
Cwmsychbant Cerdgn 43 J5
Cwmtillery Blae G 30 H3
Cwm-twrch Isaf Powys 29 L2
Cwm-twrch Uchaf
Powys 29 L2
Cwm-y-glo Carmth 28 G2
Cwm-y-glo Gwynd 67 K2
Cwmyoy Mons 45 K10
Cwmystwyth Cerdgn 54 H10
Cwrt Gwynd 54 F5
Cwrtnewydd Cerdgn 43 J5
Cwrt-y-gollen Powys 45 J11
Cyfarthfa Castle
Museum Myr Td 30 D3
Cyfronydd Powys 55 Q3
Cylibebyll Neath 29 K4
Cymau Flints 69 J3
Cymer Neath 29 N5
Cymmer Rhondd 30 D6
Cynghordy Carmth 43 R6
Cynheidre Carmth 28 E3
Cynonville Neath 29 M5
Cynwyd Denbgs 68 E6
Cynwyl Elfed Carmth 42 G9

D

Daccombe Devon 7 N5
Dacre Cumb 101 N5
Dacre N York 97 J8
Dacre Banks N York 97 J8
Daddry Shield Dur 102 G3
Dadford Bucks 49 J7
Dadlington Leics 72 C11
Dafen Carmth 28 F4
Daffy Green Norfk 76 D10
Dagenham Gt Lon 37 M4
Daglingworth Gloucs 33 J3
Dagnall Bucks 49 Q11
Dagworth Suffk 64 E9
Dailly S Ayrs 114 E7
Dainton Devon 7 M5
Dairsie Fife 135 L4
Daisy Hill Bolton 82 E4
Daisy Hill Leeds 90 H5
Dalabrog W Isls 168 c15
Dalavich Ag & B 131 K5
Dalbeattie D & G 108 H8
Dalbury Derbys 71 P8
Dalby IoM 80 b6
Dalby Lincs 87 M7
Dalby N York 98 C6
Dalcapon P & K 141 N7
Dalchalm Highld 163 L5
Dalchreichart Highld 146 H5
Dalchruin P & K 133 L4
Dalcrue P & K 134 C2
Dalderby Lincs 87 J7
Dalditch Devon 9 P8
Daldowie Crematorium
C Glas 126 B5
Dale Cumb 101 P2
Dale Derbys 72 C3
Dale Pembks 40 F9
Dale Bottom Cumb 101 J6
Dale End Derbys 84 B8
Dale End N York 96 E11
Dale Hill E Susx 26 B5
Dalehouse N York 105 L7
Dalelia Highld 138 C4
Dalgarven N Ayrs 124 H8
Dalgety Bay Fife 134 F11
Dalgig E Ayrs 115 L5
Dalginross P & K 133 M3
Dalguise P & K 141 N8
Dalhalvaig Highld 166 E6
Dalham Suffk 63 M8
Daliburgh W Isls 168 c15
Dalkeith Mdloth 127 Q4
Dallas Moray 157 L7
Dallinghoo Suffk 65 K10
Dallington E Susx 25 Q7
Dallington Nhants 60 F8
Dallow N York 97 J6
Dalmally Ag & B 131 P2
Dalmary Stirlg 132 G8
Dalmellington E Ayrs 115 J6
Dalmeny C Edin 127 L2
Dalmore Highld 156 B4
Dalmuir W Duns 125 M3
Dalnabreck Highld 138 C4
Dalnacardoch P & K 140 H3
Dalnahaitnach Highld 148 F4
Dalnaspidal P & K 140 F3
Dalnawillan Lodge
Highld 166 H8
Daloist P & K 141 J6
Dalqueich P & K 134 D7
Dalquhairn S Ayrs 114 F8
Dalreavoch Lodge
Highld 162 H5
Dalry N Ayrs 124 H8
Dalrymple E Ayrs 114 G5
Dalserf S Lans 126 D7
Dalsmeran Ag & B 120 B9
Dalston Cumb 110 G10
Dalston Gt Lon 36 H4
Dalswinton D & G 109 K3
Dalton Cumb 95 L5
Dalton D & G 109 P6
Dalton Lancs 88 F9
Dalton N York 97 P5
Dalton N York 103 M9
Dalton Nthumb 112 H6
Dalton Rothm 84 G2
Dalton-in-Furness Cumb 94 E6
Dalton-le-Dale Dur 113 P11
Dalton Magna Rothm 84 G2
Dalton-on-Tees N York 103 Q9
Dalton Parva Rothm 84 G2
Dalton Piercy Hartpl 104 E4
Dalveich Stirlg 133 J3
Dalwhinnie Highld 147 Q11
Dalwood Devon 10 E4
Damask Green Herts 50 G5
Damerham Hants 21 M11
Damgate Norfk 77 N10
Dam Green Norfk 64 E4
Damnaglaur D & G 106 F10
Danaway Kent 38 E9
Danbury Essex 52 C10
Danby N York 105 K9
Danby Bottom N York 105 J10
Danby Wiske N York 104 B11
Dandaleith Moray 157 P8
Danderhall Mdloth 127 Q4
Danebridge Ches E 83 L11
Dane End Herts 50 H6
Danegate E Susx 25 N4
Danehill E Susx 25 K5
Dane Hills C Leic 72 F10
Danemoor Green Norfk 76 F10
Danesford Shrops 57 N6
Danesmoor Derbys 84 F8
Dane Street Kent 39 J11
Daniel's Water Kent 26 G3
Danshillock Abers 158 H6
Danskine E Loth 128 F6
Danthorpe E R Yk 93 N4
Danzey Green Warwks 58 H11
Dapple Heath Staffs 71 J9
Darby Green Hants 23 M2
Darcy Lever Bolton 89 L9
Dardy Powys 45 J11
Daren-felen Mons 30 H2
Darenth Kent 37 N6
Daresbury Halton 82 C8
Darfield Barns 91 L10
Darfoulds Notts 85 J5
Dargate Kent 39 J9
Darite Cnwll 5 M8
Darland Medway 38 C8
Darland Wrexhm 69 L3
Darlaston Wsall 58 E5
Darlaston Green Wsall 58 E5
Darley N York 97 K9
Darley Abbey C Derb 72 B3
Darley Bridge Derbys 84 C8
Darley Dale Derbys 84 C8
Darley Green Solhll 59 J10
Darleyhall Herts 50 D6
Darley Head N York 97 J9
Darlingscott Warwks 47 P6
Darlington Darltn 103 Q8
Darlington
Crematorium Darltn 103 Q8
Darliston Shrops 69 Q8
Darlton Notts 85 N6
Darnford Staffs 58 H3
Darnick Border 117 Q4
Darowen Powys 55 J4
Darra Abers 158 H8
Darracott Devon 16 C8
Darracott Devon 16 H4
Darras Hall Nthumb 113 J6
Darrington Wakefd 91 M7
Darsham Suffk 65 N8
Darshill Somset 20 B6
Dartford Kent 37 M6
Dartford Crossing Kent 37 N5
Dartington Devon 7 K6
Dartmeet Devon 6 H4
Dartmoor National Park
Devon 8 G9
Dartmouth Devon 7 M8
Darton Barns 91 J8
Darvel E Ayrs 125 P10
Darwell Hole E Susx 25 Q7
Darwen Bl w D 89 K6
Datchet W & M 35 Q9
Datchworth Herts 50 G7
Datchworth Green Herts 50 G7
Daubhill Bolton 89 L9
Daugh of Kinermony
Moray 157 N9
Dauntsey Wilts 33 J8
Dava Highld 157 J10
Davenham Ches W 82 E10
Davenport Stockp 83 K7
Davenport Green Ches E 82 H9
Davenport Green Traffd 82 H7
Daventry Nhants 60 C8
Davidson's Mains C Edin 127 N2
Davidstow Cnwll 5 K4
David Street Kent 37 P8
Davington D & G 117 J10
Davington Hill Kent 38 H
Daviot Abers 151 J
Daviot Highld 156 C1
Daviot House Highld 156 C
Davis's Town E Susx 25 M
Davoch of Grange Moray 158 C
Davyhulme Traffd 82 G
Daw End Wsall 58 F
Dawesgreen Surrey 36 F1
Dawley Wrekin 57 M
Dawlish Devon 9 N
Dawlish Warren Devon 9 N
Dawn Conwy 80 B1
Daws Green Somset 18 G1
Daws Heath Essex 38 D
Daw's House Cnwll 5 N
Dawsmere Lincs 74 H
Daybrook Notts 85 J1
Day Green Ches E 70 D
Dayhills Staffs 70 H
Dayhouse Bank Worcs 58 E
Daylesford Gloucs 47 F
Ddol Flints 80 G1

Ddol-Cownwy Powys 68 D11
Deal Kent 39 Q11
Dean Cumb 100 E5
Dean Devon 7 J6
Dean Devon 17 L2
Dean Devon 17 N2
Dean Dorset 21 J11
Dean Hants 22 D8
Dean Hants 22 G11
Dean Lancs 89 P5
Dean Oxon 48 B10
Dean Somset 20 C6
Dean Bottom Kent 37 N7
Deanburnhaugh Border 117 M8
Deancombe Devon 7 J6
Dean Court Oxon 34 E3
Deane Bolton 89 K9
Deane Hants 22 F4
Dean End Dorset 21 J11
Dean Head Barns 90 H10
Deanland Dorset 21 J11
Deanlane End W Susx 15 K4
Dean Prior Devon 7 J6
Deanraw Nthumb 112 B8
Dean Row Ches E 83 J8
Deans W Loth 127 J4
Deanscales Cumb 100 E5
Deanshanger Nhants 49 L7
Deanshaugh Moray 157 M9
Deanston Stirlg 133 L7
Dean Street Kent 38 B11
Dearham Cumb 100 E3
Dearnley Rochdl 89 Q7
Debach Suffk 65 J11
Debden Essex 51 K11
Debden Essex 51 N4
Debden Green Essex 51 N4
Debenham Suffk 64 H9
Deblin's Green Worcs 46 F5
Dechmont W Loth 127 J3
Dechmont Road W Loth 127 J4
Deddington Oxon 48 E8
Dedham Essex 53 J5
Dedham Heath Essex 53 J5
Dedworth W & M 35 P9
Deene Nhants 61 K2
Deenethorpe Nhants 61 L2
Deepcar Sheff 90 H11
Deepcut Surrey 23 P3
Deepdale Cumb 95 Q4
Deepdale N York 96 C5
Deeping Gate C Pete 74 B9
Deeping St James Lincs 74 C9
Deeping St Nicholas Lincs 74 D7
Deerhurst Gloucs 46 G8
Deerhurst Walton Gloucs 46 G8
Deerton Street Kent 38 G9
Defford Worcs 46 H6
Defynnog Powys 44 C9
Deganwy Conwy 79 P9
Degnish Ag & B 130 F5
Deighton C York 91 Q2
Deighton N York 104 C10
Deiniolen Gwynd 67 K2
Delabole Cnwll 4 H5
Delamere Ches W 82 C11
Delfrigs Abers 151 P3
Delley Devon 17 J7
Delliefure Highld 157 K11
Dell Quay W Susx 15 M6
Delly End Oxon 34 C2
Delnabo Moray 149 M4
Delnashaugh Inn Moray 157 M10
Delny Highld 156 C3
Delph Oldham 90 B9
Delves Dur 112 H11
Delvin End Essex 52 C4
Dembleby Lincs 73 Q3
Demelza Cnwll 4 F9
Denaby Donc 91 M11
Denaby Main Donc 91 M11
Denbies Surrey 36 D10
Denbigh Denbgs 80 F11
Denbighshire Crematorium Denbgs 80 E10
Denbrae Fife 135 K4
Denbury Devon 7 L5
Denby Derbys 84 E11
Denby Bottles Derbys 84 E11
Denby Dale Kirk 90 G9
Denchworth Oxon 34 C6
Dendron Cumb 94 E6
Denel End C Beds 50 B3
Denfield P & K 134 B4
Denford Nhants 61 L5
Dengie Essex 52 G11
Denham Bucks 36 B3
Denham Suffk 63 N8
Denham Suffk 64 H7
Denham End Suffk 63 N8
Denham Green Bucks 36 B3
Denham Green Suffk 64 H7
Denhead Abers 159 N7
Denhead Fife 135 M5
Denhead of Gray C Dund 142 F11
Denholm Border 117 R7
Denholme C Brad 90 D4
Denholme Clough C Brad 90 D4
Denio Gwynd 66 F7
Denmead Hants 15 J4
Denmore C Aber 151 N5
Denne Park W Susx 24 E5
Dennington Suffk 65 K8
Denny Falk 133 N11
Dennyloanhead Falk 133 N11
Den of Lindores Fife 134 H4
Denshaw Oldham 90 B8
Denside Abers 151 L8
Densole Kent 27 M3
Denston Suffk 63 N10
Denstone Staffs 71 K6
Denstroude Kent 39 K9
Dent Cumb 95 Q3
Denton Cambs 61 Q3
Denton Darltn 103 P7
Denton E Susx 25 L10
Denton Kent 27 M2
Denton Kent 37 Q6
Denton Lincs 73 M4
Denton N York 96 H11
Denton Nhants 60 H9
Denton Norfk 65 K4
Denton Oxon 34 G4
Denton Tamesd 83 K5
Denver Norfk 75 M10
Denwick Nthumb 119 P8
Deopham Norfk 76 E11
Deopham Green Norfk 64 E2
Depden Suffk 63 N9

Depden Green Suffk 63 N9
Deptford Gt Lon 37 J5
Deptford Wilts 21 K7
Derby C Derb 72 B3
Derby Devon 17 K5
Derbyhaven IoM 80 c8
Derculich P & K 141 L7
Dereham Norfk 76 D9
Deri Caerph 30 F4
Derril Devon 16 E11
Derringstone Kent 27 M2
Derrington Staffs 70 F10
Derriton Devon 16 E11
Derry Hill Wilts 33 J10
Derrythorpe N Linc 92 D9
Dersingham Norfk 75 N4
Dervaig Ag & B 137 L5
Derwen Denbgs 68 E4
Derwenlas Powys 54 G5
Derwent Valley Mills Derbys 84 D9
Derwentwater Cumb 101 J6
Derwydd Carmth 43 M11
Desborough Nhants 60 H4
Desford Leics 72 D10
Deskford Moray 158 D5
Detchant Nthumb 119 L3
Detling Kent 38 C10
Deuxhill Shrops 57 M7
Devauden Mons 31 N5
Devil's Bridge Cerdgn 54 G9
Devitts Green Warwks 59 L6
Devizes Wilts 21 K2
Devonport C Plym 6 D8
Devonside Clacks 133 Q8
Devoran Cnwll 3 K6
Devoran & Perran Cnwll 3 K6
Dewarton Mdloth 128 B7
Dewlish Dorset 12 C5
Dewsbury Kirk 90 G6
Dewsbury Moor Kirk 90 G6
Dewsbury Moor Crematorium Kirk 90 G6
Deytheur Powys 68 H11
Dial N Som 31 P11
Dial Green W Susx 23 P9
Dial Post W Susx 24 E7
Dibberford Dorset 11 K4
Dibden Hants 14 D5
Dibden Purlieu Hants 14 D5
Dickens Heath Solhll 58 H9
Dickleburgh Norfk 64 H5
Didbrook Gloucs 47 L8
Didcot Oxon 34 F6
Diddington Cambs 61 Q7
Diddlebury Shrops 57 J7
Didley Herefs 45 P8
Didling W Susx 23 M11
Didmarton Gloucs 32 F7
Didsbury Manch 82 H6
Didworthy Devon 6 H6
Digby Lincs 86 E10
Digg Highld 152 H4
Diggle Oldham 90 C9
Digmoor Lancs 88 F9
Digswell Herts 50 F7
Digswell Water Herts 50 F7
Dihewyd Cerdgn 43 J3
Dilham Norfk 77 L6
Dilhorne Staffs 70 H6
Dill Hall Lancs 89 M5
Dillington Cambs 61 P7
Dilston Nthumb 112 H8
Dilton Wilts 20 G5
Dilton Marsh Wilts 20 F5
Dilwyn Herefs 45 N4
Dimple Bolton 89 L7
Dimple Derbys 84 C8
Dinas Carmth 41 Q4
Dinas Cnwll 4 E7
Dinas Gwynd 66 D7
Dinas Pembks 41 K3
Dinas Rhondd 30 D6
Dinas Dinlle Gwynd 66 G3
Dinas-Mawddwy Gwynd 67 R11
Dinas Powys V Glam 30 G10
Dinder Somset 19 Q6
Dinedor Herefs 45 Q7
Dingestow Mons 31 N2
Dingle Lpool 81 M7
Dingleden Kent 26 D5
Dingley Nhants 60 G3
Dingwall Highld 155 P6
Dinmael Conwy 68 D6
Dinnet Abers 150 D8
Dinnington N u Ty 113 K6
Dinnington Rothm 84 H3
Dinnington Somset 11 J2
Dinorwic Gwynd 67 K2
Dinton Bucks 35 L2
Dinton Wilts 21 K8
Dinwoodie D & G 109 P2
Dinworthy Devon 16 E8
Dipford Somset 18 H10
Dipley Hants 23 K3
Dippen Ag & B 120 F4
Dippen N Ayrs 121 K7
Dippenhall Surrey 23 M5
Dippermill Devon 16 B3
Dippertown Devon 8 B8
Dipple Moray 157 Q6
Dipple S Ayrs 114 D7
Diptford Devon 7 J7
Dipton Dur 113 J10
Diptonmill Nthumb 112 D8
Dirleton E Loth 128 E3
Dirt Pot Nthumb 112 C11
Discoed Powys 45 K2
Diseworth Leics 72 D6
Dishforth N York 97 N6
Disley Ches E 83 L8
Diss Norfk 64 G5
Disserth Powys 44 E3
Distington Cumb 100 D6
Distington Hall Crematorium Cumb 100 D6
Ditcham Wilts 21 L8
Ditcheat Somset 20 B7
Ditchingham Norfk 65 L2
Ditchling E Susx 24 H7
Ditherington Shrops 57 J2
Ditteridge Wilts 32 F11
Dittisham Devon 7 M7
Ditton Kent 38 B10
Ditton Green Cambs 63 L9
Ditton Priors Shrops 57 L6
Dixton Gloucs 47 J8
Dixton Mons 31 P2
Dizzard Cnwll 5 K2
Dobcross Oldham 90 B9
Dobwalls Cnwll 5 L8

Doccombe Devon 9 J7
Dochgarroch Highld 155 R9
Dockenfield Surrey 23 M6
Docker Lancs 95 M6
Docking Norfk 75 Q3
Docklow Herefs 45 R3
Dockray Cumb 101 L6
Dockray Cumb 110 E11
Dodbrooke Devon 7 J10
Doddinghurst Essex 51 N11
Doddington Cambs 62 F2
Doddington Kent 38 F10
Doddington Lincs 85 Q6
Doddington Nthumb 119 J4
Doddington Shrops 57 L9
Doddiscombsleigh Devon 9 L7
Dodd's Green Ches E 69 R6
Doddshill Norfk 75 N4
Doddy Cross Cnwll 5 N9
Dodford Nhants 60 D8
Dodford Worcs 58 D10
Dodington S Glos 32 E8
Dodington Somset 18 G6
Dodleston Ches W 69 L2
Dodscott Devon 17 J8
Dodside E Rens 125 N7
Dod's Leigh Staffs 71 J8
Dodworth Barns 91 J9
Dodworth Bottom Barns 91 J10
Dodworth Green Barns 91 J10
Doe Bank Birm 58 H5
Doe Lea Derbys 84 G7
Dogdyke Lincs 86 H9
Dogley Lane Kirk 90 F8
Dogmersfield Hants 23 L4
Dogridge Wilts 33 L7
Dogsthorpe C Pete 74 C10
Dog Village Devon 9 N5
Dolanog Powys 55 P2
Dolau Powys 55 Q11
Dolaucothi Carmth 43 N6
Dolbenmaen Gwynd 67 J6
Doley Staffs 70 C9
Dolfach Powys 55 L4
Dol-för Powys 55 J3
Dolfor Powys 55 R5
Dolgarrog Conwy 79 P11
Dolgellau Gwynd 67 N11
Dolgoch Gwynd 54 F4
Dol-gran Carmth 42 H8
Doll Highld 163 K6
Dollar Clacks 134 C8
Dollarfield Clacks 134 B8
Dolley Green Powys 56 D11
Dollwen Cerdgn 54 F8
Dolphin Flints 80 H10
Dolphinholme Lancs 95 L10
Dolphinton S Lans 127 L8
Dolton Devon 17 K9
Dolwen Conwy 80 B10
Dolwyddelan Conwy 67 N4
Dolybont Cerdgn 54 E7
Dolyhir Powys 45 J3
Domgay Powys 69 J11
Donaldson's Lodge Nthumb 118 G2
Doncaster Donc 91 P10
Doncaster Carr Donc 91 P10
Doncaster North Services Donc 91 R8
Donhead St Andrew Wilts 20 H10
Donhead St Mary Wilts 20 H10
Donibristle Fife 134 F10
Doniford Somset 18 E6
Donington Lincs 74 D3
Donington on Bain Lincs 86 H4
Donington Park Services Leics 72 D5
Donington Southing Lincs 74 D4
Donisthorpe Leics 59 M2
Donkey Street Kent 27 K5
Donkey Town Surrey 23 P2
Donnington Gloucs 47 N9
Donnington Herefs 46 D8
Donnington Shrops 57 K3
Donnington W Berk 34 E11
Donnington W Susx 15 M6
Donnington Wrekin 57 N2
Donnington Wood Wrekin 57 N2
Donyatt Somset 10 G2
Doomsday Green W Susx 24 E5
Doonfoot S Ayrs 114 F4
Dorback Lodge Highld 149 K4
Dorchester Dorset 11 P6
Dorchester-on-Thames Oxon 34 G6
Dordon Warwks 59 L4
Dore Sheff 84 D4
Dores Highld 155 Q11
Dorking Surrey 36 E11
Dorking Tye Suffk 52 F4
Dormansland Surrey 25 K2
Dormans Park Surrey 25 J2
Dormington Herefs 46 A6
Dormston Worcs 47 J3
Dorn Gloucs 47 P8
Dorney Bucks 35 P9
Dornie Highld 145 Q2
Dornoch Highld 162 H9
Dornock D & G 110 D7
Dorrery Highld 167 J6
Dorridge Solhll 59 J10
Dorrington Lincs 86 E10
Dorrington Shrops 56 H4
Dorrington Shrops 70 C6
Dorsington Warwks 47 M5
Dorstone Herefs 45 L6
Dorton Bucks 35 J2
Dosthill Staffs 59 K5
Dothan IoA 78 F10
Dottery Dorset 11 K5
Doublebois Cnwll 5 K9
Doughton Gloucs 32 G6
Douglas IoM 80 d6
Douglas S Lans 116 A4
Douglas and Angus C Dund 142 G11
Douglas Crematorium IoM 80 e6
Douglas Pier Ag & B 131 P8
Douglastown Angus 142 G8
Douglas Water S Lans 116 B3
Douglas West S Lans 116 A4
Doulting Somset 20 B6
Dounby Ork 169 b4
Doune Highld 161 Q6
Doune Stirlg 133 L7

Dounepark S Ayrs 114 C8
Dounie Highld 162 D8
Dousland Devon 6 E5
Dovaston Shrops 69 L10
Dove Dale Derbys 71 L4
Dove Green Notts 84 G10
Dove Holes Derbys 83 N9
Dovenby Cumb 100 E4
Dover Kent 27 P3
Dover Wigan 82 D4
Dover Castle Kent 27 P3
Dovercourt Essex 53 M5
Doverdale Worcs 58 C11
Doveridge Derbys 71 L8
Doversgreen Surrey 36 G11
Dowally P & K 141 P8
Dowbridge Lancs 88 E4
Dowdeswell Gloucs 47 K11
Dowlais Myr Td 30 E3
Dowland Devon 17 K9
Dowlish Ford Somset 10 H2
Dowlish Wake Somset 10 H2
Down Ampney Gloucs 33 L5
Downderry Cnwll 5 N11
Downe Gt Lon 37 K8
Downend Gloucs 32 F5
Downend IoW 14 F9
Downend S Glos 32 C9
Downend W Berk 34 E9
Downfield C Dund 142 F11
Downgate Cnwll 5 M7
Downgate Cnwll 5 P7
Downham Essex 38 B2
Downham Gt Lon 37 J6
Downham Lancs 89 M2
Downham Market Norfk 75 M10
Down Hatherley Gloucs 46 G10
Downhead Somset 19 Q9
Downhead Somset 20 C5
Downhill P & K 134 D2
Downhill Cnwll 4 D9
Downholland Cross Lancs 88 D9
Downholme N York 103 M11
Downicarey Devon 5 P3
Downies Abers 151 N9
Downing Flints 80 H9
Downley Bucks 35 M5
Down St Mary Devon 8 H4
Downs Crematorium Br & H 24 H9
Downside Somset 20 B4
Downside Somset 20 B6
Downside Surrey 36 D9
Down Thomas Devon 6 E8
Downton Hants 13 N6
Downton Wilts 21 N10
Dowsby Lincs 74 B5
Dowsdale Lincs 74 E8
Doxey Staffs 70 F10
Doxford Nthumb 119 N6
Doynton S Glos 32 D10
Draethen Caerph 30 H7
Draffan S Lans 126 B6
Dragonby N Linc 92 F8
Dragons Green W Susx 24 D6
Drakeholes Notts 85 M2
Drakelow Worcs 57 Q8
Drakemyre N Ayrs 124 H7
Drakes Broughton Worcs 46 H5
Drakewalls Cnwll 6 C4
Draughton N York 96 F10
Draughton Nhants 60 G5
Drax N York 92 A5
Drax Hales N York 91 R5
Draycot Warwks 59 P10
Draycot Foliat Swindn 33 N9
Draycott Derbys 72 C4
Draycott Gloucs 47 N7
Draycott Shrops 57 Q6
Draycott Somset 19 M4
Draycott Somset 19 Q10
Draycott in the Clay Staffs 71 M9
Draycott in the Moors Staffs 70 H6
Drayford Devon 9 J2
Drayton C Port 15 J5
Drayton Leics 60 H2
Drayton Lincs 74 D3
Drayton Norfk 76 H9
Drayton Oxon 34 E6
Drayton Oxon 48 D6
Drayton Somset 19 M10
Drayton Worcs 58 D9
Drayton Bassett Staffs 59 J4
Drayton Beauchamp Bucks 35 P2
Drayton Manor Park Staffs 59 J4
Drayton Parslow Bucks 49 M9
Drayton St Leonard Oxon 34 G5
Drebley N York 96 G9
Dreemskerry IoM 80 g3
Dreen Hill Pembks 40 H6
Drefach Carmth 28 F2
Drefach Carmth 42 F7
Drefach Cerdgn 43 J3
Drefelin Carmth 42 G7
Dreghorn N Ayrs 125 K10
Drellingore Kent 27 M3
Drem E Loth 128 E4
Dresden C Stke 70 G6
Drewsteignton Devon 8 H6
Driby Lincs 87 L6
Driffield E R Yk 99 L3
Driffield Gloucs 33 L5
Driffield Cross Roads Gloucs 33 L5
Drift Cnwll 2 C8
Drigg Cumb 100 E11
Drighlington Leeds 90 G5
Drimnin Highld 137 P5
Drimpton Dorset 11 K3
Drimsallie Highld 138 H2
Dringhouses C York 98 B11
Drinkstone Suffk 64 D9
Drinkstone Green Suffk 64 D9
Drive End Dorset 11 M3
Driver's End Herts 50 F6
Drointon Staffs 71 J9
Droitwich Spa Worcs 46 G2
Dron P & K 134 E4
Dronfield Derbys 84 E5
Dronfield Woodhouse Derbys 84 D5
Drongan E Ayrs 114 H4
Dronley Angus 142 E10

Droop Dorset 12 C3
Dropping Well Rothm 84 E2
Droxford Hants 22 H11
Droylsden Tamesd 83 K5
Druid Denbgs 68 D6
Druidston Pembks 40 G6
Druimavuic Ag & B 139 K3
Druimdrishaig Ag & B 123 M5
Druimindarroch Highld 145 L11
Drum Ag & B 124 A2
Drum P & K 134 C7
Drumalbin S Lans 116 C3
Drumbeg Highld 164 D10
Drumblade Abers 158 E9
Drumbreddon D & G 106 D9
Drumbuie Highld 153 P11
Drumburgh Cumb 110 E9
Drumburn D & G 109 J10
Drumchapel C Glas 125 N3
Drumchastle P & K 140 G6
Drumclog S Lans 125 Q10
Drumeldrie Fife 135 L7
Drumelzier Border 116 G4
Drumfearn Highld 145 L4
Drumfrennie Abers 151 J8
Drumgley Angus 142 G7
Drumguish Highld 148 D7
Drumin Moray 157 M11
Drumjohn D & G 115 K8
Drumlamford S Ayrs 107 J2
Drumlasie Abers 150 G6
Drumleaning Cumb 110 E10
Drumlemble Ag & B 120 C8
Drumlithie Abers 151 K11
Drummoddie D & G 107 L8
Drummore D & G 106 F10
Drummuir Moray 158 A9
Drumnadrochit Highld 155 P11
Drumnagorrach Moray 158 D7
Drumpark D & G 109 J5
Drumrunie Lodge Highld 161 K6
Drumshang S Ayrs 114 E5
Drumuie Highld 152 H8
Drumuillie Highld 148 G3
Drumvaich Stirlg 133 K7
Drunzie P & K 134 E6
Druridge Nthumb 119 Q10
Drury Flints 69 J2
Drybeck Cumb 102 C7
Drybridge Moray 158 B5
Drybridge N Ayrs 125 K10
Drybrook Gloucs 46 B11
Dryburgh Border 118 A4
Dry Doddington Lincs 85 Q11
Dry Drayton Cambs 62 E8
Drymen Stirlg 132 F10
Drymuir Abers 159 M8
Drynoch Highld 152 G11
Dry Sandford Oxon 34 E4
Dryslwyn Carmth 43 L10
Dry Street Essex 37 Q3
Dryton Shrops 57 K3
Dubford Abers 159 J5
Dublin Suffk 64 H8
Duchally Highld 161 P3
Duck End Bed 50 C2
Duck End Cambs 62 B8
Duck End Essex 51 Q4
Duck End Essex 51 Q5
Duckend Green Essex 52 B7
Duckington Ches W 69 N4
Ducklington Oxon 34 C3
Duck's Cross Bed 61 P9
Duddenhoe End Essex 51 L3
Duddingston C Edin 127 P3
Duddington Nhants 73 P10
Duddlestone Somset 18 H10
Duddleswell E Susx 25 L5
Duddlewick Shrops 57 M8
Duddo Nthumb 118 H2
Duddon Ches W 69 P2
Duddon Bridge Cumb 94 D3
Duddon Common Ches W 81 Q11
Dudleston Shrops 69 K7
Dudleston Heath Shrops 69 K7
Dudley Dudley 58 D6
Dudley N Tyne 113 L6
Dudley Hill C Brad 90 F4
Dudley Port Sandw 58 E6
Dudnill Shrops 57 L10
Dudsbury Dorset 13 J5
Dudswell Herts 35 Q3
Duffield Derbys 72 A2
Duffryn Neath 29 M5
Dufftown Moray 157 Q9
Duffus Moray 157 M4
Dufton Cumb 102 C5
Duggleby N York 98 H7
Duirinish Highld 153 P11
Duisdalemore Highld 145 M5
Duisky Highld 139 J3
Dukestown Blae G 30 F2
Duke Street Suffk 53 J3
Dukinfield Tamesd 83 K5
Dukinfield Crematorium Tamesd 83 K5
Dulas IoA 78 H7
Dulcote Somset 19 Q6
Dulford Devon 9 Q4
Dull P & K 141 K8
Dullatur N Lans 126 C2
Dullingham Cambs 63 K9
Dullingham Ley Cambs 63 K9
Dulnain Bridge Highld 148 H3
Duloe Bed 61 Q8
Duloe Cnwll 5 L10
Dulverton Somset 18 B9
Dulwich Gt Lon 36 H6
Dumbarton W Duns 125 L2
Dumbleton Gloucs 47 K7
Dumfries D & G 109 L5
Dumgoyne Stirlg 132 G11
Dummer Hants 22 H5
Dumpton Kent 39 Q8
Dun Angus 143 M6
Dunalastair P & K 140 H6
Dunan Ag & B 124 F3
Dunan Highld 145 J2
Dunan P & K 140 C6
Dunaverty Ag & B 120 C10
Dunball Somset 19 K6
Dunbar E Loth 128 H4
Dunbeath Highld 167 L11
Dunbeg Ag & B 138 F11
Dunblane Stirlg 133 M7
Dunbog Fife 134 H4
Dunbridge Hants 22 B9
Duncanston Highld 155 Q6
Duncanstone Abers 150 F2

268 Dunchideock – Edenhall

Dunchideock Devon 9 L7
Dunchurch Warwks 59 Q10
Duncote Nhants 49 J4
Duncow D & G 109 L4
Duncrievie P & K 134 E6
Duncton W Susx 23 Q11
Dundee C Dund 142 G11
Dundee Airport C Dund 135 K2
Dundee Crematorium C Dund 142 F11
Dundon Somset 19 N8
Dundonald S Ayrs 125 K11
Dundonnell Highld 160 H9
Dundraw Cumb 110 D11
Dundreggan Highld 147 J5
Dundrennan D & G 108 F11
Dundry N Som 31 Q11
Dunecht Abers 151 K6
Dunfermline Fife 134 D10
Dunfermline Crematorium Fife 134 E10
Dunfield Gloucs 33 M5
Dunford Bridge Barns 83 Q4
Dungate Kent 38 F10
Dungavel S Lans 126 B10
Dunge Wilts 20 G4
Dungeness Kent 27 J8
Dungworth Sheff 84 C3
Dunham Massey Traffd 82 F7
Dunham-on-the-Hill Ches W 81 P10
Dunham-on-Trent Notts 85 P6
Dunhampstead Worcs 46 H2
Dunhampton Worcs 58 B11
Dunham Town Traffd 82 F7
Dunham Woodhouses Traffd 82 F7
Dunholme Lincs 86 D5
Dunino Fife 135 N5
Dunipace Falk 133 N11
Dunkeld P & K 141 P9
Dunkerton BaNES 20 D3
Dunkeswell Devon 10 C3
Dunkeswick N York 97 M11
Dunkirk Ches W 81 M10
Dunkirk Kent 39 J10
Dunkirk S Glos 32 E7
Dunkirk Wilts 21 J2
Dunk's Green Kent 37 P10
Dunlappie Angus 143 K4
Dunley Hants 22 E4
Dunley Worcs 57 P11
Dunlop E Ayrs 125 L8
Dunmaglass Highld 147 P3
Dunmere Cnwll 4 G8
Dunmore Falk 133 P10
Dunnet Highld 167 M2
Dunnichen Angus 143 J8
Dunning P & K 134 C5
Dunnington C York 98 D10
Dunnington E R Yk 99 P10
Dunnington Warwks 47 L4
Dunnockshaw Lancs 89 N5
Dunn Street Kent 38 C9
Dunoon Ag & B 124 F2
Dunphail Moray 157 J8
Dunragit D & G 106 G6
Duns Border 129 K9
Dunsa Derbys 84 B6
Dunsby Lincs 74 B5
Dunscar Bolton 89 L8
Dunscore D & G 109 J4
Dunscroft Donc 91 Q9
Dunsdale R & Cl 104 H7
Dunsden Green Oxon 35 K9
Dunsdon Devon 16 E10
Dunsfold Surrey 24 B3
Dunsford Devon 9 K7
Dunshalt Fife 134 G5
Dunshillock Abers 159 N8
Dunsill Notts 84 G8
Dunsley N York 105 N8
Dunsley Staffs 58 C8
Dunsmore Bucks 35 N3
Dunsop Bridge Lancs 95 P11
Dunstable C Beds 50 B6
Dunstall Staffs 71 M10
Dunstall Common Worcs 46 G6
Dunstall Green Suffk 63 M8
Dunstan Nthumb 119 P7
Dunstan Steads Nthumb 119 P6
Dunster Somset 18 C6
Duns Tew Oxon 48 E9
Dunston Gatesd 113 K8
Dunston Lincs 86 E8
Dunston Norfk 77 J11
Dunston Staffs 70 G11
Dunstone Devon 6 F8
Dunstone Devon 8 H9
Dunston Heath Staffs 70 G11
Dunsville Donc 91 Q9
Dunswell E R Yk 93 J3
Dunsyre S Lans 127 K8
Dunterton Devon 5 P6
Dunthrop Oxon 48 C9
Duntisbourne Abbots Gloucs 33 J3
Duntisbourne Leer Gloucs 33 J3
Duntisbourne Rouse Gloucs 33 J3
Duntish Dorset 11 P3
Duntocher W Duns 125 M3
Dunton Bucks 49 M10
Dunton C Beds 50 F2
Dunton Norfk 76 B5
Dunton Bassett Leics 60 B2
Dunton Green Kent 37 M9
Dunton Wayletts Essex 37 Q2
Duntulm Highld 152 G3
Dunure S Ayrs 114 E4
Dunvant Swans 28 G6
Dunvegan Highld 152 D8
Dunwich Suffk 65 P7
Dunwood Staffs 70 G3
Durdar Cumb 110 H10
Durgan Cnwll 3 K8
Durham Dur 103 Q2
Durham Cathedral Dur 103 Q2
Durham Crematorium Dur 103 Q2
Durham Services Dur 104 B3
Durham Tees Valley Airport S on T 104 C8
Durisdeer D & G 116 B10
Durisdeermill D & G 116 B10
Durkar Wakefd 91 J7
Durleigh Somset 19 J7
Durley Hants 22 F11
Durley Wilts 21 P2
Durley Street Hants 22 F11
Durlock Kent 39 N10
Durlock Kent 39 P9
Durlow Common Herefs 46 B7
Durn Rochdl 89 Q7
Durness Highld 165 K3
Durno Abers 151 J2
Duror Highld 138 H6
Durran Ag & B 131 K6
Durrington W Susx 24 D9
Durrington Wilts 21 N6
Durris Abers 151 K8
Dursley Gloucs 32 E5
Dursley Cross Gloucs 46 C10
Durston Somset 19 J9
Durweston Dorset 12 E3
Duston Nhants 60 F8
Duthil Highld 148 G3
Dutlas Powys 56 C9
Duton Hill Essex 51 P5
Dutson Cnwll 5 N4
Dutton Ches W 82 C9
Duxford Cambs 62 G11
Duxford Oxon 34 C5
Duxford IWM Cambs 62 G11
Dwygyfylchi Conwy 79 N9
Dwyran IoA 78 G11
Dyce C Aber 151 M5
Dyer's End Essex 52 B4
Dyfatty Carmth 28 E4
Dyffrydan Gwynd 54 F2
Dyffryn Brdgnd 29 N6
Dyffryn Myr Td 30 E4
Dyffryn V Glam 30 E10
Dyffryn Ardudwy Gwynd 67 K10
Dyffryn Castell Cerdgn 54 H8
Dyffryn Cellwen Neath 29 N2
Dyke Lincs 74 B6
Dyke Moray 156 H6
Dykehead Angus 142 C7
Dykehead Angus 142 F6
Dykehead N Lans 126 F6
Dykehead Stirlg 132 H8
Dykelands Abers 143 N4
Dykends Angus 142 D6
Dykeside Abers 158 H9
Dylife Powys 55 K6
Dymchurch Kent 27 K6
Dymock Gloucs 46 D8
Dyrham S Glos 32 D9
Dysart Fife 135 J9
Dyserth Denbgs 80 F9

E

Eachway Worcs 58 E9
Eachwick Nthumb 112 H6
Eagland Hill Lancs 95 J11
Eagle Lincs 85 Q7
Eagle Barnsdale Lincs 85 Q7
Eagle Moor Lincs 85 Q7
Eaglescliffe S on T 104 D7
Eaglesfield Cumb 100 E5
Eaglesfield D & G 110 D6
Eaglesham E Rens 125 P7
Eagley Bolton 89 L8
Eairy IoM 80 c6
Eakring Notts 85 L8
Ealand N Linc 92 C8
Ealing Gt Lon 36 E4
Eals Nthumb 111 N9
Eamont Bridge Cumb 101 P5
Earby Lancs 96 D11
Earcroft Bl w D 89 K6
Eardington Shrops 57 N6
Eardisland Herefs 45 N3
Eardisley Herefs 45 L5
Eardiston Shrops 69 L9
Eardiston Worcs 57 M11
Earith Cambs 62 E5
Earle Nthumb 119 J5
Earlestown St Hel 82 C5
Earley Wokham 35 K10
Earlham Norfk 76 H10
Earlham Crematorium Norfk 77 J10
Earlish Highld 152 F5
Earls Barton Nhants 61 J8
Earls Colne Essex 52 E6
Earls Common Worcs 47 J3
Earl's Croome Worcs 46 G6
Earlsditton Shrops 57 L9
Earlsdon Covtry 59 M9
Earl's Down E Susx 25 P7
Earlsferry Fife 135 M7
Earlsfield Gt Lon 36 G6
Earlsford Abers 159 K11
Earl's Green Suffk 64 E8
Earlsheaton Kirk 90 H6
Earl Shilton Leics 72 D11
Earl Soham Suffk 65 J9
Earl Sterndale Derbys 83 N11
Earlston Border 117 R3
Earlston E Ayrs 125 L10
Earl Stonham Suffk 64 G10
Earlswood Surrey 36 G11
Earlswood Warwks 58 H10
Earlswood Common Mons 31 N6
Earnley W Susx 15 M7
Earnshaw Bridge Lancs 88 G6
Earsdon N Tyne 113 M6
Earsdon Nthumb 113 J2
Earsham Norfk 65 L4
Earswick C York 98 C9
Eartham W Susx 15 P5
Earthcott S Glos 32 C7
Easby N York 104 G9
Easdale Ag & B 130 E4
Easebourne W Susx 23 P10
Easenhall Warwks 59 Q9
Eashing Surrey 23 P6
Easington Bucks 35 J2
Easington Dur 104 D2
Easington E R Yk 93 Q7
Easington Nthumb 119 M4
Easington Oxon 35 J5
Easington R & Cl 105 K7
Easington Colliery Dur 104 D2
Easington Lane Sundld 113 N11
Easingwold N York 98 A7
Easole Street Kent 39 N11
Eassie and Nevay Angus 142 E9
East Aberthaw V Glam 30 D11
East Allington Devon 7 K9
East Anstey Devon 17 R6
East Anton Hants 22 C5
East Appleton N York 103 P11
East Ashey IoW 14 G9
East Ashling W Susx 15 M5
East Aston Hants 22 D5
East Ayton N York 99 K3
East Balsdon Cnwll 5 M2
East Bank Blae G 30 H3
East Barkwith Lincs 86 G4
East Barming Kent 38 B11
East Barnby N York 105 M8
East Barnet Gt Lon 50 G11
East Barns E Loth 129 J4
East Barsham Norfk 76 C5
East Beckham Norfk 76 H4
East Bedfont Gt Lon 36 C6
East Bergholt Suffk 53 J5
East Bierley Kirk 90 F5
East Bilney Norfk 76 D8
East Blatchington E Susx 25 L10
East Bloxworth Dorset 12 E6
East Boldon S Tyne 113 N8
East Boldre Hants 14 C6
East Bolton Nthumb 119 M7
Eastbourne Darltn 104 B8
Eastbourne E Susx 25 P11
Eastbourne Crematorium E Susx 25 P10
East Bower Somset 19 K7
East Bradenham Norfk 76 C10
East Brent Somset 19 K4
Eastbridge Suffk 65 P8
East Bridgford Notts 72 H2
East Briscoe Dur 103 J7
Eastbrook V Glam 30 G10
East Buckland Devon 17 M5
East Budleigh Devon 9 Q8
Eastburn C Brad 90 C2
Eastburn E R Yk 99 K9
East Burnham Bucks 35 Q8
East Burton Dorset 12 D7
Eastbury Herts 36 D2
Eastbury W Berk 34 B9
East Butsfield Dur 112 H11
East Butterwick N Linc 92 D9
Eastby N York 96 F10
East Calder W Loth 127 K4
East Carleton Norfk 76 H11
East Carlton Leeds 90 G2
East Carlton Nhants 60 H3
East Chaldon (Chaldon Herring) Dorset 12 C8
East Challow Oxon 34 C7
East Charleton Devon 7 K10
East Chelborough Dorset 11 M3
East Chiltington E Susx 25 J7
East Chinnock Somset 11 K2
East Chisenbury Wilts 21 M4
East Cholderton Hants 21 Q5
Eastchurch Kent 38 G7
East Clandon Surrey 36 C10
East Claydon Bucks 49 K9
East Clevedon N Som 31 M10
East Coker Somset 11 L2
Eastcombe Gloucs 32 G4
Eastcombe Somset 18 G8
East Compton Somset 20 B6
East Cornworthy Devon 7 L7
East Cote Cumb 109 P9
Eastcote Gt Lon 36 D3
Eastcote Nhants 49 J4
Eastcote Solhll 59 J9
Eastcott Cnwll 16 D8
Eastcott Wilts 21 K3
East Cottingwith E R Yk 92 B2
Eastcourt Wilts 21 P2
Eastcourt Wilts 33 J6
East Cowes IoW 14 F7
East Cowick E R Yk 91 R6
East Cowton N York 104 B10
East Cramlington Nthumb 113 L5
East Cranmore Somset 20 C6
East Creech Dorset 12 F8
East Curthwaite Cumb 110 F11
East Dean E Susx 25 N11
East Dean Gloucs 46 C10
East Dean Hants 21 Q9
East Dean W Susx 15 P4
East Devon Crematorium Devon 9 Q5
Eastdown Devon 7 L9
East Down Devon 17 L3
East Drayton Notts 85 N5
East Dulwich Gt Lon 36 H5
East Dundry N Som 31 Q11
East Ella C KuH 93 J5
East End Bed 61 P9
East End C Beds 49 Q6
East End E R Yk 93 L4
East End E R Yk 93 N5
Eastend Essex 38 F3
East End Essex 51 K8
East End Hants 14 C7
East End Hants 22 D2
East End Herts 51 L5
East End Kent 26 D4
East End Kent 38 G7
East End M Keyn 49 P6
East End N Som 31 N10
East End Oxon 48 C11
East End Somset 20 C5
East End Suffk 53 K4
Easter Balmoral Abers 149 P9
Easter Compton S Glos 31 Q8
Easter Dalziel Highld 156 D7
Eastergate W Susx 15 P5
Easterhouse C Glas 126 B4
Easter Howgate Mdloth 127 N5
Easter Kinkell Highld 155 Q6
Easter Moniack Highld 155 Q9
Eastern Green Covtry 59 L9
Easter Ord Abers 151 L7
Easter Pitkierie Fife 135 P6
Easter Skeld Shet 169 q9
Easter Softlaw Border 118 E4
Easterton Wilts 21 K4
Eastertown Somset 19 K4
East Everleigh Wilts 21 P4
East Farleigh Kent 38 B11
East Farndon Nhants 60 F4
East Ferry Lincs 92 D11
Eastfield N Lans 126 F5
Eastfield N York 99 L4
East Firsby Lincs 86 D3
East Fortune E Loth 128 E4
East Garforth Leeds 91 L4
East Garston W Berk 34 C9
Eastgate Dur 103 J3
Eastgate Lincs 74 B7
Eastgate Norfk 76 G7
East Ginge Oxon 34 D7
East Goscote Leics 72 G8
East Grafton Wilts 21 Q2
East Green Suffk 65 N8
East Grimstead Wilts 21 P9
East Grinstead W Susx 25 J3
East Guldeford E Susx 26 F7
East Haddon Nhants 60 E7
East Hagbourne Oxon 34 F7
East Halton N Linc 93 K7
East Ham Gt Lon 37 K4
Eastham Wirral 81 M8
Eastham Ferry Wirral 81 M8
Easthampstead Park Crematorium Br For 35 M11
Easthampton Herefs 45 N2
East Hanney Oxon 34 D6
East Hanningfield Essex 52 C11
East Hardwick Wakefd 91 M7
East Harling Norfk 64 D4
East Harlsey N York 104 D11
East Harnham Wilts 21 M9
East Harptree BaNES 19 Q3
East Hartford Nthumb 113 L5
East Harting W Susx 23 L11
East Hatch Wilts 20 H9
East Hatley Cambs 62 C10
East Hauxwell N York 97 J2
East Haven Angus 143 K10
Eastheath Wokham 35 L11
East Heckington Lincs 74 C2
East Hedleyhope Dur 103 N2
East Helmsdale Highld 163 N3
East Hendred Oxon 34 E7
East Heslerton N York 99 J5
East Hewish N Som 19 M2
East Hoathly E Susx 25 M7
East Holme Dorset 12 E7
Easthope Shrops 57 K5
Easthorpe Essex 52 F7
Easthorpe Notts 85 M10
East Horrington Somset 19 Q5
East Horsley Surrey 36 C10
East Horton Nthumb 119 K4
East Howe Bmouth 13 J5
East Huntington C York 98 C9
East Huntspill Somset 19 K5
East Hyde C Beds 50 D7
East Ilkerton Devon 17 N2
East Ilsley W Berk 34 E8
Eastington Devon 8 H3
Eastington Gloucs 32 E3
Eastington Gloucs 33 M2
East Keal Lincs 87 L8
East Kennett Wilts 33 M11
East Keswick Leeds 91 K2
East Kilbride S Lans 125 Q7
East Kimber Devon 8 C5
East Kirkby Lincs 87 K8
East Knighton Dorset 12 D7
East Knowstone Devon 17 Q7
East Knoyle Wilts 20 G8
East Lambrook Somset 19 M11
East Lancashire Crematorium Bury 89 M9
Eastlands D & G 108 H6
East Langdon Kent 27 P2
East Langton Leics 60 F2
East Lavant W Susx 15 N5
East Lavington W Susx 23 P11
East Layton N York 103 N9
Eastleach Martin Gloucs 33 P4
Eastleach Turville Gloucs 33 N3
East Leake Notts 72 F5
East Learmouth Nthumb 118 G3
East Leigh Devon 6 H8
East Leigh Devon 7 K7
East Leigh Devon 8 G3
Eastleigh Devon 16 H6
Eastleigh Hants 22 E11
East Lexham Norfk 76 B8
Eastling Kent 38 G10
East Linton E Loth 128 F4
East Liss Hants 23 L9
East Lockinge Oxon 34 D7
East London Crematorium Gt Lon 37 J4
East Lound N Linc 92 C11
East Lulworth Dorset 12 E8
East Lutton N York 99 J7
East Lydeard Somset 18 G9
East Lydford Somset 19 Q8
East Malling Kent 38 B10
East Malling Heath Kent 37 Q9
East Marden W Susx 15 M4
East Markham Notts 85 M6
East Martin Hants 21 L11
East Marton N York 96 D10
East Meon Hants 23 J10
East Mere Devon 18 C11
East Mersea Essex 52 H9
East Midlands Airport Leics 72 D5
East Molesey Surrey 36 D7
Eastmoor Norfk 75 P10
East Morden Dorset 12 F6
East Morton C Brad 90 D2
East Morton D & G 116 B10
East Ness N York 98 D5
East Newton E R Yk 93 N3
Eastney C Port 15 J7
Eastnor Herefs 46 D7
East Norton Leics 73 K10
Eastoft N Linc 92 D7
East Ogwell Devon 7 L4
Easton Cambs 61 P6
Easton Cumb 110 E9
Easton Devon 8 H7
Easton Dorset 11 P10
Easton Hants 22 F8
Easton Lincs 73 N5
Easton Norfk 76 G9
Easton Somset 19 P5
Easton Suffk 65 K10
Easton W Berk 34 D10
Easton Wilts 32 G10
Easton Grey Wilts 32 G7
Easton-in-Gordano N Som 31 P9
Easton Maudit Nhants 61 J9
Easton-on-the-Hill Nhants 73 Q10
Easton Royal Wilts 21 P2
East Orchard Dorset 20 F11
East Ord Nthumb 129 P9
East Panson Devon 5 P3
East Parley Dorset 13 J5
East Peckham Kent 37 Q11
East Pennar Pembks 41 J10
East Pennard Somset 19 Q7
East Perry Cambs 61 Q7
East Portlemouth Devon 7 K11
East Prawle Devon 7 K11
East Preston W Susx 24 C10
East Pulham Dorset 11 Q3
East Putford Devon 16 F8
East Quantoxhead Somset 18 F6
East Rainham Medway 38 D8
East Rainton Sundld 113 M11
East Ravendale NE Lin 93 M11
East Raynham Norfk 76 B6
Eastrea Cambs 74 E11
East Riding Crematorium E R Yk 99 L7
Eastriggs D & G 110 D7
East Rigton Leeds 91 K2
Eastrington E R Yk 92 C5
East Rolstone N Som 19 L2
Eastrop Swindn 33 P6
East Rounton N York 104 D10
East Rudham Norfk 76 A6
East Runton Norfk 76 H3
East Ruston Norfk 77 L6
Eastry Kent 39 P11
East Saltoun E Loth 128 D6
Eastshaw W Susx 23 N10
East Sheen Gt Lon 36 F6
East Shefford W Berk 34 C10
East Sleekburn Nthumb 113 L4
East Somerton Norfk 77 P8
East Stockwith Lincs 85 N2
East Stoke Dorset 12 E7
East Stoke Notts 85 N11
East Stour Dorset 20 F10
East Stourmouth Kent 39 N9
East Stowford Devon 17 L6
East Stratton Hants 22 F6
East Studdal Kent 27 P2
East Sutton Kent 26 D2
East Taphouse Cnwll 5 K9
East-the-Water Devon 16 H6
East Thirston Nthumb 119 N10
East Tilbury Thurr 37 Q5
East Tisted Hants 23 K8
East Torrington Lincs 86 F4
East Tuddenham Norfk 76 F9
East Tytherley Hants 21 Q9
East Tytherton Wilts 33 J10
East Village Devon 9 K3
Eastville Bristl 32 B10
Eastville Lincs 87 M9
East Wall Shrops 57 J6
East Walton Norfk 75 P7
East Water Somset 19 P4
East Week Devon 8 G6
Eastwell Leics 73 K5
East Wellow Hants 22 B10
East Wemyss Fife 135 J8
East Whitburn W Loth 126 H4
Eastwick Herts 51 K8
East Wickham Gt Lon 37 L5
East Williamston Pembks 41 L10
East Winch Norfk 75 N7
East Winterslow Wilts 21 P8
East Wittering W Susx 15 L7
East Witton N York 96 H3
Eastwood Notts 84 G11
Eastwood Sthend 38 D4
East Woodburn Nthumb 112 D3
Eastwood End Cambs 62 F2
East Woodhay Hants 22 D2
East Woodlands Somset 20 E6
East Worldham Hants 23 L7
East Wretham Norfk 64 C3
East Youlstone Devon 16 D8
Eathorpe Warwks 59 N11
Eaton Ches E 83 J11
Eaton Ches W 69 Q2
Eaton Leics 73 K5
Eaton Norfk 77 J10
Eaton Notts 85 M5
Eaton Oxon 34 D4
Eaton Shrops 56 F7
Eaton Shrops 57 J7
Eaton Bishop Herefs 45 N7
Eaton Bray C Beds 49 Q10
Eaton Constantine Shrops 57 K3
Eaton Ford Cambs 61 Q9
Eaton Green C Beds 49 Q10
Eaton Hastings Oxon 33 Q5
Eaton Mascott Shrops 57 J3
Eaton Socon Cambs 61 Q9
Eaton upon Tern Shrops 70 B10
Eaves Brow Warrtn 82 D6
Eaves Green Solhll 59 L8
Ebberston N York 98 H4
Ebbesborne Wake Wilts 21 J10
Ebbw Vale Blae G 30 G3
Ebchester Dur 112 H9
Ebdon N Som 19 L2
Ebford Devon 9 N7
Ebley Gloucs 32 F3
Ebnal Ches W 69 N5
Ebnall Herefs 45 P3
Ebrington Gloucs 47 N6
Ebsworthy Devon 8 D6
Ecchinswell Hants 22 E3
Ecclaw Border 129 K6
Ecclefechan D & G 110 C6
Eccles Border 118 E2
Eccles Kent 38 B9
Eccles Salfd 82 G5
Ecclesall Sheff 84 D4
Ecclesfield Sheff 84 E2
Eccles Green Herefs 45 M5
Eccleshall Staffs 70 E9
Eccleshill C Brad 90 F3
Ecclesmachan W Loth 127 K3
Eccles on Sea Norfk 77 N6
Eccles Road Norfk 64 E4
Eccleston Ches W 69 M2
Eccleston Lancs 88 G7
Eccleston St Hel 81 P5
Eccleston Green Lancs 88 G7
Echt Abers 151 J6
Eckford Border 118 D5
Eckington Derbys 84 F5
Eckington Worcs 46 H6
Ecton Nhants 60 H8
Ecton Staffs 71 K3
Edale Derbys 83 P7
Eday Ork 169 e3
Eday Airport Ork 169 e3
Edburton W Susx 24 F8
Edderside Cumb 109 P11
Edderton Highld 162 G10
Eddington Kent 39 L8
Eddleston Border 127 N8
Eddlewood S Lans 126 C7
Edenbridge Kent 37 K11
Edenfield Lancs 89 N7
Edenhall Cumb 101 Q4

denham Lincs 73 R6	Elcot W Berk 34 C11	Elvington C York 98 E11	Etloe Gloucs 32 C3	Fairgirth D & G 109 J9
den Mount Cumb 95 J5	Eldernell Cambs 74 F11	Elvington Kent 39 N11	Eton W & M 35 Q9	Fair Green Norfk 75 N7
den Park Gt Lon 37 J2	Eldersfield Worcs 46 E8	Elwell Devon 17 M5	Eton Wick W & M 35 P9	Fairhaven Lancs 88 C5
den Project Cnwll 3 Q3	Elderslie Rens 125 L5	Elwick Hartpl 104 E4	Etruria C Stke 70 F5	Fair Isle Shet 169 t12
ensor Derbys 84 B7	Elder Street Essex 51 N4	Elwick Nthumb 119 M3	Etteridge Highld 148 B9	Fair Isle Airport Shet 169 t12
entagart Ag & B 132 C9	Eldon Dur 103 P5	Elworth Ches E 70 C2	Ettersgill Dur 102 G5	Fairlands Surrey 23 Q4
enthorpe Donc 91 Q9	Eldwick C Brad 90 E2	Elworthy Somset 18 E8	Ettiley Heath Ches E 70 C2	Fairlie N Ayrs 124 G7
ern Gwynd 66 D7	Elerch Cerdgn 54 F7	Ely Cambs 62 H4	Ettingshall Wolves 58 D5	Fairmile Devon 10 B5
garley Somset 19 P7	Elfhill Abers 151 L10	Ely Cardif 30 F9	Ettington Warwks 47 Q5	Fairmile Surrey 36 D8
gbaston Birm 58 G8	Elford Nthumb 119 N4	Emberton M Keyn 49 N5	Etton C Pete 74 B9	Fairmilee Border 117 P4
gcombe Cnwll 3 J7	Elford Staffs 59 J2	Embleton Cumb 100 G4	Etton E R Yk 92 G2	Fair Oak Hants 22 E11
gcott Bucks 49 J10	Elgin Moray 157 N5	Embleton Dur 104 D5	Ettrick Border 117 K8	Fairoak Staffs 70 C8
ge Gloucs 32 F3	Elgol Highld 144 H5	Embleton Nthumb 119 P6	Ettrickbridge Border 117 M6	Fair Oak Green Hants 23 J2
ge Shrops 56 F3	Elham Kent 27 L3	Embo Highld 163 J8	Ettrickhill Border 117 K8	Fairseat Kent 37 P8
gebolton Shrops 69 Q10	Elie Fife 135 M7	Emborough Somset 20 B4	Etwall Derbys 71 P8	Fairstead Essex 52 C8
ge End Gloucs 31 Q2	Elilaw Nthumb 119 J9	Embo Street Highld 163 J8	Eudon George Shrops 57 M7	Fairstead Norfk 75 M6
gefield Norfk 76 F5	Elim IoA 78 F8	Embsay N York 96 F10	Euston Suffk 64 B6	Fairstead Norfk 77 K7
gefield Green Norfk 76 F5	Eling Hants 14 C4	Emery Down Hants 13 N3	Euximoor Drove Cambs 75 J11	Fairwarp E Susx 25 L5
gefold Bolton 89 L9	Elkesley Notts 85 L5	Emley Kirk 90 G8	Euxton Lancs 88 H7	Fairwater Cardif 30 F9
ge Green Ches W 69 N4	Elkstone Gloucs 33 J2	Emley Moor Kirk 90 G8	Evancoyd Powys 45 K2	Fairy Cross Devon 16 G7
gehill Warwks 48 C5	Ella Abers 158 F6	Emmbrook Wokham 35 M11	Evanton Highld 155 R4	Fakenham Norfk 76 C6
gerley Shrops 69 L11	Ellacombe Torbay 7 N6	Emmer Green Readg 35 K9	Evedon Lincs 86 E11	Fakenham Magna Suffk 64 C6
gerton Kirk 90 E7	Elland Calder 90 E6	Emmett Carr Derbys 84 G5	Evelith Shrops 57 N3	Fala Mdloth 128 C7
geside Lancs 89 N6	Elland Lower Edge Calder 90 E6	Emmington Oxon 35 K4	Evelix Highld 162 H8	Fala Dam Mdloth 128 C7
geworth Gloucs 32 H3	Ellary Ag & B 123 M4	Emneth Norfk 75 J9	Evenjobb Powys 45 K2	Falcut Nhants 48 G6
geworthy Devon 9 K2	Ellastone Staffs 71 L6	Emneth Hungate Norfk 75 J9	Evenley Nhants 48 G8	Faldingworth Lincs 86 E4
ginswell Torbay 7 M5	Ellel Lancs 95 K9	Empingham Rutlnd 73 N9	Evenlode Gloucs 47 P9	Faldouët Jersey 11 c2
giock Worcs 47 K2	Ellemford Border 129 J7	Empshott Hants 23 L8	Evenwood Dur 103 N6	Falfield S Glos 32 C6
gmond Wrekin 70 C11	Ellenabeich Ag & B 130 E4	Empshott Green Hants 23 K8	Evenwood Gate Dur 103 N6	Falkenham Suffk 53 N4
gmond Marsh Wrekin 70 C10	Ellenborough Cumb 100 D3	Emstrey Crematorium Shrops 57 J2	Evercreech Somset 20 B7	Falkirk Falk 133 P11
gton Shrops 56 F7	Ellenbrook Salfd 82 F4	Emsworth Hants 15 K5	Everingham E R Yk 92 D2	Falkirk Crematorium Falk 133 P11
gware Gt Lon 36 E2	Ellenhall Staffs 70 E9	Enborne W Berk 34 D11	Everleigh Wilts 21 P4	Falkirk Wheel Falk 133 P11
gworth Bl w D 89 L7	Ellen's Green Surrey 24 C3	Enborne Row W Berk 22 D2	Everley N York 99 K3	Falkland Fife 134 H6
nbane Highld 152 E7	Ellerbeck N York 104 D11	Enchmarsh Shrops 57 J5	Eversholt C Beds 49 Q8	Fallburn S Lans 116 D3
nburgh C Edin 127 P3	Ellerdine Heath Wrekin 69 R10	Enderby Leics 72 E11	Evershot Dorset 11 M4	Fallgate Derbys 84 E8
nburgh Airport C Edin 127 N4	Ellerhayes Devon 9 N4	Endmoor Cumb 95 L4	Eversley Hants 23 L2	Fallin Stirlg 133 N9
nburgh Castle C Edin 127 P3	Elleric Ag & B 139 J8	Endon Staffs 70 G4	Eversley Cross Hants 23 L2	Fallodon Nthumb 119 N6
nburgh Old & New Town C Edin 127 P3	Ellerker E R Yk 92 F5	Endon Bank Staffs 70 G4	Everthorpe E R Yk 92 F4	Fallowfield Manch 83 J6
nburgh Royal Botanic Gardens C Edin 127 N2	Ellerton E R Yk 92 B3	Enfield Gt Lon 51 J11	Everton C Beds 62 B10	Fallowfield Nthumb 112 D7
nburgh Zoo RZSS C Edin 127 N3	Ellerton N York 103 Q11	Enfield Crematorium Gt Lon 50 H11	Everton Hants 13 N6	Falls of Blarghour Ag & B 131 K5
ngale Highld 59 K2	Ellerton Shrops 70 C9	Enfield Lock Gt Lon 51 J11	Everton Lpool 81 L6	Falmer E Susx 25 J9
ngham D & G 108 H8	Ellesborough Bucks 35 M3	Enfield Wash Gt Lon 51 J11	Everton Notts 85 L2	Falmouth Cnwll 3 L7
ngley Notts 85 L9	Ellesmere Shrops 69 L8	Enford Wilts 21 M4	Evertown D & G 110 G5	Falnash Border 117 M9
ngthorpe Norfk 77 L5	Ellesmere Port Ches W 81 N9	Engine Common S Gloucs 32 C8	Evesbatch Herefs 46 C5	Falsgrave N York 99 L3
ngthorpe Green Norfk 77 L5	Ellingham Hants 13 K3	England's Gate Herefs 45 Q4	Evesham Worcs 47 K6	Falstone Nthumb 111 P3
ngton Border 129 M9	Ellingham Norfk 65 M3	Englefield W Berk 34 H10	Evington C Leic 72 G10	Fanagmore Highld 164 E7
ngton Nthumb 113 J4	Ellingham Nthumb 119 N5	Englefield Green Surrey 35 Q10	Ewden Village Sheff 90 H11	Fancott C Beds 50 B5
ngton Somset 19 L7	Ellingstring N York 97 J4	Engleseabrook Ches E 70 D4	Ewell Surrey 36 F8	Fanellan Highld 155 N9
ngton Wilts 20 H4	Ellington Cambs 61 Q6	English Bicknor Gloucs 46 A11	Ewell Minnis Kent 27 N3	Fangdale Beck N York 98 D2
ngton Burtle Somset 19 L6	Ellington Nthumb 113 L2	Englishcombe BaNES 20 D2	Ewelme Oxon 34 H6	Fangfoss E R Yk 98 F10
ngworth Somset 19 L4	Ellington Thorpe Cambs 61 Q6	English Frankton Shrops 69 N9	Ewen Gloucs 33 K5	Fanmore Ag & B 137 L2
stone Devon 16 D7	Elliots Green Somset 20 E5	Engollan Cnwll 4 D7	Ewenny V Glam 29 P9	Fannich Lodge Highld 154 H4
thmead Somset 19 K5	Ellisfield Hants 22 H5	Enham-Alamein Hants 22 C5	Ewerby Lincs 86 F11	Fans Border 118 B2
th Weston Rutlnd 73 N9	Ellishader Highld 153 J4	Enmore Somset 18 H7	Ewerby Thorpe Lincs 86 F11	Far Bletchley M Keyn 49 N8
lesborough Bucks 49 Q11	Ellistown Leics 72 C8	Enmore Green Dorset 20 G10	Ewhurst Surrey 24 C2	Farcet Cambs 62 B2
llingham Nthumb 119 M9	Ellon Abers 159 N11	Ennerdale Bridge Cumb 100 E7	Ewhurst Green E Susx 26 C7	Far Cotton Nhants 60 G9
mond Castle Cumb 111 J9	Ellonby Cumb 101 N4	Enniscaven Cnwll 4 F10	Ewhurst Green Surrey 24 C3	Farden Shrops 57 K9
mondsham Dorset 13 J2	Ellough Suffk 65 N4	Enochdhu P & K 141 Q5	Ewloe Flints 81 L11	Fareham Hants 14 G5
mondsley Dur 113 K11	Elloughton E R Yk 92 F5	Ensay Ag & B 137 K6	Ewloe Green Flints 81 K11	Far End Cumb 101 K11
mondthorpe Leics 73 M7	Ellwood Gloucs 31 Q3	Ensbury Bmouth 13 J5	Ewood Bl w D 89 K5	Farewell Staffs 58 G2
monton Cnwll 4 F7	Elm Cambs 75 J9	Ensdon Shrops 69 M11	Ewood Bridge Lancs 89 M6	Far Forest Worcs 57 N9
monton Gt Lon 36 H2	Elmbridge Worcs 58 D11	Ensis Devon 17 K6	Eworthy Devon 8 B5	Farforth Lincs 87 K5
mundbyers Dur 112 F10	Elmdon Essex 51 L3	Enson Staffs 70 G9	Ewshot Hants 23 M5	Far Green Gloucs 32 E4
nam Border 118 D3	Elmdon Solhll 59 J8	Enstone Oxon 48 C10	Ewyas Harold Herefs 45 M9	Faringdon Oxon 33 Q5
naston Derbys 71 N6	Elmdon Heath Solhll 59 J8	Enterkinfoot D & G 116 B10	Exbourne Devon 8 F4	Farington Lancs 88 G5
ney Common Essex 51 Q10	Elmer W Susx 15 Q6	Enterpen N York 104 E9	Exbury Hants 14 D6	Farlam Cumb 111 L9
radynate P & K 141 L7	Elmers End Gt Lon 37 J7	Enville Staffs 58 B7	Exceat E Susx 25 M11	Farleigh N Som 31 P11
rom Border 129 L8	Elmer's Green Lancs 88 G9	Eolaigearraidh W Isls 168 c17	Exebridge Somset 18 B10	Farleigh Surrey 37 J8
staston Shrops 69 P8	Elmesthorpe Leics 72 D11	Epney Gloucs 32 E2	Exelby N York 97 L3	Farleigh Hungerford Somset 20 F3
vin Loach Herefs 46 C3	Elm Green Essex 52 C10	Epperstone Notts 85 L11	Exeter Devon 9 M6	Farleigh Wallop Hants 22 H5
walton Notts 72 F3	Elmhurst Staffs 58 H2	Epping Essex 51 L10	Exeter Airport Devon 9 N6	Farlesthorpe Lincs 87 N6
wardstone Suffk 52 F3	Elmley Castle Worcs 47 J6	Epping Green Essex 51 K9	Exeter & Devon Crematorium Devon 9 M6	Farleton Cumb 95 L4
wardsville Myr Td 30 E5	Elmley Lovett Worcs 58 C11	Epping Green Herts 50 G9	Exeter Services Devon 9 N6	Farleton Lancs 95 M7
winsford Carmth 43 M8	Elmore Gloucs 46 E11	Epping Upland Essex 51 K10	Exford Somset 17 R4	Farley Derbys 84 C8
winstowe Notts 85 K7	Elmore Back Gloucs 46 E11	Eppleby N York 103 N8	Exfordsgreen Shrops 56 H3	Farley Staffs 71 K6
worth C Beds 50 F2	Elm Park Gt Lon 37 M3	Eppleworth E R Yk 92 H4	Exhall Warwks 47 M3	Farley Wilts 21 P9
wyn Ralph Herefs 46 B3	Elmscott Devon 16 C7	Epsom Surrey 36 F8	Exhall Warwks 59 N7	Farley Green Suffk 63 M10
zell Angus 143 L4	Elmsett Suffk 53 J2	Epwell Oxon 48 C6	Exlade Street Oxon 35 J8	Farley Green Surrey 36 C11
zell Woods Abers 143 L4	Elms Green Worcs 57 N11	Epworth N Linc 92 C10	Exley Head C Brad 90 C2	Farley Hill Wokham 23 K2
ail-fach Neath 29 L5	Elmstead Heath Essex 53 J7	Epworth Turbary N Linc 92 C10	Exminster Devon 9 M7	Farleys End Gloucs 32 E2
ail Isaf Rhondd 30 E8	Elmstead Market Essex 53 J7	Erbistock Wrexhm 69 L6	Exmoor National Park 17 R4	Farlington C Port 15 J5
ailnewydd Gwynd 66 F7	Elmstead Row Essex 53 J7	Erdington Birm 58 H6	Exmouth Devon 9 P8	Farlington N York 98 C7
ail-Rhyd Powys 68 G9	Elmsted Kent 27 K3	Eridge Green E Susx 25 N3	Exning Suffk 63 K7	Farlow Shrops 57 L8
ailwen Carmth 41 M5	Elmstone Kent 39 N9	Eridge Station E Susx 25 M4	Exted Kent 27 L3	Farmborough BaNES 20 C2
enechtyd Denbgs 68 F3	Elmstone Hardwicke Gloucs 46 H9	Erines Ag & B 123 Q4	Exton Devon 9 N7	Farmbridge End Essex 51 P8
fgill D & G 110 F2	Elmswell E R Yk 99 K9	Eriska Ag & B 138 G5	Exton Hants 22 H10	Farmcote Gloucs 47 L9
fingham Surrey 36 D10	Elmswell Suffk 64 D9	Eriskay W Isls 168 c17	Exton Rutlnd 73 N8	Farmcote Shrops 57 P6
flinch Staffs 71 M11	Elmton Derbys 84 H6	Eriswell Suffk 63 M5	Exton Somset 18 B8	Farmers Carmth 43 M6
ford Devon 9 L4	Elphin Highld 161 L4	Erith Gt Lon 37 M5	Exwick Devon 9 M6	Farmington Gloucs 47 M11
ford Crematorium C Plym 6 E7	Elphinstone E Loth 128 B6	Erlestoke Wilts 21 J4	Eyam Derbys 84 B5	Farmoor Oxon 34 E3
bury Hants 22 D4	Elrick Abers 151 L6	Ermington Devon 6 G7	Eydon Nhants 48 F5	Far Moor Wigan 82 B4
dean W Susx 23 Q10	Elrig D & G 107 K8	Erpingham Norfk 76 H5	Eye C Pete 74 D10	Farms Common Cnwll 2 H7
erton Bolton 89 L8	Elrington Nthumb 112 C8	Erriottwood Kent 38 F10	Eye Herefs 45 P2	Farm Town Leics 72 B7
erton Kent 26 F2	Elsdon Nthumb 112 D2	Errogie Highld 147 P3	Eye Suffk 64 G7	Farmtown Moray 158 D7
erton Forstal Kent 26 E2	Elsecar Barns 91 K11	Errol P & K 134 G3	Eye Green C Pete 74 D10	Farnah Green Derbys 84 D11
gborough N York 91 P6	Elsenham Essex 51 M5	Erskine Rens 125 M3	Eye Kettleby Leics 73 J7	Farnborough Gt Lon 37 K8
gbuckland C Plym 6 E7	Elsfield Oxon 34 F2	Erskine Bridge Rens 125 M3	Eyemouth Border 129 N7	Farnborough Hants 23 N4
gesford Devon 17 M9	Elsham N Linc 92 H8	Ervie D & G 106 D4	Eyeworth C Beds 62 C11	Farnborough W Berk 34 D8
gington C Beds 49 Q9	Elsing Norfk 76 F8	Erwarton Suffk 53 M5	Eyhorne Street Kent 38 D11	Farnborough Warwks 48 D5
ginton Derbys 71 P9	Elslack N York 96 D11	Erwood Powys 44 F6	Eyke Suffk 65 L11	Farnborough Park Hants 23 N4
glescliffe S on T 104 D8	Elson Hants 14 H6	Eryholme N York 104 B9	Eynesbury Cambs 61 Q9	Farncombe Surrey 23 Q6
gleston Dur 103 J6	Elson Shrops 69 L7	Eryrys Denbgs 68 H3	Eynsford Kent 37 M7	Farndish Bed 61 K8
ham Surrey 36 B6	Elsrickle S Lans 116 F2	Escalls Cnwll 2 B8	Eynsham Oxon 34 D3	Farndon Ches W 69 M4
ham Wick Surrey 35 Q10	Elstead Surrey 23 P6	Escomb Dur 103 N4	Eype Dorset 11 J6	Farndon Notts 85 N10
leton Rutlnd 73 M9	Elsted W Susx 23 M11	Escott Somset 18 E7	Eyre Highld 152 G7	Farne Islands Nthumb 119 P3
lingham Nthumb 119 M7	Elsthorpe Lincs 73 R6	Escrick N York 91 Q2	Eythorne Kent 27 N2	Farnell Angus 143 L6
loshayle Cnwll 4 H7	Elstob Dur 104 B6	Esgair Carmth 42 H7	Eyton Herefs 45 P2	Farnham Dorset 21 J11
loskerry Cnwll 5 M4	Elston Lancs 88 H4	Esgair Carmth 54 D11	Eyton Shrops 56 F2	Farnham Essex 51 L5
lwysbach Conwy 79 Q10	Elston Notts 85 N11	Esgairgeiliog Powys 54 H3	Eyton Shrops 56 F2	Farnham N York 97 M8
lwys-Brewis V Glam 30 D11	Elston Wilts 21 L6	Esgerdawe Carmth 43 M6	Eyton Shrops 69 M10	Farnham Suffk 65 M9
lwys Cross Wrexhm 69 N5	Elstone Devon 17 M8	Esgyryn Conwy 79 Q9	Eyton Wrexhm 69 L6	Farnham Surrey 23 M5
lwys Fach Cerdgn 54 F5	Elstow Bed 61 N11	Esh Dur 103 N2	Eyton on Severn Shrops 57 K3	Farnham Common Bucks 35 Q7
lwyswrw Pembks 41 M3	Elstree Herts 50 E11	Esher Surrey 36 E8	Eyton upon the Weald Moors Wrekin 57 M2	Farnham Green Essex 51 L5
manton Notts 85 M7	Elstronwick E R Yk 93 M4	Esholt C Brad 90 F2		Farnham Royal Bucks 35 Q7
remont Cumb 100 D8	Elswick Lancs 88 E3	Eshott Nthumb 119 P11	**F**	Farningham Kent 37 M7
remont Wirral 81 L6	Elswick N u Ty 113 K8	Eshton N York 96 D9		Farnley Leeds 90 H4
ton N York 105 M9	Elsworth Cambs 62 D8	Esh Winning Dur 103 N2	Faccombe Hants 22 C3	Farnley N York 97 K11
ton Bridge N York 105 M10	Elterwater Cumb 101 K10	Eskadale Highld 155 N9	Faceby N York 104 E10	Farnley Tyas Kirk 90 F8
ypt Bucks 49 M8	Eltham Gt Lon 37 K6	Eskbank Mdloth 127 Q4	Fachwen Powys 68 D11	Farnsfield Notts 85 K9
ypt Hants 22 E6	Eltham Crematorium Gt Lon 37 K6	Eskdale Green Cumb 100 F10	Facit Lancs 89 P7	Farnworth Bolton 89 L9
gg Highld 144 G10	Eltisley Cambs 62 C9	Eskdalemuir D & G 117 K11	Fackley Notts 84 G8	Farnworth Halton 81 Q7
an Ash Green Essex 52 F6	Elton Bury 89 M8	Eske E R Yk 93 J2	Faddiley Ches E 69 Q4	Far Oakridge Gloucs 32 H3
anreach Highld 145 P4	Elton Cambs 61 N2	Eskham Lincs 93 Q11	Fadmoor N York 98 D3	Farr Highld 148 E7
ean Donan Castle Highld 145 Q2	Elton Ches W 81 N9	Eskholme Donc 91 Q7	Faerdre Swans 29 J4	Farr Highld 156 B11
steddfa Gurig Cerdgn 54 H8	Elton Derbys 84 B8	Esperley Lane Ends Dur 103 M6	Fagwyr Swans 29 J4	Farr Highld 166 B4
an Valley Powys 44 B3	Elton Gloucs 32 D2	Esprick Lancs 88 E3	Faifley W Duns 125 M3	Farraline Highld 147 Q3
an Village Powys 44 Q2	Elton Herefs 56 H10	Essendine Rutlnd 73 Q8	Failand N Som 31 P10	Farringdon Devon 9 P6
erton S Glos 32 B7	Elton Notts 73 K3	Essendon Herts 50 G9	Failford S Ayrs 115 J2	Farrington Gurney BaNES 20 B3
oridge W Susx 15 P6	Elton S on T 104 D7	Essich Highld 156 A10	Failsworth Oldham 83 J4	Far Sawrey Cumb 101 L11
burton C Plym 6 E8	Elton Green Ches W 81 N9	Essington Staffs 58 E4	Fairbourne Gwynd 54 F2	Farsley Leeds 90 G3
combe Swindn 33 M8	Eltringham Nthumb 112 G8	Esslemont Abers 151 N2	Fairburn N York 91 L5	Farther Howegreen Essex 52 D11
	Elvanfoot S Lans 116 D4	Eston R & Cl 104 E7	Fairfield Derbys 83 N10	Farthing Green Kent 26 D2
	Elvaston Derbys 72 C4	Etal Nthumb 118 H3	Fairfield Kent 26 G6	Farthinghoe Nhants 48 F7
	Elveden Suffk 63 P4	Etchilhampton Wilts 21 L2	Fairfield Worcs 58 D9	Farthingloe Kent 27 N3
	Elvetham Heath Hants 23 M3	Etchingham E Susx 26 B6	Fairfield Park Herts 50 F4	
	Elvingston E Loth 128 D5	Etchinghill Kent 27 L3	Fairford Gloucs 33 N4	
		Etchingwood E Susx 25 M6	Fairford Park Gloucs 33 N4	
		Etling Green Norfk 76 E9		

Farthingstone Nhants 48 H4
Farthing Street Gt Lon 37 K8
Fartown Kirk 90 F7
Farway Devon 10 D5
Fasnacloich Ag & B 139 J8
Fasnakyle Highld 147 J2
Fassfern Highld 139 J2
Fatfield Sundld 113 L10
Faugh Cumb 111 K10
Fauld Staffs 71 M9
Fauldhouse W Loth 126 C5
Faulkbourne Essex 52 C8
Faulkland Somset 20 D4
Fauls Shrops 69 Q8
Faversham Kent 38 H9
Fawdington N York 97 P6
Fawdon N u Ty 113 K7
Fawdon Nthumb 119 K7
Fawfieldhead Staffs 71 K2
Fawkham Green Kent 37 N7
Fawler Oxon 48 C11
Fawley Bucks 35 L7
Fawley Hants 14 E6
Fawley W Berk 34 C8
Fawley Chapel Herefs 46 A9
Fawnog Flints 81 J11
Fawsley Nhants 60 C9
Faxfleet E R Yk 92 E6
Faygate W Susx 24 F4
Fazakerley Lpool 81 M5
Fazeley Staffs 59 K4
Fearby N York 97 J4
Fearn Highld 156 E2
Fearnan P & K 140 H9
Fearnbeg Highld 153 N6
Fearnhead Warrtn 82 D6
Fearnmore Highld 153 N5
Fearnoch Ag & B 124 A2
Featherstone Staffs 58 D3
Featherstone Wakefd 91 L7
Feckenham Worcs 47 K2
Feering Essex 52 E7
Feetham N York 103 J11
Feizor N York 96 A7
Felbridge Surrey 25 J3
Felbrigg Norfk 77 J4
Felcourt Surrey 25 J2
Felden Herts 50 B10
Felindre Carmth 42 G7
Felindre Carmth 43 L10
Felindre Carmth 43 P9
Felindre Cerdgn 43 L3
Felindre Powys 44 H10
Felindre Powys 56 B8
Felindre Swans 28 H4
Felindre Farchog Pembks 41 M3
Felin Fach Cerdgn 43 K3
Felinfach Powys 44 F8
Felinfoel Carmth 28 F4
Felingwm Isaf Carmth 43 K10
Felingwm Uchaf Carmth 43 K10
Felin-newydd Powys 44 G7
Felixkirk N York 97 Q4
Felixstowe Suffk 53 P5
Felixstowe Ferry Suffk 53 P4
Felkington Nthumb 118 H2
Felkirk Wakefd 91 K8
Felling Gatesd 113 L8
Fell Lane C Brad 90 C2
Fell Side Cumb 101 K3
Felmersham Bed 61 L9
Felmingham Norfk 77 K6
Felpham W Susx 15 P7
Felsham Suffk 64 C10
Felsted Essex 51 Q6
Feltham Gt Lon 36 D6
Felthamhill Surrey 36 C6
Felthorpe Norfk 76 H8
Felton Herefs 46 A5
Felton N Som 31 P11
Felton Nthumb 119 N10
Felton Butler Shrops 69 L11
Feltwell Norfk 63 M2
Fenay Bridge Kirk 90 F7
Fence Lancs 89 N3
Fence Rothm 84 F3
Fence Houses Sundld 113 M11
Fencott Oxon 48 G11
Fendike Corner Lincs 87 N8
Fen Ditton Cambs 62 G8
Fen Drayton Cambs 62 D7
Fen End Lincs 74 D6
Fen End Solhll 59 K10
Fenham Nthumb 119 L2
Feniscliffe Bl w D 89 K5
Feniscowles Bl w D 89 J5
Feniton Devon 10 C5
Fenland Crematorium Cambs 62 F2
Fenn Green Shrops 57 P8
Fenn Street Medway 38 C6
Fenny Bentley Derbys 71 M5
Fenny Bridges Devon 10 C5
Fenny Compton Warwks 48 D4
Fenny Drayton Leics 72 B11
Fenny Stratford M Keyn 49 N8
Fenrother Nthumb 113 J2
Fenstanton Cambs 62 D7
Fenstead End Suffk 63 P10
Fen Street Norfk 64 D2
Fen Street Suffk 64 H9
Fenton C Stke 70 F6
Fenton Cambs 62 D5
Fenton Cumb 111 K9
Fenton Lincs 85 P5
Fenton Lincs 85 Q10
Fenton Notts 85 N4
Fenton Nthumb 119 J4
Fenton Barns E Loth 128 E3
Fenwick Donc 91 P7
Fenwick E Ayrs 125 M9
Fenwick Nthumb 112 G6
Fenwick Nthumb 119 L2
Feock Cnwll 3 L6
Feolin Ferry Ag & B 122 F6
Fergushill N Ayrs 125 J9
Feriniquarrie Highld 152 B7
Fermain Bay Guern 10 c2
Fern Angus 142 H5
Ferndale Rhondd 30 C5
Ferndown Dorset 13 J4
Ferness Highld 156 H8
Fernham Oxon 33 Q6
Fernhill Heath Worcs 46 G3
Fernhurst W Susx 23 N9
Fernie Fife 135 J4
Ferniegair S Lans 126 C7
Fernilea Highld 152 F11
Fernilee Derbys 83 M9
Fernwood Notts 85 P10

Ferrensby N York 97 N8
Ferriby Sluice N Linc 92 G6
Ferrindonald Highld 145 L6
Ferring W Susx 24 C10
Ferrybridge Wakefd 91 M6
Ferrybridge Services Wakefd 91 M6
Ferryden Angus 143 N6
Ferryhill Dur 103 Q4
Ferryhill Station Dur 103 Q4
Ferry Point Highld 162 G9
Ferryside Carmth 28 C2
Ferrytown Highld 162 G9
Fersfield Norfk 64 F5
Fersit Highld 139 R2
Feshiebridge Highld 148 F7
Fetcham Surrey 36 D9
Fetlar Shet 169 t4
Fetterangus Abers 159 N7
Fettercairn Abers 143 M3
Fewcott Oxon 48 F9
Fewston N York 97 J10
Ffairfach Carmth 43 M10
Ffair Rhos Cerdgn 54 G11
Ffald-y-Brenin Carmth 43 M6
Ffawyddog Powys 45 J11
Ffestiniog Gwynd 67 N6
Ffestiniog Railway Gwynd 67 M6
Ffordd-las Denbgs 68 F2
Fforest Carmth 28 G4
Fforest Mons 45 K10
Fforest Fach Swans 28 H5
Fforest Gôch Neath 29 K4
Ffostrasol Cerdgn 42 G5
Ffrith Flints 69 J3
Ffynnonddewi Cerdgn 42 G4
Ffynnongroyw Flints 80 G8
Ffynnon-Oer Cerdgn 43 K4
Fiag Lodge Highld 165 L11
Fickleshole Surrey 37 J8
Fiddington Gloucs 46 H8
Fiddington Somset 18 H6
Fiddleford Dorset 12 D2
Fiddlers Green Cnwll 4 C10
Fiddlers Hamlet Essex 51 L10
Field Staffs 71 J8
Field Broughton Cumb 94 H4
Field Dalling Norfk 76 E4
Fieldhead Cumb 101 N3
Field Head Leics 72 D9
Fifehead Magdalen Dorset 20 E10
Fifehead Neville Dorset 12 C2
Fifehead St Quintin Dorset 12 C2
Fife Keith Moray 158 B7
Fifield Oxon 47 P11
Fifield W & M 35 P9
Fifield Wilts 21 M4
Figheldean Wilts 21 N5
Filands Wilts 32 H7
Filby Norfk 77 P9
Filey N York 99 N4
Filgrave M Keyn 49 N5
Filkins Oxon 33 P4
Filleigh Devon 8 H2
Filleigh Devon 17 M6
Fillingham Lincs 86 B3
Fillongley Warwks 59 L7
Filmore Hill Hants 23 J9
Filton S Glos 32 B9
Fimber E R Yk 98 H8
Finavon Angus 142 H6
Fincham Norfk 75 N9
Finchampstead Wokham 23 L2
Fincharn Ag & B 131 J7
Finchdean Hants 15 K4
Finchingfield Essex 51 Q4
Finchley Gt Lon 36 G2
Findern Derbys 71 Q8
Findhorn Moray 157 J5
Findhorn Bridge Highld 148 F2
Findochty Moray 158 C4
Findo Gask P & K 134 C4
Findon Abers 151 N8
Findon W Susx 24 D9
Findon Mains Highld 155 R5
Findrack House Abers 150 G7
Finedon Nhants 61 K6
Fingal Street Suffk 65 J8
Fingask P & K 134 F4
Fingest Bucks 35 L6
Finghall N York 97 J3
Fingland Cumb 110 E9
Fingland D & G 115 Q4
Finglesham Kent 39 P11
Fingringhoe Essex 52 H7
Finkle Green Essex 52 B3
Finkle Street Barns 91 J11
Finlarig Stirlg 140 E11
Finmere Oxon 48 H8
Finnart P & K 140 D6
Finningham Suffk 64 F8
Finningley Donc 91 R11
Finsbay W Isls 168 f9
Finstall Worcs 58 E10
Finsthwaite Cumb 94 H3
Finstock Oxon 48 C11
Finstown Ork 169 c5
Fintry Abers 159 J7
Fintry Stirlg 133 J10
Finzean Abers 150 G9
Fionnphort Ag & B 137 J11
Fionnsbhagh W Isls 168 f9
Firbank Cumb 95 N2
Firbeck Rothm 85 J3
Firby N York 97 L3
Firby N York 98 E7
Firgrove Rochdl 89 Q8
Firle E Susx 25 L9
Firsby Lincs 87 N8
Firsdown Wilts 21 P8
Fir Tree Dur 103 M4
Fishbourne IoW 14 G8
Fishbourne W Susx 15 M6
Fishbourne Roman Palace W Susx 15 M6
Fishburn Dur 104 C4
Fishcross Clacks 133 P8
Fisher W Susx 15 N6
Fisherford Abers 158 G10
Fisherrow E Loth 127 Q3
Fisher's Pond Hants 22 E10
Fisher's Row Lancs 95 J11
Fisherstreet W Susx 23 P8
Fisherton Highld 156 C7
Fisherton S Ayrs 114 E4
Fisherton de la Mere Wilts 21 K7
Fisherwick Staffs 59 J3

Fishery Estate W & M 35 N8
Fishguard Pembks 41 J3
Fishlake Donc 91 R8
Fishleigh Devon 8 D3
Fishmere End Lincs 74 E3
Fishnish Pier Ag & B 138 B9
Fishpond Bottom Dorset 10 H5
Fishponds Bristl 32 B9
Fishtoft Lincs 74 G2
Fishtoft Drove Lincs 87 K11
Fishwick Lancs 88 H5
Fiskavaig Highld 152 E11
Fiskerton Lincs 86 D6
Fiskerton Notts 85 M10
Fitling E R Yk 93 N4
Fittleton Wilts 21 M5
Fittleworth W Susx 24 B7
Fitton End Cambs 74 H8
Fitz Shrops 69 M11
Fitzhead Somset 18 F9
Fitzroy Somset 18 G9
Fitzwilliam Wakefd 91 L7
Five Ash Down E Susx 25 L4
Five Ashes E Susx 25 N5
Five Bells Somset 18 E6
Five Bridges Herefs 46 B5
Fivecrosses Ches W 82 B9
Fivehead Somset 19 L10
Fivelanes Cnwll 5 L5
Five Lanes Mons 31 M6
Five Oak Green Kent 37 P11
Five Oaks Jersey 11 c2
Five Oaks W Susx 24 C5
Five Roads Carmth 28 E3
Five Wents Kent 38 D11
Flack's Green Essex 52 C9
Flackwell Heath Bucks 35 N7
Fladbury Worcs 47 J5
Fladdabister Shet 169 r10
Flagg Derbys 83 P11
Flamborough E R Yk 99 Q6
Flamborough Head E R Yk 99 R6
Flamingo Land Theme Park N York 98 F5
Flamstead Herts 50 C8
Flamstead End Herts 50 H10
Flansham W Susx 15 Q6
Flanshaw Wakefd 91 J6
Flappit Spring C Brad 90 D3
Flasby N York 96 D9
Flash Staffs 83 M11
Flashader Highld 152 E7
Flaunden Herts 50 B10
Flawborough Notts 73 K2
Flawith N York 97 Q7
Flax Bourton N Som 31 P11
Flaxby N York 97 N9
Flaxley Gloucs 46 C11
Flaxmere Ches W 82 C10
Flaxpool Somset 18 F7
Flaxton N York 98 D8
Fleckney Leics 60 D2
Flecknoe Warwks 60 B8
Fledborough Notts 85 P6
Fleet Dorset 11 N8
Fleet Hants 15 K6
Fleet Hants 23 M4
Fleet Lincs 74 G6
Fleetend Hants 14 F5
Fleet Hargate Lincs 74 G6
Fleet Services Hants 23 L3
Fleetwood Lancs 94 G11
Fleggburgh Norfk 77 N9
Flemingston V Glam 30 D11
Flemington S Lans 126 B6
Flempton Suffk 63 P7
Fletchersbridge Cnwll 5 J8
Fletcher's Green Kent 37 M11
Fletchertown Cumb 100 H2
Fletching E Susx 25 K6
Fleur-de-lis Caerph 30 G5
Flexbury Cnwll 16 C10
Flexford Surrey 23 P4
Flimby Cumb 100 D4
Flimwell E Susx 26 B5
Flint Flints 81 J10
Flintham Notts 85 M11
Flint Mountain Flints 81 J10
Flinton E R Yk 93 M3
Flint's Green Solhll 59 L8
Flishinghurst Kent 26 C4
Flitcham Norfk 75 P5
Flitton C Beds 50 C3
Flitwick C Beds 50 B4
Flixborough N Linc 92 E8
Flixborough Stather N Linc 92 E8
Flixton N York 99 L5
Flixton Suffk 65 L4
Flixton Traffd 82 F6
Flockton Kirk 90 G7
Flockton Green Kirk 90 H7
Flodden Nthumb 118 H3
Flodigarry Highld 152 H3
Flookburgh Cumb 94 H5
Flordon Norfk 64 H2
Flore Nhants 60 D8
Flotterton Nthumb 119 J10
Flowers Green E Susx 25 P8
Flowton Suffk 53 J2
Flushdyke Wakefd 90 H6
Flushing Cnwll 3 L7
Fluxton Devon 10 B6
Flyford Flavell Worcs 47 J3
Fobbing Thurr 38 B5
Fochabers Moray 157 Q6
Fochriw Caerph 30 F3
Fockerby N Linc 92 E7
Foddington Somset 19 Q9
Foel Powys 55 M2
Foelgastell Carmth 28 F2
Foel y Dyffryn Brdgnd 29 M7
Foggathorpe E R Yk 92 C3
Fogo Border 129 K10
Fogwatt Moray 157 N6
Foindle Highld 164 D7
Folda Angus 142 B5
Fole Staffs 71 J7
Foleshill Covtry 59 N8
Folke Dorset 11 P2
Folkestone Kent 27 M4
Folkingham Lincs 73 R4
Folkington E Susx 25 N10
Folksworth Cambs 61 P3
Folkton N York 99 M5
Folla Rule Abers 158 H10
Follifoot N York 97 M10
Folly Gate Devon 8 E5
Folly Hill Surrey 23 M5
Fonmon V Glam 30 D11

Fonthill Bishop Wilts 20 H8
Fonthill Gifford Wilts 20 H8
Fontmell Magna Dorset 20 G11
Fontmell Parva Dorset 12 D2
Fontwell W Susx 15 N5
Font-y-gary V Glam 30 E11
Foolow Derbys 83 Q9
Foots Cray Gt Lon 37 L6
Forbestown Abers 150 B5
Forcett N York 103 N8
Ford Ag & B 130 H7
Ford Bucks 35 L3
Ford Derbys 84 F4
Ford Devon 6 C8
Ford Devon 7 K10
Ford Devon 16 H3
Ford Gloucs 47 L9
Ford Nthumb 118 H3
Ford Shrops 56 G2
Ford Somset 18 E9
Ford Somset 19 Q4
Ford Staffs 71 K4
Ford W Susx 15 Q6
Ford Wilts 21 N8
Ford Wilts 32 F9
Forda Devon 8 D6
Fordcombe Kent 25 M2
Fordell Fife 134 F10
Forden Powys 56 C4
Forder Green Devon 7 K5
Ford Green Lancs 95 K11
Fordham Cambs 63 K6
Fordham Essex 52 F6
Fordham Norfk 75 M11
Fordham Heath Essex 52 F6
Fordingbridge Hants 13 K2
Fordon E R Yk 99 L5
Fordoun Abers 143 N2
Ford's Green Suffk 64 E9
Fordstreet Essex 52 F6
Ford Street Somset 18 G11
Fordton Devon 9 K5
Fordwells Oxon 34 B2
Fordwich Kent 39 L10
Fordyce Abers 158 E5
Forebridge Staffs 70 G10
Foremark Derbys 72 A5
Forest Guern 10 b2
Forest N York 103 Q10
Forest Becks Lancs 96 A10
Forestburn Gate Nthumb 119 L9
Forest Chapel Ches E 83 L10
Forest Gate Gt Lon 37 K3
Forest Green Surrey 24 D2
Forest Hall N Tyne 113 L7
Forest Head Cumb 111 L9
Forest Hill Ox 37 J6
Forest Hill Oxon 34 G3
Forest-in-Teesdale Dur 102 H4
Forest Lane Head N York 97 M9
Forest Mill Clacks 134 B9
Forest of Bowland Lancs 95 N10
Forest of Dean Gloucs 32 B2
Forest of Dean Crematorium Gloucs 32 B2
Forest Park Crematorium Gt Lon 37 L2
Forest Row E Susx 25 K4
Forest Side IoW 14 E9
Forestside W Susx 15 L4
Forest Town Notts 85 J8
Forfar Angus 142 H7
Forgandenny P & K 134 D4
Forge Powys 54 H5
Forge Hammer Torfn 31 J5
Forge Side Torfn 30 H3
Forgie Moray 158 A7
Forgieside Moray 158 B7
Forgue Abers 158 F8
Forhill Worcs 58 G9
Formby Sefton 88 C9
Forncett End Norfk 64 G3
Forncett St Mary Norfk 64 H3
Forncett St Peter Norfk 64 H3
Fornham All Saints Suffk 64 A8
Fornham St Martin Suffk 64 B8
Fornighty Highld 156 G7
Forres Moray 157 J6
Forsbrook Staffs 70 H6
Forse Highld 167 M10
Forshaw Heath Warwks 58 G10
Forsinard Highld 166 E8
Forston Dorset 11 P5
Fort Augustus Highld 147 K6
Forteviot P & K 134 D4
Forth S Lans 126 G9
Forthampton Gloucs 46 G8
Forth Rail Bridge C Edin 127 L2
Forth Road Bridge Fife 127 L2
Fortingall P & K 140 H8
Fort le Marchant Guern 10 c1
Forton Hants 22 D6
Forton Lancs 95 K10
Forton Shrops 69 M11
Forton Somset 10 G3
Forton Staffs 70 D10
Fortrie Abers 158 G8
Fortrose Highld 156 C6
Fortuneswell Dorset 11 P10
Fort William Highld 139 L3
Forty Green Bucks 35 P6
Forty Hill Gt Lon 50 H11
Forward Green Suffk 64 G10
Fosbury Wilts 22 B3
Foscot Oxon 47 P10
Foscote Nhants 49 J5
Fosdyke Lincs 74 F4
Fosdyke Bridge Lincs 74 F4
Foss P & K 141 J6
Fossebridge Gloucs 33 L2
Foss-y-ffin Cerdgn 42 H2
Fosterhouses Donc 91 R8
Foster Street Essex 51 K9
Foston Derbys 71 M8
Foston Leics 60 D2
Foston Lincs 73 M2
Foston N York 98 D7
Foston on the Wolds E R Yk 99 N9
Fotherby Lincs 87 K3
Fothergill Cumb 100 D4
Fotheringhay Nhants 61 N2
Foula Shet 169 k10
Foula Airport Shet 169 k10
Foulbridge Cumb 110 H11
Foulby Wakefd 91 K7
Foulden Border 129 N8

Foulden Norfk 75 Q11
Foul End Warwks 59 K6
Foul Mile E Susx 25 P7
Foulness Island Essex 38 G3
Foulon Vale Crematorium Guern 10 b2
Foulridge Lancs 89 P2
Foulsham Norfk 76 E7
Fountainhall Border 128 C10
Four Ashes Solhll 59 J9
Four Ashes Staffs 58 C4
Four Ashes Staffs 58 D7
Four Ashes Suffk 64 E7
Four Cabots Guern 10 b2
Four Crosses Powys 56 C11
Four Crosses Staffs 58 D2
Four Elms Kent 37 L11
Four Foot Somset 19 Q8
Four Forks Somset 18 H7
Four Gates Bolton 89 J9
Four Gotes Cambs 75 J7
Four Lane End Barns 90 H10
Four Lane Ends Ches W 69 Q2
Four Lanes Cnwll 2 H7
Fourlanes End Ches E 70 E3
Four Marks Hants 23 J8
Four Mile Bridge IoA 78 D9
Four Oaks Birm 58 H5
Four Oaks E Susx 26 E5
Four Oaks Gloucs 46 C9
Four Oaks Solhll 59 K8
Fourpenny Highld 163 J8
Four Points W Berk 34 G9
Four Roads Carmth 28 D3
Four Shire Stone Warwks 47 P8
Fourstones Nthumb 112 C7
Four Throws Kent 26 C5
Four Wents Kent 37 P10
Fovant Wilts 21 J8
Foveran Abers 151 P3
Fowey Cnwll 5 J11
Fowley Common Warrtn 82 E6
Fowlhall Kent 37 Q11
Fowlis Angus 142 E11
Fowlis Wester P & K 133 Q3
Fowlmere Cambs 62 F11
Fownhope Herefs 46 A8
Foxbar Rens 125 M5
Foxcombe Devon 8 C7
Fox Corner Surrey 23 Q4
Foxcote Gloucs 47 K11
Foxcote Somset 20 D3
Foxdale IoM 80 C7
Foxearth Essex 52 D3
Foxendown Kent 37 P7
Foxfield Cumb 94 E3
Foxham Wilts 33 J9
Fox Hatch Essex 51 N11
Foxhills Hants 13 P3
Foxhole Cnwll 3 P3
Foxholes N York 99 J6
Foxhunt Green E Susx 25 M7
Foxley Nhants 48 H4
Foxley Norfk 76 E7
Foxley Wilts 32 G7
Foxlydiate Worcs 58 F11
Fox Street Essex 52 H6
Foxt Staffs 71 J5
Foxton Cambs 62 F11
Foxton Dur 104 C6
Foxton Leics 60 F3
Foxton N York 104 D11
Foxup N York 96 C5
Foxwist Green Ches W 82 D11
Foxwood Shrops 57 L9
Foy Herefs 46 A9
Foyers Highld 147 M3
Foynesfield Highld 156 F7
Fraddam Cnwll 2 F7
Fraddon Cnwll 4 E10
Fradley Staffs 59 J3
Fradswell Staffs 70 H8
Fraisthorpe E R Yk 99 N8
Framfield E Susx 25 L6
Framingham Earl Norfk 77 K11
Framingham Pigot Norfk 77 K11
Framlingham Suffk 65 K9
Frampton Dorset 11 N6
Frampton Lincs 74 F3
Frampton Cotterell S Glos 32 C8
Frampton Mansell Gloucs 32 H4
Frampton-on-Severn Gloucs 32 D3
Frampton West End Lincs 74 F2
Framsden Suffk 64 H10
Framwellgate Moor Dur 103 Q2
Franche Worcs 57 Q9
Frandley Ches W 82 D9
Frankaborough Devon 5 N3
Frankby Wirral 81 J7
Frankfort Norfk 77 L7
Franklands Gate Herefs 45 Q5
Frankley Worcs 58 E8
Frankley Services Worcs 58 E8
Frankton Warwks 59 N10
Frant E Susx 25 N3
Fraserburgh Abers 159 N4
Frating Essex 53 J7
Frating Green Essex 53 J7
Fratton C Port 15 J6
Freathy Cnwll 5 P11
Freckenham Suffk 63 L6
Freckleton Lancs 88 F5
Freebirch Derbys 84 D6
Freeby Leics 73 L6
Freefolk Hants 22 E5
Freehay Staffs 71 J6
Freeland Oxon 34 D2
Freethorpe Norfk 77 N10
Freethorpe Common Norfk 77 N11
Freiston Lincs 74 F2
Fremington Devon 17 J5
Fremington N York 103 K11
Frenchay S Glos 32 B9
Frenchbeer Devon 8 G7
French Street Kent 37 L10
Frenich P & K 141 J6
Frensham Surrey 23 M6
Freshfield Sefton 88 C9
Freshford Wilts 20 E2
Freshwater IoW 14 D9
Freshwater Bay IoW 14 D9
Freshwater East Pembks 41 K11
Fressingfield Suffk 65 K6
Freston Suffk 53 L4

eswick Highld....167 Q3
etherne Gloucs....32 D2
ettenham Norfk....77 J8
euchie Fife....134 H6
eystrop Pembks....41 J8
ar Park Sandw....58 F6
ar's Gate E Susx....25 L4
ars' Hill N York....98 E3
ar Waddon Dorset....11 N7
day Bridge Cambs....75 J10
day Street Suffk....65 J10
day Street Suffk....65 L11
day Street Suffk....65 M9
day Street Surrey....36 D11
daythorpe E R Yk....98 H9
den Derbys....71 M2
endly Calder....90 D6
ern Barnet Gt Lon....36 G2
esthorpe Lincs....86 E4
eston Lincs....86 B11
eth Bucks....35 L6
ezeland Notts....84 G10
lford Oxon....34 D5
lsham W Berk....34 F10
mley Surrey....23 N3
mley Green Surrey....23 N3
ndsbury Medway....38 B8
ng Norfk....75 P4
ngford Oxon....48 H9
nsted Kent....38 E10
nton-on-Sea Essex....53 M7
ockheim Angus....143 K8
og Gwynd....54 E2
sby on the Wreake Leics....72 H7
skney Lincs....87 N9
skney Eaudike Lincs....87 N9
ston E Susx....25 N11
ston Suffk....65 N9
tchley Derbys....84 E10
tham Hants....13 M2
th Bank Lincs....87 K11
th Common Worcs....57 M11
thelstock Devon....16 H8
thelstock Stone Devon....16 H8
thend Hants....23 M7
thsden Herts....50 B9
thville Lincs....87 K10
ttenden Kent....26 D3
ttiscombe Devon....7 L10
tton Norfk....65 J3
tton Norfk....77 P11
twell Oxon....48 F9
zinghall C Brad....90 E3
zington Cumb....100 D7
cester Gloucs....32 E4
odesley Shrops....57 J4
odsham Ches W....81 Q9
ogden Border....118 E5
og End Cambs....62 E11
og End Cambs....62 H9
ggatt Derbys....84 B5
oghall Staffs....71 J5
ogham Hants....13 L2
ogham Kent....39 N11
ogmore Devon....7 K10
ognall Lincs....74 C8
ogpool Cnwll....3 K5
og Pool Worcs....57 Q11
ogwell Cnwll....5 N8
olesworth Leics....60 B2
ome Somset....20 E5
ome St Quintin Dorset....11 M4
omes Hill Herefs....46 C5
on Denbgs....80 F11
on Gwynd....66 F7
on Gwynd....67 J4
on Powys....56 B5
on Powys....56 C4
oncysyllte Denbgs....69 J6
on-goch Gwynd....68 B7
on Isaf Wrexhm....69 J6
ostenden Suffk....65 P5
osterley Dur....103 K3
oxfield C Beds....49 Q8
oxfield Wilts....33 Q11
oxfield Green Hants....23 K9
vern Hill Hants....22 D10
verning Essex....51 P10
yton N York....98 D6
inary Highld....137 Q6
beck Lincs....86 B10
bourn Cambs....62 H9
brook Oxon....33 Q2
flood Hants....22 E8
iford C York....98 C11
iford Somset....18 H9
iford Staffs....70 H7
iham Gt Lon....36 G5
iking W Susx....24 F8
ilaford Devon....17 M4
ll Ayrs....125 J10
ller's End Essex....51 M5
ller's Moor Ches W....69 N4
ller Street Essex....52 B8
ller Street Kent....37 N9
llerton Hants....22 C7
lletby Lincs....87 J6
lready Warwks....47 Q5
l Sutton E R Yk....98 E9
llwood E Ayrs....125 L7
mer Bucks....35 Q7
modeston Norfk....76 D5
netby Lincs....86 E5
iney Lincs....74 E6
istone Kirk....90 F9
istow Lincs....93 P11
lwell Oxon....48 C10
lwell Sundld....113 N9
lwood Lancs....88 G4
lwood Notts....84 G9
lwood Sheff....84 D3
lwood Somset....18 H10
ndenhall Norfk....76 H2
ntington W Susx....15 M5
ntley Lincs....14 G5
ntullich P & K....133 M2
rley Devon....17 N2
rnace Ag & B....131 L7
rnace Carmth....28 F4
rnace Cerdgn....54 F5
rnace End Warwks....59 K6
rness Vale Derbys....83 M8
rneux Pelham Herts....51 K5
rther Quarter Kent....26 E4
rtho Nhants....49 L6
rzehill Dorset....12 H4
rzehills Lincs....87 J6

Furzeley Corner Hants....15 J4
Furze Platt W & M....35 N8
Furzley Hants....21 Q11
Fyfett Somset....10 E2
Fyfield Essex....51 N9
Fyfield Hants....21 Q5
Fyfield Oxon....34 D5
Fyfield Wilts....21 N2
Fyfield Wilts....33 M11
Fyfield Bavant Wilts....21 K9
Fylingthorpe N York....105 P10
Fyning W Susx....23 M10
Fyvie Abers....159 J10

G

Gabroc Hill E Ayrs....125 M7
Gaddesby Leics....72 H8
Gaddesden Row Herts....50 C8
Gadfa IoA....78 H7
Gadgirth S Ayrs....114 H3
Gadlas Shrops....69 L7
Gaer Powys....44 H10
Gaerllwyd Mons....31 M5
Gaerwen IoA....78 H10
Gagingwell Oxon....48 D9
Gailes N Ayrs....125 J10
Gailey Staffs....58 D2
Gainford Dur....103 N7
Gainsborough Lincs....85 P3
Gainsford End Essex....52 B4
Gairloch Highld....153 Q2
Gairlochy Highld....146 F11
Gairneybridge P & K....134 E8
Gaisgill Cumb....102 B9
Gaitsgill Cumb....110 G11
Galashiels Border....117 P3
Galgate Lancs....95 K9
Galhampton Somset....20 B9
Gallanachbeg Ag & B....130 G2
Gallanachmore Ag & B....130 G2
Gallantry Bank Ches E....69 P4
Gallatown Fife....134 H9
Galley Common Warwks....59 M6
Galleywood Essex....52 B11
Gallovie Highld....147 P10
Galloway Forest Park....114 H10
Gallowfauld Angus....142 G9
Gallowhill P & K....133 B10
Gallows Green Essex....52 F6
Gallows Green Worcs....46 H2
Gallowstree Common Oxon....35 J8
Galltair Highld....145 P3
Gallt-y-foel Gwynd....67 K2
Gally Hill Hants....23 M4
Gallypot Street E Susx....25 L3
Galmpton Devon....6 H10
Galmpton Torbay....7 M7
Galphay N York....97 L6
Galston E Ayrs....125 N10
Gamballs Green Staffs....83 M11
Gamblesby Cumb....102 B3
Gambles Green Essex....52 C9
Gamelsby Cumb....110 E10
Gamesley Derbys....83 M6
Gamlingay Cambs....62 B10
Gamlingay Cinques Cambs....62 B10
Gamlingay Great Heath Cambs....62 B10
Gammersgill N York....96 G4
Gamrie Abers....159 J5
Gamston Notts....72 F3
Gamston Notts....85 M5
Ganarew Herefs....45 Q11
Ganavan Bay Ag & B....138 F11
Gang Cnwll....5 N8
Ganllwyd Gwynd....67 N10
Gannachy Angus....143 K3
Ganstead E R Yk....93 K4
Ganthorpe N York....98 D6
Ganton N York....99 K5
Ganwick Corner Herts....50 G11
Gappah Devon....9 L9
Garbity Moray....157 Q7
Garboldisham Norfk....64 E5
Garbole Highld....148 D3
Garchory Abers....149 Q5
Garden City Flints....81 L11
Gardeners Green Wokham....35 M11
Garden of England Crematorium Kent....38 E8
Gardenstown Abers....159 K5
Garden Village Sheff....90 H11
Garderhouse Shet....169 q9
Gardham E R Yk....92 G2
Gare Hill Somset....20 E6
Garelochhead Ag & B....131 Q9
Garford Oxon....34 D5
Garforth Leeds....91 L4
Gargrave N York....96 D10
Gargunnock Stirlg....133 L9
Garizim Conwy....79 M9
Garlic Street Norfk....65 J5
Garlieston D & G....107 N8
Garlinge Kent....39 P8
Garlinge Green Kent....39 K11
Garlogie Abers....151 K6
Garmond Abers....159 K7
Garmouth Moray....157 Q5
Garmston Shrops....57 L3
Garnant Carmth....29 J2
Garn-Dolbenmaen Gwynd....66 H6
Garnett Bridge Cumb....101 P11
Garnfadryn Gwynd....66 D8
Garnkirk N Lans....126 B4
Garnswllt Swans....28 H3
Garn-yr-erw Torfn....30 H3
Garrabost W Isls....168 k4
Garrallan E Ayrs....115 K4
Garras Cnwll....3 J9
Garreg Gwynd....67 L6
Garrigill Cumb....102 D2
Garriston N York....97 J2
Garroch D & G....108 C4
Garrochtrie D & G....106 F10
Garrochty Ag & B....123 D7
Garros Highld....152 H5
Garsdale Cumb....95 Q3
Garsdale Head Cumb....96 A2
Garsdon Wilts....33 J7
Garshall Green Staffs....70 H6
Garsington Oxon....34 G4
Garstang Lancs....95 K11
Garston Herts....50 D10
Garston Lpool....81 N8

Gartachossan Ag & B....122 D7
Gartcosh N Lans....126 B4
Garth Brdgnd....29 N6
Garth Mons....31 K6
Garth Powys....44 D5
Garth Powys....56 D10
Garth Wrexhm....69 J6
Garthamlock C Glas....126 B4
Garthbrengy Powys....44 E8
Gartheli Cerdgn....43 L3
Garthmyl Powys....56 B5
Garthorpe Leics....73 L6
Garthorpe N Linc....92 D7
Garth Row Cumb....101 P11
Garths Cumb....95 L3
Gartly Abers....158 D11
Gartmore Stirlg....132 G8
Gartness N Lans....126 D5
Gartness Stirlg....132 G10
Gartocharn W Duns....132 K10
Garton E R Yk....93 N3
Garton-on-the-Wolds E R Yk....99 K9
Gartymore Highld....163 N4
Garva Bridge Highld....147 N9
Garvald E Loth....128 F5
Garvan Highld....138 H2
Garvard Ag & B....136 b3
Garve Highld....155 L5
Garvellachs Ag & B....130 D5
Garvestone Norfk....76 E10
Garvock Inver....124 H3
Garway Herefs....45 P10
Garway Common Herefs....45 P10
Garway Hill Herefs....45 N9
Garyvard W Isls....168 i6
Gasper Wilts....20 E8
Gastard Wilts....32 G11
Gasthorpe Norfk....64 D5
Gaston Green Essex....51 L7
Gatcombe IoW....14 E9
Gatebeck Cumb....95 L3
Gate Burton Lincs....85 P4
Gateford Notts....85 J4
Gateforth N York....91 P5
Gatehead E Ayrs....125 K10
Gate Helmsley N York....98 D9
Gatehouse Nthumb....111 Q3
Gatehouse of Fleet D & G....108 C9
Gateley Norfk....76 D7
Gatenby N York....97 M3
Gatesgarth Cumb....100 H7
Gateshaw Border....118 E6
Gateshead Gatesd....113 L8
Gates Heath Ches W....69 N2
Gateside Angus....142 G9
Gateside E Rens....125 M6
Gateside Fife....134 F6
Gateside N Ayrs....125 K7
Gateslack D & G....116 B10
Gathurst Wigan....88 G9
Gatley Stockp....82 H7
Gatton Surrey....36 G10
Gattonside Border....117 Q3
Gatwick Airport W Susx....24 G2
Gaufron Powys....55 M11
Gaulby Leics....72 H10
Gauldry Fife....135 K3
Gauldswell P & K....142 C7
Gaulkthorn Lancs....89 M5
Gaultree Norfk....75 J9
Gaunton's Bank Ches E....69 Q5
Gaunt's Common Dorset....12 H3
Gaunt's End Essex....51 N5
Gautby Lincs....86 G6
Gavinton Border....129 K9
Gawber Barns....91 J9
Gawcott Bucks....49 J8
Gawsworth Ches E....83 J11
Gawthorpe Wakefd....90 H6
Gawthrop Cumb....95 P3
Gawthwaite Cumb....94 F4
Gay Bowers Essex....52 C11
Gaydon Warwks....48 C4
Gayhurst M Keyn....49 M5
Gayle N York....96 C3
Gayles N York....103 M9
Gay Street W Susx....24 C6
Gayton Nhants....49 K4
Gayton Norfk....75 P7
Gayton Staffs....70 H9
Gayton Wirral....81 K8
Gayton le Marsh Lincs....87 M4
Gayton Thorpe Norfk....75 P7
Gaywood Norfk....75 M6
Gazeley Suffk....63 M8
Gear Cnwll....3 J9
Gearraidh Bhaird W Isls....168 i6
Geary Highld....152 D5
Gedding Suffk....64 C10
Geddington Nhants....61 J4
Gedling Notts....72 G2
Gedney Lincs....74 H6
Gedney Broadgate Lincs....74 H6
Gedney Drove End Lincs....75 J5
Gedney Dyke Lincs....74 H5
Gedney Hill Lincs....74 F8
Gee Cross Tamesd....83 L6
Geeston Rutlnd....73 P10
Geldeston Norfk....65 N3
Gelli Rhondd....30 C6
Gelli Torfn....31 J6
Gellifor Denbgs....68 F2
Gelligaer Caerph....30 F5
Gelligroes Caerph....30 G6
Gelligron Neath....29 K4
Gellilydan Gwynd....67 M7
Gellinudd Neath....29 K4
Gelly Pembks....41 L7
Gellyburn P & K....141 Q10
Gellywen Carmth....41 Q6
Gelston D & G....108 G9
Gelston Lincs....86 B11
Gembling E R Yk....99 N9
Gentleshaw Staffs....58 G2
Georgefield D & G....110 E2
George Green Bucks....35 Q8
George Nympton Devon....17 N7
Georgetown Blae G....30 G3
Georgia Cnwll....2 D6
Georth Ork....169 c4
Gerlan Gwynd....79 L11
Germansweek Devon....8 H4
Germoe Cnwll....2 F8
Gerrans Cnwll....3 M6
Gerrards Cross Bucks....36 B3
Gerrick R & Cl....105 K8

Gestingthorpe Essex....52 D4
Geuffordd Powys....56 C2
Gib Hill Ches W....82 D9
Gibraltar Lincs....87 Q9
Gibsmere Notts....85 M11
Giddeahall Wilts....32 G10
Giddy Green Dorset....12 D7
Gidea Park Gt Lon....37 M2
Gidleigh Devon....8 G7
Giffnock E Rens....125 P6
Gifford E Loth....128 E6
Giffordtown Fife....134 H5
Giggleswick N York....96 B8
Gigha Ag & B....123 K10
Gilberdyke E R Yk....92 D5
Gilbert's End Worcs....46 F6
Gilbert Street Hants....22 H8
Gilchriston E Loth....128 D6
Gilcrux Cumb....100 F3
Gildersome Leeds....90 G5
Gildingwells Rothm....85 J3
Gilesgate Moor Dur....103 Q2
Gileston V Glam....30 D11
Gilfach Caerph....30 G5
Gilfach Goch Brdgnd....30 C6
Gilfachrheda Cerdgn....42 H3
Gilgarran Cumb....100 D6
Gill Cumb....101 M5
Gillamoor N York....98 D3
Gillan Cnwll....3 K8
Gillen Highld....152 D6
Gillesbie D & G....110 C2
Gilling East N York....98 C5
Gillingham Dorset....20 F9
Gillingham Medway....38 C8
Gillingham Norfk....65 N3
Gilling West N York....103 N9
Gillock Highld....167 M5
Gillow Heath Staffs....70 F3
Gills Highld....167 P2
Gill's Green Kent....26 C5
Gilmanscleuch Border....117 L6
Gilmerton C Edin....127 N4
Gilmerton P & K....133 P3
Gilmonby Dur....103 J8
Gilmorton Leics....60 C3
Gilroes Crematorium C Leic....72 F9
Gilsland Nthumb....111 M7
Gilson Warwks....59 J7
Gilstead C Brad....90 E3
Gilston Border....128 C8
Gilston Herts....51 K8
Gilston Park Herts....51 K8
Giltbrook Notts....84 G11
Gilwern Mons....30 H2
Gimingham Norfk....77 K4
Ginclough Ches E....83 L9
Gingers Green E Susx....25 P8
Gipping Suffk....64 F9
Gipsey Bridge Lincs....87 J11
Girdle Toll N Ayrs....125 J9
Girlington C Brad....90 E4
Girlsta Shet....169 r8
Girsby N York....104 C9
Girtford C Beds....61 Q11
Girthon D & G....108 D10
Girton Cambs....62 F8
Girton Notts....85 P7
Girvan S Ayrs....114 C8
Gisburn Lancs....96 B11
Gisleham Suffk....65 Q4
Gislingham Suffk....64 F7
Gissing Norfk....64 G4
Gittisham Devon....10 C5
Gladestry Powys....45 J3
Gladsmuir E Loth....128 D5
Glais Swans....29 K4
Glaisdale N York....105 L9
Glamis Angus....142 F8
Glanaber Gwynd....67 L4
Glanafon Pembks....41 J7
Glanaman Carmth....29 J2
Glandford Norfk....76 E3
Glan-Duar Carmth....43 K6
Glandwr Pembks....41 N5
Glan-Dwyfach Gwynd....66 H6
Glandyfi Cerdgn....54 F5
Glangrwyney Powys....45 J11
Glanllynfi Brdgnd....29 N6
Glanmule Powys....56 B6
Glanrhyd Pembks....41 M2
Glan-rhyd Powys....29 L3
Glanton Nthumb....119 L8
Glanton Pike Nthumb....119 L8
Glanvilles Wootton Dorset....11 P3
Glan-y-don Flints....80 H9
Glan-y-llyn Rhondd....30 F8
Glan-y-nant Powys....55 L9
Glan-yr-afon Gwynd....68 B6
Glan-yr-afon Gwynd....68 D6
Glan-yr-afon IoA....79 L8
Glan-yr-afon Swans....28 H3
Glapthorn Nhants....61 M2
Glapwell Derbys....84 G7
Glasbury Powys....44 H7
Glascoed Denbgs....80 D10
Glascoed Mons....31 K4
Glascote Staffs....59 K4
Glascwm Powys....44 H4
Glasfryn Conwy....68 B4
Glasgow C Glas....125 P4
Glasgow Airport Rens....125 M4
Glasgow Science Centre C Glas....125 P4
Glasinfryn Gwynd....79 K11
Glasnacardoch Bay Highld....145 L8
Glasnakille Highld....144 H4
Glaspwll Powys....54 G5
Glassenbury Kent....26 C4
Glassford S Lans....126 C8
Glass Houghton Wakefd....91 L6
Glasshouse Gloucs....46 D10
Glasshouse Hill Gloucs....46 D10
Glasshouses N York....97 K8
Glasson Cumb....110 D8
Glasson Lancs....95 J9
Glassonby Cumb....101 P3
Glasterlaw Angus....143 K7
Glaston Rutlnd....73 M10
Glastonbury Somset....19 P7
Glatton Cambs....61 Q3
Glazebrook Warrtn....82 E6
Glazebury Warrtn....82 E5
Glazeley Shrops....57 N7
Gleadless Sheff....84 E4
Gleadsmoss Ches E....82 H11
Gleaston Cumb....94 E6
Glebe Highld....147 N4

Gledhow Leeds....91 J3
Gledpark D & G....108 D10
Gledrid Shrops....69 K7
Glemsford Suffk....52 D2
Glenallachie Moray....157 P9
Glenancross Highld....145 L9
Glenaros House Ag & B....137 P7
Glen Auldyn IoM....80 f3
Glenbarr Ag & B....120 C4
Glenbarry Abers....158 E7
Glenbeg Highld....137 P3
Glenbervie Abers....151 K11
Glenboig N Lans....126 C4
Glenborrodale Highld....137 Q3
Glenbranter Ag & B....131 N8
Glenbreck Border....116 F6
Glenbrittle House Highld....144 F3
Glenbuck E Ayrs....115 P2
Glencally Angus....142 F5
Glencaple D & G....109 L7
Glencarron Lodge Highld....154 E7
Glencarse P & K....134 F3
Glen Clunie Lodge Abers....149 L11
Glencoe Highld....139 L6
Glencothe Border....116 F5
Glencraig Fife....134 F9
Glencrosh D & G....115 Q10
Glendale Highld....152 B8
Glendaruel Ag & B....131 K11
Glendevon P & K....134 B7
Glendoe Lodge Highld....147 L6
Glendoick P & K....134 G3
Glenduckie Fife....134 H4
Glenegedale Ag & B....122 D9
Glenelg Highld....145 P4
Glenerney Moray....157 J8
Glenfarg P & K....134 E5
Glenfield Leics....72 E9
Glenfinnan Highld....145 R11
Glenfintaig Lodge Highld....146 G10
Glenfoot P & K....134 F4
Glenfyne Lodge Ag & B....131 Q4
Glengarnock N Ayrs....125 J7
Glengolly Highld....167 K3
Glengorm Castle Ag & B....137 L4
Glengrasco Highld....152 G9
Glenholm Border....116 G4
Glenhoul D & G....115 M10
Glenisla Angus....142 C5
Glenkin Ag & B....131 N11
Glenkindie Abers....150 C5
Glenlivet Moray....149 M2
Glenlochar D & G....108 F8
Glenlomond P & K....134 F7
Glenluce D & G....106 G6
Glenmassen Ag & B....131 N10
Glenmavis N Lans....126 D4
Glen Maye IoM....80 b6
Glen Mona IoM....80 g4
Glenmore Highld....152 G9
Glenmore Lodge Highld....148 H6
Glen Nevis House Highld....139 L3
Glenochil Clacks....133 P8
Glen Parva Leics....72 F11
Glenquiech Angus....142 G5
Glenralloch Ag & B....123 Q6
Glenridding Cumb....101 L7
Glenrothes Fife....134 H7
Glenshero Lodge Highld....147 P9
Glenstriven Ag & B....124 D2
Glentham Lincs....86 D2
Glentrool D & G....107 L2
Glen Trool Lodge D & G....114 H11
Glentruim House Highld....148 B9
Glentworth Lincs....86 B3
Glenuig Highld....138 B2
Glenvarragill Highld....152 H10
Glen Vine IoM....80 d6
Glenwhilly D & G....106 G3
Glespin S Lans....115 R2
Glewstone Herefs....45 R10
Glinton C Pete....74 C9
Glooston Leics....73 K11
Glossop Derbys....83 M6
Gloster Hill Nthumb....119 Q10
Gloucester Gloucs....46 F11
Gloucester Crematorium Gloucs....46 G11
Gloucester Services Gloucs....32 F2
Gloucestershire Airport Gloucs....46 G10
Glusburn N York....96 F11
Glutt Lodge Highld....166 H9
Gluvian Cnwll....4 E9
Glympton Oxon....48 D10
Glynarthen Cerdgn....42 F5
Glyn Ceiriog Wrexhm....68 H7
Glyncorrwg Neath....29 N5
Glynde E Susx....25 L9
Glyndebourne E Susx....25 L8
Glyndyfrdwy Denbgs....68 F6
Glynneath Neath....29 N3
Glynn Valley Crematorium Cnwll....4 H8
Glyntaff Rhondd....30 E7
Glyntaff Crematorium Rhondd....30 E7
Glyntawe Powys....44 A11
Glynteg Carmth....42 G7
Gnosall Staffs....70 E10
Gnosall Heath Staffs....70 E10
Goadby Leics....73 K11
Goadby Marwood Leics....73 K5
Goatacre Wilts....33 K9
Goathill Dorset....20 C11
Goathland N York....105 M10
Goathurst Somset....19 J8
Goathurst Common Kent....37 L10
Goat Lees Kent....26 H2
Gobowen Shrops....69 K8
Godalming Surrey....23 Q6
Goddard's Corner Suffk....65 K8
Goddard's Green Kent....26 D5
Goddards Green W Susx....24 H6
Godden Green Kent....37 N9
Godford Cross Devon....10 C4
Godington Oxon....48 H9
Godley Tamesd....83 L5
Godmanchester Cambs....62 B6
Godmanstone Dorset....11 P5
Godmersham Kent....39 J11
Godney Somset....19 N6
Godolphin Cross Cnwll....2 G7
Godre'r-graig Neath....29 L3
Godshill Hants....21 N11
Godshill IoW....14 F10
Godstone Staffs....71 J8
Godstone Surrey....37 J10

Godsworthy Devon 8 D9
Godwinscroft Hants 13 L5
Goetre Mons 31 K3
Goff's Oak Herts 50 H10
Gogar C Edin 127 N11
Goginan Cerdgn 54 F8
Golan Gwynd 67 J6
Golant Cnwll 5 J11
Golberdon Cnwll 5 N7
Golborne Wigan 82 D5
Golcar Kirk 90 D7
Goldcliff Newpt 31 L8
Golden Cross E Susx 25 M8
Golden Green Kent 37 P11
Golden Grove Carmth 43 L11
Goldenhill C Stke 70 F4
Golden Hill Pembks 41 J10
Golden Pot Hants 23 K6
Golden Valley Derbys 84 F10
Golders Green Gt Lon 36 F3
Golders Green
  Crematorium W Berk 36 G3
Goldfinch Bottom
  W Berk 22 F2
Goldhanger Essex 52 F10
Gold Hill Cambs 62 H2
Gold Hill Dorset 12 D2
Golding Shrops 57 J4
Goldington Bed 61 N10
Goldsborough N York 97 N9
Goldsborough N York 105 M8
Golds Green Sandw 58 E6
Goldsithney Cnwll 2 E7
Goldstone Kent 39 N9
Goldstone Shrops 70 C9
Goldsworth Park Surrey 23 Q3
Goldthorpe Barns 91 M10
Goldworthy Devon 16 F7
Golford Kent 26 C4
Golford Green Kent 26 C4
Gollanfield Highld 156 E7
Gollinglith Foot N York 96 H4
Golly Wrexhm 69 K3
Golsoncott Somset 18 D7
Golspie Highld 163 J6
Gomeldon Wilts 21 N7
Gomersal Kirk 90 G5
Gomshall Surrey 36 C11
Gonalston Notts 85 L11
Gonerby Hill Foot Lincs 73 N3
Gonfirth Shet 169 q7
Goodameavy Devon 6 E6
Good Easter Essex 51 P8
Gooderstone Norfk 75 Q10
Goodleigh Devon 17 L5
Goodmanham E R Yk 92 E2
Goodmayes Gt Lon 37 L3
Goodnestone Kent 38 H9
Goodnestone Kent 39 N11
Goodrich Herefs 45 R11
Goodrington Torbay 7 M7
Goodshaw Lancs 89 N5
Goodshaw Fold Lancs 89 N5
Goodstone Devon 7 K4
Goodwick Pembks 40 H3
Goodworth Clatford
  Hants 22 C6
Goodyers End Warwks 59 M7
Goole E R Yk 92 B6
Goole Fields E R Yk 92 C6
Goom's Hill Worcs 47 K4
Goonbell Cnwll 3 J4
Goonhavern Cnwll 3 K3
Goonvrea Cnwll 3 J4
Goosecruives Abers 151 K11
Gooseford Devon 8 G6
Goose Green Essex 53 K6
Goose Green Kent 26 D4
Goose Green Kent 37 P10
Goose Green S Glos 32 C10
Goose Green W Susx 24 D7
Goose Green Wigan 82 C4
Gooseham Cnwll 16 C8
Gooseham Mill Cnwll 16 C8
Goosehill Green Worcs 46 H2
Goose Pool Herefs 45 P7
Goosey Oxon 34 C6
Goosnargh Lancs 88 H3
Goostrey Ches E 82 G10
Gordano Services N Som 31 P9
Gorddinog Conwy 79 M10
Gordon Border 118 B2
Gordon Arms Hotel
  Border 117 L5
Gordonstoun Abers 158 E6
Gordonstown Abers 158 H10
Gore Powys 45 K3
Gorebridge Mdloth 127 K9
Gorefield Cambs 74 H8
Gore Pit Essex 52 E8
Gores Wilts 21 M3
Gore Street Kent 39 N8
Gorey Jersey 11 c2
Goring Oxon 34 H8
Goring-by-Sea W Susx 24 D10
Goring Heath Oxon 35 J9
Gorleston on Sea Norfk 77 Q11
Gornal Wood
  Crematorium Dudley 58 D6
Gorrachie Abers 158 H6
Gorran Churchtown
  Cnwll 3 P5
Gorran Haven Cnwll 3 Q5
Gorran High Lanes Cnwll 3 P5
Gorrig Cerdgn 42 H6
Gors Cerdgn 54 E9
Gorsedd Flints 80 H9
Gorse Hill Swindn 33 N7
Gorseinon Swans 28 G5
Gorseybank Derbys 71 P4
Gorsgoch Cerdgn 43 J4
Gorslas Carmth 28 G2
Gorsley Gloucs 46 C9
Gorsley Common Herefs 46 C9
Gorstage Ches W 82 D10
Gorstan Highld 155 L5
Gorstella Ches W 69 K2
Gorst Hill Worcs 57 N10
Gorsty Hill Staffs 71 L9
Gorten Ag & B 138 C11
Gorthleck Highld 147 N3
Gorton Manch 83 J5
Gosbeck Suffk 53 H10
Gosberton Lincs 74 D4
Gosberton Clough Lincs 74 C5
Gosfield Essex 52 C6
Gosford Devon 10 C5
Gosford Oxon 34 E2
Gosforth Cumb 100 E10
Gosforth N u Ty 113 K7
Gosling Street Somset 19 P8

Gosmore Herts 50 E5
Gospel End Staffs 58 C6
Gospel Green W Susx 23 P6
Gosport Hants 14 H7
Gossard's Green C Beds 49 Q6
Gossington Gloucs 32 D4
Goswick Nthumb 119 L2
Gotham Notts 72 E4
Gotherington Gloucs 47 J9
Gotton Somset 18 H9
Goudhurst Kent 26 B4
Goulceby Lincs 87 J5
Gourdas Abers 159 J9
Gourdie C Dund 142 F11
Gourdon Abers 143 Q3
Gourock Inver 124 G2
Govan C Glas 125 N4
Goveton Devon 7 K9
Govilon Mons 31 J2
Gowdall E R Yk 91 Q6
Gower Highld 155 P6
Gower Swans 28 F6
Gowerton Swans 28 G5
Gowkhall Fife 134 D10
Gowthorpe E R Yk 98 F10
Goxhill E R Yk 93 L2
Goxhill N Linc 93 K6
Grabhair W Isls 168 i6
Graby Lincs 74 A5
Grade Cnwll 3 J11
Gradeley Green Ches E 69 Q4
Graffham W Susx 23 P11
Grafham Cambs 61 Q7
Grafham Surrey 24 B2
Grafton Herefs 45 P7
Grafton N York 97 P8
Grafton Oxon 33 Q4
Grafton Shrops 69 M11
Grafton Worcs 46 A2
Grafton Worcs 47 J7
Grafton Flyford Worcs 47 J3
Grafton Regis Nhants 49 L5
Grafton Underwood
  Nhants 61 K4
Grafty Green Kent 26 E2
Graianrhyd Denbgs 68 H3
Graig Conwy 79 Q10
Graig Denbgs 80 F10
Graigfechan Denbgs 68 F4
Grain Medway 38 E6
Grains Bar Oldham 90 B9
Grainsby Lincs 93 N11
Grainthorpe Lincs 93 Q11
Grampound Cnwll 3 N3
Grampound Road Cnwll 3 N3
Gramsdal W Isls 168 d12
Gramsdale W Isls 168 d12
Granborough Bucks 49 L9
Granby Notts 73 K3
Grandborough Warwks 59 Q11
Grand Chemins Jersey 11 c2
Grandes Rocques Guern 10 b1
Grandtully P & K 141 M7
Grange Cumb 101 J7
Grange Medway 38 C8
Grange P & K 134 H2
Grange Wirral 81 J7
Grange Crossroads
  Moray 158 C7
Grange Hall Moray 157 K5
Grangehall S Lans 116 D2
Grange Hill Essex 37 K2
Grangemill Derbys 84 B9
Grange Moor Kirk 90 G7
Grangemouth Falk 133 Q11
Grange of Lindores Fife 134 H4
Grange-over-Sands
  Cumb 95 J5
Grangepans Falk 134 C11
Grange Park Nhants 60 G9
Grangetown R & Cl 104 F6
Grangetown Sundld 113 P10
Grange Villa Dur 113 K10
Gransmoor E R Yk 99 N9
Gransmore Green Essex 51 Q6
Granston Pembks 40 G4
Grantchester Cambs 62 F9
Grantham Lincs 73 N3
Grantham
  Crematorium Lincs 73 N3
Granton C Edin 127 N2
Grantown-on-Spey
  Highld 149 J2
Grantsfield Herefs 45 Q2
Grantshouse Border 129 L6
Grappenhall Warrtn 82 D7
Grasby Lincs 93 J10
Grasmere Cumb 101 K9
Grasscroft Oldham 83 L4
Grassendale Lpool 81 M7
Grassgarth Cumb 101 K2
Grass Green Essex 52 B4
Grassington N York 96 F8
Grassmoor Derbys 84 F7
Grassthorpe Notts 85 N7
Grateley Hants 21 Q6
Gratwich Staffs 71 J8
Graveley Cambs 62 C8
Graveley Herts 50 F5
Gravelly Hill Birm 58 H6
Gravelsbank Shrops 56 E4
Graveney Kent 39 J9
Gravesend Kent 37 Q6
Gravir W Isls 168 i6
Grayingham Lincs 92 F11
Grayrigg Cumb 101 Q11
Grays Thurr 37 P5
Grayshott Hants 23 N7
Grayson Green Cumb 100 C5
Grayswood Surrey 23 P8
Graythorp Hartpl 104 F5
Grazeley Wokham 35 J11
Greasbrough Rothm 91 L11
Greasby Wirral 81 K7
Greasley Notts 84 G11
Great Abington Cambs 62 H11
Great Addington Nhants 61 L5
Great Alne Warwks 47 M3
Great Altcar Lancs 88 C9
Great Amwell Herts 51 J8
Great Asby Cumb 102 C8
Great Ashfield Suffk 64 D8
Great Ayton N York 104 G8
Great Baddow Essex 52 B11
Great Badminton S Glos 32 F8
Great Bardfield Essex 51 Q4
Great Barford Bed 61 N10
Great Barr Sandw 58 F5
Great Barrington Gloucs 33 P2
Great Barrow Ches W 81 P11
Great Barton Suffk 64 B8

Great Barugh N York 98 E5
Great Bavington
  Nthumb 112 E4
Great Bealings Suffk 53 M2
Great Bedwyn Wilts 21 Q2
Great Bentley Essex 53 K7
Great Billing Nhants 60 H8
Great Bircham Norfk 75 Q4
Great Blakenham Suffk 64 G11
Great Blencow Cumb 101 N4
Great Bolas Wrekin 70 A10
Great Bookham Surrey 36 D10
Great Bosullow Cnwll 2 C7
Great Bourton Oxon 48 E5
Great Bowden Leics 60 F3
Great Bradley Suffk 63 L10
Great Braxted Essex 52 E9
Great Bricett Suffk 64 E11
Great Brickhill Bucks 49 P8
Great Bridgeford Staffs 70 F9
Great Brington Nhants 60 E7
Great Bromley Essex 53 J6
Great Broughton Cumb 100 E4
Great Broughton N York 104 F9
Great Budworth Ches W 82 E9
Great Burdon Darltn 104 B7
Great Burstead Essex 37 Q2
Great Busby N York 104 F9
Great Canfield Essex 51 N7
Great Carlton Lincs 87 M3
Great Casterton Rutlnd 73 Q9
Great Chalfield Wilts 20 G2
Great Chart Kent 26 G3
Great Chatwell Staffs 57 P2
Great Chell C Stke 70 F4
Great Chesterford Essex 51 M2
Great Cheverell Wilts 21 J4
Great Chishill Cambs 51 K3
Great Clacton Essex 53 L8
Great Cliffe Wakefd 91 J7
Great Clifton Cumb 100 D5
Great Coates NE Lin 93 M9
Great Comberton Worcs 47 J6
Great Comp Kent 37 P9
Great Corby Cumb 111 J10
Great Cornard Suffk 52 E3
Great Cowden E R Yk 93 M2
Great Coxwell Oxon 33 Q6
Great Cransley Nhants 60 H5
Great Cressingham
  Norfk 76 B11
Great Crosthwaite Cumb 101 J4
Great Cubley Derbys 71 M7
Great Cumbrae Island
  N Ayrs 124 F6
Great Dalby Leics 73 J8
Great Denham Bed 61 M11
Great Doddington
  Nhants 61 J8
Great Doward Herefs 45 Q11
Great Dunham Norfk 76 B9
Great Dunmow Essex 51 P6
Great Durnford Wilts 21 M7
Great Easton Essex 51 P5
Great Easton Leics 60 H2
Great Eccleston Lancs 88 G3
Great Edstone N York 98 E4
Great Ellingham Norfk 64 E2
Great Elm Somset 20 D5
Great Everdon Nhants 60 C9
Great Eversden Cambs 62 E10
Great Fencote N York 97 L2
Greatfield Wilts 33 L7
Great Finborough Suffk 64 E10
Greatford Lincs 74 A8
Great Fransham Norfk 76 B9
Great Gaddesden Herts 50 B8
Greatgate Staffs 71 K7
Great Gidding Cambs 61 P4
Great Givendale E R Yk 98 G10
Great Glemham Suffk 65 L9
Great Glen Leics 72 H11
Great Gonerby Lincs 73 M3
Great Gransden Cambs 62 C9
Great Green Cambs 50 G2
Great Green Norfk 65 K4
Great Green Suffk 64 C10
Great Green Suffk 64 C8
Great Habton N York 98 F5
Great Hale Lincs 74 B2
Great Hallingbury Essex 51 M7
Greatham Hants 23 L8
Greatham Hartpl 104 E5
Greatham W Susx 24 B7
Great Hampden Bucks 35 M4
Great Harrowden
  Nhants 61 J6
Great Harwood Lancs 89 L4
Great Haseley Oxon 34 H4
Great Hatfield E R Yk 93 L2
Great Haywood Staffs 70 H10
Great Heck N York 91 P6
Great Henny Essex 52 E4
Great Hinton Wilts 20 H3
Great Hockham Norfk 64 D3
Great Holland Essex 53 M8
Great Hollands Br For 35 N11
Great Horkesley Essex 52 G5
Great Hormead Herts 51 K5
Great Horton C Brad 90 E4
Great Horwood Bucks 49 L8
Great Houghton Barns 91 L9
Great Houghton Nhants 60 H9
Great Hucklow Derbys 83 Q9
Great Kelk E R Yk 99 N9
Great Kimble Bucks 35 M3
Great Kingshill Bucks 35 N5
Great Langdale Cumb 101 J9
Great Langton N York 103 Q11
Great Leighs Essex 52 B8
Great Limber Lincs 93 K9
Great Linford M Keyn 49 N6
Great Livermere Suffk 64 B7
Great Longstone Derbys 84 B6
Great Lumley Dur 113 L11
Great Lyth Shrops 56 H3
Great Malvern Worcs 46 E5
Great Maplestead Essex 52 D5
Great Marton Bpool 88 C3
Great Massingham Norfk 75 Q6
Great Melton Norfk 76 G10
Great Meols Wirral 81 J6
Great Missenden Bucks 35 N4
Great Mitton Lancs 89 L3
Great Mongeham Kent 39 Q11
Great Moulton Norfk 64 H3
Great Munden Herts 51 J6
Great Musgrave Cumb 102 D8
Great Ness Shrops 69 L11
Great Notley Essex 52 B7

Great Oak Mons 31 L2
Great Oakley Essex 53 L6
Great Oakley Nhants 61 J3
Great Offley Herts 50 D5
Great Ormside Cumb 102 D7
Great Orton Cumb 110 F10
Great Ouseburn N York 97 P8
Great Oxendon Nhants 60 F4
Great Oxney Green Essex 51 Q9
Great Palgrave Norfk 76 A9
Great Park N u Ty 113 K6
Great Parndon Essex 51 K9
Great Pattenden Kent 26 B3
Great Paxton Cambs 62 B8
Great Plumpton Lancs 88 D4
Great Plumstead Norfk 77 L9
Great Ponton Lincs 73 N4
Great Potheridge Devon 17 J9
Great Preston Leeds 91 L5
Great Purston Nhants 48 F7
Great Raveley Cambs 62 C4
Great Rissington Gloucs 47 N11
Great Rollright Oxon 48 B8
Great Rudbaxton
  Pembks 41 J6
Great Ryburgh Norfk 76 D6
Great Ryle Nthumb 119 K8
Great Ryton Shrops 56 H4
Great Saling Essex 51 Q5
Great Salkeld Cumb 101 Q3
Great Sampford Essex 51 P3
Great Saredon Staffs 58 E3
Great Saughall Ches W 81 M11
Great Saxham Suffk 63 N8
Great Shefford W Berk 34 C9
Great Shelford Cambs 62 G10
Great Smeaton N York 104 B9
Great Snoring Norfk 76 C5
Great Somerford Wilts 33 J8
Great Soudley Shrops 70 C9
Great Stainton Darltn 104 B6
Great Stambridge Essex 38 E3
Great Staughton Cambs 61 P8
Great Steeping Lincs 87 M8
Great Stoke S Glos 32 B8
Great Stonar Kent 39 P10
Greatstone-on-Sea Kent 27 J7
Great Strickland Cumb 101 Q6
Great Stukeley Cambs 62 B6
Great Sturton Lincs 86 H5
Great Sutton Ches W 81 M9
Great Sutton Shrops 57 J8
Great Swinburne
  Nthumb 112 D5
Great Tew Oxon 48 D9
Great Tey Essex 52 E6
Great Thurlow Suffk 63 L10
Great Torrington Devon 16 H8
Great Tosson Nthumb 119 K10
Great Totham Essex 52 E9
Great Totham Essex 52 E9
Great Tows Lincs 86 H2
Great Urswick Cumb 94 F6
Great Wakering Essex 38 F4
Great Waldingfield Suffk 52 F3
Great Walsingham Norfk 76 C4
Great Waltham Essex 51 Q8
Great Warford Ches E 82 H9
Great Warley Essex 37 N2
Great Washbourne
  Gloucs 47 J8
Great Weeke Devon 8 H7
Great Welnetham Suffk 64 B10
Great Wenham Suffk 53 J4
Great Whittington
  Nthumb 112 F6
Great Wigborough Essex 52 G8
Great Wilbraham Cambs 63 J9
Great Wilne Derbys 72 C4
Great Wishford Wilts 21 L7
Great Witchingham
  Norfk 76 G7
Great Witcombe Gloucs 32 H2
Great Witley Worcs 57 P11
Great Wolford Warwks 47 Q8
Greatworth Nhants 48 G5
Great Wratting Suffk 63 L11
Great Wymondley Herts 50 F5
Great Wyrley Staffs 58 E3
Great Wytheford Shrops 69 Q10
Great Yarmouth Norfk 77 R10
Great Yarmouth
  Crematorium Norfk 77 Q11
Great Yeldham Essex 52 C4
Grebby Lincs 87 M7
Greeba IoM 80 d5
Green Denbgs 80 F11
Green Bank Lancs 94 H4
Greenbottom Cnwll 3 K4
Greenburn W Loth 126 G5
Greencroft Hall Dur 113 J11
Green Cross Surrey 23 N7
Green Down Somset 19 Q4
Green End Bed 61 M11
Green End Bed 61 N8
Green End Bed 61 P10
Green End Bed 61 N8
Green End Cambs 61 Q4
Green End Cambs 62 E9
Green End Cambs 62 G7
Green End Cambs 62 G8
Green End Herts 50 G4
Green End Herts 50 H4
Green End Herts 51 J5
Greenend Oxon 48 B10
Green End Warwks 59 L7
Greenfield Ag & B 131 Q9
Greenfield C Beds 50 C4
Greenfield Flints 80 H9
Greenfield Highld 146 G7
Greenfield Oldham 83 L4
Greenford Gt Lon 36 E4
Greengairs N Lans 126 D3
Greengates C Brad 90 F3
Greenhalgh Lancs 88 G3
Greenham Somset 18 E11
Greenham W Berk 34 E1
Green Hammerton
  N York 97 Q9
Greenhaugh Nthumb 111 Q3
Green Head Cumb 110 G11
Greenhead Nthumb 111 N7
Green Heath Staffs 58 E2
Greenheys Salfd 82 F4
Greenhill D & G 109 P5
Greenhill Falk 126 D2
Greenhill Herefs 46 B5
Greenhill Kent 39 L8

Greenhill S Lans 116 C10
Green Hill Wilts 33 L8
Greenhillocks Derbys 84 F11
Greenhithe Kent 37 P6
Greenholm E Ayrs 125 N10
Greenholme Cumb 101 Q10
Greenhouse Border 117 Q6
Greenhow Hill N York 96 H8
Greenland Highld 167 N3
Greenland Sheff 84 E3
Greenlands Bucks 35 L7
Green Lane Devon 9
Green Lane Worcs 47 L2
Greenlaw Border 129 H10
Greenlea D & G 109 N6
Greenloaning P & K 133 N6
Green Moor Barns 90 H11
Greenmount Bury 89 M8
Green Oak E R Yk 92 D4
Greenock Inver 124 H3
Greenodd Cumb 94 G4
Green Ore Somset 19 Q4
Green Quarter Cumb 101 N10
Greensgate Norfk 76 G8
Greenshields S Lans 116 E2
Greenside Gatesd 112 H8
Greenside Kirk 90 F6
Greens Norton Nhants 49 J4
Greenstead Green Essex 52 D6
Greensted Essex 51 M10
Green Street E Susx 26 C9
Green Street Gloucs 46 G10
Green Street Herts 50 E11
Green Street Herts 51 L5
Green Street Worcs 46 G4
Green Street Green
  Gt Lon 37 L8
Green Street Green Kent 37 L6
Greenstreet Green Suffk 52 H3
Green Tye Herts 51 K7
Greenway Gloucs 46 G9
Greenway Somset 19 K11
Greenway V Glam 30 E10
Greenway Worcs 57 N11
Greenwich Gt Lon 37 J5
Greenwich Maritime
  Gt Lon 37 J5
Greet Gloucs 47 K8
Greete Shrops 57 K10
Greetham Lincs 87 K6
Greetham Rutlnd 73 N8
Greetland Calder 90 D6
Gregson Lane Lancs 88 H5
Greinton Somset 19 M8
Grenaby IoM 80 c7
Grendon Nhants 61 J8
Grendon Warwks 59 J4
Grendon Green Herefs 46 A3
Grendon Underwood
  Bucks 49 J9
Grenofen Devon 6 D4
Grenoside Sheff 84 D2
Grenoside
  Crematorium Sheff 84 D2
Greosabhagh W Isls 168 g8
Gresford Wrexhm 69 K4
Gresham Norfk 76 H4
Greshornish House
  Hotel Highld 152 E7
Gressenhall Norfk 76 D8
Gressenhall Green Norfk 76 D8
Gressingham Lancs 95 M7
Gresty Green Ches E 70 C3
Greta Bridge Dur 103 L7
Gretna D & G 110 H7
Gretna Green D & G 110 H7
Gretna Services D & G 110 H7
Gretton Gloucs 47 K8
Gretton Nhants 61 J2
Gretton Shrops 57 J5
Grewelthorpe N York 97 K5
Grey Friars Suffk 65 P7
Greygarth N York 97 J5
Grey Green N Linc 92 C9
Greylake Somset 19 L8
Greylees Lincs 73 Q2
Greyrigg D & G 109 L4
Greys Green Oxon 35 K8
Greysouthen Cumb 100 E5
Greystoke Cumb 101 M4
Greystone Angus 143 L9
Greywell Hants 23 K4
Gribb Dorset 10 H4
Gribthorpe E R Yk 92 C3
Griff Warwks 59 N7
Griffithstown Torfn 31 J5
Griffydam Leics 72 C7
Griggs Green Hants 23 M7
Grimeford Village Lancs 89 J9
Grimesthorpe Sheff 84 E3
Grimethorpe Barns 91 L9
Grimley Worcs 46 F2
Grimmet S Ayrs 114 F5
Grimoldby Lincs 87 L3
Grimpo Shrops 69 L9
Grimsargh Lancs 88 H4
Grimsby NE Lin 93 N9
Grimsby Crematorium
  NE Lin 93 N9
Grimscote Nhants 49 J4
Grimscott Cnwll 16 D10
Grimshader W Isls 168 j5
Grimshaw Bl w D 89 L5
Grimshaw Green Lancs 88 F8
Grimsthorpe Lincs 73 Q6
Grimston E R Yk 93 N3
Grimston Leics 72 H6
Grimston Norfk 75 P6
Grimstone Dorset 11 N5
Grimstone End Suffk 64 C7
Grinacombe Moor Devon 5 Q3
Grindale E R Yk 99 N6
Grindle Shrops 57 N4
Grindleford Derbys 84 C4
Grindleton Lancs 89 L2
Grindley Brook Shrops 69 P5
Grindlow Derbys 83 Q9
Grindon Nthumb 118 H2
Grindon S on T 104 D6
Grindon Staffs 71 K3
Grindon Hill Nthumb 112 B6
Grindonrigg Nthumb 118 H2
Gringley on the Hill
  Notts 85 M2
Grinsdale Cumb 110 G9
Grinshill Shrops 69 P10
Grinton N York 103 K11
Griomaisiader W Isls 168 j5
Griomsaigh W Isls 168 d12
Grishipoll Ag & B 136 F4
Grisling Common E Susx 25 L6

...thorpe N York 99 M4
...ton Norfk 64 C2
...ley Ork 169 e6
...enham Wilts 33 L8
...leton Wilts 32 G8
...beck Cumb 94 E4
...edale Cumb 94 G2
...by Leics 72 E9
...es Conwy 68 D2
...es-faen Rhondd 30 E8
...esfforrd Gwynd 66 D7
...enbgh 80 E10
...esllwyd Powys 56 C2
...eslon Gwynd 66 H3
...eslon Gwynd 67 J2
...es-Wen Caerph 30 F7
...qarry W Isls 168 c14
...gport Ag & B 120 F3
...gearraidh W Isls 168 c14
...mford Suffk 65 M10
...nant Flints 80 F8
...ombridge E Susx 25 M3
...sebay W Isls 168 g8
...smont Mons 45 N10
...ston N York 105 M9
...ton Suffk 52 G3
...ton Oldham 83 L4
...uville Jersey 11 c2
...ve Bucks 49 P10
...ve Dorset 11 P10
...ve Kent 39 M9
...ve Notts 85 M5
...ve Oxon 34 D6
...ve Pembks 41 J10
...ve Green Kent 38 C10
...venhurst Kent 26 B3
...ve Park Gt Lon 37 K6
...vesend S Glos 32 C7
...vesend Swans 28 G4
...ob Street Kent 37 N7
...nard Highld 160 E9
...nart Ag & B 122 C6
...ine Ag & B 137 N7
...a Highld 144 E2
...mbla Cnwll 2 D7
...disburgh Suffk 65 J11
...cing Shet 169 p9
...ness Shet 169 r12
...lachulain Highld 139 L8
...rdbridge Fife 135 M4
...rlford Worcs 46 F5
...y P & K 141 P8
...rnsey Guern 10 b2
...rnsey Airport Guern 10 b2
...stling Green E Susx 26 E8
...stling Thorn E Susx 26 E8
...stwick Norfk 76 H4
...le Bridge Tamesd 83 K5
...le Post Nthumb 113 L3
...den Morden Cambs 50 G2
...den Sutton Ches W 81 N11
...dford Surrey 23 Q5
...dford Crematorium Surrey 23 Q5
...stead Kent 38 D9
...dtown P & K 142 A11
...sborough Nhants 60 E6
...sfield Powys 56 C2
...ton Kent 39 N10
...creehill S Ayrs 114 G5
...eaford Devon 17 K4
...borough R & Cl 104 H7
...eley Leeds 90 F2
...t Norfk 76 E6
...ing Power Gloucs 47 L10
...ane E Loth 128 D3
...ng Green Suffk 64 A10
...al Cnwll 2 D7
...worthy Devon 6 D4
...afreston Pembks 41 M10
...ley Leics 60 E3
...amow's Shop Cnwll 4 D10
...by E R Yk 92 B3
...by Lincs 73 N6
...by Lincs 87 K7
...dleton Hants 22 H8
...Green Kent 26 C5
...Hill E Susx 25 N8
...Hill Warwks 59 L7
...n Devon 17 L5
...nerside N York 103 J11
...merton Nthumb 112 D6
...ness N Linc 92 D8
...nislake Cnwll 6 C4
...nista Shet 169 s9
...thorpe C Pete 74 C10
...thorpe N Linc 92 D11
...thorpe Norfk 76 E5
...thorpe Notts 72 H2
...ton Suffk 65 Q2
...walloe Cnwll 2 H9
...worthy Somset 18 C8
...rard IoW 14 E7
...nett Ches E 83 K10
...ney Slade Somset 20 B5
...nos Powys 29 L3
...amere Kent 38 H10
...sage All Saints Dorset 12 H2
...sage St Andrew Dorset 12 G2
...sage St Michael Dorset 12 G2
...ton Kent 27 P3
...cher Shet 169 s4
...rie Angus 143 K7
...nirn Cambs 74 H10
...nirn Gull Cambs 74 G10
...s Marsh Dorset 20 F10
...s ance Nthumb 119 P10
...chmai IoA 78 F9
...stadnant Powys 67 L3
...un-Cae-Gurwen Carmth 29 J2
...ert on Sea Cerdgn 42 C4
...alavellan Cnwll 2 G5
...ek Cnwll 3 J8
...helog Mons 31 L4
...nddwr Powys 44 F6
...nnap Mining District Cnwll 3 J5
...nt Crematorium Mons 31 K6
...nter Cnwll 3 J10
...nnaffield Flints 81 J11
...rnesney Mons 31 K4
...rnogle Carmth 43 K8

Gwernymynedd Flints 68 H2
Gwersyllt Wrexhm 69 K4
Gwespyr Flints 80 G8
Gwindra Cnwll 3 P3
Gwinear Cnwll 2 F6
Gwithian Cnwll 2 F5
Gwredog IoA 78 G7
Gwrhay Caerph 30 G5
Gwyddelwern Denbgs 68 E5
Gwyddgrug Carmth 43 J7
Gwynfryn Wrexhm 69 J4
Gwystre Powys 55 P11
Gwytherin Conwy 68 A2
Gyfelia Wrexhm 69 K5
Gyrn-goch Gwynd 66 G5

H

Habberley Shrops 56 F4
Habberley Worcs 57 Q9
Habergham Lancs 89 N4
Habertoft Lincs 87 P7
Habin W Susx 23 M10
Habrough NE Lin 93 K8
Hacconby Lincs 74 B5
Haceby Lincs 73 Q3
Hacheston Suffk 65 L10
Hackbridge Gt Lon 36 G7
Hackenthorpe Sheff 84 F4
Hackford Norfk 76 F11
Hackforth N York 97 K2
Hack Green Ches E 70 A5
Hackland Ork 169 c4
Hackleton Nhants 60 H9
Hacklinge Kent 39 P11
Hackman's Gate Worcs 58 C9
Hackness N York 99 K2
Hackness Somset 19 K5
Hackney Gt Lon 36 H4
Hackthorn Lincs 86 C4
Hackthorpe Cumb 101 P6
Hacton Gt Lon 37 N3
Hadden Border 118 E3
Haddenham Bucks 35 K3
Haddenham Cambs 62 G3
Haddington E Loth 128 E5
Haddington Lincs 86 B8
Haddiscoe Norfk 65 N2
Haddo Abers 159 K10
Haddon Cambs 61 P2
Hade Edge Kirk 83 P4
Hadfield Derbys 83 M5
Hadham Cross Herts 51 K7
Hadham Ford Herts 51 K6
Hadleigh Essex 38 D4
Hadleigh Suffk 52 H3
Hadleigh Heath Suffk 52 G3
Hadley Worcs 46 G2
Hadley Wrekin 57 M2
Hadley End Staffs 71 L10
Hadley Wood Gt Lon 50 G11
Hadlow Kent 37 P10
Hadlow Down E Susx 25 M6
Hadnall Shrops 69 P10
Hadrian's Wall 112 E7
Hadstock Essex 51 N2
Hadzor Worcs 46 H2
Haffenden Quarter Kent 26 E3
Hafodunos Conwy 80 B11
Hafod-y-bwch Wrexhm 69 K5
Hafod-y-coed Blae G 30 H4
Hafodyrynys Caerph 30 H5
Haggate Lancs 89 P3
Haggbeck Cumb 111 J6
Haggersta Shet 169 q9
Haggerston Nthumb 119 K2
Haggington Hill Devon 17 K2
Haggs Falk 126 D2
Hagley Herefs 45 R6
Hagley Worcs 58 D8
Hagmore Green Suffk 52 G4
Hagnaby Lincs 87 K8
Hagnaby Lincs 87 N5
Hagworthingham Lincs 87 K7
Haigh Wigan 89 J9
Haighton Green Lancs 88 H4
Haile Cumb 100 D3
Hailes Gloucs 47 K8
Hailey Herts 51 J8
Hailey Oxon 34 C2
Hailey Oxon 34 H7
Hailsham E Susx 25 N9
Hail Weston Cambs 61 Q8
Hainault Gt Lon 37 L2
Haine Kent 39 Q8
Hainford Norfk 77 J8
Hainton Lincs 86 G4
Hainworth C Brad 90 D3
Haisthorpe E R Yk 99 N8
Hakin Pembks 40 G9
Halam Notts 85 L10
Halbeath Fife 134 E10
Halberton Devon 9 P2
Halcro Highld 167 M4
Hale Cumb 95 L5
Hale Halton 81 P8
Hale Hants 21 N11
Hale Somset 20 D9
Hale Surrey 23 M5
Hale Traffd 82 G7
Hale Bank Halton 81 P8
Halebarns Traffd 82 G7
Hale Green E Susx 25 N8
Hale Nook Lancs 88 D2
Hales Norfk 65 M2
Hales Staffs 70 C7
Halesgate Lincs 74 F5
Hales Green Derbys 71 M6
Halesowen Dudley 58 E8
Hales Place Kent 39 K10
Hale Street Kent 37 Q11
Halesville Essex 38 F4
Halesworth Suffk 65 M6
Halewood Knows 81 P7
Halford Devon 9 L4
Halford Shrops 56 G8
Halford Warwks 47 Q5
Halfpenny Cumb 95 L3
Halfpenny Green Staffs 58 B6
Halfpenny Houses N York 97 K4
Halfway Carmth 43 M8
Halfway Carmth 43 A8
Halfway Sheff 84 F4
Halfway W Berk 34 D11
Halfway Bridge W Susx 23 P10
Halfway Houses Kent 38 G7
Halifax Calder 90 D5

Halket E Ayrs 125 L7
Halkirk Highld 167 K5
Halkyn Flints 81 J10
Hall E Rens 125 L7
Hallam Fields Derbys 72 B3
Halland E Susx 25 L7
Hallaton Leics 73 K11
Hallatrow BaNES 20 B3
Hallbankgate Cumb 111 J10
Hallbeck Cumb 95 N3
Hall Cliffe Wakefd 90 H7
Hall Cross Lancs 88 E4
Hall Dunnerdale Cumb 100 H4
Hallen S Glos 31 Q8
Hall End Bed 61 M9
Hall End C Beds 50 C3
Hallfield Gate Derbys 84 E2
Hallgarth Dur 104 B2
Hall Glen Falk 126 F2
Hall Green Birm 58 H8
Hallin Highld 152 D6
Halling Medway 38 B9
Hallington Lincs 87 K3
Hallington Nthumb 112 E5
Halliwell Bolton 89 K8
Halloughton Notts 85 L10
Hallow Worcs 46 F3
Hallow Heath Worcs 46 F3
Hallsands Devon 7 L11
Hall's Green Essex 51 K4
Hall's Green Herts 50 G5
Hallthwaites Cumb 94 D3
Hallworthy Cnwll 5 K4
Hallyne Border 116 H2
Halmer End Staffs 70 D5
Halmond's Frome Herefs 46 C5
Halmore Gloucs 32 D4
Halnaker W Susx 15 P5
Halsall Lancs 88 D8
Halse Nhants 48 G6
Halse Somset 18 F9
Halsetown Cnwll 2 E6
Halsham E R Yk 93 N5
Halsinger Devon 17 J4
Halstead Essex 52 D5
Halstead Kent 37 L8
Halstead Leics 73 K9
Halstock Dorset 11 L3
Halsway Somset 18 F7
Haltcliff Bridge Cumb 101 L3
Haltemprice Crematorium E R Yk 92 H4
Haltham Lincs 86 H8
Haltoft End Lincs 87 L11
Halton Bucks 35 N3
Halton Halton 82 B8
Halton Lancs 95 L8
Halton Leeds 91 K4
Halton Nthumb 112 E7
Halton Wrexhm 69 K7
Halton East N York 96 F10
Halton Fenside Lincs 87 M8
Halton Gill N York 96 C5
Halton Green Lancs 95 L7
Halton Holegate Lincs 87 M7
Halton Lea Gate Nthumb 111 M9
Halton Quay Cnwll 5 Q8
Halton Shields Nthumb 112 F7
Halton West N York 96 B10
Haltwhistle Nthumb 111 P8
Halvergate Norfk 77 N10
Halwell Devon 7 K8
Halwill Devon 8 B5
Halwill Junction Devon 8 B4
Ham Devon 10 E4
Ham Gloucs 32 C5
Ham Gloucs 47 J10
Ham Gt Lon 36 E6
Ham Kent 39 P11
Ham Somset 19 J9
Ham Somset 20 C5
Ham Somset 22 B2
Ham Wilts 22 B2
Hambleden Bucks 35 L7
Hambledon Hants 14 H4
Hambledon Surrey 23 Q7
Hamble-le-Rice Hants 14 E5
Hambleton Lancs 88 D2
Hambleton N York 91 P4
Hambleton Moss Side Lancs 88 D2
Hambridge Somset 19 L10
Hambrook S Glos 32 B9
Hambrook W Susx 15 L5
Ham Common Dorset 20 F9
Hameringham Lincs 87 K7
Hamerton Cambs 61 P5
Ham Green Herefs 46 E6
Ham Green Kent 26 E6
Ham Green Kent 38 D8
Ham Green N Som 31 P9
Ham Green Worcs 47 K2
Ham Hill Kent 37 Q8
Hamilton S Lans 126 C6
Hamilton Services S Lans 126 C6
Hamlet Dorset 11 M3
Hamlins E Susx 25 N9
Hammerpot W Susx 24 C9
Hammersmith Gt Lon 36 F5
Hammerwich Staffs 58 G3
Hammerwood E Susx 25 K3
Hammond Street Herts 50 H10
Hammoon Dorset 12 D2
Hamnavoe Shet 169 q10
Hampden Park E Susx 25 P10
Hamperden End Essex 51 N4
Hampnett Gloucs 47 L11
Hampole Donc 91 N8
Hampreston Dorset 13 J5
Hampsfield Cumb 95 J4
Hampson Green Lancs 95 K10
Hampstead Gt Lon 36 G3
Hampstead Norreys W Berk 34 F9
Hampsthwaite N York 97 L9
Hampton C Pete 61 Q2
Hampton Devon 10 F5
Hampton Gt Lon 36 D7
Hampton Kent 39 L8
Hampton Shrops 57 N7
Hampton Swindn 33 N6
Hampton Worcs 47 K6
Hampton Bishop Herefs 45 R7
Hampton Court Palace Gt Lon 36 E7
Hampton Fields Gloucs 32 G5
Hampton Green Ches W 69 P5
Hampton Heath Ches W 69 P5
Hampton-in-Arden Solhll 59 K8
Hampton Loade Shrops 57 N7
Hampton Lovett Worcs 58 C11
Hampton Lucy Warwks 47 Q3

Hampton Magna Warwks 59 L11
Hampton on the Hill Warwks 47 Q2
Hampton Poyle Oxon 48 F11
Hampton Wick Gt Lon 36 E7
Hamptworth Wilts 21 P11
Hamrow Norfk 76 C7
Hamsey E Susx 25 K8
Hamsey Green Surrey 37 J9
Hamstall Ridware Staffs 71 L11
Hamstead Birm 58 G6
Hamstead IoW 14 D8
Hamstead Marshall W Berk 34 D11
Hamsterley Dur 103 M4
Hamsterley Dur 112 H9
Hamstreet Kent 26 H5
Ham Street Somset 19 Q8
Hamwood N Som 19 L3
Hamworthy Poole 12 G6
Hanbury Staffs 71 M9
Hanbury Worcs 47 J2
Hanby Lincs 73 Q4
Hanchet End Suffk 63 K11
Hanchurch Staffs 70 E6
Handa Island Highld 164 D7
Handale R & Cl 105 K7
Hand and Pen Devon 9 P5
Handbridge Ches W 81 N11
Handcross W Susx 24 G5
Handforth Ches E 83 J8
Hand Green Ches W 69 P2
Handley Ches W 69 N3
Handley Derbys 84 E8
Handley Green Essex 51 Q10
Handsacre Staffs 71 K11
Handsworth Birm 58 F7
Handsworth Sheff 84 F3
Handy Cross Bucks 35 N6
Hanford C Stke 70 F6
Hanford Dorset 12 D2
Hanging Heaton Kirk 90 H6
Hanging Houghton Nhants 60 G6
Hanging Langford Wilts 21 K7
Hangleton Br & H 24 G9
Hangleton W Susx 24 C10
Hanham S Glos 32 B10
Hankelow Ches E 70 B5
Hankerton Wilts 33 J3
Hankham E Susx 25 P9
Hanley C Stke 70 F5
Hanley Castle Worcs 46 F6
Hanley Child Worcs 57 M11
Hanley Swan Worcs 46 F6
Hanley William Worcs 57 M11
Hanlith N York 96 C8
Hanmer Wrexhm 69 N7
Hannaford Devon 17 L6
Hannah Lincs 87 N5
Hannington Hants 22 F3
Hannington Nhants 60 H6
Hannington Swindn 33 N6
Hannington Wick Swindn 33 N5
Hanscombe End C Beds 50 D4
Hanslope M Keyn 49 M5
Hanthorpe Lincs 74 A6
Hanwell Gt Lon 36 E5
Hanwell Oxon 48 D6
Hanwood Shrops 56 G3
Hanworth Gt Lon 36 D6
Hanworth Norfk 76 H4
Happendon Services S Lans 116 B4
Happisburgh Norfk 77 M5
Happisburgh Common Norfk 77 M6
Hapsford Ches W 81 P10
Hapton Lancs 89 M4
Hapton Norfk 64 H2
Harberton Devon 7 K7
Harbertonford Devon 7 K7
Harbledown Kent 39 K10
Harborne Birm 58 F8
Harborough Magna Warwks 59 Q9
Harbottle Nthumb 118 H10
Harbourneford Devon 7 J6
Harbours Hill Worcs 58 E11
Harbridge Hants 13 K2
Harbridge Green Hants 13 K2
Harbury Warwks 48 C3
Harby Leics 73 J4
Harby Notts 85 Q6
Harcombe Devon 9 L8
Harcombe Devon 10 D6
Harcombe Bottom Devon 10 G5
Harden C Brad 90 D3
Harden Wsall 58 F4
Hardendale Cumb 101 Q8
Hardenhuish Wilts 32 H10
Hardgate Abers 151 K7
Hardgate D & G 108 H7
Hardgate N York 97 L8
Hardgate W Duns 125 N3
Hardham W Susx 24 B7
Hardhorn Lancs 88 D3
Hardingham Norfk 76 E11
Hardingstone Nhants 60 G9
Hardington Somset 20 D4
Hardington Mandeville Somset 11 L2
Hardington Marsh Somset 11 L2
Hardington Moor Somset 11 L2
Hardisworthy Devon 16 C7
Hardley Hants 14 D6
Hardley Street Norfk 77 M11
Hardmead M Keyn 49 P5
Hardraw N York 96 C2
Hardsough Lancs 89 M6
Hardstoft Derbys 84 F8
Hardway Hants 14 G6
Hardway Somset 20 D8
Hardwick Bucks 49 M11
Hardwick Cambs 62 E9
Hardwick Nhants 60 H7
Hardwick Norfk 65 J4
Hardwick Oxon 34 C3
Hardwick Oxon 48 G9
Hardwick Rothm 84 G3
Hardwick Wsall 58 G5
Hardwicke Gloucs 32 E2
Hardwicke Gloucs 46 H9
Hardwick Hall Derbys 84 G8
Hardy's Green Essex 52 F7
Harebeating E Susx 25 N8

Hareby Lincs 87 K7
Hare Croft C Brad 90 D3
Harefield Gt Lon 36 C2
Hare Green Essex 53 K6
Hare Hatch Wokham 35 M9
Harehill Derbys 71 M7
Harehills Leeds 91 J4
Harehope Nthumb 119 L6
Harelaw Border 117 O6
Harelaw D & G 110 H5
Harelaw Dur 113 J10
Hareplain Kent 26 D4
Haresceugh Cumb 102 B2
Harescombe Gloucs 32 F2
Haresfield Gloucs 32 E2
Hare Street Hants 22 B8
Hare Street Essex 51 K9
Hare Street Essex 51 M10
Hare Street Herts 51 J5
Harewood Leeds 97 M11
Harewood End Herefs 45 Q9
Harford Devon 6 G7
Hargate Norfk 64 G3
Hargatewall Derbys 83 P9
Hargrave Ches W 69 N2
Hargrave Nhants 61 M6
Hargrave Suffk 63 N9
Harker Cumb 110 G8
Harkstead Suffk 53 L8
Harlaston Staffs 59 K2
Harlaxton Lincs 73 M4
Harlech Gwynd 67 K8
Harlech Castle Gwynd 67 K8
Harlescott Shrops 69 N11
Harlesden Gt Lon 36 F4
Harlesthorpe Derbys 84 G5
Harleston Devon 7 K9
Harleston Norfk 65 J5
Harleston Suffk 64 E9
Harlestone Nhants 60 F8
Harle Syke Lancs 89 P3
Harley Rothm 91 K11
Harley Shrops 57 K4
Harlington C Beds 50 B4
Harlington Donc 91 M10
Harlington Gt Lon 36 C5
Harlosh Highld 152 D9
Harlow Essex 51 K8
Harlow Carr RHS N York 97 L10
Harlow Hill Nthumb 112 G7
Harlthorpe E R Yk 92 B3
Harlton Cambs 62 E10
Harlyn Cnwll 4 D6
Harman's Cross Dorset 12 G8
Harmby N York 96 H3
Harmer Green Herts 50 G7
Harmer Hill Shrops 69 N10
Harmondsworth Gt Lon 36 C5
Harmston Lincs 86 C8
Harnage Shrops 57 K4
Harnham Nthumb 112 G4
Harnhill Gloucs 33 K3
Harold Hill Gt Lon 37 M2
Haroldston West Pembks 40 G7
Haroldswick Shet 169 t1
Harold Wood Gt Lon 37 N2
Harome N York 98 C4
Harpenden Herts 50 D8
Harpford Devon 10 B6
Harpham E R Yk 99 M8
Harpley Norfk 75 Q5
Harpley Worcs 46 C2
Harpole Nhants 60 E8
Harpsdale Highld 167 K5
Harpsden Oxon 35 L8
Harpswell Lincs 86 B3
Harpurhey Manch 83 J4
Harpur Hill Derbys 83 N10
Harraby Cumb 110 H10
Harracott Devon 17 K6
Harrapool Highld 145 L3
Harrietfield P & K 134 B2
Harrietsham Kent 38 E11
Harringay Gt Lon 36 H4
Harrington Cumb 100 C5
Harrington Lincs 87 L6
Harrington Nhants 60 G4
Harringworth Nhants 73 N11
Harris Highld 144 f8
Harriseahead Staffs 70 F3
Harriston Cumb 100 G2
Harrogate N York 97 M9
Harrogate Crematorium N York 97 M10
Harrold Bed 61 K9
Harrop Dale Oldham 90 C9
Harrow Gt Lon 36 E3
Harrowbarrow Cnwll 5 Q7
Harrowden Bed 61 N11
Harrowgate Village Darltn 103 Q7
Harrow Green Suffk 64 B11
Harrow on the Hill Gt Lon 36 E3
Harrow Weald Gt Lon 36 E2
Harston Cambs 62 F10
Harston Leics 73 L4
Harswell E R Yk 92 D2
Hart Hartpl 104 E3
Hartburn Nthumb 112 G4
Hartburn S on T 104 D7
Hartest Suffk 64 A11
Hartfield E Susx 25 L3
Hartford Cambs 62 C6
Hartford Ches W 82 D10
Hartford Somset 18 C8
Hartfordbridge Hants 23 L3
Hartford End Essex 51 Q7
Hartforth N York 103 N9
Hartgrove Dorset 20 F11
Harthill Ches W 69 N3
Harthill N Lans 126 G5
Harthill Rothm 84 G4
Hartington Derbys 71 L2
Hartington Nthumb 112 F3
Hartland Devon 16 C7
Hartland Quay Devon 16 C7
Hartlebury Worcs 58 B10
Hartlepool Hartpl 104 F3
Hartlepool Crematorium Hartpl 104 F4
Hartley Cumb 102 C8
Hartley Kent 26 C5
Hartley Kent 37 P7
Hartley Nthumb 113 M5
Hartley Green Kent 37 P7
Hartley Green Staffs 70 H9
Hartley Wespall Hants 23 J3
Hartley Wintney Hants 23 L3
Hartlip Kent 38 D9

274 Hartoft End – High Bickington

Hartoft End N York 98 E2
Harton N York 98 E8
Harton S Tyne 113 N7
Harton Shrops 56 H7
Hartpury Gloucs 46 E10
Hartshead Kirk 90 F6
Hartshead Moor Services Calder 90 F6
Hartshill C Stke 70 F5
Hartshill Warwks 59 M6
Hartshorne Derbys 71 Q10
Hartside Nthumb 119 J7
Hartsop Cumb 101 M8
Hart Station Hartpl 104 E3
Hartswell Somset 18 E9
Hartwell Nhants 49 L4
Hartwith N York 97 K8
Hartwood N Lans 126 E6
Hartwoodmyres Border 117 N6
Harvel Kent 37 Q8
Harvington Worcs 47 L5
Harvington Worcs 58 C10
Harwell Notts 85 L2
Harwell Oxon 34 E7
Harwich Essex 53 N5
Harwood Bolton 89 L8
Harwood Dur 102 F4
Harwood Dale N York 105 Q11
Harwood Lee Bolton 89 L8
Harwood Park Crematorium Herts 50 G6
Harworth Notts 85 K2
Hasbury Dudley 58 E8
Hascombe Surrey 24 B3
Haselbech Nhants 60 F5
Haselbury Plucknett Somset 11 K2
Haseley Warwks 59 K11
Haseley Green Warwks 59 K11
Haseley Knob Warwks 59 K10
Haselor Warwks 47 M3
Hasfield Gloucs 46 F9
Hasguard Pembks 40 G9
Hasholme E R Yk 92 D4
Haskayne Lancs 88 D9
Hasketon Suffk 65 J11
Hasland Derbys 84 E7
Haslemere Surrey 23 P8
Haslingden Lancs 89 M6
Haslingfield Cambs 62 F10
Haslington Ches E 70 C3
Hassall Ches E 70 D3
Hassall Green Ches E 70 D3
Hassell Street Kent 27 J2
Hassingham Norfk 77 M10
Hassness Cumb 100 G7
Hassocks W Susx 24 H7
Hassop Derbys 84 B6
Haste Hill Surrey 23 P8
Haster Highld 167 P6
Hasthorpe Lincs 87 N7
Hastingleigh Kent 27 J2
Hastings E Susx 26 D10
Hastings Somset 19 K11
Hastings Crematorium E Susx 26 D9
Hastingwood Essex 51 L9
Hastoe Herts 35 P3
Haswell Dur 104 C2
Haswell Plough Dur 104 C2
Hatch C Beds 61 Q11
Hatch Beauchamp Somset 19 K10
Hatch End Bed 61 N8
Hatch End Gt Lon 36 D2
Hatchet Gate Hants 14 C6
Hatching Green Herts 50 D8
Hatchmere Ches W 82 C10
Hatcliffe NE Lin 93 M10
Hatfield Donc 91 R9
Hatfield Herefs 46 A3
Hatfield Herts 50 F9
Hatfield Worcs 46 G4
Hatfield Broad Oak Essex 51 M7
Hatfield Heath Essex 51 M7
Hatfield Peverel Essex 52 C9
Hatfield Woodhouse Donc 92 A9
Hatford Oxon 34 B6
Hatherden Hants 22 B4
Hatherleigh Devon 8 D4
Hathern Leics 72 E6
Hatherop Gloucs 33 N3
Hathersage Derbys 84 B4
Hathersage Booths Derbys 84 B4
Hatherton Ches E 70 B5
Hatherton Staffs 58 E2
Hatley St George Cambs 62 C10
Hatt Cnwll 5 Q9
Hattersley Tamesd 83 L6
Hattingley Hants 22 H7
Hatton Abers 159 Q10
Hatton Angus 142 H9
Hatton Derbys 71 N8
Hatton Gt Lon 36 C5
Hatton Lincs 86 G5
Hatton Shrops 56 H6
Hatton Warrtn 82 C8
Hatton Warwks 59 K11
Hatton Heath Ches W 69 N2
Hatton of Fintray Abers 151 L4
Haugh E Ayrs 115 J2
Haugh Lincs 87 M5
Haugh Rochdl 89 Q8
Haugham Lincs 87 K4
Haughhead E Duns 125 Q2
Haugh Head Nthumb 119 K5
Haughley Suffk 64 E9
Haughley Green Suffk 64 E9
Haugh of Glass Moray 158 B10
Haugh of Urr D & G 108 H7
Haughs of Kinnaird Angus 143 L6
Haughton Ches E 69 Q3
Haughton Notts 85 L6
Haughton Powys 69 K11
Haughton Shrops 57 M5
Haughton Shrops 57 N3
Haughton Shrops 69 L9
Haughton Shrops 69 Q11
Haughton Staffs 70 F10
Haughton Green Tamesd 83 K6
Haughton le Skerne Darltn 104 B7
Haultwick Herts 50 H6
Haunton Staffs 59 K2
Hautes Croix Jersey 11 b1
Hauxton Cambs 62 F10
Havannah Ches E 70 F2
Havant Hants 15 K5
Havant Crematorium Hants 15 K5
Haven Herefs 45 N4
Haven Bank Lincs 86 H10
Haven Side E R Yk 93 L5
Havenstreet IoW 14 G8
Havercroft Wakefd 91 K8
Haverfordwest Pembks 41 J7
Haverhill Suffk 63 L11
Haverigg Cumb 94 D5
Havering-atte-Bower Gt Lon 37 M2
Haversham M Keyn 49 M6
Haverthwaite Cumb 94 G4
Haverton Hill S on T 104 E6
Havyat N Som 19 N2
Havyatt Somset 19 P7
Hawarden Flints 81 L11
Hawbridge Worcs 46 H5
Hawbush Green Essex 52 C7
Hawcoat Cumb 94 E6
Hawen Cerdgn 42 F5
Hawes N York 96 C3
Hawe's Green Norfk 65 J2
Hawford Worcs 46 F2
Hawick Border 117 Q8
Hawkchurch Devon 10 G4
Hawkedon Suffk 63 N10
Hawkenbury Kent 26 D2
Hawkeridge Wilts 20 G4
Hawkerland Devon 9 Q7
Hawker's Cove Cnwll 4 E6
Hawkesbury S Glos 32 E7
Hawkesbury Warwks 59 N8
Hawkesbury Upton S Glos 32 E7
Hawkes End Covtry 59 L8
Hawk Green Stockp 83 L7
Hawkhill Nthumb 119 P8
Hawkhurst Kent 26 C5
Hawkhurst Common E Susx 25 M7
Hawkinge Kent 27 M4
Hawkinge Crematorium Kent 27 M3
Hawkley Hants 23 K9
Hawkley Wigan 82 C4
Hawkridge Somset 17 R5
Hawksdale Cumb 110 G11
Hawkshaw Bury 89 M7
Hawkshead Cumb 101 L11
Hawkshead Hill Cumb 101 K11
Hawksland S Lans 116 A3
Hawkspur Green Essex 51 Q4
Hawkstone Shrops 69 Q8
Hawkswick N York 96 E6
Hawksworth Leeds 90 F2
Hawksworth Notts 73 K2
Hawkwell Essex 38 E3
Hawkwell Nthumb 112 G6
Hawley Hants 23 N3
Hawley Kent 37 M6
Hawling Gloucs 47 L10
Hawnby N York 98 A3
Haworth C Brad 90 C3
Hawridge Bucks 35 P3
Hawstead Suffk 64 B10
Hawstead Green Suffk 64 B10
Hawthorn Dur 113 P11
Hawthorn Hants 23 J8
Hawthorn Rhondd 30 E7
Hawthorn Hill Br For 35 N10
Hawthorn Hill Lincs 86 H9
Hawthorpe Lincs 73 Q5
Hawton Notts 85 N10
Haxby C York 98 C9
Haxby Gates C York 98 C9
Haxey N Linc 92 C11
Haxey Carr N Linc 92 C10
Haxted Surrey 37 K11
Haxton Wilts 21 M5
Hay Cnwll 3 P3
Hay Cnwll 4 F7
Haycombe Crematorium BaNES 20 D2
Haydock St Hel 82 C5
Haydon BaNES 20 C4
Haydon Dorset 20 C11
Haydon Somset 19 J10
Haydon Bridge Nthumb 112 B8
Haydon Wick Swindn 33 M7
Haye Cnwll 5 P7
Hayes Gt Lon 36 C4
Hayes Gt Lon 37 K7
Hayes End Gt Lon 36 C4
Hayfield Ag & B 131 M3
Hayfield Derbys 83 M7
Haygate Wrekin 57 L2
Hay Green Norfk 75 K7
Hayhillock Angus 143 J9
Hayle Cnwll 2 F6
Hayle Port Cnwll 2 F6
Hayley Green Dudley 58 E8
Hayling Island Hants 15 K6
Haymoor Green Ches E 70 B4
Hayne Devon 9 J7
Hayne Devon 18 C11
Haynes (Church End) C Beds 50 C2
Haynes (Northwood End) C Beds 50 C2
Haynes (Silver End) C Beds 50 D2
Haynes (West End) C Beds 50 C2
Hay-on-Wye Powys 45 J6
Hayscastle Pembks 40 G5
Hayscastle Cross Pembks 40 H5
Haysden Kent 37 N11
Hay Street Herts 51 J5
Hayton Cumb 100 F2
Hayton Cumb 111 K9
Hayton E R Yk 98 G11
Hayton Notts 85 M4
Hayton's Bent Shrops 57 J8
Haytor Vale Devon 9 J9
Haytown Devon 16 F9
Haywards Heath W Susx 24 H6
Haywood Donc 91 P8
Haywood Herefs 45 P8
Haywood Oaks Notts 85 K9
Hazards Green E Susx 25 Q8
Hazelbank S Lans 126 E8
Hazelbury Bryan Dorset 12 B3
Hazeleigh Essex 52 D11
Hazeley Hants 23 K3
Hazelford Notts 85 M11
Hazel Grove Stockp 83 K7
Hazelhurst Tamesd 83 L4
Hazelslade Staffs 58 F2
Hazel Street Kent 25 Q3
Hazel Stub Suffk 51 Q2
Hazelton Walls Fife 135 J3
Hazelwood Derbys 84 D11
Hazlemere Bucks 35 N5
Hazlerigg N u Ty 113 K6
Hazles Staffs 71 J5
Hazleton Gloucs 47 L11
Heacham Norfk 75 N3
Headbourne Worthy Hants 22 E8
Headbrook Herefs 45 K3
Headcorn Kent 26 D3
Headingley Leeds 90 H3
Headington Oxon 34 F3
Headlam Dur 103 N7
Headlesscross N Lans 126 G6
Headless Cross Worcs 58 F11
Headley Hants 22 F2
Headley Hants 23 M7
Headley Surrey 36 F10
Headley Down Hants 23 M7
Headley Heath Worcs 58 G9
Headon Devon 16 F11
Headon Notts 85 M5
Heads Nook Cumb 111 K10
Heage Derbys 84 E10
Healaugh N York 97 R11
Healaugh N York 103 K11
Heald Green Stockp 82 H7
Heale Devon 17 L2
Heale Somset 18 H10
Heale Somset 19 L9
Healey N York 97 J4
Healey Nthumb 112 F9
Healey Rochdl 89 P7
Healey Wakefd 90 H7
Healeyfield Dur 112 G11
Healing NE Lin 93 M8
Heamoor Cnwll 2 D7
Heanor Derbys 84 F11
Heanton Punchardon Devon 17 J4
Heapham Lincs 85 Q3
Hearn Hants 23 M7
Heart of England Crematorium Warwks 59 N6
Heart of Scotland Services N Lans 126 G5
Hearts Delight Kent 38 E9
Heasley Mill Devon 17 N5
Heast Highld 145 K4
Heath Derbys 84 G7
Heath Wakefd 91 K6
Heath and Reach C Beds 49 P9
Heath Common W Susx 24 C7
Heathcote Derbys 71 L2
Heathcote Shrops 70 B9
Heath End Bucks 35 N5
Heath End Hants 22 D2
Heath End Leics 72 B6
Heath End Warwks 47 P2
Heather Leics 72 B8
Heathfield Cambs 62 G11
Heathfield Devon 9 K9
Heathfield E Susx 25 N6
Heathfield N York 96 H7
Heathfield Somset 18 G9
Heathfield Village Oxon 48 F11
Heath Green Worcs 58 G10
Heath Hall D & G 109 L5
Heath Hayes & Wimblebury Staffs 58 F2
Heath Hill Shrops 57 P2
Heath House Somset 19 M5
Heathrow Airport Gt Lon 36 C5
Heathstock Devon 10 E4
Heathton Shrops 57 Q6
Heath Town Wolves 58 D5
Heathwaite N York 104 E10
Heatley Staffs 71 K9
Heatley Warrtn 82 F7
Heaton Bolton 89 K9
Heaton C Brad 90 E3
Heaton Lancs 95 J8
Heaton N u Ty 113 L7
Heaton Staffs 70 H2
Heaton Chapel Stockp 83 J6
Heaton Mersey Stockp 83 J6
Heaton Norris Stockp 83 J6
Heaton's Bridge Lancs 88 E8
Heaverham Kent 37 N9
Heaviley Stockp 83 K7
Heavitree Devon 9 M6
Hebburn S Tyne 113 M8
Hebden N York 96 F8
Hebden Bridge Calder 90 B5
Hebden Green Ches W 82 D11
Hebing End Herts 50 H6
Hebron Carmth 41 N5
Hebron IoA 78 H8
Hebron Nthumb 113 J3
Heckfield Hants 23 K2
Heckfield Green Suffk 64 H6
Heckfordbridge Essex 52 F7
Heckington Lincs 74 B2
Heckmondwike Kirk 90 G6
Heddington Wilts 33 J11
Heddon-on-the-Wall Nthumb 112 H7
Hedenham Norfk 65 L3
Hedge End Hants 14 E4
Hedgerley Bucks 35 Q7
Hedgerley Green Bucks 35 Q7
Hedging Somset 19 K9
Hedley on the Hill Nthumb 112 G9
Hednesford Staffs 58 E2
Hedon E R Yk 93 L5
Hedsor Bucks 35 P7
Heeley Sheff 84 E4
Hegdon Hill Herefs 46 A4
Heglibister Shet 169 q8
Heighington Darltn 103 P6
Heighington Lincs 86 D7
Heightington Worcs 57 P10
Heiton Border 118 D4
Hele Devon 7 J4
Hele Devon 9 N4
Hele Devon 17 J2
Hele Somset 18 G10
Helebridge Cnwll 16 C11
Hele Lane Devon 9 J2
Helensburgh Ag & B 132 B11
Helenton S Ayrs 125 K11
Helford Cnwll 3 K8
Helford Passage Cnwll 3 K8
Helhoughton Norfk 76 B6
Helions Bumpstead Essex 51 Q2
Hellaby Rothm 84 H2
Helland Cnwll 4 H7
Hellandbridge Cnwll 4 H7
Hell Corner W Berk 22 C2
Hellescott Cnwll 5 M4
Hellesdon Norfk 77 J9
Hellesveor Cnwll 2 E5
Hellidon Nhants 60 B9
Hellifield N York 96 C9
Hellingly E Susx 25 N8
Hellington Norfk 77 L11
Helm Nthumb 119 N11
Helmdon Nhants 48 G6
Helme Kirk 90 D8
Helmingham Suffk 64 H10
Helmington Row Dur 103 N3
Helmsdale Highld 163 N3
Helmshore Lancs 89 M6
Helmsley N York 98 C4
Helperby N York 97 P7
Helperthorpe N York 99 K6
Helpringham Lincs 74 B2
Helpston C Pete 74 B9
Helsby Ches W 81 P9
Helsey Lincs 87 P6
Helston Cnwll 2 H8
Helstone Cnwll 4 H5
Helton Cumb 101 P6
Helwith N York 103 L10
Helwith Bridge N York 96 B7
Hemblington Norfk 77 L9
Hembridge Somset 19 Q7
Hemel Hempstead Herts 50 C9
Hemerdon Devon 6 F7
Hemingbrough N York 91 R4
Hemingby Lincs 86 H6
Hemingfield Barns 91 K10
Hemingford Abbots Cambs 62 C6
Hemingford Grey Cambs 62 C6
Hemingstone Suffk 64 G11
Hemington Leics 72 D5
Hemington Nhants 61 N3
Hemington Somset 20 D4
Hemley Suffk 53 N3
Hemlington Middsb 104 F8
Hempholme E R Yk 99 M10
Hempnall Norfk 65 J3
Hempnall Green Norfk 65 J3
Hempriggs Moray 157 L5
Hempstead Essex 51 P3
Hempstead Medway 38 C9
Hempstead Norfk 76 G4
Hempstead Norfk 77 N6
Hempsted Gloucs 46 F11
Hempton Norfk 76 C6
Hempton Oxon 48 D8
Hemsby Norfk 77 P8
Hemswell Lincs 86 B2
Hemswell Cliff Lincs 86 B3
Hemsworth Wakefd 91 L8
Hemyock Devon 10 C2
Henbury Bristl 31 Q9
Henbury Ches E 83 J10
Hendham Devon 7 J8
Hendomen Powys 56 C5
Hendon Gt Lon 36 F3
Hendon Sundld 113 P9
Hendon Crematorium Gt Lon 36 F2
Hendra Cnwll 3 J6
Hendra Cnwll 4 G6
Hendre Brdgnd 29 P8
Hendre Flints 80 H11
Hendre Mons 31 N2
Hendy Carmth 28 G4
Heneglwys IoA 78 G9
Henfield W Susx 24 F7
Henford Devon 5 P3
Henghurst Kent 26 G4
Hengoed Caerph 30 G6
Hengoed Powys 45 J4
Hengoed Shrops 69 J8
Hengrave Suffk 63 P7
Henham Essex 51 M5
Heniarth Powys 55 Q3
Henlade Somset 19 J10
Henley Dorset 11 P4
Henley Gloucs 46 H11
Henley Shrops 56 H7
Henley Shrops 57 J9
Henley Somset 19 M8
Henley Suffk 64 H11
Henley W Susx 23 N9
Henley Green Covtry 59 N8
Henley-in-Arden Warwks 59 J11
Henley-on-Thames Oxon 35 L8
Henley Park Surrey 23 P4
Henley's Down E Susx 26 B9
Henley Street Kent 37 Q7
Henllan Cerdgn 42 G6
Henllan Denbgs 80 E11
Henllan Amgoed Carmth 41 N7
Henllys Torfn 31 J6
Henlow C Beds 50 E3
Hennock Devon 9 K8
Henny Street Essex 52 E4
Henryd Conwy 79 P10
Henry's Moat (Castell Hendre) Pembks 41 K5
Hensall N York 91 P6
Henshaw Nthumb 111 Q8
Hensingham Cumb 100 C7
Henstead Suffk 65 P4
Hensting Hants 22 E10
Henstridge Somset 20 D11
Henstridge Ash Somset 20 D10
Henstridge Marsh Somset 20 D10
Henton Oxon 35 L4
Henton Somset 19 N5
Henwick Worcs 46 F3
Henwood Cnwll 5 M7
Henwood Oxon 34 E4
Heol-las Swans 29 J5
Heol Senni Powys 44 C10
Heol-y-Cyw Brdgnd 29 P8
Hepburn Nthumb 119 L6
Hepple Nthumb 119 J10
Hepscott Nthumb 113 K4
Heptonstall Calder 90 B5
Hepworth Kirk 90 F9
Hepworth Suffk 64 D7
Herbrandston Pembks 40 G9
Hereford Herefs 45 Q7
Hereford Crematorium Herefs 45 P6
Hereson Kent 39 Q8
Heribusta Highld 152 F3
Heriot Border 128 C9
Hermiston C Edin 127 M3
Hermitage Border 117
Hermitage Dorset 11
Hermitage W Berk 34
Hermitage W Susx 15
Hermit Hill Barns 91
Hermon Carmth 42
Hermon IoA 78
Hermon Pembks 41
Herne Kent 39
Herne Bay Kent 39
Herne Common Kent 39
Herne Hill Gt Lon 36
Herne Pound Kent 37
Herner Devon 17
Hernhill Kent 39
Herodsfoot Cnwll 5
Heronden Kent 39
Herongate Essex 37
Heronsford S Ayrs 114
Heronsgate Herts 36
Herriard Hants 23
Herringfleet Suffk 65
Herring's Green Bed 50
Herringswell Suffk 63
Herringthorpe Rothm 84
Herrington Sundld 113
Hersden Kent 39
Hersham Cnwll 16
Hersham Surrey 36
Herstmonceux E Susx 25
Herston Dorset 12
Herston Ork 169
Hertford Herts 50
Hertford Heath Herts 51
Hertingfordbury Herts 50
Hesketh Bank Lancs 88
Hesketh Lane Lancs 89
Hesket Newmarket Cumb 101
Heskin Green Lancs 88
Hesleden Dur 104
Hesleden N York 96
Hesley Donc 85
Hesleyside Nthumb 112
Heslington C York 98
Hessay C York 97
Hessenford Cnwll 5
Hessett Suffk 64
Hessle E R Yk 92
Hessle Wakefd 91
Hest Bank Lancs 95
Hestley Green Suffk 64
Heston Gt Lon 36
Heston Services Gt Lon 36
Hestwall Ork 169
Heswall Wirral 81
Hethe Oxon 48
Hethersett Norfk 76
Hethersgill Cumb 111
Hetherside Cumb 110
Hetherson Green Ches W 69
Hethpool Nthumb 118
Hett Dur 103
Hetton N York 96
Hetton-le-Hole Sundld 113
Hetton Steads Nthumb 119
Heugh Nthumb 112
Heughhead Abers 150
Heugh Head Border 129
Heveningham Suffk 65
Hever Kent 37
Heversham Cumb 95
Hevingham Norfk 76
Hewas Water Cnwll 3
Hewelsfield Gloucs 31
Hewenden C Brad 90
Hewish N Som 19
Hewish Somset 11
Hewood Dorset 10
Hexham Nthumb 112
Hextable Kent 37
Hexthorpe Donc 91
Hexton Herts 50
Hexworthy Cnwll 5
Hexworthy Devon 6
Hey Lancs 89
Heybridge Essex 51
Heybridge Essex 52
Heybridge Basin Essex 52
Heybrook Bay Devon 6
Heydon Cambs 51
Heydon Norfk 76
Heydour Lincs 73
Heyhead Manch 82
Hey Houses Lancs 88
Heylipoll Ag & B 136
Heylor Shet 169
Heyrod Tamesd 83
Heysham Lancs 95
Heyshaw N York 97
Heyshott W Susx 23
Heyside Oldham 89
Heytesbury Wilts 20
Heythrop Oxon 48
Heywood Rochdl 89
Heywood Wilts 20
Hibaldstow N Linc 92
Hickleton Donc 91
Hickling Norfk 77
Hickling Notts 72
Hickling Green Norfk 77
Hickling Heath Norfk 77
Hickling Pastures Notts 72
Hickmans Green Kent 39
Hicks Forstal Kent 39
Hickstead W Susx 24
Hidcote Bartrim Gloucs 47
Hidcote Boyce Gloucs 47
High Ackworth Wakefd 91
Higham Barns 91
Higham Derbys 84
Higham Kent 37
Higham Kent 38
Higham Lancs 89
Higham Suffk 52
Higham Suffk 63
Higham Dykes Nthumb 112
Higham Ferrers Nhants 61
Higham Gobion C Beds 50
Higham Hill Gt Lon 37
Higham on the Hill Leics 72
Highampton Devon 8
Highams Park Gt Lon 37
High Angerton Nthumb 112
High Ardwell D & G 106
High Auldgirth D & G 109
High Bankhill Cumb 101
High Beach Essex 51
High Bentham N York 95
High Bewaldeth Cumb 100
High Bickington Devon 17

h Biggins Cumb....95 N5
h Birkwith N York....96 B5
h Blantyre S Lans....126 B6
h Bonnybridge Falk....126 E2
h Borrans Cumb....101 M10
h Bradley N York....96 F11
h Bray Devon....17 M5
hbridge Hants....22 E10
hbridge Somset....19 K5
hbrook W Susx....25 J4
h Brooms Kent....25 N2
h Bullen Devon....17 J7
hburton Kirk....90 F8
hbury Gt Lon....36 H3
hbury Somset....20 C5
h Buston Nthumb....119 P9
h Callerton Nthumb....113 J6
h Casterton Cumb....95 N5
h Catton E R Yk....98 E10
hclere Hants....22 D3
hcliffe Dorset....13 M6
h Close Dur....103 N7
h Cogges Oxon....34 C3
h Common Norfk....76 D10
h Coniscliffe Darltn....103 P7
h Crosby Cumb....111 J9
h Cross Cnwll....3 J8
h Cross E Ayrs....125 L8
h Cross Hants....23 K9
h Cross Herts....51 J7
hcross Lancs....88 C3
h Cross W Susx....24 F7
h Cross Warwks....59 K11
h Drummore D & G....106 F10
h Dubmire Sundld....113 M11
h Easter Essex....51 P8
h Eggborough N York....91 P6
h Ellington N York....97 J4
her Alham Somset....20 C6
her Ansty Dorset....12 C4
her Ballam Lancs....88 D4
her Bartle Lancs....88 G4
her Berry End C Beds....49 Q8
her Bockhampton Dorset....12 B6
her Brixham Torbay....7 N8
her Burrowton Devon....9 P5
her Burwardsley Ches W....69 P3
h Ercall Wrekin....69 Q11
her Chillington Somset....10 H2
her Clovelly Devon....16 E7
hercombe Somset....18 B8
her Coombe Dorset....11 L6
her Disley Ches E....83 L8
her Folds Wigan....82 E4
her Gabwell Devon....7 N5
her Halstock Leigh Dorset....11 L3
her Harpers Lancs....89 N3
her Heysham Lancs....95 J2
her Hurdsfield Ches E....83 K10
her Irlam Salfd....82 F5
her Kingcombe Dorset....11 L4
her Kinnerton Flints....69 K2
her Marston Ches W....82 E9
her Muddiford Devon....17 K4
her Nyland Dorset....20 D10
her Ogden Rochdl....90 B8
her Pentire Cnwll....2 H8
her Penwortham Lancs....88 G5
her Prestacott Devon....5 P2
her Studfold N York....96 B6
her Town Cnwll....3 L5
her Town Cnwll....4 G9
her Town IoS....2 c1
her Tregantle Cnwll....5 Q11
her Walton Lancs....88 H5
her Walton Warrtn....82 C7
her Wambrook Somset....10 F3
her Waterston Dorset....11 Q5
her Whatcombe Dorset....12 D4
her Wheelton Lancs....89 J6
her Whitley Ches W....82 D8
her Wincham Ches W....82 E9
her Wraxall Dorset....11 M4
her Wych Ches W....69 N6
h Etherley Dur....103 N5
h Ferry Lincs....87 L11
hfield E R Yk....92 B3
hfield Gatesd....112 H9
hfield N Ayrs....125 J7
hfields Donc....91 N9
h Flats Kirk....90 G9
h Garrett Essex....52 C6
hgate Lincs....5 K4
hgate Gt Lon....36 G3
hgate Kent....25 C5
h Grange Dur....103 N4
h Grantley N York....97 K7
h Green Cumb....101 M10
h Green Kirk....90 G8
h Green Norfk....64 H4
h Green Norfk....76 G10
h Green Sheff....91 J11
h Green Shrops....57 N8
h Green Suffk....64 B9
h Green Worcs....46 G5
hgreen Manor Nthumb....112 B2
h Halden Kent....26 E4
h Halstow Medway....38 C6
h Ham Somset....19 M8
h Harrington Cumb....100 D5
h Harrogate N York....97 M9
h Haswell Dur....104 C2
h Hatton Shrops....69 R10
h Hauxley Nthumb....119 Q10
h Hawsker N York....105 P9
h Hesket Cumb....101 N2
h Hoyland Barns....90 H9
h Hunsley E R Yk....92 G3
h Hurstwood E Susx....25 L5
h Hutton N York....98 F7
h Ireby Cumb....100 H3
h Kelling Norfk....76 G3
h Kilburn N York....97 R5
h Killerby N York....99 M4
h Knipe Cumb....101 P7
h Lands Dur....103 M5
hlane Ches E....83 J11
hlane Derbys....84 F4
h Lane Stockp....83 L7

High Lanes Cnwll....2 F6
High Laver Essex....51 M9
Highlaws Cumb....109 P11
Highleadon Gloucs....46 E10
High Legh Ches E....82 F8
Highleigh W Susx....15 M7
High Leven S on T....104 E8
Highley Shrops....57 N8
High Littleton BaNES....20 B3
High Lorton Cumb....100 G5
High Marishes N York....98 G5
High Marnham Notts....85 P6
High Melton Donc....91 N10
High Mickley Nthumb....112 G8
Highmoor Cumb....110 E11
Highmoor Oxon....35 K8
Highmoor Cross Oxon....35 K8
Highmoor Hill Mons....31 N7
High Moorsley Sundld....113 M11
Highnam Gloucs....46 E11
Highnam Green Gloucs....46 E10
High Newport Sundld....113 N10
High Newton Cumb....95 J4
High Nibthwaite Cumb....94 F3
High Offley Staffs....70 D9
High Ongar Essex....51 N10
High Onn Staffs....70 E11
High Park Corner Essex....52 H7
High Pennyvenie E Ayrs....115 J6
High Post Wilts....21 N7
Highridge N Som....31 Q11
High Roding Essex....51 P7
High Row Cumb....101 L3
High Row Cumb....101 L6
High Salter Lancs....95 M8
High Salvington W Susx....24 D9
High Scales Cumb....110 C11
High Seaton Cumb....100 D4
High Shaw N York....96 C2
High Side Cumb....100 H4
High Spen Gatesd....112 H9
Highstead Kent....39 M8
Highsted Kent....38 F9
High Stoop Dur....103 M2
High Street Cnwll....3 P3
High Street Kent....26 B5
Highstreet Kent....39 J9
High Street Suffk....65 N10
High Street Suffk....65 N7
Highstreet Green Essex....52 C5
Highstreet Green Surrey....23 Q7
Hightae D & G....109 N5
Highter's Heath Birm....58 G9
High Throston Hartpl....104 E4
Hightown Ches E....70 F2
Hightown Hants....13 L4
Hightown Sefton....81 L4
High Town Staffs....58 E2
Hightown Green Suffk....64 D10
High Toynton Lincs....87 J7
High Trewhitt Nthumb....119 K9
High Urpeth Dur....113 K10
High Valleyfield Fife....134 C10
High Warden Nthumb....112 D7
Highway Herefs....45 P5
Highway Wilts....33 K10
Highweek Devon....7 L4
High Westwood Dur....112 H9
Highwood Essex....51 P10
Highwood Staffs....71 K8
Highwood Hill Gt Lon....36 F2
High Woolaston Gloucs....31 Q5
High Worsall N York....104 C9
Highworth Swindn....33 P6
High Wray Cumb....101 L11
High Wych Herts....51 L8
High Wycombe Bucks....35 N6
Hilborough Norfk....75 R10
Hilcote Derbys....84 G9
Hilcott Wilts....21 M3
Hildenborough Kent....37 N11
Hilden Park Kent....37 N11
Hildersham Cambs....62 H11
Hilderstone Staffs....70 H8
Hilderthorpe E R Yk....99 P7
Hilfield Dorset....11 N3
Hilgay Norfk....75 M11
Hill S Glos....32 B5
Hill Warwks....59 Q11
Hillam N York....91 N5
Hillbeck Cumb....102 E7
Hillborough Kent....39 M8
Hill Brow Hants....23 L9
Hillbutts Dorset....12 G4
Hill Chorlton Staffs....70 D7
Hillclifflane Derbys....71 P5
Hill Common Norfk....77 N7
Hill Common Somset....18 F9
Hill Deverill Wilts....20 G6
Hilldyke Lincs....87 K11
Hill End Dur....103 K3
Hill End Fife....134 C8
Hillend Fife....134 E11
Hill End Gloucs....46 H7
Hillend Mdloth....127 P4
Hillend N Lans....126 E4
Hillend Swans....28 D6
Hillersland Gloucs....31 Q2
Hillerton Devon....8 H5
Hillesden Bucks....49 J9
Hillesley Gloucs....32 E7
Hillfarrance Somset....18 G10
Hill Green Kent....38 D9
Hillgrove W Susx....23 N9
Hillhampton Herefs....46 A5
Hillhead Abers....158 E10
Hillhead Devon....7 N8
Hill Head Hants....14 F6
Hillhead S Lans....126 D2
Hillhead of Cocklaw Abers....159 Q9
Hilliard's Cross Staffs....59 J2
Hilliclay Highld....167 L4
Hillingdon Gt Lon....36 C4
Hillington C Glas....125 N5
Hillington Norfk....75 P5
Hillis Corner IoW....14 E8
Hillmorton Warwks....60 B6
Hillock Vale Lancs....89 M5
Hill of Beath Fife....134 F9
Hill of Fearn Highld....163 J11
Hillowton D & G....108 G7
Hillpool Worcs....58 B10
Hillpound Hants....22 G11
Hill Ridware Staffs....71 K11
Hillside Abers....151 N8
Hillside Angus....143 N5
Hillside Devon....7 J6
Hill Side Kirk....90 F7
Hill Side Worcs....46 E2
Hills Town Derbys....84 G7

Hillstreet Hants....22 B11
Hillswick Shet....169 p6
Hill Top Dur....103 J6
Hill Top Hants....14 D6
Hill Top Kirk....90 D8
Hill Top Rothm....84 E2
Hill Top Sandw....58 E6
Hill Top Wakefd....91 J7
Hillwell Shet....169 q10
Hilmarton Wilts....33 K9
Hilperton Wilts....20 G3
Hilperton Marsh Wilts....20 G3
Hilsea C Port....15 J6
Hilston E R Yk....93 N4
Hiltingbury Hants....22 D10
Hilton Border....129 M9
Hilton Cambs....62 C7
Hilton Cumb....102 D6
Hilton Derbys....71 M8
Hilton Dorset....12 C4
Hilton Dur....103 N6
Hilton Highld....156 F2
Hilton S on T....104 E8
Hilton Shrops....57 P5
Hilton Park Services Staffs....58 E4
Himbleton Worcs....46 H3
Himley Staffs....58 C6
Hincaster Cumb....95 L4
Hinchley Wood Surrey....36 E7
Hinckley Leics....59 P6
Hinderclay Suffk....64 E6
Hinderwell N York....105 L7
Hindford Shrops....69 K8
Hindhead Surrey....23 N7
Hindhead Tunnel Surrey....23 N7
Hindle Fold Lancs....89 L4
Hindley Nthumb....112 F9
Hindley Wigan....82 D4
Hindley Green Wigan....82 D4
Hindlip Worcs....46 G3
Hindolveston Norfk....76 E6
Hindon Wilts....20 H8
Hindringham Norfk....76 D4
Hingham Norfk....76 E11
Hinksford Staffs....58 C7
Hinstock Shrops....70 B9
Hintlesham Suffk....53 J3
Hinton Gloucs....32 C4
Hinton Hants....13 M5
Hinton Herefs....45 L7
Hinton S Glos....32 D9
Hinton Shrops....56 G3
Hinton Shrops....57 M8
Hinton Admiral Hants....13 M5
Hinton Ampner Hants....22 H9
Hinton Blewett BaNES....19 Q3
Hinton Charterhouse BaNES....20 E3
Hinton Green Worcs....47 K6
Hinton-in-the-Hedges Nhants....48 G7
Hinton Marsh Hants....22 G9
Hinton Martell Dorset....12 H3
Hinton on the Green Worcs....47 K6
Hinton Parva Swindn....33 P8
Hinton St George Somset....11 J2
Hinton St Mary Dorset....20 E11
Hinton Waldrist Oxon....34 C5
Hints Shrops....57 L10
Hints Staffs....59 J4
Hinwick Bed....61 K8
Hinxhill Kent....26 H3
Hinxton Cambs....62 D11
Hinxworth Herts....50 F2
Hipperholme Calder....90 E5
Hipsburn Nthumb....119 P8
Hipswell N York....103 N11
Hirn Abers....151 J7
Hirnant Powys....68 D10
Hirst Nthumb....113 L3
Hirst Courtney N York....91 Q6
Hirwaen Denbgs....68 F2
Hirwaun Rhondd....30 C3
Hiscott Devon....17 J6
Histon Cambs....62 F8
Hitcham Suffk....64 D11
Hitcham Causeway Suffk....64 D11
Hitcham Street Suffk....64 D11
Hitchin Herts....50 E5
Hither Green Gt Lon....37 J6
Hittisleigh Devon....8 H5
Hive E R Yk....92 D4
Hixon Staffs....71 J9
Hoaden Kent....39 N10
Hoar Cross Staffs....71 L10
Hoarwithy Herefs....45 Q9
Hoath Kent....39 M9
Hoathly Kent....25 Q3
Hobarris Shrops....56 E9
Hobbles Green Suffk....63 M10
Hobbs Cross Essex....51 L11
Hobbs Cross Essex....51 L8
Hobkirk Border....118 A8
Hobland Hall Norfk....77 Q11
Hobsick Notts....84 G11
Hobson Dur....113 J9
Hoby Leics....72 H7
Hoccombe Somset....18 F9
Hockering Norfk....76 F9
Hockerton Notts....85 M9
Hockley Ches E....83 K8
Hockley Covtry....59 L9
Hockley Essex....38 D3
Hockley Staffs....59 K4
Hockley Heath Solhll....59 J10
Hockliffe C Beds....49 Q9
Hockwold cum Wilton Norfk....63 M3
Hockworthy Devon....18 D11
Hoddesdon Herts....51 J9
Hoddlesden Bl w D....89 L6
Hoddom Cross D & G....110 C6
Hoddom Mains D & G....110 C6
Hodgehill Ches E....82 H11
Hodgeston Pembks....41 K11
Hodnet Shrops....69 R9
Hodsock Notts....85 K3
Hodsoll Street Kent....37 P8
Hodson Swindn....33 N8
Hodthorpe Derbys....84 H5
Hoe Hants....22 G11
Hoe Norfk....76 D8
Hoe Benham W Berk....34 D11
Hoe Gate Hants....14 H4
Hoff Cumb....102 C7
Hogben's Hill Kent....38 H10
Hoggards Green Suffk....64 B10
Hoggeston Bucks....49 M10

Hoggrill's End Warwks....59 K6
Hog Hill E Susx....26 E8
Hoghton Lancs....89 J5
Hoghton Bottoms Lancs....89 J5
Hognaston Derbys....71 N4
Hogsthorpe Lincs....87 P6
Holbeach Lincs....74 G6
Holbeach Bank Lincs....74 G5
Holbeach Clough Lincs....74 G5
Holbeach Drove Lincs....74 F8
Holbeach Hurn Lincs....74 G5
Holbeach St Johns Lincs....74 G7
Holbeach St Mark's Lincs....74 G4
Holbeach St Matthew Lincs....74 H4
Holbeck Notts....84 H6
Holbeck Woodhouse Notts....84 H6
Holberrow Green Worcs....47 K3
Holbeton Devon....6 G8
Holborn Gt Lon....36 H4
Holborough Kent....38 B9
Holbrook Derbys....72 B2
Holbrook Sheff....84 F4
Holbrook Suffk....53 L4
Holbrook Moor Derbys....84 E11
Holbrooks Covtry....59 M8
Holburn Nthumb....119 K3
Holbury Hants....14 D6
Holcombe Devon....7 P4
Holcombe Somset....20 C5
Holcombe Rogus Devon....18 E11
Holcot Nhants....60 G7
Holden Lancs....96 A11
Holdenby Nhants....60 E7
Holder's Green Essex....51 P6
Holdgate Shrops....57 K7
Holdingham Lincs....86 E11
Holditch Dorset....10 G4
Holdsworth Calder....90 D5
Holehouse Derbys....83 M6
Hole-in-the-Wall Herefs....46 B9
Holemoor Devon....16 G10
Hole Street W Susx....24 D8
Holford Somset....18 G6
Holgate C York....98 B10
Holker Cumb....94 H5
Holkham Norfk....76 B3
Hollacombe Devon....16 F11
Holland Fen Lincs....86 H11
Holland Lees Lancs....88 G9
Holland-on-Sea Essex....53 L8
Hollandstoun Ork....169 g1
Hollee D & G....110 E7
Hollesley Suffk....53 Q3
Hollicombe Torbay....7 M6
Hollingbourne Kent....38 D10
Hollingbury Br & H....24 H9
Hollingdon Bucks....49 N9
Hollingthorpe Leeds....91 K4
Hollington Derbys....71 N7
Hollington Staffs....71 K7
Hollingworth Tamesd....83 M5
Hollinlane Ches E....82 H8
Hollins Bury....89 N9
Hollins Derbys....84 D6
Hollins Staffs....70 H5
Hollinsclough Staffs....83 N11
Hollins End Sheff....84 E4
Hollins Green Warrtn....82 E6
Hollins Lane Lancs....95 K10
Hollinswood Wrekin....57 N3
Hollinwood Shrops....69 P7
Holllingrove E Susx....25 Q6
Hollocombe Devon....17 L9
Holloway Derbys....84 D9
Holloway Gt Lon....36 H3
Holloway Wilts....20 G8
Hollowell Nhants....60 E6
Hollowmoor Heath Ches W....81 P11
Hollows D & G....110 G5
Hollybush Caerph....30 G4
Hollybush E Ayrs....114 G4
Hollybush Herefs....46 E7
Holly End Norfk....75 J9
Holly Green Worcs....46 G6
Hollyhurst Ches E....69 Q6
Hollym E R Yk....93 P5
Hollywood Worcs....58 G9
Holmbridge Kirk....90 E9
Holmbury St Mary Surrey....24 D2
Holmbush Cnwll....3 Q3
Holmcroft Staffs....70 G10
Holme Cambs....61 Q3
Holme Cumb....95 L5
Holme Kirk....90 D9
Holme N Linc....92 F9
Holme N York....97 N4
Holme Notts....85 P9
Holme Chapel Lancs....89 P5
Holme Green N York....91 P2
Holme Hale Norfk....76 B10
Holme Lacy Herefs....45 R7
Holme Marsh Herefs....45 L4
Holme next the Sea Norfk....75 P2
Holme on the Wolds E R Yk....99 K11
Holme Pierrepont Notts....72 G3
Holmer Herefs....45 Q6
Holmer Green Bucks....35 P5
Holme St Cuthbert Cumb....109 P11
Holmes Chapel Ches E....82 G11
Holmesfield Derbys....84 D5
Holmes Hill E Susx....25 M8
Holmeswood Lancs....88 E7
Holmethorpe Surrey....36 G10
Holme upon Spalding Moor E R Yk....92 D3
Holmewood Derbys....84 F7
Holmfield Calder....90 D5
Holmfirth Kirk....90 E9
Holmhead E Ayrs....115 L3
Holmpton E R Yk....93 Q6
Holmrook Cumb....100 E11
Holmsford Bridge Crematorium N Ayrs....125 K10
Holmshurst E Susx....25 P5
Holmside Dur....113 K11
Holmwrangle Cumb....111 K11
Holne Devon....7 J4
Holnest Dorset....11 P3
Holnicote Somset....18 B5
Holsworthy Devon....16 E11
Holsworthy Beacon Devon....16 F10
Holt Dorset....12 H4

Holt Norfk....76 F4
Holt Wilts....20 G3
Holt Worcs....46 F2
Holt Wrexhm....69 M4
Holtby C York....98 D10
Holt End Worcs....58 G11
Holt Fleet Worcs....46 F2
Holt Green Lancs....88 D9
Holt Heath Dorset....13 J4
Holt Heath Worcs....46 F2
Holton Oxon....34 H3
Holton Somset....20 C9
Holton Suffk....65 N6
Holton cum Beckering Lincs....86 F4
Holton Heath Dorset....12 F6
Holton Hill E Susx....25 C8
Holton le Clay Lincs....93 N10
Holton le Moor Lincs....93 J11
Holton St Mary Suffk....53 J4
Holt Street Kent....39 N11
Holtye E Susx....25 L3
Holway Flints....80 H9
Holwell Dorset....11 P2
Holwell Herts....50 E4
Holwell Leics....73 J6
Holwell Oxon....33 P3
Holwick Dur....102 H5
Holworth Dorset....12 C8
Holybourne Hants....23 K6
Holy Cross Worcs....58 D9
Holyfield Essex....51 J10
Holyhead IoA....78 C8
Holy Island IoA....78 D8
Holy Island Nthumb....119 M2
Holy Island Nthumb....119 M2
Holymoorside Derbys....84 D7
Holyport W & M....35 N9
Holystone Nthumb....119 J10
Holytown N Lans....126 D5
Holytown Crematorium N Lans....126 D5
Holywell C Beds....50 B7
Holywell Cambs....62 D6
Holywell Cnwll....4 B10
Holywell Dorset....11 M4
Holywell Flints....80 H9
Holywell Nthumb....113 M6
Holywell Warwks....59 K11
Holywell Green Calder....90 D7
Holywell Lake Somset....18 F10
Holywell Row Suffk....63 M5
Holywood D & G....109 K4
Holywood Village D & G....109 L5
Homer Shrops....57 L4
Homer Green Sefton....81 L4
Homersfield Suffk....65 K4
Homescales Cumb....95 M3
Hom Green Herefs....46 A10
Homington Wilts....21 M9
Honeyborough Pembks....40 H9
Honeybourne Worcs....47 M6
Honeychurch Devon....8 F4
Honey Hill Kent....39 K9
Honeystreet Wilts....21 M2
Honey Tye Suffk....52 G4
Honiley Warwks....59 K10
Honing Norfk....77 L6
Honingham Norfk....76 G9
Honington Lincs....73 N2
Honington Suffk....64 C7
Honington Warwks....47 Q6
Honiton Devon....10 D4
Honley Kirk....90 E8
Honnington Wrekin....70 C11
Honor Oak Crematorium Gt Lon....37 J6
Hoo Kent....39 N9
Hoobrook Worcs....58 B10
Hood Green Barns....91 J10
Hood Hill Rothm....91 K11
Hooe C Plym....6 E8
Hooe E Susx....25 Q8
Hoo End Herts....50 E6
Hoo Green Ches E....82 F8
Hoohill Bpool....88 C3
Hook Cambs....62 F2
Hook Devon....10 G3
Hook E R Yk....92 C5
Hook Gt Lon....36 E8
Hook Hants....14 F5
Hook Hants....22 K4
Hook Pembks....41 J8
Hook Wilts....33 L8
Hookagate Shrops....56 H3
Hook Bank Worcs....46 F6
Hooke Dorset....11 L4
Hook End Essex....51 N10
Hookgate Staffs....70 C7
Hook Green Kent....25 Q3
Hook Green Kent....37 P6
Hook Norton Oxon....48 C8
Hook Street Gloucs....32 C5
Hook Street Wilts....33 L8
Hookway Devon....9 L5
Hookwood Surrey....24 G2
Hooley Surrey....36 G9
Hooley Bridge Rochdl....89 P8
Hoo Meavy Devon....6 E5
Hoo St Werburgh Medway....38 C7
Hooton Ches W....81 M9
Hooton Levitt Rothm....84 H2
Hooton Pagnell Donc....91 L9
Hooton Roberts Rothm....91 M11
Hopcrofts Holt Oxon....48 E9
Hope Derbys....83 Q8
Hope Devon....6 H10
Hope Flints....69 K3
Hope Powys....56 D3
Hope Shrops....56 E4
Hope Staffs....71 L4
Hope Bagot Shrops....57 K10
Hope Bowdler Shrops....56 H6
Hope End Green Essex....51 N6
Hopehouse Border....117 K7
Hopeman Moray....157 L4
Hope Mansell Herefs....46 B11
Hopesay Shrops....56 F8
Hopetown Wakefd....91 K6
Hope under Dinmore Herefs....45 Q4
Hopgrove C York....98 C10
Hopperton N York....97 P9
Hop Pole Lincs....74 C8
Hopsford Warwks....59 P8
Hopstone Shrops....57 P6
Hopton Derbys....71 P4
Hopton Shrops....69 L10
Hopton Staffs....70 G9
Hopton Suffk....64 D6

276 Hopton Cangeford – Ireby

Hopton Cangeford Shrops 57 J8
Hopton Castle Shrops 56 F9
Hoptonheath Shrops 56 F9
Hopton on Sea Norfk 65 Q2
Hopton Wafers Shrops 57 L9
Hopwas Staffs 59 J4
Hopwood Rochdl 89 P9
Hopwood Worcs 58 F9
Hopwood Park Services Worcs 58 F10
Horam E Susx 25 N7
Horbling Lincs 74 B3
Horbury Wakefd 90 H7
Horcott Gloucs 33 N4
Horden Dur 104 D2
Horderley Shrops 56 G7
Hordle Hants 13 N5
Hordley Shrops 69 L8
Horeb Carmth 28 E3
Horeb Cerdgn 42 G6
Horfield Bristl 31 Q9
Horham Suffk 65 J7
Horkesley Heath Essex 52 G6
Horkstow N Linc 92 G7
Horley Oxon 48 D6
Horley Surrey 24 G2
Hornblotton Green Somset 19 Q8
Hornby Lancs 95 M7
Hornby N York 97 K2
Hornby N York 104 C9
Horncastle Lincs 87 J7
Hornchurch Gt Lon 37 M3
Horncliffe Nthumb 129 N10
Horndean Border 129 N10
Horndean Hants 15 K4
Horndon Devon 8 D8
Horndon on the Hill Thurr 37 Q4
Horne Surrey 24 H2
Horner Somset 18 B5
Horne Row Essex 52 C11
Horners Green Suffk 52 G3
Horney Common E Susx 25 L5
Horn Hill Bucks 36 B2
Horning Norfk 77 L8
Horninghold Leics 73 L11
Horninglow Staffs 71 N9
Horningsea Cambs 62 G8
Horningsham Wilts 20 F6
Horningtoft Norfk 76 C7
Horningtops Cnwll 5 M9
Hornsbury Somset 10 G2
Hornsby Cumb 111 K10
Hornsbygate Cumb 111 K10
Horns Cross Devon 16 F7
Horns Cross E Susx 26 D7
Hornsea E R Yk 99 P11
Hornsey Gt Lon 36 H3
Horn's Green Gt Lon 37 L9
Horn Street Kent 27 L4
Hornton Oxon 48 C5
Horpit Swindn 33 P8
Horra Shet 169 r4
Horrabridge Devon 6 E5
Horringer Suffk 64 A9
Horringford IoW 14 F9
Horrocks Fold Bolton 89 L8
Horrocksford Lancs 89 M2
Horsacott Devon 17 J5
Horsebridge Devon 5 Q6
Horsebridge E Susx 25 N8
Horsebridge Hants 22 B8
Horsebridge Shrops 56 F3
Horsebridge Staffs 70 H4
Horsebrook Staffs 58 C2
Horsecastle N Som 31 M11
Horsedown Cnwll 2 G7
Horsehay Wrekin 57 M3
Horseheath Cambs 63 K11
Horsehouse N York 96 F4
Horsell Surrey 23 Q3
Horseman's Green Wrexhm 69 M6
Horsenden Bucks 35 L4
Horsey Norfk 77 P7
Horsey Somset 19 K7
Horsey Corner Norfk 77 P7
Horsford Norfk 76 H8
Horsforth Leeds 90 G3
Horsham W Susx 24 E4
Horsham Worcs 46 D3
Horsham St Faith Norfk 77 J8
Horsington Lincs 86 G7
Horsington Somset 20 D10
Horsley Derbys 72 B2
Horsley Gloucs 32 F5
Horsley Nthumb 112 G7
Horsley Nthumb 118 F11
Horsley Cross Essex 53 K6
Horsleycross Street Essex 53 K6
Horsley-Gate Derbys 84 D5
Horsleyhill Border 117 Q7
Horsley's Green Bucks 35 L6
Horsley Woodhouse Derbys 72 B2
Horsmonden Kent 26 B3
Horspath Oxon 34 G3
Horstead Norfk 77 K8
Horsted Keynes W Susx 25 J5
Horton Bucks 49 P11
Horton Dorset 12 H3
Horton Lancs 96 C10
Horton Nhants 49 M4
Horton S Glos 32 E8
Horton Shrops 69 N9
Horton Somset 10 G2
Horton Staffs 70 G3
Horton Surrey 36 E8
Horton Swans 28 E7
Horton W & M 36 B5
Horton Wilts 21 K2
Horton Wrekin 57 M2
Horton Cross Somset 19 K11
Horton-cum-Studley Oxon 34 G2
Horton Green Ches W 69 N5
Horton Heath Hants 22 E11
Horton-in-Ribblesdale N York 96 B6
Horton Kirby Kent 37 N7
Horwich Bolton 89 J8
Horwich End Derbys 83 M8
Horwood Devon 17 J6
Hoscar Lancs 88 F8
Hoscote Border 117 M8
Hose Leics 73 J5
Hosey Hill Kent 37 L10
Hosh P & K 133 P3
Hoswick Shet 169 r11
Hotham E R Yk 92 E4
Hothfield Kent 26 G3
Hoton Leics 72 F6
Hott Nthumb 111 Q3
Hough Ches E 70 C4
Hough Ches E 83 J9
Hougham Lincs 73 M2
Hough End Leeds 90 G4
Hough Green Halton 81 P7
Hough-on-the-Hill Lincs 86 B11
Houghton Cambs 62 C6
Houghton Cumb 110 H9
Houghton Hants 22 B8
Houghton Nthumb 112 H7
Houghton Pembks 41 J9
Houghton W Susx 24 B8
Houghton Conquest C Beds 50 B2
Houghton Gate Dur 113 M10
Houghton Green E Susx 26 F7
Houghton Green Warrtn 82 D6
Houghton le Side Darltn 103 P6
Houghton-le-Spring Sundld 113 M11
Houghton on the Hill Leics 72 H10
Houghton Regis C Beds 50 B6
Houghton St Giles Norfk 76 C4
Hound Green Hants 23 K3
Houndslow Border 128 G10
Houndsmoor Somset 18 F9
Houndwood Border 129 L7
Hounslow Gt Lon 36 D5
Househill Highld 156 F6
Houses Hill Kirk 90 F7
Housieside Abers 151 M2
Houston Rens 125 L4
Houstry Highld 167 L10
Houton Ork 169 c6
Hove Br & H 24 G10
Hove Edge Calder 90 E6
Hoveringham Notts 85 L11
Hoveton Norfk 77 L8
Hovingham N York 98 D5
Howbrook Barns 91 J11
How Caple Herefs 46 B8
Howden E R Yk 92 B5
Howden-le-Wear Dur 103 N4
Howe Highld 167 P4
Howe IoM 80 a8
Howe N York 97 N4
Howe Norfk 65 K2
Howe Bridge Wigan 82 E4
Howe Bridge Crematorium Wigan 82 E4
Howe Green Essex 52 B11
Howegreen Essex 52 D11
Howell Lincs 86 F11
How End C Beds 50 B2
Howe of Teuchar Abers 159 J8
Howes D & G 110 C7
Howe Street Essex 51 Q4
Howe Street Essex 51 Q8
Howey Powys 44 F3
Howgate Cumb 100 C6
Howgate Mdloth 127 N6
Howgill Lancs 96 B11
Howick Nthumb 119 Q7
Howle Wrekin 70 B10
Howle Hill Herefs 46 B10
Howlett End Essex 51 N4
Howley Somset 10 F3
How Mill Cumb 111 K9
Howmore W Isls 168 c14
Hownam Border 118 E7
Howrigg Cumb 110 F11
Howsham N Linc 92 H10
Howsham N York 98 E8
Howtel Nthumb 118 G4
Howt Green Kent 38 E8
Howton Herefs 45 N9
Howtown Cumb 101 M7
How Wood Herts 50 D10
Howwood Rens 125 K5
Hoxa Ork 169 d7
Hoxne Suffk 64 H6
Hoy Ork 169 b7
Hoylake Wirral 81 J7
Hoyland Common Barns 91 K10
Hoyland Nether Barns 91 K10
Hoyland Swaine Barns 90 H10
Hoyle W Susx 23 P11
Hoyle Mill Barns 91 K9
Hubberholme N York 96 D5
Hubberston Pembks 40 G9
Hubbert's Bridge Lincs 74 E2
Huby N York 97 L11
Huby N York 98 B7
Huccaby Devon 6 H4
Hucclecote Gloucs 46 G11
Hucking Kent 38 D10
Hucknall Notts 84 H11
Huddersfield Kirk 90 E7
Huddersfield Crematorium Kirk 90 E6
Huddington Worcs 46 H3
Hudnall Herts 50 B8
Hudswell N York 103 M10
Huggate E R Yk 98 H9
Hugglescote Leics 72 C8
Hughenden Valley Bucks 35 N5
Hughley Shrops 57 K5
Hugh Town IoS 2 c2
Huish Devon 17 J9
Huish Wilts 21 M2
Huish Champflower Somset 18 E9
Huish Episcopi Somset 19 M9
Huisinis W Isls 168 e6
Hulcote C Beds 49 P7
Hulcote Nhants 49 K5
Hulcott Bucks 49 N11
Hulham Devon 9 P8
Hulland Derbys 71 N5
Hulland Ward Derbys 71 P5
Hullavington Wilts 32 G8
Hull Bridge E R Yk 93 J2
Hullbridge Essex 38 D2
Hull, Kingston upon C KuH 93 J5
Hulme Manch 82 H5
Hulme Staffs 70 G5
Hulme Warrtn 82 D6
Hulme End Staffs 71 L3
Hulme Walfield Ches E 82 H11
Hulse Heath Ches E 82 F8
Hulton Lane Ends Bolton 89 K9
Hulverstone IoW 14 C10
Hulver Street Norfk 76 C9
Hulver Street Suffk 65 P4
Humber Devon 9 L9
Humber Herefs 45 Q3
Humber Bridge N Linc 92 H6
Humberside Airport N Linc 93 J8
Humberston NE Lin 93 P9
Humberstone C Leic 72 G9
Humberton N York 97 P7
Humbie E Loth 128 D7
Humbleton E R Yk 93 M4
Humbleton Nthumb 119 J5
Humby Lincs 73 Q4
Hume Border 118 D2
Humshaugh Nthumb 112 D6
Huna Highld 167 Q2
Huncoat Lancs 89 M4
Huncote Leics 72 E11
Hundalee Border 118 B7
Hundall Derbys 84 E5
Hunderthwaite Dur 103 J6
Hundleby Lincs 87 L7
Hundle Houses Lincs 86 H10
Hundleton Pembks 41 J10
Hundon Suffk 63 M11
Hundred End Lancs 88 E6
Hundred House Powys 44 G4
Hungarton Leics 72 H9
Hungerford Hants 13 L2
Hungerford Somset 18 D6
Hungerford W Berk 34 B11
Hungerford Newtown W Berk 34 C10
Hunger Hill Bolton 89 K9
Hunger Hill Lancs 88 G8
Hungerstone Herefs 45 N7
Hungerton Lincs 73 M5
Hungryhatton Shrops 70 B9
Hunmanby N York 99 M5
Hunningham Warwks 59 N11
Hunnington Worcs 58 E8
Hunsbury Hill Nhants 60 F9
Hunsdon Herts 51 K8
Hunsingore N York 97 P10
Hunslet Leeds 91 J4
Hunsonby Cumb 101 Q3
Hunstanton Norfk 75 N2
Hunstanworth Dur 112 D11
Hunsterson Ches E 70 B5
Hunston Suffk 64 D8
Hunston W Susx 15 N6
Hunston Green Suffk 64 D8
Hunstrete BaNES 20 B2
Hunsworth Kirk 90 F5
Hunt End Worcs 47 K2
Hunter's Inn Devon 17 M2
Hunter's Quay Ag & B 124 F2
Huntham Somset 19 K9
Hunthill Lodge Angus 142 H3
Huntingdon Cambs 62 B6
Huntingfield Suffk 65 L7
Huntingford Dorset 20 F9
Huntington C York 98 C9
Huntington Ches W 69 M2
Huntington E Loth 128 D5
Huntington Herefs 45 K4
Huntington Herefs 45 P6
Huntington Staffs 58 E2
Huntley Gloucs 46 D11
Huntly Abers 158 D10
Hunton Hants 22 E6
Hunton Kent 26 B2
Hunton N York 97 J2
Hunton Bridge Herts 50 C10
Hunt's Corner Norfk 64 F4
Huntscott Somset 18 B6
Hunt's Cross Lpool 81 N7
Hunts Green Bucks 35 N4
Hunts Green Warwks 59 J5
Huntsham Devon 18 D10
Huntshaw Devon 17 J7
Huntshaw Cross Devon 17 J7
Huntspill Somset 19 K5
Huntstile Somset 19 J8
Huntworth Somset 19 K8
Hunwick Dur 103 N4
Hunworth Norfk 76 F4
Hurcott Somset 19 L11
Hurdcott Wilts 21 N8
Hurdsfield Ches E 83 K10
Hurley W & M 35 M8
Hurley Warwks 59 K5
Hurley Bottom W & M 35 M8
Hurley Common Warwks 59 K5
Hurlford E Ayrs 125 M10
Hurlston Green Lancs 88 D8
Hurn Dorset 13 K5
Hurn's End Lincs 87 M11
Hursley Hants 22 D9
Hurst Dorset 12 C6
Hurst N York 103 K10
Hurst Somset 19 N11
Hurst Wokham 35 L10
Hurstbourne Priors Hants 22 D5
Hurstbourne Tarrant Hants 22 C4
Hurst Green E Susx 26 B6
Hurst Green Essex 53 J8
Hurst Green Lancs 89 K3
Hurst Green Surrey 37 K10
Hurst Hill Dudley 58 D6
Hurstley Herefs 45 M5
Hurstpierpoint W Susx 24 G7
Hurst Wickham W Susx 24 G7
Hurstwood Lancs 89 P4
Hurtiso Ork 169 e6
Hurtmore Surrey 23 P5
Hurworth Burn Dur 104 D4
Hurworth-on-Tees Darltn 104 B9
Hurworth Place Darltn 103 Q9
Hury Dur 103 J7
Husbands Bosworth Leics 60 D4
Husborne Crawley C Beds 49 Q7
Husthwaite N York 97 R6
Hutcherleigh Devon 7 K8
Hutcliffe Wood Crematorium Sheff 84 D4
Hut Green N York 91 P6
Huthwaite Notts 84 G9
Huttoft Lincs 87 P5
Hutton Border 129 N9
Hutton Cumb 101 M5
Hutton E R Yk 99 L10
Hutton Essex 51 P11
Hutton Lancs 88 F5
Hutton N Som 19 L3
Hutton Bonville N York 104 B10
Hutton Buscel N York 99 K4
Hutton Conyers N York 97 M6
Hutton Cranswick E R Yk 99 L10
Hutton End Cumb 101 N3
Hutton Hang N York 97 J3
Hutton Henry Dur 104 D3
Hutton-le-Hole N York 98 E2
Hutton Lowcross R & Cl 104 G8
Hutton Magna Dur 103 M8
Hutton Mulgrave N York 105 M9
Hutton Roof Cumb 95 M5
Hutton Roof Cumb 101 L4
Hutton Rudby N York 104 E9
Hutton Sessay N York 97 Q5
Hutton Wandesley N York 97 R10
Huxham Devon 9 M5
Huxham Green Somset 19 Q7
Huxley Ches W 69 P2
Huyton Knows 81 N6
Hycemoor Cumb 94 B3
Hyde Gloucs 32 G4
Hyde Hants 13 L2
Hyde Tamesd 83 K6
Hyde End Wokham 35 K11
Hyde Heath Bucks 35 P4
Hyde Lea Staffs 70 G11
Hydestile Surrey 23 Q6
Hykeham Moor Lincs 86 B7
Hylands House & Park Essex 51 Q10
Hyndford Bridge S Lans 116 C2
Hynish Ag & B 136 B8
Hyssington Powys 56 E6
Hystfield Gloucs 32 C5
Hythe Essex 52 H6
Hythe Hants 14 D5
Hythe Kent 27 L5
Hythe Somset 19 M4
Hythe End W & M 36 B6
Hyton Cumb 94 B3

I

Ibberton Dorset 12 C3
Ible Derbys 84 B9
Ibsley Hants 13 L3
Ibstock Leics 72 C9
Ibstone Bucks 35 L6
Ibthorpe Hants 22 C4
Iburndale N York 105 N9
Ibworth Hants 22 G4
Icelton N Som 31 L11
Ichrachan Ag & B 139 J11
Ickburgh Norfk 75 R11
Ickenham Gt Lon 36 C3
Ickford Bucks 34 H3
Ickham Kent 39 M10
Ickleford Herts 50 E4
Icklesham E Susx 26 E8
Ickleton Cambs 51 L2
Icklingham Suffk 63 N6
Ickornshaw N York 90 B2
Ickwell Green C Beds 61 Q11
Icomb Gloucs 47 P10
Idbury Oxon 47 P11
Iddesleigh Devon 17 K10
Ide Devon 9 L6
Ideford Devon 9 L9
Ide Hill Kent 37 L10
Iden E Susx 26 F7
Iden Green Kent 26 B4
Iden Green Kent 26 D5
Idle C Brad 90 F3
Idless Cnwll 3 L4
Idlicote Warwks 47 Q6
Idmiston Wilts 21 N7
Idole Carmth 42 H11
Idridgehay Derbys 71 P5
Idrigill Highld 152 F5
Idstone Oxon 33 Q8
Iffley Oxon 34 F4
Ifield W Susx 24 G3
Ifold W Susx 24 B4
Iford Bmouth 13 K6
Iford E Susx 25 K9
Ifton Mons 31 N7
Ifton Heath Shrops 69 K7
Ightfield Shrops 69 Q7
Ightham Kent 37 N9
Iken Suffk 65 N10
Ilam Staffs 71 L4
Ilchester Somset 19 P10
Ilderton Nthumb 119 K6
Ilford Gt Lon 37 K3
Ilford Somset 19 L11
Ilfracombe Devon 17 J2
Ilkeston Derbys 72 D2
Ilketshall St Andrew Suffk 65 M4
Ilketshall St John Suffk 65 M4
Ilketshall St Lawrence Suffk 65 M5
Ilketshall St Margaret Suffk 65 L4
Ilkley C Brad 96 H11
Illand Cnwll 5 M6
Illey Dudley 58 E8
Illidge Green Ches E 70 D2
Illingworth Calder 90 D5
Illogan Cnwll 2 H5
Illston on the Hill Leics 73 J11
Ilmer Bucks 35 L3
Ilmington Warwks 47 P6
Ilminster Somset 10 H2
Ilsington Devon 9 J9
Ilsington Dorset 12 C6
Ilston Swans 28 G6
Ilton N York 97 J5
Ilton Somset 19 L11
Imachar N Ayrs 120 G3
Immingham NE Lin 93 L8
Immingham Dock NE Lin 93 L7
Impington Cambs 62 F8
Ince Ches W 81 P9
Ince Blundell Sefton 81 L4
Ince-in-Makerfield Wigan 82 C4
Inchbae Lodge Hotel Highld 155 M4
Inchbare Angus 143 L4
Inchberry Moray 157 Q6
Incheril Highld 154 D5
Inchinnan Rens 125 M4
Inchlaggan Highld 146 F7
Inchmichael P & K 134 G2
Inchnacardoch Hotel Highld 147 K5
Inchnadamph Highld 161 M2
Inchture P & K 134 H2
Inchvuilt Highld 154 H
Inchyra P & K 134
Indian Queens Cnwll 4 E
Ingate Place Suffk 65
Ingatestone Essex 51 P
Ingbirchworth Barns 90
Ingerthorpe N York 97
Ingestre Staffs 70 H
Ingham Lincs 86
Ingham Norfk 77
Ingham Suffk 64
Ingham Corner Norfk 77
Ingleborough Norfk 75
Ingleby Derbys 72
Ingleby Arncliffe N York 104 D
Ingleby Barwick S on T 104
Ingleby Cross N York 104 E
Ingleby Greenhow N York 104
Ingleigh Green Devon 8
Inglesbatch BaNES 20
Inglesham Swindn 33
Ingleston D & G 109
Ingleton Dur 103
Ingleton N York 95
Inglewhite Lancs 88
Ingmanthorpe N York 97 P
Ingoe Nthumb 112
Ingol Lancs 88
Ingoldisthorpe Norfk 75
Ingoldmells Lincs 87
Ingoldsby Lincs 73
Ingram Nthumb 119
Ingrave Essex 37
Ingrow C Brad 90
Ings Cumb 101 M
Ingst S Glos 31
Ingthorpe Rutlnd 73
Ingworth Norfk 76
Inkberrow Worcs 47
Inkerman Dur 103
Inkhorn Abers 159 M
Inkpen W Berk 22
Inkstack Highld 167
Inmarsh Wilts 20
Innellan Ag & B 124
Innerleithen Border 117
Innerleven Fife 135
Innermessan D & G 106
Innerwick E Loth 129
Innesmill Moray 157
Innsworth Gloucs 46 G
Insch Abers 150
Insh Highld 148
Inskip Lancs 88
Inskip Moss Side Lancs 88
Instow Devon 16
Insworke Cnwll 6
Intake Sheff 84
Inver Abers 149
Inver Highld 163 K
Inver P & K 141
Inverailort Highld 145 N
Inveralligin Highld 153
Inverallochy Abers 159
Inveran Highld 162
Inveraray Ag & B 131 M
Inverarish Highld 153 K
Inverarity Angus 142 H
Inverarnan Stirlg 132
Inverasdale Highld 160 C
Inverbeg Ag & B 132
Inverbervie Abers 143
Inverboyndie Abers 158
Invercreran House Hotel Ag & B 139
Inverdruie Highld 148
Inveresk E Loth 127
Inveresragan Ag & B 138 H
Inverey Abers 149 K
Inverfarigaig Highld 147
Inverfolla Ag & B 138 H
Invergarry Highld 147
Invergeldie P & K 133
Invergloy Highld 146 G
Invergordon Highld 156
Invergowrie P & K 142 E
Inverguseran Highld 145 M
Inverhadden P & K 140
Inverherive Hotel Stirlg 132
Inverie Highld 145
Inverinan Ag & B 131
Inverinate Highld 145
Inverkeilor Angus 143 M
Inverkeithing Fife 134 E1
Inverkeithny Abers 158
Inverkip Inver 124
Inverkirkaig Highld 160
Inverlael Highld 161
Inverlair Highld 139
Inverliever Lodge Ag & B 130
Inverlochy Ag & B 131
Invermark Angus 150 C1
Invermoriston Highld 147
Invernaver Highld 166
Inverness Highld 156
Inverness Airport Highld 156
Inverness Crematorium Highld 156
Invernoaden Ag & B 131
Inveroran Hotel Ag & B 139
Inverquharity Angus 142
Inverquhomery Abers 159
Inverroy Highld 146 H1
Inversanda Highld 138
Invershiel Highld 146
Invershin Highld 162
Invershore Highld 167
Inversnaid Hotel Stirlg 132
Inverugie Abers 159
Inveruglas Ag & B 132
Inveruglass Highld 148
Inverurie Abers 151
Inwardleigh Devon 8
Inworth Essex 52
Iona Ag & B 136 H
Iping W Susx 23 N
iPort Logistics Park Donc 91 Q
Ipplepen Devon 7
Ipsden Oxon 34
Ipstones Staffs 71
Ipswich Suffk 53
Ipswich Crematorium Suffk 53
Irby Wirral 81
Irby in the Marsh Lincs 87
Irby upon Humber NE Lin 93 L
Irchester Nhants 61
Ireby Cumb 100

...by Lancs.....95 P5
...land C Beds.....50 D2
...leth Cumb.....94 E5
...shopeburn Dur.....102 G3
...ton Wood Derbys.....71 P5
...am Salfd.....57 F6
...ham Lincs.....73 Q5
...n Acton S Glos.....32 C8
...n Bridge Cambs.....75 J11
...nbridge Wrekin.....57 M4
...nbridge Gorge Wrekin.....57 M4
...n Cross Warwks.....47 L4
...nmacannie C Beds.....108 E5
...ns Bottom Surrey.....36 F11
...nville Derbys.....84 F10
...tead Norfk.....77 M7
...hington Cumb.....111 J8
...hlingborough Nhants.....61 K6
...on N York.....99 L4
...ine N Ayrs.....125 J10
...uld Highld.....166 G3
...ister Shet.....169 q4
...ister Shet.....169 s7
...ield E Susx.....25 K7
...am Nhants.....61 J6
...ton Hants.....23 L6
...ndpool Worcs.....58 C8
...ay Ag & B.....122 E4
...ay Airport Ag & B.....122 D9
...e Abbotts Somset.....19 L10
...e Brewers Somset.....19 L10
...eham Cambs.....63 K6
...e of Dogs Gt Lon.....37 J5
...e of Grain Medway.....38 E6
...e of Lewis W Isls.....168 i4
...e of Man IoM.....80 e4
...e of Man Ronaldsway Airport IoM.....80 c8
...e of Mull Ag & B.....137 G8
...e of Purbeck Dorset.....12 H8
...e of Sheppey Kent.....38 G8
...e of Skye Highld.....152 G10
...e of Thanet Kent.....39 P8
...e of Walney Cumb.....94 D7
...e of Whithorn D & G.....107 N10
...e of Wight IoW.....14 F9
...e of Wight Crematorium IoW.....14 F8
...eornsay Highld.....145 M5
...es of Scilly IoS.....2 c2
...es of Scilly St Mary's Airport IoS.....2 c2
...esteps D & G.....109 L6
...et Village Guern.....10 c1
...eworth Gt Lon.....36 E5
...ey Walton Leics.....72 C6
...bhig W Isls.....168 f5
...ington Gt Lon.....36 H4
...ington Crematorium Gt Lon.....36 G2
...p Nhants.....61 L5
...p Oxon.....34 F2
...vig W Isls.....168 f5
...mbridge Wrekin.....57 L2
...ead Rise Kent.....37 P6
...hen Abbas Hants.....22 F8
...hen Stoke Hants.....22 G8
...hingfield W Susx.....24 D5
...hington S Glos.....32 C7
...eringham Norfk.....76 G5
...on Devon.....8 G5
...on Norfk.....31 N5
...on Common Mons.....31 N5
...gill Cumb.....101 M2
...let N York.....102 H11
...er Bucks.....36 B4
...er Heath Bucks.....36 B4
...eston Cumb.....112 H10
...nghoe Bucks.....49 P11
...nghoe Aston Bucks.....49 Q11
...ington Herefs.....45 P3
...ington Green Herefs.....45 P3
...bridge Devon.....6 G7
...church Kent.....26 H6
...r Cross Dorset.....20 G10
...r Hatch Kent.....37 N10
...r Todd Norfk.....76 B10
...ade Kent.....38 F8
...erne Courtney Dorset.....12 E2
...erne Minster Dorset.....12 E2
...vorth Suffk.....64 C7
...vorth Thorpe Suffk.....64 C7

J

...ck Green Lancs.....88 H5
...ck Hill N York.....97 J10
...ck-in-the-Green Devon.....9 P5
...ck's Bush Hants.....21 Q7
...cksdale Notts.....84 F10
...ckson Bridge Kirk.....90 F9
...ckton S Lans.....125 P7
...cobstow Cnwll.....5 K2
...cobstowe Devon.....8 E4
...cobs Well Surrey.....36 B10
...meston Pembks.....41 L11
...mestown Highld.....155 N6
...mestown W Duns.....132 D11
...netstown Highld.....167 L10
...netstown Highld.....167 Q6
...rdine Hall D & G.....109 P3
...row S Tyne.....113 M8
...vis Brook E Susx.....25 M5
...sper's Green Essex.....52 B6
...wcraig Falk.....126 E2
...wick Falk.....53 L9
...alott's Hill Br For.....35 N10
...ater Houses N York.....97 P2
...dburgh Border.....118 B6
...freyston Pembks.....41 L9
...mimaville Highld.....156 C4
...bourg Guern.....10 c2
...sey Jersey.....11 b1
...sey Airport Jersey.....11 a2
...sey Crematorium Jersey.....11 b2
...sey Marine Neath.....29 K6
...rusalem Herts.....86 B6
...smond N u Ty.....113 L7
...ngle Street Mons.....31 N2
...le E Susx.....11 N10
...n Lennon Airport Lpool.....81 N8
...n o' Groats Highld.....167 Q2
...ns Cross E Susx.....26 B7
...nshaven Abers.....143 P4

Johnson Street Norfk.....77 M8
Johnston Pembks.....40 H8
Johnstone D & G.....117 J10
Johnstone Rens.....125 L5
Johnstonebridge D & G.....109 P2
Johnstown Carmth.....42 G11
Johnstown Wrexhm.....69 K5
Joppa C Edin.....127 Q3
Joppa Cerdgn.....43 J4
Joppa S Ayrs.....114 H4
Jordans Bucks.....35 Q6
Jordanston Pembks.....40 H4
Jordanthorpe Sheff.....84 E4
Joyden's Wood Kent.....37 M6
Jubilee Corner Kent.....26 D2
Jump Barns.....91 K10
Jumper's Town E Susx.....25 L4
Juniper Nthumb.....112 D9
Juniper Green C Edin.....127 M4
Jura Ag & B.....122 H3
Jurassic Coast Devon.....10 G7
Jurby IoM.....80 e2
Jurston Devon.....8 G8

K

Kaber Cumb.....102 E8
Kaimend S Lans.....126 H8
Kames Ag & B.....124 B3
Kames E Ayrs.....115 N2
Kea Cnwll.....3 L5
Keadby N Linc.....92 D8
Keal Cotes Lincs.....87 L8
Kearby Town End N York.....97 M11
Kearsley Bolton.....82 G4
Kearsley Nthumb.....112 F5
Kearsney Kent.....27 N3
Kearstwick Cumb.....95 N5
Kearton N York.....103 J11
Keasden N York.....95 Q7
Keaton Devon.....6 H6
Keckwick Halton.....82 C8
Keddington Lincs.....87 K3
Keddington Corner Lincs.....87 L3
Kedington Suffk.....63 M11
Kedleston Derbys.....71 Q6
Keelby Lincs.....93 L8
Keele Staffs.....70 E5
Keele Services Staffs.....70 E6
Keele University Staffs.....70 E5
Keeley Green Bed.....61 M11
Keelham C Brad.....90 D4
Keeres Green Essex.....51 N8
Keeston Pembks.....40 H7
Keevil Wilts.....20 H3
Kegworth Leics.....72 D5
Kehelland Cnwll.....2 G5
Keig Abers.....150 G4
Keighley C Brad.....90 D2
Keighley Crematorium C Brad.....90 C3
Keilarsbrae Clacks.....133 P9
Keillour P & K.....134 B2
Keiloch Abers.....149 M9
Keils Ag & B.....122 H6
Keinton Mandeville Somset.....19 P8
Keir Mill D & G.....109 J2
Keirsleywell Row Nthumb.....111 Q10
Keisby Lincs.....73 Q5
Keisley Cumb.....102 D6
Keiss Highld.....167 P4
Keith Moray.....158 B7
Keithick P & K.....142 C10
Keithock Angus.....143 L5
Keithtown Highld.....155 P6
Kelbrook Lancs.....89 Q2
Kelby Lincs.....73 Q2
Keld Cumb.....101 Q8
Keld N York.....102 G10
Keld Head N York.....98 F4
Keldholme N York.....98 E3
Kelfield N Linc.....92 D10
Kelfield N York.....91 P3
Kelham Notts.....85 N9
Kelhead D & G.....109 P7
Kellacott Devon.....5 Q4
Kellamergh Lancs.....88 E5
Kellas Angus.....142 H10
Kellas Moray.....157 M7
Kellaton Devon.....7 L11
Kelleth Cumb.....102 C9
Kelling Norfk.....76 F3
Kellington N York.....91 P6
Kelloe Dur.....104 B3
Kelloholm D & G.....115 P5
Kells Cumb.....100 C7
Kelly Devon.....5 P5
Kelly Bray Cnwll.....5 P7
Kelmarsh Nhants.....60 F5
Kelmscott Oxon.....33 P5
Kelsale Suffk.....65 M8
Kelsall Ches W.....81 Q11
Kelshall Herts.....51 H3
Kelsick Cumb.....110 C10
Kelso Border.....118 D4
Kelstedge Derbys.....84 D8
Kelstern Lincs.....86 H3
Kelsterton Flints.....81 K10
Kelston BaNES.....32 D11
Keltneyburn P & K.....141 J8
Kelton D & G.....109 L6
Kelty Fife.....134 E9
Kelvedon Essex.....52 E8
Kelvedon Hatch Essex.....51 N10
Kelynack Cnwll.....2 B8
Kemacott Devon.....17 M2
Kemback Fife.....135 L5
Kemberton Shrops.....57 N4
Kemble Gloucs.....33 J5
Kemble Wick Gloucs.....33 J5
Kemerton Worcs.....47 J7
Kemeys Commander Mons.....31 K4
Kemnay Abers.....151 J4
Kempe's Corner Kent.....26 H2
Kempley Gloucs.....46 C9
Kempley Green Gloucs.....46 C9
Kempsey Worcs.....46 F5
Kempsford Gloucs.....33 N5
Kemps Green Warwks.....58 H10
Kempshott Hants.....22 H4
Kempston Bed.....61 M11
Kempston Hardwick Bed.....50 B2
Kempton Shrops.....56 F8
Kemp Town Br & H.....24 H10
Kemsing Kent.....37 N9

Kemsley Kent.....38 F8
Kemsley Street Kent.....38 D9
Kenardington Kent.....26 G5
Kencot Oxon.....33 Q4
Kendal Cumb.....95 L2
Kenderchurch Herefs.....45 N6
Kendleshire S Glos.....32 C9
Kenfig Brdgnd.....29 M8
Kenfig Hill Brdgnd.....29 M8
Kenilworth Warwks.....59 L10
Kenley Gt Lon.....36 H8
Kenley Shrops.....57 K4
Kenmore Highld.....153 P6
Kenmore P & K.....141 J8
Kenn Devon.....9 M7
Kenn N Som.....31 M11
Kennacraig Ag & B.....123 P7
Kennards House Cnwll.....5 M5
Kenneggy Cnwll.....2 E7
Kennerleigh Devon.....9 K3
Kennessee Green Sefton.....81 M4
Kennet Clacks.....133 Q9
Kennethmont Abers.....150 E2
Kennett Cambs.....63 L7
Kennford Devon.....9 M7
Kenninghall Norfk.....64 E3
Kennington Kent.....26 H2
Kennington Oxon.....34 F4
Kennoway Fife.....135 K7
Kenny Somset.....19 K11
Kenny Hill Suffk.....63 L5
Kennythorpe N York.....98 F7
Kensaleyre Highld.....152 G7
Kensington Gt Lon.....36 G5
Kensington Palace Gt Lon.....36 G4
Kensworth C Beds.....50 B7
Kensworth Common C Beds.....50 B7
Kent and Sussex Crematorium Kent.....25 N3
Kentchurch Herefs.....45 N9
Kentford Suffk.....63 M7
Kent Green Ches E.....70 E3
Kentisbeare Devon.....9 Q3
Kentisbury Devon.....17 L3
Kentisbury Ford Devon.....17 L3
Kentish Town Gt Lon.....36 G4
Kentmere Cumb.....101 M10
Kenton Devon.....9 N8
Kenton Gt Lon.....36 E3
Kenton N u Ty.....113 K7
Kenton Suffk.....64 H8
Kenton Bankfoot N u Ty.....113 K7
Kentra Highld.....138 B4
Kents Bank Cumb.....94 H5
Kent's Green Gloucs.....46 D10
Kent's Oak Hants.....22 B10
Kent Street E Susx.....26 C8
Kent Street Kent.....37 Q10
Kenwick Shrops.....69 M8
Kenwyn Cnwll.....3 L4
Kenyon Warrtn.....82 D5
Keoldale Highld.....165 J3
Keppoch Highld.....145 Q3
Kepwick N York.....97 Q2
Keresley Covtry.....59 M8
Kermincham Ches E.....82 H11
Kernborough Devon.....7 K10
Kerne Bridge Herefs.....46 A11
Kerrera Ag & B.....130 G2
Kerridge Ches E.....83 K9
Kerridge-end Ches E.....83 K9
Kerris Cnwll.....2 C8
Kerry Powys.....55 Q6
Kerrycroy Ag & B.....124 E5
Kersall Notts.....85 M8
Kersbrook Devon.....9 Q8
Kerscott Devon.....17 L6
Kersey Suffk.....52 H3
Kersey Tye Suffk.....52 G3
Kersey Upland Suffk.....52 G3
Kershader W Isls.....168 i5
Kershopefoot Cumb.....111 J11
Kersoe Worcs.....47 J6
Kerswell Devon.....10 B3
Kerswell Green Worcs.....46 G5
Kerthen Wood Cnwll.....2 F7
Kesgrave Suffk.....53 M2
Kessingland Suffk.....65 Q4
Kessingland Beach Suffk.....65 Q4
Kestle Cnwll.....3 P4
Kestle Mill Cnwll.....4 C5
Keston Gt Lon.....37 K8
Keswick Cumb.....101 J6
Keswick Norfk.....77 J11
Ketsby Lincs.....87 L5
Kettering Nhants.....61 J5
Kettering Crematorium Nhants.....61 J5
Ketteringham Norfk.....76 H11
Kettins P & K.....142 C10
Kettlebaston Suffk.....64 D11
Kettlebridge Fife.....135 J6
Kettlebrook Staffs.....59 K4
Kettleburgh Suffk.....65 K9
Kettle Green Herts.....51 K7
Kettleholm D & G.....109 P5
Kettleness N York.....105 M7
Kettleshulme Ches E.....83 K9
Kettlesing N York.....97 K9
Kettlesing Bottom N York.....97 K9
Kettlestone Norfk.....76 D5
Kettlethorpe Lincs.....85 P5
Kettletoft Ork.....169 f3
Kettlewell N York.....96 E6
Ketton Rutlnd.....73 P10
Kew Gt Lon.....36 E5
Kew Royal Botanic Gardens Gt Lon.....36 E5
Kewstoke N Som.....19 K2
Kexbrough Barns.....91 J9
Kexby York.....98 E10
Kexby Lincs.....85 Q3
Key Green Ches E.....70 F2
Key Green N York.....105 M10
Keyham Leics.....72 H9
Keyhaven Hants.....13 P6
Keyingham E R Yk.....93 M5
Keymer W Susx.....24 H7
Keynsham BaNES.....32 C11
Keysoe Bed.....61 N8
Keysoe Row Bed.....61 N8
Keyston Cambs.....61 M6
Key Street Kent.....38 D9
Keyworth Notts.....72 G4
Kibbear Somset.....18 H10

Kibblesworth Gatesd.....113 K9
Kibworth Beauchamp Leics.....60 E2
Kibworth Harcourt Leics.....60 E2
Kidbrooke Gt Lon.....37 K5
Kidburngill Cumb.....100 E6
Kiddemore Green Staffs.....58 C3
Kidderminster Worcs.....58 B9
Kiddington Oxon.....48 D10
Kidd's Moor Norfk.....76 G11
Kidlington Oxon.....34 E2
Kidmore End Oxon.....35 J9
Kidsdale D & G.....107 M10
Kidsgrove Staffs.....70 E4
Kidstones N York.....96 E4
Kidwelly Carmth.....28 D3
Kiel Crofts Ag & B.....138 G10
Kielder Nthumb.....111 M2
Kielder Forest Nthumb.....111 M3
Kiells Ag & B.....122 F6
Kilbarchan Rens.....125 L5
Kilbeg Highld.....145 L6
Kilberry Ag & B.....123 M7
Kilbirnie N Ayrs.....125 J7
Kilbride Ag & B.....123 M4
Kilbride Ag & B.....124 C4
Kilbuiack Moray.....157 K5
Kilburn Derbys.....84 E11
Kilburn Gt Lon.....36 F4
Kilburn N York.....97 R5
Kilby Leics.....72 G11
Kilchamaig Ag & B.....123 P7
Kilchattan Ag & B.....124 E7
Kilchattan Ag & B.....136 b2
Kilcheran Ag & B.....138 E10
Kilchoan Highld.....137 M3
Kilchoman Ag & B.....122 B7
Kilchrenan Ag & B.....131 L3
Kilconquhar Fife.....135 M7
Kilcot Gloucs.....46 C9
Kilcoy Highld.....155 Q7
Kilcreggan Ag & B.....131 Q11
Kildale N York.....104 H9
Kildalloig Ag & B.....120 E8
Kildary Highld.....156 D3
Kildavaig Ag & B.....124 B4
Kildavanan Ag & B.....124 C4
Kildonan Highld.....163 L2
Kildonan N Ayrs.....121 K7
Kildonan Lodge Highld.....163 L2
Kildonnan Highld.....144 G10
Kildrochet House D & G.....106 E6
Kildrummy Abers.....150 D4
Kildwick N York.....96 F11
Kilfinan Ag & B.....124 A2
Kilfinnan Highld.....146 H8
Kilford Denbgs.....80 F11
Kilgetty Pembks.....41 M9
Kilgrammie S Ayrs.....114 E7
Kilgwrrwg Common Mons.....31 N5
Kilham E R Yk.....99 M8
Kilham Nthumb.....118 G4
Kilkenneth Ag & B.....136 A7
Kilkenzie Ag & B.....120 C7
Kilkerran Ag & B.....120 D8
Kilkhampton Cnwll.....16 D9
Killamarsh Derbys.....84 G4
Killay Swans.....28 H6
Killearn Stirlg.....132 G10
Killellan Highld.....156 B6
Killerby Darltn.....103 N7
Killerton Devon.....9 N4
Killichonate Highld.....146 G6
Killiechronan Ag & B.....137 N7
Killiecrankie P & K.....141 M5
Killilan Highld.....154 B11
Killimster Highld.....167 P5
Killin Stirlg.....140 E11
Killinghall N York.....97 L9
Killington Cumb.....95 N3
Killington Devon.....17 N3
Killingworth N Tyne.....113 L6
Killiow Cnwll.....3 L5
Killochyett Border.....128 D10
Kilmacolm Inver.....125 K3
Kilmahog Stirlg.....133 J6
Kilmahumaig Ag & B.....130 F9
Kilmaluag Highld.....152 G3
Kilmany Fife.....135 K3
Kilmarnock E Ayrs.....125 L10
Kilmartin Ag & B.....130 G8
Kilmaurs E Ayrs.....125 L9
Kilmelford Ag & B.....130 H5
Kilmersdon Somset.....20 C4
Kilmeston Hants.....22 G9
Kilmichael Ag & B.....120 C7
Kilmichael Glassary Ag & B.....130 H9
Kilmichael of Inverlussa Ag & B.....130 F10
Kilmington Devon.....10 F5
Kilmington Wilts.....20 E7
Kilmington Common Wilts.....20 E7
Kilmington Street Wilts.....20 E7
Kilmorack Highld.....155 N9
Kilmore Ag & B.....130 H2
Kilmore Highld.....145 L6
Kilmory Ag & B.....123 M5
Kilmory Highld.....137 N1
Kilmory N Ayrs.....121 J7
Kilmuir Highld.....152 D8
Kilmuir Highld.....152 F3
Kilmuir Highld.....156 B8
Kilmuir Highld.....156 D3
Kilmun Ag & B.....131 P11
Kilnave Ag & B.....122 C6
Kilncadzow S Lans.....126 F8
Kilndown Kent.....26 B4
Kiln Green Wokham.....35 M9
Kilnhill Cumb.....100 H4
Kilnhouses Ches W.....82 B8
Kilnhurst Rothm.....91 M11
Kiln Pit Hill Nthumb.....112 H9
Kilnsea E R Yk.....93 R7
Kilnsey N York.....96 F7
Kilnwick E R Yk.....99 K11
Kilnwick Percy E R Yk.....98 H10
Kiloran Ag & B.....136 b2
Kilpatrick N Ayrs.....120 H6
Kilpeck Herefs.....45 N8
Kilpin E R Yk.....92 C5
Kilpin Pike E R Yk.....92 C5
Kilrenny Fife.....135 N7
Kilsby Nhants.....60 C6
Kilspindie P & K.....134 G2

Kilstay D & G.....106 F10
Kilsyth N Lans.....126 F2
Kiltarlity Highld.....155 P9
Kilton R & Cl.....105 K7
Kilton Thorpe R & Cl.....105 J7
Kilvaxter Highld.....152 F4
Kilve Somset.....18 F6
Kilvington Notts.....73 L2
Kilwinning N Ayrs.....125 J9
Kimberley Norfk.....76 F11
Kimberley Notts.....72 F3
Kimberworth Rothm.....84 F2
Kimblesworth Dur.....113 L11
Kimble Wick Bucks.....35 M3
Kimbolton Cambs.....61 P7
Kimbolton Herefs.....45 Q2
Kimcote Leics.....60 C3
Kimmeridge Dorset.....12 F9
Kimmerston Nthumb.....119 J3
Kimpton Hants.....21 Q5
Kimpton Herts.....50 E7
Kimworthy Devon.....16 E9
Kinbrace Highld.....166 E10
Kinbuck Stirlg.....133 M6
Kincaple Fife.....135 M4
Kincardine Fife.....133 Q10
Kincardine Highld.....162 E9
Kincardine Bridge Fife.....133 Q10
Kincardine O'Neil Abers.....150 F8
Kinclaven P & K.....142 B10
Kincorth C Aber.....151 N7
Kincorth House Moray.....157 J5
Kincraig Highld.....148 G6
Kincraigie P & K.....141 N8
Kindallachan P & K.....141 N8
Kinerarach Ag & B.....123 L9
Kineton Gloucs.....47 L9
Kineton Warwks.....48 B4
Kinfauns P & K.....134 F3
Kingarth Ag & B.....124 D6
Kingcausie Abers.....151 N8
Kingcoed Mons.....31 M3
Kingerby Lincs.....86 D2
Kingford Devon.....16 D10
Kingham Oxon.....47 Q10
Kingholm Quay D & G.....109 L6
Kinghorn Fife.....134 H10
Kinglassie Fife.....134 G8
Kingoldrum Angus.....142 E6
Kingoodie P & K.....135 J2
King's Acre Herefs.....45 P6
Kingsand Cnwll.....6 C8
Kingsash Bucks.....35 N3
Kingsbarns Fife.....135 P5
Kingsbridge Devon.....7 J10
Kingsbridge Somset.....18 C7
Kings Bridge Swans.....28 G5
King's Bromley Staffs.....71 L11
Kingsburgh Highld.....152 F6
Kingsbury Gt Lon.....36 E3
Kingsbury Warwks.....59 K5
Kingsbury Episcopi Somset.....19 M10
King's Caple Herefs.....45 R9
Kingsclere Hants.....22 F3
King's Cliffe Nhants.....73 Q11
Kings Clipstone Notts.....85 K8
Kingscote Gloucs.....32 F5
Kingscott Devon.....17 J8
King's Coughton Warwks.....47 L3
Kingscross N Ayrs.....121 K6
Kingsdon Somset.....19 P9
Kingsdown Kent.....27 Q2
Kingsdown Swindn.....33 N7
Kingsdown Wilts.....32 F11
Kingsdown Crematorium Swindn.....33 N7
Kingseat Fife.....134 E9
Kingsey Bucks.....35 K3
Kingsfold W Susx.....24 E3
Kingsford C Aber.....151 M6
Kingsford E Ayrs.....125 L8
Kingsford Worcs.....57 Q8
Kingsgate Kent.....39 Q7
Kings Green Gloucs.....46 E8
Kingshall Street Suffk.....64 C9
Kingsheanton Devon.....17 K4
King's Heath Birm.....58 G8
Kings Hill Kent.....37 Q9
King's Hill Wsall.....58 E5
Kingshouse Hotel Highld.....139 P7
Kingshouse Hotel Stirlg.....132 H3
Kingshurst Solhll.....59 J7
Kingside Hill Cumb.....110 C10
Kingskerswell Devon.....7 M5
Kingskettle Fife.....135 J6
Kingsland Dorset.....11 K5
Kingsland Herefs.....45 N2
Kingsland IoA.....78 D8
Kings Langley Herts.....50 C10
Kingsley Ches W.....82 C10
Kingsley Hants.....23 L7
Kingsley Staffs.....71 J5
Kingsley Green W Susx.....23 N8
Kingsley Park Nhants.....60 G8
Kingslow Shrops.....57 P5
King's Lynn Norfk.....75 M6
Kings Meaburn Cumb.....102 B6
Kingsmead Hants.....14 G4
King's Mills Guern.....10 b2
King's Moss St Hel.....81 Q4
Kingsmuir Angus.....142 H8
Kingsmuir Fife.....135 N6
Kings Newnham Warwks.....59 Q9
King's Newton Derbys.....72 B5
Kingsnorth Kent.....26 H4
King's Norton Birm.....58 G9
King's Norton Leics.....72 H10
King's Nympton Devon.....17 M8
King's Pyon Herefs.....45 N4
Kings Ripton Cambs.....62 C5
King's Somborne Hants.....22 C8
King's Stag Dorset.....11 Q3
King's Stanley Gloucs.....32 F3
King's Sutton Nhants.....48 E7
Kingstanding Birm.....58 G6
Kingsteignton Devon.....7 M4
King's Sterndale Derbys.....83 N10
Kingsthorne Herefs.....45 P8
Kingsthorpe Nhants.....60 G8
Kingston Cambs.....62 D9
Kingston Cnwll.....5 P6
Kingston Devon.....6 H9
Kingston Dorset.....11 Q5
Kingston Dorset.....12 G9
Kingston E Loth.....128 E3
Kingston Hants.....13 K4
Kingston IoW.....14 E10

Kingston Kent......39 L11
Kingston W Susx......24 C10
Kingston Bagpuize Oxon....34 G5
Kingston Blount Oxon....35 K5
Kingston Deverill Wilts....20 F7
Kingstone Herefs......45 N7
Kingstone Somset......10 H2
Kingstone Staffs......71 K9
Kingstone Winslow
  Oxon......33 Q7
Kingston Lacy House &
  Gardens Dorset....12 G4
Kingston Lisle Oxon....34 B7
Kingston near Lewes
  E Susx......25 J9
Kingston on Soar Notts....72 E5
Kingston on Spey Moray...157 Q4
Kingston Russell Dorset....11 M6
Kingston St Mary
  Somset......18 H9
Kingston Seymour
  N Som......31 M11
Kingston Stert Oxon....35 K4
Kingston upon Hull
  C KuH......93 J5
Kingston upon Thames
  Gt Lon......36 E7
Kingston upon Thames
  Crematorium Gt Lon...36 E7
Kingstown Cumb......110 G9
King's Walden Herts....50 E6
Kingswear Devon......7 M8
Kingswells C Aber....151 M6
Kings Weston Bristl....31 P9
Kingswinford Dudley....58 C7
Kingswood Bucks....49 J11
Kingswood Gloucs....32 D6
Kingswood Kent......38 D11
Kingswood Powys....56 C4
Kingswood S Glos....32 B10
Kingswood Somset....18 F7
Kingswood Surrey....36 F9
Kingswood Warwks....59 J10
Kingswood Brook
  Warwks......59 J10
Kingswood Common
  Herefs......45 K4
Kingswood Common
  Staffs......58 B4
Kings Worthy Hants....22 E8
Kingthorpe Lincs....86 F5
Kington Herefs......45 K3
Kington S Glos....32 B6
Kington Worcs......47 J3
Kington Langley Wilts....32 H9
Kington Magna Dorset....20 E10
Kington St Michael Wilts....32 H9
Kingussie Highld....148 D7
Kingweston Somset....19 P8
Kinharrachie Abers....159 M11
Kinharvie D & G....109 K7
Kinkell Bridge P & K....133 Q4
Kinknockie Abers....159 P9
Kinleith C Edin....127 M4
Kinlet Shrops......57 N8
Kinloch Highld....144 F8
Kinloch Highld....164 H10
Kinloch Highld....165 N6
Kinloch P & K....142 A9
Kinlochard Stirlg....132 F7
Kinlochbervie Highld....164 F5
Kinlocheil Highld....138 H2
Kinlochewe Highld....154 D5
Kinloch Hourn Highld....146 B6
Kinlochlaggan Highld....147 N10
Kinlochleven Highld....139 M5
Kinlochmoidart Highld....138 C3
Kinlochnanuagh Highld...145 M11
Kinloch Rannoch P & K....140 G6
Kinloss Moray....157 K5
Kinmel Bay Conwy....80 D8
Kinmuck Abers....151 L4
Kinmundy Abers....151 M4
Kinnabus Ag & B....122 C11
Kinnadie Abers....159 N9
Kinnaird P & K....141 N6
Kinneff Abers....143 Q2
Kinnelhead D & G....116 E10
Kinnell Angus....143 L7
Kinnerley Shrops....69 K10
Kinnersley Herefs....45 L5
Kinnersley Worcs....46 G6
Kinnerton Powys....45 J2
Kinnerton Shrops....56 F5
Kinnerton Green Flints....69 K2
Kinnesswood P & K....134 F7
Kinninvie Dur....103 L6
Kinnordy Angus....142 F6
Kinoulton Notts....72 H4
Kinross P & K....134 E7
Kinrossie P & K....142 B11
Kinross Services P & K....134 E7
Kinsbourne Green Herts....50 D7
Kinsey Heath Ches E....70 B6
Kinsham Herefs....56 F11
Kinsham Worcs....46 H7
Kinsley Wakefd....91 L8
Kinson Bmouth....13 J5
Kintail Highld....146 B4
Kintbury W Berk....34 C11
Kintessack Moray....157 J5
Kintillo P & K....134 E4
Kinton Herefs....56 G10
Kinton Shrops....69 L11
Kintore Abers....151 K4
Kintour Ag & B....122 G9
Kintra Ag & B....122 D10
Kintra Ag & B....137 J10
Kintraw Ag & B....130 G7
Kintyre Ag & B....120 D4
Kinveachy Highld....148 G4
Kinver Staffs......58 B8
Kiplin N York....103 Q11
Kippax Leeds......91 L4
Kippen Stirlg....133 J9
Kippford D & G....108 H10
Kipping's Cross Kent....25 P2
Kirbister Ork....169 c6
Kirby Bedon Norfk....77 K10
Kirby Bellars Leics....73 J7
Kirby Cane Norfk....65 M3
Kirby Corner Covtry....59 L9
Kirby Cross Essex....53 M7
Kirby Fields Leics....72 E10
Kirby Grindalythe N York....99 J7
Kirby Hill N York....97 N7
Kirby Hill N York....103 M9
Kirby Knowle N York....97 Q3
Kirby-le-Soken Essex....53 M7
Kirby Misperton N York....98 F5
Kirby Muxloe Leics....72 E10

Kirby Sigston N York....97 P2
Kirby Underdale E R Yk....98 G9
Kirby Wiske N York....97 N1
Kirdford W Susx......24 B5
Kirk Highld......167 N5
Kirkabister Shet......161 r10
Kirkandrews D & G....108 D11
Kirkandrews upon
  Eden Cumb......110 G9
Kirkbampton Cumb....110 F9
Kirkbean D & G....109 L9
Kirk Bramwith Donc....91 Q8
Kirkbride Cumb....110 D9
Kirkbridge N York....97 L2
Kirkbuddo Angus....143 J9
Kirkburn Border....117 K3
Kirkburn E R Yk....99 K9
Kirkburton Kirk....90 F8
Kirkby Knows......81 N5
Kirkby Lincs......86 E2
Kirkby N York....104 F9
Kirkby Fleetham N York....97 L2
Kirkby Green Lincs....86 E9
Kirkby-in-Ashfield Notts....84 H9
Kirkby-in-Furness Cumb....94 E4
Kirkby la Thorpe Lincs....86 E11
Kirkby Lonsdale Cumb....95 N5
Kirkby Malham N York....96 C8
Kirkby Mallory Leics....72 D10
Kirkby Malzeard N York....97 K6
Kirkby Mills N York....98 E3
Kirkby on Bain Lincs....86 H8
Kirkby Overblow N York....97 M11
Kirkby Stephen Cumb....102 E9
Kirkby Thore Cumb....102 B5
Kirkby Underwood Lincs....73 R5
Kirkby Wharf N York....91 N2
Kirkby Woodhouse
  Notts......84 G10
Kirkcaldy Fife......134 H9
Kirkcaldy Crematorium
  Fife......134 H9
Kirkcambeck Cumb....111 K7
Kirkchrist D & G....108 E10
Kirkcolm D & G....106 D4
Kirkconnel D & G....115 P5
Kirkconnell D & G....109 L7
Kirkcowan D & G....107 K5
Kirkcudbright D & G....108 E10
Kirkdale Lpool....81 L6
Kirk Deighton N York....97 N10
Kirk Ella E R Yk....92 H5
Kirkfieldbank S Lans....116 B2
Kirkgunzeon D & G....109 J7
Kirk Hallam Derbys....72 D2
Kirkham Lancs....88 E4
Kirkham N York....98 E7
Kirkhamgate Wakefd....90 H6
Kirk Hammerton N York....97 Q9
Kirkharle Nthumb....112 F4
Kirkhaugh Nthumb....111 N11
Kirkheaton Kirk....90 F7
Kirkheaton Nthumb....112 F5
Kirkhill Highld....155 Q8
Kirkhope S Lans....116 D9
Kirkhouse Cumb....111 L9
Kirkhouse Green Donc....91 Q8
Kirkibost Highld....145 J4
Kirkinch P & K....142 E9
Kirkinner D & G....107 M7
Kirkintilloch E Duns....126 B3
Kirk Ireton Derbys....71 P4
Kirkland Cumb....100 E7
Kirkland Cumb....102 B4
Kirkland D & G....109 M3
Kirkland D & G....115 P5
Kirkland D & G....115 R9
Kirkland Guards Cumb....100 G2
Kirk Langley Derbys....71 P7
Kirkleatham
  Crematorium R & Cl....104 G6
Kirklevington S on T....104 D9
Kirkley Suffk......65 Q3
Kirklington N York....97 M4
Kirklington Notts....85 L9
Kirklinton Cumb....110 H7
Kirkliston C Edin....127 L3
Kirkmabreck D & G....107 N6
Kirkmaiden D & G....106 F10
Kirk Merrington Dur....103 Q4
Kirk Michael IoM....80 d3
Kirkmichael P & K....141 Q6
Kirkmichael S Ayrs....114 F6
Kirkmuirhill S Lans....126 D9
Kirknewton Nthumb....118 H4
Kirknewton W Loth....127 L4
Kirkney Abers....158 D11
Kirk of Shotts N Lans....126 E5
Kirkoswald Cumb....101 Q2
Kirkoswald S Ayrs....114 D6
Kirkpatrick D & G....109 K2
Kirkpatrick Durham
  D & G......108 G6
Kirkpatrick-Fleming
  D & G......110 E6
Kirk Sandall Donc....91 Q9
Kirksanton Cumb....94 C4
Kirk Smeaton N York....91 N7
Kirkstall Leeds....90 H3
Kirkstead Lincs....86 F8
Kirkstile Abers....158 D10
Kirkstile D & G....110 G2
Kirkstone Pass Inn
  Cumb......101 M9
Kirkstyle Highld....167 P2
Kirkthorpe Wakefd....91 K6
Kirkton Abers....150 G2
Kirkton D & G....109 L4
Kirkton Fife....135 K2
Kirkton Highld....145 P2
Kirkton Highld....145 B9
Kirkton P & K....134 B3
Kirkton Manor Border....117 J3
Kirkton of Airlie Angus....142 E7
Kirkton of
  Auchterhouse Angus....142 F10
Kirkton of Barevan
  Highld......156 E8
Kirkton of Collace P & K....142 B11
Kirkton of Glenbuchat
  Abers......150 B4
Kirkton of Logie
  Buchan Abers....151 P2
Kirkton of Maryculter
  Abers......151 M8
Kirkton of Menmuir
  Angus......143 J5
Kirkton of Monikie
  Angus......143 J10

Kirkton of Rayne Abers....158 G11
Kirkton of Skene Abers....151 L6
Kirkton of
  Strathmartine Angus....142 F10
Kirkton of Tealing Angus....142 G10
Kirkton of Tough Abers....150 G5
Kirktown Abers....159 N4
Kirktown Abers....159 Q7
Kirktown of Alvah Abers....158 G5
Kirktown of Bourtie
  Abers......151 L2
Kirktown of Fetteresso
  Abers......151 M10
Kirktown of Mortlach
  Moray......157 Q10
Kirktown of Slains Abers....151 Q10
Kirkurd Border....116 Q2
Kirkwall Ork....169 d5
Kirkwall Airport Ork....169 d6
Kirkwhelpington
  Nthumb......112 E4
Kirk Yetholm Border....118 F5
Kirmington N Linc....93 K8
Kirmond le Mire Lincs....86 G2
Kirn Ag & B....124 F2
Kirriemuir Angus....142 F7
Kirstead Green Norfk....65 K2
Kirtlebridge D & G....110 D6
Kirtling Cambs....63 L9
Kirtling Green Cambs....63 L9
Kirtlington Oxon....48 E11
Kirtomy Highld....166 B4
Kirton Lincs....74 F3
Kirton Notts....85 L9
Kirton Suffk....53 N3
Kirton End Lincs....74 E2
Kirtonhill W Duns....125 K2
Kirton Holme Lincs....74 E2
Kirton in Lindsey N Linc....92 F11
Kirwaugh D & G....107 M7
Kishorn Highld....153 Q10
Kislingbury Nhants....60 G9
Kitebrook Warwks....47 P8
Kite Green Warwks....59 J11
Kites Hardwick Warwks....59 Q11
Kitleigh Cnwll....5 L2
Kitt Green Wigan....88 G9
Kittisford Somset....18 E10
Kittle Swans....28 G7
Kitt's Green Birm....59 J7
Kittybrewster C Aber....151 N6
Kitwood Hants....23 J8
Kivernoll Herefs....45 P8
Kiveton Park Rothm....84 G4
Knaith Lincs....85 P4
Knaith Park Lincs....85 P3
Knap Corner Dorset....20 F10
Knaphill Surrey....23 Q3
Knapp Somset....19 K9
Knapp Hill Hants....22 D10
Knapthorpe Notts....85 M9
Knapton C York....98 B10
Knapton N York....98 H5
Knapton Norfk....77 L5
Knapton Green Herefs....45 N4
Knapwell Cambs....62 D8
Knaresborough N York....97 N9
Knarsdale Nthumb....111 N10
Knaven Abers....159 L9
Knayton N York....97 P3
Knebworth Herts....50 G6
Knedlington E R Yk....92 B5
Kneesall Notts....85 M8
Kneeton Notts....85 M11
Knelston Swans....28 E7
Knenhall Staffs....70 G7
Knettishall Suffk....64 D5
Knightacott Devon....17 M4
Knightcote Warwks....48 D4
Knightley Staffs....70 E9
Knightley Dale Staffs....70 E10
Knighton C Leic....72 G10
Knighton Devon......6 E9
Knighton Dorset....11 N2
Knighton Poole....12 H5
Knighton Powys....56 D10
Knighton Somset....18 G6
Knighton Staffs....70 C6
Knighton Staffs....70 D9
Knighton Wilts....33 Q10
Knighton on Teme
  Worcs......57 L11
Knightsbridge Gloucs....46 G9
Knightsmill Cnwll......4 H5
Knightwick Worcs....46 D3
Knill Herefs....45 K2
Knipton Leics....73 L4
Knitsley Dur....112 H11
Kniveton Derbys....71 N4
Knock Cumb....102 C5
Knock Highld....145 L6
Knock Moray....158 D7
Knock W Isls....168 j4
Knockally Highld....167 K11
Knockan Highld....161 L4
Knockando Moray....157 M9
Knockbain Highld....155 Q9
Knockbain Highld....156 A6
Knock Castle N Ayrs....124 F5
Knockdee Highld....167 L4
Knockdow Ag & B....124 E3
Knockdown Wilts....32 F5
Knockeen S Ayrs....114 F8
Knockenkelly N Ayrs....121 K6
Knockentiber E Ayrs....125 L10
Knockhall Kent....37 N6
Knockholt Kent....37 L9
Knockholt Pound Kent....37 L9
Knockin Shrops....69 K10
Knockinlaw E Ayrs....125 L10
Knockmill Kent....37 N8
Knocknain Highld....106 C5
Knockrome Ag & B....123 J2
Knocksharry IoM....80 c4
Knocksheen D & G....108 C4
Knockvennie Smithy
  D & G......108 G6
Knodishall Suffk....65 N9
Knodishall Common
  Suffk......65 N9
Knole Somset....19 N9
Knole Park S Glos....31 Q8
Knolls Green Ches E....82 H9
Knolton Wrexhm....69 L7
Knook Wilts....20 H6
Knossington Leics....73 L9
Knott End-on-Sea Lancs....94 H11
Knotting Bed....61 M8
Knotting Green Bed....61 M8
Knottingley Wakefd....91 N6
Knotty Ash Lpool....81 N6

Knotty Green Bucks....35 P6
Knowbury Shrops....57 K9
Knowe D & G....107 K3
Knowehead D & G....115 M9
Knoweside S Ayrs....114 E5
Knowle Bristl....32 B10
Knowle Devon......9 J4
Knowle Devon......9 P3
Knowle Devon......9 Q8
Knowle Devon....16 H4
Knowle Shrops....57 K10
Knowle Solhll....59 J9
Knowle Somset....18 C6
Knowle Cross Devon......9 P5
Knowlefield Cumb....110 H9
Knowle Green Lancs....89 J3
Knowle Hill Surrey....35 Q11
Knowle St Giles Somset....10 G2
Knowle Village Hants....14 G5
Knowle Wood Calder....89 Q6
Knowl Green Essex....52 C3
Knowl Hill W & M....35 M9
Knowlton Dorset....12 H3
Knowlton Kent....39 N11
Knowsley Knows....81 N5
Knowsley Safari Park
  Knows......81 P6
Knowstone Devon....17 Q7
Knox N York....97 L9
Knox Bridge Kent....26 C3
Knoydart Highld....145 P7
Knucklas Powys....56 D10
Knutsford Ches E....82 G9
Knutsford Services
  Ches E......82 F9
Knutton Staffs....70 E5
Krumlin Calder....90 D7
Kuggar Cnwll......3 J10
Kyleakin Highld....145 N2
Kyle of Lochalsh Highld....145 N2
Kylerhea Highld....145 N3
Kylesku Highld....164 F10
Kylesmorar Highld....145 P9
Kyles Scalpay W Isls....168 h8
Kylestrome Highld....164 F10
Kynaston Herefs....46 B7
Kynaston Shrops....69 L10
Kynnersley Wrekin....70 B11
Kyre Green Worcs....46 B2
Kyre Park Worcs....46 B2
Kyrewood Worcs....57 K11
Kyrle Somset....18 E10

L

La Bellieuse Guern....10 b2
Lacasaigh W Isls....168 i5
Lacasdal W Isls....168 j4
Laceby NE Lin....93 M9
Lacey Green Bucks....35 M4
Lach Dennis Ches W....82 F10
Lackenby R & Cl....104 G7
Lackford Suffk....63 N6
Lackford Green Suffk....63 N6
Lacock Wilts....32 H11
Ladbroke Warwks....48 D3
Ladderedge Staffs....70 H4
Laddingford Kent....37 Q11
Lade Bank Lincs....87 L10
Ladock Cnwll......3 M3
Lady Ork....169 f2
Ladybank Fife....135 J6
Ladycross Cnwll......5 N4
Ladygill S Lans....116 C5
Lady Hall Cumb....94 D3
Ladykirk Border....129 M10
Ladyridge Herefs....46 A8
Lady's Green Suffk....63 N9
Ladywood Birm....58 G7
Ladywood Worcs....46 G2
La Fontenelle Guern....10 c1
La Fosse Guern....10 b2
Lag D & G....109 J3
Laga Highld....138 A5
Lagavulin Ag & B....122 F10
Lagg N Ayrs....121 J6
Laggan Highld....146 H8
Laggan Highld....147 Q9
Lagganlia Highld....148 F7
La Greve Guern....10 c1
La Grève de Lecq Jersey....11 a1
La Hougue Bie Jersey....11 c2
La Houguette Guern....10 b2
Laid Highld....165 K5
Laide Highld....160 E8
Laig Highld....144 G10
Laigh Clunch E Ayrs....125 M8
Laigh Fenwick E Ayrs....125 M9
Laigh Glenmuir E Ayrs....115 M3
Laighstonehall S Lans....126 C7
Laindon Essex....37 Q3
Lairg Highld....162 D5
Laisterdyke C Brad....90 F4
Laithes Cumb....101 N3
Lake Devon......8 D7
Lake Devon....17 K5
Lake IoW....14 G10
Lake Wilts....21 M7
Lake District National
  Park Cumb....100 H9
Lakenheath Suffk....63 M4
Laker's Green Surrey....24 B3
Lakesend Norfk....75 K11
Lakeside Cumb....94 H3
Laleham Surrey....36 C7
Laleston Brdgnd....29 N9
Lamanva Cnwll......3 K7
Lamarsh Essex....52 E4
Lamas Norfk....77 J7
Lambden Border....118 D3
Lamberhurst Kent....25 Q3
Lamberhurst Down Kent....25 Q3
Lamberton Border....129 P8
Lambeth Gt Lon....36 H5
Lambeth Crematorium
  Gt Lon......36 G5
Lambfair Green Suffk....63 M10
Lambley Notts....85 K11
Lambley Nthumb....111 N9
Lambourn W Berk....34 B9
Lambourne End Essex....37 L2
Lambourn Woodlands
  W Berk......34 B9
Lamb Roe Lancs....89 L4
Lambs Green W Susx....24 F3
Lambston Pembks....40 H5
Lamellion Cnwll......5 L9
Lamerton Devon......5 C9

Lamesley Gatesd....113
Lamington S Lans....116
Lamlash N Ayrs....121
Lamonby Cumb....101
Lamorick Cnwll......4
Lamorna Cnwll......2
Lamorran Cnwll......3
Lampen Cnwll......5
Lampeter Cerdgn....43
Lampeter Velfrey
  Pembks......41
Lamphey Pembks....41
Lamplugh Cumb....100
Lamport Nhants....60
Lamyatt Somset....20
Lana Devon......16
Lana Devon......16
Lanark S Lans....116
Lancaster Lancs....95
Lancaster &
  Morecambe
  Crematorium Lancs....95
Lancaster Services Lancs....95
Lancaut Gloucs....31
Lanchester Dur....113
Lancing W Susx....24
L'Ancresse Guern....10
Landbeach Cambs....62
Landcross Devon....16
Landerberry Abers....151
Landford Wilts....21
Land-hallow Highld....167
Landican Crematorium
  Wirral......81
Landimore Swans....28
Landkey Devon....17
Landore Swans....29
Landrake Cnwll......5
Landscove Devon......7
Land's End Cnwll......2
Land's End Airport Cnwll....2
Landshipping Pembks....41
Landue Cnwll......5
Landulph Cnwll......5
Landwade Suffk....63
Lane Cnwll......4
Laneast Cnwll......5
Lane Bottom Lancs....89
Laneham Notts....85
Lane End Bucks....35
Lane End Cnwll......4
Lane End Hants....22
Lane End Kent....37
Lane End Lancs....96
Lane End Warrtn....82
Lane End Wilts....20
Lane Ends Derbys....71
Lane Ends Lancs....89
Lane Ends N York....90
Lane Green Staffs....58
Laneham Notts....85
Lanehead Dur....102
Lane Head Dur....103
Lanehead Nthumb....111
Lane Head Wigan....82
Lane Head Wsall....58
Lane Heads Lancs....88
Laneshaw Bridge Lancs....89
Lane Side Lancs....89
Langaller Devon......5
Langaller Somset....19
Langar Notts....73
Langbank Rens....125
Langbar N York....96
Langbaurgh N York....104
Langcliffe N York....96
Langdale End N York....99
Langdon Cnwll......5
Langdon Beck Dur....102
Langdown Hants....14
Langdyke Fife....135
Langenhoe Essex....52
Langford C Beds....50
Langford Devon......9
Langford Essex....52
Langford N Som....19
Langford Notts....85
Langford Oxon....33
Langford Budville
  Somset......18
Langham Dorset....20
Langham Essex....52
Langham Norfk....76
Langham Rutlnd....73
Langham Suffk....64
Langho Lancs....89
Langholm D & G....110
Langland Swans....28
Langlee Border....117
Langley Ches E....83
Langley Derbys....84
Langley Gloucs....47
Langley Hants......9
Langley Herts....50
Langley Kent....38
Langley Nthumb....112
Langley Oxon....47
Langley Rochdl....89
Langley Slough....36
Langley Somset....18
Langley Warwks....47
Langley Burrell Wilts....32
Langley Castle Nthumb....112
Langley Common Derbys....71
Langley Green Derbys....71
Langley Green Essex....52
Langley Green Warwks....47
Langley Lower Green
  Essex......51
Langley Marsh Somset....18
Langley Mill Derbys....84
Langley Moor Dur....103
Langley Park Dur....113
Langley Street Norfk....77
Langley Upper Green
  Essex......51
Langney E Susx....25
Langold Notts....85
Langore Cnwll......5
Langport Somset....19
Langrick Lincs....87
Langridge BaNES....32
Langridgeford Devon....17
Langrigg Cumb....110
Langrish Hants....23
Langsett Barns....90
Langside P & K....133
Langstone Hants....15
Langstone Newpt....31
Langthorne N York....97
Langthorpe N York....97

gthwaite N York..........103 K10
gtoft E R Yk..........99 L7
gtoft Lincs..........74 B8
gton Dur..........103 N7
gton Lincs..........86 H7
gton Lincs..........87 L6
gton N York..........98 F7
gton by Wragby
　Lincs..........86 F5
gton Green Kent..........25 M3
gton Green Suffk..........64 G7
gton Herring Dorset..........11 N8
gton Long
　Blandford Dorset..........12 F3
gton Matravers
　Dorset..........12 H9
gtree Devon..........16 H8
gtree Week Devon..........16 H8
gwathby Cumb..........101 Q4
gwell House Highld..........163 Q2
gwith Derbys..........84 H7
gwith Junction
　Derbys..........84 H7
gworth Lincs..........86 E5
hydrock House &
　Gardens Cnwll..........4 H9
ivet Cnwll..........4 G9
jeth Cnwll..........3 P3
k Cnwll..........4 H6
livery Cnwll..........4 H10
oy Cnwll..........5 M6
reath Cnwll..........5 K10
sallos Cnwll..........5 K11
teglos Cnwll..........4 H5
teglos Highway
　Cnwll..........5 J11
ton Border..........118 B6
ton Nthumb..........118 H4
Passee Guern..........10 b1
ford Devon..........8 H3
hroaig Ag & B..........122 E10
ley Staffs..........58 C2
Pulente Jersey..........11 a2
worth Warwks..........59 J10
achbeg Highld..........138 B8
breck Lancs..........88 E2
gie Abers..........158 F11
giemore Ag & B..........131 J10
goward Fife..........135 M6
gs N Ayrs..........124 G6
gybeg N Ayrs..........121 K7
gymore N Ayrs..........121 K7
kbeare Devon..........9 Q5
kfield Inver..........124 C2
kfield Kent..........38 B10
khall S Lans..........126 D7
khill Wilts..........21 M6
ling Norfk..........64 D4
Rocque Jersey..........11 c2
Rousaillerie Guern..........10 b1
tington Dur..........103 K7
borough Gloucs..........32 F6
ham Hants..........23 J6
hbrook Devon..........8 B3
hbrook Devon..........16 G10
henden Kent..........26 D3
k Edge Staffs..........70 G3
swade Mdloth..........127 Q4
tingham N York..........98 E2
cham Somset..........19 M5
chford Herts..........51 J6
chford Oxon..........35 J4
chford Warrtn..........82 D7
chingdon Essex..........52 E11
chley Cnwll..........5 Q7
ely Common Warrtn..........82 E5
hbury M Keyn..........49 N6
heron Highld..........167 M10
heronwheel Highld..........167 L10
imer Bucks..........50 B11
teridge S Glos..........32 C8
tiford Somset..........20 C9
ton Wilts..........33 L5
der Border..........128 E10
gharne Carmth..........28 B2
ghterton Lincs..........85 P5
ighton E Susx..........25 L8
ighton Leics..........60 E3
ighton Lincs..........74 A4
ighton Lincs..........92 D11
ighton-en-le-
　Morthen Rothm..........84 H3
ncells Cnwll..........16 C10
ncells Cross Cnwll..........16 D10
nceston Cnwll..........5 N5
nton Oxon..........48 H10
rrencekirk Abers..........143 N3
rieston D & G..........108 E8
rieston Falk..........126 G2
rendon M Keyn..........49 P4
enham Staffs..........52 F2
ernock V Glam..........30 G11
ersdale Cumb..........111 J8
erstock Wilts..........21 N8
erstoke Hants..........22 E5
erton Gloucs..........47 L7
erton N York..........97 K6
erton Somset..........20 E4
villette Guern..........10 b2
ister Wrexhm..........69 L3
S Lans..........126 E7
vers P & K..........140 G10
vford Essex..........53 J5
vford Somset..........18 F7
Hill S Lans..........126 E7
vhitton Cnwll..........5 P5
vkland N York..........97 R7
vkland Green N York..........96 A7
vley Wrekin..........57 M3
vnhead Staffs..........70 E9
vns Wood
　Crematorium Leeds..........90 H3
vrenny Pembks..........41 K9
vshall Suffk..........64 B11
vshall Green Suffk..........64 B11
vton Herefs..........45 N3
ay W Isls..........168 i5
dale W Isls..........168 j4
IoM..........80 f5
field Suffk..........65 K7
ford Bridge Highld..........164 F7
o Shet..........169 r7
ton E R Yk..........92 C5
ton Nhants..........73 P11
ton Notts..........85 M7
cock C Brad..........90 C2
er Breton Essex..........52 F8
er-de-la-Haye Essex..........52 G7

Layer Marney Essex..........52 F8
Layham Suffk..........52 H3
Layland's Green W Berk..........34 C11
Laymore Dorset..........10 H4
Layter's Green Bucks..........35 Q6
Laytham E R Yk..........92 B3
Laythes Cumb..........110 D9
Lazenby R & Cl..........104 G7
Lazonby Cumb..........101 P3
Lea Derbys..........84 D9
Lea Herefs..........46 C10
Lea Lincs..........85 P3
Lea Shrops..........56 F7
Lea Shrops..........56 G3
Lea Wilts..........33 J7
Lea Marston Warwks..........59 K6
Leachkin Highld..........156 A9
Leadburn Border..........127 N6
Leaden Roding Essex..........51 N8
Leadgate Dur..........112 H10
Leadgate Nthumb..........112 H10
Leadhills S Lans..........116 B7
Leadingcross Green Kent..........38 E11
Leadmill Derbys..........84 B4
Leafield Oxon..........48 B11
Leagrave Luton..........50 C6
Leahead Ches W..........70 B2
Lea Heath Staffs..........71 J9
Leake N York..........97 P2
Leake Common Side
　Lincs..........87 L10
Lealholm N York..........105 L9
Lealholm Side N York..........105 L9
Lealt Highld..........153 J5
Leam Derbys..........84 B5
Lea Marston Warwks..........59 K6
Leamington Hastings
　Warwks..........59 P11
Leamington Spa Warwks..........59 M11
Leamside Dur..........113 M11
Leap Cross E Susx..........25 N8
Leasgill Cumb..........95 K4
Leasingham Lincs..........86 E11
Leasingthorne Dur..........103 Q4
Leatherhead Surrey..........36 E9
Leathley N York..........97 K11
Leaton Shrops..........69 N11
Leaton Wrekin..........57 L2
Lea Town Lancs..........88 F4
Leaveland Kent..........38 H11
Leavenheath Suffk..........52 G4
Leavening N York..........98 F8
Leaves Green Gt Lon..........37 K8
Lea Yeat Cumb..........95 R3
Lebberston N York..........99 M4
Le Bigard Guern..........10 b2
Le Bourg Guern..........10 b2
Le Bourg Guern..........11 c2
Lechlade on Thames
　Gloucs..........33 P5
Lecht Gruinart Ag & B..........122 C6
Leck Lancs..........95 N5
Leckbuie P & K..........140 H9
Leckford Hants..........22 C7
Leckhampstead Bucks..........49 K7
Leckhampstead W Berk..........34 D9
Leckhampstead
　Thicket W Berk..........34 D9
Leckhampton Gloucs..........46 H11
Leckmelm Highld..........161 K9
Leckwith V Glam..........30 G10
Leconfield E R Yk..........92 H2
Ledaig Ag & B..........138 G10
Ledburn Bucks..........49 P10
Ledbury Herefs..........46 D7
Leddington Gloucs..........46 C8
Ledgemoor Herefs..........45 N4
Ledicot Herefs..........45 N2
Ledmore Junction
　Highld..........161 L4
Ledsham Ches W..........81 M10
Ledsham Leeds..........91 M5
Ledston Leeds..........91 L5
Ledstone Devon..........7 J7
Ledston Luck Leeds..........91 L4
Ledwell Oxon..........48 D9
Lee Devon..........16 H2
Lee Gt Lon..........37 J5
Lee Hants..........22 C11
Lee Shrops..........69 M8
Leebotwood Shrops..........56 H5
Lee Brockhurst Shrops..........69 P9
Leece Cumb..........94 E7
Lee Chapel Essex..........37 Q3
Lee Clump Bucks..........35 P4
Lee Common Bucks..........35 P4
Leeds Kent..........38 D11
Leeds Leeds..........90 H4
Leeds Bradford Airport
　Leeds..........90 G2
Leeds Castle Kent..........38 D11
Leedstown Cnwll..........2 G7
Lee Green Ches E..........70 B2
Leek Staffs..........70 H3
Leek Wootton Warwks..........59 L11
Lee Mill Devon..........6 F7
Leeming C Brad..........90 C4
Leeming N York..........97 L3
Leeming Bar N York..........97 L3
Lee Moor Devon..........6 F6
Lee-on-the-Solent Hants..........14 G6
Lees C Brad..........90 C3
Lees Derbys..........71 P7
Lees Oldham..........83 L4
Lees Green Derbys..........71 P7
Leesthorpe Leics..........73 K8
Lee Street Surrey..........24 F2
Leeswood Flints..........69 J2
Leetown P & K..........134 G3
Leftwich Ches W..........82 E10
Legar Powys..........45 J11
Legbourne Lincs..........87 L4
Legburthwaite Cumb..........101 K7
Legerwood Border..........118 A2
Legoland W & M..........35 P10
Le Gron Guern..........10 b2
Legsby Lincs..........86 F3
Le Haguais Jersey..........11 c2
Le Hocq Jersey..........11 c2
Leicester C Leic..........72 F10
Leicester Forest East
　Leics..........72 E10
Leicester Forest East
　Services Leics..........72 E10
Leigh Devon..........17 N9
Leigh Dorset..........11 N3
Leigh Gloucs..........46 G9
Leigh Kent..........37 M11
Leigh Shrops..........56 E4
Leigh Surrey..........36 F11
Leigh Wigan..........82 E5

Leigh Wilts..........33 L6
Leigh Worcs..........46 E4
Leigh Beck Essex..........38 D5
Leigh Delamere Wilts..........32 G9
Leigh Delamere
　Services Wilts..........32 G9
Leigh Green Kent..........26 F5
Leigh Knoweglass S Lans..........125 P6
Leighland Chapel
　Somset..........18 D7
Leigh-on-Sea Sthend..........38 D4
Leigh Park Dorset..........12 H5
Leigh Park Hants..........15 K5
Leigh Sinton Worcs..........46 E4
Leighswood Wsall..........58 G4
Leighterton Gloucs..........32 F6
Leighton N York..........97 J5
Leighton Powys..........56 C3
Leighton Shrops..........57 L3
Leighton Somset..........20 D6
Leighton Bromswold
　Cambs..........61 P5
Leighton Buzzard C Beds..........49 P9
Leigh upon Mendip
　Somset..........20 C5
Leigh Woods N Som..........31 Q10
Leinthall Earls Herefs..........56 G11
Leinthall Starkes Herefs..........56 G11
Leintwardine Herefs..........56 G10
Leire Leics..........60 B3
Leiston Suffk..........65 N9
Leith C Edin..........127 P2
Leitholm Border..........118 E2
Lelant Cnwll..........2 E6
Lelley E R Yk..........93 M4
Lem Hill Worcs..........57 N9
Lempitlaw Border..........118 E4
Lemreway W Isls..........168 i6
Lemsford Herts..........50 F8
Lenchwick Worcs..........47 K5
Lendalfoot S Ayrs..........114 B9
Lendrick Stirlg..........132 H6
Lendrum Terrace Abers..........159 R9
Lenham Kent..........38 E11
Lenham Heath Kent..........26 F2
Lenie Highld..........147 N2
Lennel Border..........118 G2
Lennox Plunton D & G..........108 D10
Lennoxtown E Duns..........125 Q2
Lent Bucks..........35 P8
Lenton C Nott..........72 F3
Lenton Lincs..........73 Q4
Lenwade Norfk..........76 F8
Lenzie E Duns..........126 B3
Leochel-Cushnie Abers..........150 E5
Leomansley Staffs..........58 H3
Leominster Herefs..........45 P3
Leonard Stanley Gloucs..........32 F4
Leoville Jersey..........11 a1
Lepe Hants..........14 D7
Lephin Highld..........152 B8
Leppington N York..........98 F8
Lepton Kirk..........90 G7
Lerags Ag & B..........130 H2
Lerryn Cnwll..........5 K9
Lerwick Shet..........169 r9
Les Arquêts Guern..........10 b2
Lesbury Nthumb..........119 P8
Les Hubits Guern..........10 c2
Leslie Abers..........150 F3
Leslie Fife..........134 H7
Les Lohiers Guern..........10 b2
Lesmahagow S Lans..........126 E10
Les Murchez Guern..........10 b2
Lesnewth Cnwll..........5 J3
Les Nicolles Guern..........10 b2
Les Quartiers Guern..........10 c1
Les Quennevais Jersey..........11 a2
Les Sages Guern..........10 b2
Lessingham Norfk..........77 M6
Lessonhall Cumb..........110 D10
Lestowder Cnwll..........3 K9
Les Villets Guern..........10 b2
Leswalt D & G..........106 D5
L'Etacq Jersey..........11 a1
Letchmore Heath Herts..........50 E11
Letchworth Garden
　City Herts..........50 F4
Letcombe Bassett Oxon..........34 C4
Letcombe Regis Oxon..........34 C7
Letham Angus..........143 J8
Letham Border..........118 C9
Letham Falk..........133 P10
Letham Fife..........135 J5
Letham Grange Angus..........143 L8
Lethenty Abers..........150 F3
Lethenty Abers..........159 K9
Letheringham Suffk..........65 K10
Letheringsett Norfk..........76 E3
Lettaford Devon..........8 H8
Letterewe Highld..........154 C3
Letterfearn Highld..........145 Q3
Letterfinlay Lodge
　Hotel Highld..........146 H9
Lettermorar Highld..........145 M10
Letters Highld..........161 K9
Lettershaw S Lans..........116 B6
Letterston Pembks..........40 H5
Lettoch Highld..........149 J4
Lettoch Highld..........157 L11
Letton Herefs..........45 L5
Letton Herefs..........56 F10
Lett's Green Kent..........37 L9
Letty Green Herts..........50 G9
Letwell Rothm..........85 J3
Leuchars Fife..........135 M3
Leumrabhagh W Isls..........168 i6
Leurbost W Isls..........168 i5
Levalsa Meor Cnwll..........3 Q4
Levedale Staffs..........70 F11
Level's Green Essex..........51 L6
Leven E R Yk..........99 N11
Leven Fife..........135 K7
Levens Cumb..........95 K3
Levens Green Herts..........51 J6
Levenshulme Manch..........83 J6
Levenwick Shet..........169 r11
Leverburgh W Isls..........168 f9
Leverington Cambs..........74 H8
Leverstock Green Herts..........50 C9
Leverton Lincs..........87 M11
Le Villocq Guern..........10 b1
Levington Suffk..........53 M4
Levisham N York..........98 G2
Lew Oxon..........34 B3
Lewannick Cnwll..........5 N5
Lewdown Devon..........8 C7
Lewes E Susx..........25 K8
Leweston Pembks..........40 H6

Lewisham Gt Lon..........37 J6
Lewisham
　Crematorium Gt Lon..........37 J6
Lewiston Highld..........147 N2
Lewistown Brdgnd..........29 P7
Lewis Wych Herefs..........45 L3
Lewknor Oxon..........35 K5
Leworthy Devon..........16 E11
Leworthy Devon..........17 M4
Lewson Street Kent..........38 G9
Lewth Lancs..........88 F3
Lewtrenchard Devon..........8 C7
Lexden Essex..........52 G6
Lexworthy Somset..........19 J7
Ley Cnwll..........5 K8
Leybourne Kent..........37 Q9
Leyburn N York..........96 H2
Leycett Staffs..........70 D5
Leygreen Herts..........50 E6
Ley Hill Bucks..........35 Q4
Leyland Lancs..........88 G6
Leyland Green St Hel..........82 C4
Leylodge Abers..........151 K5
Leys P & K..........142 D10
Leys Abers..........159 P7
Leysdown-on-Sea Kent..........38 H7
Leysmill Angus..........143 L8
Leys of Cossans Angus..........142 F8
Leysters Herefs..........45 R2
Leyton Gt Lon..........37 J3
Leytonstone Gt Lon..........37 J3
Lezant Cnwll..........5 N6
Lezerea Cnwll..........2 H7
Lhanbryde Moray..........157 P5
Libanus Powys..........44 D9
Libberton S Lans..........116 D2
Liberton C Edin..........127 P4
Lichfield Staffs..........58 H3
Lichfield & District
　Crematorium Staffs..........59 J2
Lickey Worcs..........58 E10
Lickey End Worcs..........58 E10
Lickey Rock Worcs..........58 E10
Lickfold W Susx..........23 P9
Liddaton Green Devon..........8 C8
Liddesdale Highld..........138 D6
Liddington Swindn..........33 P8
Lidgate Derbys..........84 D5
Lidgate Suffk..........63 M9
Lidget Donc..........91 R10
Lidgett Notts..........85 K7
Lidham Hill E Susx..........26 D8
Lidlington C Beds..........49 Q7
Lidsey W Susx..........15 P6
Lidsing Kent..........38 C9
Liff Angus..........142 E11
Lifton Devon..........5 P4
Liftondown Devon..........5 P4
Lighthorne Warwks..........48 B3
Lighthorne Heath
　Warwks..........48 C3
Lightwater Surrey..........23 P2
Lightwater Valley
　Theme Park N York..........97 L5
Lightwood C Stke..........70 G5
Lightwood Green Ches E..........70 A6
Lightwood Green
　Wrexhm..........69 L6
Lilbourne Nhants..........60 C5
Lilburn Tower Nthumb..........119 K6
Lilleshall Wrekin..........70 C11
Lilley Herts..........50 D5
Lilley W Berk..........34 D9
Lilliesleaf Border..........117 Q5
Lillingstone Dayrell
　Bucks..........49 K7
Lillingstone Lovell Bucks..........49 K6
Lillington Dorset..........11 N2
Lilliput Poole..........12 H7
Lilstock Somset..........18 G5
Lilyhurst Shrops..........57 N2
Limbrick Lancs..........89 J7
Limbury Luton..........50 C6
Limebrook Herefs..........56 F11
Limefield Bury..........89 N8
Limekilnburn S Lans..........126 C7
Limekilns Fife..........134 E11
Limerigg Falk..........126 F3
Limerstone IoW..........14 D10
Limestone Brae Nthumb..........111 Q11
Lime Street Worcs..........46 F9
Limington Somset..........19 P10
Limmerhaugh E Ayrs..........115 M2
Limpenhoe Norfk..........77 M11
Limpley Stoke Wilts..........20 E2
Limpsfield Surrey..........37 K10
Limpsfield Chart Surrey..........37 K10
Linby Notts..........84 H10
Linchmere W Susx..........23 N8
Lincluden D & G..........109 L5
Lincoln Lincs..........86 C6
Lincoln Crematorium
　Lincs..........86 C6
Lincomb Worcs..........57 Q11
Lincombe Devon..........7 J10
Lincombe Devon..........16 H2
Lindale Cumb..........95 J4
Lindal in Furness Cumb..........94 E5
Lindfield W Susx..........24 H5
Lindford Hants..........23 M7
Lindley Kirk..........90 E7
Lindley N York..........97 K11
Lindores Fife..........134 H4
Lindridge Worcs..........57 M11
Lindsell Essex..........51 P5
Lindsey Suffk..........52 G3
Lindsey Tye Suffk..........52 G3
Liney Somset..........19 L7
Linford Hants..........13 L3
Linford Thurr..........37 Q5
Lingbob C Brad..........90 D3
Lingdale R & Cl..........105 J7
Lingen Herefs..........56 F11
Lingfield Surrey..........25 J2
Lingwood Norfk..........77 M10
Liniclate W Isls..........168 c13
Linkend Worcs..........46 F8
Linkenholt Hants..........22 C3
Linkhill Kent..........26 D7
Linkinhorne Cnwll..........5 N7
Linktown Fife..........134 H9
Linkwood Moray..........157 N5
Linley Shrops..........56 F6
Linley Green Herefs..........46 C4
Linleygreen Shrops..........57 M5
Linlithgow W Loth..........126 H2
Linn Crematorium
　E Rens..........125 P6
Linshiels Nthumb..........118 G9

Linsidemore Highld..........162 C7
Linslade C Beds..........49 P9
Linstead Parva Suffk..........65 L6
Linstock Cumb..........110 H9
Linthurst Worcs..........58 E10
Linthwaite Kirk..........90 E8
Lintlaw Border..........129 L8
Lintmill Moray..........158 D4
Linton Border..........118 E5
Linton Cambs..........63 J11
Linton Derbys..........71 P11
Linton Herefs..........46 C9
Linton Kent..........38 C11
Linton Leeds..........97 N11
Linton N York..........96 E8
Linton N York..........103 L2
Linton Heath Derbys..........71 P11
Linton Hill Herefs..........46 C10
Linton-on-Ouse N York..........97 Q8
Linwood Hants..........13 L3
Linwood Lincs..........86 F3
Linwood Rens..........125 L5
Lionacleit W Isls..........168 c13
Lional W Isls..........168 k1
Lions Green E Susx..........25 N7
Liphook Hants..........23 M8
Lipley Shrops..........70 C8
Liscard Wirral..........81 K6
Liscombe Somset..........18 A8
Liskeard Cnwll..........5 M9
Lismore Ag & B..........138 E9
Liss Hants..........23 L9
Lissett E R Yk..........99 N9
Liss Forest Hants..........23 L9
Lissington Lincs..........86 F4
Liston Essex..........52 E3
Lisvane Cardif..........30 G8
Liswerry Newpt..........31 K7
Litcham Norfk..........76 B8
Litchard Brdgnd..........29 P8
Litchborough Nhants..........48 H4
Litchfield Hants..........22 E4
Litherland Sefton..........81 L5
Litlington Cambs..........50 H2
Litlington E Susx..........25 M10
Little Abington Cambs..........62 H11
Little Addington Nhants..........61 L6
Little Airies D & G..........107 M8
Little Almshoe Herts..........50 F5
Little Alne Warwks..........47 M2
Little Altcar Sefton..........88 C9
Little Amwell Herts..........51 J8
Little Asby Cumb..........102 C9
Little Aston Staffs..........58 G5
Little Atherfield IoW..........14 E11
Little Ayton N York..........104 G8
Little Baddow Essex..........52 C10
Little Badminton S Glos..........32 F8
Little Bampton Cumb..........110 E9
Little Bardfield Essex..........51 Q4
Little Barford Bed..........61 Q9
Little Barningham Norfk..........76 G5
Little Barrington Gloucs..........33 P2
Little Barrow Ches W..........81 P11
Little Barugh N York..........98 F5
Little Bavington Nthumb..........112 E5
Little Bealings Suffk..........53 M2
Littlebeck N York..........105 N10
Little Bedwyn Wilts..........33 Q11
Little Bentley Essex..........53 K6
Little Berkhamsted
　Herts..........50 G9
Little Billing Nhants..........60 H8
Little Billington C Beds..........49 P10
Little Birch Herefs..........45 Q8
Little Bispham Bpool..........88 C2
Little Blakenham Suffk..........53 K2
Little Blencow Cumb..........101 N4
Little Bloxwich Wsall..........58 F4
Little Bognor W Susx..........24 B6
Little Bolehill Derbys..........71 P4
Little Bollington Ches E..........82 F7
Little Bookham Surrey..........36 D10
Littleborough Devon..........9 K2
Littleborough Notts..........85 P4
Littleborough Rochdl..........89 Q7
Littlebourne Kent..........39 M10
Little Bourton Oxon..........48 E6
Little Bowden Leics..........60 F3
Little Bradley Suffk..........63 L10
Little Brampton Herefs..........45 L2
Little Brampton Shrops..........56 F8
Little Braxted Essex..........52 D9
Little Brechin Angus..........143 K5
Littlebredy Dorset..........11 M7
Little Brickhill M Keyn..........49 P8
Little Bridgeford Staffs..........70 F9
Little Brington Nhants..........60 E8
Little Bromley Essex..........53 J6
Little Broughton Cumb..........100 E4
Little Budworth Ches W..........82 C11
Littleburn Highld..........156 A7
Little Burstead Essex..........37 Q2
Littlebury Essex..........51 M3
Littlebury Green Essex..........51 L3
Little Bytham Lincs..........73 Q7
Little Canfield Essex..........51 N6
Little Carlton Lincs..........87 L3
Little Carlton Notts..........85 N9
Little Casterton Rutlnd..........73 Q9
Little Catwick E R Yk..........93 K2
Little Catworth Cambs..........61 P6
Little Cawthorpe Lincs..........87 L4
Little Chalfont Bucks..........35 Q5
Little Chart Kent..........26 F2
Little Chesterford Essex..........51 M2
Little Cheveney Kent..........26 B3
Little Cheverell Wilts..........21 J4
Little Chishill Cambs..........51 K3
Little Clacton Essex..........53 L8
Little Clanfield Oxon..........33 Q4
Little Clifton Cumb..........100 E5
Little Coates NE Lin..........93 M9
Little Comberton Worcs..........47 J6
Little Common E Susx..........26 B10
Little Comp Kent..........37 P9
Little Compton Warwks..........47 Q8
Little Corby Cumb..........111 J9
Little Cornard Suffk..........52 F4
Littlecott Wilts..........21 M4
Little Cowarne Herefs..........46 B4
Little Coxwell Oxon..........33 Q6
Little Crakehall N York..........97 K2
Little Cransley Nhants..........60 H5
Little Cressingham Norfk..........76 B11
Little Crosby Sefton..........81 L4
Little Crosthwaite Cumb..........100 H5
Little Cubley Derbys..........71 M7
Little Dalby Leics..........73 K8
Littledean Gloucs..........32 C2
Little Dewchurch Herefs..........45 Q8

Little Ditton Cambs....63 L9
Little Doward Herefs....45 Q11
Littledown Hants....22 B3
Little Downham Cambs....62 H4
Little Driffield E R Yk....99 L9
Little Dunham Norfk....76 B9
Little Dunkeld P & K....141 P9
Little Dunmow Essex....51 Q6
Little Durnford Wilts....21 M8
Little Easton Essex....51 P6
Little Eaton Derbys....72 B2
Little Ellingham Norfk....64 E2
Little Elm Somset....20 D5
Little Everdon Nhants....60 C9
Little Eversden Cambs....62 E10
Little Faringdon Oxon....33 P4
Little Fencote N York....97 L2
Little Fenton N York....91 N3
Little Fransham Norfk....76 C9
Little Gaddesden Herts....35 Q2
Little Garway Herefs....45 N10
Little Gidding Cambs....61 P4
Little Glemham Suffk....65 L10
Little Gorsley Herefs....46 C10
Little Gransden Cambs....62 C9
Little Green Notts....73 J2
Little Green Somset....20 D5
Little Grimsby Lincs....87 K2
Little Gringley Notts....85 M4
Little Habton N York....98 E5
Little Hadham Herts....51 K6
Little Hale Lincs....74 B3
Little Hallam Derbys....72 D2
Little Hallingbury Essex....51 M7
Littleham Devon....9 P8
Littleham Devon....16 Q7
Little Hampden Bucks....35 N4
Littlehampton W Susx....24 B10
Little Hanford Dorset....12 D2
Little Harrowden Nhants....61 J6
Little Haseley Oxon....34 H4
Little Hatfield E R Yk....93 L2
Little Hautbois Norfk....77 K7
Little Haven Pembks....40 G8
Littlehaven W Susx....24 E4
Little Hay Staffs....58 H4
Little Hayfield Derbys....83 M7
Little Haywood Staffs....71 J10
Little Heath Staffs....70 F11
Little Heath W Berk....35 J10
Littlehempston Devon....7 L6
Little Hereford Herefs....57 K11
Little Horkesley Essex....52 G5
Little Hormead Herts....51 K5
Little Horsted E Susx....25 L7
Little Horton C Brad....90 F4
Little Horton Wilts....21 K2
Little Horwood Bucks....49 L8
Little Houghton Barns....91 L9
Little Houghton Nhants....60 H9
Littlehoughton Nthumb....119 P7
Little Hucklow Derbys....83 Q9
Little Hulton Salfd....82 F4
Little Hungerford W Berk....34 F10
Little Hutton N York....97 Q5
Little Irchester Nhants....61 K7
Little Kelk E R Yk....99 M9
Little Keyford Somset....20 E5
Little Kimble Bucks....35 M3
Little Kineton Warwks....48 B4
Little Kingshill Bucks....35 N5
Little Knox D & G....108 H8
Little Langdale Cumb....101 K10
Little Langford Wilts....21 K7
Little Laver Essex....51 M9
Little Leigh Ches W....82 D9
Little Leighs Essex....52 B8
Little Lever Bolton....89 M9
Little Linford M Keyn....49 M6
Little Load Somset....19 N10
Little London Bucks....34 H2
Little London Cambs....74 H11
Little London E Susx....25 N6
Little London Essex....51 L5
Little London Essex....51 Q3
Little London Gloucs....46 D11
Little London Hants....22 C5
Little London Hants....22 H3
Little London Leeds....90 G3
Little London Lincs....74 D6
Little London Lincs....74 H6
Little London Lincs....87 K6
Little London Norfk....75 L6
Little London Powys....55 N7
Little Longstone Derbys....83 Q10
Little Madeley Staffs....70 D5
Little Malvern Worcs....46 E6
Little Mancot Flints....81 L11
Little Maplestead Essex....52 D5
Little Marcle Herefs....46 C7
Little Marland Devon....17 J9
Little Marlow Bucks....35 N7
Little Massingham Norfk....75 Q6
Little Melton Norfk....76 H10
Littlemill Abers....150 Q8
Littlemill Highld....156 G7
Little Mill Mons....31 K4
Little Milton Oxon....34 H4
Little Missenden Bucks....35 P5
Littlemoor Derbys....84 E8
Little Moor Somset....19 K8
Littlemore Oxon....34 F4
Little Musgrave Cumb....102 E8
Little Ness Shrops....69 M11
Little Neston Ches W....81 K9
Little Newcastle Pembks....41 J5
Little Newsham Dur....103 M7
Little Norton Somset....19 N11
Little Oakley Essex....53 M6
Little Oakley Nhants....61 J3
Little Odell Bed....61 L9
Little Offley Herts....50 D5
Little Ormside Cumb....102 D7
Little Orton Cumb....110 G9
Little Ouse Cambs....63 K3
Little Ouseburn N York....97 P8
Littleover C Derb....72 A4
Little Oxendon Nhants....60 F4
Little Packington Warwks....59 K8
Little Pattenden Kent....26 B2
Little Paxton Cambs....61 Q8
Little Petherick Cnwll....4 E7
Little Plumpton Lancs....88 D4
Little Plumstead Norfk....77 L9
Little Ponton Lincs....73 N4
Littleport Cambs....63 J3
Littleport Bridge Cambs....63 J3
Little Posbrook Hants....14 F6
Little Potheridge Devon....17 J9

Little Preston Leeds....91 K4
Little Preston Nhants....48 G4
Littler Ches W....82 D11
Little Raveley Cambs....62 C5
Little Reedness E R Yk....92 D6
Little Ribston N York....97 N10
Little Rissington Gloucs....47 N11
Little Rollright Oxon....47 Q8
Little Rowsley Derbys....84 C7
Little Ryburgh Norfk....76 D6
Little Ryle Nthumb....119 K8
Little Ryton Shrops....56 H4
Little Salkeld Cumb....101 Q3
Little Sampford Essex....51 Q4
Little Sandhurst Br For....23 M2
Little Saredon Staffs....58 D3
Little Saughall Ches W....81 M11
Little Saxham Suffk....63 P8
Little Scatwell Highld....155 L6
Little Shelford Cambs....62 G10
Little Shrewley Warwks....59 K11
Little Silver Devon....9 M3
Little Singleton Lancs....88 D3
Little Skipwith N York....91 R3
Little Smeaton N York....91 N7
Little Snoring Norfk....76 D5
Little Sodbury S Glos....32 E8
Little Sodbury End S Glos....32 D8
Little Somborne Hants....22 C8
Little Somerford Wilts....33 J8
Little Soudley Shrops....70 C9
Little Stainforth N York....96 B7
Little Stainton Darltn....104 B6
Little Stanion Nhants....61 J3
Little Stanney Ches W....81 N10
Little Staughton Bed....61 P8
Little Steeping Lincs....87 M8
Little Stoke Staffs....70 G8
Littlestone-on-Sea Kent....27 J7
Little Stonham Suffk....64 G9
Little Stretton Leics....72 H10
Little Stretton Shrops....56 G6
Little Strickland Cumb....101 Q7
Little Stukeley Cambs....62 B5
Little Sugnall Staffs....70 E8
Little Sutton Ches W....81 M9
Little Sutton Shrops....57 J8
Little Swinburne Nthumb....112 D5
Little Sypland D & G....108 F10
Little Tew Oxon....48 C9
Little Tey Essex....52 E7
Little Thetford Cambs....62 H5
Little Thirkleby N York....97 Q5
Little Thornage Norfk....76 F4
Little Thornton Lancs....88 D2
Little Thorpe Dur....104 D2
Littlethorpe Leics....72 E11
Littlethorpe N York....97 M7
Little Thurlow Suffk....63 L10
Little Thurlow Green Suffk....63 L10
Little Thurrock Thurr....37 P5
Littleton Angus....142 E7
Littleton BaNES....19 Q2
Littleton Ches W....81 N11
Littleton D & G....108 D9
Littleton Dorset....12 E4
Littleton Hants....22 E8
Littleton Somset....19 N8
Littleton Surrey....23 Q5
Littleton Surrey....36 C7
Littleton Drew Wilts....32 F8
Littleton-on-Severn S Glos....31 Q7
Littleton Pannell Wilts....21 K4
Little Torrington Devon....16 H8
Little Totham Essex....52 E9
Little Town Cumb....100 H7
Littletown Dur....104 B2
Little Town Lancs....89 K3
Little Town Warrtn....82 D6
Little Twycross Leics....72 A9
Little Urswick Cumb....94 F6
Little Wakering Essex....38 F4
Little Walden Essex....51 M2
Little Waldingfield Suffk....52 F2
Little Walsingham Norfk....76 C4
Little Waltham Essex....52 B9
Little Warley Essex....37 P2
Little Washbourne Gloucs....47 J8
Little Weighton E R Yk....92 G4
Little Welnetham Suffk....64 B10
Little Welton Lincs....87 K3
Little Wenham Suffk....53 J4
Little Wenlock Wrekin....57 L3
Little Weston Somset....20 B9
Little Whitefield IoW....14 G9
Little Whittingham Green Suffk....65 K6
Little Whittington Nthumb....112 E7
Littlewick Green W & M....35 M9
Little Wilbraham Cambs....62 H9
Littlewindsor Dorset....11 J4
Little Witcombe Gloucs....46 H11
Little Witley Worcs....46 E2
Little Wittenham Oxon....34 G6
Little Wolford Warwks....47 Q7
Littlewood Staffs....58 E3
Little Woodcote Ct Lon....36 G8
Littleworth Bucks....49 N10
Littleworth Oxon....34 B5
Littleworth Staffs....58 F2
Littleworth Staffs....70 G10
Littleworth W Susx....24 E6
Littleworth Worcs....46 G4
Littleworth Worcs....47 J2
Littleworth Common Bucks....35 P7
Little Wratting Suffk....63 L11
Little Wymington Bed....61 L9
Little Wymondley Herts....50 F5
Little Wyrley Staffs....58 F3
Little Wytheford Shrops....69 Q11
Little Yeldham Essex....52 C4
Litley Green Essex....51 Q7
Litton Derbys....83 Q9
Litton N York....96 D6
Litton Somset....19 Q4
Litton Cheney Dorset....11 L6
Liurbost W Isls....168 i5
Liverpool Lpool....81 L6
Liverpool Maritime Mercantile City Lpool....81 L7
Liversedge Kirk....90 F6
Liverton Devon....9 K9
Liverton R & Cl....105 K7
Liverton Mines R & Cl....105 K7
Liverton Street Kent....26 E11

Livingston W Loth....127 K4
Livingston Village W Loth....127 J4
Lixwm Flints....80 H10
Lizard Cnwll....3 J11
Llaingoch IoA....78 C8
Llaithddu Powys....55 P8
Llan Powys....55 K4
Llanaber Gwynd....67 L11
Llanaelhaearn Gwynd....66 F6
Llanafan Cerdgn....54 F10
Llanafan-Fawr Powys....44 D3
Llanafan-fechan Powys....44 D4
Llanallgo IoA....79 J7
Llanarmon Gwynd....66 G7
Llanarmon Dyffryn Ceiriog Wrexhm....68 G8
Llanarmon-yn-Ial Denbgs....68 G3
Llanarth Cerdgn....42 H3
Llanarth Mons....31 L2
Llanarthne Carmth....43 K11
Llanasa Flints....80 G8
Llanbabo IoA....78 F7
Llanbadarn Fawr Cerdgn....54 E8
Llanbadarn Fynydd Powys....55 P9
Llanbadarn-y-garreg Powys....44 G5
Llanbadoc Mons....31 L5
Llanbadrig IoA....78 F6
Llanbeder Newpt....31 L6
Llanbedr Gwynd....67 K9
Llanbedr Powys....44 G5
Llanbedr Powys....45 J10
Llanbedr-Dyffryn-Clwyd Denbgs....68 F3
Llanbedrgoch IoA....79 J8
Llanbedrog Gwynd....66 E8
Llanbedr-y-Cennin Conwy....79 P11
Llanberis Gwynd....67 K2
Llanbethèry V Glam....30 D11
Llanbister Powys....55 Q10
Llanblethian V Glam....30 C10
Llanboidy Carmth....41 P6
Llanbradach Caerph....30 F6
Llanbrynmair Powys....55 K4
Llancadle V Glam....30 D11
Llancarfan V Glam....30 D10
Llancayo Mons....31 L4
Llancloudy Herefs....45 P10
Llancynfelyn Cerdgn....54 E6
Llandaff Cardif....30 G9
Llandanwg Gwynd....67 K9
Llandarcy Neath....29 K5
Llandawke Carmth....41 Q8
Llanddaniel Fab IoA....78 H10
Llanddarog Carmth....43 K11
Llanddeiniol Cerdgn....54 D10
Llanddeiniolen Gwynd....79 J11
Llandderfel Gwynd....68 C7
Llanddeusant Carmth....43 Q10
Llanddeusant IoA....78 E7
Llanddew Powys....44 F8
Llanddewi Swans....28 E7
Llanddewi Brefi Cerdgn....43 N3
Llanddewi'r Cwm Powys....44 E5
Llanddewi Rhydderch Mons....31 L2
Llanddewi Velfrey Pembks....41 M7
Llanddewi Ystradenni Powys....55 Q11
Llanddoget Conwy....67 Q2
Llanddona IoA....79 K9
Llanddowror Carmth....41 Q8
Llanddulas Conwy....80 C9
Llanddwywe Gwynd....67 K10
Llanddyfnan IoA....79 J9
Llandecwyn Gwynd....67 L7
Llandefaelog Powys....44 E8
Llandefaelog-Tre'r-Graig Powys....44 G9
Llandefalle Powys....44 F7
Llandegfan IoA....79 K10
Llandegla Denbgs....68 G4
Llandegley Powys....44 G2
Llandegveth Mons....31 K5
Llandegwning Gwynd....66 D9
Llandeilo Carmth....43 M10
Llandeilo Graban Powys....44 F6
Llandeilo'r Fan Powys....44 B8
Llandeloy Pembks....40 G5
Llandenny Mons....31 M4
Llandevaud Newpt....31 M6
Llandevenny Mons....31 M7
Llandinabo Herefs....45 Q9
Llandinam Powys....55 N7
Llandissilio Pembks....41 M6
Llandogo Mons....31 P4
Llandough V Glam....30 C10
Llandough V Glam....30 G10
Llandovery Carmth....43 P5
Llandow V Glam....29 P10
Llandre Carmth....43 N6
Llandre Cerdgn....54 E7
Llandre Isaf Pembks....41 M5
Llandrillo Denbgs....68 D7
Llandrillo-yn-Rhos Conwy....79 Q8
Llandrindod Wells Powys....44 F2
Llandrinio Powys....69 J11
Llandudno Conwy....79 P8
Llandudno Junction Conwy....79 P9
Llandulas Powys....44 B6
Llandwrog Gwynd....66 H3
Llandybie Carmth....43 M11
Llandyfaelog Carmth....28 D2
Llandyfan Carmth....43 M11
Llandyfriog Cerdgn....42 F6
Llandyfrydog IoA....78 G7
Llandygai Gwynd....79 K10
Llandygwydd Cerdgn....41 P2
Llandynan Denbgs....68 G5
Llandyrnog Denbgs....80 G11
Llandyssil Powys....56 B5
Llandysul Cerdgn....42 H6
Llanedeyrn Cardif....30 H8
Llanedi Carmth....28 G3
Llaneglwys Powys....44 F7
Llanegryn Gwynd....54 E3
Llanegwad Carmth....43 K10
Llaneilian IoA....78 H6
Llanelian-yn-Rhôs Conwy....80 B10
Llanelidan Denbgs....68 F4
Llanelieu Powys....44 H8
Llanellen Mons....31 K2
Llanelli Carmth....28 F4

Llanelli Crematorium Carmth....28 F4
Llanelltyd Gwynd....67 N11
Llanelly Mons....30 H2
Llanelwedd Powys....44 E4
Llanenddwyn Gwynd....67 K10
Llanengan Gwynd....66 D9
Llanerch Gwynd....68 A11
Llanerch Powys....56 E6
Llanerchymedd IoA....78 G8
Llanerfyl Powys....55 N3
Llanfachraeth IoA....78 E8
Llanfachreth Gwynd....67 P10
Llanfaelog IoA....78 E10
Llanfaelrhys Gwynd....66 C9
Llanfaenor Mons....31 N11
Llanfaes IoA....79 L9
Llanfaes Powys....44 E9
Llanfaethlu IoA....78 E7
Llanfair IoA....67 K9
Llanfair Caereinion Powys....55 Q3
Llanfair Clydogau Cerdgn....43 M4
Llanfair Dyffryn Clwyd Denbgs....68 F3
Llanfairfechan Conwy....79 M10
Llanfair Kilgeddin Mons....31 L3
Llanfair-Nant-Gwyn Pembks....41 N3
Llanfairpwllgwyngyll IoA....79 J10
Llanfair Talhaiarn Conwy....80 C10
Llanfair Waterdine Shrops....56 C9
Llanfairynghornwy IoA....78 E6
Llanfair-yn-Neubwll IoA....78 E9
Llanfallteg Carmth....41 N6
Llanfallteg West Carmth....41 M7
Llanfarian Cerdgn....54 D9
Llanfechain Powys....68 G10
Llanfechell IoA....78 F6
Llanferres Denbgs....68 G2
Llanfflewyn IoA....78 F7
Llanfigael IoA....78 E8
Llanfihangel-ar-arth Carmth....43 J7
Llanfihangel Glyn Myfyr Conwy....68 C5
Llanfihangel Nant Bran Powys....44 C8
Llanfihangel-nant-Melan Powys....44 H3
Llanfihangel Rhydithon Powys....56 B11
Llanfihangel Rogiet Mons....31 N7
Llanfihangel Tal-y-llyn Powys....44 G9
Llanfihangel-uwch-Gwili Carmth....43 J10
Llanfihangel-y-Creuddyn Cerdgn....54 F9
Llanfihangel-yng-Ngwynfa Powys....68 E11
Llanfihangel yn Nhowyn IoA....78 E9
Llanfihangel-y-pennant Gwynd....54 F3
Llanfihangel-y-pennant Gwynd....67 J6
Llanfihangel-y-traethau Gwynd....67 K8
Llanfilo Powys....44 G8
Llanfoist Mons....31 J2
Llanfor Gwynd....68 B7
Llanfrechfa Torfn....31 K6
Llanfrothen Gwynd....67 L6
Llanfrynach Powys....44 F9
Llanfwrog Denbgs....68 F3
Llanfwrog IoA....78 E8
Llanfyllin Powys....68 F11
Llanfynydd Carmth....43 L9
Llanfynydd Flints....69 J3
Llanfyrnach Pembks....41 P4
Llangadfan Powys....55 N2
Llangadog Carmth....28 D3
Llangadog Carmth....43 P9
Llangadwaladr IoA....78 F11
Llangadwaladr Powys....68 G8
Llangaffo IoA....78 G11
Llangain Carmth....42 G11
Llangammarch Wells Powys....44 C5
Llangan V Glam....30 C9
Llangarron Herefs....45 Q10
Llangasty-Talyllyn Powys....44 G9
Llangathen Carmth....43 L10
Llangattock Powys....45 J11
Llangattock Lingoed Mons....45 M10
Llangattock-Vibon-Avel Mons....45 P11
Llangedwyn Powys....68 G10
Llangefni IoA....78 H9
Llangeinor Brdgnd....29 P7
Llangeitho Cerdgn....43 M3
Llangeler Carmth....42 G7
Llangelynin Gwynd....54 D3
Llangendeirne Carmth....28 E2
Llangennech Carmth....28 G4
Llangennith Swans....28 D6
Llangenny Powys....45 J11
Llangernyw Conwy....80 B11
Llangian Gwynd....66 D9
Llangiwg Neath....29 K3
Llangloffan Pembks....40 H4
Llanglydwen Carmth....41 N5
Llangoed IoA....79 L9
Llangoedmor Cerdgn....42 D5
Llangollen Denbgs....68 H6
Llangolman Pembks....41 M5
Llangors Powys....44 G9
Llangovan Mons....31 N3
Llangower Gwynd....68 B8
Llangranog Cerdgn....42 F4
Llangristiolus IoA....78 G10
Llangrove Herefs....45 M9
Llangua Mons....45 M10
Llangunllo Powys....55 L9
Llangunnor Carmth....42 H10
Llangurig Powys....55 L8
Llangwm Conwy....68 C6
Llangwm Mons....31 M5
Llangwm Pembks....41 J9
Llangwnnadl Gwynd....66 C8
Llangwyfan Denbgs....80 G11
Llangwyllog IoA....78 G9
Llangwyryfon Cerdgn....54 D10
Llangybi Cerdgn....43 M4
Llangybi Gwynd....66 G6

Llangybi Mons....31 L6
Llangyfelach Swans....28 H4
Llangynhafal Denbgs....68 F2
Llangynidr Powys....44 H11
Llangynin Carmth....41 Q6
Llangynllo Cerdgn....42 G6
Llangynog Carmth....28 C2
Llangynog Powys....55 Q2
Llangynwyd Brdgnd....29 N7
Llanhamlach Powys....44 F9
Llanharan Rhondd....30 D8
Llanharry Rhondd....30 D8
Llanhennock Mons....31 L5
Llanhilleth Blae G....30 H3
Llanidan IoA....78 H11
Llaniestyn Gwynd....66 D8
Llanigon Powys....44 H7
Llanilar Cerdgn....54 E9
Llanilid Rhondd....30 C8
Llanina Cerdgn....42 H3
Llanio Cerdgn....43 M2
Llanishen Cardif....30 G9
Llanishen Mons....31 M3
Llanllechid Gwynd....79 L11
Llanlleonfel Powys....44 C5
Llanllowell Mons....31 L5
Llanllugan Powys....55 P3
Llanllwch Carmth....42 G11
Llanllwchaiarn Powys....55 Q5
Llanllwni Carmth....42 H6
Llanllyfni Gwynd....66 H4
Llanmadoc Swans....28 D6
Llanmaes V Glam....30 C11
Llanmartin Newpt....31 M7
Llanmerewig Powys....56 B4
Llanmihangel V Glam....30 C10
Llanmiloe Carmth....41 P7
Llanmorlais Swans....28 F5
Llannefydd Conwy....80 D11
Llannon Carmth....28 F4
Llannor Gwynd....66 F7
Llanon Cerdgn....54 C11
Llanover Mons....31 K4
Llanpumsaint Carmth....42 H9
Llanrhaeadr-ym-Mochnant Powys....68 F10
Llanrhian Pembks....40 F4
Llanrhidian Swans....28 E6
Llanrhos Conwy....79 P8
Llanrhychwyn Conwy....67 P2
Llanrhyddlad IoA....78 E6
Llanrhystud Cerdgn....54 C11
Llanrothal Herefs....45 P11
Llanrug Gwynd....67 K2
Llanrumney Cardif....30 H7
Llanrwst Conwy....67 P2
Llansadurnen Carmth....41 Q7
Llansadwrn Carmth....43 M7
Llansadwrn IoA....79 K9
Llansaint Carmth....28 D2
Llansamlet Swans....29 J5
Llansanffraid Glan Conwy Conwy....79 Q8
Llansannan Conwy....80 C11
Llansannor V Glam....30 C10
Llansantffraed Powys....44 G9
Llansantffraed-Cwmdeuddwr Powys....55 M10
Llansantffraed-in-Elvel Powys....44 F4
Llansantffraid Cerdgn....54 C11
Llansantffraid-ym-Mechain Powys....68 H10
Llansawel Carmth....43 M7
Llansilin Powys....68 G11
Llansoy Mons....31 M4
Llanspyddid Powys....44 E9
Llanstadwell Pembks....40 H10
Llansteffan Carmth....28 D2
Llanstephan Powys....44 G6
Llantarnam Torfn....31 K6
Llanteg Pembks....41 N8
Llanthewy Skirrid Mons....45 L11
Llanthony Mons....45 K9
Llantilio-Crossenny Mons....31 L11
Llantilio Pertholey Mons....45 L11
Llantood Pembks....41 N2
Llantrisant IoA....78 F7
Llantrisant Mons....31 L5
Llantrisant Rhondd....30 D8
Llantrithyd V Glam....30 D10
Llantwit Fardre Rhondd....30 E7
Llantwit Major V Glam....30 C11
Llantysilio Denbgs....68 G5
Llanuwchllyn Gwynd....68 B8
Llanvaches Newpt....31 M6
Llanvair Discoed Mons....31 M7
Llanvapley Mons....45 M11
Llanvetherine Mons....45 M11
Llanveynoe Herefs....45 L10
Llanvihangel Crucorney Mons....45 L11
Llanvihangel Gobion Mons....31 L2
Llanvihangel-Ystern-Llewern Mons....31 N11
Llanwarne Herefs....45 Q9
Llanwddyn Powys....68 D11
Llanwenarth Mons....31 J2
Llanwenog Cerdgn....43 J5
Llanwern Newpt....31 L7
Llanwinio Carmth....41 Q6
Llanwnda Gwynd....66 H3
Llanwnda Pembks....40 H4
Llanwnnen Cerdgn....43 J5
Llanwnog Powys....55 N5
Llanwonno Rhondd....30 D6
Llanwrda Carmth....43 P7
Llanwrin Powys....54 H3
Llanwrthwl Powys....44 D4
Llanwrtyd Powys....44 B6
Llanwrtyd Wells Powys....44 B6
Llanwyddelan Powys....55 P3
Llanyblodwel Shrops....68 H11
Llanybri Carmth....42 G11
Llanybydder Carmth....43 J5
Llanycefn Pembks....41 L5
Llanychaer Pembks....41 J4
Llanycrwys Carmth....43 M5
Llanymawddwy Gwynd....68 B11
Llanymynech Powys....68 H11
Llanynghenedl IoA....78 E8
Llanynys Denbgs....80 F11
Llan-y-pwll Wrexhm....69 K4
Llanyre Powys....44 E3
Llanystumdwy Gwynd....66 H6
Llanywern Powys....44 G9
Llawhaden Pembks....41 L7
Llawnt Shrops....68 H9

wryglyn Powys....55 L6
y Wrexhm....69 K3
chcynfarwy IoA....78 F8
chfaen Powys....44 F9
chrhyd Caerph....30 F3
chryd Cerdgn....41 P2
chylched IoA....78 E9
drod Cerdgn....54 E10
yn Peninsula Gwynd....66 E7
rdiau Gwynd....68 A7
iartnenog Carmth....43 K7
iart-y-parc Denbgs....68 F6
hfaen Gwynd....66 F6
c Flints....80 G9
wes Powys....44 H6
rydcoed Rhondd....30 C4
ydcoed
 Crematorium Rhondd....30 C3
ydiarth Powys....68 D11
yn Denbgs....68 E2
yncelyn Cerdgn....42 H3
yndafydd Cerdgn....42 G3
ynderw Powys....56 C4
ryn-drain Pembks....41 Q4
ryn-du Mons....45 K11
yngwril Gwynd....54 D3
ynhendy Carmth....28 F5
yn mawr Wrexhm....68 H7
yn-on Myr Td....30 D2
yn-y-brain Carmth....41 N8
yn-y-groes Cerdgn....43 L3
ynypia Rhondd....30 C6
nclys Shrops....69 J10
nfaes IoA....78 G9
n-y-pandy Flints....81 J11
sfaen Conwy....80 B9
swen Cerdgn....43 J2
swen Powys....44 G7
sworney V Glam....30 C10
s-y-frân Pembks....41 K6
wel Powys....44 B8
d Brook Sheff....84 C3
an Falk....126 H2
anend Nthumb....129 N9
anhead Mdloth....127 P4
nningfoot D & G....109 L9
ns S Ayrs....125 J11
b Devon....16 H4
hillcross Devon....8 C7
hailort Highld....145 N11
haline Highld....138 B9
hans D & G....106 E6
harbriggs D & G....109 L4
havich Ag & B....131 J4
hawe Ag & B....131 N2
h Baghasdail W Isls....168 c16
hboisdale W Isls....168 c16
hbuie Highld....137 Q10
hcarron Highld....154 A10
hdar W Isls....168 c13
hdon D & G....138 C11
hdonhead Ag & B....138 C11
head Ag & B....123 N4
hearnhead Stirlg....132 H3
hee C Dund....142 F11
heilside Station
 Highld....138 H2
hend Highld....155 Q10
heport W Isls....168 d11
hfoot D & G....109 J6
hgair Ag & B....131 J9
hgelly Fife....134 F9
hgilphead Ag & B....130 H10
hgoilhead Ag & B....131 Q7
hieheads Fife....134 H5
hill Moray....157 P5
hindorb Lodge
 Highld....156 H10
hinver Highld....160 H2
h Lomond and The
 Trossachs National
 Park....132 E5
hluichart Highld....155 K5
hmaben D & G....109 N4
hmaddy W Isls....168 e11
h Maree Hotel Highld....154 B3
h nam Madadh W Isls....168 e11
h Ness Highld....147 N2
hore Fife....134 F8
hranza N Ayrs....124 A7
hside Abers....143 N5
hside D & G....109 L5
hside Highld....156 E7
hslin Highld....163 J10
hton S Ayrs....107 J2
hty Abers....143 J5
hty Fife....135 N6
huisge Highld....138 D6
hwinnoch Rens....125 K6
hwood D & G....116 F11
kengate Cnwll....4 G9
kerbie D & G....109 P4
keridge Wilts....33 M11
kerley Hants....22 B9
king N Som....19 L3
king Stumps Warrtn....82 D6
kington E R Yk....99 K11
kington Leics....72 D5
kleywood Shrops....70 B9
ksbottom Gt Lon....37 K7
ksgreen IoW....14 D8
ks Heath Hants....14 F5
kton N York....98 G3
dington Leics....73 K10
dington Nhants....60 H5
diswell Devon....7 J9
don Norfk....65 M2
e Cambs....62 H8
e Heath Solhll....59 J8
iers Dorset....11 K6
ge Hill
 Crematorium Birm....58 F8
dsworth W Susx....20 P10
thouse Leeds....91 J5
thouse N York....96 H6
thouse Gate Wakefd....91 J6
tus R & Cl....105 K7
gan E Ayrs....115 L3
ieback Cumb....94 D2
anlea W Loth....126 H5
gerheads Staffs....70 C7
ie Angus....143 M5
ie Moray....157 J7
ie Pert Angus....143 M5
ie Newton Abers....158 G10
ierait P & K....141 N7
ierieve Abers....151 N2

Login Carmth....41 N6
Lolworth Cambs....62 E8
Lonbain Highld....153 M7
Londesborough E R Yk....98 H11
London Gt Lon....36 H4
London Apprentice
 Cnwll....3 Q4
London Beach Kent....26 E4
London Colney Herts....50 E10
Londonderry N York....97 M3
London End Nhants....61 K7
London Gateway
 Services Gt Lon....36 E2
Londonthorpe Lincs....73 P3
London Zoo ZSL Gt Lon....36 G4
Londubh Highld....160 D10
Lonemore Highld....153 P2
Long Ashton N Som....31 P10
Long Bank Worcs....57 P10
Long Bennington Lincs....73 L2
Longbenton N Tyne....113 L7
Longborough Gloucs....47 N9
Long Bredy Dorset....11 M6
Longbridge Birm....58 F9
Longbridge Warwks....47 Q2
Longbridge Deverill
 Wilts....20 G6
Long Buckby Nhants....60 D7
Longburgh Cumb....110 F9
Longburton Dorset....11 N2
Long Cause Devon....7 K4
Long Clawson Leics....73 J5
Longcliffe Derbys....84 B9
Longcombe Devon....7 L7
Long Common Hants....14 F4
Long Compton Staffs....70 F10
Long Compton Warwks....47 Q8
Longcot Oxon....33 Q6
Long Crendon Bucks....35 J3
Long Crichel Dorset....12 G3
Longcroft Cumb....110 D9
Longcross Surrey....35 Q11
Longden Shrops....56 G3
Longden Common
 Shrops....56 G3
Long Ditton Surrey....36 E7
Longdon Staffs....58 G2
Longdon Worcs....46 F7
Longdon Green Staffs....58 G2
Longdon Heath Worcs....46 F7
Longdon upon Tern
 Wrekin....69 R11
Longdown Devon....9 L6
Longdowns Cnwll....3 J7
Long Drax N York....92 A5
Long Duckmanton
 Derbys....84 F6
Long Eaton Derbys....72 D4
Longfield Kent....37 P7
Longford Covtry....59 N7
Longford Derbys....71 N7
Longford Gloucs....46 F10
Longford Gt Lon....36 C5
Longford Kent....37 M9
Longford Shrops....70 A8
Longford Wrekin....70 C11
Longforgan P & K....134 H2
Longformacus Border....128 H8
Long Green Ches W....81 P10
Long Green Worcs....46 F8
Longham Dorset....13 J5
Longham Norfk....76 C8
Long Hanborough Oxon....34 D2
Longhaven Abers....159 R10
Long Hedges Lincs....87 L11
Longhirst Nthumb....113 K3
Longhope Gloucs....46 C11
Longhope Ork....169 c7
Longhorsley Nthumb....112 H2
Longhoughton Nthumb....119 P7
Long Itchington Warwks....59 P11
Longlands Cumb....101 J3
Longlane Derbys....71 N7
Long Lawford Warwks....59 Q9
Long Meadowend
 Shrops....56 G8
Long Melford Suffk....52 E2
Longmoor Camp Hants....23 L8
Longmorn Moray....157 N6
Longmoss Ches E....83 J10
Long Newnton Gloucs....32 H6
Longnewton Border....118 A5
Long Newton E Loth....128 E7
Longnewton S on T....104 C7
Longney Gloucs....32 E2
Longniddry E Loth....128 C4
Longnor Shrops....56 H4
Longnor Staffs....71 K2
Longparish Hants....22 D5
Longpark Cumb....110 H8
Long Preston N York....96 B9
Longridge Lancs....89 J3
Longridge Staffs....70 G11
Longridge W Loth....126 G5
Longriggend N Lans....126 E3
Long Riston E R Yk....93 K2
Longrock Cnwll....2 E7
Longsdon Staffs....70 H4
Longshaw Wigan....82 B4
Longside Abers....159 P8
Long Sight Oldham....89 Q9
Longslow Shrops....70 B7
Longstanton Cambs....62 E7
Longstock Hants....22 C7
Longstone Pembks....41 M9
Longstowe Cambs....62 D10
Long Stratton Norfk....64 H3
Long Street M Keyn....49 L5
Longstreet Wilts....21 M4
Long Sutton Hants....23 K5
Long Sutton Lincs....74 H6
Long Sutton Somset....19 N9
Longthorpe C Pete....74 C11
Long Thurlow Suffk....64 E8
Longthwaite Cumb....101 M6
Longton C Stke....70 G6

Longton Lancs....88 F5
Longtown Cumb....110 G7
Longtown Herefs....45 L9
Longueville Jersey....11 c2
Longville in the Dale
 Shrops....57 J6
Long Waste Wrekin....69 R11
Long Whatton Leics....72 D6
Longwick Bucks....35 L3
Long Wittenham Oxon....34 F6
Longwitton Nthumb....112 H3
Longwood D & G....108 F8
Longworth Oxon....34 C5
Longyester E Loth....128 E7
Lôn-las Swans....29 K5
Lonmay Abers....159 P6
Lonmore Highld....152 D8
Looe Cnwll....5 M11
Loose Kent....38 C11
Loosebeare Devon....8 H3
Loosegate Lincs....74 F5
Loosley Row Bucks....35 M4
Lootcherbrae Abers....158 F7
Lopcombe Corner Wilts....21 Q7
Lopen Somset....11 J2
Loppington Shrops....69 N9
Lorbottle Nthumb....119 K9
Lordington W Susx....15 L5
Lordsbridge Norfk....75 L8
Lordshill C Sotn....22 C11
Lords Wood Medway....38 C9
Lornty P & K....142 B8
Loscoe Derbys....84 F11
Loscombe Dorset....11 K5
Losgaintir W Isls....168 f9
Lossiemouth Moray....157 N3
Lostford Shrops....69 R8
Lostock Gralam Ches W....82 E10
Lostock Green Ches W....82 E10
Lostock Hall Lancs....88 G5
Lostock Hall Fold Bolton....89 K9
Lostock Junction Bolton....89 K9
Lostwithiel Cnwll....5 J10
Lothbeg Highld....163 L4
Lothersdale N York....96 E11
Lothmore Highld....163 M4
Loudwater Bucks....35 P6
Loughborough Leics....72 E7
Loughborough
 Crematorium Leics....72 E7
Loughor Swans....28 G5
Loughton Essex....51 K11
Loughton M Keyn....49 M7
Loughton Shrops....57 L8
Lound Lincs....73 R7
Lound Notts....85 L3
Lound Suffk....65 Q2
Lounston Devon....9 J9
Lount Leics....72 B7
Louth Lincs....87 K3
Love Clough Lancs....89 N5
Lovedean Hants....15 J4
Lover Wilts....21 P10
Loversall Donc....91 P11
Loves Green Essex....51 P10
Lovesome Hill N York....104 C11
Loveston Pembks....41 L9
Lovington Somset....19 Q8
Low Ackworth Wakefd....91 M7
Low Angerton Nthumb....112 H3
Lowbands Gloucs....46 E8
Low Barbeth D & G....106 D4
Low Barlings Lincs....86 E6
Low Bell End N York....105 K11
Low Bentham N York....95 N7
Low Biggins Cumb....95 N5
Low Borrowbridge
 Cumb....102 B10
Low Bradfield Sheff....84 C2
Low Bradley N York....96 F11
Low Braithwaite Cumb....101 M2
Low Burnham N Linc....92 C10
Low Buston Nthumb....119 P9
Lowca Cumb....100 C6
Low Catton E R Yk....98 E10
Low Coniscliffe Darltn....103 Q8
Low Crosby Cumb....110 H9
Lowdham Notts....85 L11
Low Dinsdale Darltn....104 B8
Lowe Shrops....69 N8
Lowe Hill Staffs....70 H3
Lower Ellington N York....97 K4
Lower Aisholt Somset....18 H7
Lower Ansty Dorset....12 C4
Lower Apperley Gloucs....46 G9
Lower Arncott Oxon....48 H11
Lower Ashton Devon....9 K8
Lower Assendon Oxon....35 K8
Lower Ballam Lancs....88 D4
Lower Bartle Lancs....88 F4
Lower Basildon W Berk....34 H9
Lower Bearwood Herefs....45 M3
Lower Beeding W Susx....24 F5
Lower Benefield Nhants....61 L3
Lower Beobridge Shrops....57 P6
Lower Birchwood
 Derbys....84 F10
Lower Boddington
 Nhants....48 E4
Lower Boscaswell Cnwll....2 B7
Lower Bourne Surrey....23 M6
Lower Brailes Warwks....48 B7
Lower Breakish Highld....145 L3
Lower Bredbury Stockp....83 K6
Lower Broadheath
 Worcs....46 F3
Lower Broxwood Herefs....45 M4
Lower Buckenhill Herefs....46 B8
Lower Bullingham
 Herefs....45 Q7
Lower Burgate Hants....21 N11
Lower Burrowton Devon....9 P5
Lower Burton Herefs....45 N3
Lower Caldecote C Beds....61 Q4
Lower Cam Gloucs....32 D4
Lower Canada N Som....19 L3
Lower Catesby Nhants....60 B9
Lower Chapel Powys....44 E7
Lower Chicksgrove Wilts....21 J9
Lower Chute Wilts....22 B4
Lower Clapton Gt Lon....36 H3
Lower Clent Worcs....58 D9
Lower Common Hants....23 L2
Lower Creedy Devon....9 K4
Lower Crossings Derbys....83 M8
Lower Cumberworth
 Kirk....90 G9
Lower Darwen Bl w D....89 K5
Lower Dean Bed....61 N7
Lower Denby Kirk....90 G9

Lower Diabaig Highld....153 P5
Lower Dicker E Susx....25 N8
Lower Dinchope Shrops....56 H8
Lower Down Shrops....56 E8
Lower Dunsforth N York....97 P8
Lower Egleton Herefs....46 B5
Lower Elkstone Staffs....71 K3
Lower Ellastone Staffs....71 L6
Lower End Bucks....35 J3
Lower End M Keyn....49 P7
Lower End Nhants....60 H9
Lower End Nhants....61 J8
Lower Everleigh Wilts....21 N4
Lower Exbury Hants....14 D7
Lower Eythorne Kent....27 N2
Lower Failand N Som....31 P10
Lower Farringdon Hants....23 K7
Lower Feltham Gt Lon....36 C6
Lower Fittleworth
 W Susx....24 B7
Lower Foxdale IoM....80 c6
Lower Frankton Shrops....69 L8
Lower Freystrop
 Pembks....41 J8
Lower Froyle Hants....23 L6
Lower Gabwell Devon....7 N5
Lower Gledfield Highld....162 D8
Lower Godney Somset....19 N6
Lower Gornal Dudley....58 D6
Lower Gravenhurst
 C Beds....50 D3
Lower Green Herts....50 E4
Lower Green Herts....51 K4
Lower Green Kent....25 N2
Lower Green Kent....25 P2
Lower Green Norfk....76 D4
Lower Green Staffs....58 D3
Lower Green Suffk....63 M7
Lower Hacheston Suffk....65 L10
Lower Halliford Surrey....36 C7
Lower Halstock Leigh
 Dorset....11 L3
Lower Halstow Kent....38 E8
Lower Hamworthy
 Poole....12 G6
Lower Hardres Kent....39 L11
Lower Harpton Herefs....45 K2
Lower Hartlip Kent....38 D9
Lower Hartshay Derbys....84 E10
Lower Hartwell Bucks....35 L2
Lower Hatton Staffs....70 E7
Lower Hawthwaite
 Cumb....94 E3
Lower Hergest Herefs....45 K3
Lower Heyford Oxon....48 E10
Lower Heysham Lancs....95 J8
Lower Higham Kent....38 B7
Lower Holbrook Suffk....53 L4
Lower Hordley Shrops....69 L9
Lower Horncroft W Susx....24 B7
Lowerhouse Lancs....89 N4
Lower Houses Kirk....90 F7
Lower Howsell Worcs....46 E5
Lower Irlam Salfd....82 F6
Lower Kilburn Derbys....72 B2
Lower Kilcott Gloucs....32 E7
Lower Killeyan Ag & B....122 C11
Lower Kingcombe
 Dorset....11 M5
Lower Kingswood
 Surrey....36 F10
Lower Kinnerton Ches W....69 K2
Lower Langford N Som....19 N2
Lower Largo Fife....135 L7
Lower Leigh Staffs....71 J7
Lower Lemington Gloucs....47 P8
Lower Llanfadog Powys....55 M11
Lower Lovacott Devon....17 J6
Lower Loxhore Devon....17 L4
Lower Lydbrook Gloucs....46 A11
Lower Lye Herefs....56 G11
Lower Machen Newpt....30 H7
Lower Maes-coed Herefs....45 L8
Lower Mannington
 Dorset....13 J4
Lower Marston Somset....20 E6
Lower Meend Gloucs....31 Q4
Lower Merridge Somset....18 H8
Lower Middleton
 Cheney Nhants....48 F5
Lower Milton Somset....19 P5
Lower Moor Worcs....47 J5
Lower Morton S Glos....32 B6
Lower Nazeing Essex....51 J9
Lower Norton Warwks....47 P2
Lower Nyland Dorset....20 D10
Lower Penarth V Glam....30 G11
Lower Penn Staffs....58 C5
Lower Pennington Hants....13 P6
Lower Penwortham
 Lancs....88 G5
Lower Peover Ches E....82 F10
Lower Place Rochdl....89 Q8
Lower Pollicott Bucks....35 K2
Lower Quinton Warwks....47 N5
Lower Rainham Medway....38 D8
Lower Raydon Suffk....52 H4
Lower Roadwater
 Somset....18 D7
Lower Salter Lancs....95 N8
Lower Seagry Wilts....33 J8
Lower Sheering Essex....51 L8
Lower Shelton C Beds....49 Q6
Lower Shiplake Oxon....35 L9
Lower Shuckburgh
 Warwks....48 E2
Lower Slaughter Gloucs....47 N10
Lower Soothill Kirk....90 H6
Lower Soudley Gloucs....32 C3
Lower Standen Kent....27 M3
Lower Stanton St
 Quintin Wilts....32 H8
Lower Stoke Medway....38 D6
Lower Stone Gloucs....32 C6
Lower Stonnall Staffs....58 G4
Lower Stow Bedon
 Norfk....64 D3
Lower Street Dorset....12 D5
Lower Street E Susx....26 B9
Lower Street Norfk....77 K4
Lower Street Suffk....63 N10
Lower Street Suffk....64 G11
Lower Stretton Warrtn....82 D8
Lower Stroud Dorset....11 K5
Lower Sundon C Beds....50 C5
Lower Swanwick Hants....14 E5
Lower Swell Gloucs....47 N9
Lower Tadmarton Oxon....48 D7
Lower Tale Devon....9 Q4
Lower Tean Staffs....71 J7
Lower Thurlton Norfk....65 N2

Lower Town Cnwll....2 H8
Lower Town Devon....7 J4
Lower Town Herefs....46 B6
Lower Town Pembks....41 J3
Lower Trebullett Cnwll....5 N6
Lower Treluswell Cnwll....3 K6
Lower Tysoe Warwks....48 B5
Lower Ufford Suffk....65 K11
Lower Upcott Devon....9 L8
Lower Upham Hants....22 F11
Lower Upnor Medway....38 C7
Lower Vexford Somset....18 F7
Lower Walton Warrtn....82 D7
Lower Waterston Dorset....12 D4
Lower Weare Somset....19 M4
Lower Weedon Nhants....60 D9
Lower Welson Herefs....45 K4
Lower Westmancote
 Worcs....46 H7
Lower Whatcombe
 Dorset....12 D4
Lower Whatley Somset....20 D5
Lower Whitley Ches W....82 D9
Lower Wick Gloucs....32 D5
Lower Wick Worcs....45 F4
Lower Wield Hants....22 H6
Lower Willington E Susx....25 N10
Lower Withington
 Ches E....82 H11
Lower Woodend Bucks....35 M7
Lower Woodford Wilts....21 M7
Lower Wraxall Dorset....11 M4
Lower Wyche Worcs....46 E6
Lower Wyke C Brad....90 F5
Lowesby Leics....73 J9
Lowestoft Suffk....65 Q3
Loweswater Cumb....100 F6
Low Fell Gatesd....113 L9
Lowfield Heath W Susx....24 G3
Low Gartachorrans Stirlg....132 F10
Low Gate Nthumb....112 D8
Low Gettbridge Cumb....111 K9
Lowgill Cumb....102 B11
Lowgill Lancs....95 P8
Low Grantley N York....97 K6
Low Green N York....97 K9
Low Habberley Worcs....57 Q9
Low Ham Somset....19 M9
Low Harrogate N York....97 L9
Low Hawsker N York....105 P9
Low Hesket Cumb....111 J11
Low Hutton N York....98 F7
Lowick Cumb....94 F3
Lowick Nhants....61 L4
Lowick Nthumb....119 K3
Lowick Bridge Cumb....94 F3
Lowick Green Cumb....94 F3
Low Knipe Cumb....101 P7
Low Laithe N York....97 J8
Lowlands Dur....103 M5
Lowlands Torfn....31 J5
Low Langton Lincs....86 G5
Low Leighton Derbys....83 M7
Low Lorton Cumb....100 G5
Low Marishes N York....98 G5
Low Marnham Notts....85 P7
Low Middleton Nthumb....119 M3
Low Mill N York....105 J11
Low Moor C Brad....90 F5
Low Moorsley Sundld....113 M11
Low Moresby Cumb....100 C6
Low Newton Cumb....95 J4
Low Row Cumb....100 G2
Low Row Cumb....101 L3
Low Row Cumb....111 L8
Low Row N York....103 J11
Low Salchrie D & G....106 D4
Low Santon N Linc....92 F8
Lowsonford Warwks....59 J11
Low Street Norfk....77 L7
Low Street Thurr....37 Q5
Low Tharston Norfk....64 H2
Lowther Cumb....101 P6
Lowther Castle Cumb....101 P6
Lowthorpe E R Yk....99 M8
Lowton Devon....8 G4
Lowton Somset....18 G11
Lowton Wigan....82 D5
Lowton Common Wigan....82 D5
Lowton St Mary's Wigan....82 D5
Low Torry Fife....134 C10
Low Toynton Lincs....87 J6
Low Valley Barns....91 L10
Low Wood Cumb....94 G4
Low Worsall N York....104 C9
Low Wray Cumb....101 L10
Loxbeare Devon....18 B11
Loxhill Surrey....23 B3
Loxhore Devon....17 L4
Loxhore Cott Devon....17 L4
Loxley Warwks....47 Q4
Loxley Green Staffs....71 K8
Loxter Herefs....46 D6
Loxton N Som....19 L3
Loxwood W Susx....24 B4
Loyal Lodge Highld....165 P7
Lubenham Leics....60 F3
Lucasgate Lincs....87 M11
Lucas Green Surrey....23 P2
Luccombe Somset....18 B6
Luccombe Village IoW....14 G11
Lucker Nthumb....119 N4
Luckett Cnwll....5 P7
Lucking Street Essex....52 D5
Luckington Wilts....32 F8
Lucklawhill Fife....135 L3
Lucknam Wilts....32 F10
Luckwell Bridge Somset....18 B7
Lucton Herefs....45 N2
Lucy Cross N York....103 P8
Ludag W Isls....168 c16
Ludborough Lincs....93 N11
Ludbrook Devon....6 H8
Ludchurch Pembks....41 M8
Luddenden Calder....90 C5
Luddenden Foot Calder....90 C5
Luddenham Court Kent....38 G9
Luddesdown Kent....37 Q7
Luddington N Linc....92 D7
Luddington Warwks....47 N4
Luddington in the
 Brook Nhants....61 P4
Ludford Lincs....86 G3
Ludford Shrops....57 J10
Ludgershall Bucks....35 J11
Ludgershall Wilts....21 Q4
Ludgvan Cnwll....2 E7
Ludham Norfk....77 M8
Ludlow Shrops....57 J9
Ludney Somset....10 H2
Ludwell Wilts....20 H10

282 Ludworth – Medway Services

Ludworth Dur 104 C2
Luffenhall Herts 50 G5
Luffincott Devon 5 N3
Luffness E Loth 128 D4
Lugar E Ayrs 115 L3
Luggate Burn E Loth 128 F5
Lugg Green Herefs 45 N2
Luggiebank N Lans 126 D3
Lugton E Ayrs 125 L7
Lugwardine Herefs 45 R6
Luib Highld 145 J2
Luing Ag & B 130 E5
Lulham Herefs 45 N6
Lullington Derbys 59 K2
Lullington E Susx 25 M10
Lullington Somset 20 E4
Lulsgate Bottom N Som 31 P11
Lulsley Worcs 46 D3
Lulworth Camp Dorset 12 D8
Lumb Calder 90 C6
Lumb Lancs 89 N6
Lumbutts Calder 90 B6
Lumby N York 91 M4
Lumloch E Duns 125 Q3
Lumphanan Abers 150 F7
Lumphinnans Fife 134 F9
Lumsden Abers 150 D3
Lunan Angus 143 M7
Lunanhead Angus 142 H7
Luncarty P & K 134 D2
Lund E R Yk 99 K11
Lund N York 91 R4
Lundie Angus 142 D10
Lundin Links Fife 135 L7
Lundin Mill Fife 135 L7
Lundy Devon 16 A2
Lundy Green Norfk 65 J3
Lunga Ag & B 130 E6
Lunna Shet 169 r7
Lunsford Kent 37 Q9
Lunsford's Cross E Susx 26 B9
Lunt Sefton 81 L4
Luntley Herefs 45 M3
Luppitt Devon 10 D3
Lupridge Devon 7 J8
Lupset Wakefd 91 J7
Lupton Cumb 95 M4
Lurgashall W Susx 23 P9
Lurley Devon 18 B11
Lusby Lincs 87 K7
Luscombe Devon 7 K7
Luson Devon 6 G8
Luss Ag & B 132 D9
Lussagiven Ag & B 130 C10
Lusta Highld 152 D6
Lustleigh Devon 9 J8
Luston Herefs 45 P2
Luthermuir Abers 143 M4
Luthrie Fife 135 J4
Lutley Dudley 58 D8
Luton Devon 9 M9
Luton Devon 10 B4
Luton Luton 50 C6
Luton Medway 38 C8
Luton Airport Luton 50 D6
Lutterworth Leics 60 B4
Lutton Devon 6 F7
Lutton Devon 6 H6
Lutton Lincs 74 H5
Lutton Nhants 61 P3
Luxborough Somset 18 C7
Luxulyan Cnwll 4 H10
Luxulyan Valley Cnwll 4 H10
Luzley Tamesd 83 L4
Lybster Highld 167 M9
Lydbury North Shrops 56 E7
Lydcott Devon 17 M4
Lydd Kent 26 H7
Lydd Airport Kent 27 J7
Lydden Kent 27 N2
Lydden Kent 39 Q8
Lyddington Rutlnd 73 M11
Lydeard St Lawrence Somset 18 F8
Lyde Green Hants 23 K3
Lydford Devon 8 D7
Lydford on Fosse Somset 19 Q8
Lydgate Calder 89 Q5
Lydgate Rochdl 90 B7
Lydham Shrops 56 E6
Lydiard Green Wilts 33 L7
Lydiard Millicent Wilts 33 L7
Lydiard Tregoze Swindn 33 M8
Lydiate Sefton 81 M4
Lydiate Ash Worcs 58 E9
Lydlinch Dorset 12 B2
Lydney Gloucs 32 B4
Lydstep Pembks 41 L11
Lye Dudley 58 D8
Lye Cross N Som 19 N2
Lye Green Bucks 35 Q4
Lye Green E Susx 25 M4
Lye Green Warwks 59 J11
Lye Head Worcs 57 P10
Lye's Green Wilts 20 F5
Lyford Oxon 34 C6
Lymbridge Green Kent 27 K3
Lyme Regis Dorset 10 G6
Lyminge Kent 27 L3
Lymington Hants 13 P5
Lyminster W Susx 24 B10
Lymm Warrtn 82 E7
Lymm Services Warrtn 82 E8
Lympne Kent 27 K4
Lympsham Somset 19 K4
Lympstone Devon 9 N8
Lynbridge Devon 17 N2
Lynchat Highld 148 D7
Lynch Green Norfk 76 H10
Lyndhurst Hants 13 P3
Lyndon Rutlnd 73 N10
Lyndon Green Birm 58 H7
Lyne Border 117 J2
Lyne Surrey 36 B7
Lyneal Shrops 69 M8
Lyne Down Herefs 46 B8
Lyneham Devon 9 L9
Lyneham Oxon 47 Q10
Lyneham Wilts 33 K9
Lyneholmford Cumb 111 K6
Lynemouth Nthumb 113 L2
Lyne of Skene Abers 151 K5
Lynesack Dur 103 L5
Lyness Ork 169 c7
Lyng Norfk 76 F8
Lyng Somset 19 K9
Lynmouth Devon 17 N2
Lynn Staffs 58 G4
Lynn Wrekin 70 D11
Lynsted Kent 38 F9
Lynstone Cnwll 16 C10
Lynton Devon 17 N2
Lyon's Gate Dorset 11 P3
Lyonshall Herefs 45 L3
Lytchett Matravers Dorset 12 F5
Lytchett Minster Dorset 12 G6
Lyth Highld 167 N4
Lytham Lancs 88 D5
Lytham St Anne's Lancs 88 C5
Lythbank Shrops 56 H3
Lythe N York 105 M8
Lythmore Highld 167 J3

M

Mabe Burnthouse Cnwll 3 K7
Mablethorpe Lincs 87 P4
Macclesfield Ches E 83 K10
Macclesfield Crematorium Ches E 83 K10
Macduff Abers 158 H5
Macharioch Ag & B 120 D10
Machen Caerph 30 H7
Machrie N Ayrs 120 G5
Machrihanish Ag & B 120 B7
Machrins Ag & B 136 b3
Machynlleth Powys 54 G4
Machynys Carmth 28 F5
Mackworth Derbys 71 Q7
Macmerry E Loth 128 C5
Maddaford Devon 8 D6
Madderty P & K 134 B3
Maddington Wilts 21 L6
Maddiston Falk 126 G2
Madehurst W Susx 15 Q4
Madeley Staffs 70 D6
Madeley Wrekin 57 M4
Madeley Heath Staffs 70 D5
Madford Devon 10 C2
Madingley Cambs 62 E8
Madley Herefs 45 N7
Madresfield Worcs 46 F5
Madron Cnwll 2 D7
Maenaddwyn IoA 78 H8
Maenan Conwy 79 P11
Maenclochog Pembks 41 L5
Maendy V Glam 30 D9
Maenporth Cnwll 3 K8
Maentwrog Gwynd 67 M6
Maen-y-groes Cerdgn 42 G3
Maer Cnwll 16 C10
Maer Staffs 70 D7
Maerdy Carmth 43 N9
Maerdy Rhondd 30 C5
Maesbrook Shrops 69 K10
Maesbury Shrops 69 K9
Maesbury Marsh Shrops 69 K9
Maes-glas Newpt 31 J7
Maesgwynne Carmth 41 P6
Maeshafn Denbgs 68 H2
Maesllyn Cerdgn 42 G6
Maesmynis Powys 44 E5
Maesmynis Powys 44 E5
Maesteg Brdgnd 29 N6
Maesybont Carmth 43 L11
Maesycwmmer Caerph 30 G6
Magdalen Laver Essex 51 M9
Maggieknockater Moray 157 Q8
Maggots End Essex 51 L5
Magham Down E Susx 25 P8
Maghull Sefton 81 M4
Magna Park Leics 60 B4
Magor Mons 31 M7
Magor Services Mons 31 M7
Maidenbower W Susx 24 G3
Maiden Bradley Wilts 20 F7
Maidencombe Torbay 7 N5
Maidenhayne Devon 10 F5
Maiden Head N Som 31 Q11
Maidenhead W & M 35 N8
Maiden Law Dur 113 J11
Maiden Newton Dorset 11 M5
Maidens S Ayrs 114 D6
Maiden's Green Br For 35 P10
Maidenwell Lincs 87 K5
Maiden Wells Pembks 41 J11
Maidford Nhants 48 H4
Maids Moreton Bucks 49 K7
Maidstone Kent 38 C10
Maidstone Services Kent 38 D10
Maidwell Nhants 60 F5
Mail Shet 169 r9
Maindee Newpt 31 K7
Mainland Ork 169 d6
Mainland Shet 169 r8
Mainsforth Dur 104 B4
Mains of Balhall Angus 143 J5
Mains of Balnakettle Abers 143 L3
Mains of Dalvey Highld 157 L11
Mains of Haulkerton Abers 143 N3
Mains of Lesmoir Abers 150 D2
Mains of Melgunds Angus 143 J6
Mainsriddle D & G 109 K9
Mainstone Shrops 56 D7
Maisemore Gloucs 46 F10
Major's Green Worcs 58 H9
Makeney Derbys 72 B2
Malborough Devon 7 J11
Malcoff Derbys 83 N8
Malden Rushett Gt Lon 36 E8
Maldon Essex 52 E10
Malham N York 96 D8
Maligar Highld 152 H5
Mallaig Highld 145 L8
Mallaigvaig Highld 145 L8
Malleny Mills C Edin 127 M4
Mallows Green Essex 51 L5
Malltraeth IoA 78 G11
Mallwyd Gwynd 55 K2
Malmesbury Wilts 32 H7
Malmsmead Devon 17 P2
Malpas Ches W 69 N5
Malpas Cnwll 3 L5
Malpas Newpt 31 K6
Malshanger Hants 22 G4
Malswick Gloucs 46 D10
Maltby Lincs 87 K4
Maltby Rothm 84 H2
Maltby S on T 104 E8
Maltby le Marsh Lincs 87 N4
Malting Green Essex 52 G7
Maltman's Hill Kent 26 F3
Malton N York 98 F6
Malvern Worcs 46 E5
Malvern Hills 46 E6
Malvern Link Worcs 46 E5
Malvern Wells Worcs 46 E6
Mamble Worcs 57 M10
Mamhilad Mons 31 K4
Manaccan Cnwll 3 K9
Manafon Powys 55 Q4
Manais W Isls 168 g9
Manaton Devon 9 J8
Manby Lincs 87 L3
Mancetter Warwks 59 M5
Manchester Manch 82 H5
Manchester Airport Manch 82 H8
Manchester Crematorium Manch 82 H6
Mancot Flints 81 L11
Mandally Highld 146 H7
Manea Cambs 62 G3
Maney Birm 58 H5
Manfield N York 103 P8
Mangerton Dorset 11 K5
Mangotsfield S Glos 32 C9
Mangrove Green Herts 50 D6
Manhay Cnwll 2 H7
Manish W Isls 168 g9
Mankinholes Calder 90 B6
Manley Ches W 81 Q10
Manmoel Caerph 30 G4
Mannel Ag & B 136 B7
Manningford Bohune Wilts 21 M3
Manningford Bruce Wilts 21 M3
Manningham C Brad 90 E3
Manning's Heath W Susx 24 F5
Mannington Dorset 13 J3
Manningtree Essex 53 K5
Mannofield C Aber 151 N7
Manorbier Pembks 41 L11
Manorbier Newton Pembks 41 K10
Manordeilo Carmth 43 N9
Manorhill Border 118 C4
Manorowen Pembks 40 H3
Manor Park Gt Lon 37 K3
Manor Park Crematorium Gt Lon 37 K3
Mansell Gamage Herefs 45 M6
Mansell Lacy Herefs 45 N5
Mansergh Cumb 95 N4
Mansfield E Ayrs 115 M5
Mansfield Notts 84 H8
Mansfield & District Crematorium Notts 84 H9
Mansfield Woodhouse Notts 84 H8
Mansriggs Cumb 94 F4
Manston Dorset 20 F11
Manston Kent 39 P8
Manston Leeds 91 K4
Manswood Dorset 12 G3
Manthorpe Lincs 73 N3
Manthorpe Lincs 73 R7
Manton N Linc 92 F10
Manton Notts 85 K5
Manton Rutlnd 73 M10
Manton Wilts 33 N11
Manuden Essex 51 L5
Manwood Green Essex 51 M8
Maperton Somset 20 C9
Maplebeck Notts 85 M8
Maple Cross Herts 36 B2
Mapledurham Oxon 35 J9
Mapledurwell Hants 23 J4
Maplehurst W Susx 24 E6
Maplescombe Kent 37 N8
Mapleton Derbys 71 M5
Mapleton Kent 37 L11
Mapperley Derbys 72 C2
Mapperley Park C Nott 72 F2
Mapperton Dorset 11 L5
Mappleborough Green Warwks 58 G11
Mappleton E R Yk 93 M2
Mapplewell Barns 91 J8
Mappowder Dorset 12 B3
Marazanvose Cnwll 3 K3
Marazion Cnwll 2 E7
Marbury Ches E 69 Q5
March Cambs 74 H11
March S Lans 116 D8
Marcham Oxon 34 E5
Marchamley Shrops 69 Q9
Marchamley Wood Shrops 69 Q8
Marchington Staffs 71 L8
Marchington Woodlands Staffs 71 L9
Marchros Gwynd 66 E9
Marchwiel Wrexhm 69 L5
Marchwood Hants 14 C4
Marcross V Glam 29 P11
Marden Herefs 45 Q5
Marden Kent 26 B3
Marden Wilts 21 L3
Marden Ash Essex 51 N10
Marden Beech Kent 26 B3
Mardens Hill E Susx 25 M4
Marden Thorn Kent 26 C3
Mardlebury Herts 50 G7
Mardy Mons 45 L11
Marefield Leics 73 J9
Mareham le Fen Lincs 87 J8
Mareham on the Hill Lincs 87 J7
Marehay Derbys 84 E11
Marehill W Susx 24 C7
Maresfield E Susx 25 L6
Marfleet C KuH 93 K5
Marford Wrexhm 69 L3
Margam Neath 29 L7
Margam Crematorium Neath 29 L7
Margaret Marsh Dorset 20 F11
Margaret Roding Essex 51 N8
Margaretting Essex 51 Q10
Margaretting Tye Essex 51 Q10
Margate Kent 39 Q7
Margnaheglish N Ayrs 121 K5
Margrie D & G 108 C10
Margrove Park R & Cl 105 J7
Marham Norfk 75 P9
Marhamchurch Cnwll 16 C11
Marholm C Pete 74 B10
Marian-glas IoA 79 J8
Mariansleigh Devon 17 N7
Marine Town Kent 38 F7
Marionburgh Abers 151 J6
Marishader Highld 152 H5
Maristow Devon 6 D6
Marjoriebanks D & G 109 N4
Mark Somset 19 L5
Markbeech Kent 25 L2
Markby Lincs 87 N5
Mark Causeway Somset 19 L5
Mark Cross E Susx 25 N4
Markeaton C Derb 72 A3
Markeaton Crematorium C Derb 72 A3
Market Bosworth Leics 72 C10
Market Deeping Lincs 74 B8
Market Drayton Shrops 70 B8
Market Harborough Leics 60 F3
Market Lavington Wilts 21 K4
Market Overton Rutlnd 73 M7
Market Rasen Lincs 86 F3
Market Stainton Lincs 86 H5
Market Warsop Notts 85 J7
Market Weighton E R Yk 92 E2
Market Weston Suffk 64 D6
Markfield Leics 72 D9
Markham Caerph 30 G4
Markham Moor Notts 85 M6
Markinch Fife 134 H7
Markington N York 97 L7
Markle E Loth 128 F4
Marksbury BaNES 20 C2
Mark's Corner IoW 14 E8
Marks Tey Essex 52 F7
Markwell Cnwll 5 P10
Markyate Herts 50 C7
Marlborough Wilts 33 N11
Marlbrook Herefs 45 Q4
Marlbrook Worcs 58 E10
Marlcliff Warwks 47 L4
Marldon Devon 7 M6
Marle Green E Susx 25 N7
Marlesford Suffk 65 L10
Marley Kent 39 L11
Marley Kent 39 P11
Marley Green Ches E 69 Q5
Marley Hill Gatesd 113 K9
Marlingford Norfk 76 G10
Marloes Pembks 40 E9
Marlow Bucks 35 M7
Marlow Herefs 56 G9
Marlow Bottom Bucks 35 M7
Marlpit Hill Kent 37 K11
Marlpits E Susx 25 L5
Marlpits E Susx 26 B9
Marlpool Derbys 84 F11
Marnhull Dorset 20 E11
Marple Stockp 83 L7
Marple Bridge Stockp 83 L7
Marr Donc 91 N9
Marrick N York 103 L11
Marros Carmth 41 P9
Marsden Kirk 90 C8
Marsden S Tyne 113 N8
Marsden Height Lancs 89 P3
Marsett N York 96 D3
Marsh Bucks 35 M3
Marsh C Brad 90 C3
Marsh Devon 10 F2
Marshall's Heath Herts 50 E8
Marshalswick Herts 50 E9
Marsham Norfk 76 H7
Marsh Baldon Oxon 34 G5
Marsh Benham W Berk 34 D11
Marshborough Kent 39 P10
Marshbrook Shrops 56 G7
Marshchapel Lincs 93 Q11
Marsh Farm Luton 50 C5
Marshfield Newpt 31 J8
Marshfield S Glos 32 E10
Marshgate Cnwll 5 K3
Marsh Gibbon Bucks 48 H10
Marsh Green Devon 9 P6
Marsh Green Kent 25 K2
Marsh Green Wrekin 57 L2
Marshland St James Norfk 75 K9
Marsh Lane Derbys 84 F5
Marsh Lane Gloucs 31 Q3
Marshside Sefton 88 D7
Marsh Street Somset 18 C6
Marshwood Dorset 10 H5
Marske N York 103 M10
Marske-by-the-Sea R & Cl 104 H6
Marsland Green Wigan 82 E5
Marston Ches W 82 E9
Marston Herefs 45 M3
Marston Lincs 73 M2
Marston Oxon 34 F3
Marston Staffs 58 B2
Marston Staffs 70 G9
Marston Warwks 59 K6
Marston Wilts 21 J3
Marston Green Solhll 59 J7
Marston Jabbet Warwks 59 N7
Marston Magna Somset 19 Q10
Marston Meysey Wilts 33 M5
Marston Montgomery Derbys 71 L7
Marston Moretaine C Beds 49 Q6
Marston on Dove Derbys 71 N9
Marston St Lawrence Nhants 48 F6
Marston Stannett Herefs 45 R3
Marston Trussell Nhants 60 E3
Marstow Herefs 45 R11
Marsworth Bucks 35 P2
Marten Wilts 21 Q2
Marthall Ches E 82 G9
Martham Norfk 77 P8
Martin Hants 21 L11
Martin Kent 27 P2
Martin Lincs 86 F9
Martin Lincs 86 H7
Martindale Cumb 101 M7
Martin Dales Lincs 86 G8
Martin Drove End Hants 21 L10
Martinhoe Devon 17 M2
Martin Hussingtree Worcs 46 G2
Martinscroft Warrtn 82 E7
Martinstown Dorset 11 N7
Martlesham Suffk 53 M2
Martlesham Heath Suffk 53 M2
Martletwy Pembks 41 K8
Martley Worcs 46 E2
Martock Somset 19 N11
Marton Ches E 83 J11
Marton Ches W 82 D11
Marton Cumb 94 E5
Marton E R Yk 93 L3
Marton E R Yk 99 Q7
Marton Lincs 85 P4
Marton Middsb 104 F7
Marton N York 97 P8
Marton N York 98 E
Marton Shrops 56 D
Marton Warwks 59 P1
Marton-le-Moor N York 97 N
Martyr's Green Surrey 36 C
Martyr Worthy Hants 22 F
Marwell Wildlife Hants 22 F1
Marwick Ork 169 b
Marwood Devon 17 J
Marybank Highld 155 N
Maryburgh Highld 155 P
Marygold Border 129 L
Maryhill C Glas 125 P
Maryhill Crematorium C Glas 125 P
Marykirk Abers 143 M
Maryland Mons 31 P
Marylebone Gt Lon 36 G
Marylebone Wigan 88 H
Marypark Moray 157 M1
Maryport Cumb 100 D
Maryport D & G 106 F1
Marystow Devon 8 B
Mary Tavy Devon 8 D
Maryton Angus 143 M
Marywell Abers 150 F
Marywell Abers 151 N
Marywell Angus 143 M
Masham N York 97 K
Mashbury Essex 51 Q
Mason N u Ty 113 K
Masongill N York 95 P
Masonhill Crematorium S Ayrs 114 G
Mastin Moor Derbys 84 C
Matching Essex 51 M
Matching Green Essex 51 M
Matching Tye Essex 51 M
Matfen Nthumb 112 F
Matfield Kent 25 Q
Mathern Mons 31 P
Mathon Herefs 46 D
Mathry Pembks 40 G
Matlask Norfk 76 H
Matlock Derbys 84 D
Matlock Bank Derbys 84 D
Matlock Bath Derbys 84 C
Matlock Dale Derbys 84 C
Matson Gloucs 46 G1
Matterdale End Cumb 101 L
Mattersey Notts 85 L
Mattersey Thorpe Notts 85 L
Mattingley Hants 23 K
Mattishall Norfk 76 F
Mattishall Burgh Norfk 76 F
Mauchline E Ayrs 115 J
Maud Abers 159 M
Maufant Jersey 11 c
Maugersbury Gloucs 47 P
Maughold IoM 80 g
Mauld Highld 155 M1
Maulden C Beds 50 C
Maulds Meaburn Cumb 102 B
Maunby N York 97 N
Maund Bryan Herefs 45 R
Maundown Somset 18 E
Mautby Norfk 77 P
Mavesyn Ridware Staffs 71 K1
Mavis Enderby Lincs 87 L
Mawbray Cumb 109 N1
Mawdesley Lancs 88 F
Mawdlam Brdgnd 29 M
Mawgan Cnwll 3 J
Mawgan Porth Cnwll 4 D
Maw Green Ches E 70 C
Mawla Cnwll 3 J
Mawnan Cnwll 3 K
Mawnan Smith Cnwll 3 K
Mawsley Nhants 60 H
Mawthorpe Lincs 87 N
Maxey C Pete 74 B
Maxstoke Warwks 59 K
Maxted Street Kent 27 K
Maxton Border 118 B
Maxton Kent 27 P
Maxwell Town D & G 109 L
Maxworthy Cnwll 5 M
Mayals Swans 28 H
May Bank Staffs 70 F
Maybole S Ayrs 114 E
Maybury Surrey 36 B
Mayes Green Surrey 24 D
Mayfield E Susx 25 N
Mayfield Mdloth 128 B
Mayfield Staffs 71 M
Mayford Surrey 23 Q
May Hill Gloucs 46 D1
Mayland Essex 52 F1
Maylandsea Essex 52 F1
Maynard's Green E Susx 25 N
Maypole Birm 58 G
Maypole Kent 39 M
Maypole Mons 45 P1
Maypole Green Norfk 65 N
Maypole Green Suffk 64 C1
Maypole Green Suffk 65 K
May's Green Oxon 35 K
May's Green Surrey 36 C
Mead Devon 16 C
Meadgate BaNES 20 C
Meadle Bucks 35 M
Meadowfield Dur 103 P
Meadowtown Shrops 56 E
Meadwell Devon 5 Q
Meaford Staffs 70 F
Meal Bank Cumb 101 P1
Mealrigg Cumb 109 P1
Mealsgate Cumb 100 H
Meanwood Leeds 90 H
Mearbeck N York 96 B
Meare Somset 19 N
Meare Green Somset 19 J1
Meare Green Somset 19 K
Mearns E Rens 125 N
Mears Ashby Nhants 60 H
Measham Leics 72 A
Meathop Cumb 95 J
Meaux E R Yk 93 J
Meavy Devon 6 E
Medbourne Leics 60 H
Meddon Devon 16 D
Meden Vale Notts 85 J
Medlam Lincs 87 K
Medlar Lancs 88 E
Medmenham Bucks 35 M
Medomsley Dur 112 H1
Medstead Hants 23 J
Medway Crematorium Kent 38 B
Medway Services Medway 38 D

eerbrook Staffs 70 H2
eer Common Herefs 45 M4
eesden Herts 51 K4
eeson Wrekin 70 A10
eeth Devon 17 J10
eeting Green Suffk 63 M9
eeting House Hill Norfk 77 J6
eidrim Carmth 41 Q6
eifod Powys 56 F2
eigle P & K 142 D9
eikle Carco D & G 115 Q5
eikle Earnock S Lans 126 C7
eikle Kilmory Ag & B 124 D5
eikle Obney P & K 141 P10
eikleour P & K 142 B10
eikle Wartle Abers 158 H11
einciau Carmth 28 E2
eir C Stke 70 G6
eir Heath Staffs 70 G6
elbourn Cambs 51 J2
elbourne Derbys 72 B5
elbourne E R Yk 92 C2
elbur Cnwll 3 N3
elbury Dorset 16 F8
elbury Abbas Dorset 20 G10
elbury Bubb Dorset 11 M3
elbury Osmond Dorset 11 M3
elbury Sampford Dorset 11 M3
elchbourne Bed 61 M7
elcombe Bingham Dorset 12 C4
eldon Devon 8 E6
eldon Nthumb 112 H4
eldon Park Nthumb 112 H3
eldreth Cambs 62 E11
eldrum Stirlg 133 L8
elfort Ag & B 130 C5
eliden Denbgs 80 F8
elinau Powys 41 N8
elin-byrhedyn Powys 55 J5
elincourt Neath 29 M4
elin-y-coed Conwy 67 Q2
elin-y-ddol Powys 55 P3
elin-y-wig Denbgs 68 D5
elkinthorpe Cumb 101 Q5
elkridge Nthumb 111 P8
elksham Wilts 20 H2
ellangoose Cnwll 2 H8
ell Green W Berk 34 E9
ellguards Cumb 110 H11
elling Lancs 95 M6
elling Sefton 81 M4
elling Mount Sefton 81 N4
ellis Suffk 64 F7
ellon Charles Highld 160 C8
ellon Udrigle Highld 160 D7
ellor Lancs 89 K4
ellor Stockp 83 L7
ellor Brook Lancs 89 J4
ells Somset 20 D5
ells Suffk 65 N6
elmerby Cumb 102 B3
elmerby N York 96 G3
elmerby N York 97 M5
elness Highld 165 N4
elon Green Suffk 64 A10
elplash Dorset 11 K5
elrose Border 117 Q4
elsetter Ork 169 b8
elsonby N York 103 N9
eltham Kirk 90 E8
eltham Mills Kirk 90 E8
elton E R Yk 92 E5
elton Suffk 65 K11
eltonby E R Yk 98 F10
elton Constable Norfk 76 E5
elton Mowbray Leics 73 K7
elton Ross N Linc 93 J8
elvaig Highld 160 A9
elverley Shrops 69 K11
elverley Green Shrops 69 K11
elvich Highld 166 E4
embury Services W Berk 34 B9
emsie Abers 159 N5
emus Angus 142 G6
enabilly Cnwll 4 H11
enagissey Cnwll 3 J4
enai Bridge IoA 79 K10
endip Crematorium Somset 19 Q6
endip Hills 19 P4
endlesham Suffk 64 G8
endlesham Green Suffk 64 F9
enheniot Cnwll 5 M9
enithwood Worcs 57 N11
enna Cnwll 3 N3
ennock D & G 115 N4
enston C Brad 90 F2
enstrie Clacks 133 P8
enthorpe N York 92 B4
eoble Highld 145 N10
eole Brace Shrops 56 H2
eonstoke Hants 22 H11
eopham Kent 37 P7
eopham Green Kent 37 P7
eopham Station Kent 37 P7
epal Suffk 52 F4
eppershall C Beds 50 D3
erbach Herefs 45 L5
ere Ches E 82 F8
ere Wilts 20 F8
ere Brow Lancs 88 E7
ereclough Lancs 89 P4
ere Green Birm 59 H5
ere Green Worcs 47 J2
ere Heath Ches W 82 E10
eresborough Medway 38 D9
ereworth Kent 37 Q10
eriden Solhll 59 K8
erkadale Highld 152 F11
erley Poole 12 H5
erley Green Suffk 64 F9
errington Shrops 40 H11
errion Pembks 40 H11
erriott Somset 11 J2
errivale Devon 8 D9
erry Field Hill Dorset 12 H4
erry Hill Herts 36 D2
erry Lees Leics 72 D9
erryhill Wolves 58 C5
errymeet Cnwll 5 M8
ersea Island Essex 52 H4
ersey Crossing Halton 81 Q8
ersham Kent 27 J3

Merstham Surrey 36 G10
Merston W Susx 15 N6
Merstone IoW 14 F9
Merther Cnwll 3 M5
Merthyr Carmth 42 G10
Merthyr Cynog Powys 44 D7
Merthyr Dyfan V Glam 30 F11
Merthyr Mawr Brdgnd 29 N9
Merthyr Tydfil Myr Td 30 D3
Merthyr Vale Myr Td 30 E5
Merton Devon 17 J9
Merton Gt Lon 36 G6
Merton Norfk 64 C2
Merton Oxon 48 G11
Meshaw Devon 17 P8
Messing Essex 52 E8
Messingham N Linc 92 E10
Metfield Suffk 65 K5
Metherell Cnwll 5 Q8
Metheringham Lincs 86 D8
Methil Fife 135 K8
Methilhill Fife 135 K7
Methley Leeds 91 K5
Methley Junction Leeds 91 K5
Methlick Abers 159 L10
Methven P & K 134 C2
Methwold Norfk 63 M2
Methwold Hythe Norfk 63 M2
Mettingham Suffk 65 M4
Metton Norfk 76 J4
Mevagissey Cnwll 3 Q5
Mexborough Donc 91 M10
Mey Highld 167 N2
Meyllteyrn Gwynd 66 C8
Meysey Hampton Gloucs 33 M4
Miabhig W Isls 168 f4
Miavaig W Isls 168 f4
Michaelchurch Herefs 45 Q9
Michaelchurch Escley Herefs 45 L8
Michaelchurch-on-Arrow Powys 45 J4
Michaelstone-y-Fedw Newpt 30 H8
Michaelstone-le-Pit V Glam 30 G10
Michaelstow Cnwll 4 H6
Michaelwood Services Gloucs 32 D5
Michelcombe Devon 6 H5
Micheldever Hants 22 F7
Micheldever Station Hants 22 F6
Michelmersh Hants 22 B9
Mickfield Suffk 64 G9
Micklebring Donc 84 H2
Mickleby N York 105 M8
Micklefield Leeds 91 L4
Micklefield Green Herts 50 B11
Mickleham Surrey 36 E10
Mickleover C Derb 71 Q8
Micklethwaite C Brad 90 E2
Micklethwaite Cumb 110 E10
Mickleton Dur 103 J6
Mickleton Gloucs 47 N6
Mickletown Leeds 91 L5
Mickle Trafford Ches W 81 N11
Mickley Derbys 84 D5
Mickley N York 97 L5
Mickley Green Suffk 64 A10
Mickley Square Nthumb 112 G8
Mid Ardlaw Abers 159 M5
Midbea Ork 169 d2
Mid Beltie Abers 150 G7
Mid Bockhampton Dorset 13 L5
Mid Calder W Loth 127 K4
Mid Clyth Highld 167 N9
Mid Culbeuchly Abers 158 G5
Middle Assendon Oxon 35 K7
Middle Aston Oxon 48 E9
Middle Barton Oxon 48 D9
Middlebie D & G 110 D5
Middlebridge P & K 141 L4
Middle Chinnock Somset 11 K2
Middle Claydon Bucks 49 K9
Middlecliffe Barns 91 L9
Middlecott Devon 8 H7
Middle Duntisbourne Gloucs 33 J3
Middleham N York 96 H3
Middle Handley Derbys 84 F5
Middle Harling Norfk 64 D4
Middlehill Cnwll 5 M8
Middlehill Wilts 32 F11
Middlehope Shrops 56 H7
Middle Kames Ag & B 131 J10
Middle Littleton Worcs 47 L5
Middle Madeley Staffs 70 D5
Middle Maes-coed Herefs 45 L8
Middlemarsh Dorset 11 P3
Middle Mayfield Staffs 71 L6
Middle Mill Pembks 40 F5
Middlemore Devon 6 D4
Middle Quarter Kent 26 E4
Middle Rasen Lincs 86 E3
Middle Rocombe Devon 7 N5
Middle Salter Lancs 95 N8
Middlesbrough Middsb 104 E7
Middlesceugh Cumb 101 M2
Middleshaw Cumb 95 M3
Middlesmoor N York 96 G6
Middle Stoford Somset 18 G10
Middle Stoke Medway 38 D6
Middlestone Dur 103 Q4
Middlestone Moor Dur 103 P4
Middle Stoughton Somset 19 M6
Middlestown Wakefd 90 H7
Middle Street Gloucs 32 E4
Middle Taphouse Cnwll 5 K9
Middlethird Border 118 C2
Middleton Ag & B 136 A7
Middleton Cumb 95 N3
Middleton Derbys 71 M2
Middleton Derbys 84 C9
Middleton Essex 52 E4
Middleton Hants 22 C6
Middleton Herefs 57 J11
Middleton Lancs 95 J11
Middleton Leeds 91 J5
Middleton N York 96 H1
Middleton N York 98 F3
Middleton Nhants 60 H3
Middleton Norfk 75 N7
Middleton Nthumb 112 G4
Middleton Nthumb 119 M3
Middleton P & K 134 D2
Middleton Rochdl 89 P9
Middleton Shrops 57 J9

Middleton Shrops 69 K9
Middleton Suffk 65 N8
Middleton Swans 28 D7
Middleton Warwks 59 J5
Middleton Cheney Nhants 48 E6
Middleton Crematorium Rochdl 89 P9
Middleton Green Staffs 70 H7
Middleton Hall Nthumb 119 J5
Middleton-in-Teesdale Dur 102 H5
Middleton Moor Suffk 65 N8
Middleton One Row Darltn 104 C8
Middleton-on-Leven N York 104 E9
Middleton-on-Sea W Susx 15 Q6
Middleton on the Hill Herefs 45 Q2
Middleton on the Wolds E R Yk 99 J11
Middleton Park C Aber 151 N5
Middleton Priors Shrops 57 L6
Middleton Quernhow N York 97 M5
Middleton St George Darltn 104 B8
Middleton Scriven Shrops 57 M7
Middleton Stoney Oxon 48 F10
Middleton Tyas N York 103 P9
Middletown Cumb 100 C9
Middletown N Som 31 N10
Middletown Powys 56 E2
Middle Tysoe Warwks 48 B6
Middle Wallop Hants 21 Q7
Middlewich Ches E 82 F11
Middle Winterslow Wilts 21 P8
Middlewood Cnwll 5 M6
Middlewood Herefs 45 K6
Middle Woodford Wilts 21 M7
Middlewood Green Suffk 64 F9
Middleyard E Ayrs 125 N11
Middle Yard Gloucs 32 F4
Middlezoy Somset 19 L8
Middridge Dur 103 P5
Midford BaNES 20 E2
Midge Hall Lancs 88 G6
Midgeholme Cumb 111 M9
Midgham W Berk 34 G11
Midgley Calder 90 C5
Midgley Wakefd 90 H8
Mid Holmwood Surrey 36 E11
Midhopestones Sheff 90 G11
Midhurst W Susx 23 N10
Mid Lavant W Susx 15 N5
Midlem Border 117 Q3
Mid Mains Highld 155 M10
Midney Somset 19 N9
Midpark Ag & B 124 D5
Midsomer Norton BaNES 20 D4
Midtown Highld 165 N4
Midville Lincs 87 L9
Mid Warwickshire Crematorium Warwks 48 B3
Midway Ches E 83 K8
Mid Yell Shet 169 s4
Migvie Abers 150 C6
Milborne Port Somset 20 C11
Milborne St Andrew Dorset 12 D5
Milborne Wick Somset 20 C10
Milbourne Nthumb 112 H5
Milbourne Wilts 33 J7
Milburn Cumb 102 C5
Milbury Heath S Glos 32 C4
Milby N York 97 P7
Milcombe Oxon 48 D8
Milden Suffk 52 G2
Mildenhall Suffk 63 M6
Mildenhall Wilts 33 P11
Milebrook Powys 56 E10
Milebush Kent 26 C2
Mile Elm Wilts 33 J11
Mile End Essex 52 G6
Mile End Gloucs 31 Q2
Mile End Suffk 65 L4
Mile Oak Br & H 24 F9
Mile Oak Kent 25 Q2
Mile Oak Staffs 59 J4
Miles Hope Herefs 45 R2
Milesmark Fife 134 D10
Mile Town Kent 38 F7
Milfield Nthumb 118 H4
Milford Derbys 84 E11
Milford Devon 16 C7
Milford Powys 55 P6
Milford Staffs 70 H10
Milford Surrey 23 P6
Milford Haven Pembks 40 H9
Milford on Sea Hants 13 N6
Milkwall Gloucs 31 Q3
Millais Jersey 11 a1
Milland W Susx 23 M9
Milland Marsh W Susx 23 M9
Mill Bank Calder 90 C6
Millbeck Cumb 101 J5
Millbreck Abers 159 P9
Millbridge Surrey 23 M6
Millbrook C Beds 50 B3
Millbrook C Sotn 14 C4
Millbrook Cnwll 5 C8
Millbrook Jersey 11 b2
Millbrook Tamesd 83 L5
Mill Brow Stockp 83 L7
Millbuie Abers 151 K3
Millbuie Highld 155 Q7
Millcombe Devon 7 K8
Mill Common Norfk 77 L11
Mill Common Suffk 65 N5
Millcorner E Susx 26 D7
Millcraig Highld 156 B3
Mill Cross Devon 7 J5
Milldale Staffs 71 L4
Mill End Bucks 35 L7
Mill End Cambs 62 H9
Millend Gloucs 32 D5
Mill End Herts 50 H4
Millerhill Mdloth 127 Q4
Miller's Dale Derbys 83 P10
Millers Green Derbys 71 P4
Millerston C Glas 125 Q4
Millgate Lancs 89 P7
Mill Green Cambs 63 K11
Mill Green Essex 51 P10

Mill Green Herts 50 F8
Mill Green Lincs 74 D6
Mill Green Norfk 64 G5
Millgreen Shrops 70 B9
Mill Green Staffs 58 G4
Mill Green Staffs 71 K10
Mill Green Suffk 52 G3
Mill Green Suffk 64 D10
Mill Green Suffk 64 G9
Mill Green Suffk 65 L9
Millhalf Herefs 45 K5
Millhayes Devon 10 E4
Millhead Lancs 95 K6
Millheugh S Lans 126 C7
Mill Hill E Susx 25 P9
Mill Hill Gt Lon 36 F2
Millhouse Ag & B 124 B3
Millhousebridge D & G 109 P3
Millhouse Green Barns 90 G10
Millhouses Barns 91 L10
Millhouses Sheff 84 D4
Milliken Park Rens 125 L5
Millin Cross Pembks 41 J9
Millington E R Yk 98 G10
Millmeece Staffs 70 E8
Millness Cumb 95 L4
Mill of Drummond P & K 133 N4
Mill of Haldane W Duns 132 D11
Millom Cumb 94 D4
Millook Cnwll 5 K2
Millpool Cnwll 2 F7
Millpool Cnwll 5 J7
Millport N Ayrs 124 F7
Mill Side Cumb 95 J4
Mill Street Kent 37 Q9
Mill Street Norfk 76 F8
Mill Street Suffk 64 F7
Millthorpe Derbys 84 D5
Millthrop Cumb 95 P2
Milltimber C Aber 151 M7
Milltown Abers 149 P6
Milltown Abers 150 D4
Milltown Cnwll 5 J10
Milltown D & G 110 F5
Milltown Derbys 84 E8
Milltown Devon 17 K4
Milltown of Auchindoun Moray 157 R9
Milltown of Campfield Abers 150 H7
Milltown of Edinvillie Moray 157 P9
Milltown of Learney Abers 150 G7
Milnathort P & K 134 E7
Milngavie E Duns 125 P3
Milnrow Rochdl 89 Q8
Milnthorpe Cumb 95 K4
Milnthorpe Wakefd 91 J7
Milovaig Highld 152 B8
Milson Shrops 57 L10
Milstead Kent 38 F10
Milston Wilts 21 N5
Milthorpe Lincs 74 B4
Milton C Stke 70 G4
Milton Cambs 62 G8
Milton Cumb 111 L8
Milton D & G 106 H7
Milton D & G 108 H6
Milton Derbys 71 Q9
Milton Highld 153 M9
Milton Highld 155 N11
Milton Highld 155 Q8
Milton Highld 156 D3
Milton Highld 167 P6
Milton Inver 125 K4
Milton Kent 37 Q8
Milton Moray 149 M4
Milton Moray 158 D5
Milton N Som 19 K2
Milton Newpt 31 L7
Milton Notts 85 M6
Milton Oxon 34 E6
Milton Oxon 48 E7
Milton P & K 141 Q5
Milton Pembks 41 K10
Milton Somset 19 L10
Milton Stirlg 132 G7
Milton W Duns 125 L3
Milton Abbas Dorset 12 D4
Milton Abbot Devon 5 Q6
Milton Bridge Mdloth 127 P5
Milton Bryan C Beds 49 Q8
Milton Clevedon Somset 20 C7
Milton Combe Devon 6 D5
Milton Common Oxon 35 J4
Milton Damerel Devon 16 F9
Milton End Gloucs 32 D2
Milton End Gloucs 33 M4
Milton Ernest Bed 61 M9
Milton Green Ches W 69 N3
Milton Hill Oxon 34 E6
Milton Keynes M Keyn 49 N7
Milton Lilbourne Wilts 21 N1
Milton Malsor Nhants 60 F9
Milton Morenish P & K 140 F10
Milton of Auchinhove Abers 150 F7
Milton of Balgonie Fife 135 J7
Milton of Buchanan Stirlg 132 E9
Milton of Campsie E Duns 126 B2
Milton of Leys Highld 156 B9
Milton of Murtle C Aber 151 M7
Milton of Tullich Abers 150 B8
Milton on Stour Dorset 20 E9
Milton Regis Kent 38 F9
Milton Street E Susx 25 M10
Milton-under-Wychwood Oxon 47 Q11
Milverton Somset 18 F9
Milverton Warwks 59 M11
Milwich Staffs 70 H8
Milwr Flints 80 H10
Minard Ag & B 131 K8
Minchington Dorset 12 G2
Minchinhampton Gloucs 32 G4
Mindrum Nthumb 118 F4
Minehead Somset 18 C6
Minera Wrexhm 69 J4
Minety Wilts 33 K6
Minffordd Gwynd 67 K7
Mingarrypark Highld 138 D3
Miningsby Lincs 87 K8
Minions Cnwll 5 M7
Minishant S Ayrs 114 F5
Minllyn Gwynd 55 L2
Minnigaff D & G 107 M4

Minnonie Abers 159 J5
Minshull Vernon Ches E 70 B2
Minskip N York 97 N8
Minstead Hants 13 N2
Minsted W Susx 23 N10
Minster Kent 38 G7
Minster Kent 39 P9
Minsterley Shrops 56 F3
Minster Lovell Oxon 34 B2
Minsterworth Gloucs 46 E11
Minterne Magna Dorset 11 P4
Minterne Parva Dorset 11 P4
Minting Lincs 86 G6
Mintlaw Abers 159 N8
Mintlyn Crematorium Norfk 75 N7
Minto Border 117 R6
Minton Shrops 56 G6
Minwear Pembks 41 K8
Minworth Birm 59 J6
Mirehouse Cumb 100 C7
Mireland Highld 167 P4
Mirfield Kirk 90 G7
Miserden Gloucs 32 H3
Miskin Rhondd 30 D5
Miskin Rhondd 30 D8
Misson Notts 85 L2
Misterton Leics 60 C4
Misterton Notts 85 N2
Misterton Somset 11 K3
Mistley Essex 53 K5
Mistley Heath Essex 53 K5
Mitcham Gt Lon 36 G7
Mitcheldean Gloucs 46 C11
Mitchell Cnwll 3 M3
Mitchellslacks D & G 116 D11
Mitchel Troy Mons 31 N2
Mitford Nthumb 113 J3
Mithian Cnwll 3 J3
Mitton Staffs 70 F11
Mixbury Oxon 48 H8
Mixenden Calder 90 D5
Moats Tye Suffk 64 E10
Mobberley Ches E 82 G9
Mobberley Staffs 71 J6
Moccas Herefs 45 M6
Mochdre Conwy 79 Q9
Mochdre Powys 55 P7
Mochrum D & G 107 K8
Mockbeggar Hants 13 L3
Mockbeggar Kent 26 B2
Mockerkin Cumb 100 E6
Modbury Devon 6 H8
Moddershall Staffs 70 G7
Moelfre IoA 79 J7
Moelfre Powys 68 C9
Moel Tryfan Gwynd 67 J3
Moffat D & G 116 F9
Mogador Surrey 36 F10
Moggerhanger C Beds 61 P11
Moira Leics 71 Q11
Molash Kent 38 H11
Mol-chlach Highld 144 G5
Mold Flints 68 H2
Moldgreen Kirk 90 F7
Molehill Green Essex 51 N6
Molehill Green Essex 52 B7
Molescroft E R Yk 92 H2
Molesden Nthumb 112 H4
Molesworth Cambs 61 N5
Molland Devon 17 Q6
Mollington Ches W 81 M10
Mollington Oxon 48 D5
Mollinsburn N Lans 126 C3
Monachty Cerdgn 43 K2
Mondynes Abers 143 P2
Monewden Suffk 2 J10
Moneydie P & K 134 D2
Moneyrow Green W & M 35 N9
Moniaive D & G 115 Q9
Monifieth Angus 142 H11
Monikie Angus 142 H10
Monimail Fife 134 H5
Monington Pembks 41 M2
Monk Bretton Barns 91 K9
Monken Hadley Gt Lon 50 F11
Monk Fryston N York 91 N5
Monkhide Herefs 46 B6
Monkhill Cumb 110 F9
Monkhopton Shrops 57 L6
Monkland Herefs 45 P3
Monkleigh Devon 16 H7
Monknash V Glam 29 P10
Monkokehampton Devon 8 E3
Monkseaton N Tyne 113 M6
Monks Eleigh Suffk 52 G2
Monk's Gate W Susx 24 F5
Monks Heath Ches E 82 H10
Monk Sherborne Hants 22 H3
Monks Horton Kent 27 K3
Monksilver Somset 18 E7
Monks Kirby Warwks 59 Q8
Monk Soham Suffk 65 J8
Monkspath Solhll 58 H9
Monks Risborough Bucks 35 M4
Monksthorpe Lincs 87 M7
Monk Street Essex 51 P5
Monkswood Mons 31 K4
Monkton Devon 10 D4
Monkton Kent 39 N9
Monkton S Ayrs 114 G2
Monkton S Tyne 113 M8
Monkton V Glam 29 P10
Monkton Combe BaNES 20 E2
Monkton Deverill Wilts 20 G7
Monkton Farleigh Wilts 32 F11
Monkton Heathfield Somset 19 J9
Monkton Up Wimborne Dorset 12 H2
Monkton Wyld Dorset 10 G5
Monkwearmouth Sundld 113 N9
Monkwood Hants 23 J8
Monmore Green Wolves 58 D5
Monmouth Mons 31 P2
Monnington on Wye Herefs 45 M6
Monreith D & G 107 L9
Montacute Somset 19 N11
Montcliffe Bolton 89 K8
Montford Shrops 56 G2
Montford Bridge Shrops 69 M11
Montgarrie Abers 150 F4
Montgomery Powys 56 C5
Monton Salfd 82 G5
Montrose Angus 143 N6
Mont Saint Guern 10 b2
Monxton Hants 22 B6
Monyash Derbys 83 Q11

Monymusk Abers ... 150 H4
Monzie P & K ... 133 P2
Moodiesburn N Lans ... 126 B3
Moonzie Fife ... 135 J4
Moor Allerton Leeds ... 91 J3
Moorbath Dorset ... 11 J5
Moorby Lincs ... 87 J8
Moorcot Herefs ... 45 M3
Moor Crichel Dorset ... 12 G3
Moordown Bmouth ... 13 J6
Moore Halton ... 82 C8
Moor End C Beds ... 49 Q10
Moor End Calder ... 90 D5
Moor End Devon ... 17 M10
Moorend Gloucs ... 32 D4
Moor End Lancs ... 88 D2
Moor End N York ... 91 Q3
Moorends Donc ... 92 A7
Moorgreen Hants ... 22 E11
Moor Green Herts ... 50 H5
Moorgreen Notts ... 84 G11
Moorhall Derbys ... 84 D6
Moorhampton Herefs ... 45 M5
Moorhead C Brad ... 90 E3
Moor Head Leeds ... 90 G5
Moorhouse Cumb ... 110 E10
Moorhouse Cumb ... 110 F9
Moorhouse Donc ... 91 M8
Moorhouse Notts ... 85 N7
Moorhouse Bank Surrey ... 37 K10
Moorland Somset ... 19 K8
Moorlinch Somset ... 19 L7
Moor Monkton N York ... 97 R9
Moor Row Cumb ... 100 D8
Moor Row Cumb ... 110 D11
Moorsholm R & Cl ... 105 J8
Moorside Dorset ... 20 E11
Moor Side Lancs ... 88 E4
Moor Side Lancs ... 88 F3
Moorside Leeds ... 90 G3
Moor Side Lincs ... 87 J9
Moorside Oldham ... 89 Q9
Moor Side Sefton ... 81 M4
Moorstock Kent ... 27 K4
Moor Street Birm ... 58 E8
Moor Street Medway ... 38 D8
Moorswater Cnwll ... 5 L9
Moorthorpe Wakefd ... 91 M8
Moortown Devon ... 8 E4
Moortown Hants ... 13 L4
Moortown IoW ... 14 D10
Moortown Leeds ... 90 H3
Moortown Lincs ... 93 J11
Moortown Wrekin ... 69 R11
Morangie Highld ... 162 H10
Morar Highld ... 145 L9
Moray Crematorium Moray ... 158 A5
Morborne Cambs ... 61 P2
Morchard Bishop Devon ... 9 J3
Morcombelake Dorset ... 11 J6
Morcott Rutlnd ... 73 N10
Morda Shrops ... 69 J9
Morden Dorset ... 12 F5
Morden Gt Lon ... 36 G7
Mordiford Herefs ... 45 R7
Mordon Dur ... 104 B5
More Shrops ... 56 E6
Morebath Devon ... 18 C9
Morebattle Border ... 118 E6
Morecambe Lancs ... 95 J8
Moredon Swindn ... 33 M7
Morefield Highld ... 161 J7
Morehall Kent ... 27 M4
Moreleigh Devon ... 7 K8
Morenish P & K ... 140 F10
Moresby Parks Cumb ... 100 C7
Morestead Hants ... 22 F9
Moreton Dorset ... 12 D7
Moreton Essex ... 51 M9
Moreton Herefs ... 45 Q2
Moreton Oxon ... 35 J4
Moreton Staffs ... 70 D11
Moreton Staffs ... 71 L9
Moreton Wirral ... 81 K7
Moreton Corbet Shrops ... 69 Q10
Moretonhampstead Devon ... 9 J7
Moreton-in-Marsh Gloucs ... 47 P8
Moreton Jeffries Herefs ... 46 B5
Moretonmill Shrops ... 69 Q10
Moreton Morrell Warwks ... 48 B3
Moreton on Lugg Herefs ... 45 Q5
Moreton Paddox Warwks ... 48 B4
Moreton Pinkney Nhants ... 48 G5
Moreton Say Shrops ... 70 A8
Moreton Valence Gloucs ... 32 E3
Morfa Cerdgn ... 42 F4
Morfa Bychan Gwynd ... 67 J7
Morfa Dinlle Gwynd ... 66 G3
Morfa Glas Neath ... 29 N3
Morfa Nefyn Gwynd ... 66 D6
Morganstown Cardif ... 30 F8
Morgan's Vale Wilts ... 21 N10
Morham E Loth ... 128 F5
Moriah Cerdgn ... 54 E9
Morland Cumb ... 102 B6
Morley Ches E ... 82 H8
Morley Derbys ... 72 B2
Morley Dur ... 103 M5
Morley Leeds ... 90 H5
Morley Green Ches E ... 82 H8
Morley St Botolph Norfk ... 64 F2
Mornick Cnwll ... 5 N7
Morningside C Edin ... 127 N3
Morningside N Lans ... 126 E6
Morningthorpe Norfk ... 65 J3
Morpeth Nthumb ... 113 J3
Morphie Abers ... 143 N5
Morrey Staffs ... 71 L11
Morridge Side Staffs ... 71 J4
Morriston Swans ... 29 J5
Morston Norfk ... 76 E3
Mortehoe Devon ... 16 H2
Morthen Rothm ... 84 G3
Mortimer W Berk ... 23 J2
Mortimer Common W Berk ... 35 J11
Mortimer's Cross Herefs ... 45 N2
Mortimer West End Hants ... 22 H2
Mortlake Gt Lon ... 36 F5
Mortlake Crematorium Gt Lon ... 36 E5
Morton Cumb ... 101 N3
Morton Cumb ... 110 G10
Morton Derbys ... 84 F8
Morton IoW ... 14 H9
Morton Lincs ... 74 A6
Morton Lincs ... 85 P2
Morton Notts ... 85 M11

Morton Shrops ... 69 J10
Morton Hall Lincs ... 85 Q8
Mortonhall Crematorium C Edin ... 127 P4
Morton-on-Swale N York ... 97 M2
Morton on the Hill Norfk ... 76 G8
Morton Tinmouth Dur ... 103 N6
Morvah Cnwll ... 2 C6
Morval Cnwll ... 5 M10
Morvich Highld ... 146 B3
Morville Shrops ... 57 M6
Morville Heath Shrops ... 57 M6
Morwenstow Cnwll ... 16 C8
Mosborough Sheff ... 84 F4
Moscow E Ayrs ... 125 M9
Mose Shrops ... 57 P6
Mosedale Cumb ... 101 L4
Moseley Birm ... 58 G8
Moseley Wolves ... 58 D5
Moseley Worcs ... 46 F3
Moses Gate Bolton ... 89 L9
Moss Ag & B ... 136 B7
Moss Donc ... 91 P8
Moss Wrexhm ... 69 K4
Mossat Abers ... 150 D4
Mossbank Shet ... 169 r6
Moss Bank St Hel ... 81 Q5
Mossbay Cumb ... 100 C5
Mossblown S Ayrs ... 114 H3
Mossbrow Traffd ... 82 F7
Mossburnford Border ... 118 C7
Mossdale D & G ... 108 E6
Mossdale E Ayrs ... 115 J7
Moss Edge Lancs ... 88 E2
Mossend N Lans ... 126 C5
Mosser Mains Cumb ... 100 F5
Mossley Ches E ... 70 F2
Mossley Tamesd ... 83 L4
Mosspaul Hotel Border ... 117 M11
Moss Side Cumb ... 110 C10
Moss-side Highld ... 156 F6
Moss Side Lancs ... 88 D4
Moss Side Sefton ... 81 M4
Mosstodloch Moray ... 157 Q6
Mossyard D & G ... 107 P7
Mossy Lea Lancs ... 88 G8
Mosterton Dorset ... 11 K3
Moston Manch ... 83 J4
Moston Shrops ... 69 Q9
Moston Green Ches E ... 70 C2
Mostyn Flints ... 80 H8
Motcombe Dorset ... 20 G9
Mothecombe Devon ... 6 G9
Motherby Cumb ... 101 M5
Motherwell N Lans ... 126 C6
Motspur Park Gt Lon ... 36 F7
Mottingham Gt Lon ... 37 K6
Mottisfont Hants ... 22 B9
Mottistone Hants ... 22
Mottistone IoW ... 14 D10
Mottram in Longdendale Tamesd ... 83 L5
Mottram St Andrew Ches E ... 83 J9
Mouilpied Guern ... 10 b2
Mouldsworth Ches W ... 81 Q10
Moulin P & K ... 141 M6
Moulsecoomb Br & H ... 24 H9
Moulsford Oxon ... 34 G8
Moulsoe M Keyn ... 49 P6
Moultavie Highld ... 156 A3
Moulton Ches W ... 82 E11
Moulton Lincs ... 74 F6
Moulton N York ... 103 P10
Moulton Nhants ... 60 G7
Moulton Suffk ... 63 L8
Moulton V Glam ... 30 E11
Moulton Chapel Lincs ... 74 E7
Moulton St Mary Norfk ... 77 M10
Moulton Seas End Lincs ... 74 F5
Mount Cnwll ... 4 B10
Mount Cnwll ... 5 J8
Mount Kirk ... 90 D7
Mountain C Brad ... 90 D4
Mountain Ash Rhondd ... 30 D5
Mountain Cross Border ... 127 M8
Mountain Street Kent ... 39 J11
Mount Ambrose Cnwll ... 3 J5
Mount Bures Essex ... 52 F5
Mountfield E Susx ... 26 B7
Mountgerald House Highld ... 155 Q5
Mount Hawke Cnwll ... 3 J4
Mount Hermon Cnwll ... 2 H10
Mountjoy Cnwll ... 4 D9
Mount Lothian Mdloth ... 127 P6
Mountnessing Essex ... 51 P11
Mounton Mons ... 31 P6
Mount Pleasant Ches E ... 70 E3
Mount Pleasant Derbys ... 71 P11
Mount Pleasant Derbys ... 84 D11
Mount Pleasant Dur ... 103 Q4
Mount Pleasant E R Yk ... 93 N3
Mount Pleasant E Susx ... 25 K7
Mount Pleasant Norfk ... 64 D3
Mount Pleasant Suffk ... 63 M11
Mount Pleasant Worcs ... 47 K2
Mountsett Crematorium Dur ... 113 J10
Mountsorrel Leics ... 72 F8
Mount Sorrel Wilts ... 21 K10
Mount Tabor Calder ... 90 D5
Mousehole Cnwll ... 2 D8
Mouswald D & G ... 109 N6
Mow Cop Ches E ... 70 F3
Mowhaugh Border ... 118 F6
Mowmacre Hill C Leic ... 72 F9
Mowsley Leics ... 60 D3
Moy Highld ... 147 L11
Moy Highld ... 156 D11
Moyle Highld ... 145 Q4
Moylegrove Pembks ... 41 M2
Muasdale Ag & B ... 120 C3
Muchalls Abers ... 151 N9
Much Birch Herefs ... 45 N8
Much Cowarne Herefs ... 46 B5
Much Dewchurch Herefs ... 45 P8
Muchelney Somset ... 19 M10
Muchelney Ham Somset ... 19 M10
Much Hadham Herts ... 51 K7
Much Hoole Lancs ... 88 F6
Much Hoole Town Lancs ... 88 F6
Muchlarnick Cnwll ... 5 L10
Much Marcle Herefs ... 46 C8
Much Wenlock Shrops ... 57 L5
Muck Highld ... 144 F12
Mucking Thurr ... 37 Q4
Muckingford Thurr ... 37 Q5
Muckleburgh Collection Norfk ... 76 G3

Muckleford Dorset ... 11 N6
Mucklestone Staffs ... 70 C7
Muckley Shrops ... 57 L5
Muckton Lincs ... 87 L4
Muddiford Devon ... 17 K4
Muddles Green E Susx ... 25 M8
Mudeford Dorset ... 13 L6
Mudford Somset ... 19 Q11
Mudford Sock Somset ... 19 Q11
Mudgley Somset ... 19 N5
Mud Row Kent ... 38 H7
Mugdock Stirlg ... 125 P2
Mugeary Highld ... 152 G10
Mugginton Derbys ... 71 P6
Muggintonlane End Derbys ... 71 P6
Muggleswick Dur ... 112 F11
Muirden Abers ... 158 H7
Muirdrum Angus ... 143 K10
Muiresk Abers ... 158 G8
Muirhead Angus ... 142 E11
Muirhead Fife ... 134 H6
Muirhead N Lans ... 126 B4
Muirkirk E Ayrs ... 115 N2
Muirmill Stirlg ... 133 L11
Muir of Fowlis Abers ... 150 F5
Muir of Miltonduff Moray ... 157 M6
Muir of Ord Highld ... 155 P7
Muirshearlich Highld ... 146 E11
Muirtack Abers ... 159 N10
Muirton P & K ... 133 Q5
Muirton Mains Highld ... 155 N7
Muirton of Ardblair P & K ... 142 B9
Muker N York ... 102 H11
Mulbarton Norfk ... 76 H11
Mulben Moray ... 157 R7
Mulfra Cnwll ... 2 D7
Mull Ag & B ... 137 Q9
Mullacott Cross Devon ... 17 J3
Mullion Cnwll ... 2 H10
Mullion Cove Cnwll ... 2 H10
Mumby Lincs ... 87 P6
Munderfield Row Herefs ... 46 B4
Munderfield Stocks Herefs ... 46 C4
Mundesley Norfk ... 77 L4
Mundford Norfk ... 63 P2
Mundham Norfk ... 65 L2
Mundon Hill Essex ... 52 E11
Mundy Bois Kent ... 26 F2
Mungrisdale Cumb ... 101 L4
Munlochy Highld ... 156 A7
Munnoch N Ayrs ... 124 H8
Munsley Herefs ... 46 C6
Munslow Shrops ... 57 J7
Murchington Devon ... 8 G7
Murcot Worcs ... 47 L6
Murcott Oxon ... 48 G11
Murcott Wilts ... 33 J6
Murkle Highld ... 167 L3
Murlaggan Highld ... 146 C9
Murrell Green Hants ... 23 K3
Murroes Angus ... 142 H10
Murrow Cambs ... 74 G9
Mursley Bucks ... 49 M9
Murston Kent ... 38 F9
Murthill Angus ... 142 H6
Murthly P & K ... 141 R10
Murton C York ... 98 C10
Murton Cumb ... 102 D6
Murton Dur ... 113 N11
Murton N Tyne ... 113 M6
Murton Nthumb ... 129 P10
Murton Swans ... 28 G7
Musbury Devon ... 10 F6
Muscoates N York ... 98 D5
Musselburgh E Loth ... 127 Q3
Muston Leics ... 73 L3
Muston N York ... 99 M5
Mustow Green Worcs ... 58 C10
Muswell Hill Gt Lon ... 36 G3
Mutehill D & G ... 108 E11
Mutford Suffk ... 65 P4
Muthill P & K ... 133 P4
Mutterton Devon ... 9 P3
Muxton Wrekin ... 57 N2
Mybster Highld ... 167 L6
Myddfai Carmth ... 43 Q8
Myddle Shrops ... 69 N10
Mydroilyn Cerdgn ... 43 J3
Myerscough Lancs ... 88 F3
Mylor Cnwll ... 3 L6
Mylor Bridge Cnwll ... 3 L6
Mynachlog ddu Pembks ... 41 M4
Mynydd-Ilan Flints ... 80 H10
Myndtown Shrops ... 56 F7
Mynydd-bach Mons ... 31 N6
Mynydd-Bach Swans ... 29 J5
Mynydd Buch Cerdgn ... 54 G9
Mynyddgarreg Carmth ... 28 D3
Mynydd Isa Flints ... 69 J2
Mynydd Llandygai Gwynd ... 79 L11
Mynytho Gwynd ... 66 E8
Myrebird Abers ... 151 J8
Myredykes Border ... 118 A11
Mytchett Surrey ... 23 N3
Mytholm Calder ... 90 B5
Mytholmroyd Calder ... 90 C5
Mythop Lancs ... 88 D4
Myton-on-Swale N York ... 97 P7

N

Naast Highld ... 160 C10
Nab's Head Lancs ... 89 J5
Na Buirgh W Isls ... 168 f8
Naburn C York ... 98 B11
Nab Wood Crematorium C Brad ... 90 E3
Naccolt Kent ... 27 J3
Nackington Kent ... 39 L11
Nacton Suffk ... 53 M3
Nafferton E R Yk ... 99 M9
Nag's Head Gloucs ... 32 G5
Nailbridge Gloucs ... 46 B11
Nailsbourne Somset ... 18 H9
Nailsea N Som ... 31 N10
Nailstone Leics ... 72 C9
Nailsworth Gloucs ... 32 F5
Nairn Highld ... 156 F6
Nalderswood Surrey ... 36 F11
Nancegollan Cnwll ... 2 G7
Nancledra Cnwll ... 2 D7
Nanhoron Gwynd ... 66 D8
Nannerch Flints ... 80 H11
Nanpantan Leics ... 72 E7

Nanpean Cnwll ... 4 F10
Nanquidno Cnwll ... 2 B8
Nanstallon Cnwll ... 4 G8
Nant-ddu Powys ... 30 D2
Nanternis Cerdgn ... 42 G3
Nantgaredig Carmth ... 43 J10
Nantgarw Rhondd ... 30 F7
Nant-glas Powys ... 55 M11
Nantglyn Denbgs ... 68 D2
Nantgwyn Powys ... 55 M9
Nantle Gwynd ... 67 J4
Nantmawr Shrops ... 69 J10
Nantmel Powys ... 55 N11
Nantmor Gwynd ... 67 L4
Nant Peris Gwynd ... 67 L3
Nantwich Ches E ... 70 B4
Nant-y-Bwch Blae G ... 30 F2
Nant-y-caws Carmth ... 43 J11
Nant-y-derry Mons ... 31 K3
Nantyffyllon Brdgnd ... 29 M6
Nantyglo Blae G ... 30 G2
Nant-y-gollen Shrops ... 68 H9
Nant-y-moel Brdgnd ... 29 P6
Nant-y-pandy Conwy ... 79 M10
Naphill Bucks ... 35 M5
Napleton Worcs ... 46 G5
Nappa N York ... 96 C10
Napton on the Hill Warwks ... 48 E2
Narberth Pembks ... 41 M8
Narborough Leics ... 72 E11
Narborough Norfk ... 75 P8
Narkurs Cnwll ... 5 N10
Nasareth Gwynd ... 66 H5
Naseby Nhants ... 60 E5
Nash Bucks ... 49 L8
Nash Gt Lon ... 37 K8
Nash Herefs ... 45 L2
Nash Newpt ... 31 K8
Nash Shrops ... 57 L10
Nash End Worcs ... 57 P8
Nash Lee Bucks ... 35 M3
Nash's Green Hants ... 23 J5
Nash Street Kent ... 37 P7
Nassington Nhants ... 73 R11
Nastend Gloucs ... 32 E3
Nasty Herts ... 51 J6
Nateby Cumb ... 102 E9
Nateby Lancs ... 88 F2
National Memorial Arboretum Staffs ... 59 J2
National Motor Museum (Beaulieu) Hants ... 14 C6
National Space Centre C Leic ... 72 F9
Natland Cumb ... 95 L3
Naughton Suffk ... 52 H2
Naunton Gloucs ... 47 M10
Naunton Worcs ... 46 G7
Naunton Beauchamp Worcs ... 47 J4
Navenby Lincs ... 86 C9
Navestock Essex ... 51 M11
Navestock Side Essex ... 51 N11
Navidale House Hotel Highld ... 163 N3
Navity Highld ... 156 D5
Nawton N York ... 98 D4
Nayland Suffk ... 52 G5
Nazeing Essex ... 51 K9
Nazeing Gate Essex ... 51 K9
Neacroft Hants ... 13 L5
Neal's Green Warwks ... 59 M8
Neap Shet ... 169 s8
Near Cotton Staffs ... 71 K5
Near Sawrey Cumb ... 101 L11
Neasden Gt Lon ... 36 F3
Neasham Darltn ... 104 B8
Neath Neath ... 29 L5
Neatham Hants ... 23 K6
Neatishead Norfk ... 77 L7
Nebo Cerdgn ... 54 C11
Nebo Conwy ... 67 Q3
Nebo Gwynd ... 66 H4
Nebo IoA ... 78 H6
Necton Norfk ... 76 B10
Nedd Highld ... 164 D10
Nedderton Nthumb ... 113 K4
Nedging Suffk ... 52 G2
Nedging Tye Suffk ... 52 H2
Needham Norfk ... 65 J5
Needham Market Suffk ... 64 F10
Needham Street Suffk ... 63 M7
Needingworth Cambs ... 62 D6
Neen Savage Shrops ... 57 L9
Neen Sollars Shrops ... 57 M10
Neenton Shrops ... 57 L7
Nefyn Gwynd ... 66 E6
Neilston E Rens ... 125 M6
Nelson Caerph ... 30 F5
Nelson Lancs ... 89 P3
Nemphlar S Lans ... 116 B2
Nempnett Thrubwell BaNES ... 19 P2
Nenthall Cumb ... 111 Q11
Nenthead Cumb ... 102 E2
Nenthorn Border ... 118 C3
Neopardy Devon ... 9 J5
Nep Town W Susx ... 24 F7
Nercwys Flints ... 68 H2
Nereabolls Ag & B ... 122 B8
Nerston S Lans ... 125 Q6
Nesbit Nthumb ... 119 J4
Nesfield N York ... 96 G11
Ness Ches W ... 81 L9
Nesscliffe Shrops ... 69 L11
Neston Ches W ... 81 K9
Neston Wilts ... 32 G11
Netchwood Shrops ... 57 L6
Nether Alderley Ches E ... 82 H9
Netheravon Wilts ... 21 M5
Nether Blainslie Border ... 117 Q3
Netherbrae Abers ... 159 J6
Nether Broughton Leics ... 72 H6
Netherburn S Lans ... 126 D8
Netherbury Dorset ... 11 K5
Netherby N York ... 97 M11
Nether Cerne Dorset ... 11 P5
Nethercleuch D & G ... 109 P3
Nether Compton Dorset ... 19 Q11
Nethercote Warwks ... 60 B8
Nethercott Devon ... 16 H4
Nether Crimond Abers ... 151 L3
Nether Dallachy Moray ... 157 R5
Netherend Gloucs ... 31 Q4
Nether Exe Devon ... 9 N4
Netherfield E Susx ... 26 B8

Netherfield Leics ... 72 F7
Netherfield Notts ... 72 F7
Nether Fingland S Lans ... 116 C8
Nethergate N Linc ... 92 C11
Nethergate Norfk ... 76 F6
Netherhampton Wilts ... 21 M8
Nether Handley Derbys ... 84 F6
Nether Handwick Angus ... 142 F9
Nether Haugh Rothm ... 91 L11
Netherhay Dorset ... 11 J3
Nether Headon Notts ... 85 M6
Nether Heage Derbys ... 84 E10
Nether Heyford Nhants ... 60 E9
Nether Howcleugh S Lans ... 116 E8
Nether Kellet Lancs ... 95 L7
Nether Kinmundy Abers ... 159 Q9
Netherland Green Staffs ... 71 L8
Nether Langwith Notts ... 84 H6
Netherlaw D & G ... 108 F12
Netherley Abers ... 151 M9
Nethermill D & G ... 109 M3
Nethermuir Abers ... 159 N9
Netherne-on-the-Hill Surrey ... 36 G9
Netheroyd Hill Kirk ... 90 E7
Nether Padley Derbys ... 84 B6
Netherplace E Rens ... 125 N6
Nether Poppleton C York ... 98 B10
Nether Row Cumb ... 101 K3
Netherseal Derbys ... 59 L4
Nether Silton N York ... 97 Q2
Nether Skyborry Shrops ... 56 D10
Nether Stowey Somset ... 18 G7
Netherstreet Wilts ... 21 J2
Netherthong Kirk ... 90 F8
Netherthorpe Derbys ... 84 F6
Netherton Angus ... 143 J7
Netherton Devon ... 7 M4
Netherton Dudley ... 58 D7
Netherton Hants ... 22 C3
Netherton Herefs ... 45 Q8
Netherton Kirk ... 90 E8
Netherton N Lans ... 126 D7
Netherton Nthumb ... 119 J9
Netherton Oxon ... 34 D5
Netherton P & K ... 142 A7
Netherton Sefton ... 81 L5
Netherton Shrops ... 57 N8
Netherton Stirlg ... 125 Q3
Netherton Wakefd ... 90 H7
Netherton Worcs ... 47 J5
Nethertown Cumb ... 100 C9
Nethertown Highld ... 167 C9
Nethertown Lancs ... 89 Q5
Nethertown Staffs ... 71 L11
Netherurd Border ... 116 G2
Nether Wallop Hants ... 22 C8
Nether Wasdale Cumb ... 100 F10
Nether Welton Cumb ... 110 H10
Nether Westcote Gloucs ... 47 P10
Nether Whitacre Warwks ... 59 K6
Nether Whitecleuch S Lans ... 116 A7
Nether Winchendon Bucks ... 35 K2
Netherwitton Nthumb ... 112 G2
Nethy Bridge Highld ... 149 J4
Netley Hants ... 14 E5
Netley Marsh Hants ... 13 N4
Nettlebed Oxon ... 35 J7
Nettlebridge Somset ... 20 C5
Nettlecombe Dorset ... 11 L5
Nettlecombe IoW ... 14 F11
Nettleden Herts ... 50 B8
Nettleham Lincs ... 86 D5
Nettlestead Kent ... 37 Q10
Nettlestead Green Kent ... 37 Q10
Nettlestone IoW ... 14 H8
Nettlesworth Dur ... 113 L11
Nettleton Lincs ... 93 K10
Nettleton Wilts ... 32 F9
Nettleton Shrub Wilts ... 32 F9
Netton Devon ... 6 G9
Netton Wilts ... 21 M7
Neuadd Carmth ... 43 P11
Neuadd-ddu Powys ... 55 L9
Nevendon Essex ... 38 C3
Nevern Pembks ... 41 L2
Nevill Holt Leics ... 60 H3
New Abbey D & G ... 109 L7
New Aberdour Abers ... 159 L5
New Addington Gt Lon ... 37 J8
Newall Leeds ... 97 J11
New Alresford Hants ... 22 G8
New Alyth P & K ... 142 C8
Newark C Pete ... 74 D10
Newark Ork ... 169 g2
Newark-on-Trent Notts ... 85 N10
New Arram E R Yk ... 92 H2
Newarthill N Lans ... 126 D6
New Ash Green Kent ... 37 P8
New Balderton Notts ... 85 P10
Newbarn Kent ... 27 L3
New Barn Kent ... 37 P7
New Barnet Gt Lon ... 50 G11
New Barton Nhants ... 61 J8
Newbattle Mdloth ... 127 Q4
New Bewick Nthumb ... 119 L6
Newbie D & G ... 110 C7
Newbiggin Cumb ... 94 H3
Newbiggin Cumb ... 101 N5
Newbiggin Cumb ... 101 Q5
Newbiggin Cumb ... 111 L11
Newbiggin Dur ... 112 H11
Newbiggin N York ... 96 E2
Newbiggin N York ... 96 H2
Newbiggin-by-the-Sea Nthumb ... 113 M3
Newbigging Angus ... 142 G9
Newbigging Angus ... 142 H10
Newbigging Angus ... 142 H11
Newbigging S Lans ... 127 J3
Newbigging-on-Lune Cumb ... 102 D11
New Bilton Warwks ... 59 Q9
Newbold Derbys ... 84 E6
Newbold Leics ... 72 C7
Newbold on Avon Warwks ... 59 Q8
Newbold on Stour Warwks ... 47 Q5
Newbold Pacey Warwks ... 47 Q3
Newbold Revel Warwks ... 59 Q7
Newbold Verdon Leics ... 72 C10
New Bolingbroke Lincs ... 87 K9
Newborough C Pete ... 74 D9
Newborough IoA ... 78 G11

Newborough Staffs...71 L9
Newbottle Nhants...48 F7
Newbottle Sundld...113 M10
New Boultham Lincs...86 C6
Newbourne Suffk...53 N3
New Bradwell M Keyn...49 M6
New Brampton Derbys...84 E6
New Brancepeth Dur...103 P2
Newbridge C Edin...127 L3
Newbridge Caerph...30 H5
Newbridge Cerdgn...43 K3
Newbridge Cnwll...2 C7
Newbridge D & G...109 K5
Newbridge Hants...21 Q11
Newbridge IoW...14 D9
New Bridge N York...98 G3
Newbridge Oxon...34 D4
Newbridge Wrexhm...69 J6
Newbridge Green Worcs...46 F7
Newbridge-on-Usk Mons...31 L6
Newbridge-on-Wye Powys...44 E3
New Brighton Flints...81 K11
New Brighton Wirral...81 L6
New Brinsley Notts...84 G10
New Brotton R & Cl...105 J6
Newbrough Nthumb...112 C7
New Broughton Wrexhm...69 K4
New Buckenham Norfk...64 F3
Newbuildings Devon...9 J4
Newburgh Abers...151 P2
Newburgh Abers...159 N6
Newburgh Fife...134 G4
Newburgh Lancs...88 F8
Newburgh Priory N York...98 A5
Newburn N u Ty...113 J7
Newbury Bolton...82 F4
Newbury Somset...20 C5
Newbury W Berk...34 E11
Newbury Wilts...20 F6
Newbury Park Gt Lon...37 K3
Newby Cumb...101 Q6
Newby Lancs...96 B11
Newby N York...95 Q7
Newby N York...99 L2
Newby N York...104 F8
Newby Bridge Cumb...94 H3
Newby Cross Cumb...110 G10
Newby East Cumb...111 J9
Newby Head Cumb...101 Q6
Newby West Cumb...110 G10
Newby Wiske N York...97 N5
Newcastle Mons...45 N11
Newcastle Shrops...56 D8
Newcastle Airport Nthumb...113 J6
Newcastle Emlyn Carmth...42 F6
Newcastleton Border...111 J3
Newcastle-under-Lyme Staffs...70 E5
Newcastle upon Tyne N u Ty...113 K8
Newchapel Pembks...41 N4
Newchapel Staffs...70 F4
Newchapel Surrey...25 J2
Newchurch Blae G...30 G2
Newchurch Herefs...45 M4
Newchurch IoW...14 G9
Newchurch Kent...27 J5
Newchurch Mons...31 N5
Newchurch Powys...45 J4
Newchurch Staffs...71 L10
Newchurch in Pendle Lancs...89 N3
New Costessey Norfk...76 H9
New Cowper Cumb...109 P11
Newcraighall C Edin...127 Q3
New Crofton Wakefd...91 K7
New Cross Cerdgn...54 E9
New Cross Gt Lon...37 J5
New Cross Somset...19 M11
New Cumnock E Ayrs...115 M5
New Cut E Susx...26 D8
New Deer Abers...159 L8
New Delaval Nthumb...113 L5
New Denham Bucks...36 B4
Newdigate Surrey...24 E2
New Duston Nhants...60 F8
New Earswick C York...98 C9
New Eastwood Notts...84 G11
New Edlington Donc...91 N11
New Elgin Moray...157 N5
New Ellerby E R Yk...93 L3
Newell Green Br For...35 N10
New Eltham Gt Lon...37 K6
New End Worcs...47 L2
Newenden Kent...26 D6
New England C Pete...74 C10
New England Essex...52 B3
Newent Gloucs...46 D9
New Farnley Leeds...90 H4
New Ferry Wirral...81 L7
Newfield Dur...103 P4
Newfield Dur...113 K10
Newfield Highld...156 D2
New Fletton C Pete...74 C11
New Forest National Park...13 N3
Newfound Hants...22 G4
New Fryston Wakefd...91 M5
Newgale Pembks...40 G6
New Galloway D & G...108 D5
Newgate Norfk...76 E3
Newgate Street Herts...50 H9
New Gilston Fife...135 L6
New Grimsby IoS...2 b1
Newhall Ches E...69 R5
Newhall Derbys...71 P10
Newham Nthumb...119 N6
New Hartley Nthumb...113 M5
Newhaven C Edin...127 P2
Newhaven E Susx...25 K10
New Haw Surrey...36 C8
New Hedges Pembks...41 M9
New Herrington Sundld...113 M10
Newhey Rochdl...89 Q8
New Holkham Norfk...76 B4
New Holland N Linc...93 J6
Newholm N York...105 N8
New Houghton Derbys...84 G7
New Houghton Norfk...75 Q5
Newhouse N Lans...126 D5
New Houses N York...96 B6
New Houses Wigan...82 C4
New Hutton Cumb...95 M2
New Hythe Kent...38 B10

Newick E Susx...25 K6
Newingreen Kent...27 K4
Newington Kent...27 L4
Newington Kent...38 E9
Newington Oxon...34 H5
Newington Shrops...56 G8
Newington Bagpath Gloucs...32 F6
New Inn Carmth...43 J7
New Inn Torfn...31 K5
New Invention Shrops...56 D9
New Lakenham Norfk...77 J10
New Lanark S Lans...116 B2
New Lanark Village S Lans...116 B2
Newland C KuH...93 J4
Newland Cumb...94 G3
Newland E R Yk...92 D5
Newland Gloucs...31 Q3
Newland N York...92 A6
Newland Oxon...34 C3
Newland Somset...17 Q4
Newland Worcs...46 E5
Newlandrig Mdloth...128 B7
Newlands Border...111 K2
Newlands Cumb...101 K3
Newlands Nthumb...112 G9
Newlands of Dundurcas Moray...157 P7
New Lane Lancs...88 E8
New Lane End Warrtn...82 D6
New Langholm D & G...110 G4
New Leake Lincs...87 M9
New Leeds Abers...159 N7
New Lodge Barns...91 K9
New Longton Lancs...88 G5
New Luce D & G...106 G5
Newlyn Cnwll...2 D8
Newmachar Abers...151 M4
Newmains N Lans...126 E6
New Malden Gt Lon...36 F7
Newman's End Essex...51 M8
Newman's Green Suffk...52 E3
Newmarket Suffk...63 K8
Newmarket W Isls...168 j4
New Marske R & Cl...104 H6
New Marston Oxon...34 F3
New Mill Abers...151 K11
Newmill Border...117 P8
New Mill Cnwll...2 D7
New Mill Herts...35 P2
Newmill Kirk...90 F9
Newmill Moray...158 B7
Newmillerdam Wakefd...91 J7
Newmill of Inshewan Angus...142 G5
Newmills C Edin...127 M4
New Mills Cnwll...3 M3
New Mills Derbys...83 M7
Newmills Fife...134 C10
Newmills Mons...31 P3
New Mills Powys...55 P4
Newmiln P & K...142 A11
Newmilns E Ayrs...125 N10
New Milton Hants...13 M5
New Mistley Essex...53 K5
New Moat Pembks...41 L5
Newnes Shrops...69 L8
Newney Green Essex...51 Q9
Newnham Hants...23 K4
Newnham Herts...50 F3
Newnham Kent...38 G10
Newnham Nhants...60 C9
Newnham Worcs...57 L11
Newnham on Severn Gloucs...32 C2
New Ollerton Notts...85 L7
New Oscott Birm...58 G6
New Pitsligo Abers...159 L6
New Polzeath Cnwll...4 E6
Newport Cnwll...5 N4
Newport Dorset...12 E5
Newport E R Yk...92 E4
Newport Essex...51 M4
Newport Gloucs...32 D5
Newport Highld...163 Q2
Newport IoW...14 F9
Newport Newpt...31 K7
Newport Norfk...77 Q8
Newport Pembks...41 L3
Newport Wrekin...70 C11
Newport-on-Tay Fife...135 L2
Newport Pagnell M Keyn...49 N6
Newport Pagnell Services M Keyn...49 N6
Newpound Common W Susx...24 C5
New Prestwick S Ayrs...114 F3
New Quay Cerdgn...42 G3
Newquay Cnwll...4 C9
New Quay Essex...52 H7
Newquay Zoo Cnwll...4 C9
New Rackheath Norfk...77 K9
New Radnor Powys...45 J2
New Rent Cumb...101 N3
New Ridley Nthumb...112 G9
New Road Side N York...90 B2
New Romney Kent...27 J7
New Rossington Donc...91 Q11
New Row Cerdgn...54 G10
New Row Lancs...89 J3
New Sauchie Clacks...133 P9
Newsbank Ches E...82 H11
Newseat Abers...158 H11
Newsham Lancs...88 G3
Newsham N York...97 N4
Newsham N York...103 M8
Newsham Nthumb...113 M5
New Sharlston Wakefd...91 K7
Newsholme E R Yk...92 B5
Newsholme Lancs...96 B10
New Shoreston Nthumb...119 N4
New Silksworth Sundld...113 N10
New Skelton R & Cl...105 J7
Newsome Kirk...90 F8
New Somerby Lincs...73 N3
New Southgate Crematorium Gt Lon...36 G4
New Springs Wigan...88 H9
Newstead Border...117 R4
Newstead Notts...84 H10
Newstead Nthumb...119 N5
New Stevenston N Lans...126 D6
New Street Herefs...45 L3
New Swannington Leics...72 C7
Newthorpe N York...91 M4
Newthorpe Notts...84 G11
New Thundersley Essex...38 C4
Newtimber W Susx...24 G8
Newtoft Lincs...86 D3

Newton Ag & B...131 L8
Newton Border...118 B6
Newton Brdgnd...29 M9
Newton C Beds...50 F2
Newton Cambs...62 F11
Newton Cambs...74 H8
Newton Cardif...30 H9
Newton Ches W...69 P3
Newton Ches W...81 N11
Newton Ches W...82 B9
Newton Cumb...94 E6
Newton Derbys...84 F9
Newton Herefs...45 L8
Newton Herefs...45 Q4
Newton Herefs...56 F11
Newton Highld...155 Q7
Newton Highld...156 C8
Newton Highld...156 D4
Newton Highld...167 P7
Newton Lancs...88 C3
Newton Lancs...95 M6
Newton Lincs...73 Q3
Newton Mdloth...127 Q4
Newton Moray...157 M5
Newton Moray...157 Q5
Newton N York...98 H6
Newton Nhants...61 J4
Newton Norfk...76 A8
Newton Notts...72 H2
Newton Nthumb...112 F8
Newton Nthumb...118 H9
Newton S Lans...116 C4
Newton S Lans...126 B5
Newton Sandw...58 F6
Newton Shrops...69 M8
Newton Somset...18 F7
Newton Staffs...71 J9
Newton Suffk...52 F3
Newton W Loth...127 K2
Newton Warwks...60 B5
Newton Wilts...21 P10
Newton Abbot Devon...7 M4
Newton Arlosh Cumb...110 D9
Newton Aycliffe Dur...103 Q6
Newton Bewley Hartpl...104 E5
Newton Blossomville M Keyn...49 P4
Newton Bromswold Nhants...61 L7
Newton Burgoland Leics...72 B9
Newton-by-the-Sea Nthumb...119 P5
Newton by Toft Lincs...86 D3
Newton Ferrers Devon...6 F9
Newton Ferry W Isls...168 d10
Newton Flotman Norfk...65 J2
Newtongrange Mdloth...127 Q5
Newton Green Mons...31 P6
Newton Harcourt Leics...72 G11
Newtonhill Abers...151 N9
Newton Hill Wakefd...91 J6
Newton-in-Bowland Lancs...95 P10
Newton Kyme N York...91 M2
Newton-le-Willows N York...97 K3
Newton-le-Willows St Hel...82 C5
Newtonloan Mdloth...127 Q5
Newton Longville Bucks...49 M8
Newton Mearns E Rens...125 N6
Newtonmill Angus...143 L5
Newtonmore Highld...148 C8
Newton Morrell N York...103 P9
Newton Mountain Pembks...41 J9
Newton Mulgrave N York...105 L7
Newton of Balcanquhal P & K...134 F5
Newton of Balcormo Fife...135 N7
Newton-on-Ouse N York...97 R9
Newton-on-Rawcliffe N York...98 G2
Newton on the Hill Shrops...69 N10
Newton-on-the-Moor Nthumb...119 N9
Newton on Trent Lincs...85 P6
Newton Poppleford Devon...10 B7
Newton Purcell Oxon...48 H8
Newton Regis Warwks...59 L3
Newton Reigny Cumb...101 N4
Newton St Cyres Devon...9 L5
Newton St Faith Norfk...77 J8
Newton St Loe BaNES...20 D2
Newton St Petrock Devon...16 G8
Newton Solney Derbys...71 P9
Newton Stacey Hants...22 D6
Newton Stewart D & G...107 M4
Newton Tony Wilts...21 P6
Newton Tracey Devon...17 J6
Newton under Roseberry R & Cl...104 G8
Newton Underwood Nthumb...112 H3
Newton upon Derwent E R Yk...98 E11
Newton Valence Hants...23 K8
Newton Wamphray D & G...109 P2
Newton with Scales Lancs...88 F4
Newtown Blae G...30 G4
Newtown Ches W...82 B9
Newtown Cnwll...2 F8
Newtown Cnwll...5 M6
Newtown Cumb...101 P6
Newtown Cumb...109 P11
Newtown Cumb...110 C8
Newtown Cumb...111 K8
Newtown D & G...115 Q3
Newtown Derbys...83 L8
Newtown Devon...9 M6
Newtown Devon...17 Q9
Newtown Dorset...11 K4
Newtown Dorset...12 G3
Newtown Dorset...21 J11
New Town Dorset...21 J11
New Town E Susx...25 L6
Newtown Gloucs...32 C4
Newtown Hants...13 N2
Newtown Hants...14 H4
Newtown Hants...22 E2
Newtown Herefs...45 P3
Newtown Herefs...45 Q8
Newtown Herefs...46 B5

Newtown Herefs...46 D7
Newtown Highld...147 K3
Newtown IoW...14 D8
Newtown Lancs...88 G7
New Town Nhants...61 L5
Newtown Nthumb...119 J4
Newtown Nthumb...119 K10
Newtown Nthumb...119 K5
Newtown Poole...12 H6
Newtown Powys...55 Q6
Newtown Rhondd...30 E5
Newtown Shrops...69 M10
Newtown Somset...10 N8
Newtown Somset...18 E4
Newtown Staffs...58 E4
Newtown Staffs...70 G2
Newtown Wigan...82 C4
Newtown Wilts...20 H9
Newtown Wilts...21 Q2
New Town Wilts...33 Q10
Newtown Worcs...46 G3
Newtown Worcs...58 D9
Newtown-in-St Martin Cnwll...3 J7
Newtown Linford Leics...72 E9
Newtown of Beltrees Rens...125 K6
Newtown St Boswells Border...117 R4
Newtown Unthank Leics...72 D10
New Tredegar Caerph...30 F4
New Trows S Lans...126 E10
New Tupton Derbys...84 E7
Newtyle Angus...142 E9
New Walsoken Cambs...75 J9
New Waltham NE Lin...93 N10
New Whittington Derbys...84 E5
New Winton E Loth...128 C5
New Yatt Oxon...34 C2
Newyears Green Gt Lon...36 C3
Newyork Ag & B...131 K5
New York Lincs...86 H9
New York N Tyne...113 M6
New York N York...97 J8
Nextend Herefs...45 L3
Neyland Pembks...41 J9
Niarbyl IoM...80 b6
Nibley Gloucs...32 C3
Nibley S Glos...32 C8
Nibley Green Gloucs...32 D5
Nicholashayne Devon...18 F11
Nicholaston Swans...28 F7
Nickies Hill Cumb...111 K7
Nidd N York...97 M8
Nigg C Aber...151 N7
Nigg Highld...156 E3
Nigg Ferry Highld...156 D4
Nimlet BaNES...32 D10
Ninebanks Nthumb...111 Q10
Nine Elms Swindn...33 M7
Nine Wells Pembks...40 E6
Ninfield E Susx...26 B9
Ningwood IoW...14 C9
Nisbet Border...118 C5
Nisbet Hill Border...129 K9
Niton IoW...14 F11
Nitshill C Glas...125 N5
Noah's Ark Kent...37 N9
Noak Bridge Essex...37 Q2
Noak Hill Gt Lon...37 M2
Noblethorpe Barns...90 H9
Nobold Shrops...56 H2
Nobottle Nhants...60 E8
Nocton Lincs...86 E8
Nogdam End Norfk...77 M11
Noke Oxon...34 F2
Nolton Pembks...40 G7
Nolton Haven Pembks...40 G7
No Man's Heath Ches W...69 P5
No Man's Heath Warwks...59 L3
No Man's Land Cnwll...5 M10
Nomansland Devon...9 K2
Nomansland Wilts...21 Q11
Noneley Shrops...69 N9
Nonington Kent...39 N11
Nook Cumb...95 L4
Nook Cumb...111 J5
Norbiton Gt Lon...36 E7
Norbreck Bpool...88 C2
Norbridge Herefs...46 D6
Norbury Ches E...69 Q5
Norbury Derbys...71 L6
Norbury Gt Lon...36 H7
Norbury Shrops...56 F6
Norbury Staffs...70 D10
Norbury Common Ches E...69 Q5
Norbury Junction Staffs...70 D10
Norchard Worcs...58 B11
Norcott Brook Ches W...82 D8
Norcross Lancs...88 C2
Nordelph Norfk...75 L10
Norden Rochdl...89 P8
Nordley Shrops...57 M5
Norfolk Broads Norfk...77 P10
Norham Nthumb...129 N10
Norland Town Calder...90 D6
Norley Ches W...82 C10
Norleywood Hants...14 C7
Norlington E Susx...25 K8
Normanby Lincs...86 C3
Normanby N Linc...92 E7
Normanby N York...98 E4
Normanby R & Cl...104 F7
Normanby le Wold Lincs...93 K11
Norman Cross Cambs...61 Q2
Normandy Surrey...23 P4
Normans Bay E Susx...25 Q9
Norman's Green Devon...9 Q4
Normanton C Derb...72 A4
Normanton Leics...73 N2
Normanton Notts...85 M10
Normanton Rutlnd...73 N9
Normanton Wakefd...91 K6
Normanton Wilts...21 M6
Normanton le Heath Leics...72 B8
Normanton on Cliffe Lincs...86 B11
Normanton on Soar Notts...72 E6
Normanton on the Wolds Notts...72 G4
Normanton on Trent Notts...85 N7
Normoss Lancs...88 C3
Norney Surrey...23 P6
Norrington Common Wilts...20 G2
Norris Green Cnwll...5 Q8
Norris Green Lpool...81 N6

Norris Hill Leics...72 A7
Norristhorpe Kirk...90 G6
Northacre Norfk...64 C2
Northall Bucks...49 Q10
Northallerton N York...97 N3
Northall Green Norfk...76 D9
Northam C Sotn...14 D4
Northam Devon...16 H6
Northampton Nhants...60 G8
Northampton Worcs...58 B11
Northampton Services Nhants...60 F9
North Anston Rothm...84 H4
North Ascot Br For...35 P10
North Aston Oxon...48 E9
Northaw Herts...50 G10
Northay Somset...10 F2
North Baddesley Hants...22 C10
North Ballachulish Highld...139 K5
North Barrow Somset...20 B9
North Barsham Norfk...76 C4
North Benfleet Essex...38 C4
North Berwick E Loth...128 E3
North Bitchburn Dur...103 N4
North Blyth Nthumb...113 M4
North Boarhunt Hants...14 H4
North Bockhampton Dorset...13 L5
Northborough C Pete...74 C9
Northbourne Kent...39 P11
North Bovey Devon...8 H9
North Bradley Wilts...20 G3
North Brentor Devon...8 C8
North Brewham Somset...20 D7
North Bridge Surrey...23 Q7
Northbridge Street E Susx...26 B7
Northbrook Hants...22 F7
Northbrook Oxon...48 E10
North Buckland Devon...16 H3
North Burlingham Norfk...77 M10
North Cadbury Somset...20 B9
North Carlton Lincs...86 B5
North Carlton Notts...85 J4
North Cave E R Yk...92 E4
North Cerney Gloucs...33 K3
North Chailey E Susx...25 J6
Northchapel W Susx...23 Q9
North Charford Hants...21 N11
North Charlton Nthumb...119 N6
North Cheam Gt Lon...36 F7
North Cheriton Somset...20 C9
North Chideock Dorset...11 J6
Northchurch Herts...35 Q3
North Cliffe E R Yk...92 E3
North Clifton Notts...85 P6
North Close Dur...103 Q4
North Cockerington Lincs...87 L2
North Connel Ag & B...138 G11
North Cornelly Brdgnd...29 M8
North Corner Cnwll...3 K10
North Cotes Lincs...93 P10
Northcott Devon...5 N3
Northcott Devon...10 B2
Northcott Devon...10 C3
North Country Cnwll...2 H5
Northcourt Oxon...34 E5
North Cove Suffk...65 P4
North Cowton N York...103 Q10
North Crawley M Keyn...49 P6
North Cray Gt Lon...37 L6
North Creake Norfk...76 B4
North Curry Somset...19 K9
North Dalton E R Yk...99 J11
North Deighton N York...97 N10
North Devon Crematorium Devon...17 J5
Northdown Kent...39 Q7
North Downs...38 F10
North Duffield N York...92 A3
North Duntulm Highld...152 G3
North East Surrey Crematorium Gt Lon...36 F7
Northedge Derbys...84 E7
North Elham Kent...27 L3
North Elkington Lincs...87 J2
North Elmham Norfk...76 D7
North Elmsall Wakefd...91 M8
Northend Bucks...35 K6
North End C Port...15 J4
North End Cumb...110 F9
North End Dorset...20 F9
North End E R Yk...93 L2
North End E R Yk...93 N4
North End Essex...51 Q7
North End Hants...21 M11
North End Hants...22 G9
North End Leics...72 F7
North End Lincs...74 D2
North End Lincs...87 M3
North End Lincs...92 H11
North End Lincs...93 H10
North End N Linc...93 K6
North End N Som...31 M11
North End Nhants...61 L7
North End Norfk...64 D3
North End Nthumb...119 M10
North End Sefton...81 L4
North End W Susx...15 Q6
North End W Susx...24 D9
Northend Warwks...48 C4
Northenden Manch...82 H7
Northend Woods Bucks...35 P7
North Erradale Highld...160 A10
North Evington C Leic...72 G10
North Fambridge Essex...38 E2
North Featherstone Wakefd...91 L6
North Ferriby E R Yk...92 G5
Northfield Birm...58 F9
Northfield C Aber...151 N6
Northfield E R Yk...92 H5
Northfields Lincs...73 Q9
Northfleet Kent...37 P6
North Frodingham E R Yk...99 M10
North Gorley Hants...13 L2
North Green Norfk...65 J4
North Green Suffk...65 L9
North Green Suffk...65 M8
North Greetwell Lincs...86 D6
North Grimston N York...98 G7
North Halling Medway...38 B8
North Haven Shet...169 t12
North Hayling Hants...15 K6
North Hazelrigg Nthumb...119 L4
North Heasley Devon...17 N5
North Heath W Susx...24 C6

North Hele Devon...18 D10
North Hertfordshire Memorial Park & Crematorium Herts...50 E4
North Hill Cnwll...5 M6
North Hillingdon Gt Lon...36 C4
North Hinksey Village Oxon...34 E3
North Holmwood Surrey...36 E11
North Huish Devon...7 J7
North Hykeham Lincs...86 B7
Northiam E Susx...26 D7
Northill C Beds...61 P11
Northington Gloucs...32 D3
Northington Hants...22 G7
North Kelsey Lincs...92 H10
North Kessock Highld...156 B8
North Killingholme N Linc...93 K7
North Kilvington N York...97 P3
North Kilworth Leics...60 D4
North Kingston Hants...13 L4
North Kyme Lincs...86 G10
North Lancing W Susx...24 E9
North Landing E R Yk...99 Q6
Northlands Lincs...87 K10
Northleach Gloucs...33 M2
North Lee Bucks...35 M3
North Lees N York...97 L6
Northleigh Devon...10 D5
Northleigh Devon...17 L5
North Leigh Kent...27 K2
North Leigh Oxon...34 C2
North Leverton with Habblesthorpe Notts...85 N4
Northlew Devon...8 D5
North Littleton Worcs...47 L5
Northload Bridge Somset...19 N7
North Lopham Norfk...64 E5
North Luffenham Rutlnd...73 N10
North Marden W Susx...23 M11
North Marston Bucks...49 L10
North Middleton Mdloth...128 B8
North Middleton Nthumb...119 J6
North Millbrex Abers...159 K9
North Milmain D & G...106 E7
North Molton Devon...17 N6
Northmoor Oxon...34 D4
North Moreton Oxon...34 G7
Northmuir Angus...142 F7
North Mundham W Susx...15 N6
North Muskham Notts...85 N9
North Newbald E R Yk...92 F3
North Newington Oxon...48 D6
North Newnton Wilts...21 M3
North Newton Somset...19 K8
Northney Hants...15 K6
North Nibley Gloucs...32 D5
North Oakley Hants...22 F4
North Ockendon Gt Lon...37 N3
Northolt Gt Lon...36 D4
Northop Flints...81 J11
Northop Hall Flints...81 K11
North Ormesby Middsb...104 F7
North Ormsby Lincs...87 J2
Northorpe Kirk...90 G6
Northorpe Lincs...74 A7
Northorpe Lincs...74 D3
Northorpe Lincs...92 E11
North Otterington N York...97 N3
Northover Somset...19 N7
Northover Somset...19 P10
North Owersby Lincs...86 E2
Northowram Calder...90 E5
North Perrott Somset...11 K3
North Petherton Somset...19 J8
North Petherwin Cnwll...5 M4
North Pickenham Norfk...76 B10
North Piddle Worcs...47 J4
North Poorton Dorset...11 L5
Northport Dorset...12 F7
North Poulner Hants...13 L3
North Queensferry Fife...134 E11
North Radworthy Devon...17 P5
North Rauceby Lincs...86 D11
Northrepps Norfk...77 J4
North Reston Lincs...87 L4
North Rigton N York...97 L11
North Ripley Hants...13 L5
North Rode Ches E...83 J11
North Ronaldsay Ork...169 g1
North Ronaldsay Airport Ork...169 g1
North Row Cumb...100 H4
North Runcton Norfk...75 M7
North Scale Cumb...94 D7
North Scarle Lincs...85 P7
North Seaton Nthumb...113 L3
North Seaton Colliery Nthumb...113 L3
North Shian Ag & B...138 G9
North Shields N Tyne...113 N7
North Shoebury Sthend...38 F4
North Shore Bpool...88 C3
North Side C Pete...74 E11
North Side Cumb...100 C5
North Skelton R & Cl...105 J7
North Somercotes Lincs...93 R11
North Stainley N York...97 L5
North Stainmore Cumb...102 F8
North Stifford Thurr...37 P4
North Stoke BaNES...32 D11
North Stoke Oxon...34 H7
North Stoke W Susx...24 B8
Northstowe Cambs...62 F7
North Street Cambs...63 J7
North Street Hants...21 N11
North Street Hants...21 H8
North Street Kent...38 H10
North Street Medway...38 D7
North Street W Berk...34 H10
North Sunderland Nthumb...119 P4
North Tamerton Cnwll...5 M2
North Tawton Devon...8 G4
North Third Stirlg...133 M10
North Thoresby Lincs...93 N11
North Togston Nthumb...119 P10
Northton W Isls...168 e9
North Town Devon...17 J10
North Town Somset...19 Q6
North Town W & M...35 N8
North Tuddenham Norfk...76 E9
North Uist W Isls...168 C10
Northumberland National Park Nthumb...118 G10
North Walbottle N u Ty...113 J7
North Walsham Norfk...77 K6

North Waltham Hants...22 G5
North Warnborough Hants...23 K4
Northway Somset...18 F9
North Weald Bassett Essex...51 L10
North Wheatley Notts...85 N3
North Whilborough Devon...7 M5
Northwich Ches W...82 K10
North Wick BaNES...31 Q11
Northwick S Glos...31 Q7
Northwick Somset...19 L5
Northwick Worcs...46 F3
North Widcombe BaNES...19 Q3
North Willingham Lincs...86 G3
North Wingfield Derbys...84 F7
North Witham Lincs...73 N6
Northwold Norfk...75 Q11
Northwood C Stke...70 F5
Northwood Derbys...84 C8
Northwood Gt Lon...36 C2
Northwood IoW...14 E8
Northwood Shrops...69 N8
Northwood Green Gloucs...46 D11
North Wootton Dorset...11 P2
North Wootton Norfk...75 M6
North Wootton Somset...19 Q6
North Wraxall Wilts...32 F9
North Wroughton Swindn...33 M8
North York Moors National Park...105 K10
Norton Donc...91 N7
Norton E Susx...25 L10
Norton Gloucs...46 G10
Norton Halton...82 C8
Norton Herts...50 F4
Norton IoW...13 P7
Norton Mons...45 N10
Norton N Som...19 K2
Norton N Nhants...60 C8
Norton Notts...85 J6
Norton Powys...56 E11
Norton S on T...104 D6
Norton Sheff...84 E4
Norton Shrops...56 H8
Norton Shrops...57 K3
Norton Shrops...57 L8
Norton Shrops...57 N4
Norton Suffk...64 D8
Norton Swans...28 H7
Norton W Susx...15 P5
Norton Wilts...32 G8
Norton Worcs...46 G4
Norton Worcs...47 K5
Norton Bavant Wilts...20 H6
Norton Bridge Staffs...70 F8
Norton Canes Staffs...58 F3
Norton Canes Services Staffs...58 F3
Norton Canon Herefs...45 M5
Norton Corner Norfk...76 F6
Norton Disney Lincs...85 Q9
Norton Ferris Wilts...20 E7
Norton Fitzwarren Somset...18 G9
Norton Green IoW...13 P7
Norton Hawkfield BaNES...19 Q2
Norton Heath Essex...51 P10
Norton in Hales Shrops...70 C7
Norton in the Moors C Stke...70 F4
Norton-Juxta-Twycross Leics...59 M3
Norton-le-Clay N York...97 P6
Norton Lindsey Warwks...47 N2
Norton Little Green Suffk...64 D8
Norton Malreward BaNES...20 B2
Norton Mandeville Essex...51 N10
Norton-on-Derwent N York...98 F6
Norton St Philip Somset...20 E3
Norton Subcourse Norfk...65 N2
Norton sub Hamdon Somset...19 N11
Norton Wood Herefs...45 M5
Norwell Notts...85 N8
Norwell Woodhouse Notts...85 M8
Norwich Norfk...77 J10
Norwich Airport Norfk...77 J9
Norwich (St Faith) Crematorium Norfk...77 J8
Norwick Shet...169 t2
Norwood Clacks...133 P9
Norwood Derbys...84 G4
Norwood Kent...27 J5
Norwood End Essex...51 N9
Norwood Green Calder...90 E5
Norwood Green Gt Lon...36 D5
Norwood Hill Surrey...24 F2
Norwoodside Cambs...74 H11
Noseley Leics...73 J11
Noss Mayo Devon...6 F9
Nosterfield N York...97 L4
Nosterfield End Cambs...51 P2
Nostie Highld...145 Q2
Notgrove Gloucs...47 M10
Nottage Brdgnd...29 M9
Notter Cnwll...5 P9
Nottingham C Nott...72 F3
Nottington Dorset...11 P8
Notton Wakefd...91 J8
Notton Wilts...32 H11
Nounsley Essex...52 C9
Noutard's Green Worcs...57 Q11
Nowton Suffk...64 B9
Nox Shrops...56 G2
Nuffield Oxon...35 J7
Nunburnholme E R Yk...98 G11
Nuncargate Notts...84 H10
Nunclose Cumb...111 J11
Nuneaton Warwks...59 N6
Nuneham Courtenay Oxon...34 G5
Nunhead Gt Lon...36 H5
Nunkeeling E R Yk...99 N11
Nun Monkton N York...97 R9
Nunney Somset...20 D5
Nunney Catch Somset...20 D6
Nunnington Herefs...45 R6
Nunnington N York...98 D5
Nunsthorpe NE Lin...93 N9
Nunthorpe C York...98 C10
Nunthorpe Middsb...104 F8
Nunthorpe Village Middsb...104 F8
Nunton Wilts...21 N9

Nunwick N York...97 M6
Nunwick Nthumb...112 C6
Nupdown S Glos...32 B5
Nup End Bucks...49 N11
Nupend Gloucs...32 E3
Nuptown Br For...35 N10
Nursling Hants...22 C11
Nursted Hants...23 L10
Nurston V Glam...30 E11
Nurton Staffs...58 B4
Nutbourne W Susx...15 L5
Nutbourne W Susx...24 C7
Nutfield Surrey...36 H10
Nuthall Notts...72 E2
Nuthampstead Herts...51 K4
Nuthurst W Susx...24 D5
Nutley E Susx...25 K5
Nutley Hants...22 H6
Nuttall Bury...89 M7
Nutwell Donc...91 Q10
Nybster Highld...167 Q4
Nyetimber W Susx...15 N7
Nyewood W Susx...23 M10
Nymans W Susx...24 G6
Nymet Rowland Devon...17 N10
Nymet Tracey Devon...8 H4
Nympsfield Gloucs...32 F4
Nynehead Somset...18 F10
Nythe Somset...19 M8
Nyton W Susx...15 P5

● O

Oadby Leics...72 G10
Oad Street Kent...38 E9
Oakall Green Worcs...46 F2
Oakamoor Staffs...71 J6
Oakbank W Loth...127 K4
Oak Cross Devon...8 D5
Oakdale Caerph...30 G5
Oake Somset...18 G9
Oaken Staffs...58 C4
Oakenclough Lancs...95 L11
Oakengates Wrekin...57 N2
Oakenholt Flints...81 K10
Oakenshaw Dur...103 N3
Oakenshaw Kirk...90 F5
Oakerthorpe Derbys...84 E10
Oakford Cerdgn...43 J3
Oakford Devon...18 B10
Oakfordbridge Devon...18 B10
Oakgrove Ches E...83 K11
Oakham Rutlnd...73 M9
Oakhanger Ches E...70 D4
Oakhanger Hants...23 L7
Oakhill Somset...20 B5
Oakhurst Kent...37 N10
Oakington Cambs...62 F8
Oaklands Powys...44 E4
Oakle Street Gloucs...46 E11
Oakley Bed...61 M10
Oakley Bucks...34 H2
Oakley Fife...134 C10
Oakley Hants...22 G4
Oakley Oxon...35 L4
Oakley Poole...12 H5
Oakley Suffk...64 H6
Oakley Green W & M...35 P9
Oakley Park Powys...55 M7
Oakridge Lynch Gloucs...32 H4
Oaks Lancs...89 K4
Oaks Shrops...56 G4
Oaksey Wilts...33 J6
Oaks Green Derbys...71 M8
Oakshaw Ford Cumb...111 K5
Oakshott Hants...23 K9
Oakthorpe Leics...59 M2
Oak Tree Darltn...104 C8
Oakwood C Derb...72 B3
Oakwood Nthumb...112 D7
Oakworth C Brad...90 C3
Oare Kent...38 H9
Oare Somset...17 P2
Oare Wilts...21 N2
Oasby Lincs...73 Q3
Oath Somset...19 L9
Oathlaw Angus...142 H6
Oatlands Park Surrey...36 C7
Oban Ag & B...130 H2
Oban Airport Ag & B...138 G10
Obley Shrops...56 E9
Obney P & K...141 P10
Oborne Dorset...20 C11
Obthorpe Lincs...74 A8
Occold Suffk...64 H7
Occumster Highld...167 N9
Ochiltree E Ayrs...115 K3
Ockbrook Derbys...72 C3
Ocker Hill Sandw...58 E6
Ockeridge Worcs...46 E2
Ockham Surrey...36 C9
Ockle Highld...137 P1
Ockley Surrey...24 D2
Ocle Pychard Herefs...46 A5
Octon E R Yk...99 L7
Odcombe Somset...19 P11
Odd Down BaNES...20 D2
Oddendale Cumb...101 Q8
Oddingley Worcs...46 H3
Oddington Gloucs...47 P9
Oddington Oxon...48 G11
Odell Bed...61 L9
Odham Devon...8 C4
Odiham Hants...23 K4
Odsal C Brad...90 F5
Odsey Cambs...50 G3
Odstock Wilts...21 M9
Odstone Leics...72 B9
Offchurch Warwks...59 N11
Offenham Worcs...47 L5
Offerton Stockp...83 K7
Offerton Sundld...113 M9
Offham E Susx...25 K8
Offham Kent...37 Q9
Offham W Susx...24 B9
Offleymarsh Staffs...70 D9
Offord Cluny Cambs...62 B7
Offord D'Arcy Cambs...62 B7
Offton Suffk...53 J2
Offwell Devon...10 D5
Ogbourne Maizey Wilts...33 N10
Ogbourne St Andrew Wilts...33 N10
Ogbourne St George Wilts...33 P10
Ogden Calder...90 D4
Ogle Nthumb...112 H5
Oglet Lpool...81 N8
Ogmore V Glam...29 N9

Ogmore-by-Sea V Glam...29 N9
Ogmore Vale Brdgnd...29 P6
Ogwen Bank Gwynd...79 L11
Okeford Fitzpaine Dorset...12 D2
Okehampton Devon...8 E6
Oker Side Derbys...84 C8
Okewood Hill Surrey...24 D3
Olchard Devon...9 L9
Old Hants...60 G6
Old Aberdeen C Aber...151 N6
Old Alresford Hants...22 G8
Oldany Highld...164 C10
Old Auchenbrack D & G...115 Q8
Old Basford C Nott...72 F2
Old Basing Hants...23 J4
Old Beetley Norfk...76 D8
Oldberrow Warwks...58 H11
Old Bewick Nthumb...119 L6
Old Bolingbroke Lincs...87 L7
Old Bramhope Leeds...90 G2
Old Brampton Derbys...84 D6
Old Bridge of Urr D & G...108 G7
Old Buckenham Norfk...64 F3
Old Burghclere Hants...22 E3
Oldbury Kent...37 N9
Oldbury Sandw...58 E7
Oldbury Shrops...57 N6
Oldbury Warwks...59 M6
Oldbury Naite S Glos...32 B6
Oldbury-on-Severn S Glos...32 B6
Oldbury on the Hill Gloucs...32 F7
Old Byland N York...98 B3
Old Cantley Donc...91 Q10
Old Cassop Dur...104 B3
Old Castle Brdgnd...29 P9
Oldcastle Mons...45 L10
Oldcastle Heath Ches W...69 N5
Old Catton Norfk...77 J9
Old Churchstoke Powys...56 D6
Old Clee NE Lin...93 N9
Old Cleeve Somset...18 D6
Old Colwyn Conwy...80 B9
Oldcotes Notts...85 J3
Old Dailly S Ayrs...114 D8
Old Dalby Leics...72 H6
Old Dam Derbys...83 P9
Old Deer Abers...159 N8
Old Ditch Somset...19 P5
Old Edlington Donc...91 N11
Old Eldon Dur...103 P4
Old Ellerby E R Yk...93 L3
Old Felixstowe Suffk...53 P4
Oldfield C Brad...90 C3
Oldfield Worcs...46 F2
Old Fletton C Pete...74 C11
Oldford Somset...20 E4
Old Forge Herefs...45 R11
Old Furnace Herefs...45 P10
Old Glossop Derbys...83 M6
Old Goole E R Yk...92 B6
Old Grimsby IoS...2 b1
Old Hall Green Herts...51 J6
Oldhall Green Suffk...64 B10
Old Hall Street Norfk...77 L5
Oldham Oldham...83 K4
Oldham Crematorium Oldham...83 K4
Oldhamstocks E Loth...129 J5
Old Harlow Essex...51 L8
Old Heath Essex...52 H7
Old Hunstanton Norfk...75 N2
Old Hurst Cambs...62 D5
Old Hutton Cumb...95 M3
Old Inns Services N Lans...126 D2
Old Kea Cnwll...3 L5
Old Kilpatrick W Duns...125 M3
Old Knebworth Herts...50 F6
Old Lakenham Norfk...77 J10
Oldland S Glos...32 C10
Old Langho Lancs...89 L3
Old Laxey IoM...80 f5
Old Leake Lincs...87 M10
Old Malton N York...98 F6
Oldmeldrum Abers...151 L2
Oldmill Cnwll...5 P7
Old Milverton Warwks...59 L11
Old Newton Suffk...64 F9
Old Oxted Surrey...37 J10
Old Portlethen Abers...151 N8
Old Quarrington Dur...104 B3
Old Radford C Nott...72 F2
Old Radnor Powys...45 K3
Old Rayne Abers...150 H2
Old Romney Kent...26 H7
Old Shoreham W Susx...24 F9
Oldshoremore Highld...164 F5
Old Soar Kent...37 P10
Old Sodbury S Glos...32 E8
Old Somerby Lincs...73 P4
Old Stratford Nhants...49 L6
Old Struan P & K...141 K4
Old Swarland Nthumb...119 N10
Old Swinford Dudley...58 D8
Old Tebay Cumb...102 B9
Old Thirsk N York...97 P4
Old Town Calder...90 C5
Old Town Cumb...95 M4
Old Town Cumb...101 N2
Old Town E Susx...25 N11
Old Town IoS...2 c2
Old Trafford Traffd...82 H5
Old Tupton Derbys...84 E7
Oldwall Cumb...111 J3
Oldwalls Swans...28 E6
Old Warden C Beds...50 E2
Oldways End Somset...17 R7
Old Weston Cambs...61 N5
Old Wick Highld...167 Q6
Old Windsor W & M...35 Q10
Old Wives Lees Kent...39 J11
Old Woking Surrey...36 B9
Old Wolverton M Keyn...49 M6
Old Woodhall Lincs...86 H7
Old Woods Shrops...69 N10
Olgrinmore Highld...167 J6
Olive Green Staffs...71 L11
Oliver's Battery Hants...22 E9
Ollaberry Shet...169 q5
Ollach Highld...153 J10
Ollerton Ches E...82 G9
Ollerton Notts...85 L8
Ollerton Shrops...70 A9
Olmarch Cerdgn...43 M3
Olmstead Green Cambs...51 P2
Olney M Keyn...49 N4
Olrig House Highld...167 L3

Olton Solhll...58 H8
Olveston S Glos...32 B8
Ombersley Worcs...46 F2
Ompton Notts...85 L7
Once Brewed Nthumb...111 N6
Onchan IoM...80 e6
Onecote Staffs...71 J3
Onehouse Suffk...64 E10
Onen Mons...31 M2
Ongar Street Herefs...56 F11
Onibury Shrops...56 H8
Onich Highld...139 J5
Onllwyn Neath...29 M4
Onneley Staffs...70 D6
Onslow Green Essex...51 Q7
Onslow Village Surrey...36 A9
Onston Ches W...82 C10
Openwoodgate Derbys...84 E11
Opinan Highld...153 N5
Orbliston Moray...157 Q6
Orbost Highld...152 D9
Orby Lincs...87 N7
Orchard Portman Somset...18 H10
Orcheston Wilts...21 L5
Orcop Herefs...45 P9
Orcop Hill Herefs...45 P9
Ord Abers...158 F6
Ordhead Abers...150 H4
Ordie Abers...150 D7
Ordiequish Moray...157 Q7
Ordley Nthumb...112 D9
Ordsall Notts...85 M5
Ore E Susx...26 D9
Oreleton Common Herefs...56 H11
Oreton Shrops...57 M8
Orford Suffk...65 N11
Orford Warrtn...82 D6
Organford Dorset...12 F6
Orgreave Staffs...71 L11
Orkney Islands Ork...169 d6
Orkney Neolithic Ork...169 c5
Orlestone Kent...26 H5
Orleton Herefs...56 H11
Orleton Worcs...57 N11
Orlingbury Nhants...61 J6
Ormathwaite Cumb...101 J5
Ormesby R & Cl...104 F7
Ormesby St Margaret Norfk...77 P9
Ormesby St Michael Norfk...77 P9
Ormiscaig Highld...160 D8
Ormiston E Loth...128 C6
Ormsaigmore Highld...137 M3
Ormsary Ag & B...123 P4
Ormskirk Lancs...88 E8
Ornsby Hill Dur...113 J11
Oronsay Ag & B...136 b4
Orphir Ork...169 c6
Orpington Gt Lon...37 L7
Orrell Sefton...81 L5
Orrell Wigan...88 G8
Orrell Post Wigan...88 G8
Orrisdale IoM...80 d3
Orroland D & G...108 G11
Orsett Thurr...37 P4
Orsett Heath Thurr...37 P4
Orslow Staffs...70 E11
Orston Notts...73 J2
Orthwaite Cumb...101 J4
Ortner Lancs...95 L10
Orton Cumb...102 B9
Orton Nhants...60 H5
Orton Staffs...58 C5
Orton Longueville C Pete...74 C11
Orton-on-the-Hill Leics...59 M4
Orton Rigg Cumb...110 F10
Orton Waterville C Pete...74 C11
Orwell Cambs...62 E10
Osbaldeston Lancs...89 J3
Osbaldeston Green Lancs...89 J3
Osbaldwick C York...98 C10
Osbaston Leics...72 C10
Osbaston Shrops...69 K10
Osborne IoW...14 F8
Osborne House IoW...14 F8
Osbournby Lincs...73 R3
Oscroft Ches W...81 R11
Ose Highld...152 E9
Osgathorpe Leics...72 C7
Osgodby Lincs...86 F2
Osgodby N York...99 M4
Osgodby N York...92 B4
Oskaig Highld...153 J10
Oskamull Ag & B...137 M6
Osmaston Derbys...71 M6
Osmington Dorset...11 Q8
Osmington Mills Dorset...12 B8
Osmondthorpe Leeds...91 J4
Osmotherley N York...104 E11
Osney Oxon...34 F3
Ospringe Kent...38 H9
Ossett Wakefd...90 H6
Ossington Notts...85 N8
Ostend Essex...38 F2
Osterley Gt Lon...36 D5
Oswaldkirk N York...98 C5
Oswaldtwistle Lancs...89 L5
Oswestry Shrops...69 J9
Otford Kent...37 N9
Otham Kent...38 C11
Otham Hole Kent...38 D11
Othery Somset...19 L9
Otley Leeds...90 H2
Otley Suffk...65 J10
Otley Green Suffk...65 J10
Otterbourne Hants...22 E10
Otterburn N York...96 C9
Otterburn Nthumb...112 C4
Otter Ferry Ag & B...131 N1
Otterham Cnwll...5 J4
Otterhampton Somset...18 H6
Otterham Quay Kent...38 D9
Otterham Station Cnwll...5 J4
Otternish W Isls...168 d10
Ottershaw Surrey...36 B8
Otterswick Shet...169 s5
Otterton Devon...10 B7
Otterwood Hants...14 D6
Ottery St Mary Devon...10 C5
Ottinge Kent...27 L3
Ottringham E R Yk...93 M5
Oughterby Cumb...110 F9
Oughtershaw N York...96 E4
Oughterside Cumb...100 F3
Oughtibridge Sheff...84 D2
Oughtrington Warrtn...82 E7
Oulston N York...98 B6

ulton Cumb....110 D10
ulton Leeds....91 K5
ulton Norfk....76 G6
ulton Staffs....70 D10
ulton Staffs....70 G7
ulton Suffk....65 Q3
ulton Broad Suffk....65 Q3
ulton Street Norfk....76 H6
undle Nhants....61 M3
unsdale Staffs....58 C6
ur Dynamic Earth
  C Edin....127 P3
usby Cumb....102 B4
usden Suffk....63 M9
usefleet E R Yk....92 D6
uston Dur....113 L10
utchester Nthumb....119 M4
ut Elmstead Kent....39 M11
utgate Cumb....101 L11
uthgill Cumb....102 E10
uthill Warwks....58 H11
utlands Staffs....70 D8
utlane Kirk....90 D7
ut Newton E R Yk....93 Q6
ut Rawcliffe Lancs....88 E2
utwell Norfk....75 K10
utwick Hants....21 M11
utwood Surrey....36 H11
utwood Wakefd....91 J6
utwood Gate Bury....89 M9
utwoods Leics....72 C7
utwoods Staffs....70 D11
uzlewell Green Leeds....91 J3
venden Calder....90 D5
ver Cambs....62 E8
ver Ches W....82 D11
ver Gloucs....46 F11
ver S Glos....31 Q8
ver Burrows Derbys....71 P7
verbury Worcs....47 J7
vercombe Dorset....11 P8
ver Compton Dorset....19 Q11
verdale Crematorium
  Bolton....89 K9
ver End Cambs....61 N2
vergreen Derbys....84 D6
ver Green Warwks....59 J6
ver Haddon Derbys....84 B7
ver Kellet Lancs....95 L7
ver Kiddington Oxon....48 D10
verleigh Somset....19 N7
verley Staffs....71 M11
ver Monnow Mons....31 P2
ver Norton Oxon....48 B9
ver Peover Ches E....82 G10
verpool Ches W....81 M9
verscaig Hotel Highld....161 Q2
verseal Derbys....71 P11
ver Silton N York....97 P2
versland Kent....39 J10
versley Green Warwks....47 L3
verstone Nhants....60 G7
ver Stowey Somset....18 G7
verstrand Norfk....77 J3
ver Stratton Somset....19 M11
verstreet Wilts....21 L7
ver Tabley Ches E....82 F9
verthorpe Nhants....48 E6
verton C Aber....151 M5
verton Ches W....81 Q9
verton Hants....22 F5
verton Lancs....95 J9
verton N York....98 B9
verton Shrops....57 J10
verton Swans....28 E7
verton Wakefd....90 H7
verton Wrexhm....69 L6
verton Bridge Wrexhm....69 L6
verton Green Ches E....70 E2
vertown Lancs....95 N5
vertown N Lans....126 E7
vertown Swindn....33 N9
vertown Wakefd....91 K7
ver Wallop Hants....21 Q7
ver Whitacre Warwks....59 L6
ver Woodhouse Derbys....84 G6
ver Worton Oxon....48 D9
very Oxon....34 G6
ving Bucks....49 L10
ving W Susx....15 P6
vingdean Br & H....25 J10
vingham Nthumb....112 G8
vington Dur....103 M8
vington Essex....52 C3
vington Hants....22 G8
vington Norfk....76 C11
vington Nthumb....112 G8
wer Hants....14 E6
wer Hants....22 B11
wermoigne Dorset....12 C7
wlbury Shrops....56 E6
wlerton Sheff....84 D3
wlpen Gloucs....32 E5
wl's Green Suffk....65 K8
wlsmoor Br For....23 M2
wlswick Bucks....35 L3
wmby Lincs....86 D3
wmby Lincs....93 J10
wslebury Hants....22 F10
wston Donc....91 P8
wston Leics....73 K9
wston Ferry N Linc....92 D10
wstwick E R Yk....93 N4
wthorpe E R Yk....93 P5
wthorpe Notts....72 H4
wton Manor Hartpl....104 E5
xborough Norfk....75 P10
xbridge Dorset....11 K5
xcombe Lincs....87 K5
xcroft Derbys....84 G6
xen End Essex....51 Q9
xenholme Cumb....95 L3
xen Pen C Brad....90 C4
xen Park Cumb....94 G3
xenpill Somset....19 M6
xenton Gloucs....47 J8
xenwood Wilts....22 B3
xford Oxon....34 F3
xford Oxon....48 E11
xford Crematorium
  Oxon....34 G4
xford Services Oxon....34 H4
xhey Herts....50 D10
xhill Dur....113 J10
xhill Warwks....48 B5
xley Wolves....58 D4
xley Green Essex....52 F2
xley's Green E Susx....25 Q6
xlode Cambs....62 G3
xnam Border....118 C7
xnead Norfk....77 J7

Oxshott Surrey....36 D8
Oxshott Heath Surrey....36 D8
Oxspring Barns....90 H10
Oxted Surrey....37 J10
Oxton Border....128 D9
Oxton N York....91 N2
Oxton Notts....85 K10
Oxton Wirral....81 L7
Oxwich Swans....28 E7
Oxwich Green Swans....28 E7
Oxwick Norfk....76 C6
Oykel Bridge Hotel
  Highld....161 P6
Oyne Abers....150 H2
Oystermouth Swans....28 H7
Ozleworth Gloucs....32 E6

P

Pabail W Isls....168 k4
Packers Hill Dorset....11 P2
Packington Leics....72 B8
Packmoor C Stke....70 F4
Packmores Warwks....59 L11
Padanaram Angus....142 G7
Padbury Bucks....49 K8
Paddington Gt Lon....36 G4
Paddington Warrtn....82 D7
Paddlesworth Kent....27 L4
Paddlesworth Kent....37 Q8
Paddock Wood Kent....25 Q2
Paddolgreen Shrops....69 P8
Padfield Derbys....83 M5
Padgate Warrtn....82 D7
Padhams Green Essex....51 P11
Padiham Lancs....89 M4
Padside N York....97 J9
Padstow Cnwll....4 E6
Padworth W Berk....34 H11
Page Bank Dur....103 P3
Pagham W Susx....15 N7
Paglesham Essex....38 F3
Paignton Torbay....7 M6
Pailton Warwks....59 Q8
Paine's Cross E Susx....25 P6
Painleyhill Staffs....71 J8
Painscastle Powys....44 H5
Painshawfield Nthumb....112 G8
Painsthorpe E R Yk....98 G9
Painswick Gloucs....32 G3
Painter's Forstal Kent....38 G10
Paisley Rens....125 M5
Paisley Woodside
  Crematorium Rens....125 M5
Pakefield Suffk....65 Q3
Pakenham Suffk....64 C8
Pale Gwynd....68 C7
Pale Green Essex....51 Q2
Palestine Hants....21 Q6
Paley Street W & M....35 N9
Palfrey Wsall....58 F5
Palgrave Suffk....64 G6
Pallington Dorset....12 C6
Palmersbridge Cnwll....5 K6
Palmers Green Gt Lon....36 H2
Palmerston E Ayrs....115 K4
Palmerstown V Glam....30 F11
Palnackie D & G....108 N9
Palnure D & G....107 N5
Palterton Derbys....84 G7
Pamber End Hants....22 H3
Pamber Green Hants....22 H3
Pamber Heath Hants....22 H2
Pamington Gloucs....46 H8
Pamphill Dorset....12 G4
Pampisford Cambs....62 G11
Panborough Somset....19 N5
Pancrasweek Devon....16 D10
Pancross V Glam....30 D11
Pandy Caerph....30 G7
Pandy Gwynd....54 E4
Pandy Gwynd....68 A9
Pandy Mons....45 L10
Pandy Powys....55 L4
Pandy Wrexhm....68 G7
Pandy'r Capel Denbgs....68 E4
Pandy Tudur Conwy....67 R2
Panfield Essex....52 B6
Pangbourne W Berk....34 H9
Pangdean W Susx....24 H8
Panks Bridge Herefs....46 B5
Pannal N York....97 M10
Pannal Ash N York....97 L10
Pannanich Wells Hotel
  Abers....150 C8
Pant Shrops....69 J10
Pantasaph Flints....80 H9
Panteg Pembks....40 H4
Pantersbridge Cnwll....5 K8
Pant-ffrwyth Brdgnd....29 P8
Pant Glas Gwynd....66 H5
Pantglas Powys....54 H5
Pant-Gwyn Carmth....43 L9
Pant-lasau Swans....29 J4
Pant Mawr Powys....55 J8
Panton Lincs....86 G5
Pant-pastynog Denbgs....68 D2
Pantperthog Gwynd....54 G4
Pant-y-dwr Powys....55 M10
Pant-y-ffridd Powys....56 B4
Pantyffynnon Carmth....28 H2
Pantygaseg Torfn....31 J5
Pant-y-gog Brdgnd....29 P6
Pantymenyn Carmth....41 M5
Pant-y-mwyn Flints....68 G2
Panxworth Norfk....77 M9
Papa Stour Airport Shet....169 n8
Papa Westray Airport Ork....169 d1
Papcastle Cumb....100 F4
Papigoe Highld....167 Q6
Papple E Loth....128 F5
Papplewick Notts....84 H10
Papworth Everard
  Cambs....62 C8
Papworth St Agnes
  Cambs....62 C8
Par Cnwll....3 R3
Paramount Street Kent....39 N9
Parbold Lancs....88 F8
Parbrook Somset....19 Q7
Parbrook W Susx....24 C5
Parc Gwynd....68 C6
Parc Gwyn
  Crematorium Pembks....41 M8
Parcllyn Cerdgn....42 D4
Parc Seymour Newpt....31 M6
Pardshaw Cumb....100 E6
Parham Suffk....65 L9

Park D & G....109 K2
Park Nthumb....111 N8
Park Bottom Cnwll....2 H5
Park Bridge Tamesd....83 K4
Park Corner E Susx....25 M3
Park Corner Oxon....35 J7
Park Corner W & M....35 N8
Park Crematorium Hants....23 N5
Park Crematorium Lancs....88 D5
Park End Bed....49 Q4
Parkend Gloucs....32 B3
Park End Nthumb....112 C5
Parkers Green Kent....37 P11
Parkeston Essex....53 M5
Parkeston Quay Essex....53 M5
Park Farm Kent....26 H4
Parkgate Ches W....81 K9
Parkgate Cumb....110 D11
Parkgate D & G....109 M3
Parkgate E Susx....26 B9
Parkgate Essex....51 Q5
Park Gate Hants....14 F5
Parkgate Kent....26 E5
Parkgate Kent....37 M8
Park Gate Leeds....90 F2
Parkgate Surrey....24 F2
Park Gate Worcs....58 D10
Park Green Essex....51 L5
Park Green Suffk....64 G9
Parkgrove
  Crematorium Angus....143 L8
Parkhall W Duns....125 M3
Parkham Devon....16 F7
Parkham Ash Devon....16 F7
Park Head Derbys....84 E10
Park Hill Gloucs....31 Q5
Parkhouse Mons....31 P4
Parkmill Swans....28 F7
Park Royal Gt Lon....36 E4
Parkside Dur....113 P11
Parkside N Lans....126 E6
Parkside Wrexhm....69 L3
Parkstone Poole....12 H6
Park Street Herts....50 D10
Park Street W Susx....24 D4
Parkway Herefs....46 D7
Park Wood
  Crematorium Calder....90 E6
Parley Green Dorset....13 K5
Parmoor Bucks....35 L7
Parndon Wood
  Crematorium Essex....51 K9
Parracombe Devon....17 M2
Parrog Pembks....41 L3
Parsonby Cumb....100 F3
Parson Cross Sheff....84 D2
Parson Drove Cambs....74 G9
Parson's Heath Essex....52 H6
Parson's Hill Derbys....71 P9
Partick C Glas....125 N4
Partington Traffd....82 F6
Partney Lincs....87 M7
Parton Cumb....100 C6
Partridge Green W Susx....24 E7
Partrishow Powys....45 K10
Parwich Derbys....71 M4
Paslow Wood Common
  Essex....51 N10
Passenham Nhants....49 L7
Passfield Hants....23 M8
Passingford Bridge
  Essex....51 M11
Paston C Pete....74 C10
Paston Norfk....77 L5
Pasturefields Staffs....70 H10
Patchacott Devon....8 C5
Patcham Br & H....24 H9
Patchetts Green Herts....50 D11
Patching W Susx....24 C9
Patchole Devon....17 L3
Patchway S Glos....32 B8
Pateley Bridge N York....97 J7
Paternoster Heath Essex....52 F8
Pathe Somset....19 L8
Pathhead Fife....134 H7
Pathhead Mdloth....128 B7
Pathlow Warwks....47 N3
Path of Condie P & K....134 D5
Patmore Heath Herts....51 K5
Patna E Ayrs....114 H5
Patney Wilts....21 L3
Patrick IoM....80 b5
Patrick Brompton
  N York....97 K2
Patricroft Salfd....82 G5
Patrington E R Yk....93 P6
Patrington Haven E R Yk....93 P6
Patrixbourne Kent....39 L10
Patterdale Cumb....101 L7
Pattingham Staffs....57 Q5
Pattishall Nhants....49 J4
Pattiswick Green Essex....52 D7
Patton Shrops....57 K5
Patton Bridge Cumb....101 Q11
Paul Cnwll....2 D8
Paulerspury Nhants....49 K5
Paull E R Yk....93 L5
Paul's Dene Wilts....21 M8
Paulton BaNES....20 C3
Paunton Herefs....46 C4
Pauperhaugh Nthumb....119 M11
Pave Lane Wrekin....70 D11
Pavenham Bed....61 L9
Pawlett Somset....19 J6
Pawston Nthumb....118 G4
Paxford Gloucs....47 N7
Paxton Border....129 N9
Payden Street Kent....38 F11
Payhembury Devon....10 B4
Paynter's Lane End
  Cnwll....2 H5
Paythorne Lancs....96 B10
Paytoe Herefs....56 G10
Peacehaven E Susx....25 K10
Peak Dale Derbys....83 N9
Peak District National
  Park Derbys....83 Q6
Peak Forest Derbys....83 P9
Peak Hill Lincs....74 C9
Peakirk C Pete....74 C9
Pearson's Green Kent....25 Q2
Peartree Green Herefs....46 A8
Peasedown St John
  BaNES....20 D3
Peasehill Derbys....84 F11
Peaseland Green Norfk....76 F8
Peasemore W Berk....34 E9
Peasenhall Suffk....65 M8
Pease Pottage W Susx....24 G4
Pease Pottage Services
  W Susx....24 G4

Peaslake Surrey....24 C2
Peasley Cross St Hel....81 Q6
Peasmarsh E Susx....26 E7
Peasmarsh Somset....10 G2
Peasmarsh Surrey....23 Q5
Peathill Abers....159 M4
Peat Inn Fife....135 M6
Peatling Magna Leics....60 C2
Peatling Parva Leics....60 C3
Peaton Shrops....57 J7
Pebmarsh Essex....52 E5
Pebworth Worcs....47 M5
Pecket Well Calder....90 B5
Peckforton Ches E....69 P3
Peckham Gt Lon....36 H5
Peckleton Leics....72 D10
Pedairffordd Powys....68 F10
Pedlinge Kent....27 K4
Pedmore Dudley....58 D8
Pedwell Somset....19 M7
Peebles Border....117 K2
Peel IoM....80 b5
Peel Lancs....88 D4
Peel Common Hants....14 G6
Peel Green
  Crematorium Salfd....82 F5
Peene Kent....27 L4
Peening Quarter Kent....26 E6
Peggs Green Leics....72 C7
Pegsdon C Beds....50 D4
Pegswood Nthumb....113 K3
Pegwell Kent....39 Q3
Peinchorran Highld....153 J11
Peinlich Highld....152 G6
Pelcomb Pembks....40 H7
Pelcomb Bridge Pembks....40 H7
Pelcomb Cross Pembks....40 H7
Peldon Essex....52 G8
Pell Green E Susx....25 P4
Pelsall Wsall....58 F4
Pelsall Wood Wsall....58 F4
Pelton Dur....113 L10
Pelton Fell Dur....113 L10
Pelutho Cumb....109 P11
Pelynt Cnwll....5 L10
Pemberton Carmth....28 F4
Pemberton Wigan....82 C4
Pembles Cross Kent....26 E2
Pembrey Carmth....28 D4
Pembridge Herefs....45 M3
Pembroke Pembks....41 J10
Pembroke Dock Pembks....41 J10
Pembrokeshire Coast
  National Park Pembks....40 F6
Pembury Kent....25 P2
Pen-allt Herefs....45 R9
Penallt Mons....31 P2
Penally Pembks....41 M11
Penare Cnwll....3 P5
Penarth V Glam....30 G10
Penblewin Pembks....41 M7
Pen-bont
  Rhydybeddau Cerdgn....54 F8
Penbryn Cerdgn....42 E4
Pencader Carmth....42 H7
Pencaenewydd Gwynd....66 G6
Pencaitland E Loth....128 C6
Pencarnisiog IoA....78 F10
Pencarreg Carmth....43 K5
Pencarrow Cnwll....5 J5
Pencelli Powys....44 F9
Penclawdd Swans....28 F5
Pencoed Brdgnd....30 C8
Pencombe Herefs....46 A4
Pencoyd Herefs....45 Q9
Pencraig Herefs....45 R10
Pencraig Powys....68 D9
Pendeen Cnwll....2 B7
Penderyn Rhondd....29 P3
Pendine Carmth....41 P9
Pendlebury Salfd....82 G4
Pendleton Lancs....89 M3
Pendock Worcs....46 E8
Pendoggett Cnwll....4 H5
Pendomer Somset....11 L2
Pendoylan V Glam....30 E9
Pendre Brdgnd....29 P8
Penegoes Powys....54 H4
Penelewey Cnwll....3 L5
Pen-ffordd Pembks....41 L6
Pengam Caerph....30 G5
Pengam Cardif....30 H9
Penge Gt Lon....37 J6
Pengelly Cnwll....4 H5
Pengorffwysfa IoA....78 H6
Pengover Green Cnwll....5 M8
Pen-groes-oped Mons....31 K3
Pengwern Denbgs....80 E9
Penhale Cnwll....2 H10
Penhale Cnwll....4 E10
Penhale Cnwll....4 H9
Penhale Cnwll....5 Q11
Penhallow Cnwll....3 K3
Penhalurick Cnwll....3 J6
Penhalvean Cnwll....3 J6
Penhill Swindn....33 N7
Penhow Newpt....31 M6
Penhurst E Susx....25 Q7
Peniarth Gwynd....54 E3
Penicuik Mdloth....127 N6
Peniel Carmth....42 H10
Peniel Denbgs....68 D2
Penifiler Highld....152 H9
Peninver Ag & B....120 E7
Penisarwaun Gwynd....67 K2
Penistone Barns....90 G10
Penjerrick Cnwll....3 K7
Penketh Warrtn....82 C7
Penkill S Ayrs....114 D8
Penkridge Staffs....58 D2
Penlean Cnwll....5 L2
Penleigh Wilts....20 G4
Penley Wrexhm....69 M6
Penllergaer Swans....28 H5
Pen-llyn IoA....78 F8
Pen-lôn IoA....78 G11
Penmachno Conwy....67 P4
Penmaen Caerph....30 G5
Penmaen Swans....28 F7
Penmaenan Conwy....79 N9
Penmaenmawr Conwy....79 N9
Penmaenpool Gwynd....67 M11
Penmark V Glam....30 E11
Penmon IoA....79 L8
Penmorfa Gwynd....67 J6
Penmount
  Crematorium Cnwll....3 L4
Penmynydd IoA....79 J10
Penn Bucks....35 P6
Penn Wolves....58 C5

Pennal Gwynd....54 F4
Pennan Abers....159 K3
Pennant Cerdgn....43 K2
Pennant Denbgs....68 D8
Pennant Powys....55 K5
Pennant-Melangell
  Powys....68 D9
Pennard Swans....28 G7
Pennerley Shrops....56 F5
Pennicott Devon....9 L4
Pennines....90 B3
Pennington Cumb....94 F5
Pennington Hants....13 P5
Pennington Green
  Wigan....89 J9
Pennorth Powys....44 G9
Penn Street Bucks....35 P5
Pennsylvania S Glos....32 D10
Penny Bridge Cumb....94 G4
Pennycross Ag & B....137 N10
Pennygate Norfk....77 L7
Pennyghael Ag & B....137 N10
Pennyglen S Ayrs....114 E5
Penny Green Derbys....84 H5
Penny Hill Lincs....74 G5
Pennymoor Devon....9 L2
Pennywell Sundld....113 N9
Penparc Cerdgn....42 D5
Penparcau Cerdgn....54 D8
Penpedairheol Caerph....30 F5
Penpedairheol Mons....31 K4
Penperlleni Mons....31 K4
Penpethy Cnwll....4 H10
Penpillick Cnwll....3 L6
Penpol Cnwll....3 L6
Penpoll Cnwll....5 J11
Penponds Cnwll....2 G6
Penpont Cnwll....4 H7
Penpont D & G....108 H2
Penpont Powys....44 D9
Penquit Devon....6 G8
Penrest Cnwll....5 N6
Penrherber Carmth....41 Q3
Pen-rhiw Pembks....41 P2
Penrhiwceiber Rhondd....30 E3
Pen Rhiwfawr Neath....29 K2
Penrhiwllan Cerdgn....42 G5
Penrhiw-pal Cerdgn....42 F5
Penrhos Gwynd....66 E8
Penrhos IoA....78 D8
Penrhos Mons....31 M2
Penrhos Powys....29 M2
Penrhos garnedd Gwynd....79 K10
Penrhyn Bay Conwy....79 Q8
Penrhyncoch Cerdgn....54 E8
Penrhyn-coch Cerdgn....54 E8
Penrhyndeudraeth
  Gwynd....67 L7
Penrhyn-side Conwy....79 Q8
Penrice Swans....28 F7
Penrioch N Ayrs....120 G3
Penrith Cumb....101 P4
Penrose Cnwll....4 D7
Penruddock Cumb....101 M5
Penryn Cnwll....3 K7
Pensarn Conwy....80 D9
Pensax Worcs....57 N11
Pensby Wirral....81 K8
Penselwood Somset....20 E8
Pensford BaNES....20 B2
Pensham Worcs....46 H6
Penshaw Sundld....113 M10
Penshurst Kent....25 M2
Penshurst Station Kent....37 M11
Pensilva Cnwll....5 M7
Pensnett Dudley....58 D7
Penstone Devon....9 J4
Penstrowed Powys....55 Q4
Pentewan Cnwll....3 Q4
Pentir Gwynd....79 K11
Pentire Cnwll....4 B9
Pentlepoir Pembks....41 M9
Pentlow Essex....63 P11
Pentlow Street Essex....63 P11
Pentney Norfk....75 P8
Pentonbridge Cumb....110 H5
Penton Grafton Hants....22 B5
Penton Mewsey Hants....22 B5
Pentraeth IoA....79 J9
Pentre Denbgs....68 E2
Pentre Flints....81 L11
Pentre Mons....31 K3
Pentre Mons....31 M4
Pentre Powys....55 P7
Pentre Powys....56 B7
Pentre Powys....56 D6
Pentre Rhondd....30 C5
Pentre Shrops....69 L11
Pentre Wrexhm....69 J6
Pentre bâch Cerdgn....43 L5
Pentre Bach Flints....81 J9
Pentrebach Myr Td....30 E4
Pentre-bach Powys....44 C8
Pentrebeirdd Powys....56 B2
Pentre Berw IoA....78 H10
Pentre-bont Conwy....67 N4
Pentrebychan
  Crematorium Wrexhm....69 K5
Pentre-cagel Carmth....42 F6
Pentrecelyn Denbgs....68 F4
Pentre-celyn Powys....55 K3
Pentre-chwyth Swans....29 J6
Pentre-clawdd Shrops....69 J8
Pentre-cwrt Carmth....42 G7
Pentredwr Denbgs....68 G5
Pentrefelin Gwynd....67 J7
Pentrefelin IoA....78 G6
Pentre Ffwrndan Flints....81 K10
Pentrefoelas Conwy....67 N4
Pentregat Cerdgn....42 F4
Pentre-Gwenlais Carmth....43 M11
Pentre Gwynfryn Gwynd....67 K9
Pentre Halkyn Flints....81 J10
Pentre Hodrey Shrops....56 E9
Pentre Isaf Conwy....80 D10
Pentre Llanrhaeadr
  Denbgs....68 E2
Pentre Llifior Powys....56 B5
Pentre-llwyn-llwyd
  Powys....44 D4
Pentre-llyn Cerdgn....54 E9
Pentre-llyn-cymmer
  Conwy....68 C4
Pentre-Maw Powys....55 K4
Pentre Meyrick V Glam....30 C9
Pentre-piod Torfn....31 J4
Pentre-poeth Carmth....31 J4
Pentre'rbryn Cerdgn....42 G4
Pentre'r-felin Cerdgn....43 M5

288 Pentre'r Felin – Potters Marston

Pentre'r Felin Conwy 79 Q11
Pentre'r-felin Powys 44 C8
Pentre Saron Denbgs 68 D2
Pentre-tafarn-y-fedw Conwy 67 Q2
Pentre ty gwyn Carmth 43 R7
Pentrich Derbys 84 E10
Pentridge Dorset 21 K11
Pen-twyn Caerph 30 H4
Pen-twyn Mons 31 P3
Pen-twyn Torfn 31 J4
Pentwynmaur Caerph 30 G5
Pentyrch Cardif 30 F8
Penwithick Cnwll 4 G10
Penwood Hants 22 D2
Penwyllt Powys 44 B11
Penybanc Carmth 43 M10
Penybont Powys 44 G2
Pen-y-bont Powys 68 H10
Pen-y-bont-fawr Powys 68 E10
Pen-y-bryn Pembks 41 N2
Pen-y-cae Powys 29 M2
Penycae Wrexhm 69 J5
Pen-y-cae-mawr Mons 31 M5
Penycaerau Gwynd 66 B9
Pen-y-cefn Flints 80 G9
Pen-y-clawdd Mons 31 N3
Pen-y-coedcae Rhondd 30 E7
Penycwn Pembks 40 G6
Pen-y-fai Brdgnd 29 N8
Pen-y-felin Flints 80 H11
Penyffordd Flints 69 K2
Penyffridd Gwynd 67 J3
Pen-y-garn Cerdgn 54 E7
Pen-y-Garnedd Powys 68 F10
Pen-y-genffordd Powys 44 H9
Pen-y-graig Gwynd 66 C8
Penygraig Rhondd 30 D6
Penygroes Carmth 28 G2
Penygroes Gwynd 66 H4
Pen-y-Gwryd Gwynd 67 M3
Pen-y-lan V Glam 30 C9
Pen-y-Mynydd Carmth 28 E4
Penymynydd Flints 69 K2
Pen-y-pass Gwynd 67 L3
Pen-yr-Heol Mons 31 M2
Pen-yr-Heolgerrig Myr Td 30 D3
Penysarn IoA 78 H6
Pen-y-stryt Denbgs 68 H4
Penywaun Rhondd 30 C4
Penzance Cnwll 2 D7
Peopleton Worcs 46 H4
Peover Heath Ches E 82 G10
Peper Harow Surrey 23 P6
Peplow Shrops 70 A10
Pepper's Green Essex 51 P8
Pepperstock C Beds 50 C7
Perceton N Ayrs 125 K9
Percyhorner Abers 159 N4
Perelle Guern 10 b2
Perham Down Wilts 21 Q5
Periton Somset 18 C5
Perivale Gt Lon 36 E4
Perkins Village Devon 9 P6
Perkinsville Dur 113 L10
Perlethorpe Notts 85 K6
Perranarworthal Cnwll 3 K6
Perranporth Cnwll 3 K3
Perranuthnoe Cnwll 2 E8
Perranwell Cnwll 3 K3
Perranwell Cnwll 3 K6
Perran Wharf Cnwll 3 K6
Perranzabuloe Cnwll 3 K3
Perrott's Brook Gloucs 33 K3
Perry Birm 58 G6
Perry Barr Birm 58 G6
Perry Barr Crematorium Birm 58 G6
Perry Green Essex 52 D7
Perry Green Herts 51 K7
Perry Green Wilts 33 J7
Perrystone Hill Herefs 46 B9
Perry Street Somset 10 G3
Pershall Staffs 70 E9
Pershore Worcs 46 H5
Pertenhall Bed 61 N7
Perth P & K 134 E3
Perth Crematorium P & K 134 D2
Perthy Shrops 69 L8
Perton Herefs 46 A6
Perton Staffs 58 C5
Pertwood Wilts 20 G7
Peterborough C Pete 74 C11
Peterborough Crematorium C Pete 74 C10
Peterborough Services Cambs 61 P2
Peterchurch Herefs 45 L7
Peterculter C Aber 151 L7
Peterhead Abers 159 R8
Peterlee Dur 104 D2
Petersfield Hants 23 K10
Peter's Green Herts 50 D7
Petersham Gt Lon 36 E6
Peters Marland Devon 16 H9
Peterstone Wentlooge Newpt 31 J9
Peterston-super-Ely V Glam 30 E9
Peterstow Herefs 45 R10
Peters Village Kent 38 B9
Peter Tavy Devon 8 D9
Petham Kent 39 K11
Petherwin Gate Cnwll 5 M4
Petrockstow Devon 17 J10
Petsoe End M Keyn 49 N5
Pet Street Kent 27 J2
Pett E Susx 26 E9
Pettaugh Suffk 64 H10
Pett Bottom Kent 39 L11
Petterden Angus 142 G9
Pettinain S Lans 116 D2
Pettistree Suffk 65 L10
Petton Devon 18 D10
Petton Shrops 69 M9
Petts Wood Gt Lon 37 L7
Pettycur Fife 134 H10
Petty France S Glos 32 E7
Pettymuk Abers 151 N3
Petworth W Susx 23 Q10
Pevensey E Susx 25 P9
Pevensey Bay E Susx 25 Q10
Pewsey Wilts 21 N2
Pheasant's Hill Bucks 35 L7
Phepson Worcs 46 H3
Philadelphia Sundld 113 M10
Philham Devon 16 D7
Philiphaugh Border 117 N5
Phillack Cnwll 2 F6
Philleigh Cnwll 3 M6
Philpot End Essex 51 P7
Philpstoun W Loth 127 K2
Phocle Green Herefs 46 B9
Phoenix Green Hants 23 L3
Phones Highld 148 C9
Pibsbury Somset 19 M9
Pica Cumb 100 D6
Piccadilly Warwks 59 K5
Piccotts End Herts 50 B9
Pickburn Donc 91 N9
Pickering N York 98 F4
Picket Piece Hants 22 C5
Picket Post Hants 13 L3
Picket Twenty Hants 22 C5
Pickford Covtry 59 L8
Pickford Green Covtry 59 L8
Pickhill N York 97 M4
Picklescott Shrops 56 G5
Pickmere Ches E 82 E9
Pickney Somset 18 G9
Pickstock Wrekin 70 C10
Pickup Bank Bl w D 89 L6
Pickwell Devon 16 H3
Pickwell Leics 73 K8
Pickwick Wilts 32 G10
Pickworth Lincs 73 Q4
Pickworth Rutlnd 73 P8
Picton Ches W 81 N10
Picton Flints 80 G8
Picton N York 104 D9
Piddinghoe E Susx 25 K10
Piddington Bucks 35 M6
Piddington Nhants 49 M4
Piddington Oxon 48 H11
Piddlehinton Dorset 11 Q5
Piddletrenthide Dorset 11 Q5
Pidley Cambs 62 D5
Piercebridge Darltn 103 P7
Pierowall Ork 169 d2
Piff's Elm Gloucs 46 H9
Pigdon Nthumb 113 J3
Pigeon Green Warwks 47 P2
Pig Oak Dorset 12 H4
Pig Street Herefs 45 M5
Pikehall Derbys 71 M3
Pilford Dorset 12 H4
Pilgrims Hatch Essex 51 N11
Pilham Lincs 85 Q2
Pill N Som 31 P9
Pillaton Cnwll 5 P9
Pillatonmill Cnwll 5 P9
Pillerton Hersey Warwks 47 Q5
Pillerton Priors Warwks 47 Q5
Pilleth Powys 56 D11
Pilley Barns 91 J10
Pilley Hants 13 P5
Pilley Bailey Hants 13 P5
Pillgwenlly Newpt 31 K7
Pillhead Devon 16 H6
Pilling Lancs 95 J11
Pilling Lane Lancs 94 H11
Pilning S Glos 31 Q7
Pilot Inn Kent 27 J8
Pilsbury Derbys 71 L2
Pilsdon Dorset 11 J5
Pilsgate C Pete 73 R9
Pilsley Derbys 84 B6
Pilsley Derbys 84 F8
Pilson Green Norfk 77 M9
Piltdown E Susx 25 K6
Pilton Devon 17 K5
Pilton Nhants 61 M4
Pilton Rutlnd 73 N10
Pilton Somset 19 Q6
Pilton Green Swans 28 D7
Pimbo Lancs 81 P4
Pimlico Herts 50 C9
Pimlico Lancs 89 L2
Pimlico Nhants 48 H6
Pimperne Dorset 12 F3
Pinchbeck Lincs 74 D5
Pinchbeck Bars Lincs 74 C5
Pincheon Green Donc 91 R7
Pinchinthorpe R & Cl 104 G8
Pincock Lancs 88 G7
Pinfold Lancs 88 D8
Pinford End Suffk 64 A10
Pinged Carmth 28 D4
Pingewood W Berk 35 J11
Pin Green Herts 50 G5
Pinhoe Devon 9 N6
Pinkett's Booth Covtry 59 L8
Pinkney Wilts 32 G7
Pinkneys Green W & M 35 N8
Pinley Covtry 59 N9
Pinley Green Warwks 59 K11
Pin Mill Suffk 53 M4
Pinminnoch S Ayrs 114 C9
Pinmore S Ayrs 114 D9
Pinn Devon 10 C7
Pinner Gt Lon 36 D3
Pinner Green Gt Lon 36 D3
Pinsley Green Ches E 69 Q5
Pinvin Worcs 47 J5
Pinwherry S Ayrs 114 D10
Pinxton Derbys 84 G10
Pipe and Lyde Herefs 45 Q6
Pipe Aston Herefs 56 H10
Pipe Gate Shrops 70 C6
Pipehill Staffs 58 G3
Piperhill Highld 156 F7
Pipers Pool Cnwll 5 M5
Pipewell Nhants 60 H3
Pippacott Devon 17 J4
Pippin Street Lancs 88 H6
Pipton Powys 44 H7
Pirbright Surrey 23 P3
Pirbright Camp Surrey 23 P3
Pirnie Border 118 C5
Pirnmill N Ayrs 120 G3
Pirton Herts 50 D4
Pirton Worcs 46 G5
Pisgah Cerdgn 54 F9
Pishill Oxon 35 K7
Pistyll Gwynd 66 E6
Pitagowan P & K 141 K4
Pitblae Abers 159 N5
Pitcairngreen P & K 134 D2
Pitcalnie Highld 156 E3
Pitcaple Abers 151 J2
Pitcarity Angus 142 E4
Pitchcombe Gloucs 32 G3
Pitchcott Bucks 49 L10
Pitcher Row Lincs 74 E4
Pitchford Shrops 57 J4
Pitch Green Bucks 35 L4
Pitch Place Surrey 23 N7
Pitch Place Surrey 23 Q4
Pitchroy Moray 157 M10
Pitcombe Somset 20 C8
Pitcot V Glam 29 N10
Pitcox E Loth 128 G5
Pitfichie Abers 150 H4
Pitglassie Abers 158 G9
Pitgrudy Highld 162 H8
Pitlessie Fife 135 J6
Pitlochry P & K 141 M6
Pitmachie Abers 150 H2
Pitmain Highld 148 C7
Pitmedden Abers 151 M2
Pitmedden Garden Abers 151 M2
Pitminster Somset 18 H11
Pitmuies Angus 143 K8
Pitmunie Abers 150 H5
Pitney Somset 19 N9
Pitroddie P & K 134 G2
Pitscottie Fife 135 L5
Pitsea Essex 38 B4
Pitses Oldham 83 K4
Pitsford Nhants 60 G7
Pitstone Bucks 49 P11
Pitt Devon 18 D11
Pitt Hants 22 E9
Pittarrow Abers 143 N3
Pitt Court Gloucs 32 D5
Pittenweem Fife 135 P7
Pitteuchar Fife 134 H8
Pittington Dur 104 B2
Pittodrie House Hotel Abers 150 H3
Pitton Wilts 21 P8
Pitt's Wood Kent 37 P11
Pittulie Abers 159 N4
Pityme Cnwll 4 F6
Pity Me Dur 113 L11
Pivington Kent 26 F2
Pixey Green Suffk 65 J6
Pixham Surrey 36 E10
Plains N Lans 126 D4
Plain Street Cnwll 4 F6
Plaish Shrops 57 J5
Plaistow Gt Lon 37 K4
Plaistow W Susx 24 B4
Plaitford Hants 21 Q11
Plank Lane Wigan 82 D5
Plas Cymyran IoA 78 D9
Plastow Green Hants 22 F2
Platt Bridge Wigan 82 D4
Platt Lane Shrops 69 P7
Platts Heath Kent 38 E11
Plawsworth Dur 113 L11
Plaxtol Kent 37 P10
Playden E Susx 26 F7
Playford Suffk 53 M2
Play Hatch Oxon 35 K9
Playing Place Cnwll 3 L5
Playley Green Gloucs 46 E8
Plealey Shrops 56 G3
Plean Stirlg 133 N10
Pleasance Fife 134 G5
Pleasington Bl w D 89 J5
Pleasington Crematorium Bl w D 89 J5
Pleasley Derbys 84 H8
Pleasleyhill Notts 84 H8
Pleasurewood Hills Suffk 65 Q2
Pleck Dorset 11 Q2
Pledgdon Green Essex 51 N5
Pledwick Wakefd 91 J7
Pleinheaume Guern 10 b1
Plemont Jersey 11 a1
Plemstall Ches W 81 P10
Plenmeller Nthumb 111 P8
Pleshey Essex 51 Q8
Plockton Highld 153 Q11
Plowden Shrops 56 F7
Plox Green Shrops 56 F4
Pluckley Kent 26 F2
Pluckley Station Kent 26 F3
Pluckley Thorne Kent 26 F3
Plucks Gutter Kent 39 N9
Plumbland Cumb 100 G3
Plumgarths Cumb 95 K2
Plumley Ches E 82 F10
Plumpton Cumb 94 G5
Plumpton Cumb 101 N3
Plumpton E Susx 25 J8
Plumpton Nhants 48 G5
Plumpton End Nhants 49 K6
Plumpton Green E Susx 25 J7
Plumpton Head Cumb 101 P3
Plumstead Gt Lon 37 K5
Plumstead Norfk 76 G5
Plumstead Green Norfk 76 G4
Plumtree Notts 72 G4
Plumtree Green Kent 26 D2
Plungar Leics 73 K4
Plurenden Kent 26 F4
Plush Dorset 11 Q4
Plusha Cnwll 5 M5
Plushabridge Cnwll 5 N7
Plwmp Cerdgn 42 G4
Plymouth C Plym 6 D8
Plymouth Airport C Plym 6 E6
Plympton C Plym 6 E7
Plymstock C Plym 6 E8
Plymtree Devon 9 Q4
Pockley N York 98 C3
Pocklington E R Yk 98 G11
Pode Hole Lincs 74 D6
Podimore Somset 19 P10
Podington Bed 61 K8
Podmore Staffs 70 D7
Point Clear Essex 53 K9
Pointon Lincs 74 B4
Pokesdown Bmouth 13 K6
Polbain Highld 160 F4
Polbathic Cnwll 5 N10
Polbeth W Loth 127 J5
Polbrock Cnwll 4 G8
Poldark Mine Cnwll 2 H7
Polebrook Nhants 61 N3
Pole Elm Worcs 46 F4
Polegate E Susx 25 N10
Pole Moor Kirk 90 D7
Polesden Lacey Surrey 36 D10
Polesworth Warwks 59 L4
Polgigga Cnwll 2 B9
Polglass Highld 160 G5
Polgooth Cnwll 3 P3
Polgown D & G 115 P7
Poling W Susx 24 B10
Poling Corner W Susx 24 B9
Polkerris Cnwll 4 H11
Pollard Street Norfk 77 L5
Pollington E R Yk 91 Q7
Polloch Highld 138 D4
Pollokshaws C Glas 125 P5
Pollokshields C Glas 125 P5
Polmassick Cnwll 3 P4
Polmear Cnwll 4 H11
Polmont Falk 126 G2
Polnish Highld 145 N11
Polperro Cnwll 5 L11
Polruan Cnwll 5 J11
Polsham Somset 19 P6
Polstead Suffk 52 G4
Polstead Heath Suffk 52 G3
Poltalloch Ag & B 130 G8
Poltescoe Cnwll 3 J10
Poltimore Devon 9 N5
Polton Mdloth 127 P5
Polwarth Border 129 J9
Polyphant Cnwll 5 M5
Polzeath Cnwll 4 E6
Pomathorn Mdloth 127 N6
Pomeroy Derbys 83 P11
Ponde Powys 44 G7
Pondersbridge Cambs 62 C2
Ponders End Gt Lon 51 J11
Ponsanooth Cnwll 3 K6
Ponsonby Cumb 100 E9
Ponsongath Cnwll 3 K10
Ponsworthy Devon 7 J4
Pont Abraham Services Carmth 28 G3
Pontac Jersey 11 c2
Pontamman Carmth 28 H2
Pontantwn Carmth 28 D2
Pontardawe Neath 29 K4
Pontarddulais Swans 28 G4
Pont-ar-gothi Carmth 43 K10
Pont-ar-Hydfer Powys 44 B9
Pont-ar-llechau Carmth 43 P10
Pontarsais Carmth 42 H9
Pontblyddyn Flints 69 J2
Pont Cyfyng Conwy 67 N3
Pontcysyllte Aqueduct Wrexhm 69 J6
Pont Dolgarrog Conwy 79 P11
Pontdolgoch Powys 55 N6
Pont-Ebbw Newpt 31 J7
Pontefract Wakefd 91 M6
Pontefract Crematorium Wakefd 91 L6
Ponteland Nthumb 113 J6
Ponterwyd Cerdgn 54 G8
Pontesbury Shrops 56 F3
Pontesbury Hill Shrops 56 F3
Pontesford Shrops 56 G3
Pontfadog Wrexhm 68 H7
Pontfaen Pembks 41 K4
Pont-faen Powys 44 D8
Pontgarreg Cerdgn 42 F4
Pontgarreg Pembks 41 M2
Ponthenry Carmth 28 E3
Ponthir Torfn 31 K6
Ponthirwaun Cerdgn 42 E5
Pontllanfraith Caerph 30 G5
Pontlliw Swans 28 H5
Pontlottyn Caerph 30 F3
Pontlyfni Gwynd 66 G4
Pont Morlais Carmth 28 F3
Pontnêddféchan Neath 29 P3
Pontnewydd Torfn 31 J5
Pontnewynydd Torfn 31 J4
Pont Pen-y-benglog Gwynd 67 M2
Pontrhydfendigaid Cerdgn 54 G11
Pont Rhyd-sarn Gwynd 67 R9
Pont Rhyd-y-cyff Brdgnd 29 N7
Pont-rhyd-y-fen Neath 29 L6
Pontrhydygroes Cerdgn 54 G10
Pontrhydyrun Torfn 31 J5
Pontrilas Herefs 45 M9
Pont Robert Powys 55 Q2
Pont-rug Gwynd 67 J2
Ponts Green E Susx 25 Q7
Pontshaen Cerdgn 42 H5
Pontshill Herefs 46 B10
Pontsticill Myr Td 30 E2
Pont Walby Neath 29 N3
Pontwelly Carmth 42 H6
Pontyates Carmth 28 E3
Pontyberem Carmth 28 F2
Pont-y-blew Wrexhm 69 K7
Pontybodkin Flints 69 J3
Pontyclun Rhondd 30 D8
Pontycymer Brdgnd 29 P6
Pontyglasier Pembks 41 M3
Pontygwaith Rhondd 30 D6
Pontygynon Pembks 41 M3
Pont-y-pant Conwy 67 P4
Pontypool Torfn 31 J4
Pontypool Road Torfn 31 K5
Pontypridd Rhondd 30 E7
Pont-yr-hafod Pembks 40 H5
Pont-yr-Rhyl Brdgnd 29 P7
Pontywaun Caerph 30 H6
Pool Cnwll 2 H5
Pool IoS 2 b2
Pool Leeds 97 K11
Poole Poole 12 H6
Poole Crematorium Poole 12 H5
Poole Keynes Gloucs 33 J5
Poolewe Highld 160 D10
Pooley Bridge Cumb 101 N6
Pooley Street Norfk 64 F5
Poolfold Staffs 70 F3
Pool Head Herefs 45 R4
Poolhill Gloucs 46 D9
Pool of Muckhart Clacks 134 C7
Pool Quay Powys 56 D2
Pool Street Essex 52 C4
Pooting's Kent 37 L11
Popham Hants 22 G6
Poplar Gt Lon 37 J4
Poplar Street Suffk 65 N8
Porchfield IoW 14 D8
Poringland Norfk 77 K11
Porkellis Cnwll 2 H7
Porlock Somset 18 A5
Porlock Weir Somset 17 R2
Portachoillan Ag & B 123 N8
Port-an-Eorna Highld 153 P11
Port Appin Ag & B 138 G8
Port Askaig Ag & B 122 F6
Portavadie Ag & B 124 A4
Port Bannatyne Ag & B 124 D4
Portbury N Som 31 P9
Port Carlisle Cumb 110 D8
Port Charlotte Ag & B 122 C8
Portchester Hants 14 H5
Portchester Crematorium Hants 14 H5
Port Clarence S on T 104 E6
Port Driseach Ag & B 124 B3
Port Ellen Ag & B 122 E10
Port Elphinstone Abers 151 K3
Portencalzie D & G 106 D3
Portencross N Ayrs 124 F8
Port Erin IoM 80 a8
Portesham Dorset 11 N7
Portessie Moray 158 B4
Port e Vullen IoM 80 g3
Port Eynon Swans 28 E7
Portfield Gate Pembks 40 H7
Portgate Devon 5 Q4
Port Gaverne Cnwll 4 G5
Port Glasgow Inver 125 J3
Portgordon Moray 158 A5
Portgower Highld 163 N4
Porth Cnwll 4 C9
Porth Rhondd 30 D6
Porthallow Cnwll 3 K9
Porthallow Cnwll 5 L11
Porthcawl Brdgnd 29 M9
Porthcothan Cnwll 4 D7
Porthcurno Cnwll 2 B9
Porthdinllaen Gwynd 66 D6
Port Henderson Highld 153 P3
Porthgain Pembks 40 F4
Porthgwarra Cnwll 2 B9
Porthill Staffs 70 E5
Porthkea Cnwll 3 L5
Porthkerry V Glam 30 E11
Porthleven Cnwll 2 G8
Porthmadog Gwynd 67 K7
Porthmeor Cnwll 2 C6
Porth Navas Cnwll 3 K8
Portholland Cnwll 3 P5
Porthoustock Cnwll 3 L9
Porthpean Cnwll 3 Q3
Porthtowan Cnwll 2 H4
Porthwgan Wrexhm 69 L5
Porthyrhyd Carmth 43 K11
Porth-y-Waen Shrops 69 J10
Portincaple Ag & B 131 Q9
Portinfer Jersey 11 a1
Portington E R Yk 92 C4
Portinnisherrich Ag & B 131 K5
Portinscale Cumb 101 J6
Port Isaac Cnwll 4 F5
Portishead N Som 31 N9
Portknockie Moray 158 C4
Portland Dorset 11 P10
Portlethen Abers 151 N8
Portling D & G 109 J10
Portloe Cnwll 3 N6
Port Logan D & G 106 E9
Portlooe Cnwll 5 L11
Portmahomack Highld 163 L10
Portmeirion Gwynd 67 K7
Portmellon Cnwll 3 Q5
Port Mor Highld 144 F12
Portmore Hants 13 P5
Port Mulgrave N York 105 L7
Portnacroish Ag & B 138 G8
Portnaguran W Isls 168 k4
Portnahaven Ag & B 122 A9
Portnalong Highld 152 E11
Port nan Giuran W Isls 168 k4
Port nan Long W Isls 168 d10
Port Nis W Isls 168 k1
Portobello C Edin 127 Q3
Portobello Gatesd 113 L9
Portobello Wolves 58 E5
Port of Menteith Stirlg 132 H7
Port of Ness W Isls 168 k1
Porton Wilts 21 N7
Portontown Devon 5 Q6
Portpatrick D & G 106 C7
Port Quin Cnwll 4 F5
Port Ramsay Ag & B 138 F8
Portreath Cnwll 2 H4
Portreath Harbour Cnwll 2 H4
Portree Highld 152 H9
Port St Mary IoM 80 b8
Portscatho Cnwll 3 M6
Portsea C Port 14 H6
Portskerra Highld 166 E3
Portskewett Mons 31 N7
Portslade Br & H 24 G9
Portslade-by-Sea Br & H 24 G9
Portslogan D & G 106 C6
Portsmouth C Port 14 H7
Portsmouth Calder 89 Q5
Portsmouth Dockyard C Port 14 H6
Port Soderick IoM 80 d7
Port Solent C Port 14 H5
Portsonachan Hotel Ag & B 131 L3
Portsoy Abers 158 E4
Port Sunlight Wirral 81 L8
Portswood C Sotn 14 D4
Port Talbot Neath 29 L7
Port Tennant Swans 29 J6
Portuairk Highld 137 L2
Portway Herefs 45 P6
Portway Herefs 45 P7
Portway Sandw 58 E7
Portway Worcs 58 G10
Port Wemyss Ag & B 122 A9
Port William D & G 107 K9
Portwrinkle Cnwll 5 P11
Portyerrock D & G 107 N10
Posbury Devon 9 K5
Posenhall Shrops 57 M4
Poslingford Suffk 63 N11
Posso Border 117 J4
Postbridge Devon 8 G9
Postcombe Oxon 35 K5
Post Green Dorset 12 G6
Postling Kent 27 K4
Postwick Norfk 77 K10
Potarch Abers 150 G8
Potsgrove C Beds 49 Q8
Potten End Herts 50 B9
Potten Street Kent 39 N8
Potter Brompton N York 99 K5
Pottergate Street Norfk 64 H3
Potterhanworth Lincs 86 E7
Potterhanworth Booths Lincs 86 E7
Potter Heigham Norfk 77 N8
Potterne Wilts 21 J3
Potterne Wick Wilts 21 J3
Potter Row Bucks 35 P4
Potters Bar Herts 50 F10
Potters Brook Lancs 95 K10
Potter's Cross Staffs 58 B8
Potters Crouch Herts 50 D9
Potter's Forstal Kent 26 E2
Potters Green Covtry 59 N8
Potter's Green E Susx 25 M6
Potter's Green Herts 51 J6
Pottersheath Herts 50 F7
Potters Marston Leics 72 D11

Potter Somersal – Rheindown 289

otter Somersal Derbys 71 L7
otterspury Nhants 49 L6
otter Street Essex 51 L9
otterton Abers 151 N4
otterton Leeds 91 L3
otthorpe Norfk 76 C7
ottle Street Wilts 20 F6
otto N York 104 E10
otton C Beds 62 B11
ott Row Norfk 75 P6
ott's Green Essex 52 F7
ott Shrigley Ches E 83 K9
oughill Cnwll 16 C10
oughill Devon 9 L3
ouiner Hants 13 L3
oulshot Wilts 21 J3
oulton Gloucs 33 L4
oulton Wirral 81 L6
oulton-le-Fylde Lancs 88 C3
oulton Priory Gloucs 33 L5
ound Bank Worcs 57 N10
oundbury Dorset 11 P6
oundffald Swans 28 G6
oundgate E Susx 25 L5
ound Green E Susx 25 M6
ound Green Suffk 63 M10
ound Green Worcs 57 P9
ound Hill W Susx 24 G3
oundon Bucks 48 H9
oundsbridge Kent 25 M2
oundsgate Devon 7 J4
oundstock Cnwll 5 L2
ound Street Hants 22 E2
ounsley E Susx 25 M6
outon D & G 107 N8
ouy Street Suffk 65 M7
ovey Cross Surrey 24 G2
owburn Nthumb 119 L7
owderham Devon 9 N8
owerstock Dorset 11 L5
owfoot D & G 109 P7
ow Green Herefs 46 D6
owhill Cumb 110 D9
owick Worcs 46 F4
owmill P & K 134 C8
oxwell Dorset 12 B8
oyle Slough 36 B5
oynings W Susx 24 G8
oyntington Dorset 20 C10
oynton Ches E 83 K8
oynton Wrekin 69 Q11
oynton Green Wrekin 69 Q11
oyston Cross Pembks 41 J7
oystreet Green Suffk 64 D10
raa Sands Cnwll 2 F8
ratt's Bottom Gt Lon 37 L8
raze-an-Beeble Cnwll 2 G6
redannack Wollas Cnwll 2 H10
rees Shrops 69 Q8
reesall Lancs 94 H11
rees Green Shrops 69 Q8
reesgweene Shrops 69 J7
rees Heath Shrops 69 Q7
rees Higher Heath Shrops 69 Q7
rees Lower Heath Shrops 69 Q8
rendwick Nthumb 119 K8
ren-gwyn Cerdgn 42 H6
renteg Gwynd 67 K6
renton Wirral 81 L7
rescot Knows 81 P6
rescott Devon 10 B2
rescott Shrops 57 M8
rescott Shrops 69 M10
resnerb Angus 142 B4
ressen Nthumb 118 F3
restatyn Denbgs 80 F8
restbury Ches E 83 J9
restbury Gloucs 47 J10
resteigne Powys 45 L2
restleigh Somset 20 B6
restolee Bolton 89 M9
reston Border 129 K8
reston Br & H 24 H9
reston Devon 7 M4
reston Dorset 11 Q8
reston E R Yk 93 L4
reston Gloucs 33 K4
reston Herts 50 E6
reston Kent 38 H9
reston Kent 39 M9
reston Lancs 88 G5
reston Nthumb 119 N5
reston Rutlnd 73 M10
reston Shrops 57 J2
reston Somset 18 E7
reston Torbay 7 M6
reston Wilts 33 K9
reston Wilts 33 Q10
reston Bagot Warwks 59 J11
reston Bissett Bucks 49 J9
reston Bowyer Somset 18 F9
reston Brockhurst Shrops 69 P10
reston Brook Halton 82 C8
reston Candover Hants 22 H6
reston Capes Nhants 48 G4
reston Crematorium Lancs 88 H4
reston Crowmarsh Oxon 34 H6
reston Deanery Nhants 60 G9
reston Green Warwks 59 J11
reston Gubbals Shrops 69 N11
reston Montford Shrops 56 G2
reston on Stour Warwks 47 P5
reston on Tees S on T 104 D7
reston on the Hill Halton 82 C8
reston on Wye Herefs 45 M6
restonpans E Loth 128 B5
reston Patrick Cumb 95 L4
reston Plucknett Somset 19 P11
reston St Mary Suffk 64 C11
reston Street Kent 39 N9
reston-under-Scar N York 96 G2
reston upon the Weald Moors Wrekin 70 B11
reston Wynne Herefs 45 R5
restwich Bury 82 H4
restwick Nthumb 113 J6
restwick S Ayrs 114 G2
restwick Airport S Ayrs 114 G2
restwood Bucks 35 N4
restwood Staffs 58 C7
Price Town Brdgnd 29 P6
Prickwillow Cambs 63 J4
Priddy Somset 19 P4
Priestacott Devon 8 B3
Priestcliffe Derbys 83 P10
Priestcliffe Ditch Derbys 83 P10
Priest Hutton Lancs 95 L6
Priestland E Ayrs 125 P10
Priestley Green Calder 90 E5
Priest Weston Shrops 56 D5
Priestwood Green Kent 37 Q8
Primethorpe Leics 60 B2
Primrose Green Norfk 76 F8
Primrosehill Border 129 K8
Primrose Hill Cambs 62 E3
Primrose Hill Derbys 84 F9
Primrose Hill Dudley 58 D7
Primrose Hill Lancs 88 D9
Primsidemill Border 118 F5
Princes Gate Pembks 41 M8
Princes Risborough Bucks 35 M4
Princethorpe Warwks 59 P10
Princetown Devon 6 F4
Prinsted W Susx 15 L5
Prion Denbgs 68 E2
Prior Rigg Cumb 111 J7
Priors Halton Shrops 56 H9
Priors Hardwick Warwks 48 E3
Priorslee Wrekin 57 N2
Priors Marston Warwks 48 E3
Priors Norton Gloucs 46 G10
Priory Wood Herefs 45 K5
Prisk V Glam 30 D9
Priston BaNES 20 C2
Pristow Green Norfk 64 G4
Prittlewell Sthend 38 E4
Privett Hants 23 J9
Prixford Devon 17 K4
Probus Cnwll 3 M4
Prora E Loth 128 E4
Prospect Cumb 100 F2
Prospidnick Cnwll 2 G7
Protstonhill Abers 159 K5
Prudhoe Nthumb 112 G8
Prussia Cove Cnwll 2 F8
Publow BaNES 20 B2
Puckeridge Herts 51 J6
Puckington Somset 19 L11
Pucklechurch S Glos 32 C9
Puckrup Gloucs 46 G7
Puddinglake Ches W 82 F11
Puddington Ches W 81 L10
Puddington Devon 9 K2
Puddledock Norfk 64 F3
Puddletown Dorset 12 C6
Pudleston Herefs 45 R3
Pudsey Leeds 90 G4
Pulborough W Susx 24 B7
Puleston Wrekin 70 C10
Pulford Ches W 69 L3
Pulham Dorset 11 Q3
Pulham Market Norfk 64 H4
Pulham St Mary Norfk 65 J4
Pullens Green S Glos 32 B6
Pulloxhill C Beds 50 C4
Pulverbatch Shrops 56 G4
Pumpherston W Loth 127 K4
Pumsaint Carmth 43 N6
Puncheston Pembks 41 K5
Puncknowle Dorset 11 L7
Punnett's Town E Susx 25 P6
Purbrook Hants 15 J5
Purfleet Thurr 37 N5
Puriton Somset 19 K6
Purleigh Essex 52 D11
Purley Gt Lon 36 H8
Purley W Berk 35 J9
Purlogue Shrops 56 D9
Purlpit Wilts 32 G11
Purls Bridge Cambs 62 G3
Purse Caundle Dorset 20 C11
Purshull Green Worcs 58 C10
Purslow Shrops 56 F8
Purston Jaglin Wakefd 91 L7
Purtington Somset 10 H3
Purton Gloucs 32 C3
Purton Gloucs 32 C4
Purton Wilts 33 L7
Purton Stoke Wilts 33 L6
Pury End Nhants 49 K5
Pusey Oxon 34 C5
Putley Herefs 46 B7
Putley Green Herefs 46 B7
Putloe Gloucs 32 E3
Putney Gt Lon 36 F6
Putney Vale Crematorium Gt Lon 36 F6
Putsborough Devon 16 G3
Puttenham Herts 35 N2
Puttenham Surrey 23 P5
Puttock End Essex 52 D3
Putton Dorset 11 N8
Puxley Nhants 49 L6
Puxton N Som 19 M2
Pwll Carmth 28 E4
Pwllcrochan Pembks 40 H10
Pwll-du Mons 30 H2
Pwll-glâs Denbgs 68 F4
Pwllgloyw Powys 44 E8
Pwllheli Gwynd 66 F7
Pwllmeyric Mons 31 P6
Pwll Trap Carmth 41 Q7
Pwll-y-glaw Neath 29 L6
Pydew Conwy 79 Q9
Pye Bridge Derbys 84 F10
Pyecombe W Susx 24 G8
Pye Corner Newpt 31 K7
Pye Green Staffs 58 E2
Pyle Brdgnd 29 M8
Pyleigh Somset 18 F8
Pylle Somset 20 B7
Pymoor Cambs 62 G3
Pymore Dorset 11 K6
Pyrford Surrey 36 B9
Pyrton Oxon 35 J5
Pytchley Nhants 61 J6
Pyworthy Devon 16 E11

Q

Quabbs Shrops 56 C8
Quadring Lincs 74 D4
Quadring Eaudike Lincs 74 D4
Quainton Bucks 49 K10
Quaker's Yard Myr Td 30 E5
Quaking Houses Dur 113 J10
Quantock Hills Somset 18 G7
Quarff Shet 169 r10
Quarley Hants 21 Q6
Quarndon Derbys 72 A2
Quarr Hill IoW 14 G8
Quarrier's Village Inver 125 K4
Quarrington Lincs 73 R2
Quarrington Hill Dur 104 B3
Quarrybank Ches W 82 C11
Quarry Bank Dudley 58 D7
Quarrywood Moray 157 M5
Quarter N Ayrs 124 F5
Quarter S Lans 126 C7
Quatford Shrops 57 N6
Quatt Shrops 57 P7
Quebec Dur 103 N2
Quedgeley Gloucs 32 F2
Queen Adelaide Cambs 63 J4
Queenborough Kent 38 F7
Queen Camel Somset 19 Q10
Queen Charlton BaNES 32 B11
Queen Dart Devon 17 Q8
Queen Elizabeth Forest Park Stirlg 132 G7
Queenhill Worcs 46 G7
Queen Oak Dorset 20 E8
Queen's Bower IoW 14 G10
Queensbury C Brad 90 E4
Queensferry Flints 81 L11
Queensferry Crossing Fife 134 E11
Queen's Head Shrops 69 K9
Queenslie C Glas 126 B4
Queen's Park Bed 61 M11
Queen's Park Nhants 60 G8
Queen Street Kent 37 Q11
Queen Street Wilts 33 K7
Queenzieburn N Lans 126 B2
Quendon Essex 51 M4
Queniborough Leics 72 G8
Quenington Gloucs 33 M4
Quernmore Lancs 95 L9
Queslett Birm 58 G6
Quethiock Cnwll 5 N9
Quick's Green W Berk 34 G9
Quidenham Norfk 64 E4
Quidhampton Hants 22 F4
Quidhampton Wilts 21 M8
Quina Brook Shrops 69 P8
Quinbury End Nhants 48 H4
Quinton Dudley 58 E8
Quinton Nhants 49 L4
Quinton Green Nhants 49 L4
Quintrell Downs Cnwll 4 C9
Quixhall Staffs 71 L6
Quixwood Border 129 K7
Quoditch Devon 5 Q2
Quoig P & K 133 N3
Quorn Leics 72 F7
Quothquan S Lans 116 D3
Quoyburray Ork 169 e6
Quoyloo Ork 169 b4

R

Raasay Highld 153 K9
Rabbit's Cross Kent 26 C2
Rableyheath Herts 50 F7
Raby Cumb 110 C10
Raby Wirral 81 L9
Rachan Mill Border 116 G4
Rachub Gwynd 79 L11
Rackenford Devon 17 R8
Rackham W Susx 24 B8
Rackheath Norfk 77 K9
Racks D & G 109 M6
Rackwick Ork 169 b7
Radbourne Derbys 71 P7
Radcliffe Bury 89 M9
Radcliffe Nthumb 119 Q10
Radcliffe on Trent Notts 72 G3
Radclive Bucks 49 J8
Radcot Oxon 33 Q5
Raddery Highld 156 C6
Raddington Somset 18 D9
Radernie Fife 135 M6
Radford Covtry 59 M8
Radford Semele Warwks 48 B2
Radlet Somset 18 H7
Radlett Herts 50 E10
Radley Devon 17 N7
Radley Oxon 34 F5
Radley W Berk 34 C11
Radley Green Essex 51 P9
Radmore Green Ches E 69 Q3
Radnage Bucks 35 L5
Radstock BaNES 20 C4
Radstone Nhants 48 G6
Radway Warwks 48 C5
Radwell Bed 61 M9
Radwell Herts 50 F3
Radwinter Essex 51 P3
Radwinter End Essex 51 P3
Radyr Cardif 30 F8
RAF College (Cranwell) Lincs 86 D11
Rafford Moray 157 K6
RAF Museum Cosford Shrops 57 P3
RAF Museum Hendon Gt Lon 36 F2
Ragdale Leics 72 H7
Ragdon Shrops 56 H6
Raginnis Cnwll 2 D8
Raglan Mons 31 M3
Ragnall Notts 85 P6
Raigbeg Highld 148 E2
Rainbow Hill Worcs 46 G3
Rainford St Hel 81 P4
Rainham Gt Lon 37 M4
Rainham Medway 38 D8
Rainhill St Hel 81 P6
Rainhill Stoops St Hel 81 Q6
Rainow Ches E 83 K9
Rainsbrook Crematorium Warwks 60 B6
Rainsough Bury 82 H4
Rainton N York 97 N5
Rainworth Notts 85 J9
Raisbeck Cumb 102 B9
Raise Cumb 111 P11
Raisthorpe N York 98 H8
Rait P & K 134 G2
Raithby Lincs 87 K4
Raithby Lincs 87 L7
Raithwaite N York 105 N8
Rake Hants 23 M9
Rakewood Rochdl 89 Q8
Ralia Highld 148 C8
Ram Carmth 43 L5
Ramasaig Highld 152 B9
Rame Cnwll 3 J7
Rame Cnwll 6 C9
Ram Hill S Glos 32 C9
Ram Lane Kent 26 G2
Rampisham Dorset 11 M4
Rampside Cumb 94 E7
Rampton Cambs 62 F7
Rampton Notts 85 P5
Ramsbottom Bury 89 M7
Ramsbury Wilts 33 Q10
Ramscraigs Highld 167 K11
Ramsdean Hants 23 K10
Ramsdell Hants 22 G3
Ramsden Oxon 48 C11
Ramsden Worcs 46 H5
Ramsden Bellhouse Essex 38 B3
Ramsden Heath Essex 38 B2
Ramsey Cambs 62 C3
Ramsey Essex 53 M5
Ramsey IoM 80 g3
Ramsey Forty Foot Cambs 62 D3
Ramsey Heights Cambs 62 B4
Ramsey Island Essex 52 F10
Ramsey Island Pembks 40 D6
Ramsey Mereside Cambs 62 C3
Ramsey St Mary's Cambs 62 C3
Ramsgate Kent 39 Q8
Ramsgill N York 96 H6
Ramshaw Dur 103 M5
Ramshaw Dur 112 E11
Ramsholt Suffk 53 P3
Ramshope Nthumb 118 D10
Ramshorn Staffs 71 K5
Ramsley Devon 8 G6
Ramsnest Common Surrey 23 P8
Ranby Lincs 86 H5
Ranby Notts 85 L4
Rand Lincs 86 F5
Randalls Park Crematorium Surrey 36 E9
Randwick Gloucs 32 F3
Ranfurly Rens 125 K4
Rangemore Staffs 71 M10
Rangeworthy S Glos 32 C7
Rankinston E Ayrs 115 J5
Ranksborough Rutlnd 73 L8
Rank's Green Essex 52 B8
Rannoch Station P & K 140 B6
Ranscombe Somset 18 B6
Ranskill Notts 85 L3
Ranton Staffs 70 F10
Ranton Green Staffs 70 E10
Ranworth Norfk 77 M9
Raploch Stirlg 133 M9
Rapness Ork 169 e2
Rapps Somset 19 K11
Rascarrel D & G 108 G11
Rashfield Ag & B 131 N11
Rashwood Worcs 58 D11
Raskelf N York 97 Q6
Rassau Blae G 30 G2
Rastrick Calder 90 E6
Ratagan Highld 145 R4
Ratby Leics 72 E9
Ratcliffe Culey Leics 72 A11
Ratcliffe on Soar Notts 72 D5
Ratcliffe on the Wreake Leics 72 G8
Ratfyn Wilts 21 N6
Rathen Abers 159 N5
Rathillet Fife 135 K3
Rathmell N York 96 B9
Ratho C Edin 127 L3
Ratho Station C Edin 127 L3
Rathven Moray 158 B4
Ratlake Hants 22 D10
Ratley Warwks 48 C5
Ratling Kent 39 M11
Ratlinghope Shrops 56 G5
Rattar Highld 167 N2
Ratten Row Cumb 101 K2
Ratten Row Cumb 110 G11
Ratten Row Lancs 88 E2
Rattery Devon 7 J6
Rattlesden Suffk 64 D10
Ratton Village E Susx 25 N10
Rattray P & K 142 B8
Raughton Cumb 110 G11
Raughton Head Cumb 110 G11
Raunds Nhants 61 L6
Ravenfield Rothm 91 M11
Ravenglass Cumb 100 E11
Ravenhills Green Worcs 46 D4
Raveningham Norfk 65 M2
Ravenscar N York 105 Q10
Ravenscraig N Lans 126 D6
Ravensdale IoM 80 e3
Ravensden Bed 61 N10
Ravenseat N York 102 G10
Ravenshead Notts 85 J10
Ravensmoor Ches E 69 R4
Ravensthorpe Kirk 90 G6
Ravensthorpe Nhants 60 E6
Ravenstone Leics 72 C8
Ravenstone M Keyn 49 M4
Ravenstonedale Cumb 102 D10
Ravenstruther S Lans 126 G8
Ravensworth N York 103 M9
Raw N York 105 P9
Rawcliffe C York 98 B10
Rawcliffe E R Yk 92 A6
Rawcliffe Bridge E R Yk 92 A6
Rawdon Leeds 90 G3
Rawdon Crematorium Leeds 90 G3
Rawling Street Kent 38 F10
Rawmarsh Rothm 91 L11
Rawnsley Staffs 58 F2
Rawreth Essex 38 C3
Rawridge Devon 10 E3
Rawtenstall Lancs 89 N6
Raydon Suffk 52 H4
Raylees Nthumb 112 D2
Rayleigh Essex 38 D3
Raymond's Hill Devon 10 G5
Rayne Essex 52 B7
Raynes Park Gt Lon 36 F7
Reach Cambs 63 J7
Read Lancs 89 M4
Reading Readg 35 K10
Reading Crematorium Readg 35 K9
Reading Services W Berk 35 J11
Reading Street Kent 26 F5
Reading Street Kent 39 Q8
Reagill Cumb 102 B7
Realwa Cnwll 2 G6
Rearquhar Highld 162 G8
Rearsby Leics 72 H8
Rease Heath Ches E 70 A4
Reay Highld 166 G4
Reculver Kent 39 M8
Red Ball Devon 18 E11
Redberth Pembks 41 L10
Redbourn Herts 50 D8
Redbourne N Linc 92 G11
Redbrook Gloucs 31 P3
Redbrook Wrexhm 69 P6
Redbrook Street Kent 26 F4
Redburn Highld 156 G8
Redburn Nthumb 111 Q8
Redcar R & Cl 104 H6
Redcastle D & G 108 H7
Redcastle Highld 155 Q8
Red Dial Cumb 110 E11
Redding Falk 126 G2
Reddingmuirhead Falk 126 G2
Reddish Stockp 83 J6
Redditch Worcs 58 F11
Redditch Crematorium Worcs 58 F11
Rede Suffk 63 P9
Redenhall Norfk 65 K5
Redenham Hants 22 B5
Redesmouth Nthumb 112 C4
Redford Abers 143 P3
Redford Angus 143 K9
Redford W Susx 23 N9
Redfordgreen Border 117 M7
Redgate Rhondd 30 D7
Redgorton P & K 134 D2
Redgrave Suffk 64 E6
Redhill Abers 151 K7
Red Hill Bmouth 13 J5
Redhill Herts 50 H4
Redhill N Som 19 N2
Redhill Surrey 36 G10
Red Hill Warwks 47 M3
Redisham Suffk 65 N5
Redland Bristl 31 Q9
Redland Ork 169 c4
Redlingfield Suffk 64 H7
Redlingfield Green Suffk 64 H7
Red Lodge Suffk 63 L6
Red Lumb Rochdl 89 N7
Redlynch Somset 20 D8
Redlynch Wilts 21 P10
Redmain Cumb 100 F4
Redmarley Worcs 57 P11
Redmarley D'Abitot Gloucs 46 E8
Redmarshall S on T 104 C6
Redmile Leics 73 K3
Redmire N York 96 F2
Redmyre Abers 143 P2
Rednal Birm 58 F9
Rednal Shrops 69 L9
Redpath Border 118 A3
Redpoint Highld 153 N4
Red Post Cnwll 16 D10
Red Rock Wigan 88 H9
Red Roses Carmth 41 P8
Red Row Nthumb 119 Q11
Redruth Cnwll 2 H5
Redstocks Wilts 20 H2
Redstone P & K 142 B11
Redstone Cross Pembks 41 M7
Red Street Staffs 70 E4
Redvales Bury 89 N9
Red Wharf Bay IoA 79 J8
Redwick Newpt 31 M8
Redwick S Glos 31 P7
Redworth Darltn 103 P6
Reed Herts 51 J3
Reedham Norfk 77 N11
Reedness E R Yk 92 C6
Reeds Beck Lincs 86 H7
Reeds Holme Lancs 89 N6
Reepham Lincs 86 D6
Reepham Norfk 76 G7
Reeth N York 103 K11
Reeves Green Solhll 59 L9
Regaby IoM 80 f2
Regil N Som 19 P2
Reiff Highld 160 F4
Reigate Surrey 36 G10
Reighton N York 99 N5
Reisque Abers 151 M4
Reiss Highld 167 P6
Rejerrah Cnwll 4 B10
Releath Cnwll 2 H7
Relubbus Cnwll 2 F7
Relugas Moray 156 H8
Remenham Wokham 35 L8
Remenham Hill Wokham 35 L8
Rempstone Notts 72 F6
Rendcomb Gloucs 33 K3
Rendham Suffk 65 L9
Rendlesham Suffk 65 L11
Renfrew Rens 125 N4
Renhold Bed 61 N10
Renishaw Derbys 84 G5
Rennington Nthumb 119 P7
Renton W Duns 125 K2
Renwick Cumb 101 Q2
Repps Norfk 77 N8
Repton Derbys 71 Q9
Resaurie Highld 156 C8
Rescassa Cnwll 3 P5
Rescorla Cnwll 3 P4
Resipole Highld 138 C5
Reskadinnick Cnwll 2 G5
Resolis Highld 156 B4
Resolven Neath 29 M4
Rest and be thankful Ag & B 131 Q6
Reston Border 129 M7
Restronguet Cnwll 3 L6
Reswallie Angus 143 J7
Reterth Cnwll 4 E9
Retford Notts 85 M4
Retire Cnwll 4 G9
Rettendon Essex 38 C2
Retyn Cnwll 4 D10
Revesby Lincs 87 J8
Rew Devon 7 J11
Rew Devon 7 K4
Rewe Devon 9 M5
Rew Street IoW 14 E8
Rexon Devon 5 Q4
Reydon Suffk 65 P6
Reymerston Norfk 76 E10
Reynalton Pembks 41 L9
Reynoldston Swans 28 E7
Rezare Cnwll 5 P6
Rhadyr Mons 31 L4
Rhandirmwyn Carmth 43 Q6
Rhayader Powys 55 M11
Rheindown Highld 155 P8

Rhes-y-cae Flints 80 H10
Rhewl Denbgs 68 F2
Rhewl Denbgs 68 G6
Rhewl-fawr Flints 80 G8
Rhewl Mostyn Flints 80 H8
Rhicarn Highld 164 C11
Rhiconich Highld 164 G6
Rhicullen Highld 156 B3
Rhigos Rhondd 29 P3
Rhireavach Highld 160 G7
Rhives Highld 163 J6
Rhiwbina Cardif 30 G8
Rhiwbryfdir Gwynd 67 M5
Rhiwderyn Newpt 31 J7
Rhiwen Gwynd 67 K2
Rhiwinder Rhondd 30 D7
Rhiwlas Gwynd 68 B7
Rhiwlas Gwynd 79 K11
Rhiwlas Powys 68 G8
Rhiwsaeson Rhondd 30 E8
Rhode Somset 19 J8
Rhoden Green Kent 37 Q11
Rhodesia Notts 85 J5
Rhodes Minnis Kent 27 L3
Rhodiad-y-brenin Pembks 40 E5
Rhonehouse D & G 108 F9
Rhoose V Glam 30 E11
Rhos Carmth 42 G7
Rhos Denbgs 68 F2
Rhos Neath 29 K4
Rhosbeirio IoA 78 F6
Rhoscefnhir IoA 79 J9
Rhoscolyn IoA 78 D9
Rhoscrowther Pembks 40 H10
Rhos-fawr Gwynd 66 F7
Rhosgadfan Gwynd 67 J3
Rhosgoch IoA 78 G7
Rhosgoch Powys 44 H5
Rhos Haminiog Cerdgn 42 K2
Rhoshill Pembks 41 N2
Rhoshirwaun Gwynd 66 C9
Rhoslan Gwynd 66 H6
Rhoslefain Gwynd 54 D3
Rhosllanerchrugog Wrexhm 69 J5
Rhôs Lligwy IoA 78 H7
Rhosmaen Carmth 43 M10
Rhosmeirch IoA 78 H9
Rhosneigr IoA 78 E10
Rhosnesni Wrexhm 69 L4
Rhôs-on-Sea Conwy 79 Q8
Rhosrobin Wrexhm 69 K4
Rhossili Swans 28 D7
Rhostryfan Gwynd 66 H3
Rhostyllen Wrexhm 69 K5
Rhosybol IoA 78 G7
Rhos y-brithdir Powys 68 F10
Rhosygadfa Shrops 69 K8
Rhos-y-garth Cerdgn 54 E10
Rhos-y-gwaliau Gwynd 68 B8
Rhos-y-llan Gwynd 66 C7
Rhosymedre Wrexhm 69 J6
Rhos-y-meirch Powys 56 D11
Rhu Ag & B 132 B11
Rhualit Denbgs 80 F9
Rhubodach Ag & B 124 C3
Rhuddall Heath Ches W 69 Q2
Rhuddlan Cerdgn 43 J6
Rhuddlan Denbgs 80 E9
Rhulen Powys 44 G5
Rhunahaorine Ag & B 123 M10
Rhyd Gwynd 67 L6
Rhydargaeau Carmth 42 H9
Rhydcymerau Carmth 43 L7
Rhydd Worcs 46 F5
Rhyd-Ddu Gwynd 67 K4
Rhydding Neath 29 K5
Rhydgaled Conwy 68 C2
Rhydlanfair Conwy 67 Q4
Rhydlewis Cerdgn 42 F5
Rhydlios Gwynd 66 B9
Rhyd-lydan Conwy 68 A4
Rhydowen Cerdgn 42 H5
Rhydrosser Cerdgn 54 D11
Rhydspence Herefs 45 J5
Rhydtalog Flints 68 H4
Rhyd-uchaf Gwynd 68 B7
Rhyd-y-clafdy Gwynd 66 E8
Rhydycroesau Shrops 68 H8
Rhydyfelin Cerdgn 54 D9
Rhydyfelin Rhondd 30 E7
Rhyd-y-foel Conwy 80 C9
Rhydyfro Neath 29 K3
Rhyd-y-groes Gwynd 79 K11
Rhydymain Gwynd 67 Q10
Rhyd-y-meirch Mons 31 K3
Rhydymwyn Flints 81 J11
Rhyd-y-pennau Cerdgn 54 E7
Rhyd-yr-onnen Gwynd 54 E4
Rhyd-y-sarn Gwynd 67 M6
Rhyl Denbgs 80 E8
Rhymney Caerph 30 F3
Rhynd P & K 134 F3
Rhynie Abers 150 D2
Rhynie Highld 163 J11
Ribbesford Worcs 57 P10
Ribbleton Lancs 88 H4
Ribby Lancs 88 E4
Ribchester Lancs 89 K3
Riber Derbys 84 D9
Riby Lincs 93 L9
Riccall N York 91 Q3
Riccarton Border 111 K2
Riccarton E Ayrs 125 L10
Richards Castle Herefs 56 H11
Richings Park Bucks 36 B5
Richmond Gt Lon 36 E6
Richmond N York 103 N10
Richmond Sheff 84 F3
Richmond Fort Guern 10 b2
Rich's Holford Somset 18 F7
Rickerscote Staffs 70 G10
Rickford N Som 19 N3
Rickham Devon 7 K11
Rickinghall Suffk 64 E6
Rickling Essex 51 L4
Rickling Green Essex 51 M5
Rickmansworth Herts 36 C2
Riddell Border 117 Q6
Riddings Derbys 84 F10
Riddlecombe Devon 17 J9
Riddlesden C Brad 90 D2
Ridge BaNES 19 Q3
Ridge Dorset 12 F7
Ridge Herts 50 F10
Ridge Wilts 21 J8
Ridgebourne Powys 44 F2
Ridge Green Surrey 36 H11
Ridge Lane Warwks 59 L6

Ridge Row Kent 27 M3
Ridgeway Derbys 84 F4
Ridgeway Worcs 47 K2
Ridgeway Cross Herefs 46 D5
Ridgewell Essex 52 B3
Ridgewood E Susx 25 L7
Ridgmont C Beds 49 Q7
Riding Mill Nthumb 112 F8
Ridley Kent 37 P8
Ridley Nthumb 111 Q8
Ridley Green Ches E 69 Q4
Ridlington Norfk 77 L5
Ridlington Rutlnd 73 L10
Ridlington Street Norfk 77 L5
Ridsdale Nthumb 112 D4
Rievaulx N York 98 B3
Rigg D & G 110 E7
Riggend N Lans 126 D3
Righoul Highld 156 F7
Rigmadon Park Cumb 95 N4
Rigsby Lincs 87 M5
Rigside S Lans 116 B3
Riley Green Lancs 89 J3
Rileyhill Staffs 58 H2
Rilla Mill Cnwll 5 M7
Rillaton Cnwll 5 M7
Rillington N York 98 H6
Rimington Lancs 96 B11
Rimpton Somset 20 B10
Rimswell E R Yk 93 P5
Rinaston Pembks 41 J5
Rindleford Shrops 57 N5
Ringford D & G 108 E9
Ringinglow Sheff 84 C4
Ringland Norfk 76 G9
Ringles Cross E Susx 25 L6
Ringlestone Kent 38 E10
Ringley Bolton 89 M9
Ringmer E Susx 25 K8
Ringmore Devon 6 H9
Ringmore Devon 7 N4
Ring o'Bells Lancs 88 F8
Ringorm Moray 157 P9
Ring's End Cambs 74 G10
Ringsfield Suffk 65 N4
Ringsfield Corner Suffk 65 N4
Ringshall Herts 35 Q2
Ringshall Suffk 64 E11
Ringshall Stocks Suffk 64 F11
Ringstead Nhants 61 L5
Ringstead Norfk 75 P2
Ringwood Hants 13 L3
Ringwould Kent 27 Q2
Rinmore Abers 150 C4
Rinsey Cnwll 2 F9
Rinsey Croft Cnwll 2 G8
Ripe E Susx 25 M8
Ripley Derbys 84 E10
Ripley Hants 13 L5
Ripley N York 97 L8
Ripley Surrey 36 C9
Riplingham E R Yk 92 G4
Riplington Hants 23 J10
Ripon N York 97 M6
Rippingale Lincs 74 A5
Ripple Kent 27 Q2
Ripple Worcs 46 G7
Ripponden Calder 90 C7
Risabus Ag & B 122 D11
Risbury Herefs 45 Q4
Risby N Linc 92 F8
Risby Suffk 63 P7
Risca Caerph 30 H6
Rise E R Yk 93 L2
Riseden E Susx 25 P4
Riseden Kent 26 B4
Risegate Lincs 74 D5
Riseholme Lincs 86 C5
Risehow Cumb 100 D4
Riseley Bed 61 M8
Riseley Wokham 23 K2
Rishangles Suffk 64 H8
Rishton Lancs 89 L4
Rishworth Calder 90 C7
Rising Bridge Lancs 89 M5
Risley Derbys 72 D3
Risley Warrtn 82 E6
Risplith N York 97 K7
Rivar Wilts 22 B2
Rivenhall Essex 52 D8
Rivenhall End Essex 52 D8
River Kent 27 N3
River W Susx 23 P10
River Bank Cambs 62 H7
Riverford Highld 155 P7
Riverhead Kent 37 M9
Rivers Corner Dorset 12 C2
Rivington Lancs 89 J8
Rivington Services Lancs 89 J8
Roachill Devon 17 R7
Roade Nhants 49 L4
Road Green Norfk 65 K3
Roadhead Cumb 111 K6
Roadmeetings S Lans 126 F8
Roadside E Ayrs 115 L4
Roadside Highld 167 L4
Roadwater Somset 18 D7
Roag Highld 152 D9
Roa Island Cumb 94 E7
Roan of Craigoch S Ayrs 114 E7
Roast Green Essex 51 L4
Roath Cardif 30 G9
Roberton Border 117 N8
Roberton S Lans 116 C5
Robertsbridge E Susx 26 B7
Robertstown Kirk 90 F6
Robeston Wathen Pembks 41 L7
Robgill Tower D & G 110 D6
Robin Hill Staffs 70 G3
Robin Hood Lancs 88 G8
Robin Hood Leeds 91 J5
Robin Hood Crematorium Solhll 58 H8
Robin Hood Doncaster Sheffield Airport Donc 91 R11
Robinhood End Essex 52 B4
Robin Hood's Bay N York 105 Q9
Roborough Devon 6 E6
Roborough Devon 17 K8
Roby Knows 81 N6
Roby Mill Lancs 88 G9
Rocester Staffs 71 L7
Roch Pembks 40 G6
Rochdale Rochdl 89 P8
Rochdale Crematorium Rochdl 89 P8
Roche Cnwll 4 F9
Rochester Medway 38 B8
Rochester Nthumb 118 F11
Rochford Essex 38 E3

Rochford Worcs 57 L11
Roch Gate Pembks 40 G6
Rock Cnwll 4 E7
Rock Neath 29 L6
Rock Nthumb 119 P6
Rock W Susx 24 D8
Rock Worcs 57 N10
Rockbeare Devon 9 P6
Rockbourne Hants 21 M11
Rockcliffe Cumb 110 G8
Rockcliffe D & G 108 H10
Rockcliffe Cross Cumb 110 F8
Rock End Staffs 70 F3
Rockend Torbay 7 N6
Rock Ferry Wirral 81 L7
Rockfield Highld 163 L10
Rockfield Mons 31 N2
Rockford Devon 17 P2
Rockford Hants 13 L3
Rockgreen Shrops 57 J9
Rockhampton S Glos 32 C6
Rockhead Cnwll 4 H5
Rockhill Shrops 56 D9
Rock Hill Worcs 58 E11
Rockingham Nhants 61 J2
Rockland All Saints Norfk 64 D2
Rockland St Mary Norfk 77 L11
Rockland St Peter Norfk 64 D2
Rockley Notts 85 M6
Rockley Wilts 33 N10
Rockliffe Lancs 89 P6
Rockville Ag & B 131 Q5
Rockwell End Bucks 35 L7
Rockwell Green Somset 18 F10
Rodborough Gloucs 32 F4
Rodbourne Swindn 33 M7
Rodbourne Wilts 32 H8
Rodd Herefs 45 L2
Roddam Nthumb 119 K6
Rodden Dorset 11 N8
Roddymoor Dur 103 N3
Rode Somset 20 F4
Rode Heath Ches E 70 E3
Rode Heath Ches E 83 J11
Rodel W Isls 168 f9
Roden Wrekin 69 Q11
Rodhuish Somset 18 D7
Rodington Wrekin 57 K2
Rodington Heath Wrekin 57 K2
Rodley Gloucs 32 D2
Rodley Leeds 90 G3
Rodmarton Gloucs 32 H5
Rodmell E Susx 25 K9
Rodmersham Kent 38 F9
Rodmersham Green Kent 38 F9
Rodney Stoke Somset 19 N5
Rodsley Derbys 71 N6
Rodway Somset 19 J6
Roecliffe N York 97 N7
Roe Cross Tamesd 83 L5
Roe Green Herts 50 F9
Roe Green Herts 50 H4
Roe Green Salfd 82 F4
Roehampton Gt Lon 36 F6
Roffey W Susx 24 E4
Rogart Highld 162 G6
Rogate W Susx 23 M10
Roger Ground Cumb 101 L11
Rogerstone Newpt 31 J7
Roghadal W Isls 168 f9
Rogiet Mons 31 N7
Roke Oxon 34 H6
Roker Sundld 113 P9
Rollesby Norfk 77 N8
Rolleston Leics 73 J10
Rolleston Notts 85 M10
Rolleston on Dove Staffs 71 N9
Rolston E R Yk 93 N2
Rolstone N Som 19 L2
Rolvenden Kent 26 D5
Rolvenden Layne Kent 26 E5
Romaldkirk Dur 103 J6
Romanby N York 97 N2
Romanno Bridge Border 127 M8
Romansleigh Devon 17 N7
Romden Castle Kent 26 E3
Romesdal Highld 152 G7
Romford Dorset 13 J3
Romford Gt Lon 37 M3
Romiley Stockp 83 K6
Romney Street Kent 37 N8
Romsey Cambs 62 G9
Romsey Hants 22 C10
Romsley Shrops 57 P8
Romsley Worcs 58 E8
Rona Highld 153 L6
Ronachan Ag & B 123 M9
Rood Ashton Wilts 20 G3
Rookhope Dur 102 H2
Rookley IoW 14 F10
Rookley Green IoW 14 F10
Rooks Bridge Somset 19 L4
Rooks Nest Somset 18 E8
Rookwith N York 97 K3
Roos E R Yk 93 N4
Roose Cumb 94 E7
Roosebeck Cumb 94 F7
Roothams Green Bed 61 N9
Ropley Hants 22 H8
Ropley Dean Hants 22 H8
Ropley Soke Hants 23 J8
Ropsley Lincs 73 P4
Rora Abers 159 Q7
Rorrington Shrops 56 E4
Rosarie Moray 158 A7
Rose Cnwll 3 J3
Roseacre Lancs 88 E3
Rose Ash Devon 17 P7
Rosebank S Lans 126 E8
Rosebush Pembks 41 L5
Rosecare Cnwll 5 K2
Rosecliston Cnwll 4 C10
Rosedale Abbey N York 105 K11
Rose Green Essex 52 F6
Rose Green Suffk 52 F4
Rose Green Suffk 52 G3
Rose Green W Susx 15 P7
Rosehall Highld 162 B6
Rosehearty Abers 159 M4
Rose Hill E Susx 25 L7
Rose Hill Lancs 89 N4
Rosehill Shrops 69 N11
Rose Hill Crematorium Donc 91 Q10
Roseisle Moray 157 L4
Roselands E Susx 25 P10
Rosemarket Pembks 41 J9
Rosemarkie Highld 156 C6
Rosemary Lane Devon 10 D2

Rosemount P & K 142 B9
Rosenannon Cnwll 4 F8
Rosenithon Cnwll 3 L9
Roser's Cross E Susx 25 M6
Rosevean Cnwll 4 D9
Rosevine Cnwll 3 M6
Rosewarne Cnwll 2 G6
Rosewell Mdloth 127 P5
Roseworth S on T 104 D6
Roseworthy Cnwll 2 G6
Rosgill Cumb 101 P7
Roskestal Cnwll 2 B9
Roskhill Highld 152 D9
Roskorwell Cnwll 3 K9
Rosley Cumb 110 F11
Rosliston Derbys 71 N11
Rosneath Ag & B 132 B11
Ross D & G 108 D12
Ross Nthumb 119 M3
Rossett Wrexhm 69 L3
Rossett Green N York 97 L10
Rossington Donc 91 Q11
Rossland Rens 125 L3
Ross-on-Wye Herefs 46 A10
Roster Highld 167 N9
Rostherne Ches E 82 F8
Rosthwaite Cumb 101 J8
Roston Derbys 71 L6
Rosudgeon Cnwll 2 F8
Rosyth Fife 134 E11
Rothbury Nthumb 119 L10
Rotherby Leics 72 H7
Rotherfield E Susx 25 N5
Rotherfield Greys Oxon 35 K8
Rotherfield Peppard Oxon 35 K8
Rotherham Rothm 84 F2
Rotherham Crematorium Rothm 84 G2
Rotherwick Hants 23 K3
Rothes Moray 157 P8
Rothesay Ag & B 124 D5
Rothiebrisbane Abers 158 H10
Rothiemay Moray 158 E8
Rothiemurchus Lodge Highld 148 H6
Rothienorman Abers 158 H10
Rothley Leics 72 F8
Rothley Nthumb 112 F3
Rothmaise Abers 158 G11
Rothwell Leeds 91 J5
Rothwell Lincs 93 K11
Rothwell Nhants 60 H4
Rotsea E R Yk 99 M10
Rottal Lodge Angus 142 F4
Rottingdean Br & H 25 J10
Rottington Cumb 100 C8
Roucan D & G 109 M5
Roucan Loch Crematorium D & G 109 M5
Roud IoW 14 F10
Rougham Norfk 76 A7
Rougham Suffk 64 C9
Rough Close Staffs 70 G7
Rough Common Kent 39 K10
Roughlee Lancs 89 N2
Roughpark Abers 149 Q5
Roughton Lincs 86 H8
Roughton Norfk 77 J4
Roughton Shrops 57 P6
Roughway Kent 37 P10
Roundbush Essex 52 E11
Round Bush Herts 50 D11
Roundbush Green Essex 51 N8
Round Green Luton 50 D6
Roundham Somset 11 J3
Roundhay Leeds 91 J3
Rounds Green Sandw 58 E7
Round Street Kent 37 Q7
Roundstreet Common W Susx 24 C5
Roundswell Devon 17 J5
Roundway Wilts 21 K2
Roundyhill Angus 142 F7
Rousay Ork 169 c3
Rousdon Devon 10 F6
Rousham Oxon 48 E10
Rous Lench Worcs 47 K4
Routenburn N Ayrs 124 F5
Routh E R Yk 93 J2
Rout's Green Bucks 35 L5
Row Cnwll 4 H6
Row Cumb 95 K3
Row Cumb 102 B4
Rowanburn D & G 110 H5
Rowardennan Stirlg 132 D8
Rowarth Derbys 83 M7
Row Ash Hants 14 F4
Rowberrow Somset 19 N3
Rowborough IoW 14 E10
Rowde Wilts 21 J2
Rowden Devon 8 F5
Rowen Conwy 79 P10
Rowfield Derbys 71 M5
Rowfoot Nthumb 111 N8
Rowford Somset 18 H9
Row Green Essex 52 B7
Rowhedge Essex 52 H7
Rowhook W Susx 24 D4
Rowington Warwks 59 K11
Rowland Derbys 84 B6
Rowland's Castle Hants 15 K4
Rowlands Gill Gatesd 113 J9
Rowledge Surrey 23 M6
Rowley Dur 112 G11
Rowley E R Yk 92 G4
Rowley Shrops 56 E3
Rowley Regis Sandw 58 E7
Rowley Regis Crematorium Sandw 58 E7
Rowlstone Herefs 45 M9
Rowly Surrey 24 B2
Rowner Hants 14 F6
Rowney Green Worcs 58 F10
Rownhams Hants 22 C11
Rownhams Services Hants 22 C11
Rowrah Cumb 100 E7
Rowsham Bucks 49 M11
Rowsley Derbys 84 C7
Rows of Trees Ches E 82 H9
Rowstock Oxon 34 E7
Rowston Lincs 86 E9
Rowthorne Derbys 84 G8
Rowton Ches W 69 M2
Rowton Shrops 56 F2
Rowton Shrops 56 G8
Rowton Wrekin 69 R11

Row Town Surrey 36 B8
Roxburgh Border 118 C4
Roxby N Linc 92 F7
Roxby N York 105 L7
Roxton Bed 61 Q10
Roxwell Essex 51 Q9
Royal Leamington Spa Warwks 59 M1
Royal Oak Darltn 103 P6
Royal Oak Lancs 81 N4
Royal's Green Ches E 69 R6
Royal Sutton Coldfield Birm 58 H6
Royal Tunbridge Wells Kent 25 N3
Royal Wootton Bassett Wilts 33 L8
Royal Yacht Britannia C Edin 127 P2
Roy Bridge Highld 146 H1
Roydhouse Kirk 90 G5
Roydon Essex 51 K9
Roydon Norfk 64 G5
Roydon Norfk 75 Q6
Roydon Hamlet Essex 51 K9
Royston Barns 91 K8
Royston Herts 51 J2
Royton Oldham 89 Q9
Rozel Jersey 11 c1
Ruabon Wrexhm 69 K6
Ruaig Ag & B 136 D6
Ruan High Lanes Cnwll 3 N6
Ruan Lanihorne Cnwll 3 L5
Ruan Major Cnwll 3 J10
Ruan Minor Cnwll 3 J10
Ruardean Gloucs 46 B11
Ruardean Hill Gloucs 46 B11
Ruardean Woodside Gloucs 46 B11
Rubery Birm 58 E9
Rubha Ban W Isls 168 c16
Ruckcroft Cumb 101 P2
Ruckhall Herefs 45 P7
Ruckinge Kent 26 H5
Ruckland Lincs 87 K5
Ruckley Shrops 57 J3
Rudby N York 104 F9
Rudchester Nthumb 112 H7
Ruddington Notts 72 F4
Ruddle Gloucs 32 C2
Ruddlemoor Cnwll 3 Q3
Rudford Gloucs 46 E10
Rudge Somset 20 F4
Rudgeway S Glos 32 B7
Rudgwick W Susx 24 C4
Rudhall Herefs 46 B9
Rudheath Ches W 82 F10
Rudheath Woods Ches E 82 F10
Rudley Green Essex 52 D11
Rudloe Wilts 32 F10
Rudry Caerph 30 H7
Rudston E R Yk 99 M8
Rudyard Staffs 70 H3
Ruecastle Border 118 C4
Rufford Lancs 88 F7
Rufford Abbey Notts 85 L8
Rufforth C York 98 A10
Rug Denbgs 68 B5
Rugby Warwks 60 B5
Rugeley Staffs 71 J11
Ruishton Somset 19 J9
Ruislip Gt Lon 36 C3
Rùm Highld 144 E8
Rumbach Moray 158 F9
Rumbling Bridge P & K 134 C8
Rumburgh Suffk 65 L5
Rumby Hill Dur 103 N4
Rumford Cnwll 4 D7
Rumford Falk 126 G2
Rumney Cardif 30 H9
Rumwell Somset 18 G10
Runcorn Halton 81 Q8
Runcton W Susx 15 N6
Runcton Holme Norfk 75 M9
Runfold Surrey 23 N6
Runhall Norfk 76 F10
Runham Norfk 77 P10
Runham Norfk 77 Q10
Runnington Somset 18 F10
Runsell Green Essex 52 C10
Runshaw Moor Lancs 88 G7
Runswick N York 105 M7
Runtaleave Angus 142 C3
Runwell Essex 38 C3
Ruscombe Wokham 35 L9
Rushall Herefs 46 B7
Rushall Norfk 64 H4
Rushall Wilts 21 M3
Rushall Wsall 58 F4
Rushbrooke Suffk 64 B9
Rushbury Shrops 57 J5
Rushden Herts 50 H4
Rushden Nhants 61 L8
Rushenden Kent 38 F7
Rusher's Cross E Susx 25 P5
Rushford Devon 5 P4
Rushford Norfk 64 C4
Rush Green Essex 53 L8
Rush Green Gt Lon 37 M3
Rush Green Herts 50 F6
Rush Green Warrtn 82 E6
Rushlake Green E Susx 25 P7
Rushmere Suffk 65 P4
Rushmere St Andrew Suffk 53 L2
Rushmoor Surrey 23 N6
Rushock Herefs 45 L3
Rushock Worcs 58 C10
Rusholme Manch 83 J4
Rushton Ches W 69 Q2
Rushton Nhants 60 H4
Rushton Shrops 57 L3
Rushton Spencer Staffs 70 G2
Rushwick Worcs 57 Q3
Rushyford Dur 103 Q5
Ruskie Stirlg 133 J7
Ruskington Lincs 86 E10
Rusland Cumb 94 G3
Rusper W Susx 24 F3
Ruspidge Gloucs 32 C2
Russell Green Essex 52 B9
Russell's Water Oxon 35 K7
Russel's Green Suffk 65 K7
Russ Hill Surrey 24 F2
Rusthall Kent 25 N3
Rustington W Susx 24 B10
Ruston N York 99 K4
Ruston Parva E R Yk 99 M8
Ruswarp N York 105 N9
Ruthall Shrops 57 K6
Rutherford Border 118 C4

...utherglen S Lans 125 Q5
...uthernbridge Cnwll 4 G8
...uthin Denbgs 68 F3
...uthrieston C Aber 151 N7
...uthven Abers 158 D8
...uthven Angus 142 D8
...uthven Highld 148 D8
...uthven Highld 156 E11
...uthvoes Cnwll 4 E9
...uthwaite Cumb 100 H3
...uthwell D & G 109 N7
...uxley Corner Gt Lon 37 L6
...uxton Green Herefs 45 Q11
...uyton-XI-Towns Shrops 69 L10
...val Nthumb 112 F6
...vall Dorset 11 J5
...vall Worcs 46 G6
...varsh Kent 37 Q8
...vcote Oxon 35 J3
...vdal Cumb 101 L9
...vde IoW 14 G8
...vebank Shrops 69 P8
...veford Herefs 46 B10
...ve Foreign E Susx 26 E7
...ve Harbour E Susx 26 F8
...vehill E R Yk 93 M5
...veish Green Wokham 35 K11
...ve Street Worcs 46 E7
...vhall Rutlnd 73 Q8
...vhill Wakefd 91 K8
...vhope Sundld 113 P10
...vlah Derbys 84 G7
...vland Lincs 86 D5
...vlands Notts 72 E3
...vlstone N York 96 E9
...vme Intrinseca Dorset 11 M2
...vther N York 91 P3
...vton Gatesd 113 J8
...vton N York 98 F5
...vton Shrops 57 P4
...vton Warwks 59 P7
...vton-on-Dunsmore
    Warwks 59 N10
...vton Woodside Gatesd 112 H8
...SS Edinburgh Zoo
    C Edin 127 N3

S

...abden Lancs 89 M3
...abine's Green Essex 51 M11
...acombe Herts 50 H7
...acombe Green Herts 50 H7
...acriston Dur 113 K11
...adberge Darltn 104 B7
...addell Ag & B 120 E5
...addington Leics 60 E2
...addlebow Norfk 75 M7
...addlescombe W Susx 24 G8
...adgill Cnwll 101 N9
...affron Walden Essex 51 M3
...ageston Pembks 41 L10
...agham Hills Norfk 76 C11
...agham Toney Norfk 76 B11
...aighton Ches W 69 M2
...t Abbs Border 129 N6
...t Agnes Border 128 H7
...t Agnes Cnwll 3 J3
...t Agnes IoS 2 b3
...t Agnes Mining
    District Cnwll 3 J4
...t Albans Herts 50 D9
...t Allen Cnwll 3 L3
...t Andrew Guern 10 b2
...t Andrews Fife 135 N4
...t Andrews Botanic
    Garden Fife 135 N4
...t Andrew's Major
    V Glam 30 F10
...t Andrews Well Dorset 11 K6
...t Anne's Lancs 88 C5
...t Ann's D & G 109 N2
...t Ann's Chapel Cnwll 5 Q7
...t Ann's Chapel Devon 6 H9
...t Anthony Cnwll 3 K8
...t Anthony's Hill E Susx 25 P10
...t Arvans Mons 31 P5
...t Asaph Denbgs 80 E10
...t Athan V Glam 30 D11
...t Aubin Jersey 11 b2
...t Austell Cnwll 3 Q3
...t Bees Cumb 100 C8
...t Blazey Cnwll 3 R3
...t Blazey Gate Cnwll 3 R3
...t Boswells Border 118 A4
...t Brelade Jersey 11 a2
...t Brelade's Bay Jersey 11 a2
...t Breock Cnwll 4 F7
...t Breward Cnwll 4 H6
...t Briavels Gloucs 31 Q4
...t Brides Pembks 40 F8
...t Bride's Major V Glam 29 N10
...t Brides Netherwent
    Mons 31 M7
...t Brides-super-Ely
    V Glam 30 E9
...t Brides Wentlooge
    Newpt 31 J8
...t Budeaux C Plym 6 D7
...t Buryan Cnwll 2 B8
...t Catherine BaNES 32 E11
...t Catherines Ag & B 131 N6
...t Chloe Gloucs 32 F4
...t Clears Carmth 41 Q7
...t Cleer Cnwll 5 L8
...t Clement Cnwll 5 M5
...t Clement Jersey 11 c2
...t Clether Cnwll 5 L5
...t Colmac Ag & B 124 C4
...t Columb Major Cnwll 4 E9
...t Columb Minor Cnwll 4 C9
...t Columb Road Cnwll 4 E10
...t Combs Abers 159 Q5
...t Cross South Elmham
    Suffk 65 K5
...t Cyrus Abers 143 N11
...t David's P & K 133 Q3
...t Davids Pembks 40 E5
...t Davids Cathedral
    Pembks 40 E5
...t Day Cnwll 3 J5
...t Decumans Somset 18 D8
...t Dennis Cnwll 4 F10
...t Devereux Herefs 45 N6
...t Dogmaels Pembks 42 C5
...t Dogwells Pembks 41 J5
...t Dominick Cnwll 5 Q8

St Donats V Glam 29 P11
St Edith's Marsh Wilts 21 J2
St Endellion Cnwll 4 F6
St Enoder Cnwll 4 D10
St Erme Cnwll 3 L4
St Erney Cnwll 5 P10
St Erth Cnwll 2 F6
St Erth Praze Cnwll 2 F6
St Ervan Cnwll 4 D8
St Eval Cnwll 4 D8
St Ewe Cnwll 3 N4
St Fagans Cardif 30 F9
St Fagans: National
    History Museum
    Cardif 30 F9
St Fergus Abers 159 Q7
St Fillans P & K 133 K3
St Florence Pembks 41 L10
St Gennys Cnwll 5 J2
St George Conwy 80 D9
St Georges N Som 19 L2
St George's V Glam 30 F9
St George's Hill Surrey 36 C8
St Germans Cnwll 5 P10
St Giles in the Wood
    Devon 17 J8
St Giles-on-the-Heath
    Devon 5 P3
St Gluvia's Cnwll 3 K7
St Harmon Powys 55 M10
St Helen Auckland Dur 103 N5
St Helens Cumb 100 D4
St Helen's E Susx 26 D9
St Helens IoW 14 H9
St Helens St Hel 81 Q5
St Helens Crematorium
    St Hel 81 P5
St Helier Gt Lon 36 G7
St Helier Jersey 11 b2
St Hilary Cnwll 2 E7
St Hilary V Glam 30 D10
Saint Hill Devon 10 B3
Saint Hill W Susx 25 J3
St Illtyd Blae G 30 H4
St Ippollitts Herts 50 E5
St Ishmael's Pembks 40 F9
St Issey Cnwll 4 E7
St Ive Cnwll 5 N8
St Ive Cross Cnwll 5 N8
St Ives Cambs 62 D6
St Ives Cnwll 2 E5
St Ives Dorset 13 K4
St James Norfk 77 K7
St James's End Nhants 60 F8
St James South
    Elmham Suffk 65 L5
St Jidgey Cnwll 4 E8
St John Cnwll 5 Q11
St John Jersey 11 b1
St Johns Dur 103 L4
St John's IoM 80 c5
St John's Kent 37 M9
St Johns Surrey 23 Q3
St Johns Worcs 46 F4
St John's Chapel Devon 17 J4
St John's Chapel Dur 102 G3
St John's Fen End Norfk 75 K8
St John's Highway Norfk 75 K8
St John's Kirk S Lans 116 D3
St John's Town of Dalry
    D & G 108 D4
St John's Wood Gt Lon 36 G4
St Jude's IoM 80 e2
St Just Cnwll 2 B7
St Just-in-Roseland
    Cnwll 3 L6
St Just Mining District
    Cnwll 2 B7
St Katherines Abers 159 J11
St Keverne Cnwll 3 K9
St Kew Cnwll 4 G6
St Kew Highway Cnwll 4 G6
St Keyne Cnwll 5 L9
St Lawrence Cnwll 4 G8
St Lawrence Essex 52 G11
St Lawrence IoW 14 F11
St Lawrence Jersey 11 b1
St Lawrence Kent 39 Q8
St Leonards Bucks 35 P3
St Leonards Dorset 13 K4
St Leonards E Susx 26 D10
St Leonard's Street Kent 37 Q9
St Levan Cnwll 2 B9
St Lythans V Glam 30 F10
St Mabyn Cnwll 4 G7
St Madoes P & K 134 F3
St Margarets Herefs 45 M8
St Margarets Herts 51 J8
St Margaret's at Cliffe
    Kent 27 Q3
St Margaret's Hope Ork 169 d7
St Margaret South
    Elmham Suffk 65 L5
St Marks IoM 80 c7
St Martin Cnwll 3 J9
St Martin Cnwll 5 M10
St Martin Guern 10 b2
St Martin Jersey 11 c1
St Martin's IoS 2 c1
St Martin's P & K 142 B11
St Martin's Shrops 69 K7
St Martin's Moor Shrops 69 K7
St Mary Jersey 11 a1
St Mary Bourne Hants 22 D4
St Marychurch Torbay 7 N5
St Mary Church V Glam 30 D10
St Mary Cray Gt Lon 37 L7
St Mary Hill V Glam 30 C9
St Mary in the Marsh
    Kent 27 J6
St Marylebone
    Crematorium Gt Lon 36 G3
St Mary's IoS 2 c2
St Mary's Ork 169 d6
St Mary's Bay Kent 27 J6
St Mary's Grove N Som 31 N11
St Mary's Hoo Medway 38 D6
St Mary's Platt Kent 37 P9
St Maughans Mons 45 P11
St Maughans Green
    Mons 45 P11
St Mawes Cnwll 3 L7
St Mawgan Cnwll 4 D8
St Mellion Cnwll 5 P8
St Mellons Cardif 30 H8
St Merryn Cnwll 4 D7
St Mewan Cnwll 3 Q3
St Michael Caerhays
    Cnwll 3 P5
St Michael Church
    Somset 19 K8

St Michael Penkevil
    Cnwll 3 M5
St Michaels Kent 26 E4
St Michaels Worcs 57 K11
St Michael's Mount Cnwll 2 E8
St Michael's on Wyre
    Lancs 88 F2
St Michael South
    Elmham Suffk 65 L5
St Minver Cnwll 4 F6
St Monans Fife 135 N7
St Neot Cnwll 5 K8
St Neots Cambs 61 Q8
St Newlyn East Cnwll 4 C10
St Nicholas Pembks 40 H3
St Nicholas V Glam 30 E10
St Nicholas-at-Wade
    Kent 39 N8
St Ninians Stirlg 133 M9
St Olaves Norfk 65 P2
St Osyth Essex 53 K8
St Ouen Jersey 11 a1
St Owens Cross Herefs 45 Q10
St Paul's Cray Gt Lon 37 L7
St Paul's Walden Herts 50 E6
St Peter Jersey 11 a1
St Peter Port Guern 10 c2
St Peter's Guern 10 b2
St Peter's Kent 39 Q8
St Peter's Hill Cambs 62 B6
St Petrox Pembks 41 J11
St Pinnock Cnwll 5 L9
St Quivox S Ayrs 114 G3
St Ruan Cnwll 3 J10
St Sampson Guern 10 c1
St Saviour Guern 10 b2
St Saviour Jersey 11 b2
St Stephen Cnwll 3 N3
St Stephens Cnwll 5 N8
St Stephens Cnwll 5 Q10
St Teath Cnwll 4 H5
St Margaret's Bay Kent 27 Q3
St Tudy Cnwll 4 H6
St Twynnells Pembks 41 J11
St Veep Cnwll 5 J10
St Vigeans Angus 143 L9
St Wenn Cnwll 4 E9
St Weonards Herefs 45 P10
St y-Nyll V Glam 30 E9
Salcombe Devon 7 J11
Salcombe Regis Devon 10 D7
Salcott-cum-Virley Essex 52 F7
Sale Traffd 82 G6
Saleby Lincs 87 N5
Sale Green Worcs 46 H3
Salehurst E Susx 26 C7
Salem Carmth 43 M9
Salem Cerdgn 54 F8
Salen Ag & B 137 P7
Salen Highld 138 B5
Salesbury Lancs 89 K4
Salford C Beds 49 P7
Salford Oxon 47 Q9
Salford Salfd 82 H5
Salford Priors Warwks 47 L4
Salfords Surrey 36 G11
Salhouse Norfk 77 L9
Saline Fife 134 C9
Salisbury Wilts 21 M9
Salisbury Crematorium
    Wilts 21 N8
Salisbury Plain Wilts 21 L6
Salkeld Dykes Cumb 101 P3
Salle Norfk 76 G7
Salmonby Lincs 87 K6
Salperton Gloucs 47 L10
Salph End Bed 61 N10
Salsburgh N Lans 126 E5
Salt Staffs 70 H9
Salta Cumb 109 N11
Saltaire C Brad 90 E3
Saltaire C Brad 90 E3
Saltash Cnwll 6 C7
Saltburn Highld 156 C3
Saltburn-by-the-Sea
    R & Cl 105 J6
Saltby Leics 73 M5
Salt Coates Cumb 110 C10
Saltcoats Cumb 100 E11
Saltcoats N Ayrs 124 G9
Saltcotes Lancs 88 D5
Saltdean Br & H 25 J10
Salterbeck Cumb 100 C4
Salterforth Lancs 96 C11
Salterswall Ches W 82 D11
Salterton Wilts 21 M7
Saltfleet Lincs 87 N2
Saltfleetby All Saints
    Lincs 87 N2
Saltfleetby St Clement
    Lincs 87 N2
Saltfleetby St Peter
    Lincs 87 M3
Saltford BaNES 32 C11
Salthouse Norfk 76 F3
Saltley Birm 58 H7
Saltmarsh Newpt 31 K8
Saltmarshe E R Yk 92 C6
Saltney Flints 69 L2
Salton N York 98 E5
Saltrens Devon 16 H7
Saltwell Crematorium
    Gatesd 113 L8
Saltwick Nthumb 113 J4
Saltwood Kent 27 L4
Salvington W Susx 24 D9
Salwarpe Worcs 46 G2
Salway Ash Dorset 11 K5
Sambourne Warwks 47 L2
Sambrook Wrekin 70 C10
Samlesbury Lancs 88 H4
Samlesbury Bottoms
    Lancs 89 J5
Sampford Arundel
    Somset 18 F11
Sampford Brett Somset 18 E6
Sampford Courtenay
    Devon 8 G4
Sampford Moor Somset 18 F11
Sampford Peverell
    Devon 9 P2
Sampford Spiney Devon 6 E4
Samsonlane Ork 169 f4
Samson's Corner Essex 53 J8
Samuelston E Loth 128 D5
Sanaigmore Ag & B 122 B5
Sancreed Cnwll 2 C8
Sancton E R Yk 92 E3
Sand Somset 19 M5
Sandaig Highld 145 M7
Sandale Cumb 100 H2

Sandal Magna Wakefd 91 J7
Sandavore Highld 144 G11
Sanday Ork 169 f2
Sanday Airport Ork 169 f2
Sandbach Services
    Ches E 70 D2
Sandbank Ag & B 131 P11
Sandbanks Poole 12 H7
Sandend Abers 158 E4
Sanderstead Gt Lon 36 H8
Sandford Cumb 102 D7
Sandford Devon 9 K4
Sandford Dorset 12 F7
Sandford Hants 13 L4
Sandford IoW 14 F10
Sandford N Som 19 M3
Sandford S Lans 126 C9
Sandford Shrops 69 K10
Sandford Shrops 69 Q8
Sandford-on-Thames
    Oxon 34 F4
Sandford Orcas Dorset 20 B10
Sandford St Martin Oxon 48 D9
Sandgate Kent 27 M4
Sandhaven Abers 159 N4
Sandhead D & G 106 E8
Sandhill Rothm 91 L11
Sandhills Dorset 11 M4
Sandhills Dorset 11 P2
Sandhills Leeds 91 K3
Sandhills Oxon 34 G3
Sandhills Surrey 23 P7
Sandhoe Nthumb 112 E7
Sandhole Ag & B 131 L8
Sand Hole E R Yk 92 D3
Sandholme E R Yk 92 D4
Sandholme Lincs 74 F3
Sandhurst Br For 23 M2
Sandhurst Gloucs 46 F10
Sandhurst Kent 26 D6
Sandhurst Cross Kent 26 C6
Sandhutton N York 97 N4
Sand Hutton N York 98 D9
Sandiacre Derbys 72 D3
Sandilands Lincs 87 P4
Sandiway Ches W 82 D10
Sandleheath Hants 21 M11
Sandleigh Oxon 34 E4
Sandley Dorset 20 E10
Sandling Kent 38 C10
Sandlow Green Ches E 82 G11
Sandness Shet 169 n8
Sandon Essex 52 B11
Sandon Herts 50 H4
Sandon Staffs 70 G9
Sandon Bank Staffs 70 G9
Sandown IoW 14 G10
Sandplace Cnwll 5 M10
Sandridge Herts 50 E8
Sandridge Wilts 32 H11
Sandringham Norfk 75 N5
Sands Bucks 35 M6
Sandsend N York 105 N8
Sand Side Cumb 94 E4
Sandside Cumb 95 K4
Sandtoft N Linc 92 B9
Sandway Kent 38 E11
Sandwell Valley
    Crematorium Sandw 58 F6
Sandwich Kent 39 P10
Sandwick Cumb 101 M7
Sandwick Shet 169 r11
Sandwick W Isls 168 j4
Sandwith Cumb 100 C8
Sandwith Newtown
    Cumb 100 C8
Sandy C Beds 61 Q11
Sandy Bank Lincs 87 J9
Sandycroft Flints 81 L11
Sandy Cross E Susx 25 N6
Sandy Cross Herefs 46 C3
Sandyford D & G 110 D2
Sandygate Devon 7 M4
Sandygate IoM 80 e2
Sandy Haven Pembks 40 G9
Sandyhills D & G 109 J9
Sandylands Lancs 95 J8
Sandy Lane C Brad 90 E3
Sandylane Staffs 70 C7
Sandylane Swans 28 G7
Sandy Lane Wilts 33 J11
Sandy Lane Wrexhm 69 M6
Sandy Park Devon 8 H7
Sandysike Cumb 110 G8
Sandyway Herefs 45 P9
Sangobeg Highld 165 K3
Sangomore Highld 165 K3
Sankey Bridges Warrtn 82 C7
Sankyn's Green Worcs 57 P11
Sanna Bay Highld 137 L2
Sanndabhaig W Isls 168 j4
Sannox N Ayrs 124 C8
Sanquhar D & G 115 Q6
Santon Cumb 100 F10
Santon IoM 80 d7
Santon Bridge Cumb 100 F10
Santon Downham Suffk 63 P3
Sapcote Leics 59 Q6
Sapey Common Herefs 46 D2
Sapiston Suffk 64 C6
Sapley Cambs 62 B6
Sapperton Derbys 71 M8
Sapperton Gloucs 32 H4
Sapperton Lincs 73 Q4
Saracen's Head Lincs 74 F5
Sarclet Highld 167 P8
Sarisbury Hants 14 F5
Sarn Brdgnd 29 P8
Sarn Gwynd 66 C8
Sarn Powys 55 M9
Sarn Powys 56 C6
Sarnau Carmth 42 F11
Sarnau Cerdgn 42 F4
Sarnau Gwynd 68 C7
Sarnau Powys 44 H11
Sarnau Powys 68 H11
Sarn Bach Gwynd 66 E9
Sarnesfield Herefs 45 M4
Sarn Park Services
    Brdgnd 29 P8
Sarn-wen Powys 69 J11
Saron Carmth 28 H2
Saron Carmth 42 G7
Saron Gwynd 66 H3
Saron Gwynd 79 J11
Sarratt Herts 50 B11
Sarre Kent 39 N8
Sarsden Oxon 47 Q10
Sarson Hants 22 B6
Satley Dur 103 M2

Satmar Kent 27 N4
Satron N York 102 H11
Satterleigh Devon 17 M7
Satterthwaite Cumb 94 G2
Satwell Oxon 35 K8
Sauchen Abers 151 J5
Saucher P & K 142 B11
Sauchieburn Abers 143 M4
Saul Gloucs 32 D3
Saundby Notts 85 N3
Saundersfoot Pembks 41 M10
Saunderton Bucks 35 L4
Saunderton Station
    Bucks 35 M5
Saunton Devon 16 H4
Sausthorpe Lincs 87 L7
Saverley Green Staffs 70 H7
Savile Town Kirk 90 G6
Sawbridge Warwks 60 B7
Sawbridgeworth Herts 51 L8
Sawdon N York 99 J4
Sawley Derbys 72 D4
Sawley Lancs 96 A11
Sawley N York 97 K7
Sawston Cambs 62 G11
Sawtry Cambs 61 Q4
Saxby Leics 73 L7
Saxby Lincs 86 D3
Saxby All Saints N Linc 92 G7
Saxelbye Leics 72 H6
Saxham Street Suffk 64 F9
Saxilby Lincs 85 Q5
Saxlingham Norfk 76 E4
Saxlingham Green Norfk 65 J2
Saxlingham
    Nethergate Norfk 65 J2
Saxlingham Thorpe
    Norfk 65 J2
Saxmundham Suffk 65 M9
Saxondale Notts 72 H3
Saxon Street Cambs 63 L9
Saxtead Suffk 65 K8
Saxtead Green Suffk 65 K9
Saxtead Little Green
    Suffk 65 J8
Saxthorpe Norfk 76 G5
Saxton N York 91 M3
Sayers Common W Susx 24 G7
Scackleton N York 98 C6
Scafell Pike Cumb 100 H9
Scaftworth Notts 85 L2
Scagglethorpe N York 98 G6
Scalasaig Ag & B 136 B3
Scalby E R Yk 92 D5
Scalby N York 99 L2
Scald End Bed 61 M9
Scaldwell Nhants 60 G6
Scaleby Cumb 110 H8
Scalebyhill Cumb 110 H8
Scales Cumb 94 F6
Scales Cumb 101 K5
Scalesceugh Cumb 110 H11
Scalford Leics 73 K6
Scaling N York 105 K8
Scaling Dam R & Cl 105 K8
Scalloway Shet 169 r10
Scalpay Highld 153 L11
Scambleby Lincs 87 J5
Scammonden Kirk 90 D7
Scamodale Highld 138 E3
Scampston N York 98 H5
Scampton Lincs 86 C5
Scaniport Highld 156 A10
Scapegoat Hill Kirk 90 D7
Scarba Ag & B 130 D7
Scarborough N York 99 L3
Scarcewater Cnwll 3 N3
Scarcliffe Derbys 84 G7
Scarcroft Leeds 91 K2
Scarfskerry Highld 167 N2
Scargill Dur 103 L8
Scarinish Ag & B 136 C7
Scarisbrick Lancs 88 D8
Scarness Cumb 100 H4
Scarning Norfk 76 D9
Scarrington Notts 73 J2
Scarth Hill Lancs 88 E9
Scarthingwell N York 91 M3
Scartho NE Lin 93 N9
Scatsta Airport Shet 169 q6
Scaur D & G 108 H10
Scawby N Linc 92 G9
Scawby Notts 91 N10
Scawthorpe Donc 91 P9
Scawton N York 98 A4
Scayne's Hill W Susx 25 J6
Scethrog Powys 44 G9
Scholar Green Ches E 70 E3
Scholemoor
    Crematorium C Brad 90 E4
Scholes Kirk 90 F5
Scholes Kirk 90 F9
Scholes Leeds 91 K3
Scholes Rothm 91 K11
Scholes Wigan 88 H9
School Aycliffe Dur 103 Q6
School Green C Brad 90 E4
School Green Ches W 70 A2
Schoolgreen Wokham 35 K11
School House Dorset 10 H4
Scissett Kirk 90 G8
Scleddau Pembks 40 H4
Scofton Notts 85 K4
Scole Norfk 64 H6
Scone P & K 134 E2
Sconser Highld 153 J11
Scoonie Fife 135 K7
Scopwick Lincs 86 E9
Scoraig Highld 160 G2
Scorborough E R Yk 99 L11
Scorrier Cnwll 3 J5
Scorriton Devon 7 J5
Scorton Lancs 95 L11
Scorton N York 103 Q10
Sco Ruston Norfk 77 K7
Scotby Cumb 110 H9
Scotch Corner N York 103 P9
Scotch Corner Rest
    Area N York 103 P9
Scotforth Lancs 95 K9
Scot Hay Staffs 70 D5
Scothern Lincs 86 D5
Scotland Lincs 73 Q4
Scotland Gate Nthumb 113 L4
Scotlandwell P & K 134 F7
Scot Lane End Bolton 89 J9
Scotscalder Station
    Highld 167 J5
Scotsdike Cumb 110 G6
Scot's Gap Nthumb 112 F3

Scotsmill Abers...150 F4
Scotstoun C Glas...125 N4
Scotswood N u Ty...113 K8
Scotter Lincs...92 E10
Scotterthorpe Lincs...92 E10
Scottish Seabird Centre E Loth...128 F2
Scottish Wool Centre Stirlg...132 G7
Scottlethorpe Lincs...73 R6
Scotton Lincs...92 E11
Scotton N York...97 M9
Scotton N York...103 N11
Scottow Norfk...77 K7
Scott Willoughby Lincs...73 R3
Scoulton Norfk...76 D11
Scounslow Green Staffs...71 K9
Scourie Highld...164 E8
Scourie More Highld...164 D8
Scousburgh Shet...169 q12
Scouthead Oldham...90 B9
Scrabster Highld...167 K2
Scraesburgh Border...118 C7
Scrafield Lincs...87 K7
Scrainwood Nthumb...119 J9
Scrane End Lincs...74 G2
Scraptoft Leics...72 G9
Scratby Norfk...77 Q8
Scrayingham N York...98 E9
Scrays E Susx...26 C8
Scredington Lincs...74 A2
Scremby Lincs...87 M7
Scremerston Nthumb...129 Q10
Screveton Notts...73 J2
Scrivelsby Lincs...87 J7
Scriven N York...97 M9
Scrooby Notts...85 L2
Scropton Derbys...71 M8
Scrub Hill Lincs...86 H9
Scruton N York...97 L2
Scuggate Cumb...110 H6
Scullomie Highld...165 P4
Sculthorpe Norfk...76 B5
Scunthorpe N Linc...92 E8
Scurlage Swans...28 E7
Sea Somset...10 G2
Seaborough Dorset...11 J3
Seabridge Staffs...70 E6
Seabrook Kent...27 L4
Seaburn Sundld...113 P9
Seacombe Wirral...81 L6
Seacroft Leeds...91 K3
Seacroft Lincs...87 Q8
Seadyke Lincs...74 F3
Seafield Highld...152 H9
Seafield W Loth...127 J4
Seafield Crematorium C Edin...127 P2
Seaford E Susx...25 L11
Seaforth Sefton...81 L5
Seagrave Leics...72 G7
Seagry Heath Wilts...33 J8
Seaham Dur...113 P11
Seahouses Nthumb...119 P4
Seal Kent...37 N9
Sealand Flints...81 M11
Seale Surrey...23 N5
Seamer N York...99 L4
Seamer N York...104 E8
Seamill N Ayrs...124 G8
Sea Palling Norfk...77 N6
Searby Lincs...93 J9
Seasalter Kent...39 J9
Seascale Cumb...100 D10
Seathwaite Cumb...100 H11
Seathwaite Cumb...100 H8
Seatle Cumb...94 H4
Seatoller Cumb...100 H8
Seaton Cnwll...5 N11
Seaton Cumb...100 D4
Seaton Devon...10 E6
Seaton Dur...113 N11
Seaton E R Yk...99 P11
Seaton Kent...39 M10
Seaton Nthumb...113 M5
Seaton Rutlnd...73 N11
Seaton Burn N Tyne...113 K6
Seaton Carew Hartpl...104 F5
Seaton Delaval Nthumb...113 M5
Seaton Ross E R Yk...92 C2
Seaton Sluice Nthumb...113 M5
Seatown Dorset...11 J6
Seave Green N York...104 G10
Seaview IoW...14 H8
Seaville Cumb...110 C10
Seavington St Mary Somset...11 J2
Seavington St Michael Somset...19 M11
Sebastopol Torfn...31 J5
Sebergham Cumb...101 L2
Seckington Warwks...59 L3
Second Severn Crossing Mons...31 P7
Sedbergh Cumb...95 P2
Sedbury Gloucs...31 P6
Sedbusk N York...96 C2
Sedgeberrow Worcs...47 K7
Sedgebrook Lincs...73 M3
Sedge Fen Suffk...63 L4
Sedgefield Dur...104 C5
Sedgeford Norfk...75 P3
Sedgehill Wilts...20 G9
Sedgemoor Crematorium Somset...19 J6
Sedgemoor Services Somset...19 L4
Sedgley Dudley...58 D6
Sedgley Park Bury...82 H4
Sedgwick Cumb...95 L3
Sedlescombe E Susx...26 C8
Sedrup Bucks...35 M2
Seed Kent...38 F10
Seend Wilts...20 H2
Seend Cleeve Wilts...20 H2
Seer Green Bucks...35 Q6
Seething Norfk...65 L2
Sefton Sefton...81 M4
Seghill Nthumb...113 L6
Seighford Staffs...70 F9
Seion Gwynd...79 J11
Seisdon Staffs...58 B5
Selattyn Shrops...69 J8
Selborne Hants...23 K8
Selby N York...91 Q4
Selham W Susx...23 P10
Selhurst Gt Lon...36 H7
Selkirk Border...117 P5
Sellack Herefs...45 R9
Sellafield Station Cumb...100 D10
Sellafirth Shet...169 s4

Sellan Cnwll...2 C7
Sellick's Green Somset...18 H11
Sellindge Kent...27 J4
Selling Kent...38 H10
Sells Green Wilts...20 H2
Selly Oak Birm...58 F8
Selmeston E Susx...25 M9
Selsdon Gt Lon...37 J8
Selsey Gloucs...32 F4
Selsey W Susx...15 N8
Selsfield Common W Susx...24 H4
Selside Cumb...101 P11
Selside N York...96 A5
Selsted Kent...27 M3
Selston Notts...84 G10
Selworthy Somset...18 B5
Semer Suffk...52 G2
Semington Wilts...20 G2
Semley Wilts...20 G9
Sempringham Lincs...74 B4
Send Surrey...36 B9
Send Marsh Surrey...36 B9
Senghenydd Caerph...30 F6
Sennen Cnwll...2 B8
Sennen Cove Cnwll...2 B8
Sennybridge Powys...44 C9
Serlby Notts...85 K3
Sessay N York...97 Q5
Setchey Norfk...75 M8
Setley Hants...13 P4
Seton Mains E Loth...128 C4
Settle N York...96 B8
Settrington N York...98 G6
Seven Ash Somset...18 G8
Sevenhampton Gloucs...47 K10
Sevenhampton Swindn...33 P6
Seven Hills Crematorium Suffk...53 M3
Seven Kings Gt Lon...37 L3
Sevenoaks Kent...37 M9
Sevenoaks Weald Kent...37 M10
Seven Sisters Neath...29 M3
Seven Springs Gloucs...47 J11
Seven Star Green Essex...52 F6
Severn Beach S Glos...31 P8
Severn Bridge S Glos...31 Q6
Severn Stoke Worcs...46 G6
Severn View Services S Glos...31 Q7
Sevick End Bed...61 N10
Sevington Kent...26 H3
Sewards End Essex...51 N3
Sewardstonebury Essex...51 J11
Sewell C Beds...49 Q10
Sewerby E R Yk...99 P7
Seworgan Cnwll...3 J7
Sewstern Leics...73 M6
Sexhow N York...104 E9
Sezincote Gloucs...47 N8
Sgiogarstaigh W Isls...168 k1
Shabbington Bucks...35 J3
Shackerley Shrops...57 Q3
Shackerstone Leics...72 B9
Shacklecross Derbys...72 C4
Shackleford Surrey...23 P5
Shade Calder...89 Q6
Shader W Isls...168 i2
Shadforth Dur...104 B2
Shadingfield Suffk...65 N5
Shadoxhurst Kent...26 G4
Shadwell Leeds...91 J3
Shadwell Norfk...64 C5
Shaftenhoe End Herts...51 K3
Shaftesbury Dorset...20 G10
Shaftholme Donc...91 P9
Shafton Barns...91 K8
Shafton Two Gates Barns...91 K8
Shakerley Wigan...82 E4
Shalbourne Wilts...22 B2
Shalcombe IoW...14 C9
Shalden Hants...23 J6
Shalden Green Hants...23 K6
Shaldon Devon...7 N4
Shalfleet IoW...14 D9
Shalford Essex...52 B6
Shalford Surrey...36 B11
Shalford Green Essex...52 B6
Shallowford Staffs...70 F9
Shalmsford Street Kent...39 J11
Shalstone Bucks...48 H7
Shamley Green Surrey...24 B2
Shandford Angus...142 H5
Shandon Ag & B...132 B10
Shandwick Highld...156 F2
Shangton Leics...73 J11
Shankhouse Nthumb...113 L5
Shanklin IoW...14 G10
Shap Cumb...101 Q7
Shapinsay Ork...169 e5
Shapwick Dorset...12 F4
Shapwick Somset...19 M7
Shard End Birm...59 J7
Shardlow Derbys...72 C4
Shareshill Staffs...58 D3
Sharlston Wakefd...91 K7
Sharlston Common Wakefd...91 K7
Sharman's Cross Solhll...58 H9
Sharnal Street Medway...38 C7
Sharnbrook Bed...61 L9
Sharneyford Lancs...89 P6
Sharnford Leics...59 Q6
Sharnhill Green Dorset...11 Q3
Sharoe Green Lancs...88 G4
Sharow N York...97 M6
Sharpenhoe C Beds...50 C4
Sharperton Nthumb...119 J10
Sharp Green Norfk...77 M7
Sharpness Gloucs...32 C4
Sharpthorne W Susx...25 J4
Sharptor Cnwll...5 M7
Sharpway Gate Worcs...58 E11
Sharrington Norfk...76 E4
Shatterford Worcs...57 P7
Shatterling Kent...39 N10
Shatton Derbys...84 B4
Shaugh Prior Devon...6 E6
Shave Cross Dorset...11 J5
Shavington Ches E...70 B4
Shaw C Brad...90 C3
Shaw Oldham...89 Q9
Shaw Swindn...33 M7
Shaw W Berk...34 E11
Shaw Wilts...32 G11
Shawbirch Wrekin...57 L2
Shawbost W Isls...168 h3
Shawbury Shrops...69 Q10
Shawclough Rochdl...89 P8
Shaw Common Gloucs...46 C9

Shawdon Hill Nthumb...119 L8
Shawell Leics...60 B4
Shawford Hants...22 E9
Shawforth Lancs...89 P6
Shaw Green Herts...50 H4
Shaw Green Lancs...88 G7
Shaw Green N York...97 L8
Shawhead D & G...109 J5
Shaw Mills N York...97 L8
Shawsburn S Lans...126 D7
Shear Cross Wilts...20 G6
Shearington D & G...109 M7
Shearsby Leics...60 D2
Shearston Somset...19 J8
Shebbear Devon...16 G10
Shebdon Staffs...70 D9
Shebster Highld...166 H4
Sheddens E Rens...125 P6
Shedfield Hants...14 G4
Sheen Staffs...71 L2
Sheepbridge Derbys...84 E6
Sheep Hill Dur...113 J9
Sheepridge Kirk...90 F7
Sheepscar Leeds...91 J4
Sheepscombe Gloucs...32 G2
Sheepstor Devon...6 F5
Sheepwash Devon...8 C3
Sheepwash Nthumb...113 L3
Sheepway N Som...31 N9
Sheepy Magna Leics...72 A10
Sheepy Parva Leics...72 A10
Sheering Essex...51 M8
Sheerness Kent...38 F7
Sheerwater Surrey...36 B8
Sheet Hants...23 L9
Sheffield Cnwll...2 D8
Sheffield Sheff...84 E3
Sheffield Bottom W Berk...34 H11
Sheffield City Road Crematorium Sheff...84 E3
Sheffield Green E Susx...25 K5
Sheffield Park E Susx...25 K6
Shefford C Beds...50 D3
Shefford Woodlands W Berk...34 C10
Sheigra Highld...164 E4
Sheinton Shrops...57 L4
Shelderton Shrops...56 G9
Sheldon Birm...58 J8
Sheldon Derbys...83 Q11
Sheldon Devon...10 C3
Sheldwich Kent...38 H10
Sheldwich Lees Kent...38 H10
Shelf Calder...90 E5
Shelfanger Norfk...64 G5
Shelfield Warwks...47 M2
Shelfield Wsall...58 F4
Shelfield Green Warwks...47 M2
Shelford Notts...72 H2
Shelford Warwks...59 P7
Shellacres Nthumb...118 G2
Shelley Essex...51 N9
Shelley Kirk...90 G8
Shelley Suffk...52 H4
Shelley Far Bank Kirk...90 G8
Shellingford Oxon...34 B6
Shellow Bowells Essex...51 P9
Shelsley Beauchamp Worcs...46 D2
Shelsley Walsh Worcs...46 D2
Shelton Bed...61 M7
Shelton Norfk...65 J3
Shelton Notts...73 K2
Shelton Shrops...56 H2
Shelton Green Norfk...65 J3
Shelton Lock C Derb...72 B4
Shelton Under Harley Staffs...70 E7
Shelve Shrops...56 E5
Shelwick Herefs...45 Q6
Shenfield Essex...51 P11
Shenington Oxon...48 C6
Shenley Herts...50 E10
Shenley Brook End M Keyn...49 M7
Shenleybury Herts...50 E10
Shenley Church End M Keyn...49 M7
Shenmore Herefs...45 M7
Shennanton D & G...107 K5
Shenstone Staffs...58 H4
Shenstone Worcs...58 C10
Shenstone Woodend Staffs...58 H4
Shenton Leics...72 B11
Shenval Moray...149 N2
Shepeau Stow Lincs...74 F8
Shephall Herts...50 G6
Shepherd's Bush Gt Lon...36 F4
Shepherd's Green Oxon...35 K8
Shepherds Patch Gloucs...32 D4
Shepherdswell Kent...27 N2
Shepley Kirk...90 F9
Shepperdine S Glos...32 B5
Shepperton Surrey...36 C7
Shepperton Green Surrey...36 C7
Shepreth Cambs...62 D11
Shepshed Leics...72 D7
Shepton Beauchamp Somset...19 M11
Shepton Mallet Somset...20 B6
Shepton Montague Somset...20 C8
Shepway Kent...38 C11
Sheraton Dur...104 D3
Sherborne Dorset...20 B11
Sherborne Gloucs...33 N2
Sherborne Somset...19 Q3
Sherborne St John Hants...22 H3
Sherbourne Warwks...47 Q2
Sherburn Dur...104 B2
Sherburn N York...99 K5
Sherburn Hill Dur...104 B2
Sherburn in Elmet N York...91 M4
Shere Surrey...36 C11
Shereford Norfk...76 B6
Sherfield English Hants...21 Q10
Sherfield on Loddon Hants...23 J3
Sherfin Lancs...89 M5
Sherford Devon...7 K10
Sherford Dorset...12 F6
Sheriffhales Shrops...57 P2
Sheriff Hutton N York...98 D7
Sheringham Norfk...76 H3
Sherington M Keyn...49 N5
Shermanbury W Susx...24 F7
Shernborne Norfk...75 P4
Sherrington Wilts...21 J7

Sherston Wilts...32 G7
Sherwood C Nott...72 F2
Sherwood Forest Notts...85 K8
Sherwood Forest Crematorium Notts...85 L7
Shetland Islands Shet...169 r8
Shettleston C Glas...125 Q5
Shevington Wigan...88 G9
Shevington Moor Wigan...88 G8
Shevington Vale Wigan...88 G9
Sheviock Cnwll...5 P10
Shibden Head C Brad...90 D5
Shide IoW...14 F9
Shidlaw Nthumb...118 F3
Shiel Bridge Highld...146 A4
Shieldaig Highld...153 Q7
Shieldhill D & G...109 M3
Shieldhill Falk...126 F2
Shieldhill House Hotel S Lans...116 E2
Shields N Lans...126 D6
Shielfoot Highld...138 B3
Shielhill Angus...142 G6
Shielhill Inver...124 G3
Shifford Oxon...34 C4
Shifnal Shrops...57 N3
Shilbottle Nthumb...119 N9
Shildon Dur...103 P5
Shillford E Rens...125 M6
Shillingford Devon...18 C10
Shillingford Oxon...34 G6
Shillingford Abbot Devon...9 M7
Shillingford St George Devon...9 M7
Shillingstone Dorset...12 D2
Shillington C Beds...50 D4
Shillmoor Nthumb...118 G9
Shilton Oxon...33 Q3
Shilton Warwks...59 P8
Shimpling Norfk...64 H5
Shimpling Suffk...64 B11
Shimpling Street Suffk...64 B11
Shincliffe Dur...103 Q2
Shiney Row Sundld...113 M10
Shinfield Wokham...35 K11
Shingay Cambs...62 D11
Shingle Street Suffk...53 Q3
Shinnersbridge Devon...7 K6
Shinness Highld...162 C4
Shipbourne Kent...37 N10
Shipdham Norfk...76 D10
Shipham Somset...19 M3
Shiphay Torbay...7 M5
Shiplake Oxon...35 L9
Shiplake Row Oxon...35 K9
Shiplate N Som...19 L3
Shipley C Brad...90 F3
Shipley Derbys...72 C2
Shipley Shrops...57 Q5
Shipley W Susx...24 D6
Shipley Bridge Surrey...24 H2
Shipley Hatch Kent...26 H4
Shipmeadow Suffk...65 M3
Shippea Hill Station Cambs...63 K4
Shippon Oxon...34 E5
Shipston-on-Stour Warwks...47 Q6
Shipton Bucks...49 L9
Shipton Gloucs...47 K11
Shipton N York...98 B9
Shipton Shrops...57 K6
Shipton Bellinger Hants...21 P5
Shipton Gorge Dorset...11 K6
Shipton Green W Susx...15 M7
Shipton Moyne Gloucs...32 G7
Shipton-on-Cherwell Oxon...48 E11
Shiptonthorpe E R Yk...92 E2
Shipton-under-Wychwood Oxon...47 Q11
Shirburn Oxon...35 J5
Shirdley Hill Lancs...88 D8
Shire Cumb...102 B3
Shirebrook Derbys...84 H7
Shiregreen Sheff...84 E2
Shirehampton Bristl...31 P9
Shiremoor N Tyne...113 M6
Shirenewton Mons...31 N6
Shire Oak Wsall...58 G4
Shireoaks Notts...85 J4
Shirkoak Kent...26 H4
Shirland Derbys...84 F9
Shirlett Shrops...57 L5
Shirley C Sotn...14 D4
Shirley Derbys...71 N6
Shirley Gt Lon...37 J7
Shirley Solhll...58 H9
Shirl Heath Herefs...45 N3
Shirrell Heath Hants...14 G4
Shirvan Ag & B...123 Q3
Shirwell Devon...17 L4
Shiskine N Ayrs...120 H6
Shittlehope Dur...103 K3
Shobdon Herefs...45 N2
Shobley Hants...13 L3
Shobrooke Devon...9 L4
Shoby Leics...72 H6
Shocklach Ches W...69 M5
Shocklach Green Ches W...69 M5
Shoeburyness Sthend...38 F4
Sholden Kent...39 Q11
Sholing C Sotn...14 E4
Sholver Oldham...89 Q9
Shoot Hill Shrops...56 G2
Shop Cnwll...16 C9
Shop Cnwll...4 C7
Shopwyke W Susx...15 N5
Shore Rochdl...89 Q7
Shoreditch Gt Lon...36 H4
Shoreditch Somset...18 H10
Shoreham Kent...37 M8
Shoreham Airport W Susx...24 E9
Shoreham-by-Sea W Susx...24 F9
Shoreswood Nthumb...129 N10
Shorley Hants...22 H8
Shorncote Gloucs...33 K5
Shorne Kent...37 Q6
Shorta Cross Cnwll...5 M10
Shortbridge E Susx...25 L6
Shortfield Common Surrey...23 M6
Shortgate E Susx...25 L7
Short Heath Birm...58 G6
Shortheath Hants...23 L7
Short Heath Wsall...58 E4
Shortlanesend Cnwll...3 L4
Shortlees E Ayrs...125 L11
Shortstown Bed...61 N11
Shorwell IoW...14 E10

Shoscombe BaNES...20 D3
Shotesham Norfk...65 J2
Shotgate Essex...38 C3
Shotley Suffk...53 M4
Shotley Bridge Dur...112 G10
Shotleyfield Nthumb...112 G10
Shotley Gate Suffk...53 M5
Shottenden Kent...38 H11
Shottermill Surrey...23 M7
Shottery Warwks...47 N4
Shotteswell Warwks...48 D5
Shottisham Suffk...53 P3
Shottle Derbys...71 Q5
Shottlegate Derbys...71 Q5
Shotton Dur...104 D3
Shotton Dur...104 B3
Shotton Flints...81 L11
Shotton Nthumb...113 M5
Shotton Nthumb...118 F3
Shotton Colliery Dur...104 C2
Shotts N Lans...126 E5
Shotwick Ches W...81 L10
Shougle Moray...157 N6
Shouldham Norfk...75 N8
Shouldham Thorpe Norfk...75 N8
Shoulton Worcs...46 F3
Shover's Green E Susx...25 Q4
Shraleybrook Staffs...70 D5
Shrawardine Shrops...69 L11
Shrawley Worcs...57 Q11
Shreding Green Bucks...36 B4
Shrewley Warwks...59 K11
Shrewsbury Shrops...56 H2
Shrewton Wilts...21 L6
Shripney W Susx...15 P6
Shrivenham Oxon...33 Q7
Shropham Norfk...64 D3
Shroton Dorset...12 E2
Shrub End Essex...52 F7
Shucknall Herefs...46 A6
Shudy Camps Cambs...51 P2
Shuna Ag & B...130 F3
Shurdington Gloucs...46 H11
Shurlock Row W & M...35 M10
Shurnock Worcs...47 K2
Shurrery Highld...166 H5
Shurrery Lodge Highld...166 H5
Shurton Somset...18 H6
Shustoke Warwks...59 K6
Shute Devon...9 P5
Shute Devon...10 F5
Shutford Oxon...48 C5
Shut Heath Staffs...70 F10
Shuthonger Gloucs...46 G7
Shutlanger Nhants...49 K5
Shutterton Devon...9 N8
Shutt Green Staffs...58 C3
Shuttington Warwks...59 L3
Shuttlewood Derbys...84 G6
Shuttleworth Bury...89 N7
Siabost W Isls...168 h3
Siadar W Isls...168 i2
Sibbertoft Nhants...60 E4
Sibdon Carwood Shrops...56 G7
Sibford Ferris Oxon...48 C6
Sibford Gower Oxon...48 C6
Sible Hedingham Essex...52 C4
Sibley's Green Essex...51 P4
Siblyback Cnwll...5 L7
Sibsey Lincs...87 L10
Sibsey Fenside Lincs...87 K10
Sibson Cambs...74 A11
Sibson Leics...72 B10
Sibster Highld...167 P6
Sibthorpe Notts...85 M6
Sibthorpe Notts...85 M2
Sibton Suffk...65 M8
Sicklesmere Suffk...64 B9
Sicklinghall N York...97 N11
Sidbrook Somset...19 J9
Sidbury Devon...10 D6
Sidbury Shrops...57 M7
Sid Cop Barns...91 K9
Sidcot N Som...19 M3
Sidcup Gt Lon...37 L5
Siddick Cumb...100 D4
Siddington Ches E...82 H10
Siddington Gloucs...33 K4
Sidemoor Worcs...58 E10
Sidestrand Norfk...77 K4
Sidford Devon...10 D6
Sidlesham W Susx...15 N7
Sidlesham Common W Susx...15 M7
Sidley E Susx...26 B10
Sidmouth Devon...10 D7
Siefton Shrops...56 H8
Sigford Devon...7 K4
Sigglesthorne E R Yk...99 P11
Sigingstone V Glam...30 C10
Signet Oxon...33 Q2
Silchester Hants...22 H2
Sileby Leics...72 F7
Silecroft Cumb...94 D3
Silfield Norfk...64 G2
Silian Cerdgn...43 L3
Silkstead Hants...22 D10
Silkstone Barns...90 H9
Silkstone Common Barns...90 H10
Silk Willoughby Lincs...73 R2
Silloth Cumb...109 P10
Silpho N York...99 K1
Silsden C Brad...96 F11
Silsoe C Beds...50 C3
Silton Dorset...20 D8
Silverburn Mdloth...127 N5
Silverdale Lancs...95 K6
Silverdale Staffs...70 E5
Silver End Essex...52 D7
Silverford Abers...159 J5
Silvergate Norfk...76 H6
Silverley's Green Suffk...65 K6
Silverstone Nhants...48 H5
Silver Street Kent...38 E9
Silver Street Somset...19 N9
Silverton Devon...9 M4
Silverwell Cnwll...3 K4
Silvington Shrops...57 L9
Simister Bury...82 H4
Simmondley Derbys...83 M5
Simonburn Nthumb...112 C6
Simonsbath Somset...17 N5
Simonstone Lancs...89 M4
Simonstone N York...96 D3
Simprim Border...129 J11
Simpson M Keyn...49 N7
Simpson Cross Pembks...40 G6

nclair's Hill Border....129 L9
nclairston E Ayrs 115 J4
nderby N York....97 M4
nderhope Nthumb....112 B10
nderland Green Traffd....82 K7
ndlesham Wokham....35 L11
nfin C Derb....72 A4
ngle Street Gt Lon....37 K9
ngleton Kent....26 H3
ngleton Lancs....88 D3
ngleton W Susx....15 N4
nglewell Kent....37 G6
nkhurst Green Kent....26 D3
nnarhard Abers....150 D5
nnington N York....98 E3
nope Leics....72 C7
nton Worcs....46 F2
nton Worcs....46 F2
nton Green Worcs....46 F2
nson Gt Lon....36 C5
nhowy Blae G....30 D2
ssinghurst Kent....26 C4
ston S Glos....32 C9
scott Devon....5 P3
chney Cnwll....2 G8
chney Common Cnwll....2 G8
chney Green Cnwll....2 G8
ctingbourne Kent....38 F9
ck Ashes Shrops....57 P7
ck Bells Blae G....30 H4
ckhills Lincs....86 G3
ck Mile Bottom Cambs....63 J9
ckmile Cottages Kent....27 K3
ckpenny Handley Dorset....21 J11
k Rues Jersey....11 b1
rewell Suffk....65 P9
aill Ork....169 e6
ara Brae Ork....169 b5
ares E Ayrs....115 K4
ateraw Abers....151 N9
ateraw E Loth....129 J5
eabost Highld....152 G8
eeby N York....103 N10
effington Leics....73 J10
effling E R Yk....93 Q7
egby Notts....84 G8
egby Notts....85 N7
egness Lincs....87 Q8
elbo Highld....162 H7
elbo Street Highld....162 H8
elbrooke Donc....91 N8
eldyke Lincs....74 F3
ellingthorpe Lincs....86 B6
ellorn Green Ches E....83 K8
ellow Donc....91 N8
elmanthorpe Kirk....90 G8
elmersdale Lancs....88 F9
elmorlie N Ayrs....124 F4
elpick Highld....166 B5
elston D & G....108 H3
elton C York....98 B9
elton Cumb....101 M8
elton E R Yk....92 C5
elton N York....103 L10
elton R & Cl....105 J7
elton on Ure N York....97 N7
elwith Bridge Cumb....101 K10
endleby Lincs....87 M7
ene House Abers....151 K5
enfrith Mons....45 P10
erne E R Yk....99 L9
erray Highld....165 Q4
erricha Highld....164 F6
erries Airport Shet....169 t6
erton Lancs....95 K8
etchley Leics....59 P6
etty Swans....28 H6
ewen Neath....29 K5
ewsby N York....98 C6
eyton Norfk....77 J6
eyton Corner Norfk....77 K6
all Highld....166 N3
dbrooke Lincs....87 M2
dbrooke North End Lincs....93 R11
dby E R Yk....92 H4
igersta W Isls....168 k1
ilgate Somset....18 C9
illington Lincs....73 M5
inburness Cumb....109 P9
inidin N York....97 J4
inners Green W Berk....34 D11
inningrove N Ayrs....105 K7
ipness Ag & B....123 R8
ipper's Bridge D & G....110 G4
iprigg Cumb....110 G11
ipsea E R Yk....99 P10
ipsea Brough E R Yk....99 P10
ipton N York....96 E10
ipton-on-Swale N York....97 N5
ipwith N York....91 R3
irlaugh E R Yk....93 K3
irling Border....116 F3
irmett Bucks....35 L6
irpenbeck E R Yk....98 E9
irwith Cumb....102 B4
irwith N York....95 Q6
irza Highld....167 Q3
itby Cumb....110 H7
ittle Green Bucks....35 L4
okholm Island Pembks....40 D10
omer Island Pembks....40 D9
ulamus Highld....145 L3
yborry Green Shrops....56 D10
ye Green Essex....52 E7
ye of Curr Highld....148 H3
yreholme N York....96 G8
ck Calder....90 B5
ckcote Oldham....90 B9
ck Head Cumb....95 K5
cks of Cairnbanno Abers....159 K8
d Gloucs....32 G3
de Devon....10 C3
de Devon....17 J2
de Devon....17 Q6
de Oxon....34 G6
de Green Gt Lon....37 M5
de Heath Staffs....58 D3
de Hooton Rothm....84 H3
desbrook Cnwll....4 G7
iggburn Lancs....95 Q10
ithwaite Kirk....90 D8
ley Derbys....84 C9
ley Nthumb....112 E9

Slamannan Falk....126 F3
Slapton Bucks....49 P10
Slapton Devon....7 L9
Slapton Nhants....48 H5
Slattocks Rochdl....89 P9
Slaugham W Susx....24 G5
Slaughterford Wilts....32 F10
Slawston Leics....60 G2
Sleaford Hants....23 M7
Sleaford Lincs....86 E11
Sleagill Cumb....101 Q2
Sleap Shrops....69 N9
Sleapford Wrekin....70 A11
Sleapshyde Herts....50 E9
Sleasdairidh Highld....162 E7
Slebech Pembks....41 K7
Sledge Green Worcs....46 F8
Sledmere E R Yk....99 J8
Sleetbeck Cumb....111 K5
Sleight Dorset....12 G5
Sleightholme Dur....103 J8
Sleights N York....105 N9
Slepe Dorset....12 F6
Slickly Highld....167 N3
Sliddery N Ayrs....120 H7
Sligachan Highld....144 G2
Sligrachan Ag & B....131 P9
Slimbridge Gloucs....32 D4
Slindon Staffs....70 E8
Slindon W Susx....15 Q5
Slinfold W Susx....24 D4
Sling Gwynd....79 L11
Slingsby N York....98 D6
Slip End C Beds....50 C7
Slip End Herts....50 G3
Slipton Nhants....61 L5
Slitting Mill Staffs....71 J11
Slockavullin Ag & B....130 G8
Sloley Norfk....77 K7
Sloncombe Devon....8 H7
Sloothby Lincs....87 N6
Slough Slough....35 Q9
Slough Crematorium Bucks....35 Q8
Slough Green Somset....19 J11
Slough Green W Susx....24 G5
Slumbay Highld....154 A10
Slyfield Green Surrey....23 Q4
Slyne Lancs....95 K7
Smailholm Border....118 B3
Smallbridge Rochdl....89 Q7
Smallbrook Devon....9 L5
Smallbrook Gloucs....31 Q4
Smallburgh Norfk....77 L7
Smalldale Derbys....83 N9
Smalldale Derbys....83 Q8
Small Dole W Susx....24 F8
Smalley Derbys....72 C2
Smalley Common Derbys....72 C2
Smalley Green Derbys....72 C2
Smallfield Surrey....24 H2
Small Heath Birm....58 H7
Small Hythe Kent....26 E5
Smallridge Devon....10 G4
Smallthorne C Stke....70 F4
Smallways N York....103 M8
Smallwood Ches E....70 E2
Small Wood Hey Lancs....94 H11
Smallworth Norfk....64 E5
Smannell Hants....22 C5
Smardale Cumb....102 D9
Smarden Kent....26 E3
Smarden Bell Kent....26 E3
Smart's Hill Kent....25 M2
Smeafield Nthumb....119 L3
Smearisary Highld....138 A2
Smeatharpe Devon....10 D2
Smeeth Kent....27 J4
Smeeton Westerby Leics....60 E2
Smelthouses N York....97 J8
Smerral Highld....167 L10
Smestow Staffs....58 C6
Smethwick Sandw....58 F7
Smethwick Green Ches E....70 E2
Smisby Derbys....72 A7
Smitheclose IoW....14 F8
Smith End Green Worcs....46 E4
Smithfield Cumb....110 H7
Smith Green Lancs....95 K9
Smithies Barns....91 K9
Smithincott Devon....9 Q2
Smith's Green Essex....51 K3
Smith's Green Essex....51 N6
Smithstown Highld....160 B11
Smithton Highld....156 C8
Smithy Bridge Rochdl....89 Q7
Smithy Green Ches E....82 F10
Smithy Green Stockp....83 J7
Smithy Houses Derbys....84 E11
Smockington Leics....59 Q7
Smoo Highld....165 K3
Smythe's Green Essex....52 F8
Snade D & G....108 H3
Snailbeach Shrops....56 F4
Snailwell Cambs....63 K7
Snainton N York....99 J4
Snaith E R Yk....91 Q6
Snake Pass Inn Derbys....83 P6
Snape N York....97 L4
Snape Suffk....65 M10
Snape Green Lancs....88 D8
Snape Street Suffk....65 M10
Snaresbrook Gt Lon....37 K3
Snarestone Leics....72 A9
Snarford Lincs....86 D4
Snargate Kent....26 G6
Snave Kent....26 H6
Sneachill Worcs....46 H4
Snead Powys....56 E6
Sneath Common Norfk....64 H4
Sneaton N York....105 N9
Sneatonthorpe N York....105 P9
Snelland Lincs....86 E4
Snelson Ches E....82 H10
Snelston Derbys....71 M6
Snetterton Norfk....64 D3
Snettisham Norfk....75 N4
Snibston Leics....72 C8
Snig's End Gloucs....46 E9
Snitter Nthumb....119 K10
Snitterby Lincs....86 C2
Snitterfield Warwks....47 P3
Snitterton Derbys....84 C8
Snitton Shrops....57 K9
Snoadhill Kent....26 F3
Snodhill Herefs....45 L6
Snodland Kent....38 B9
Snoll Hatch Kent....37 Q10
Snowden Hill Barns....90 H10
Snowdon Gwynd....67 L4

Snowdon Kent....39 M11
Snowdonia National Park....67 Q9
Snow End Herts....51 K4
Snowshill Gloucs....47 L8
Snow Street Norfk....64 F5
Soake Hants....15 J4
Soar Cardif....30 E8
Soar Devon....7 J11
Soar Powys....44 D8
Soay Highld....144 F5
Soberton Hants....22 H11
Soberton Heath Hants....14 H4
Sockbridge Cumb....101 N5
Sockburn Darltn....104 B9
Sodom Denbgs....80 F10
Sodylt Bank Shrops....69 K7
Soham Cambs....63 J6
Soham Cotes Cambs....63 J5
Solas W Isls....168 d10
Solbury Pembks....40 G8
Soldon Devon....16 E9
Soldon Cross Devon....16 E9
Soldridge Hants....23 J7
Sole Street Kent....27 J2
Sole Street Kent....37 Q8
Solihull Solhll....59 J9
Sollers Dilwyn Herefs....45 N3
Sollers Hope Herefs....46 B8
Sollom Lancs....88 E9
Solva Pembks....40 F6
Solwaybank D & G....110 F5
Somerby Leics....73 K8
Somerby Lincs....93 J9
Somercotes Derbys....84 F10
Somerford Dorset....13 L6
Somerford Keynes Gloucs....33 K5
Somerley W Susx....15 M7
Somerleyton Suffk....65 P2
Somersal Herbert Derbys....71 L7
Somersby Lincs....87 K6
Somersham Cambs....62 E5
Somersham Suffk....53 J2
Somerton Oxon....48 E9
Somerton Somset....19 N9
Somerton Suffk....63 P10
Somerwood Shrops....57 K2
Sompting W Susx....24 E9
Sompting Abbotts W Susx....24 E9
Sonning Wokham....35 L9
Sonning Common Oxon....35 K8
Sonning Eye Oxon....35 K9
Sontley Wrexhm....69 K5
Sopley Hants....13 L5
Sopwell Herts....50 E9
Sopworth Wilts....32 F7
Sorbie D & G....107 M8
Sordale Highld....167 K4
Sorisdale Ag & B....136 H3
Sorn E Ayrs....115 L2
Sortat Highld....167 N4
Sotby Lincs....86 H5
Sots Hole Lincs....86 F8
Sotterley Suffk....65 N5
Soughton Flints....81 J11
Soulbury Bucks....49 N9
Soulby Cumb....101 N5
Soulby Cumb....102 D8
Souldern Oxon....48 F8
Souldrop Bed....61 L8
Sound Ches E....70 A5
Sound Muir Moray....157 R7
Soundwell S Glos....32 C9
Sourton Devon....8 D6
Soutergate Cumb....94 E3
South Acre Norfk....75 R8
South Alkham Kent....27 M3
Southall Gt Lon....36 D5
South Allington Devon....7 K11
South Alloa Falk....133 P9
Southam Gloucs....47 J9
Southam Warwks....48 D2
South Ambersham W Susx....23 P10
Southampton C Sotn....14 D4
Southampton Airport Hants....22 E11
Southampton Crematorium Hants....22 D11
South Anston Rothm....84 H4
South Ascot W & M....35 P11
South Ashford Kent....26 H3
South Baddesley Hants....14 C7
South Ballachulish Highld....139 K6
South Bank C York....98 B10
South Bank R & Cl....104 F6
South Barrow Somset....20 B9
South Beddington Gt Lon....36 G8
South Beer Cnwll....5 N3
South Benfleet Essex....38 C4
South Bockhampton Dorset....13 L5
Southborough Gt Lon....37 K7
Southborough Kent....25 N2
Southbourne Bmouth....13 K6
Southbourne W Susx....15 L5
South Bowood Dorset....11 J5
South Bramwith Donc....91 Q8
South Brent Devon....6 H6
South Brewham Somset....20 D7
South Bristol Crematorium Bristl....31 Q11
South Broomhill Nthumb....119 P11
Southburgh Norfk....76 E10
South Burlingham Norfk....77 M10
Southburn E R Yk....99 K10
South Cadbury Somset....20 B9
South Carlton Lincs....86 B5
South Carlton Notts....85 J4
South Cave E R Yk....92 F4
South Cerney Gloucs....33 K5
South Chailey E Susx....25 J7
South Chard Somset....10 G3
South Charlton Nthumb....119 N6
South Cheriton Somset....20 C10
South Church Dur....103 P5
Southchurch Sthend....38 F4
South Cleatlam Dur....103 M7
South Cliffe E R Yk....92 E3
South Clifton Notts....85 P6
South Cockerington Lincs....87 L3
South Cornelly Brdgnd....29 M8
Southcott Cnwll....5 K2
Southcott Devon....8 D5
Southcott Devon....9 J8

Southcott Devon....16 G8
Southcott Wilts....21 N3
Southcourt Bucks....35 M2
South Cove Suffk....65 P5
South Creake Norfk....76 B4
South Crosland Kirk....90 E8
South Croxton Leics....72 H8
South Dalton E R Yk....99 K11
South Darenth Kent....37 N7
South Dell W Isls....168 j1
South Downs National Park....25 J9
South Duffield N York....92 A4
South Earlswood Surrey....36 G11
Southease E Susx....25 K9
South Elkington Lincs....87 J3
South Elmsall Wakefd....91 M8
Southend Ag & B....120 C10
South End E R Yk....93 J2
South End Hants....21 M11
South End Herefs....46 D6
South End N Linc....93 K6
South End Norfk....64 D3
Southend Wilts....33 N10
Southend Airport Essex....38 E4
Southend Crematorium Sthend....38 E4
Southend-on-Sea Sthend....38 E4
Southernby Cumb....101 L3
Southernden Kent....26 E2
Southerndown V Glam....29 N10
Southerness D & G....109 L10
South Erradale Highld....153 N3
Southerton Devon....10 B6
Southery Norfk....63 K2
South Essex Crematorium Gt Lon....37 N3
South Fambridge Essex....38 E3
South Fawley W Berk....34 C8
South Ferriby N Linc....92 G6
South Field E R Yk....92 H5
Southfield Falk....126 E3
Southfleet Kent....37 P6
Southgate Gt Lon....36 G2
Southgate Norfk....75 N4
Southgate Norfk....76 B4
Southgate Norfk....76 G7
Southgate Swans....28 G7
South Godstone Surrey....37 J11
South Gorley Hants....13 L2
South Gosforth N u Ty....113 K7
South Green Essex....37 Q2
South Green Essex....52 H8
South Green Kent....38 E9
South Green Norfk....76 F9
South Green Norfk....64 H6
South Gyle C Edin....127 M3
South Hanningfield Essex....38 B2
South Harting W Susx....23 L11
South Hayling Hants....15 K7
South Hazelrigg Nthumb....119 L4
South Heath Bucks....35 P4
South Heighton E Susx....25 K10
South Hetton Dur....113 N11
South Hiendley Wakefd....91 K8
South Hill Cnwll....5 N7
South Hill Somset....19 N9
South Hinksey Oxon....34 F4
South Hole Devon....16 C7
South Holmwood Surrey....24 E2
South Hornchurch Gt Lon....37 M4
South Horrington Somset....19 Q5
South Huish Devon....6 H10
South Hykeham Lincs....86 B8
South Hylton Sundld....113 N9
Southill C Beds....50 E2
Southington Hants....22 F5
South Kelsey Lincs....92 H11
South Kessock Highld....156 B8
South Killingholme N Linc....93 K6
South Kilvington N York....97 P4
South Kilworth Leics....60 D4
South Kirkby Wakefd....91 L8
South Knighton Devon....7 J3
South Kyme Lincs....86 G11
South Lanarkshire Crematorium S Lans....126 B6
South Leicestershire Crematorium Leics....72 F11
Southleigh Devon....10 E6
South Leigh Oxon....34 C3
South Leverton Notts....85 N4
South Lincolnshire Crematorium Lincs....74 D5
South Littleton Worcs....47 L5
South London Crematorium Gt Lon....36 G7
South Lopham Norfk....64 E5
South Luffenham Rutlnd....73 N10
South Lynn Norfk....75 M7
South Malling E Susx....25 K8
South Marston Swindn....33 N7
South Merstham Surrey....36 G10
South Middleton Nthumb....119 J6
South Milford N York....91 M4
South Milton Devon....6 J10
South Mimms Herts....50 F10
South Mimms Services Herts....50 F10
Southminster Essex....38 G2
South Molton Devon....17 N6
South Moor Dur....113 J10
Southmoor Oxon....34 C5
South Moreton Oxon....34 G7
Southmuir Angus....142 F7
South Mundham W Susx....15 N6
South Muskham Notts....85 N9
South Newbald E R Yk....92 G4
South Newington Oxon....48 D8
South Newton Wilts....21 L8
South Normanton Derbys....84 F9
South Norwood Gt Lon....36 H7
South Nutfield Surrey....36 H11
South Ockendon Thurr....37 N4
Southoe Cambs....61 Q8
Southolt Suffk....64 H7
South Ormsby Lincs....87 L5
Southorpe C Pete....74 A10
South Ossett Wakefd....90 H7
South Otterington N York....97 N3
Southover Dorset....11 N3
Southover E Susx....25 Q5

South Owersby Lincs....86 E2
Southowram Calder....90 E6
South Oxfordshire Crematorium Oxon....34 D6
South Park Surrey....36 F11
South Perrott Dorset....11 K3
South Petherton Somset....19 M11
South Petherwin Cnwll....5 N5
South Pill Cnwll....5 Q10
South Pool Devon....7 K10
South Poorton Dorset....11 L5
Southport Sefton....88 C7
Southport Crematorium Lancs....88 D8
South Queensferry C Edin....127 L2
South Radworthy Devon....17 N5
South Rauceby Lincs....86 D11
South Raynham Norfk....76 B7
South Reddish Stockp....83 J6
Southrepps Norfk....77 K4
South Reston Lincs....87 M4
Southrey Lincs....86 F7
South Ronaldsay Ork....169 d10
Southrop Gloucs....33 N4
South Runcton Norfk....75 M9
South Scarle Notts....85 P8
Southsea C Port....15 J7
Southsea Wrexhm....69 K4
South Shian Ag & B....138 G9
South Shields S Tyne....113 N7
South Shields Crematorium S Tyne....113 M8
South Shore Bpool....88 C4
Southside Dur....103 M5
South Somercotes Lincs....87 M2
South Stainley N York....97 M8
South Stifford Thurr....37 N5
South Stoke BaNES....20 D2
South Stoke Oxon....34 G8
South Stoke W Susx....24 B9
South Stour Kent....26 H4
South Street Kent....37 P8
South Street Kent....39 J10
South Street Kent....39 K8
South Tarbrax S Lans....127 J7
South Tawton Devon....8 G6
South Tehidy Cnwll....2 G6
South Thoresby Lincs....87 M5
South Thorpe Dur....103 M8
South Town Hants....23 J7
Southtown Norfk....77 Q10
Southtown Somset....19 K11
South Uist W Isls....168 d14
Southwaite Cumb....110 H11
Southwaite Services Cumb....110 H11
South Walsham Norfk....77 M9
Southwark Gt Lon....36 H5
South Warnborough Hants....23 K5
Southwater W Susx....24 E5
Southwater Street W Susx....24 D5
Southway Somset....19 P6
South Weald Essex....37 N2
Southwell Dorset....11 P10
Southwell Notts....85 L10
South West Middlesex Crematorium Gt Lon....36 D6
South Weston Oxon....35 K5
South Wheatley Cnwll....5 L3
South Wheatley Notts....85 N3
Southwick Hants....14 H5
Southwick Nhants....61 M2
Southwick Somset....19 L5
Southwick Sundld....113 N9
Southwick W Susx....24 F9
Southwick Wilts....20 F3
South Widcombe BaNES....19 Q3
South Wigston Leics....72 F11
South Willesborough Kent....26 H3
South Willingham Lincs....86 G4
South Wingate Dur....104 D4
South Wingfield Derbys....84 E9
South Witham Lincs....73 N7
Southwold Suffk....65 Q6
South Wonston Hants....22 E7
Southwood Norfk....77 M10
Southwood Somset....19 Q8
South Woodham Ferrers Essex....38 D2
South Wootton Norfk....75 M6
South Wraxall Wilts....20 F2
South Zeal Devon....8 G6
Sovereign Harbour E Susx....25 P10
Sowerby Calder....90 C6
Sowerby N York....97 P4
Sowerby Bridge Calder....90 D6
Sowerby Row Cumb....101 L3
Sower Carr Lancs....88 D2
Sowerhill Somset....18 A10
Sowhill Torfn....31 J4
Sowley Green Suffk....63 M10
Sowood Calder....90 D7
Sowton Devon....6 E5
Sowton Devon....9 N6
Soyland Town Calder....90 C6
Spa Common Norfk....77 K5
Spain's End Essex....51 Q3
Spalding Lincs....74 D6
Spaldington E R Yk....92 C4
Spaldwick Cambs....61 P6
Spalford Notts....85 P7
Spanby Lincs....74 A3
Spanish Green Hants....23 J3
Sparham Norfk....76 F8
Sparhamill Norfk....76 F8
Spark Bridge Cumb....94 G4
Sparket Cumb....101 M5
Sparkford Somset....20 B9
Sparkhill Birm....58 H8
Sparkwell Devon....6 F7
Sparrow Green Norfk....76 C9
Sparrowpit Derbys....83 N8
Sparrows Green E Susx....25 P4
Sparsholt Hants....22 D8
Sparsholt Oxon....34 B7
Spartylea Nthumb....112 C11
Spath Staffs....71 K7
Spaunton N York....98 E3
Spaxton Somset....18 H7
Spean Bridge Highld....139 G11
Spear Hill W Susx....24 D7
Spearywell Hants....22 B9
Speen Bucks....35 M5
Speen W Berk....34 E11

Speeton N York..........99 P6
Speke Lpool..........81 N8
Speldhurst Kent..........25 N2
Spellbrook Herts..........51 L7
Spelmonden Kent..........26 B4
Spelsbury Oxon..........48 B10
Spen Kirk..........90 F5
Spencers Wood Wokham..........35 K11
Spen Green Ches E..........70 E2
Spennithorne N York..........96 H3
Spennymoor Dur..........103 Q4
Spernall Warwks..........47 L2
Spetchley Worcs..........46 G4
Spetisbury Dorset..........12 F4
Spexhall Suffk..........65 M5
Spey Bay Moray..........157 R4
Speybridge Highld..........149 J2
Speyview Moray..........157 P9
Spilsby Lincs..........87 M7
Spindlestone Nthumb..........119 N4
Spinkhill Derbys..........84 G5
Spinningdale Highld..........162 F9
Spion Kop Notts..........85 J7
Spirthill Wilts..........33 J9
Spital Wirral..........81 L8
Spital Hill Donc..........85 K2
Spital in the Street Lincs..........86 C2
Spithurst E Susx..........25 K7
Spittal E Loth..........128 D4
Spittal E R Yk..........98 F10
Spittal Highld..........167 L6
Spittal Nthumb..........129 Q9
Spittal Pembks..........41 J6
Spittalfield P & K..........141 R9
Spittal of Glenmuick
  Abers..........149 Q10
Spittal of Glenshee P & K..........141 N4
Spittal-on-Rule Border..........118 A7
Spixworth Norfk..........77 J8
Splatt Cnwll..........4 F3
Splatt Cnwll..........5 L4
Splatt Devon..........8 F3
Splayne's Green E Susx..........25 K6
Splottlands Cardif..........30 H9
Spofforth N York..........97 N10
Spondon C Derb..........72 C3
Spon Green Flints..........69 J2
Spooner Row Norfk..........64 F2
Sporle Norfk..........76 A9
Spott E Loth..........128 H4
Spottiswoode Border..........128 G10
Spratton Nhants..........60 F7
Spreakley Surrey..........23 M6
Spreyton Devon..........8 G3
Spriddlestone Devon..........6 E8
Spridlington Lincs..........86 D4
Springburn C Glas..........125 Q4
Springfield D & G..........110 F7
Springfield Essex..........52 B10
Springfield Fife..........135 J5
Springhill Staffs..........58 E4
Springhill Staffs..........58 G3
Springholm D & G..........108 H6
Springside N Ayrs..........125 K10
Springthorpe Lincs..........85 Q3
Spring Vale Barns..........90 H10
Springwell Sundld..........113 L9
Springwood
  Crematorium Lpool..........81 N7
Sproatley E R Yk..........93 L4
Sproston Green Ches W..........82 F11
Sprotbrough Donc..........91 N10
Sproughton Suffk..........53 K3
Sprouston Border..........118 E3
Sprowston Norfk..........77 K9
Sproxton Leics..........73 M6
Sproxton N York..........98 C4
Spunhill Shrops..........69 M8
Spurstow Ches E..........69 Q3
Spyway Dorset..........11 L6
Square & Compass
  Pembks..........40 F7
Stableford Shrops..........57 P5
Stableford Staffs..........70 E7
Stacey Bank Sheff..........84 C2
Stackhouse N York..........96 B7
Stackpole Pembks..........41 J11
Stackpole Elidor Pembks..........41 J11
Stacksford Norfk..........64 F3
Stacksteads Lancs..........89 P6
Staddiscombe C Plym..........6 E8
Staddlethorpe E R Yk..........92 D5
Staden Derbys..........83 N10
Stadhampton Oxon..........34 H5
Stadhlaigearraidh W Isls..........168 c14
Staffield Cumb..........101 P2
Staffin Highld..........152 H4
Stafford Staffs..........70 G10
Stafford Crematorium
  Staffs..........70 H10
Stafford Services
  (northbound) Staffs..........70 F8
Stafford Services
  (southbound) Staffs..........70 F8
Stagsden Bed..........49 Q5
Stainborough Barns..........91 J10
Stainburn Cumb..........100 D5
Stainburn N York..........97 L11
Stainby Lincs..........73 N6
Staincross Barns..........91 J8
Staindrop Dur..........103 M6
Staines-upon-Thames
  Surrey..........36 B6
Stainfield Lincs..........74 A6
Stainfield Lincs..........86 F5
Stainforth Donc..........91 Q8
Stainforth N York..........96 B7
Staining Lancs..........88 C3
Stainland Calder..........90 D7
Stainsacre N York..........105 P9
Stainsby Derbys..........84 G5
Stainton Cumb..........95 L3
Stainton Cumb..........101 N5
Stainton Cumb..........110 C9
Stainton Donc..........85 J2
Stainton Dur..........103 J7
Stainton Middsb..........104 E8
Stainton N York..........103 M11
Stainton by Langworth
  Lincs..........86 E5
Staintondale N York..........105 Q11
Stainton le Vale Lincs..........86 G2
Stainton with Adgarley
  Cumb..........94 E6
Stair Cumb..........100 H6
Stair E Ayrs..........114 H3
Stairfoot Barns..........91 K9
Stairhaven D & G..........106 H7
Staithes N York..........105 L7
Stakeford Nthumb..........113 L3
Stake Pool Lancs..........95 J11

Stakes Hants..........15 J5
Stalbridge Dorset..........20 D11
Stalbridge Weston
  Dorset..........20 D11
Stalham Norfk..........77 M6
Stalham Green Norfk..........77 M7
Stalisfield Green Kent..........38 G11
Stalland Common Norfk..........64 E2
Stallen Dorset..........20 B11
Stallingborough NE Lin..........93 L8
Stalling Busk N York..........96 D3
Stallington Staffs..........70 G7
Stalmine Lancs..........94 H11
Stalmine Moss Side
  Lancs..........94 H11
Stalybridge Tamesd..........83 L5
Stambourne Essex..........52 B4
Stambourne Green
  Essex..........51 Q3
Stamford Lincs..........73 Q9
Stamford Nthumb..........119 P7
Stamford Bridge Ches W..........81 P11
Stamford Bridge E R Yk..........98 E3
Stamfordham Nthumb..........112 G6
Stamford Hill Gt Lon..........36 H3
Stanah Lancs..........88 D2
Stanborough Herts..........50 F8
Stanbridge C Beds..........49 Q10
Stanbridge Dorset..........12 H4
Stanbury C Brad..........90 C3
Stand Bury..........89 M9
Stand N Lans..........126 D4
Standburn Falk..........126 G3
Standeford Staffs..........58 D3
Standen Kent..........26 E5
Standen Street Kent..........26 D5
Standerwick Somset..........20 F4
Standford Hants..........23 M8
Standingstone Cumb..........100 E4
Standish Gloucs..........32 E3
Standish Wigan..........88 H8
Standish Lower Ground
  Wigan..........88 H9
Standlake Oxon..........34 C4
Standon Hants..........22 D9
Standon Herts..........51 J6
Standon Staffs..........70 E7
Standon Green End
  Herts..........51 J7
Standwell Green Suffk..........64 G8
Stane N Lans..........126 F6
Stanfield Norfk..........76 C7
Stanford C Beds..........50 E2
Stanford Kent..........27 K4
Stanford Shrops..........56 E2
Stanford Bishop Herefs..........46 C4
Stanford Bridge Worcs..........57 N11
Stanford Bridge E R Yk..........70 C10
Stanford Dingley W Berk..........34 G10
Stanford in the Vale
  Oxon..........34 B6
Stanford le Hope Thurr..........37 Q4
Stanford on Avon
  Nhants..........60 C5
Stanford on Soar Notts..........72 E6
Stanford on Teme Worcs..........57 N11
Stanford Rivers Essex..........51 M10
Stanfree Derbys..........84 G6
Stanghow R & Cl..........105 J7
Stanground C Pete..........74 D11
Stanhill Lancs..........89 L5
Stanhoe Norfk..........75 R3
Stanhope Border..........116 G5
Stanhope Dur..........103 J3
Stanhope Kent..........26 H3
Stanhope Bretby Derbys..........71 P10
Stanion Nhants..........61 K3
Stanklin Worcs..........58 C10
Stanley Derbys..........72 C2
Stanley Dur..........113 J10
Stanley Notts..........84 G8
Stanley P & K..........141 R11
Stanley Shrops..........57 N8
Stanley Staffs..........70 G4
Stanley Wakefd..........91 J6
Stanley Common Derbys..........72 C2
Stanley Crook Dur..........103 N3
Stanley Ferry Wakefd..........91 K6
Stanley Gate Lancs..........88 E9
Stanley Moor Staffs..........70 G4
Stanley Pontlarge
  Gloucs..........47 K8
Stanmer Br & H..........24 H9
Stanmore Gt Lon..........36 E2
Stanmore Hants..........22 E9
Stanmore W Berk..........34 E9
Stannersburn Nthumb..........111 P3
Stanningfield Suffk..........64 B10
Stanningley Leeds..........90 G4
Stannington Nthumb..........113 K5
Stannington Sheff..........84 C3
Stannington Station
  Nthumb..........113 K4
Stansbatch Herefs..........45 L2
Stansfield Suffk..........63 N10
Stanshope Staffs..........71 L4
Stanstead Suffk..........52 D2
Stanstead Abbotts Herts..........51 J8
Stansted Kent..........37 P8
Stansted Airport Essex..........51 N6
Stansted Mountfitchet
  Essex..........51 M5
Stanton Derbys..........71 P11
Stanton Gloucs..........47 L8
Stanton Mons..........45 L10
Stanton Nthumb..........112 H2
Stanton Staffs..........71 L5
Stanton Suffk..........64 D7
Stanton by Bridge
  Derbys..........72 B5
Stanton by Dale Derbys..........72 D3
Stanton Drew BaNES..........19 Q2
Stanton Fitzwarren
  Swindn..........33 N6
Stanton Harcourt Oxon..........34 D3
Stanton Hill Notts..........84 G8
Stanton in Peak Derbys..........84 B8
Stanton Lacy Shrops..........56 H7
Stanton Lees Derbys..........84 C8
Stanton Long Shrops..........57 K6
Stanton-on-the-Wolds
  Notts..........72 G4
Stanton Prior BaNES..........20 C2
Stanton St Bernard Wilts..........21 L2
Stanton St John Oxon..........34 G3
Stanton St Quintin Wilts..........32 H9
Stanton Street Suffk..........64 D8
Stanton under Bardon
  Leics..........72 D8
Stanton upon Hine
  Heath Shrops..........69 Q10

Stanton Wick BaNES..........20 B2
Stantway Gloucs..........32 D2
Stanwardine in the
  Field Shrops..........69 M10
Stanwardine in the
  Wood Shrops..........69 M9
Stanway Essex..........52 F7
Stanway Gloucs..........47 L8
Stanway Green Essex..........52 G7
Stanway Green Suffk..........65 J7
Stanwell Surrey..........36 C6
Stanwell Moor Surrey..........36 B6
Stanwick Nhants..........61 L6
Stanwick St John N York..........103 N8
Stanwix Cumb..........110 H9
Staoinebrig W Isls..........168 c14
Stape N York..........98 F2
Stapehill Dorset..........13 J4
Stapeley Ches E..........70 B5
Stapenhill Staffs..........71 P10
Staple Kent..........39 N10
Staple Cross Devon..........18 D10
Staplecross E Susx..........26 C7
Staplefield W Susx..........24 G5
Staple Fitzpaine Somset..........19 J11
Stapleford Cambs..........62 G10
Stapleford Herts..........50 H7
Stapleford Leics..........73 L7
Stapleford Lincs..........85 Q9
Stapleford Notts..........72 D3
Stapleford Wilts..........21 L7
Stapleford Abbotts
  Essex..........37 M2
Stapleford Tawney
  Essex..........51 M11
Staplegrove Somset..........18 H9
Staplehay Somset..........18 H10
Staple Hill Worcs..........58 E10
Staplehurst Kent..........26 C3
Staplers IoW..........14 F9
Staplestreet Kent..........39 J9
Stapleton Cumb..........111 K6
Stapleton Herefs..........56 E11
Stapleton Leics..........72 C11
Stapleton N York..........103 Q8
Stapleton Shrops..........56 H4
Stapleton Somset..........19 N10
Stapley Somset..........10 D2
Staploe Bed..........61 Q8
Staplow Herefs..........46 C6
Star Fife..........135 J7
Star IoA..........79 J10
Star Pembks..........41 P4
Star Somset..........19 M3
Starbeck N York..........97 M9
Starbotton N York..........96 E6
Starcross Devon..........9 N8
Stareton Warwks..........59 M10
Starkholmes Derbys..........84 D9
Starlings Green Essex..........51 L4
Starr's Green E Susx..........26 C8
Starston Norfk..........65 J5
Start Devon..........7 L10
Startforth Dur..........103 K7
Startley Wilts..........32 H8
Statenborough Kent..........39 P10
Statham Warrtn..........82 E7
Stathe Somset..........19 L9
Stathern Leics..........73 K4
Station Town Dur..........104 D3
Staughton Green Cambs..........61 P7
Staughton Highway
  Cambs..........61 P8
Staunton Gloucs..........31 Q2
Staunton Gloucs..........46 E9
Staunton in the Vale
  Notts..........73 L2
Staunton on Arrow
  Herefs..........45 M2
Staunton on Wye Herefs..........45 M4
Staveley Cumb..........94 H3
Staveley Cumb..........101 N11
Staveley Derbys..........84 F6
Staveley N York..........97 N8
Staverton Devon..........7 K6
Staverton Gloucs..........46 G10
Staverton Nhants..........60 B8
Staverton Wilts..........20 G2
Staverton Bridge Gloucs..........46 G10
Stawell Somset..........19 L7
Stawley Somset..........18 E10
Staxigoe Highld..........167 Q6
Staxton N York..........99 L5
Staylittle Cerdgn..........54 E7
Staylittle Powys..........55 K6
Staynall Lancs..........88 D2
Staythorpe Notts..........85 N10
Stead C Brad..........96 H11
Stean N York..........96 G6
Stearsby N York..........98 C6
Steart Somset..........19 J5
Stebbing Essex..........51 Q6
Stebbing Green Essex..........51 Q6
Stechford Birm..........58 H7
Stede Quarter Kent..........26 E4
Stedham W Susx..........23 N10
Steel Nthumb..........112 F9
Steel Cross E Susx..........25 M4
Steelend Fife..........134 C9
Steele Road Border..........111 K2
Steel Green Cumb..........94 D5
Steel Heath Shrops..........69 P7
Steen's Bridge Herefs..........45 Q3
Steep Hants..........23 K9
Steephill IoW..........14 F11
Steep Lane Calder..........90 C6
Steeple Dorset..........12 F8
Steeple Essex..........52 F11
Steeple Ashton Wilts..........20 H3
Steeple Aston Oxon..........48 E9
Steeple Barton Oxon..........48 D10
Steeple Bumpstead
  Essex..........51 Q2
Steeple Claydon Bucks..........49 K9
Steeple Gidding Cambs..........61 P4
Steeple Langford Wilts..........21 K7
Steeple Morden Cambs..........50 G2
Steep Marsh Hants..........23 L9
Steeton C Brad..........90 C2
Stein Highld..........152 D6
Stella Gatesd..........113 J8
Stelling Minnis Kent..........27 K2
Stembridge Somset..........19 M10
Stenalees Cnwll..........4 G10
Stenhouse D & G..........115 P9
Stenhousemuir Falk..........133 P11
Stenigot Lincs..........86 H4
Stenscholl Highld..........152 H4
Stenson Fields Derbys..........72 A4
Stenton E Loth..........128 G5
Steornabhagh W Isls..........168 j4

Stepaside Pembks..........41 M9
Stepford D & G..........109 J4
Stepney Gt Lon..........37 J4
Stepping Hill Stockp..........83 K7
Steppingley C Beds..........50 B3
Stepps N Lans..........126 B4
Sternfield Suffk..........65 M9
Stert Wilts..........21 K3
Stetchworth Cambs..........63 K9
Stevenage Herts..........50 F5
Steven's Crouch E Susx..........26 B8
Stevenston N Ayrs..........124 H3
Steventon Hants..........22 F5
Steventon Oxon..........34 E6
Steventon End Essex..........51 N2
Stevington Bed..........49 Q4
Stewartby Bed..........50 B2
Stewartfield S Lans..........125 Q6
Stewarton Ag & B..........120 C8
Stewarton E Ayrs..........125 L8
Stewkley Bucks..........49 N9
Stewley Somset..........19 K11
Stewton Lincs..........87 L3
Steyne Cross IoW..........14 H9
Steyning W Susx..........24 E8
Steynton Pembks..........40 H9
Stibb Cnwll..........16 C9
Stibbard Norfk..........76 D6
Stibb Cross Devon..........16 G9
Stibb Green Wilts..........21 P2
Stibbington Cambs..........74 A11
Stichill Border..........118 D3
Sticker Cnwll..........3 P3
Stickford Lincs..........87 L8
Sticklepath Devon..........8 F6
Sticklepath Somset..........18 D7
Stickling Green Essex..........51 L4
Stickney Lincs..........87 K9
Stiffkey Norfk..........76 D3
Stifford Clays Thurr..........37 P4
Stifford's Bridge Herefs..........46 D5
Stile Bridge Kent..........26 C2
Stileway Somset..........19 N6
Stilligarry W Isls..........168 c14
Stillingfleet N York..........91 P2
Stillington N York..........98 B7
Stillington S on T..........104 C6
Stilton Cambs..........61 Q3
Stinchcombe Gloucs..........32 D5
Stinsford Dorset..........11 Q6
Stiperstones Shrops..........56 F4
Stirchley Birm..........58 G8
Stirchley Wrekin..........57 M3
Stirling Abers..........159 R9
Stirling Stirlg..........133 M9
Stirling Castle Stirlg..........133 M9
Stirling Services Stirlg..........133 N10
Stirtloe Cambs..........61 Q7
Stirton N York..........96 E10
Stisted Essex..........52 D7
Stitchcombe Wilts..........33 P11
Stithians Cnwll..........3 J6
Stivichall Covtry..........59 M9
Stixwould Lincs..........86 G7
Stoak Ches W..........81 N10
Stobo Border..........116 H3
Stoborough Dorset..........12 F7
Stoborough Green
  Dorset..........12 F7
Stobs Castle Border..........117 Q9
Stobswood Nthumb..........119 P11
Stock Essex..........51 Q11
Stock N Som..........19 N2
Stockbridge Hants..........22 C7
Stockbriggs S Lans..........126 D10
Stockbury Kent..........38 D9
Stockcross W Berk..........34 D11
Stockdalewath Cumb..........110 H3
Stocker's Hill Kent..........38 G11
Stockerston Leics..........73 L11
Stock Green Worcs..........47 J3
Stocking Herefs..........46 B8
Stockingford Warwks..........59 M6
Stocking Pelham Herts..........51 L5
Stockland Devon..........10 E4
Stockland Bristol Somset..........18 H6
Stockland Green Kent..........25 N2
Stockleigh English
  Devon..........9 L3
Stockleigh Pomeroy
  Devon..........9 L4
Stockley Wilts..........33 J11
Stockley Hill Herefs..........45 M7
Stocklinch Somset..........19 L11
Stockmoor Herefs..........45 M4
Stockport Stockp..........83 J6
Stockport
  Crematorium Stockp..........83 K7
Stocksbridge Sheff..........90 H11
Stocksfield Nthumb..........112 G8
Stockton Herefs..........45 Q2
Stockton Norfk..........65 M3
Stockton Shrops..........56 D4
Stockton Shrops..........57 N5
Stockton Warwks..........48 D2
Stockton Wilts..........21 J7
Stockton Wrekin..........70 D11
Stockton Brook Staffs..........70 G4
Stockton Heath Warrtn..........82 D7
Stockton-on-Tees S on T..........104 D7
Stockton on Teme Worcs..........57 N11
Stockton on the Forest
  C York..........98 D9
Stockwell Gloucs..........32 H2
Stockwell End Wolves..........58 C4
Stockwell Heath Staffs..........71 K10
Stockwood Bristl..........32 B11
Stockwood Dorset..........11 M3
Stock Wood Worcs..........47 K3
Stoddat Lancs..........95 K9
Stodmarsh Kent..........39 M9
Stody Norfk..........76 F4
Stoer Highld..........164 B11
Stoford Somset..........11 L7
Stoford Wilts..........21 L7
Stogumber Somset..........18 E7
Stogursey Somset..........18 H6
Stoke Covtry..........59 N9
Stoke Devon..........16 C7
Stoke Hants..........15 K6
Stoke Hants..........22 D4
Stoke Medway..........38 D7
Stoke Abbott Dorset..........11 K4
Stoke Albany Nhants..........60 H3
Stoke Ash Suffk..........64 G8
Stoke Bardolph Notts..........72 G3
Stoke Bliss Worcs..........46 C2
Stoke Bruerne Nhants..........49 K5
Stoke-by-Clare Suffk..........52 C3
Stoke-by-Nayland Suffk..........52 G4

Stoke Canon Devon..........9 M[?]
Stoke Charity Hants..........22 E[?]
Stoke Climsland Cnwll..........5 [?]
Stoke Cross Herefs..........46 B[?]
Stoke D'Abernon Surrey..........36 D[?]
Stoke Doyle Nhants..........61 M[?]
Stoke Dry Rutlnd..........73 M[?]
Stoke Edith Herefs..........46 B[?]
Stoke End Warwks..........59 J[?]
Stoke Farthing Wilts..........21 L[?]
Stoke Ferry Norfk..........75 P[11]
Stoke Fleming Devon..........7 [?]
Stokeford Dorset..........12 E[?]
Stoke Gabriel Devon..........7 [?]
Stoke Golding Leics..........72 B[?]
Stoke Goldington
  M Keyn..........49 M[?]
Stoke Green Bucks..........35 Q[?]
Stoke Hammond Bucks..........85 N[?]
Stoke Hammond Bucks..........49 N[?]
Stoke Heath Shrops..........70 B[?]
Stoke Heath Worcs..........58 D[11]
Stoke Holy Cross Norfk..........77 J[?]
Stokeinteignhead Devon..........7 N[?]
Stoke Lacy Herefs..........46 B[?]
Stoke Lyne Oxon..........48 C[?]
Stoke Mandeville Bucks..........35 M[?]
Stokenchurch Bucks..........35 L[?]
Stoke Newington Gt Lon..........36 H[?]
Stokenham Devon..........7 L[?]
Stoke Orchard Gloucs..........46 H[?]
Stoke Poges Bucks..........35 Q[?]
Stoke Pound Worcs..........58 E[?]
Stoke Prior Herefs..........45 Q[?]
Stoke Prior Worcs..........58 D[?]
Stoke Rivers Devon..........17 L[?]
Stoke Rochford Lincs..........73 N[?]
Stoke Row Oxon..........35 J[?]
Stoke St Gregory Somset..........19 K[?]
Stoke St Mary Somset..........19 J[?]
Stoke St Michael Somset..........20 C[?]
Stoke St Milborough
  Shrops..........57 K[?]
Stokesay Shrops..........56 G[?]
Stokesby Norfk..........77 N[?]
Stokesley N York..........104 F[?]
Stoke sub Hamdon
  Somset..........19 N[11]
Stoke Talmage Oxon..........35 J[?]
Stoke Trister Somset..........20 D[?]
Stoke upon Tern Shrops..........70 B[?]
Stoke-upon-Trent C Stke..........70 F[?]
Stoke Wake Dorset..........12 C[?]
Stoke Wharf Worcs..........58 D[?]
Stolford Somset..........18 H[?]
Stondon Massey Essex..........51 N[10]
Stone Bucks..........35 L[?]
Stone Gloucs..........32 C[?]
Stone Kent..........37 N[?]
Stone Rothm..........85 J[?]
Stone Somset..........19 C[?]
Stone Staffs..........70 G[?]
Stone Worcs..........58 C[?]
Stonea Cambs..........62 G[?]
Stone Allerton Somset..........19 M[?]
Ston Easton Somset..........20 B[?]
Stonebridge N Som..........19 L[?]
Stonebridge Norfk..........64 C[?]
Stonebridge Warwks..........59 J[?]
Stone Bridge Corner
  C Pete..........74 E[1]
Stonebroom Derbys..........84 F[?]
Stone Chair Calder..........90 F[?]
Stone Cross E Susx..........25 M[?]
Stone Cross E Susx..........25 P[?]
Stone Cross E Susx..........25 P[?]
Stone Cross Kent..........25 P[?]
Stone Cross Kent..........27 L[?]
Stone Cross Kent..........39 P[?]
Stonecross Green Suffk..........63 N[?]
Stonecrouch Kent..........26 B[?]
Stone-edge-Batch
  N Som..........31 N[1]
Stoneferry C Kull..........93 K[?]
Stonefield Castle Hotel
  Ag & B..........123 C[?]
Stonegate E Susx..........25 C[?]
Stonegate N York..........105 L[?]
Stonegrave N York..........98 C[?]
Stonehall Worcs..........46 G[?]
Stonehaugh Nthumb..........111 P[?]
Stonehaven Abers..........151 M[?]
Stonehenge Wilts..........21 M[?]
Stone Hill Donc..........92 A[?]
Stonehouse C Plym..........6 D[?]
Stone House Cumb..........95 R[?]
Stonehouse Gloucs..........32 F[?]
Stonehouse Nthumb..........111 N[?]
Stonehouse S Lans..........126 C[?]
Stone in Oxney Kent..........26 F[?]
Stoneleigh Warwks..........59 M[11]
Stoneley Green Ches E..........69 R[?]
Stonely Cambs..........61 P[?]
Stoner Hill Hants..........23 K[?]
Stonesby Leics..........73 L[?]
Stonesfield Oxon..........48 C[1]
Stones Green Essex..........53 L[?]
Stone Street Kent..........37 N[?]
Stone Street Suffk..........52 H[?]
Stone Street Suffk..........65 N[?]
Stonethwaite Green Kent..........27 J[?]
Stonethwaite Cumb..........101 J[?]
Stonewells Moray..........157 P[?]
Stonewood Kent..........37 P[?]
Stoneybridge W Isls..........168 c[1]
Stoneybridge Worcs..........58 D[?]
Stoneyburn W Loth..........126 H[?]
Stoney Cross Hants..........13 N[?]
Stonegate C Leic..........72 G[?]
Stoneyhills Essex..........38 C[?]
Stoneykirk D & G..........106 E[?]
Stoney Middleton
  Derbys..........84 B[?]
Stoney Stanton Leics..........59 Q[?]
Stoney Stoke Somset..........20 D[?]
Stoney Stretton Somset..........20 H[?]
Stoney Stretton Shrops..........56 F[?]
Stoneywood C Aber..........151 M[?]
Stoneywood Falk..........133 M[?]
Stonham Aspal Suffk..........64 G[?]
Stonnall Staffs..........58 G[?]
Stonor Oxon..........35 L[?]
Stonton Wyville Leics..........73 J[?]
Stony Cross Herefs..........46 D[?]
Stony Cross Herefs..........57 M[?]
Stonyford Hants..........13 N[?]
Stony Houghton Derbys..........84 G[?]
Stony Stratford M Keyn..........49 [?]

Stonywell – Tan-y-Bwlch 295

onywell Staffs 58 G2
oodleigh Devon 17 M5
oodleigh Devon 18 B11
op 24 Services Kent 27 K4
opham W Susx 24 B7
opsley Luton 50 D6
optide Cnwll 4 E6
oreton Wirral 81 L8
oreyard Green Herefs 46 D6
orey Arms Powys 44 D10
ornoway W Isls 168 j4
ornoway Airport W Isls 168 j4
orridge Herefs 46 E5
orrington W Susx 24 C8
orth Cumb 95 K5
orwood E R Yk 92 B2
otfield Moray 157 N3
otfold C Beds 50 F3
ottesdon Shrops 57 M8
oughton Leics 72 G10
oughton Surrey 23 Q4
oughton W Susx 15 M4
oulton Worcs 46 H5
ourbridge Dudley 58 C8
ourbridge Crematorium Dudley 58 C8
ourhead Wilts 20 E8
ourpaine Dorset 12 E3
ourport-on-Severn Worcs 57 Q10
our Provost Dorset 20 E10
our Row Dorset 20 F10
ourton Leeds 91 J4
ourton Staffs 58 C8
ourton Warwks 47 Q7
ourton Wilts 20 E8
ourton Caundle Dorset 20 D11
out Somset 19 M8
ove Shet 169 r11
oven Suffk 65 N5
ow Border 117 P2
ow Lincs 85 Q4
ow Bardolph Norfk 75 M9
ow Bedon Norfk 64 D2
owbridge Norfk 75 M9
ow-cum-Quy Cambs 62 H8
owe Gloucs 31 Q3
owe Shrops 56 E10
owe by Chartley Staffs 71 J9
owehill Nhants 60 D9
owell Somset 20 C10
owey BaNES 19 Q3
owford Devon 8 B5
owford Devon 8 B7
owford Devon 10 C7
owford Devon 17 M3
owlangtoft Suffk 64 D8
ow Longa Cambs 61 P6
ow Maries Essex 38 D2
owmarket Suffk 64 E10
ow-on-the-Wold Gloucs 47 N9
owting Kent 27 K3
owting Common Kent 27 K3
owupland Suffk 64 F9
raanruie Highld 148 H4
rachan Abers 150 H9
rachur Ag & B 131 M7
radbroke Suffk 65 J7
radbrook Wilts 20 H4
radishall Suffk 63 N10
radsett Norfk 75 N9
ragglethorpe Lincs 86 B10
ragglethorpe Notts 72 H3
raight Soley Wilts 34 B10
raiton Mdloth 127 P4
raiton S Ayrs 114 G7
raloch Abers 151 M3
raloch P & K 141 P5
ramshall Staffs 71 K7
rang IoM 80 e6
rangeways Salfd 82 H5
rangford Herefs 46 A9
ranraer D & G 106 E5
rata Florida Cerdgn 54 G11
ratfield Mortimer W Berk 23 J2
ratfield Saye Hants 23 J2
ratfield Turgis Hants 23 J3
ratford C Beds 61 Q11
ratford Gt Lon 37 J4
ratford St Andrew Suffk 65 M9
ratford St Mary Suffk 52 H5
ratford sub Castle Wilts 21 M8
ratford Tony Wilts 21 L9
ratford-upon-Avon Warwks 47 P3
rath Highld 160 B11
rathan Highld 160 H2
rathan Highld 165 N4
rathaven S Lans 126 C9
rathblane Stirlg 125 P2
rathcanaird Highld 161 K6
rathcarron Highld 154 B9
rathcoil Ag & B 138 B11
rathdon Abers 150 B5
rathkinness Fife 135 M4
rathloanhead W Loth 126 G3
rathmashie House Highld 147 P9
rathmiglo Fife 134 G6
rathpeffer Highld 155 N6
rathtay P & K 141 M7
rathwhillan N Ayrs 121 K4
rathy Highld 166 D4
rathy Inn Highld 166 D3
rathyre Stirlg 132 H4
ratton Cnwll 16 C10
ratton Dorset 11 P6
ratton Gloucs 33 K4
ratton Audley Oxon 48 H9
ratton-on-the-Fosse Somset 20 C4
ratton St Margaret Swindn 33 N7
ratton St Michael Norfk 65 J3
ratton Strawless Norfk 77 J7
ream Somset 18 E7
reat E Susx 25 J7
reatham Gt Lon 36 H6
reatley C Beds 50 C5
reatley W Berk 34 G8
reet Devon 10 D7
reet Lancs 95 L10
reet N York 105 K10
reet Somset 19 N7
reet Ashton Warwks 59 Q8
reet Dinas Shrops 69 K7
Street End E Susx 25 P6
Street End Kent 39 K11
Street End W Susx 15 N7
Street Gate Gatesd 113 K9
Streethay Staffs 58 H2
Street Houses N York 98 A11
Streetlam N York 104 B11
Street Lane Derbys 84 E11
Streetly Wsall 58 G5
Streetly Crematorium Wsall 58 G5
Streetly End Cambs 63 K11
Street on the Fosse Somset 20 B7
Strefford Shrops 56 G7
Strelitz P & K 142 B10
Strelley Notts 72 E2
Strensall C York 98 C8
Strensham Worcs 46 H6
Strensham Services (northbound) Worcs 46 G6
Strensham Services (southbound) Worcs 46 H6
Stretcholt Somset 19 J6
Strete Devon 7 L9
Stretford Herefs 45 N3
Stretford Herefs 45 Q3
Stretford Traffd 82 G6
Strethall Essex 51 L3
Stretham Cambs 62 H6
Strettington W Susx 15 N5
Stretton Ches W 69 M4
Stretton Derbys 84 E8
Stretton Rutlnd 73 N7
Stretton Staffs 58 C2
Stretton Staffs 71 P9
Stretton Warrtn 82 D8
Stretton en le Field Leics 59 M2
Stretton Grandison Herefs 46 B6
Stretton-on-Dunsmore Warwks 59 P10
Stretton on Fosse Warwks 47 P7
Stretton Sugwas Herefs 45 P6
Stretton under Fosse Warwks 59 Q8
Stretton Westwood Shrops 57 K5
Strichen Abers 159 M6
Strines Stockp 83 L7
Stringston Somset 18 G6
Strixton Nhants 61 K8
Stroat Gloucs 31 Q5
Stroma Highld 167 Q1
Stromeferry Highld 153 R11
Stromness Ork 169 b6
Stronachlachar Stirlg 132 E5
Stronafian Ag & B 131 L11
Stronchrubie Highld 161 L3
Strone Ag & B 131 P11
Strone Highld 146 E11
Strone Highld 147 N2
Stronenaba Highld 146 G11
Stronmilchan Ag & B 131 P2
Stronsay Ork 169 f4
Stronsay Airport Ork 169 f4
Strontian Highld 138 E5
Strood Kent 26 E5
Strood Medway 38 B8
Strood Green Surrey 36 F11
Strood Green W Susx 24 B6
Stroud Gloucs 32 G3
Stroud Hants 23 K10
Stroude Surrey 36 B7
Stroud Green Essex 38 E3
Stroud Green Gloucs 32 F3
Stroxton Lincs 73 N4
Struan Highld 152 E10
Struan P & K 141 K4
Strubby Lincs 87 N4
Strumpshaw Norfk 77 L10
Strutherhill S Lans 126 D8
Struthers Fife 135 K6
Struy Highld 155 M9
Stryd-y-Facsen IoA 78 E8
Stryt-issa Wrexhm 69 J5
Stuartfield Abers 159 N8
Stubbers Green Wsall 58 F4
Stubbington Hants 14 G6
Stubbins Lancs 89 M7
Stubbs Green Norfk 65 K2
Stubhampton Dorset 12 F2
Stubley Derbys 84 D5
Stubshaw Cross Wigan 82 C5
Stubton Lincs 85 Q11
Stuckton Hants 13 L2
Studfold N York 96 B7
Stud Green W & M 35 N9
Studham C Beds 50 B7
Studholme Cumb 110 E9
Studland Dorset 12 H8
Studley Warwks 47 L2
Studley Wilts 33 J10
Studley Common Warwks 47 L2
Studley Roger N York 97 L7
Studley Royal N York 97 L6
Studley Royal Park & Fountains Abbey N York 97 L7
Stuntney Cambs 63 J5
Stunts Green E Susx 25 P8
Sturbridge Staffs 70 E8
Sturgate Lincs 85 Q3
Sturmer Essex 51 Q2
Sturminster Common Dorset 12 C2
Sturminster Marshall Dorset 12 G4
Sturminster Newton Dorset 12 C2
Sturry Kent 39 L9
Sturton N Linc 92 G10
Sturton by Stow Lincs 85 Q4
Sturton le Steeple Notts 85 N4
Stuston Suffk 64 G6
Stutton N York 91 M2
Stutton Suffk 53 L5
Styal Ches E 82 H8
Stydd Lancs 89 K3
Stynie Moray 157 Q5
Styrrup Notts 85 K2
Succoth Ag & B 132 B6
Suckley Worcs 46 D4
Suckley Green Worcs 46 D4
Sudborough Nhants 61 L4
Sudbourne Suffk 65 N11
Sudbrook Lincs 73 P2
Sudbrook Mons 31 P7
Sudbrooke Lincs 86 D5
Sudbury Derbys 71 M8
Sudbury Gt Lon 36 E3
Sudbury Suffk 52 E3
Sudden Rochdl 89 P8
Sudgrove Gloucs 32 H3
Suffield N York 99 K2
Suffield Norfk 77 J5
Sugdon Wrekin 69 R11
Sugnall Staffs 70 D8
Sugwas Pool Herefs 45 P6
Suisnish Highld 145 J4
Sulby IoM 80 e3
Sulgrave Nhants 48 G6
Sulham W Berk 34 H10
Sulhamstead W Berk 34 H11
Sulhamstead Abbots W Berk 34 H11
Sulhamstead Bannister W Berk 34 H11
Sullington W Susx 24 C8
Sullom Shet 169 q6
Sullom Voe Shet 169 r6
Sully V Glam 30 G11
Sumburgh Airport Shet 169 q12
Summerbridge N York 97 K8
Summercourt Cnwll 4 D10
Summerfield Norfk 75 Q3
Summerfield Worcs 58 B10
Summer Heath Bucks 35 K6
Summerhill Pembks 41 N9
Summerhill Staffs 58 G3
Summer Hill Wrexhm 69 K4
Summerhouse Darltn 103 P7
Summerlands Cumb 95 L3
Summerley Derbys 84 E5
Summersdale W Susx 15 N5
Summerseat Bury 89 M8
Summertown Oxon 34 F3
Summit Oldham 89 Q9
Summit Rochdl 89 Q7
Sunbiggin Cumb 102 C9
Sunbury-on-Thames Surrey 36 D7
Sundaywell D & G 108 H4
Sunderland Ag & B 122 B7
Sunderland Cumb 100 G3
Sunderland Lancs 95 J9
Sunderland Sundld 113 N9
Sunderland Bridge Dur 103 Q3
Sunderland Crematorium Sundld 113 N9
Sundhope Border 117 L5
Sundon Park Luton 50 C5
Sundridge Kent 37 L9
Sunk Island E R Yk 93 N7
Sunningdale W & M 35 Q11
Sunninghill W & M 35 P11
Sunningwell Oxon 34 E4
Sunniside Dur 103 M3
Sunniside Gatesd 113 K9
Sunny Brow Dur 103 N4
Sunnyhill C Derb 72 A4
Sunnyhurst Bl w D 89 K6
Sunnylaw Stirlg 133 M8
Sunnymead Oxon 34 F3
Sunton Wilts 21 P4
Surbiton Gt Lon 36 E7
Surfleet Lincs 74 E5
Surfleet Seas End Lincs 74 E5
Surlingham Norfk 77 L10
Surrex Essex 52 E7
Surrey & Sussex Crematorium W Susx 24 G3
Sustead Norfk 76 H4
Susworth Lincs 92 D10
Sutcombe Devon 16 E9
Sutcombemill Devon 16 E9
Suton Norfk 64 F2
Sutterby Lincs 87 L6
Sutterton Lincs 74 E3
Sutton C Beds 62 B11
Sutton C Pete 74 A11
Sutton Cambs 62 F5
Sutton Devon 7 J10
Sutton Devon 8 H4
Sutton Donc 91 P8
Sutton E Susx 25 L11
Sutton Gt Lon 36 G8
Sutton Kent 27 P2
Sutton N York 91 M5
Sutton Norfk 77 M7
Sutton Notts 73 K3
Sutton Oxon 34 D3
Sutton Pembks 40 H7
Sutton Shrops 57 J2
Sutton Shrops 57 N7
Sutton Shrops 69 L9
Sutton Shrops 70 B8
Sutton St Hel 82 B6
Sutton Staffs 70 D10
Sutton Suffk 53 P2
Sutton W Susx 23 Q11
Sutton Abinger Surrey 36 D11
Sutton-at-Hone Kent 37 N7
Sutton Bassett Nhants 60 G2
Sutton Benger Wilts 32 H9
Sutton Bingham Somset 11 L2
Sutton Bonington Notts 72 E6
Sutton Bridge Lincs 75 J6
Sutton Cheney Leics 72 C10
Sutton Coldfield Birm 58 H5
Sutton Coldfield Crematorium Birm 58 H5
Sutton Courtenay Oxon 34 F6
Sutton Crosses Lincs 74 H6
Sutton cum Lound Notts 85 L4
Sutton Fields Notts 72 D5
Sutton Green Surrey 36 B10
Sutton Green Wrexhm 69 M5
Sutton Howgrave N York 97 M5
Sutton-in-Ashfield Notts 84 G9
Sutton-in-Craven N York 90 C2
Sutton in the Elms Leics 60 B2
Sutton Lane Ends Ches E 83 K10
Sutton Maddock Shrops 57 N4
Sutton Mallet Somset 19 L7
Sutton Mandeville Wilts 21 J9
Sutton Manor St Hel 81 Q6
Sutton Marsh Herefs 45 R6
Sutton Montis Somset 20 B10
Sutton-on-Hull C KuH 93 K4
Sutton on Sea Lincs 87 P4
Sutton-on-the-Forest N York 98 B8
Sutton on the Hill Derbys 71 N8
Sutton on Trent Notts 85 N7
Sutton Poyntz Dorset 11 Q8
Sutton St Edmund Lincs 74 G8
Sutton St James Lincs 74 G7
Sutton St Nicholas Herefs 45 Q5
Sutton Scotney Hants 22 E7
Sutton Street Kent 38 D10
Sutton-under-Brailes Warwks 48 B7
Sutton-under-Whitestonecliffe N York 97 Q4
Sutton upon Derwent E R Yk 98 E11
Sutton Valence Kent 26 D2
Sutton Veny Wilts 20 H6
Sutton Waldron Dorset 20 G11
Sutton Weaver Ches W 82 B9
Sutton Wick BaNES 19 Q3
Sutton Wick Oxon 34 E6
Swaby Lincs 87 L5
Swadlincote Derbys 71 P11
Swaffham Norfk 75 R9
Swaffham Bulbeck Cambs 63 J8
Swaffham Prior Cambs 63 J8
Swafield Norfk 77 K5
Swainby N York 104 E10
Swainshill Herefs 45 P6
Swainsthorpe Norfk 77 J11
Swainswick BaNES 32 E11
Swalcliffe Oxon 48 C7
Swalecliffe Kent 39 K8
Swallow Lincs 93 L10
Swallow Beck Lincs 86 B7
Swallowcliffe Wilts 21 J9
Swallowfield Wokham 23 K2
Swallownest Rothm 84 G3
Swallows Cross Essex 51 P11
Swampton Hants 22 D4
Swanage Dorset 12 H9
Swanbourne Bucks 49 M9
Swanbridge V Glam 30 G11
Swancote Shrops 57 N6
Swan Green Ches W 82 F10
Swanland E R Yk 92 G5
Swanley Kent 37 M7
Swanley Village Kent 37 M7
Swanmore Hants 22 G11
Swannington Leics 72 C7
Swannington Norfk 76 G8
Swanpool Lincs 86 C7
Swanscombe Kent 37 P6
Swansea Swans 29 J6
Swansea Airport Swans 28 G6
Swansea Crematorium Swans 29 J5
Swansea West Services Swans 28 H5
Swan Street Essex 52 E6
Swanton Abbot Norfk 77 K6
Swanton Morley Norfk 76 E8
Swanton Novers Norfk 76 E5
Swanton Street Kent 38 E10
Swan Valley Nhants 60 F9
Swan Village Sandw 58 E6
Swanwick Derbys 84 F10
Swanwick Hants 14 F5
Swarby Lincs 73 Q2
Swardeston Norfk 77 J11
Swarkestone Derbys 72 B5
Swarland Nthumb 119 N10
Swarraton Hants 22 G7
Swartha C Brad 96 G11
Swarthmoor Cumb 94 F5
Swaton Lincs 74 B3
Swavesey Cambs 62 E7
Sway Hants 13 N5
Swayfield Lincs 73 P6
Swaythling C Sotn 22 D11
Sweet Green Worcs 46 B2
Sweetham Devon 9 L5
Sweethaws E Susx 25 M5
Sweetlands Corner Kent 26 C2
Sweets Cnwll 5 K2
Sweetshouse Cnwll 4 H9
Swefling Suffk 65 L9
Swepstone Leics 72 B8
Swerford Oxon 48 C8
Swettenham Ches E 82 H11
Swffryd Blae G 30 H5
Swift's Green Kent 26 E3
Swilland Suffk 64 H11
Swillbrook Lancs 88 F4
Swillington Leeds 91 K4
Swimbridge Devon 17 L5
Swimbridge Newland Devon 17 L5
Swinbrook Oxon 33 Q2
Swincliffe Kirk 90 G5
Swincliffe N York 97 K9
Swincombe Devon 17 M3
Swinden N York 96 C10
Swinderby Lincs 85 Q8
Swindon Gloucs 46 H9
Swindon Nthumb 119 J11
Swindon Staffs 58 C6
Swindon Swindn 33 M8
Swine E R Yk 93 K3
Swinefleet E R Yk 92 C6
Swineford S Glos 32 C11
Swineshead Bed 61 N7
Swineshead Lincs 74 D2
Swineshead Bridge Lincs 74 D2
Swiney Highld 167 M9
Swinford Leics 60 C5
Swinford Oxon 34 D3
Swingfield Minnis Kent 27 M3
Swingfield Street Kent 27 M3
Swingleton Green Suffk 52 G2
Swinhoe Nthumb 119 P5
Swinhope Lincs 93 M11
Swinithwaite N York 96 F3
Swinmore Common Herefs 46 C6
Swinscoe Staffs 71 L5
Swinside Cumb 100 H6
Swinstead Lincs 73 Q6
Swinthorpe Lincs 86 E4
Swinton Border 129 L10
Swinton N York 97 K5
Swinton N York 98 F6
Swinton Rothm 91 M11
Swinton Salfd 82 G4
Swithland Leics 72 F8
Swordale Highld 155 Q4
Swordland Highld 145 N9
Swordly Highld 166 B4
Sworton Heath Ches E 82 E8
Swyddffynnon Cerdgn 54 F11
Swyncombe Oxon 35 J6
Swynnerton Staffs 70 F7
Swyre Dorset 11 L7
Sycharth Powys 68 H9
Sychnant Powys 55 M9
Sychtyn Powys 55 M3
Sydallt Wrexhm 69 K3
Syde Gloucs 33 J2
Sydenham Gt Lon 37 J6
Sydenham Oxon 35 K4
Sydenham Damerel Devon 5 Q6
Sydenhurst Surrey 23 Q8
Syderstone Norfk 76 A5
Sydling St Nicholas Dorset 11 N5
Sydmonton Hants 22 E3
Sydnal Lane Shrops 57 Q3
Syerston Notts 85 M11
Syke Rochdl 89 P7
Sykehouse Donc 91 Q7
Syleham Suffk 65 J6
Sylen Carmth 28 F3
Symbister Shet 169 s7
Symington S Ayrs 125 K11
Symington S Lans 116 D3
Symondsbury Dorset 11 J6
Symonds Yat (East) Herefs 45 R11
Symonds Yat (West) Herefs 45 R11
Sympson Green C Brad 90 F3
Synderford Dorset 10 H4
Synod Inn Cerdgn 42 H4
Syre Highld 165 Q8
Syreford Gloucs 47 K10
Syresham Nhants 48 H6
Syston Leics 72 G8
Syston Lincs 73 N2
Sytchampton Worcs 58 B11
Sywell Nhants 60 H7

T

Tabley Hill Ches E 82 F9
Tackley Oxon 48 E11
Tacolneston Norfk 64 G2
Tadcaster N York 91 M2
Taddington Derbys 83 P10
Taddington Gloucs 47 L8
Taddiport Devon 16 H8
Tadley Hants 22 H2
Tadlow Cambs 62 C11
Tadmarton Oxon 48 C7
Tadwick BaNES 32 D10
Tadworth Surrey 36 F9
Tafarnaubach Blae G 30 F2
Tafarn-y-bwlch Pembks 41 L4
Tafarn-y-Gelyn Denbgs 68 G2
Taff's Well Rhondd 30 F8
Tafolwern Powys 55 K4
Taibach Neath 29 L7
Tain Highld 162 H10
Tain Highld 167 M3
Tai'n Lôn Gwynd 66 G4
Tairbeart W Isls 168 g7
Tai'r Bull Powys 44 D9
Takeley Essex 51 N6
Takeley Street Essex 51 M6
Talachddu Powys 44 F8
Talacre Flints 80 G8
Talaton Devon 9 Q5
Talbenny Pembks 40 F8
Talbot Green Rhondd 30 D8
Talbot Village Bmouth 13 J6
Taleford Devon 10 B5
Talerddig Powys 55 L4
Talgarreg Cerdgn 42 H4
Talgarth Powys 44 H8
Talisker Highld 152 E11
Talke Staffs 70 E4
Talke Pits Staffs 70 E4
Talkin Cumb 111 L9
Talladale Highld 154 B3
Talla Linnfoots Border 116 G6
Tallaminnock S Ayrs 114 H8
Tallarn Green Wrexhm 69 M6
Tallentire Cumb 100 F3
Talley Carmth 43 M8
Tallington Lincs 74 A9
Tallwrn Wrexhm 69 J5
Talmine Highld 165 N4
Talog Carmth 42 F9
Talsarn Cerdgn 43 K3
Talsarnau Gwynd 67 L7
Talskiddy Cnwll 4 E8
Talwrn IoA 78 H9
Talwrn Wrexhm 69 L5
Tal-y-bont Cerdgn 54 F7
Tal-y-Bont Conwy 79 P11
Tal-y-bont Gwynd 67 K10
Tal-y-bont Gwynd 79 L10
Talybont-on-Usk Powys 44 G10
Tal-y-Cafn Conwy 79 P10
Tal-y-coed Mons 45 N11
Tal-y-garn Rhondd 30 D9
Tal-y-llyn Gwynd 54 G3
Talysarn Gwynd 66 H4
Tal-y-Waun Torfn 31 J4
Talywern Powys 55 J4
Tamar Valley Mining District Devon 6 C5
Tamer Lane End Wigan 82 D4
Tamerton Foliot C Plym 6 D6
Tamworth Staffs 59 K4
Tamworth Green Lincs 74 G2
Tamworth Services Warwks 59 K4
Tancred N York 97 Q9
Tancredston Pembks 40 G5
Tandridge Surrey 37 J10
Tanfield Dur 113 J9
Tanfield Lea Dur 113 J10
Tangiers Pembks 41 J7
Tangley Hants 22 B4
Tangmere W Susx 15 P5
Tangusdale W Isls 168 b17
Tan Hill N York 102 G9
Tankerness Ork 169 e6
Tankersley Barns 91 J11
Tankerton Kent 39 K8
Tannach Highld 167 P7
Tannachie Abers 151 K11
Tannadice Angus 142 H6
Tanner's Green Worcs 58 G10
Tannington Suffk 65 J8
Tannochside N Lans 126 C5
Tansley Derbys 84 D9
Tansor Nhants 61 N2
Tantobie Dur 113 J10
Tanton N York 104 F8
Tanwood Worcs 58 D10
Tanworth in Arden Warwks 58 H10
Tan-y-Bwlch Gwynd 67 M6

Tan-y-fron Conwy 68 C2
Tan-y-fron Wrexhm 69 J4
Tan-y-grisiau Gwynd 67 M5
Tan-y-groes Cerdgn 42 E5
Taobh Tuath W Isls 168 e9
Taplow Bucks 35 P8
Tarbert Ag & B 123 L9
Tarbert Ag & B 123 Q6
Tarbert W Isls 168 g7
Tarbet Ag & B 132 C7
Tarbet Highld 145 N9
Tarbet Highld 164 E7
Tarbock Green Knows 81 P7
Tarbolton S Ayrs 114 H2
Tarbrax S Lans 127 J6
Tardebigge Worcs 58 E11
Tarfside Angus 142 H2
Tarland Abers 150 D7
Tarleton Lancs 88 F6
Tarlscough Lancs 88 E8
Tarlton Gloucs 33 J5
Tarnock Somset 19 L4
Tarns Cumb 109 P11
Tarnside Cumb 95 J2
Tarporley Ches W 69 Q2
Tarr Somset 17 R5
Tarrant Crawford Dorset 12 F4
Tarrant Gunville Dorset 12 F2
Tarrant Hinton Dorset 12 F2
Tarrant Keyneston Dorset 12 F4
Tarrant Launceston Dorset 12 F3
Tarrant Monkton Dorset 12 F3
Tarrant Rawston Dorset 12 F3
Tarrant Rushton Dorset 12 F3
Tarring Neville E Susx 25 K10
Tarrington Herefs 46 B6
Tarskavaig Highld 145 J5
Tarves Abers 159 L11
Tarvin Ches W 81 P11
Tarvin Sands Ches W 81 P11
Tasburgh Norfk 64 H2
Tasley Shrops 57 M6
Taston Oxon 48 C10
Tatenhill Staffs 71 N10
Tathall End M Keyn 49 M5
Tatham Lancs 95 N7
Tathwell Lincs 87 K4
Tatsfield Surrey 37 K9
Tattenhall Ches W 69 N3
Tatterford Norfk 76 B6
Tattersett Norfk 76 A6
Tattershall Lincs 86 H9
Tattershall Bridge Lincs 86 G9
Tattershall Thorpe Lincs 86 H9
Tattingstone Suffk 53 K4
Tattingstone White Horse Suffk 53 K4
Tatton Park Ches E 82 F8
Tatworth Somset 10 G3
Tauchers Moray 157 N8
Taunton Somset 18 H10
Taunton Deane Crematorium Somset 18 H10
Taunton Deane Services Somset 18 G10
Taverham Norfk 76 H9
Taverners Green Essex 51 N7
Tavernspite Pembks 41 N8
Tavistock Devon 6 D4
Tavistock Devon 6 D4
Taw Green Devon 8 G5
Tawstock Devon 17 K6
Taxal Derbys 83 M9
Tay Bridge C Dund 135 L2
Taychreggan Hotel Ag & B 131 L3
Tay Forest Park P & K 141 J5
Tayinloan Ag & B 123 L10
Taynton Gloucs 46 D10
Taynton Oxon 33 P2
Taynuilt Ag & B 139 J11
Tayport Fife 135 M2
Tayvallich Ag & B 130 E10
Tealby Lincs 86 G2
Tealing Angus 142 G10
Team Valley Gatesd 113 K9
Teangue Highld 145 L6
Teanord Highld 155 Q5
Tebay Cumb 102 B10
Tebay Services Cumb 102 B9
Tebworth C Beds 49 Q9
Tedburn St Mary Devon 9 K6
Teddington Gloucs 47 J8
Teddington Gt Lon 36 E6
Tedstone Delamere Herefs 46 C3
Tedstone Wafer Herefs 46 C3
Teesport R & Cl 104 F6
Teesside Crematorium Middsb 104 E7
Teesside Park S on T 104 E7
Teeton Nhants 60 E6
Teffont Evias Wilts 21 J8
Teffont Magna Wilts 21 J8
Tegryn Pembks 41 P4
Teigh Rutlnd 73 M7
Teigncombe Devon 8 G7
Teigngrace Devon 7 M4
Teignmouth Devon 7 N4
Teindside Border 117 N9
Telford Wrekin 57 M3
Telford Crematorium Wrekin 57 N2
Telford Services Shrops 57 N3
Tellisford Somset 20 F3
Telscombe E Susx 25 K10
Telscombe Cliffs E Susx 25 K10
Tempar P & K 140 G6
Templand D & G 109 N3
Temple Cnwll 5 J7
Temple Mdloth 127 Q6
Temple Balsall Solhll 58 K9
Temple Bar Cerdgn 43 K4
Temple Cloud BaNES 20 B3
Templecombe Somset 20 D10
Temple End Suffk 63 L10
Temple Ewell Kent 27 N3
Temple Grafton Warwks 47 M3
Temple Guiting Gloucs 47 L9
Temple Herdewyke Warwks 48 C4
Temple Hirst N York 91 Q6
Temple Normanton Derbys 84 F7
Temple of Fiddes Abers 151 L11
Temple Sowerby Cumb 102 B5
Templeton Devon 9 L2
Templeton Pembks 41 M8
Templetown Dur 112 H10

Tempsford C Beds 61 Q10
Tenbury Wells Worcs 57 K11
Tenby Pembks 41 M10
Tendring Essex 53 K7
Tendring Green Essex 53 K6
Tendring Heath Essex 53 K6
Ten Mile Bank Norfk 75 L11
Tenpenny Heath Essex 53 J7
Tenterden Kent 26 E5
Terling Essex 52 C8
Tern Wrekin 69 R11
Ternhill Shrops 70 A8
Terregles D & G 109 K5
Terrington N York 98 D6
Terrington St Clement Norfk 75 L6
Terrington St John Norfk 75 K8
Terry's Green Warwks 58 H10
Teston Kent 38 B11
Testwood Hants 14 C4
Tetbury Gloucs 32 G6
Tetbury Upton Gloucs 32 G5
Tetchill Shrops 69 L8
Tetcott Devon 5 N2
Tetford Lincs 87 K6
Tetney Lincs 93 P10
Tetney Lock Lincs 93 P10
Tetsworth Oxon 35 J4
Tettenhall Wolves 58 C4
Tettenhall Wood Wolves 58 C5
Teversal Notts 84 G8
Teversham Cambs 62 G9
Teviothead Border 117 N9
Tewin Herts 50 G7
Tewin Wood Herts 50 G7
Tewkesbury Gloucs 46 G8
Teynham Kent 38 G9
Thackley C Brad 90 F3
Thackthwaite Cumb 100 F6
Thackthwaite Cumb 101 M5
Thainstone Abers 151 K4
Thakeham W Susx 24 D7
Thame Oxon 35 K3
Thames Ditton Surrey 36 E7
Thamesmead Gt Lon 37 L4
Thamesport Medway 38 E7
Thanet Crematorium Kent 39 Q8
Thanington Kent 39 K10
Thankerton S Lans 116 D3
Tharston Norfk 64 H3
Thatcham W Berk 34 F11
Thatto Heath St Hel 81 Q6
Thaxted Essex 51 P4
Theakston N York 97 M3
Thealby N Linc 92 E7
Theale Somset 19 N5
Theale W Berk 34 H10
Thearne E R Yk 93 J3
The Bank Ches E 70 E3
The Bank Shrops 57 L5
The Beeches Gloucs 33 K4
Theberton Suffk 65 N8
The Blythe Staffs 71 J9
The Bog Shrops 56 F5
The Bourne Worcs 47 J3
The Braes Highld 153 J11
The Bratch Staffs 58 C6
The Broad Herefs 45 P2
The Broads 77 P10
The Brunt E Loth 128 H5
The Bungalow IoM 80 e4
The Burf Worcs 57 Q11
The Butts Gloucs 46 G11
The Camp Gloucs 32 H3
The Chequer Wrexhm 69 N6
The City Bed 61 P9
The City Bucks 35 L5
The Common Oxon 47 Q9
The Common Wilts 21 P8
The Common Wilts 33 K7
The Corner Kent 26 B3
The Cronk IoM 80 d2
Theddingworth Leics 60 E3
Theddlethorpe All Saints Lincs 87 N3
Theddlethorpe St Helen Lincs 87 N3
The Deep C KuH 93 J5
The Den N Ayrs 125 J7
The Forge Herefs 45 L3
The Forstal Kent 26 H4
The Fouralls Shrops 70 B8
The Green Cumb 94 D4
The Green Essex 52 C8
The Green N York 105 J8
The Green Wilts 20 G8
The Grove Worcs 46 G6
The Haven W Susx 24 C4
The Haw Gloucs 46 F9
The Headland Hartpl 104 F4
The Hill Cumb 94 D4
The Holt Wokham 35 M9
The Hundred Herefs 45 Q2
Thelbridge Cross Devon 9 J2
The Leacon Kent 26 G5
The Lee Bucks 35 P4
The Lhen IoM 80 e1
Thelnetham Suffk 64 E6
The Lochs Moray 157 Q5
Thelveton Norfk 64 H5
Thelwall Warrtn 82 E7
The Marsh Powys 56 E5
Themelthorpe Norfk 76 F7
The Middles Dur 113 K10
The Moor Kent 26 C6
The Mumbles Swans 28 H7
The Murray S Lans 125 Q7
The Mythe Gloucs 46 G8
The Narth Mons 31 P3
The Neuk Abers 151 J8
Thenford Nhants 48 F6
Theobald's Green Wilts 33 K11
The Quarry Gloucs 32 D5
The Quarter Kent 26 E3
The Reddings Gloucs 46 H10
Therfield Herts 50 H4
The Rhôs Powys 44 H8
The Ross P & K 133 M3
The Sands Surrey 23 N5
The Shoe Wilts 32 F10
The Smithies Shrops 57 M5
The Spring Warwks 59 L10
The Square Torfn 31 J5
The Stair Kent 37 P11
The Stocks Kent 26 F6
The Straits Bucks 35 N4
The Strand Wilts 20 H3
Thetford Norfk 64 B3
Thetford Forest Park 63 P3
Thethwaite Cumb 101 L2

The Towans Cnwll 2 F6
The Vauld Herefs 45 Q5
The Wyke Shrops 57 N3
Theydon Bois Essex 51 K11
Theydon Mount Essex 51 L11
Thicket Priory N York 92 A2
Thickwood Wilts 32 F10
Thimbleby Lincs 86 H6
Thimbleby N York 104 D11
Thingwall Wirral 81 K8
Thirkleby N York 97 Q5
Thirlby N York 97 Q4
Thirlestane Border 128 F10
Thirn N York 97 K3
Thirsk N York 97 P4
Thirtleby E R Yk 93 L4
Thistleton Lancs 88 E3
Thistleton Rutlnd 73 N7
Thistley Green Suffk 63 L5
Thixendale N York 98 G8
Thockrington Nthumb 112 E5
Tholomas Drove Cambs 74 H9
Tholthorpe N York 97 Q7
Thomas Chapel Pembks 41 M9
Thomas Close Cumb 101 M2
Thomastown Abers 158 E10
Thomas Town Warwks 47 L2
Thompson Norfk 64 C2
Thong Kent 37 Q6
Thongsbridge Kirk 90 F9
Thoralby N York 96 F3
Thoresby Notts 85 K6
Thoresthorpe Lincs 87 N5
Thoresway Lincs 93 L11
Thorganby Lincs 93 M11
Thorganby N York 92 A2
Thorgill N York 105 K11
Thorington Suffk 65 N7
Thorington Street Suffk 52 H4
Thorlby N York 96 E10
Thorley Herts 51 L7
Thorley IoW 14 C9
Thorley Houses Herts 51 L6
Thorley Street IoW 14 C9
Thormanby N York 97 Q6
Thornaby-on-Tees S on T 104 E7
Thornage Norfk 76 F4
Thornborough Bucks 49 K8
Thornborough N York 97 L5
Thornbury C Brad 90 F4
Thornbury Devon 16 G10
Thornbury Herefs 46 B3
Thornbury S Glos 32 B6
Thornby Cumb 110 E10
Thornby Nhants 60 E5
Thorncliff Staffs 71 J3
Thorncliffe Crematorium Cumb 94 D6
Thorncombe Dorset 10 H4
Thorncombe Street Surrey 23 Q6
Thorncott Green C Beds 61 Q11
Thorncross IoW 14 D10
Thorndon Suffk 64 G8
Thorndon Cross Devon 8 D6
Thorne Donc 92 A8
Thorne Coffin Somset 19 P11
Thornecroft Devon 7 K5
Thornehillhead Devon 16 G8
Thorner Leeds 91 K2
Thornes Staffs 58 G4
Thornes Wakefd 91 J7
Thorne St Margaret Somset 18 F10
Thorney Bucks 36 B5
Thorney C Pete 74 E10
Thorney Notts 85 Q6
Thorney Somset 19 M10
Thorney Hill Hants 13 M5
Thorney Island W Susx 15 L6
Thorney Toll Cambs 74 F10
Thornfalcon Somset 19 J10
Thornford Dorset 11 N2
Thorngrafton Nthumb 111 Q7
Thorngrove Somset 19 L8
Thorngumbald E R Yk 93 M5
Thornham Norfk 75 P2
Thornham Magna Suffk 64 G7
Thornham Parva Suffk 64 G7
Thornhaugh C Pete 73 R10
Thornhill C Sotn 14 E4
Thornhill Caerph 30 G8
Thornhill Cumb 100 D3
Thornhill D & G 116 B11
Thornhill Derbys 83 Q8
Thornhill Kirk 90 H7
Thornhill Stirlg 133 K7
Thornhill Lees Kirk 90 G7
Thornhills Calder 90 F6
Thornholme E R Yk 99 N8
Thornicombe Dorset 12 E4
Thornington Nthumb 118 G4
Thornley Dur 103 M3
Thornley Dur 104 C3
Thornley Gate Nthumb 112 B9
Thornliebank E Rens 125 P6
Thornsett Derbys 83 M7
Thorns Green Ches E 82 G8
Thornthwaite Cumb 100 H5
Thornthwaite N York 97 J9
Thornton Angus 142 F8
Thornton Bucks 49 K7
Thornton C Brad 90 D4
Thornton E R Yk 98 F11
Thornton Fife 134 H8
Thornton Lancs 88 C2
Thornton Leics 72 D9
Thornton Lincs 86 H7
Thornton Middsb 104 E8
Thornton Nthumb 129 P10
Thornton Pembks 40 H9
Thornton Sefton 81 L4
Thornton Curtis N Linc 93 J7
Thornton Garden of Rest Crematorium Sefton 81 L4
Thorntonhall S Lans 125 P6
Thornton Heath Gt Lon 36 H7
Thornton Hough Wirral 81 L8
Thornton-in-Craven N York 96 D11
Thornton in Lonsdale N York 95 P6
Thornton-le-Beans N York 97 N2
Thornton-le-Clay N York 98 D7
Thornton-le-Dale N York 98 H4
Thornton le Moor Lincs 92 H11
Thornton-le-Moor N York 97 N3

Thornton-le-Moors Ches W 81 N10
Thornton-le-Street N York 97 P3
Thorntonloch E Loth 129 K5
Thornton Rust N York 96 E3
Thornton Steward N York 97 J3
Thornton Watlass N York 97 K3
Thornwood Common Essex 51 L10
Thornydykes Border 128 G10
Thornythwaite Cumb 101 L6
Thoroton Notts 73 K2
Thorp Arch Leeds 97 P11
Thorpe Derbys 71 M4
Thorpe E R Yk 99 K11
Thorpe Lincs 87 N4
Thorpe N York 96 F8
Thorpe Norfk 65 N2
Thorpe Notts 85 N11
Thorpe Surrey 36 B7
Thorpe Abbotts Norfk 64 H6
Thorpe Acre Leics 72 E7
Thorpe Arnold Leics 73 K6
Thorpe Audlin Wakefd 91 M7
Thorpe Bassett N York 98 H6
Thorpe Bay Sthend 38 F4
Thorpe by Water Rutlnd 73 M11
Thorpe Common Rothm 91 K11
Thorpe Constantine Staffs 59 L3
Thorpe End Norfk 77 K9
Thorpe Green Essex 53 L7
Thorpe Green Lancs 88 H6
Thorpe Green Suffk 64 C11
Thorpe Hesley Rothm 91 K11
Thorpe in Balne Donc 91 P8
Thorpe Langton Leics 60 F2
Thorpe Larches Dur 104 C5
Thorpe Lea Surrey 36 B6
Thorpe le Fallows Lincs 86 B4
Thorpe-le-Soken Essex 53 L7
Thorpe le Street E R Yk 92 D2
Thorpe Malsor Nhants 60 H5
Thorpe Mandeville Nhants 48 F6
Thorpe Market Norfk 77 J4
Thorpe Marriot Norfk 76 H8
Thorpe Morieux Suffk 64 C11
Thorpeness Suffk 65 P10
Thorpe on the Hill Leeds 91 J5
Thorpe on the Hill Lincs 86 B7
Thorpe Park Surrey 36 B7
Thorpe St Andrew Norfk 77 K10
Thorpe St Peter Lincs 87 N8
Thorpe Salvin Rothm 84 H4
Thorpe Satchville Leics 73 J8
Thorpe Thewles S on T 104 C6
Thorpe Tilney Lincs 86 F9
Thorpe Underwood N York 97 Q9
Thorpe Underwood Nhants 60 G4
Thorpe Waterville Nhants 61 M4
Thorpe Willoughby N York 91 P4
Thorpland Norfk 75 M9
Thorrington Essex 53 J8
Thorverton Devon 9 M4
Thrales End C Beds 50 D7
Thrandeston Suffk 64 G6
Thrapston Nhants 61 L5
Threapland Cumb 100 G3
Threapland N York 96 E8
Threapwood Ches W 69 M6
Threapwood Staffs 71 J6
Threapwood Head Staffs 71 J6
Threave S Ayrs 114 F6
Three Ashes Herefs 45 Q10
Three Bridges W Susx 24 G3
Three Burrows Cnwll 3 J4
Three Chimneys Kent 26 D4
Three Cocks Powys 44 H7
Three Counties Crematorium Essex 52 C6
Three Crosses Swans 28 G6
Three Cups Corner E Susx 25 P6
Three Gates Worcs 46 C2
Threehammer Common Norfk 77 L8
Three Hammers Cnwll 5 L4
Three Holes Norfk 75 K10
Threekingham Lincs 74 A3
Three Leg Cross E Susx 25 Q4
Three Legged Cross Dorset 13 J3
Three Mile Cross Wokham 35 K11
Threemilestone Cnwll 3 K4
Three Miletown W Loth 127 K2
Three Oaks E Susx 26 D9
Threlkeld Cumb 101 K5
Threshers Bush Essex 51 L9
Threshfield N York 96 E8
Thrigby Norfk 77 P9
Thringarth Dur 102 H6
Thringstone Leics 72 C7
Thrintoft N York 97 M2
Thriplow Cambs 62 F11
Throapham Rothm 84 H3
Throckenhalt Lincs 74 G9
Throcking Herts 50 H4
Throckley N u Ty 113 J7
Throckmorton Worcs 47 J4
Throop Bmouth 13 K5
Throop Dorset 12 D6
Throphill Nthumb 112 H3
Thropton Nthumb 119 K10
Throsk Stirlg 133 P9
Througham Gloucs 32 H3
Throughgate D & G 109 J3
Throwleigh Devon 8 G6
Throwley Kent 38 G10
Throwley Forstal Kent 38 G11
Thrumpton Notts 72 E4
Thrumpton Notts 85 M4
Thrumster Highld 167 P7
Thrunscoe NE Lin 93 P9
Thrunton Nthumb 119 L8
Thrup Oxon 33 Q5
Thrupp Gloucs 32 G4
Thrupp Oxon 48 E11
Thrushelton Devon 8 C7
Thrussington Leics 72 H7
Thruxton Hants 21 Q5
Thruxton Herefs 45 N7
Thrybergh Rothm 91 M11
Thulston Derbys 72 C4

Thundersley Essex 38 C3
Thurcaston Leics 72 F8
Thurcroft Rothm 84 G4
Thurgarton Norfk 76 H5
Thurgarton Notts 85 L11
Thurgoland Barns 90 H11
Thurlaston Leics 72 E11
Thurlaston Warwks 59 Q11
Thurlbear Somset 19 J10
Thurlby Lincs 74 A8
Thurlby Lincs 86 B8
Thurlby Lincs 87 P7
Thurleigh Bed 61 N9
Thurlestone Devon 6 H10
Thurloxton Somset 19 J9
Thurlstone Barns 90 G11
Thurlton Norfk 65 N2
Thurlwood Ches E 70 E2
Thurmaston Leics 72 G9
Thurnby Leics 72 G10
Thurne Norfk 77 N8
Thurnham Kent 38 D10
Thurning Nhants 61 N4
Thurning Norfk 76 F6
Thurnscoe Barns 91 M9
Thurrock Services Thurr 37 P5
Thursby Cumb 110 F10
Thursden Lancs 89 P4
Thursford Norfk 76 D5
Thursley Surrey 23 P7
Thurso Highld 167 K3
Thurstaston Wirral 81 J8
Thurston Suffk 64 C8
Thurston Clough Oldham 90 C9
Thurstonfield Cumb 110 F9
Thurstonland Kirk 90 F8
Thurston Planch Suffk 64 C8
Thurton Norfk 77 L11
Thurvaston Derbys 71 N5
Thuxton Norfk 76 E10
Thwaite N York 102 H11
Thwaite Suffk 64 G8
Thwaite Head Cumb 94 G2
Thwaite St Mary Norfk 65 L2
Thwaites C Brad 90 D3
Thwaites Brow C Brad 90 D3
Thwing E R Yk 99 L6
Tibbermore P & K 134 C2
Tibbers D & G 116 B11
Tibberton Gloucs 46 F10
Tibberton Worcs 46 H3
Tibberton Wrekin 70 B10
Tibbie Shiels Inn Border 117 J4
Tibenham Norfk 64 G3
Tibshelf Derbys 84 F8
Tibshelf Services Derbys 84 F8
Tibthorpe E R Yk 99 K10
Ticehurst E Susx 25 Q4
Tichborne Hants 22 G8
Tickencote Rutlnd 73 P8
Tickenham N Som 31 N11
Tickford End M Keyn 49 N5
Tickhill Donc 85 J2
Ticklerton Shrops 56 H5
Ticknall Derbys 72 B6
Tickton E R Yk 93 K2
Tidbury Green Solhll 58 H9
Tidcombe Wilts 21 Q3
Tiddington Oxon 34 H4
Tiddington Warwks 47 P3
Tiddleywink Wilts 32 G9
Tidebrook E Susx 25 P5
Tideford Cnwll 5 P10
Tideford Cross Cnwll 5 N9
Tidenham Gloucs 31 Q5
Tideswell Derbys 83 Q9
Tidmarsh W Berk 34 H10
Tidmington Warwks 47 Q7
Tidpit Hants 21 L11
Tidworth Wilts 21 Q5
Tiers Cross Pembks 40 H8
Tiffield Nhants 49 J4
Tigerton Angus 143 J7
Tigh a Ghearraidh W Isls 168 c11
Tigharry W Isls 168 c11
Tighnabruaich Ag & B 124 B3
Tigley Devon 7 K6
Tilbrook Cambs 61 N7
Tilbury Thurr 37 P5
Tilbury Dock Thurr 37 P5
Tilbury Green Essex 52 B3
Tilbury Juxta Clare Essex 52 B3
Tile Cross Birm 59 J7
Tile Hill Covtry 59 M9
Tilehouse Green Solhll 59 J10
Tilehurst Readg 35 J10
Tilford Surrey 23 N6
Tilgate W Susx 24 G3
Tilgate Forest Row W Susx 24 G4
Tilham Street Somset 19 P8
Tillers Green Gloucs 46 C7
Tillicoultry Clacks 133 Q8
Tillietudlem S Lans 126 E8
Tillingham Essex 52 G11
Tillington Herefs 45 N5
Tillington W Susx 23 Q10
Tillington Common Herefs 45 P5
Tillybirloch Abers 150 H6
Tillyfourie Abers 150 H5
Tillygreig Abers 151 M3
Tillyrie P & K 134 E5
Tilmanstone Kent 39 P11
Tilney All Saints Norfk 75 K7
Tilney High End Norfk 75 K7
Tilney St Lawrence Norfk 75 K8
Tilshead Wilts 21 K6
Tilstock Shrops 69 P7
Tilston Ches W 69 N4
Tilstone Bank Ches W 69 Q3
Tilstone Fearnall Ches W 69 Q3
Tilsworth C Beds 49 Q9
Tilton on the Hill Leics 73 J9
Tiltups End Gloucs 32 F5
Tilty Essex 51 P5
Timberland Lincs 86 F9
Timbersbrook Ches E 70 F2
Timberscombe Somset 18 C6
Timble N York 97 J10
Timewell Devon 18 C9
Timpanheck D & G 110 E5
Timperley Traffd 82 G7
Timsbury BaNES 20 C3
Timsbury Hants 22 C9
Timsgarry W Isls 168 f4
Timsgearraidh W Isls 168 f4
Timworth Suffk 64 B7
Timworth Green Suffk 64 B8

ncleton Dorset.........12 C6
ndale Cumb.........111 M9
ngewick Bucks.........49 J8
ngley Leeds.........90 H5
ngrith C Beds.........50 B4
ngwell Ork.........169 d4
nhay Devon.........5 P4
nker's Hill Hants.........22 D5
nkersley Derbys.........84 C8
nsley Sheff.........84 F2
nsley Green W Susx.........24 C3
ntagel Cnwll.........4 H4
ntern Parva Mons.........31 P4
ntinhull Somset.........19 N11
ntwistle Derbys.........83 M5
nwald D & G.........109 M4
nwell Rutlnd.........73 Q9
ppacott Devon.........17 P2
pp's End Norfk.........75 K11
ptoe Hants.........13 N5
pton Sandw.........58 E6
pton Green Sandw.........58 E6
pton St John Devon.........10 B6
ptree Essex.........52 E8
ptree Heath Essex.........52 E8
rabad Powys.........44 B6
ree Ag & B.........136 C7
ree Airport Ag & B.........136 C7
retigan Ag & B.........123 M7
rley Gloucs.........46 F9
roran Ag & B.........137 M10
rphil Caerph.........30 F4
ril Cumb.........101 P5
r-y-fron Flints.........69 J3
sbury Wilts.........20 H9
sman's Common
  W Susx.........24 C4
ssington Derbys.........71 M4
tchberry Devon.........16 C6
tchfield Hants.........14 F5
tchfield Common
  Hants.........14 F5
tchmarsh Nhants.........61 M5
tchwell Norfk.........75 Q2
tchby Notts.........72 H3
tley Herefs.........45 L2
tmore Green Herts.........50 F5
tsey Surrey.........37 K10
tson Cnwll.........16 C11
ttensor Staffs.........70 F7
ttleshall Norfk.........76 B7
tton Worcs.........58 B11
verton Ches W.........69 Q2
verton Devon.........9 N2
vetshall St Margaret
  Norfk.........64 H4
vetshall St Mary Norfk.........64 H4
vington Somset.........18 B5
vy Dale Barns.........90 H9
xall Staffs.........70 H10
xover Rutlnd.........73 P10
ab Shet.........169 q12
adhole Derbys.........84 E9
admoor Derbys.........84 D10
bermory Ag & B.........137 N4
beronochy Ag & B.........130 E6
bha Mor W Isls.........168 c14
cher Abers.........158 G11
chieneal Moray.........158 D4
ckenham Wilts.........33 K9
ckenham Wick Wilts.........33 K8
cketts R & Cl.........104 H7
ckholes Bl w D.........89 K6
ckington S Glos.........32 B7
ckwith N York.........97 Q10
dber Dorset.........20 E11
dburn Nthumb.........119 M11
ddington C Beds.........50 B5
ddington Gloucs.........47 K8
ddington Services
C Beds.........50 B5
dds Green Herts.........50 F5
denham Gloucs.........47 P7
dhills Angus.........142 G10
dhills Cumb.........110 G8
dhills Dur.........103 P4
dhills Rest Area Cumb.........110 G8
dmorden Calder.........89 Q6
dwick Rothm.........84 G4
ft Cambs.........62 E9
ft Ches E.........82 G9
ft Lincs.........73 R7
ft Warwks.........59 Q10
ft Hill Dur.........103 N5
ft Hill Lincs.........86 H8
ft Monks Norfk.........65 N3
ft next Newton Lincs.........86 D3
ftrees Norfk.........76 B6
ftwood Norfk.........76 D9
gston Nthumb.........119 P10
kavaig Highld.........145 K5
kers Green Oxon.........35 K9
lastadh W Isls.........168 K3
ldish Cnwll.........4 E10
ll W Isls.........168 j4
lland Somset.........18 F8
llard Farnham Dorset.........21 J11
llard Royal Wilts.........20 H11
ll Bar Devon.........91 P9
ller Fratrum Dorset.........11 M5
ller Porcorum Dorset.........11 M5
llerton N York.........97 N4
llerton Notts.........72 G4
ller Whelme Dorset.........11 L4
llesbury Essex.........52 G9
lleshunt D'Arcy Essex.........52 F9
lleshunt Knights Essex.........52 F9
lleshunt Major Essex.........52 F9
llingham E R Yk.........92 D3
lpuddle Dorset.........12 C6
lsta W Isls.........168 k3
lworth Gt Lon.........36 E7
lmatin Hghld.........148 E2
lmchrasky Hghld.........146 H5
lmdoun Hghld.........146 F7
lmich Hghld.........147 J2
lmich Hghld.........155 P8
lmich Hghld.........156 B3
lmich Hghld.........162 E5
lmintoul Moray.........149 M4
lmlow Warwks.........48 D5
lnacross Hghld.........155 P9
lnavoulin Moray.........149 N2
lmpkin Staffs.........70 g4
n Mons.........31 K4
n Mons.........31 L5
nbridge Kent.........37 N11
ndu Brdgnd.........29 N8

Tonedale Somset.........18 F10
Ton fanau Gwynd.........54 D4
Tong C Brad.........90 G4
Tong Kent.........38 G10
Tong Shrops.........57 P3
Tonga W Isls.........168 j4
Tonge Lincs.........72 C6
Tong Green Kent.........38 G11
Tongham Surrey.........23 N4
Tongland D & G.........108 E10
Tong Norton Shrops.........57 P3
Tongue Highld.........165 N5
Tongue End Lincs.........74 C7
Tongwynlais Cardif.........30 F8
Tonmawr Neath.........29 M5
Tonna Neath.........29 L5
Ton-teg Rhondd.........30 F7
Tonwell Herts.........50 H7
Tonypandy Rhondd.........30 D6
Tonyrefail Rhondd.........30 D7
Toot Baldon Oxon.........34 G4
Toot Hill Essex.........51 M10
Toothill Hants.........22 C11
Toothill Swindn.........33 M8
Tooting Gt Lon.........36 G6
Tooting Bec Gt Lon.........36 G6
Topcliffe N York.........97 N5
Topcroft Norfk.........65 K3
Topcroft Street Norfk.........65 K3
Top End Bed.........61 M8
Topham Donc.........91 Q7
Top of Hebers Rochdl.........89 P9
Toppesfield Essex.........52 B4
Toprow Norfk.........64 H2
Topsham Devon.........9 N7
Torbeg N Ayrs.........120 G6
Torboll Highld.........162 H1
Torbreck Highld.........156 A9
Torbryan Devon.........7 L5
Torcastle Highld.........139 L2
Torcross Devon.........7 L10
Tore Highld.........155 R7
Torfrey Cnwll.........5 J11
Torinturk Ag & B.........123 P7
Torksey Lincs.........85 P5
Tormarton S Glos.........32 E9
Tormore N Ayrs.........120 G5
Tornagrain Highld.........156 D7
Tornaveen Abers.........150 G6
Torness Highld.........147 P2
Toronto Dur.........103 N4
Torpenhow Cumb.........100 H3
Torphichen W Loth.........126 H3
Torphins Abers.........150 G7
Torpoint Cnwll.........6 C7
Torquay Torbay.........7 N6
Torquay Crematorium
  Torbay.........7 N5
Torquhan Border.........128 C10
Torr Devon.........6 F8
Torran Highld.........153 K8
Torrance E Duns.........125 Q3
Torranyard N Ayrs.........125 K9
Torre Somset.........18 D7
Torridon Highld.........154 B6
Torridon House
  Highld.........153 R6
Torrin Highld.........145 J3
Torrisdale Ag & B.........120 E4
Torrisdale Highld.........165 Q4
Torrish Highld.........163 M3
Torrisholme Lancs.........95 K8
Torrobull Highld.........162 D6
Torry C Aber.........151 N6
Torryburn Fife.........134 C10
Torteval Guern.........10 a2
Torthorwald D & G.........109 M5
Tortington W Susx.........24 B10
Torton Worcs.........58 B10
Tortworth S Glos.........32 D6
Torvaig Highld.........152 H9
Torver Cumb.........94 F2
Torwood Falk.........133 N10
Torwoodlee Border.........117 P3
Torworth Notts.........85 L3
Tosberry Devon.........16 D7
Toscaig Highld.........153 N10
Toseland Cambs.........62 B8
Tosside Lancs.........95 R9
Tostock Suffk.........64 D9
Totaig Highld.........152 C9
Tote Highld.........152 G8
Tote Highld.........153 J5
Tote Hill W Susx.........23 N10
Totford Hants.........22 G7
Tothill Lincs.........87 M4
Totland IoW.........13 P7
Totley Sheff.........84 D5
Totley Brook Sheff.........84 D4
Totnes Devon.........7 L6
Toton Notts.........72 E4
Totronald Ag & B.........136 F4
Totscore Highld.........152 F4
Tottenham Gt Lon.........36 H2
Tottenhill Norfk.........75 M8
Totteridge Gt Lon.........36 F2
Totternhoe C Beds.........49 Q10
Tottington Bury.........89 M8
Tottleworth Lancs.........89 L4
Totton Hants.........14 C4
Touchen End W & M.........35 N9
Toulston N York.........91 M2
Toulton Somset.........18 G8
Toulvaddie Highld.........163 N10
Tovil Kent.........38 C11
Towan Cnwll.........3 Q4
Towan Cnwll.........4 D7
Toward Ag & B.........124 E4
Toward Quay Ag & B.........124 E4
Towcester Nhants.........49 J5
Towednack Cnwll.........2 D6
Tower of London Gt Lon.........36 H4
Towersey Oxon.........35 K3
Towie Abers.........150 C5
Tow Law Dur.........103 M3
Town End Cambs.........74 H1
Town End Cumb.........95 J4
Town End Cumb.........101 K9
Town End Cumb.........101 B5
Townend W Duns.........125 K2
Towngate Cumb.........111 K11
Towngate Lincs.........74 B8
Town Green Lancs.........88 E9
Town Green Norfk.........77 M9
Townhead Barns.........83 Q4
Townhead Cumb.........100 E3
Town Head Cumb.........101 M10
Townhead Cumb.........102 B4
Townhead D & G.........109 M3
Town Head N York.........96 B9

Townhead of Greenlaw
  D & G.........108 F8
Townhill Fife.........134 E10
Town Kelloe Dur.........104 C3
Townlake Devon.........5 Q7
Town Lane Wigan.........82 E5
Town Littleworth E Susx.........25 K7
Town of Lowton Wigan.........82 D5
Town Row E Susx.........25 N4
Towns End Hants.........22 G3
Townsend Somset.........10 H2
Townshend Cnwll.........2 F7
Town Street Suffk.........63 N3
Townwell S Glos.........32 D6
Town Yetholm Border.........118 F5
Towthorpe C York.........98 C9
Towthorpe E R Yk.........98 H8
Towton N York.........91 M3
Towyn Conwy.........80 D9
Toxteth Lpool.........81 M7
Toynton All Saints Lincs.........87 L8
Toynton Fen Side Lincs.........87 L8
Toynton St Peter Lincs.........87 M8
Toy's Hill Kent.........37 L10
Trabboch E Ayrs.........114 H3
Trabbochburn E Ayrs.........115 J3
Traboe Cnwll.........3 J9
Tracebridge Somset.........18 E10
Tradespark Highld.........156 F6
Trafford Park Traffd.........82 G5
Trallong Powys.........44 D9
Tranent E Loth.........128 C5
Tranmere Wirral.........81 L7
Trantelbeg Highld.........166 E6
Trantlemore Highld.........166 E6
Tranwell Nthumb.........113 J4
Trap Carmth.........43 N11
Traprain E Loth.........128 F4
Trap's Green Warwks.........58 H11
Trapshill W Berk.........22 C2
Traquair Border.........117 L4
Trash Green W Berk.........35 J11
Trawden Lancs.........89 Q3
Trawscoed Cerdgn.........54 F10
Trawsfynydd Gwynd.........67 N7
Trealaw Rhondd.........30 D6
Trealear Lancs.........88 E4
Trearddur Bay IoA.........78 D9
Treaslane Highld.........152 F7
Treator Cnwll.........4 E6
Tre Aubrey V Glam.........30 D10
Trebanog Rhondd.........30 D6
Trebanos Neath.........29 K4
Trebartha Cnwll.........5 M6
Trebarwith Cnwll.........4 H4
Trebeath Cnwll.........4 M6
Trebetherick Cnwll.........4 E6
Treborough Somset.........18 D7
Trebudannon Cnwll.........4 D9
Trebullett Cnwll.........5 N6
Treburgett Cnwll.........4 H6
Treburley Cnwll.........5 P6
Treburrick Cnwll.........4 D7
Trebyan Cnwll.........4 H9
Trecastle Powys.........44 B9
Trecogo Cnwll.........5 N5
Trecott Devon.........8 F4
Trecwn Pembks.........41 J4
Trecynon Rhondd.........30 C4
Tredaule Cnwll.........5 L5
Tredavoe Cnwll.........2 D8
Tredegar Blae G.........30 F3
Tredethy Cnwll.........4 H7
Tredington Gloucs.........46 H9
Tredington Warwks.........47 Q6
Tredinnick Cnwll.........4 E7
Tredinnick Cnwll.........4 G10
Tredinnick Cnwll.........5 K8
Tredinnick Cnwll.........5 L10
Tredinnick Cnwll.........5 M10
Tredomen Powys.........44 G8
Tredrissi Pembks.........41 L2
Tredrizzick Cnwll.........4 F6
Tredunnock Mons.........31 L6
Tredustan Powys.........44 G8
Treen Cnwll.........2 B9
Treen Cnwll.........2 C6
Treesmill Cnwll.........4 H10
Treeton Rothm.........84 F3
Trefasser Pembks.........40 G3
Trefdraeth IoA.........78 G10
Trefecca Powys.........44 G8
Trefeglwys Powys.........55 M6
Trefenter Cerdgn.........54 E11
Treffgarne Pembks.........41 J6
Treffgarne Owen
  Pembks.........40 G5
Trefforest Rhondd.........30 E7
Treffynnon Pembks.........40 G5
Trefil Blae G.........30 F2
Trefilan Cerdgn.........43 K3
Trefin Pembks.........40 F4
Treflach Wood Shrops.........69 J9
Trefnannau Powys.........68 H11
Trefnant Denbgs.........80 E10
Trefonen Shrops.........69 J9
Trefor Gwynd.........66 F5
Trefor IoA.........78 F8
Trefrew Cnwll.........4 J5
Trefriw Conwy.........67 P2
Tregadillett Cnwll.........5 M5
Tre-gagle Mons.........31 P3
Tregaian IoA.........78 H8
Tregare Mons.........31 M2
Tregarne Cnwll.........3 K9
Tregaron Cerdgn.........43 N3
Tregarth Gwynd.........79 L11
Tregaswith Cnwll.........4 D9
Tregatta Cnwll.........4 H4
Tregawne Cnwll.........4 G8
Tregeare Cnwll.........5 L4
Tregeiriog Wrexhm.........68 G9
Tregele IoA.........78 F6
Tregellist Cnwll.........4 G6
Tregenna Cnwll.........4 M5
Tregeseal Cnwll.........2 B7
Tre-Gibbon Rhondd.........30 C3
Tregiskey Cnwll.........3 Q4
Tregolls Cnwll.........3 J6
Tregonce Cnwll.........4 E7
Tregonetha Cnwll.........4 F9
Tregonning & Gwinear
  Mining District Cnwll.........2 F7
Tregony Cnwll.........3 N5
Tregoodwell Cnwll.........5 J5
Tregorrick Cnwll.........3 Q3
Tregoss Cnwll.........4 F9

Tregoyd Powys.........44 H7
Tregrehan Mills Cnwll.........3 Q3
Tre-groes Cerdgn.........42 H6
Tregullon Cnwll.........4 H9
Tregunna Cnwll.........4 F7
Tregunnon Cnwll.........5 L5
Tregurrian Cnwll.........4 D8
Tregynon Powys.........55 P5
Tre-gynwr Carmth.........42 H11
Trehafod Rhondd.........30 D6
Trehan Cnwll.........5 Q10
Treharris Myr Td.........30 E5
Treharrock Cnwll.........4 G6
Trehemborne Cnwll.........4 D7
Treherbert Carmth.........43 L5
Treherbert Rhondd.........29 P5
Trehunist Cnwll.........5 N9
Trekenner Cnwll.........5 N6
Treknow Cnwll.........4 H4
Trelan Cnwll.........3 J10
Trelash Cnwll.........5 K3
Trelassick Cnwll.........3 L6
Trelawne Cnwll.........5 L11
Trelawnyd Flints.........80 F9
Treleague Cnwll.........3 K9
Treleaver Cnwll.........3 K10
Trelech Carmth.........41 Q4
Trelech a'r Betws
  Carmth.........42 F9
Treleddyd-fawr Pembks.........40 E5
Trelew Cnwll.........3 L6
Trelewis Myr Td.........30 F5
Treligga Cnwll.........4 G5
Trelights Cnwll.........4 F6
Trelill Cnwll.........4 G6
Trelinnoe Cnwll.........5 N5
Trelion Cnwll.........3 N3
Trelissick Cnwll.........3 L6
Trellech Mons.........31 P3
Trellech Grange Mons.........31 N4
Trelogan Flints.........80 G8
Trelow Cnwll.........4 E8
Trelowarren Cnwll.........3 J9
Trelowia Cnwll.........5 M10
Treluggan Cnwll.........3 M6
Trelystan Powys.........56 D4
Tremadog Gwynd.........67 K7
Tremail Cnwll.........5 K4
Tremain Cerdgn.........42 D5
Tremaine Cnwll.........5 M8
Tremar Cnwll.........5 M8
Trematon Cnwll.........5 P10
Trembraze Cnwll.........5 M8
Tremeirchion Denbgs.........80 F10
Tremethick Cross Cnwll.........2 C7
Tre-Mostyn Flints.........80 G9
Trenance Cnwll.........4 L9
Trenance Cnwll.........4 D8
Trenance Cnwll.........4 E7
Trenarren Cnwll.........3 Q4
Trench Wrekin.........57 M2
Trench Green Oxon.........35 J9
Trendeal Cnwll.........3 M3
Trendrine Cnwll.........2 D6
Treneague Cnwll.........4 F7
Trenear Cnwll.........2 H7
Treneglos Cnwll.........5 L4
Trenerth Cnwll.........2 G6
Trenewan Cnwll.........5 K11
Trenewth Cnwll.........4 H6
Trengune Cnwll.........5 K3
Treninnick Cnwll.........4 C9
Trenoweth Cnwll.........4 B10
Trenoweth Cnwll.........3 K7
Trent Dorset.........19 Q11
Trentham C Stke.........70 F6
Trentishoe Devon.........17 L2
Trentlock Derbys.........72 D4
Trent Port Lincs.........85 P4
Trent Vale C Stke.........70 F6
Trenwheal Cnwll.........2 G7
Treoes V Glam.........29 P9
Treorchy Rhondd.........30 C5
Trequite Cnwll.........4 G6
Tre'r-ddol Cerdgn.........54 F6
Trerhyngyll V Glam.........30 D9
Trerulefoot Cnwll.........5 N10
Tresaith Cerdgn.........42 E4
Tresawle Cnwll.........3 M4
Tresco IoS.........2 b2
Trescott Staffs.........58 C5
Trescowe Cnwll.........2 F7
Tresean Cnwll.........4 B10
Tresham Gloucs.........32 E6
Treshnish Isles Ag & B.........136 G7
Tresillian Cnwll.........3 M4
Tresinney Cnwll.........5 J5
Treskinnick Cross Cnwll.........5 L2
Tresmeer Cnwll.........5 L4
Tresparrett Cnwll.........5 J3
Tressait P & K.........141 K5
Tresta Shet.........169 q8
Tresta Shet.........169 t4
Treswell Notts.........85 N5
Treswithian Cnwll.........2 G5
Treswithian Downs
  Crematorium Cnwll.........2 G5
Tre Taliesin Cerdgn.........54 F6
Trethevey Cnwll.........4 H4
Trethewey Cnwll.........2 B9
Trethomas Caerph.........30 G7
Trethosa Cnwll.........3 N4
Trethurgy Cnwll.........4 G10
Tretio Pembks.........40 E5
Tretire Herefs.........45 Q9
Tretower Powys.........44 H10
Treuddyn Flints.........69 J3
Trevadlock Cnwll.........5 M6
Trevalga Cnwll.........4 H3
Trevalyn Wrexhm.........69 L3
Trevanger Cnwll.........4 F6
Trevanson Cnwll.........4 F7
Trevarrack Cnwll.........2 D7
Trevarren Cnwll.........4 E9
Trevarrian Cnwll.........4 D8
Trevarrick Cnwll.........3 P5
Trevarth Cnwll.........3 J6
Trevaughan Carmth.........42 G3
Tre-Vaughan Carmth.........42 G10
Treveal Cnwll.........2 D6
Treveal Cnwll.........4 B10
Treveighan Cnwll.........4 H6
Trevellas Downs Cnwll.........3 J5
Trevelmond Cnwll.........5 L9
Trevemper Cnwll.........4 C10
Treveor Cnwll.........3 P5
Treverbyn Cnwll.........3 M4
Treverbyn Cnwll.........5 L9
Treverva Cnwll.........3 K7
Trevescan Cnwll.........2 B9

Trevethin Torfn.........31 J4
Trevia Cnwll.........4 H5
Treviglio Cnwll.........5 N8
Trevilla Cnwll.........3 L6
Trevilson Cnwll.........4 C10
Treviscoe Cnwll.........4 E10
Treviskey Cnwll.........4 N5
Trevithick Cnwll.........3 P4
Trevithick Cnwll.........4 D9
Trevoll Cnwll.........4 C10
Trevone Cnwll.........4 D6
Trevor Wrexhm.........69 J6
Trevorgans Cnwll.........2 C8
Trevorrick Cnwll.........4 E7
Trevose Cnwll.........4 D6
Trew Cnwll.........2 G8
Trewalder Cnwll.........4 H5
Trewalkin Powys.........44 H8
Trewarmett Cnwll.........4 H4
Trewassa Cnwll.........5 J4
Trewavas Cnwll.........2 F8
Trewavas Mining
  District Cnwll.........2 F8
Treween Cnwll.........5 L5
Trewellard Cnwll.........2 B7
Trewen Cnwll.........5 M5
Trewennack Cnwll.........2 H8
Trewent Pembks.........41 K11
Trewern Powys.........56 D2
Trewetha Cnwll.........4 G5
Trewethern Cnwll.........4 G6
Trewidland Cnwll.........5 M10
Trewillis Cnwll.........3 K10
Trewint Cnwll.........5 L5
Trewithian Cnwll.........3 M9
Trewoodloe Cnwll.........5 M6
Trewoon Cnwll.........2 H10
Trewoon Cnwll.........3 P3
Treworga Cnwll.........3 M5
Treworgan Cnwll.........3 L4
Treworlas Cnwll.........3 M6
Treworld Cnwll.........5 J3
Treworthal Cnwll.........3 M6
Tre-wyn Mons.........45 L10
Treyarnon Cnwll.........4 D7
Treyford W Susx.........23 M11
Trickett's Cross Dorset.........13 J4
Triermain Cumb.........111 L7
Triffleton Pembks.........41 J6
Trillacott Cnwll.........5 M4
Trimdon Dur.........104 C4
Trimdon Colliery Dur.........104 C3
Trimdon Grange Dur.........104 C3
Trimingham Norfk.........77 K4
Trimley Lower Street
  Suffk.........53 N4
Trimley St Martin Suffk.........53 N4
Trimley St Mary Suffk.........53 N4
Trimpley Worcs.........57 P9
Trimsaran Carmth.........28 E4
Trims Green Herts.........51 L7
Trimstone Devon.........17 J3
Trinafour P & K.........140 H5
Trinant Caerph.........30 H5
Tring Herts.........35 P2
Tringford Herts.........35 P2
Tring Wharf Herts.........35 P2
Trinity Angus.........143 L5
Trinity Jersey.........11 b1
Trinity Gask P & K.........134 B4
Triscombe Somset.........18 G7
Trislaig Highld.........139 K3
Trispen Cnwll.........3 L5
Tritlington Nthumb.........113 K2
Troan Cnwll.........4 D10
Trochry P & K.........141 N9
Troedrhiwfuwch Caerph.........30 F4
Troedyraur Cerdgn.........42 F5
Troedyrhiw Myr Td.........30 E4
Trofarth Conwy.........80 B10
Trois Bois Jersey.........11 b1
Troon Cnwll.........2 H6
Troon S Ayrs.........125 J11
Tropical World
  Roundhay Park Leeds.........91 J3
Trossachs Stirlg.........132 G6
Trossachs Pier Stirlg.........132 F6
Troston Suffk.........64 B7
Troswell Cnwll.........5 M3
Trotshill Worcs.........46 G3
Trottiscliffe Kent.........37 P8
Trotton W Susx.........23 M10
Troughend Nthumb.........112 C2
Trough Gate Lancs.........89 P6
Troutbeck Cumb.........101 L8
Troutbeck Cumb.........101 M10
Troutbeck Bridge Cumb.........101 M10
Troway Derbys.........84 E5
Trowbridge Wilts.........20 G3
Trowell Notts.........72 D3
Trowell Services Notts.........72 D2
Trowle Common Wilts.........20 F3
Trowley Bottom Herts.........50 C8
Trowse Newton Norfk.........77 J10
Troy Leeds.........90 G3
Trudoxhill Somset.........20 D6
Trull Somset.........18 H10
Trumfleet Donc.........91 Q8
Trumpan Highld.........152 C5
Trumpet Herefs.........46 C7
Trumpington Cambs.........62 F10
Trumpsgreen Surrey.........35 Q11
Trunch Norfk.........77 K5
Trunnah Lancs.........88 C2
Truro Cnwll.........3 L5
Truscott Cnwll.........5 M4
Trusham Devon.........8 L8
Trusley Derbys.........71 P7
Trusthorpe Lincs.........87 P4
Trysull Staffs.........58 C6
Tubney Oxon.........34 D5
Tuckenhay Devon.........7 L7
Tuckhill Shrops.........57 P7
Tuckingmill Cnwll.........2 H5
Tuckingmill Wilts.........20 H9
Tuckton Bmouth.........13 K6
Tucoyse Cnwll.........3 P4
Tuddenham Suffk.........63 N6
Tuddenham Suffk.........63 M6
Tudeley Kent.........37 P11
Tudhoe Dur.........103 Q3
Tudorville Herefs.........45 A10
Tudweiliog Gwynd.........66 C7
Tuesley Surrey.........23 Q6
Tuffley Gloucs.........32 F2
Tufton Hants.........22 E5
Tufton Pembks.........41 K5
Tugby Leics.........73 K10
Tugford Shrops.........57 K7
Tughall Nthumb.........119 P5

Tullibody Clacks 133 P8
Tullich Highld 147 Q2
Tullich Highld 156 F6
Tulliemet P & K 141 P7
Tulloch Abers 159 K11
Tullochgorm Ag & B 131 K8
Tulloch Station Highld 147 K11
Tullymurdoch P & K 142 B7
Tullynessle Abers 150 F4
Tulse Hill Gt Lon 36 H6
Tumble Carmth 28 F2
Tumbler's Green Essex 52 B6
Tumby Lincs 86 H9
Tumby Woodside Lincs 87 J3
Tunbridge Wells Kent 25 N3
Tundergarth D & G 110 C4
Tungate Norfk 77 K6
Tunley BaNES 20 C3
Tunstall E R Yk 93 P4
Tunstall C Stke 70 F4
Tunstall Kent 38 E9
Tunstall Lancs 95 N6
Tunstall N York 103 P11
Tunstall Norfk 77 N10
Tunstall Staffs 70 D9
Tunstall Suffk 65 M10
Tunstall Sundld 113 N10
Tunstead Derbys 83 P10
Tunstead Norfk 77 K7
Tunstead Milton Derbys 83 M8
Tunworth Hants 23 J5
Tupsley Herefs 45 Q6
Turgis Green Hants 23 J3
Turkdean Gloucs 47 M11
Tur Langton Leics 60 F2
Turleigh Wilts 20 F2
Turleygreen Shrops 57 P7
Turn Lancs 89 N7
Turnastone Herefs 45 M7
Turnberry S Ayrs 114 D6
Turnchapel C Plym 6 D8
Turnditch Derbys 71 P5
Turner Green Lancs 89 J4
Turner's Green E Susx 25 P7
Turner's Green Warwks 59 J11
Turner's Hill W Susx 24 H3
Turners Puddle Dorset 12 C6
Turnford Herts 51 J10
Turnhouse C Edin 127 M3
Turnworth Dorset 12 D3
Turriff Abers 158 H7
Turton Bottoms Bl w D 89 L7
Turves Cambs 74 F11
Turvey Bed 49 P4
Turville Bucks 35 L6
Turville Heath Bucks 35 K6
Turweston Bucks 48 H7
Tushielaw Inn Border 117 L7
Tutbury Staffs 71 N9
Tutnall Worcs 58 E10
Tutshill Gloucs 31 P6
Tuttington Norfk 77 J6
Tutwell Cnwll 5 P6
Tuxford Notts 85 M6
Twatt Ork 169 b4
Twatt Shet 169 q8
Twechar E Duns 126 B2
Tweedbank Border 117 Q4
Tweedmouth Nthumb 129 P9
Tweedsmuir Border 116 G6
Twelveheads Cnwll 3 K5
Twelve Oaks E Susx 25 Q6
Twemlow Green Ches E 82 G11
Twenty Lincs 74 C6
Twerton BaNES 20 D2
Twickenham Gt Lon 36 E6
Twigworth Gloucs 46 F10
Twineham W Susx 24 G6
Twineham Green W Susx 24 G6
Twinhoe BaNES 20 E3
Twinstead Essex 52 E4
Twitchen Devon 17 P5
Twitchen Shrops 57 F9
Twitham Kent 39 N10
Two Bridges Devon 6 G4
Two Dales Derbys 84 C8
Two Gates Staffs 59 K4
Two Mile Oak Cross Devon 7 L5
Two Pots Devon 17 J3
Two Waters Herts 50 C9
Twycross Leics 72 A10
Twycross Zoo Leics 59 M3
Twyford Bucks 49 J9
Twyford Hants 22 E10
Twyford Leics 73 J8
Twyford Lincs 73 N6
Twyford Norfk 76 E7
Twyford Wokham 35 L9
Twyford Common Herefs 45 Q7
Twyn-carno Caerph 30 F3
Twynholm D & G 108 G10
Twyning Green Gloucs 46 H7
Twynllanan Carmth 43 Q10
Twyn-yr-Odyn V Glam 30 F10
Twyn-y-Sheriff Mons 31 M3
Twywell Nhants 61 L5
Tyberton Herefs 45 M7
Tyburn Birm 58 H6
Tycroes Carmth 28 H2
Ty Croes IoA 78 E10
Tycrwyn Powys 68 F11
Tydd Gote Lincs 75 J7
Tydd St Giles Cambs 74 H7
Tydd St Mary Lincs 74 H7
Tye Hants 15 K6
Tye Green Essex 51 M6
Tye Green Essex 51 N3
Tye Green Essex 52 C7
Tyersal C Brad 90 F4
Tyldesley Wigan 82 E4
Tyler Hill Kent 39 K9
Tylers Green Bucks 35 P6
Tyler's Green Essex 51 M9
Tylers Green Surrey 36 H10
Tylorstown Rhondd 30 D5
Tylwch Powys 55 M8
Ty-nant Conwy 68 C6
Ty-nant Gwynd 68 B9
Tyndrum Stirlg 139 Q11
Ty'n-dwr Denbgs 69 H6
Tyneham Dorset 12 E8
Tynemouth N Tyne 113 N7
Tynemouth Crematorium N Tyne 113 M7
Tyne Tunnel S Tyne 113 M7
Tynewydd Rhondd 29 P5
Tyninghame E Loth 128 G4
Tynron D & G 115 R9

Ty'n-y-bryn Rhondd 30 D7
Ty'n-y-coedcae Caerph 30 G7
Tynygongl IoA 79 J8
Tynygraig Cerdgn 54 F11
Ty'n-y-Groes Conwy 79 P10
Tyn-y-nant Rhondd 30 E7
Tyseley Birm 58 H8
Tythegston Brdgnd 29 N9
Tytherington Ches E 83 K9
Tytherington S Glos 32 C7
Tytherington Somset 20 E6
Tytherington Wilts 20 H6
Tytherleigh Devon 10 G4
Tytherton Lucas Wilts 32 H10
Tyttenhanger Herts 50 E9
Tywardreath Cnwll 4 H11
Tywardreath Highway Cnwll 4 H10
Tywyn Conwy 79 P9
Tywyn Gwynd 54 D4

U

Ubbeston Green Suffk 65 L7
Ubley BaNES 19 P3
Uckerby N York 103 P10
Uckfield E Susx 25 L6
Uckinghall Worcs 46 G7
Uckington Gloucs 46 H10
Uckington Shrops 57 K2
Uddingston S Lans 126 B5
Uddington S Lans 126 B4
Udimore E Susx 26 E8
Udny Green Abers 151 M2
Udny Station Abers 151 N3
Uffcott Wilts 33 M9
Uffculme Devon 9 Q2
Uffington Lincs 73 R9
Uffington Oxon 34 B7
Uffington Shrops 57 J2
Ufford C Pete 74 A10
Ufford Suffk 65 K11
Ufton Warwks 48 C2
Ufton Nervet W Berk 34 H11
Ugadale Ag & B 120 E6
Ugborough Devon 6 H7
Uggeshall Suffk 65 N5
Ugglebarnby N York 105 N9
Ughill Sheff 84 C2
Ugley Essex 51 M5
Ugley Green Essex 51 M5
Ugthorpe N York 105 L8
Uibhist A Deas W Isls 168 d14
Uibhist A Tuath W Isls 168 C10
Uig Ag & B 136 F5
Uig Highld 152 B7
Uig Highld 152 F5
Uig W Isls 168 f4
Uigshader Highld 152 G8
Uisken Ag & B 137 K12
Ulbster Highld 167 P8
Ulcat Row Cumb 101 M6
Ulceby Lincs 87 M6
Ulceby N Linc 93 K8
Ulceby Skitter N Linc 93 K7
Ulcombe Kent 26 D2
Uldale Cumb 100 H3
Uley Gloucs 32 E5
Ulgham Nthumb 113 K2
Ullapool Highld 161 J8
Ullenhall Warwks 58 H11
Ullenwood Gloucs 46 H11
Ulleskelf N York 91 N3
Ullesthorpe Leics 60 B3
Ulley Rothm 84 G3
Ullingswick Herefs 46 A5
Ullinish Lodge Hotel Highld 152 E10
Ullock Cumb 100 E6
Ullswater Cumb 101 M6
Ullswater Steamers Cumb 101 L7
Ulpha Cumb 94 D2
Ulpha Cumb 95 K4
Ulrome E R Yk 99 P9
Ulsta Shet 169 r5
Ulting Wick Essex 52 D10
Ulva Ag & B 137 K7
Ulverley Green Solhll 58 H8
Ulverston Cumb 94 F5
Ulwell Dorset 12 H8
Ulzieside D & G 115 Q6
Umberleigh Devon 17 L7
Unapool Highld 164 F10
Underbarrow Cumb 95 K2
Under Burnmouth Border 111 J4
Undercliffe C Brad 90 F4
Underdale Shrops 57 J2
Underling Green Kent 26 C2
Underriver Kent 37 N10
Underwood Notts 84 G10
Undley Suffk 63 L4
Undy Mons 31 M7
Union Mills IoM 80 e6
Union Street E Susx 26 B5
Unst Shet 169 s3
Unstone Derbys 84 E5
Unstone Green Derbys 84 E5
Unthank Cumb 101 N3
Unthank Cumb 102 B2
Unthank Cumb 110 G11
Unthank Derbys 84 D5
Unthank Nthumb 129 P10
Upavon Wilts 21 M4
Up Cerne Dorset 11 P4
Upchurch Kent 38 D8
Upcott Devon 17 P6
Upcott Herefs 45 L4
Upend Cambs 63 M9
Up Exe Devon 9 M4
Upgate Norfk 76 G8
Upgate Street Norfk 64 F3
Upgate Street Norfk 65 K3
Uphall Dorset 11 M4
Uphall W Loth 127 K3
Upham Devon 9 L3
Upham Hants 22 F10
Uphampton Herefs 45 M2
Uphampton Worcs 46 F2
Uphill N Som 19 K3
Up Holland Lancs 88 G9
Uplawmoor E Rens 125 L6
Upleadon Gloucs 46 E9
Upleatham R & Cl 104 H7
Uplees Kent 38 H9
Uploders Dorset 11 L6
Uplowman Devon 18 D11

Uplyme Devon 10 G6
Up Marden W Susx 15 L4
Up Mudford Somset 19 Q11
Up Nately Hants 23 J4
Up Pottery Devon 10 E3
Upper Affcot Shrops 56 G7
Upper Ardchronie Highld 162 E11
Upper Arley Worcs 57 P8
Upper Arncott Oxon 48 H11
Upper Astrop Nhants 48 F7
Upper Basildon W Berk 34 G9
Upper Batley Kirk 90 G5
Upper Beeding W Susx 24 E8
Upper Benefield Nhants 61 L3
Upper Bentley Worcs 58 E11
Upper Bighouse Highld 166 E5
Upper Birchwood Derbys 84 F9
Upper Boat Rhondd 30 F7
Upper Boddington Nhants 48 E4
Upper Borth Cerdgn 54 E7
Upper Brailes Warwks 48 B7
Upper Breakish Highld 145 L3
Upper Breinton Herefs 45 P6
Upper Broadheath Worcs 46 F3
Upper Broughton Notts 72 H5
Upper Bucklebury W Berk 34 F11
Upper Burgate Hants 21 N11
Upper Bush Medway 37 Q7
Upperby Cumb 110 H10
Upper Caldecote C Beds 61 Q11
Upper Canada N Som 19 L3
Upper Canterton Hants 13 N2
Upper Catesby Nhants 60 B9
Upper Catshill Worcs 58 E10
Upper Chapel Powys 44 E6
Upper Cheddon Somset 18 H9
Upper Chicksgrove Wilts 21 J9
Upper Chute Wilts 21 Q4
Upper Clapton Gt Lon 36 H3
Upper Clatford Hants 22 C4
Upper Coberley Gloucs 47 J11
Upper Cotton Staffs 71 K5
Upper Cound Shrops 57 K3
Upper Cudworth Barns 91 K9
Upper Cumberworth Kirk 90 G9
Upper Dallachy Moray 157 P5
Upper Deal Kent 39 Q11
Upper Dean Bed 61 M7
Upper Denby Kirk 90 G9
Upper Denton Cumb 111 M7
Upper Dicker E Susx 25 N9
Upper Dinchope Shrops 56 H8
Upper Dounreay Highld 166 H3
Upper Dovercourt Essex 53 M5
Upper Drumbane Stirlg 133 K6
Upper Dunsforth N York 97 P8
Upper Eashing Surrey 23 Q6
Upper Eathie Highld 156 E11
Upper Egleton Herefs 46 B6
Upper Elkstone Staffs 71 K3
Upper Ellastone Staffs 71 L6
Upper End Derbys 83 N9
Upper Enham Hants 22 C4
Upper Farmcote Shrops 57 P6
Upper Farringdon Hants 23 K7
Upper Framilode Gloucs 32 E2
Upper Froyle Hants 23 L6
Upperglen Highld 152 E7
Upper Godney Somset 19 N6
Upper Gravenhurst C Beds 50 D3
Upper Green Mons 45 M11
Upper Green Suffk 63 M8
Upper Green W Berk 22 C2
Upper Grove Common Herefs 45 R9
Upper Hackney Derbys 84 C8
Upper Hale Surrey 23 M5
Upper Halliford Surrey 36 C7
Upper Halling Medway 37 Q8
Upper Hambleton RutInd 73 N9
Upper Harbledown Kent 39 K10
Upper Hardres Court Kent 39 L11
Upper Hardwick Herefs 45 N3
Upper Hartfield E Susx 25 L4
Upper Hartshay Derbys 84 E10
Upper Hatherley Gloucs 46 H10
Upper Hatton Staffs 70 E7
Upper Haugh Rothm 91 L11
Upper Hayton Shrops 57 J8
Upper Heaton Kirk 90 F7
Upper Helmsley N York 98 D9
Upper Hergest Herefs 45 K4
Upper Heyford Nhants 60 E9
Upper Heyford Oxon 48 E9
Upper Hill Herefs 45 P4
Upper Hockenden Kent 37 M7
Upper Hopton Kirk 90 F7
Upper Howsell Worcs 46 E5
Upper Hulme Staffs 71 J2
Upper Ifold Surrey 24 B4
Upper Inglesham Swindn 33 P5
Upper Kilcott Gloucs 32 E7
Upper Killay Swans 28 G6
Upper Kinchrackine Ag & B 131 P2
Upper Knockando Moray 157 M9
Upper Lambourn W Berk 34 B8
Upper Landywood Staffs 58 E3
Upper Langford N Som 19 N3
Upper Langwith Derbys 84 H7
Upper Largo Fife 135 L7
Upper Leigh Staffs 71 J7
Upper Littleton N Som 19 Q2
Upper Lochton Abers 150 H9
Upper Longdon Staffs 58 G2
Upper & Lower Stondon C Beds 50 E4
Upper Ludstone Shrops 57 Q5
Upper Lybster Highld 167 N9
Upper Lyde Herefs 45 P6
Upper Lye Herefs 56 F11
Upper Maes-coed Herefs 45 L8
Uppermill Oldham 90 B9
Upper Milton Worcs 57 Q10
Upper Minety Wilts 33 K6
Upper Moor Worcs 47 J5
Upper Moor Side Leeds 90 G4
Upper Mulben Moray 157 R7
Upper Netchwood Shrops 57 L6

Upper Nobut Staffs 71 J7
Upper Norwood W Susx 23 P11
Upper Padley Derbys 84 B5
Upper Pennington Hants 13 P5
Upper Pollicott Bucks 35 K2
Upper Poppleton C York 98 B10
Upper Quinton Warwks 47 N5
Upper Ratley Hants 22 B10
Upper Rissington Gloucs 47 P11
Upper Rochford Worcs 57 L11
Upper Ruscoe D & G 108 C8
Upper Sapey Herefs 46 C2
Upper Saxondale Notts 72 H3
Upper Seagry Wilts 32 H8
Upper Shelton C Beds 49 Q6
Upper Sheringham Norfk 76 G3
Upper Skelmorlie N Ayrs 124 C4
Upper Slaughter Gloucs 47 N10
Upper Soudley Gloucs 32 C2
Upper Spond Herefs 45 L4
Upper Standen Kent 27 M3
Upper Staploe Bed 61 P9
Upper Stoke Norfk 77 K11
Upper Stowe Nhants 60 D9
Upper Street Hants 21 N11
Upper Street Norfk 64 H6
Upper Street Norfk 77 L8
Upper Street Norfk 77 M8
Upper Street Suffk 53 K5
Upper Street Suffk 63 N10
Upper Street Suffk 64 G11
Upper Strensham Worcs 46 H7
Upper Sundon C Beds 50 B5
Upper Swell Gloucs 47 N9
Upper Tankersley Barns 91 J11
Upper Tasburgh Norfk 65 J2
Upper Tean Staffs 71 J7
Upperthong Kirk 90 E9
Upperthorpe Derbys 84 G4
Upperthorpe N Linc 92 C10
Upper Threapwood Ches W 69 M5
Upperton W Susx 23 Q10
Uppertown Derbys 71 N4
Uppertown Derbys 84 D8
Uppertown Dur 103 L3
Upper Town Herefs 46 A5
Uppertown Highld 167 Q1
Upper Town N Som 31 P11
Upper Town Suffk 64 C8
Upper Tumble Carmth 28 F2
Upper Tysoe Warwks 48 B6
Upper Ufford Suffk 65 K11
Upperup Gloucs 33 K5
Upper Upham Wilts 33 P9
Upper Upnor Medway 38 C7
Upper Victoria Angus 143 J10
Upper Vobster Somset 20 D5
Upper Wardington Oxon 48 E5
Upper Weald M Keyn 49 M7
Upper Weedon Nhants 60 D9
Upper Welland Worcs 46 E6
Upper Wellingham E Susx 25 K8
Upper Weston BaNES 32 D11
Upper Weybread Suffk 65 J6
Upper Wick Worcs 46 F4
Upper Wield Hants 22 H7
Upper Winchendon Bucks 35 K2
Upperwood Derbys 84 C9
Upper Woodford Wilts 21 M7
Upper Wootton Hants 22 G4
Upper Wraxall Wilts 32 F10
Upper Wyche Worcs 46 E6
Uppincott Devon 9 M3
Uppingham RutInd 73 M11
Uppington Dorset 12 H3
Uppington Shrops 57 K3
Upsall N York 97 Q3
Upsettlington Border 129 M10
Upshire Essex 51 K10
Up Somborne Hants 22 C7
Upstreet Kent 39 M9
Up Sydling Dorset 11 N4
Upthorpe Suffk 64 D7
Upton Bucks 35 L2
Upton C Pete 74 B10
Upton Cambs 61 Q5
Upton Ches W 81 N11
Upton Cnwll 5 M7
Upton Cnwll 16 C11
Upton Cumb 101 K3
Upton Devon 7 J10
Upton Devon 10 B4
Upton Dorset 12 B8
Upton Dorset 12 G6
Upton E R Yk 99 N10
Upton Halton 81 P7
Upton Hants 22 C11
Upton Hants 22 C3
Upton Leics 72 B11
Upton Lincs 85 Q3
Upton Nhants 60 F8
Upton Norfk 77 M9
Upton Notts 85 M10
Upton Notts 85 M5
Upton Oxon 33 P2
Upton Oxon 34 F7
Upton Pembks 41 K10
Upton R & Cl 105 K7
Upton Slough 35 Q9
Upton Somset 18 C9
Upton Somset 19 N9
Upton Wakefd 91 M8
Upton Warwks 47 M3
Upton Wilts 20 G8
Upton Wirral 81 K7
Upton Bishop Herefs 46 C9
Upton Cheyney S Glos 32 C10
Upton Cressett Shrops 57 M6
Upton Crews Herefs 46 C9
Upton Cross Cnwll 5 M7
Upton End C Beds 50 D4
Upton Grey Hants 23 J5
Upton Heath Ches W 81 N11
Upton Hellions Devon 9 K4
Upton Lovell Wilts 20 H6
Upton Magna Shrops 57 K2
Upton Noble Somset 20 D7
Upton Pyne Devon 9 M5
Upton St Leonards Gloucs 46 G11
Upton Scudamore Wilts 20 G5
Upton Snodsbury Worcs 46 H4
Upton Towans Cnwll 2 F5
Upton-upon-Severn Worcs 46 G6
Upton Warren Worcs 58 D11
Upwaltham W Susx 15 P4

Upware Cambs 62 H
Upwell Norfk 75 J1
Upwey Dorset 11 P
Upwick Green Herts 51 L
Upwood Cambs 62 C
Urchfont Wilts 21 L4
Urdimarsh Herefs 45 Q
Ure Bank N York 97 M
Urlay Nook S on T 104 D
Urmston Traffd 82 G
Urpeth Dur 113 L1
Urquhart Moray 157 P
Urquhart Castle Highld 147
Urra N York 104 G1
Urray Highld 155 P
Usan Angus 143 N
Ushaw Moor Dur 103 P
Usk Mons 31 L
Usselby Lincs 86 F
Usworth Sundld 113 M
Utkinton Ches W 82 B
Utley C Brad 90 D
Uton Devon 9
Utterby Lincs 87 K
Uttoxeter Staffs 71
Uwchmynydd Gwynd 66 B
Uxbridge Gt Lon 36
Uyeasound Shet 169 s
Uzmaston Pembks 41

V

Vale Guern 10 C
Vale Crematorium Luton 50 C
Vale of Glamorgan Crematorium V Glam 30 F1
Valley IoA 78 D
Valley End Surrey 23
Valley Truckle Cnwll 4
Valtos Highld 153 J
Valtos W Isls 168 J
Vange Essex 38 B
Varteg Torfn 31 J
Vatsetter Shet 169 s
Vatten Highld 152 D
Vaynor Myr Td 30 D
Vazon Bay Guern 10 b
Veensgarth Shet 169 s
Velindre Powys 44 H
Vellow Somset 18 E
Velly Devon 16 D
Venngreen Devon 16 H
Vennington Shrops 56 F
Venn Ottery Devon 10 B
Venny Tedburn Devon 9 K
Venterdon Cnwll 5 P
Ventnor IoW 14 G1
Venton Devon 6 F
Vernham Dean Hants 22 B
Vernham Street Hants 22 B
Vernolds Common Shrops 56 H
Verwood Dorset 13 J
Veryan Cnwll 3 N
Veryan Green Cnwll 3 N
Vicarage Devon 10 E
Vickerstown Cumb 94 D
Victoria Barns 90 F
Victoria Blae G 30 G
Victoria Cnwll 4 F
Vidlin Shet 169 s
Viewfield Moray 157 P
Viewpark N Lans 126 C
Vigo Kent 37 P
Village de Putron Guern 10 c
Ville la Bas Jersey 10 a
Villiaze Guern 10 b
Vinehall Street E Susx 26 C
Vines Cross E Susx 25 N
Vinters Park Crematorium Kent 38 C1
Virginia Water Surrey 36 B
Virginstow Devon 5 P
Vobster Somset 20 D
Voe Shet 169 r
Vowchurch Herefs 45 M
Vulcan Village St Hel 82 C

W

Waberthwaite Cumb 94 C
Wackerfield Dur 103 N
Wacton Norfk 64 H
Wadborough Worcs 46 H
Waddesdon Bucks 35 K
Waddesdon Manor Bucks 49 K1
Waddeton Devon 7 M
Waddicar Sefton 81 N
Waddingham Lincs 92 G1
Waddington Lancs 89 L
Waddington Lincs 86 C
Waddon Devon 9 M
Waddon Dorset 11 N
Wadebridge Cnwll 4 F
Wadeford Somset 10 G
Wadenhoe Nhants 61 M
Wadesmill Herts 51 J
Wadhurst E Susx 25 P
Wadshelf Derbys 84 D
Wadsworth Calder 90 C
Wadworth Donc 91 P1
Waen Denbgs 68 C
Waen Denbgs 80 G1
Waen Powys 68 C
Waen Fach Powys 68 H1
Waen-pentir Gwynd 79 K1
Waen-wen Gwynd 79 K1
Wagbeach Shrops 56 H
Wainfelin Torfn 31 J
Wainfleet All Saints Lincs 87 M
Wainfleet Bank Lincs 87 M
Wainfleet St Mary Lincs 87 N
Wainford Norfk 65 L
Wainhouse Corner Cnwll 5 K
Wainscott Medway 38 C
Wain's Hill N Som 31 L1
Wainstalls Calder 90 D
Waitby Cumb 102 E
Waithe Lincs 93 N1
Wakefield Wakefd 91 J
Wakefield Crematorium Wakefd 91 J
Wake Green Birm 58 H
Wakehurst Place W Susx 24 H
Wakerley Nhants 73 P1
Wakes Colne Essex 52 F

Walberswick Suffk	65	P7
Walberton W Susx	15	Q5
Walbottle N u Ty	113	J7
Walbutt D & G	108	F7
Walby Cumb	110	H8
Walcombe Somset	19	Q5
Walcot Lincs	73	R3
Walcot N Linc	92	E6
Walcot Shrops	56	C7
Walcot Shrops	57	K2
Walcot Swindn	33	N8
Walcot Warwks	47	M3
Walcote Leics	60	C4
Walcott Lincs	86	F9
Walcott Norfk	77	M5
Walden N York	96	F4
Walden Head N York	96	E4
Walden Stubbs N York	91	N7
Walderslade Medway	38	C9
Walderton W Susx	15	L4
Walditch Dorset	11	K6
Waldley Derbys	71	L7
Waldridge Dur	113	L11
Waldringfield Suffk	53	N2
Waldron E Susx	25	M7
Wales Rothm	84	G4
Wales Somset	19	Q10
Walesby Lincs	86	F2
Walesby Notts	85	L6
Walford Herefs	46	A4
Walford Herefs	56	F10
Walford Shrops	69	M10
Walford Staffs	70	E8
Walford Heath Shrops	69	M11
Walgherton Ches E	70	B5
Walgrave Nhants	60	H6
Walhampton Hants	13	P5
Walkden Salfd	82	F4
Walker N u Ty	113	L8
Walkerburn Border	117	M3
Walker Fold Lancs	89	K2
Walkeringham Notts	85	N2
Walkerith Lincs	85	N2
Walkern Herts	50	G5
Walker's Green Herefs	45	Q5
Walker's Heath Birm	58	G9
Walkerton Fife	134	G7
Walkford Dorset	13	M6
Walkhampton Devon	6	E5
Walkington E R Yk	92	G3
Walkley Sheff	84	D3
Walk Mill Lancs	89	P5
Walkwood Worcs	47	K2
Wall Nthumb	112	D7
Wall Staffs	58	H3
Wallacetown S Ayrs	114	E7
Wallacetown S Ayrs	114	F3
Wallands Park E Susx	25	K8
Wallasey Wirral	81	K4
Wallasey (Kingsway) Tunnel Wirral	81	L6
Wall End Cumb	94	E4
Wall End Herefs	45	N3
Wallend Medway	38	C6
Waller's Green Herefs	46	C7
Wallhead Cumb	111	J8
Wall Heath Dudley	58	C7
Wall Houses Nthumb	112	H7
Wallingford Oxon	34	H7
Wallington Gt Lon	36	G8
Wallington Hants	14	G5
Wallington Herts	50	E4
Wallington Heath Wsall	58	E4
Wallis Pembks	41	K5
Wallisdown Poole	13	J6
Walliswood Surrey	24	D3
Walls Shet	169	p9
Wallsend N Tyne	113	L7
Wallthwaite Cumb	101	L6
Wall under Haywood Shrops	57	J6
Wallyford E Loth	128	B5
Walmer Kent	39	Q11
Walmer Bridge Lancs	88	F6
Walmersley Bury	89	N8
Walmestone Kent	39	N10
Walmley Birm	58	H6
Walmley Ash Birm	58	H6
Walmsgate Lincs	87	L5
Walpole Somset	19	K6
Walpole Suffk	65	M7
Walpole Cross Keys Norfk	75	K7
Walpole Highway Norfk	75	K8
Walpole St Andrew Norfk	75	K7
Walpole St Peter Norfk	75	K7
Walrow Somset	19	K5
Walsall Wsall	58	F5
Walsall Wood Wsall	58	F4
Walsden Calder	89	Q6
Walsgrave on Sowe Covtry	59	N8
Walsham le Willows Suffk	64	E7
Walshaw Bury	89	M8
Walshford N York	97	N9
Walsoken Norfk	75	J8
Walston S Lans	127	L4
Walsworth Herts	50	E4
Walter's Ash Bucks	35	M5
Walters Green Kent	25	M2
Walterston V Glam	30	E10
Walterstone Herefs	45	L9
Waltham Kent	27	K2
Waltham NE Lin	93	N10
Waltham Abbey Essex	51	J10
Waltham Chase Hants	14	G4
Waltham Cross Herts	51	J10
Waltham on the Wolds Leics	73	L6
Waltham St Lawrence W & M	35	M9
Waltham's Cross Essex	51	Q4
Walthamstow Gt Lon	37	J3
Walton C Pete	74	C10
Walton Cumb	111	K8
Walton Derbys	84	E7
Walton Leeds	97	P11
Walton Leics	60	C3
Walton M Keyn	49	N7
Walton Powys	45	K3
Walton Shrops	56	H9
Walton Somset	19	N7
Walton Staffs	70	F8
Walton Staffs	70	G6
Walton Suffk	53	N4
Walton W Susx	15	M5
Walton Wakefd	91	K7
Walton Warwks	47	Q4
Walton Wrekin	69	Q11
Walton Cardiff Gloucs	46	H8
Walton East Pembks	41	K4
Walton Elm Dorset	20	E11
Walton Grounds Nhants	48	F8
Walton Highway Norfk	75	J8
Walton-in-Gordano N Som	31	M10
Walton Lea Crematorium Warrtn	82	D7
Walton-le-Dale Lancs	88	H5
Walton-on-Thames Surrey	36	D7
Walton-on-the-hill Staffs	70	H10
Walton on the Hill Surrey	36	F9
Walton-on-the-Naze Essex	53	N7
Walton on the Wolds Leics	72	F7
Walton-on-Trent Derbys	71	N11
Walton Park N Som	31	M10
Walton West Pembks	40	G8
Waltonwrays Crematorium N York	96	E10
Walwen Flints	80	G9
Walwen Flints	80	H10
Walwen Flints	81	J9
Walwick Nthumb	112	D6
Walworth Darltn	103	P7
Walworth Gt Lon	36	H5
Walworth Gate Darltn	103	P6
Walwyn's Castle Pembks	40	G8
Wambrook Somset	10	F3
Wampool Cumb	110	D10
Wanborough Surrey	23	P5
Wanborough Swindn	33	P8
Wandon End Herts	50	D6
Wandsworth Gt Lon	36	G6
Wangford Suffk	65	P6
Wanlip Leics	72	F8
Wanlockhead D & G	116	B8
Wannock E Susx	25	N10
Wansford C Pete	73	R11
Wansford E R Yk	99	M9
Wanshurst Green Kent	26	C2
Wanstead Gt Lon	37	K3
Wanstrow Somset	20	D6
Wanswell Gloucs	32	C4
Wantage Oxon	34	C7
Wants Green Worcs	46	E3
Wapley S Glos	32	D9
Wappenbury Warwks	59	N11
Wappenham Nhants	48	H5
Warbleton E Susx	25	P7
Warborough Oxon	34	G6
Warboys Cambs	62	D4
Warbreck Bpool	88	C3
Warbstow Cnwll	5	L3
Warburton Traffd	82	F7
Warcop Cumb	102	D7
Warden Kent	38	H7
Warden Nthumb	112	D7
Ward End Birm	58	H7
Warden Street C Beds	50	D2
Ward Green Suffk	64	E9
Ward Green Cross Lancs	89	J3
Wardhedges C Beds	50	C3
Wardington Oxon	48	E5
Wardle Ches E	69	R3
Wardle Rochdl	89	Q7
Wardley Gatesd	113	M8
Wardley Rutlnd	73	L10
Wardley Salfd	82	G4
Wardlow Derbys	83	Q10
Wardsend Ches E	83	K8
Wardy Hill Cambs	62	G4
Ware Herts	51	J8
Wareham Dorset	12	F7
Warehorne Kent	26	G5
Warenford Nthumb	119	M5
Waren Mill Nthumb	119	M4
Warenton Nthumb	119	M4
Wareside Herts	51	J7
Waresley Cambs	62	C10
Waresley Worcs	58	B10
Ware Street Kent	38	C10
Warfield Br For	35	N10
Warfleet Devon	7	M8
Wargate Lincs	74	D4
Wargrave Wokham	35	L9
Warham Herefs	45	P7
Warham Norfk	76	D3
Wark Nthumb	112	C5
Wark Nthumb	118	F3
Warkleigh Devon	17	L7
Warkton Nhants	61	J5
Warkworth Nhants	48	E6
Warkworth Nthumb	119	P9
Warlaby N York	97	M2
Warland Calder	89	Q6
Warleggan Cnwll	5	K8
Warleigh BaNES	20	E2
Warley Town Calder	90	D6
Warlingham Surrey	37	J9
Warmbrook Derbys	71	P4
Warmfield Wakefd	91	K6
Warmingham Ches E	70	C2
Warmington Nhants	61	N2
Warmington Warwks	48	D5
Warminster Wilts	20	G5
Warmley S Glos	32	C10
Warmsworth Donc	91	N10
Warmwell Dorset	12	C7
Warndon Worcs	46	G3
Warner Bros Studio Tour Herts	50	C10
Warnford Hants	22	H10
Warnham W Susx	24	E4
Warnham Court W Susx	24	E4
Warningcamp W Susx	24	B9
Warninglid W Susx	24	F5
Warren Ches E	83	J10
Warren Pembks	40	H11
Warrenby R & Cl	104	G5
Warren Row W & M	35	M8
Warren's Green Herts	50	G5
Warren Street Kent	38	F11
Warrington M Keyn	49	N4
Warrington Warrtn	82	D7
Warriston C Edin	127	P2
Warriston Crematorium C Edin	127	P2
Warsash Hants	14	E5
Warslow Staffs	71	K3
Warsop Vale Notts	84	H7
Warter E R Yk	98	H10
Warthermaske N York	97	K5
Warthill N York	98	D9
Wartling E Susx	25	Q9
Wartnaby Leics	73	J6
Warton Lancs	88	E5
Warton Lancs	95	K6
Warton Nthumb	119	K10
Warton Warwks	59	L4
Warwick Warwks	59	L11
Warwick Bridge Cumb	111	J9
Warwick Castle Warwks	47	Q2
Warwick-on-Eden Cumb	111	J9
Warwick Services Warwks	48	B3
Wasbister Ork	169	c3
Wasdale Head Cumb	100	G9
Wash Derbys	83	N8
Washall Green Herts	51	K4
Washaway Cnwll	4	G8
Washbourne Devon	7	K8
Washbrook Somset	19	M4
Washbrook Suffk	53	K3
Washfield Devon	18	B11
Washfold N York	103	L10
Washford Somset	18	E6
Washford Pyne Devon	9	K2
Washingborough Lincs	86	D6
Washington Sundld	113	M9
Washington W Susx	24	D8
Washington Services Gatesd	113	L9
Washwood Heath Birm	58	H7
Wasing W Berk	22	G2
Waskerley Dur	112	F11
Wasperton Warwks	47	Q3
Wasps Nest Lincs	86	E8
Wass N York	98	B5
Wast Water Cumb	100	G9
Watchet Somset	18	E6
Watchfield Oxon	33	P6
Watchfield Somset	19	K5
Watchgate Cumb	101	P11
Watchill Cumb	100	G2
Watcombe Torbay	7	N5
Watendlath Cumb	101	J7
Water Devon	7	J8
Water Lancs	89	N5
Waterbeach Cambs	62	G7
Waterbeach W Susx	15	N5
Waterbeck D & G	110	D5
Waterden Norfk	76	B4
Water Eaton Oxon	34	F2
Water Eaton Staffs	58	D2
Water End Bed	61	P10
Water End Bed	61	P11
Water End C Beds	50	C3
Waterend Cumb	100	F6
Water End E R Yk	92	C3
Water End Essex	51	N2
Water End Herts	50	C5
Water End Herts	50	F10
Waterfall Staffs	71	K4
Waterfoot Ag & B	120	F4
Waterfoot E Rens	125	P6
Waterford Herts	50	H8
Water Fryston Wakefd	91	M5
Watergate Cnwll	5	J7
Waterhead Cumb	101	L10
Waterheads Border	127	N7
Waterhouses Dur	103	N2
Waterhouses Staffs	71	K4
Wateringbury Kent	37	Q10
Waterlane Gloucs	32	H4
Waterloo Cnwll	5	J7
Waterloo Derbys	84	F8
Waterloo Herefs	45	L5
Waterloo Highld	145	L3
Waterloo N Lans	126	E7
Waterloo Norfk	77	J8
Waterloo P & K	141	Q10
Waterloo Pembks	41	J10
Waterloo Sefton	81	L5
Waterloo Cross Devon	9	Q2
Waterloo Port Gwynd	66	H2
Waterlooville Hants	15	J5
Watermead Bucks	49	M11
Watermillock Cumb	101	M6
Water Newton Cambs	74	B11
Water Orton Warwks	59	J6
Waterperry Oxon	34	H3
Waterrow Somset	18	E9
Watersfield W Susx	24	B7
Waterside Bl w D	89	L6
Waterside Bucks	35	Q4
Waterside Cumb	110	D11
Waterside Donc	91	R8
Waterside E Ayrs	114	H6
Waterside E Ayrs	125	M9
Waterside E Duns	126	B3
Water's Nook Bolton	89	K9
Waterstein Highld	152	A8
Waterstock Oxon	34	H3
Waterston Pembks	40	H9
Water Stratford Bucks	49	J8
Water Street Neath	29	M8
Waters Upton Wrekin	70	A11
Water Yeat Cumb	94	F3
Watford Herts	50	D11
Watford Nhants	60	D7
Watford Gap Services Nhants	60	D7
Wath N York	96	H7
Wath N York	97	M5
Wath upon Dearne Rothm	91	L10
Watlington Norfk	75	M8
Watlington Oxon	35	J6
Watnall Notts	84	H11
Watten Highld	167	M6
Wattisfield Suffk	64	E7
Wattisham Suffk	64	E11
Watton Dorset	11	K6
Watton E R Yk	99	L10
Watton Norfk	76	C11
Watton-at-Stone Herts	50	H7
Watton Green Norfk	76	C11
Wattons Green Essex	51	M11
Wattston N Lans	126	D3
Wattstown Rhondd	30	D6
Wattsville Caerph	30	H6
Wauldby E R Yk	92	G5
Waulkmill Abers	150	G9
Waunarlwydd Swans	28	H5
Waunfawr Cerdgn	54	E8
Waunfawr Gwynd	67	J3
Waungron Swans	28	G4
Waunlwyd Blae G	30	G3
Wavendon M Keyn	49	P7
Waveney Crematorium Suffk	65	P4
Waverbridge Cumb	110	D11
Waverton Ches W	69	N2
Waverton Cumb	110	D11
Wawne E R Yk	93	J3
Waxham Norfk	77	N6
Waxholme E R Yk	93	P5
Way Kent	39	P8
Waye Devon	7	K4
Wayford Somset	11	J3
Waytown Dorset	11	K5
Way Village Devon	9	L2
Way Wick N Som	19	L2
Weacombe Somset	18	F6
Weald Oxon	34	B4
Wealdstone Gt Lon	36	E3
Weardley Leeds	90	H2
Weare Somset	19	M4
Weare Giffard Devon	16	H7
Wearhead Dur	102	G3
Wearne Somset	19	M9
Wear Valley Crematorium Dur	103	Q4
Weasdale Cumb	102	C10
Weasenham All Saints Norfk	76	A7
Weasenham St Peter Norfk	76	B7
Weaste Salfd	82	H5
Weatheroak Hill Worcs	58	G10
Weaverham Ches W	82	D10
Weaverslake Staffs	71	L11
Weaverthorpe N York	99	K6
Webbington Somset	19	L3
Webb's Heath S Glos	32	C10
Webheath Worcs	58	F11
Webton Herefs	45	N7
Wedderlairs Abers	159	L11
Wedding Hall Fold N York	96	D11
Weddington Kent	39	N10
Weddington Warwks	59	N6
Wedhampton Wilts	21	L3
Wedmore Somset	19	M5
Wednesbury Sandw	58	E5
Wednesfield Wolves	58	D4
Weecar Notts	85	P7
Weedon Bucks	49	M11
Weedon Bec Nhants	60	D9
Weedon Lois Nhants	48	H5
Weeford Staffs	58	H4
Week Devon	7	K6
Week Devon	17	K6
Week Devon	17	N8
Weeke Devon	9	J3
Weeke Hants	22	E8
Weekley Nhants	61	J4
Week St Mary Cnwll	5	L2
Weel E R Yk	93	J3
Weeley Essex	53	K7
Weeley Crematorium Essex	53	K7
Weeley Heath Essex	53	L7
Weem P & K	141	K8
Weeping Cross Staffs	70	G10
Weethley Warwks	47	L3
Weeting Norfk	63	N3
Weeton E R Yk	93	Q6
Weeton Lancs	88	D4
Weeton N York	97	L11
Weetwood Leeds	90	H3
Weir Lancs	89	P5
Weirbrook Shrops	69	K10
Weir Quay Devon	6	C5
Weisdale Shet	169	q8
Welborne Norfk	76	F9
Welbourn Lincs	86	C10
Welburn N York	98	E7
Welbury N York	104	C10
Welby Lincs	73	P3
Welches Dam Cambs	62	G3
Welcombe Devon	16	C8
Weldon Nhants	61	K3
Weldon Bridge Nthumb	119	M11
Welford Nhants	60	D4
Welford W Berk	34	D10
Welford-on-Avon Warwks	47	M4
Welham Leics	60	G2
Welham Notts	85	M4
Welham Bridge E R Yk	92	C4
Welham Green Herts	50	F9
Well Hants	23	L5
Well Lincs	87	M6
Well N York	97	L4
Welland Worcs	46	E6
Wellbank Angus	142	H10
Well End Bucks	35	N7
Well End Herts	50	F11
Wellesbourne Warwks	47	Q3
Wellesbourne Mountford Warwks	47	Q3
Well Head Herts	50	E5
Well Hill Kent	37	L8
Wellhouse W Berk	34	F10
Welling Gt Lon	37	L5
Wellingborough Nhants	61	J7
Wellingham Norfk	76	B7
Wellingore Lincs	86	C9
Wellington Cumb	100	E10
Wellington Herefs	45	P5
Wellington Somset	18	F10
Wellington Wrekin	57	M2
Wellington Heath Herefs	46	D6
Wellington Marsh Herefs	45	P5
Wellow BaNES	20	D3
Wellow IoW	14	C9
Wellow Notts	85	L7
Wellpond Green Herts	51	K6
Wells Somset	19	P5
Wellsborough Leics	72	B10
Wells Green Ches E	70	B4
Wells Head C Brad	90	D4
Wells-next-the-Sea Norfk	76	C3
Wellstye Green Essex	51	P7
Well Town Devon	9	M3
Welltree P & K	134	B3
Wellwood Fife	134	D10
Welney Norfk	62	H2
Welshampton Shrops	69	M7
Welsh Bicknor Herefs	46	A11
Welsh End Shrops	69	P7
Welsh Frankton Shrops	69	L8
Welsh Hook Pembks	40	H4
Welsh Newton Herefs	45	Q11
Welshpool Powys	56	D3
Welsh St Donats V Glam	30	D9
Welton Cumb	101	L2
Welton E R Yk	92	G5
Welton Lincs	86	D5
Welton Nhants	60	C7
Welton le Marsh Lincs	87	M7
Welton le Wold Lincs	87	J3
Welwick E R Yk	93	P6
Welwyn Herts	50	F7
Welwyn Garden City Herts	50	F8
Wem Shrops	69	P9
Wembdon Somset	19	J7
Wembley Gt Lon	36	E3
Wembury Devon	6	E9
Wembworthy Devon	17	M10
Wemyss Bay Inver	124	F4
Wenallt Cerdgn	54	F10
Wendens Ambo Essex	51	M3
Wendlebury Oxon	48	G11
Wendling Norfk	76	C9
Wendover Bucks	35	N3
Wendron Cnwll	2	H7
Wendron Mining District Cnwll	2	H7
Wendy Cambs	62	D11
Wenfordbridge Cnwll	4	H6
Wenhaston Suffk	65	N6
Wennington Cambs	62	B5
Wennington Gt Lon	37	M4
Wennington Lancs	95	N7
Wensley Derbys	84	C8
Wensley N York	96	G3
Wentbridge Wakefd	91	M7
Wentnor Shrops	56	F6
Wentworth Cambs	62	G5
Wentworth Rothm	91	K11
Wenvoe V Glam	30	F10
Weobley Herefs	45	N4
Weobley Marsh Herefs	45	N4
Wepham W Susx	24	B9
Wereham Norfk	75	N10
Wergs Wolves	58	C4
Wern Gwynd	67	J7
Wern Powys	44	G11
Wern Powys	56	D2
Wern Shrops	69	J8
Werneth Low Tamesd	83	L8
Wernffrwd Swans	28	F6
Wern-y-gaer Flints	81	J11
Werrington C Pete	74	C10
Werrington Cnwll	5	N4
Werrington Staffs	70	G5
Wervin Ches W	81	N10
Wesham Lancs	88	E4
Wessex Vale Crematorium Hants	22	E11
Wessington Derbys	84	E9
West Aberthaw V Glam	30	D11
West Acre Norfk	75	Q7
West Allerdean Nthumb	129	P10
West Alvington Devon	7	J10
West Amesbury Wilts	21	M6
West Anstey Devon	17	R6
West Appleton N York	97	K2
West Ashby Lincs	87	J6
West Ashling W Susx	15	M5
West Ashton Wilts	20	G3
West Auckland Dur	103	N5
West Ayton N York	99	K4
West Bagborough Somset	18	G8
West Bank Blae G	30	H3
West Bank Halton	81	Q8
West Barkwith Lincs	86	G4
West Barnby N York	105	M8
West Barns E Loth	128	H4
West Barsham Norfk	76	C5
West Bay Dorset	11	K6
West Beckham Norfk	76	G4
West Bedfont Surrey	36	C6
Westbere Kent	39	L9
West Bergholt Essex	52	G6
West Berkshire Crematorium W Berk	34	F11
West Bexington Dorset	11	L7
West Bilney Norfk	75	P7
West Blatchington Br & H	24	G9
West Boldon S Tyne	113	N8
Westborough Lincs	73	M2
Westbourne Bmouth	13	J6
Westbourne W Susx	15	L5
West Bourton Dorset	20	E9
West Bowling C Brad	90	F4
West Brabourne Kent	27	J3
West Bradenham Norfk	76	C10
West Bradford Lancs	89	L2
West Bradley Somset	19	Q7
West Bretton Wakefd	90	H8
West Bridgford Notts	72	F3
West Briscoe Dur	103	J7
West Bromwich Sandw	58	F6
Westbrook Kent	39	P7
Westbrook W Berk	34	D10
Westbrook Wilts	33	J11
West Buckland Devon	17	M5
West Buckland Somset	18	G10
West Burrafirth Shet	169	p8
West Burton N York	96	F3
West Burton W Susx	15	Q4
Westbury Bucks	48	H7
Westbury Shrops	56	F3
Westbury Wilts	20	G4
Westbury Leigh Wilts	20	G5
Westbury on Severn Gloucs	32	D2
Westbury-on-Trym Bristl	31	Q9
Westbury-sub-Mendip Somset	19	P5
West Butsfield Dur	103	M3
West Butterwick N Linc	92	D9
Westby Lancs	88	D4
West Byfleet Surrey	36	B8
West Cairngaan D & G	106	F12
West Caister Norfk	77	Q9
West Calder W Loth	127	J5
West Camel Somset	19	Q10
West Challoch Dorset	12	C8
West Challow Oxon	34	C7
West Charleton Devon	7	K10
West Chelborough Dorset	11	L3
West Chevington Nthumb	119	P11
West Chiltington W Susx	24	C7
West Chinnock Somset	11	K2
West Chisenbury Wilts	21	M4
West Clandon Surrey	36	B10
West Cliffe Kent	27	P3
Westcliff-on-Sea Sthend	38	E4
West Coker Somset	11	L2
West Combe Devon	7	K6
Westcombe Somset	19	Q6
West Compton Somset	19	Q6
West Compton Abbas Dorset	11	M6
Westcote Gloucs	47	P9
Westcote Barton Oxon	48	D9
Westcott Bucks	49	K11

Westcott Devon.....9 P4
Westcott Surrey.....36 D11
West Cottingwith N York..92 A2
Westcourt Wilts.....21 P2
West Cowick E R Yk.....91 Q6
West Cross Swans.....28 H7
West Curry Cnwll.....5 M3
West Curthwaite Cumb..110 F11
Westdean E Susx.....25 M11
West Dean N Susx.....15 N4
West Dean Wilts.....21 Q9
West Deeping Lincs.....74 B9
West Derby Lpool.....81 M6
West Dereham Norfk.....75 N10
West Ditchburn Nthumb..119 M6
West Down Devon.....17 J3
Westdown Camp Wilts.....21 K5
Westdowns Cnwll.....4 H5
West Drayton Gt Lon.....36 C5
West Drayton Notts.....85 M6
West Dunnet Highld.....167 M2
Wested Kent.....37 M7
West Ella E R Yk.....92 H5
West End Bed.....49 Q4
West End Br For.....35 N10
West End Caerph.....30 H5
West End Cambs.....62 D7
West End Cumb.....110 F9
West End E R Yk.....92 F4
West End E R Yk.....93 L4
West End E R Yk.....93 N5
Westend Gloucs.....32 E3
West End Hants.....14 E4
West End Hants.....22 H7
West End Herts.....50 G9
West End Herts.....50 H9
West End Lancs.....89 L5
West End Leeds.....90 G3
West End Lincs.....93 Q11
West End N Som.....31 N11
West End N York.....91 N2
West End Norfk.....76 C10
West End Norfk.....77 Q9
West End Oxon.....34 G7
West End S Glos.....32 D7
West End Somset.....20 C8
West End Surrey.....23 P2
West End Surrey.....36 D8
West End W & M.....35 M9
West End W Susx.....24 F7
West End Wilts.....20 H10
West End Wilts.....21 J10
West End Wilts.....33 J9
West End Green Hants.....23 J2
Westend Town Nthumb..111 Q7
Westenhanger Kent.....27 K4
Wester Aberchalder
  Highld.....147 P3
Westerdale Highld.....167 K6
Westerdale N York.....105 J9
Westerfield Suffk.....53 L2
Westergate W Susx.....15 P5
Westerham Kent.....37 K10
Westerhope N u Ty.....113 J7
Westerland Devon.....7 M6
Westerleigh S Glos.....32 C9
Westerleigh
  Crematorium S Glos.....32 D9
Western Isles W Isls.....168 f8
Wester Ochiltree W Loth..127 J3
Wester Pitkierie Fife.....135 P6
Wester Ross Highld.....160 F11
Westerton W Susx.....15 N5
Westerton of Rossie
  Angus.....143 M7
Westerwick Shet.....169 p9
West Ewell Surrey.....36 F8
West Farleigh Kent.....38 B11
West Farndon Nhants.....48 F4
West Felton Shrops.....69 K9
Westfield BaNES.....20 C4
Westfield Cumb.....100 C5
Westfield E Susx.....26 D8
Westfield Highld.....167 J4
Westfield N Lans.....126 C3
Westfield Norfk.....76 D10
Westfield W Loth.....126 G3
Westfields Dorset.....12 B3
Westfields Herefs.....45 P6
Westfields of Rattray
  P & K.....142 B8
Westfield Sole Kent.....38 C9
West Flotmanby N York..99 M5
Westford Somset.....18 F10
Westgate Dur.....102 H3
Westgate N Linc.....92 C9
Westgate Norfk.....76 D3
Westgate Hill C Brad.....90 G5
Westgate-on-Sea Kent.....39 P7
Westgate Street Norfk.....76 H7
West Ginge Oxon.....34 D7
West Grafton Wilts.....21 P2
West Green Hants.....23 K3
West Grimstead Wilts.....21 P9
West Grinstead W Susx..24 E6
West Haddlesey N York..91 P5
West Haddon Nhants.....60 D6
West Hagbourne Oxon.....34 F7
West Hagley Worcs.....58 D8
Westhall Suffk.....65 N5
West Hallam Derbys.....72 C2
West Hallam Common
  Derbys.....72 C2
West Halton N Linc.....92 F6
Westham Dorset.....11 P9
Westham E Susx.....25 P10
West Ham Gt Lon.....37 J4
Westham Somset.....19 M5
Westhampnett W Susx.....15 N5
West Handley Derbys.....84 E5
West Hanney Oxon.....34 D6
West Hanningfield Essex..38 B2
West Harnham Wilts.....21 M9
West Harptree BaNES.....19 Q3
West Harting W Susx.....23 L10
West Hatch Somset.....19 J10
West Hatch Wilts.....20 H9
West Haven Angus.....143 K10
Westhay Somset.....19 M6
Westhead Lancs.....88 E9
West Head Norfk.....75 L9
West Heath Birm.....58 F9
West Heath Hants.....22 G3
West Helmsdale Highld..163 N3
West Hendred Oxon.....34 D7
West Hertfordshire
  Crematorium Herts.....50 D10
West Heslerton N York..99 J5
West Hewish N Som.....19 L2
Westhide Herefs.....46 A6
Westhill Abers.....151 M5

West Hill Devon.....9 Q6
West Hoathly W Susx.....25 J4
West Holme Dorset.....12 D7
Westhope Herefs.....45 P4
Westhope Shrops.....56 H7
West Horndon Essex.....37 P3
Westhorp Nhants.....48 F4
Westhorpe Lincs.....74 D4
Westhorpe Suffk.....64 E8
West Horrington Somset..19 Q5
West Horsley Surrey.....36 C10
West Horton Nthumb.....119 K4
West Hougham Kent.....27 N3
Westhoughton Bolton.....89 K9
Westhouse N York.....95 P6
Westhouses Derbys.....84 F9
West Howe Bmouth.....13 J5
West Howetown Somset..18 B8
Westhumble Surrey.....36 E10
West Huntingtower
  P & K.....134 D3
West Huntspill Somset.....19 K6
West Hyde C Beds.....50 D7
West Hyde Herts.....36 B2
West Hythe Kent.....27 K5
West Ilkerton Devon.....17 N2
West Ilsley W Berk.....34 E8
West Itchenor W Susx.....15 L6
West Keal Lincs.....87 K8
West Kennett Wilts.....33 M11
West Kilbride N Ayrs.....124 G3
West Kingsdown Kent.....37 N8
West Kington Wilts.....32 F9
West Kirby Wirral.....81 J7
West Knapton N York.....98 H5
West Knighton Dorset.....12 B7
West Knoyle Wilts.....20 G8
West Kyloe Nthumb.....119 L2
Westlake Devon.....6 G8
West Lambrook Somset..19 M11
West Lancashire
  Crematorium Lancs.....88 E8
Westland Green Herts.....51 K6
West Langdon Kent.....27 P2
West Lavington W Susx..23 N10
West Lavington Wilts.....21 K4
West Layton N York.....103 M8
West Leake Notts.....72 E5
West Learmouth
  Nthumb.....118 F3
West Lees N York.....104 E10
West Leigh Devon.....8 G3
Westleigh Devon.....16 H6
Westleigh Devon.....18 E11
West Leigh Somset.....18 F8
Westleton Suffk.....65 N8
West Lexham Norfk.....76 A4
Westley Shrops.....56 F3
Westley Suffk.....63 P8
Westley Waterless
  Cambs.....63 K9
West Lilling N York.....98 C8
Westlington Bucks.....35 L2
West Linton Border.....127 M7
Westlinton Cumb.....110 G8
West Littleton S Glos.....32 E9
West Lockinge Oxon.....34 D7
West London
  Crematorium Gt Lon..36 F4
West Lothian
  Crematorium W Loth..127 J3
West Lulworth Dorset.....12 D8
West Lutton N York.....99 J7
West Lydford Somset.....19 Q8
West Lyn Devon.....17 N2
West Lyng Somset.....19 K9
West Lynn Norfk.....75 M6
West Malling Kent.....37 Q9
West Malvern Worcs.....46 E5
West Marden W Susx.....15 L4
West Markham Notts.....85 M6
Westmarsh Kent.....39 N9
West Marsh NE Lin.....93 N9
West Marton N York.....96 C10
West Melbury Dorset.....20 G10
West Melton Rothm.....91 L10
West Meon Hants.....22 H10
West Meon Hut Hants.....23 J9
West Meon Woodlands
  Hants.....22 H9
West Mersea Essex.....52 H9
Westmeston E Susx.....24 H8
West Mickley Nthumb....112 G8
West Midland Safari
  Park Worcs.....57 Q9
Westmill Herts.....50 H7
Westmill Herts.....51 J5
West Milton Dorset.....11 L5
Westminster Gt Lon.....36 G5
Westminster Abbey &
  Palace Gt Lon.....36 G5
West Molesey Surrey.....36 D7
West Monkton Somset....19 J9
West Moors Dorset.....13 J4
West Morden Dorset.....12 F5
West Morriston Border..118 B2
West Morton C Brad.....90 D2
West Mudford Somset....19 Q10
Westmuir Angus.....142 F7
West Ness N York.....98 D5
West Newbiggin Darltn..104 C7
West Newton Cumb.....100 F11
West Newton E R Yk.....93 M3
West Newton Norfk.....75 N5
West Newton Somset.....19 J9
West Norwood Gt Lon...36 H6
West Norwood
  Crematorium Gt Lon..36 H6
Westoe S Tyne.....113 N7
West Ogwell Devon.....7 L4
Weston BaNES.....32 D11
Weston Ches E.....70 C4
Weston Devon.....10 C4
Weston Devon.....10 D7
Weston Dorset.....11 P10
Weston Halton.....81 Q8
Weston Hants.....23 K10
Weston Herefs.....45 M3
Weston Herts.....50 G4
Weston Lincs.....74 E6
Weston N York.....97 J11
Weston Nhants.....48 G5
Weston Notts.....85 N7
Weston Shrops.....56 H10
Weston Shrops.....57 L6
Weston Shrops.....69 J9
Weston Staffs.....70 H9
Weston W Berk.....34 C10
Weston Beggard Herefs..46 A6
Westonbirt Gloucs.....32 G7

Weston by Welland
  Nhants.....60 G2
Weston Colley Hants.....22 F7
Weston Colville Cambs..63 K10
Weston Corbett Hants.....23 J5
Weston Coyney C Stke....70 G6
Weston Favell Nhants.....60 G8
Weston Green Cambs.....63 K10
Weston Heath Shrops.....57 P2
Weston Hills Lincs.....74 E6
Weston in Arden Warwks..59 N7
Westoning C Beds.....50 B4
Weston-in-Gordano
  N Som.....31 M10
Westoning Woodend
  C Beds.....50 B4
Weston Jones Staffs.....70 D10
Weston Longville Norfk..76 G8
Weston Lullingfields
  Shrops.....69 M10
Weston Mill
  Crematorium C Plym.....6 D7
Weston-on-Avon Warwks..47 N4
Weston-on-the-Green
  Oxon.....48 F5
Weston Park Staffs.....57 Q2
Weston Patrick Hants.....23 J5
Weston Rhyn Shrops.....69 J7
Weston-sub-Edge Gloucs..47 M6
Weston-super-Mare
  N Som.....19 K2
Weston-super-Mare
  Crematorium N Som.....19 L2
Weston Turville Bucks.....35 N2
Weston-under-Lizard
  Staffs.....57 Q2
Weston under Penyard
  Herefs.....46 B10
Weston-under-
  Redcastle Shrops.....69 Q9
Weston under
  Wetherley Warwks.....59 N11
Weston Underwood
  Derbys.....71 P6
Weston Underwood
  M Keyn.....49 N4
Weston-upon-Trent
  Derbys.....72 C5
Westonzoyland Somset..19 L8
West Orchard Dorset.....20 F11
West Overton Wilts.....33 M11
Westow N York.....98 F7
West Panson Devon.....5 N3
West Park Abers.....151 K8
West Parley Dorset.....13 J5
West Peckham Kent.....37 P10
West Peeke Devon.....5 N3
West Pelton Dur.....113 K10
West Pennard Somset.....19 P7
West Pentire Cnwll.....4 B9
West Perry Cambs.....61 P7
West Pinchbeck Lincs.....74 D6
West Porlock Somset.....17 R2
Westport Somset.....19 L10
West Pulham Dorset.....11 Q3
West Putford Devon.....16 F8
West Quantoxhead
  Somset.....18 F6
Westquarter Falk.....126 G2
Westra V Glam.....30 F10
West Raddon Devon.....9 L4
West Rainton Dur.....113 M11
West Rasen Lincs.....86 E3
West Ravendale NE Lin..93 M11
Westray Ork.....169 d2
Westray Airport Ork.....169 d1
West Raynham Norfk.....76 B6
West Retford Notts.....85 L4
Westridge Green W Berk..34 G9
Westrigg W Loth.....126 G3
West Road
  Crematorium N u Ty..113 K7
Westrop Swindn.....33 P6
West Rounton N York..104 D10
West Row Suffk.....63 L5
West Rudham Norfk.....75 R5
West Runton Norfk.....76 H3
Westruther Border.....128 C8
Westry Cambs.....74 H11
West Saltoun E Loth.....128 C6
West Sandford Devon.....9 K4
West Sandwick Shet.....169 r5
West Scrafton N York.....96 G4
West Sleekburn Nthumb..113 L4
West Somerton Norfk.....77 P7
West Stafford Dorset.....11 Q7
West Stockwith Notts.....92 C11
West Stoke W Susx.....15 M5
West Stonesdale N York..102 G10
West Stoughton Somset..19 M6
West Stour Dorset.....20 E10
West Stourmouth Kent....39 N9
West Stow Suffk.....63 P6
West Stowell Wilts.....21 M2
West Stratton Hants.....22 F6
West Street Kent.....38 F11
West Street Kent.....39 P11
West Street Medway.....38 B6
West Street Suffk.....64 D7
West Suffolk
  Crematorium Suffk.....63 P7
West Tanfield N York.....97 L5
West Taphouse Cnwll.....5 J9
West Tarbert Ag & B.....123 P6
West Tarring W Susx.....24 D10
West Thirston Nthumb..119 N11
West Thorney W Susx.....15 L6
West Thorpe Notts.....72 G5
West Thurrock Thurr.....37 N5
West Tilbury Thurr.....37 Q5
West Tisted Hants.....23 J9
West Torrington Lincs.....86 F4
West Town BaNES.....19 P2
West Town Hants.....15 K7
West Town Herefs.....45 N2
West Town N Som.....31 N1
West Town Somset.....19 P7
West Town Somset.....20 D6
West Tytherley Hants.....21 Q9
West Walton Norfk.....75 J8
Westward Cumb.....101 J2
Westward Ho! Devon.....16 G6
Westwell Kent.....26 G2
Westwell Oxon.....33 P3
Westwell Leacon Kent.....26 G2
West Wellow Hants.....21 Q11
West Wembury Devon.....6 E9
West Wemyss Fife.....135 J2
Westwick Cambs.....62 F7
Westwick Dur.....103 L7

West Wick N Som.....19 L2
Westwick Norfk.....77 K6
West Wickham Cambs..63 K11
West Wickham Gt Lon.....37 J7
West Williamston
  Pembks.....41 K9
West Wiltshire
  Crematorium Wilts.....20 H3
West Winch Norfk.....75 M7
West Winterslow Wilts....21 P8
West Wittering W Susx....15 L7
West Witton N York.....96 G3
Westwood Devon.....9 P5
Westwood Kent.....37 P6
Westwood Kent.....39 Q8
Westwood Notts.....84 G10
Westwood Nthumb.....111 Q7
Westwood Wilts.....20 F3
West Woodburn
  Nthumb.....112 C3
West Woodhay W Berk....22 C2
Westwood Heath Covtry..59 L9
West Woodlands Somset..20 E6
West Woodside N Linc...92 B10
West Worldham Hants...23 K7
West Worthing W Susx..24 D10
West Wratting Cambs....63 K10
West Wycombe Bucks.....35 M6
West Wylam Nthumb....112 H8
West Yatton Wilts.....32 G9
West Yoke Kent.....37 P7
West Youlstone Cnwll.....16 D8
Wetham Green Kent.....38 D8
Wetheral Cumb.....111 J10
Wetherby Leeds.....97 P11
Wetherby Services
  N York.....97 P10
Wetherden Suffk.....64 E9
Wetheringsett Suffk.....64 G8
Wethersfield Essex.....52 B5
Wetherup Street Suffk.....64 G9
Wetley Rocks Staffs.....70 H5
Wettenhall Ches E.....69 R2
Wetton Staffs.....71 L3
Wetwang E R Yk.....99 J9
Wetwood Staffs.....70 D8
Wexcombe Wilts.....21 Q3
Wexham Slough.....35 Q8
Wexham Street Bucks.....35 Q8
Weybourne Norfk.....76 G3
Weybourne Surrey.....23 N5
Weybread Suffk.....65 J5
Weybread Street Suffk....65 J5
Weybridge Surrey.....36 C8
Weycroft Devon.....10 G5
Weydale Highld.....167 L4
Weyhill Hants.....22 B5
Weymouth Dorset.....11 P9
Weymouth
  Crematorium Dorset.....11 P9
Whaddon Bucks.....49 M8
Whaddon Cambs.....62 E11
Whaddon Gloucs.....32 F2
Whaddon Gt Lon.....36 H8
Whaddon Wilts.....20 G2
Whaddon Wilts.....21 N9
Whale Cumb.....101 P6
Whaley Derbys.....84 H6
Whaley Bridge Derbys....83 M8
Whaley Thorns Derbys....84 H6
Whaligoe Highld.....167 P8
Whalley Lancs.....89 L3
Whalley Banks Lancs.....89 L3
Whalsay Shet.....169 s7
Whalton Nthumb.....112 H4
Whaplode Lincs.....74 F6
Whaplode Drove Lincs....74 F8
Wharf Warwks.....48 D4
Wharfe N York.....96 A7
Wharles Lancs.....88 E3
Wharley End C Beds.....49 P6
Wharncliffe Side Sheff..84 C2
Wharram-le-Street
  N York.....98 H7
Wharton Ches W.....82 E11
Wharton Herefs.....45 Q3
Whashton N York.....103 N9
Whasset Cumb.....95 L4
Whatcote Warwks.....47 Q6
Whateley Warwks.....59 K5
Whatfield Suffk.....52 H2
Whatley Somset.....20 H3
Whatley Somset.....20 D5
Whatley's End S Glos.....32 C8
Whatlington E Susx.....26 C8
Whatsole Street Kent.....27 K3
Whatstandwell Derbys....84 D10
Whatton Notts.....73 J3
Whauphill D & G.....107 M8
Whaw N York.....103 J10
Wheal Peevor Cnwll.....3 J5
Wheal Rose Cnwll.....3 J5
Wheatacre Norfk.....65 P3
Wheatfield Oxon.....35 J3
Wheathampstead Herts..50 E8
Wheathill Shrops.....57 L8
Wheathill Somset.....19 Q8
Wheatley Calder.....90 D5
Wheatley Hants.....23 L6
Wheatley Oxon.....34 G3
Wheatley Hill Dur.....104 C3
Wheatley Hills Donc.....91 P10
Wheatley Lane Lancs.....89 N3
Wheaton Aston Staffs.....58 C2
Wheatsheaf Wrexhm.....69 K4
Wheddon Cross Somset..18 B7
Wheelbarrow Town
  Kent.....27 K2
Wheeler End Bucks.....35 M6
Wheeler's Green
  Wokham.....35 L10
Wheeler's Street Kent.....26 D3
Wheelerstreet Surrey.....23 P6
Wheelock Ches E.....70 D3
Wheelock Heath Ches E..70 D3
Wheelton Lancs.....89 J5
Wheldale Wakefd.....91 M5
Wheldrake C York.....92 A3
Whelford Gloucs.....33 N5
Whelpley Hill Bucks.....35 Q4
Whelpo Cumb.....101 K3
Whelston Flints.....81 J9
Whempstead Herts.....50 H6
Whenby N York.....98 C7
Whepstead Suffk.....64 A10
Wherstead Suffk.....53 L3
Wherwell Hants.....22 C6
Wheston Derbys.....83 P9
Whetsted Kent.....37 Q11
Whetstone Gt Lon.....36 G2
Whetstone Leics.....72 F11

Wheyrigg Cumb.....110 C11
Whicham Cumb.....94 C4
Whichford Warwks.....48 B8
Whickham Gatesd.....113 K8
Whiddon Devon.....8 C5
Whiddon Down Devon.....8 H4
Whigstreet Angus.....142 H9
Whilton Nhants.....60 D8
Whimble Devon.....16 F11
Whimple Devon.....9 P5
Whimpwell Green Norfk..77 M6
Whinburgh Norfk.....76 E10
Whin Lane End Lancs.....88 D2
Whinnie Liggate D & G..108 F10
Whinnow Cumb.....110 F10
Whinnyfold Abers.....159 Q9
Whinny Hill S on T.....104 C7
Whippingham IoW.....14 F8
Whipsnade C Beds.....50 B7
Whipsnade Zoo ZSL
  C Beds.....50 B7
Whipton Devon.....9 N5
Whirlow Sheff.....84 D4
Whisby Lincs.....86 B7
Whissendine Rutlnd.....73 L8
Whissonsett Norfk.....76 C7
Whistlefield Ag & B.....131 Q9
Whistlefield Inn Ag & B..131 P11
Whistley Green Wokham..35 L10
Whiston Knows.....81 P6
Whiston Nhants.....60 H8
Whiston Rothm.....84 F3
Whiston Staffs.....58 C2
Whiston Staffs.....71 J4
Whiston Cross Shrops.....57 P4
Whiston Eaves Staffs.....71 J3
Whitacre Fields Warwks..59 L4
Whitbeck Cumb.....94 C4
Whitbourne Herefs.....46 D3
Whitburn S Tyne.....113 P8
Whitburn W Loth.....126 G5
Whitby Ches W.....81 M8
Whitby N York.....105 M8
Whitbyheath Ches W.....81 M10
Whitchester Border.....129 J8
Whitchurch BaNES.....32 B11
Whitchurch Bucks.....49 M10
Whitchurch Cardif.....30 G9
Whitchurch Devon.....6 D4
Whitchurch Hants.....22 E5
Whitchurch Herefs.....45 R11
Whitchurch Oxon.....34 H9
Whitchurch Pembks.....40 D4
Whitchurch Shrops.....69 Q6
Whitchurch
  Canonicorum Dorset.....10 H5
Whitchurch Hill Oxon.....34 H9
Whitcombe Dorset.....11 Q7
Whitcot Shrops.....56 F6
Whitcott Keysett Shrops..56 D8
Whiteacre Kent.....27 K2
Whiteacre Heath Warwks..59 K6
Whiteash Green Essex....52 C5
White Ball Somset.....18 F11
Whitebridge Highld.....147 M4
Whitebrook Mons.....31 P3
Whitebushes Surrey.....36 G11
Whitecairns Abers.....151 N4
Whitechapel Gt Lon.....36 H4
White Chapel Lancs.....88 H2
Whitechurch Pembks.....41 L3
Whitecliffe Gloucs.....31 Q3
White Colne Essex.....52 E6
White Coppice Lancs.....89 J7
Whitecraig E Loth.....127 Q3
Whitecroft Gloucs.....32 B3
Whitecrook D & G.....106 F6
Whitecross Cnwll.....2 H6
White Cross Cnwll.....2 H7
Whitecross Cnwll.....4 F7
Whitecross Falk.....126 F3
White End Worcs.....46 E8
Whiteface Highld.....162 H8
Whitefarland N Ayrs.....120 G3
Whitefaulds S Ayrs.....114 E6
Whitefield Bury.....89 N9
Whitefield Devon.....17 N4
Whitefield Somset.....18 E9
Whitefield Lane End
  Knows.....81 P7
Whiteford Abers.....151 J2
Whitegate Ches W.....82 D11
Whitehall Hants.....23 J4
Whitehall Ork.....169 f4
Whitehall W Susx.....24 C5
Whitehaven Cumb.....100 C7
Whitehill Kent.....38 H10
Whitehill Leics.....72 C8
Whitehill and Bordon
  Hants.....23 L8
Whitehills Abers.....158 G4
Whitehouse Abers.....150 G5
Whitehouse Ag & B.....123 Q5
Whitehouse Common
  Birm.....58 H5
Whitekirk E Loth.....128 F3
White Kirkley Dur.....103 J3
White Lackington Dorset..11 Q4
Whitelackington Somset..19 L11
White Ladies Aston
  Worcs.....46 H4
Whiteleaf Bucks.....35 M4
White-le-Head Dur.....113 J10
Whiteley Hants.....14 F5
Whiteley Bank IoW.....14 G10
Whiteley Green Ches E..83 K9
Whiteley Village Surrey..36 C8
Whitemans Green
  W Susx.....24 H5
White Mill Carmth.....43 J10
Whitemire Moray.....156 H7
Whitemoor C Nott.....72 E2
Whitemoor Cnwll.....3 P4
Whitemoor Derbys.....84 D11
Whitemoor Staffs.....70 F4
Whiteness Shet.....169 r8
White Notley Essex.....52 C8
Whiteoak Green Oxon.....34 B2
White Ox Mead BaNES..20 D3
Whiteparish Wilts.....21 P10
White Pit Lincs.....87 L5
Whiterashes Abers.....151 M3
White Roding Essex.....51 N8
Whiterow Highld.....167 Q6
Whiterow Moray.....157 J6
Whiteshill Gloucs.....32 F3
Whitesmith E Susx.....25 N8
White Stake Lancs.....88 G5
Whitestaunton Somset..10 F2
Whitestone Devon.....9 L6
White Stone Herefs.....45 R4

Whitestone Cross – Woodford 301

hitestone Cross Devon 9 L6
hitestreet Green Suffk 52 G4
hitewall Corner N York 98 F7
hite Waltham W & M 35 M9
hiteway BaNES 20 D2
hiteway Gloucs 32 H2
hitewell Lancs 95 P11
hiteworks Devon 6 G4
hitfield C Dund 142 G11
hitfield Kent 27 P2
hitfield Nhants 48 H7
hitfield Nthumb 111 Q9
hitfield S Glos 32 C6
hitfield Hall Nthumb 111 Q9
hitford Devon 10 F5
hitford Flints 80 G9
hitgift E R Yk 92 D6
hitgreave Staffs 70 G9
hithorn D & G 107 M9
hiting Bay N Ayrs 121 K6
hitkirk Leeds 91 K4
hitland Carmth 41 N7
hitlaw Border 117 Q8
hitletts S Ayrs 114 G3
hitley N York 91 P6
hitley Readg 35 K10
hitley Sheff 84 D2
hitley Wilts 32 G11
hitley Bay N Tyne 113 N6
hitley Bay
Crematorium N Tyne 113 M6
hitley Chapel Nthumb 112 D9
hitley Heath Staffs 70 E9
hitley Lower Kirk 90 G7
hitley Row Kent 37 L10
hitlock's End Solhll 58 H9
hitminster Gloucs 32 E3
hitmore Dorset 13 J3
hitmore Staffs 70 E6
hitnage Devon 18 D11
hitnash Warwks 48 B2
hitney-on-Wye Herefs 45 K5
hitrigg Cumb 100 H3
hitrigg Cumb 110 D9
hitrigglees Cumb 110 D9
hitsbury Hants 21 M11
hitsome Border 129 M9
hitson Newpt 31 L8
hitstable Kent 39 K8
hitstone Cnwll 5 M2
hittingham Nthumb 119 L8
hittingslow Shrops 56 G7
hittington Derbys 84 E5
hittington Gloucs 47 K10
hittington Lancs 95 N5
hittington Norfk 75 P11
hittington Shrops 69 K8
hittington Staffs 58 C8
hittington Staffs 59 J3
hittington Warwks 59 L5
hittington Worcs 46 G4
hittington Moor
Derbys 84 E6
hittlebury Nhants 49 J6
hittle-le-Woods Lancs 88 H6
hittlesey Cambs 74 E11
hittlesford Cambs 62 G11
hittlestone Head
Bl w D 89 L7
hitton N Linc 92 F6
hitton Nthumb 119 L10
hitton Powys 56 D11
hitton S on T 104 C6
hitton Shrops 57 K10
hitton Suffk 53 K2
hittonditch Wilts 33 Q10
hittonstall Nthumb 112 G9
hitway Hants 22 E3
hitwell Derbys 84 H5
hitwell Herts 50 E6
hitwell IoW 14 F11
hitwell N York 103 Q11
hitwell Rutlnd 73 N9
hitwell-on-the-Hill
N York 98 E7
hitwell Street Norfk 76 G7
hitwick Leics 72 C7
hitwood Wakefd 91 L6
hitworth Lancs 89 P7
hixall Shrops 69 P8
hixley N York 97 P9
horlton Dur 103 M8
horlton N York 104 E10
hyle Herefs 45 R2
hyteleafe Surrey 36 H9
ibdon Gloucs 31 Q5
ibsey C Brad 90 E4
ibtoft Warwks 59 Q7
chenford Worcs 46 E2
chling Kent 38 F10
ck Bmouth 13 L6
ck Devon 10 D4
ck Highld 167 Q6
ck S Glos 32 D10
ck Somset 18 H6
ck Somset 19 M9
ck V Glam 29 P10
ck W Susx 24 B10
ck Wilts 21 N10
ck Worcs 47 J5
cken Cambs 63 J6
cken Nhants 49 K7
cken Bonhunt Essex 51 L4
ckenby Lincs 86 E4
ck End Bed 49 Q4
cken Green Village
Norfk 76 A5
ckersley Rothm 84 G2
cker Street Green
Suffk 52 G3
ckford Essex 38 B3
ckham Hants 14 G4
ckham W Berk 34 C10
ckham Bishops Essex 52 D9
ckhambreaux Kent 39 M10
ckhambrook Suffk 63 N10
ckhamford Worcs 47 L6
ckham Green Suffk 64 F8
ckham Green W Berk 34 D10
ckham Heath W Berk 34 D11
ckham Market Suffk 65 L10
ckhampton Norfk 77 N10
ckham St Paul Essex 52 D4
ckham Skeith Suffk 64 F8
ckham Street Suffk 63 N10
ckham Street Suffk 64 F8
ckhurst Green W Susx 24 D4
ck John o' Groats
Airport Highld 167 Q6
cklewood Norfk 76 F11
ckmere Norfk 76 H5
Wick St Lawrence N Som 31 L11
Wicksteed Park Nhants 61 J5
Wickstreet E Susx 25 M9
Wickwar S Glos 32 D7
Widdington Essex 51 M4
Widdop Calder 89 Q4
Widdrington Nthumb 119 Q11
Widdrington Station
Nthumb 113 K2
Widecombe in the
Moor Devon 8 H9
Widegates Cnwll 5 M10
Widemouth Bay Cnwll 16 C11
Wide Open N Tyne 113 K6
Widford Essex 51 Q10
Widford Herts 51 K7
Widham Wilts 33 L7
Widley Hants 15 J5
Widmer End Bucks 35 N5
Widmerpool Notts 72 G5
Widmore Gt Lon 37 K7
Widnes Halton 81 Q7
Widnes Crematorium
Halton 81 Q7
Widworthy Devon 10 E5
Wigan Wigan 88 H9
Wigan Crematorium
Wigan 82 C4
Wigborough Somset 19 M11
Wiggaton Devon 10 C6
Wiggenhall St Germans
Norfk 75 L8
Wiggenhall St Mary
Magdalen Norfk 75 L8
Wiggenhall St Mary the
Virgin Norfk 75 L8
Wiggenhall St Peter
Norfk 75 M8
Wiggens Green Essex 51 Q2
Wiggenstall Staffs 71 K2
Wiggington Shrops 69 K7
Wigginton C York 98 C9
Wigginton Herts 35 P2
Wigginton Oxon 48 C8
Wigginton Staffs 59 K3
Wigginton Bottom Herts 35 P3
Wigglesworth N York 96 B9
Wiggonby Cumb 110 E10
Wiggonholt W Susx 24 C7
Wighill N York 97 Q11
Wighton Norfk 76 C4
Wightwick Wolves 58 C5
Wigley Derbys 84 D6
Wigley Hants 22 B11
Wigmore Herefs 56 G11
Wigmore Medway 38 C9
Wigsley Notts 85 Q6
Wigsthorpe Nhants 61 M4
Wigston Leics 72 G11
Wigston Fields Leics 72 G10
Wigston Parva Leics 59 Q7
Wigthorpe Notts 85 J4
Wigtoft Lincs 74 E3
Wigton Cumb 110 E11
Wigtown D & G 107 M6
Wigtwizzle Sheff 90 G11
Wike Leeds 91 J2
Wilbarston Nhants 60 H3
Wilberfoss E R Yk 98 E10
Wilburton Cambs 62 G5
Wilby Nhants 61 J7
Wilby Norfk 64 E4
Wilby Suffk 65 J7
Wilcot Wilts 21 M2
Wilcott Shrops 69 L11
Wilcrick Newpt 31 M7
Wilday Green Derbys 84 D6
Wildboarclough Ches E 83 L11
Wilden Bed 61 N9
Wilden Worcs 58 B10
Wilde Street Suffk 63 M5
Wildhern Hants 22 C4
Wildhill Herts 50 G9
Wildmanbridge S Lans 126 E7
Wildmoor Hants 23 J3
Wildmoor Worcs 58 E9
Wildsworth Lincs 92 D11
Wilford C Nott 72 F3
Wilford Hill
Crematorium Notts 72 F3
Wilkesley Ches E 70 A6
Wilkhaven Highld 163 L9
Wilkieston W Loth 127 L4
Wilkin's Green Herts 50 E9
Wilksby Lincs 87 J8
Willand Devon 9 P2
Willards Hill E Susx 26 B7
Willaston Ches E 70 B4
Willaston Ches W 81 L9
Willen M Keyn 49 N6
Willenhall Covtry 59 N9
Willenhall Wsall 58 E5
Willerby E R Yk 92 H4
Willerby N York 99 L5
Willersey Gloucs 47 M7
Willersley Herefs 45 L5
Willesborough Kent 26 H3
Willesborough Lees Kent 26 H3
Willesden Gt Lon 36 F4
Willesleigh Devon 17 K5
Willesley Wilts 32 G7
Willett Somset 18 F8
Willey Shrops 57 M5
Willey Warwks 59 Q8
Willey Green Surrey 23 P4
Williamscot Oxon 48 E5
Williamstown Rhondd 30 D6
Willian Herts 50 F4
Willicote Warwks 47 N5
Willingale Essex 51 N9
Willingdon E Susx 25 N10
Willingham Cambs 62 F6
Willingham by Stow
Lincs 85 Q4
Willingham Green
Cambs 63 K10
Willington Bed 61 P10
Willington Derbys 71 P9
Willington Dur 103 N3
Willington Kent 38 C11
Willington N Tyne 113 M7
Willington Warwks 47 Q7
Willington Corner
Ches W 82 B11
Willitoft E R Yk 92 B4
Williton Somset 18 E6
Willoughby Lincs 87 N6
Willoughby Warwks 60 B7
Willoughby Hills Lincs 87 L11
Willoughby-on-the-
Wolds Notts 72 G5
Willoughby Waterleys
Leics 60 C2
Willoughton Lincs 86 B2
Willow Green Ches W 82 D9
Willows Green Essex 52 B8
Willsbridge S Glos 32 C10
Willsworthy Devon 8 D8
Willtown Somset 19 L10
Wilmcote Warwks 47 N3
Wilmington BaNES 20 C2
Wilmington Devon 10 E5
Wilmington E Susx 25 M10
Wilmington Kent 37 M6
Wilmslow Ches E 82 H8
Wilnecote Staffs 59 K4
Wilpshire Lancs 89 K4
Wilsden C Brad 90 D3
Wilsford Lincs 73 Q2
Wilsford Wilts 21 M3
Wilsford Wilts 21 M7
Wilsham Devon 17 P2
Wilshaw Kirk 90 E9
Wilsill N York 97 J8
Wilsley Green Kent 26 C4
Wilsley Pound Kent 26 C4
Wilson Herefs 45 R10
Wilson Leics 72 C6
Wilsontown S Lans 126 G6
Wilstead Bed 50 C2
Wilsthorpe Lincs 74 A8
Wilstone Herts 35 P2
Wilstone Green Herts 35 P2
Wilton Cumb 100 D8
Wilton Herefs 46 A10
Wilton N York 98 H4
Wilton R & Cl 104 G7
Wilton Wilts 21 L8
Wilton Wilts 21 Q2
Wilton Dean Border 117 P8
Wimbish Essex 51 N3
Wimbish Green Essex 51 P3
Wimbledon Gt Lon 36 F6
Wimblington Cambs 62 F2
Wimboldsley Ches W 70 B2
Wimborne Minster
Dorset 12 H5
Wimborne St Giles
Dorset 12 H2
Wimbotsham Norfk 75 M9
Wimpole Cambs 62 E11
Wimpstone Warwks 47 P5
Wincanton Somset 20 D9
Winceby Lincs 87 K7
Wincham Ches W 82 E9
Winchburgh W Loth 127 K3
Winchcombe Gloucs 47 K9
Winchelsea E Susx 26 F8
Winchelsea Beach E Susx 26 F8
Winchester Hants 22 E9
Winchester Services
Hants 22 F7
Winchet Hill Kent 26 B3
Winchfield Hants 23 L4
Winchmore Hill Bucks 35 P5
Winchmore Hill Gt Lon 36 H2
Wincle Ches E 83 L11
Wincobank Sheff 84 E2
Winder Cumb 100 D7
Windermere Cumb 101 M11
Windermere
Steamboats &
Museum Cumb 101 M11
Winderton Warwks 48 B6
Windhill Highld 155 P8
Windlehurst Stockp 83 L7
Windlesham Surrey 23 P2
Windmill Cnwll 4 D7
Windmill Derbys 83 Q9
Windmill Hill E Susx 25 P8
Windmill Hill Somset 19 K11
Windrush Gloucs 33 N2
Windsole Abers 158 E5
Windsor W & M 35 Q9
Windsor Castle W & M 35 Q9
Windsoredge Gloucs 32 F4
Windsor Green Suffk 64 B11
Windygates Fife 135 J7
Windyharbour Ches E 82 H10
Windy Hill Wrexhm 69 K4
Wineham W Susx 24 F6
Winestead E R Yk 93 N6
Winewall Lancs 89 Q2
Winfarthing Norfk 64 G4
Winford IoW 14 G10
Winford N Som 19 P2
Winforton Herefs 45 K5
Winfrith Newburgh
Dorset 12 D8
Wing Bucks 49 N10
Wing Rutlnd 73 M10
Wingate Dur 104 D3
Wingates Bolton 89 K9
Wingates Nthumb 119 L11
Wingerworth Derbys 84 E7
Wingfield C Beds 50 B5
Wingfield Suffk 65 J6
Wingfield Wilts 20 F3
Wingfield Green Suffk 65 J6
Wingham Kent 39 M10
Wingland Lincs 75 J6
Wingmore Kent 27 L2
Wingrave Bucks 49 N11
Winkburn Notts 85 M9
Winkfield Br For 35 P10
Winkfield Row Br For 35 N10
Winkhill Staffs 71 K4
Winkhurst Green Kent 37 L11
Winkleigh Devon 17 L10
Winksley N York 97 L6
Winkton Dorset 13 L5
Winlaton Gatesd 113 J8
Winlaton Mill Gatesd 113 J8
Winless Highld 167 P6
Winllan Powys 68 H10
Winmarleigh Lancs 95 K11
Winnall Hants 22 E9
Winnersh Wokham 35 L10
Winnington Ches W 82 D10
Winscales Cumb 100 D5
Winscombe N Som 19 M3
Winsford Ches W 82 E11
Winsford Somset 18 B8
Winsham Devon 17 J4
Winsham Somset 10 H3
Winshill Staffs 71 P10
Winshwen Swans 29 J5
Winskill Cumb 101 Q4
Winslade Hants 23 J5
Winsley Wilts 20 E2
Winslow Bucks 49 L9
Winson Gloucs 33 L3
Winsor Hants 13 P2
Winster Cumb 95 J2
Winster Derbys 84 B8
Winston Dur 103 M7
Winston Suffk 64 H9
Winstone Gloucs 33 J3
Winswell Devon 16 H9
Winterborne Came
Dorset 11 Q7
Winterborne Clenston
Dorset 12 D4
Winterborne
Herringston Dorset 11 P7
Winterborne
Houghton Dorset 12 D4
Winterborne Kingston
Dorset 12 E5
Winterborne Monkton
Dorset 11 P7
Winterborne Stickland
Dorset 12 D4
Winterborne Tomson
Dorset 12 E5
Winterborne
Whitechurch Dorset 12 D4
Winterborne Zelston
Dorset 12 E5
Winterbourne S Glos 32 B8
Winterbourne W Berk 34 E10
Winterbourne Abbas
Dorset 11 N6
Winterbourne Bassett
Wilts 33 L10
Winterbourne
Dauntsey Wilts 21 N8
Winterbourne Earls Wilts 21 N8
Winterbourne Gunner
Wilts 21 N7
Winterbourne
Monkton Wilts 33 L10
Winterbourne
Steepleton Dorset 11 N7
Winterbourne Stoke
Wilts 21 L6
Winterbrook Oxon 34 H7
Winterburn N York 96 D9
Winteringham N Linc 92 F6
Winterley Ches E 70 C3
Wintersett Wakefd 91 K7
Winterslow Wilts 21 P8
Winterton N Linc 92 F7
Winterton-on-Sea Norfk 77 P8
Winthorpe Lincs 87 Q7
Winthorpe Notts 85 P9
Winton Bmouth 13 J6
Winton Cumb 102 E8
Winton E Susx 25 M10
Winton N York 104 D11
Wintringham N York 98 H6
Winwick Cambs 61 P4
Winwick Nhants 60 D6
Winwick Warrtn 82 D6
Wirksworth Derbys 71 P4
Wirral 81 K7
Wirswall Ches E 69 P6
Wisbech Cambs 75 J9
Wisbech St Mary Cambs 74 H9
Wisborough Green
W Susx 24 C5
Wiseman's Bridge
Pembks 41 M9
Wiseton Notts 85 M3
Wishanger Gloucs 32 H3
Wishaw N Lans 126 D6
Wishaw Warwks 59 J6
Wisley Surrey 36 C9
Wisley Garden RHS
Surrey 36 C9
Wispington Lincs 86 H6
Wissenden Kent 26 F3
Wissett Suffk 65 M6
Wissington Norfk 75 N11
Wissington Suffk 52 G5
Wistanstow Shrops 56 G7
Wistanswick Shrops 70 B9
Wistaston Ches E 70 B4
Wistaston Green Ches E 70 B4
Wisterfield Ches E 82 H10
Wiston Pembks 41 K7
Wiston S Lans 116 D4
Wiston W Susx 24 D8
Wistow Cambs 62 C4
Wistow Leics 72 G11
Wistow N York 91 P3
Wiswell Lancs 89 L3
Witcham Cambs 62 G4
Witchampton Dorset 12 G3
Witchford Cambs 62 H5
Witcombe Somset 19 N10
Witham Essex 52 D9
Witham Friary Somset 20 D6
Witham on the Hill Lincs 73 R7
Witham St Hughs Lincs 85 Q8
Withcall Lincs 87 J4
Withdean Br & H 24 H9
Witherenden Hill E Susx 25 P5
Witheridge Devon 9 K2
Witherley Leics 72 A11
Withern Lincs 87 M4
Withernsea E R Yk 93 P5
Withernwick E R Yk 93 L2
Withersdale Street Suffk 65 K5
Withersfield Suffk 63 L11
Witherslack Cumb 95 J4
Withiel Cnwll 4 F8
Withiel Florey Somset 18 C8
Withielgoose Cnwll 4 G8
Withington Gloucs 47 K11
Withington Herefs 45 R6
Withington Manch 82 H6
Withington Shrops 57 K2
Withington Staffs 71 J7
Withington Green
Ches E 82 H10
Withington Marsh
Herefs 45 R6
Withleigh Devon 9 M2
Withnell Lancs 89 J6
Withybed Green Worcs 58 F10
Withybrook Warwks 59 P8
Withycombe Somset 18 D6
Withyham E Susx 25 L3
Withy Mills BaNES 20 C3
Withypool Somset 17 Q4
Withywood Bristl 31 Q11
Witley Surrey 23 P7
Witnesham Suffk 64 H11
Witney Oxon 34 C2
Wittering C Pete 73 R10
Wittersham Kent 26 F6
Witton Birm 58 G6
Witton Norfk 77 L10
Witton Norfk 77 L5
Witton Gilbert Dur 113 K11
Witton Green Norfk 77 N11
Witton le Wear Dur 103 M4
Witton Park Dur 103 N4
Wiveliscombe Somset 18 E9
Wivelrod Hants 23 J7
Wivelsfield E Susx 24 H6
Wivelsfield Green E Susx 25 J7
Wivelsfield Station
W Susx 24 H7
Wivenhoe Essex 52 H7
Wivenhoe Cross Essex 52 H7
Wiveton Norfk 76 E3
Wix Essex 53 L6
Wixams Bed 50 C2
Wixford Warwks 47 L4
Wix Green Essex 53 L6
Wixhill Shrops 69 Q9
Wixoe Suffk 52 B3
Woburn C Beds 49 P8
Woburn Safari Park
C Beds 49 Q8
Woburn Sands M Keyn 49 P7
Wokefield Park W Berk 35 J11
Woking Surrey 36 B9
Woking Crematorium
Surrey 23 Q3
Wokingham Wokham 35 M11
Wolborough Devon 7 M4
Woldingham Surrey 37 J9
Wold Newton E R Yk 99 L6
Wold Newton NE Lin 93 M11
Wolfclyde S Lans 116 E3
Wolferlow Herefs 46 C2
Wolferton Norfk 75 N5
Wolfhampcote Warwks 60 B7
Wolfhill P & K 142 B11
Wolf Hills Nthumb 111 P9
Wolf's Castle Pembks 41 J5
Wolfsdale Pembks 40 H6
Wollaston Dudley 58 C8
Wollaston Nhants 61 K8
Wollaston Shrops 56 E2
Wollaton C Nott 72 E3
Wollaton Hall & Park
C Nott 72 E3
Wolleigh Devon 9 K8
Wollerton Shrops 69 R8
Wollescote Dudley 58 D8
Wolseley Bridge Staffs 71 J10
Wolsingham Dur 103 L3
Wolstanton Staffs 70 F5
Wolstenholme Rochdl 89 N8
Wolston Warwks 59 P9
Wolsty Cumb 109 P10
Wolvercote Oxon 34 E2
Wolverhampton Wolves 58 D5
Wolverhampton
Halfpenny Green
Airport Staffs 58 B6
Wolverley Shrops 69 N8
Wolverley Worcs 58 B9
Wolverton Hants 22 G3
Wolverton Kent 27 N3
Wolverton M Keyn 49 M6
Wolverton Warwks 47 P2
Wolverton Wilts 20 E8
Wolverton Common
Hants 22 G3
Wolvesnewton Mons 31 N5
Wolvey Warwks 59 P7
Wolvey Heath Warwks 59 P7
Wolviston S on T 104 E5
Wombleton N York 98 D4
Wombourne Staffs 58 C6
Wombwell Barns 91 L10
Womenswold Kent 39 M11
Womersley N York 91 N7
Wonastow Mons 31 N2
Wonersh Surrey 36 B11
Wonford Devon 9 M6
Wonson Devon 8 G7
Wonston Dorset 12 B3
Wonston Hants 22 E7
Wooburn Bucks 35 P7
Wooburn Green Bucks 35 P7
Wooburn Moor Bucks 35 P7
Woodacott Devon 16 F10
Woodale N York 96 F5
Woodall Rothm 84 G4
Woodall Services Rothm 84 G4
Woodbank Ches W 81 M10
Woodbastwick Norfk 77 L8
Woodbeck Notts 85 N5
Wood Bevington Warwks 47 L4
Woodborough Notts 85 K11
Woodborough Wilts 21 M3
Woodbridge Devon 10 D5
Woodbridge Dorset 20 G11
Woodbridge Suffk 53 N2
Wood Burcote Nhants 49 J5
Woodbury Devon 9 P7
Woodbury Salterton
Devon 9 P7
Woodchester Gloucs 32 F4
Woodchurch Kent 26 F5
Woodchurch Wirral 81 K7
Woodcombe Somset 18 C5
Woodcote Gt Lon 36 G8
Woodcote Oxon 34 H8
Woodcote Wrekin 70 D11
Woodcote Green Worcs 58 D10
Woodcott Hants 22 D4
Woodcroft Gloucs 31 P5
Woodcutts Dorset 21 J11
Wood Dalling Norfk 76 F6
Woodditton Cambs 63 L9
Woodeaton Oxon 34 F2
Wood Eaton Staffs 70 E11
Wooden Pembks 41 M9
Wood End Bed 61 M11
Wood End Bed 61 N7
Wood End C Beds 49 Q6
Wood End Cambs 62 E5
Wood End Gt Lon 36 D4
Wood End Herts 50 H5
Woodend Highld 138 D5
Woodend Nhants 48 H5
Woodend Staffs 71 M9
Woodend W Loth 126 G4
Woodend W Susx 15 M5
Wood End Warwks 58 H10
Wood End Warwks 59 K5
Wood End Warwks 59 L7
Wood End Wolves 58 D4
Wood Enderby Lincs 87 J8
Woodend Green Essex 51 N5
Woodfalls Wilts 21 N10
Woodford Cnwll 16 C9

Woodford Devon......7 K8
Woodford Gloucs......32 C5
Woodford Gt Lon......37 K2
Woodford Nhants......61 L5
Woodford Stockp......83 J8
Woodford Bridge Gt Lon......37 K2
Woodford Green Gt Lon......37 K2
Woodford Halse Nhants......48 F4
Woodford Wells Gt Lon......37 K2
Woodgate Birm......58 E8
Woodgate Devon......18 F11
Woodgate Norfk......76 B8
Woodgate Norfk......76 E8
Woodgate W Susx......15 P6
Woodgate Worcs......58 E11
Wood Green Gt Lon......36 H2
Woodgreen Hants......21 N11
Woodgreen Oxon......34 C2
Woodhall N York......96 E2
Woodhall Hill Leeds......90 G3
Woodhall Spa Lincs......86 G8
Woodham Bucks......49 K11
Woodham Dur......103 Q5
Woodham Surrey......36 B8
Woodham Ferrers Essex......38 C2
Woodham Mortimer
Essex......52 D11
Woodham Walter Essex......52 D10
Wood Hayes Wolves......58 D4
Woodhead Abers......159 J10
Woodhill Shrops......57 N8
Woodhill Somset......19 L9
Woodhorn Nthumb......113 L3
Woodhorn Demesne
Nthumb......113 M3
Woodhouse Leeds......90 H4
Woodhouse Leics......72 E8
Woodhouse Sheff......84 F4
Woodhouse Wakefd......91 K6
Woodhouse Eaves Leics......72 E8
Woodhouse Green Staffs......70 G2
Woodhouselee Mdloth......127 N5
Woodhouselees D & G......110 G6
Woodhouse Mill Sheff......84 F3
Woodhouses Cumb......110 F10
Woodhouses Oldham......83 K4
Woodhouses Staffs......58 G3
Woodhouses Staffs......71 M11
Woodhuish Devon......7 N8
Woodhurst Cambs......62 D5
Woodingdean Br & H......25 J9
Woodkirk Leeds......90 H5
Woodland Abers......151 M3
Woodland Devon......6 G7
Woodland Devon......7 K5
Woodland Dur......103 L4
Woodland Kent......27 K3
Woodland S Ayrs......114 C8
Woodland Head Devon......9 J5
Woodlands Abers......151 K8
Woodlands Donc......91 N9
Woodlands Dorset......13 J3
Woodlands Hants......13 P2
Woodlands Kent......37 N8
Woodlands N York......97 M10
Woodlands Somset......18 G6
Woodlands (Coleshill)
Crematorium Warwks......59 J7
Woodlands Park W & M......35 N9
Woodlands St Mary
W Berk......34 B9
Woodlands
(Scarborough)
Crematorium N York......99 L3
Woodlands
(Scunthorpe)
Crematorium N Linc......92 E8
Woodland Street Somset......19 P7
Woodland View Sheff......84 D3
Wood Lane Shrops......69 M8
Wood Lane Staffs......70 E5
Woodleigh Devon......7 J3
Woodlesford Leeds......91 K5
Woodley Stockp......83 K6
Woodley Wokham......35 L10
Woodmancote Gloucs......32 E5
Woodmancote Gloucs......33 K3
Woodmancote Gloucs......47 J9
Woodmancote W Susx......15 L5
Woodmancote W Susx......24 F8
Woodmancote Worcs......46 H6
Woodmancott Hants......22 G6
Woodmansey E R Yk......93 J3
Woodmansgreen W Susx......23 N9
Woodmansterne Surrey......36 C9
Woodmanton Devon......9 P7
Woodmarsh Wilts......20 G3
Woodmill Staffs......71 L10
Woodminton Wilts......21 K10
Woodnesborough Kent......39 P10
Woodnewton Nhants......61 M2
Woodnook Notts......84 G10
Wood Norton Norfk......76 E6
Woodplumpton Lancs......88 F4
Woodrising Norfk......76 D11
Wood Row Leeds......91 K5
Woodrow Worcs......58 C9
Wood's Corner E Susx......25 Q7
Woods Eaves Herefs......45 K5
Woodseaves Shrops......70 B8
Woodseaves Staffs......70 D9
Woodsend Wilts......33 P9
Woodsetts Rothm......84 H4
Woodsford Dorset......12 C6
Wood's Green E Susx......25 P4
Woodside Br For......35 P10
Woodside Cumb......100 D4
Woodside Essex......51 L10
Woodside Fife......135 L6
Woodside Gt Lon......36 H7
Woodside Hants......13 P6
Woodside Herts......51 F9
Woodside P & K......142 C10
Woodside
Crematorium Inver......124 H2
Woodside Green Kent......38 F11
Woodstock Oxon......48 D2
Woodstock Pembks......41 K5
Woodston C Pete......74 C11
Wood Street Norfk......77 M7
Wood Street Village
Surrey......23 Q4
Woodthorpe Derbys......84 G6
Woodthorpe Leics......72 E7
Woodthorpe Lincs......87 M4
Woodton Norfk......65 K3
Woodtown Devon......16 G7
Woodvale Sefton......88 C8
Woodvale
Crematorium Br & H......24 H9
Woodville Derbys......71 Q11

Woodwall Green Staffs......70 D8
Wood Walton Cambs......62 B4
Woodyates Dorset......21 K11
Woody Bay Devon......17 M2
Woofferton Shrops......57 J11
Wookey Somset......19 P5
Wookey Hole Somset......19 P5
Wool Dorset......12 D7
Woolacombe Devon......16 H3
Woolage Green Kent......27 M2
Woolage Village Kent......39 M11
Woolaston Gloucs......31 Q5
Woolaston Common
Gloucs......31 Q4
Woolavington Somset......19 K6
Woolbeding W Susx......23 N10
Woolbrook Devon......10 C7
Woolcotts Somset......18 C4
Wooldale Kirk......90 F9
Wooler Nthumb......119 J5
Woolfardisworthy
Devon......9 K3
Woolfardisworthy
Devon......16 E7
Woolfold Bury......89 M8
Woolfords S Lans......127 L6
Woolhampton W Berk......34 G11
Woolhope Herefs......46 B7
Woolland Dorset......12 C3
Woollard BaNES......20 B2
Woollensbrook Herts......51 J9
Woolley BaNES......32 D11
Woolley Cambs......61 Q6
Woolley Cnwll......16 D8
Woolley Derbys......84 E8
Woolley Wakefd......91 J8
Woolley Bridge Derbys......83 M6
Woolley Edge Services
Wakefd......91 J8
Woolley Green W & M......35 M8
Woolmere Green Worcs......47 J2
Woolmer Green Herts......50 G8
Woolmerston Somset......19 J8
Woolminstone Somset......11 J3
Woolpack Kent......26 E4
Woolpit Suffk......64 D9
Woolpit Green Suffk......64 D9
Woolscott Warwks......60 B7
Woolsgrove Devon......9 J4
Woolsington N u Ty......113 J7
Woolstaston Shrops......56 H5
Woolsthorpe Lincs......73 L4
Woolsthorpe-by-
Colsterworth Lincs......73 N6
Woolston C Sotn......14 D4
Woolston Devon......7 J10
Woolston Devon......7 J8
Woolston Shrops......56 G7
Woolston Shrops......69 K10
Woolston Somset......18 D4
Woolston Somset......20 C9
Woolston Warrtn......82 D7
Woolstone Gloucs......47 J8
Woolstone M Keyn......49 N7
Woolstone Oxon......33 Q7
Woolston Green Devon......7 J5
Woolton Lpool......81 N7
Woolton Hill Hants......22 D2
Woolverstone Suffk......53 L4
Woolverton Somset......20 E4
Woolwich Gt Lon......37 K5
Woonton Herefs......45 M4
Woonton Herefs......45 R2
Wooperton Nthumb......119 K6
Woore Shrops......70 C6
Wootten Green Suffk......65 J7
Wootton Bed......50 B2
Wootton Hants......13 M5
Wootton Herefs......45 L4
Wootton IoW......14 F8
Wootton Kent......27 M2
Wootton N Linc......93 J7
Wootton Nhants......60 G9
Wootton Oxon......34 E4
Wootton Oxon......48 D11
Wootton Shrops......69 K9
Wootton Staffs......70 E9
Wootton Staffs......71 L6
Wootton Bassett Wilts......33 L8
Wootton Bridge IoW......14 F8
Wootton Broadmead
Bed......50 B2
Wootton Common IoW......14 F8
Wootton Courtenay
Somset......18 B6
Wootton Fitzpaine
Dorset......10 H5
Wootton Rivers Wilts......21 N2
Wootton St Lawrence
Hants......22 G4
Wootton Wawen
Warwks......47 N2
Worcester Worcs......46 G4
Worcester
Crematorium Gt Lon......46 G3
Worcester Park Gt Lon......36 F7
Wordsley Dudley......58 C7
Worfield Shrops......57 P5
Worgret Dorset......12 F7
Workhouse End Bed......61 P10
Workhouse Green Suffk......52 F4
Workington Cumb......100 D5
Worksop Notts......85 J5
Worlaby Lincs......87 K5
Worlaby N Linc......92 H8
Worlds End Bucks......35 N3
Worlds End Hants......14 H4
World's End W Berk......34 E9
Worlds End W Susx......24 H6
Worle N Som......19 L2
Worleston Ches E......70 B3
Worlingham Suffk......65 N4
Worlington Devon......9 J2
Worlington Suffk......63 L6
Worlingworth Suffk......65 J8
Wormald Green N York......97 M7
Wormbridge Herefs......45 N8
Wormegay Norfk......75 N8
Wormelow Tump Herefs......45 P8
Wormhill Derbys......83 P10
Wormhill Herefs......45 N7
Wormingford Essex......52 F5
Worminghall Bucks......34 H3
Wormington Gloucs......47 K7
Worminster Somset......19 Q6
Wormit Fife......135 L2
Wormleighton Warwks......48 E4
Wormley Herts......51 J9
Wormley Surrey......23 P7
Wormleybury Herts......51 J9
Wormley Hill Donc......91 R7

Wormshill Kent......38 E10
Wormsley Herefs......45 N5
Worplesdon Surrey......23 Q4
Worrall Sheff......84 D2
Worrall Hill Gloucs......32 B2
Worsbrough Barns......91 K10
Worsbrough Bridge
Barns......91 K10
Worsbrough Dale Barns......91 K10
Worsley Salfd......82 G4
Worstead Norfk......77 L6
Worsthorne Lancs......89 P4
Worston Devon......6 H7
Worston Lancs......89 M2
Worth Kent......39 P10
Worth Somset......19 P6
Worth W Susx......24 H3
Wortham Suffk......64 F6
Worthen Shrops......56 E4
Worthenbury Wrexhm......69 M5
Worthing Norfk......76 D8
Worthing W Susx......24 D10
Worthing Crematorium
W Susx......24 D9
Worthington Leics......72 C6
Worth Matravers Dorset......12 G9
Worthybrook Mons......31 N2
Worting Hants......22 G4
Wortley Barns......91 J11
Wortley Leeds......90 H4
Worton N York......96 E3
Worton Wilts......21 J3
Wortwell Norfk......65 K5
Wotherton Shrops......56 D4
Wothorpe C Pete......73 Q9
Wotter Devon......6 F6
Wotton Surrey......36 D11
Wotton-under-Edge
Gloucs......32 E6
Wotton Underwood
Bucks......49 J11
Woughton on the
Green M Keyn......49 N7
Wouldham Kent......38 B9
Woundale Shrops......57 P6
Wrabness Essex......53 L5
Wrafton Devon......16 H4
Wragby Lincs......86 F5
Wragby Wakefd......91 L7
Wramplingham Norfk......76 G10
Wrangaton Devon......6 H7
Wrangbrook Wakefd......91 M8
Wrangle Lincs......87 M10
Wrangle Common Lincs......87 M10
Wrangle Lowgate Lincs......87 M10
Wrangway Somset......18 F11
Wrantage Somset......19 K10
Wrawby N Linc......92 H9
Wraxall N Som......31 N10
Wraxall Somset......20 B7
Wray Lancs......95 N7
Wray Castle Cumb......101 L10
Wraysbury W & M......36 B6
Wrayton Lancs......95 N6
Wrea Green Lancs......88 D4
Wreaks End Cumb......94 E3
Wreay Cumb......101 M6
Wreay Cumb......110 H10
Wrecclesham Surrey......23 M6
Wrekenton Gatesd......113 L9
Wrelton N York......98 F3
Wrenbury Ches E......69 Q5
Wrench Green N York......99 K3
Wreningham Norfk......64 H2
Wrentham Suffk......65 P5
Wrenthorpe Wakefd......91 J6
Wrentnall Shrops......56 G4
Wressle E R Yk......92 B4
Wressle N Linc......92 G9
Wrestlingworth C Beds......62 C11
Wretton Norfk......75 N10
Wrexham Wrexhm......69 K4
Wrexham Industrial
Estate Wrexhm......69 L4
Wribbenhall Worcs......57 P9
Wrickton Shrops......57 L7
Wrightington Bar Lancs......88 G8
Wright's Green Essex......51 M7
Wrinehill Staffs......70 D5
Wrington N Som......19 N2
Writhlington BaNES......20 C4
Writtle Essex......51 Q9
Wrockwardine Wrekin......57 L2
Wroot N Linc......92 B10
Wrose C Brad......90 F4
Wrotham Kent......37 P9
Wrotham Heath Kent......37 P9
Wrottesley Staffs......58 B4
Wroughton Swindn......33 M8
Wroxall IoW......14 G11
Wroxall Warwks......59 K10
Wroxeter Shrops......57 K3
Wroxham Norfk......77 L8
Wroxton Oxon......48 D6
Wyaston Derbys......71 M6
Wyatt's Green Essex......51 N11
Wyberton East Lincs......74 E2
Wyberton West Lincs......74 F2
Wyboston Bed......61 Q9
Wybunbury Ches E......70 B5
Wychbold Worcs......58 D11
Wych Cross E Susx......25 K4
Wychnor Staffs......71 M11
Wyck Hants......23 L7
Wyck Rissington Gloucs......47 N10
Wycliffe Dur......103 M8
Wycoller Lancs......89 Q3
Wycomb Leics......73 K6
Wycombe Marsh Bucks......35 N6
Wyddial Herts......51 J4
Wye Kent......27 J2
Wyesham Mons......31 P2
Wyfordby Leics......73 K7
Wyke C Brad......90 F5
Wyke Devon......9 J5
Wyke Devon......10 F5
Wyke Dorset......20 E8
Wyke Shrops......57 L4
Wyke Surrey......23 P4
Wyke Champflower
Somset......20 C8
Wykeham N York......99 K4
Wyken Covtry......59 N8
Wyken Shrops......57 P5
Wyke Regis Dorset......11 P9
Wykey Shrops......69 L10
Wykin Leics......72 C11
Wylam Nthumb......112 H8
Wylde Green Birm......58 H6
Wylye Wilts......21 K7
Wymeswold Leics......72 G6

Wymington Bed......61 L8
Wymondham Leics......73 L7
Wymondham Norfk......76 G11
Wyndham Brdgnd......29 P6
Wynford Eagle Dorset......11 M5
Wynyard Park S on T......104 D5
Wynyard Village S on T......104 D5
Wyre Forest
Crematorium Worcs......57 Q10
Wyre Piddle Worcs......47 J5
Wysall Notts......72 G5
Wyson Herefs......57 J11
Wythall Worcs......58 G9
Wytham Oxon......34 E3
Wythburn Cumb......101 K8
Wythenshawe Manch......82 H7
Wythop Mill Cumb......100 G5
Wyton Cambs......62 C6
Wyton E R Yk......93 L4
Wyverstone Suffk......64 E8
Wyverstone Street Suffk......64 E8
Wyville Lincs......73 M5

Y

Yaddlethorpe N Linc......92 E9
Yafford IoW......14 D10
Yafforth N York......97 M2
Yalberton Torbay......7 M7
Yalding Kent......37 Q10
Yanwath Cumb......101 P5
Yanworth Gloucs......33 L2
Yapham E R Yk......98 F10
Yapton W Susx......15 Q6
Yarborough N Som......19 L3
Yarbridge IoW......14 H9
Yarburgh Lincs......87 L2
Yarcombe Devon......10 E3
Yard Devon......17 P7
Yardley Birm......58 H7
Yardley Crematorium
Birm......58 H8
Yardley Gobion Nhants......49 L6
Yardley Hastings Nhants......61 J9
Yardley Wood Birm......58 H9
Yardro Powys......45 J3
Yarford Somset......18 H9
Yarkhill Herefs......46 B6
Yarley Somset......19 P6
Yarlington Somset......20 C9
Yarm S on T......104 D8
Yarmouth IoW......14 C9
Yarnacott Devon......17 L5
Yarnbrook Wilts......20 G4
Yarner Devon......9 J9
Yarnfield Staffs......70 F8
Yarnscombe Devon......17 K7
Yarnton Oxon......34 E2
Yarpole Herefs......45 P2
Yarrow Border......117 M5
Yarrow Somset......19 L5
Yarrow Feus Border......117 L5
Yarrowford Border......117 N4
Yarsop Herefs......45 N5
Yarwell Nhants......73 R11
Yate S Glos......32 D8
Yateley Hants......23 M2
Yatesbury Wilts......33 L10
Yattendon W Berk......34 G10
Yatton Herefs......56 G11
Yatton N Som......31 M11
Yatton Keynell Wilts......32 G9
Yaverland IoW......14 H9
Yawl Devon......10 G6
Yawthorpe Lincs......85 Q2
Yaxham Norfk......76 E9
Yaxley Cambs......61 Q2
Yaxley Suffk......64 G7
Yazor Herefs......45 N5
Yeading Gt Lon......36 D4
Yeadon Leeds......90 G2
Yealand Conyers Lancs......95 L6
Yealand Redmayne
Lancs......95 L5
Yealand Storrs Lancs......95 K5
Yealmbridge Devon......6 F8
Yealmpton Devon......6 F8
Yearby R & Cl......104 G6
Yearngill Cumb......100 F2
Yearsley N York......98 B6
Yeaton Shrops......69 M11
Yeaveley Derbys......71 M6
Yeavering Nthumb......118 H4
Yedingham N York......98 H5
Yelford Oxon......34 C4
Yell Shet......169 r5
Yelland Devon......16 H5
Yelling Cambs......62 C8
Yelvertoft Nhants......60 C5
Yelverton Devon......6 E4
Yelverton Norfk......77 K11
Yenston Somset......20 D10
Yeoford Devon......9 J5
Yeolmbridge Cnwll......5 N4
Yeo Mill Devon......17 Q6
Yeo Vale Devon......16 G7
Yeovil Somset......19 Q11
Yeovil Crematorium
Somset......19 P11
Yeovil Marsh Somset......19 P11
Yeovilton Somset......19 P10
Yerbeston Pembks......41 L9
Yesnaby Ork......169 b5
Yetlington Nthumb......119 K9
Yetminster Dorset......11 M2
Yetson Devon......7 L7
Yettington Devon......9 Q7
Yetts o'Muckhart Clacks......134 C7
Yews Green C Brad......90 D4
Yew Tree Sandw......58 F5
Yielden Bed......61 M7
Yieldingtree Worcs......57 C9
Yieldshields S Lans......126 F7
Yiewsley Gt Lon......36 C4
Y Maerdy Conwy......68 D6
Y Nant Wrexhm......69 J4
Ynysboeth Rhondd......30 E5
Ynysddu Caerph......30 G6
Ynysforgan Swans......29 J5
Ynyshir Rhondd......30 D6
Ynyslas Cerdgn......54 E6
Ynysmaerdy Rhondd......30 D8
Ynysmeudwy Neath......29 K3
Ynystawe Swans......29 J4
Ynyswen Powys......29 M2

Ynyswen Rhondd......30
Ynysybwl Rhondd......30
Ynysymaengwyn Gwynd......54
Yockenthwaite N York......96
Yockleton Shrops......56
Yokefleet E R Yk......92
Yoker C Glas......125
York C York......98 C4
York Lancs......89
York City Crematorium
C York......98 B3
Yorkletts Kent......39
Yorkley Gloucs......32
Yorkshire Dales National
Park......96
York Town Surrey......
Yorton Heath Shrops......69 P
Youlgreave Derbys......84
Youlthorpe E R Yk......98
Youlton N York......97
Youngsbury Herts......51
Young's End Essex......52
Yoxall Staffs......71 L
Yoxford Suffk......65
Y Rhiw Gwynd......66
Ysbyty Cynfyn Cerdgn......54
Ysbyty Ifan Conwy......67
Ysbyty Ystwyth Cerdgn......54 G
Ysceifiog Flints......80 H
Ysgubor-y-Coed Cerdgn......54
Ystalyfera Neath......29
Ystrad Rhondd......30
Ystrad Aeron Cerdgn......43
Ystradfellte Powys......29
Ystrad Ffin Carmth......43
Ystradgynlais Powys......29
Ystrad Meurig Cerdgn......54 G
Ystrad Mynach Caerph......30
Ystradowen V Glam......30
Ystumtuen Cerdgn......54
Ythanbank Abers......159 M
Ythanwells Abers......158 F
Ythsie Abers......159 L

Z

Zeal Monachorum
Devon......8
Zeals Wilts......20
Zelah Cnwll......3
Zennor Cnwll......2
Zoar Cnwll......3 K
Zouch Notts......72
ZSL London Zoo Gt Lon......36
ZSL Whipsnade Zoo
C Beds......50

Distances and journey times

The mileage chart shows distances in miles between two towns along AA-recommended routes. Using motorways and other main roads this is normally the fastest route, though not necessarily the shortest.

The journey times, shown in hours and minutes, are average off-peak driving times along AA-recommended routes. These times should be used as a guide only and do not allow for unforeseen traffic delays, rest breaks or fuel stops.

For example, the 378 miles (608 km) journey between Glasgow and Norwich should take approximately 7 hours 28 minutes.

Journey tim

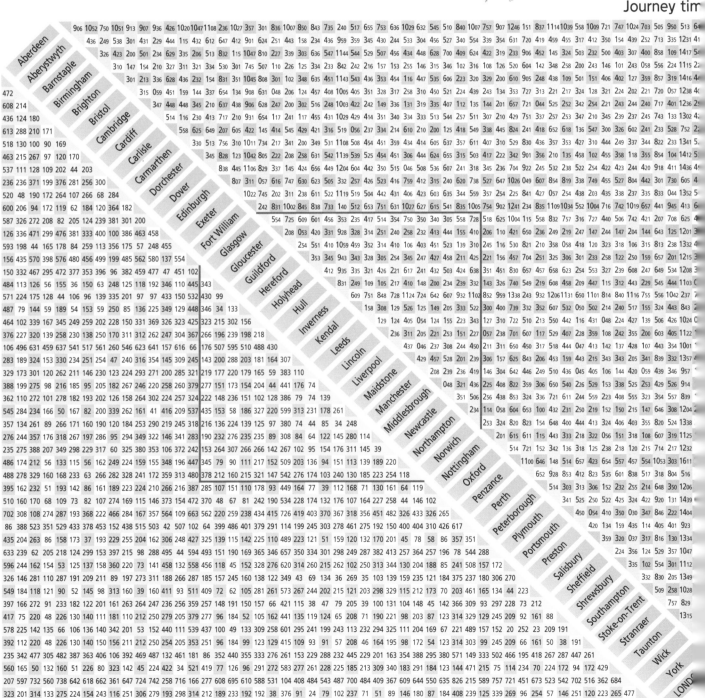

Distances in miles (one mile equals 1.6093 km)